WALLENSTEIN

WALLENSTEIN

his life narrated by
GOLO MANN

Translated by Charles Kessler

HOLT, RINEHART AND WINSTON
NEW YORK

Original German title: *Wallenstein.*
Sein Leben erzählt von Golo Mann
Copyright © 1971 by S. Fischer Verlag GmbH, Frankfurt am Main
English translation © 1976 by
André Deutsch Limited, London, and
Holt, Rinehart & Winston, New York.

Published simultaneously in Canada by Holt, Rinehart and Winston of Canada, Limited.

Library of Congress Cataloging in Publication Data

Mann, Golo, 1909–
    Wallenstein, his life narrated.

    1.   Wallenstein, Albrecht Wenzel Eusebius von,
Herzog zu Friedland, 1583-1634.
D270.W19M313   943'.04'0924   [B]   76-4721
ISBN 0-03-091884-7

First published in the United States in 1976

Designer: Robert Eames

Printed in Great Britain

10 9 8 7 6 5 4 3 2 1

Contents

6 WALLENSTEIN

Foreword
to the English-Language Edition

THE English-language edition of my book has had to forgo the scholastic backing found in the original. Instead I would like briefly to comment here on what my method of work has been. I have used the sources. All published ones – there are over twenty volumes of letters by Wallenstein, to Wallenstein, about Wallenstein – as well as unpublished ones located in the Prague State Archives. These would indeed have provided much else which is now being gradually disclosed, but hardly anything that could materially affect my delineation. My ambition was to write the definitive Wallenstein biography. A number of German critics have remarked that the book is also literature. To that I raise no objection. Should it however be claimed that it is simply literature, then I must protest. Literature lets the reader off more lightly than I can. This is a true story, not an invented one. In the original there is one annotation for every five sentences. The two "Nocturnal Fantasies", attempts at the art of interior monologue, are the exception. They amount to not half a per cent of the whole.

The historian has always to try to do two different things simultaneously. He must swim with the stream of events, allowing himself to be carried along as though he had been present. He must from outside converge on his subject from various directions, a later, better-informed observer, and catechize it, yet never quite have it in the hollow of his hand. How to combine these two methods so as to yield a semblance of homogeneity and without the narrative falling apart, that would be a man of letters' concern.

In this book the first approach preponderates. It even colours the language, which dallies distantly with that of the seventeenth century. In the text I have abstained from argument with my precursors. Illusion would have been destroyed. A few "discoveries" were made. That, for example, Wallenstein's famous "Contract with the Emperor", in 1632 and the all too favourite subject of donnish investigation, never existed but, like so much in the case of this life, is sheer legend. The kind of thing said as in an aside. Amidst the flow of facts it did not play the part which lay within the scope of the abstract personality elaborated by its proud detector. Another instance. During the last year of his life Wallenstein, aware of the great war imminent between France and Spain, wanted to keep Germany out of those hostilities. Nevertheless this strand of motivation was in his mind so entangled with others that I allowed it only discreet reverberation. At no point have I portrayed Wallenstein's character. His career, as he dealt and was dealt by, his actions and reactions, constitutes his character. Of course that holds good for every historical figure. For this one in particular, though, because the issue is an individuality at once very strong and exuberant, eventually erupting into forfeiture of his own identity. I have given no summing up, no final verdict. Reality knows none.

Marx, I am convinced, was in error. There is no single secret gist behind, nor clue to, historical phenomena. Words and deeds show what men are and how events take shape. Narration and elucidation synchronize.

Should my book leave the English-language reader discontent, the responsibility lies squarely on the shoulders of the author, not the translator. The latter has performed a difficult task in a way that could neither have been bettered nor more happily accomplished. I wish to thank him for it.

GOLO MANN

Childhood: A Mosaic
with Many Stones Missing

Yes, he started so small and is now so great.
At school in Altdorf he caused quite a scandal,
If I may speak so, acting the Vandal
And carrying on at a high old rate

SCHILLER

THE village of Hermanitz lies by the Elbe where, in the east of lovely Bohemia, it follows a southerly course. The setting, with meadows, rippling water and surrounding beechwood heights, still pleases the eye even though it is not quite the same as in the days when only a few outhouses and villeins' homes fringed the castle. This has long since disappeared. A farm stands on the site. From 1548 to 1623 Hermanitz and five neighbouring villages were Waldstein domain, then changed hands in quick succession: the Trčkas of Lípa gave way to the Danish Ulefelds, the Piccolomini from Siena, the Czernins with their Drslawitz ancestry, and finally the Hospitaller Order of St John of God. An account, dating from 1713, tells us about the manorial church: " . . . in Hermanitz there is a church by the name of St Mary Magdalene the Sinner, an old stone structure, but the bell-tower, wherein are three bells, large, medium, and small, is wholly dilapidated, so that now they can scarce be rung." A few years later German settlers demolished the church, but the tombstones on either side of the altar were left in their original position when a new one was built. They portray in white marble, carved to somewhat less than life-size, a knight and his lady. The knight, with moustache and pointed beard, is bare-headed. In his right hand he has a sword. In life, as we know, he never wielded such. Its tip rests on a coat-of-arms with a device of four lions. The inscription, in Czech and running around the relief-work, reads: "In the Year of the Lord 1595, on Friday, St Matthew's Day, there died the high-born lord, Lord Vilim the Elder, of Valdšteyn upon Hermanitz, and here his body doth rest unto the joyous Resurrection." On the altar's farther side the lady, with coif and big ruff, looks a little humpbacked. She holds a prayer-book. The inscription defines the escutcheon at her feet: "In

the Year of the Lord 1593, on St Mary Magdalene's Day, there died
the high-born lady, Lady Markyta of Smiřice, wife to the high-born
lord, Lord Vilim the Elder, of Valdšteyn and upon Hermanitz, and
here her body doth rest unto the joyous Resurrection."

Albrecht Wenzel Eusebius, the only surviving son, had these monuments erected in 1602 on his return from abroad. At nineteen, although
not quite certain what now to do with himself, he was in the advantageous situation of early independence and a comfortable heritage. So
long had he been away from home that to him it was hardly still home.
He found only the dead on hand – his parents, his brothers Jan Jiři and
Adam, his sisters Hedvika and Magdalena, whose weathered tombstones
are today to be seen by the church's outer wall. Two other sisters, Maria
Buhumila and Katharina Anna, were living elsewhere under the care of
an aunt, the noble Damozel Jitka of Valdšteyn.

He had come from Italy, having previously been in France. Some say
in Spain too, or in England, but that is untrue. The travel which
pertained to the education of the Bohemian nobility could include
England or Spain, or both these realms, and there are cases where it did,
but this was not one of them. For the rest we really know very little about
Albrecht Wallenstein's grand tour. He wrote no letters, or at any rate
none has survived. Much of his later conversation has been transmitted
to us, but the contents are confined to matters of war and state. Never, or
hardly ever, do they deal with personal affairs. If he savoured first love
and friendship, the facts remain hidden. Maybe he did not. At the turn
of the sixteenth and seventeenth centuries little emphasis was laid on
what we term emotions. Those that were none the less experienced, and
for which the names current among us did not exist, were kept concealed or at best confided to one's father confessor, a spiritual adviser
who had for his part to be practised in taciturnity. Were diaries written,
which did happen, they recorded events and observations on outside
matters, not reactions, much less personal reactions. There were
exceptions, there always are, and in the course of our narrative we shall
encounter some. Wallenstein is not, however, among them. If he presents
an exception, then it is rather in the opposite direction in as much as
he subsequently pushed reticence, about what passed through his
mind and what had moulded him into the man that he was, to a point
beyond that exercised by most of his fellows.

So he came from Italy, from Padua. There, according to more or less
contemporary accounts, he is supposed to have studied politics, mathematics, astronomy and astrology, which played a part in his later life.

We believe that he was at Padua because all the early sources agree on this. Anything more is already dubious. Definite is only that he stayed long enough to learn the language. At the juncture when he emerges from obscurity, a little light falling upon him, then ever more, and ever more glaringly, he has an elegant turn of Italian phrase and likes to scatter Italian proverbs through his letters.

THE NAME

The name, properly speaking, is Waldstein and was originally Waldnstein. As the Czech tongue finds it easy to accumulate consonants at the start of a word, but difficult to do so in the middle, it was pronounced Walstein. The Germans added a consonant or a syllable (Wallstein, Wallenstein, Wahlenstein) according to taste during a period when people were not too particular about consistency of spelling. Albrecht himself wrote Waldstein until such time as he betook himself into circles where signature is confined to Christian name or initials.

That Slav stock should have a German name is not hard to explain. The gentry often called themselves after castles built by German master-masons who gave them German names: Sternberg, Rosenberg, Michelsberg, Wartenberg, Löwenberg, Rotstein and plenty more, and hence too Waldstein. When that happened, in the thirteenth century, the notion of seeing it as national betrayal crossed nobody's mind.

The ruins of Castle Waldstein are not far from Turnau. The name derived from the three boulders or rocks, linked by bridges, on which it was erected; the surrounding forest consisted of birches, pines and beeches. He who had it built was dubbed Zdenek and lacked any other name until he called himself, or was called, Waldstein after his new fortress. At that date the construction of stone castles commended itself because the atrocities of the Mongol invasions which had devastated Silesia and Moravia, lands with kindred destinies, lingered in living memory. Their sovereigns, moreover, were once again weak and the laws no protection.

The man who was simply dubbed Zdenek was the descendant of a widely ramified, old, rich and powerful family which for its part had no name. In the nineteenth century historians called them the Markwarts because their alleged twelfth-century founder was a knight by the name of Markwart. So Bohemian gentry were not shy of German names and one of this Markwart's sons was called Hermann. Slav names like Benesh, Hawel, Zawisch, Zdenko and Jaroslav were however more frequent among the Markwarts. They ruled in the Iser valley of north-east Bohemia without anyone knowing how and when they acquired their dominion, Slav proto-aristocracy. Remarkable is that from the outset they ruled there where four hundred, even seven hundred, years later the properties of the Waldsteins continued to be, and we shall yet hear of Markwart foundations like the town and monastery of München-grätz. In the late thirteenth century they split into a variety of clans who began to foster individual identities.

In a letter of recommendation on behalf of young Albrecht Wallen-stein, his Moravian brother-in-law, Karl von Zierotin wrote, "He is high-born, as you know, and related to all the great houses of Bohemia," which was true. Not only had one of his ancestors been Lord Chamber-lain at the court of the powerful Czech monarch George of Podiebrad, but he was himself descended from this sovereign in as much as one of his maternal great-grandmothers, a Silesian duchess of Münsterberg, was the great-granddaughter of the King, making the latter Wallen-stein's forefather in the seventh generation. As for his contemporary kin, the Smiřickýs, Slawatas, Wartenbergs, Zierotins, Lobkowiczs, and others with equally resounding names, they resided in the castles of Bohemia and the margraviate of Moravia; in frontier fortresses facing Germany and Hungary, ancient structures perched on crags and en-larged, according to need and current taste, by way of corner-towers, outer baileys and curtain-walls; in great houses in the new Italian style, long rows of stone halls set around arcaded courtyards and richly decorated with panelling, gilded carvings, weapons, costly materials, pictures with figures from fable and myth and ancestral portraits; in the market-place of their own towns, in the lanes of Prague's Lesser Town, or between tree-topped heights and river-valley. There they lived, surrounded by artists whose immediate task might be to paint the knights' hall with frescoes or to embellish the park with statues and fountains, by doctors and chaplains, French, Italian and German secretaries, and served by equerries, masters of hounds, major-domos, chefs and cooks, pastry-makers and confectioners, valets, lackeys, runners and mounted couriers. Sovereigns to the extent of their do-mains, masters over life and death of their vassals. Patriots too, govern-ors of their provinces, active members of the Prague Diet, holders of the senior state appointments, but patriots after their own fashion, namely, the equation of national liberty with their own liberties, which were prodigious privileges extracted in the course of centuries from kings and burghers. They remained privileged even in death, lying in their own chapels, husband and wife cheek by jowl, their likenesses hewn from white stone, stern-faced, clear-eyed, waiting with hands held high in prayer, awaiting the eternity that would mete out to them yet ampler glory.

Bearers of a couple of dozen names, they always intermarried so as to keep their properties for ever in the same circle and because connection with inferior rank would have demeaned their nobility. Albrecht's grandfather, for example, was married three times: to a Slawata, a Zierotin and a Lobkowicz. He had six daughters and thirteen sons to provide for, which meant that the individual's portion was bound to be small. But the third son of the first marriage, Vilim or Wilhelm, had the luck to be adopted as heir by a childless uncle, and that is how Hermanitz came into his possession.

THE PRECOCIOUS CHILD

Conditions at Hermanitz, although consonant with status, were by no means so splendid as the life led by the Bohemian lords as a whole, or at least by their leaders. Splendid is what they were at neighbouring Castle Nachod, a name supposed to signify "access", access into Silesia. That was where Markyta Smiřický, the handsomely endowed wife of Vilim of Waldstein, came from. There too, it seems, originated the proneness to ailments of all kind, physical and mental harassments hitherto unknown among the robust Waldsteins. One of the Smiřickýs was unsound of mind, "simple". That four among Albrecht's brothers and sisters died in childhood does not mean much, children then having more reason to succumb than to survive. But soon after her marriage another of his remaining sisters perished of consumption and eclampsia, and his mother passed away young. He himself is described as sturdy, at any rate as a youth. His recovery from some severe illnesses supports the case. Born on 14 September 1583 Old Style (at that time the Julian calendar prevailed in Bohemia), or 24 September New Style, he was a seven-months-child who is alleged immediately upon arrival to have startled his parents on the score of *vultus severitate, oculorum gravitate* (stern visage, grave aspect). So the tale goes, just as it does that in early years he concentrated on playing at soldiers and drilled the peasant children in battle-formation, proclaimed to willing and unwilling listeners alike how he would one day be a ruler, and, though this at a later date, let his schoolfellows in the Latin class know about the dream wherein the willows beneath which he slept bowed before him. Tales we pass on without warranty.

At ten he witnessed his mother's death. Lord Vilim, notwithstanding that he was in his prime, hereupon made his will, as still being in full possession of his faculties. He appointed his brother-in-law, Lord Heinrich of Slawata-upon-Koschumberg, to be the guardian of his children and bequeathed to his beloved son Albrecht Wenzel Eusebius the castle and demesne of Hermanitz, a large golden vessel capable of being dismantled into salt cellars, dishes, candlesticks and smaller-sized cups, and a chain comprising 411 gold ducats. The daughters were to be suitably settled out of the income from the estate. Having seen to these matters, Lord Vilim died too and Uncle Slawata came to conduct the twelve-year-old Albrecht to Koschumberg. It was a good thing that Lord Heinrich had a son of approximately the same age as his ward. There was also a nephew, Wilhelm von Slawata, but he was eleven years Albrecht's senior. I had better explain about him immediately. He is the one who on 23 May 1618 was thrown out of a window of the Prague citadel and who played a hostilely sneaking role in Wallenstein's career. Wilhelm claimed to have known his kinsman only too well in his early days. True maybe, but hard to say how true. Wilhelm Slawata turned Catholic soon after the dejected orphan's arrival at Koschumberg. From what we know of Lord Heinrich, an apostate from the faith of his fathers would have been unwelcome in his castle.

The Waldensteins, as good Czechs, had become adherents of John Hus in his lifetime and remained such. Their preference was, however, for the gentry's temperate compliance with his reformist spirit, not the social inferences drawn from his preaching by the turbulent lower orders. Divine service at Hermanitz, if I have got it right, was performed in accordance with the "Bohemian Confession", a mixture of Hussite and Lutheran tradition adopted by the Diet in the decade before Wallenstein's birth and grown since into a sort of national creed. The principle of church authority through the crown was wholly missing. On the contrary, the creed professed was not the crown's and none of its province to meddle with. Profession was made with greater, lesser or total absence of devotional ardour. Let us assume a state of piety in rural Hermanitz and that young Albrecht listened wide-eyed as an old family retainer, Hans Graf, gave him his first scriptural as well as secular lessons.

A different matter was the community of the Bohemian Brethren, to which Heinrich of Slawata belonged. Really pious, yet well-organized, a sect and the core of a political party, one of the outstanding attempts at a revival and fortification of fervour. In Bohemia and Moravia, which latterly had evolved into its true centre, many of the higher nobility were community members. At Eibenschitz there was a school, supported by contributions from well-off co-religionists, for the education of youth in the proper spirit. The community's discipline was strict. Lords who in other respects yielded to none submitted to the ecclesiastical penances imposed by the elected "elders". Doctrine fluctuated. The Lutherans had been the prime favourites, but with disappointment at the human frailty which they displayed in Bohemia the influence of the Calvinists rose. Not so much on the score of doctrine, which was not the Brethren's main concern, but because their theologians at Basle and Geneva, Strasbourg and Heidelberg were thought to be more pious. Purity of conduct, the importance of education, taking seriously such Christian pledges as the fraternity which discerned in a villein a human being too, and more of this kind may have been enunciated by the elder who taught a couple of patrician lads in Castle Koschumberg. Had Albrecht Wallenstein become or stayed a zealous member of the community, we might perhaps know a little more about his boyhood. Its leaders, not unlike the Jesuits with whom they stood in hostile rivalry, were experts in the spiritual business of how to thwart the Devil's temptations and to purge the soul through confession. This did not however occur in the seclusion of a box, but in letters addressed to learned fellow-Brethren.

What influence the precepts had on the twelve-, thirteen-, fourteen-year-old Albrecht, whether they had any at all, is impossible to say. Conceivably his spirit was infertile soil for this seed. No more than a guess can be hazarded as to what other cud was furnished for his young intellect to chew on.

Bohemia was a large and mighty kingdom. Other lands, Silesia, Lusatia, Moravia, whose lords made much of an imaginary independence, belonged to it. The King, Rudolf, resided three days' journey from Koschumberg in his castle in the great city of Prague which comprised three towns, the Old, the New and the Lesser. Its founder had been the heathen princess and sorceress Libussa, a name shared by one of Albrecht's aunts, so numerous he could hardly know them all. A queer character, the King, as everybody agreed, and a bad ruler. Nevertheless, seeing that he was King, elected by the lords and knights of the land, and his father and grandfather had been too, he would remain so until he died. He did not even speak Czech and was a Papist, though associating with Protestants as well. His Principal Master of the Horse was Uncle Adam, Adam von Waldstein, a Catholic despite having a Protestant father. Catholics were not to be trusted. They were mischievous and rejoiced when Protestants met with bad luck. It could happen that a cousin and a gentleman, like Wilhelm Slawata, would suddenly present himself as a Catholic. That had to be put up with. Religion was a dividing factor, but in the long run class and kin were more important.

The Estates were the lords and the knights. The towns had representation in the Diet, but the burgesses were not entitled to advise the King, for all that he, alas, as gossip maintained, took advice from quite impossible people, valets and fire-layers. The peasants were entitled to nothing at all. If they were disobedient, banded together and fundamentally misconstrued Protestant dogma, just punishment was meted out to them in the same way as at Linz, where when Albrecht was fourteen, a peasant leader was quartered. Lords existed too in countries which did not belong to Bohemia, in Austria and in Hungary, but where the King of Bohemia none the less ruled. Alliances could be formed with them, all the more so as they were almost all Protestant. The King had many kinsmen, closer and more distant, members without exception of the exalted archducal Habsburg House and regents or governors elsewhere, at Vienna and Innsbruck, in Styria and Spain. King Philip, the second of his name, had been ruling that country for almost fifty years.

The Germans obeyed a multitude of princes and also the King in Prague, who was the Holy Roman Emperor. The number of Germans in Bohemia was high. Hard-working, the best craftsmen, miners and merchants, they were not always popular. The towns of Silesia had gradually become German, those of Moravia nearly so. But not in Bohemia. Where the Waldsteins had their properties, there had formerly been more Germans than now. In Prague, the capital, the total was increasing, with two large churches unable to hold them all, and whenever in the crush of the lanes a welcome occasion for violence arose, the cry of "Kill the German dogs" resounded. The cry of the rabble, not the nobility, who held German civilization in esteem and had not been left unaffected by it. Albrecht was Czech. How should he be anything else? But I think that his first teacher, Hans Graf, whom he subsequently created Lord of Ehrenfeld, was a German and that he had already learned the language from him.

The real enemies of the country and of Christianity were not, of course not, the Germans. They were the Turks, and the Sultan was the mightiest potentate on earth. He never kept quiet. Lord Vilim of Waldstein, only shortly before he died, equipped four foot-soldiers against him and, together with his brother Karl, four mounted ones. What, though, were these against the five hundred thousand men waiting in the Sultan's camp for the next campaign? This camp was not at all far. The Sultan was master of most of Hungary and could at any moment launch his pashas against Moravia and Silesia, or Styria, or wherever he pleased. When Turks took Christians prisoner, they sold them into slavery. Evil events like a Turkish foray or the death of a king were heralded by a comet. Sometimes blood rained from the sky. At others loud trumpet blasts were heard, nobody knew whence, the clouds parted, and up in the heavens two hosts were seen in conflict. The significance of such a manifestation was uncertain, but it boded no good. Maladies which must quickly prove mortal abounded. The worst was the plague, then a typhoid called the "Hungarian sickness". Gout, painful but not fatal, was the lot of most older men, particularly among the nobility. The spirits of the dead were to be shunned; bad things could be heard about them. For instance, an unfaithful servant of King Rudolf who took his own life had after a while to be disinterred and his corpse burned to cinders because Rucky (the malefactor's name) had been seen in the palace at night, astride a ram and accompanied by six grey cats, ghosts too. . . . Prayer was a protection, like the castle which was home and the family to which one belonged. There was another form of protection against the world's wicked disorders and lurking dangers, but that Albrecht found out only later.

He stayed two years at Koschumberg. Then, some say, he was sent to the Jesuit college at Olmütz. Others assert that it was the Latin school at Goldberg in Silesia, which is the right version. Not that the first is inherently impossible. With their well-planned curricula designed to render learning a pleasure and to substitute *honesta aemulatio* for uncouth penal discipline, their healthy, broad-minded physical exercises like swimming, fencing and dancing, Jesuit educational establishments were the best anywhere. Even non-Catholics, whose children the sagacious· and adroit fathers readily admitted, though not as boarders, had to grant as much. It would however have been difficult to fathom if, of all people, a member of the community of Bohemian Brethren had entrusted his ward to the Jesuits. Historians who believe it explain the process, artificially enough, by an illness or mental blank on the part of Heinrich Slawata. No explanation is needed. Incontrovertible is that in 1597 Albrecht Wallenstein arrived at Goldberg. Between his stay at Koschumberg and at Goldberg no time is left for him to have been at Olmütz. At this point a reader may ask how this fact comes to be known, how indeed anything comes to be known about the lad's circumstances. Let me answer the question as concisely as possible.

A WORD ABOUT SOURCES

Available are a few letters written by Wallenstein when he was fourteen and sixteen respectively. They are, as we shall discover, of official character but informative enough. This is the least muddied of sources. The more the pity that the spring's flow is not more abundant.

Furthermore there are marginal notes, set down much later. Again in his own hand, they deal with his horoscope, predictions by one well-versed in the science of the stars, and they include some which look back so as to compare the actual course of events. But these notes start only in 1605 and are witness to the years after attainment of majority, not those of orphanhood.

Finally we have the biographies composed shortly subsequent to Wallenstein's death. That by Gualdo Priorato was published in 1643 at Lyons and dedicated to the King of France. Priorato served under Wallenstein. He may therefore have seen him – he describes him as "pale, fair rather than dark" – or at any rate have heard about him from such as knew him, since on occasion he refers to informants. Priorato's account contains inaccuracies as well as much that is correct. When he is inaccurate, he seems to have misunderstood matters or to be passing on fallacious traditions rather than exercising his inventive powers. In addition he is fond of flowery elaborations and observations of the most general kind.

The other contemporary biography is Count Khevenhüller's. Indeed he wrote two short monographs on Wallenstein's life.

Senior Hereditary Master of the Horse in Carinthia and Senior General Commanding the Slovene-Croat Frontier, imperial Carver, Senior Keeper of the imperial Silver, Lord Chamberlain to the Holy Roman Emperors Matthias and Ferdinand, Count Franz Christoph Khevenhüller was, as his titles indicate, a great courtier and diplomat, although, as his titles fail to indicate, not always to his own advantage. When he was ambassador in Madrid, for example, his salary was so far in arrears that one day he could no longer buy bread and had to sell off his own and his wife's clothes at ludicrous prices. A not unusual fate for those who served the House of Austria, which Khevenhüller none the less continued to do. Five years Wallenstein's junior, he survived him by seventeen. Death did not right away furnish this extremely active man with the rest he deserved. "That Count Khevenhüller is said to show himself grieves me. 'Tis surely not he, but a spirit in his shape. God grant him salvation," wrote his sister-in-law. That Wallenstein and Khevenhüller met during their attendance at court is certain on one occasion, probable as regards others. Khevenhüller had access to official documents and made ample use of his opportunities for the purpose of his *Brief Lives*, as well as for his main and monumental work, *Annales Ferdinandei*, a political history of his age in twelve folio volumes. He spent his life in surroundings which enabled him to glean much authentic material about the renowned persons of his day and class, that Austrian and Bohemian nobility which, previously separate, was merged under Ferdinand II into a single caste. Khevenhüller used authentic material and mere rumour too. His was an age strangely reckless in the fabrication of events that then were dragged along in text after text until, towards the end of the nineteenth century, some sharp-witted brain proved their non-existence.

Neither Priorato nor Khevenhüller know anything about Albřecht's residence at the Jesuit college in Olmütz and his conversion there to Catholicism. Knowledge of this is to be gained from a third biographer, the Jesuit father and Bohemian historian Boheslas Balbinus. A godchild of Wallenstein and a warm admirer, Balbinus belonged to another generation. He began work on his history of the seminary at Gitschin, weaving into it the life-story of its princely founder, thirty-four years after Wallenstein's death. His was a labour of love. In Castle Koschumberg he asked to see the room where seventy or more years ago lessons were given. He studied carefully the diaries and annual registers kept by the fathers at Olmütz. They did not contain anything about young Wallenstein's stay and conversion, nor could any witness to a happening seventy years ago still be living. It was a story current at the college that Balbinus took over, one which he had perhaps heard as a child and never doubted, like that about how two champions of the Catholic faith, Lord Jan Kawka of Ričan, another uncle of Albrecht by marriage, and Father Veit Pachta, took up the cause of the boy because they recognized his high talent and tore him away from the Bohemian Brethren. Being brought into the care of the Order of the Society of Jesus at Olmütz, the scales soon fell from his eyes and he adhered to the true religion. All that could have been true and was for long held to be so by those who accepted it from Balbinus. In fact, though, Albřecht was still Protestant when at fourteen he entered the Latin school at Goldberg. He arrived there from Koschumberg, not from Olmütz.

THE LATIN SCHOLAR

The school had been chosen by Lord Heinrich on the advice of a friend, Baron Karl von Zierotin, a great man in Moravia and a respected Brethren communicant. This is the conclusion to be drawn from a letter by Wallenstein wherein he says that his admission to Goldberg was due to the good offices of learned Master Laurenz Circlerus. Headmaster at Goldberg for a short period in the 1580s, Circlerus had been Zierotin's tutor and accompanied him to Strasbourg and Basle. The beliefs of the Swiss reformers were for the Baron, of whose austere character we shall glean a few examples, his prop and his stay; he called Basle his second home. So Albrecht, attended by preceptor and servant, journeyed across the Riesengebirge into richly wooded Silesia to the little town which the map shows lying close to Liegnitz and took up residence in the house of learned Laurenz Circlerus's nephew. His meals he had with one who was to become his stern instructor, Precentor Fechner.

What did they teach at Goldberg? A possible answer is to refer to the requirements Wallenstein laid down when he himself came to found a school. "See to it," writes the Duke of Friedland in 1625 to his provincial governor, "that from time to time they ride out once a week with the riding-master so that they accustom themselves to sit astride a horse, diligently apply themselves to arithmetic, and perhaps play a musical instrument. The organist will be able to teach them . . . and a clavichord may be purchased in their behalf." And four years later, "Pray, have yourself a diligent care and, if 'tis not done, advise me, that the boys keep themselves clean in all respects, go early to school, are versed in the Latin tongue, of an afternoon learn to write in German and Italian, as also arithmetic, and to dance and strike the lute." Conceivably there is here an element of the Jesuit style of upbringing. At Goldberg matters may have proceeded along less aesthetic lines. The school anyhow enjoyed a laudable tradition. The pupils must never dare to avail themselves of German. Even at the end of the day their conversations had to be in Latin. The authors whose prose and poetry they had to be able to imitate were Romans: Terence and Plautus, Cicero, Virgil, Ovid. This poet's *Ars amatoria*, though, will hardly have been included in the curriculum: the school regulations imposed strict continence and forbade any sort of intercourse with young women. Propriety was writ large. No intoxicating drinks, no nocturnal outings, sobriety of dress, politeness to one and all, especially masters. Lying was of all offences the most heinous.

Goldberg was a Latin school of the classical type. The region was German. The Dukes of Liegnitz were descended from the old Polish Piast dynasty, but had in time become German like their neighbours and peers, the Dukes of Brieg, Münsterberg, Jägerndorf and the like, whom they met at the Silesian assembly of rulers, German and Protestant. The same held good for their subjects. But there were others, in the villages and east of the Oder in the towns, whose native tongue was Polish. Sons of the Polish nobility as well as Germans studied at Goldberg. In the town hall's cellar tavern Latin invective flowed freely between the nationalities, Catholics and Lutherans, patricians and burghers. Albrecht, neither German nor Pole, looked on. Subsequently, as imperial Generalissimo, he came for well-considered reasons to attach importance to alliance with Poland. It did not inhibit him from dropping the uncannily modern remark, "Poles are Germans' natural enemies." Memories of Goldberg lingered.

He too experienced animosity. How people like to call others names, threaten and pretend to hate them, is as familiar as how strangers furnish a welcome target for such an itch. Albrecht, walking proud of mien through the little town's streets, his servant following with his books, was not spared such humiliation. One occasion is the subject of the first letter in his own hand that we possess. The superscription runs, "To the Noble Puissant Honourable and Well-Named Lord Wencelao of Czedlitz, Governor of the Principality of Liegnitz, My Lord and Friend," and the letter sets out how he was not merely showered with abuse, but at night had stones thrown through the windows of his bedroom until finally, after suffering other indignities, he was pursued over the threshold of Precentor Fechner's house by a stupid bully of a soldier with drawn sword.

The letter is Albrecht's own composition. Had his host helped him, the German would be better. Instead it is still rather bungling and tangled, displaying none of the terse mastery of the language which he gained later. What emanates however is that, mature for his fourteen years on account of his early orphanhood and frequent change of surroundings he knows, although feeling defenceless in a foreign land, what is due to the dignity of his name. He has suffered affront until the cup is full to overflowing. Now he has no other recourse than to complain to authority and to see whether a stranger is wholly without protection. In this instance, because the provincial governor knew what was owing to a member of the Bohemian nobility, protection was not lacking.

Our knowledge of Wallenstein the Latin scholar nears its end. In August 1599 he left Goldberg, perhaps rather sooner than originally intended, as the plague began to ravage the region. His odyssey next took him to Franconia. Koschumberg was no longer important since Lord Heinrich Slawata, a second father to him, had died at the beginning of the year. Damozel Jitka of Waldstein had assumed his guardianship, but the old maid will hardly have been able to exercise much authority over the nearly grown lad. On 29 August we find him inscribed as a student of the Nürnberg Academy at Altdorf: "*Albertus a Waldstein, Baro Boh., Johannes Heldreich, praeceptor Görlicensis Lusatus, Wenceslaus Metrouski fam.*" Whether these two were the same attendants who had accompanied him to Goldberg must remain an unanswered question. In any case his mentor was now a German, and one saddled with a hopeless task.

THE UNRULY STUDENT

The academy had a good reputation. Originally the Nürnberg *gymnasium*, its university status dated only from the 1570s after its removal to Altdorf, where the scholars were meant to be freer from the agreeable temptations of the big city. With some fifteen professors and two hundred students, an atmosphere of intimacy prevailed. The alumni included numerous sons of the Protestant Austrian and Bohemian nobility. From 1580 to 1584, for instance, Georg Erasmus von Tschernembl, eloquent leader of the Upper Austrian Estates, had pursued his education at Altdorf, and pursued it to good purpose, bringing home with him a medal of honour, profound knowledge of the law and many a learned book dedicated to him by professorial hand. At Altdorf knowledge was there for the taking by those who wanted it.

Perhaps rather more in Tschernembl's days than two decades later. Student generations and their dominant mood succeed one another quickly. Before dealing with Wallenstein's experiences and behaviour at Altdorf, something should probably be interpolated about contemporary university habits as a whole. The exemplary Ingolstadt academies, its college and its university, under Jesuit direction and attracting pupils from as far afield as Poland, Denmark, England, Switzerland and Spain, were the only exceptions to the rule.

Habits were distinctly rowdy. A satirical verse of 1617 –

> From Tübingen sans wench,
> From Leipzig, sound of paunch,
> From Helmstädt without cracks,
> From Jena without chaps,
> From Marburg still alive,
> He hath not studied at all five

held good for the other seats of learning too. At Dillingen manslaughter among students was so frequent that the wearing of swords had to be forbidden. The Marburg Annals for 1619 lauded the fact that a whole year had passed without murder. The records teem with tales of accidental pregnancies, dissolute drinking-bouts and bloody frays, the last of these partly between students, partly between students and the university towns' citizens. As for the professors, who should have been pictures of propriety, as we now say, they often presented a tarnished image. The example of Dr Scipio Gentilis, teacher of jurisprudence and in 1598 Rector of Altdorf, who liked to rampage at night through the town as the ringleader of drunken students, thrashing harmless citizens, gashing them with sword-thrusts, smashing tables and chairs, and who, when he had in virtue of his office to act against the sinners led astray by him, frankly confessed that what he was doing he did not believe in, need be regarded neither as typical nor yet as a glaring exception. Else the incongruous jurist would not in 1613 have again been elected His Magnificence the Rector.

Albrecht Wallenstein quickly and cordially welcomed this state of affairs. Recently, it was alleged, Herr Wolf Reipp, chief alderman of the town council, had been "vexed to death" by students. How they managed that is not quite clear, but at any rate Wallenstein was prepared to participate in whatever they were up to. In fresh surroundings, with the sap of his sixteen years, attired in the splendour of the patrician student's dress with its military touch, supervised on the spot by a preceptor who evidently soon ran off (not one word more is heard about him) and at a distance by a helpless female guardian who could not sustain the role for long, would it not have been surprising if he had not played the ruthless adult? He was one of the party when, three months after his arrival, students paid off a certain Dr Schopper for we know not what offence. They marched in the small hours to the man of learning's home, presented him with their jeering compliments, splintered his door, shattered his windows and promised to return the following night.

The Nürnberg Superintendence, its aid implored by the terrified pedagogue, instructed the Altdorf Superintendent to protect Schopper's life and limb as well as "discreetly" to inquire "who the wanton spirits are". Their names, those of the ringleaders, turned out to be Baron Waldstein, Gottfried Sebisch from Beslau, Jaroslaus Sokolintzky and Johann Lopes. They had to appear before the academy's senate. Scipio Gentilis did his best to defend them, but they seem to have been sentenced to a brief period of duress.

In vain, if the intention was to inculcate repentance. On 23 December Wallenstein, Sebisch, Hans Hartmann of Steinau and a few more devotees of scholarship encountered during their evening stroll Ensign Wolf Fuchs, citizen of Altdorf. A dispute ensued, became fiercer and culminated in Hartmann of Steinau running his blade through the soldier. Fuchs died on the spot. The same night Steinau made his escape, the gates being closed, across the town's roofs and walls. The annals of the university record that Wallenstein "played his part" in Fuchs' demise. He and his friend Sebisch, again summoned before the senate, were severely reprimanded and their respective relatives requested by letter to remove as soon as possible trouble-makers who evidently had no intention of taking their studies seriously. These measures did not, however, satisfy the indignant citizens of Altdorf or the Nürnberg magistracy, all the more for the suspicion that Steinau was still hiding in Altdorf. Searches of student quarters were instituted; their inhabitants offered armed resistance. The Superintendent called out the citizens and had reinforcements brought from Nürnberg. A battle between the arrogant aliens and the doughty locals, with swords, daggers and halberds being wielded to the sound of tocsins, seemed imminent, but the energetic intervention of commissioners from Nürnberg put a stop to the commotion. They promised that justice should be done and began a fresh inquiry into the murder. While they were still sitting, Wallenstein stabbed a fellow-student in the leg. That was on 9 January 1600. Events now followed so fast upon one another that it becomes difficult to put them in their proper order. On 10 and 11 January Wallenstein, Sebisch and another malefactor are inmates of the Nürnberg prison-keep. Next day Wallenstein is released, though with the injunction to remain at Altdorf and with an extremely severe reprimand. It refers not only to "every kind of irresponsible action", but blasphemous conduct too: by unheard-of impiety he has "not spared the Holy Trinity derision and abuse" and he should ponder whether he has not really earned corporal punishment. Perhaps he had tried to alarm the commissioners themselves with imprecations and been lacking in respect in every other way. On 14 January, back in Altdorf, he thrashed Johan Reheberger, his German servant, and left the lad in such appalling condition that he had to be sent to Nürnberg for exhibition of his bruises to the highest academic authorities. Wallenstein excused his behaviour by reference to his servant's laziness – he had found him idling by a window. The authorities refused to entertain the explanation, ordering the Baron to pay a fine of thirty gulden and "to arrange a settlement with the lad's friends". For Reheberger was not entirely without protectors. His guardian, the baker Christoff Amberger, and his friends, the butcher Hans Bauer and the tailor Hans Vestner, took up his cause with a will. Especially the butcher's wife decided to make the most of the matter. She demanded, in addition to the fine and apart from the doctor's fee, no less than a hundred gulden compensation. So we see the young patrician engaged in highly embarrassing negotiation with the menacingly deployed townsmen, prepared to pay because he must, but not the whole amount. He offers forty-five gulden, three taler outstanding wages and four gulden for a new suit, from which conclusions may be drawn as to the state of the old. The townsmen declare themselves satisfied with the offer (it was probably more than satisfactory), but the butcher's wife only "howls and cries". Wallenstein paid five gulden on account and the rest the following month. The time-lag clearly shows that he had to send home for the sum.

Bearing in mind that the cases of Dr Schopper, Ensign Fuchs, Gotthard Livo or Livon (the student wounded in the leg) and Johan Reheberger all occurred within the space of five weeks, it is intelligible that the government of the Free City of Nürnberg had had enough of the Bohemian Baron. In a letter to Rector Dr Taurellus, its council decreed: "We therefore herewith enjoin you on account of the foregoing causes to confine your Lord of Walstein [sic] to his rooms where he shall have his meals served and be denied egress until such time as he shall by payment be exempt of the debts he hath incurred at Altdorf and, when this same hath happened, to tell him forthwith to remove himself from Altdorf and seek abode elsewhere." The order is dated 12 January. If our dates are right, it did not even include the Reheberger affair and the reference is to other debts.

The unruly youngster now sat confined in his quarters with, we assume, a moustachioed guard in front of the door and, we would like to assume, something of a smile, though mixed with haughtiness, playing over his face as he at once sent two fellow-students to Nürnberg to plead for the remission of his punishment. This he was not granted, but at least some "ventilation". For his meals the Baron was allowed to resort to his usual host and, if he wanted, he could attend lectures and sermons. He must however continue to abstain from every sort of roving about the town or the precincts before the gates. The council's amiability encouraged the quarter-prisoner to make another move. In a letter carefully holding the scales between contrition and gentlemanly pride, he thanked his "gracious friends" for their measures of relaxation. Their edict did none the less contain something that unfortunately could not be construed as other than unspoken proscription from the university. Such could not but redound to the shame and detriment not only of himself, but also those high-born lords, Karl and Adam von Waldstein, Privy Councillors to His Imperial Majesty, and indeed of his whole honourable house. Wherefore he ardently solicited that the unspoken relegation as well as the remaining portion of his confinement be entirely repealed and the day upon which he should leave Altdorf left to his own discretion. For his part he promised to satisfy his creditors, never again to vex the council and ever more to behave in a manner behooving a gentleman: "Yr obedient Albrecht Waldstein." The name is spelt with a "d" in the signature, a "t" in the body of the text. The signature is Wallenstein's own; the letter was written and, I suspect, drafted by someone else. Scipio Gentilis? The German is the officialese of the time and the argumentation, for all its humility, comprises a threat, though shrewdly veiled.

The distance from the republic of Nürnberg to "golden" Prague was not great, but the magistracy could have little more than a very approximate notion of how things stood there, what part the two Waldsteins did or did not play as Privy Councillors, and with what kinds of unpleasantness they were capable of wreaking vengeance for an affront to their house. The council's reply was consequently couched in evasive terms, simultaneously giving ground and maintaining its rights: proscription had never been mentioned, but the confinement must be upheld. Albrecht killed time in his mildly restricted freedom until his debts were paid. Then, after a six-month stay, he shook the dust of Franconia from his feet at the end of February or the beginning of March 1600.

For successful men at the height of their careers to meet again old teachers, or their successors, and to derive a certain titillation from the occurrence is not unusual. In the same way Wallenstein had subsequent contact with Goldberg and Altdorf. In 1626, when the Generalissimo paused at Goldberg, he ordered the aged Fechner to appear before him, expressed in generous terms his gratitude for the Precentor's former well-merited, beneficial strictness, presented him with a hundred taler, and had a guard posted in front of his house. Fechner's receipt for the money is preserved in the Breslau city archives, or it was, prior to the disorders of recent decades. The old man probably attached more value to the guard than to the silver.

Six years later, when the great duel between Wallenstein and the Swedish King was being enacted in Franconia, Croats took captive Nüssler, Rector of Altdorf and a physician. Wallenstein put him to work as military surgeon. Nüssler had no liking for the role and asked the university to submit a petition which the Generalissimo would undoubtedly sanction if it were properly phrased, meaning along the following lines: Seeing that to the Duke's well-known reputation for heroic qualities there had recently been added that for a noble magnanimity to which so many prisoners owed their freedom, how could it be otherwise than that he, the Rector, too should come to know this magnanimity and the university receive a fresh pledge of His Grace's old-established princely disposition towards it . . .? All that in Latin.

Another memorial penned in Latin, dated 1633 and one of many well-informed but fundamentally hostile papers passed by Wilhelm von Slawata to the Emperor Ferdinand, states that what people thought of the Commander-in-Chief before he attained high office was no secret. He had commonly been called (at this point the writer breaks into German quotation) "Mad Wallstein". *When* was he called so? Surely not as a child at Hermanitz nor at Koschumberg, where commonly no German was spoken and the ten- or thirteen-year-old boy can hardly have given occasion for such a nickname? It seems best suited to the Altdorf days. But how did Slawata know what the Altdorf stick-in-the-muds called their short-term guest? "Mad Wallstein" is what he certainly was then. This aggressive *joie de vivre* of Altdorf was later replaced by a restrained, stately manner. Now and again, though, the violent temper he contained and which poor Johan Reheberger had been the first to experience, was loosed in oaths and gruesome orders. The trait stayed with him to his last hour, when he is supposed to have cursed more terribly than ever before. It is the way we change in life, slipping into another skin, yet flesh and blood beneath remain the same.

After Altdorf followed the two-year trip through France and Italy; the residence at Padua (Europe's contemporary Athens) and the homeward journey. He had the monuments to his parents erected and donated a bell, piously inscribed, for the Hermanitz church. These actions betokened that he was now of age and bore responsibility for the domain. They furnished no answer to the question assuming an ever sharper edge: what should he do with his life?

He grew a beard, Spanish fashion, and wore his hair short. Some say it was dark, others that it tended to reddish. The latter I doubt, for he subsequently showed a horror of red hair, as also of overlong noses and other physical peculiarities offensive to his aesthetic sense. In his youth he was handsome, with a high and noble brow, darkly glowing eyes, a slender frame standing about five foot eight. The fact has been confirmed apart from descriptions and portraits of the day. For his ups and downs, turbulent as they were in life, continued beyond death, whether as regards the immortal part of him or his mortal remains, and in this century, his coffin, already changed several times, was once more opened. What survived of the skeleton was handed to anthropologists for examination. The bones showed traces of illness late in life. They also attested to what, in good health, his dimensions had been.

The World in which he will have to Live

IN the dawn of history the predicate had been Pharaoh, "the great house", Lord of the Realms, Builder of the Pyramids. Now it was "I and my House", "I and my worshipful Arch-House". For the elected Holy Roman Emperor, King of Hungary and Bohemia, Archduke of Austria, to discuss politics was to speak of matters pertaining to his own and his family's wide-ranging interests, also such as touched on God and the Holy Faith, more rarely about those concerning christendom, because this word included, or could seem to include, religious communities whom there was no intention whatever of including. Almost never was there any reference to the public weal. Thus it had been four thousand years ago. Thus it remained for ever after.

The House of Habsburg has a big part to play in our story, and it is no unknown quantity, this power hatched from a series of marital alliances and accidental heritages. By this time it was considered to be by far the strongest in Europe. It was divided into two branches, the Spanish and the Austro-German, yet in such a way as to ensure that through the marriage of near relatives their boughs criss-crossed again and again. The Emperor Rudolf, since 1576 head of the German branch, was the great-grandson of Johanna the Mad twice over, through his father, the son of Ferdinand who had been the Emperor Charles V's German brother, and once more through his mother, who had been Charles V's daughter. From his twelfth to his eighteenth year he had been brought up in Madrid at the court of his uncle, King Philip II, and he was slightly mad too.

The feeling of divinely ordained unity which cemented the dynasty did not prevent cracks, of estrangement or even hostility, running through its structure. Rudolf at Prague listened to the Spanish party – the ambassador, envoys of a less regular calibre, and native magnates adhering to the Spaniards as a matter of rigidly conservative conviction. He listened, and he did not listen. He had need of it in his stealthy conflict with the instigators of intellectual and social unrest, the Protestants, who in their various breeds amounted to nine-tenths of all

Bohemians. But he mistrusted it, partly because he felt himself to be German, partly and more particularly because he was an excessively suspicious individual, jealously watchful of his royal rights. In 1599, a Princess of the German branch, Margaret, sister of the young Archduke Ferdinand, Regent of Styria, married King Philip III. Her journey to her new home, with ceremonial halts on the way, lasted six months. That was long. Couriers normally took a month. Her mother accompanied the Princess. Neither of them liked Spain at all. "Everything they say is untrue," was the new Queen's verdict on her subjects. Madam Mamma held a similar opinion: to get on with the Spaniards it was necessary "to put on airs and graces".

She hailed from Bavaria, this mother, Maria, sister of Duke William V and aunt to Duke Maximilian, a man with a cold, distant look and reserved manner concealing a fervently devout soul, who in 1597 had taken over his country's rule. The Bavarian House of Wittelsbach could almost be regarded as a collateral of the Habsburgs. The same multifarious kinship linked by common interest, the same internal tensions. By origin the Wittelsbachs could consider themselves to be Habsburg's betters, but, hemmed in by the latter's might and nearness, they were now incomparably the lesser.

How a single family calling itself the exalted Arch-House and consisting of two monarchs plus a couple of dozen generally very mediocrely gifted princes came to hold sway over a major part of Europe is a question claiming an answer. It runs something like this. The Habsburgs were at the top of a stratum where each layer simultaneously bolstered the one above and pressed on that below, until the last and broadest endured the load alone. Social structure by Estate rested on community of dominating interest. No king without secular and spiritual sub-heads – magnates, landowners, bishops; no magnates without king. Whether a minor nobility, whether a privileged and wealthy middle class were feasible without magnates and king had yet to be seen. Those few free republics which did exist furnished no conclusive proof for or against. At any rate, the newly founded republic of the Netherlands, uniting the Seven Provinces, did not think that it could do without a semi-monarch, its Stadtholder, the Prince of Orange. If a king made any encroachment upon the lords, the landowning nobility which was the estate closest to the top of the stratum, he had to proceed warily, divide the enemy, win over one group or at least be certain of strong outside help, else the days of his rule were numbered. Possessed of determination, diligence, sagacity and tenacity, he could to a considerable extent

clinch matters in his own favour. Without such endowment he would
merely preside, leave the reins of government in the hands of cliques
whose members came from the highest ranks of the nobility and sometimes from somewhere totally different, and play them off against each
other. Should he show himself to be wholly unsuited to office, an
eccentric, a misanthrope, a fool, his subjects' patience was great, though
not infinite.

Their patience was great because they believed in the sanctity of the
office and whoever held it. Their belief was of its essence. Lacking this
magical mortar and based only on the strength of self-interest and
hidden or open force, the hierarchy would not have held. To be sovereign
by God's grace, anointed and crowned, that was something. It imbued
the potentates with a feeling of eminence and security in circumstances
where others' courage would have waned. A monarch who lacked belief
in the sanctity of his rights would have been lost. We find no example of
it.

The creed of the House of Habsburg, like that of its smaller collateral,
Bavaria, was Roman Catholicism. Had this been what it formerly was,
catholic in the word's exact sense of universal, it would not have lent the
dynasty the support and identity that it did. The creed of no longer
more than half of Europe, a creed with antagonists and therefore itself
characterized by antagonism, a creed threatened and aggressively
defensive in the Austrian part of Germany as well as ferociously threatening to those suspected of betraying it inside the Spanish domain, it was
in this newly pugnacious, exalted manifestation the bastion of Habsburg.
It was the creed of the Jesuits, the Soldiers of God. Where God has
need of such soldiers, soldiers with another style of play will not be
lacking, nor sparks to fly and ignite their game.

Great was the distance separating Spain from Austro-Bohemia. Did
the consequently protracted exchange of communications admit of
common planning and action? The question could just as well apply to
the whole of Europe. The latter resembled a magnetic field, with every
power in direct or indirect touch with every other, regardless of bad
roads, dangerous sea-lanes, the months or seasons keeping them apart.
Politician corresponded with politician, merchant with merchant,
intellect with intellect. Vivid, packed with itch for knowledge and
psychological insight, were the reports arriving from afar. Now and
again a writer's impatience, almost despair, at the ignorance and indifference of those at home would break through. The more difficult contact
was to foster, the more determined must have been the energy of those

who fostered it, considerably more determined indeed than nowadays and intensely more serious. Politicians looked far ahead and had long to wait until the plans which they had concocted evoked response and came to fruition. The calculation they displayed was not on that account any the less circumspect, intransigent or malicious than what we meet today. Maps might be clumsily drawn, but Spanish commanders knew very well what roads led from Italy to eastern Switzerland and the Tirol, the Rhine, the Netherlands. Diplomats and monks in diplomatic mission took care of the political traffic, merchants of the economic, natural philosophers, erudite humanists, astronomers of the intellectual. Art was thoroughly European, no nook or cranny strange to it. Regional relationships were close, making of many lands a kind of bloc akin in ways of life, sentiments and visions, and they existed where today we should not go in quest of them. Scandinavia and the Netherlands constituted one; Upper Hungary – later termed Slovakia – Austria, Moravia, Bohemia, Silesia and Cracow another. There were transverse connections, especially of a religious kind, between every one of the provinces mentioned. From Bohemia to Amsterdam and The Hague, Geneva, Basle, Heidelberg, Oxford and the Huguenot parts of France. From Poland and the Catholic territories of Germany to Rome. From the courts of Prague and Vienna to Madrid. Exchanges between the two Habsburg branches were facilitated by the Spanish Empire's far-flung but permanent forward posts in Brussels and Milan.

Considering the impediments, the amount that Europeans knew about one another is astonishing, although too little in the light of what their amicable and inimical designs upon each other were. He hardly knew Sweden by name, said learned Duke William of Bavaria, so how should he pass judgement on its policy? Barely fifty years later the king of that country was to ride into the Bavarian capital as conqueror. Because economics, power politics, seafaring and wayfaring, not to mention community of creeds which recognized no frontier, were linked throughout the continent, its conflicts, internal, international and longstanding, tended to proceed via combination to magnification. Because information was inadequate, grave and rash mistakes would be made, a distant enemy underrated, as Gustavus Adolphus of Sweden was at first greatly underrated by Maximilian of Bavaria, William's son, or the other way about, a distant friend overrated and help expected from whence none came, as matters were not as had fondly been imagined.

Not altogether beside the mark was what those in the know thought about Spain – that the empire was on the decline and poor, despite gold and silver carried in galleons from the newly discovered world, that the stony heartland of Castile was incapable of pumping fresh life-blood into the ponderous body and later, that the son and grandson of Philip II were totally unequal to their royal calling. When an empire like the Spanish decays, it decays long. Ruled by a caste accustomed to govern and to enjoy the most splendid advantages from government, defended by a chain of forbidding fortresses from northern Italy to the southern Rhine, past master of the art of war, Spain continued to be for Europe's politicians the epicentre of fateful decisions, and what the Spanish ambassador advised the King-Emperor at Prague was generally acted on. Neither the French nor the British were Spain's arch-enemy. Enemies, yes, but such with whom from time to time it was possible and imperative to come to terms. The arch-enemy were the Netherlanders, the States-General, called for short the Dutch, seceded provinces and at Wallenstein's birth rebels of fifteen years' standing.

The struggle, it has been said, was between two civilizations with no choice but to belabour each other until one of them was down. The one static, still medieval, dominated by landowners, monks and soldiers. The other, dynamic, already middle-class, brilliantly successful in its orientation towards profit-making enterprises of a new type. Radically contrasting qualities which found intellectual expression in the latter's adoption of Calvin's teaching. We shall not spend much time brooding on the validity of this explanation. Anything can lead to war. Nothing need lead to war. Between the Spaniards and the Dutch existed a state of war so incessant that in 1600 a man had to be elderly, in 1630 hoary, to recall its beginnings. The Spaniards conducted it under the illusion of restoring their empire and subduing insolent republicans. The Dutch fought initially for their lives and bare existence, gradually for expansion, then enrichment round about and on the Seven Seas. Theirs was a totally different Europe. From the gable-roofed town-houses, from the bleak naves, from the piled-up decks of the warships and merchantmen riding at anchor in the harbours, from the parade-grounds where soldiers were drilled in the most modern techniques of discipline, from the rich pastures of the Rhine delta radiated stimuli whose effect was felt throughout the continent, whether in cognate societies such as the German coastal cities or ones with an entirely dissimilar structure, Bohemia, for example. Those who were of Protestant faith looked to Holland. Those who belonged to a chafing, discontent estate and wrangled with their king, especially if their king was a Habsburg, pinned their hopes upon Holland. Hopes which the Dutch at least did not discourage, because they could not be other than agreeable to them. Spain personified Habsburg. Austro-Bohemia was under Habsburg domination – for the present. The empire, still styled Roman and Holy, lay under a species of Habsburg mandate difficult to define. The more of these territories that were alienated from the dynasty, the better. The Dutch, without knowing it, followed an imperialistic path full of promise for the future. Some of its milestones were the launching in 1602 of the East India Company, the inauguration in 1613 of the Amsterdam stock exchange together with activity in and the terminology of "shares", the conclusion in 1613 of a commercial treaty with the most distant realm in the world, Japan, and the foundation in 1616 and 1626 respectively of the cities Batavia, on the island of Java, and New Amsterdam, on the island of Manhattan. We are slightly anticipating events, as such a cursory inventory and perspective surely permit. When Batavia began to be built, Wallenstein was young yet, just on his way, far from arriving. The Dutch were soon to be his concern; Java and Manhattan, never.

The springboard from which Spain's imperialist politicians hoped to suppress the great middle-class uprising was the southern Netherlands, the portion that Philip II had been able to retain: Luxembourg, Flanders, Brabant, the city of Brussels. Shortly before his death the King, wiser than tradition has it, awarded these "Spanish Netherlands" – again a convenient misnomer – a measure of autonomy. They were to transact their affairs through their own councils and Estates and be bound to Spain solely through the person of the regent and the inexorable laws relating to religion. This step did not prevent Spanish policy being pursued at Brussels in a manner sometimes cloaked and slightly mellowed, but in a crisis undisguised, vigorous and brusque. The regent was Philip's daughter, the Infanta Isabella Clara Eugenia. Her intended had been none other than her cousin Rudolf, the Holy Roman Emperor. He however had no serious inclination for marriage. For eighteen years he put off the Spanish court with promises until the last thread of Philip's patience finally snapped and he wedded his over-ripe daughter to Rudolf's brother, the Archduke Albrecht. The move is the easier to understand if it is borne in mind how awkward it was for the ageing maid to play her part at Brussels without the help of a male co-regent. None the less Rudolf did not understand it and now was embittered at his brother's gain, which he had trifled away by eighteen years' frivolity. The archducal pair of regents conducted their business as sensibly and well-meaningly as they were allowed. Eventually, in 1609, they even accommodated themselves to ending the war with the seceded north as being "free Provinces and States to which" they laid "no claim". Whether that signified international recognition of the States-General was obscure. If it did, the pronouncement was that of the regents in Brussels, not of the King in Madrid. The peace was to last twelve years. Simply an armistice, even if for so long that none could foretell how affairs would proceed afterwards. Such limited conclusions of peace, although they subsequently went out of fashion, were not unusual and were more often than not respected. Affirmed in the name of God, seal and signature afforded necessary protection in a dangerous world. Whoever denounced an armistice before its expiry stood in bad shape before his peers and the gazetteers. "Afterwards" depended on internal Spanish developments, on whether the imperialist party, the *partido militar*, would gain the upper hand, or that which pleaded for a policy of renunciation abroad and remedial treatment of the ever more palpable social malaise at home. It also depended on the Netherlands. For one thing is certain – in a long-term perspective it always takes two to wage a war.

Peace, lasting, not limited, had since 1598 supervened between France and Spain. To be sure, anyone properly acquainted with the political map and knowing how Spanish power constricted the French to south, east and north could predict that this peace would none the less not prove lasting. King Henry IV himself predicted it during a confidential talk in 1609. The reconciliation of France and Spain, he expounded, was a chimera: the greatness of the one was the ruin of the other, with the converse holding equally good. Marriage alliances – such took place shortly after this conversation – or good will could achieve nothing against the power of facts. France, he continued, had been put on the right road, but it was not yet at its journey's end. Certain territorial coping-stones were still essential: in the north, Flanders; in the east, Lorraine. Inside the country the source of all order was the royal authority. Hence the military and financial resources which he had so diligently accumulated to make him, and after him his son, *absolute*. Hence too why in the long run only *one* religion was admissible, the Catholic, things being what they were. He took Protestants like Catholics into his service and saw to it that they received their full due, but he hoped to bring them back, step by step and peacefully, to the Old Faith. Thus spake the ruler who had been a Calvinist champion, for worldly reasons put up with his attendance at mass, and again for worldly reasons granted Huguenots the most unheard-of privileges, making them a state within the state, with levies, fortresses and treasuries to be filled

by the King and with their own synods, general assemblies and ecclesi-
archs. The capitulation was supposed to have permanent validity, but
by Henry's reading it would have but temporary duration, for as long as
need be. It contradicted the principle he wished to effect – a unitary
realm inside firm boundaries with a unitary state of order, religious
uniformity constituting a part of that too. He who adhered to the
ruler's creed was his obedient servant. He who did not adhere was not
his obedient servant, or stood at least in suspicion of latent disobedience
in secular matters as well. Why should a unitary realm, such solitary
source of order, really have to be? Kings are seldom philosophers. They
head for an objective. Reaching it, they head for another. "Why" is not
a word in their vocabulary.

The conflict between France and Spain, its apparent alleviation during
the first two decades of the new century simply the prelude to a fiercer
eruption, was not, however, one between civilizations. The differences
between these two societies were not as radical as that. Nor was the issue
one of religion, but of power, between states and their usufructuaries.
That is why Henry IV and even more his successors, keenly though they
aspired to a national unity of Catholic orientation, felt no scruples
whatever about lending support as best they could to Protestants and
rebels outside their realm. Piety was a motive capable of inspiring
mundane acts. Theological dogmatism constituted a power, often
malevolent and eating into the souls of men. Court chaplains, pulpit
preachers and priestly pamphleteers baited each other in the lewdest
terms. But if a political question was at stake, confessors and pastors
alike subsided and discovered some ground or other why in this specific
instance reasons of state outweighed God's enigmatic will. The example
set by Henry IV, conversion from one denomination to another when an
enticing heritage or similar advantage beckoned, was copied by numerous princes, particularly Germans, on a smaller scale. For a monarch to
regard his subjects' and his own salvation as a transcendent responsibility
and be ready to lose country and people rather than yield an inch of his
divine duty did occur, but it was the exception. Such an attitude may be
thought praiseworthy; its consequences were not.

As France helped the Dutch in the new century, so England under
Queen Elizabeth had in the old. Aid at first dissembled, then open to the
point of provoking Spain into its hideously shattered attempt at invasion.
Nor had religion been the main cause at that time. The link between
militantly democratic Calvinism dominant in the Netherlands and
purged, pope-less semi-Catholicism in England was tenuous. James I,

Elizabeth's Stuart successor and ruler over what was now the United Kingdom, was laxly loquacious about the spiritual problem. The difference between the denominations was fundamentally not so deep, he assured his listeners, and "no bishop, no king" – a notion whose confirmation the future held in store for his House. James was a distinctly continental, distinctly political animal, political in the notorious Machiavellian sense, bent on alliances which had nothing to do with religious controversy. England's gradual divorce from Europe, under his own government and his son's, was not his fault. The responsibility lay with the growing dispute between crown and middle class, not wholly incomparable with that between the Spanish Empire and the Netherlands.

Every state competed with every other – the closer, the more fiercely – and no amount of common creed, enmities, perils and resultant leagues were of much avail. The struggle was for coveted territories, commercial routes, fishing rights, trade as such; sovereignty of the seas, which served trade, security and greatness; titles and forms which denoted the greatness. So it was between England and Spain; England and the Netherlands, despite their old association; Denmark–Norway* and Sweden. The last two kingdoms belonged to the same cultural sphere if ever neighbours did. Lutheranism's uncontested preponderance flourished there with a vigour scarcely met anywhere in its land of origin. They should surely have been friends. They were, up to a point, but friends constantly eyeing one another with suspicion and sometimes going to war, as from 1611 to 1613 as well as once more later, because each would dearly have liked to turn the Baltic into its own *mare nostrum*.

The struggle for the Baltic was not new. As long back as 1563 an Elector of Saxony complained that Sweden's treatment of German shipping was rough, "all for the purpose of engrossing the cargo and the commerce with the Muscovites, the sway and mastery of the entire sea, and ousting the Holy Empire's estates and cities from there." A manifold struggle. Between Sweden and Denmark which, still controlling a part of Sweden's southern coast and the Sound, demanded a high toll of all those plying the salt waters. Between these nations and Poland. Between the three of them and Muscovy, as yet without a foothold on the Baltic but worldly wise pressing towards it. A detached, northern and eastern struggle, nevertheless bound up with the other main antipode whose

---

* Denmark and Norway were at this date under a single ruler, the former being the predominant partner. See also note on p. 39 (translator's note).

centre lay on the Rhine and concerned Spanish Habsburg, France, the western German princes and cities, the Netherlands and England, because in the European lists all were in quest of confederates and foes. In 1614 King Gustavus Adolphus concluded an alliance with the States-General. In the eyes of the Spaniards a faraway country, Poland, constituted a power suited to its partnership.

That had not always been the case. Not during the second third of the preceding century when young Polish nobles acquired their education at Wittenberg and Geneva as well as in Huguenot France and the cry "Away from Rome" was echoed among the middle classes. Polish links with German and Latin intellectual life were profound. No line of art and thought failed to find creative reflection there, Lutheranism deriving from the north, varieties of Bohemian religiosity in the south, humanism at Cracow's thriving university. Towards the end of the century the forces of the Old Church rallied for counter-attack, spear-headed by the King, prosperous noblemen prepared for material sacrifice, and Jesuits winning over souls through their academic foundations, practical assistance, persuasive sermons, scholarship and presentation of beautiful or entertaining spectacles. Success held out the promise of more success. At the date our tale begins Poland, seen from without, was a Catholic power even if among its refractory nobility Protestantism of the Genevese brand survived.

A great realm, Poland, with a key-position in eastern Europe. It brought together the far north and the far south, touching here on the area of Hungarian–Turkish troubles and often dragged into them, there on Sweden and the Swedish possessions on the southern littoral of the Baltic. It brought together east and centre, stretching into regions as distant as Vitebsk, Kiev and Cossack territory later subject to the Tsar. At the outset of the new century it could still hanker to have Moscow for its vassal while possessing as liege-lord a sort of sovereignty over Prussia. It shared frontiers with the lands of the Bohemian crown. The elective Polish kingship was moreover as much in demand as the German, and more easily won. A French prince, a Magyar magnate owing fealty to the Sultan, the Prince of Transylvania and a Swedish Vasa had succeeded one another upon the throne. Power fantasies veered from south to east to north according to the inclination of the ruling dynasty. In the 1590s it looked as though Poland and Sweden would become united: Sigismund Vasa, elected King of Poland, of Catholic sympathies and a Habsburg relative by marriage, was also King of Sweden. An entirely different northern empire would have replaced the dissolved Scandinavian Union:* Sweden, Finland, Livonia and Poland, with Warsaw as the focal point. At the end of the sixteenth century such a structure was thought feasible. It illustrates how flexible political and national identities were, or at any rate appeared to be. A mistake, in this case. Sweden's nobility and peasants did not want to be Poles, much less Catholics. A senior Vasa, Duke Charles, rose against his Polish nephew, become a stranger in his own country, and forced him to abdicate. Gustavus Adolphus, Charles' son and successor, saw Poland as his arch-enemy until such time as there arose another whom he regarded as even more dangerous. Having wrangled profitably with the Muscovites and deprived them of Karelia, he sought their friendship against Poland. Therewith began an elastic and not very effective relationship, but one outlasting the years of our story.

All these power conglomerations lacked many of the qualities constituting what was later termed a state. They were harassed, often brought to a condition of apparent paralysis, by the separatist ambitions of provinces and cities, by insurgent vassals, religious wars and the struggle for division of power between monarchy and polyarchy, King and Estates. None the less they were on the way, indeed well advanced, to becoming states of the new stamp, each in a different manner: Sweden, Denmark, the Netherlands, France and England. Two institutions had, however, relinquished hardly a jot of their claims which derived from the Middle Ages (as awareness of undergoing major changes now led the past to begin to be called): the Pope's spiritual regiment at Rome, operative everywhere and combined with carrying on the practical politics of a secular Italian state; and the Emperor's Empire, Holy and Roman. It was not allowed to be dubbed German, and it scarcely ever was. People talked of Germany, but not of the German Empire, because this Empire was meant to afford law and protection to more nations than just the German and its Emperor to be the head of Christendom. The dream of this dignity was a favourite with Rudolf II, all the more the less it corresponded to reality.

The Empire's structure was a tangled mass of precedents, resolutions, judgements and election capitulations.† The Emperor was chosen by

---

* Also called the Union of Kalmar (1397–1523), whereby Denmark, Norway, and Sweden were brought together under the Danish crown. The Swedes always represented an element of dissidence. A war of independence (1520–23) was successfully fought by Gustavus Vasa, founder of the royal dynasty and ancestor of Gustavus Adolphus (translator's note).

† Election oaths by the Emperors, of varied formula, swearing to maintain certain traditional privileges of their subjects, to rule only through the Diet,

seven Electors. Three, the Catholic Archbishops of Mainz, Cologne and Trèves, were themselves elective. Four were the temporal rulers of the Palatinate, Saxony, Brandenburg and Bohemia. The participation of the last was an anomaly. Not only did the King of Bohemia belong to the dynasty from which for centuries the Emperor had regularly proceeded, but lawyers could not decide whether Bohemia was an Estate and member-state of the Empire at all. The Emperor acted in agreement with the Electors, who looked on themselves as a second imperial government; with the Diet, the motley and hierarchical joint representative body of the Estates; with the *Reichskammergericht* (the imperial court of appeal), whose members were nominated on an ingeniously confederate basis; with the Aulic Council, whose members he picked on his own and who were more accommodating to his interests. To those of the Empire too? That might have been the case if the Emperor had been no more than its personification, sovereign, and supreme representative, equally so in all provinces. Instead he was, in terms of square miles, its most powerful territorial prince and what he could do to its advantage or disadvantage depended more on his own resources than on those that the Empire was prepared to furnish. Some of his territories – Bohemia, Croatia, Hungary – were neither German nor imperial. He was a member of a supra-national dynasty whose interests comprehended Germany without being concentrated there. He was Catholic and this did not, as in France, mean an agent of the state over against a militant minority, but champion of one religious party *vis-à-vis* another which in the interior, Germany proper, could claim to be by far the stronger. That is why he was no clear fount of imperial pacificatory authority. At a distance, on the northern coasts, he was a very shadowy figure about whom, seeing that he could neither give nor take, hardly anyone bothered. The Catholic Estates trusted him only within very narrowly drawn limits; the Protestants not at all. The more scrupulously he viewed his antiquated imperial duty, the worse were the troubles he must cause. The failing and the merit of Maximilian II, Rudolf's father, had been that his conscience permitted him patience, tolerance and scepticism.

Below the Emperor were the Estates – the principal dukedoms and margraviates, with or without electoral right; the bishoprics, holding

keep foreigners out of imperial appointments, and neither declare war nor put anyone to the imperial ban, i.e. outlaw him, without general agreement (translator's note).

sway over wide regions; the imperial towns,* middle-class republics, fortresses and trade centres, without fuss more than a match for many a prince as regards money and capacity for self-defence: imperial abbeys, tiny imperial municipalities,* imperial villages* and imperial knights. The Estates were divided by mundane and spiritual interests as well as a blend of each. Catholic members, estranged in other respects, were united on religion; among the Protestants disharmony prevailed even in that, Lutherans and Calvinists harbouring for one another an acrimony even more venomous than both together against the Catholics. The settlement of 1555 was still the basis for Catholics and Protestants living side by side.† It had stood the test of time better than could have been anticipated. The trouble was that the things it was supposed to settle had meanwhile changed and not remained in balance. The teachings of Luther and Calvin might be lacking in their original depth and passion, but they had spread in ever-broadening circles, partly as an expression of class aspirations, partly because the princes sought means to aggrandize their incomes. If the subjects of an abbot or bishop became alienated from the church, the temptation to secularize such ecclesiastical domain was manifest. During the course of decades rich lands had fallen into the lap of Protestant Estates, whether by simple annexation or by the appointment of so-called administrators, members of important Protestant families, in the place of bishops. To restore to the church what it had lost was a postulate of the Catholic Estates. To retain such property and to apply the principle behind its acquisition further and further was that of the opposition. Both sides were now in a defensive stance which did not fall far short of an offensive one. An ideological dispute, started nearly a century ago and thought to have been half-bereft of its explosive force forty years earlier, was moving towards a fresh climax. One indication followed upon another. In 1605 the *Reichskammergericht* ceased to function on account of a Lutheran's election as its president. The Catholics were not prepared to recognize his jurisdiction. In the same year Protestant princes, led by the Elector Palatine, once more left a session of the Diet in protest, declaring that the controversy about restitution of ecclesiastical properties could never be subject to majority resolutions. And again in the same year the Emperor put Donauwörth‡

---

* Also termed free cities, towns, villages (translator's note).

† The Peace of Augsburg. It recognized the Lutheran creed on equal terms with the Roman Catholic, but excluded all others (e.g. Calvinists). The imperial Estates received the privilege of deciding which should prevail in their territories, leading to the formula *cujus regio, ejus religio* (translator's note).

‡ A free city (translator's note).

to the imperial ban because its citizens' behaviour to a neighbouring, provocatively pious Catholic community had been all too flagrant. The Duke of Bavaria was entrusted with implementing the edict. Maximilian had the town occupied, first by soldiers, then by Jesuit proselytizers, and finally kept it as a pawn to compensate for his outlays. Rudolf II had in this instance conscientiously acted out his imperial role to the point of breaching imperial law. A bad omen. To discuss this, and how the consequences might nevertheless be averted, proved a favourite topic for debate in honeyed tones sticky with attachment to peace. No one, however, came forward to put a brake on the course of affairs slowly but surely approaching a crisis. Indeed no one could come forward short of being a god endowed with power to bring order at a stroke into the bedevilled German body politic. It was not a land divided into two parties where one was capable of defeating the other or both were susceptible to working out a new productive compromise. It was a chaos, with groups of aspirations fighting, colliding with and mutually exclusive of one another, in so far as those behind such aspirations merged into any grouping and had any idea of what was left to aspire to. Everyone wanted to preserve "the meritorious imperial constitutions", mainly because change, while known by experience, as a matter of principle was strange and repugnant to them. What the ancient constitution provided, though, was a point about which there existed as many versions as there were parties and politicians concocting schemes.

EMPEROR RUDOLF AND THE HEREDITARY LANDS

The Archduchy of Austria divided into four parts: the Lands Above and Below the Enns; Inner Austria, consisting of Carinthia, Styria, Carniola and Gorizia; the Tirol; and the glacis provinces of Alsace and Breisgau; these together constituted the territories of the German Habsburgs called, for simplicity's sake, the Hereditary Lands. With perilous inaccuracy Hungary and Bohemia were included in the term, in the case of Bohemia with all the regions theoretically attached in perpetuity to the crown of St Wenceslas – Moravia, Lusatia, Silesia. The inaccuracy arose from the Habsburg arrogation of hereditary rights which the Estates there denied or at best allowed with reservations. The whole complex of lands originated in a way similar to the Spanish–Burgundian–Netherlands one, although over the years it proved an incomparably firmer structure. Rudolf II resided at Prague.

An unsuitable hereditary ruler comes as less of a surprise to our habits of thought than one who fails after being summoned to office by electors with a choice in the matter. That happens too. At all events Rudolf, anointed inheritor in a line of heirs, ruined his heritage. Not that he was lacking in fine qualities. He had a keen intelligence provided that it was not clouded by some momentary urge, all too decided an opinion of his high responsibility, tenacity and an extremely subtle artistic sense. Prague, thanks to his presence, became an international centre, a city of inspiration for people of many nationalities as well as the most various tastes and talents. The fact that Rudolf was half-Spanish, and that when a decision in politics was unavoidable he regularly sided with the Spanish party, did not inhibit him from tolerating a swarm of foreign Protestants in his vicinity. Painters from Holland and Italy, doctors and humanists from Silesia and Upper Hungary, Tycho Brahe from Denmark, with and after him Johannes Kepler from Swabia, the most celebrated astronomer of the day, not to mention all kinds of eccentrics and imposters. The border-line between science and magic was as yet blurred. Rudolf was an amateur of astronomy, physics and medicine. Versed in wood-carving and clock-making, his taste was eclectic. He loved what was already regarded as old and classic; he would pay any price for a Dürer. He was equally receptive to the most modern, daring explorations into the world of dreams and that which touched on the demented. Such labyrinthine arts may have been safe enough for those expert in them, but they were dangerous for one of Rudolf's basically precarious mental condition.

Insanity is usually said to "break out", a description which rightly implies that it takes root long before its manifestation. Rudolf's nature was known to his contemporaries to be enigmatic when at twenty-four he became King of Bohemia and shortly afterwards Emperor. Around 1600 word spread that he was mad. The Elector Palatine, on whom it would fall to act with his Saxon colleague as imperial regent if there was an interregnum, thought it his duty to obtain an unofficial opinion on the Emperor's state. His spy reported that there could be no gain-saying His Majesty's grasp of politics in unclouded moments. He was however the victim of a severe melancholy. Its recurrent bouts rendered him incapable of all action and entirely dependent on creatures of obscure origin and even more obscure character. His attitude to those in holy orders and to spiritual consolation was also strange. This remark was more than amply borne out by the Prague Nuncio, who told Rome that out of the Emperor spake the Devil. Further causes of astonishment were the monarch's sensitivity to noise, and a shyness which led him to avoid the company of the most distinguished councillors, let alone people in the mass such as, for instance, the Estates assembled in Diet. There were too his sudden rages and, a repeated feature, morose exhibitions of faith or lack of faith. In that age, it should be added, the personality of kings, due to the glamour of their office, could mould patterns of behaviour, especially where imaginative youngsters were concerned. So here and there some of them – we have one particularly in mind – may later to some extent have unconsciously taken Rudolf for their model.

Of his brothers one, Albrecht, lived in Brussels, entirely absorbed by his delicate duties as regent. A second, Maximilian, a boor with a strong political streak, held court at Innsbruck. The eldest, Matthias, resided as the royal governor in Austria. From the outset jealousy, that trite passion, had been responsible for dissensions between him and the head of the dynasty. Nothing of his brother's gifts and their concomitant hazards was to be found in Matthias, although other common characteristics were not lacking. He shared Rudolf's love of power without the strength to exercise it. He was spiteful, sluggish, and could not be bothered to read the most important dispatches. They were passed to Melchior Khlesl, his principal adviser, provost of St Stephen's cathedral and chancellor of Vienna university, son of a baker, later a bishop, still later a cardinal. Khlesl, crafty man of God and political craftsman, had the presumption to lecture his master: "To know people, to take an interest in affairs, to act, to proceed prudently, *that* is to reign and to rule, *that* stirs people to deeds, inspires respect for a prince. But everyone relies on Your Majesty" – he was writing after Rudolf's death – "asking for nothing and letting matters take what course they will." Both brothers had been unmarried so long that this, for a prince, unbecoming condition could not now appear other than final. It will be recalled what a procrastinating game Rudolf had for eighteen years played with the Infanta Isabella. When that was done, and his aged mother would not stop plaguing him to provide for legitimate offspring, he talked vaguely of his devotion to a Muscovite princess, though no one had or in future would have any more precise details about this barbaric lady.

The melancholic's unwedded state rendered all the more urgent the problem of the succession in the Hereditary Lands and in the Empire. Its traditional settlement was by election of a King of the Romans, as he was styled in the Middle Ages, with status as imperial deputy and subsequent entitlement to the crown. To pick a candidate for this dignity from his own family and have him voted by the Electoral College was the demand with which all, Spanish and papist politicians to the fore, concerned for the House of Habsburg and Germany's Catholic future did not cease to importune the Emperor. As long as the question was not settled, they urged, catastrophic consequences remained possible. The most various outsiders, like the Duke of Bavaria (a mistake), the King of France, indeed even Protestants like the King of Denmark and the Elector Palatine, were not free from suspicion of casting a speculative eye on the imperial diadem. Rudolf, however, hated any reference to the delicate subject, much as old egotists in fear of death do not want to hear anything about composing a will. He espied in it an attempt to infringe his privileges, a secret plan to wrest from him in his lifetime the sceptre which brought him little happiness but which he enjoyed threatening to relinquish voluntarily, while simultaneously clutching it to him with trembling hand. When his ministers tried to pave the way for a Spanish envoy who came to Prague on this mission, he chased them away with a furious cry of "I shall have no peace as long as these people are about me! Go, tell them to be off, that I may no longer have the sight of them!" Here was an outbreak of neurotic suspicion that similarly caused his brother's fearful, un-concerted efforts always to miscarry.

There remained the Emperor's younger cousin, Archduke Ferdinand, regent of Inner Austria. A specimen of mankind totally different from the difficult brothers. On the best of terms with God Our Father, which was the main thing, a happily married man, a good son, a conscientious father to his people. Kind-hearted, provided piety did not demand cruelty, full of the joy of life and fit as a fiddle. His mother, Maria of Bavaria, had borne fifteen children, twelve of whom escaped death in infancy. Regardless of the Burgundian–Spanish pomp prevailing at the Habsburg courts, she brought them up in a lively, straightforward, practical manner. She saw three of her daughters become queens, two of Poland, one of Spain. Before her eldest son reached his majority she effectively acted as regent, taking the sound approach to this task that has often been displayed by women of vigour and good sense. Ferdinand, prior to assuming the reins of government in 1598, made a pilgrimage to Loreto, where he entered the confessional, inspected the chapel's treasures and watched a woman being exorcized of a demon who was forced to articulate his name, Insalata. The prince, happy to see her delivered and devout, talked to the woman. On his return he promised his mother that he would rather lose all the world's wealth than do hurt to God's religion. "That the eternal is ever to be preferred to the temporary" was the principle which to the end of his days he truly took for his guide in all his acts. At first the Graz townsfolk, Protestant to the core, laughed when this youth marched with his priests through the streets behind the Host. The spectacle was soon to cease to be funny.

In 1600 Ferdinand married the Bavarian princess Maria Anna, sister to Duke Maximilian, his cousin. The marriage forged another link between them. Their school-days together at the Jesuit college in Ingoldstadt had not been without friction. Once there was a squabble about precedence when, the seventeen-year-old Bavarian having taken top place in church, twelve-year-old Ferdinand stepped in front of him. The upshot was a prolix, pungent correspondence between parents and kinsmen of both princes. The incident illustrates their relationship – lifelong companions in fortune and a friendship never free from tensions. Maximilian was incomparably more outstanding, meaning stronger-minded, graver and more penetrating, made more of less, and on occasion laid down the law to the Habsburg while always preserving the forms appropriate to one a grade lower in degree. His piety appears as not merely the outcome of Jesuit methods of education, but a quality immanent and vibrant in the depths of his soul. In utmost privacy he practised penances, fasts which alone would have tried his cousin in Styria hard enough, and flagellations. He wore hair-shirts beneath his robes of state. Later, on the opening of a tabernacle bequeathed to the monastery of Altötting, it was found to contain a slip of paper whereon was written in the Duke's own blood the dedication to the Holy Virgin of his life and the long years of hard work ahead of him. Ferdinand, on a reliable footing with the Heavenly Powers as long as he faithfully performed everything the dictates of his conscience demanded, would never have gone to such lengths.

A retinue of twelve hundred horsemen accompanied Maximilian to the wedding at Graz, a capital beautified at the hands of Mantuan architects. The festivities lasted a week, with triumphal arches raised in the streets, the court church alight with fresh resplendence, stirring sermons, dramatic spectacles presented by the Jesuits, entertainments by musicians from Milan, banquets, and dancing from noon to night. The Styrian Estates grumblingly footed the bill. The bridal pair's apostolic blessing was conveyed by Cardinal-Legate Franz von Dietrichstein, Bishop of Olmütz.

All Habsburgs cherished fundamentally the same views about the right order of things. Inside the Empire the Protestants were not to be

allowed to extend their progress beyond what they had attained before
1555. Any advances since were unlawful. They should be forced to
surrender them whenever and wherever possible. In Habsburg territories the task was to reduce the power of the Estates, representing the
nobility and the cities, to a measure consonant with the majesty of the
ruling House. This programme compounded worldly and spiritual
ambition because the Estates, in Bohemia and its subsidiary lands as well
as in Austria and Hungary, were in the main not Catholic. The realization of these aims had, however, a long way to go. The Estates were
firmly entrenched behind their rights and their economic power. Money,
needed at every hand's turn, particularly for the everlasting Turkish
hostilities, was not to be had without them. They, for their part,
wavered between their duty towards their countries' defence and the
worry that an army under Habsburg control might one day not be
incapable of doing something other than tussling with the Turk. Another
factor was that the rivalry secretly smouldering between Rudolf and
Matthias forced them both to woo the favour of respectively the
Bohemian and Austrian Estates, a process during which they pretended
to be more broad-minded than they were and scattered promises that
they had no intention of keeping.

The first to venture a frontal attack, not against the Estates but against
the non-Catholics, was Ferdinand of Styria. Hardly did the reins of
government lie in his hands before he had the Lutheran preachers
expelled, their churches closed and their dangerous books (ten thousand
in number) burnt in front of Graz's city gate. On this followed the strict
order that all citizens – for the present he spared the nobility – would
within the space of three Sundays at the latest wait on their local priests
and enter their names in the mass-book, or leave the country. And behold,
some emigrated, the vast majority acquiesced, and soon no land was more
Catholic than Styria. The Archduke had little money and few soldiers.
The Lutherans would not have been very hard put to it to overpower
him and his supporters. Mysteriously they did not, did not even try to
do so. His success was as instructive for the young Archduke as for his
family in Austria and Bohemia. Since the turn of the century the
Catholic party had taken the offensive with fresh courage. For Austria
the "Catholic party" signified, simplifying matters a little, Habsburg and
the dynasty's allies, the majority of the nobility, against the majority of
the middle class. For Bohemia and Moravia, where constitutional law
was of a finer weft and the sense of history keener, where two nations
lived in jumbled juxtaposition, where the ruling House was alien and the

King also the Emperor, where Spain had its hand in the game, where the Empire was multifariously represented, with Prague a European centre and politics practically a profession – for lands in such circumstances no simplification is admissible.

BOHEMIA AND MORAVIA

Franz von Dietrichstein was born at Madrid, where his father was imperial envoy, in the same year as the Archduke Ferdinand. His education was put in the hands of the Jesuits who conducted the Collegium Germanicum at Rome, and this enterprising establishment would have abundant reason for pride in its pupil. He was Cardinal and Prince-Bishop of Olmütz at twenty-one, the latter dignity entitling him to a seat in the *Landrecht*, Moravia's highest court of justice and, in practice, a committee of the Estates assembly. The German prelate's presence immediately sparked off a critical squabble. Never, he was told, had anything but Czech been spoken here, he too must not use any language other than the one he was not master of, and to have to communicate this to him in German was in itself preposterous enough. An old nobleman recalled his father's rebuke, when he had as a child uttered some words in German, that he might as well bark like a dog and have done with it. This had been the way of their fathers; this was the proper spirit. Dietrichstein retorted that he could, if they preferred, address them in Latin, but he would not let himself be degraded to a dumb clod. He read the oath in Czech. His pronunciation was thought not at all bad, his gesture in swearing by the Mother of God and all the Saints as offensive as it was illegal. At subsequent meetings the Cardinal employed the services of an interpreter until, diligent as he was, he had mastered the native tongue.

If initially it was the intruder's speech which irritated the Protestant lords, soon it was his conduct too. None surpassed Dietrichstein in the zeal with which he threw himself into the task of reclaiming souls for the Old Faith. Severe in Olmütz, where he could afford to be severe, he set an example of how to woo adherents in places where for the time being severity could not be applied. With what ardour the young Bishop scurried through the land, praying, teaching, making friends, here thrusting a mediocre speaker from the pulpit and continuing his sermon for him, there leading a procession barefoot; exorcizing the Devil, receiving confession from plain folk, giving absolution in large assemblies to contrite heretics; consecrating priests, feeding the poor, daily and hourly performing tasks not normally associated with the duties of a high ecclesiastic. His sermons were so exciting, enticing and menacing that many a Protestant, of the nobility too, and especially their ladies, did not disdain to be numbered among his audiences. Not a few of his listeners sooner or later appeared in His Eminence's anteroom with serious supplication. Indeed conversion became the fashion. Under Dietrichstein's influence the freshly converted competed in the fulfilment of their duty with such as had never abandoned it. Some lords, it was alleged, were not content with chasing their vassals to mass with hounds, but also had their jaws torn apart with pincers to force the Host down their throats. Not that the proselytizers were really as tactless as that. It was a cheerful invention of their enemies. . . . Only a few years after his ungracious reception in the *Landrecht* Dietrichstein was deputy-governor of Moravia. Neither the favour of the court at Prague, which he frequently visited, nor the favour of the Pope, whose principal agent at Prague he had risen to be, furnish sufficient explanation. Neither the Emperor nor the Pope could interfere directly with the Estates' privileges. Adroit push, follow-up, pressure and placing as well as bold action at the right moment gave a minority, which in the circumstances was bound always to remain a small minority, a growing influence incommensurate with its numbers. Those who had been circumvented, the majority of nine out of ten, watched the process with impotent bitterness.

A comparable trend was to be observed in Bohemia, on and from which Moravia must be envisaged as being dependent and independent. The Margrave of Moravia, with his capital at Brünn, was the King of Bohemia at Prague. The Bohemian Chancellery found ways and means of intervening in the affairs of the collateral lands. The Moravians, however, still held their autonomy dear. The Estates elected their own governor or demanded at least the right to advise the King on his nomination. He had to be a member of the Moravian nobility, his election made him the representative of the crown and his country's highest dignitary, he was the presiding functionary in the *Landrecht* and Estates assembly, and he was the head of a body of officials. Bohemia did not have complete freedom of religion. Moravia did, leaving aside the territory of the Bishop of Olmütz. If landowners forced their religion on their vassals, their action was illegal. Persuasion was permissible, coercion was not. In practice the distinction was blurred.

For all the political separation between the two countries, the links between them were close. Links of religious community and the multifarious interests connected therewith. Of language in any case, but even more of a language whose future both sides held to be endangered. And of family. Bohemian lords either were at the same time Moravian or became such by marriage. Wilhelm of Slawata, for example, turned into a wealthy member of Moravian society by allying himself with the last heiress of the Neuhaus stock, and, within the limits allowed him, amply endowed his tenants with religious instruction. Of the equally well-off politician Karl Liechtenstein it would have been difficult to say where he belonged. In 1599 he was a chief justice of Moravia, in 1600 a privy councillor at Prague, in 1604 the Governor of Moravia. He had been one of the first to surrender to the glowing blandishments of the Bishop of Olmütz, although the fire in his own soul burned low. His was a cool, calculating brain. He retained contact with his former co-religionists just as long as politics allowed, completing the breach the moment he realized that they no longer did. So vigorous an opportunist is difficult to assign to any party, more particularly as the Spanish party, to which since his conversion he belonged, was not a party in today's sense of the word. Even assuming that an individual's attitude to party is not subject to fluctuation or the state of passing power and advantage, to identify a personality with specific views is quite often wrong because, leaving aside the most exceptional characters, views are assumed, modified and cast aside without his personality coming to grief.

The Spanish party, this much is clear, consisted of the Spaniards at Prague, those constantly resident and those visiting there with instructions. For the Habsburg German–Slav dominion not to fall apart into a heap of Estates-ruled bodies politic could not but be a principal interest of Spanish politicians. Also of the Papacy. To that degree the envoys of the Pope and the King of Spain played the same game. To them should be added a small minority of the Bohemian and Moravian nobility: families or portions of families which had remained or again become Catholic and, with bland Jesuit assistance, introduced Spanish brides into the country; the Lobkowiczs, Liechtensteins, Slawatas, Martinitzs, Rosenbergs, Neuhaus and Pernštejns, although the last three houses died out at the turn of the century. The party could have counted on the Catholic clergy if that body's moral probity had been greater than it was. It could count on the Jesuits.

On the King-Emperor it had to count because what it aspired to was, so to speak, an aspiration on his behalf. He was, inherent in the logic of the matter, its chief. Rudolf II, they say, was essentially a man of peace, in favour of acceptable compromises, and did not for his part like the

Spaniards. We are prepared to believe it. There are remarks, actions, or at least samples of dilatory behaviour, which point in this direction. They were, however, sham liberties which he allowed himself, who had no real liberty. For to him, like all Habsburgs, heresy and rebellion were ultimately the same. Nor, even if he had wanted, would he have been permitted to abandon the identification at a time when the urge to break away from one another and fall into a hostile clinch was growing in both Germany and Bohemia. Half-pushing, half-driven, he tolerated that the struggle for key positions should regularly go in favour of the Spanish party. The appointment in 1599 of Zdenko Lobkowicz, Jesuit pupil and a "Spaniard" of the most rigid school, to head the Bohemian Chancellery amounted to no less than a well-prepared *coup d'état*. Liechtenstein's summons to Prague served a similar purpose. This unfanatical convert seems in the long run, though, to have been too little Spanish for the Spaniards.

Whether the issue was religion or power and its amenities is a retrospective differentiation. It was in religion that individuality and freedom, pride and hope in life were sought. Now a decree by the new administration, proclaimed in Prague by imperial heralds to the roll of drums and the blare of trumpets, proscribed every member of the nobility, the middle class, and the peasants who was not Catholic or Utraquist. That meant three-quarters of Bohemia's population. The Utraquists, or Old Hussites, had long since lost their fighting character and were reckoned almost as Catholics. The decree struck at the Lutherans, who were very numerous, particularly in the towns, and at the Bohemian Brethren. This matchlessly pious, zealous sect was fewer in numbers than even the Catholics, but the strongest in influence and probably in riches too. For a century and a half the Brethren had rendered the most estimable contributions to the country's theological, humanistic and political education. The decree signified outlawry. Their debtors no longer needed to pay them; their marriages and their wills lacked validity. The *Landrecht* contested its construction, an act whereby Bohemia's supreme court took sides against the King. There was prodigious speech-making in the assemblies of the Estates, orations full of erudition and passion. Utterly in vain. But because the decree was neither rescinded nor consistently implemented, the troubles it was supposed to abate were merely augmented.

Among Protestants it had become customary to lay the main blame for the slowly and steadily more envenomed situation at the door of the Jesuits – "these blood-thirsty, throughout the world justly abominated *turbatores publicae pacis* and through their lethally indited scrawls more than all too well-known windbags," as they were described in a Bohemian pamphlet of later date. Catholic historians have retorted that the blame lay not with the Jesuits, but with the fanatical agitation against them. Were not tales told of how they chopped little boys into pieces, how one of them had had a child, and how their scheme was to massacre all Protestants on the pattern of St Bartholomew's Eve in Paris? The age, like every age, was credulous. We know better. The Jesuits fostered the sciences and helped their needy adepts even when, like Kepler, they were not Catholic and did not become so. Their schools and colleges, whether like the Clementinum at Prague, intended as a counterpart to the Protestant Carolinum, or the new Olmütz university, were outstanding seats of learning. A particularly commendable feature of their teaching was that at all levels it was free of charge. Morally the Jesuits were impeccable, which could not always be said as regards some of the older Orders. Far too true were stories of abbots who squandered the bequests to their monasteries, of monks who shared their cells with mistresses or partook in lay dress of night-life in the towns, where encounters with nuns on similar expeditions caused them no surprise. That kind of tale, if told of Jesuits, was empty slander. They were on hand where there was danger. They nursed those sick of the plague and died in the process, God's dutiful soldiers. In many spheres they inspired enlightenment rather than obscurantism. Why, then, the loathing of them? They were a sworn community with their own secrets, partly real, partly imaginary ones deduced by outsiders from the success of their activities. Intellectual weapons are of all weapons the most dangerous. Protestants outside Bohemia could not, even at several removes, compete with Jesuit calibre. While not despising ordinary folk, the Society's practical principle was to stick to the rich and powerful, to the heirs to resounding names and fortunes who had to be secured at a tender age, to those lords over many souls, the princes. Appropriate them and, sooner or later, their subjects would be appropriated too, as the example given by Ferdinand of Styria showed. The Jesuits, ran the rumour in Bohemia, incited important potentates against each other, governments against their subjects, subjects against their governments. By their threat of eternal damnation they coerced sovereigns into following their evil counsel. All secrets became theirs through the confessional, and their domination was such that even good could be done only with their permission. They had also amassed lands, as formerly happened with the Templars. That faith need not be kept with heretics was their notorious tenet. The Order's members defended themselves with dignity. It was regrettably true, was the tenor of their answer, that all kinds of dissension existed and must inevitably exist where more than one creed subsisted under single rule. That was not their fault, they continued, nor could they help the jealousy and hate that their zeal for the propagation of the Catholic faith aroused among dissenters. How could they abandon their duty to serve God and instruct the young? It was a dispute in which each felt himself to be in the right. Insoluble, but the observer standing above party cannot fail at least to concede that the proposition Them or Us, pregnant with calamity, was formulated most trenchantly by those whose education and resources for catching souls were the most refined.

CONVERGENT DISORDER

Every land had its own forms of government. In each the objectives which parties tried to achieve in the teeth of opposition were different. None the less everything that happened between Transylvania and Amsterdam, Stockholm and Rome did hang together, and everywhere restless, resourceful minds who perceived this coherence of affairs brooded deeply upon it. The Lutheran Estates of Austria kept in close touch with those of Bohemia and Moravia. They also kept in close touch with western German Protestants. They ignored the fact that the most active among them, those in the Palatinate, swore by the teachings of Calvin, that German Lutherans (particularly at Dresden) regarded Calvinists as a more hateful pack than Catholics, Turks or heathens, and that Germany's Protestant Estates consisted of princes (monarchs, properly speaking) who curtailed the rights of their own representative assemblies whenever they could, whereas the Austrian and Bohemian Estates voiced the views of a large nobility in confrontation with their sovereign. Far-flung, discrepant, precarious alliances. If the Kings of France and Spain made peace with one another, the Pope and all good Catholics jubilated. Had they really good reason to do so? Henry IV's foreign policy was determined by considerations having nothing to do with religion. Given peace in the south, he saw improved opportunity to extend eastward, conspire with the Protestant princes and foment trouble in Germany in order to break the chain of Habsburg positions around his kingdom. Not that his chosen friends were very effective. The German Protestants were capable of bringing the Empire's ancient constitutional machinery to a standstill by drawing out issues for years, producing hair-splitting memoranda and in an emergency leaving Diet meetings with a passable show of unanimity. What they were incapable of doing was to consolidate their strength for vigorous action. In 1597 a Spanish general, Mendoza by name and on his way to conferring once again a final lesson on the Dutch, marched his army through the Rhineland. His troops, quartered in Jülich and elsewhere, wreaked havoc like soldiers of Satan. The General presumed, moreover, to Catholicize in Spanish style the towns that he occupied in breach of international law. All the same it took two years for the Empire's local defence machinery to pull itself together and set resistance on foot.

Central Europe's structure was crumbling. Fragments that fell away sought to cement themselves with such as fell away in other parts. Nobody placed any reliance on the duration of the existing order. Everybody hoped that, if it did not endure, change would in their own case bring gain.

How different things would have been if the two parties had, without secret reservations, recognized each other as possessing legitimate aims and being there to stay. That they had basically never done. A distinction should at least have been drawn between political recognition and spiritual recognition. In Germany the staunchly conservative Lutherans, headed by the Elector of Saxony, were recognized by their Catholic fellow-princes and the Emperor. In Bohemia recognition was accorded to the Utraquists. But now in Bohemia and Moravia it had been withdrawn from the Brethren. In Germany and Austria the Calvinists had never enjoyed it. The existence of non-Catholics was in the eyes of the Catholic church something intrinsically inadmissible. Should they die unconverted, their abode in hell was assured. Their complete elimination remained, in this perspective, an immutable purpose which would sooner or later be attained. In their heart of hearts Catholic princes and politicians, as sons of the church and therefore in spiritual bond to it, either were or had to be credited with being unable to understand the matter otherwise. This applied even though, for as long as could be seen ahead, they were fighting simply for the preservation of what was left to them and, in their own eyes, were the party attacked. That was precisely why every advance by the Catholic party, in Bohemia and Moravia for example, was felt to be not merely a step forward, but headway towards its ineluctable aim – as in the case of a militant missioner like Cardinal Dietrichstein it admittedly was. Germany's Protestant princes generally displayed little more tolerance than Catholic ones, on occasions less. They did not, however, maintain that the

Catholic church was an institution which should in principle be abolished altogether. They could not. The spiritual movement they turned to their advantage was from its outset imbued with the axiom of heterogeneity, and this had inevitably to extend in all directions. The most recent instance was the impassioned dispute among Austrian Lutherans as to whether original sin was inherent in the stuff of man or an accidental property. The protagonists loathed each other, like the Calvinists and Lutherans in western Germany.

Disentangling the main question from the mass of incidental squabbles, the issue in the Habsburg Hereditary Lands was that of monarchy or aristocracy, Catholic monarchy or Protestant rule by Estates. In the Empire, sprawling and multifarious, rule by Estates had long since prevailed. Real power consequently lay in the hands of an oligarchy of semi-sovereign princes ruling over regions the largest of which in fact were, or unconsciously were tending to becomes states. Nevertheless even the most important of them, whether the ruler of Bavaria, Saxony or the Palatinate, could not be rid of the Empire. Partly because, for all their selfishness, they were not lacking in a sense of loyalty to it as an entity. Partly because their own future, expansion or diminution, continued to depend on what happened throughout the Empire. If a resolution to impose a Turkish campaign tax was passed with a bare majority at one of the quarrelsome Diet meetings, the minority was faced with deciding whether or not the Catholic majority could force it to pay. Let the "Circles", districts organized for the Empire's protection, prove inadequate to fend off an impudent breach of international law by the Spaniards, and the problem of whether the Empire was a community in any way still capable of defending itself, or whether it was not much more a matter of each state having to seek refuge in its own preparedness or through special alliances, was raised in a form that could no longer be concealed behind a flow of patriotic phrases. The impulse towards negation and dissolution won every time. Not that this was what its leaders wanted, not at least the majority, not all of whom were unwilling to compromise. It resulted from the prevailing state of mind. Each of the two main camps was convinced that the other was determined on its annihilation, not immediately but gradually, and correspondingly interpreted in that light everything that the other did.

In 1608 mainly southern German Protestant princes and cities, the Palatinate, Württemberg, Baden, Hesse, Darmstadt, Ulm and Nürnberg concluded an alliance known as the "Union". Its object was the preservation of peace and justice, no more, and its foundation was not without precedent. But one combination evokes another. Next year Duke Maximilian constituted a Catholic counter-union, subsequently called the "League", an assemblage of southern German and Rhenish spiritual rulers under Bavaria's leadership. Its term was limited to nine years, that of the Union to ten, and it also had for its sole aim the preservation of what was sound and traditional. The question was what the two sides understood by preservation. Thanks to the vigour of its president and his well-lined coffers, the League was the better organized and soon had a strong army at its disposal. The Empire was still whole. Now, though, it contained two armed and jealously watchful parties, both involved in alliances and antagonisms outside, but encircling, the imperial borders.

Among the projects on a German and European scale whose purpose was to subvert the existing framework of power one of the most dangerous was that which centred on the future of Bohemia. The idea was old, dating from the 1580s, when Henry of Navarre was struggling as a Huguenot for his right to the French succession, but it had never been forgotten. Bohemia's crown, so ran the argument, was elective, not as the Habsburgs who ruled there understood the word, but according to the time-honoured convention of the Bohemian Estates. Should it prove possible to revive the usage and to oust the Habsburgs from Prague, the Arch-House would sustain a defeat of immeasurable importance. The preponderantly Protestant Austrian Estates would perhaps dislodge their unpopular rulers. A Protestant majority would perhaps, no, surely, ensue in the German Electoral College. Driven out of Bohemia, the head of Habsburg must lose the imperial dignity. Its directly effective power might be small, but the benefits it could confer on the "Enlarger of the Empire", deriving from the weight of ancient sanctified authority attaching to his tenure of this office, were inestimable. No longer in Austrian hands, what would remain of France's encirclement by the Empire and Spanish world dominion? Precisely this analysis should have told politicians with a sense of responsibility that, even in the conflict of sentiments, everything affecting the affairs of the Roman church and the Arch-House forbade trifling with Bohemia. He who tried to promote revolution there was playing with European fire. But where were such unselfish politicians to be found? What prince, Privy Councillor, leader of Estates did not play with fire?

Let us take one, at random, as an example, from among those who did so as their main vocation – Prince Christian of Anhalt–Bernburg, offspring of a minor princely family, no more really than an official of the

Palsgrave, for whom he acted as governor in the Upper Palatinate, bordering on Bohemia. From 1595 to 1620 Anhalt advised on or conducted Palatine policy along what he liked to imagine was a Palatine–French–Dutch–Calvinist line. In the last-named year his papers fell into enemy hands. His secret correspondence was eagerly ploughed through. "In time," wrote a Bavarian publicist commenting on his plans, "all Europe would have succumbed thereto", and the remark was no exaggeration. Convinced that the Spanish world power either would achieve its aim or must be blasted apart, Anhalt's resourceful mind had hatched an inexhaustible stock of intrigues and woven a string of plots wherein every conceivable ally had his place. A system of castles in the air and fatal booby-traps which encompassed the whole continent. The Habsburg Hereditary Lands played an important part.

Personally Prince Christian was of a sanguine temperament, a commanding figure fond of the delights of life, sophisticatedly conversant with the ways of Europe's courts. Indeed it would be wrong to fancy that gloom was the prevailing temper of those who, merely self-seeking or ambitiously meddling with the major issues, worked busily at the preparations for a large-scale conflagration. Politics gave them intrinsic pleasure. Political visits and conferences in small groups, at country seats or town-houses, were frequent, occasions when everything passed off very merrily, what with hunting, carousals and fireworks tracing mythological patterns in the air.

Who footed the bill? To say "the princes" would be shallow. A prince was neither peasant, craftsman, miner, seaman nor merchant. He plied no trade. He took from those who plied one, partly on his own lands, partly in the towns and on the estates of his nobility. In Bohemia approximately one-tenth of the land belonged to the King. The rest was divided among the nobility of 254 lords and 1128 knights, "royal" towns directly subject to the sovereign without a feudatory intermediary, unfree towns (whose share was small) and free peasants (with very little indeed). The wealth of the nobility was incomparably greater than that of the towns. The latter augmented theirs with, among other things, land, woods and ponds beyond their walls. Since the nobility neither sowed nor reaped the properties they owned, the answer to the question is clear. The money spent usefully or uselessly by the princes came preponderantly from the peasants. They carried the burden without being asked how much they could or were willing to bear. They had no vote, they were no Estate, neither in Bohemia nor anywhere else except in Sweden. They were their landlord's vassals and bound to the soil,

unable either to leave or to sell their farm without their lord's permission. It might be given, particularly if he wanted outright possession
of what was his, by seigniorial privilege, without his being able to call it
his property. For domicile on their lord's territory the peasants had to
perform service, on average ten days a year – seventy days a century
later – and pay an annual tribute in money or natural produce to the
value of three or four taler. Those who had nothing, the lacklands, did
direct service for their lords, on a daily payment basis, in his flour mills,
breweries, vegetable gardens, linen mills, sheep-farms and whatever
other enterprises he operated. If he could not obtain enough workers
within his own domain, he had to entice them from elsewhere. From this
resulted a certain freedom of movement comprising a relationship
between landlord and labourer which no longer corresponded to the
feudal, patriarchal one. Thus too there arose villages, especially in
mountainous districts, resembling small towns whose inhabitants would
be working in mines, iron production, glass-works and forestry.

It does not sound too barbarous and was certainly better than conditions in neighbouring Poland, Hungary and Austria. Much depended
on the nature of the overlordship. Peasants situated by a large town could
deal with its citizens on their own. At a distance from a town, the lord
arbitrarily fixed the prices for which he would buy and sell. Should
landlords or their stewards have heard of new economic methods, tried
in the Netherlands, and be both intelligent and receptive to experimentation, they would care little for their vassals' payments and service.
Instead they would let them work on their own initiative, buy what they
had to offer, whether wheat, linen or flax, as cheaply as possible and sell
wholesale, a form of exploitation conducing to the lords' greatest advantage and the vassals' least constraint. That was how the Smiřickýs,
with estates stretching from Prague to the edge of Silesia, had acquired
and multiplied their riches. We mention the fact at this point because
in time someone else was to take possession of their property and adopt
their economic methods. Others, iike the Trčkas, stuck to the older
tradition of rigorously squeezing out of their vassals whatever possible.
Those were the estates on which insurrections broke out soonest and
were fought with the utmost desperation. But let the peasants band
together and storm castles, as they did in the 1590s in Austria and once
more thirty years later in Bohemia as well as Austria, and they would have
against them all the classes squabbling among themselves and pursuing
politics as a pastime, princes and Estates alike. The peasants were always
the losers.

On one occasion Wilhelm Kinsky, a spokesman for the Bohemian knightage, member of a politically very active family and surpassing even Christian of Anhalt in love of intrigue, ordered that two escaped and recaptured vassals "shall each have two fingers hacked off on the bench by the hangman, then be strangled, their punishment serving as an example to others". Eventually, because his wife beseeched him so earnestly, this champion of the liberties of the Estates conceded that his sentence should not be implemented – an instance of seigniorial mercy.

So much for the world, at close and farther quarters, with which Wallenstein had gradually to familiarize himself. We return now to our central figure. We shall often have to cast a glance at matters still little of his concern. They had an effect on him, but not as yet he on them.

He Seeks his Course and Finds Help

A N early tradition alleges that Wallenstein was for a time a page
at the court of the Margrave of Burgau. It could, and could
really only in 1603, have been the case. The story is not improbable. False legends may easily accrue from some happening which
becomes embellished, misinterpreted, and twisted, but in this instance
it is not palpable what should have been twisted. Wallenstein either
served the Habsburg prince or he did not. For him to have done so at
the age of twenty as a "page" need cause no surprise. The title simply
signified the lowest rung of the court ladder.

If however Wallenstein attended the Margrave, it will not have been
in the little Upper Swabian country town of Burgau, where there is
now a small street called after him, but in the Tirolese hill-castle of
Ambras. That was where the Margrave, doughty warrior-grandson of
Emperor Ferdinand I and son to the beautiful Augsburg burgher's
daughter Philippine Welser, held court amidst his father's amazing
collection of fossilized dragons, snakes, and scorpions, Chinese musical
instruments, gorgeous Aztec robes, automata, and cunningly devised
clocks, giant gewgaws and Brobdingnagian beakers, misshapen creatures,
Bacchus grottoes, beauties' galleries, voluptuous bath-room installations,
ghastly death depictions, and a thousand other oddities. Ferdinand of
Tirol and his nephew the Emperor Rudolf both had collection-mania,
but the former showed a greater sense of humour and less artistic
perception than the latter. Let us at any rate assume that our hero, at
moments when he did not with downcast eyes have to stand at attention
on the entry of his prince, did gaze in wonderment at these things which
we can today still see for ourselves.

A straightforward fairy-tale, though, is the story of his conversion.
One day, so it goes, he fell asleep by the window of a high-up chamber
and had a nasty fall into the depths below. He did not however sustain
any injury and, believing thanks for such a marvellous delivery to be due
to the Holy Virgin, he drew the appropriate conclusion. This is nonsense.
In the first place a grown man does not in his sleep fall out of a window.

Secondly, it is not the way people change their religion. Conversion was at that time a fashion, catching and of advantage to those who followed it, without any need for dramatic explanation in particular cases. Starting with Cardinal Khlesl, the puissant adviser of Emperor Matthias, and Ferdinand II's minister Prince Eggenberg, we shall soon meet converts in the immediate entourage of more than one Apostolic Majesty. A return to the faith of one's fathers proceeded moreover not, as now, after serious instruction and solemn ceremony, a second baptism, but by going to mass a couple of times and making an affirmation. That was enough to put matters right. Wallenstein took this very practical step, but in all probability not before 1606. That the precise date is not known is explicable in terms of the discreet, clear-headed manner of the accepted procedure.

Burgau-Ambras is the last episode in Wallenstein's youth which those who want to do so can call into question on the score of lack of documentary evidence. Henceforward the ground is firm.

THE SOLDIER

Apart perhaps from rattling their swords threateningly during their assemblies, Bohemian lords took little pleasure in the profession of arms. They were content to live in their castles, go hunting, wassail, collect their dues and play politics. For their officers, especially senior ones, the Habsburgs had to go where such were to be found – to the Netherlands, Germany, Italy, Spain. When in 1604 Wallenstein reported for duty against the Turks, his action was an exception, not the rule. The orphaned young man, master of a free and indeterminate fate, wanted to have a taste of what did not interest most of the members of his class.

Military schools did not exist, but a number of publications dealing with the theory of the subject were available: Dilich's *Book of War*, Wallhausen's *Art of Infantry Warfare*, and more of the kind. Georg Basta, the Albanian-born imperial commander-in-chief in Hungary, had written a pamphlet about cavalry. Ambitious officers might make use of such works, but on the whole they preferred to ignore the innocent notions of pen-pushers. A young nobleman would serve "from the pike up", as the pertinent phrase had it. That is, he would begin in the ranks as a pikeman, where his merits, his money, or hints from above ensured that he did not long remain. It could also happen the other way about, the recruit starting as a colonel because the establishment and pay of a regiment demanded more mercantile than military acumen, the completion of a business contract with the commissioning ruler. The rest came by experience.

Wallenstein began as an ensign. His regiment was one that the Bohemian Estates had, like it or not, granted the King and paid for. Like it or not. Besides the fact that a regiment cost several hundred thousand gulden a year, it was never certain why that witless fool on the Hradschin (site of Prague's royal palace) needed soldiers, whether for the ostensible, plausible reason or an obscure one inimical to the country's liberties. War with the Turks had on previous occasions furnished the Habsburgs with such excuse; it could do so again. Yet the war was all too much of a reality and a genuine danger to the lands of the Bohemian crown. The head of the House of Habsburg was called King of Hungary, but the portion of Hungary over which he ruled, in so far as he ruled there, was only a narrow strip of the kingdom – Upper Hungary as far as Kaschau (Košice), the Danube valley from Pressburg (Bratislava) to Gran (Esztergom), and an approximately corresponding stretch on the southern bank of the river. The fortresses supposed to defend this fragment, Raab, Gran, Canissa, were sometimes in the hands of the Christians, then back with the infidels, opening for them the road to Brünn (Brno), Vienna or Graz. "In the hands of the Christians" meant, depending on the blood in their veins and the language they spoke, in the hands of Germans, Walloons, Italians, Czechs, liberators whom the Magyar nobility only in an emergency relished more, and sometimes rather less, than the Turks. Arrogant, brutalized by war, proud to excess of their nation, they only just desired to be defended, and certainly not to be ruled, by Germans. Religion, as an expression of independence and an item in the struggle for power, played a part everywhere in central Europe. Rudolf, astray but stubborn as always, cared not a fig for the country's way of thinking. Where his mercenaries provided protection, Calvinist preachers were expelled, priests and bishops brought back. The Turks permitted freedom of belief as well as sometimes allowing their vassals a meed of autonomy. This, to quote one example, applied to the Prince of Transylvania. His multilingual, fertile principality, situated in the south-east of Upper Hungary, was regarded by both the Sultan and the King of Hungary as belonging to their sphere of influence. The treaties between the two sovereigns were regularly so formulated as to admit of different interpretations and to give rise to incessant guerilla skirmishes and frontier forays. That was the reason why it did not fundamentally much matter whether there was an armistice or not. Within living memory no Turkish campaign had been decided in open battle. Wearisome sieges, castles taken by storm, brief blood-baths resulting from ambushes, pillage and laying waste of the countryside by friend and foe was what it always came to.

The year 1604 proved no different. At the beginning of July Bohemian infantry departed in the direction of the Danube, followed by cavalry under Count Heinrich Matthias von Thurn. Sundry imperial and royal forces converged on Gran from north and west, out to besiege something or be besieged. Their commander-in-chief was Georg Basta, his Brabant deputy Johann Tserclaes von Tilly. The paths of a small knot of men destined to re-encounter one another later crossed at Gran – Tilly, forty-five and well on the road to fame; the Bohemian (or assimilated Bohemian) fighting-cock Mathias Thurn; twenty-one-years-old Wallenstein; and another young Czech, Johann von Bubna. During the course of a night in May 1633 Wallenstein would say of him, "He has known me too for so many years. . . ."

Hardly, by the middle of September, had the imperial troops moved into Gran and provisioned the fortress when the Turks, commanded by a certain Ali Pasha and allegedly sixty thousand in number, with horrid tumult arrived in front of it. They encamped along the Danube. The siege was on and lasted slightly over three weeks. First there was the Turks' direct assault, repulsed by Tilly's well-sited quarter-cannon.* Then, to the accompaniment of jeering ululations and a variety of catapulted missiles, attacks on the approaches, sallies by the besieged, scrimmages below the walls, and a murderous fight for an outwork. On 11 October Ali Pasha left, his army badly shrunken. Wallenstein had risen to captain. The year's campaign was, it seemed, already over. Its place was taken by a new calamity.

Precisely during this October occurred the uprising of Istvan Bocskay. Its precedents, a Transylvanian or Hungarian lord making common front with the arch-enemy, were countless. But the Lord of Debreczen and Grossvardin had cause enough for dissatisfaction with his Christian liege-lord. When recently he had been in Prague to urge encouragement upon the King, not only had Rudolf not received him – he hardly received anyone any more – but impudent pages in the antechambers took delight in tossing balls at his head. Moreover, while he was losing time at Prague, imperial troops quartered on his estates were not wasting theirs. They behaved with a vileness no Turk could rival.

* Twenty-four-pounder guns (translator's note).

Bocskay received the news, withdrew from the precincts of the crazy court, hurried home, concluded a pact with the Grand Vizier, and summoned Hungarians at large to fight for freedom and religion. The plot was well prepared. Hungarian mercenaries serving under Basta suddenly turned upon their companions-in-arms. The whole of Upper Hungary appeared likely to fall into Bocskay's hands. He assumed the title Prince of Hungary and Transylvania. Sultan Achmed addressed him as King of Hungary in letters from Constantinople which suggested that they should pursue the war against the Germans together and divide the booty.

Basta and Tilly knew where their duty lay. A province belonging to their master which was also a door to his key Bohemian territories could not be surrendered without fight. The autumn campaign saw its run unexpectedly extended into winter. Attended by cold, danger, and dire exigencies, the setting was transferred north-east from its initial scene on the Danube. That was when Wallenstein for the first time got to know war properly. Not on a major scale nor in conformity with the rules of military art as conducted by the Spaniards and the Dutch, but none the less war. Camp-fires guarded by sentry-posts and sudden shots out of the dark. Foraging and the search for food – flour, lard, pickled meat, geese cooked with cabbage, and pork which the peasants hid on the approach of troops. Plundering and the seizure of loot – money, clothes, horses. Growing distress on arrival in devastated districts. The merger of two or three units into one as they dwindled through desertion, sickness, and cold. Perhaps he was happy in spite of it all. To be twenty-one and a soldier goes well together. Or at any rate he was not unhappy at the experience, else he would not a few years later have been so eager to repeat it.

Hans Wild of Nürnberg went through this campaign, finding it fun at first, less so later, and his description includes the action at the small fortress of St Andrea, seven miles from Kaschau, when Wallenstein sustained a wound in the hand. A grazing shot. It cannot have been severe, seeing that soon he was fit to undertake a lengthy journey.

In the second half of December Georg Basta decided that for the duration of winter nothing more could be achieved. He withdrew the remainder of his force into the mountains, from Kaschau in the direction of Prešov. What hampered him more than cold and the country's dearth and hostility was his inability to pay his troops. An inveterate lament. This age and this society were basically too poor to conduct war in the style that they did. However, because rulers were as blind and egotistic as the more powerful of their subjects, they waged it not-withstanding. Because society was poor, it was easy to find soldiers and for the same reason impossible to foot the bill. Those who had been cheated thereupon paid themselves back in whatever way they could, which was no different whether they were still with or dismissed from the colours. And again society, because it was poor, incohesive, and vulnerable, could not defend itself against the spirits it had invoked, the marauding soldiery. Batches, ridiculously petty in our eyes, of mercenaries laid waste tracts of the countryside. Sheer necessity and greed for booty augmented that instinctive cruelty which feeds on itself. So it was everywhere and always. The first move was for the unpaid hirelings to refuse performance of their service – money had been the sole induce-ment for their promise to risk their lives, and General Basta knew it all too well. As he wrote in his cavalry treatise, "Give me but an army with all these commodities [meaning pay and supplies] and at once it will be corrupted, so I should venture upon reform and to set it aright. Yet I could not promise, nay, it would be impossible, that if it were deprived of its essential commodities I should be able to maintain a good army in proper and good discipline." I do not know whether Wallenstein read the treatise. At Prešov he was at all events a witness to this state of affairs.

One officer, it was decided, should be dispatched from each regiment to where it had been mustered and there request funds. Without pay the campaign could not in spring be resumed. Wallenstein was selected to go on behalf of the Czech infantry, a Lord Hysrle von Chodu for the cavalry. That the choice fell on Wallenstein suggests that he had cut a good figure during the past three months, but the explanation may also lie in the name he bore. With a seat and a vote in the assembly of the nobility, the young captain stood a better chance of obtaining a hearing than another officer might have done.

Escorted by twenty horsemen and sleighs, Wallenstein and Chodu began their journey by coach. They did not travel the road that they had come, this now being barred to them, but took their way due west via Zips or Spiš, then north to where the High Tatra's peaks strain heaven-ward in desperate supplication, and finally across Polish territory into Silesia. Chodu commemorated the adventure in his *Reminiscences*, recounting how pitifully they suffered from the cold in the mountains, struggling through storms and snow-drifts. In Poland they met with every kind of calamity, being mistaken in turn for enemies of some sort, robbers, and merchants trying to defraud the King of his dues. In their overnight quarters they kept awake by telling tales while outside hostile soldiery prowled noisily around the house. Once the ice over a river broke beneath their feet. Rescue proved possible only by hauling each other out by the hairs of the head. Their delight at setting foot on their own soil again was correspondingly great. Reaching the capital after survival of so many hazards, Wallenstein collapsed. We know it from Chodu as well as from a note written in his own hand: "In my twenty-second year I had the Hungarian sickness and the plague, anno 1605, in January." The plague, starting with heart-quakes, bouts of fever and excruciating thirst, generated the black glandular boils which gave rise to the term "bubonic". It cannot however have befallen Wallenstein with all its frightfulness. He mentions only January. The Estates entrusted him in February with a new appointment. That would hardly have happened if he had continued to be dangerously ill.

Chodu had to try and fulfil alone his general's instructions. He achieved nothing. "My remarks," he closes, "were for the most part ridiculed or falsely construed." The exertion had been wholly in vain, as is so often the case in war, and in peace too.

The office entrusted by the Estates to Wallenstein, together with a Count Fürstenberg, was that of a military commissioner. Instead of carrying fresh funds to his anxiously waiting, hungry comrades in distant Slovakia, he was to investigate what had been the fate of earlier grants, what was the effective manpower state in the Bohemian border-fortresses, and what was the position as regards their pay. His report was to be rendered to the next Diet. The task, if he fulfilled it, must have entailed considerable travel and interrogation. When the situation in Hungary and Moravia took a turn for the worse and the Bohemians tardily resolved upon defensive measures, the youthful commissioner was transformed into the colonel of a "regiment of German soldiers". We owe the information to no less a source than the Emperor Rudolf; he mentioned it in a letter to his brother, Archduke Albrecht, at Brussels. Both his appointments testify to the fact that Wallenstein, after barely six months' active service, was viewed by his equals as being an experienced officer and that competition in this field was not crippling. However, before he could prove his mettle as a regimental commander, peace was made with the Hungarian rebels and the Turks.

Istvan Bocskay had envisaged an alliance with the Bohemian, or at least the Moravian, Estates. This notion of a general Estates and Protestant rising against the misrule of the King-Emperor hung in the air and continued for a long time to come. Its full materialization came late, properly speaking never, because the principle on which it was based was a contradiction in terms. The leading Estates, the lords and knights, were composed of groups of selfish individuals or families barely capable of attaining effectual coherence among themselves, much less of collaborating in an opportune, durable alliance with similarly disposed, refractory, ill-defined factions in other Habsburg lands. That the Protestant nobility in Moravia had cause for concern at the progress of militant Catholicism was correct. The Old church, under the leadership of the cool-headed convert Karl von Liechtenstein and the Bishop of Olmütz, was distinctly on the offensive. Liechtenstein was however the governor of the margraviate and Dietrichstein the doyen of his Estate. The Protestants had no wish for a break with their Catholic peers. They were very proud and insistent on their rights, but, precisely versed in constitutional affairs, at the same time keenly aware of their obligations to their Margrave, Rudolf II. Their respect for royal authority was deep, however shaky might be the hands which held it. Therefore, instead of taking up Bocskay's tempting offers, they transmitted them with utmost loyalty to Prague and requested instructions. Bocskay, unable to obtain the Moravian Estates' friendship, decided to let them have a taste of his enmity. He sent his hordes, *hajduk*,* Tartars, and even Turks, into the southern parts of the margraviate. What he really had in mind with this invasion, I have been unable to discover. It was hardly the way to make an ally of the Moravians.

The Estates at Brünn formed a security committee, granted a special war tax, called up peasants totally unsuited to the soldier's trade, and appointed Liechtenstein and the Bishop of Olmütz commanders-in-chief. Of Liechtenstein it was bruited that the country's violation did not particularly distress him as long as his own properties were spared, and he is supposed to have gone so far as to say that it was less than a thousand pities about heretics being killed by Hungarians. The Cardinal learned his new role with fiery energy, fondling visions of himself as a bishop in olden days, cross in one hand, sword in the other. His nerves, though, would appear to have been not quite steady enough for the pageant of his dreams. Certain noblemen were not prepared to serve under a prelate, and very soon there was bickering between the two

---

* *Hajduk* was the Turkish term for bands of robbers or brigands who had roamed south-eastern Europe already prior to the Ottoman occupation. By reason of the latter, the name became among Balkan Slavs that given to nationalist guerillas. In Hungarian party warfare of the sixteenth and seventeenth centuries the word (Magyar by origin) was applied to native mercenary infantry. In 1605 Istvan Bocskay made them grants of land east of the Tisza where they constituted a county of their own. *Hajduk* is the plural (translator's note).

generals, who could not stand each other. Whenever Bocskay's swift, elusive riders came on the scene, they left behind them ruined harvests, burnt-out villages, death, and the plague. In those circumstances Liechtenstein's strategic concept – to get round the back of the Hungarians (a very feasible proposition) and to do the same in their own country – was not without merit. Once villages were ablaze and their inhabitants as well as animals being slaughtered, Bocskay agreed on an armistice with the security committee at Brünn. Implementation, as can be imagined, was difficult. None the less it was the beginning of peace.

THE ARCHDUKES

The foregoing will not have left the impression that Bohemia, Moravia, or any of the Habsburg territories were in good shape to protect their borders and pursue with determination any particular policy. The principle of rule by Estates, as it had evolved in terms of the human weakness of those upon whom it was incumbent to carry it through, was responsible for this state of affairs. Yet no other principle was to hand. Monarchy in the proper sense of the word did not exist. The royal command, if there was such at all, was not sole command. The personality of Rudolf II was moreover a deplorable hindrance to the opportunities for action open to a crowned head.

Not that princes of the House of Habsburg were excessively sensitive to the sufferings of their subjects. No, not that. But they were alive to the dynasty's greatness and had long been aware that its head was endangering its future. What in the present instance made reform at the top seem a matter of urgency were the Turkish war and the disorders in Hungary and Moravia. Twice during 1605 an archducal deputation, led by the Princes Matthias and Ferdinand, journeyed to Prague. Matthias, like his brother, was growing old without heirs. Ferdinand was young and his marriage was blessed by children. It explains why all was not entirely well between him and Matthias, suspicious that Ferdinand might be animated by the ambition to succeed the Emperor directly by leapfrogging his cousin. Ferdinand denied that, but in such matters many a denial has been uttered with eyes glued to the project in view. The man from Graz, as we know, thought along rigidly legalistic Catholic lines. Curtailment of the powers of the King appointed by the Grace of God, let alone his deposition, an act intrinsically contrary to all the most sacred principles, must in this instance benefit parties with whom

Ferdinand stood in heated altercation – the Estates as such, the Protestant Estates in particular. For this reason Ferdinand sympathized only partially with the object of their missions. Co-operation based on mutual confidence between him and Matthias was never achieved. Rudolf received the Archdukes neither on their first nor on their second visit to Prague, but at least the upshot of the second was that Matthias was empowered to wage war and conclude peace in the south-east to the best of his ability. Matthias, familiar with his brother's spitefulness, placed no reliance on the mandate.

In April 1606, during the time of the negotiations with Istvan Bocskay, a further move, indeed by strict definition an archducal plot, occurred. A document couched in Latin dealt with the Emperor's condition, alleging that this severely impaired his ability to rule, and declared Matthias head of the family. The wording was deliberately obscure and the paper was meant as a strictly secret family compact. So ran Ferdinand's interpretation. When the conspiracy none the less became known, not without Matthias's connivance, the young Archduke hurried to make his excuses to the Emperor. He had gone to Vienna, he maintained, because he thought the issue was simply that of quenching the Hungarian uprising. Once there, he had had to listen to exaggerated accounts of the Emperor's physical and mental infirmity and he signed the document mainly to be absolved from Matthias's suspicion that he wanted to deprive him of the crown, but also with a specific proviso against notifying the Pope and the King of Spain about the transaction. He remained, he assured Rudolf, ready as ever to pledge himself entirely on behalf of His Imperial Majesty's life and person. It lay in Rudolf's own interest to bring over the head of the junior dynastic line into his camp. He stated himself satisfied with Ferdinand's avowal. The Archduke's shrewd Bavarian mother, on the other hand, was displeased: "My child ... I only fear that the Emperor doth promise you much so that you shall be goaded against the Archduke Matthias and that then he will desert you. What if he doth indeed make you King of the Romans and provides no wherewithal? *In summa*, 'tis a perilous business."

Furnished with official proxy and his House's secret compact, Matthias was able to give an impetus to the negotiations with Hungary. In June 1606 they ended, a peace concluded alike by Habsburg and the Estates. Deputies from Moravia, Protestants principally, partook in the discussions and had to guarantee to the Hungarian nobles the observance of what was agreed – the exclusion of all non-Magyars from official posts and representation of the King *in absentia* by a viceroy, a Palatine to be elected by the country's magnates. Bocskay was recognized as Prince of Transylvania. The article in hottest dispute was that dealing with freedom of religion. On this Matthias's outlook accorded with that of the Habsburgs as a whole, and his spiritual adviser, Melchior Khlesl, had in duty bound drawn his attention to the prospective pains and penalties in hell if he were to yield on this question of cardinal gravity. That was the theoretical background. In practice the Hungarian magnates were Protestant, the Moravian ones too, and at present the means were lacking to compel them to save their souls, an argument that Khlesl eventually allowed. They would, he wrote to his friend Dietrichstein, *"in puncto religionis* have to swallow a bitter pill"*. It tasted most bitter of all to the King at Prague. Rudolf ratified the treaty which he regarded as a victory for Protestantism, an act of defiance by the Estates, and a piece of treachery on the part of his brother, without any intention of keeping it. He also ratified the succeeding treaty with the Turks. The two signatory sovereigns took the unprecedented step of adopting one another as father and son, exchanged gifts of which it was stipulated that much the more valuable should be presented by the German side, and promised to effect for twenty years no change in the current state of territorial possessions as well as to erect no new fortresses against each other, but at most to strengthen existing ones. If the Peace of Zsitva-Torok proved long-lived, the reason is to be sought less in the wisdom of its negotiators than the course of events in Persia whose inhabitants had for years been a source of trouble to the Grand Turk on the eastern flank of his realm. The circumstance provisionally moderated Constantinople's policy towards the West.

Istvan Bocskay died within a few weeks of his triumph. He was soon to have a still shrewder, still more daring successor.

ZIEROTIN

In August 1604 Wallenstein's sister Katharina Anna married the Moravian Lord Karl von Zierotin upon Náměšt and Rošicze. Wallenstein was on his way to the Hungarian theatre of war and could not be present at the ceremony. But next year, when she was said to be suffering from consumption, he visited his sister. A few weeks later he followed her coffin to the grave. His connection with Zierotin did not hereupon end. The lonely grandee continued to take an interest in his nineteen years junior brother-in-law. Seeing that Zierotin was by far the most outstanding personality Wallenstein met in his younger days, the reader has a claim to know more about him.

Karl von Zierotin – or, better, Karel Žerotín – was the head of one of the margraviate's richest, most eminent, pious families. Not since the days of Hus had there been a Papist among it. "For 140 years," wrote Zierotin, "we can prove it documentarily, our ancestors have been the Word of God's most zealous defenders in this land." An assiduous member of the Moravian Brethren, a scholar, a man of deep meditation and an earnest patriot, he could count himself of their company. He loved music, provided that it was of an elevated character. Once, as he shamefacedly admitted, he had imbibed wine to the point of inebriation, but never again. He dressed in sombre velvet, only shedding it for a brighter silk on the anniversary of his wedding-day. He spoke many languages and kept up profuse correspondence in them with friends all over Europe. In his youth (as previously mentioned) he sought instruction at Geneva from Pastor Theodor Beza, Calvin's assistant and successor, without being unduly disturbed at what is inevitably repugnant to us, Beza's vigorous defence of Michel Servet's martyrdom. Other times, other customs. Beza's temper was less wrathful than Calvin's, Zierotin far more tolerant than Beza, whom he none the less admired. His links with Geneva and Basle brought him into contact with the international circle of Protestant partisans which included Heidelberg savants and politicians as well as the group around the King of Navarre. To help the latter in his fight against Spain and the League, Zierotin in 1591 out of his own pocket equipped a body of cavalry and sailed with it from Holland to Normandy. The great-hearted adventure ended in disappointment. The King received his Slav co-religionist with less warmth of confidence than he had anticipated. He soon realized that in the French civil war religion was less at stake than temporal power and the succession to the throne. His partiality for France evaporated, a fact which was of help to the policy he advocated. It could have helped the Moravians too if his policy had prevailed. Now, although continuing in contact with leading figures of the Calvinist alliance like the Prince of Anhalt, his opinion was that the Protestant Estates in Moravia and other Habsburg territories should defend their cause alone. If they allowed themselves to be dragged into the main European conflict between France and Spain, they would incur the danger of being used as pawns and ground to dust in the process. That was why he was for moderation. Open resistance to the King was admissible, but only in direst emergency. Which was not the case, not *yet* the case. . . . The distinction drawn at that time in the Habsburg lands between "politicians" and "extremists" was between those in both camps who insisted, particularly where questions of religion were concerned, on having the whole of their own way at any price and those who for the sake of peace were prepared to be content with a reasonable share. Zierotin was a "politician", a man of compromise because he was genuinely devout, a devotion having nothing to do with the narrow pride and fanaticism of the "extremists". His type was bound to meet with difficulties and eventually founder, as Zierotin sensed. He was a defender, not an aggressor. His allegiance was to the traditional body politic of free Estates to which the monarch belonged as *primus inter pares*. The sovereign was the Estates, the lords, the knights, the prelates, and the King-Margrave in one. There is much to suggest that this fissured oligarchy could not have been saved, not even if the religious conflict had not existed and the majority of Zierotin's peers had been of his stamp.

Nationality and language were factors in the defence of the traditional body politic. Zierotin spoke French, German, and Italian in addition to Czech. He pretended, though, that he knew German worst in so far as he understood it at all. He once took exception to and rejected receipt of an official document sent him in German from Olmütz. He had friends in Germany, where princes received this Moravian lord as an equal. He thought German cities cleaner and more prosperous than Slav ones. None the less in his eyes Bohemia and Moravia should remain separate, crowned republics distinguished by their nationality and noble native tongue. It could have been objected that in Moravia the time for this was gone because the population of its major cities was preponderantly German and a relationship of real trust no longer subsisted between the municipal communes and the oligarchy, while at Prague the "German party" was identical with that of the court, the Catholics, and the Spaniards. Zierotin regarded it as a hostile element. "The privy councillors are Germans, our foes of old, and not conversant with Moravian affairs."

Zierotin was small of build and plagued by illnesses which in part were specifically diagnosed as gout, in part vaguely as *febris erratica*. He also suffered from something he called *morbus imaginationis* – an anxious disposition. Reference has already been made to contemporary self-containment and inner loneliness of spirit, a want of skill in intimate communication with others and oneself. That could easily lead to a frame of mind which, long familiar because it could not but become manifest, had been given the name still current for it – melancholy.

Morbus imaginationis, the hatching of harrowing thoughts and imaginary perils, is unlikely to have been much different. Not that Zierotin was a harsh egotist like others who, presumably in this way, unknowingly provided their own punishment. He hankered for exchange of ideas and discussion. He wrote letters, he sought friends, but he found small response.

When Wallenstein first entered on a closer relationship with Zierotin, their respective sister and wife was lying on her death-bed. During the succeeding years he was a frequent guest in his brother-in-law's sumptuous homes. Zierotin's magnificent, though sober, style of life cannot fail to have impressed and to some small extent have formed him, for when we are young we imitate what we admire. How should he have been able to counterfeit two such fundamentally disparate characters as Zierotin and the Emperor Rudolf? We accept the paradoxes of life as we encounter them, which in this instance is not difficult. The real Wallenstein had nothing in common with Karl von Zierotin and not much with Rudolf II.

THE ADVANTAGE OF GOOD CONNECTIONS

Wallenstein's reconciliation to the Catholic church probably took place during the course of 1606. If this day of quietly consummated change does not with certainty lie in 1606 at the earliest, that is certainly where it lies at the latest. At the beginning of 1607 Zierotin is writing about his brother-in-law, *"Il va à la messe."*

Specimens from the chronicle of contemporary young nobles' conversion reach from instances of burning conviction, exemplified by Wilhelm von Slawata, to those of the coolly practical deliberation displayed by Karl von Liechtenstein. So much is clear. We have however no means of deducing Wallenstein's feelings, least of all at this period. Was he moved by a spiritual discontent? Did he find, as has many a man since, that Protestant sects are all very well if participation in their communion takes place with real humility and effort, but not otherwise, whereas under the canopy of the Old Church peace comes by way of simple obedience and acceptance? Was it Father Veit Pachta, that shrewd member of the Society of Jesus, who during illuminating conversations at the seat of his uncle Jan von Ričan convinced him of the truth of the Roman faith? That Pachta had a hand in the game and that Wallenstein remained grateful to him has been confirmed, although the gratitude could have other grounds. But very little else has been confirmed. Wallenstein stayed a loyal, punctiliously practising Catholic for the rest of his life. He fulfilled the duties, including the spiritual ones, of a wealthy Catholic landowner as long as that was all that he was. He maintained very close, though anything but frictionless, relations with the Jesuits. He founded monasteries, he made pious endowments. When, on the other hand, at a later stage he objected to the violence accompanying Counter-Reformation on the grand scale, it was the politician pronouncing a political, and in politics a realistic judgement.

He wanted to make a career for himself. In this respect, and in so far as his friendship with Father Veit was determined by this wish, it speaks for his political instinct that he backed the future of Catholicism. During the Emperor Rudolf's final years the cause of Catholicism and the Habsburgs, seen through less perceptive eyes, was in poor shape, in Bohemia still poorer than in Moravia. He may have surmised what later he definitely knew – the cause of the Protestant oligarchy was secretly in yet poorer shape.

And finally, because we are at the beginning what we are at the end, the will to lead, the gift of leadership, such strong compulsions in Wallenstein, harmonized better with Catholic than Protestant principle. Theory, if thought worth study, taught that. Practice taught it too. The King of Spain's command was absolute. The King of Bohemia, whose predecessors had permitted the Reformed faith to spread, could by himself command nothing. The Lutheran princes of Germany, become their own popes, had indeed power of command. That was however a special case, known to Bohemia at best from neighbouring Saxony. Here and now, in the Habsburg hereditary possessions in the year 1606, Protestant principle came close to republicanism and rebellion; the Catholic was its diametrical opposite. Wallenstein hated rebellion, then and always.

Karl von Zierotin forgave his brother-in-law the change. Fitting into his gloomy picture of the way of the world, it could not do otherwise than depress him, but he forgave him and furthermore acceded to Wallenstein's request to furnish him with introduction to the Archduke Matthias's court. He did it in three letters which we possess. One, dated from the beginning of February 1607, he sent to Vienna. The other two, from April, he gave Wallenstein to take with him. The first, in French, was addressed to Johann von Mollard, the Archduke's minister; the second, to Mollard again; and the third, in Italian, to a gentleman at the archducal court.

He was writing, he said, on behalf of a young man full of good and praiseworthy qualities who had already delivered varied proof of his merit. Of excellent family, pleasing manners, well-educated and, keeping in mind his youth, discriminatingly mature. Incidentally, and not really requiring mention since this was known to make no difference to His Serene Highness, he attended mass. His keenest desire was to belong to the company of gentlemen in attendance on His Highness, partly on account of his special devotion to the latter, partly because he was seeking a master "whose authority and whose greatness may serve as a foothold and a ladder for his ascent in the world." Why not? Such approaches and formulations were a staple of chivalric form. On receipt of the Privy Councillor's reply, Zierotin sent his brother-in-law off to Vienna with more letters and good advice. The new letters played variations on the earlier theme, especially as regards the aspect of maturity. "His assessment cannot be as mellow as that of a man of advanced age nor his understanding so certain, but the gifts bestowed on him by nature are good and the manner of his thinking and acting admirable for his years." He was not one of those who "from presumption wish to intervene in all things and be the first", which was the reason for his needing friendly introduction. One point had admittedly to be feared: "He is so on fire to practise the trade of war that, should it please His Serene Highness to accept him into the service of His Chamber, he will not let be until he hath leave to serve some time with the Archduke Albrecht in Flanders," though this was possibly more laudable than reprehensible. So much for the substance of the letters. They are written by a man who, at forty-three, has no illusions about his own thoroughly mature insight into matters and nevermore in his life will utter a lie. He tells the truth and nothing but the truth. The whole truth? That, if utterable at all, is seldom uttered even by a strict moralist like Zierotin. His letters are at any rate carefully weighed, not painted in too bright colours, not overstrained. Had Wallenstein at this date still been "wild Wallenstein" and rendered Bohemia's castles as unsafe a place to be as seven years ago the little town of Altdorf, the letters would assuredly not have been written.

He obtained the Chamberlain appointment. He presumably also kept his ears open as to what were prevailing court views and whose sympathies it was important to gain, whether of Cardinal Khlesl or jovial Karl von Harrach whose star in the archducal firmament was in the ascendant. The nature of his appointment, particularly when it concerned the Silver and the Vestment Chambers, did not demand his constant presence. Leave could be had at any time. The main onus on a chamberlain was occasionally to form part of the prince's escort when travelling or hunting and to be among his entourage at official ceremonies. For a wealthy man court service perhaps held prospects, but as yet Wallenstein was not wealthy. We have no idea how long at this stage his stay in Vienna lasted.

It was towards the end of the following year, in 1608, that his new friend in the Society of Jesus, Father Veit, asked him to come to Olmütz on urgent business.

THE HOROSCOPE

He was still young, in the eyes of his brother-in-law Zierotin still very young. At twenty-five he was none the less farther along the course, this unknown but only available course, than he would be today. He owned an estate that interested him solely to the extent of the modest income he drew from it. He was the colonel of a regiment of "German soldiers" which at present did not exist. He held a court appointment such as was enjoyed by many others, including quite mediocre personalities. Around him prevailed a state of pull devil, pull baker disorder. In the sky there suddenly twinkled a star not previously seen. The world groaned at a trail of wars, now here, now there, finely contrived intrigues, hate-laden wranglings, agreements never viewed as more than temporary, fear in plenty, greed in plenty, penury faced by unjust enrichment. Pent up in his soul was the muffled feeling that, given the chance, he could perform more than others.

Some time in 1608 the notion crossed Wallenstein's mind that he should have his horoscope cast. Were it to be done, then by Johannes Kepler, mathematician to His Imperial Roman Majesty and the most famous astrologer of the day. The idea was not abstruse. People turned to astrology, an ancient science, in the same way as to physic or spiritual consolation. On the one hand they wanted to learn what they were and what fate they must expect, on the other to obtain tips on what they should currently do or not do in order, as it were, nevertheless to dodge their destiny. For centuries the practice of astrology, although of anything but Christian origin, had not been accounted impious. Recently, since the Council of Trent, to be precise, it had been condemned and forbidden. Strictly orthodox potentates like Ferdinand of Styria respected the veto. Emperor Rudolf, like other great lords before and after him, ignored it.

Kepler did not perform his subsidiary profession which was probably what he was principally paid for, if he was paid, purely sceptically as a matter of material necessity. That is established fact. Without anyone giving him money for his pains, he had cast his own, his parents', and his wife's horoscopes, with avid interest checking the doleful experiences of terrestrial existence with the portents of the constellations. Where he differed from his colleagues was not in misgivings about immemorial traditions, but in certain doubts and discriminations, problems which in his profoundly honest fashion he courageously faced and tackled even if he did not entirely get the best of them. The first related to the determination of an individual's character by the position of the planets at the moment of birth – but not by that alone. Other elements left their mark, and Kepler was too deeply versed in the phenomena of nature to be the man to overlook them. The next concerned the individual's different times of life, what befell him from year to year. This unlatched the gate to a truly intricate maze. What a person, especially one with strongly delineated characteristics, did in certain circumstances derived from his inmost nature, consequently also from the constellation reigning at his hour of birth.

> Once I have probed the heart's core of a man
> I know his wishes. . . .*

Yet the situation of the planets in the passage of time, that is, the more or less potent, the more or less favourable angles of their current position, complementally to that at the moment of birth, could not be left out of calculation because these were operative. How exactly were they operative? Kepler had no wish to enter too closely into details, whether about this illness, that profit, or this loss. Those wanting to know the particulars of life beforehand should avail themselves of the services of others. "There are many astrologers who take pleasure and who believe in such sport. He who would be deceived open-eyed may voluntarily suffer their pains and pastimes. Philosophy, and thus true astrology, is a witness unto God's works and so a sacred, in no wise wanton thing that for my part I do not desire to dishonour . . ." (from Wallenstein's second horoscope). A conscientious observer could not fail to heed the power of purely terrestrial, human, and deliberately produced causes. If an ailment was contracted through love, as happened

* Schiller, *Wallenstein, a Historical Drama in Three Parts,* tr. Charles E. Passage (Frederick Ungar Publishing Co., N.Y., revised edition, 4th printing, 1965).

only too easily to young widowers, that was merely the terrestrial Lady Venus taking a hand in the game and should not be laid to the score of the noble celestial body of that name. Kepler shunned the question of occult correspondence between terrestrial and stellar agencies, contenting himself with drawing a distinction between them. He did not shun another, extremely onerous problem – the affinity between fate in general and that of the individual. If a land endured war, insurrection, or plague, then what was not to be foreseen in his own horoscope could well happen to an individual and in an unanticipated manner throw him out of his course. Fate in general, though, was as much subject to the law of twofold cause, the fortuitous terrestrial and the celestial, as the individual. And Kepler's astrological activity was not confined to casting horoscopes for individual paying clients. He dealt with the future, at least that within nearer range, of entire regions and kingdoms. He had made a start on this kind of work as a young mathematician at Graz. In old age he continued it at Linz in the service of the Upper Austrian Estates, uttering predictions of which later he could with reason be sadly proud. They affected the fate of whole nations, who after all were only individuals in the aggregate. None the less it is evident that, despite his pluck in facing problems, the question of what shapes individual fate was not probed by him in quite so divorced and then re-integrated a way as our more sophisticated era would demand. The latter has admittedly not made all that progress with the dilemma either.

There has certainly never been an augur who took his responsibility more seriously than Kepler. He wanted to do no harm, not to confuse and frighten people, not to lead them into temptation. Once indeed, as he confirmed in a letter to an unnamed adviser of Emperor Rudolf, he did not shrink from deliberately prophesying contrary to his knowledge of the stars so that no mischief should ensue from his more unerring interpretation. That occurred when, a few years after the events with which we are dealing here, the quarrel between the Emperor and Archduke Matthias was reaching its climax. He distrusted, if not his craft, the effects of his craft. Very few were qualified to receive the benediction of his skill. Thus it came about that, prior to casting a horoscope, he invariably made inquiries whether his client was sufficiently versed in philosophy to discern what was and what was not within the scope of a sophisticated stellar exegesis. Because he was not allowed to know, or at least the fiction was that he did not know, who a client was, such personal knowledge had to be obtained by devious means. Dr Stromaier, a Prague medical man, and Lieutenant Gerhard von Taxis, now and later one of Wallenstein's confidential agents, were the two intermediaries in his case.

Kepler went to work and found the results interesting. The "noble lord" had been born under the constellation of Aquarius and the sign of Saturn and Jupiter, the two most eminent planets farthest removed from the sun. They stood in ascension and therefore in the first house, always the dominant one, still more dominant than the other corner-houses, the fourth, the seventh and the tenth. A meeting of Saturn with Jupiter in the same house, a *conjunctio magna*, occurred only every twenty years. In the seventh house the sun stood under the constellation of Libra at the precise moment when day and night became equal. Next to the sun, Mercury. Not far off, in the eighth house which was that of death, Mars, at its zenith. Four planets, Saturn, Jupiter, Mercury and Venus, showed themselves bound by strong links: in conjunction, in opposition or reflection, in sextile and in trine. Unfavourable, to be sure, was the situation of the moon, the heavenly body significant of the fair sex, friendship and sociability. It was not only invisible and wholly out of place in the twelfth house, but under the sign of Capricorn, the constellation inimical and harmful to it – as other astrologers main-tained, Kepler added. For that was the way he compromised: "Other astrologers are wont to say here," as though it were not in fact he who was stating it. What delineation of character could on the basis of these calculations be ventured? Something like the following: "I may in truth write of this lord that he is of an alert, animated, assiduous, restless temper, with a keen appetite for novelties of every kind, without liking for common human conduct and action, but striving after new, untried, or at least otherwise singular means, yet with much more in his mind than he doth let outwardly be seen and apprehended. For Saturn in ascension maketh for leisured, melancholy, always vigilant thinking, induces an inclination to alchemy, sorcery, incantation, communion with spirits, contempt and disregard for human precepts and practices and all religions, rendereth everything that God or men do suspect and equivo-cal as though 'twere all nothing but deceit and much more of other matter lies behind than is admitted. And, because the moon is out of place, this nature of his will accrue to his grievous hurt and disparagement among those whose company he must keep, in that he will be deemed an aloof, disdainful, hard-hearted wretch. His character will also be prone to lack mercy, brotherly or marital love, with esteem for none, devoted alone to himself and his pleasures, harsh to those beneath him, rapacious, covetous, deceptive, fickle in manner, usually silent, oft vehement, disputatious too, intrepid, man and woman together, albeit Saturn rots his fancies so that oft he feeleth fear in vain. But the best of this birth is that Jupiter doth follow and giveth hope that, with the mellowness of age, most of these failings will be worn away and thus his exceptional nature be suited to perform great and important deeds." Great thirsting after honour as well as aspiration for power and temporal dignities were clearly visible. Concomitantly he would incur dangerous enmities, although mostly emerging victorious. He would be superstitious too and perhaps by superstitious means one day set himself up as head and ringleader of a malcontent faction. Horrid and dreadful disorders might be linked with his person, particularly in the year 1613 or before or after, if he was still living. So much for what was of general and continuous application. There followed what probably interested the client, though not his counsellor, most – a cautious investigation into the details of different periods, past as well as future. Between the subject's eleventh and thirteenth years conditions had been troubled and gone against the grain. From then until his twentieth year they may have proceeded quite satisfactorily, except that there may have been a falling out with scholars and learned doctors. The indications for the twenty-first year were of a dangerous sickness. The present year – 1608 – and the next harboured few hopeful prospects. The auspices for the thirty-third year were however excellent and would afford opportunity for a splendid marriage. "The astronomers are wont to add that it will be a widow, and not beautiful, but rich in lands, buildings, cattle, and coin. Although it cannot be claimed as celestial writ, I hold that he will content himself with such a one rather than all others because, with me, his nature and bent count for more than his constellation. . . ." On the whole, concluded Kepler, the horoscope of the individual in question was similar to that of the English Queen Elizabeth and that of the 'former chancellor in Poland'. The significance of this was that Great Chancellor and Royal Field-Marshal Jan Zamoyski had been an exceedingly energetic statesman and leader of the Swedish party at Cracow which, when Wallenstein was a child, had by force prevented the accession of a Habsburg to the Polish throne.

It would be pleasant at this point to deliver the reader from this somewhat hypothetical business so as to allow him to arrive the more quickly at those stretches of time where more colourful happenings occur. Yet there are problems which, if they cannot be solved, should at least be purged of their dross because they bear on the plot of our narrative.

Kepler, it has been asserted, was aware from the outset whose nativity he was casting. True, he wrote in cipher on his own copy the name "Waltstein". Nobody, though, can say when he inscribed it, and that after 1614 he knew the identity of his client is common knowledge. Let us assume that, perhaps through Dr Stromaier, this was also the case in 1608. What help would it have been to him? Who was this unknown, modest, well-mannered but not yet fully mature young man that he should have such a perilously grandiose fate predicted for him? If Kepler investigated what there was to investigate, the "agitation between the eleventh and the thirteenth year" could refer to the death of his parents and the crusty relationship with dons and doctors to the incidents at Altdorf; the sickness in the twenty-first year, which was really his twenty-second, might have been an allusion to Wallenstein's collapse in January 1605. It is remotely conceivable that Dr Stromaier nursed the patient or, since any outbreaks of plague inevitably interested all the capital's medical men, heard of the event from colleagues. But these are simply speculations. They could only just be judged plausible if proof were forthcoming that such terrestrial detective wok formed part of an astrologer's professional practice. Kepler would never have done anything considered dishonest. And what student, a patrician to boot, has not fallen foul of dons and doctors? The planets' faintest wink in this direction would comfortably justify the assumption.

What subsequently impressed Wallenstein most was the forecast of his marriage to a rich widow. "In May of the year 1609," he noted in the margin of his copy, "I entered into this marriage with a widow as described here *ad vivum*." One critical historian has thereby been led to comment that Kepler had information about Wallenstein's being involved in matrimonial negotiations – the urgent business on which Father Veit had summoned him to Olmütz. Well, the Jesuits were not in the habit of trumpeting their secrets abroad beforehand. How Kepler should have come to be initiated into this one is difficult to follow. If he was, why did he predict the rich marriage for the thirty-third instead of the twenty-sixth year? Did he suppose that the youth and the ageing woman would prolong the anticipatory pleasures of engagement for seven years?

The same perspicacious historian (he devoted a wealth of painstaking labour to research into Wallenstein's younger years) has put forward a suggestion with more solid ingredients. The subject of the horoscope, he says, must in the first thirty-four years of his life have been a comparatively idle, politically uninterested and by no means markedly ambitious individual. Wallenstein reads that his life is constituted under the same stars as the life of the great Queen and that of the great

Chancellor. He reads that it is composed of this and that element, that he will do this and that. And, after reading it all, what does he do? He marries and for the next eight years, while thrones quake and nations, classes, religious communities savage one another, he is content to administer his estates by marriage, enjoy the fat of the land, and fill a small number of indifferently important official appointments with no particular distinction. The driving passion for greatness came suddenly and late after long somnolence. Not even Kepler's predictions could arouse him.... Our critic, however, overlooked one detail. The horoscope was cast in 1608, but Wallenstein did not then read it because not until five or six years later did he receive it. It was in December 1614 that Lieutenant von Taxis wrote to Kepler that several years ago he had asked him to cast his nativity "as well as that of the well-born Lord Albrecht von Wallenstein". At this moment, if not sooner, Kepler learned the name of his client in 1608. Taxis wrote again on 1 May 1615, repeating his request. Wallenstein, he stated, had "recently" received his horoscope, but unfortunately he, the lieutenant, not yet his. "Recently" means a number of weeks ago, at the most a few months. Why delivery should have taken so long is anybody's guess. Possibly Kepler had been defrauded too often and did not want to hand it over until he had his promised fee, and maybe that was delayed. When another ten years had passed and Taxis once more applied to Kepler, this time for amendments and amplifications, he also once more resumed the pretence that the Great Unknown was still the Great Unknown, the "Bohemian lord". In those days people remained mystery-mongers even when a secret had long been babbled away.

Turning from the problem of name and date to that of content, was Kepler's portrayal of Wallenstein correct? If not, we need spend no time on it. If yes, how did he hit on it? Were I to say that there is something to the art of astrology, provided the right man does it, I would no doubt provoke a smile on the part of many a reader. I would happily tolerate that if only I were offered a better explanation. To ascribe the entire proceeding to a lucky guess would be stupid – the character of an unknown individual is not guessed that way. But how could Kepler *know*? Even had he indulged in the indiscreet showmanship displayed in their work by our contemporary daily prophets, had he visited Hermanitz, Koschumberg, Goldberg, and Altdorf, had he eavesdropped among regimental comrades, relations, Viennese courtiers, from nowhere and nobody would he have obtained the information of which in his paper he believed himself to be in possession. It lends fresh colour to the surmise that he not only knew the name of his client but encountered him personally, surveying him with his sad, shrewd eyes. One historian has therefore supposed that Wallenstein rode straight to Prague and introduced himself to Kepler. That however is not the manner in which matters were handled. Proof of the mystification in which the identity of the "Bohemian lord" was steeped and of mediation on the part of Taxis and Stromaier is twofold. Kepler had no idea of his client's disposition, intellect, spirit, ability, and appearance. None the less he was reasonably confident about his analysis and the more so when sixteen years later the world at large had learned sundry things about Wallenstein. That was how he came to reply, not without an undercurrent of sarcasm, "The individual in question will best know how I hit the mark with the delineation of his nature." He had cause to be content with the likeness he had drawn.

Disregarding certain details, such as a bent towards alchemy with which Wallenstein was never reproached, it remained the accepted portrait of him in his own lifetime and after. To quote one example, in 1626 one of his numerous well-disposed enemies and a great dissector of souls commented: "Indeed his innate slyness and cunning border – this can be said with assurance – on the unbelievable. Behind the rough exterior of his demeanour, which as a rule is more artificially than naturally harsh, he conceals and buries the designs and purposes he has in mind. ... Unless it be through conjecture and presentiment from long familiarity, none but God delves to the bottom of his heart. ..." And the first short monograph by Count Khevenhüller, a contemporary, begins: "Lord Albrecht von Wallenstein, a meditative and melancholic, ever restless, generous, resourceful, magnanimous gentleman, though hard and harsh of temper...." The impression survived until it reached its culmination in Schiller, who makes self-concealment, ambiguity, and brooding profundity of his hero's essence.

Can the original of what for centuries was written about Wallenstein be ascribed to Kepler's horoscope? It is not improbable. Astrologers kept secrets learned professionally no better than did medical men, who kept theirs badly enough. Kepler was an honest, but also a talkative man. When Wallenstein had become rich, powerful, and dangerous, everyone of course knew *who* had cast his nativity. He will have been asked. He will have shown his copy or described the contents. If he told no more than a single individual, things like that spread quickly and backed by Kepler's fame, did not fail of their effect.

How was the key figure affected? With what avidity did he gulp the mathematician's assessment when at last he had it in his hands? A guess can be hazarded. Earth-bound as he was, he believed in the precision and exact legibility of the nocturnal sky's inordinately fitful writing, though without a scrap of Kepler's more delicate scruples. This went to such an extent that, foretold events being approximately confirmed but not at the times prognosticated, he had the astrologer after sixteen years once again quest'oned whether, on the basis of this and that happening at a date earlier or later than anticipated, it were not with hindsight perhaps possible to correct the minutes and hour of his birth, especially as "clocks do not at all times go right". Kepler replied that this was demanding too much of the art. What was in a person's fate could perchance be accelerated, as in the case of premature birth caused by a mother's fall downstairs – there was nothing the stars could do about that. But, notwithstanding that he had thrown cold water on Wallenstein's unreasonable request, he fulfilled it by taking note of the fact that his client's severe illness occurred in 1605 instead of 1604. His conclusion, after laborious calculations, was that the birth must have happened almost a quarter of an hour later than stated by the parents. It altered nothing of vital significance in the original horoscope except that the moon's position was now in the eleventh house in place of the last, which could signify a certain mitigation in the passage relating to "manners in company". The exchange demonstrates Wallenstein's absolute faith in Kepler's deductions, similar to that which we attach to the skilled analysis of an x-ray picture. Could he then do other than trust to Kepler's delineation of his character, compare it with the results that self-examination showed, and find it all the truer the longer he scrutinized, with shuddering curiosity, its points of resemblance? So that Kepler's study would have as formative an effect on him as, in Kepler's view, the stars had at the moment of his birth? Precisely. For Kepler saw formative and formed as in a mirror! The nature of the evolving personality responded to the effect of the planets by simultaneous incorporation and modification. Had Wallenstein been a cheerful child under Jupiter, and nothing but that, he would not have been able to play the saturnine role that scientific exposition allotted him.

He never did strictly adhere to it and never quite fulfilled it. In the end he did not brace himself to play the part of ringleader of a malcontent faction. He oppressed those beneath him rather less harshly than others of his class. He was not a hard-hearted wretch. His conversation, which people feared as though they had indeed read Kepler's horoscope, could be amiable, not to say easy-going and jovial. Nevertheless, as this tale unfolds, we shall ever again be reminded of Kepler, and in particular of the incompatibilities in his delineation. It is not a straightforward picture that he draws, in a way that could be expected from a more primitive form of psycho-analysis. His subject is suspicious and reserved, but also vehement, disputatious, and intrepid, yet timorous and imagining perils where none exist. Saturn's influence is mitigated by Jupiter's.

We shall often be reminded of these and other factors. Let it for the present remain open with what precision they fall into place. Only the story as a whole can show what kind of a man our hero was, which would be impossible to do in a mosaic of a few hundred words. It must, I fear, for ever remain an unanswered question whence Kepler derived his insights, in so far as they were correct and, again, how far they came to be correct because he wrote them down.

MARRIAGE

The preceding section included the remark that the business which led Father Veit to summon Wallenstein to Olmütz was matrimonial. That was it: a matter of marriage and a matter of business.

Father Veit, a robust preacher and spiritual guide to the rich of Moravia, as well as director of the Jesuit seminar at Olmütz, had among his penitents one who caused him anxiety – Lucretia, daughter to Sigmund Nekeš von Landek, widow of the lately deceased Arkleb von Vičkov, Lady upon Vsetín, Lukov, Rymnice, and Milotice. Any mention of Hermanitz in the same context as these estates, valued at over four hundred thousand gulden and supporting several thousand souls, would have been sheer mockery. Lady Lucretia had inherited them mainly from her father's family, of which she was the sole survivor. She had no children. She did have Protestant relations. The duty of her father confessor was plain – to find her another husband, firm of faith and, if possible, sufficiently energetic to put in repair on the estates what had hitherto been left neglected there. To the shrewd priest Wallenstein seemed his man. Wallenstein thought so too. The rest of the essentials, settlement of the patrimonial affairs and bringing the couple together, was discreetly and speedily done.

Hardly one among Wallenstein's many biographers omits to say that Lucretia von Landek was well advanced in years. Few fail to add to her ripe age the misfortune of ugliness. Perhaps it derives from Kepler's forecast about the widow with poor looks. The first historian to make the allegation was Gualdo Priorato. His information was also that the new

Lady Waldstein tried to prompt her husband's deficient love with a magic potion of which he nearly died. Privy Councillor Herchenhahn, a scribbler of the 1780s who dealt with Wallenstein and was a source for Schiller, took over the story: "A wealthy old Moravian widow of the Wickova clan, skilfully fished resilient Wallenstein for her second spouse, preferring him above numerous other suitors to her shrivelled hand. Her love grew with the days of her new marriage, but the canker of jealousy stole into her heart. The enamoured old lady demanded many tokens of reciprocal love and, to kindle this, had recourse to unnatural means. A love-philtre . . .", and so on. The wedded pair's cohabitation may have been what it will. The unemotional preliminaries to the marriage tells us nothing about it. Marriage arrangements, in the class to which Wallenstein belonged, almost always were impassive transactions. The only special feature was that, whereas riches were usually joined to riches, in this instance a relatively leanly endowed young man obtained a very wealthy woman. As for Lucretia's age, her skull escaped modern scientific investigation as little as Wallenstein's did and the conclusion has been that at the time of her death she can have been thirty-five at the most. So she was thirty or thereabouts when she married again. The dates of her parents likewise make it impossible for their daughter to have been any older. This lady seems to have suffered almost as great injustice as Xantippe. Wallenstein, who honoured her memory, was as little to blame for that as Socrates.

For the rest, matters proceeded smoothly and entirely in accordance with the notions of the marriage-broker. After Lady Lucretia had paid off the manager of the estates, her brother-in-law, with a piece of land and eight thousand gulden, she made her husband joint-owner and sole legatee of her vast fortune. After four years she died, supported by the religious consolations administered by Carthusian monks. Thirteen years later, when Wallenstein founded the Carthusian monastery of Walditz near Gitschin, he expressly recalled "the especial propensity of his late deceased wife, Lady Lucretia Nekeš von Landek, for this Order", and it was to Walditz that he then had Lucretia's coffin transferred.

> At Gitschin, in the cloister he himself
> Once founded, rests the Countess Wallenstein.
> Beside her, who created his first fortunes,
> He wished some day, from gratitude, to sleep.*

* Schiller, *Wallenstein, A Historical Drama in Three Parts*, tr. Charles E. Passage.

She can truly be said to have been the founder of his first fortune. He, one of some thirty Waldsteins, had been an insignificant Bohemian gentleman. Now he belonged to Moravia's wealthiest gentry. However, as he wrote of his monks when once again he had cause to be irritated by them, "The more they have, the more they want."

He Observes the Ways of the World and Cautiously Obtrudes

WHEN Wallenstein installed himself with his "randy gammer" – a slightly later chronicler's epithet for his young wife – on her Moravian estates, the margraviate had just broken its link with Bohemia. Its sovereign was no longer the Emperor Rudolf, but Prince Matthias, Archduke of Austria and King of Hungary. The tale that hung thereby was as follows.

The game in which the privileged classes indulged in the Habsburg lands was of dual character, a contest between the Estates, preponderantly the Protestant ones, and the ruler on the one hand, between the rancorous brothers Matthias and Rudolf inside the ruling House on the other. The Catholic and royal power, moving towards absolutism without being rightly aware of it, was divided within itself. The same held good for the Estates in Austria, Moravia, and Bohemia in as much as the Protestants were faced by a growing Catholic minority. Nor could it with certainty be said which of two motives stirred more forcibly the souls of Catholic lords: religion dovetailed with blind allegiance to the head of the dynasty, as exemplified by Wallenstein's cousin Wilhelm von Slawata, or religion brought passably into line with national and class interests, in the way that Karl von Liechtenstein tried to achieve in Moravia when and for as long as he judged it to be to his own advantage. An eye to the latter was in general the strongest motive of all. It accounts, leaving aside completely honest or fanatical believers and a few unselfish politicians, for the remarkable tergiversations on the part of the nobility.

Emperor Rudolf had never really accepted the treaties of 1606, the peace with the Sultan, Hungarian autonomy, his brother's regency in Austria. He intrigued, and he permitted his followers to intrigue, against them. The result was that the Protestant Hungarians, Austrians, and Moravians veered towards alliance with the Archduke. The step lay in the nature of this struggle for ascendancy, just as the alliance could inherently not be other than insincere and short-lived. Both parties, the Estates and the Archduke, intended to use one another in the contest with Rudolf while keeping their later options open. Spanish policy, supporting the Archduke on the border-line of rebellion rather than the rightful King-Emperor because Madrid had finally recognized the bane that Rudolf was to Habsburg, spells out plainest the combination's temporary character. But then how could King Philip III's advisers have been expected to sustain for long a radical Calvinist, properly speaking a republican, like Erasmus von Tschernembl, spokesman for the Austrian Estates, and a statesman of so un-Catholic a piety as Zierotin?

In April 1608, after copious public discussion in the Diets and conspiracy in castles lent by Karl von Zierotin, Matthias undertook with hired troops and Estates' recruited regiments what was in effect a campaign against his brother. At Lieben, then close to Prague, now a suburb of it, this essentially less than forceful, enterprising prince compelled King Rudolf to renounce all Habsburg lands to the south and east of Bohemia. The Hungarians would accept Matthias as King, the Moravians as Margrave, and he should be styled King-designate of Bohemia provided that was agreeable to the Bohemian Estates.

This second compromise was as little serviceable as the first had been and the next would be. As long as Rudolf remained King of Bohemia and Holy Roman Emperor, invested with the nimbus attached to that office and all its concomitant links to Germany's Catholic princes, the sick legatee's fantasies continued to imperil the fresh state of peace as they had done the old. Both brothers were now faced by the need to contrive a reconciliation with the Diets of their Estates through an arrangement which would in any case be meant to be as ambivalent, spurious, and ephemeral as all the political moves of those years. Thanks to the Protestants, the one Habsburg had won a victory over the other. Thanks to the dispute between the two, the Protestants, indeed the Estates as a whole, could extend their sphere of influence to the point where the Kings retained but a shred of their dignity.

In the summer of the following year, 1609, the Bohemians, left alone with their broken King, deprived to three-quarters of his authority, achieved what they wanted, and wanted almost to the exclusion of everything else. The other Habsburg lands were not their worry. There was indeed a good deal that, in the light of Rudolf's pitiful weakness, they could have had on friendly terms. Instead, partly because they did not trust him, partly because they enjoyed their superiority, and their spokesmen for all their piety were very power-greedy, they inflated their grievances to the verge of mendacity, breathed threats, elected ten representatives from each Estate to constitute a committee of thirty directors, and began to collect troops headed by a lieutenant-general, Count Thurn, swearing, regardless of the fact that at the moment they were not the party attacked, either to resist unto death or be allowed to live by their rights. The document bearing the royal signature and eventually, on 9 July, transmitted to them was in form a "Letter of Majesty". Its authors were not however the King's advisers, but the Estates themselves, their lawyers and lords versed in religious affairs. Its talk of love and harmony, humble pleas and due humility, that was empty formality. Terrified of the men thronging his chamber and furious at the humiliations which the text contained, Rudolf left the room without a word even as the draft was read to him. Then he conceded the demands, bit by bit, only for appearance's sake sticking at a bagatelle. "Utraquists", that is, those who participated in Holy Communion *sub utraque specie*, not "Evangelicals", was what the bullying suppliants should be called. It signified a confusion of terms because the real Utraquists were quasi-Catholics and the capture of their institutions, Prague university and the consistory, was precisely one of the Protestants' main demands. They, Lutherans and Brethren in league, could hereupon take possession of these centres of spiritual order and place them under the administration of elective "defensors". They obtained everything – the right to establish schools, to build churches, to ordain priests and to bury their dead in consecrated ground to the toll of bells wheresoever upholders of the purged creed dwelt. Furthermore the peasants should not "be ousted from their religion either by their overlords or other person else, whether spiritual or temporal, and constrained to adhere by force or any other device to another religion". The application was restricted to Bohemia, but because religion was a subject affecting the two creeds' adherents in the Estates as well as the King and the Protestants, an Estates treaty was signed on the same day. Under the eagle-eyed scrutiny of the lawyers, both documents were very precisely worded, although still not meticulously enough for those who were skilled and tractable in the art of interpretation.

The country's spiritual government signified virtually its entire government, its spiritual freedom virtually its entire freedom. What had occurred was an upheaval, and one which could not be other than vexatious to the Spanish party. The intervention of foreign powers on behalf of the Protestants had been disconcerting. The Letter of Majesty alluded to "highly placed intercession", a reference to the Elector of Saxony. Prince Christian von Anhalt, from whom the Bohemians had sought help in the shape of arms and munitions, travelled to Prague to partake actively in the occasion he regarded as "the House of Austria's fatal day" (*terminus fatalis Austriae domus*). He arrived to find the matter settled. The Protestant nobility, firmly in the saddle under a shadow-king, lacked inclination to join the French-Palatine-Estates confederacy, that mundane political net at whose creation he had been busy for a decade but whose meshes ever and again came apart between his diligent fingers. Zdenko Lobkowicz, the Catholic Grand Chancellor, had refused to put his name to the Letter of Majesty. Berserk members of the Protestant nobility were for defenestration, throwing him out of the window. The notion heralds an early theme in our drama.

What Rudolf endured in Bohemia befell Matthias in the lands now subject to him. In Moravia his concessions went willy-nilly so far as effectively to turn the margraviate into a republic of nobles. Complete freedom of religion for them and their tenantry; freedom too for the burghers in the royal towns to practise their creed at least beyond the municipal precincts; declarations of war, conclusions of peace, and appointments to the highest offices to take place only with the consent of the Estates; Moravian jurisdiction to be operative at all levels under the auspices of the elected governor, not the Margrave, but the latter bound to let his children (if he had any) learn Czech. This did not complete the list of obligations and abrogations of power imposed upon him. Karl von Zierotin answered in a letter to his Austrian fellow-conspirator Tschnernembl the question as to why in these circumstances a prince remained necessary at all – to fortify the unity of the commonwealth and to afford the safeguard of legitimacy in a dangerous world, especially against the indubitably incessant machinations of that wicked old fellow on the Hradschin. Not until he had agreed to everything was Matthias allowed, to the accompaniment of magnificent festivities, to have homage paid to him at Brünn. The Archduke was the guest of Cardinal Dietrichstein at a banquet of three hundred courses served by eighteen barons and vassals of his bishopric. Matthias expressed his thanks with a feast of still more surpassing splendour. At one table sat the host, the Cardinal, and the national office-holders; at a second, the lords of Austria and Moravia; at a third, the burghers of Brünn.

Albrecht Wallenstein was on hand in his capacity as the Archduke's Chamberlain. That can be confidently assumed. He had also been on hand earlier, from the start, and knew of the plots culminating in the campaign against Prague, for Zierotin used his brother-in-law as a link to Matthias. When Rudolf dispatched commissioners to his brother, to try and persuade him to desist from his designs, Wallenstein was among those who fruitlessly negotiated with the imperial delegates. His cousin, Wilhelm Slawata, sat opposite him. He kept fully abreast of these complicated conflicts. At twenty-five, and for all that in 1608 he was still a Bohemian lord, he had become so deeply engaged in the archducal and Estates' revolution as to be expressly named, when it came to the Treaties of Lieben, among those to whom King Rudolf had to promise not to hold their conduct against them. In the following year, during the wrangling at Prague about the Letter of Majesty, his marriage had led him to move to Moravia, but he was too much of a stranger there and too young to participate actively in its new order of things.

LANDLORD

The tangles of the Habsburg fraternal dissension were by no means over. They were, personified through the accident of succession by two incompetent old men's mutual loathing, nothing other than a series of struggles for power at Estate and national level. These in turn were simply subsidiary skirmishes in the major European conflict and furnished Spaniards, Frenchmen, and Germans with highly welcome opportunity to put out their feelers. There will be more to say on this subject. Wallenstein, as a Moravian lord and Diet member, was inevitably involved, but for the present these affairs were not his main preoccupation. Primarily he was the owner and administrator of large estates, on behalf of his wife and jointly with her, subsequently on his own; secondly, a Viennese courtier; thirdly, and lastly, a Moravian politician. He and Lady Lucretia lived part of the time at Castle Lukov, now in ruins, and the rest in that at Vsetín, with meadows and woods rising behind and facing even steeper heights, a grey pile which survives to perform an unattractive function. From Vsetín to Olmütz is a day's hard riding, at first along a pleasant path beside the river, later across flat and dreary country.

At certain intervals, Khevenhüller says, Wallenstein went to Vienna, established house on a sumptuous scale, "and when he had exhausted his resources, he returned home and remained there until he had amassed enough to come to court again." In other words, he was thrifty in the country so as to spend grandly in town, not in Brünn nor in Olmütz, Moravia's principal cities – what was Moravia to him? – but in resplendent Vienna, the residence of his King who would soon be his Emperor.

What was Bohemia to him? Not much either, it seems, for in 1610 he sold Hermanitz, the family seat, together with its church and his parents' vault, to an uncle by the name of Hannibal, thus forfeiting his status as a Bohemian noble. On his Moravian properties the convert energetically prosecuted what was termed religious reformation. Jesuits from Olmütz, Father Veit Pachta, Father Dingelauer, and others, assisted him. One of them, Father Grissus, preached and reformed so ardently that, the report goes, he suffered a mental breakdown. Neither preaching nor expulsions of pastors and vassals were the end of it. Tales were told of "soldierly operations", meaning that armed retainers drove the peasants to mass. Zierotin thought such methods inadmissible. In a stern, though not unkindly, letter he drew his brother-in-law's attention to the fact that the visitation of armed force upon disobedient members of society was a prerogative reserved to Moravia's margrave or his governor. The landlord moderated his methods without desisting from his purpose. Why? The pricks of a pious conscience? Worldly calculations? How sharp was the line of division? At this juncture, other than later, he was certainly susceptible to Jesuit spiritual influence. He sought advice from the Society's fathers and he performed the devotions imposed on him. Balbinus relates how in 1612 he undertook a pilgrimage to Loreto. He was, at any rate, in Italy then.

Having little information about his activities as a man of property during this period, buying and selling, hunting, building, stud-farming, but plenty as to a subsequent one, we can hold over description of this aspect of his life. He had occasionally to raise loans, for three thousand gulden or six thousand gulden, once even having to dispose of a homestead in consequence of all too lavish expenditure at Vienna. One of his marginal notes on Kepler's horoscope hints at economic vexations: in 1611 he had had "inconveniences in plenty". In 1614 his wife died. The following year he fell dangerously ill and "barely escaped with his life". He stayed a widower for nine years – a decidedly exorbitant span, bearing in mind his age and position. Whether celibacy mattered little to him even in his youth, as some believe, or whether he made shift with mistresses, as canny Kepler unhesitatingly assumed, is an unresolved point.

As well as bestowing on his Jesuits money and victuals, Wallenstein promised to build them a college in eastern Moravia. For the present nothing came of the project, probably because they asked for more than he was prepared to give. Instead the modest Carthusians became the beneficiaries of his ambition to found; in 1617 a monastery was erected for them on his Lukov estate. It was the first of a protracted series of endowments by means of which later he tried to make his mark as a great lord and to bend the clergy to his will.

CONCERNING THE MACHIAVELLIAN ACTIVITY
OF THE PASSAU RABBLE

Archduke Leopold, Bishop of Passau, was not exactly one of the most seasoned intriguers of his day. He was too stupid for that. His grief at the decline and the impotence of the Habsburg dynasty, at the decay of the divinely ordained order, was genuine. We know it from his letters, in particular those to Ferdinand of Styria, his elder brother. Emperor Rudolf liked the young dolt, who at least had what he himself lacked – youth, self-confidence, high spirits and drive. He would have liked best to make Leopold his successor, in Bohemia and the Empire, had it only been to upset Matthias. For the present Leopold was appointed Imperial Commissioner for the Rhineland dukedoms Jülich and Berg whose sovereignty was in abeyance through the extinction of the ruling house. This responsibility, thought the archducal bishop, was not without potentialities.

The imposition of imperial administration on the dukedoms was sound imperial law. Only thorough investigation could establish which claimant, Saxony, Brandenburg, or Palatine Neuburg, had the best title. Neither the Elector of Brandenburg, who for technical considerations relating to the inheritance flitted from Lutheranism to Calvinism, nor the Palatine Neuburg prince, who for the same purpose had rediscovered the Catholic faith of his ancestors, had awaited the judgement of imperial justice. They occupied the territories, for that reason being termed the "Possessing" Princes. Rudolf, the greybeard just humiliatingly expelled from the preponderant part of his Hereditary Lands, regarded it as his imperial duty to drive them out.

The interest attaching to the Rhenish dukedoms derived from their proximity to the western territories of the Netherlands, France, and Spain. The Protestants held that Berg and Jülich must therefore not be allowed to fall into Habsburg hands, not even on the plea of a temporary imperial arrangement. Thanks to Christian von Anhalt's customary good services, the Union princes quickly forged an alliance with France: King Henry would in person lead a contingent as large as theirs (which promised to be considerable), the Dutch were to be of the party, and international Catholicism would suffer a decisive defeat, although of a kind to please rather than offend the Pope because, rumour ran, he was on France's side. The seeds of a Rhineland and European war sown here did not ripen. François Ravaillac's dagger-thrusts saw to that. After Henry IV's assassination France sank back into its former state of disorder and for some years failed to play an active role abroad. The sole outcome of small-scale campaigning which none the less took place – French, Dutch, and Germans against Spaniards and other Germans – was that the Possessing Princes remained in possession. Archduke Leopold, who had planned mighty operations stretching from Alsace to the Lower Rhine, had to abandon the field.

Yet whenever the House of Habsburg or one of its princes mobilized to perform this or that meritorious act, whether to fight the Turks or the French or to uphold the Empire's laws, it always secretly included some ulterior motive or other indeterminate objective. Supposing it to be impossible to do anything against the external foe, then maybe something could be done against the internal one, the Protestants, the Estates, those with whom oaths of good faith had just been exchanged. That was the way, too, that Protestant fellow-gamesmen always interpreted the matter, consequently not knowing whether it was better to contribute to the external military undertaking, prepare a counter-position, or with a distrustful squint combine both these moves. That the Passauers – the nickname for Leopold's troops because they obeyed the Bishop of Passau and now were stationed in his domain – had in reality never been meant to dislodge the Possessing Princes and the French, but to serve King Rudolf's highly personal designs for vengeance on extraction of the Letter of Majesty and against Austria's, Bohemia's, and Moravia's newly-won freedom, was the Estate politicians' instant suspicion. Moravia's governor, Zierotin, always a pessimist and always circumspect, carried through the Diet a vote for increased armaments. In June 1610 Albrecht Wallenstein was selected to command a regiment of musketeers. Colonel in Moravia by grace of the Estates is what he continued to be during nine years abounding in change. He was allowed to remain so in spite of being a Papist and having caused scandal by the spiritual government of his properties. The coming conflict, signalized by ever fresh eruptions, was not viewed in a religious light. No one wanted to view it as such. How could it be viewed as such when Moravia's greatest, reputedly loyal lords, the Bishop of Olmütz and Karl von Liechtenstein, were Catholics, when in the currently brewing crisis it was the Habsburg Matthias who was being backed, when everything was so thoroughly, endlessly tangled?

There happened what was expected and in part it happened because it was expected. In December the Passauers, nine thousand infantry and four thousand cavalry, swarmed into Upper Austria and down the Danube under the command of a fellow called Ramé. The Viennese were all a-tremble, but he was really intent on reaching Prague, where Leopold at the Emperor's side was waiting for him, and suddenly his incendiaries wheeled northward into the Bohemian lands. Lots of lies and some quarter-truths were as usual spread about the operation's object. One version ascribed it to nothing but a search for winter quarters, warmth, and rations, which the small bishopric could not continue to furnish, as well as lack of money to disband the mercenaries. A not improbable tale. There was always money enough to recruit troops, never to send them home. On the other hand their leaders had announced in their cups that their arms would be turned against all who were concerting harm to the Emperor. Later they qualified this, again ambivalently, as being rough rankers' talk which only those with a bad conscience had reason to fear. What emerged was that Leopold had ordered the invasion of Bohemia for the purpose of reversing the 1608–9 train of events and that Rudolf, knowing this, half approved, half shrank back in fright. Visions of vengeance were one thing. Their materialization by means of a campaign which the foxiest jurisprudent could not proclaim legal was another. Rudolf wrote to Leopold that, having heard with great displeasure and reluctantly given credence to the invasion, he not only enjoined Ramé's prompt withdrawal, but insisted that in no circumstances must he be allowed to reach Prague. An alibi and an expression of real fright at the spirits he had allowed to be summoned. He urged the Bohemian Estates moreover to take defensive measures. No more than an incoherent bundle of utterly disparate fears and desires, he had now inspired the formation of two armies about to set upon one other.

Ramé's unpaid bands, boasting how they would tear to bits the Letter of Majesty, surged northward through Bohemia. They are hardly likely to have known what the Letter of Majesty was. The Bohemian peasants, men and women whom they drove naked, noses and ears lopped off, out of their burning houses into the wintry night, will have known it as little. Eventually the Passauers reached Prague. They succeeded in establishing themselves in the Little Quarter, but were unable to storm the barricaded Charles Bridge into the Old and New Towns. For some three weeks the city was divided. Leopold and Ramé's hordes pillaged the Little Quarter while the leaders of the Estate forces, Count Matthias Thurn, Lord Colonna von Fels, and the knight Wenzel

Kinsky, dominated it on the other bank of the Moldau. "Dominated" is hardly the right word. However much Kinsky, in the character of military man, politician, and demagogue, strove to gain the ears of the masses, to set them right, and to keep them under control, he and his compeers could not prevent the rage, fright, and superstition of the closely confined populace, usually so very patient, so very passive, from being vented in the most horrible murders, particularly of Catholic clergy. We are convinced that their victims were innocent. We are not convinced that the collective instinct of the murderers was altogether erroneous. There exists, for instance, the correspondence of two Bohemian abbots whose Latin demonstrates distinct sympathy for the Passauers. Notorious too is the highly confidential relationship with the speakers for the militant wing of Bohemian Catholicism, Privy Councillors Slawata and Martinitz, cultivated by Archduke Leopold from the Little Quarter.

Amid the madhouse to which the capital and the country had been reduced, the Spanish ambassador, Don Baltasar Zúñiga, adopted a clear stance. He declined all contact with the Archduke Leopold, vigorously imputing unqualified responsibility to the reckless young man and hinting at the Emperor's too. Madrid should tell the world that it had nothing to do with this bloody scandal, ruinous to the Catholic cause. He made no bones about threatening his departure. At the same time he thought it his duty as a Spanish diplomat to protest against the murderous attacks by the Estates on the Church's consecrated representatives, and in this he was joined by the Nuncio. The Estates' reply was meek – they had been sincerely grieved at such inhuman gruesomeness on the part of the common herd and would punish the criminals, but the true blame lay with the Passauer rabble and its abettors. This was to the point. The nobility was in control of neither the city mob nor the countryside. "Master Omnis", as the popular phrase went, began with a variety of outrages to wreak destruction upon the owners of castles and forests. If order was ignominiously crumbling through the fault of its beneficiaries, why should those cling to it who most frequently were its victims?

The knot was cut by Matthias. He manifested a power of decision that no one any longer suspected his indolent personality to be capable of. With his own hand he wrote to the Bohemian grandees that the long-concealed, shameful fraud of Leopold and his pack was now revealed; the brigands and their adherents must be punished. He would march on Prague and free the city with his faithful followers. Archbishop Khlesl made arrangements to let it be known that the Protestants' opinion of him was quite mistaken: he had long grasped that there could not be anything other than complete freedom of religion in Bohemia and the Empire. Perhaps at that instant he really meant it. Politicians of his calibre do mean the momentarily feasible and then later something else again.

In the Bohemian camp Baron Wenzel Kinsky, yesterday but a knight, managed to win over the majority of his peers to the moderate solution which kept matters within Habsburg bounds. Kinsky had six brothers. One of them, Wilhelm, approximately toed his line. Another, Ulrich, was not ashamed to hold a commission as captain under Ramé. With Wenzel's collusion? Possibly, for at one stage Wenzel made approaches to the Archduke Leopold, suggesting that the Emperor and Catholicism ought to be saved by a bold stroke. His secret intention was to produce the situation whose victims now cried to heaven – the Passauers would be the ruin of Rudolf and his supporters. Excessively subtle and abhorrent as the scheme strikes us, it was not Kinsky's only one, just as spies sometimes no longer know which side they are really serving. He had long curried favour with the Emperor and at this very time had, with his six brothers, been raised to the peerage. If Rudolf, he argued, on his own initiative and voluntarily made generous concessions to the Estates, he could maintain himself on his throne despite his enemies. His alleged reply to the objection of a minister, that the King of Bohemia would in such case play no more than the shadowy role fulfilled by Poland's ruler, is worth recording: Poles and Czechs were brothers anyway. An early instance of pan-Slav feeling with a feudal savour. While in this manner trying to save Rudolf, he coincidentally worked towards his downfall and Matthias' succession. He had done so for years, but never more ardently than at this juncture of unsurpassed crisis when he conducted the correspondence of the Estates with the Archduke. Barely however was Matthias' coronation at Prague performed, before the Baron pronounced that now they had swopped one old fool for another and soon would have a younger, Ferdinand. Why should they be so stupid as always to elect a Habsburg? Kinsky, like other politicians of his day, must have been ruled by the irresistible urge to tinker with the disposition of things the minute that they were settled. In his case, though, it was paired with comparatively rational egotism – the one firm point in this intricate, oscillating web of intrigue. Kinsky knew that Matthias, once become King of Bohemia, would out of gratitude shower him with riches. Which is what happened.

And so once more the inevitable, inevitably dishonest alliance between the Protestant peers and Matthias, the rigorously Catholic Habsburg with a rigorously Habsburg perspective. He needed the Estates because they had money and soldiers. They needed him because he had in his gift the phantom of lawfulness without which they still thought that they were unable to manage. Once more the expedition to Prague, augmented along its stages by the accretion of Moravian lords and mercenaries. Once more the attempts by Rudolf's supporters to delay approaching destiny, to negotiate and achieve any kind of ostensible peace. In this instance Adam von Waldstein acted as Rudolf's emissary. In vain. Whatever was in store for the pious Emperor, a Prague gazette proclaimed, he would nevermore be able to retain the Bohemian throne, "and it will henceforth help His Majesty little to say that the fault for this and the other hitherto aforegone wrongdoings has not been his. He can in all particulars be convicted of them by his own hand. He hath these days indeed himself indited a brief epistle unto King Matthias, but now it is too late." When on 24 March 1611 Matthias, on horseback and in scarlet attire with a spray of herons' feathers in his hat, made his entry into Prague amidst a mighty cavalcade consisting of his own court, Austrian lords, Moravian lords, Bohemian lords who had ridden out to meet him, the cavalry regiments of the Estates dressed each in their colours and bearing their insignia, including such proud ones as *virescit vulnere virtus, constantes pro patria*, better death than life without honour, and when Adam von Waldstein's greeting of the Archduke in Czech had been relayed by another lord into German, the enforced change of sovereignty was a settled affair with only such details left for clarification as what Rudolf's income and the relationship between the Estates and their new monarch should be, a business not easy of clarification. Ramé, with the remainder of his troops, had taken to his heels. Leopold excused all the misery which he had caused on the score of his extreme youth, a notion that should surely have crossed his mind earlier. Rudolf, quite incapable of admitting mistakes, signed his abdication with a shower of curses upon ingrate Prague. He was bought off with money. He also remained Emperor. He would doubtless have continued to play his hand as before, particularly since Christian of Anhalt, difficult though this is to credit, with his creation, the Protestant Union, swung over to his side and taking advantage of Rudolf's unbalanced state of mind, was unsparing of unseemly proposals solely so that the fires in the Hereditary Lands should not cease to glimmer. But Rudolf died at the beginning of 1612. At Matthias's court, Khevenhüller tells us, "the planned pleasures [though late, the King was about to marry] were transformed into mourning apparel, though not heartfelt hurt."

The upshot of it all? Habsburg remained Habsburg, the Catholic and Protestant factions remained what they had been, the Estates remained the Estates. The age and inertia of Bohemia's new King, with Archbishop Khlesl's present alacrity to allow that crooked was straight, seemed at best to promise a respite. That the aims of the Estates' kingmakers and the King's party were not the same had already emerged during the negotiations preceding Matthias's coronation. To say that it emerged is to say that it had been emerging for nearly a century, only temporarily concealed by the fraternal Habsburg strife. During their stay in Prague Matthias's ministers met in secret conference with certain Bohemian Catholics, Martinitz, Slawata, Zdenko von Lobkowicz, who by reason of the Passauer invasion were regarded as severely compromised. The principle to which the Bohemians attached greatest importance, that Matthias attained his crown through election by the Estates and not on the strength of hereditary entitlement, was never conceded by the Viennese politicians. Just as little were they prepared to allow the validity of other rights claimed by the Estates: "confederation" with the Estates of all other Habsburg lands; "defension", an army common to all Estates; "hereditary union", the revival of old Bohemian alliances with Saxony, Brandenburg, and Poland. All of these institutions, whatever their justificative background, were to prove unrealistic when serious issues were at stake, as Saxony's lukewarm attitude in the recent crisis should have been able to convince the Bohemian nobility. To want to be deceived is the way of the world. Yet those who are called on to deal with the world do not care to acknowledge this and to take it for what it is. Carefully scrutinized, the Estates' claims amounted to no more than a sign that, from the outset, there was no agreement between them and the new régime because neither side desired that there should be. The question as to why in that case they had arrived at their accommodation persists.

During the crisis Albrecht Wallenstein had been one of those to whom Moravia entrusted its military security. His regiment of foot was only intended for defensive purposes and had not participated in the advance on Bohemia. He, alike in his capacity as Chamberlain to Matthias and a Moravian nobleman, must have done so. It taught him a fresh political lesson. To chronicle all such lessons, all significant accounts gathered by him from the gazettes, and all major ceremonies that he attended in a minor capacity is impossible. This one has however had to be described

because it catches the tone of many a matter indicative of the future as
regards political forces, motives and practices. We have had a glimpse of
men whom later we shall see acting according to their specific character.
Count Matthias Thurn, for example, and Wilhelm Kinsky. Their deeds
and designs twenty years afterwards, when Wallenstein wrought their
ruin or they his, are unintelligible without familiarity with the tortuous
paths they travelled around 1611.

Rudolf II's death made necessary an imperial election in the proper
sense of the word because malice had prompted him to ensure to the last
that no designated successor should be on hand. Matthias's choice by the
Electors was unanimous but listless. In the following year, 1613, Wallenstein accompanied the new Emperor to the Diet held at Regensburg
where he saw conditions simmering, though in a larger, gaudier pot, in
the same way as in the Hereditary Lands – a union of states who no
longer recognized the rules of the game which cemented their unity,
taxpayers refusing to pay their dues, quarrels about competing compe-
tences, the breakdown of justice under the burden of mutually exclusive
power interests. Karl von Zierotin warned his brother-in-law that his
place was in Moravia, not Germany, but Wallenstein could not let the
chance to take a first close look at the German condition of affairs escape
him. His purpose accomplished, he did not protract his stay. He did not
await the fiddlers' departure when the discords of problems long talked
to death were left in the air so as to be brought into harmony (it was
hoped) on the occasion of a subsequent, more intimate festivity.

HELPER IN NEED ON HIS OWN ACCOUNT

The condition of neighbourliness is akin to that of enmity. Neighbours
have to rub along somehow, and the odds on a bad relationship are as
high as those on a good one. The complex of lands inherited by Archduke Ferdinand, not simply Styria and Carinthia, but Carniola, Gorizia,
and parts of Istria including the cities of Trieste and Grado, comprised a
portion of the Adriatic littoral as well. The Republic of Venice would
not have been averse to making of this what the Swedes would so dearly
have loved to make of the Baltic, their exclusive preserve. Had they not
suffered many minor provocations permitting the promotion of a major
strategy? Such are never lacking. At the southern end of Croatia, a
collateral territory belonging to the Hungarian crown, not to Ferdinand,
dwelt the bold and fierce Uskoks. In the German-speaking world this
tribe was reputed to be, if rather unruly, a fine people, good Christians,

and with an aristocracy of its own. Their settlement in Croatia, particularly in the region around the port of Zengg, had sprung from their desire to escape the brutal bondage of the Turks. If now and again they did pillage a Venetian ship, there were worse things than that, particularly as these vessels mostly engaged in arms deliveries to the Turks. And the Archduke, after all, was not responsible for what happened in Croatia. The Venetians however took a different view. Their reprisals included the infliction of damage in Istria, blockading the port of Trieste, or moving boundary-stones eastward into the archducal domain. Whether they did it to obtain justice by the possession of certain trump cards or, as suspected at Graz, to drive the Germans out of Italy and become sole masters of the Adriatic is a point that can be left open. These skirmishes had persisted for years, in the lifetime already of Ferdinand's predecessor, and were suspended only by treaties which were not kept. If in 1615 the Republic resorted to warlike measures, the ultimate reason probably was that an outbreak of hostilities hung in the political air. Naturally the Republic was on the look-out for allies so as to cope with all eventualities. Naturally those who would be glad to be allies, because Habsburg was the enemy, sent embassies: England, the States-General, the Duke of Savoy, and even the Turks who, despite their former hint of being nothing loth to divide the whole of Venetia with Austria, in practice supported the Republic and, it was said, mouthed the same phrases as the Dutch. The German Union princes also cocked half an ear at the Republic's proposals. But Venice's most dangerous ally was the confederacy of the Three Leagues, the Grey Leagues or Grisons, in command of the eastern Swiss passes to Italy, rugged Rhaetians whose internal conflicts were not enough to deter them from external adventures and who, like Savoy, had the Spaniards in unwelcome juxtaposition. Is it surprising that the Archduke looked for help from where, in these circumstances, it must come, from Spanish Lombardy, Bavaria, Vienna? On the other hand, with money so desperately short and conditions in the Hereditary Lands and the Empire so tense, Emperor Matthias and his adviser Khlesl did not want to hear a word about war against Venice. Other sovereigns too, Khlesl wrote consolingly, had had to put up with all sorts of things.

To put up with what he considered an injustice ran entirely contrary to Archduke Ferdinand's high opinion of his House and position. Peaceful counter-reprisals, like the expulsion of Venetian subjects from his harbours and closure of the overland trade route to merchants, had proved too blunt a weapon. The issue of orders to burn down precisely as many Venetian villages as had been set on fire in his own territory, sparing only the churches, initiated counter-hostilities without calling them such. For two years, from December 1615 onward, war prevailed between Venice and the collateral Habsburg line which inevitably would soon be the main one. Although the conflict was set in sufficiently remote a cranny of north-eastern Italy to nullify the possibility of its expansion into a European war, yet it was too interesting for Europe not to attract to the scene representatives from most of its nationalities, here Britons, Dutch, French, Savoyards, Swiss, Corsicans, Cretans, Albanians, and there Spaniards, Walloons, Germans, as well as those savage South Slavs, the Uskoks, who were supposed to be the mischievous cause of it all. If anywhere on the continent two opponents for however idosyncratic motives tilted and shot at one another, the main antagonists of the day intervened directly or indirectly, to extend, to prolong, and to make of the specific issue a microcosm or incidental scene of the general one. Into local disorders was gathered the inflammation of the entire body politic, preceding its convulsion. So it was in the collision between Spain and the Netherlands, in Jülich-Berg, in the internal chaos of the Hereditary Lands, and in the present instance.

Nothing whatever was achieved and eventually, with ostensible settlement of the ostensible cause, the parties dispersed in the same way as two years earlier their encounter began. Talk of more comprehensive war aims was better suppressed; not having been consummated, they had never existed. Thanks to the good services of the Pope, the Kings of France and Spain, and the Spanish regent in Milan, the process of mediation was during the period of hostilities never for a moment interrupted. Conditions of peace and a precise time-table for their fulfilment would be set out in writing – for a start the resettlement of Uskoks away from the coast, then evacuation by the Venetians of their unlawfully occupied positions, followed by a general armistice, and thereafter unimpeded navigation of the Adriatic, exchange of prisoners, and an amnesty. One belligerent, though, would accuse the other of having begun the hostilities and not sincerely wanting peace. Besides, supposing this to be signed, where was the pledge for its fulfilment? Peace and justice was all that one side wanted. Unfortunate that, for the present, the other did not, particularly at a juncture when it had just attained a military advantage.

The contenders fought for the advantage represented by possession of Gradisca, the fortress-town on the western bank of the Isonzo, with a double chain of ramparts and walls constructed from huge blocks of hewn stone, its northern flank protected by marshy and reedy ground, its south dominated by a fort accessible to wary attackers only from the west. The energies of Europe in miniature, temporarily concentrated on this war and on Gradisca with its garrison of two thousand men, were more drastically sapped by wintry cold and summer heat, drought, pestilence, lack of water, lack of money, and every other kind of lack than by the occasional slinging of shot and shell. The Venetians' objective was to achieve a breakthrough in the east or at least to prove their definite superiority by capture of the fortified town. To hold it, provision it from the east, harass and demoralize the enemy in the fortress's vicinity was the task of the Archduke's forces. The more stubbornly Gradisca was defended, the more troops the Venetians had to put into action and the more Ferdinand's generals had to think about reinforcements. What could not be indefinitely concealed was that in this game the Republic held the stronger hand – mastery of the sea-lanes, money, more resolute allies. Success in turning his private war into the Empire's, based on the argument that Turkish aid to the Venetians constituted a breach of the imperial peace, eluded Ferdinand. The help derived from certain German princes' contributions of gulden and gunpowder was hardly more than symbolic. As for Vienna, it never mustered anything but warnings of growing danger and pleas of insurmountable financial difficulties.

In this emergency the Archduke turned to the nobility of Austria and Bohemia-Moravia, invoking spontaneous action and a sense of chivalry as in the olden days. Very olden days. The times when the king's vassals with their men-at-arms thronged in good cheer and at their own expense to their liege-lord's side lay far back. It does not appear that this clarion call from the south effected much reverberation in the north. We know of only a single case. On 6 April 1617 a message from Prague stated: "Lord Albrecht von Wallenstein will for his own account place 180 cuirassiers and 80 musketeers at Archduke Ferdinand's disposal in the camp." He had sent out his agents, had had the recruiting-sergeant's drum beaten in Moravia's small towns and villages, bought horses, cuirasses and helmets, pistols and lances, examined volunteers with the trained eye of an officer, settled terms of pay with those who satisfied his purpose and drilled them into a unit. At the beginning of June he arrived at Gradisca. A long march and a romantic, almost quixotic act of chivalry not unlike that which Karl von Zierotin once wanted to render King Henry, but one to be crowned by greater success.

As for its military aspect, a distinction has of course to be drawn between what historians say, arising from one treading blindly in the footsteps of another, and what the only safe source has to offer. There must therefore be no talk of Wallenstein decisively affecting the course of the Venetian campaign. In the first place nothing decisive was ever achieved, the contestants at the end desisting from mutual attack in a state of exhaustion. Secondly, Wallenstein's cavalry was much too small in numbers, a couple of hundred against sundry ten thousand, to perform any outstanding feats. He was however of the party when during a summer's night Dampierre, the archducal commander-in-chief, launched a dangerous surprise sortie to prevent at the last moment the fortress's encirclement to the east, which would have involved the garrison's starvation, and to bring provisions of corn into the town. And that was possible only after a murderous skirmish with the Grisons fighting in the service of the Republic. Such was Wallenstein's contribution and proficiency of command that in the next order of the day he was singled out for special mention. "On this occasion," Khevenhüller reports in his annals, "Lord Albrecht von Wallenstein (hereinafter Duke of Friedland) . . . conducted himself honourably and judiciously." The present chronicler has extracted this quotation from an official document in the Vienna military archives. It still lies there along with another which, referring to a similar engagement on 22 September, says: "Albrecht von Wallenstein especially distinguished himself by intrepid daring and valour." So he had progressed to becoming a cavalry officer, and not a particularly young one at that, who amidst nocturnal scuffles knew how to give his men appropriate orders and set them an appropriate example. The suggestion that he intervened in the negotiations with Venice or drafted a manual of cavalry organization, martial law, strategy, is either misunderstanding or embellishment on the part of historians wanting to make a great man of him when he was not yet one. Moreover he arrived late on the scene of action, at a moment when it was mere pretence not to know that the negotiations pursued at Madrid would drag to their appointed end.

That happened during the succeeding winter. In substance the peace was a restoration of the *status quo* except for the banishment of the guiltiest among the Uskoks and the reduction to ashes of their piratical navy. Madrid, to be sure, was a long way off. There was a laborious passage between its stipulations and their performance on the spot, where neither side failed to accuse the other's followers of dishonesty or debility. It was summer 1618 before everything was implemented, evacuated, restituted, and pardoned. Summer 1618. That was the summer when the Venetians would have been able to find a fresh ally at the heart of the Habsburg Hereditary Lands and whom they now wished well without going so far as to merge their resources with him. It was a circumstance which would recur often enough. Let one party just be emerging from the fray and the other would be plunging in.

Wallenstein had by then returned home, possibly in December. He had earned the enduring gratitude of Ferdinand of Styria, subsequent Holy Roman Emperor. In the successive patents which set out the reasons for the rescuer's promotions, the Friulian campaign and how "he placed at Our disposal two companies of horse on his own account," was regularly noted. Gradisca, like his marriage to the rich widow, laid the basis for Wallenstein's good fortune. He had long been Catholic and pro-Habsburg. Henceforward he was Ferdinand's man. His good fortune would increase in ratio as Ferdinand experienced any. There is, incidentally, a link between these two incipient decisions of his. Without Lady Lucretia's wealth he would never have been able to pay for the two mounted companies. Who knows? Perhaps he would none the less not have raised them if in the previous year Kepler's horoscope, which promised him such a splendid, perilous life, had not at last reached him.

The Bohemian Revolution

THE Habsburg fraternal strife had brought the nobility and the burghers gains utterly loathed by the losers, in so far as they recognized the concessions at all, which in the case of certain important claims by the Estates they never did. Freedom of religion had indeed been solemnly confirmed in writing. For the time being there was nothing to be done about that. Nobody wanted to be a lawbreaker, although everybody was a legal glossarist, a legal rigger. A direct breach of covenant, wrote Karl von Liechtenstein, was unfortunately not possible. For the present it was a matter of raising an army on the pretext of danger from the Turks, keeping it in being, and (this seemed to him a very promising aspect) dividing the commonalty from the nobility by way of paternalistic government reliefs. It was a line of thought with which both sides toyed, and would continue to toy for a long time ahead. Both were however equally incapable of implementing it because the peasants were the one joint, exploited adversary left to them. A Moravian Diet resolution once again forbade the peasantry on pain of corporal punishment to carry arms or to appeal over the heads of their lords to the royal courts. As for freedom of religion, the position was that it had become law and yet could not be allowed to be law because God's will and the sovereign's most sacred duty ran counter to it. Fire and water might somehow be made to mix in words on paper, but what did anyone suppose the outcome to be?

The Bohemians cannot be said to have played their hand skilfully. Their efforts at confederation with the Estates of other Habsburg territories bore no fruit. The strange discussion or, more accurately, non-discussion of this lofty project occurred in 1615 at Prague during a General Diet, a meeting of all the lands belonging to the crown of St Wenceslas, to which the Austrians were invited. When their representatives had bowingly made their entrance, they were haughtily asked what was their desire; their hosts craved nothing. Simply because Bohemia's nobility deemed it beneath its dignity to be the first to propose alliance.

The Austrians, astounded and disgusted, left empty-handed. The same meeting passed a motion for preservation of the Czech tongue. In future nobody should be allowed to live in the land or become a citizen of one of its towns unless conversant with the language. This is an occasion when the national element, which in all the disputes emerges far less often, clearly or dominatingly than seems usually to be assumed, does come to the fore. The spokesmen for the Bohemian nobility, who between 1606 and 1612 had taken Matthias's part and now with dreary inevitability gathered against him, were by no means all of Czech origin and fluent Czech speakers. The brothers Kinsky; Lord Peter von Rosenberg, the richest man in southern Bohemia until his death a short while before; Lord Albrecht Smiřický upon Nachod, the richest man in eastern Bohemia; Lord Wenzel von Budowa, one of the few clean among the crowd of unclean; these, and others, yes. But Lord Colonna von Fels came from the Tirol, Count Friedrich Fürstenberg from the Alemannic regions, and Count Heinrich Matthias Thurn, loudest-mouthed, most pushing of them all, from Gorizia in the southern sector of Ferdinand's domains. His Czech sounded pitiable, his German not much better. Loquaciously choleric and perfervidly eager to perform great feats, he was an abnormally stupid man. Only a certain gullible probity, together with the miserable turns of fate and repeatedly broken hopes in store for him, will stop us in the course of this narrative from laughing at him. Alas, it says little for the Bohemians' cause that they could find no better leader than this.

The succession. All too soon the succession was again the issue. Admittedly Matthias, when elected King of Bohemia, had had to promise not to raise the problem, this of all problems the most important, during the years that remained to him. Reality, though, revolted against the extorted pledge. German traditions as much as Czech ones flew in the face of reason. The former, even if unwritten, demanded that the Holy Roman Emperor should at the same time be King of Bohemia. Consequently the Empire could have no designated successor without there being one for Bohemia and, in the absence of such, for practical purposes none for Austria and Hungary either. Seeing that Matthias, childless, was so plagued by illnesses as hardly to be able to enjoy his newly won sovereignties and that his brothers Albrecht and Maximilian were approaching an age when the future holds out no other prospects than sorrow, Habsburg loyalists could not help asking what was to happen in Bohemia, irrespective of whether the Prague election capitulation allowed it or not.* The candidate upon whom the Habsburgs had agreed among themselves was Ferdinand, the young, the pious, the strict upholder of the law, the phlegmatically energetic, the lucky dog. Cardinal Khlesl did not like the idea. He tried to postpone its realization by arguing that first there must take place the "composition", the major easing of tension in the Empire and the Hereditary Lands as well as the settlement of all the main points of dissension there; afterwards the succession would prove capable of completely smooth solution. The motive which he did not let out of the bag was that Ferdinand, if he became successor, would in view of Matthias's wasting sickness be very nearly master, one with whom it would not be so easy to deal as with the present monarch. The prince of the church instinctively hated the militant young Archduke. That may in some small part explain why in the Venetian campaign he prevented a single scrap of aid reaching him. He wanted the war to consume Ferdinand as a fever consumes the human body. He should scream until the water ran in his mouth. Those were the words imputed to the Cardinal. Whether sheer enjoyment of power or a judicious love of peace and foresight really guided Khlesl's carefully spun policy, contemporaries unhesitatingly assumed the first to be the case. So he and Ferdinand were bitter enemies, like Khlesl and Liechtenstein, Duke Max of Bavaria and Khlesl, Khlesl and old Archduke Maximilian whose downright advice once was to have the Cardinal "put out of the way by poison". Murder, resolved upon by the august dynasty, was law-enforcement even when performed by the most secret lethal means and without benefit of sentence.

Finally Khlesl could no longer delay the royal election. The reason was partly Matthias's illness, deemed hopeless, and still more the appearance on the scene of Oñate, the new ambassador from Madrid, thirsting for action, who forthwith entered into alliance with Ferdinand and brought Spain's prodigious authority to bear on his behalf. In spring 1617 the critical moment arrived. Emperor Matthias, a last time up and about, introduced his adopted son Ferdinand to the Bohemian Estates as their future King. The sequel constitutes one of the most difficult episodes to understand in a tale by no means deficient in episodes difficult to understand.

Was Bohemia an elective kingdom? That had long been the Estates' contention and in western Europe it was the key to the Palatine-French party's long-term speculation. The point is a moot one, the question

* See p. 39 on imperial capitulations. The Bohemian ones extracted before coronation belonged to the same category of pledges (translator's note).

being at what date back in time to call a halt and how far the old traditions had been overlaid by new. Beyond dispute was the Diet's privilege of "acceptance". The reigning sovereign could propose his choice for the throne, but rejection of his candidate meant that he could not become King. Indisputable precedents proved it. No more determined Catholic reformer and no more unbending enemy to heresy existed outside Spain than the Archduke of Styria. The world knew it, the Bohemians knew it. If there was one man who did not fit into their seething state of affairs, it was Ferdinand, swear what he would. All the boasted determination and all the real power on the part of the Protestant nobility and the towns' representatives could have been expected to concentrate on the objective of "not this man". Which, then? Here matters became intricate because, straining our eyes as hard as we can, we are ourselves unable to espy near or afar another Habsburg who could have been acceptable to the Bohemians. Therefore the question facing the nobility with staggering suddenness was basically whether, taking into account imponderable consequences, they should now expel the Habsburg dynasty or yet again put it to the test. Disunited despite all their boasted cabals, the latter is what they did, as though in a state of trance and dazed coercion. More than one of those who voted for the candidate's acceptance were four years later to die by the sword of Emperor Ferdinand II's executioner. Properly speaking, they all voted in favour, Colonna von Fels and Matthias Thurn excepted. Thurn, the stupidest of the lot, had in the end the only shrewd inspiration: acceptance of a king did not involve the Bohemian Estates alone, but all those belonging to St Wenceslas's crown; Moravia, Silesia and Lusatia should be summoned to a fresh General Diet. The Catholic Habsburg party's well-greased diplomacy, thoroughly familiar with all the ins and outs of constitutional law, slid around this obstacle too. In the twinkling of an eye Ferdinand was accepted, proclaimed, anointed and crowned. His behaviour at the banquet which afterwards he gave for his subjects was jovial, modest, and sincere towards Catholics and non-Catholics alike.

After the Spanish *coup d'état* of 1599 followed the Letter of Majesty, the Protestant Bohemian triumph of 1609; on this, the atrocities of the Passauer folk, Rudolf's effort to regain what he had lost, and his fall; on this, an unserviceable compromise between King Matthias and the Bohemians; and on this, Ferdinand's election, which meant a new, incomparably greater victory for the Spanish party.

Matthias had had to promise not to put forward any successor during the years that remained to him. His successor, on being crowned, had

had to promise not to meddle in Bohemian affairs during the years that remained to Matthias. The second promise was kept as little as the first. A prince still young, with pride of position and deeply held convictions, could not act as though the realm of which he would shortly be ruler did not concern him. Even had he wanted to do so, his followers there, numerous enough, would not have let him. The Catholic party in Bohemia and Moravia re-formed and, sure of a legitimate, strong protector in Austria, went over to the attack. The Protestants went over to resistance and counter-attack. Soon, finally, and at a high price, the situation would arise which recently could have been had a little more cheaply. It was one thing on the basis of law and tradition not to permit a Habsburg pretender to mount the throne, another to topple him when he had acquired it by prescription and to declare war on the dynasty holding the reins of power over a large part of Europe, from Silesia to Spain. In his augury for 1618 Kepler predicted that "truly May will not pass away without great difficulty at those places and in those disputes because everything hath previously already been prepared, and especially where the community hath in other respects great free-dom." Where everything was previously already prepared – Kepler knew his Bohemians. Playing at squabbles cannot be protracted in-definitely. One day the game turns serious. The question who first started being serious is then fairly irrelevant.

The Emperor had quitted the Hradschin to die in Vienna. He left behind ten governors, at any rate three of them Protestant. Immediately Ferdinand's influence, or that of Bohemians who saw in him their protector, was felt. A decree issued at Prague placed all printed matter hitherto supervised by the "defensors" of the Protestant church under the Lord Chancellor's control – what later generations would have called a censorship law. A second decree stripped the Prague municipal authorities of their power. Simultaneously a dispute burst into flame which had been smouldering for years and had been ventilated in thorough historical debate – were domains in the possession of the Catholic church ecclesiastical or really royal property, on no more than loan to the church? If the latter, the Protestants living on them could in accordance with the Letter of Majesty freely build churches there. If the former, their souls also were in bondage to abbots and bishops. The Protestant interpretation appears in this instance to have come closer to the truth. It was however an instance in which the leaning towards pugnacity by both parties lay at the back of the lawyers' chain of argu-ments. Whoever had the might took the course he thought right. When, the citizens of Braunau having refused to surrender the keys of their church to the abbot, their representatives next met in the dungeons of Prague's White Tower and when the church built at Klostergrab was torn down at the Bishop's order, the defensors recognized what from the outset had been clear to Count Thurn's not precisely eagle eye: Ferdinand's election had delivered them, hands bound, into the power of Church and King.

An assembly of Protestant office-holders was summoned to Prague. A memorial submitted to His Imperial Majesty received the trenchant reply that nothing whatever illegal had occurred, the sovereign's patience was exhausted, and the initiators of impudent and highly unauthorized meetings must expect to incur the full severity of the law. At Prague the suspicion was instant that the enemy within the walls, Wilhelm von Slawata, supreme justiciary and royal governor, had fathered this bleak missive. Slawata swore that Khlesl, not he, was its progenitor. Perfectly true. The Cardinal, usually no friend of frontal assaults, felt that this time it was essential to pounce like a lion and not slink like a fox. Perhaps he genuinely believed that a roar would save the situation. Perhaps he was sly enough to scent which way the wind was blowing since Ferdinand had moved to Vienna. His advice was in any case unsound. In May the defensors summoned a second protest meeting, the mood of the nobility and a part of the towns being such that they had no choice. At this session, held in the turret-chamber of wealthy Albrecht Smiřický's mansion and not of course in public, the exploit was planned – the strong-arm, ultimate demonstration – that has in histories of Europe become legendary: the Defenestration. The meeting took place on 22 May. What happened next day – the entry by force into the governors' council-chamber on the Hradschin of the sword-clanking nobility, Matthias Thurn, Albrecht Smiřický, Count Andreas Schlick, Wenzel von Ruppa, two Ričan brothers, two Kinsky brothers, a Slawata who was no less than Wilhelm's own brother, Colonna von Fels, Wilhelm von Lobkowicz, and others; the long wrangle with the four governors, Sternberg, Diepold von Lobkowicz, Jaroslaw von Martinitz, and Wilhelm von Slawata, whom they found there; the conspirators' menacing question as to who in March had framed the imperial note; the beseeching answer of the royal officials, recognizing their danger, that they could and must not reveal this, but authorship had assuredly not lain with them; the fulmination to the point of self-exhaustion, hesitation, and talking themselves into new and better fulminations by the intruders because what they proposed to do was impossible to perform without fulmination; the reading of the sentence which condemned Slawata and Martinitz as enemies of the Estates and their country; its implementation by throwing the precipitately damned, with their secretary, into the castle-moat fifty feet below – all that is so much a part of general history that we can presumably spare the reader its dramatic details. Question, answer, and sentence were shadow-play. The sentence or, more correctly, the murderous decision based on a vague concept of chivalric lynch-law had been taken irrevocably the day before. Its execution was farcical. The three victims, as everyone knows, escaped with mortal fright, their lives, and a few bruises. How they managed it nobody knows. The sequel – that was neither shadow-play nor farce.

It could have proved much less than lurid if the deed had happened in a fit of irrationality provoked by the circumstances of the moment, if muzzy-brained Count Thurn had not known perfectly well what he was persuading his compeers to do and why. At Vienna news of the Defenestration created confusion rather than a feeling that it called for action. Matthias was not a man of quick decisions. Archduke, or King, Ferdinand was in Pressburg, wooing the Hungarian Diet for St Stephen's crown. Cardinal Khlesl's position was roughly that, while his permanent policy was none other than the restoration of Catholic power and any obstacle to this objective purely temporary, the temporary could last a long time. Since 1611 his policy had factually amounted to accommodation, postponement, and relaxation, a policy rendered unconstructive cnly by being provisional and dishonestly meant. Up against such resistance as the governors' attempted murder intimated, Khlesl's grim inclination was to wait and display flexibility. "I am an Austrian," he said soothingly to a leader of the Austrian Estates. "My advice has always lain on the side of peace, never on that running counter to the Emperor's seal and signature, nor am I any longer so young as to yearn for the feel of a sword. Therefore I do not advise bloodshed, but peace, provided it is conformable with the Emperor's good name." The Letter of Majesty must not be torn asunder. He wanted as long as practicable to interpret the defenestration as something other than it had been intended to be, not as a far-reaching design, but a sudden access of passion. One thing the experienced diplomat nevertheless immediately and rightly saw. The more the Bohemians' assertion of an act of religiously, purely religiously motivated rebellion was left uncontradicted, the juster their cause in the eyes of Europe's heretics. The stronger the accent placed on profanely political and social aspects, with proof forthcoming that "the present Bohemian mischief doth not touch on that which it is most superficially given out to be", the better the chance of bringing over at least the more conservative Protestants into one's own camp. The Elector of Saxony, for example. From that minute forward, down to the present day, whether political writers, and subsequently historians, have treated the question as a religious or secular conflict has been the surest criterion of their pro- or anti-Bohemian attitude.

In the first instance an imperial commission was sent to Prague to establish what had precisely happened. Special couriers rode off to Madrid, Rome, and the most important German princes, the Duke of Bavaria, the Archbishops of Cologne and Mainz, the Elector Palatine and Saxony's Elector, who in turn began to conduct an excited correspondence among themselves. Expert opinions were solicited or unsolicited expert opinions sympathetically studied. They cancelled each other out, of course. One set recommended giving way in order to avoid terrible consequences and to save what remained to be saved. Adam von Waldstein, Principal Lord Chamberlain, still at Prague in a somewhat cheerless position, supported this thesis. The Upper Austrian Estates (their spokesmen, Erasmus von Tschernembl, is a figure well known to us) let it be understood as their view that war is easy to start, laborious and intricate in conduct, and problematic as to its conclusion, with at best the ruler's commanders and ministers, not he himself, benefiting from even the greatest victory. In short, forgiveness and redress of grievances would preserve Bohemia for the Emperor, not rough treatment, certainly not war. Different was the counsel contained in a paper presented by the group close to Ferdinand. Sponsored by the Bohemian Lord Great Chancellor Lobkowicz, the Spanish ambassador Count Oñate, and Ferdinand's personal intimate Eggenberg, it termed the Bohemian insurrection a downright stroke of luck. This was the time to cauterize the cancerous growth and once for all to be rid of the unbearable enslavement to rule-by-Estates. There was everything to win, nothing to lose, for what value attached in such demeaning circumstances to what was still held in Bohemia? Emperor Matthias read the opinions with a staring, melancholy expression and fell asleep in the process. Khlesl carried on with their perusal and, in as much as he reserved his decision, found them all equally right or equally wrong.

What poured ever fresh oil on the flames of those who burned for action was the behaviour of the Estates at Prague. They certainly wrote to Vienna, Munich and Dresden that they were struggling for nothing else than the maintenance of their prescriptive rights and that they were, and wished to remain, their King's loyal subjects. But how they acted, with astonishing promptitude on the very day after the Defenestration, was different – the establishment of what amounted to a revolutionary government of thirty members, ten from each Estate, and comprising such familiar personalities as Wenzel von Budowa the pious, Albrecht Smiřický the rich, and Wilhelm Kinsky the arch-intriguer. Thurn was not included. He, with his reputed strategic gifts, was put in command of a hastily raised army. Under him served Lord Colonna von Fels with the rank of lieutenant-general and Johann von Bubna, Wallenstein's fellow-soldier in the Turkish campaign, as major-general. The army was to be composed partly of a national levy, wherein every tenth feudal dependant as well as every eighth citizen would have to enlist, and partly of volunteers. High taxes were imposed without being collected. The great lords, with a few laudable exceptions, were readier to revolt than to pay. What, incidentally, was the purpose of an army whose organizers desired none other than to be their King's loyal, peaceful subjects? Self-defence, of course. A state of preparedness for all eventualities. We shall see in a moment when an eventuality was assumed to have occurred.

The King's loyal subjects decreed the expulsion of the King's dearest comforters, the Jesuits. In sadly ceremonial procession the members of the Order left city and land. On their heels followed, voluntarily but presumably knowing why, the highest ecclesiastical dignitaries, at their head the Archbishop of Prague. The beginning of an emigration, an event of which the future would witness many a variety, as also of the numerous confiscations which were now initiated in order to obtain ready money. Requisitioned were the fortunes of such traitors as Wilhelm von Slawata and Paul Michna, Secretary to the Bohemian Chancellery, busy at Vienna stoking the fires. A dangerous expedient, confiscations. We observe here what we shall so often have occasion to observe, an age when war and preparations for war did not render society more productive; they rendered it poorer. Where anything was paid for, *if* it was paid for, someone had to suffer confiscation. No one was rewarded except at the expense of another. The thirty directors decided on a moratorium for all debtors. The law was meant to stop economic breakdowns, but merely brought about economic breakdown. Who lends or sells on credit when defaulters are covered by a general amnesty? No more than a few days had passed before the more intelligent among the Estates' leaders clearly saw that their skiff was rushing on a torrent towards perilous cataracts. There were such as would gladly have headed for shore again if it had been at all possible.

This did not apply to rumbustious Count Thurn. The Defenestration was not a month old before he tore out of Prague with three thousand infantry and a thousand cavalry at his back. The objectives were Bohemian towns like Budweis and Krumau in the south of the country who refused to co-operate. Perfectly obvious that the whole of Bohemia should and must obey the new government, else what would things come to? Yet whoever moved into southern Bohemia moved in the direction of the Austrian frontier. Moreover it hardly sounded pacific when Thurn let the inhabitants of Budweis know that, short of their voluntary surrender, he would smash his way into the town unsparing of the child in its mother's womb.

Of what use, in the light of so rapid and unequivocal a development of affairs, were the equivocal documents exchanged between the parties, the apologias going from Prague to Vienna, the edicts from Vienna to Prague, self-righteous and threatening, then again less harsh in tone and admitting certain Bohemian complaints to be in some degree well-founded? What use was it that the imperial court refused to hear anything about a Bohemian directory, but, like it or not, negotiated with "the personages from all three Estates assembled in the Palace at Prague"? Negotiation was no longer serious, simply a matter of erecting a paper screen while the search for money, soldiers, and allies was on. None the less the warmongering business was pursued more energetically at Prague than at Vienna. "Most dearly beloved Lord Brother," the Elector of Cologne wrote to the Duke of Bavaria, "this cunctation of His Majesty doth seem to me entirely unseasonable." Duke Max replied that this was his sentiment too and the whole of the Prague proceedings could be laid at the door of those who had all too delicately played their political hand.

The anxiety of the two Wittelsbachs was shared by the two Habsburgs, Maximilian and Ferdinand. They could not be rid of the Emperor, not this time, and they therefore decided to eliminate the man whom they regarded as the chief temporizer, chief appeaser, and chief culprit. Count Oñate, the Spaniard, took a hand in the game while emphasizing that officially he must not know of anything. The plot was precisely planned, cleverly contrived. Ferdinand suddenly began writing Khlesl letters so flattering that they could not fail to put the enemy into an amiable frame of mind. The two princely conspirators went so far as to pay the Cardinal a courtesy visit. The tenor of the conversation is not known, but it went pleasantly enough to lure Khlesl next day into a return call. He drove to the imperial palace in the nuncio's coach, staying in it a short time to complete his absorbing talk with the Roman dignitary. The latter, uninitiated into the plot, seems to have inveighed against the prevailing peace policy, for the Cardinal's expression is said to have been thoughtful, indeed troubled, as he mounted the stairs. But how painfully put out of countenance was the prince of the church when in the antechamber three officers, Counts Dampierre, Collalto, and Montecuccoli, intercepted him, declared him to be under arrest, overwhelmed him with abuse, and forced him to exchange his purple robe of office for an ordinary priestly gown. He was instructed to keep quiet, do as he was told, climb into the coach waiting at a back-door, and stop uttering protests which were of no avail because everything was happening on the orders of Their Serene Highnesses. These, and Oñate, lurked hidden in the offing. While his fate slowly dawned on Khlesl and he shuddered with chagrin at being so stupid for all his shrewdness, the coach bore him helter-skelter, day in, day out, to Castle Ambras in distant Tirol. There the prisoner could play with the marvels which Wallenstein had – possibly – seen in his days as a page at court.

A *coup d'état* on the part of the Archdukes, as well as once more a Spanish *coup d'état*, against the Emperor. Breaking the news to him was not effected without scenes of rage and tears (these shed by the Empress), without humble pleas of vindication, prostrations, and appeals for forgiveness, without retrospective accusations of the unheard condemned. Had the past witnessed a rising against an intolerable monarch, Rudolf, how much more was this surely permissible and imperative in the case of an intolerable minister. After a few days Matthias gave way, pretending to be convinced of his favourite's knavery, because he had no choice. But he never recovered from the injury to his dignity. During the three-quarters of a year left to him, he was a resigned and broken old man. Power remained in the hands of Ferdinand and the individuals of his choice. That meant the party determined to pursue the Bohemian business, and thereafter presumably also other business, to the bitter end.

Khlesl, politically dead, was allowed to stay alive and, after many years, even received some indemnification. That was thanks to his ecclesiastical dignity. Had he not been a member of the Sacred College, he would probably not have left the Archduke's antechamber other than with perforated chest and wrapped in a carpet.*

* See p. 844.

THE BEGINNING OF THE THIRTY YEARS

What the Bohemians had started on 23 May 1618 was their affair and theirs alone. First, action based on vague hopes. Then the search for a sheet anchor against whatever was to come.

Even in Moravia, the most important of the collateral lands of St Wenceslas, nobody had been told beforehand and nobody afterwards knew what would in the near future be done. By now the principal members of the nobility were Catholic – the royal governor Lobkowicz, Prince Liechtenstein, and the Bishop of Olmütz. Liechtenstein enjoyed a threefold role as a member of his Moravian Estate, an Austrian, and a friend of the Habsburgs; Dietrichstein's was fourfold as a member of his Estate, a cardinal, a spiritual and secular adviser to the Emperor, and "Colonel-General" of the margraviate. The two of them took their duty as Estate members seriously. For as long as it could be managed, they did not want to be bad Moravians. And they had no wish for the war which was looming between Habsburg and Bohemia because either way it must put Moravia, including themselves, in a dangerous position. Still less was it the wish of the leading personality among the Protestant nobility, Karl von Zierotin. The three made common cause in trying to restore peace through Moravian mediation. Dietrichstein's motive was fear; Liechtenstein's, cool political calculations; Zierotin's, love of peace and a Christianity tinged with pessimism. In the course of the years his hopes dwindled more and more. He had voluntarily relinquished the royal governorship and his influence had receded. But, invested with a halo of melancholy wisdom, he still commanded attention. For the present, during the summer following the Defenestration, the Diet resolved once more upon a state of military preparedness manifested by the current establishment of two thousand cavalry under Georg von Nachod and three thousand musketeers under Albrecht Wallenstein. His commission as colonel, dating from 1610 and 1615 repectively, was therefore renewed. An appointment as colonel on behalf of the Estates, be it noted.

The crowned republic of nobles, as an institution, held no appeal for Wallenstein. By this time his peers should have known that. Nor did he share their feelings for what they called freedom. He was a convert, a founder of monasteries, a harrier of pastors, and a friend of the Jesuits. He belonged to Ferdinand of Austria's party. Of course, and the fact was notorious. He was only six months back from Gradisca. Why then did the majority of Moravia's nobility entrust a considerable part of its forces to him? Well, if the Bohemians had accepted distrusted Ferdinand as King, why should not the Moravians appoint Lord von Wallenstein, a compatriot and one of their few experienced soldiers, colonel? Here was no choice between one loyalty and another, but in theory a batch of loyalties which was by some means intended to be kept intact, loyalty to Estate and nation, to Estate over and beyond national border, to religion, and to the country's sovereign or royal authority.

Wallenstein's turn of mind was less complex. From the outset he made no secret of his disdain for the Bohemian revolution, his disbelief in, and lack of desire for, its happy consummation. The future, he felt in the marrow of his bones, lay in a different direction, one he had already encountered and wanted to follow. Seven years later he wrote that he had only taken over the command "for the speedier subjection and extinction of the ignited insurgency". A near enough description. Hardly had he assumed command before he was planning another of a totally different kind. In August he borrowed twenty thousand gulden from a certain Václav Mol of Modřelice. What for? The names of the sureties embellishing the promissory note, none less than the princely ones of Liechtenstein and Dietrichstein, prove it at any rate to have been a political loan and that, at the same time as the Moravian Estates as a whole were engaged on a course of national, supra-confessional unity, a secret Catholic separatist movement was forming.

The imperialists mobilized. The Bohemians continued to mobilize. The imperialists, completely under the driving influence of Ferdinand and his circle, obtained the services as commander-in-chief of Count Buquoy, a well-known Spanish Netherlands career officer. He knew his market value. He demanded and received three thousand gulden per month, not to speak of an enormous sum for his equipment. At his side were two important veterans from the Italian campaign, Count Dampierre and Don Baltasar Marradas, a Spaniard by origin. In addition to Thurn, the Bohemians acquired another general hailing from the Empire, Count Hohenlohe. They also gained their first ally. Count Peter Ernst von Mansfeld, bastard of an eminent Netherlands noble, poor and disinherited from the cradle, was a sombre personality. One of Archduke Leopold's mercenary leaders in the struggle for Jülich-Berg, he had since retained under his standard several thousand soldiers whom he never disbanded because they were his sole possession. Haughty, notwithstanding a reputation for dirty dealings in matters of honour, embittered, disloyal, and for ever on the search for his heritage, he pined to punish those who had done hardly by him, amounting in his eyes to almost the whole world. For some time past he had been serving the Duke of Savoy. In the Italian campaign the latter had sided with the Venetians against Spain and Ferdinand. Now, aspiring to the Bohemian throne, the Duke persuaded the Bohemians that he could procure them Venetian, not to mention other, support. As a first step he ordered Mansfeld to proceed with his troops to Bohemia. This was however top secret because, peace reigning between him and the Emperor, he wanted the matter to look like an arrangement between the thirty directors and Mansfeld, not himself. Mansfeld besieged Pilsen, another of the towns which had not wished to participate. Buquoy, with his Walloons, such forces as had been enlisted in Austria, and remnants from the army at Gradisca, invaded southern Bohemia. Ferdinand had what he had been seeking since June – armed action against the rebels. The Moravians had what they would so gladly have averted. A commission to negotiate peace – Liechtenstein, Zierotin, and Dietrichstein, a strange trio – travelled to Vienna. It also travelled to Prague, right through the theatre of war, and the sights that met Zierotin's eyes – burnt-out villages, fleeing peasants, starved animals, the corpses of those savaged to death – shattered him to the depths of his soul. At Prague he pleaded with the tongue of a despairing angel. A little sense, a little humility! Acceptance of the mediation proffered! Armistice! Peace, peace!

He received a glum hearing. How should arms be laid down when the imperialists were making themselves so provocatively at home in southern Bohemia? Who stood behind the negotiators? Who guaranteed, in view of all past experience of treaties, what was negotiated? Better, far better for the Moravian Estates to do at last what the Silesian ones were about to do and close ranks with the just cause of the heartland. Were it really to come to a pacifically minded intervention, interposition, composition by the German princes, the Duke of Bavaria, the Palsgrave, and the Electors of Mainz and Saxony, whose good services the Emperor had sought, they would enter the negotiations incomparably stronger in unison than if split among themselves. It never did come to the interposition of the German princes. Duke Max of Bavaria and the Palsgrave, each for his own reasons, wanted no intervention. Mainz possessed the electoral title, but no power. John George of Saxony, close to Bohemian affairs, of sound Lutheran and sound imperial disposition alike, stood alone with his desire to negotiate. On the score of his position he could have proved useful, not on that of his talents. To have saved the peace at this stage would have required a statesman of superhuman calibre.

Zierotin was in the last resort not that. His efforts in Bohemia proved unavailing, a few months later in Moravia too. In January 1619 he wrote that Moravia's coalition with Bohemia would never compel the Emperor to compromise. On the contrary, it would drive the Catholic party "into such desperation or, better said, into such fierce determination that not this land alone, but all surrounding lands, aye, the whole Empire, must be brought to their ultimate end and utter destruction". It once more demonstrated his foresight as a political observer and true Christian. Unhappily those who possess penetration can usually not act, while those who act usually lack penetration.

Albrecht Wallenstein saw quite clear-eyed and now was also determined on action, though of an unconstructive, military kind. From September forward he kept in touch by letter, from Iglau in northwestern Moravia where his regiment was stationed, with General Buquoy, rendering him services which an officer of neutral Moravia's Estates should not have been allowed to render. In October he went to Vienna with his twenty thousand borrowed gulden and another twenty thousand which he drew from his own money-chests. His proposal to have a thousand cuirassiers or heavy cavalry recruited in the Spanish Netherlands with the assistance of this sum and to place them under his own command as an imperial colonel was eagerly accepted. His temporary appointment followed promptly. The precise terms of agreement date from March 1619. No mention any longer of expenditure on his part. The colonel was granted 1440 gulden per month for "pay for his own person, table-money, a lieutenant-colonel, sergeant, quartermaster, chaplain, clerk, provost-officer and his people, trumpeter, military drummer, cook, coach, all of which he shall be obliged to maintain, and others of the colonel's servants"; the regiment's captains, lieutenants and cornets were conceded correspondingly graduated wages. Interestingly enough, the expedition leader received in addition an *ajuto di costa*, supplementary annual pay of eight thousand gulden, practically half as much again as laid down in the agreement, although with the reservation that this exceptional act of grace should not be taken as applying to any other colonel. Why should Wallenstein have been its beneficiary? Hardly because of earlier services. They had derived their merit from being, and being meant to remain, unrewarded. More likely with an eye to the future. As early as November 1618 the Vienna Privy Council was keen to know "what is the disposition of the Wallenstein military in Moravia and whether reliance may in an eventuality be placed upon it?" This referred not to the new, still to be recruited imperial force, but to the unit belonging to the Estates. Did it appear worth while to make a special gesture to please the man who in an emergency might transform it from an Estates into an imperial regiment? At any rate he took the money; he may even have asked for it. As for the forty thousand gulden, they were no present. He insisted on the receipt of a royal promissory note. It was the first transaction of this kind between Wallenstein and Ferdinand II, of a modest order, but far from the last.

Now he was both, an imperial and an Estates colonel. Formally this could pass muster because as yet Moravia had neither declared itself against the Emperor nor for Bohemia. But, regardless of Zierotin's efforts to inculcate good sense, everyone felt the way that the wind was blowing. Let the storm break and Wallenstein, taking matters to their logical conclusion, would have to lead two regiments against each other in the same fashion as in 1611 Emperor Rudolf had two opposing armies situated right and left of the Moldau. He would certainly not do that. When in November Buquoy's troops, badly mauled by Thurn and his men, retired towards the Moravian frontier, the colonel commanding at Iglau lent them support with victuals and ammunition – a fresh, severer breach of the neutrality painstakingly maintained by his employers. The Bohemian army leaders drew the Moravians' attention to this provocation, complaining that their colonel was not only behaving directly contrary to what the Estates had resolved, but that he had insultingly "announced to his cousins and kin who serve with us that he will lay a rod in pickle for them and, had he a say in the matter, long ere this would have joined with the imperial folk". We do not know whether Wallenstein really wrote such a letter, perhaps to his uncle Hannibal who was on the side of the rebels. To me it seems nonsensical, but possibly that is how he talked. The Estates none the less left him at his important, dangerous post. They put no obstacles in the way of his journeys to Vienna in January from Iglau and in March from Olmütz, his regiment having been moved inland. He appears to have been in Vienna when Emperor Matthias finally sank back into the nirvana – "What is happening to me? I can no longer see my right hand!" – from which this luckless potentate had better never have emerged. The Emperor died on 20 March 1619. Four days later Wallenstein's commission as imperial colonel was confirmed. It was one of the first official acts undertaken by Ferdinand, now de facto successor everywhere in spite of being it de jure scarcely anywhere. In Bohemia everything was in a state of bloodily indeterminate flux; Ferdinand had yet to be elected Emperor; even the Austrian Estates disputed his right of succession.

During these winter months little occurred because of the cold, the famine, and the gruesome epidemics which destroyed half the Bohemian army. As long as hostilities were suspended, negotiations proceeded, whether in official and hopeless exchanges of notes between Prague, Brünn, and Vienna or in secret correspondence, bloated with illusory secrets, between Prague, Turin, Heidelberg, and, it may be presumed, London, the Hague, and Venice. Bloodshed and flames in fine weather; inky paper, couriers, and conferences in the bad season of the year.

AN UNSUCCESSFUL BUT DECISIVE STEP

With the return of spring the Bohemians recovered their courage. The Thirty ordered Count Thurn to win over Moravia by force to that which any amount of talking and writing had not been able to win it over – bundling the righteous-minded, undoubtedly in the majority, into the revolutionary camp and putting a spoke in the wheel of the unrighteous. And a Saxon agent was able to report: "The project is to take Colonel von Wallenstein, as an arch-papist, prisoner. Since Lord Carol von Zierotin could also be caught, the same may happen to him too." A few days later: "Sundry Latin verses against Lord Carol von Zierotin have been publicly affixed there [in Olmütz] at the town hall. He is said to be very fearful and to have made ready his last possessions to flee to Austria. . . ." During recent months this noble patriot had become a stranger to his own country. The balance of his peace policy was tilted towards the Habsburg scale. This was due to the situation. The more obviously his countrymen inclined to Bohemia, the more must he appear as a royal retainer and legitimist because he was unable any longer to maintain the equilibrium he so ardently desired. But he made no move, for he would never have actively betrayed his compeers. He remained where he was, entreated his countrymen without hope of being heeded, and was derided as one who, formerly a great man, was hopelessly out of date.

In April Thurn marched with ten thousand men into Moravia. On the twenty-third of the month he was in Iglau where the citizens cheered him as their liberator. So at least it seemed to his sanguine temperament. He proceeded to Znaim. The Protestant nobility rode out to meet the Bohemians as friends; so did the Catholic, which had reason to fear for its property. Indeed the leading Habsburg supporters, Princes Dietrich-stein and Liechtenstein, sent envoys to Thurn to tell him that they no longer had any objection to an alliance between the two lands, an act of which later they were tactfully not reminded. The Cardinal, who after all was "Colonel-General", had not given the Moravian forces instructions of any sort. A session of the Estates was summoned to Brünn. What would in the circumstances be solved politically and militarily was perfectly clear. Nevertheless the Catholic magnates and Protestant neutralist Zierotin attended. Perhaps in Zierotin's case it was a matter of conscience, the patriot's inflexible feeling for propriety. With Liechtenstein and Dietrichstein it is more likely that they thought the Habsburg cause lost.

Different and on their own responsibility was the conduct of Zierotin's son-in-law, Colonel Georg von Nachod, commanding the Moravian cavalry, and of Zierotin's brother-in-law, Albrecht Wallenstein, commanding the Moravian infantry. They struck their blow on the same day, 30 April, doubtless in concert.

Nachod ordered his cavalry to leave Brünn in the direction of Olmütz. After a while his second-in-command asked at whose behest they were travelling. The royal governor's, Lobkowicz, replied Nachod. That would not do, his officers retorted, the Estates must issue the directive, there was something fishy, an odour of treachery, the colonel a traitor. The soldiers growled agreement, brandishing their colours over Nachod's head and reviling him for a dishonourable young wretch. Their behaviour rendered him glad to escape safe and sound of limb and able to flee to Austria. That was the speedy end to the first part of this colonels' conspiracy.

Wallenstein and Nachod, it has been alleged, planned for their militia units to join with the rest of the Habsburg army under Dampierre's command situated on the Hungarian – the Slovak – frontier, turn about, dissolve the meeting of the Diet at Brünn, and effectively launch a counter-revolution. An implausible tale. The way that matters had developed in Moravia, the nobility and the towns throwing themselves into the arms of the rebels, no longer permitted of such a swift and facile stroke with the forces at best available. The objective must have been more modest – for the time being to preserve the Moravian regiments on Ferdinand's behalf. An element of sheer self-defence played a part in the game too. How would the "arch-papist" Wallenstein have fared if rabid Thurn had caught him?

At midday, 30 April, Wallenstein at Olmütz instructed Major Khuen to march with nine companies in the direction of Lundenburg on the Hungarian border; he would join them later with the tenth company. Khuen obeyed, but in the evening he returned, saying that the business seemed irregular to him, he did not even have a billet requisition. Wallenstein, on horseback, listened to the stammerings of his subordin- ate, also mounted, tore his sword from its scabbard, and ran him through the chest. Khuen toppled, mortally wounded. Whether Wallenstein's was an act of blind rage, on the Altdorf pattern, or a rapid calculation of how best to restore wavering discipline, or both, towering passion in the service of sound sense, let decide who will. A fresh major was immediately appointed and displayed greater tractability. At ten o'clock Wallenstein, with a large escort of musketeers, paid a call on Biryta, the Moravian Treasurer, and summoned him straightway to surrender the contents of his money-chests. Biryta pleaded the impossibility of this without Estates' sanction. The sword which he had just turned to such bloody advantage in hand, the colonel warned the official to cut the tomfoolery short – the keys or a rope round his neck. What was Biryta to do? In the exchequer Wallenstein found 96,000 taler. He had wagons loaded, eight in all, and did not overlook the inclusion of some ammuni- tion from the arsenal. During the night the transport trundled out of Olmütz. Wallenstein was in the saddle. The goal was the Hungarian frontier, or, if necessary, Vienna. It turned out to be Vienna.

From Olmütz to Brünn is not far. Soon the assembled Estates learned of Wallenstein's defection. So did Count Thurn who had just come to terms of ebullient fraternization with them. Nobody enjoyed his fits of rage more than Thurn did. In this instance he had good reason for self-indulgence. He sent nearly 1800 horsemen after the renegade's force, another 400 Moravians for good measure, and a proclamation of outlawry to be read to the Wallensteiners. Thurn's delighted fury found outlet too in a private letter: "There sits the proud beast, hath lost his honour, goods and chattels, besides his soul, and doth he not do penance is like to go to Purgatory." Thurn's cavalry did not overtake the colonel, his officers and wagons, but most of his slower-moving musket- eers whom they effortlessly persuaded to retrace their steps. These men were no ordinary mercenaries, but Moravians with some notions per- taining to patriotism and Estates.

At Brünn Wallenstein's most eminent friends were in a situation not dissimilar to that which in the preceding year Slawata and Martinitz had on the Hradschin tasted to the full. Karl von Zierotin in particular. He was the only one to behave with his accustomed dignity although, we are told, he already "looked out of the window". The intercession of the original defenestrators, the Bohemians, alone saved him from the fate of the Prague governors. Prince Liechtenstein was not content with protesting his innocence, he swore to remain forthwith, in life and death, loyal to the Estates. Of this pledge it can be said that it was given under duress and did not count. At any rate Liechtenstein seems subsequently to have understood it that way. The Cardinal and Colonel-General broke down completely. On his knees, and not without spilling tears, he begged for mercy. He offered, to the accompaniment of raucous laughter from the nobility, to abandon all his offices, withdraw to Rome, and never again meddle with politics. Scarcely back on his feet, and still a prisoner of the Estates, he scribbled to Ferdinand, "What the use hath been of Colonel von Wallenstein's extremely troublesome and, that I may not term it otherwise, unconsidered decision is something that we unfortunately experience every hour. 'Tis to be feared that Your Majesty's own person may yet suffer harm in all lands on account of this enterprise which will not find the least approbation from any man, be he Catholic or of other religion." The Estates must have their money returned without delay, else he could not answer for the consequences. The contempt for the Cardinal which Wallenstein later liked often to display – "Let Cardinal von Dietrichstein not soil his breeches for fear" – dated from this episode.

A few days later the Moravian Diet pronounced sentence upon its former colonel of infantry. Found guilty of vicious treason, unmindful of the dictates of honour, he was banished for ever from the margraviate and expropriated from his possessions which would be used for the good of his country. In August the judgement was confirmed.

Wallenstein, with his eight wagons, the regimental colours, and some two hundred mercenaries who had continued loyal to him, arrived in Vienna late on the night of 5 May. Next morning he had an audience of Ferdinand. We may assume that his reception was gracious. To Dietrichstein the King wrote that he had known nothing about the undertaking and by no means approved of it, but that the Colonel's argument, about the inadmissibility of letting the Bohemian rebels have the money to consummate their revolt, was one that merited at least a kindly hearing. ... Ninety-six thousand taler was an amount that the Habsburg had seldom seen all at once. How glad he would have been to keep it, how urgently he could have used it. He forcibly deliberated the subject with his ministers. Eggenberg was for retention, the majority against, and the sum was indeed restored. Count Dietrichstein, a cousin of the Cardinal, came in great secrecy to fetch the coffers with their iron hinges and conducted them back to Olmütz. At that very moment Moravia was in a state of wild insurrection, directors on the Prague model took over power, and the Jesuits, Wallenstein's friends, were chased out of the country with a brutality even greater than that shown them earlier by the Bohemians. No state of war either did or could exist between Ferdinand and Moravia. The situation was simply that of wrong on the one side, the implementation of right on the other. The latter must therefore itself do no wrong. Everything had to proceed on the basis of impeachment and conviction in accordance with the law. That would duly provide for the expropriation of more, much more than ninety-six thousand taler.

One more point: in the patents which subsequently recorded Wallenstein's promotions and recounted in detail his services no reference was ever made to the Olmütz exploit. He himself mentioned it with complacency in the constitution which he gave his dukedom. The Emperor's legal draftsmen refrained from mention.

Bílá Hora

B Y April 1619 rabid Count Thurn had revolutionized and swept along Moravia. By the first week of June he stood with his troops in front of Vienna. Had they been well-equipped, sufficient in numbers, well fed, and imbued with firmness of spirit, he would have been able to take the city, about half of whose population sympathized with his undertaking. Whether it would have been a decisive blow is difficult to say. Ferdinand, holding out under the most provoking circumstances, could always have escaped to the south, secure in the justice of his cause and in the knowledge that aid was slowly on its way from widely different sources. Count Thurn, on the other hand, had difficulties with his soldiers. Mostly of German origin, unpaid, hungry, and sometimes, we are told, running about naked, they had little liking for the business for which they were supposed to fight. There was a lack of both artillery and the numbers necessary to lay siege to Vienna. Thurn hoped to win it as he had won Moravia a couple of months ago. That did not seem intrinsically impossible. He was entitled to expect from the Upper Austrians at least hindrance to the passage of Spanish relief forces. The Hungarian Diet, hostile to the Habsburgs, was in session at Pressburg, very close to Vienna. The Lower Austrian Estates, with a stronger Catholic representation, were more divided than the Upper Austrian. Their Protestant element had protracted debates with Thurn, promised to send delegates to a General Diet at Prague, and gave offence to Ferdinand, their ruler whom for the present they did not recognize as such, by making demands which that obstinate Prince would never fulfil. But they neither lent the Bohemians effective assistance nor were they as adequately organized as would have been essential for the purpose. After a few days Thurn ordered withdrawal to Bohemia.

The decision was all the more vital because Ferdinand's forces under Count Buquoy had meanwhile invaded south-west Bohemia, bereft of protection, and were behaving as abominably there as Thurn's troops did in Upper Austria. Ernst von Mansfeld, war entrepreneur and uncertain ally, was stationed inactive at Pilsen. Sent against Buquoy, he walked into the trap set for him at Netolitz by his opponent, superior in numbers, and lost all he had with him, close on three thousand dead and prisoners, his provision train, and even his fine silver table-ware. The victory delivered the region into Habsburg hands.

At this date, June 1619, thirteen months after the beginning of the insurrection, the state of Bohemian affairs was already unfavourable enough – the onslaught on Austria dispersed, an entire army corps annihilated, a part of the country in enemy hands. Bohemia is not so large that it is from any point very far to the capital. The condition of morale and the economy was even more parlous than the military, with the third dependent primarily on the second and all the more directly the worse morale was. The ruling party's conduct implied however that its plans were for an eternity, with a re-organization of the rights appertaining to the crown of St Wenceslas being briskly undertaken at midsummer.

There were three main issues: the constitution of the kingdom and its collateral territories, the relationship with the other Habsburg lands, and the person of the monarch. Negotiations on the constitution took place between the directors and the representatives of the collateral territories. The upshot was the so-called "Act of Confederation", resolved on 31 July in a ceremony of solemn political and religious character. This act breathed a spirit of boldness. The kingdom was turned for legislative purposes into a federation. Financial and army matters were administered according to their own wishes by the member republics within whose borders towns were allowed complete autonomy and the Protestant peasantry was conceded freedom of religious practice. The sole common component would be the King, elective, and in the appointment of his officials, the command of his army, the formation of his foreign policy as well as the effectual realization of his ecclesiastical policy to such a degree controlled by the Estates and so threatened by their right to oppose and depose him, that the question as to why he should have been necessary any more at all may obtrude. The answer is that he was needed because the unity of the federated lands was supplied through the crown alone. He was needed, or it was hoped that he would be needed, for practical purposes because Protestant, predominantly monarchic Europe would be more likely to furnish aid for this head, this crowned head of state, than for mere republicans. If, though, Ferdinand spread the tale that the Bohemians were unblushing republicans, the Act of Confederation vindicated him. No one with any feeling for power would ever have worn this fictive, shadowy crown.

If the Czechs wanted a state composed of their nationals, they had no choice but to want segregation, logically from the collateral German-speaking lands too, definitely from sovereign territories which did not have the crown in common with them, only its current holders, the Habsburg family. Their real aim however was the precise opposite. What they desired to create was a large commonwealth of republics comprising the Estates of Bohemia, Austria, and Hungary, a Protestant confederation, with Prague as its focal point if possible. Treaties with the lords of Upper and Lower Austria did indeed come to pass, but in such fashion as explicitly to negate the pre-eminence of one treaty partner, namely Bohemia. For the rest, the wording of the agreements was promising enough.

They had hardly been signed before the Bohemians on their own initiative undertook something that the Austrians had by no means advised – they declared Ferdinand to be rid of the crown once and for all. The detailed explanation published with this resolution contained everything to be said about the King's character and deeds, including much of what could well have been known when three years ago he had been "accepted". He had, for example, during Matthias's lifetime never been entitled to present himself for acceptance and from the outset his kingship was a usurpation. Or that he had shown himself in his own Styria to be an inexorable persecutor of Protestants. Perfectly correct. Unfortunately the view expressed at this juncture by a German potentate, the Archbishop of Cologne, was not wrong either: "If it should be that the Bohemians are about to depose Ferdinand and elect a counter-King, let everyone be straightway prepared for a twenty, thirty or forty years' war." This prince of the church, brother to Maximilian of Bavaria, had a proper appreciation of Bohemia's importance in the power-game.

A new king had yet to be found, but the search for him had of course long been on. Three candidates were under discussion: Duke Charles Emmanuel of Savoy, Elector John George of Saxony, and Frederick, Elector Palatine. The Duke of Savoy had the merit of being reckoned a foe of the Habsburgs, particularly the Spanish line, and having arranged the first assistance received by the Bohemians, that on the part of Ernst von Mansfeld, man of business in the trade of war. The Duke moreover had recently come to an agreement with the grand-intriguer Christian von Anhalt. Each month he would pay the handsome sum of a hundred thousand ducats and induce his ally Venice to do the same, provided that he was not attacked by Spain and on the understanding that the sympathies prevailing at Prague in favour of the Elector Palatine would be transferred to him, whereupon he would no doubt consent to accept the elective crown. This pact, for whose sake Anhalt had made one of his many hasty and lengthy journeys, was not worth the paper on which it was written. The Bohemians would not again elect a Catholic king; Anhalt, who had all along been backing another candidate, was determined to prevent precisely that which he had just promised the Duke to effect. He was barely back from Italy before setting down in a memorandum the warning that Charles Emmanuel "lacks nerve and vigour".

John George of Saxony, the most powerful of the three Protestant Electors, head of the Lutherans, Bohemia's neighbour, a wealthy and influential personality, was or could have been a more serious possibility. He was however the man of whom Wallenstein would once say, "What a brute he is and what a life he leads," a view upheld at the General Diet by those who knew him, especially the lords from Silesia and Lusatia, who cautioned against having a drunkard as king. John George would in secret not have taken unkindly to being elected and in any case regarded another candidate's selection as insult. Nevertheless he would neither have accepted the crown nor, because he was conservative to the core and intent on preservation of the good old imperial order, did he attempt to conceal this fact from the Bohemian delegates. Whether torpid from beer or comparatively clear-headed, his outlook never wavered for a moment. Bluff, crude and simple-minded, a German patriot after his fashion, he believed in the "Empire" and was not at all of a mind to understand that it had for long been on the brink of breaking apart and that he, as the most powerful among the Protestants, must somewhen and somehow take sides. He honestly wanted peace, his advice to the Bohemians to reach agreement with Ferdinand was honest. Yet he was sly enough to surmise that, were the conflict to be fought to its end, his own advantage was to be sought in the camp to which by religion he did not belong. With such leanings the Elector of Saxony was really out of the question as a choice for the revolutionary shadow-throne. The Bohemians should have known that. Indeed when the day of election came, the great majority of them had realized it, although one Prague party continued to sham importance by flourishing the Saxon colours.

This left the third candidate. From the outset his election had represented the sole serious contingency. Only idle talk and specious alternatives had been able to call it into question. At Prague it was noted in the Elector Palatine's favour that he was modest and of agreeable character, rich and amply capable of furnishing funds, surely in a position to count on having England, France, the States-General, Sweden, Venice, Switzerland, Hungary, and Transylvania on his side, as head of the Protestant Union the real master of Germany, on good terms with Saxony and more particularly Bavaria which he could neutralize, and, in short, the best bet far and wide. Rarely has a proposition been threaded by so many illusions. On 26 and 27 August Frederick was elected by the Bohemians, Moravians, Silesians and Lusatians, their lords, knights, and burgesses, with an overwhelming majority and only seven votes for John George.

Far too long and deeply involved in the affair to be able honourably to escape from it, the Elector Palatine would none the less have keenly preferred the election's postponement in order first to assure himself of his father-in-law's, the King of England's, goodwill and assistance. The Bohemians did not postpone the election, and the reason was not simply because the thirty Directors wanted to be rid of their ever more unpleasantly burdensome responsibility. In the summer of this year another process of election was drawing to its conclusion. While at Prague the search was for a king, the Electors were searching for an emperor. The interregnum had lasted since old Matthias's death in March. Despite many years' chatter and correspondence about other eligible personalities, for the imperial election there too existed only one serious candidate. Yet let Ferdinand once be invested with the potent aura of privileges and titles attaching to the imperial crown and it would be much more difficult to act against him in Prague. Hence the urgency.

The election process at Frankfurt required more, although quite fruitlessly more, time than that at Prague. First there was some discussion of the problem whether, prior to the election, an attempt should be made to compose the Bohemian business. This, they decided, could just as well happen afterwards. Then there was a debate on whether to receive a Bohemian embassy which had arrived in the vicinity of Frankfurt with orders to protest against the presence and vote of the expelled King-Elector. They resolved not to hear the embassy. "They" was the quorum of representatives of the three secular Electors, who had preferred not to appear in person, and the three spiritual ones who made their appearance. During these deliberations, whose theme was his own disputed position, Ferdinand remained tactfully in the background. Only the Palatine representatives pleaded on the Bohemian's behalf. The Saxons, wavering at the start, received instructions from Dresden to adhere to the loyal majority. Only the Palatine representatives tried for the election of another candidate, the Duke of Bavaria, a manoeuvre bereft of much hope as Maximilian had long before let it be known that a vote for him must count as one for Ferdinand. When finally the Elector of Bohemia's turn came, he stated modestly that, as his fellow-Electors with one exception were for him, he did not want to do less than as much on his own account and would therefore vote for himself. Hereupon, to ensure unanimity, the Palatine representatives withdrew their earlier choice. The lawyers in the Heidelberg cabinet ought to have understood the ceremony's fatal legal significance. By not challenging Ferdinand's right to vote, they recognized him as King of Bohemia. They ought also to have appreciated the political significance of the process. The Empire, in the shape of its seven Electors, or at any rate six of them, solemnly took the side of the Habsburg candidate, abandoning that of Bohemia. The decision, scrutinized more closely, was that of those on whom the issue really depended because they alone could conceivably have changed their minds – Saxony and Brandenburg.

That Ferdinand accepted election was a matter of course, but, a pious man conscious of his sacred charge, he was honestly moved. The news of his deposition by the Bohemians, which reached him at Frankfurt, stirred him less deeply. Only "idiots and cranks", he told himself, could do a thing like that. He was threefold confident of his cause: *dei gratia*, thanks to the help of God, on which he relied; through pride of lineage, which was identical with pride of title; through knowledge of the actual balance of power in Europe, about which he did not lack innate flair.

That the Elector Palatine accepted the Bohemian election was not a matter of course, one would have thought. His advisers could tell the inexperienced, very shallow young man how matters stood in Bohemia and with the Bohemians. There was no encouragement forthcoming from London. His own Protestant Union did embolden him with a lukewarm majority, but the loose alliance of minor Protestant dominions was far less militarily prepared than Prague and Heidelberg liked to believe. The support of France, on which for decades Christian von Anhalt had for the currently emergent train of events relied, formerly with some justice, now fell away altogether.

Judgement comes easily to us because we know the upshot. There were however more than a few contemporaries whose verdict was the same at a time when the upshot was as yet unknown. The Duke of Bavaria, for example. The letter which on 24 September 1619 he wrote to his young Palatine cousin deserves mention on more than one score. It demonstrates among other things that, whatever Maximilian's subsequent attitude in the great conflict and whatever evil advantages he extracted from it, he by no means wanted to see the conflagration lit. On the contrary, he bent all his lucid intelligence to advancing arguments which would extinguish the spark. The Bohemian unrest, he said, signified for many fine lands, indeed the Empire and almost the whole of Christendom, far greater perils than many seemed to imagine. The greatest misery, though, was reserved for him who accepted the allegedly elective crown. Bohemia was one of Europe's most interesting realms, but disorder there had often spread beyond its borders. Particularly those of its rulers who were not of native descent had fared badly. The stringent conditions the Bohemians were attaching to the tenure of their throne were known. Was his cousin not disconcerted that, for the time being, the only discernible ally of the Bohemian Estates should be the Prince of Transylvania, a vassal almost in thrall to the Turks? Did he not see that, by acceptance of the election, he would be affording the most dangerous assistance to Christendom's arch-enemy? Let him bear in mind that Austria, a powerful dynasty, would be everlastingly aggrieved and snatch at opportunity for revenge. Such opportunity often occurred overnight. At the same time one should never do unto others what one did not wish to have done unto oneself. Where would matters end if subjects expelled their princes without more ado and a brother-prince, as well as sanctioning highly inadmissible procedure of that kind, sat himself in the place of him who contrary to all justice had been robbed of his sovereign authority? The widely prevalent view regrettably held among the Empire's Protestant Estates that the Catholics were planning their destruction was false. He implored the Elector to believe that it was false. Frederick replied that the letter from his cousin and friend had undoubtedly been inspired by upright German feeling. But matters did not lie that way; they lay differently in every respect. That was his reply, or the reply that he had sent, since he was quite incapable of composing a letter with political content. If he had to answer the address of an envoy, either he ran off something learnt by heart, often irrelevant to what had just been said, or he sought whispered aid from his ministers. This twenty-three-years-old was not the man to lead a revolution for all that he had to follow its call. On 23 October he made his ceremonial entry into Prague. Four days later the bejewelled and doom-laden crown of St Wenceslas, highest symbol of a foreign land blessed by nature but lacerated in spirit, was set upon his curly ringlets.

It happened at a moment when for the last time the cause of the Estates appeared to have a favourable breeze behind it, in the shape of a sudden hope at which Duke Maximilian had in his letter to Frederick hinted and against whose deceptive, hazardous character he had warned. It centred on Gabor Bethlen or, as he is imprecisely called in history-books, Bethlen Gabor, Prince of Transylvania.

Bethlen had been a brother-in-arms and was now the next successor but one to that Istvan Bocskay who, fifteen years back, had given Wallenstein his first taste of war. Bethlen, like Bocskay, was a Magyar and a firm Calvinist, but fickle in worldly affairs and for ever turning over new political projects in his mind. Given the geographical situation of Transylvania, there was nothing he could do against the Sultan nor anything he could do unless with the Sultan's at least tacit acquiescence. That was the sole stable rule in his policy which otherwise, like all policy, aimed at his own aggrandizement and enrichment. For that there seemed to be considerable scope through a sort of blackmailing collaboration with the Habsburgs. Yet power politics and religious sympathies drew him more strongly to the side of the Estates. If in the late summer of 1619 he offered help to the Bohemians, so as on the strength of this to unite Hungary with his political semi-entity, he was simply repeating Bocskay's own attempt which had come to grief through the loyalty of the Moravians. His country, he wrote to the Directors at Prague, lay between the jaws of the Turks. Their counsels fluctuated like the waves of the ocean and at present they represented all the greater a danger for Christendom because they were at peace with the Persians. None the less he had succeeded in gaining the favour of the Ottoman Emperor and securing the flank of his territory. For the honour of God he would launch a mighty army westward and before the autumn was out he would be standing upon Moravia's border.

Which he did. His campaign, taking in imposing distances, was planned on a grand scale and executed with swift success – a pincer movement against Kaschau (Košice) in north-eastern Upper Hungary and against Pressburg. This city was of twofold importance to him. It is a key to Hungary, Austria, and Moravia; from its heights the view stretches far into all three countries. It was the capital of Hungary where the Diets met and in whose citadel was kept the crown of St Stephen. He had to have it to make right of might. He really did manage to get Hungary's Protestant nobility to brandish their swords on his behalf.

Bethlen's advance on Pressburg threw the Viennese into panic. The grandest *émigrés*, with Cardinal Dietrichstein in the lead, fled in a cloud of dust to Upper Austria. Ferdinand, just become Emperor, just returned from Frankfurt, conducted his court under harassing conditions to Graz. Buquoy, whose troops had hitherto driven the Bohemians back and forth like a herd of sheep, was summoned south, a retreat which must have proved catastrophic if Count Thurn's mercenaries and their masters had been other than they were. The Bohemian–Moravian and the Transylvanian–Hungarian forces joined hands. Buquoy, close to Vienna, had under their pressure to undertake a hazardous withdrawal across the Danube, seeing to it that his pontoon bridge was destroyed ahead of the enemy's approach. The allies none the less crossed the river near Pressburg and, to the affliction of towns and villages on the right bank, marched on Vienna. A prodigiously expanded host, this time in superior strength, probably close on fifty thousand. The imperialists lay within the city to which, as his residential capital, and being a true father of his country, Ferdinand had thought it his duty to return. Now he would gladly have been away from it again. All that he saw, heard, sensed, the hunger, the disease, the overcrowding, the pillaging, all the reports brought to him of what was happening outside, the torments of his subjects, the wails of lamentation, death, fire, icy cold, if all that was proceeding the way that it apparently must for the maintenance of his sacred right, then it was better not to be there. For the moment he sat trapped in his palace. A single major thrust, one bold attack, and Emperor and imperial capital would be in the rebels' hands, with Count Thurn and Gabor Bethlen able to dictate their terms.

None was made, much as in the preceding June. On top of familiar hardship, lack of artillery, lack of money, lack of discipline, arrived news which Bethlen interpreted as compelling him to abandon his part in the siege. Sigismund, King of Poland and Ferdinand's brother-in-law, had sent a few thousand Cossacks, the incorrect term for Polish cavalry, across the Carpathians into Upper Hungary. Bethlen would have done better to leave the Cossacks to wreak their havoc, for they would not have got so very far, and to have clinched matters where they could be clinched. But as soon as he felt unsafe in the rear, he forsook the breakthrough in the front. For his purposes, not entirely coincident with the Bohemians', it was enough to hold Pressburg. Bethlen alone had rendered possible this second, and late, offensive. The Bohemian host too rolled back from Vienna as it had come. Or, more accurately, not as it had come, because pestilence had ravaged its ranks worse than the enemy's.

The last chance was squandered. The helper in need from the southeast had on this occasion proved as unreliable as he was subsequently often to prove – swift to the spot with his barbarian horde, arousing hope, enigmatic, and away again. What the confederated states now still did, whether they knew or hid it from themselves, was really to await their destruction.

Max of Bavaria had with eight well-considered arguments impressively warned his Palatine cousin against acceptance of the Wenceslas crown. He could have added a ninth, even more impressive one.

Relations between the Bavarian branch of the Wittelsbachs and the Austrian Habsburgs were not quite so straightforward as hitherto our narrative has perhaps allowed to appear. Maximilian held the head of the Empire in honour; his feeling for the great territorial lord to the east was another matter. Where the autonomy of his own, as yet small but compact and razor-sharp administered political entity seemed menaced, even from afar, there was no joking with him. Jokiness was indeed a quality with which he could not in the least be reproached. The alliance of Catholic princes earlier formed by him, the League, had been ambiguous in character. Under Bavarian leadership and of emphatically native German composition, it was a foil thrust at the Protestant Union, yet not without an edge capable of being turned against the encircling supranational power of the Habsburgs. This was the conjunction, the veiled distinction, on which Palatine policy staked its attempt to play the imperial dignity into Maximilian's hands, a bid for which the Duke was not too lacklustre of ambition but too shrewd. He knew his limits. Under Habsburg pressure he had, as it were, let his League doze off. In spring 1619, this time at the wish of his cousin and brother-in-law Ferdinand, he re-awakened it to life. Sought out by a secretary from the Spanish embassy at Vienna who urged him to pursue a more active course in the conflict rending the lands of the German Habsburgs, he took an evasive line: the Protestant Union and what it might do in the future was something of his business, Bohemia none really. Should the head of the Union set upon his brows the Bohemian crown, begetting a confluence of German and Bohemian affairs, this attitude of a statesman keeping strictly within his prescribed sphere of interest was incapable of being upheld. Maximilian knew it; he should duly have drawn the Palsgrave's attention to the fact. Exactly a fortnight after he had written him his insufficiently clear warning letter, a treaty was concluded at Munich between Maximilian, Ferdinand, and the King of Spain, the latter represented by his ambassador at Vienna, Count Oñate.

Bavaria undertook to prepare for war and to support the Emperor with all the means at its own and the League's disposal. It was to receive full compensation for its outlay, with a lien upon all Habsburg lands seized from the rebels until repayment to the last farthing had been effected. Spain would support the League with a fixed number of cavalry in addition to Spanish troops already stationed in Bohemia. Archduke Albrecht, regent at Brussels, would moreover launch a diversion against the Palatinate to keep the Union in check. The precision of the stipulations shows how Maximilian liked to play safe, "*ex naturali instinctu* concerned for his own defence", as he put it. He was concerned for more as well. The answer to the delicate question as to what should be his reward was only given verbally and without similar precision. The Duke was to become Elector at the Palsgrave's expense after the latter had been put to the imperial ban and stripped of his electoral dignity. He should be allowed to retain such Palatine lands as he obtained by force of arms – whether permanently or, like the Austrian ones, in lien is not clear.

By signing the Munich treaty Ferdinand relinquished the conduct of German affairs and placed them in the hands of an incomparably more capable man at the head of an incomparably more cohesive political entity. He, the Emperor, would probably benefit, although drawbacks would not be lacking. And the Empire? What perils arising from the divulged conditions and the undivulged promises plighted before covetous witnesses lay in wait for it?

Maximilian went to work, step by step, as his practice was. He sent his councillors to Madrid and to Rome to spur Pope Paul V into accelerating his covenanted aid. He entered into correspondence with the regent at Brussels. He mobilized, and he saw to it that his allies mobilized or paid their contributions. Unhurriedly he spun the toils of a Europe-wide Catholic coalition in which during the following year, or at the latest the one after, 1621, the Bohemian rebellion and all connected with it should be strangled.

Nothing of the kind happened on the opposing side. Ferdinand's alliance took more concrete shape and his allies' plans became more synchronized with every month that passed. Those on whom the Bohemians had pinned their hopes drew back, were non-committal, or even turned into foes.

One of the favourite arguments for Frederick's election had been his affiliation with the British crown. James I however disapproved of his son-in-law's adventure and very bluntly said so. His diplomacy was directed towards friendship with Spain. Not that this corresponded to any national requirements. He was animated simply by royal caprice, the indulgence of a ruler's whim to try for once the exact opposite of national tradition and to do what his recalcitrant Parliament disliked. Resistance by subjects to their monarch, no matter where it occurred, was deeply offensive to his feeling for the common craft of kingship. In the Bohemian case the sentiment was aggravated by awareness that this must result in a Catholic counter-front which would be awkward for his personal policy. He therefore tried to negotiate. During 1619 his personal ambassador extraordinary, a Lord Doncaster, travelled about Europe, had audiences with the regent Albrecht, the Palsgrave, Duke Maximilian, and Ferdinand, put in an appearance wherever anything (the imperial election, for instance) was on foot, and everywhere created a slightly ludicrous impression on account of his ignorance of continental affairs. The extent to which Maximilian's flattery made rings around his judgement can be seen from his report to London that the Duke was not in the least as his enemies depicted him, distinctly liberal in his ideas and thoroughly hostile to the Jesuits, reptiles that he would long ago have chased out of his land if it were not for the respect that he owed his retired, greybeard father. The British sage's instructions were however to arrange matters in such a way that "the Bohemian Estates should be surpassed by no one in obedience to the Emperor and render themselves by their reasonable attitude deserving of peaceful terms whose concession would be neither demeaning to their overlord nor their acceptance a cause of regret to his subjects." A marvellous formulation, although it demanded the squaring of the circle. No wonder that Lord Doncaster was treated with a politely concealed contempt barely accorded to his successors.

The French knew conditions in central Europe better. But the days of Henry IV were over, those of the great Cardinal not yet begun. During the intervening period fumbling, uncertainty, and internal troubles were the rule. To make use of the Bohemian revolution for a vigorous thrust against Habsburg was neither the policy nor indeed, given circumstances at home, practical politics. On the other hand Ferdinand's complete triumph, transformation of the tangled constitution of Estates into a unitary state such as France approximated to, also did not seem desirable. The French aim, like the British, was therefore "mediation", a friendly settlement, where there was nothing left to mediate. More familiar with southern Germany than Bohemia, French efforts at pacification concentrated on the two conflicting German associations, Catholic League and Protestant Union. In June 1620 a French mission arrived for that purpose in the nick of time.

This was the season, a contemporary noted, when "not only in Germany, but in all neighbouring lands, so great were the preparations and readiness for war that a man could easily reckon how a great shedding of blood was inescapable." Readiness for war applied particularly to the League and the Union, the latter under the leadership of the Margrave of Ansbach in the absence of its head. From June onward the troops of the two alliances faced each other in the region of Ulm. Were Duke Maximilian to withdraw his forces in order to lead them against Bohemia, he would leave a powerful force of the enemy in his rear – an uncomfortable situation which this ever cautious prince would certainly not venture. Instead he proposed a treaty on the following lines: the League and the Union should not attack one another, but both should be free to fight as they pleased for or against third parties – for or against Bohemia, for or against the Emperor. The regent of the Netherlands would moreover remain unaffected by the treaty and consequently free to do what he was openly proposing to do, to conquer the native country of the head of the Union, the Rhenish Palatinate. And finally, were the Duke, not as head of the League, but on instruction from the Emperor and the Empire, to put into effect the outlawry pronounced upon the pretended King of Bohemia and in the course of its execution to occupy the Palatinate, then he should be allowed to do this without the slightest opposition. Maximilian's demand amounted to Germany's neutralization at the expense of the entire confederation of Estates in the Habsburg lands and of the Palatinate which, after all, was a flourishing constituent of Germany. Acceptance of these conditions by the princes comprising the Union was to purchase an extremely provisional peace through a grave, extremely unilateral concession on the part of those incapable of rendering Bohemia direct aid, but able to help it indirectly by a blow against the League. They behaved like a man who plugs up a well at the very moment his house starts to burn, and it was the French mission of mediation led by the Duke of Angoulême who persuaded them. He achieved, with the assistance of frightened, vacillating members of the Union, what the Duke of Bavaria alone could not have accomplished. The Treaty of Ulm, drafted by the French, was an easily won imperial victory. It gave Duke Max all the security he needed, the Union simply that which it did not now need and which would later do it little good, although the French, to be sure, took a totally different view of what "later" would involve. To complete the work of pacification begun at Ulm, they travelled down the Danube to Vienna. They had not been there long before they were told of an event which made their presence as superfluous as it was embarrassing. No one however knows what would have happened if they had not mediated the false semi-peace of Ulm. The affairs of Bohemia stood under a peculiarly unfortunate star – even those who wanted within moderation to extend help contributed directly to its downfall.

The States-General, at the instance of Prince Maurice, sent fifty thousand gulden a month to Prague, a drop in the ocean. For all the intellectual and indirectly political influence of the Dutch, the practical assistance that they could offer to Bohemia across the breadth of Germany was almost nil, more especially since they had at all times to fear a re-kindling of their old war with Spain. Like Venice, Sweden and Denmark, they recognized the new King *de jure*. "Recognition", though, does not add as much to reality as is apparently believed.

So there was a mighty Catholic coalition and no Protestant one. Worse, worst of all, in spring 1620 the head of Germany's Lutherans made up his mind in his own fashion. Elector John George, he on whom the Bohemians had looked as their natural protector and possible future King, promised to do in the north what the Duke would do in the west and the south – bring Silesia and Lusatia back within the folds of obedience. Of course he insisted on booty in lien, being the margraviates of Upper and Lower Lusatia, a transaction which was to prove permanent. For the rest – he was, let it be understood, not without conscience – he had himself assured in the usual precarious, malleable provisos that his co-religionists of the Augsburg Confession would go unharmed in Bohemia and the collateral lands.

The hand was close on played. During the winter the King attended all kinds of Prague galas; in the spring he proceeded to Brünn and Breslau to receive ceremonial homage. Nevertheless beneath this thin veneer of brilliance gloom prevailed, a lack of confidence between the King and his subjects who no longer wanted to be such, bickering between Palatines and Czechs, bickering between the Estates, unrest among the plagued peasantry, disruption of the finances accelerated by the minting of bad coin, a presentiment of approaching evil. During the winter, which the Palsgrave-King spent quite merrily, seven-eighths of the soldiers in a single Bohemian regiment, nearly 3500 men, either starved or froze to death. What can the leaders of troops who suffered that in the bad season of the year have expected from them in the good?

Evil omens augured evil realities. The most horrendous was reported from Hamburg. On a bright August day a dragon, breathing fire in a north-easterly direction from its wide-open jaws, appeared in the south-westerly sector of the sky. Ahead of it moved a host of horsemen, four in a row, while below its tail lay seven cities with truncated towers, not far off another little town, and then four more cities with pointed turrets. Towards this frightful manifestation now advanced yet another from the north-east, again a large dragon, accompanied by three smaller specimens, all stretching their tongues towards that from the south-west. These creatures had with them a multitude of infantry who began to skirmish with the cavalry. Just then a giant, with a long white face and clad in white armour, came on the scene from the south-west, helped the horsemen and laid the infantry low. Gradually the manifestation from the north-east vanished into air, but that from the south-west remained visible for close on two hours, and very disagreeably too, for the dragon never ceased from afflicting the towns below it with fire from its jaws and lashing them with its tail. . . . Did the westerly dragon's triumph relate to the armed array which was marching against King Frederick from the west?

The Duke of Bavaria had declined to attack Bohemia directly. He neither wanted to venture across difficult passes into a devastated land nor to leave an equally culpable enemy, the Austrians, unpunished behind him. Having neutralized the Union, his first priority was to put Upper Austria into place, make an example that would discourage other rebels, and incidentally allow for the possibility of effecting a junction with the imperial forces. He detached men in the direction of Furth-im-Wald. They would serve, apart from other purposes, to deter the Bohemians from thinking of paying him a complementary visit in Bavaria. With the bulk of his army, 25,000 musketeers, 5200 cavalry, and horse artillery whose finest cannon bore the names of the Apostles, he moved from Regensburg down the Danube towards Linz. The commander on the ground was Tserclaes von Tilly, that monkish veteran expert whom Maximilian, shrewdly modest, left to deal with immediate military responsibilities. Policy he looked after himself.

He met with no resistance. Only Upper Austrian delegations who inquired what, seeing that peace and neighbourliness reigned between his and their lands, he was really at. Protests, yes; resistance, no. He entered Linz without trouble, compelling the Estates to do him homage as the imperial commissary and forthwith to dismiss their troops, whereupon he strengthened his own numbers from their ranks. Everything else they should arrange subsequently with their legitimate ruler. For the time being he was regent, acting in the Emperor's name. "With exchanges of letters," Maximilian blandly remarked, "they would for ten

years have been able to carry matters along and have meanwhile remained masters of the land. But let, besides quills, blotting-powder of
the like that each caster has to be dragged by thirty to forty horses" –
he meant his Apostle cannon – "come into a land and speedy resolutions
will be brought about."

The leaders of the Upper Austrian Estates, who knew that no mercy
awaited them, fled to Prague. Erasmus von Tschernembl, the most
capable, was not sparing of good advice to the King. For example: "Let
the freedom of subjects be proclaimed in the land and villeinage be
abolished. . . . The common man would sooner die for his freedom."
The nobility should in this extreme emergency contribute what it
possessed, while military management should at last be entrusted to
honest people. . . . The nobility, who had begun it all and bore the
responsibility, wished to forgo their villein peasants as little as their
silver and gold.

The Bavarians turned towards Prague, not in a straight line, but by
way of all sorts of movements meant to deceive the enemy. Contact with
the imperial forces was made on Lower Austrian soil. The Bohemians
or those on the Bohemian side – not too many among them could speak
Czech – withdrew into Moravia. That threw up the question whether they
should be attacked there or the advance on Prague continued, giving
them the opportunity once again with Gabor Bethlen to threaten Vienna.
And if so? Twice already they had threatened it. Were they to do it a
third time, under incomparably less advantageous circumstances, they
would not achieve anything decisive either. Probably, though, they would
not start on this enterprise, but try and save their own royal capital. The
calculation proved correct. Christian von Anhalt, now King Frederick's
supreme commander, dashed to Bohemia as soon as he recognized the
enemy's objective. Who does not know the melancholy end?

During the night of 7 to 8 November, after a certain amount of to and
fro and round about, the armies faced one another a few kilometres west
of Prague. On the morning of 8 November occurred the battle called
Bílá Hora, or White Mountain, after the ridge on which Anhalt not
unskilfully stationed his regiments. The hero of our narrative was not
present. His Walloon regiment, but not he. As we have yet to describe
battles which, if it is true that generals conduct battles, were conducted
by Wallenstein, we may on this occasion spare the reader a delineation
of what has so often been portrayed, although it must be conceded that
not one of the many other battles in the Thirty Years War ever completely, lastingly, and finally decided anything, whereas the battle of the

White Mountain decided Bohemia's history for centuries. So we say – and doubt the words before they are out of our mouth. Can a single battle have effected that? A single hour's fighting in which one side, Czechs, Germans, Hungarians, and Austrians, did not, leaving aside a few notable individual exceptions, really fight but allowed itself simply to be scattered and chased apart, so that the victors suffered barely 250 dead? Not the numerical superiority of the Bavarian-imperialist force – 28,000 against 21,000 men – decided the outcome. That could probably have been overcome if the Bohemians had used their favourable position for a timely attack. What could not be retrieved in an hour was what for two and a half years had been let slip, neglected, and wasted. The battle of the White Mountain was the death of something long ripe to die, the collapse of this "feeble, ailing regiment", to quote the words of an English observer, a mere endorsement.

The outcome was final because the weak authorities at Prague accepted it as final. During the first night of hectically conflicting council the King and Queen sought refuge in the Old Town; next morning by escape to Breslau. To organize the beaten mercenaries, unpaid pillagers, and mutineers into fresh resistance proved more than could be done. Whoever advised it, like the imperturbable Austrian Tschernembl, gave good but impossible advice. The victors entered the city only a few hours after the defeated had left. The leaders of the Estates, at the start still talking of conditions but coolly admonished to have regard for the actual state of affairs, appeared again before the Duke of Bavaria three days after the battle. Lord Wilhelm von Lobkowicz, on behalf of them all, made a fine speech "with dewy eye and tearful voice": they knew how greatly they had transgressed against His Imperial Majesty, were now bitter sore of heart at it, and bade most humbly for forgiveness; never, nevermore would they recognize a sovereign other than Ferdinand II and him they would forthwith venerate with inviolable fidelity; the Duke should be pleased to be good enough to be a gracious interceder with His Majesty. Thus these statesmen abruptly tore away, or thought that they could, the mask of gravity so wantonly and brazenly assumed so many years. To throw strongly into relief triumph and subjection, victory and defeat by word and pantomime was a general contemporary tendency: the one through gorgeous processions in gold and scarlet, thanksgiving services to tumultuous organ peals, strident speeches; the other through weeping, kneeling, and remorseful self-accusations. A third form of emphasis was the derision in which the mass of outsiders, no more than gaping bystanders, took delight. The broadsheets hastily flung on the market, jeering with greater or lesser degree of wit at the Winter King, do not particularly surprise us. But what are we to say to the Frenchman seen riding through the streets of Prague, naked, facing and holding his horse's tail, while three fiddlers accompanied his obscene abuse of King and Country with the whining of their strings? The citizens of Prague, formerly so proud, bore it without murmur. They had quite different distress to bear. Of which shortly. The dragon, with sack and murder in its train, straddled the city. When the victors eventually put things in order, it was an order in which the kingdom's centuries-old nature was no longer to be discerned.

Victors' Return

"**H**IS great moment past, von Walstein rested" [*post magnum momentum quiescit von Walstein*] "because the burden of bringing up ninety-six thousand taler from the Olmütz treasury had been very heavy," a Saxon agent reported satirically. Sufficiently rested, the Colonel betook himself to the southern Bohemian theatre of war. He fought, and his regiment fought, in the battle of Netolitz which went so badly for the Bohemians. On Mansfeld's defeat followed the devastation of the countryside by the imperialists, the conquest of strong towns and castles. A member of the Waldstein clan, a Slawata, defended Castle Nové Hrad. Ordered to accept ignominious terms of surrender, he sought his uncle's intervention. It left Wallenstein cold. He had no compassion for kith and kin, just as they would in identical circumstances have had none for him. There are no indications that the gruesome war which he helped to wage against his countrymen caused him any scruples, either now or later.

The colonel of a regiment, with his staff of lieutenant-colonel, major, adjutant, stores commissary, baggage-master, and quartermaster, had a considerable amount of executive work to do. The payment and feeding of his mercenaries in so far as they did not support themselves by plunder, the finding of replacements for those killed, the sick, and deserters, the procurement of arms and equipment, the allocation of quarters, all this was his business because in practice no formation higher than a regiment existed. The administrative importance of a head-quarters would be very considerably extended by Wallenstein, and more will be said about that later, but at the outset of his career it was small. The foregoing does not however mean that a regimental commander was purely an orderly-room officer. He was expected, his own men expected him, to fight alongside his unit. The battle of the White Mountain cost the Bavarians and imperialists only 250 dead. Nevertheless these included three colonels and probably a dozen captains.

Cavalry was of two kinds, cuirassiers and arquebusiers. Cuirassiers wore heavy armour and helmets with visors. In illustrations they resemble the knights of olden days. Their weapons were the pistol and a short sword. Arquebusiers were meant to be more mobile and capable of quicker deployment. Their defence was a firelock, the arquebus from which they derived their name, and the lance. Because they were frequently or originally of Croat nationality, Croats or "Krabats" is what they were generally called even if they did not come from that border-land.

When a colonel gave the signal for attack, he normally led the charge towards the enemy, who did well not to wait but to sound the counter-attack. Of the succeeding skirmish it would not be quite correct to say that it dissolved into a series of hand-to-hand combats; it was a multi-plicity of such from the start. A cuirassier would rush past his opposite number, and veering, shoot him in the back as being the part of the body regarded as more vulnerable. Or he would try to ram his foe's steed, thus – with luck – jolting its rider out of the saddle to slay him on the ground. Or he would endeavour to pull him off by his bandoleer. Alternatively, two cavalrymen coming sufficiently close together would enclose each other in their arms and both be torn from their mounts, after which they crashed their heavy pistols against one another's skulls. This is not to mention skilled manoeuvres like training a horse to lash out its heels behind, and so hold off a pursuer, or having such control over it that it would spring at and bite its counterpart, furnishing a good opportunity to thrust a sword into an adversary's visor-opening or the unprotected area between cuisse and greave. But if musketeers were the target of the cavalry's charge, the former did better to wait, with their long lances pointed at the quadrupeds, or at the right moment to trigger off the muskets resting on their stands. If they missed their aim, they were in a poor way. In the throng friend might well strike down friend as, apart from the colours of scarves and agreed battle-cries, unifying recognition-marks were lacking. The multiplication of individual slaughterings accumulated somehow into a result of a psychological nature. Panic would spread, flight became infectious. The attacker broke through the front of the defence, fell upon its rear and flanks. Only at this point would a second regiment, held in reserve and consisting of so and so many companies, each a hundred strong, be launched into the fray. The encircled enemy flung away their weapons and begged for quarter. That, or something like it, was how matters went. That Wallenstein in those years, 1619 and 1620, in his capacity as colonel of cuirassiers more than once headed a cavalry assault is beyond doubt. He was not wounded, neither then nor later, the last serious occasion having been in 1604.

He participated too in the withdrawal of his badly attenuated unit to Austria, a move necessitated by Gabor Bethlen's march on Pressburg. At Ulrichskirchen, in the vicinity of Vienna, he helped to cover the dangerous retreat across the Danube. We shall not argue with his admirers and detractors whether he respectively performed exceptional deeds of valour or simply did his duty like the rest. During the siege he was inside Vienna and emerged after Bethlen's departure, but with so few of his men that he had to launch a fresh recruiting campaign in the Spanish Netherlands. A letter on this subject has survived. Dated the last day of the year 1619 and addressed to the Emperor, its starkly matter-of-fact tone is startling. Whereas letters generally, and those to the Emperor in particular, usually consisted to a good half of fine flourishes, Wallenstein states in his first sentence what he needs, why he needs it, and what instructions the Emperor should issue to enable him to obtain his needs. At the beginning of 1620 he was given a second command composed of 1500 cuirassiers and five hundred arquebusiers. A double regiment, counting a thousand horsemen as the normal strength. More soldiers, more influence. And more business. A regimental commander received (if anyone did) the overall amount of pay to be divided among his subordinates. That furnished opportunities for dubious profit. In the first place came devices for curtailing the mercenaries' wages. Secondly, colonels were in the habit of concealing for as long as possible the number of missing, whether through death or desertion, so that soldiers appeared on the pay-roll who no longer existed. Thirdly, warfare often provided booty, levies, and ransom money. Commanders took their share, sometimes the whole, sometimes little; no law settled the proportion. At the end of 1620 an anonymous publication at Prague declared that Wallenstein aimed at the removal of all other troops from Bohemia "so that he should then be able to govern here with his own according to his pleasure." Nonsense as yet, of course. It shows, though, of what he was thought capable.

In spring 1620, while he was taking part in the mere containment action and preliminary skirmishing of the campaign in Austria he had his first bout of the affliction which during the following fourteen years was to sour his life. "Gout beset me in the year 1620, in April, but until now doth treat me right graciously." Worse was to come in summer. "In the year 1620, in July, I was sick unto death, and I believe that I brought on the illness myself through drinking; was expected to become the Hungarian malady, but the experience and diligence of the physician methinks prevented that." He thought so because Kepler had predicted for him around this date venereal disease and complaints deriving from falls, vaults, fights, and alcoholic as well as gastronomic excesses.

The troops belonging to his double command fought on the White Mountain, but not their colonel. He had himself detailed to proceed with a small number of men towards Laun, a town fifty-five miles north-west of Prague, and from there to see to the submission of the Bohemian communities bordering on Saxony. This meant treading on Elector John George's preserve. However detestably Bohemia's false friend had behaved, waiting to distrain upon Lusatia until he could be certain that all went smoothly in the main theatre of war, the northern Bohemian communities were none the less anxious to surrender to him, if surrender they must, and to slide under Saxon protection because the Elector had agreed to concede more generous terms, freedom of religion, and the maintenance of ancient privileges, than Duke Max would. Wallenstein, on the other hand, was there to insist on the Emperor's prerogative. For the burghers of such towns as Saatz, Brüx, Aussig, Leitmeritz, Ellenbogen, and more of the kind, to do homage to the Elector was all right, but it did not release them from the obligation to take an oath of fealty in the presence of His Majesty's representative. "Wherefore I once more admonish you not to venture a jot of dilatoriness, but forthwith to swear the oath you owe, a failure you would much rue, but too late." That was how he addressed the burghers of Brüx, and that was now his style. The town's emissaries related how "Lord Albrecht von Waldstein is a right amiable lord, but over and above this so severe and stern that whatever he is set upon must take its course, nor would he relinquish. . . ." "Right amiable" will have meant understanding of their situation and a measure of politeness; the rest signified manner of command, laconic refusal to tolerate evasive talking around the point and pedantic subterfuges (both favourite tactics), and threats. These last he could at present implement only on paper. But after the battle of the White Mountain most towns knew what hour had struck.

He was in Prague among those attendant upon the Duke of Bavaria when on 11 November the Bohemian Estates, with Lobkowicz for their mouthpiece, so pitiably begged forgiveness. With what sensations did he look on and listen? Contempt? Malicious satisfaction? Embarrassment, compassion, shame? With very little feeling, I would imagine, and that of gentleness least of all. With awareness, though, that in the coming months an enormous opportunity, properly managed, was at hand.

In December he inspected fleetingly a chain of estates not far from his birth-place, property of the Smiřickýs, his close relatives and a family badly compromised by the events of the rebellion. At the beginning of January he had 1300 barrels of wine brought from Moravia and sold in conquered Prague, anxious about supplies. We do not know the amount of his profit. He was in bed at the time or was, as he wrote in Italian to Buquoy, his commander-in-chief, undergoing a cure. That did not stop him from extremely assiduous activity in several directions.

THE NEW MASTERS

In November the report by an emissary of the Elector of Saxony, whose onus for what now transpired was heavy, ran, "All they crave is money and blood." A month later an unidentified personality wrote from Prague, "Murder is now also afoot and everyone rues that resistance was not made to the last man." The enjoyment to its utmost of a victory too easily gained was the particularly repugnant feature. The defeated had fought neither properly nor effectively nor yet with the earnestness which their enterprise demanded. Their revolution had not been genuine. The counter-revolution was.

Nevertheless we cannot concur with the judgement which alleges that liberal undertakings, later not kept, were responsible for cessation of the fighting. If illusions existed, the blame lay with those who chose to indulge them. At the moment when Duke Maximilian magnanimously told the Estates' representatives that he thought it possible at any rate to promise them their lives, they had already surrendered. The Duke, acting simply as the Emperor's delegate, was moreover in no position to stipulate anything positive. For his own part he said in a letter to Ferdinand that, even though he might in public seek mercy from him on the rebels' behalf, this was purely a matter of form and His Majesty should in no wise allow himself to be misled thereby. The iron must be struck while it was hot, once and for all an example made. Furthermore matters did not stand in Bohemia as well as the collapse of the rebellion would let them appear. Tempers were still smouldering and what the imperial officers and soldiery were indiscriminately doing to Catholics and Protestants was not likely to calm them. This reproof was of a mould that would henceforward be tossed back and forth for many years, the Bavarians accusing the imperialists of "exorbitances", looting, arson, and murder, the imperialists reproaching the Bavarians with precisely the same. Having thus simultaneously encouraged and warned his principal, as well as in his own view done an excellent piece of work all round, Maximilian returned to Munich. As his deputy, the indirect deputy or sub-delegate of the King-Emperor, he appointed Prince Karl von Liechtenstein.

This experienced Estates politician, courtier, and cold, clever fox had accompanied the imperial army during its march on Prague in the capacity, as it were, of head of a future military government. His right-hand man was Lord Paul von Michna, prior to 1618 and now again Secretary to the Bohemian Exchequer. Son of a butcher and Serb by birth, Michna had his obnoxiously suitable talents to thank for having been able to crawl into the position of next but one in power. During Emperor Matthias's days he had already proved his mettle as a Catholic agitator. So manfully did he help to fan the flames of conflict that emigrants of a more moderate calibre, Adam von Waldstein, for instance, frankly held this intriguing fanatic responsible for their common misfortune. Now misfortune was no longer the lot of Michna or of Waldstein who was able to resume office as Principal Lord Chamberlain. Now they all indulged in a taste for advice on how most effectively to tame the country and punish the rebels. Now they were full of plans for reparation of the injury which they had suffered, not to mention the spiritual martyrdom which they had sustained and that could, if at all, only be made good with a great deal of money. Jaroslav von Martinitz and Wilhelm von Slawata, the two grandees hurled from the Hradschin window, Archbishop Lobel of Prague and Abbot Caspar Questenberg von Strachow, the expelled and now homing Jesuits, Franciscans and Minors, all of them inspected their run-down properties with a certain satisfaction; there would be plenty forthcoming to recompense and reward them. Wallenstein too was able to present a bill with respect to the ruin of his Moravian estates, the loss of income in years past. When in December the margraviate also made its submission, its fate was similar to Bohemia's. Cardinal von Dietrichstein, the former frightened rabbit leaping from one funk-hole to another, was now able to play the role that his old friend and opponent Liechtenstein was impersonating at Prague. He revelled in it and performed it thoroughly.

Soon more equivocal characters joined the throng of those who, whether by losses, exile, danger to life and limb or by achievement had a clear claim to the victor's reward. At Prague, apart from those queuing in the antechamber of greedy, impudent Secretary Michna, the enormously rich knight Rudolf Trčka importuned the military government with good wishes and demands while expatiating on the agonies he had had to endure at the hands of the rebels. In the ears of the initiated it sounded strange – they had never heard other than that Trčka had under King Frederick also been a hale and hearty, or at least unscathed, member of the *Landrecht*. Nevertheless the Trčkas, husband, wife, and their young son Adam Erdmann too, managed to manoeuvre themselves across to the side of the winners and new masters, benefiting greatly in the process. No less extraordinary was how the Kinsky brothers fared. One of them, Ulrich, had died a hero's death *pro patria*. Lucky for him, seeing that there were no two ways about his active participation in the Defenestration. The arch-intriguer Wenzel Kinsky could prove the trouble that really, and fortunately, had existed between him and the Estates at the time when illegal rule prevailed. Not that it had had anything to do with loyalty to the crown, being simply the upshot of his private knaveries and arrogant behaviour. Wilhelm Kinsky had been a member of the principal guilty party, the thirty Directors, but had neither belonged to it very long nor been distinguished by great zeal. At any rate, whatever additional extenuating circumstances he was able to adduce, the wind was tempered to him and Wenzel. Finally, what is to be said about Colonel Count Heinrich von Schlick who on the White Mountain fought for the rebels and only thereafter, but immediately thereafter, was allowed to come to such terms with the imperial house and imperial church as to be on the brink of a brilliant career in the imperial army? Schlick's cousin, Count Joachim Andreas, was shortly expedited at the hands of the executioner from life to death. Count Heinrich died in the fullness of time as a field-marshal, president of the imperial War Council at Vienna, and Knight of the Golden Fleece. In the concourse of trials set on foot it was not *only* a question of guilt that decided how an individual got on, away, or not away. Luck, audacity, adroitness, and connections had also something to do with it.

Emperor Ferdinand and his councillors, Eggenberg, Harrach, Trautt-mansdorff, and others with whom the reader will become familiar, had no plan for the settlement of Bohemian affairs. The most practical approach was not to lay down any hard-and-fast rules. No conclusion of peace followed on the heels of a war which, as understood by international law, had not been one. It was not even, strictly speaking, at an end. Gabor Bethlen was still in Upper Hungary and much embittered at what he regarded as betrayal by the Bohemians and Moravians. That enterprising warrior Ernst von Mansfeld remained in the area of Pilsen and in the Upper Palatinate. Most, but not all, Bohemian towns had capitulated. The fugitive Palsgrave refused to recognize accomplished facts and to beg forgiveness from His Affronted Majesty. Silesia had not yet made up its mind. At least one of its notables, the Margrave of Jägerndorf, was grimly determined to turn defeat into victory. The same applied to Matthias von Thurn. He fled south, not north. First to Brünn, then to Bethlen's camp, eventually to Constantinople in order to incite the Grand Turk to war. There was too the German Union which had not, but *could* have, intervened in Bohemia. Its leaders were discounted, but not yet disarmed. And, finally, Bohemia was still simmering. In the streets of its towns civilians timidly kept out of the soldiers' way, but the country's temper was becoming gloomier in proportion to the severity of the new rulers' decrees. The battle of the White Mountain had been a decisive victory, a momentous one, but also cheaply gained. The worry that it might have been only an apparent victory was never out of the minds of politicians, like the Duke of Bavaria, concerned for the future. In such a situation the practical course probably was not to say what was going to be done and not to be tied down by any type of proclamation. But also dangerous because it increased the general uncertainty as to the legal position. Hundreds of thousands had by the most slender tenure of office become implicated with the rebellious government and the Winter King. They did not know whether and what punishment they faced. That, in turn, was bad for business.

On the other hand the King-Emperor was in financial straits, head over heels in debt to the Duke of Bavaria, who was entitled to expect payment of his entire military outlay, and the colonels of his own army. Consequently the decision to confiscate the rebels' estates had been taken long before battle occurred. There were of course sly abettors who suggested that it might be better to leave even the guiltiest in possession of their properties, or a part of them, and to impose instead a heavy tribute which, to facilitate payment, the gentlemen would then squeeze to the utmost out of their lands. The victors would harvest a finer yield than the promise held out by sale, in all likelihood well below par and attended by variously displeasing circumstances, of the confiscated goods. The proponents of these economic speculations were however outvoted. Confiscation was the simpler procedure, the more ample revenge, and would moreover (although this was ventilated only in the tiniest of high circles) once and for all sap the Bohemian Protestant nobility's will to survive.

No doubt existed about the cessation in principle of the old order, including Rudolf's Letter of Majesty, except in so far as authority chose to tolerate its continuance. All legal transactions, appointments, and registrations of statutory character effected under the rebels were to be quashed.

Not quite so certain was the position of what was pious Ferdinand's most zealous interest – the solution of the religious problem. The rebels' argument had constantly been how the issue turned on religion and nothing else, whereas the imperialists constantly harped on religion having nothing whatever to do with the issue which was purely one of secular insurrection. Consequently their approach to religious affairs, having regard also for their ally, Elector John George, had to be cautious, more cautious than was to the victor's liking. Nevertheless anyone knowing Ferdinand of Styria's character and his earlier history could surmise how the matter would end. That was the way that it did end, though only years later. Step by step, the solution involved the Calvinists, the Brethren, the adherents of the "Bohemian Confession", eventually the Lutherans; it involved the vassals on the spiritual domains, the royal towns, the nobility's vassals, the nobility itself; and the reason regularly given was that not the faith, but the insurrectionary temporal ideas and deeds to which the faith gave rise were meant to be involved.

Prince Liechtenstein felt rather lonely in his office, despite the lucrative opportunities it afforded and of which he fully availed himself. For all that the appointment soon was transformed from that of a mere sub-delegate into that of a royal governor, effectively a viceroy, a dignity hitherto completely unknown in Bohemia, he remained simply the executor of orders from Vienna. Too long personally and politically connected with the proceedings of the Bohemian and Moravian Estates not to feel some embarrassment at the nobility's economic or physical annihilation, too intelligent not to ponder the outcome of the severest acts of punishment and vengeance, he none the less regularly yielded to instructions from the "most gracious" and "most puissant". What lay beyond the King's power to bestow on those who were complaisant? What had the defeated to offer?

On 20 February, three and a half months after the battle of the White Mountain, the governor was commanded to take into safe custody without further delay the former Directors and thirty-two other political offenders. Assisted by the Bavarian Lieutenant-General Tilly and Colonel Wallenstein, he did so on the afternoon of the same day. Tradition has it that at the last moment Tilly had a warning conveyed to those in danger. If that was the case, he behaved more nobly than

Wallenstein; it is possible. Not that his tips could help the victims any more, just as the often reiterated question why they should "under incomprehensible delusion" have so long remained in Prague is of little use. Flight would have had to have been immediately after the battle, and very far at that, to Constantinople like Thurn, to Denmark like Christian von Anhalt, to Berlin, Holstein, and ultimately The Hague like King Frederick and his Palatine advisers. The Elector extradited remorselessly those who tarried in Saxony.

At Prague was constituted a special court with its own terms of reference and a questionnaire containing 236 points. The Bohemian *Landrecht*, in any case inappropriate to the task, had been dissolved. For appearances' sake a reasonably large number of Bohemian assessors were appointed, not all those invited to participate were prepared to comply. Neither Slawata nor Martinitz, although Adam von Waldstein did. Prince Liechtenstein presided. A few learned lawyers, imperial councillors and reliable Austrian administrative officials ensured legal process – in so far as lawyers on the winning side could ensure anything like that. As it did not make good sense to condemn to death those who had died during the rebellion, their entire property was proclaimed forfeit. Sentence of death and confiscation was meted out summarily against those alive and successfully flown.

Some had flown, but not from Bohemia, and were in hiding. Count Joachim Andreas Schlick, for example, previously spokesman for the Saxon party, sought refuge with Lord Redern, his relative, in the castle of Friedland. This stout fortress lies in north-eastern Bohemia on a steep basalt spur covered with woods and approachable only from the north. Two miles from Saxon Zittau, it also borders on Silesia. A strategically important spot whose walls ensured peace. Schlick's men made no resistance when the Saxons forced their way in, and it availed Schlick nothing that in 1619 it had been he who came to Dresden to offer the Elector the Bohemian crown. Now he had to visit Dresden again, as a prisoner, and was brought from there to Prague. Redern escaped to Poland.

Wallenstein stationed a garrison in Friedland and duly obeyed the order to arrest Lord Christoph von Harrant, a widely travelled man, musician and author who had written a work on *The Path to the Holy Land*. Although a Catholic, he had partaken in the rebellion on the losing side. At the gate of Castle Pecka Wallenstein invited his fellow-peer to enter his coach, surrounded by armed riders. It is not known what the two gentlemen discussed during the journey, but that they chatted is likely – members of the nobility observed the social courtesies even when one was driving another to his death. Their way lay via Gitschin, not far from Hermanitz, Wallenstein's birthplace.

THE DOWNFALL OF THE HOUSE OF SMIŘICKÝ

Gitschin was the main seat of one of the domains belonging to the Smiřickýs of Smiřice, the powerful family so closely related to the hero of our tale. Now it was plunging to its fall, a fact partially explicable in political terms, partially through internal events. A short tale within our tale and one which takes us back a little in time.

At the beginning of the century the House of Smiřický, divided into two main branches, was probably the richest in Bohemia. Its domestic needs were supplied from its seventeen enormously spacious estates situated principally in eastern Bohemia in the region today called the "Bohemian Paradise". Manor houses like ancient Nachod, recently extended on Italian lines, Skal, Castle Trosky perched high on two grotesquely conic-shaped rises seen from afar, Schwarzkosteletz, gloomy Kumburg, the mansion on the market-square at Gitschin, Aulibitz, Dub, and Friedstein attested to the fortune of the Smiřickýs. Their property consisted of allodial estates, meaning such as could be freely bequeathed or sold, and an entail centring in the town of Schwarz-kosteletz, an asset which therefore passed in turn to whoever was the senior member of the family, males enjoying priority. This arrangement was established by Jaroslaw, of the Skal branch, who died in 1597. Markyta, the daughter of his brother Albrecht who had his seat at Nachod, was the mother of Wallenstein. Marital alliances between Waldsteins and Smiřickýs are likely also to have occurred earlier. The pristine Castle Waldstein was situated in, or bordered on, "Paradise". Among other families marrying into the Smiřickýs or becoming connected with them through marriage we find the Hasenburgs, Slawatas, and Wartenbergs, all of them components of a single Greater Bohemian clan, regardless of its members' indifferent and often remarkably antipathetic behaviour towards one another.

When the Skal branch died out, the whole property came into the hands of Sigmund Smiřický upon Nachod. He was so rich and so adroit in the augmentation of his riches that he was able, in spite of what the refinements of his household cost, annually to set aside a hundred thousand taler. In 1608, at point of death, his hoard of gold must have run into millions. The allodial estates passed to his sons Jaroslaw,

Heinrich, and Albrecht while the entail also devolved upon Jaroslaw. Three years later the latter died, as after another three years did his uncle Albrecht Wenzel who had been the successor to his fat of the land. The sole survivors of the house which not long ago had so many collaterals were Sigmund's two sons Heinrich and Albrecht, his two daughters Elisabeth and Margareta Salomena.

All was not well with Heinrich Georg. Generally called "the simpleton" and regularly referred to as such by his cousin Wallenstein, he should have succeeded to the entail. It is probable that he was not so much weak in the head, as suggested by the word "simple", as incurably deranged. Albrecht Jan, the younger brother, stepped into the entail, whether as guardian for the simpleton or as holder on his own behalf is not quite clear. That is how he was entered in the Bohemian land registry and that is what mattered. The allodial estates should have been shared between the two brothers, the bright and the dim, but being of no practical significance it did not happen. One sister received money.

The brilliance, talent, and virtues of the Bohemian nobility three centuries ago, but now extinct, shone forth once more in the personality of young Albrecht Jan. We shall not account it a reproach to him that it should have been in *his* palace at Prague that the Defenestration was planned and that he participated in the attempted murder on the Hradschin. His concern with religion and country was genuine, as he proved by hazarding his fortune, setting up a regiment and punctually paying his men, probably the sole Bohemian unit to which this happened. Despite his extreme youth – he was only twenty-two – he was elected to the Directory. Some indeed wished immediately to make him King. That he would have been a better one than the Palsgrave is certain. Taking physical risks with as reckless daring as he staked his fortune in politics, Albrecht Jan fell ill from inflammation of the lungs caught in the damp cold of the field. On a late autumn day, because at that date there was no cure for his malady, he lay on his death-bed, in baggy breeches, velvet cloak, and lace ruff, hands folded upon a bible, so handsome that the delicately waxen-coloured mask of death framed by a youthful beard was still full of seductive charm. Had anyone, I remain convinced, been able to lead the Bohemian revolt to victory, Albrecht Jan Smiřický was the man. His death was mourned, as the saying goes, by his sisters, Elisabeth and Margareta, and the simpleton in so far as he noted it, as well as abroad by a cousin, or second cousin, Wallenstein.

Eleven years ago Elisabeth had unfortunately so compromised and degraded herself as to start an affair with the son of a peasant. Since discovery of this disgrace she had lived as a family prisoner in Castle Kumburg, though whether in the tower-dungeon like common folk or in a few sparsely furnished chambers is not known.

The younger sister, Margareta, is described as a possibly foolish but entirely innocent creature. This is especially the case where chroniclers are hostile to Wallenstein and enjoy venting indignation over the manner in which he is alleged to have cheated the young woman out of her fortune. Margareta Salomena cannot however have been quite such a dear person. If she had been, she would have seen to it, with her stern father and chivalric brother dead, that Elisabeth was at last released after more than sufficient mortification for the weakness of her flesh. That was something Margareta Salomena very prudently did not do. As long as her elder sister sat incarcerated and deemed unworthy of inheritance, she, Margareta, was the simpleton's guardian and beneficiary of all the house of Smiřický's possessions. Despite her youth she was sufficiently shrewd and hard-hearted to appreciate the connection. Possibly her husband, Heinrich von Slawata, breathed the appropriate arguments into her ears. Brother to the defenestrated Wilhelm Slawata, Lord Heinrich had watched Wilhelm being dragged to the window and either not heard or retorted derisively when brother called to brother for pity. As unbecoming was the Slawata couple's behaviour after Albrecht Jan's death. In order to enter on sole possession of the inheritance, Lord Heinrich brought into play the political influence that he enjoyed as a meritorious revolutionary; Margareta exercised financial persuasion by bribing the principal Director, Wenzel von Ruppa, with fifty thousand taler. That amount did the trick. Elisabeth remained in prison; Heinrich and Margareta could choose in which of the Smiřický castles they wanted to live.

Not long without vexation. For now there entered on the scene Otto von Wartenberg, an old widower and swashbuckler of ill-repute nick-named "the hobbler" since being wounded in the Turkish war. His plan was to rescue the imprisoned Elisabeth, marry her, and demand at least half the inheritance. He may secretly have arranged this beforehand with the damsel in distress because, when he scaled a wall of the feebly defended castle with a small number of armed retainers and penetrated to the captive, she was ready without ado to follow the rogue as his bride.

The marriage bells had hardly ceased pealing and Elisabeth von Wartenberg was barely accustomed to her new-won freedom before she made overtures to her sister which we cannot call other than equitable. Her first proposal was to share the inheritance. On the rejection of this amicable offer she suggested that the whole of the property should be put in the hands of a trustee until such time as the government at Prague reached a decision on the matter. These sensible approaches none the less remained unavailing. The Wartenbergs hereupon resorted to force. Taking advantage of the fact that the Slawatas could not be in simultaneous residence on all their domains, the rival claimants one day appeared at Gitschin and required the vassals to do homage to them, an exaction performed with indifference. A squad of soldiers, a private garrison, was stationed in the town. The castle, more mansion than fortress, was put in a state of makeshift defence, with a considerable supply of munitions accumulated there in preparation for all events.

Meanwhile Palsgrave Frederick, when he became King of Bohemia, was faced with the repugnant task of reaching a decision on a legal squabble totally foreign to him. It attested to potentialities and customs such as he had never experienced in his well-administered Rhenish Palatinate. Entirely dependent on Bohemian advisers who were in turn fellow-revolutionaries and fellows in corruption of Heinrich Slawata, he decreed what they wanted: Elisabeth Smiřický must immediately evacuate every piece of territory rightly belonging to her sister. An imposing commission, a lord, two knights, Heinrich Slawata, and several justiciaries to boot, set out for Gitschin, not to pronounce once more upon the already decided case, but to evict Lady Elisabeth with the prescribed ritual.

In the town hall of Gitschin all went smoothly. The citizens obeyed the King's order and did homage to Lord von Slawata just as willingly as six months earlier they had to the Lady von Wartenberg. Presumably it made no difference who ruled and pestered them. When the commissioners' summons to afford access to the castle fell on pretended deaf ears, Slawata's possession of the key to a back-door effected entry. At once the party began to draw up an inventory to ensure that no valuables should disappear or had already disappeared. The Lady von Wartenberg found them at this business, a wrangle ensued, and the Lady was so affronted that, to avoid further torment and perhaps temporarily to find shelter on another Gitschin property, she ordered horses to be harnessed. Slawata was not ready to make even this concession: the fine horses were his and must not leave the stables. Elisabeth, beside herself with rage and distress, returned to her apartment, enticed there the mercenaries who had sworn fealty to her husband, and liberally indulged them with drink, probably meaning to spur them to action against the commissioners. Whether the soldiery, torches in hand, forced the powder-magazine to obtain ammunition and behaved with drunken folly or, as I am inclined to believe, the Lady Elisabeth, who had been heard screaming that she had rather die than suffer more such humiliation, ignited the powder so that everything would go to rack and ruin for good and all, she, her persecutors, and the disputed ownership – whatever the facts, the mansion went up in the air with a thundering roar, burying in flame and ashes every living creature within. The shock and horror of Gitschin's vassals, not unmixed with pleasure, can be imagined. When after hours they undertook a search of the site, they found all the commissioners and Lord von Slawata dead, the majority of the soldiers and servants, some fifty in all, slain. The Lady von Wartenberg was half buried alive, with burns at hands and feet. She was not given the aid for which she pleaded, instead even viler treatment of which she died. Daughter of Sigmund Smiřický and sister to noble Albrecht Jan, she was put naked into ground outside the precincts of the town.

The Gitschin catastrophe cast a deep depression over King Frederick and the country at large. This made however no difference to the established legal position, only that Margareta Salomena was now rid of sister and husband alike. She remained in possession and the simpleton's guardian.

As for Otto von Wartenberg, the hobbler, he was twice lucky, third time unlucky. In the first place that, having been at Prague and by King Frederick's orders not allowed to leave, he was not at Gitschin on the day of the explosion. In the second place that, after secretly fleeing the capital, making for Saxony and fighting stoutly against the Bohemians, he was enabled to return as one of the new masters, even though of the third rank, and, by accommodating himself to Mass, to enjoy a fragment of the riches that he had vainly sought at the Lady Elisabeth's side. Unlucky in that, parvenu man of property and parvenu Catholic zealot, he drove his peasants too far. They stormed his castle and slew him gruesomely. Wallenstein's chief steward, who was in a position to know, wrote to his master that the hobbler had only himself to thank for his ugly end.

THE STRUGGLE FOR THE INHERITANCE

After the battle of the White Mountain Margareta fled from Bohemia with as much money and jewellery as she could hurriedly lay her hands on, first to the Electorate of Brandenburg, then Hamburg, the powerful free city which held out promise of safety. Gindely, the historian whose researches are on other occasions so useful to us, thinks that an evil spirit in the shape of Wallenstein must have inspired her to flight because this was unnecessary – in general no steps were taken against the wives of rebels if they remained, but their possessions were seized if they left the country. At that moment, however, Margareta could not have had any idea of these two rules which emerged only gradually. What she could not fail to know was that if one individual in the whole kingdom was quite definitely not in danger of punishment, then it was her simpleton of a ward. Even the most partisan royal prosecutor could raise no charge of rebellion against a madman who for years past had spent his twilit days in a castle among keepers. None the less Margareta took the simpleton with her. Why? Why burden herself with this awkward load? Doubtless in the same frame of mind as someone unable physically to transfer a valuable takes with him the title-deed to it. The incapacitated owner embodied her own title to both the Schwarzkosteletz entail and half the Smiřický allodial properties. Which shows again that Margareta cannot have been so naïve as is asserted. Quite definitely, though, it was not Wallenstein who advised her to take her ward on her flight because it was he who forthwith had himself appointed by his senior fellow-profiteer from victory, the governor Liechtenstein, as Heinrich Georg Smiřický's guardian. From that moment forward his concern was to see to the simpleton's return to Bohemia. On this subject a mass of autograph letters and postscripts exists. "I request my lord to send me also the order to the Elector of Brandenburg that the simpleton Smiřický shall be delivered unto me . . .". The hypothesis that he drove his little cousin to ruin by way of treacherous counsel therefore lacks any basis of probability. Moreover, constituted as he was and the political circumstances being what they were, he would have brought her to her knees even had she been in the land. Had he known, he would have put an abrupt stop to the simpleton's flight by a *coup de main*. As it was, he could take proper possession of his new property only seven years later by having his cousin Heinrich Georg seized at Hamburg and brought to Bohemia. He provided, once more in Castle Skal, accommodation appropriate to his station, but he declined to see him. People of normal understanding could prove a strain on Wallenstein's nerves; he had no desire whatever to traffic with madmen.

He can now be observed approaching one and the same objective by various routes. To comprehend his tactics it has to be borne in mind that condemnation of the dead Albrecht Jan as an arch-rebel automatically involved the confiscation of his holdings, just as in April 1621 the memory of him was ceremonially sentenced to eternal execration. The value of his and simpleton Heinrich's real estate can be estimated as having been close on two million gulden – four to five times more than had sufficed to make Wallenstein one of Moravia's wealthy men.

His first step was to have the dominion of Gitschin made over to him as collateral. The Emperor and the imperial Exchequer needed money like a man dying of thirst needs water. To produce it was one of Liechtenstein's top priorities. Two months after the battle of the White Mountain Wallenstein offered a loan of sixty thousand gulden, one of the many projects on which he worked while "taking a cure" at Prague. Ten of the sixty thousand were to be in cash, the rest represented by his valuable silver table-ware stored at Vienna. Whether these ornamental items derived from his deceased wife's collection or from war booty must remain a moot point. If from the latter source, special indignation would not be called for. Nests were feathered at others' expense whenever possible. Even Maximilian of Bavaria, the most moral prince of his day, returned from Prague with a splendid haul from the possessions of his cousin, the Palsgrave. As for the grant of liens, sometimes to obtain money, m.re often as temporary indemnity for money owed, that was the usual practice in Bohemia. Formerly Wallenstein had been content to advance money on the strength of mere promissory notes. Now the sums involved were of an order where he could demand security. Nevertheless Vienna hesitated, not on the score of principle but because the scale of the demand was in this instance so brazen. The three towns, sixty-seven villages, four manorial seats, thirteen farms belonging to the dominion of Aulibitz or Gitschin, with breweries and other thriving enterprises, would yield a product that, so calculated a ledger clerk in the imperial Exchequer, whoever pocketed it year after year for a loan of only sixty thousand gulden could easily obtain fifteen per cent interest at a time when more than six per cent was already in excess of the normal figure. What would happen if interest rates were driven up to that level? Not that he, the ledger clerk, wished any possible detriment to ensue for Colonel Wallenstein as a result of such calculation, "for who is not aware that he hath abandoned his property in Moravia through these tumults" and had risked life, limb, and fortune for His Majesty? The quill-driver for his part miserably underpaid, wavered between two worries, the duty he owed to the Exchequer, the fear with which Wallenstein inspired him. "Who is not aware . . ." meant the position of power already held directly and indirectly by the colonel, thanks to his connections with the court at Vienna and the Viceroy at Prague. The Emperor, even had he been more industrious than he was, could never alone have coped with the mass of intricate business showered upon his desk from Bohemia. He had to rely on his advisers, in this case on the counsel of his poor quill-driver. He wrote to Liechtenstein that the offer seemed a sound one, but the stipulation very onerous, not least because of the bad example that it set, and he could therefore not grant the money-lending colonel the whole of the Gitschin receipts. He could however, in lieu of his instrinsic entitlement, probably concede him 3600, 4000, or 4500, indeed 5000 gulden per annum. Ferdinand can be observed raising the figure in the process of dictation, and it can be sensed how even he, the King-Emperor, is beginning to fall under the spell of the colonel whose name he has recently so often encountered. The deal was barely settled before it was repeated – a further loan of fifty thousand gulden, a further lien, and again, it so happened, in the shape of Smiřický estates, Aicha, Klein-Skal, and others. The premise was that everything previously belonging to the Smiřickýs now belonged to the Exchequer.

While Wallenstein by this means slowly gained a hold on the heritage, he simultaneously experimented with a method which led in another, precisely opposite direction – he disputed the justice of any claim by the Emperor on the assets of his relations. This he did as trustee for the simpleton, a function it had been all the easier to confer on him in so far as all proceedings dating from the period when the rule of law was inoperative, including therefore that of the trusteeship by the fugitive Margareta, were null and void.

On this front Wallenstein the lawyer adopted the following strategy. The entail of Schwarzkosteletz, belonging to the simpleton, could not have been confiscated from his dead brother Jan Albrecht because it had never been settled upon him; he had merely had the usufruct in his capacity as guardian. Half of the allodial assets would have been his if they had ever been really divided. That never having happened, they must be regarded as a single whole whose subsequent dismantlement to the prejudice of his ward Wallenstein would not permit. There existed moreover a prerogative from the days of Emperor Rudolf II, of blessed memory, providing that Bohemian lords who committed the crime of lese-majesty could indeed be punished by loss of life but not be robbed of their possessions. These had in such case to devolve on the next-of-kin in the paternal line. From there to where? Prince Liechtenstein, the viceroy, closely collaborating with Wallenstein in the entire business, took these legal considerations very seriously, or pretended to take them seriously. After consultation with a number of not exactly uninterested authorities like Jaroslaw von Martinitz and the rich, ever richer Rudolf Trčka, he gave his own expert opinion. The first point must without qualification be conceded: the entail belonged, and continued to belong, to the simpleton because it was obvious that the latter could not, having regard to his state of simplicity, have had any hand in the rebellion. This, it had better be stated right away, was a lie on Liechtenstein's part, and no pointless lie either. The entail having really and truly belonged to the dead Albrecht, it soon belonged to the governor by advantageous purchase from Wallenstein and continued to belong to the Liechtensteins until the Year of Our Lord 1945. As for the second point, the opinion went on, the colonel, it must reluctantly be said, was probably also in a position to win that too, if the matter were taken to court. Therefore it was advisable to come to an amicable settlement with him over this and he, the governor, thought he had cause to believe that Wallenstein would be prepared to agree on a compromise. The third point was however totally untenable. Prerogative or no prerogative, if this were now to be brought forward and countenanced, the whole process of confiscation would break down, with brothers, sisters, great-aunts of rebels succeeding to their possessions in place of the Emperor, and how was the war then to be paid for? The Emperor subscribed to the sagacity of his viceroy in this very comprehensive matter in the same way as he had to that of his quill-driver in the above-mentioned small one. The allodial assets were divided between the Colonel and the Exchequer. Wallenstein, after a precise study of the map of Bohemia, chose on his ward's behalf those segments which fitted into his large-scale plan, shortly to be revealed. Nachod, handsome though it was, he did not take because he did not need it. Subsequently it was bought by the Trčka family. He did however require a small counter-favour for having acceded to division of the assets, namely, the right to dispose at will over the property of the simpleton, whether by sale or barter. The governor found this condition odd, but on careful consideration not inordinate, seeing that Wallenstein was not only the simpleton's trustee but successor and universal heir. He would scarcely do anything which harmed his ward to his own detriment. Ferdinand II, with a bewildered shake of the head, agreed.

Now comes the third method that Wallenstein employed. The colonel who as a tyro-financier had vast pledges assigned to him for little money and the guardian who fought on his ward's behalf with the sharp weapons of the law sought at the same time to become sole heir by achieving an arrangement with every conceivable rival. Katharina von

Ričan, for instance, an old aunt who, born Smiřický, was a sister of his mother. After the simpleton's death she would be likely to have been able to lay better claim to the entail than Wallenstein. The rules of succession provided that Smiřický females followed in succession to males, but in the case of relatives bearing other names age alone was the deciding factor. There were also two cousins, sons of Anna Slawata, his other maternal aunt, with one of whom he had spent childhood years at Castle Koschumberg. Michael Slawata, as rebel and refugee, did not count. Johann Albrecht, who had remained, followed Aunt Katharina's example and ceded all his hereditary rights. Whether Wallenstein had these relatives handed a ducat-filled purse, whether he dangled before the eyes of implicated family members any prospect of only too badly needed favours if they proved tractable, or whether he merely expressed his wishes in a cutting voice tantamount to commands, we do not know. I incline, though, to think that the settlement was amicable. An arrangement made with an appearance of freedom would last longer than one imposed by force; it would be more economical.

That left the last Smiřický daughter, refugee Margareta Salomena, who had a boy. Bohemian historians say that she was no more than fifteen when she fled the country. Surprising, in view of her energy and cunning. Even more surprising by light of the calculation that she would then, at her brother Albrecht Jan's death, have had to have been a good business woman and hard-hearted wife at thirteen. Such abnormalities do occur, but would have deserved remark. Whatever the truth about her character and age, the fact is that Wallenstein wanted to come to terms even with this claimant. To anticipate matters chronologically, he made the effort in 1624. She was living in Hamburg and had appealed to King Christian of Denmark whether, ever gracious, he could not assist her to recover her home and property. In those days princes liked to intervene on behalf of this or that individual deprived of his rights, and more especially if he or she was not one of their own subjects. They were continually writing to one another about such cases. It cost nothing and was hardly ever of any use, but it gave the writer a reputation for liberality and importance. In the present one it may have been Christian's mediation which led Wallenstein to advance to his cousin a few conciliatory proposals, no matter whether to be obliging to the King, or once and for all to be rid of this remote inheritance worry too, or just from good nature. Ferdinand II exempted her from the overall applicable death penalty, giving permission for her free and safe return to Bohemia; Wallenstein declared his readiness to provide for her in accordance with her station. Should she prefer to live abroad, he would not be un-sympathetic to the idea of making a purchase in Holland to furnish the wherewithal for her and her family. Margareta would have done well to content herself with this offer of something. Insisting on everything, she got nothing and remained in penury.

In June, against the background of a fresh loan of 58,000 gulden or, probably more literally, to compensate for outlay on his regiments, Wallenstein was granted a fresh lien, this time on the dominions of Friedland and Reichenberg, part of the confiscated real estate belonging to the refugee Lord von Redern. Looking at the map, the reader will see that Friedland and Gitschin are separated by some fifty miles of beautiful countryside, the "Bohemian Paradise", with its sand-strewn rocks, firs, rolling hills, rich meadows, and the wooded spurs of the Giant Mountains.

HE SEES TO GOOD ORDER

The occurrence of another event has attached sad renown to 21 June 1621, the day on which Wallenstein obtained a lien on Friedland. On that date, in front of the town hall of Prague's Old Town, twenty-seven of the forty rebels convicted of high treason, those forty wrecked on the 236-points questionnaire, died at the executioner's hand. The terrible spectacle lasted four and a half hours because only one headsman was available. Responsible for good order, seeing to it that the condemned should not at the last moment make unsuitable speeches, that the spectators who would undoubtedly appear in large numbers, whether out of grief or from some other spark of interest, did not give vent to too loud lamentation, that indeed no *coup de main* to rescue the felons was attempted, responsible for these things was an infantry regiment belong-ing to Colonel Wallenstein. As the governor, seated under a canopy, had to attend the execution and as Wallenstein was in Prague in charge of matters on that day, we must assume him to have been present on the wooden dais and in immediate proximity of the governor. The fact excited no comment, and of those who had to bare their neck to the sword it has to be said that more horrible acts had come to pass in Bohemia under their rule.

None the less Prince Liechtenstein was not wholly at his ease. We know it from a letter that five years later he wrote to the Emperor's father-confessor, a strangely agitated screed of self-vindication whose sentences, page upon page, start with the question "Who . . .?" and frequently fling out the challenge "Let Prince Waldstein be asked. . . ." Included is the plaintive demand, "Who accomplished such harsh execution without ensuing trouble and danger to life and limb, incurring the burden of many persons' and families' enmity and in the eyes of posterity the character of tyrant because nothing of the kind befell else-where, as though 'twas not His Majesty's, but alone my will and pleasure?" These political murders were not Liechtenstein's will and pleasure. He had effected many a reprieve for such of the condemned as had been no more than "pure idiots" or too old properly to know what they were doing or participated only reluctantly out of fright. He had dallied with the execution until he was not allowed to dally any longer. The Emperor is also reported to have hesitated. After a sleepless night he asked his father confessor for advice, but was refused – the business was within His Majesty's discretion and Holy Writ prescribed nothing here. He signed the sentences tearfully and with a quivering hand.

He ratified them, not with pleasure, but with a will. Unless his good-nature was a mere mask, his soul held another layer which was different. And then, what now really depended still on his will? When it was a matter of deciding whether Bohemia should be allowed to go its way or whether to obtain the better of it with violence, he had helped to tilt the balance of decision. Now there was no choice any more. If on occasion the Emperor wanted to exercise clemency or promised such, he could not keep his pledge. A victory like that of the White Mountain has an immanent logic. What is inherent in it, cannot be repressed. It must come out, not all at once, but bit by bit.

A few days later the Emperor's representative and his military abettors watched the performance of what they had in detail prepared. They saw, unwinkingly and stony-faced, the blood spurting and head laid by head. The cool morning had turned into a hot forenoon before they could at last proceed to an early soup. As they drained it, they may more strongly than at any time since the battle on the White Mountain have had the feeling how considerable was the difference between being on the winning or the losing side.

The heads of twelve of the executed were nailed to the bridge-tower of the Old Town. For ten years they could be seen as a warning to all, a manifestation of the archaic ritualistic quality pervading the whole affair and from which the concept of penalty and vengeance has still not quite departed.

Had the death of these twenty-seven men closed this chapter of criminal justice, it would perhaps have been possible to say that the price exacted for the subjection and reorganization of a state was, though severe, not too high. It was but the beginning. The work of the Expropriation Council with its whole, half, and quarter confiscations according to scale of guilt, the labours of the Commissioners-General for Reformation, the collective punishment imposed on towns, their depopulation and economic ruin, the expulsion of preachers, the emigration and flight of laymen, and the sanctions intended to dissuade them, it was all unending, dragged on for years, decades. Absolutism as a form of government which now for the first time befell central Europe is claimed to have been superior in efficacy to rule by the Estates. It is the claim of historians who see such things in the perspective of eras and like to deal with comprehensive denominators. They may, from their point of view, be perfectly right. But talk to a Bohemian in the 1620s, to a Lutheran mineworker, a member of the petty nobility, a burgess of Tabor or Königgrätz, enlighten him on the lines of "Don't you understand, man, that at last you are living under an up-to-date régime productive for the future?", and – what eyes he would have made.

Major Matters

CHRISTIAN VON ANHALT, that international politician, supranational general, never disheartened fabricator of grand designs, and at the last, on the White Mountain, commander-in-chief of the Bohemian forces, was now no longer any of these things. After the defeat he had in the first place betaken himself to Sweden, then to Danish-held Holstein. Not, though, to spin further intrigues and continue to assist the Palsgrave, who was by no means ready to abandon his cause. On the contrary, the Prince wrote to Ferdinand. He had, he admitted, on occasion probably gone rather far in his zeal for the Reformed faith, but where on this earth was to be found the man who did not at one time or another commit a folly? Was not God alone without blemish, but His creatures always fallible? Let therefore His Majesty spread the cloak of clemency over his, the Prince's, trivial errors and forgive him.

After a quarter of a century's fanaticism, Christian von Anhalt was suddenly filled with longing for only one thing – to put himself on a right footing with the Emperor and Empire, enjoy the quiet of old age on his beloved Bernburg and become a thoroughly sober, still, withdrawn spectator of events. There are more people like that than is generally imagined. They act a character without having one and are capable of changing the part when its continued performance promises to be increasingly irksome.

Prince Christian had a son of the same name, commonly called "young Anhalt". To judge from his journals, he was a likeable young man, more modest and stable than his father, and at least the latter's equal in perspicacity. In the battle before the gates of Prague he led a strong cavalry attack against the Bavarians. With a pistol-shot wound in the arm-pit, he was captured and at first passed himself off for an ordinary captain. However, even if the red tippet he wore over his armour and his golden hat-badge had not given the lie to this pretence, his bearing aroused all the more suspicion when during the course of the night respectively Neapolitan, German, French, and Walloon barber-surgeons clumsily rummaged in his wound. Whoever bore that without a groan must indeed be of very noble blood, and so he came to be recognized for who he was. There followed a period of chivalric arrest while a number of officers belonging to the Bavarian–imperial–Spanish camp squabbled for possession of the Prince, partly on account of the antici- pated ransom, partly out of sheer well-bred rivalry for his guardianship and because he was a prisoner of political importance. After a while the Emperor decided that Anhalt, an imperial prince who had fought against his liege-lord, belonged to him and he ordered his removal to Vienna. On parole, the young man spent the winter of 1621–2 in dignified semi- freedom, paying and receiving the most formal calls, participating in the most various celebrations as though he were not in custody, let alone the son of an outlaw, and noting down in his diary acute observations of what went on at court and among the politicians.

We see the prince wooed by courtiers whose advice is to prostrate himself before the Emperor; it will redound to his advantage. We hear him protesting against this exaction that on the occasion of an audience he will behave as is proper. It leaves the imperial Vice-Chancellor, a Herr von Ulm or Ulmer, unsatisfied. A prostration it must be, as the rules of jousting prescribe for imperial princes who are captives of the Emperor. A prostration unconditionally agreed and voluntarily per- formed, else no audience. Anhalt finally submits. Conducted into the Chamber of State, he makes on the threshold two deep bows, two again on reaching the middle of the hall, and four paces from the Emperor a fifth. This time the bow is accompanied by a backward movement of the left hip so that his knee touches the ground. In this position he utters the form of address "Most Gracious Emperor and Lord", rises, and in eloquent words tells his story, the story of an inno- cent and wholly unpolitical individual. Ferdinand signs to him to approach, raises his hat, gives him his hand, and apostrophizes him as "Your Dilection",* the appellation appropriate to his rank. During the succeeding weeks the prisoner frequently meets the Emperor, goes hunting with him, sails with him, and is thought worthy of receiving the most exalted, indeed political confidences. The monarch confides that he is not so ferocious as abroad they make him out to be; let the Prince at a later date impart that to those whom it concerns. He has no wish to rob anyone of his own, but neither does he want to be robbed himself.

---

* This designation was invented in 1867 by Thomas Carlyle, writing his essay on *Frederick the Great*, to convey the flavour of an archaic title used among German princes (translator's note).

The imperial Vice-Chancellor talks in a similar vein – the Emperor's honest desire is to exercise indulgence rather than severity and to settle matters amicably with the Palsgrave if only the latter is prepared to do the same. Should Spain be of different mind, there is no disposition to sail in its wake. The President of the Aulic Council, Count Hohenzollern, goes still further. Vienna, this important dignitary assures the young Protestant, contains no more mischievous and harmful personality than Count Oñate, the Spanish ambassador. Remarkable candour to be employed towards a twenty-years-old captured rebel. Without a trace of embarrassment a member of one party reviles a man belonging to the other, its ally and rival. Love of peace is the phrase that they all mouth. The words are as true as they can be when action and accomplished facts gainsay them. For the past year the Palsgrave has had the ban of outlawry pronounced upon him. His electoral office and his land, at least a part of his land, the Upper Palatinate, has been promised to the Duke of Bavaria. At this very moment the Spaniards are waging war in the Rhenish Palatinate without a thought being given to stopping them. How then, quite apart from what has happened and continues to happen in Bohemia, should there be peace in the Empire, amicable composition?

The marks of favour shown to Anhalt at the top focus on him the attention of those just below, the grandees, the ministers, the foreign representatives whose stamping-ground is Vienna. Prince Liechtenstein, on a visit to the capital, sends him his card. The wife of the Bohemian Grand Chancellor Lobkowicz invites him to her drawing-room. The Lobkowicz family, it must be realized, is like most Bohemian families split within itself. Wilhelm von Lobkowicz is that "sheer idiot" who, thanks to Liechtenstein's efforts, has been reprieved to life-long fortress confinement. Zdenko von Lobkowicz, the Chancellor, is Catholic. His wife, a little past the brink of autumn, espouses the attractive young Prince's cause. She would "like to wrap him in the cocoon of Catholic religion", though it may be all that she can wrap him in; alas, then, that greater youth than hers should apparently be essential for even this. Anhalt resolves to visit the most mischievous and harmful personality in Vienna, Count Oñate. They have not been speaking Italian long before Colonel Wallenstein, the soldier of whom there is now so much talk, joins them. Soon the conversation turns to the Bohemian campaign, the encounter on the White Mountain. The imperialists had no more than fourteen thousand men, says Wallenstein. Forty thousand Anhalt retorts (which is nearer the truth). The loss on both sides amounted to no more than eight hundred, Wallenstein continues. Five thousand

Anhalt claims (again he is closer to the mark). From a military point of view, Wallenstein comments, the battle was by no means outstanding, the number who fell outside Prague no greater than succumb in many a skirmish about which not much fuss is made, its importance purely political because here in a single hour an entire kingdom was conquered. And at that point the Colonel is very hard upon the target, for all that he may merely mean to minimize an action in which he had no part.

During the next few weeks Anhalt encountered Wallenstein on more than one occasion, including the wedding of Lord Max von Waldstein to the Lady Katharina, daughter of Privy Councillor Karl Leonhart von Harrach.

Perhaps a marriage of mutual attraction, definitely a political marriage with whose arrangement Wallenstein had not been unconcerned. Maximilian, son of the Principal Lord Chamberlain Adam, was a distant cousin of Albrecht by virtue of a common great-great-grandfather. He was also probably some fifteen years his junior. Wallenstein liked him. The liking grew so palpably that, sparing though he was with giving his confidence, he nevertheless in time came to trust his cousin completely, a gift which cannot have been owing to the depth of his personality – Maximilian's portrait carries no hint of that – but must have been owing to the smooth surface of an adroit, amiable courtier. As for Lord Harrach, his position was such that any man of ambition could be congratulated upon becoming his son-in-law. The marital festivities, with cavalcades, banquets, dancing, and witty lampoonings of the guests, lasted two days. The Emperor himself participated, dining at a separate table. The presents tendered by the ambassadors of the Pope, Spain, Denmark, Saxony and Brandenburg showed that the political significance of the match had not been lost upon them. How merry one can be in one place while at others, not so far distant, hunger and fear and every other sort of misery prevail.

GOVERNOR OF BOHEMIA

Wallenstein had not come to Vienna only for the sake of his cousin's blue eyes. On 17 January 1622, the date of Lord Maximilian's wedding, the Emperor handed Prince Liechtenstein letters patent which transformed the mere "sub-delegate" into his regent or viceroy. The next day saw Wallenstein's appointment as "Commandant of Prague". The title and office were new creations, a sign of the times. There never had been nor, for as long as the old constitution prevailed, could there ever have been somebody like a royal commanding officer at Prague and thus for the whole country, a military "Governor of Bohemia". Wallenstein's rights and obligations corresponded in the military field to Liechtenstein's political function, yet in such a way as to keep him subordinate to the Viceroy. He became the executant of what Vienna and Prague devised.

What he himself wanted, in accordance with his turn of mind and temperament, was order – order in a state of disorder. Let the dispute he had had in the second half of 1622 with Cardinal Dietrichstein, Prefect (or perverter) of Moravia, serve as example. It necessitates a brief retrospect.

Gabor Bethlen had refused to recognise the conclusion of peace with Bohemia, which was not in fact one at all. He went on corresponding with the expelled Palsgrave. He lent an ear to the whisperings of fugitive Matthias Thurn. He was not prepared to abandon the dignity of King of Hungary. He and his hordes still exercised their pleasure in and upon Upper Hungary. In short, he was continuing the war in the way that it was being continued, or only just properly starting, on the Rhine. At the same time things were not going well in Silesia. Elector John George had indeed concluded a "General Accord" with the Silesian Estates, but its liberality was not to Vienna's taste. When the Margrave of Jägerndorf, a Protestant, warned his countrymen that a government on Spanish lines, demonstrated by the horrible, tyrannic, and surpassingly barbarous executions at Prague, was also meant to be their lot and that they should resist, his sounding of the tocsin was not simply and entirely an outpouring of deep-seated venom and malicious disposition, not simply and wholly without foundation, as the Emperor caused to be pronounced in a counter-proclamation. Immediately after the bloody spectacle in front of the town hall in Prague's Old Town, Wallenstein had been ordered to proceed to Silesia and there to undertake all kinds of things which were not in the spirit of the general amnesty granted by the Elector. Arrest of "the principals", for instance. He did not however get far before he received fresh instructions to proceed urgently to Moravia. The country was in a situation not unlike that of 1605, threatened by the Hungarians and Transylvanians, but threatened in such a way as to cause many Moravians' sympathies to lie with the enemy. The latter's conquest of the province could prove the signal for the constantly feared "general uprising" against Habsburg rule. The pattern is familiar – the need to keep in mind the possible loss of all recently acquired possession precisely because it had been so very easily acquired and was being administered in so exceedingly barbaric a manner.

During the confused manoeuvrings of these late summer and autumn months Buquoy, the imperial commander-in-chief, had been killed. Wallenstein managed to hold the Moravian capital, but he could not prevent the Hungarians laying waste the flat countryside in the customary fashion. It was on the question of how to finance defence measures that Colonel and Cardinal-Governor collided. Wallenstein demanded the imposition of a general levy on the nobility and towns in proportion to their capacity to pay. The Cardinal did not want a tax which would have forced him too to dip deeply into his pocket. Wallenstein flew into a rage compounded of impatience and resignation. "Had Your Princely Grace not ceased the land levy, it would have been possible to give the military folk tolerable subsistence, though in deduction of their pay, and the country folk would have found it far easier to contribute than to let themselves be wholly and utterly ruined. . . . Let Your Princely Grace be assured that a general uprising will much sooner be caused by whole-sale confiscation than orderly levy. . . . *Basta*, I have done my part and will not be responsible if disturbances occur . . . I desire nothing for myself, but have a care for His Majesty's service and the country's preservation." These are the arguments and this is the tone which will reverberate for a good ten years more. Wallenstein issues orders where he is in a position to issue orders. When he cannot order, in negotiations with the court, the imperial War Council, the imperial Exchequer, and in this instance the Cardinal, he tenders his views with a swiftly spent irritability which is the reflection of a superior intellect lacking the power to carry his point, but deeply loathing the constant to and fro of debate. How often we shall experience the recurrence of this!

In the end Bethlen, for all that the fortune of war fluctuated uncertainly in Moravia and Upper Hungary, condescended to make peace. As usual, the political and legal skirmishes parallel to the military havoc took months. First, the question of where negotiations should take place. Secondly, how the exchange of which hostages should guarantee the safety of the negotiators. Thirdly, the subject of the negotiations as such. With winter approaching, the Transylvanian took what he could get – a part of Hungary including hotly coveted Kaschau as a spring-board, a few Silesian principalities, and money. As consideration he surrendered the crown of St Stephen. Count Thurn travelled to Constantinople with Bethlen's greetings to the Grand Vizier and the message that, were the pashas of Pest and Bosnia in future to support him more effectively, he would yet teach the Emperor manners. If the promise had a pleasing ring in the Sultan's ear, it echoed still more pleasantly in Holland in that of the Palsgrave, whom Thurn informed of what had transpired. The enciphered letters carried by secret emissaries, posting right across Europe and putting incredible distances behind them, boded ill for the common man everywhere. The Empire's two most powerful princes, Lutheran John George and Catholic Duke Max, had thought that rapid suffocation of the Bohemian rebellion could save the peace, the old constitution, and imperial independence of dangerous allies. Their calculation was not even stupid, simply wrong. They drew up the bill without allowing for the host and outside guests.

THE COINERS

The year 1622 was in Bohemia, Moravia and Lower Austria a monetary *annus mirabilis*. Some few individuals had the most lucrative experience with their currency, the majority only evil. Recently robbed of their trust in many a matter which had seemed solid, secure in perpetuity, they now lost it too in the universally coveted silver gulden. Mercenaries no longer wanted to accept it and tradesmen no longer to give anything for it. Inflation was on hand, steered by the state, but very laxly steered so as to shed a burden of debts. When inflation happens, there are, as we know, winners and losers. The winners are those controlling the levers of political and economic power, the pushers, the artful, the impudent – the birds of prey. The lame duck is the average man.

Debasement of the coinage, meaning secret diminution of its silver content, had already proved a necessity in the days of the Estates and the Palsgrave. With the victors' return it continued. At the same time the rate of silver output from the mines at Kuttenberg and the large-scale purchase of silver scrap, old silverware to be melted down, quickened. Jakob Bassevi, the Prague Jew and merchant, was a prominent figure in the sphere of collection and supply. The object of all this activity was to furnish more gulden for the King-Emperor who had the mint monopoly. Seeing that the quantity of wares on sale did not match the increased money in circulation, quite to the contrary indeed, we cannot help suspecting that price increases, and considerable ones at that, would in any case have occurred even if the ratio of the gulden to silver had been left as before. This aspect failed to be realized because at that date progress in the knowledge pertaining to the wealth of nations was not as yet far advanced.

The higher output of silver solved nothing. Soon we see the *sub-commissarius*, the subsequent governor, Liechtenstein adopting the method tried by the Estates. From one mark of silver – about half a pound – twenty-seven gulden are minted instead of nineteen, then thirty-nine, then forty-seven. To export silver or unadulterated coinage is strictly forbidden. Exchange control. The price of silver rises of course and it has to be bought with the new, "long" or "small" specie. The hoax is that the price does not rise correspondingly fast, does not immediately react to the discrepancy in content, and that the imperial coiners have a lead, leaving the Exchequer with a profit potential.

But why not equal opportunity for private individuals too if they are prepared to undertake the whole minting business? There would not be anything intrinsically new about that. The grant of minting rights had precedents in the same way as the circulation of base coinage was truly no fresh invention. New in this instance was only the scale of the operation. The notion of completely relieving the Emperor of his money management worries by the formation of a "consortium" of "interested persons" first appears to have crossed the mind of grasping Secretary Michna, now Privy Councillor Lord Weizenhofen. He wins Prince Liechtenstein over to the idea. The participation of Bassevi, the wholesale silver dealer is a palpable move, but the Jew does not have the status to head such an enterprise. For this there is another, the only really appropriate, personality available: Hans de Witte, Bohemia's richest financier. Arriving as a young man in Prague from Antwerp, he settled down to become an apprentice, enter into commercial partnership, and make his fortune as an independent trader, a dealer in all kinds of costly goods given on credit, a court supplier, a money-lender of sums large and small. De Witte has a lucky hand, an excellent reputation, the best connections throughout Europe. In point of religion he is an unrepentant Calvinist and, because he is so rich, he can afford to remain such all the more safely for having acted with the greatest circumspection during the days of the insurrectionary government. Bankers, Jewish or Calvinist, are seldom friends to revolutionaries; they cherish legitimate authority.

Michna, Bassevi, Liechtenstein, and de Witte are names pleasing to the ear in Vienna, with each striking a different note in the scale. Wallenstein's, that of the second must powerful man in Bohemia, is added to that of the first and to these five are joined another ten, the so-called "unknown parties". Their identity has remained an enigma. Whether Lords Eggenberg and Harrach, loyal enough politicians not averse to making money, or von Polheim, President of the Exchequer, or three other Treasury officials, or Baron Meggau, the newly appointed Governor of Lower Austria who is believed to have had a splendid talent for getting rich quickly, were among the partners is neither so certain nor so important because the ten unknown played but a minor role in the business. The agreement between "Hans de Witte and his partners" on the one side and the imperial Exchequer on the other is however signed on the same day, 18 January 1622, as Wallenstein is promoted to Governor of Bohemia. The terms are as follows.

For a period of one year, starting on 1 February 1622, the consortium is granted the right to mint coinage for Bohemia, Moravia, and Lower Austria. A veto will be imposed on the circulation and import of all foreign coinage and a duty to surrender such at fixed prices be proclaimed. Inside the three territories the partners will have a monopoly over the purchase at fixed prices of freshly mined Bohemian silver and the acquisition of silver scrap. Other would-be purchasers of silver must furnish proof of domestic requirement. Seventy-nine gulden will be minted per silver mark on the understanding that each partner obtains and issues coinage in ratio to the amount of silver he contributes. In exchange for the foregoing the King-Emperor will receive payment of six million gulden due in weekly instalments. This sum is the profit margin which the mintage business affords, although in this particular case it is assessed at a lump sum, quickly earned, guaranteed, and exceptionally high. That is why Ferdinand's councillors recommended the scheme's acceptance at the moment when so very much is required for expenditure, apart from other matters, on the war which is supposed to be over but refuses to stop. Naturally, even if there is no mention of it in the agreement, the partners are to obtain a return. Discounting all the talk of laudable zeal on the community's behalf, no patriot will enter into such a dangerous enterprise unless he has hopes of gaining something by it.

Wallenstein, landholder and soldier, has hitherto not known much more about money than that it is always good to have some. He is in this affair neither the driving force nor by a long way its outstanding beneficiary. From the evidence which has survived, meagre, fragmentary, and confusing, there does at least emerge who during the year of the agreement contributed how much: Liechtenstein, 797 silver marks; Wallenstein, 5000; Michna, 2932; de Witte, 402,652; Bassevi, 146,353; and the ten unknowns 4848 together. More than 42 million gulden were minted from this total of 561,682 silver marks. The statistics show that the unknowns contributed very little, Wallenstein more than all of them, and de Witte almost a hundred times more than Wallenstein. A pride of lions, it seems at a first glance, but then seen to be one in which the lions have the smallest share. For the table also reveals who received how much per silver mark: Bassevi, 46 gulden; de Witte, 78; Wallenstein, 123; Michna, 248; the unknowns, on average 440; Prince Liechtenstein, 569. Strange figures. The only conclusion to be drawn is that the value of a silver mark varied with the status of its purveyor. Wallenstein, the "Governor of Bohemia", it is worth noting, obtains more than the Jewish and the Calvinist bankers, less than the intriguer Michna. For the Viceroy to have rated highest is no surprise, and the calculation has been made that, had de Witte paid himself as highly per mark as he did Liechtenstein, he would have had to pocket 229 million gulden instead of the 31 million he booked to his account. For practical purposes the consortium is an enterprise run by de Witte and Bassevi. The rest are political props and embellishments. They gather their profit in proportion to the support and ornamental quality they have to offer. An embellishment of society, incidentally, is what the least ornamental member of the company becomes. In recognition of his services he is raised to the nobility under the surpassingly handsome name of "von Treuenberg", Lord Mountfaithful, heading the long list of Semitic tradesmen upon whom the Habsburgs conferred the accolade.

An inundation of forty-two million gulden during the course of a single year, thirty of them flooding the money market in the first two months, exceeds the capacity of the three territories' long-shattered economies. They could probably not absorb such an amount even if the money were good. Instead, bad at the start, it gets worse. According to the agreement with the Exchequer, the gulden is to retain the silver content which still remains to it, about a quarter of the original. When after eighteen months the inevitable currency reform takes place, the new gulden is reduced to one sixth of its nominal value. That is an uncertain indicator, but none the less an indicator, of the measure of its progressive adulteration in the preceding period. Responsibility for that does not basically lie with the partners in the consortium because they have to reap as they have sown. The Exchequer is dissatisfied with the instalment payments; it demands advances. The Emperor is dissatisfied with his six millions; de Witte and Bassevi have to furnish him with a loan out of their own pockets. De Witte is dissatisfied with the quantity of silver available in the three territories; he has to apply for permission to buy the coveted metal wherever he can find it and at whatever prices demanded. In Germany and in the Netherlands illusions about the new Habsburg gulden are fewer even than in Bohemia. If at the outset the supply of silver needs time to accommodate itself to the spiral of inflation, towards the end of the year the tendency to run ahead of and anticipate it is evident. The point is reached where de Witte has to pay eighty-five gulden per mark. When to this are added the costs of administration, mintage, and licence, as well as the profit which the partners want to make, any layman will appreciate how at least 110 gulden have to be extracted per mark, a calculation which the subsequent currency reform confirms to the hilt. For de Witte to publish a statement that all talk of a further loss of standard content is nothing but "false and envious accusations" is no proof to the contrary. He must, though it is in vain, publish such a statement. In vain too for Prince Liechtenstein to term rumour of an impending devaluation an "evil, unfounded delusion" and to express astonishment that the ordinary man should no longer be able to purchase the basic necessities with the only and enduringly valid national currency when, God be praised, there is no shortage of victuals in Bohemia. Maybe there is no famine, but victuals are long since scarce and anyhow, scarce or plentiful, slink away from the bad money to be secreted in exchange for the old, the forbidden, and the good. Threat of capital punishment for hoarding and trafficking in it at dizzy rates against the new gulden, as well as for participation in the butchers' and other shopkeepers' strikes, is ineffective. Where money and an unnatural impediment to its flow are concerned, penal decrees are useless. When the year is up, the Emperor's advisers are prepared to prolong the agreement on stricter conditions. Prince Liechtenstein presents counter-proposals. They do not meet with approval. At heart he and his partners are probably glad to escape from this ever more perilously labyrinthine business and to be able to make off with the profit that it has brought them.

Like it or not, the Emperor takes charge again of the coinage. For a few months he allows matters to drift along their course. Then he undertakes the operation whose mere notion Prince Liechtenstein as recently as six months ago condemned as delusion and treason. In the summer of 1623 a start is made with the mintage of money containing the standard weight and alloy. To pay the soldiers, sound imperial taler formerly worth one and a half gulden are bought at the price of eight new ones each. December sees a more radical step. People are told to exchange their inflationary money against the newest issue, which is the old, at the rate of six gulden to one. In the case of kreutzer, sixty to the gulden, the ratio is even more depressing. The process of conversion and recall duly face the rulers with problems for whose solution neither history nor text-books furnish precepts.

Since our concern is biography, not numismatology, there is no need to pursue further either the rate of the Bohemian, Moravian, and Austrian coinages or the later history of the consortium. The latter continued another forty years. Ferdinand II was undoubtedly lazy, not versed in the fiscal sciences, heartily glad if he could be told that this or that debt had, however temporarily, been settled, and that for one or another favourite, one or another pleasure excursion the means were, in spite of everything, available. In his Exchequer, on the other hand, sat men who were austere, sticklers for the rules, and unwilling to have their department cheated. They did not cease, during the Emperor's lifetime and thereafter, to burrow into the conduct of the consortium's partners. It caused them no little irritation to note how now and then most important files mysteriously disappeared. It prevented the "Royal Bohemian Effectuation and Implementation Commission on General Mintage and Encashment Infringement" from properly attaining its objective. Nevertheless it got as far as finding such scraps of evidence as have been mentioned. It even got so far as demanding from Prince Liechtenstein's heirs an indemnity of thirty-one million gulden plus forty years' accumulated interest, a claim that it can hardly itself have taken seriously. In 1665 Emperor Leopold, grandson of Ferdinand, was content to accept 275,000 gulden. That however is neither here nor there.

In one of the surviving enigmatic tables Wallenstein's investment in the coinage business is given as 220,000 gulden, his profit as 240,000. If the two figures are to be taken the way that a professional understands them, which is to deduct the smaller from the larger figure in order to arrive at the net profit, the latter would on the whole undertaking be twenty thousand gulden. A dividend of less than ten per cent. A contemptible trifle. It is not impossible that the world at large, like the Exchequer, had a false notion of the partners' "millions of profits the whole world knows about". The whole world knows about a number of things that are untrue. During 1622, the year of inflation, the emphasis of Wallenstein's attention to economic activities was not in the direction of the consortium. This was the year of his breakthrough to enormous wealth, though not by the delivery to de Witte's private central bank of a small amount of silver or, as was probably the case, of a couple of hundred thousand gulden booked to his account as silver. His new connections with Bassevi and that splendid financier de Witte opened up quite different possibilities. The inflation gulden flitted lightly and swiftly from hand to hand. Snatch at it, in his capacity as commander-in-chief in Bohemia, and with the assistance of the country's cleverest bankers he could both obtain and extend credits of so far undreamt extent. Given the circumstances and the unique legal or political conditions, he was in a position to buy what no devaluation ever threatens – land. So much land that its owner would be no mere landowner, but a lord paramount, a prince, a sovereign lord.

FIEFS IN PLENTY

The process by which half Bohemia changed hands took place in several stages and under several heads. Immediate and unqualified was the expropriation of the principal guilty parties who were deceased, like Albrecht Jan Smiřický, who had been executed at Prague, like Wenzel von Budowa, and who had fled the country, like Christoph von Redern, Lord of Friedland. Expropriated to their entirety, to half, to a quarter or a fifth were those who felt guilty in smaller or greater degree and, according to imperial decree, had of their own free will to appear before the Court of Confiscation. The proper use of their own free will was advisable. The Court, under the presidency of Adam von Waldstein, was constituted on 18 January, the day when the agreement on the coinage consortium was signed and Wallenstein appointed Governor of Bohemia. This was no coincidence. A strong hand was needed to maintain the subjugated kingdom in the anguish of obedience. Gulden in plenty were needed to implement the semi- and quarter-confiscations because the intention was to take the whole of their land even from those classified as less than principally guilty, paying them to relinquish the portions which as a matter of grace they had been allowed to retain. That was why, although it proved insufficient, the inflation money of 1622–3 was required. At best the semi-expropriated received depreciated cash or, when the currency became harder again, interest on the money promised, interest payment which continued some forty years. In 1665 it was discontinued. Enough, it was said, is enough.

Wallenstein was by far the most successful among those who stood to gain by this process.

He had long had his eye on Friedland. Hardly had Liechtenstein tipped him off that the property was ripe for purchase before he hurried to Prague from the Moravian theatre of war in order to complete the deal. Unlikely, wrote Liechtenstein to the Emperor, that anyone would match the Colonel's offer of 150,000 gulden. None the less negotiations dragged. The Exchequer demanded a precise valuation, then agreed to the tender as commensurate. In June 1622 the domains of Friedland and Reichenberg with their appurtenant castles, towns, villages, and inhabitants, with their dairy-farms, sheep-farms, mills, carp-ponds, and woods, with their mines, forges, and tin-works passed to Wallenstein in perpetual fee. The payment for such a haul, more especially when we consider that de Witte gulden were involved, was slight. But the government, inveighing against price increases and grimly clinging to the fiction of equation between the new gulden and the old, could not be party to demanding allowance for inflation. Nor, of course, could Wallenstein, commander-in-chief in Bohemia and member of the coinage consortium, pay other than in the solely legitimate currency. . . . The purchase of Friedland made of him what he had long ago decided to become, a Bohemian magnate. The relinquishment a little later of his seat in the Moravian Upper House was a matter of indifference to him. He sold Vsetín. Its surrounding countryside had for nine years been his domestic background, but he belonged to a nobility to whom real property was what subsequently industrial shares were to be, not hearth and home, simply an investment commutable at all times.

The next step was to unite the Smiřický estates in the south and the Friedland ones in the north by becoming indisputable master of the inheritance and accumulating whatever lay between the focal points of Gitschin and Friedland. The first part was achieved in 1623 by way of a strange legal process. Wallenstein, with the Smiřický allodial estates already secured to him twice and three times over, now bought them from his simpleton ward, properly speaking from himself. The purchase price of 500,000 gulden, now belonging to the madman and again in reality to himself, he made over to the Emperor as a loan, for the latter's convenience and as a surety for the sick heir, in such manner that he himself was to enjoy the interest through cancellation of the tax assessments on his estates and vassals; but, if this amount was not ample enough, through supplementation from other sources. The purchase price or loan, be it clearly understood, would on the simpleton's death be inherited by none else than Wallenstein. A confoundedly cunning idea – to appear magnanimous, create confidence, and deeply involve the Exchequer in the issue which he had at heart, the construction of his principality. If however it was to be a rich and handsome principality, it still needed to be rounded off in all directions.

So now followed the whirligig of purchases, exchanges, and resales, the purchases of confiscated estates from the authorities, the purchases from those in possession, the re-sales even to such as had been victims of the confiscations. Planning journeys hither and thither, inspections, and valuations were the concomitant features. A frenzy lasting more than eighteen months and one of which Wallenstein, as though addicted to a drug, was nevermore quite rid. Pecka was obtained from the widow of the executed Lord von Harrant whom he had arrested there. Arnau, once the estate of his grandfather whose descendants took their name from it, was acquired from the authorities: they had seized it from the condemned Johann Fünfkircher. Neuschloss and the town of Böhmisch-Leipa had been the possessions of Johann Georg von Wartenberg. Kopidlno with Bartaušov and Silvar were exchanged for Neustadt-on-Mettau and other lands owned by the Lady Magdalena Trčka, wife to Rudolf Trčka and a woman with a sharp nose for business. Were we to list all the estates which Wallenstein bought, mainly now but later too, unceasingly, constantly, and almost to the end, the estates he bought and kept, he bought but instead of making payment temporarily allowed the vendor to retain, he re-sold, he gave away, he settled in entail, he conferred in fee, and were we to list the names which he noted down, underlined, and struck out again, we would arrive at a total of a hundred and seventy-nine, not counting the original Moravian property complex. Moreover another dozen names should be added to most of these, because any such property did not exist on its own but consisted of a structure of possessions and rights, just as it developed into a favourite occupation of their new owner to complement this and that domain with tempting neighbouring fragments, woods, farms, urban districts held in other hands. At the beginning of 1624, with the main task provisionally, always only provisionally, done, Wallenstein was lord over a hundred square miles stretching from the northern frontier of Bohemia to its centre, not all too far from Prague, and in the east cutting deep into the Giant Mountains. How this territory was sub-divided and administered, which parts its ruler and supreme overlord reserved directly to himself, namely the best, and which he bestowed in feudal tenure, expended on pious endowments, and used as gifts for useful servitors will be told later.

The process of leviathan creation did not proceed without hardships. Herewith one example, probably the worst instance. Hans Georg von Wartenberg, brother to Otto Heinrich of ill fame in connection with the Gitschin explosion catastrophe, although he had, like most of his class, initially participated in the rebellion, long before the battle of the White Mountain made his submission to the Elector of Saxony (and thus to the Emperor), for this purpose especially travelling to Dresden to collect attestations to his good conduct. He obtained them in plenty as well as the assurance of the general amnesty promised for precisely such cases as his. Yet none of this stopped the Confiscation Court from passing a sentence of expropriation, and *in toto* at that. In vain did Wartenberg assail Liechtenstein and the Emperor with suits to repeal such a palpable judicial error. He was married to a German princess, which seemed to enhance his chances. No less than thirty-five imperial princes, including such considerable ones as the Duke of Bavaria, entered pleas on his behalf. Advised to possess himself in patience, sent from one major official department to another, he found himself at every step beating upon the air. Soon he knew why. Wallenstein wanted his domains of Neuschloss and Böhmisch-Leipa to the west and had already bought them from the Exchequer. The origination of the unjust sentence became manifest. Did not Adam von Waldstein preside over the Court? Did it require more than a wink on the part of the Viceroy to have a sentence so framed as he or his covetous friends desired? Hans Georg von Wartenberg died abroad in dire poverty. He and his brother, the vile Otto Heinrich, were the last of a formerly great family, one which moreover belonged to the same stock as the Waldsteins.

Wartenberg's experience has been recounted because we wish neither to hide anything nor to make our hero out to have been better than he was. As a matter of principle, though, it also holds good that, had he not done what he did, others would have done it in his stead. He played the game as all of them played it who could. He however played it best and to the most grandiose purposes. Consequently it came about that he soared higher than them all, including finally Prince Liechtenstein, to the latter's vexed surprise since he had always looked on him as his creature. Wallenstein was by far the most constructive among the major brigands of the second Bohemian revolution. His vassals derived more benefit than detriment from falling under his dominion. He made something of his booty.

There were two sides to this, one more palpable than the other. The first is that, when we speak of his buying from the state, he was in fact one of the pillars on which the new state rested and which was expropriating the Bohemian nobility. The second aspect is less obvious. Wallenstein, according to a widely held proposition, paid for his estates far below their actual value if only because he was paying, not for all but many of them, with inflationary money. The properties, it is further alleged, were rated too low because the assessors were interested parties, about which the Exchequer at Vienna complained, and Wallenstein's bids fell below even the feeblest ratings but were never rebuffed. The instances quoted are nevertheless not outrageous, remaining usually within the range of a few per cent. And here too he did what all of them did who sat at the fount of victory and spoils. In contrast to his competitors, however, he was in 1625 magnanimous and shrewd enough to offer a supplementary lump payment of two hundred thousand gulden in sound currency. On this score he earned Emperor Ferdinand's express commendation, was held up as an example to his peers, and pronounced free and exempt from all further obligations. Had the dynasty "Waldstein and Friedland" prospered, that gesture would have spared it the tedious troubles which during the course of the century the Liechtenstein dynasty had to sustain.

With what did he pay for it all? How did someone become one of the richest men in christendom when, after the battle of the White Mountain, his assets in money and real estate amounted to only about half a million? We are faced with a mound of documented guess-work, not a pile of tidily corroborated facts. If in our own day it has not proved other than very unsatisfactorily possible to explain in court the accumulation of a politician's affluence because of confusing contradictory evidence, the disappearances of file, refusals to testify, lapses of memory, etc, etc, it is questionable whether the origin of a personal fortune three hundred and fifty years ago is a task that can be expected of a historian.

There exists a letter, dated September 1622, from Ferdinand II to Prince Liechtenstein in which he speaks of a highly desirable project that has come to his ears, the advance of "divers millions" to the Exchequer on the strength of the confiscations to be taken in hand. The opposite number to this imperial missive is a tentative agreement drawn up in December of the same year by Prince Liechtenstein. According to this, "Lord von Waldstein and his associates" offer to ease the Emperor's indebtedness by a loan of three and a half million gulden. In return they would in due time be granted appropriately rated properties. If the contract did enter into effect, Wallenstein would have stood at the head of a second, a loan consortium. The properties would have devolved upon him, but the moneys would have been furnished preponderantly by his "associates", certainly de Witte, probably Bassevi, Michna, and others, whom he would sooner or later have had to compensate for their assistance. Another contract or draft contract between Wallenstein and the Viceroy, also dating from December 1622, tells us about a loan of two millions without any mention of "associates". Finally there is a "Wallenstein Files Index" which lists among its five hundred important documents "Prince Liechtenstein's Composition on Three and a Half Million Rhenish Gulden, His Serene Grace the Duke of Friedland having furnished these against thus many Confiscated Properties as He shall receive. At Prague, the 13th day of January, 1623". So runs the docket. The file, with the Viceroy's receipt, had disappeared in the way that papers do disappear or because later there were those who wanted to let it disappear. The inferences are uncertain, but they are clear enough to permit the conclusion that in the winter of 1622–3 Wallenstein must have advanced to the Emperor a loan so large that he could by no means raise it all at once. He therefore borrowed, inflationary money at that, what he transmitted. The link between coinage consortium and loan consortium becomes an established fact. The question is, seeing that he stood alone in the purchase of properties on a grand scale, a practice followed by neither de Witte nor Bassevi von Treuenberg, how, when, and with what he satisfied the claims of his "associates". By way of a deceitful, dizzy inflation-deflation profit margin? Wilhelm von Slawata thought that he knew. In 1624 the Defenestration victim asserted, in a Latin memorandum consisting of no less than forty-two counts against Wallenstein, that his hated cousin had purposely postponed disbursement of the major part of the loan of "three, or at least two, millions" until the last few days before currency reform. Then he borrowed sound ducats from Prague's Jewry and deposited them with the Exchequer at the exorbitant prevailing rate in order to have them set off at the reverse entry on his behalf at the gulden's new depressed rate following the reform. So if for example, Wallenstein lent 10,000 ducats, Slawata explained to the slow-witted Privy Councillors, he would claim to have provided 160,000 gulden; but the same 10,000 ducats being returned to him after reform, in any manner whatsoever, his receipt would run for only 23,000 instead of 160,000 gulden. Whether he really played this game with gulden and ducats, with bad and reformed gulden, or, as I believe, Slawata simply echoed rumours, contemporaneously current about great lords' behaviour but difficult to make tally with the habits of Exchequer officials who on other occasions were sharply on the watch, that is again something indeterminable. More than one point relating to the origination of this particular fortune will never prove capable of elucidation.

SECOND MARRIAGE

He had become a great lord. The status required a lady. The entail which comprehended his new estates demanded an heir. In the summer of 1623 Wallenstein, a widower for nine years, married again. His chosen was Lady Isabella, daughter of Lord von Harrach, sister to the Katharina whom Wallenstein called "Lady Kit-Cat" and who had recently wedded his cousin Max. Everyone agreed that the bride was as pious as pretty and charming as clever. She was twenty-one, Wallenstein thirty-nine. Love? Among members of the nobility the word had a formal ring. We have however grounds for assuming that Isabella was attached by bonds of real love to her grand husband and that Wallenstein was not left cold by this sentiment. On the other hand the marriage was political too, just as had been that of Lord Max and Lady Kit-Cat. Both nuptials lifted the Waldstein clan from its specifically Bohemian background and shifted it towards the Viennese and Austro-German one. Through them Wallenstein unlocked for himself the most private openings to the imperial court, setting his foot between door and threshold.

Karl Leonhart, Lord of Harrach, Lord upon Rohrau, Lord in Stauff and Aschau, and holder of the lien upon Bruck-on-the-Leitha, was as commanding as he was friendly. Emperor Ferdinand, the chronicler relates, called him "loyalty personified". "His friends could rely on him, the younger nobility respected him like a father, foreigners saw in him their protector. His courtesy, courage, and candour were inveterate. What he said and what he felt were in harmony. The common folk loved him and sang the praise that he invested the imperial court with grace and glory." Leonhart, or Lienhart, the eldest of his five sons, was married to the daughter of Lord von Eggenberg, the one imperial councillor who exceeded Harrach in influence. Ernst Adalbert, the second, twenty-four years old, had just been consecrated Prince-Archbishop of Prague and would not have to wait long for the cardinal's hat. Wallenstein himself undertook the military training of the youngest son, Franz. Two of Harrach's daughters were now wedded to Wallensteins. The third, Maximiliana, later married Lord Adam Erdmann, son to the rich Trčka couple. It is she, "sister to the Duchess", whom Schiller transformed into his "Countess Terzky" by lending her some of her mother-in-law's qualities, her ambition, and her energy, as well as inventing certain others. A sister of young Trčka was wife to Wilhelm Kinsky, the arch-intriguer. These marital knots manifested the constitution and intersection of two clans. One, Habsburg, Catholic, and German, was composed of the Eggenberg–Harrach–Wallenstein elements. The other, Wallenstein–Trčka–Kinsky, must be regarded as preponderantly Bohemian and Protestant, for Adam Trčka's conversion will not have been one of conviction and Kinsky, though glad to help himself from the Bohemian confiscation pile, remained Protestant. Between these two incongruous family alliances stood Wallenstein in a central position which at the moment caused him no difficulty. The Austrian clan was by far the more important to him.

Its outstanding figure was Lord and newly created Prince Eggenberg, father-in-law to Wallenstein's brother-in-law Lienhart. Chairman of the imperial Privy Council, a sort of head of government, he gave from afar the impression of being Fortune's favourite, a man who succeeded in whatever he attempted without it even costing him excessive effort. Born lucky, he was the type of convert who was not too deadly serious about religion, a striking contrast to those who regarded rekindled faith as their sole spark of happiness. As a politician, he sided with the establishment through support for the House of Habsburg of German nationality as represented by the Hereditary Lands. Eggenberg's wish was to steer an Austrian course in not too close dependence on Munich, Madrid, or Rome. In the Bohemian business he belonged from the outset to those who favoured a stringent policy, not so much because of the spiritual issue as that he recognized the irreconcilability of the Estates' claims with the principle of monarchy. That was why he approved of the *coup d'état* against Cardinal Khlesl although he made, and this was characteristic of him, an attempt to save the Cardinal by imploring him "through loyal warning and admonition" to change his line. The prince of the church, according to Eggenberg, would have spared himself and others keen embarrassment "had not arrogance, contempt for all others, and his own passions blinded him so utterly". The new state of affairs in Bohemia also brought Eggenberg, entirely without exertion on his part, a fine profit. The Emperor bestowed on him the enormous complex of properties formerly the possession of the now extinct Rosenberg family. The latter had owned approximately as much land in south-western Bohemia as the Smiřickýs had in the north-east. Eggenberg's own estates lay in Styria. He was not a native Austrian, like Harrach, but had come from Graz to Vienna with Ferdinand, the friend of his youth. Whenever he returned to his old home or went to a spa for treatment of his gout, the Emperor felt helpless: "Hence I do await you here, with God's help, with positive certainty, for as usual such important business daily doth ensue that I dispense with you, Lord knows, all too hardly. . . ." His master addressed his minister by his Christian name – "Illustrious Prince! Beloved Hans Ulrich!" Rare intimacy in an age when the holders of great public office maintained an unhealthy distance between each other and gave expression to it in the arabesques of mutual address. That anyone should have apostrophized Wallenstein, at the stage of his life which we have now reached, as "Beloved Albrecht" is simply impossible to conceive.

The application of such a form did not occur to the Lady Isabella. Her letters to her husband begin, "Illustrious Prince! Lord most dear to my Heart". Or, "Illustrious Lord and Master! Lord most dear to my Heart". The text which follows is of a fine spontaneity and tenderness. A series of letters dating from August 1624, no less than eight during this single month, have survived. She waits and waits for her lord and master's return, is deeply grieved that his sick leg causes him pain again and retards his journey home from Vienna. She is disappointed because the post has brought her no letter from him, and when one arrives she is delighted. "Our Lord knows, how nothing in the world affects me more hardly than not to see him so long, but because that is as yet not his wish, I must await with patience and listlessness until he shall send intelligence that it doth happen. I am grieved to the heart that his foot pains him again; but I hope in God that it will soon be better. This is indeed no time for him to suffer illness. I would to God that I could for but a few hours be beside him and sit by his bed upon the ground; I would indeed stay attentively beside him." And so on, throughout eight little letters. Wallenstein, it shows, was capable of inspiring love, and of inspiring it in so fine a specimen of womanhood. A pity that no one drew Master Johann Kepler's attention to this aspect of his subject's nature. A pity too that Wallenstein's letters to Isabella are lost. She did collect and neatly bundle them, but after her death they were surrendered to imperial officials and disappeared into some Vienna archive. I have indeed heard of someone seeing such a letter, and that it began "Beloved Wife", but I have not myself been able to find it or its fellows.

RAISED STATUS

In 1623 Wallenstein was invested with the ancient dignity, dating from Carolingian or late Roman days, of *Comes Palatinus*, a Count Palatine or Palsgrave. It ranked higher than a simple Count, but it did not carry with it the appellation. For another three quarters of a year the Palsgrave continued to sign his name as "A. Waldstein" or, more formally, "Albrecht, Ruler of the House of Waldstein and Friedland". That was because the same patent, drafted with full legal circumstance, which proclaimed his Palatine status also turned him into the "ruler" or head of his family, forthwith allowed to call itself "Waldstein and Friedland". In the same breath there was sanctioned the creation for all his estates of an entail that would forestall the possibility of the ancient House of Waldstein being wasted away through disputes about inheritance and the division of properties.

A Palsgrave had originally been an itinerant or resident royal proxy. From this derived the powers he still enjoyed and which the patent enumerated. Such as being able to confer nobility on those deserving of it, appoint judges and notaries, legitimize those born outside holy wedlock, free villeins, and enfeoff superior and inferior vassals. In Wallenstein's case the dignity was moreover accompanied by useful material privileges: the prerogative to work mines, the franchise to hold markets, a licence to trade or to permit commerce and trade to be pursued within his territory at his own discretion. Truly royal rights, or, allowing for the relative modesty of the domain, at any rate princely ones. And three-quarters of a year after investment with the Palatine dignity came the welcome elevation to princely status, first fruit of the new Viennese family alliance.

At this stage readers, be they few or many, who are interested in the long-eroded and now entirely crumbled grades of the old hierarchy will be grateful for an explanation. Whoever in 1623 became a German prince could only be a prince of the Holy Roman Empire, created such by the Emperor. The degree of Austrian, Bavarian, Brandenburg-Prussian prince was a later invention. All German potentates above the rank of count were princes; the landgraves and margraves, the prince-bishops and the prince-abbots, as well as the dukes, including those exceptional seven bishops, margraves, dukes who had arrogated to themselves the privilege of electing the Emperor. Their style was the royal "We", prefaced with proud piety "By God's Grace". All princes were entitled to the designation "Illustrious" and the alternative form of address "Your Dilection", "Your princely Grace", or both. Respecting the attribute "Serenity", a claim only recently advanced by the secular Electors, the Vienna imperial Chancellery was making difficulties. For the Emperor every prince was "Our Cousin", a fiction of royal relationship deriving from France or Spain. In the seventeenth century the first to receive the princely coronet, at the hands of Emperor Matthias, was

Karl von Liechtenstein. On his heels followed the President of the Aulic Council, a Count von Hohenzollern in the Swabian line, Eggenberg, Wallenstein, and the Bohemian Chancellor Zdenko von Lobkowicz. About him Lady Isabella, herself only just transformed into the Princess of Friedland, wrote to her husband, "The Lord Chancellor will surely be well pleased that he is become prince, and in particular his lady because her satisfaction is set so high." The Liechtensteins are to this day princes, the Hohenzollerns too, and neither of them, one hears, are badly off. The Eggenbergs died out in the eighteenth century. In our own age the Lobkowiczs first landed in political company which was against all titles and then into such as was against all private owner-ship, so that nothing of either has remained to them and they are back where they were a thousand years ago, on the same level as everyone else.

The German princes, meaning the old ones, were pained by the accretions to their number and disconcerted as to how their new, dubious peers should be treated. Four years after Wallenstein's elevation the subject was thoroughly ventilated among the Electors' assembled delegates. The cause was Wallenstein's claim to the salutation "Lord and Friend". Mainz protested that this was not the practice even between Electors. Saxony informed the meeting that missives from Dresden to the General began "Illustrious, especially dear Lord and Friend" or some-times though rarely with the attribute "Your Dilection", and this was the way that it was proposed to continue to proceed in future. All were unanimous that a distinction should be drawn between the old and the new princes. Bavaria moreover wanted it made more specific between those whose domains at least lay within the Empire, like the Zollerns, and those whose estates were situated only in the Habsburg Hereditary Lands. Brandenburg decidedly rejected the form "Lord"; "Prince" and "Friend" were more than enough. Each was of course entitled to make his own choice, but a compromise had to be found for such occasions as when the Electors wrote to Wallenstein in a body. Eventually the formula consisted of "Especially dear Friend, as also gracious Prince and Lord". So the "Lord" was conceded, but placed at the end as inconspicuously as possible. Wallenstein, at that time at the zenith of his power, was extremely sensitive in matters of style. "How it doth pain me that the Emperor, who is my lord, treats me as an imperial prince, but that this man, who neither is nor will be my lord, treats me as a puppy. . . ." That was when Archduke Leopold, Ferdinand's brother, would not salute him as "Your Dilection". As much annoyed at his claims as were

Wallenstein's new peers were his former ones, whom he now held at such a distance. Adam von Waldstein, for instance, his cousin or second cousin.

The new prince selected as his motto a distinctly challenging one: *Invita Invidia* – Envy Defying.

Europe's Feeble Resistance

A PRICKED bubble, the Bohemians' hopes of their allies. Europe looked on. True, not everyone everywhere, in The Hague or in Copenhagen nor in Stockholm, was so blind as to believe that only the fate of the Bohemians, Moravians, and Austrians was at stake. What rendered recognition ineffective was the size of the stage on which the drama was enacted, the intricacy of antagonisms elsewhere, the fluctuations of views which hamstrung one another. So long, albeit for just so long, as Ferdinand of Habsburg proceeded against rebellious subjects within the borders of his Hereditary Lands, he had to be left to proceed as he pleased, a principle to which French policy was retrospectively to attach importance. Moreover, if the German Protestants, so close to Bohemia and the first to be threatened by like disaster, in cowardly perplexity made no move, how should those farther removed help?

In 1620 Gustavus Adolphus, King of Sweden, pious and pugnacious soldier as well as the ruler with more vision than any other of his day, a luminous, enchanting personality who radiated mastery, strength, and joy of living, visited Germany incognito, staying at Berlin, Heidelberg, and elsewhere. The motive for his journey was marriage to Maria Eleonora, a sister of the Brandenburg Elector, but as a by-product the monarch was collecting personal impressions of the Germans. At Erfurt he is said to have stolen into a Catholic church, attended Mass, and with repugnance had his notions of idolatry and papal mummery confirmed. Confirmed, at any rate, was his suspicion about the paltriness and impotence of the German Protestants. Axel Oxenstierna, his Chancellor, summarized the matter with an elegant turn of Latin phrase: "Most of them in these parts seem to foster neutrality as being the safest course; the wisdom of that let them observe for themselves. Where can there be possibility of relief here when in the Empire there is no authority [*cum in imperio nullum sit imperium*], no order, no energy, indeed no feeling at all for the public weal?" That was the season when Duke Max was putting the last touch to his preparations for the Bohemian campaign. None of the Union princes at Ulm felt any inclination to salvage matters by leaping into the breach and they all had rings made around them by the French. At Prague the Elector-King helplessly awaited presentation of the bill. Gustavus Adolphus would have liked to visit both Ulm and Prague, but it never came to that.

The Brandenburg marriage made the King member of a European–German–Protestant grouping of sovereigns who were all related. Elector George William of Brandenburg, for instance, had a brother who was the refractory Margrave of Jägerndorf, rebel friend and ally of Gabor Bethlen, while his wife was sister to Elector Frederick and one of his own sisters wife to the Duke of Brunswick-Wolfenbüttel. The latter had a brother, Christian, of whom more will soon be heard. The two of them were nephews to the King of Denmark, the King of England's brother-in-law who for his part was father-in-law to the Elector and King of Bohemia, nephew of the Prince of Orange. Strange clan. None the less reasons of state and domestic ties, ambition and greed, fear and weakness counted for more.

They weighed more than affinity of stock, religion, and neighbourly intercourse. Denmark–Norway and Sweden could in loyal alliance have constituted a power of crucial effectiveness and capable of imposing order. On the tablets of history stood engraved that it was something which during this long, long period of crisis they would never do, for all that or precisely because they were governed by rulers of more than average energy and with ambition to match. Christian IV was an imposing figure of a king, immensely rich since half Denmark belonged to him personally, a renowned seaman and warrior under whom his nobility had something to say, his citizens little, and his peasants nothing at all. Nevertheless in the cathedral at Roskilde his wish to protect the silent Estate against the vocal and the great is attested by the pictures, scenes of chivalrous and Solomon-like acts of justice, around his tomb, its lid heavy with cross and sword. Monuments in stone are witness to his love of endowment and building: the exchange at Copenhagen for the new money men, harbours for his men-of-war and merchant vessels, homes for long-serving old sailors, and splendid castles like Friederichsburg and Rosenburg for the King. As Duke of Holstein and Prince of the Empire, German and Bohemian affairs concerned Christian more closely than Sweden did. But Sweden was a vexatious obstacle to the calculations of Danish ambition. Geographically still cramped by Danish possessions, politically still far away and outlandish for the moulders of opinion, the talkers, and the letter-writers of central Europe, Sweden was in reality stronger already than Denmark, more successfully expansive already thanks to its copper and iron ore, its peasant soldiers and its ships, its shrewdly applied and augmented wealth. Let one of the two Nordic monarchs venture anything and he could never be sure what the other would do while the venture was in progress.

During the first year of Bohemia's abasement, in 1621, Gustavus Adolphus ventured once more on a war with Poland which – in his words – had lain buried under the ashes of an armistice. A Swedish operation directed towards the protection and extension of what Sweden possessed on the southern shore of the Baltic. To pass it off as aid for Bohemia was mere rhetoric. King Sigismund certainly did belong to the system of Catholic powers which, loose enough, was at any rate tighter than the Protestant one and he had indeed rendered his Styrian brother-in-law quite discreetly a little help against the rebels. His Cossacks, who enjoyed pestering the Prince of Transylvania, were in the habit of spiking the latter's schemes at the very moment when they were reaching their zenith. In that sense a community of interest, but tenuous and wide-meshed, existed between Gabor Bethlen, Gustavus Adolphus, and the Bohemian *émigrés*. For the Swede to wage war against the Poles and seize Riga, their finest harbour, was something that could only mildly disconcert the beneficiaries of the victory on the White Mountain.

Disconcertment was the Elector of Brandenburg's lot. He had recently inherited the Duchy of Prussia, a Polish fief and a circumstance that had caused him to hesitate before agreeing to his sister's Swedish marriage. Brother-in-law and vassal of respectively the King of Sweden and the King of Poland, he could find no better counsel than, with miserable modesty, to offer his services as mediator in case of conflict between them. John George of Saxony, the neighbour with whom he was on closest terms, had warned him in good time. John George had no love for Swedes or foreigners of any ilk. Brandenburg, on the other hand, was weaker than Saxony, more on the periphery, with possessions to the east and north, not to mention hopes of another inheritance, Pomerania, which would give it a Baltic coast. Brandenburg was attracted to the rising Nordic star. The trouble was that George William, its Elector, was a feeble, inoffensive personality who would have liked to live in a world free of dangerous decisions.

Back once more to the clan. James Stuart, King of England and of Scotland, was a monarch increasingly irritated by the members of his

Parliament whom, as a stranger, he was inherently incapable of understanding, but a sly, coarse-grained master of his royal trade and not
without a secret partiality for its new, absolutist form. James had thought
Elector Frederick's usurpation of the Bohemian throne distinctly
improper and made little attempt to help the youth out of the exigency
in which he had landed himself. He did in fact less than his English
subjects, with whom Protestant Bohemia traditionally counted for
something, would have been willing to pay for. When however
Frederick's own land, the Palatinate, was drawn into the game, occupied
by enemy forces, and confiscated from the Palsgrave, the King was
faced with a different situation. He could not but feel humiliated in the
person of his daughter, and a humiliated king divested of his god-like
appearance is an emperor without clothes. To reinstate his daughter
and his son-in-law at Heidelberg was a more legitimate purpose than to
maintain them on the throne of Bohemia. It had less of the common
English touch because it was a purely dynastic concept, with
something of legalism about it but no attachment to freedom and
religion. James underlined this facet of his policy and royal arbitrariness
by proposing to achieve his aim through alliance with Spain rather than
with Protestant powers prepared to join with him. Such a scheme, for all
that politicians at Madrid also seriously considered its feasibility, went
against the nature of things, English and Spanish. The plot, spun for
years on end only to be eventually broken off, thwarted, even if in other
conditions it had been capable of realization, the formation of an over-all
Protestant front.

Had the plan materialized, intensifying the sombre folly of the
struggle between the powers, it would have inevitably had to be directed
against the free part of the Netherlands called for concision Holland, the
States-General. For it was precisely in 1621, the year in which the long
Swedish-Polish armistice ended, that on 9 April the Dutch-Spanish one
also came to an end. This was no longer a surprise. When Philip III's
regiments helped in the overthrow of Bohemia, the protagonists of the
imperialist dream at Madrid had already won against the party of peace
and domestic recovery. What otherwise would a Spain which cared for
nothing but Spain have been seeking in Bohemia? The last demands
presented to the States-General – to renounce all commerce with India
and the Indies as well as to allow their secret and dangerous Catholic
subjects liberty to practise their religion – were of so unsuitable a sort
as not to permit Madrid to place expectations of success on them. A
change of sovereigns exacerbated the imperialist policy, not so much on

account of the character of the young successor, Philip IV (he is not worth elaboration), but because of his new chief minister's designs. Count Olivares was a splendidly deleterious dreamer whose vision beheld a unitary Spanish state comprising a merger of all Iberian lands and the restoration of pan-Spanish power over the continent. In other words the old, old war anew. Not that this was so utterly unwelcome to certain important parties on the other side, least of all to Prince Maurice of Orange, honorary president and Generalissimo of the republican confederation, specialist in foreign affairs and professional soldier, the career ruler who gave the United Provinces that degree of unity which they possessed. War often looks a desirable means to fortify fragile internal unity.

The death in Brussels of the co-regent, Archduke Albrecht, occurred but a few months after the armistice ran out. His widow, Isabella, daughter of Philip II, continued to perform or have performed what Madrid wanted to see performed, so that the Spanish Netherlands, whatever its population's feelings, cannot for the purposes of our narrative be reckoned other than an outpost, indeed forward headquarters, of Spanish imperialist policy. Ambrogio di Spinola, scion of a Genoese aristocratic and moneyed family, Spain's outstanding army commander, operated from Brussels. The city was the home of a crowd of diplomats and soldiers, part Spanish, part Walloon, always freely available. The Spanish leaders knew what they wanted and what they did not want. No less the Dutch. With Madrid so distant and confusion prevailing everywhere else, Europe's chaotic conflict found its focus in Brussels and The Hague, so close to one another.

The Hague was where, under the protection of his mother's brothers, the Orange princes Maurice and Frederick Henry, the expelled King of Bohemia settled after a certain amount of roaming and visits to hoped-for friends. His court was a sorry affair. In the querulous words of one of his privy councillors, Camerarius, to another, "The English and other lackeys daily run after me, demanding pence for their board and other things, just as the tradesmen and artisans do. That is why I cannot issue orders and have neither information nor money. . . ." The members of the government-in-exile with which Frederick surrounded himself had to see how they could earn small change by doing jobs on the side for other gentlemen. In its composition his government was, because the King had given the Bohemians all too little reason to hold him in respect, more Palatine than Bohemian and, so one would have thought, entirely in leading strings, totally impotent. That, in spite of everything, it was not.

It personified an element of unrest, capable of being exploited by others and conscious of its value, which included the justice or fancied justice of its cause, as a bargaining counter.

Just as a reader who scans a novel thinks that the author has had to accept this and that twist to his plot to prevent his tale from stopping short, so in the true and bloody narration recounted here many a thing had to happen as it did if it was to continue. Had the Elector Palatine agreed to the bagatelle required of him by Ferdinand II, had he asked for forgiveness and bent his knee to the Emperor as the young Prince of Anhalt did, then, as witnesses corroborate, he would not have been robbed of his Electorate and a crucial motive for the war's extension would have evaporated. The objection can be raised that war and peace do not depend on a genuflexion, that Ferdinand had in Germany as little as in Bohemia the strength to brake the dynamic of victory, that the Spaniards and the Bavarians, the Dutch as well, and later others too, would have seen to its continuation. Possibly. But at least the Elector could have forced the Emperor to manifest to all the world his lack of will or power to pursue the path of peace. He did not do so.

THE FREEBOOTERS

Many another piece fell into place. That of the Protestant powers who procrastinated and vacillated was temporarily taken by petty, properly speaking private powers who did not vacillate and who played their part in keeping the flame aglow.

Ernst von Mansfeld, bastard count and military entrepreneur, with the inflexibility, solitude, and bitterness of the age concentrated in his person, had at the right moment led his mercenaries, his sole possession, out of Bohemia. That was something that he knew how to do. More destined for defeat than victory, he stood straight up again when believed to be irretrievably down. It was how he held his soldiery, men below him in the social scale but clamped in the same spiritual misery. He deserved their trust. That of his employers, hardly. Perish the thought that Mansfeld might have felt any obligation of loyalty to Palsgrave Frederick. He had often enough made manifest his readiness to sell himself to others, better paymasters, not excluding Emperor Ferdinand. Because such overtures did not meet with success, in the last resort he always remained on the side of those hostile to Habsburg and accepted patronage where he could find it – from the Palatines, Dutch, British, French or Venetians. He did not much care whose general he

EUROPE'S FEEBLE RESISTANCE 199

was for the moment called. He never belonged to anyone except himself, faithful only to his own luckless lot and bitter fortune. He would never have sailed his craft, had christendom sprung fewer leaks. But, given the condition its parts were in, the wanton fighting quality inherent in any man represented a power potential with which every ruler reckoned.

Of a different calibre from Mansfeld, the hater and the hated, was Margrave Georg Friedrich von Baden-Durlach. A learned, pious old man, he had read the Bible fifty-eight times right through. Presumably he carefully counted the number of times and made no secret of the total. Ashamed of his fellows in the Protestant Union who after the battle of the White Mountain unobtrusively withdrew from the scene, he, one for all, stepped into the breach. An altruist in days of savage egotism. An idealist fated for wretchedness in the same way as the lone wolf Mansfeld. So far he had been content to recruit troops, professing to hold them in readiness against the contingency of his own small territory being invaded. What he really had in mind was to slip their leash as soon as the dogs of war approached the Rhine. For all his great stout-heartedness, he too cannot be absolved of guilt. Had no Protestant armed force stirred in Germany at all any more, there could have been no further hostilities. Any form of peace, as we of a later and wiser era know, would have been better than what was now brewing. The Margrave of Baden did not know it.

To these two disparate personalities, Mansfeld and Georg Friedrich, must be added a third. Impelled by his own fantastic vision of things, Duke Christian of Brunswick was generally known as "The Halberstädter" or "the mad Halberstädter" because he "administered" the bishopric of Halberstadt, a pious task for which nobody could have been less suited than this particular Protestant. A gentleman with a fist better adapted to striking than pushing a pen was how the Margrave of Cassel, his neighbour, described him. Yet he could write the most gallantly phrased French letter, this prince who, knight and brigand chief, delighted in the most boorish manner of speech (presumably to emphasize his manliness) when wine had flushed his pale complexion. Those were the occasions for his calling King James "that old shit-in-his-pants", "that old English bed-pisser", and "the world's biggest scoundrel" whose daughter's excrement was worth more than he. No less biting was his contempt for the "German scoundrels" whom he would not allow to be termed "princes" in his presence and who, he alleged, were the Emperor to order him to put paid to this pack, would in the event make an imperialist of him. Regardless of such bandit's rhetoric, soon to be followed by bandit's action in the shape of plundered churches, raped nuns, and rafters burning to the sound of tocsins, I know of at least three poets or historians of the female sex who centuries later have been captivated by this lanky, tousled youth. He for his part fancied himself in love with Elizabeth of England and the Palatinate, an entirely voluntary conclusion reached before his darting eyes ever came to rest on the exalted refugee. His army served neither like Georg Friedrich's the serious Protestant cause nor, like Mansfeld's, the self-sufficient purpose of going to war because in peace he must go under. Its dedication was to violent and quixotic adventure. The heterogeneous motives behind the recruitment of their regiments made little difference, though, to the afflicted common folk.

Christian von Brunswick was not the only young German prince who took advantage of prevailing disorder to mount his steed, brandish his sword, and revel in the confusion to the full. His was only the most spectacular case. Dynasties with too many descendants to be supported without the wherewithal to support them abounded. Eight Saxe-Weimar brothers, for example, and six Saxe-Lauenburg ones. They lived close together in castles where stuffed bruins and boars bared their teeth while a few weather-beaten ancestral portraits constituted the rest of the decor, cold corridors smelt of spiders' webs and rot, and they had no wish to stay for the rest of their lives. Constantly revised family compacts meant that they had to divide among themselves the paltry incomes squeezed from their estates. A regnant duke was glad to have eleven thousand gulden a year allotted to him and his court, with his brothers receiving six thousand each – as much as a senior officer would pocket per month. They sought their fortune in war. At this date three Saxe-Lauenburg brothers, Heinrich Julius, Rudolf Maximilian, and Franz Albrecht, the last of whom had a nimble brain, were in the service of the Emperor. A fourth, Franz Karl, had pitched his tent in the camp of the Emperor's opponent, Mansfeld. Three of the Saxe-Weimar brood enlisted under the Winter King. One of them, more high-minded than was customary, followed Frederick to The Hague. There was a younger brother, Duke Bernhard, born in 1604.

A component of Protestant policy and strategy, in so far as such existed at all, was a power in farthest south-eastern Europe. Not Turkey, although in the logic of power politics it should have been. But no Christian ruler wanted openly to ally himself with Christendom's hereditary foe and the masters of Constantinople did not envisage the future of their empire along such lines as to deem it advisable to venture a new frontal attack on Vienna. Their preference was for a proxy, Gabor Bethlen, Prince of Transylvania, on whom the Protestants could count and with whom they could conspire without anyone being able to utter shrill reproaches. Bethlen we have encountered more than once before. Indeed we are on a certain footing with him, but not to so intimate a degree that his introduction at this point, rendering the extent of our *dramatis personae* tolerably complete, would be inappropriate.

Misapprehensions about Bethlen are frequent. He has been called a barbarian and stranger to European ways, a circumcised and clandestine Mohammedan, a Tartar, and many things else. In fact he derived from an old Magyar aristocratic family which in our own century has contined to furnish Hungary with statesmen. His first wife was a Countess Károlyi; his second, a Brandenburg agnate, brought him his dearly desired recognition of status as a European prince. Now a member of that great clan, he was the butt for Wallenstein's wit – "Lord Brother-in-Law". None the less he remained a Turkish vassal, thoroughly familiar with the corrupt workings of the grand despotism in whose capital he formerly lived for years. He had to pay tribute, keep the peace with his neighbouring pashas, and was in no position to be a prince without the consent of the Sublime Porte. Three ethnic groups, Magyars, Germans, and Szeklers, who were half Turks, lived in his principality. The demarcation of the borders was blurred. Bethlen would have liked to extend their circumference to take in the whole, or the lion's share, of Hungary as well as Moldavia and Wallachia to the south-east, creating a Magyar-Slav empire. A fevered fantasy born of rambling ambition and fear, for Bethlen also belonged among those who sought security through attack and expansion. He knew that there could never be a balanced peace between himself and the Habsburgs, his neighbours to the west, between Calvinist and arch-Catholic, between the Magyar who had constantly to be ready to ally himself with rebellious Magyar kin and the Emperor who in effect counted Hungary as part of his hereditary territories. There was no room for both, the Habsburg Danubian monarchy and a half-Protestant, half-Orthodox kingdom of Dacia. That is why all conclusions of peace between Ferdinand and Bethlen were simply armistices, their conditions were never fulfilled, and the Transylvanian ever again broke loose when trouble in the north-west boiled over.

Then he would wage war in one of three ways. The least considerable was alliance with the Estates of the Habsburg lands. At a high level lay the stratagem to be performed in consort with Protestant friends in the

Empire – an advance by them on Bohemia or Moravia through Silesia and by him from some south-eastern corner, the two parties meeting in the middle. The major manoeuvre, and the dream of Palatine politicians was a gigantic pincer movement whereby he would join with no less a person than the King of Sweden who would be marching through Poland towards Moravia. The first method was tried in 1620–1 and found too brittle. The second thereafter. The third and most daring remained a concept. Bethlen's soldiery, wild Turks and Magyars consisting in the main of light cavalry, were characteristic of his campaigns and himself – quickly come, quickly gone. The pincer movement was never of sufficient strength and duration.

The good and the bad adventurers, Mansfeld, Baden, Halberstadt, Bethlen, were incapable of filling the place of the Powers whom they screened – Holland, England, Denmark, Sweden. Neither Germany's many princes nor its many moneyed municipal republics between Strasbourg and Lübeck – doing nothing to attract attention to themselves, only wanting to live in peace and to follow their trade, simply frightened – could for their part put things right again.

This was the time, in 1621, when King Gustavus Adolphus wrote to the Duke of Mecklenburg, a German prince who believed himself to be far from the scene of action, "What is now happening in the Palatinate will tomorrow happen to you" – *Hodie illi, cras tibi*. The Duke thought the warning strange.

THE SPARKS SPREAD TO GERMANY

A Spanish attack on the Rhenish Palatinate, led by Spinola, had begun in the summer of 1620 even before the battle of the White Mountain. In the following spring, when the prolonged Dutch-Spanish armistice ran out, the war on the middle reaches of the Rhine coalesced with that on its lower reaches. With the embers of rebellion in Bohemia buried under ashes, the Rhenish theatre of war temporarily held the centre of the scene. The evil having spread from Bohemia prior to its suppression there, it continued on its course.

The Protestant Union's task, and the plea on which it had abandoned Bohemia, was defence of the Palatinate. Now it shrank back, alike from this and everything else. The princes and city republics resolved by an overwhelming majority that here too it was better to remain outside the conflict. They found excuses, such as the publication of the highly compromising correspondence belonging to Prince von Anhalt, the so-called "Anhalt Chancellery" captured by the Bavarians at Prague, and the pronouncement of outlawry against the Palsgrave. This archaic and macabre ceremony, with threats directed against all who should render aid to the individual thrust beyond the pale, was of dubious validity to those versed in German constitutional law. But real power, fortified by hallowed titles, lay behind it. As the months of 1621 slipped past, the Union ceased for practical purposes to exist – in the light of which it would have been better for it never to have existed. An alliance lustily contributing to the division of Germany into hostile camps and then beating a cowardly retreat when the advance was sounded, it created all the harm usually inflicted by alliances without conferring any of their benefits.

The Spaniards wanted to occupy the Palatinate in order to reduce the Palsgrave to utter impotence, turning him into an embarrassment rather than trump card for the Dutch. Thereafter they would quite have liked to re-establish their victim, humiliated and dependent on them, in his petty principality because protracted fighting in Germany must interfere with their war against Holland and because they hoped for good relations with England. Those were not to be had if they treated its ruler's son-in-law too roughly. Ingeniously spun, as always, the thread of consanguinity was entangled with the rest.

Recently the Emperor had slid deeply into the Duke of Bavaria's debt. In the first place on account of the Bohemian expeditionary force, then for a second campaign conducted by Maximilian in the Upper Palatinate. The Duke, strict man of business, was in a position to present a bill for twelve million gulden. Had he been a man of superior sagacity instead of merely clever, cunning, and pious, he would have possessed himself in patience in regard to its reimbursement. He had had the money, else it could not have been spent, and his treasure-chests were presumably not short of more. However we cannot expect from even one of the most able and sober of contemporary princes that he should have looked beyond, and set himself above, the age in which he lived. So he demanded from the Emperor land for the millions the latter could not repay, with Upper Austria as security and the Upper Palatinate as security too, but with the second of these to pass subsequently into his definite ownership. This, in turn a breach of imperial law, he was promised. Ferdinand, to finance the war, had already confiscated properties in Bohemia. Henceforth the practice was extended for the same purpose to entire imperial principalities. By this time his pledge to invest the Duke with electoral dignity was an open secret. Ernst von

Mansfeld had seized letters – a so-called "Spanish Chancellery" whose publication was the exiled Palatine government's jeering retort to the "Anhalt" disclosures – in which this was to be read. What the Spaniards did west of the Rhine and the Bavarians did in the Upper Palatinate produced, despite dual intent, the same result.

Soon Tilly and the Bavarian forces were also on the Rhine. He was in pursuit of Mansfeld who, unable to hold his position in the Upper Palatinate, had with customary skill extracted himself and his mercenaries from the trap and marched them right across southern Germany to the Rhenish Palatinate. During the winter months the campaign dropped off, to the distress of those under whose roofs it drowsed. When it re-awakened in 1622, Spinola and Tilly faced three venturesome opponents: the upright Margrave of Baden, the sinister Mansfeld, and the wild Christian von Halberstadt approaching from the north-west. Each successively succumbed to Spanish strategy, behind its real, unlike their factitious, power. By the end of 1622 the whole of the Rhenish Palatinate was under foreign occupation, the Bavarians holding the territory east of the Rhine, the Spaniards that to the west. The Margrave of Baden had temporarily desisted from his loyal and lonely undertaking. Mansfeld and Halberstadt made a fighting retreat to Holland. There, not without help from the States-General, they set about repairing their strength so as next year to start something somewhere and continue it until such time as the great powers bestirred themselves.

The situation left the politicians at Vienna a free hand to implement the long-planned constitutional violation – transference to his Bavarian cousin of the outlawed Palsgrave's electoral dignity. On 23 January the Emperor conferred on the matter with the German princes, or at any rate a select number of them. The congress summoned to Regensburg had been meant to be a *Deputationstag*, that is to say, a meeting of all the Electors plus delegations from important Estates like Bavaria, Brunswick, Pomerania, and others. But the Protestants either did not attend at all or, like Saxony and Brandenburg, dispatched delegates whose instructions were more in line with suspicious supervision than co-operation. In the event the Catholics kept to themselves, impotent to pass binding resolutions. They certainly wanted to take advantage of the opportunity to drive Protestantism still farther back, yet simultaneously were afraid of the consequences arising from excessive use of such passing advantage. They agreed on the principle and disclaimed responsibility for its effectuation – His Imperial Majesty knew what was best for the Empire. Duke Maximilian became Elector. An idealized

depiction of the act of transference hangs at Munich. For a fact the
ceremony took place in an atmosphere of gloom. The Saxon and
Brandenburg representatives refused to attend. So did the Spanish
ambassador, an event bound to excite remark and confusion. While the
Duke kneelingly received the insignia of his new dignity, the old Elector
of Mainz, Arch-Chancellor of the Empire, pensively scratched his head.
When it came to Maximilian's turn to speak, his utterance was "quite
timid". That was due to his bad conscience. He knew the precedents too
well to be deceived about the breach of law on which his elevation was
founded. He knew German and European politics too well not to surmise
that what was happening would harm the state of peace. It was the
conflict between his greed and his conscience, as well as his knowledge of
affairs, that caused him to stutter at the moment when he was meant to
express his gratitude. The Bavarian electoral status was a fresh declaration of war on international Protestantism just as previously the bloody
scene in front of Prague's Old Town town hall, the conquest of the
Palatinate, and the Counter-Reformation in Bohemia had been. The
Electoral College now had four Catholic as against two Protestant
members. In so far as this highest imperial advisory body was still live
and legal, it would henceforward presumably act in whatever manner
pleased best the Emperor or His Holiness's nuncio.

Not that the great powers retaliated in any effective way. They simply
exchanged embassies about desirable coalitions. But they looked with
more favour than hitherto on what the freebooters, Mansfeld and
Christian von Brunswick, stood for and gave them a little money so that
they should be able in the coming campaign season to stand up for it
again.

In those circumstances Christian von Halberstadt's own forces and all
others available to him were inadequate for his planned summer
strategy. He had envisaged a march from Lower Saxony, on whose
borders he was perpetrating his normal mischief, to Silesia. There he
hoped to rouse the inhabitants to fresh rebellion and defection. He would
then continue into Bohemia, convinced that a torch-bearer of freedom
in his shape was earnestly awaited, in order finally to join Gabor Bethlen
somewhere in Moravia. No one was more delighted at the prospect than
the fugitive government at The Hague. Diligent correspondence on the
topic was exchanged with the Transylvanian potentate and Count
Thurn, never discouraged in his thirst for action.

The project did not even get under way. The conduct of the mercenaries had drawn the real power behind the Catholic League, Bavaria's

armed might, step by step to northern Germany. At the end of August Bethlen with fifty thousand cavalry and infantry, thirty thousand of them Turks, advanced into Hungary. He would hardly have done so if he had known that eighteen days earlier Halberstadt had once more suffered annihilating defeat at Tilly's hands and been thrust back towards Holland.

GÖDING

From the outset Wallenstein regarded the dangers attaching to this second coalition as grave. No one could tell who would participate and how, who not. That the imperial war establishment, particularly with its best troops dispatched to assist Tilly in Germany, was in poor shape he did know. The remaining forces barely sufficed to keep the towns in a state of obedience and fear. Should the structure built up since November 1620 collapse, His Princely Grace the Grand Proprietor would face the fate he had previously only just escaped and the bitterness of which the Protestant members of his clan were experiencing to the full. He on whom good fortune breathes so swiftly and so hotly will be afraid of getting his fingers burned. When Bethlen began to fulfil his part in the all-too-bold strategic concept, no more than nine thousand men could be mustered against him, not a fifth of the strength at the Transylvanian's disposal. The depressingly outnumbered force lacked any light cavalry unit (their employment was Bethlen's favourite method of surprise), ammunition and fuses, carts and horses, fodder and victuals. These, had Wallenstein been in charge, were things that he would have seen to, knowing the business from experience. He was however still a subordinate who could on his own authority neither issue orders nor impose penalties although "they – the stores commissaries – lie to the Emperor, cheat him, and say that there are stocks on hand when there is not a word of truth in it, and they are not punished." Why at the approach of the storm he, as military governor of Bohemia and the driving spirit behind its defence, was not entrusted with the supreme command remains unknown. Instead it was given to an old Neapolitan, Montenegro by name. A question of Spanish influence, perhaps. Next came Marradas. Wallenstein was only third in the scale.

The imperial War Council concluded that to safeguard Austria and Vienna had top priority. Montenegro's instruction therefore was to move southwards down the March and take up his position at Pressburg as being Vienna's advance bastion. "No doubt we shall have to obey His

Majesty's command to go to Pressburg, but Bohemia, Moravia, and Silesia will surely be lost to us," Wallenstein objected. Had not Bethlen in a manifesto sworn that he would not rest until freedom of religion and former proprietorial rights were restored in those lands? Was not his cavalry swarming round the neighbourhoods of Olmütz and Brünn? Swarming too in a more south-easterly direction, between the Waag and the March, in such numbers that the imperial troops proceeding slowly on meagre rations and through downpours along the latter river did not dare to make contact with them. Rather did the commanders – "the Lord General, Don Baltasar, and I" – deem the most prudent course a withdrawal into a fortified town, Göding (Hodonín), advantageously situated on the March. Wallenstein hoped for an enemy attack. "It is said that they propose to assault our camp. Would to God that it were true, for in our stronghold they will assuredly do us no harm." Next day he had to abandon the comparatively pleasing prospect. The foe refused to stir and "*in summa*, he is sharp-witted and means to starve us out".

For the twenty-two days of the siege we have twenty letters in Wallenstein's own hand, all addressed to h's father-in-law Harrach at Vienna. In cipher, they were carried by messengers who at night rowed across the stream or stole through the woods. Harrach's answers, though there are fewer of them, also reached their destination. The dangerous exchanges took respectively six days in all.

Were Harrach to ask his plans, Wallenstein wrote, they certainly did not include leading a sally. The imperial cavalry was at the end of its tether. "So our resolution must be to perish in this place, one eating the other, but I am uneasy that the soldiery's resolution will be another and that from necessity they will seize us officers by the hairs of our head, deliver us to the enemy, and themselves remain in his service. ..."
"We officers shall do what behoves honest folk."

His uneasiness, he emphasized, was not for his own life, for "on any occasion we can easily be put along our road by an arqbusier". His fear was on the score of his young wife, Harrach's daughter. Granted, there would be an outcry and malicious tongues encouraged to wag if the Princess of Friedland openly fled from Prague. That was none the less what he advised, pleaded for, and repeated seven times in these letters, smuggled out at such peril. His cousin Max should conduct the Lady Isabella from Prague to Upper Austria, though on no account straight across Bohemia because it was too hazardous, but along foot-paths into Bavaria and then by ship down the Danube. Alternatively, he should convey her to Dresden down the Elbe. Tenderness permeated these constantly reiterated requests, and how relieved he was on receipt of the longed-for news is patent: "A hundred thousand times I express thanks to my lord for inducing my wife to leave Prague and I am thereby assuredly rid of my greatest care." The range of his political and military preoccupations was extensive. Prince von Liechtenstein should be prodded into recruiting more troops and laying in provisions for the towns. All suspect individuals and unnecessary mouths should be expelled from Prague "because they do nothing but consume the victuals". A completely fresh army should be assembled under such and such colonels and brought into action only after proper preparation so that "if we are in any case to perish, the Emperor will not lose his position".

The one direct ray of hope derived from the rumour of six thousand "Polacks" or "Cossacks" coming at King Sigismund's behest through Silesia to the rescue of the besieged. (They never arrived.) Wallenstein worried, however, about the possibility of deficiencies resulting in their dispersal on the way. Flour supplies ought to be stored for them at Olmütz, at Nikolsburg, at Eisgrub, at Lundenberg, and no ear lent to liars who maintained that sufficient was on hand, just as he for his part no longer trusted his stores commissaries. "Sometimes I threaten to hang them, at others to enrich them, and, did I not see to it myself, we would long ago have had nothing to eat." He was driven to raving impatience by the feeling of matters being left undone if he did not perform them in person. Confined to the fortress, what was there of any importance that he could do? "Spend thousands on spies", to discover Bethlen's plans as well as to pacify a starving garrison on the verge of mutiny. And outside, in the broad acres of the imperilled land? Why would no one believe him? Why was credence given to Cardinal von Dietrichstein whenever he "blethered" how well things stood? Of the fresh preparations being made in Vienna "the one set is in my opinion so poor and the other so slow that they will scarcely be of help to us because the new and comprehensive recruitments will not be able to reach us in time".

The writer of these letters is enraged at not being in charge of the war's over-all conduct. He is contemptuous of what his principals do, do not do, or do too late. They should not have let go the Polish cavalry whose return is now vainly awaited. They should have accepted his offer in early summer to set up an army, should have seen in good time to the essential war supplies, should have begun earlier on the forward defences and schemes for counter-attack. Justifiable criticisms, put to paper by candlelight and penned by a man of foresight, although also of high-strung temperament and inclined to pessimistic overstatements. For in our view he interpreted the situation at Göding as more forbidding than it really was. "The Emperor stands in greater danger than ever before of losing his lands." It is unlikely that that was truly the Emperor's plight. What three years ago Bethlen had failed to achieve in alliance with the Bohemian rebels, he was incapable at this juncture of accomplishing on his own. He relied on assistance from the north which did not materialize. His light cavalry, a fickle instrument, was suited to snatching quick successes, but, far from its base, not to their long-term consolidation. At Vienna however there were also moments of panic when the city, Prague, or even Munich was thought to be threatened – as though the Transylvanian's perseverance would have been commensurate with that. The propensity of Habsburg politicians and strategists, which Wallenstein so despised, was first to let the military machine rust, undertaking no more than bravado actions bound to provoke counter-attacks, and then, when these occurred, to fall into a state of belated, debilitated excitement. The expectation of a new rebellion in Bohemia aggravated this bias. Not that any such thing happened, not even now, with the country practically stripped of troops.

A final point: Wallenstein's outlook was clouded by his isolation among hungry marauders in a fortress surrounded by an enemy in overwhelming superiority. The momentousness of an actual location, especially if impossible to escape from, is always apt to be exaggerated. In this instance Wallenstein could from his confinement look into three lands, Austria, Moravia, and Bohemia, whose circumstances he well knew, whether the tenuous, uncertain threads linking their destinies were concerned or the hopes for a change cherished by the many sufferers at Prague, and his knowledge was steeped in the hue of his immediate environment.

At the same time the Transylvanian was finding his stamping-ground too chilly and barren. His Turkish cavalry, loaded with booty and averse to a winter campaign, wanted to go home. On this aspect Wallenstein was wrongly informed, just as Bethlen did not rightly know what might be happening in that broad no-man's-land termed the Empire. Was it inconceivable that a powerful force, led by Tilly in person, could surprise and utterly rout him at the instant when his own men had sunk into hibernation? Was it worth continuing to make a show outside this hovel Göding when its compulsory lodgers would not, in spite of every incitement, let themselves be lured into a skirmish? On 19

November Wallenstein could report to Harrach that, thanks to the mediation of the Hungarian palatine, an armistice would be concluded and the enemy soon take their departure. Next day Bethlen, on horseback and splendidly attired, met old Montenegro in front of the fortress. The Prince made a movement as though to dismount; the imperial commander hastened to anticipate him. Duped, he found himself on the ground while Bethlen remained in the saddle. To the accompaniment of march music and the thunder of cannon, they proceeded, Montenegro on foot and Bethlen riding, to the spot selected for signature of the document. If, as may be assumed, Wallenstein was on hand, he for the first and last time saw "Bethlehem" in person. Then the garrison was able to regale itself on a profusion of food. The peace treaty concluded six months later was simply of regional character and even there anything but conclusive. There was too much inflammable material about and too much tinder, too much cinder, not to render the condition of affairs combustible. A compromise between Bethlen and Ferdinand was a little water, a little sand thrown upon a single, small burning bush. Bethlen left with his old, though no new, booty. He honourably refused to extradite the Bohemian *émigrés* in his following. Count Thurn in particular would have fared badly. In these tangled encounters his luck continued to hold, though I am not certain whether for the countries of central Europe it could have been called luck.

This was the end of the war in 1623, the sixth year of hostilities since the beginning of the Bohemian rising – *post bohemos commotus*, as the usual epistolary turn of phrase was. The second coalition, unsatisfactory from its inception, had been brought low. The Prince of Transylvania wrote a dignified letter to the Palsgrave. He had, he said, performed far beyond what could be expected from him, sacrificing much blood and money as well as maintaining his Turks at the onset of winter longer in the field than any Sultan had ever succeeded in doing. Had Duke Christian kept his promise or anyone else in Germany afforded the slightest aid, the greatest and ultimate objectives would probably have been capable of achievement.

In January 1624 Wallenstein rode back to Prague. He found standing below the Hradschin a palace, in the Italian style, where previously there had been none. His. Why not at last enjoy what had been acquired?

Duke and Duchy

WE possess few authentic, lifelike portraits of Wallenstein. The one most frequently reproduced is that from van Dyck's practised master brush. But the artist never saw his model and simply had a few second-hand impressions from which to add a speedily drawn piece to his collection of the great of his day. It conforms to a pattern – a mountain range in the background, breastplate, sash, field-marshal's baton, and the stern traits appurtenant to a ruler. Its fidelity to delineations made directly is none the less unmistakable. The rendering of the physiognomy ennobled by van Dyck is grim, indeed ugly in the work by an unknown painter which hangs in the museum at Eger (Cheb). That really was drawn from life, I am inclined to think, although not in the sense that Wallenstein sat for the picture because he would have had neither time nor taste for such a proceeding. The face is indisputably that of one accustomed to command, alive with intelligence but not endearing. Everything about it is strong and hard, with deep-set smouldering eyes below arched brows, a high and fur-rowed forehead, hollow cheeks, prominent cheek-bones, pointed beard below thick lips. This portrait corresponds to what was said about him – that he seldom smiled, spoke little, was reserved and haughty towards equals, formidable towards inferiors: "arrogant von Waldstein", a "proud beast". Painted from life is Christian Kaulfersch's depiction of him in cavalry dress, now hanging over a mantelpiece in the Waldstein Palace at Prague, and another by the same painter in Castle Friedland. The features are finer, more lined with suffering than they are shown at Eger, due perhaps to the portrayal being of later date, in 1631, when its subject was already a very sick man. The mask-like quality to be observed in all representations of him, although part of an artistic convention, may in this particular instance also be explicable in terms of Wallenstein's habit, common to many high-strung individuals, of keeping a tight hold on himself, an acquired self-restraint that deserted him only when he felt exceptionally well or flew into one of his rages. There were those who alleged his abrupt manners and fits of fury to be sheer play-acting. Well, there is no reason why natural disposition should not be made to serve a purpose.

He is generally shown as wearing armour, which in fact he wore only on rare martial occasions. His tailor's bills reveal that for civilian appearances he had a distinct preference for red: "eighteen ells long carmine fringes for His Princely Grace's gloves", "a robe of scarlet thickly edged in carmine, and a doublet of red satin. . . " In addition there is mention of "buff", "nail-brown", and "ashen". So the tradition that copying his brother-in-law Zierotin, he mostly wore black and always only displayed a trace of red (for which there were superstitious reasons) can hardly be correct. His high boots had to be lined with fur.

He was a distinctly clean person in an age which normally went un-washed and smelt worse. He loved baths and the feel of water. At Genoa he had a silver bath and bench made for himself. At Prague a goldsmith manufactured a "large tub" for him. Perhaps when he lay in it, the water fragrant with fine herbs, the stern mask slipped from his face. In his household, observers reported with astonishment, tablecloths and napkins were never allowed to be used more than once.

His health was poor. Above all he was tormented by gout, an afflic-tion which to the accompaniment of burning pains caused the toes to swell, moved up into the joints and formed knots, dried up the skin until it cracked and generated ulcers as well as digestive complaints, could cause colics and finally did not leave the heart unaffected. At forty he was not yet that far, but it would happen. For a long time to come his handwriting would be firm and bold. We must therefore assume that the suffering was confined to his feet and did not spread to his fingers. Nor does he make any other mention of it: ". . . the villainy is once again at my feet" and, a few months later, "Now I lie more than I stir." When he did stir, that was the reason for the fur-lined boots.

Sufferers from gout should abstain from alcohol. Formerly Wallenstein had been a friend of, and expert on, wine. Even now, though very rarely, it occurred that in good humour he would surrender to its delights: "Today the envoy and I fuddled ourselves in our cups." When his brother-in-law, the youthful Archbishop of Prague, had in his absence been in charge of his cellar, he bantered, "If Cardinal von Harrach is no better versed in the *ceremoniis Romanis* than in wine, he will have to be unfrocked, for the wine is bad and I have already grumbled soundly because of it." Soon he had altogether to abandon Tokay, Melnik, and Gumpoldskirchen, Rhenish and Burgundian vintages

and confine himself to the light, pricklingly tart Valtellina which
he imagined did him least harm. He was however far fonder of beer,
especially if made from wheaten malt, than wine. "I must complain
that in Brandenburg there is no pale ale to be had and I therefore have to
slake my thirst with wine; beer brewed from barley malt I cannot
imbibe." Wine does not assuage thirst whereas beer, we know, lends it a
touch of splendour and, particularly where high-strung, hoarse, and
parched individuals with easily upset stomachs are concerned, has a
beneficent, soothing effect. Wherever Wallenstein was, there beer had
to be. He turned brewing into one of his duchy's most flourishing
industries. Mainly of course because it brought in money, but in
addition the brewers supplied his own needs. "An order has gone to the
governor of Neuschloss to convey without delay a barrel of pale ale, so
well laid down that there be no taste of cask, for His Princely Grace's
own draught." All the stewards of his estates had "on pain of corporeal
punishment" to have several such barrels ready for him. Wallenstein
was quicker to issue such threats of reprisals, which could signify a
thrashing, maiming, or even death, than to implement them.

He liked to maintain a liberal board – orders and bills attest to the fact
– but by this time he had to be as frugal with food as with wine. His fare
consisted of pheasants, partridges, young vegetables, fruit and other
light victuals. "I pray too that my lord let My Wife be advised that I am
well and learn to eat gammon and broths." *Schunken*, the word he used
here, was a conglomeration of Czech *šunka* and German *Schinken*, one
of the rare examples of his native tongue infiltrating his German.

The latter he now wrote better, meaning tauter, more fluently and
wittily, than any German-born personality of his day. To say that is not
to pronounce any verdict on whether he had a natural bent for German
or, supposing his fate had been bound up with Sweden, that he would
have acquired Swedish just as well, whether indeed his restless genius,
concentrated wholly on matters in hand, would have allowed him to
master any language whatever. German at any rate was the one in which
he was adept, German with a faintly Austrian tinge, just as we must
presumably think of him articulating it with an Austro-Bohemian accent.

I do not know of any letter in which he expressly extolled the Germans.
His endorsement was indirect, by way of what two centuries later would
have been termed his language policy. His Court was German and his
households were German. A servant asked for his discharge "because
he is not versed in German speech". The justice dispensed in his duchy
was administered in German. "You must have a German clerk in the

chancery, for I do not wish that anything should be handled in Czech."
That in a domain whose north was predominantly populated by Germans, but in its south and capital, Gitschin, by Czechs. Wallenstein
hardly felt himself any longer to be a Czech, as Wilhelm von Slawata and
Adam von Waldstein, in spite of everything, continued to do. Catholic
and loyalists, they none the less remained Bohemian nobles. Wallenstein,
Prince of the Holy Roman Empire, had grown away from his native
hearth and status, for hearth depends solely on status. He retained his
familiarity with it, but as an outside observer, a renegade. "I know the
Bohemians all too well. . . ." "I could wish that for once Count Slawata
would cease to use his Bohemian knavery against me. . . ." To that degree
he was German, had become so German as not really to hold any other
nationality in much regard. He liked to give vent to his contempt for
Magyars – "the Hungarians will tell Vienna some lie or other," for theirs
is "a country of scoundrels". No less held good for Poland or at least the
"Polacks", that truly good-for-nothing pack of rascals, the Polish
cavalry for whom he cried out when they were not there and regularly
wished to the devil when they were. "As for the Polacks, let my lord
send them away as soon as may be, for they are more noxious to us than
the enemy." About the Italians – well, being a gentleman he spoke their
language, the language of civilized Europe. He decreed moreover that it
should be taught in his schools. And he had buildings erected in the
Italian style, mostly by Italian architects. All that was a foregone
conclusion. But the nation was not, as some believed, a special favourite
of his. "That's all the gratitude the Duke can claim/For always having
put these Latins first" – Schiller). They were by no means "always
preferred" by him. He employed them as his commanders, men like
Collalto, Gallas, Gonzaga, Piccolomini, because they were sent him by
the imperial court and because they were reckoned, to an even greater
extent than the Spaniards, to be the outstanding strategists of the day.
His liking for, indifference to, or hate of them was in ratio to the way they
matched up to that reputation. Of their language he sometimes talked
in terms befitting the most boorish German burgess – the "rapscallion
Italian tongue". "I doubt not that the court resounds with all kinds of
gossip by women, priests, and sundry Italian rapscallions."

All of which does not signify that Germans accepted him as one of
themselves or that he was ever able to get Bohemia out of his system.
That is not so easy.

He continued to have a Bohemian secretary for official intercourse
with Prague because, let it be said again, reorganization by the trium-

phant Habsburg party did not include the banishment of Czech from the country's capital. Occasionally too he dashed down a few personal notes in Czech, but ninety-nine out of a hundred of his letters were now in German. He must have had a team of German scriveners scrawling down, as needs they must, whatever he dictated and reproducing it in fair copy below which he put his initials, AHZF, later AHZM,* in bold and unruly lineaments covering half the page. The greater a man's position in the world the more flourishes he added to his signature. In the case of the King of Sweden and the Duke of Bavaria these were so many as to render it almost inconceivable how such models of artistic embroidery can ever have become blind habit to their writers.

He wrote an astonishing amount in his own hand, ten or twelve letters a day, everything of a confidential nature and to confidential agents, everything wherein he gave free rein to his feelings and which was inappropriate to secretaries' ears. Over every letter he drew a cross, as pious Spaniards still do. Nearly every letter had a postscript – there was always something more that occurred to him. Punctuation worried him even less than most of his contemporaries. Sentences were often tele-scoped into one another, clauses always, and the subscription "But for my part I remain . . ." too, investing the whole with a quality of haste and breathlessness. He used no envelopes, instead folding the paper and sealing it with a small red signet-ring. It was the letters of state written by clerkly pens which displayed on the back the large coat-of-arms whose quarterings, surmounted by the ducal bonnet, would in time be filled galore. For the present they contained only the four Waldstein lions and Friedland eagle. He was the Lady Isabella's devoted correspondent, but unfortunately not one of his letters to her has survived.

He loved her, within the bounds imposed by class and personal constitution, and made generous provision for her possible widowhood. Whenever war approached Bohemia's frontiers, he sent her where she would be safest. His strange career entailed that for long periods, a year or eighteen months, he never saw her. But let him at last be in her vicinity again and he would be impatient of delay at their reunion. "I could not answer for it to my wife, should I saunter abroad ere I came to her. She would then indeed receive me evilly." Among the many descriptions of his public appearances there are none, as far as I know, which include any in the company of his Duchess. Admittedly the reports stem from diplomats and military men. One, by an ecclesiastic,

---

* A(lbrecht) H(erzog = duke) Z(u = of) F(riedland), AHZM(ecklenburg).

alleges that Wallenstein trusts nobody, not even his own wife, and speaks to her only after most careful consultation of the stars. That, supposing it to have been true, must have provided for cheerless family meals.

During campaigns he filled his bed alone. That, like the lower orders, he should have had anything to do with the strumpets who accompanied the army can be dismissed as out of the question. Had he had mistresses of commensurate rank, those who spied on him would have known about it and tried to exert influence over such ladies. Wallenstein despised womanizers as he despised drunkards, and his caustic suspicion that they might qualify as the former fell upon many. About the Augustinian fraternity at Böhmisch-Leipa he remarked, "That the monks at Leipp should this year have used up two thousand gulden surprises me. Used them up, I doubt not, on whoring and loose company, as their habit is." Cardinal von Dietrichstein he bluntly calls "a whore-ridden little priest" – whether with reason or not I leave open.

From the fact that the fair sex preoccupied him less than most men does not follow that like King James of England he was attracted to his own, or indeed even capable of close friendships. He needed many to serve him, each at his own level, from door-keeper to Lord High Steward, provincial governor, and general. No more. Count Max Waldstein, his cousin, possessed a skilled courtier's ways and Wallenstein liked to use him for all kinds of delicate business, but he too counted for no more than that. He was a lonely man, sometimes from solitude confidentially loquacious to those undeserving of confidence. An observer of mankind rather than of his individual fellow-men. He knew only two means to incite his servants and helpers: reward and punishment. His whole life he adhered to what he wrote from beleaguered Göding: "My threats are in part of hanging, in part of gifts." It was the guiding principle of his time. Count Khevenhüller, chronicler of Ferdinand II, calls "*poena* and *praemium* the core of government". Wallenstein earned notoriety simply by taking the principle further than the rest. Whether he bared his soul to his father confessors remains unknown; they gave nothing away.

The monkish politician just quoted also speaks of Wallenstein's "exact knowledge of history" and "a corresponding familiarity with the political and martial events which have transpired from the happenings that, some years ago in Germany and particularly in Bohemia, had for their consequence the transition from one sovereign to another". The latter is indubitably correct. From the outset of the quarrel between Rudolf and Matthias, both long in their graves, he had had opportunity to observe in minutest detail both the political and warlike turn of events in the Habsburg territories. He was moreover fond of referring to the practical knowledge of affairs which since 1604 he had gained. "For Us, who know full well what it lies in the power of war to achieve, this is not Our first year of soldiering." He drew on early memories, experiences vividly present and tidily ordered in his mind, rather than on books. He can be seen becoming better and better acquainted, through personal encounters and discussions, a constantly growing range of correspondence, the information of his agents and spies, with the state of Europe. Historical knowledge, though, would qualify under a different head. Conrad Ferdinand Meyer, in his tale *Gustav Adolf's Page*, puts into Wallenstein's mouth the words, "In bed, when sleep eludes me, it is my habit to read." The older and more ailing he was, the more tormentingly sleep will undoubtedly have eluded him. But the evidence that he read much is missing. A modest bill for books dates from the time of his brief, enforced retirement: "Twenty gulden sent to Prague for two books bought on His Princely Grace's behalf." He never collected a library, for none is mentioned in the precise inventory of his Prague palace made after his death. It contains (I have counted them) fifteen hundred and fifty-two items in all, from the rose damask-hung ceiling in the Knights' Hall, the Turkish carpets, and blue or gold leather tapestries to the commodes with copper basins, and only a single book is listed, *Architecturae militariae*, whose subject would have been siege strategy. There was no contemplative streak in Wallenstein. He, who fell into a raging impatience at the compulsory perusal of his political correspondence because its writers were usually so elaborate whereas his habit was to dive with his first sentence into the middle of matters and with the last to break away again, had no time for reading. Only for astrology did he have time because he thought it indispensable to his calling. But there too he wanted results, not mere theory. A personality of that sort, fleeing before its inner self into externals, is of course defenceless if illness or other cirumstances paralyse its pleasure in activity. How shall his mind occupy itself to any profit?

He had to have order around him. Beauty too in so far as it was combined with utility: spaciousness, airiness, moisture, fragrance. His buildings, next to power and horses, were the things most important to him. On the one hand he was interested in their dimensions, the nobility of their exteriors, and the grounds and annexes surrounding them, on the other in their practical, their sanitary qualities. Not really, though, in their interiors, furniture, ornaments, pictures. In this respect he only issued instructions of the most general kind. "So see to it also that the rooms are made ready, provided with furnishings and fine paintings." Fine paintings – in the Prague palace there hung, as was proper, portraits of the Emperor and Empress, the King of Spain and other rulers, "heathen Emperors", and a few "landscapes". The artists remained anonymous and Wallenstein in his correspondence never once mentioned the name of any painter belonging either to former ages or to his own, which was artistically not wholly despicable. To absorb himself in an artistic achievement and to derive strength as well as peace of mind from it was not in his nature. To take delivery of decently fashioned decorations sufficed him.

He had game preserves in plenty and he organized hunting-parties as every prince did, although his heart was not in them. Possibly he did not care for the killing of animals, in any case not in the numbers which were usual, and certainly he was contemptuous of the hours his master, the Emperor, wasted thereon. He admitted to being no expert in the chase: "I am no past master at it, but you shall so arrange matters with the chief ranger that I shall have satisfaction." He hated dogs. Wherever he was, they had to be locked away and he is never shown with the speckled quadrupeds who were customarily a ruler's companions. His letters never speak of hounds. Only once do his letters contain a mention of dogs, such as would be strong enough to attack wolves. To say that he cared too greatly for wildlife to love the chase would incite sportsmen to protest, and so we refrain from saying it. He did however really love animals, wild and tame alike – cows, sheep, deer, birds, and swans, down to the goldfish in the basins in his gardens, as well as the "sick, silly capons and chicks" which he ordered to be "distributed among the farmsteads so that they shall be restored to health by the fresh blades of the meadows". When he went from Gitschin to his zoo to watch the noble red deer and when, supporting himself on an Indian cane, he sauntered in the park of his Prague palace to stop in front of the leaf-embowered cages where faery-like birds shrilled fancy-free, those were moments when he may indeed have been content.

His happiest hours were among his horses. They were his delight and his passion, the last a quality which grew with the years rather than reaching satiety. Bays, greys, and black-coated steeds, they came from Spain, Naples, Friesland, Pomerania or wherever else the handsomest were to be found. "Let them cost what they will, I shall gladly pay, but they must stand high." For a stallion he would disburse as much as a thousand gulden. He had to wage war and play politics, occupations which once assumed were impossible to shed, but had he been a free man maybe he would have confined himself to breeding bloodstock. At Prague his horses stood "in a stabling which was marvellously prepared, the mangers of marble, and by each manger a spring of clear water to give drink". Thus wrote the Irish adventurer Thomas Carve after he had seen it all with his own eyes. His description included the stud-farm at Smrkowitz, near Gitschin. "In its midst was a tower from which, in the morning and in the evening, a guard gave a signal apprising the stable-hands to curry, to clean and to feed the horses. He kept here at least three hundred costly steeds." Wallenstein, however weary from the strain of command and the exercise of power, always found time, pleasure, and temper to vent upon their care. "I hear that the foals have this year been so installed, so filled with fodder, that their appearance is more of swine than chargers. I had not deemed the stud-groom such an ass that he would not have given heed to what is of foremost importance, that the foals should not over-feed themselves. I shall on that account severely reprimand him." Believing the death of a pair of foals to be ascribable to the fault of his servants, he stormed. "A single foal concerns me more than two butteries." Whether his instruction that "during the covering of the mare *ipso actu* the mare be freed so that it shall see the stallion and conceive according to its form", whether indeed the prescription was practicable, let experts decide. He would not have veterans reduced to rough tillage labour, but when they had become useless through war-service appointed a chivalric death for them. The charger shot beneath him at Lützen he had stuffed and mounted, with the result that it can today still be seen in his palace at Prague, most recently stored in a lumber-room.

Wallenstein, whether at his army headquarters or in his principality, never asked, never proposed, never recommended that things should be done; he ordered them. "I have no longer any use for the dean at Friedland. He wants to be supplicated. That I neither care nor am accustomed to do." Whatever it might be that he ordered, it had to be executed "*in furia*", "*subito*", "without losing a minute", possibly because there was so much that he wanted done, possibly because he had a presentiment that there was not much time left to him. He never jested, it was said. That was untrue. His letters contain plenty of jokes and good-humoured banter. But he was determined that everyone should know his orders to be no joke. "*Sciunt mei ministri, me nugare non solere et quae volo serio velle*" – "my officials know that it is not my habit to trifle and that what I want is meant seriously." "Do not suppose that I write for the sake of amusement, but that I wish it to be done so." All engaged in his affairs, manifold as these were and bursting at the seams, had to labour and be worthy of their hire. "My instruction is to heed that the gardener no longer makes merry and that you punish him severely if he be in the least neglectful, or it is you who will suffer. See to it that he looks to his work rather than drinks and goes roaming." People, in his view, were willing to work, but had to be offered something in return. "In the duchy there are peasants enough who will gladly toil, epecially those in the mountainous districts, provided that they are paid." Practical good sense, not compassion with the poverty-stricken hill-farmers, is here the key-note – both sides will have something to gain. Good workers received good wages. They and, after their deaths, their children. "Until my arrival give the builder's sons their father's keep, which it is my intent to continue, for he served me well." Later, as the shadows over his life lengthen, the tone of his orders became harsher. He wrote more of malefactions than benefactions.

He had a reputation for moodiness, irascibility, singularity, formidableness. Perhaps he was not loth to see this reputation, which his enemies in any case busily propagated, spread. Of course he had enemies, their numbers increasing in proportion to his own might. "The Duke of Friedland," was Emperor Ferdinand's mollifying admission to the envoy of a German prince, "doth incline in talk and manners to be somewhat rough," adding that this should not be taken too tragically. Friends also complained, and not only in later years when his state of nerves and mind could not be termed other than ailing. This feature began earlier and grew gradually worse. "Our General is in the grip of his gout. My brother can conceive how he deals with those around him. There is not a man more impatient and morose. Hardly one in the town durst other than whisper in his neighbour's ear lest he disturb the Prince by the clamour of his speech." Gerhard von Questenberg, the Vienna privy councillor who wrote those words, was Wallenstein's own creature, his agent, friend, and defender almost to the last. A man disposed to be sensitive to his own condition can least tolerate physical sufferings. When smitten with pain, Wallenstein possessed the displeasing though redoubtable capacity for letting not only his entire household but the whole city share in his affliction.

The reverse held equally good. He could be enchanting, whether to serve a particular purpose or because that was his temporary mood. The greater was the surprise of those who had heard so much to the contrary. "I must tell Your Highness," wrote a princess of Brandenburg to the Elector, "that we had the honour of seeing the Duke of Friedland. He is verily a fine gentleman, and thus not as various people have made him out to be, of truly great courtesy and has shown us all much honour. He was of very good cheer. . . . I shall ever have cause to regard him as my best of friends." So that was also the impression he could create, not merely of politeness, with concomitant bows and flatteries, but of laughter, and being at his ease, and in his Austro-Bohemian tone of voice spinning yarns about his past. His life held tales in plenty.

What was the stuff of his dreams? Did he, with all the urgent business on hand, have time to dream? There is always time for dreams, whether when out riding (as he continued to do for as long as gout permitted) or during contemplation of his marvellous birds or at night when he lay sleepless. All his actions stemmed from his dreams. He had learned that he was capable of more, incomparably more, than others and that something in him made people obey. He wanted money, a great deal of money. Whatever he obtained, it was never enough. He wanted a domain which would be his own, where he could issue commands and whose centres would diffuse order and beauty. That he had now, but it was never entirely secure. Whether its extent was broad or narrow depended on perspective. Broad, as compared with the properties of mere vassals. Narrow, if likened to the lands of rulers. He wanted to be a man who had only equals, above him only the Emperor, this fanatical, indolent, mentally limited, yet shrewd and inevitable imperial Majesty. For the present there were still some below whom he stood. Perhaps he would be able to attain to their level; it was a matter of opportunity. Nobody, for all the progress made in astrology, could forecast that. The oracular pronouncements were so often indistinct, so full of ifs and buts. He had done well with the Habsburg dynasty, with the Church of Rome too, and he would stick to both, particularly since there was no choice any more. Loyalty paid off. Rebellion – he had seen how that paid off. And if there was one thing that was impossible, it was that he should ever return to the camp of the murdered, beaten, and humiliated Bohemians. Not that on this account his relationships with his compatriots, or former compatriots, ceased to preoccupy him. He was a Bohemian. If he was no longer that, he was properly speaking no longer anything other than himself, his dream of a kind that simply turned upon himself. He could join in a general cause, Habsburg's or the Empire's, but those were ties of mind and volition, not inherent.

At the outset already, in 1625, he had had mounted on the ceiling of his Prague palace's great banqueting-hall a painting which is still to be seen there today – the depiction of a victor in his triumphal chariot, drawn by four steeds through a light bank of clouds, a star shining above his head. Some say that it is a portrayal of him. Others argue that it is simply Phoebus. The Greek sun-god, albeit with a beard; a rarity. Maybe too it is Mars. If he who commissioned it really had himself in mind, it must have been in a moment of joyous self-confidence, effervescent high spirits, such as are not very characteristic in his case. "Character", as the epithet goes, though he was. And what a variety of mutually alien qualities rubbed shoulders there.

THE COURT

Wallenstein, it will be remembered, had in the early autumn of 1623 been raised to the status of Prince of the Empire. Let us be as strict in this matter as people in those days were. His elevation did not turn Friedland into a principality. It was perfectly possible personally to enjoy princely status without being possessed of property. Six months later, though, Friedland was "established, elevated, and confirmed as a principality peculiar". Soon the process was repeated at a stage higher. From June 1625 onwards Wallenstein was entitled to call himself Duke. A duke was more than a prince. Every duke was a prince, but not every prince was a duke. That made Friedland for practical purposes a duchy; in January 1627 legalization of the position ensued. The family settlement was that the tenant in tail, the "ruler of the House of Waldstein and Friedland", should be the Duke; his children bore the title "prince". This was apparently what Wallenstein had in mind when he disputed the right of Liechtenstein agnates to claim ducal status: "From my lord's letter I understand that all chancelleries have been instructed neither to extend the ducal title to those who simply bear the name of Liechtenstein nor to accept their use of it. That, in my opinion, is not enough. If justice is to be done, they must be forbidden their subscription of themselves as duke ... for it is prejudicial to me." He need not have been so deadly serious about the matter. Of the three new dukes, Liechtenstein, Wallenstein, and Eggenberg, he was at bottom the only real one. The other two had estates, not states. They were surrounded by no court and themselves were but courtiers. The Duke of Friedland, on the other hand, gradually assembled a court so graded, numerous, well-paid, and glittering that the Elector's embittered comment was that not one of them, neither King nor Emperor, had ever had one to compare. A provocation, undeniably, and dangerous too – a Bohemian baron, seven years earlier so small and obscure, seriously playing at being a monarch.

The nominal roll of his court was impressively long and meant to impress. The Lord High Steward, Count Liechtenstein; the Lord High Chamberlain, Count Harrach; the Lord High Equerry, Count Hardegg; his deputy, Lord von Breuner. Below these came no less than twenty-four chamberlains, including such resonant names as Solms, Limburg, Hoyos, and Khevenhüller. The domestic establishment functioned as a three-pronged instrument, with the kitchen, silver closet, and stablings sections each having its own staff hierarchy, such as master cook, assistant master cook, senior steward, senior table-setter, not to mention lower orders like wardrobe-keepers, court bakers, valets, musicians, doorkeepers, dancing masters, pages with their tutors, fencing masters, trumpeters, donkey-drivers, and letter-carriers. Finally there was the executioner, with his assistants, because a court composed of 899 individuals needed at all times, as much as a regiment of musketeers, to have on hand the man with axe and rope. At any rate 899 individuals at the zenith of Wallenstein's power. The figure's bulge derived from each of the top officials having a host of helpers. The lord high steward alone had forty-five. The kitchen section, with its French cooks, pastrycooks, roasting masters, ornamental gardeners, capon keepers, meat-carvers, bakers, pewter-scrubbers, scriveners, and controllers, had sixty-five. The section heads were moreover entitled to have at least as many horses as helpers. The ducal court, whether on the move or resident, consequently never managed with less than 1072 horses. It had to be looked after and, under the supervision of the major dignitaries, this was done by the master cook with his buyers, the butler, and the chief huntsman with his assistant huntsmen. Two good oxen, 20 sheep, 10 lambs, 4 calves, 1 good pig, 1 ton of butter, 40 young and 15 grown chickens, 600 small loaves of white bread, 400 small loaves of rye-bread, 8 barrels of good beer, 2 casks of Rhine wine, 4 pails of Franconian wine as well as 1 pound of saffron, 2 pounds of pepper, corresponding amounts of ginger, cloves, cinnamon, almonds, raisins, currants, candied lemon peel, olives, capers, lemons, oranges, coriander seeds, pistachios, ordinary gingerbread, and Nürnberg gingerbread, 20 pounds of white sugar, 20 pounds of kitchen sugar, ice, 10 pounds of soap, 6 pounds of starch, 2 wagons of coal, and wood according to need – so runs the list of haphazardly chosen items of kitchen requirements for a single day. The whole was consumed to the greater glory of one who contented himself with half a young pheasant, artichokes, strawberries of various breed, and a couple of beakers of pale ale. A rough estimate of the outlay, enormous in any case, requires an appreciation of the economic factors involved. All goods of a rare and sumptuous sort were expensive – silver table-ware from Genoa, tapestries from the Netherlands, carpets from Venice, gold-coloured leather wall-hangings, damask table-linen, light blue cloth, and crimson fabric from England for the lackeys and the pages who strutted in a blue-red livery, as well as finery of other kinds. But food and drink, expensive for the poor, was not expensive for the rich. When Wallenstein held court at Gitschin or Prague, it cost him little because he could draw on his estates for as many oxen, sheep, chickens, and as much beer he required. Labour, even of the most exclusive class, was cheap. Wallenstein had a reputation for being a punctual, open-handed paymaster. That explains the number of ancient aristocratic offspring who vied to serve him. For a thoroughbred he disembursed a thousand gulden. His Lord High Steward he gave two hundred, his Lord High Equerry a hundred, his chamberlains thirty gulden each per month. The vast majority of his 899 employees was glad to work for him or to stand about ceremonially in return for a roof over their heads, plentiful keep, and a gratuity. The entire establishment, in its red and blue and blue and gold array, including the horses and the carriages upholstered in red leather, did not cost the mint of money which a modern reader would suppose. The actual amounts are quite indeterminate, but an early historian who dealt carefully with documentary evidence states that Wallenstein during the first year of maintaining his princely household spent 1342 gulden, at a later date 4673 gulden per month. That assessment is certainly too low. In 1630 he requisitioned and received monthly from his bankers 20,000 taler solely for his court's food and drink, which would mean 240,000 taler or some 350,000 gulden per year. This figure comes fairly close to the estimate of a Prince Hohenlohe who at some place or other watched the entry of Wallenstein's cavalcade and concluded that such a show could not be put on for less than 200,000 imperial taler per annum. Alongside this military outlay has to be calculated the upkeep of his court at Prague (in charge of "The Lady" during the master's absence) and the building or reconstruction work on the palace at Gitschin and castles elsewhere, which never ceased. If to all this are added his wholesale purchases, generous gifts, and expenditure on bribery, Wallenstein can for his personal and secret political purposes – excluding his military budget – hardly have spent less than half a million taler per year. What does that signify? Well, let us take into consideration that he was regarded as a man of substance after his marriage into an overall fortune of 300,000 taler. Let us recall that ruling Duke of Saxe-Weimar who was, or had to be, satisfied with 11,000 gulden a year. And let us at this point take note of the fact that the Elector of Bavaria incurred for himself, for his by no means unpretentious court, for the administration of a state exceeding in area and population Wallenstein's duchy many times over, as well as for a war which he waged as a European power, costs amounting to 1,500,000 taler each year. Comparative figures like that help to put matters into perspective.

Why did Wallenstein insist on quite such pomp? From pleasure at orderly beauty amid chaos? Behind the ramparts of his park to enjoy protection from the vulgar, noisy world through his followers and silent, on tiptoe moving pages? To convince himself of his own power? To impress others, his former equals, and his new, uneasy, afflicted, and harassed subjects?

Whenever he and his court set out to take the waters, the selected spa was months beforehand thrown into a condition of nervously busy excitement akin to that of an ant-heap. On such occasions the Duke of Friedland did not have a suite, an inn, or several inns, but the whole town reserved on his behalf. The famous Karlsbad shall serve as an example. The specific date does not matter.

On 4 March the ducal commissary for the court's quartering affairs requisitions for a week after Easter "almost all the lodgings on the Market Square", including for the use of Wallenstein and his immediate entourage two houses which belong to an attorney's widow. On 5 March the town council meets and after thorough discussion decides that with the utmost dispatch all chimneys shall be swept and, if defective, repaired; dunghills, particularly that in the market square, cobbles, and rubble shall be removed; drains and sewers shall be cleaned; dogs are to be kept day and night locked indoors, "so that no complaint shall be caused through their misconduct and baying"; every citizen shall be on his guard, behave with due diffidence, and especially during the Duke's stay abstain from drinking to excess; nocturnal discharge from windows is strictly forbidden; and the attorney's widow shall see to it that in her two houses she has in all haste everything done to facilitate the distinguished guest's necessary comfort. Tension rises as, almost a month after the date announced, Wallenstein still does not come, although paying for the reservations made. It is the beginning of May before he finally arrives. Into and through the spa moves a lengthy procession of fifty carriages each drawn by six horses, forty-four horse vehicles for the kitchen section, plus ten baggage-wagons each drawn by six horses. The coach which is the cynosure of all eyes halts in front of the widow's house. The square has earlier been lined with halberdiers and enclosed with chains. In the vicinity wait the mayor and council, dressed in all their finery, not quite certain how to behave; the mayor has at all events prepared an address. But he who now descends somewhat laboriously from the coach, this tall, sallow-complexioned nobleman leaning on the arm of his cousin, Count Max, raises briefly and just once his hat with a red feather, then disappears behind the Lord High Steward hurrying ahead of him into the house. A few more lords who, it is whispered, are respectively Count Berchtold, Max's brother, immensely wealthy old Trčka, and young Trčka follow. Soon the curtains in the rooms on the first floor can be seen drawn; His Princely Grace must presumably rest after the long journey. Police are deployed and chase citizens from the surrounding streets. The boots of the guards marching up and down are wrapped in sackcloth. Silence falls upon the market square. . . . A normal excursion to a spa, not a large-scale entry, "only half the princely household". Yet imposing enough to show people who it is that will now for three weeks take the waters here. And it has to be demonstrated again and again. A monarchy which like a magic castle has arisen out of nothing and like such could again vanish into nothing must constantly re-assert itself through the sheer tangibility of its manifestation. It really is, and is for keeps – Envy Defying.

THE DUCHY

Lord von Wolkenstein, Habsburg financial official, felt impelled to compose a memorial. Not to the Emperor, because that would probably be hopeless, but to the Emperor's son, the young and ambitious Prince Ferdinand, King-designate of Bohemia and Hungary. The memorial dealt with the condition of Bohemia. More properly, with the condition of the two Bohemias, for it could no longer be concealed that Bohemia was divided into two parts, a *terra deserta* and a *terra felix*. How pleasurable it would have been if he, the memorialist, could most humbly have accounted the *terra felix* a portion of His Royal Majesty's realms. Alas, he could not. "The contrary prevails." In that part of the country where the King was still king there could nowhere be seen anything but ruination of buildings on a Trojan, devastation of forests on an Ethiopian scale. "Towns, precious castles, markets, villages – all tumble down and

the so cherished, fruitful soil is overgrown with thistle and thorns."
Whole towns were depopulated. In Prague alone almost 1400 houses
stood desolate. In Leitmeritz it was difficult to find thirty houses intact.
Was it any wonder that the fiscal authorities of the royal cities, formerly
such gems, had no prospects of revenue from them? As for the *terra
felix*, the official continued, that, as was well known, belonged "to the
praiseworthy and victorious prince and lord, Lord Albrecht, Duke of
Friedland, and his hereditarily joined and maritally related *consanguineis*"
by which he must have meant to refer to Count Max and the two Trčkas
whose properties lay close to as well as right inside the duchy. "To
proceed *ad subjectam materiam*, in this part a general state of peace,
delectable and beneficial, predominates. The military is not in the least
allowed passage, and still less billeting in any wise, whereby not only are
the vassals left to their undisturbed existence, but it daily elevates the
entire land to marked betterment and everything is to be found in a
condition of greatest prosperity." The administration was economically
so well organized that "it is no matter for surprise that this pricely
status has in such brief time so powerfully and flourishingly taken root.
Not to be doubted but that this Friedland *status* will shortly stretch even
to the Elbe." And thus His Royal Majesty was losing, bit by bit, the finest
domains, many thousands of vassals, and an annual income of millions,
all of which were accruing to the *statui Friedlandico* and being abstracted
from His Own Noble Kingdom in such manner that, if things went a
little further, the ruling house would have nothing left to it other than a
stretch of desert and an impotent title. The memorial dates from the
year 1633. It delineates the *terra deserta*'s plight in perhaps stronger
terms than it would have done in 1625, but its description of the
state of affairs in the fairy-tale duchy is certainly no more rosy than
they already were in that same year. On the contrary. For various
reasons Friedland in 1633 was not as happily off as it had been eight
years earlier.

Friedland's creator was so often called "the Friedlander" by his
contemporaries that the ignorant believed it to be his cognomen –
"General Friedlander". A strange name derived from a place that until
recently had been simply that of an unknown spot on the northern
border of Bohemia. People sensed what Friedland meant to Wallenstein
– his most treasured invention, his hearth, his pride, his self-manifesta-
tion. And the main source of his wealth. Friedland had to furnish him
with the money and the materials to wage war. In Friedland he demonstrated what till then public finance and administration had been unaware

of – that war can enrich a country provided that it is employed in it, but is not the scene of hostilities, and that all its productive resources are entirely harnessed to war production.

Here a glance at the duchy's organization.

At the head of it, deputizing for the Duke who was absent most of the time, stood the Governor. From 1625 until 1631 he was that Gerhard von Taxis who in 1608 requested Kepler to cast his own and Wallenstein's horoscope and had since, with certain interruptions, remained an agent of the slowly rising star. His antecedents were hazy. Whether he was entitled to call himself "von Taxis" is a matter of doubt. Seeing that he was now Governor, Wallenstein procured him baronial status, the least that by way of rank the Duke's senior representative must be. That for six years Taxis was able to hold his position, as interesting and lucrative as it was dangerous, speaks for his adroitness. With the Duke far away, in Hungary, Mecklenburg, or Jutland, correspondence took weeks during which the Governor had to act on his own initiative. That was precisely what Wallenstein expected. "Do not later excuse yourself that it was not the Chamber's wish, for you know that it has indeed to tender advice, but that you must decide." Was it always possible to tell which moves would meet with his formidable master's approval? In spite of all his cunning and experience, things would ultimately turn out badly for Taxis.

Below the Governor were the two central authorities, Chamber and Chancellery. Constituted on a collegiate basis, their respective chairmen were the Governor and the Chancellor. Chamber councillors managed or controlled the economy and collected the revenues; Chancellery lawyers sat and passed judgements in common. A clear separation between administration and justice. In regard to the latter, Wallenstein's aim was complete severance between Bohemia's and his own. This bold design was achieved in 1627 when the Emperor conceded "the institution of a law and tribunal peculiar". Hereafter no subject of Wallenstein could appeal to or be summoned before a royal court outside Friedland's border. The Duke himself, as an imperial prince, could still in theory be required to appear in front of the Aulic Council or the *Reichskammergericht* and, as a vassal of the Bohemian crown, a royal court. Forms without sanction. His objective, pursued with utmost discretion, was the division of Friedland from Bohemia, the *terra felix* from the *terra deserta*. After 1627 it had for all practical purposes been achieved.

The ducal properties, the fat of the land concentrated into large-scale centrally administered estates and the possession of the ruling house in

perpetuity, were subordinate to the Chamber. At the apogee of Wallenstein's power there were twenty-four such estates, each with a bailiff
responsible for the health of their men and beasts, sowing and reaping,
brewing and storage, buying and selling, performance and compliance.
The bailiffs were the Chamber's employees and had each week to render
an account, once a year to report in person. In addition they had over
them a Chief Bailiff, a kind of inspector-general but not a member of the
Chamber: "Seeing that the Chamber is to adjudge upon his commission
and omission, it is not proper that he shall sit upon the Chamber's
board." The motive is palpable – Chamber and Chief Bailiff are to act as
mutual observers.

Then there were the mesne fiefs; lands, villages, and castles which
Wallenstein sold and in the course of years re-sold or bestowed but
always in such manner as to remain their liege-lord. The practical effect
was the Duke's retention of certain rights, particularly in respect of
game preserves, and reversion by escheat if the tenant did not fulfil the
terms of his tenure, died without direct heirs or intestate, or failed in the
obligation to discharge his bill of enfeoffment through payment of a fee
indicative of his vassalage. Many tenants, to the detriment of their
heirs, did neglect this errand to the Chancellery. "From your letter I
learn that Garosch has died *ab intestato* and that you have had his
holdings sequestered. There you have done rightly, for most of my
tenants have not discharged their bill of enfeoffment with the Chancellery. Therefore I bid you, if one or other of them shall depart this
life, leave sons, and not have discharged his bill of enfeoffment, so shall
you enter upon aforesaid holdings, for it contravenes my will that this
should take root and the bill of enfeoffment lie undischarged, as though
'twere not respected, at the Chancellery." There was clearly something
more to the game, a legal or political stake. Otherwise of what consequence would it have been to him, immensely rich as he was, the fee on
this or that petty holding? No, people were simply not to be allowed to
suppose that his decrees were to be trifled with or that perhaps the entire
dukedom was a trifling matter. These vassals were his tenants, just as he
was the Emperor's vassal and tenant. The association of ideas was of
utmost importance to him.

There were six Waldsteins among the holders of these mesne fiefs,
starting with Count Max. Their powerful relative would not tolerate any
sort of impertinence on the part of these cognates. "Distrain upon that
frivolous sozzler, Zdenko von Waldstein, the amount that he owes for
beer and refuses to pay." His court and administrative officials also

became land-holders on such terms. So did numerous of his officers (whom he thereby tried to bind to himself twice over), nobles who formerly already had been resident in these parts, burgesses, and, last but not least, members of the spiritual orders, Jesuits, Carthusians, Augustinians. They were to cause him more vexation than satisfaction, but at no point was either party, duke or clergy, prepared to renounce the other.

In a different class were the towns. There were such as were to be counted as mesne fiefs, and such, more important ones like Gitschin, Friedland, Böhmisch-Leipa, Arnau, Aicha, Turnau, Weisswasser, and Reichenberg, which were raised successively to the status of free ducal towns. They had their mayors and corporations, owned real property, and were even allowed, as in the case of Gitschin, to become feudatories. A political stake, this too. The conferment of privileges on their communes was meant to make the burgesses proud of their state and turn them into Friedland patriots. They were moreover to constitute a free Estate. Popular representation through Estates was to be the consummation of the whole structure. A Wallenstein letter of 1632 shows that he had "some years ago" instructed his Chancellor to draw up a constitution. The draft foresaw three Estates: clergy, nobility, and municipal communes. "The duty of these three Estates is that, as often as general exigency demands, they shall upon Our writ obediently appear through their representatives to the Diet which shall on each occasion be held in Our city of Gitschin in the place appointed by Us, hear the Diet's proposition, deliberate and resolve upon it, with each Estate invested for such consultations with a collegiate vote." A means to political integration, not a Magna Charta for Estates such as the 1618 rebels dreamt of. Wallenstein's sympathies for aspirations of that calibre could be enlisted as little now as then.

When his nobility approached him with a petition which sounded unseemly in his ears, they were advised that they would be guilty of self-deception if they fancied themselves able to turn Friedland "into a free republic, as it were". For the future they should choose a befitting tone towards authority or it would be all over with their "highly extolled liberty".

In the palace at Gitschin visitors are shown a two-tiered hall where the Estates should have assembled. But, the guide explains, "Wallenstein lacked the time to implement the plan" – a phrase of frequent recurrence in his capital.

THE ECONOMY

He is the great economist of his day – *il grand economo*, as one of his early biographers calls him. Neither the largest nor the smallest matter is spared the spur of his determination, whether it concerns the magnificence of the towns he builds or the yield that cows must annually furnish – in the lowlands a ton of butter and four hundredweight of cheese between five of them, in the mountainous regions six. That is what he enjoins, and woe betide the bailiff who does not adhere to the regulation.

He rules over wooded mountains, medium altitudes, and plains. Each region has its part to play. The mountains provide timber, game, and pastures for cattle and sheep; the medium altitudes, oats and rye; the plains, barley and wheat, fruit and hops, flax and hemp. Mines supply silver, copper, lead, tin, and iron. Mill-wheels are turned by running waters, fish are bred in still ones. Towns are the sire of industry, handicrafts, and trade; villages, of cottage labour. No room for idlers in this state. Vagrants are apprehended, cleansed, clothed, and forced to work or, if no longer fit enough, lodged in almshouses. The guiding principle is that everything capable of being produced inside the country shall be produced there and that it is the crafts in which it lacks experience, not their products, that shall be imported.

To have artisans brought from Parma who are specialists in manufacture of the city's cheese is cheaper than to have this article transported from Italy. To have a French tailor in Gitschin is cheaper than to order court costumes from Paris. "The cloth for the clothes and the shoes too are to be bought in the duchy; I wish no other interest to prevail than that the money for wares finds use among its people." "I would sooner that Friedlanders have it than outsiders rob me." The phrase is somewhat more magnanimous than genuine because nobody would be allowed to rob him. Pheasant-keepers suspected of delivering the leaner birds to the court kitchen and secretly selling the fatter ones are threatened with the gallows, whereas the discoverer of the crime will receive a hundred gulden. A brewer expiates with a hundred strokes of the rod the bad taste his beer left in His Princely Grace's mouth.

An *Economic System*, published in 1628, lays down in twenty-one articles concocted by expert hand – "On Grain", "On Flax", "On Orchards" – how work is to proceed everywhere. More thoroughly, more productively, and under more rigid superintendence. Arable land may not lie fallow, no area may become derelict, only the best seed may be sown, the crop from such and such soil must be so and so. A similar note is struck in all the articles. Hay being needed for the constantly growing number of horses, substitute fodder like malt refuse, leaves, and rushes must be obtained for stall-feeding cattle. No by-product may be left unturned to account. Five times the quantity of beer is brewed in the duchy than prior to Wallenstein's time; hops cultivation has therefore to be forced. Not enough flax can be harvested to meet the requirements of the spinning and weaving guilds and the cottage workers. Not enough sheep can be shorn to supply sufficient wool for tunics. Not enough trees can be felled for construction in the towns and props for the mines whose iron ore is needed for cannon-balls, entrenching tools, and horseshoes. Never can enough be grown, enough produced. The sternly supervised, incentive-stimulated and penalty-driven working collective that is the Duchy of Friedland comes near to bursting at the seams. More timber is demanded of the woods than the foresters can answer for. The farms have to accommodate more cattle than there is fodder or stabling available because the carpenters are otherwise engaged. The iron output is inadequate to meet the claims on it for armaments, building machines, fire-guards, bird cages, and conduits for fountains and grottoed bathing pools. To an increasing degree the economy is on a war footing and engaged in the production of war essentials: meat, bread, biscuits, beer; uniforms, stockings, boots; weapons, powder, and shot. It was not so at the outset, only after autumn 1625, but it explains the insatiability of the demand. What indeed will not be needed when the commander-in-chief is at the same time his army's food, dress, and armaments purveyor?

On the other hand the economic miracle that is Friedland must not be thought explicable purely in terms of war or viewed as based exclusively on that condition. It is not even certain whether the state's founder ever waged war gladly or would not rather have dwelt in peace amidst his finest creation. What, after a brief interval, again drove him afar and into danger has yet to be narrated. But his determination to turn Friedland into something worth while that would arouse the world's admiration existed already before, in the summer of 1625, he became the Emperor's principal commander and would in any case have been fulfilled. Consequently too the arts of peace were continued in the midst of war: the erection of sumptuous buildings as well as such as were of utilitarian kind and the pursuit of refined crafts like glass-making, paper-making, and ceramics. For whatever the army did not take delivery of, butter, for instance, wholesalers with a market in Prague and farther afield were to be found. Whatever could not be sold with profit abroad had to be consumed at home, whether the Duke's subjects liked it or not. Its quality would see to it that their hands were voluntarily forced.

Beer is one example. The licence to brew had been the Estates', nobles and towns alike, most lucrative source of income. Wallenstein, wherever his writ ran, took it from them by a stroke of the pen until such time as he had got his state together. Henceforward brewing was a ducal monopoly. Henceforward Friedlanders were not allowed to drink other than ducal beer except "if they travel, when now and then a draught must at need be quaffed, though otherwise positively not". As for the penalties attaching to consumption of non-Wallenstein beer, they amounted to no less than one hundred talers for the publican and a thousand ducats for the village's feudal lord who might be accessory to the fact.

A detail. But Wallenstein's annual revenue from his duchy, in round figures seven hundred thousand gulden, was compounded of a multitude of items. Out of the many small sums grew the aggregates he needed in order to be able to spend them again as quickly as possible. In this context the least amount could as little afford to be neglected as the largest.

No miner himself, Wallenstein can none the less be deemed a patron of mining in so far as such existed in his day. Whatever may lie beneath the soil by way of ores, gold, copper, silver, lead, tin, iron, has to be found, excavated, put to use. The ownership and operation arrangements vary. There are mines which are the Duke's own property and he alone exploits, others which he leases, still others in which he participates on a kind of consortium basis. The hallmark of all his undertakings, employment of experts, applies equally to his mine-working and metallurgical enterprises. The experts are in this case drawn mainly from Italy. The methods include more rigorous extraction processes so as to cause something to be yet gained from what has formerly been discarded as barren rock. The pay is high and premiums are awarded as incentive. Application or sale of the yields is prompt. A special mining office administers this important sector of industry.

Gold, the dream of all princes, is rarely discovered. Silver manifests itself in rather more considerable quantities – for a single year the value of the workings runs to 17,000 gulden the preponderant part of which admittedly is engulfed by production costs, with an outlay of 6000 gulden alone on wages. On copper and tin there is some return. The most precious metal is iron, although not so much in cash value. For the lease to two Italian ironmasters of the mine and foundry at Raspenau near Friedland, in whose neighbourhood today still or today again the blast furnaces can be seen standing against the skyline, Wallenstein receives annually 2400 gulden, a couple of drops in the ocean of those 700,000 gulden he pockets every year. No, indigenous iron is an asset other than of straightforward monetary value. The Duke-General is his lessees' sole purchaser at prices over which we may assume that he also has some say. What he builds up all around Raspenau, and then extends to the area of the neighbouring towns Reichenberg and Böhmisch-Leipa, is an enormous armaments smithy. Herein again lies profit potentiality because the army he leads is never his own, for all that towards the end he will in deplorable error fancy it to be such; it is the Emperor's. Whatever he supplies to the army, cannon-balls or biscuits, account is kept of it and sooner or later the Emperor must pay. If not in money, which he does not have, then in money's worth. So ultimately the entire Friedland war economy is a means to expansion of the grand economist's power. The dukedom had to produce duchies.

It was not what he had originally purposed. Instead the unpredictable course of things brought it with them. Originally it had been an end in itself, and the most agreeable achievements are always those which are related to a self-sufficient end. The promotion of trade and communications by road construction, the standardization of weights and measures, a rapid mounted postal service, removal of internal customs barriers to the state's borders, toleration for Jews ("It pleases me to hear that the Jew wishes to traffic at Gitschin; let him"), the encouragement of trade in general through his court's requirements of livery, candles, food, drink, and their appurtenant receptacles, the straining of every nerve and the fulfilment of every moment with activity, the ferreting out of every possible profit. A substance has been found in the neighbourhood of Jeseney, reports the Governor to the Duke, which is called cinnabar and (he adds in explanation) "is red in colour". In the margin of the letter Wallenstein scrawls, "Take me not for such a fool. I know very well what cinnabar is. Let it work for me."

THIS TIME GOOD MONEY

He has the right to coin money, in gold and silver, which will carry his likeness, coat of arms, and mint-master's mark. It must, though, accord in size, fineness, crude weight, value, constituents, final weight with the ordinances of the imperial mint. He has the right – that is to say, he has arrogated it to himself since acquisition of the ducal title. Not until 1628 is he formally invested with the *jus monetandi* which he has long practised.

The mint at Gitschin is managed under Wallenstein's control. Another, subsequently established at Sagan, he leases. To him, so he claims, the matter is simply one of his repute, of letting the world know in gold and silver that he is an imperial prince, acquaint itself with his features, full face, half-face, and profile, and see how he wears his hair and beard, how stern he looks. An opportunity also for it to familiarize itself with his armorial bearings and the growing dominion that they represent. First, the Waldstein lions and Friedland eagle; later, the crowned buffalo head with antlers and nose-rings, betokening Mecklenburg, and an angel, signifying Sagan.

Coins spread renown, particularly if they are not debased. That is here the case, with a single exception. In 1629 experts at Dresden discover that the Friedland ducats for the current year do not correspond precisely to their face value. The mint-master is immediately thrown into jail and subsequently expelled.

This is not an enterprise which Wallenstein regards as a source of profit for himself, much less his officials. On one occasion he says that he is prepared "not only to have no advantage from it, but to sustain a loss", on another that he seeks no gain, but desires no detriment. On the early taler issues the Governor has the motto *Dominus Meus Protector* engraved. What, he is asked, can have put it into his head "when my device is *Invita Invidia*? Therefore omit the first and make it thus". Two days later there is a change of mind. "In my foregoing letter I wrote that you should place upon the reverse of my coin the device that I bear, namely *Invita Invidia*. Now I have bethought me otherwise and, whereas upon the obverse stands *Albertus D G Dux Fridlandiae,* let upon the reverse stand *Sac. Imperii princeps* and omit *Invita Invidia*." But it is to be done quickly, the mint-master is to deliver one thousand gold ducats a month, the purchase of silver for gulden and half-gulden is to proceed even if the prices paid are higher than those acceptable to the Royal Chamber at Prague. The Chamber regards this as annoying competition and accuses the Duke of driving up the rate of silver; parity must obtain not only in respect of the coins, but in the metal's purchase price too. Wallenstein does not allow such obstacles to block his path. Having decided to avail himself of his privilege, it must go ahead *in furia.* "See that the minting proceeds and that I have no reason for reproof. It stinks in my nostrils to hear how what I have commanded is not compiled with. I am not accustomed to uttering orders more than once." In 1633 he demands delivery of forty thousand ducats all at once, then as many as a hundred thousand. That is well beyond the realm of possibility.

Just as it requires hard work to construct a state where there was previously none, so the foundation of a new coinage system runs into a variety of difficulties. From where is the equipment to be obtained? Mainly Prague, which can also furnish the essential experience. Where is the metallurgical artist capable of portraying the Duke's features impressively and with some degree of verisimilitude? The one first chosen engraves them so horribly that the die has to be discarded. Wallenstein attaches importance to his appearance on the coins. He is right. In a single year the mint at Sagan issues 682,000 groschen. They will pass through millions of hands. Millions of eyes, precisely because they are new, will scrutinize them.

A few examples of the different denominations, ten and five ducat pieces, double ducats and ducats, double taler and taler, gulden, half-gulden, and groschen have survived and can be seen in the coin collections at Munich, Prague, Vienna, Zurich, and elsewhere. But there are not many of them, for this coinage was too good. Consequently they found their way into the crucible again, to be multiplied and embellished there with other portrayals. And, as likely as not, to obliterate as far as possible remembrance of the first and last Duke of Friedland. The residue were in such demand by collectors that a shrewd nineteenth-century operator had the idea of forging Wallenstein specie. Groschen of the years 1629, 1630 and 1632 are particularly to be bewared of.

PATRON OF BUILDING

Wallenstein, had he been of single-minded purpose, would have behaved in relation to Prague as he wanted Friedland to stand in relation to Bohemia. He would, in other words, have severed his connection with the capital. But he had no centre of gravity, not even his favourite creation served him as such, and he who was to collect dukedoms as a real estate speculator collects properties saw no incompatibility between his feeling of sovereignty and living as a vassal of the King, albeit the greatest of kings, in the shadow of the Hradschin. Today still "Friedland House", subsequently called the Waldstein Palace, remains an adornment of the Mala Strana (Little Quarter).

The purchase of houses, twenty-five in all, to make room for this structure began soon after the battle of the White Mountain, much to the annoyance of Wilhelm Slawata who not only begrudged the loss of so many excellent tax-payers but also alleged that his cousin shamelessly commandeered soldiers as construction workers. If true, there was worse employment on which they could have been engaged. The architects were Italian. First, a certain Spezza, then one by the name of Pieroni who also did well at Gitschin. By 1626 the main, residential tract was complete in so far as anything that Wallenstein undertook was ever complete. He was for ever making improvements, for ever adding. In 1634 work on Friedland House or its annexes was still continuing.

Its front is a Bohemian version of contemporary Italian style, copied from the Palazzo Farnese, but, according to experts, on less slender lines and, owing to the heaviness of the roof, the closeness of the windows to one another – eighteen of them on each of the two storeys – and the thrusting interposition of the portal, squatter. On an amateur the effect is pleasing and by no means leaves an impression of excess or defiance as the later Czernin Palace does. Its real size is not realized until the interior courtyards and the park have been examined. Only the façade can be seen from the square in which it stands; winding lanes which flank it hide the rest from view.

The house was no ordinary nobleman's mansion, a slice of autonomous territory rather, amidst the patchwork of the city a miniature realm enclosed by outbuildings and a park wall like a circumvallation. When Wallenstein's coach had rolled into the courtyard to the left of the front, he had all that he needed – a chapel, a riding-ground at the lower end of the park, and (the absolute essential) a bathing pool, in a grotto bedizened with crystals, shells, and stalactites, as well as walks between statues and fountains. There was even a covered way to the adjoining monastery of St Thomas. To imagine him moving freely through the city, cheered by his fellow-citizens, is impossible. He had no fellow-citizens, he was probably detested. He ruled over the multitude without coming into contact with it, ruled so as not to have to come into contact with it. We cannot even properly visualize him as host, not as one who with a smile of welcome received guests who were his equals. The state rooms must have served some purpose, but a detailed description of their use is rare. Certainly for the reception of ambassadors, imperial ministers, delegations come to woo or plead, and in any event for family festivities. Nevertheless in the last resort the palace, its stonework, gilt leather hung halls, gardens, cool courtyards and splashing waters, was there "for me", those two words which so often recur in his written orders.

At Gitschin, where he was his own master, not the imperial sheriff, things were different, as they also were in the lands that he subsequently acquired. Everywhere, of course, castles, pleasances, and zoos had to be set aside "for me". Yet at Gitschin, while the whole town and the whole countryside became his plaything, that was not only to the enjoyment of the prince, but his subjects' too, and their descendants' today still. The town had less than two hundred houses when his reign began. There were five hundred when his assassination bloodily put paid to all plans. From a backward peasant community, to whose dung-heaps in front of their homes all contributed, it had turned into a shiny capital and a centre for crafts and commerce. Late, though, in Wallenstein's life. Always torn between various scenes of activity and always tempted or forced to go far afield, he was at first content with simple repairs to the dilapidated Smiřický mansion. Only "sundry rooms" were to be restored to the degree that "stench does not fill the air". He wanted moreover a stream, "fairly big", to flow through the garden. More costly plans followed, but they underwent reduction when in 1627 the duchy of Sagan fell into his lap and he seemed temporarily to prefer his Silesian to his Bohemian seat. "Meanwhile, as it is not my intent to build so much at Gitschin, I bid you see that all the burgesses so array their houses that they resemble citizens', not peasants', habitations." At Sagan even more houses than at Prague, close on eighty, were demolished for the erection of a castle which, according to Thomas Carve, would have proved the world's eighth wonder. Construction never proceeded beyond the foundation-walls. None the less these are sufficient to indicate that what its begetter had in mind would have proved more of a bombardment-resistant, moated citadel than placid residence. Wallenstein's mind switched back from Sagan to Gitschin, but, a year later, with the duchy of Mecklenburg conferred on him, he proposed to shift his capital in a northerly direction – "I am resolved to build at Wismar the palace that I had meant to build at Gitschin" – and he did not transform his earliest acquisition into a teeming construction site until, with Mecklenburg again lost to him, he was living in enforced retirement. During the warmer seasons of the year five thousand carters, shovellers, masons, tilers, plumbers, stucco-workers, and decorators are said to have been simultaneously engaged there. The new palace remained even more incomplete than the one at Prague, but it was at least habitable. Its original appearance, with three towers, was different from how it now looks, due to alterations in the eighteenth century. On the other hand the square before it, as we can see from old prints, had in Wallenstein's day exactly the same aspect as in our own, a spacious quadrilateral bordered on each side by Late Renaissance, gabled houses. The town's new founding-father loved homogeneity. For Sagan he ordained that "they are to see that the house-fronts which they build there shall be fabricated of stone or brick, executed finely and neatly". I think that he had two models in mind, Nové Meso in Bohemia, not far from Nachod, and Telč in Moravia. Both had been laid out by their respective owners with the most splendid sense of symmetry. They are an even more delightful sight than Gitschin. The latter is however bigger, and big is what Wallenstein wanted it to be, another Prague, consisting like Prague of three towns, the seat of a bishop and a university. He wanted the Iser, the duchy's river, to flow through the city and, had a start been made on digging its channel, would doubtless have demanded that this be finished *in furia* without the loss of more than several minutes. Matters did not get that far. There were limits to what he, whose life had not seriously begun before he was nearing the end of his thirties, who died at fifty and spent most of this solitarily glittering decade in distant theatres of war, could achieve. Of his designs a torso remains – the town with its two noble principal buildings, the palace and the college, the cathedral, the main square, the suburbs, the avenue of lime trees between the town and the Carthusian monastery or, more accurately, between the stablings, pleasure-garden and town, for there was not time to bring the avenue quite as far as the monastery. Here is the instruction, dated 1632, to the municipal building supervisor: "We doubt not that you will make your zealous concern what We have ordered for the buildings at Gitschin, in particular to advance what is needful upon the palace work. . . . Touching the Capuchin monastery, We adhere to Our wish that this shall not stand within the city, but one for the Dominicans in its place, and that for the Capuchins one be built without the city where a traveller takes the road to Aulowitz. You will then make this your utmost concern, as also to undertake all the dismantlements, so that when We come at the beginning of the impending month of April you will be able to show Us these. . . . No less than with the lime trees which line the way, those in the garden shall be replaced, if they perish through winter, with others and these, that they may grow straight and furnish a fine vista, shall be left to attain their height unimpeded. Also urge upon Our Chamber that, as We have heretofore ordered that at all times a guard shall be appointed to prevent the spoliation of the lime trees by the folk coming from the city, this same be done. You will in like wise attend to it that the tiles are diligently baked, so that everywhere in the town can the houses be roofed with tiles, in particular as it is Our desire that nowhere shall shingle roofs obtain." Wallenstein was preparing for his decisive battle with the King of Sweden when he penned this letter. It is much longer, sterner in tone, and imbued with sensitive solicitude than our quotation indicates.

Whoever wished to stand well with him built, or had to build, at Gitschin. Such included his Waldstein cousins, his young brother-in-law Adam Trčka – although his castle Opočno was situated quite near – and the gentlemen of his court. The citizens were among those who had to build there or "His Princely Grace will expel them". Later he decided "in no way to force the burghers to build better houses, but to have assessed the old houses of those who do not want to build, pay them, and at ducal expense have others erected there". As for those who were ready to do so of their own accord, they should be loaned funds and receive materials at a cheap rate. Sanitation was an ever recurrent subject. Water was to be laid through the town. The "squares and streets are to be cleansed of dung and filth". His orders were issued from afar, without hope of seeing his elected home and creation either that month or that year. About the town and castle of Friedland, as though having an inward aversion to the place whose name he bore, he hardly bothered, did not truly bother at all, and took up quarters there no more than fleetingly a couple of times. Otherwise he had extensions, modernizations, and embellishments made whenever his eye fell upon a castle or palace belonging to him if it appealed to his sense of beauty. Such were Lämberg, not far from Friedland, and Castle Kost, all alone and barely defensible in an entrancing valley of eastern Bohemia. He would never live there, but it was a source of comfort to him to learn that his behest was being fulfilled.

> Gladly do I recall the olden days.
> His happiness lay as yet in building. . . .

Schiller put the words into his duchess's mouth. The truth is that his happiness in building was as great at later date as at earlier. Death did not strike him down while he was busy waging war. At the time he was slain he hardly waged war any longer and his wish was for peace. He wanted to go on building.

ECCLESIASTICAL AFFAIRS

In vanquished Bohemia the official venture called by Protestant historians "the Counter-Reformation", but by those who effected it "the Reformation", proceeded only gradually by way of jerks and jolts. When imperial fortunes of war wavered, fear of a "general uprising" put a brake on the undertaking. Had the Transylvanian, Mansfeld, and the mad Halberstadter been once more driven back into their haunts and an anti-Habsburg coalition again suffered shipwreck, the enterprise would have acquired fresh impetus. The objective was clear. As previously in Styria, no non-Catholic, whether Calvinist or Lutheran, pastor or layman, nobleman or commoner, was to be allowed to remain in the country. Certain essential considerations, especially in regard to Saxony, slowed progress and protracted fulfilment over a period of some eight years after the battle of the White Mountain. Not until 1628 was so great a lord as Wilhelm Kinsky, Wallenstein's relation who made no secret of his Lutheranism, forced to seek residence in Saxony. He was allowed to keep his estates in the neighbourhood of Teplitz, draw his income from them, and occasionally obtained restricted permission to visit his home. A very wealthy man with connections in high and top places will even in exile be better off than most of his fellow-refugees.

Heretical clergy could be expelled, with Lutherans last in the line. For laymen the lie of the land was different. The most clouded ministerial gaze, including that of Bohemia's regent, Prince Liechtenstein, whose gaze we know was not so clouded, could perceive the valuelessness of a depopulated state. Liechtenstein would have preferred to accomplish the sacred task more tardily and without all too rigorous consistency. The piety of the Emperor had unfortunately decided otherwise, the Nuncio Caraffa preached acceleration without attention to mundane interests, and a reform commission not lacking in defenestrated Privy Councillor Martinitz's membership received instruction to take all action necessary. It hit on two methods of procedure – benevolent instruction or, failing success by reason of the catechumen's spiteful obduracy, force. The instruction, given in churches or town halls by delegated divines, was shrewdly allowed to concede many a point, such as that the widespread profligacy of the Roman clergy in Bohemia could not be denied. But what was to have been expected of a land wherein for two hundred years heresy had prevailed? The issues were twofold: salvation of souls and the prevention of fresh rebellions catastrophic, like that of 1618, for the country. That was what those *in statu pupillari* were invited to bear in mind. If after reasonable reprieve they proved still unwilling to entertain the idea, other approaches were brought into play – fines, withdrawal of licence to trade, the requisition of billets. Whole regiments were diverted to Bohemia for the last purpose, a plague which (according to expert opinion) would illumine the insight of their involuntary hosts.

Members of the Society of Jesus were among the most eager to devote themselves to the task of reformation. Their paucity was alleviated by reinforcements from Italy, Spain, France, and the Netherlands. Bohemia, hitherto linked to Austria in the Society's organization, was raised to the status of an independent province of the Order. New schools, new academies were founded by the Society and it succeeded in bringing under its wing the ancient Carolina, the capital's Charles University, Bohemia's pride, and merging it with its own Prague academy into a single establishment, henceforward to be called the Carolina-Ferdinandea. The step did not prove feasible without a long inter-Catholic altercation because, as usually happens even among the most pious of mankind, the powerful human constellation seeking to convert Bohemia broke in two parties, one with traditional Catholic, Roman, and universalist sympathies, the other with a novel Catholic, politically and dynastically centred outlook not oblivious of its own interest. This was the party of the Jesuits. On their side they had the court at Vienna and the Emperor. The latter now trusted his confessor, Father Lamormaini, to the point of blind obedience, and all archdukes were urged by him to appoint their own confessors from the ranks of the Society. The opposition party rallied to Caraffa. "What is certain", the Nuncio wrote to Rome, "is that the Jesuits, thanks to the unimaginable favour granted them by the Emperor, have achieved a position of influence which transcends all other Orders and excludes these from the exercise of any effect upon matters of political or spiritual weight with the Jesuits. Their sway is not confined to ascendancy over the Orders, but extends to all. They will enter into contest with the most prominent minister if their will be not done. . . . One of the most important and trusted ministers, Eggenberg, has recently told me that the great favour shown the Jesuits by the Emperor will lead to their undoing." Father Lamormaini, the report continued, had behaved to the Nuncio with a chilly impertinence only too clearly demonstrative of his true sentiments towards Rome and the Holy Father. . . . On the side of the Nuncio was Wallenstein's brother-in-law, Cardinal Harrach, the young Archbishop

of Prague, in the main probably because he felt his own authority
infringed by the spiritual and secular presumptions of the Jesuits. For
all that he belonged to the Vienna court coterie, Harrach struggled
stoutly against the Jesuit take-over of the Charles University. His
argument, to no purpose, that the Emperor was unable to revoke its
charter because, although Hussite for two centuries, it had been a papal
foundation, owed its inspiration to his confessor, the Capuchin Valeriano
Magni, of noble Lombard descent and hostile to the Jesuits, yet so
respected as to be able whenever he wished to stalk into the court at
Vienna, head held high. So impregnable was the position of this count in
friar's habit that Father Lamormaini contribed all kinds of schemes to
win him for the Jesuit cause. A brother of Magni, for example, was
colonel in the imperial army. The most splendid career was open to him,
Lamormaini insinuated, should the Cardinal's confessor desist a little
from his intransigence. Magni was the wrong choice for such barter.

And Wallenstein? In the Moravian chapter of his life he had been a
vigorous reformer, friend and patron of the Jesuits. Was he not one of the
court party, his Emperor's most faithful servitor, risen high with him?
The more experienced and the more powerful he grew, the more
independent grew his train of thought. The moment had inevitably
come (and in our narrative has already arrived) when it would be a
mistake to associate him with any particular party. The church in
general, the Jesuits especially, suited him where educational tasks were
to be performed or the maintenance of order was to be upheld. But let
them excite rather than appease tempers and his ruler's instinct turned
against them.

The Jesuit college at Gitschin was his first spiritual endowment in the
duchy. Attached to it was a boys' boarding-school. Letters exchanged in
1623–5 between the founder and its rector, Valentin Coronius, have
survived. They are business letters, although the subject of their correspondence was no profit-making business. They show Wallenstein as
prepared to allocate the Jesuits the income from certain specified estates,
but no more, and prepared to grant them at Gitschin a particular plot of
ground, but not the one that they want, and he never yields.

Balbinus, chronicler of the Gitschin college and godson of Wallenstein
who in his early boyhood days witnessed the town's splendid reconstruction, heard old men tell how the Duke liked to visit his foundation,
frequently did so, and on such occasions was relaxed in mood, chatting
gaily or seriously as might befit the matter in hand. When the toll of a
bell chased the fathers away to a service, he would ask to be included in

their prayers. All undoubtedly true, just as other things were true too. The Jesuits knew what they wanted as well as he did. When their aims did not coincide, whether in private or public affairs, friction ensued.

The youngest of Wallenstein's brothers-in-law, Franz von Harrach, was put for a couple of years into the boarding-school prior to military training. The priests conceived other notions as to his future. "I understand," said Wallenstein in a letter to his Governor, "that the Jesuits have persuaded little Franz von Harrach to become a Jesuit. His father handed him to me to make a soldier, not a Jesuit, of him. It pains me that, after the receipt of so many benefactions, this is the way in which they seek to requite me and practice deception as to this boy. Since they are wont to abduct such boys and, against the will of their friends, send them secretly to become novitiates, as happened to Doctor Wilhelm. . . ." There followed the order immediately to carry off little Franz, another Harrach boy, and a Waldstein one, from Gitschin and bring all three to Böhmisch-Aicha where they could pursue their studies just as well. To be done without the loss of an hour, even though "my wife or who may be there speaks out against it. Their words must not be heeded, for they do not understand." The high-handed action succeeded. Little Franz did not turn Jesuit, but was "brought up in the profession of arms and has on many occasions been of chivalrous behaviour".

As for public affairs, there existed a divergence of outlook in regard to the Catholic "Reformation", which could also have been termed deformation. Wallenstein, no longer the inexperienced young man he had been in 1619, was basically against it. He claimed, as he must, to be for it and no more than against the harshness of its methods. "The Reformation I esteem as good, the roughness as evil. That is why I wish that the procedure shall be cirumspect." Yet without the "roughness" and the "vexation", the means advocated by Jesuits to illumine the discernment of heretics, the objective could not be attained. Next to the higher nobility, who did not suffer all that badly, the staunchest resistance came from poor folk, miners, cloth-makers, glass-blowers, peasants, the fruit of whose labour the Duke of Friedland had no desire to forgo. The supervisors of his estates moreover included Protestants of various denominations and he retained them as long as he could. "If Your Princely Grace wishes Your vassals to be Catholics, then they must have Catholic supervisors," Taxis told the Duke, "for the peasants and other vassals say, Shall we become of other faith whilst our supervisors, whose wits are sharper than ours, do not?" The Chancellor of Friedland, Ilgen von Ilgenau, a Protestant, remained in office as late as 1628, when

Wallenstein had finally to dismiss him. Or at least pretend to do so, seeing that secretly he none the less retained him. "As now after the Reformation my Chancellor will no doubt have to go, see that you find another, but await my confirmation." The instruction illustrates what we shall repeatedly observe – that Wallenstein was even at the height of his power never omnipotent. He could slow down the pace of the Reformation, but not bring it to a halt, not at least that portion of it visible to all the world. As regards his army, matters were different. There the Reform Commission officials were not permitted to pry and he employed Protestant senior officers from start to finish.

Summarily, whereas the Jesuits constituted the party of an arch-Catholic dynasty and their own, Wallenstein represented (if he must be classified) the party of order. He went to mass and, whether from conviction or propriety, scrupulously adhered to all the religious rules. Apart from that, his mode of government was and remained, as shortly his conduct of policy would, an as yet inarticulate application of the future principle that subjects should be allowed to achieve blessedness after their own fashion. Fanatical Ferdinand alleged that the issue throughout this endless dispute was solely one of secular law, not religion. Out of his mouth the utterance was an untruth, but the proposition was the essence of Wallenstein's concern. No wonder that in the eyes of the Bohemian grand inquisitors Martinitz, Slawata and Dietrichstein he cut the figure of a Reformation obstructionist. He repaid their enmity in their own coin. "Prithee that they cease in Bohemia to proceed so frightfully on the Lutherans' account, else credit will be lost with one and all. These are Jesuit or that mischievous lickspittle Martinitz's inventions. If evil supervene, Jesuits will find another college, the Emperor no other land."

The effect produced by the activities of this notable Order was always charged with ambivalence, creating both an atmosphere of human understanding and of unrest. Since Wallenstein did not lack mental penetration and thought objectively, his relationship with the Jesuits could not be other than ambivalent too. For him the unrest which they inspired in Bohemia and European policy at large was unforgivable. The time was to come when two influential members of the Society would be among his grimmest adversaries and he would be reproached with the most repulsive pronunciations against it. That did not impede his continued collaboration with its representatives as well as the foundation or planning of colleges on its behalf whenever he was in a position to act a sovereign role. The Jesuits, for their part, rendered the subsequent memory of him more service than disservice. The affinity between them remained a tense one, half friendly, half hostile, not lacking in humorous aspects, and indissoluble on both sides.

Something similar held good for all other Orders whom Wallenstein accorded settlement in his territories: the Franciscans at Castle Welisch, the Augustinians at Böhmisch-Leipa, the Dominicans and Capuchins at Gitschin, the Carthusians at Walditz. His endowments were always imposing, he always displayed an actively pious paternal solicitude, and there was for ever the admixture of half contemptuous, half mocking distrust. He demanded that the monks pay taxes. A pure feint, as they owed all their possessions to him. But he was furious when they claimed that he had promised them exemption. "A lie. I have never promised nor exempted them. See to it that they pay, or subtract from the wherewithal they were given to build. The more they have, the more they want to have." Nothing was easier than to enforce these pseudo-levies. He only needed to reduce what he had promised them. As for the Augustinians at Böhmisch-Leipa, he remained convinced, and he returned repeatedly to the subject in correspondence with his Governor, that they had stolen or turned to highly iniquitous purposes the gulden which they had been granted for the construction of their monastery. The fine formulation of their endowment deeds often contrasted strangely with the terms in which he expressed himself about those endowed.

The consummation of the work of creating a hierarchy in the duchy was meant to have been the foundation of a Friedland see. As early as 1624 imperial licence for this was obtained and plans were drawn up which foresaw a palace at Gitschin for a bishop, prior, dean, archdeacon, ten canons, fourteen curates, organists, choir boys, and sextons – all for twenty thousand gulden a year. The scheme, in common with the rest of Wallenstein's schemes, was at once precise and on an imposing scale, particularly so on the question of finance. Under the pressure of business which overwhelmed its progenitor, it was never implemented. Only the cathedral church, with a flying buttress linking it to the palace, remains. Its design was based on Santiago de Compostela, but I have been told at Gitschin that it too was never entirely completed because four bell-towers in all should have been erected and it has no more than one.

Why did Wallenstein plunge into such constant, expensive outlays on behalf of the church? Those who believe in straightforward motives, straightforward convictions, and straightforward qualities of character will have a clear answer to the question. According to them, individuals are either selfish or love their neighbours, religious or irreligious, Christian or un-Christian, Catholic or un-Catholic, good or bad. For our part we cannot side with such black-and-white psychology, especially in the case of one who not merely excluded others from prying into the recesses of his soul but himself shrank from the process, concentrating wholly upon externals in order to find in unending activity the happiness that his innermost being lacked. Why should such a man not at the same time have held in esteem and scorned the Orders and their salvationist contrivances? Not at the same time have feared, derided, and disbelieved in God? Not have had the most various reasons for his ecclesiastical foundations? Because of the seemliness of such action for the princely identification that he sought. Because the monasteries were, or were intended to be, centres of humane education. Because planning, directing, and building always gave him pleasure. Because of the benefit to his reputation and, possibly, his spiritual welfare. Remarks of comparatively early date reflect reservations in his respect for the Papacy's ultramundane as well as mundane military powers: "If the Pope desires to achieve anything in this matter, let him give money and hold back his folk with their indulgences." All periods of his life furnish proof of his wish for peace between the denominations. This did not prevent his preference for a monopoly in Bohemia and his own land on the part of only one of them, had it been possible without paying the price of disorder and vexatious economic losses. Even when such consequences were not entailed, he inclined to connive in so far as imperial policy left him scope. "From the enclosure you will see what it is that the Widow Raschmin petitions me. I saw, when I was in Bohemia, that there they do not proceed so strictly with widows. You shall therefore see to it that she is left on her little property until Our Lord give her better thoughts whereby she may understand the true faith." Good nature? Just indifference? Is he really serious about "the true faith"? Does he really know what he takes seriously? I attempt no conclusion. About a personality like Wallenstein no conclusion can be attempted except in the light of what he did. And, depending on frame of mind and circumstances, he did a multitude of different things.

More unsophisticated intellects could not but view the problem otherwise. In 1633 Wilhelm Slawata, old foe and kinsman, wrote to the Emperor that the Duke's claim to be Catholic rested on confession and communion once a year. "For the rest, he reeks of atheism *magis Atheismum redolet* and troubles not about God, often utters the most horrendous blasphemies and oaths, and seeks support for his decisions over war and peace in the counsel of astrologers." Respecting his endowments of various Orders, he was himself in the habit of saying that he made these not for the increase of religion or out of piety, but only for political reasons. It was from Slawata, whose memorial was passed to him, that the Elector of Bavaria took over a specific misgiving: what blessing could be expected from the leadership of a general who, "as all men know, insults the Divine omnipotence with such frightful, exorbitant old and newly fabricated oaths, abuse of God, and blasphemies, gives great example and source for such abuse to the common soldiery who, thanks to the articles of war, are forbidden it on pain of corporal punishment and loss of life, and directs his actions and the welfare of Catholic religion more by the light of deceitful astrology than trust in God"? All the benefactions Wallenstein had showered on the clergy could not hinder his ultimately being regarded by his adversaries as a godless, totally depraved creature.

THE EDUCATIONIST

In 1927 the German secondary school at Böhmisch-Leipa, in the ownership of the Albrecht Eusebius Count Waldstein, Duke of Friedland, Education Endowment, celebrated its third centenary. It was now a state school, no longer a monastic one, and the Augustinians had had to submit to ceding to the Endowment a dairy-farm with which Wallenstein had provided them in order to be able to finance their educational work. So long had Wallenstein's school survived, and still would a little while longer yet. Only recently I met a German town councillor who had been a pupil there. Voluntarily, no doubt. In Wallenstein's days the inhabitants of Leipa and the vicinity *had* to send their children to the new school on pain otherwise of "unrelenting penalty". Henceforward piety, the liberal arts, and foreign languages could be learned at Leipa as well as anywhere else; studies pursued abroad involved heavy, now totally unjustifiable costs; all children who were to receive instruction should be registered forthwith at the Governor's office; no equivocation or excuse would be tolerated. ... The Leipa school was not the Duke's sole scholastic foundation. The one to which he attached most importance was the Jesuit educational establishment at Gitschin. For its sake, in spite of all irritations, he preferred not to renounce his link with the Order.

Political policy influenced this aspect of his activity too, the determination to produce in his own land an educated, loyal younger generation sprung from the ranks of the nobility and middle class as well as, incidentally, to replenish his army with officers genuinely devoted to him. When the youngsters had completed their studies, he would have them asked whether perhaps they wished to serve under him. The tone of the question rendered a negative reply inadvisable. In the selection of pupils he gave preference to Germans over "doltish Bohemian whiners". All had to have a "taste for probity" and they must be "spirited", else he did not want them. Well-to-do parents had to pay for their children; for others the fee came out of his pocket. Those who left with commendation received a present of money to invest in "clothes and other things" or sometimes, if they were to become pages at court, even an estate and a loan of a thousand gulden. From the most distant theatres of war, preoccupied with military and political worries, he still issued his educational instructions, sometimes dealing with the subject in general, at others with problems relating to individual pupils. "Send me a list of nobly born boys who are at school, how many they are, and give me the name of each, how old he is, which school he attends, what hopes are placed in him for the future." "At New Year I instructed you at Gitschin to furnish, as the endowment says, clothes for the boys whom I am having educated and, as the endowment lays down, provide all necessaries. You will see that this is truly and unerringly conformed to. Let the doctor who, as the endowment prescribes, is to heal them, be liberal with his physic and pay what is expended in the apothecary's shop. And since they are wont to have scabs from sheer dirtiness, see that they are kept cleaner than heretofore and that the doctor heals with baths and other requisite remedies those who are scabious. See also that they learn everything that the endowment says."

What they were to learn was German, Italian, and Latin; mathematics; fencing, riding, and dancing, and to play a musical instrument. No public performance was to be given. Presumably Wallenstein regarded this as unsuited to their status. His educational precepts were always addressed to the Governor, responsible in turn for their appropriate onward transmission. Never did the Duke refer to his own boyhood experiences at Goldberg and Altdorf. His early days seem to have been erased from his memory.

He never jested, an eighteenth-century historian wrote about him. "But when all around him fell in ruins, smoke and dust filled the air, and the moans of mortal agony beat upon the ear, when all grovelled with terror shriekingly on their knees before him and he tore aside his hand from mothers and children who, clinging to him, implored their lives,

then speechless satisfaction gleamed upon his face." Wallenstein as the
third in a trio composed of Attila and Jenghis Khan as they live in the
memory of the western world. Well, the military leader remains for
discussion in more detail at a later stage. In that capacity he behaved, or
tolerated behaviour, as it was customary in his own time and much later
too, though with differences that speak for rather than against him. As a
ruler he was no ruthless tyrant. Haughty, yes, but not like most of his
peers who, seated glassy-eyed over their cups, with no more than a wave
of the hand bade them be filled. His haughtiness was that of one who,
risen by his own strength, now stood high above the common herd. He
used his subjects for his own purposes. They had always to labour "for
me", not the country or the common weal, concepts which would have
been foreign to him. Nevertheless he was shrewd enough to appreciate
the reciprocity between his and their material welfare. If war taxes had
to be raised, the wealthy should pay more than the needy; the latter's
share should be a "contribution endurable and proportionate for the
poor man". He had it constantly bruited abroad that his love for his
people was so great that his desire was for their domestic and bodily
welfare. If therefore those who had left the land for such and such
reason were now to return and re-occupy their holdings, he would
declare them free for three years of all services and levies. Enlightened
self-interest. When however he decreed that the corn upon the fields
belonging to those who recently had died of the plague could be gathered
by any who chose, "because it is better that some person shall enjoy it
than that it rot", then it was no longer self-interest that spoke, but the
voice of plain economic good sense with an undertone of compassion.
He had at his own expense bread distributed to the poor. He had almshouses erected in every town, their maintenance to be derived from
income of the Chamber estates and fiefs. (A simple order did not
suffice him. He insisted on seeing an exact plan which must take proper
account of essential hygienic and spatial requirements.) Not intrinsically
anything unusual. The better among the German princes were fully
capable of taking similar steps. Yet with Wallenstein there is an element
of good nature in these actions which does not quite fit the fact that he
was not really a philanthropist or friend to individuals. The paradox
is not irreconcilable – there can be beneficence without personal contact,
a lonely man's fellow-feeling, goodness without warmth. He heard of an
old servant whose malady arose "purely and simply from the melancholy
of poverty" and ordered, "not as wage, but as pension", the donation to
him of two hundred gulden a year instead of fourteen as hitherto. A

stable-boy who became blind received four gulden a month. A ducal worker who broke his leg is "for his better balm to be paid a hundred gulden from our rents. On the doctor and the surgeon shall be impressed that they apply the utmost diligence that he shall not alone not lose his life, but be truly healed and no palsy follow upon it." Such were the instructions proceeding from the distant commander-in-chief who, had he wished, could daily have witnessed and heard how wounded mercenaries had limbs amputated with no anodyne other than, at best, an utterly besotting draught and who mentioned only in passing how pillaged peasants in their penury were casting themselves into the sea. That was war. At home, in the duchy, he thought every individual instance of distress worth trouble.

Happiness lay within his grasp. The flowering meadows and lush pastures, the throng of workers at the mines, the scaffolding in towns which grew more beautiful with every year, the clatter of mill-wheels, the chants of the monks, the bustle of students on horseback and scurrying pages, the humble greetings of well-fed, cleanly clad vassals as the ducal column of carriages rolled by, it was all his achievement, all his own. What more did he need? The events of his age which, thanks to his unsurpassed skill in turning them to his own advancement, had borne him high brought him no peace. Even if they had done so, he would not have acquiesced in it because there was none in him, no peace of soul. That may have been the presentiment of Christina Poniatowska, the pious hysteric who one winter's day appeared at the palace in Gitschin. Or did politics, propaganda, and the hatred of Bohemian *émigrés* towards him who had to the greatest degree exploited their misery lie behind her mission?

Christina Poniatowska was a religious ecstatic, subject sometimes to trances, at others to visions. She was also a disciple and confidant of Jan Amos Comenius, that noble humanist, educationist, denunciator of the atrocities of his age, and Bohemia's glory to this day. Sympathetic to the Brethren, he had after the battle of the White Mountain been protected and hidden by Wallenstein's brother-in-law, Zierotin. He did not leave his native country until January 1628, precisely the time when his pious associate was fulfilling her divine mission to travel to Gitschin and hand "the raving dog, him of Wallenstein", or in the Duke's absence his wife, the sealed letter which He Himself had dictated to her. The Duke was indeed not at home. The Jesuits and ducal councillors were disinclined to give her access to the Duchess. Gentle Isabella none the less received the emissary and accepted the missive. There was still time, she read, for the bloodhound and godless man to turn aside and repent his sins, the door of mercy was still held open for him. But let him continue on his present path and believe God's warnings jests, then the steely sword to slay him was already ground, the bow to wreak vengeance upon him already strung, and the miscreant committed like a lamb to everlasting slaughter. While the Duchess studied the document, Christina Poniatowska fell into a rapture wherein she was commanded immediately to leave this accursed house which was not worthy of the godly presence. Then she experienced another vision: "I saw in a dream how Wallenstein entered in a bloody gown and sought swiftly to climb a ladder into the clouds, but it had broken and so he fell to earth. As he lay stretched upon the ground, flames belched with a horrid roar from his mouth whilst poison and pitch were ejaculated from his heart until this was pierced by a bolt sent from Heaven and an angel spoke the words, 'This is the day when this wicked man wholly without pity shall perish.'" Such unpropitious omens were reported in a German *Little Tract of Miracles* published during Wallenstein's own lifetime, in 1632, and Comenius subsequently thought the incident worth mention.

What was Wallenstein's reaction to the warning? Ho ho ho, he is supposed to have shouted, "My Lord the Emperor gets letters from Rome and Constantinople, Madrid and Paris, but I receive them from Heaven!" Maybe he was really amused. Maybe, maybe not.

The Offer

A YEAR of peace, the twelve months of 1624 during which Wallenstein built up his duchy. The end of an act which the shortsighted may have mistaken for the final curtain. The Bohemian–Austrian revolution lay choked in blood while hard, greedy men were at work to exploit the changes flowing from it. In the Empire the Catholic forces, imperial, Bavarian and Spanish contingents, had everywhere been successful. The Palatinate was occupied by the Bavarians and Spaniards. The upright Margrave of Baden had been expelled from his own territory. The freebooters Mansfeld, Halberstadt, and Bethlen were beaten. Count Tilly, lieutenant-general of the Duke, or rather, Elector, of Bavaria, stood deep in northern Germany close to the borders of the Lower Saxon Circle.* The German Estates, loth to follow the Palsgrave's example, trembled lest his fate was being prepared for them. The old balance of parties had been radically destroyed. Elector Maximilian, principal beneficiary of the new order of things, was quite disposed to enjoy the grievously longed for peace on condition that he could keep what he had acquired. Peaceably inclined too were the Emperor and his councillors, victors also, but beggars amidst their victory. Not the councillors as individuals, because in that capacity they had of late won fortunes, but as members of the imperial Chancellery, administrators of the state. For that purpose the twenty gulden necessary to pay a courier were sometimes lacking. Fresh armaments? No one at court had such in mind. On the contrary, disarmament was not only the motto but the need. A reduction of regimental establishments, a repatriation of units and their colonels. Disarmament admittedly presented greater immediate financial difficulty than a retention under arms. Those on active service could be consoled with promises of pay and the

---

* The Empire was divided for fiscal and military purposes into ten Circles. Each had a Diet and elected President. The Emperor had only extremely indirect and ineffective control over the Circles' military affairs. One or more of them could be engaged in war without official knowledge on his part (translator's note).

indebtedness to them allowed to become bloated. Those with cancelled contracts would want to see the colour of their money.

Yet not much more than a year later there was a spreading fear that this swift and voluntary reduction had been untimely. Victory, to be final, should have been universal. That it had never been. Partial victories which have a bearing on the overall situation do no more than bring into the field new enemies who inject fresh courage into old, humiliated and pillaged ones. Bohemia, isolated though it might be through duress, remained a part of Europe; Germany, so much bigger, all the more so. At issue was no single source of conflict, a quarrel between two powers or expansion by one. What existed was a jumble of antagonistic aims too incompatible ever to be able to constitute, as was claimed for some of them, a common front against another common front. The scene resembled a tournament, with single pairs jousting. All of a sudden they merge into two lines moving against each other, although even while this is happening cases of disloyalty occur in both ranks. One man breaks out, withdraws into a corner, gesticulates encouragingly to the party against which he has just been fighting, insinuates himself between the two sides, and tries to play the mediator. Another wants to lure one contestant from this faction, another from that, and together form a third. Illusion, error, quackery are constant elements. The participants know too little about each other, some not enough about themselves. One of the requisites for the art of politics is ability to keep secrets and to stow away as many of them as possible.

Challenged to name one prime European apple of discord amidst all this confusion, its selection at this stage would be easy – that blessed, now accursed strip of land on both sides of the central reaches of the Rhine, the Palatinate. Suppression of the Bohemian revolution could have been accepted by the Protestants. At a very severe pinch, assignation of the electoral dignity to Bavaria too, for all that the balance of power inside Germany was thereby abrogated. But to see Spain in possession of the Palatinate, that was too much. For France, for the States-General, for England. The case of a politically motivated world, where injustice went down like water, refusing recognition of such injustice out of a sense of justice? To some small degree, in so far as it was unexampled for an old dynasty to be expropriated like a fractious noble or a Jew chased by the Treasury for his shekels. Nevertheless this sense of justice would probably not have proved so tenacious if power interests had not acted as an accessory.

In spring movement crept into what, at the end of 1623, when

Wallenstein returned from Göding, had seemed to have become inert.

The British were no longer friends with the Spaniards. Just before inclined to curb the free Netherlands in company with the protectors of the Holy Office, they were now making themselves agreeable at The Hague. Family feeling decided the matter for King James, a greybeard at fifty-eight. Spain had refused the boon that he had hoped of it – restitution of the Palatinate. In April he received the sinister freebooter and bandit-in-chief Count Mansfeld. He gave (or promised) him money to recruit in England a force with which to help "Our dearest Children", the Palsgrave and his wife, to recover their dignities, although in such manner as not to impinge too nearly upon the lawful possessions of Our dear Brother the King of Spain and Our dear Sister and Cousin the Infanta at Brussels. Not an easy task, but Mansfeld had to take what he could get. London's welcome of him, whose record was far richer in failures than triumphs, as a "great prince or saint" was balm upon the scabs of his soul. Members of Parliament, on bad terms with the King and worse ones with Buckingham, his favourite, succumbed to the wave of Mansfeld enthusiasm. Their objective was however not that of their king, a balanced dynastic continental alliance, but a good old war against Spain waged on the pattern of the preceding century – a war at sea, a trade war, a war with loot. A pack of English agents was sent to the Protestant capitals – The Hague, Stockholm, Copenhagen – and to northern Germany as well. Its princes and coastal cities had obviously to form part of the game if the Dutch and Scandinavians were to undertake an enterprise in common. The emissaries met with difficulties –the strife between Sweden and Denmark, the fears of German rulers unable to decide which way to face, the incisive and clear demands of the Swedish monarch. The House of Commons kept King James short where the nerve-centre of supply lay. "I am not so great or rich a Prince as to do so much," he modestly deplored. "I am only the King of two poor little islands."

April, the month during which Mansfeld had himself feasted at London, was precisely that in which Richelieu entered the Council of the King of France. Not yet as First Minister, but as a political craftsman whose mastery of his trade from the bottom up would soon become apparent. He received his summons a year before that of Wallenstein to a different role.

Under the aegis of the new ministry the King of France's couriers carried in their saddle-bags dispatches of more robust character than had formerly been the case. An alliance was forged between Paris,

London, and The Hague, only of a defensive kind and not so headstrong as the English would now have liked, but at least unequivocal as to what was to be defended. A swarm of French emissaries was loosed upon Germany to enlighten its Protestant princes on the threat hanging over them and to draw the attention of its Catholic ones to the unpalatable fact that victory had been attained not so much by their party as primarily and far more by the Emperor, secondly by the Spaniards. With the Elector of Bavaria this point could not fail of effect. His fondness for Spaniards had sensibly cooled since they had voted against his elevation, and whom he disliked he suspected. What could not help but confuse him was that Richelieu, at the same time as he wooed the Elector, took into his pay the Palsgrave's old partisan, Count Mansfeld, already hired by the British. The two financial engagements served different purposes. On King James's behalf Mansfeld was to liberate the Palatinate, an objective of no such great attraction for Richelieu because it would impinge on Bavarian interests. What the Cardinal wanted was military support against the Spaniards. They had occupied the Val Telline.

What had this southern mountain valley to do with major political matters? Simply that some roads out of it led to the Tirol and thence to Bavaria, others into the Engadine and thence to Vorarlberg, the Lake of Constance, and Alsace. Here was a bridge between the two Habsburg camps, that of the Spaniards dominant in Lombardy and that of their German cousins, a passage from Italy to the Rhine. The population of the Val Telline was Catholic, subject to the Grey Leagues, and a confederation divided within itself by gruesome feuds. The rising of the valley's inhabitants against their barbaric, foreign, and Protestant overlords gave the viceroy at Milan the chance to obtain mastery over the strongholds of the Val Telline. A prince of the church who thought along religious lines could only approve of this step. But the new French minister's thoughts on the world's affairs were mundane and his thinking ran on strategic lines. The Spanish occupation was in his view a new link in the chain meant to shackle, constrain, and throttle France. To the slack northern alliance, France–States-General–England, he added a tauter southern one, France–Savoy–Venice. In the winter of 1624–5 French forces clashed with Spanish ones in the Val Telline. Not that this signified a formal state of war between the two monarchies. The Duke of Savoy and the Signory of Venice, it will be recalled, were old enemies of Ferdinand of Styria.

Large-scale plans continued however to flap unfulfilled in the wind either because their initiators were inept or the means insufficient or the champions could not agree among themselves. For all his highly anti-Spanish ideas, Cardinal Richelieu could not put France at the head of a big Protestant coalition. He was all the less able to do so when, in 1625, the Huguenots began to stoke his domestic hearth to an uncomfortable pitch again. Had the Protestant powers come to terms without him, that would from his perspective have been perfectly satisfactory provided that their fortunes of war did not carry them too far. A Germany which was neither rook, knight, nor bishop on the Spanish chessboard was what he would very much have preferred to see. But Germany was too massive, too coveted, in its division too desirable to be capable of being neutralized. It lacked the internal peace without which there can be no neutrality, and the Cardinal overestimated the freedom of action open to individual German rulers. Now, five years too late, King James would for his part have dearly wished to bring about a grand coalition, indeed the greatest conceivable, for restoration of the *status quo ante*: Britain, Sweden, Denmark, the States-General, the considerable principality of Brandenburg, a benevolent France in the background, and Bethlen, as well as possibly the Muscovite Tsar, who would put Poland in a vice or at least lend money. (This point went awry over the rate of interest demanded by the Russians.) Elector George William of Brandenburg did in the summer of 1624 try to stretch a hand towards the incipient coalition and he sent his diplomats to Scandinavia to hawk yet another scheme among the many already hatched. The key question always was which line of attack the alliance should adopt. For example, and most important of all, where in practical terms was the King of Sweden's landing to occur in order to march on which objective? From the Palatine to Livonia, there were possible targets in plenty. Eventually the grand coalition dwindled after all into a petty one. What Gustavus Adolphus demanded before launching into the German deeps – sole and supreme command (highly offensive to Denmark), two first-class and secure ports on the Baltic and the North Sea (Wismar and Bremen, for instance), an Anglo-Dutch fleet in the North Sea (to safeguard him against Denmark), and mounds of money – all that was more than the artificers of alliance had to offer. Thereupon Gustavus broke off the negotiations and renewed his private war with Poland, which he chose to regard as part of the overall European state of hostilities. Sweden's defection involved Brandenburg's secession, not to mention that of Tsar Michael Romanov, a strange confederate anyway. That left Denmark. (The participation of the States-General, since 1620 the driving force behind all anti-Spanish, anti-Habsburg movements, was a matter of course.) With Denmark, more modest in its claims than Sweden, King James was able to come to terms. Strategy was to have been agreed in the spring at a conference to be held between the Protestant powers at The Hague. This had to be postponed until the late autumn because in April there died the Dutch leader, Prince Maurice of Orange, and King James too. The death of the latter was a blow to Christian of Denmark, for the new king, Charles I, if only to show that he was not the same as the old, had other plans.

Why should Denmark, more precisely, the King of Denmark, seeing that his councillors were against it, want to wage war in Germany? Out of the ambition and craving for aggrandizement lodged in every potentate's soul. His judgement can nevertheless be allowed to have been sound in so far as requirements of state are taken seriously, a duty by which kings in the first place earn their keep. Were Germany to have become completely subject to the Catholic party, with the Spaniards and imperialists firmly entrenched along its coasts, Denmark's independence would have been lost. To save German Protestantism was a vital interest of the Northern monarchs. That, in principle, was how both Gustavus Adolphus and Christian understood the matter. The question was what resources the latter had at his disposal. He counted, correctly, upon the United Netherlands, but these could not assume the whole burden and were currently engaged in fending off a Spanish offensive. He thought that he could count on England or at any rate on its new general, Count Mansfeld. Hopes, though unreliable hopes, could be pinned on Bethlen, a new revolt in Bohemia and Moravia, possibly on Venice and the Francophile party which had taken shape in Italy. The prime essential was participation by that section of Germany bordering on Denmark, the Lower Saxon Circle. It had, with the Bavarian Elector's troops menacing its frontiers, better reason than the rest for falling in with the king's project. The trouble was that the Emperor, and the Elector of Bavaria acting on his behalf, had the law on their side, the "beneficent imperial constitutions", although nothing whatever was laid down as to exactly what action they did entitle them. A further difficulty was created by the Hanseatic cities' primary interest in peace and none in an expansion of Danish trade. By a narrow majority King Christian was elected commander-in-chief of the Lower Saxon Circle. His supporters were the two Dukes of Mecklenburg, Mecklenburg-Schwerin and Mecklenburg-Güstrow, a collateral Duke of Holstein, and Christian Wilhelm, Administrator of episcopal Magdeburg who was a member of the House of Brandenburg. The rest of the Estates representatives would have preferred a less aggressive commanding officer, but at least the Diet's resolutions had an inaggressive ring. Its armaments were to be refurbished solely for defensive purposes and its army, reinforced by Danish auxiliaries, was to be employed nowhere outside the Circle's limits. Such were the formulae by which the Estates hid from themselves that they had joined a European coalition, having affirmed in one breath what they denied in the next.

Of course Brussels, Madrid, Vienna and Munich either knew or surmised something of all this. Apart from ambassadors and roving clerics, the good relations subsisting between Paris and Bavaria saw to that. Elector Max was a vigilant politician, eyes and ears open in all directions. At the outset of 1625 the probability that he would once more have to fight on behalf of his all too handsome acquisitions crystallized in his mind into certainty. Indeed he inclined to overestimate the danger, for Sweden's late, abrupt secession from the coalition could not be anticipated and the news took months to spread.

The reports of ambassadors and spies were more than amply confirmed by the occurrence of natural phenomena. The winter was warm, so warm that almond-trees blossomed, but in summer they decayed from cold. In February the bishopric of Bamberg experienced an earthquake, a mountain heaved in its entirety and came to rest elsewhere, far away. At Hamburg the spring floods rose higher than for seventy years and carried off ships, houses, humans, and cattle as well as two thousand chests of sugar. During the coronation of the Emperor's young son as King of Hungary no less than three suns were seen shining over Ödenburg and afterwards, when there was no sun at all, a rainbow hung in the sky. Did it signify that one day the Archduke would wear all three crowns, the Hungarian, the Bohemian, and the Roman? Alas no, more likely it meant calamity, war again, and all the misery that war brought with it, as such abnormal portents usually did. These were harbingers of destiny, and destiny was evil. Was it not something, though, for which those were responsible who, if they had wished, could have ensured a happier course of events? No, destiny would be what it must inexorably be, whether deriving from quarrelsome kings or the heavens above.

KEPLER, AGAIN

A multitude of business, personal, relating to his duchy (that alone could have filled the whole of his time), and public, occupied the Commandant of Prague during 1624, the year of pseudo-peace. He was, for instance, intent on presenting the citizens of the capital with a citadel. It had nothing to do with the town's fortifications, the system of defensive walling. Citadels could in an emergency serve against external attack, but their principal purpose, the one that Wallenstein had here and now as well as later and elsewhere in mind, was to discipline a city's inhabitants. The embodiment of provocation, a symbol of domination hewn in iron and stone. Construction was begun on Vyšehrad, Prague's oldest acropolis, but whether it was ever completed is uncertain and no traces remain. Prince Liechtenstein, always rather more stylish in his intercourse with the subjugated nation, had been no friend of the project and dallied over its execution.

Protracted legal labours produced a new constitution for the kingdom. The old one no longer held good. While the victors tasted their victory to the full, nothing held good. In 1623 it was however decided that matters could not continue for ever without a constitution. Two years later a commission was entrusted with its drafting. The members were Karl von Liechtenstein, the Duke of Friedland, imperial Vice-Chancellor Stralendorf, Privy Councillor Werdenberg, the Bohemian Vice-Chancellor von Nostitz, and three lawyers. The latter may be assumed to have contributed most; it should not be assumed that Wallenstein's attendance at the commission's sessions was assiduous. This kind of employment was unsuited to his temperament. It may even have been that he never studied the long-winded document published in 1627. None the less its basic principles appealed to him. The monarchy was without any reservations declared hereditary. The right to legislate became a royal monopoly. The Estates had no say except where money was concerned. Their number was raised to four, with the clergy as in ancient times the First Estate. Political alliances within the assembly of Estates, the formation of parties, and common voting were forbidden, the penalties of treason attached. Nomination of senior officials was an unrestricted royal prerogative. So was conferment of civil rights, a change of intrinsic importance to the many new nationals, new property-owners, and alien new masters who both now and later settled in Bohemia. The army was the King's alone – no Estate regiments any more. There was but one religion. The officially recognized languages, on equal footing, were Czech and German. And plenty more along the same pattern. Put succinctly, the new constitution forbade what had been the nobility's and the towns' favourite game, politics. In that respect it went further than even trusty friends of the Spanish party, however sympathetic to the House of Habsburg, wanted if they still felt

themselves to be Bohemians. It did not, though, go further than Wallenstein's overbearing, impatient outlook approved. Let the King be absolute in Bohemia if that was his own position in Friedland, and step by
step he was sundering Friedland from Bohemia.

In December 1624 he dictated his will. During the same month he
turned once again to Johannes Kepler, now resident at Linz in the service
of the Upper Austrian Estates. The subject of his request, it will be
recalled, was whether a correction of his natal hour was possible in the
light of details pertaining to his experiences since 1608. He also wanted
more exact information about his future than Kepler had formerly been
prepared to give. Would he die of apoplexy, away from home, as other
astrologers thought? Would he attain dignities and properties *extra
patriam*? Should he continue his military career and, if yes, in what
countries and with what success would it be crowned? Whom should he
regard as his friends and was it true, what other mathematicians had
calculated, that his Bohemian compatriots would be his worst enemies?
Gerhard von Taxis, who acted as intermediary as he had done sixteen
years ago, added that the Bohemian lord desired no flatteries, but the
truth, let it be what it might.

For another three-quarters of a year, although now quite senselessly,
he continued to play at secrecy as formerly. Christoph von Hochkircher,
a young officer stationed at Vienna, was charged with transmission of the
letters and putting himself at Kepler's disposal in order to spur him to
his task, yet "*celato nomine Principis*", under concealment of the Prince's
name. Suddenly, in September 1625, Taxis behaved as though there
had never been any obfuscation: "His Princely Grace the Duke of
Friedland" had instructed this and that. Kepler's retort was that at last
he could see clearly. True, he had already had a suspicion of how matters
lay, but Hochkircher's ambiguity had made it difficult to trust his
presentiment. A paltry dissimulation. He had known long since, eight
years at least. He knew who Taxis was, no longer a lieutenant, but risen
to lieutenant-colonel, baron, and governor, and whose governor he knew
too. This second horoscope furnishes therefore fewer riddles than the
first. The Duke of Friedland, Governor of Bohemia, was a man about
whom worldly-wise Kepler had heard more than enough. Nevertheless
he maintained the pretence of simply making inferences, to a smaller
degree from the planets, to a larger from intimations contained in Taxis's
letters.

The behest not to flatter his highly placed employer he fulfilled
punctiliously. Whoever wanted to know of the stars what Wallenstein

asked, he scolded, had never properly gone to school nor ever properly cleaned the light of reason which God had ignited for him. Could the Bohemian lord not finally abandon the folly of seeking the source of all events in the heavens? Terrestrial occurrences had terrestrial causes; full stop. A military appointment forecast for such and such a year had not come to pass? How could it when there was no war in that particular year? Did his questioner imagine that he was the sole pivot of affairs and the entire universe must accommodate itself to the destiny of his own person? Many, very many men existed on this earth besides him, each born under an individual constellation. How could anyone tell when and under what circumstances theirs would encounter his? To try to do so would ultimately involve the exploration of a single, all-embracing nativity comprehending probably the whole of christendom, a task well beyond the scope of any scientific skill. Granted, the trends for heads of state enjoyed comparably a universal significance: had the Emperor not won the war in Bohemia, the destiny of many, including Wallenstein, would have been quite different. Whether the inquirer would continue in a military career depended in the first place on whether the state of war continued, a problem that had nothing to do with his own birth. Since he was manifestly a very eminent lord, it was reasonably probable that he would administer, if his King so pleased, offices outside his own country. Death supervened either in a man's native land or not, within or without its borders. Such "yes" or "no" questions always presented the prospect of guessing one of the two halves correctly, but no serious astrologer spent time on them. The same applied to the manner of death. In any case gout (to which Wallenstein admitted) usually brought about a bitter end through apoplexy. Seeing that the Bohemian lord was still engaged in a military career, but that for the Bohemian rebels affairs had taken such a sad turn, he was palpably a loyal adherent of the Bohemian crown and had intrinsically no disfavour to fear from its wearer. His relationship with his compatriots was a different matter, "for whoever is a Bohemian and conducts himself within the kingdom as I forecast (seventeen years ago), he will doubtlessly be nowhere better known or more hated than quite certainly in Bohemia". These feelings were probably not confined to the defeated because innumerable "birds of prey and tale-bearers" customarily hovered over and around situations such as prevailed in Bohemia. He who had greatly exploited the victory to his own advantage would do well to be on his guard against them, especially as the nativities of Wallenstein and the Emperor indicated little mutual affection and inclination and the horoscope of the royal successor was not lacking in disagreeable configurations inimical to his questioner. A hint to be careful? A warning? Yes and no. Seventeen years had changed neither Kepler's way of thought nor method. Notwithstanding that in the main he rejected Wallenstein's demands on his science as sheer absurdity, he proceeded to comply with them as far as, possibly slightly farther than, his conscience allowed. As he wrote at a later date, he had done his utmost. He undertook the correction with regard to the moment of birth. Considerable changes ensued. Wallenstein's most auspicious period now lay between his fortieth and forty-fifth, not as previously between his forty-seventh and fifty-second, years. Kepler also subjected the "revolutions", the run of seasons between the birth-hour anniversaries, to fresh, expert examination. From September 1624 to September 1625, exceptionally good omens. For 1625–6, important dealings, vexatious impediments. The years 1626–7 are "akin to a revolution in the nativity's nature, for if he succeeds in augmentation of his authority and of power in respect of money and goods, doubtlessly it happens to the world's injury and that of many people, wherefore it will also arouse against him enmity, resistance, impediment, and doubtlessly through embitterment also the gout". For 1627–8, more evil than good. "If success in all things came immediately to the nativity, he would still not be satisfied, but feed upon himself, let alone the opponents he would stir against him. None the less this revolution is eruptive and victorious." In 1628–9 things would become worse or at any rate more obscure, less certain. They would continue to do so until 1634. Then, for March, the signs were horror-laden. Better to break off at this point, all the more so since what lay so far in the future was incapable of inspiring acute feeling . . . Was not the nativity in any case, as emerged from his queries, tolerably tired of the toilsome, ruinous ways of war, more especially as the gout's itch gave his nights no rest from spasms? What better could the astronomer wish him than an understanding of his science purged of superstition, peace, convalescence and joy? For himself, he hoped for generous payment from the coffers of his wealthy client because, through no fault of his own, he found himself again in the most dire circumstances.

Poor Kepler, not a penny did he receive. Taxis did dispatch to him a sackful of devaluated coin through Ensign Hochkircher, but the latter overflowed with prevarications: the sack was too heavy, the highway too dangerous, far better for the money for the time being to remain at home in his trust. When Kepler found an attorney willing to arrange the transfer, the sack was empty, its contents cast upon the waters of the Ensign's needs and pleasures.

Wallenstein disregarded alike the phantasmagoria and the impertinences of Kepler's appraisal. He heeded only the "revolutions", henceforth comparing them year by year with actual events. His notes in the margin of the horoscope prove it. "In August Denmark beaten." "Denmark driven out of Holstein, Jutland, Mecklenburg." "Fief of Sagan obtained. Possession taken of Mecklenburg. Stralsund besieged." One, though inconspicuously placed, remark must have struck him more than all the rest. For its sake it would not have been improper to reward the astronomer with gold rather than devalued copper. "A ruler . . . who knew all this would doubtlessly send such a commander with such an impressive constellation, if he was sure of his loyalty, against his present foreign enemies." This passage dealt with here and now, the year 1625. The foreign enemies were on hand. Should it not occur to the ruler to send the commander against them, the idea could be put into his mind.

BAVARIA

The undisclosed, never altogether secret negotiations between Paris and Munich continued. Nothing would have pleased Elector Maximilian better than the conclusion of a general peace, provided that he could keep his gains. His polity had been increased in a way that only his subjective wish could see as legal. His objective intelligence could not but warn him that it had been dangerous. He therefore played at power politics on more European than German lines and he welcomed in France a factor to counterbalance his Spanish friends and semi-foes. None the less Richelieu and Maximilian, in the discussions conducted on their behalf by lay and ecclesiastical envoys, constantly talked past and were mistaken in one another. What Richelieu wanted of Bavaria, that it should break with the Emperor and adopt complete neutrality towards not merely France, but England, the States-General – Maximilian was anyway determined to keep out of that hornets' nest – Sweden, Denmark, Lower Saxony, and even Count Mansfeld, was impossible. What Maximilian wanted of France, that it should abandon precisely these powers, the incipient northern coalition, to their own devices or proceed against them, was also impossible. That was why the transactions between Cardinal and Elector ever and again came to grief even, as was later the case, when they had been put on paper, sealed, and sworn.

It takes two sides to play a game. This one would not have been complete without the Spaniards and imperialists attempting what England and, more deviously, France were trying to do – to concoct a coalition and, on the strength of it, preserve the present state of affairs. For this purpose France was out of the question for them. The new Pope, Urban VIII, a scion of the Barberini family, was engaged in a policy inspired by more mundane motives than the struggle against heresy. Elector Max therefore remained the only practicable ally. Vienna and Madrid were Maximilian's suitors as well as Paris. The grandee acting on behalf of the first two, Don Balthasar Marradas, Wallenstein's old comrade-in-arms, was sent in February 1625 to Munich to snaffle the Elector with intimations of the common danger and by gross flattery. Maximilian proved evasive. A specific tripartite alliance he called a matter for "some scruple, partly unnecessary too". Scruple, because such an alliance would implicate him in all kinds of troubles with which he did not want to have anything to do, those in the Val Telline, the Franco–Spanish disagreement, and the Spanish–Dutch affair. Unnecessary, he objected, because the three parties already stood shoulder to shoulder, fighting on the same extended front, each in his place and fulfilling his appropriate task – the Spaniards in the Netherlands, His Imperial Majesty wherever he deemed right, and he himself within the Empire. Why awkwardly formalize this natural, elastic, and salutary division of labour through a treaty? Notwithstand'ng that the fox refused to be lured from his hole, he did not cease to warn Vienna against untimely disarmament and urgently to recommend strong preparations for hostilities. Peril, in his eyes, threatened from every direction – England, Denmark, Sweden, Mansfeld, malcontents within the Empire, Bethlen, the Turks, the Bohemian émigrés. At the same time he wavered between two desires difficult to reconcile, retention of the supreme command in Germany, granted him six years earlier and with such handsome returns to show for it, but on the other hand shelter if the sun should cease to shine. Did Vienna not take rearmament seriously, he was put out. Response to his adjurations through a recruitment of troops, though, plunged him into minute examination as to whom they might be turned against and where they might be employed. His primary concern, should an emergency arise, in Lower Saxony, for instance, was for imperial auxiliaries in conjunction with a mandate to occupy, in the name of Emperor and Empire, every stitch of German land. A mandate which he obtained.

Ferdinand II, weak, good-natured, harassed by financial worries, inclined even less to fresh bloodshed. During the winter and early spring he and his councillors sounded an even more optimistic note than the Elector did. There had been missives to Denmark and the German princes, warnings against unconstitutional steps. Reassuring replies had been received. Peace, so essential, still prevailed. If the worst came to pass, there would still be time enough for defensive measures. Not until the second week in May was Maximilian the recipient of a disconcertingly vigorous announcement from Vienna. Although "Our hereditary kingdoms and territories, with their subjects, are to the uttermost degree exhausted, drained, and deteriorated," it had none the less been decided to heed the Bavarian admonitions and not simply to restore to shape the six regiments remaining with the colours, each with a strength of three thousand men, but to raise a new force of fifteen thousand infantry and six thousand cavalry "under the command of Our high-born Cousin, Prince of the Empire, dear and faithful Albrecht Wenzel Eusebius, Ruler of the House of Waldstein and Prince of Friedland, Our military councillor, chamberlain, and colonel". The task of this new army would be to safeguard the Hereditary Lands against the Turks and Bethlen as well as "to act alongside of Your own dear Highness's and the faithful, obedient Electors', Princes', and Estates' forces", should Sweden and Denmark make any hostile move. The information is likely to have left the Elector in a divided frame of mind. He was being offered what he wanted. More than he wanted.

THE OFFER

Kepler had counselled it. Hedged with provisos, as was his habit. But that one sentence stood there. The state of affairs impelled it. Wallenstein knew of the northern coalition as well as Maximilian did. Friedland lay nearer and was more endangered by the centre of troubles than Bavaria. Let matters take an evil turn and Bavaria, although diminished, would still remain Bavaria. Let the enemy come to Bohemia, the Danes through Lusatia, Gustavus Adolphus through Silesia, Mansfeld from the west, and Friedland would dissolve into nothing. The interests of the Emperor and the Empire, as understood by the Emperor, and those of Wallenstein coincided. At any rate in politics, signifying the abstract power-game. As far as gross materialism was concerned, the Austrian Estates' warning in 1618 to the late Emperor Matthias held good: wars enrich ministers and military men, not monarchs. Kepler had in his second horoscope been sneering about a "good, lucrative war". Had not in fact the Bohemian war been lucrative for Wallenstein? If hostilities were now resumed, and they probably would be resumed with or without him, and if he placed himself at the head of them, could he not venture entirely different stakes than on the first occasion? Bring Friedland's industries to their finest pitch? Furnish advances which the Emperor would never be able to repay and would therefore have to repay many times over? Was that Wallenstein's principal motive? The Venetian ambassador at the imperial court, shrewd, gossipy Signor Padavin, thought so. "The Prince wishes to disburse little and to have security for his disbursement. He has his eye on the possession of certain lands in Bohemia and this is the sole ultimate purpose of all his proposals." I think the ambassador was mistaken at least as to the extent of Wallenstein's greed – if the mainsprings of his conduct could any longer be termed greed at all.

His offer was not his first. As early as 1623 he had hinted at the establishment of a force of fifteen thousand men under his command, and he must in the next year have again suggested something of the kind because the imperial councillors made reference to it during their thorough investigation into the present project. He had already bitterly criticized the custom of groping for means of defence only when invasion had occurred. To his mind a condition of constant preparedness, a standing army, was ineluctable. It complemented his concept of the state, especially when the state was simply a dynasty ruling a number of always restless nationalities more or less prone to rebellion.

A document clearly formulating his propositions has not been traced. Probably none ever existed. In the winter and spring he was often in Vienna to press his convictions on his influential friends. In January rumours were rife that certain matters turned on his person. In March they thickened. In April the imperial War Council informed him secretly that he had been selected as *capo*, or commander, of all forces which might be dispatched into the Empire and he should hold himself in readiness. Not yet an appointment or a licence to begin recruitments, merely a harbinger of such. To his father-in-law Harrach he wrote a plea for help "that His Majesty shall not temporize with recruitment while the enemy does not wassail but daily musters more soldiery and will sooner be in Silesia and these lands than we expect. That is why there is assuredly not a minute to be lost. I have indeed offered to be of service to His Majesty . . . but if I come to see that boldness is lost and recruitment intended only when the enemy is at our throats, then I shall not venture into such a labyrinth."

Quite a number of minutes were lost. The Privy Council sessions to decide what should in general be done and whether in particular "Prince Wallenstein's offer of recruitment be put into execution" dragged on two months and longer, from 25 April until 21 June. The Emperor's heavy-footed advisers, First Minister Eggenberg, the President of the imperial War Council, Count Rombaldo Collalto, the President of the imperial Exchequer Abbot Antonius of Kremsmünster, Prince Gundakar Liechtenstein (brother of the Bohemian viceroy), and the Lords von Meggau, Stralendorf, Slawata, Harrach, and Werdenberg, the last acting as secretary, met seven times. Because hard-working Harrach made notes which have survived, we know what was discussed and how opinions fluctuated. Wallenstein's character and capacity were never called in question. Wilhelm von Slawata, who would only too keenly have liked to do so, stayed silent because he saw himself hopelessly outnumbered. The embittered twitchings at the corners of his mouth can be imagined. Outnumbered too was Eggenberg, which attests to the deliberations having been democratic rather than autocratic. The chairman asked his colleagues to reflect that danger was not yet certain, but untimely rearmament would make it so. The majority took a different view. Danger was certain, certain indeed from so many different quarters that it was downright impossible to say against which aspect of it to turn first. That was also the view of Bavaria and of Saxony. The latter was demanding deeds instead of words. Deeds with what objective? On that the Emperor's faithful councillors were not quite clear in their mind. In one breath they advised something like a preventive war, arguing that it was better to make things hot for the enemy at home than to await an undesired visitation. In another they contended something that at a later date would have been called negotiation from a position of strength – whereas now the enemy enjoyed superiority and could dictate conditions, "when equality has been achieved, everything is susceptible of discussion and composition". Peace through armaments! This ruinous war would continue for ever unless one became strong and bared one's teeth to the wicked. That too would instil the neutrals with a feeling of security. A bargain must be struck with the Turks – there had been friction again – even at the cost of a hundred thousand gulden. (An agreement was concluded while the meetings were still proceeding.) The Prince of Transylvania must either with Turkish assistance be completely ruined or, seeing how erratic he was, used in a positive way by "inciting him against the Venetians". Spain should cause France a liberal dose of domestic trouble. His Holiness the Pope should be asked for subsidies.

Not only was the defence of Italy involved, but the issue was primarily a struggle against the heretics. Was not perhaps an accord with England and the Palatine government-in-exile after all feasible? Many an inept illusion was muttered, many a contradiction in terms unashamedly ventilated. Once, at the beginning of May, Wallenstein was summoned to Vienna to be interrogated about his plans. Then, in the second week of June, the whole party went to Nikolsburg because they did not want to finalize anything without the Governor of Moravia, Cardinal Dietrich-stein. Hardly more love was lost between the Cardinal and Wallenstein than between the latter and Slawata. None the less it was in Dietrich-stein's castle that the matter was settled which had practically been decided at Vienna – the establishment of a new imperial army of twenty-four thousand men. That too was when and where Wallenstein was raised to ducal status, either to underline his superiority over all the other dignitaries with whom he would have to deal or as a sop for the lack of unanimity about the military title that he should be given. A comparatively simple solution was found to the problem of how to define the enemy: "His Majesty regards as his foes all those who have taken or take or do not lay down their arms against him."

Precisely at the moment when the imperialists were preparing to fulfil completely the demands of the Elector, he began to tack about, secretly, crookedly. Peace with the Turks was the more welcome as Gabor Bethlen would hardly be able to undertake anything without Turkish help. The latest news from the Netherlands theatre of war, the fall of Breda to the Spaniards, had a more ambivalent edge to it. A splendid triumph for Catholic arms, it could nevertheless cause Mansfeld, who had tried to relieve the city, possibly to switch his nefarious activities to the Palatinate or even Bohemia. His, Maximilian's, commander, Lieu-tenant-General von Tilly, was however well equipped to meet such eventualities, manoeuvring within the Empire neither too far north nor too far south so as to be able to defy both Mansfeld and the Dane. Therefore it was merely prudent and necessary to have a few imperial regiments as auxiliaries. Were it not such an imposing host as recently planned, that would, "considering the present swift course of affairs", probably be no misfortune. To Wallenstein the Elector wrote a letter. We do not have it, but the addressee reported to Collalto, "I observe that he is not happy about the business". The hand that was now to be played for a good eight years between Wallenstein and Maximilian began even before the beginning of hostilities.

They were begun by the Elector. It was he who, on 15 July, ordered

his commander not to dally any longer, but by crossing into the Lower
Saxon Circle to make sure and certain of what had hitherto only menacingly become more probable. In vain the warning of the irresolute
Emperor that while the danger in the north was indisputable, yet "in the
circumstances prevailing at this time We regard an immediate and
unprepared invasion of the Lower Saxon Circle as very dangerous
because hereby a new war would be engaged . . ." The letter arrived at
Munich after the orders to march had been given. If war was inevitable
and on this occasion to be of incalculable dimensions, Ferdinand had no
desire for the fault to lie with him, an attitude most likely prompted by
Eggenberg.

Why then did he accept Wallenstein's plan? A ruler will under such
pressure do many a thing which cancels out preceding action, and will
tie himself down when he still fancies himself not to have done so.
During the first seven months of 1625 central Europe was overshadowed
by a diplomatic crisis of the type which since the days of Thucydides
had usually preceded a great war, a convention which was to remain
unchanged. Why it lasted seven months rather than seven weeks, seven
days, or seven hours is explicable in the ratio of time to distance. The
"pleas", the lies and self-complacent protestations, were carried back
and forth at the pace of steeds. The later "mobilization" was in Wallenstein's era the "muster". The two were in principle not unlike each
other. In one case the reservists were summoned to the colours according
to a lovingly elaborated plan; in the other men were drummed together,
hastily examined for suitability, and hired, some with previous experience of active service, others trying out for the first time whether or not
there was a balance of advantage in being the plunderer in place of the
plundered. On 23 June Ferdinand asked Wallenstein whether the venture should not be postponed, indeed called off. He was in receipt of
pacificatory communications from Denmark. In that direction, it
seemed, all might not be lost, whereas too energetic a muster would
signify abandonment of the implements of peace. Wallenstein replied
chillingly, "For Denmark and the others now to return fairer words –
they are right to do so. If we are right to trust them, that I doubt."
Nothing came of the notion of demobilization. Matters had gone too far
on both sides.

Maximilian and Wallenstein basically assessed the situation alike, and
correctly alike. The northern coalition's preparations were not, he
thought, meant as a feint. They agreed moreover that Bavaria could not
by itself withstand a north German–European attack. The view of the

War Council at Munich stated that "Tilly cannot gain superiority alone. The Danes have great advantages. They will be the moving spirits and consume us." The Elector, though, wanted what was not to be had – to benefit from strong imperial aid and nevertheless not to lose the cherished supreme command. Consequently when Wallenstein's troops reached Lower Saxony, he reacted like a dog into whose garden another has strayed.

WHO IS TO PAY?

The Exchequer, the imperial ministry of finance, later made the disclaimer that "with respect to maintenance of the Wallenstein armada, not only was nothing ever known, but it was, as it were, ensured that without any remuneration on the part of His Imperial Majesty it was the Duke of Friedland's intention to provide his armada with all its needs until such time as a state of peace might again be attained". That was not strictly accurate. Abbot Antonius, President of the Exchequer, had attended the crucial meetings of the Privy Council and listened to its members hoodwinking one another with notions that two and a half million gulden could probably be realized from special taxes, loans, fines, and "anticipations". Hot air against which the fiscal abbot should have raised timely protest. The gentlemen of the Exchequer knew that they did not have the money for maintenance of a new army. They must have known that Wallenstein did not have it either. The annual cost of an infantry regiment, on a stringent calculation, was 500,000 gulden. The question here, looking matters squarely in the eye, was of twenty regiments – for a start. From where should the Duke whose income in lucky years ran to 700,000 gulden, an amount always earmarked in advance, take ten to fifteen million gulden? Even had the Devil played them into his hands, was he the man to pass on such a gift for nothing? Those concerned slunk around the thorny problem and during its discussion evaded each other's glances. Both parties knew that neither could afford what was at stake and therefore new, loathsome methods of financing must be adopted. Sometimes they were mentioned, but in an undertone.

The "Instruction" to Wallenstein, drawn up at the end of June, touched on a number of matters, some of them splendid, others not quite so splendid. First, definition of the objective – the achievement of peace, salutary and longed for by all pious souls, and the extirpation at the roots of all harmful distrust and mutual bitterness. Secondly, elucidation of the grievous point that the wickedness of the rebels, who shrank not even from seeking to inveigle the arch-enemy of christendom into association with their godless arms, rendered it the Emperor's purely bounden paternal duty to defend the faithful Estates. Thirdly, religion. That was not what was at stake, as the instigators mendaciously alleged, because one and all were to be allowed to continue to abide by the Augsburg Confession and, as hitherto, retain seized abbeys and monasteries, although this promise did not hold good for such as would refuse to lay down their guilty weapons. Fourthly, mention of the need for good relations with all loyal princes and allies, the Infanta at Brussels, the three spiritual Electors, the Elector of Saxony, and above all the Bavarian Elector and Palsgrave. Fifthly, reference to military discipline which regrettably had fallen into a state of almost total deterioration, but without which wars were no better than predatory expeditions. The General would earn eternal fame if through the imposition of exemplary penalties he would put an end to unchristian burnings, ruinations, and plunderings as well as the rape of respectable women and maids, and if the armed forces hereupon ceased also in enemy country to take from the citizenry anything more "than daily need demands". "None the less we sanction . . . the levy in conquered places and territories of sufferable contributions and loans. . . ." Sufferable contributions.

According to an old tradition reaching back to Khevenhüller's *Annals*, Wallenstein during the early summer startled the Emperor and his Privy Council with the paradoxical assertion that he would be able to sustain an army of fifty thousand but not of twenty thousand men. Such superiority alone would enable him to exact the sums of money he needed. The legend contains a grain of truth. Lord von Harrach scribbled on a letter from his son-in-law, dated 10 June, a note which really amounted to a fourteen-point programme. One of them ran, "If His Majesty rearms strongly, he will be able to make terms and to compel his people in the Empire to agree to everything and he will thereby accelerate peace." Room had always to be found for the theme of peace, particularly with so clement a cavalier as Karl von Harrach. The train of thought is however clear and inclement – the greater the Emperor's military power, the severer the compulsion on the Empire to finance it.

On the other hand there was no notion, with the economy as inadequate and the tax system as irrational as each was, that the princes and towns, the enemy ones, be it understood, which represented as yet the smaller part of the Empire, could have borne the entire burden of fifty, eighty or a hundred thousand men. Even Count Mansfeld never took the field without subsidies, whether Savoyard, Dutch, French, or English. No army lived only on booty. Even if it was feasible – perhaps the hitherto untried was feasible – it is an established fact that Wallenstein did not assent to this. What did he assent to? That emerged gradually from the complaints and protests he sent during the course of 1626 to Vienna.

"He complains," noted Harrach, "of the court's belief that he should and can conduct the whole war out of his pocket, says that he never promised more than to set up the army and bring it into position, has hitherto sustained it, but that such a war cannot be conducted by other than a great potentate and not a private person." Which reveals exactly how matters stood. The big businessman had offered to build the factory, not to keep it running at his own expense. Its construction, in the shape of clothing, arming, and finding the first month's pay as well as the "enticement money" for fifty thousand men, required far more means than he had or could raise. The small businessmen, colonels who organized regiments and captains who formed companies, had to contribute their share with the prospect of being subsequently compensated. Plus profit, else what turn would it have served them? A "reimbursement of what You will indispensably have to incur in Our service" was also Emperor Ferdinand's undertaking to Wallenstein. Where were the funds to come from? How were the daily outlays for the army to be met in so far as they went beyond what could be extorted from the Empire? Impatient to be launched on his life's crowning adventure, Wallenstein did not ask, and his employers were glad that he did not ask. At a later stage he would improvise, possibly make a little on it too. He would have preferred a well-paid soldiery, smaller in numbers, to large masses without pay. "But as that cannot now be," he wrote to Harrach, "we must needs go *a la desparata* and take what we can get."

DEPARTURE

He sat in his Prague palace, where the masons were at work, dictating, writing, waiting. For artillery, promised by the imperial War Council. For the new troops marching in long columns from Moravia and Austria, Swabia and Franconia towards Eger, the rendezvous on Bohemia's northern frontier. For his "Instruction". For the designation of his rank. Was it not possible somewhat to accelerate these procedures? It would be late in the season before northern Germany was reached, too late to be able to undertake anything of a large-scale nature.

His appointment was transmitted in July, with his title that of General, the salary to be fixed later. Hitherto rulers had invested their senior commanders only with proxy for their own authority, making Lieutenant-Generals of them. For one to become a general was a novelty, although soon it would be manifest that this was still not enough. For the moment there were no general officers at all under the one, sole general. Those holding such rank, old, useless Montenegro, and the Major-Generals over cavalry and artillery, Marradas and Prince Max Liechtenstein, had tactfully resigned their appointments as token of a changed régime. Naturally it was unwelcome to these gentlemen that he who so recently had stood far below them should now stand far above. Marradas expected fresh employment consonant with his dignity. To his no small astonishment none was foreseen. Did the new star in the martial firmament think that he could command such an army all alone?

Marradas was in collusion with Colonel Rudolf Colloredo, who was hoping for promotion and could rely on court connections. "Express my humble thanks to His Majesty that he has taken no decision on Colloredo's appointment as Major-General, but wishes to have my opinion. Had it transpired, I would assuredly not have remained. The army with him would have been like a village with a fatuous shaveling. Never in my life, I can take my oath, have I met a greater recreant. His regiment is in such a state of disorder that it gives me more trouble than the whole armada." Wallenstein was writing to Harrach about the colonel. He and his brother Hieronimus were Germanized Italians until, favoured by the fortunes of war as others were not, they settled sumptuously in Bohemia.* This was the time when many a name cropped up in Wallenstein's circle which would not again drop out of it – Colonels Duke Franz Albrecht von Sachsen-Lauenburg, Isolani (of the Croat contingent), Tiefenbach, Aldringen, Schlick, Desfours, and a number more. The General scrutinized them closely. "Colonel Wratislaw has borne himself well." "Prithee, my lord, tell Secretary Questenberg that Colonel Hebron, his appointee, does not bear himself as well as he might." Formidable introductions were no guarantee of advancement. One who made no headway was the Marquis Caretto di Grana. He never forgot the fact. "The Marquis di Grana shows great resentment that I refuse him regimental command. His mouth will not remain inactive. Prithee, my lord, forestall it with His Majesty and with the ministers that he is recommended to me, for I

* The Colloredos were beneficiaries of Wallenstein's murder in that they received one of his estates as reward for their services (translator's note).

swear that I would rather betake me to an almshouse than have him by me. I like him less from day to day."

The man most useful to him at this stage was Johann von Aldringen, a Luxemburger by birth which, wicked tongues wagged, was so low that he began as a lackey or valet. Empty slander. His origin was noble but penurious. He started in the soldier's trade as a pikeman, but thanks to his gift for writing letters and doing sums rendered himself indispensable to orderly-rooms. His rise was rapid. By 1622 he was a regimental commander, a year later senior recruitment, payment, and billeting commissary entrusted with the reduction of establishments. Nothing more natural than that he should switch from disarmament to rearmament when this was current policy. His was a twofold delicate task. He had to lay down recruitment areas and see that the military entrepreneurs did not poach on each others' preserves. The German Estates, particularly those in no position seriously to refuse and resist, the imperial towns, had to be coerced into not only inviting their unwelcome military guests but rendering financial contributions. Aldringen performed this staff work with the identical skill that formerly had rendered him popular with his company commander. Not that he really made himself popular with Wallenstein. The General did not care to have the "ink-swiller", as he called him, too near. "From my lord's letter I perceive that Colonel Aldringen corresponds much with the court. It is well that he does so, for he is of the quill profession, while for me it is impossible to report all bagatelles. I know that the Emperor delights in them, but I have other food for thought." (To Harrach.)

When matters had proceeded sufficiently far, with officers galloping up and down the columns of luckless fortune-seekers plodding in dust and stench towards the frontier-town, the baggage train, the powder-carts, the victualling and camp-followers' wagons in the rear, when the quarter-cannon and culverins were in place and some, though far too little, money was in the commissaries' iron chests, when, in short, all had in exactly four months been done that in such circumstances could be done, Wallenstein left Prague with his household and two companies of cuirassiers as bodyguard. On 31 July he arrived at the gates of Eger. He was received by a town council deputation. The Duke spoke words of encouragement, promising to see to good order. Gifts were presented on the part of the town: two pails of wine for each colonel; a stag, wine, beer, and mead for the General. Did the city fathers think that such trifles could constitute a ransom? On 12 August Wallenstein summons the mayors and orders payment of thirty thousand talers into the war-chest. A meeting of the town council declared this an impossibility: Eger had already paid forty thousand gulden, and that at the price of the city patriciate's wives and daughters selling their jewellery. A fresh meeting with the General. "See that the money decreed by Commissary Aldringen is paid, else I cannot be on the march. I have spared you billeting of the soldiery and seen that discipline is maintained. Go!" The town council meets again, another meeting with Aldringen. Suddenly he is all affability. Last night, he tells them, he saw His Princely Grace in as good a humour as has long not been the case – an intimation as to how familiar Aldringen is with the Duke – and seized the chance to discuss the town's difficult situation, obtaining permission not only to reduce its contribution to a mere ten thousand gulden, but a free hand to come to any sensible agreement. Hereupon the town council offers five thousand gulden. Aldringen raises the figure to seven thousand. Tolerable satisfaction on both sides. An invitation to the ducal table, kept in any case at the town's expense. The Duke chats agreeably. Two mayoral offspring volunteer for the imperial colours. The pattern would often be repeated. The design's execution would not always run so comparatively smoothly.

Wallenstein remained at Eger the whole of August. Better not to ask what the town had to pay for his household's support in addition to the seven thousand gulden. He inspected the regiments (four old, three new, and fifty-three cavalry units), whereafter they moved westwards into the Empire by various routes. His orders were to leave for the present not only the Catholic, but also the neutral Protestant Estates as far as possible unmolested by the army's passage. As he wrote to Trauttmansdorff, "The reason I have to divide them [the regiments] is that around Schweinfurt all is Saxon, Würzburg, and Fulda territory which has to be spared." On 3 September he left Eger. The coaches rolled into Franconia, with Schweinfurt as their destination.

By now he was commander of a force exceeding fifty thousand mercenaries, a number far in excess of what Tilly had at his disposal. That such a main force should be assembled against the main enemy, Denmark, leader of the northern coalition, and not against Mansfeld, making forays eastwards from the Netherlands, was logical, however much it annoyed Elector Maximilian. When five years later the Electors sounded the general attack against Wallenstein, one of the charges was that, without their knowledge and to the ruin of the Empire, an imperial army of previously unwitnessed magnitude had been raised at a time when almost no enemy was any longer on hand. That has to be understood in the perspective of spring 1630. Affairs lay otherwise in 1625. Then it had been particularly Bavaria which had keenly espied the armed opposition to all that since the battle of the White Mountain had happened in central Europe, a real, not simply possible threat, and had demanded counter-measures. Was it, though, a reality which demanded *such* counter-measures? Wallenstein, on the threshold of the adventure, was in unbending and arrogant mood. "This is not the time for kind words to Lower Saxony's princes. They are atrociously caught in the net, so that the Emperor can do with them what he will, and eventually it must assuredly happen that they will pay the Emperor his armada." If it did not now march against them, where should the new army go? Out of desperation it would either turn on the Empire's faithful Estates or seek quarters in Bohemia, to the disaster of this kingdom. That was just what Eggenberg had feared. Excessive rearmament created two enemies – the foreign one who might otherwise not have come on the scene and the domestic one. An army could in four months be conjured up, but it was not an entity which could within four months be made to disappear again. Let alone he who commanded it.

The First Generalate

THINGS lay askew. Absolute monarchy, which obtained in Spain and was the German Habsburgs' unconscious, half-conscious objective, may not altogether have been salutary in its effects, but the principle of rule by Estates could certainly wear a look of archaic, inflexible feudalism. It did in Bohemia, not in the Netherlands. Two of the states leaning towards the great coalition against Habsburg were at home engaged in a struggle for tighter, absolutist rule, unsuccessfully where the Stuart kings were concerned, soundly successful as regards the Bourbons. Cardinal Richelieu, Wallenstein's more fortunate fellow in fate, did indeed still distinguish between celestial and terrestrial matters, pursuing the overthrow of the Protestants in politics but countenancing feeedom of faith for them if otherwise they behaved as obedient subjects. After him, though, that changed too, and France does not fit easily into the picture of two ways of life at grips with one another. The Pope, Urban VIII, was a foe to heretics and Spaniards alike. Within the Empire no Emperor could cling more closely to its clumsy institutions than Saxony, principal power among German Lutherans. Bavaria, the arch-Catholic protagonist, took an amiable view of France, an unamiable one of Spain. Two of the monarchs belonging to the Protestant, maritime camp, the Swede and the Dane, were former foes always ready to renew their enmity. The backward Muscovites were on the progressive party's side, the Swedish, Dutch and English, but the Persians on the periphery opted for the Spaniards in so far as they fought against the Turks, the Austrians' adversary. A thread of sense runs through these complexities of war, but it is frail, obscure, a will-o'-the-wisp. Need or caprice constantly made for the strangest bedfellows.

Certain states had at any rate reached a stage where, however great their inner diversity, they were able to prosecute a broad foreign policy. The Empire was unable to do so and never would attain that point. In theory the imperial Diet had to decide on a war waged by the Empire, although in an emergency this could be done by the Emperor and the Electors acting together. No resolution was, however, passed about the war conducted by Wallenstein. How could it have been, seeing that primarily and for a long time to come it was undertaken against Estates of the Empire? Formally it was no more than a series of executive proceedings ordered by the head of the Empire against "proscribed outlaws" like the Palsgrave, Mansfeld, Mad Christian, rebels, and "abominable persons". Even a foreign ruler, the King of Denmark, who entered the lists against the House of Habsburg, was accounted a rebel on the same footing as at Madrid the Dutch were still held to be rebels. Nothing, they said at Vienna, was known about hostilities against His Royal Grace the King of Denmark and Norway, only about legal action against "a Duke of Holstein", who unfortunately was also the commanding officer of the Lower Saxon Circle. In principle neither a condition of war nor parleys for peace could supervene in the case of such an opponent. The abominable person should lay down his arms, confess his error and with true German fealty submit to divinely appointed authority. That done, it would perhaps not prove impossible to achieve indulgent understanding; the Emperor was merciful and sore of heart at all this bloodshed, ruinous to the Empire. These types of fiction were not conducive to real peace.

The pretence did not render any easier the existence of neutrals. There genuinely were some, and bluff John George, Elector of Saxony, is familiar to us as their leader. Strictly speaking, in the light of the mere police actions on which the Emperor embarked first in Bohemia, then in southern Germany and now in northern Germany, there was no room for the status. It was a sufferance of facts when even at Vienna the talk was of neutrals who should be won over or at least kept neutral. In practice this was made difficult enough, and sooner or later intolerable for them. Their territories lay open and undefended. Let one of the fighting cocks betake himself into them, the other could but follow. The passage of troops, depending on the lie of the border, was anyhow unavoidable. If enemy soil was too ravaged to be capable of feeding an army, where should lodging be found other than with neutrals, friends? An additional point was the all too often fluctuating, Janus-headed, more than suspicious character of the neutrals' neutrality, like that of the Elector of Brandenburg.

In respect of foreign powers proper, England or France, no state of belligerency prevailed. Their ambassadors resided in appropriate pomp at Vienna. The matter was simply one of envoys from Paris and London passing over to the "abominable persons", as did, in accordance with secret agreements, also money and forces, or simply the matter of a prince as loyal to the Empire as the Elector of Bavaria entering into negotiations with the French, conduct strangely incompatible with his duty to Emperor and Empire as well as his actual community of interest with the House of Habsburg. Neither the Empire nor its princes were at war with the Dutch, but the Spaniards were. They stood in the western half of the Empire, the Emperor was to a good half a Spaniard and, without his having asked the Electors for advice on the subject, a number of his sparse regiments helped the Infanta at Brussels against the Dutch. Can a worse confusion be imagined, a confusion compounded of appalling, short-sighted egotism, immature heroics, opinionatedness and cant?

One of the pieces of cant was that the war was no war of religion and had no aim other than that everyone should have his due and what he had always had. Why then war at all, a never-ending war at that? Because this side wanted only justice, the other injustice. At no point was Emperor Ferdinand out to breach the Augsburg religious settlement; he repeated the assurance over and over again. More ambiguous was the position relating to everything subsequent to the Augsburg compromise and whose occurrence formed part of the bulk of a mutable, not immobile process of pacification. Bohemia, however bitter its fate, could be let be: changes there affected only indirectly the Empire and its equilibrium. A subject of direct concern was the deprivation and outlawry of the Palsgrave, all the more as Elector Maximilian in the conquered Palatinate and in Upper Austria, which the Emperor had granted him in lien, was with utmost severity pushing forward the deformation called the Counter-Reformation. With the war spreading to northern Germany, the great and lucrative imperial foundations of Magdeburg, Halberstadt, Hildesheim, Osnabrück, Bremen, long *de facto* Protestant but in the eyes of Viennese politicians not *de jure*, became the objects of fright and greed. Were they to be re-Catholicized, there would remain of former powerful German Protestantism a mere residue capable of being chopped small or blown away at will. It was the avowed principle of Habsburg policy, set down too in Wallenstein's instructions as General, that the old settlement had validity in the case of those, and only those, who submitted in good time. Too late a compliance forfeited any claim. But when was in good time? Is it any wonder that the Protestant princes and republics never quite knew how to safeguard themselves, whether by submission or alliance with those prepared to fight?

Running counter to the conflict between the confessions was the fact that army commanders never asked after the faith of their officers and men. To no one did this apply more than to Wallenstein. In the first place he had to take soldiers where he could find them. *"Capite, rapide"*, as he once wrote. Secondly, in antithesis to his principals, he denied from start to finish the war's religious ingredients, knowing that no war of that kind could ever be brought to an end. A third element may also have lain behind the interdenominational character of his troops. Just as the states in conflict, all part of the same pie, at no point became wholly divided from one another and the warring rulers continued to exchange letters larded with love of peace and petulance, so the sects stuck together through, and regardless of, their scuffles. Their nature was not such as to render possible the demarcation of distinct fronts between them. Soldiers ran away and ran over to the enemy whenever it suited them. Among the smaller war entrepreneurs, the colonels and the captains, it was termed change of service, a process undertaken with dizzying frequency. Colonel Hans Georg von Arnim, a Brandenburger by birth, served successively the King of Sweden, the King of Poland, Count Mansfeld, the King of Sweden again, the Emperor of Wallenstein, the Elector of Saxony, and again the Emperor. He was moreover an exception, not in changing his masters like his clothes, but as a man given to serious, religious, political reflection. What, in these pernicious circumstances, could the average officer be after other than his own interest, booty, possessions, and fame?

So much for how the European scene was set when Wallenstein first entered upon it as imperial general. Before dealing with this fresh chapter of his life, it appears commendable to say in the same way as earlier a word about our sources.

For the years between 1625 and 1628 his letters to Harrach are of incomparable value. There were occasions when he wrote him two, four, five letters in a single day. Father-in-law and son-in-law were formal in their modes of address: "Illustrious and Beloved Prince" on the one hand, "Noble Lord" on the other. Protocol observed, Wallenstein was completely frank with Harrach, indeed to such an extent that the minister, whether with posterity in mind or because he wanted to show the missive to highest authority, often saw fit to make a few phrases illegible. More guarded, diplomatically worried, but still copiously frank was the Duke's correspondence with other courtiers, Privy Councillor Max von Trauttmansdorff (the Emperor's most capable adviser after Eggenberg and Harrach) in particular, Count Collalto (President of the imperial War Council), Gerhard von Questenberg (secretary to the same body), and others. That with Eggenberg is missing because the preponderant portion of the latter's epistolary collection has been lost. Letters to the Emperor have survived. They are astonishing for their directness, positive abruptness of style. And then there is the flood of dictated, purely political, purely military communications, imperious orders, inquiries, answers, reports by, to, about him, exchanges of courtesies and opinions, conference minutes, secret tale-bearing, and public news-letters. One investigator was able to fill ten volumes with such Wallensteiniana and others have succeeded in producing ten times that amount. In archives, especially Bohemian ones, much lies as yet unlocked. What has come to light is a cornucopia of good things.

ONE YEAR, TWO CAMPAIGNS

First of all, a bare outline of events.

During the late autumn of 1625 and winter 1626 not much happened in the new Lower German theatre of war. Only what was customary at those seasons, meaning that the armies' main preoccupations were as far as possible to keep warm, as far as possible to survive with full bellies. Alongside this a bit of politics, some effort at making peace, on this occasion before hostilities had properly begun. Well-wishing mediators, Saxony at their head, were never lacking. Was it not feasible, seeing that all parties to the quarrel wanted no more than justice, no gains, no conquests, not to harm a fly, was it not in those circumstances feasible to find a golden mean? Envoys met at Brunswick. Their instructions served as *démarches* into thin air. Each acting as though his side had already won, they put forward quite impossible demands so as then to reduce them by a little, though far from enough. Each accused the other of not really wanting a peaceful solution, of false play, and of simply using the interval to increase his armaments, the last point perfectly correct. Each expressed his readiness to disarm if the other made a start. Each blamed the other for the breakdown of negotiations which no one ever doubted would be the outcome. "I have small hope of peace", wrote Wallenstein to Harrach. Indeed, what would otherwise have been the purpose of all the costly preparations? Not that anybody could pay for them unless it were the wretched common man who had already after his own fashion begun to pay.

The King of Denmark experienced a good deal of annoyance with his German allies, the members of the Lower Saxon Circle. No more than a narrow majority had voted for common defence measures. Those who had not, the Duke of Lüneburg, the wealthy maritime cities, felt no obligation to participate. The Duke of Brunswick, weak and unable to make up his mind, vacillated. His brother, Mad Christian, succeeded however in usurping dominion over Brunswick, whereupon this free-booter, now pledged to Denmark, managed to assume in some sort the appearance of a ruler in his own right. Count Mansfeld, having marched from Friesland via Lübeck into Lower Saxon territory, was also on the scene again, this time in the shape of an excellently accoutred ally, dispatched by the Kings of Great Britain and France to the Lower Saxon Circle without the latter ever having actually asked for his services. To these two adventurers was added a third, Duke Johann Ernst von Weimar, undoubtedly the soundest of them as far as character went. Actors all three in the raw, as yet chaotic drama performed by Germany's and Europe's polities, they were not exactly allied to any legitimate power, but none the less needed to be taken seriously as long as mercenaries flocked to their colours. It was they who, because they had most to win and nothing to lose, brought life into the stagnant state of hostilities.

There was friction too between Tilly and Wallenstein, Wallenstein and Tilly. The one old and crowned with laurels, the other young by comparison and unproved. Their two armies operated side by side and were condemned to live from the same lean soil. Their two supreme commanders were closely related, confederates, and stalking the same game, for all that in secret it was not quite the same. Wallenstein's first, facile military move had been to occupy Magdeburg and Halberstadt. His palpable purpose was to furnish his troops with winter quarters and victual them at the expense of both bishoprics. Confidential letters revealed his further aim – to keep out Bavaria. Where Elector Max came, there he stayed, as witness the fate of the Upper Palatinate and the Palatinate right bank of the Rhine. The Emperor's advisers, on the other hand, regarded Magdeburg and Halberstadt as arch-Catholic territories doubly forfeit to their sovereign – the Protestant administrator of Halberstadt was none other than Mad Christian, his Magdeburg neighbour was Christian Wilhelm von Brandenburg, in any case not on the spot and a sympathizer with the Danes. Let Magdeburg and Halberstadt become benefices for the Emperor's younger son? Wallenstein had discussed the point with Father Lamormaini, the imperial confessor, before he set out. Colonel Aldringen, ever ready to be obliging to Vienna, sounded the same note. "That would be a titbit for the son of His Majesty," he told Collalto. "Or at least the pie could be shared." Wallenstein's observation to Harrach about the Elector, "It does not accord with reasons of state to make him mightier to the Emperor's cost", went to the heart of the matter.

Tilly held the Weser, Wallenstein the Elbe, a strategic division of labour satisfactory to the latter. The Elbe was his home stream down which grain could be floated from Bohemia – not that any arrived except from his duchy. A bridgehead on its right bank ensured him a return route to the Hereditary Lands, Silesia, Bohemia, Moravia. Such security he accounted precaution's first commandment. He thought the free-booters, particularly Mansfeld, capable of attempting what three years ago had been planned, the big south-eastern pincer movement. He was prepared to credit the Danes with an attempt at the project too, or the Swedes, since his spies gave him reason to anticipate their landing some-where in Pomerania or Mecklenburg. As the Emperor's continental commander-in-chief he had to be on the look-out in all directions, including the Netherlands, France, and Italy. It may be said, with requisite chariness, that his nose for the east, Brandenburg, Silesia, Prussia, Poland, was the sharper. That was due to his origins; the Rhine-land was foreign country to him. Although, for as long as he was sta-tioned in Lower Germany, his direct confrontation was with the Danes and the Danes' venturesome friends, his task remained to defend the Habsburg Hereditary Lands and to keep in being the new rule of force and order in Bohemia against its many afflicted foes.

One factor in the positions taken up was the strategy that it was proposed to follow when the weather would smile more kindly. This subject, with the question of a junction between their forces, was debated by Wallenstein and Tilly in dispatches as well as personal dis-cussions during meetings at a half-way meeting place. Agreement was long delayed because the one was always trying to bring the other closer to his side or to obtain a loan of troops, each fancying his theatre of war to be the more important or imperilled. When finally, in early summer, an understanding on a major plan of campaign was reached, with each to move separately and then launch a united attack, it was again too late.

King Christian had his base at Wolfenbüttel, well inside the triangle formed by Wallenstein's and Tilly's forces. Fortresses like Minden, Northeim, and Göttingen, within the imperial-Bavarian radius of activ-ity, lay in his hands. His freebooters' quest for food and plunder took them southwards into Hesse. Their ability to sweep intact through even such a narrow strip of country is explicable only in terms of the thinness of contingents on the ground which distinguished the conduct of contemporary warfare. There were no fronts. Several hundred or a thousand horsemen would infiltrate a sprinkling of strong-points, sometimes successfully, sometimes caught in the act. Guerrilla warfare, with friend and foe everywhere, the sallies unplanned and inspired or interrupted by passing circumstances. Thanks to Wallenstein, a little order was introduced into this mess and muddle of military activity. At an early stage he had seized the town of Dessau as well as the bridges across the Mulde and Elbe leading to it. During the winter thousands of mercenaries and impressed peasants worked on the erection of a small fort on the right, fortifications on the left banks of the Elbe. The Dessau bridge became the strongest link in the chain connecting Wallenstein with the Hereditary Lands. As Count Mansfeld advanced with his Dutchmen, Germans, Danes, Scots, and French up the eastern side of the Elbe, ignoring the anyhow dubious neutrality of Brandenburg, it occurred to him to attack the Emperor's new general precisely where he was established at his prickliest. Nobody knows why. He could have achieved what was thought to be his intention without tackling the Elbe bridge. Maybe he did not care to leave an undefeated enemy in his rear. Maybe he wanted, after so many discomfitures, once more to prove to his paymasters the stuff he was made of. Whatever his motive, at the beginning of April he settled down opposite the bridgehead, surrounded it with redoubts on which he mounted cannon, and had approaches dug. The officer commanding the bridgehead was Colonel Aldringen, the "quillpusher" and Wallenstein's paymaster-general. He now showed that his skill went beyond collecting tributes. Although effectively supported by eighty-six quarter cannon, the two regiments available to him were far outnumbered by Mansfeld's twenty thousand men. For three weeks he held his own by way of nocturnal sorties and artillery fire by day. Messenger after messenger was posted to his commander-in-chief, at this date preparing an offensive against King Christian directly from his headquarters at Aschersleben. Mansfeld compelled him to relinquish the plan, first by reinforcing Aldringen, then by leading in person the main part of his army to Dessau. The crucial day was 25 April 1626. The battle, lasting longer than was usual, raged six hours. There is said to have been a moment when Wallenstein had a mind to surrender the bridgehead and blow up the pontoons, but he was dissuaded by Aldringen. Whether true or merely rumour which Aldringen was at no pains to deny, that can be left open. The battle-plan depicted by Merian demonstrates at any rate remarkably clear-headed determination. The sally from the bridgehead, at the most critical moment the thrust across the bridge by the imperialist infantry under Wallenstein's own command at the same time as the cannonade against Mansfeld's left wing by a battery posted on the left bank of the Elbe, and the attack of Count Schlick's cuirassiers from a concealed position when Mansfeld had already ordered withdrawal, these four operations constituted an articulated whole for which connoisseurs of the military art cannot withhold their admiration. Mansfeld's withdrawal would probably have degenerated from a well-controlled retreat into a slaughter and wild flight if, to cap everything, his powder-train had not exploded and his men imagined themselves to be completely surrounded. Three to four thousand of them were left dead on the field. No difficulty was experienced in enticing the prisoners, almost fifteen hundred in all, to enter Wallenstein's service. Mansfeld rode away with barely five thousand survivors. By nightfall Wallenstein had chased him as far as Zerbst, but next morning desisted from the pursuit, returning across the Elbe to Aschersleben. His reports, to the Emperor on the day of battle, to the Elector of Bavaria, the Infanta, and the Archdukes on the day after, have a proud ring about them. "In duty bound I cannot leave Yr Imperial Majesty unapprised how God, the Supporter at all times of Yr Majesty's just Cause, has today given me the good fortune to smite Mansfeld upon the head."

Smite Mansfeld upon the head, yes. But soon there were murmurs at Vienna that he had not exploited his triumph to polish off finally the vilest of the freebooter leaders. It was what Wallenstein expected. "I doubt not that there will be all kinds of chatter by scolds, priestlings, and sundry Italian rapscallions that the victory against Mansfeld is not prosecuted, territory has not been seized, and other steps possible upon the attainment of victory are not taken." Were the critics in his place, they would adopt a different tone. Mansfeld was not his sole adversary. The Dane was preparing a widespread attack. Mad Christian and his 3500 horsemen were also in the vicinity. From Tilly, whose host lay encamped unmolested beside the Weser, he was receiving no help at all. As for conducting a campaign into the blue while the corn was still green, "whoever wishes to be a fool and wreck an army in a fortnight, let him do it, particularly since there cannot be done with an unpaid army what a paid one will do." His strength sufficed for a battle, but it was insufficient to turn success to account because his men were exhausted, listless to the verge of mutiny. Proceeding farther, they would not have found the necessities of life. The situation was such as sub-

sequently would incline him sometimes to suppress news of the favourable outcome of a passage of arms "because I know how they are at
court when a good report arrives". And he did not believe that during
the rest of this year Mansfeld would be back on his feet. A mistake.

For a last time the old death-merchant did what he had so often done
before – he refused to acknowledge defeat. Making himself at home in
the Brandenburg Marches, he waited for reinforcements, from Scots,
Danes, and Duke Johann Ernst von Weimar's private army, and six
weeks later had brought his strength up again to the twenty thousand
men under his command before the battle at the Dessau bridgehead.
His guests, the Elector of Brandenburg conveyed to Wallenstein, were
unwelcome, but unfortunately he could not be rid of them. Which was
both true and untrue. The presence of Mansfeld's mercenaries was even
more of a disaster than that of all other war-lords' troops. Although he
could offer his subjects no proper protection, the Elector's heart bled for
them. Yet Brandenburg policy had for long past been pro-Danish, or
pro-Dutch, or pro-Swedish, and it still retained those sympathies, a fact
to which Wallenstein often drew the Emperor's attention. "I beseech
that no trust be reposed in the Elector of Brandenburg." To George
William he addressed the warning that he would respect Brandenburg
neutrality as long as the other side did, but that the enemy must be
sought where he was to be found.

During the second half of June he was engaged in drafting a major
plan to end the war in northern Germany. The Bavarian and imperial
armies should march down both banks of the Elbe in the direction of
Hamburg and Holstein. The Danish king should be constrained either
to fight or to be squeezed off imperial soil, "for it is time". The meeting
of the two generals on 30 June at Duderstadt was as ceremonial as
always, but the upshot was more fruitful than on earlier occasions.
Wallenstein made a concession. He would relinquish to Tilly two of his
own regiments and the auxiliary corps of eight thousand men promised
by the Infanta. The Spaniards had never abandoned their dream of
linking the German war with their own and a splendid idea had been
hatched at Brussels – an attack on the Dutch, whom it proved again and
again impossible to beat on land, at their most sensitive point, their
commercial lines of communication. To this end it was necessary to
bring under control, with the imperialists, the most important German
coastal *entrepôts*, such as Lübeck. For the Empire this design held the
danger that its implementation would inextricably involve it in the
Spanish–Dutch war. That was precisely why the Elector of Bavaria,

unfriendly to the Spaniards, was no friend of it. The generals, though, longing "to spatter the enemy before Swedish help arrives" (Wallenstein), eagerly accepted the Spanish offer while they politely declined to have their strategy and policy dictated by Brussels.

Three or four unanticipated vexations intervened. Affairs suddenly went so badly for the Spaniards that they had to drop their naval warfare project into a drawer and await its later re-discovery. The promise of an auxiliary corps was not kept. In Upper Austria the peasants rose against Elector Maximilian's hated overlordship. This was a serious business, prepared long beforehand, comprising every house in every village, under the leadership of a yeoman, Stephan Fadinger, with a gift for military organization and the composition of perfectly formulated letters, a rebellion complete with committees to open negotiations and a parliament constituted on the right lines, a patriotic and a religious uprising. The peasants' enemies propagated the lie that they had republican leanings on the Swiss pattern. On the contrary, they thought that they had the Emperor's support, which was not altogether an illusion in so far as their movement was aimed against the loathed Bavarian administration and exploitation. Vienna, already warned that Maximilian might keep for ever his extorted lien, resented that too. Where the matter turned on religious coercion, the expulsion of Protestant ministers and their supersession by "Italian, incompetent, provocative preachers", resisted by the peasants, Emperor and Elector were of the same mind, the second performing what the first was unflinchingly intent upon. Belatedly the Bavarian governor presented himself to the peasants as "not the tyrant he has baselessly been proclaimed and calumniated as being", but as one who "prefers amiability to severity". However, beaten by them in battle, he had to flee in disgrace back to Linz, the only larger place not in league with the rebels. Vienna and Munich called for troops. They could only be taken from the force at Wallenstein's disposal, if not in northern Germany, then from among the regiments stationed in Austria and Bohemia.

He was loth to let them go. That poor, scattered little cloud of dust which Mansfeld was at the beginning of May had gathered anew into an eastward coursing thundercloud. Gabor Bethlen, the south-eastern veteran was showing those signs of military restiveness which he always displayed at exactly the moment when something Protestant, something anti-Habsburg was stirring in the direction of Silesia and Moravia. Would he and Mansfeld descend, as schemed three years ago, in a cloudburst on the Habsburg territories, kindling in Moravia and Bohemia insurrections similar to that in the Land above the Enns?* The situation was familiar. On the one hand the Emperor's power triumphant, on the other the grave insecurity and danger to its structure. A few weeks after the discussions at Duderstadt Wallenstein knew that all the planning had been in vain. He sent a few regiments to Silesia. He improved the Silesian defence machinery, intrinsically the responsibility of the Estates and princes but, like all Estate military organization, useless. Gradually he faced the fact that he must proceed in person to a region which he knew and where he hated waging war. Moravia, that was feasible. But Hungary, Upper Hungary, its Slovak component, or even Lower Hungary, Pannonia proper? With unpaid, grim-faced mercenaries, without assured provisions?

As late as 3 July Wallenstein thought Mansfeld incapable of performing such an enterprise as the Silesian–Hungarian one. Yet ten days afterwards he was talking about four theatres of war – "here, in Silesia, in Hungary, and in the Land above the Enns". Mansfeld and Danish forces were able to advance into Silesia only because a large part of its population was hostile to the Emperor. In their train came Bohemian *émigrés*. The peasant revolt in the Land above the Enns was the answer by Austrian Protestants to what hopes they reposed in the Danes. So was Gabor Bethlen's manoeuvring. It was not coincidence that the four theatres of war ensued simultaneously. On 17 July panic befell him. "Our affairs stand at a worse juncture than ever before. If we suffer the slightest reverse, the entire Empire will move against us." "My lord will see how the blaze will spread all around." The day after next he had decided to undertake the long journey, preceding it by a nocturnal ride to meet Tilly. He could not leave the scene of operations, accompanied by the bulk of his army, in the way that he would have left a spa. He agreed to transfer eighty-five companies of foot and horse under the command of Colonels Aldringen, Desfours, and the Duke of Lüneburg. "Not one whit more," Tilly grumbled bitterly. The Bavarians were in exchange to hold, if they could, Wallenstein's former Elbe positions. During the last few days of the month he put the rest of the army, infantry, cavalry, and artillery totalling some twenty thousand men, across that river.

On 28 July he shifted his headquarters from Aschersleben to Zerbst. There he stayed a fortnight, still not quite certain what he should do.

---

* "The Land above the Enns", "The Land below the Enns" were and are traditional names for Upper and Lower Austria whose border south of the Danube is constituted by the river Enns (translator's note).

"If I go from here, all the places occupied are lost, the soldiers whom I leave behind will be slaughtered, the Elector of Saxony will have to side with the enemy, all the noxious spirits in the Empire will rise. . . . If I do not go, I am apprehensive at the peril to the Emperor and all his lands. . . . For a while I must necessarily still dally here." During that interval one task was to recruit Polish cavalry, at first hand, not through King Sigismund. Since Poland was an elective monarchy, with many magnates Calvinist and opposed to the Emperor, negotiations for alliance would prove too protracted. The cavalry was required with utmost speed and must join him somewhere in Silesia. It was all the more essential on account of the Hungarians' unreliability, attested twenty-two years ago. He had had experience of their behaviour in such a crisis. "They busy their heads with religion." He needed moreover money, those paltry hundred thousand talers that he had been promised long past. He also needed flour, to be distributed at points all along his line of advance. What would his soldiers otherwise do if they arrived somewhere towards nightfall and found no food on hand? Thought should be given to what was to happen to the Transylvanian, once his horde was routed. Furthermore the Governor of Moravia, Cardinal Dietrichstein, had proposed the recruitment of twelve thousand men. That was something that he should not be allowed to try because he would only use them for the protection of his own properties. Waste, not gain. Or let him attempt it on condition that the whoring little priest went to Rome as ambassador, thereby removed from the scene. Prescient, teeming ideas, dashed down on paper and sent scurrying to Vienna. If he has money, bread, eight thousand Cossacks from Poland, and is met by Hungarian cavalry at the border, then he will be ready to overthrow Bethlen, Mansfeld, Weimar, uphold order in the Hereditary Lands, and – this in a moment of euphoria which sometimes seizes him – next year proceed to Prussia in order, together with Poland, to ban the Swedish danger before Germany falls victim to it.

On 8 August he broke up his camp at Zerbst. "I shall make vigorous marches by day and take but little rest." His marches were indeed vigorous. From Zerbst to Olmütz, in Moravia, is over 370 miles. Along this stretch he drove in twenty-two days the enormous serpentine train of his army, with its gipsies, women, thousand baggage-wagons and guards in addition to the cursing soldiers dragging themselves forward in their tattered boots. The rate, without the inevitable days of rest, was more than eighteen miles every twenty-four hours. Is there in modern times anything to compare? Wallenstein's fate was to arouse suspicion

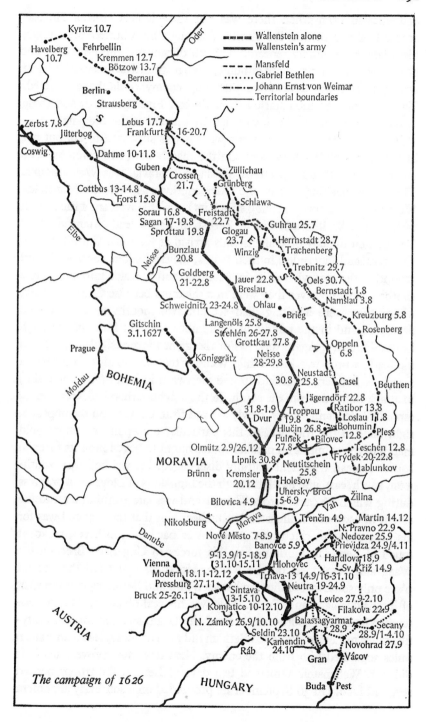

The campaign of 1626

and chagrin even when there was not the slightest reason. He was accused of progressing too slowly. Although he rebutted the charge, historians have blindly repeated it. Such distances could obviously not be covered in such time with impunity. Exhaustion, dysentery, and plague wrought far more devastation than any enemy could have inflicted. Twenty thousand men started from Zerbst. Five thousand, and those in the shape to be expected, were left by the end of the campaign.

It was a spectral one, achieving what it was supposed to do, but not in any gloriously strategic way. On the march were two columns. The inner, passing through western Silesia to Moravia, was Wallenstein's. The outer, pushing east of the Oder southwards, was the Mansfeld–Weimar–Danish force. Having struck its tents at Havelberg a full month earlier than Wallenstein did at Zerbst, it had a lead. Mansfeld took Teschen on the day of Wallenstein's arrival at Kottbus. With Teschen, Troppau, and Jägerndorf in their hands, the freebooters controlled good ground in the area where Silesia, Moravia, and Slovakia impinge on one another. Now however they were in a dilemma because Gabor Bethlen, whom they were awaiting, had set out two months after their own departure and in the middle of September was still fumbling through Lower Hungary. Again the jaws of the giant pincer failed to close and the lead in time was lost. While Weimar took the road to Hungary in search of Bethlen, Mansfeld turned westward in order (as some claim) to attack Bohemia from the south. In the neighbourhood of Kremsier he espied Wallenstein's army, newly arrived from Olmütz, on the opposite, right bank of the Morawa. At this particular map-point the month-old march of the columns on parallel course ought to have found its focus in battle. Instead Mansfeld skilfully disengaged. He writhed east, south-west, south, east, and north through the highlands of Slovakia, a progress during which he came across Weimar and was successful at least to the extent of escaping Wallenstein's clutches. Not that the General was for his part trying to catch him. At a slower pace than hitherto, he spent much of September bringing up his forces to Ungarisch-Brod on the Waag and Neuhäusel on the Neitra. He knew that from this second place only some forty miles lay between him and Bethlen's encampment of Transylvanians and Turks. This was his real objective. On 27 September he moved south-east, crossed the Gran, and continued twenty-five miles to Levice. Provided Bethlen did not run away, less than sixteen miles separated him from the enemy. Next day must prove crucial. It did not. Wallenstein remained two days at Levice; the troops needed rest and food. On 30 September he proceeded on a southerly alignment through the Hungarian plain. His advance guard had a brush with Bethlen's cavalry, but not until close on evening did he make contact with the main Transylvanian body. Although in the dusk the two armies faced each other in battle array, there was no battle. Next morning Bethlen had disappeared. "Three hours more light and I would have had a splendid victory," Wallenstein wrote to Harrach on a somewhat subdued note, "for the foe was so dejected as never yet has happened to Lord Bethlehem [sic]." A more detailed excuse was proffered to the Emperor – the enemy had, during the lull and under cover of darkness, ignominiously taken to his heels. He had left his baggage-train and artillery behind at Neuhäusel. Without them, without victuals, without cash, he regarded it as impossible, and his officers gladly concurred with him, to plunge in pursuit deep into the plain. He therefore returned slowly the way that he had come, back to Levice, back over the Neitra and the Waag, to Turnau. It was now the middle of October, almost two and a half months since he had left his camp at Zerbst.

The south-eastern campaign ended because no one was capable of continuing it. Had Wallenstein's army not kept on its parallel course to Mansfeld's and crept towards the Transylvanian lines, Bethlen and the German freebooters would have been able to do whatever they liked in the Habsburg lands. Wallenstein's five-hundred-miles march put a stop to that. All parties concerned were frustrated in the achievement of their objective by the distances involved and their own shortcomings. Nevertheless those who were the attackers can be regarded as the losers. Bethlen admitted as much, for no more than ten days after he had declined battle with Wallenstein he put forward peace proposals. That was what he had done in 1621 and again in 1623. As in the latter year, Wallenstein advised their acceptance. A treaty was ratified in December. A last, a final one? That would have been improbable, had Bethlen's fate not already been sealed in the shape of dropsy.

Similarly dismal, but further gone, was the state of the German freebooters. Mansfeld, his battered army abandoned to make his way to Ragusa and thence to Paris and London for fresh subsidies and reinforcements, suffered a fatal haemorrhage near Sarajevo. A fortnight later Johann Ernst von Weimar, a youngster broken by the destructive strain of contemporary war, was laid in the soil. When in early summer the firebrand Mad Christian of Brunswick, Halberstadt's ecclesiastic administrator, had been quenched, Wallenstein exclaimed with indecorous boisterousness, "Good luck along the road!" All three of them ended as failures, racked by bodily pain, and not as they would have wished.

They had however faithfully fulfilled their mission to keep the embers of war glimmering until those who were mightier than they threw fresh logs upon the glow. It now happened of its own accord. They were no longer needed.

A swift retrospective glance elsewhere. In August Count Tilly, master veteran, defeated the King of Denmark in the Battle of Lutter which lasted barely a couple of hours. Wallenstein's auxiliaries proved useful to him. Not that this affray put paid to King Christian, as little as the battle for the Elbe bridge had done to Mansfeld. The reason was always the same – the capacity to withdraw, in spite of grievous losses, in a north-easterly direction, reassemble the scattered troops, and take up new positions between the estuary of the Elbe and the Weser, whereas Tilly was unable to cling to his heels. Nevertheless Lutter had more important consequences than Dessau for the Lower Saxon Circle and neighbouring territories. The Dane was a principal in the deal; Mansfeld had merely been a weathercock collateral. Those who still could, broke away. Brunswick was one. Its Duke submitted to the imperial authority. Brandenburg was another. Its false neutrality veered weakly towards loyalty to Emperor and Empire.

In late autumn the peasant uprising in Upper Austria finished in the way that ultimately peasant insurrections always finished – with the rebels' capitulation and penal tribunals. The peasants had achieved remarkable victories, negotiated with the imperial commissioners on equal footing, and attained agreement to all kinds of alleviations. But Maximilian took fright at the possibility of matters being decided over his own head. He ignored the armistice. His local commander, Gottfried Heinrich von Pappenheim, a seasoned campaigner, had to concede that never had he encountered resistance as stout as was offered him by these "frantic, fanatical beasts". It availed them nothing that before the battle they sang Luther's "A Safe Stronghold is Our God" and that at the time of their success they had practised saintly moderation. The rule applied was as eternal as the mundane order of things. The social pyramid rested on the peasants' backs: they furnished their lords with food, they paid the taxes, and if they tried to tamper with the order they were massacred. The harvest gleaned in this instance was scanty. Maximilian lost his taste for the land which had shown such recalcitrance and, half devastated, half depopulated, promised no profit any more. He relinquished his lien in exchange for the Upper Palatinate and the Palatine territories east of the Rhine. The peasant survivors could once again be the pious Emperor's subjects. Sombre good fortune.

By the close of the year the affairs of the group interests called for brevity's sake the Catholic party stood more favourably than they had at the beginning. That may or may not be applauded as a good thing or simply registered as a fact. It brought no end to the war. For as long as Denmark held out, King Gustavus Adolphus fought the Poles in distant Prussia, the politicians at Madrid and Brussels persisted in their megalomania, the Palatine government-in-exile spun its threads of intrigue from The Hague, the King of England was prepared to give money to Habsburg's foes, and Cardinal Richelieu pursued the same policy, for so long would fresh fires be lit.

The contribution of the new Wallenstein army to the martial events of 1626, intrinsically difficult to assess, lay under a shadow. The Duke had been forced, against his wish and will, to leave the northern German theatre of war at the precise moment when something could have been undertaken there. No similar laurels were in Hungary for the plucking. The assistance he gave Tilly shrivelled in the eyes of his critics as compared with what he should have done. In his own opinion he had fulfilled his duty to the utmost – "Had I served God as well, I would assuredly be the foremost saint in Heaven." The view taken at Vienna, let alone Munich, was different. It had been so almost from the outset and, with visibly growing ill-humour, became more so in the months succeeding the battle at the Dessau bridge. The doubts among courtiers, diplomats, and rivals whether Wallenstein was really the man to command a large army culminated at the time when the Hungarian campaign atrophied into nothing.

THE GENERAL

He had barely set foot upon the boards before he wished himself back in the wings. As yet he lacked the assurance that in the next three years he would display to such imposing effect. Consequently he provoked irritation, disappointment and suspicion, reactions which he sensed to be right but which only served to increase his uncertainty.

During 1626 weariness, ill humour, complaints of bad health were the outstanding features of his correspondence. "I am far too tired." "The effort is too much for me." "I cannot do this alone." "I become daily more indisposed." "From downright repugnance I know not what I do." For months on end these expressions recur in nearly every letter to his father-in-law. He was plagued by gout. This, though, is a progressive malady and should in the succeeding years have become worse. It did

not. The failure to do so suggests that psychological factors, exactly as
forecast by Kepler, played an important part in its onsets. His declarations of tiredness were accompanied in the first instance, and with his
characteristic insistence, by requests for a senior assistant, a lieutenant-
general. When one was sent him, their relations briefly went well, then
very badly. Harmony with his deputy's successor was middling.

His burden of work must have been immense. Acceptance of the
overall command had landed him in a deeper bed of nettles than he had
imagined. To squeeze money out of territories which did not want, and
often were unable, to pay; the assignment of billets, in constant argument with the rival Bavarian army and the Spaniards in occupation of
the Rhine sector; to procure provisions, uniforms and boots, weapons
and munitions, and that without the help of those whose task should
have been to supply the imperial army; to move regiments back and
forth, working out their respective distances if they were required in
emergency; the imposition of a minimum of discipline on the common
soldier and the predatory colonels; to keep together the whole tangled
human apparatus against an enemy who was everywhere and nowhere –
what strong nerves would have been requisite for all that even without
"my learned lords", "those bald-pated fellows", as he termed the
Emperor's ministers and councillors of war, continually intervening with
suggestions, instructions, and demands for explanations. He had to
concern himself with the most important matters (Spanish policy,
Sweden's probable eastern strategy) and the most trivial ("Have ten
thousand pairs of boots made for the soldiers, so that I can have them
distributed among the regiments. . . . The boots must be carefully tied
together, pair by pair, so that it will be known which belong to each
other"). He, who had already become so great a lord enjoying his life on
so grand a scale, might with reason ask why he should have entered this
maze. He did ask and wanted, or as sceptics thought pretended to want,
to extricate himself. We cannot share the sceptics' view and have on our
side Lord von Harrach. He took seriously enough his son-in-law's
repeated requests to obtain his release in the coming spring, late autumn,
winter, and again spring: "Therefore I conclude, as I know the Duke
and he also *ad partem* expressly writes me, that he will certainly not be
possible to hold beyond the summer." But he did not take his suit
further than entering his plea and notifying his intention. He never
completed the process by handing in a formal application to His Imperial
Majesty.

Generally moody, generally in a state of umbrage, he inclined to see in sombre colours the cause he served. "We must regard it as a maxim that we can trust absolutely no one." He hoped to bring the war to an end this year still "else our affairs stand dismally". "Those who advised His Imperial Majesty to resort to war now see into what a labyrinth they have led Him and us all," he deplored when he was reluctantly bracing himself for the south-eastern campaign. He placed the blame on "divers priests" and, he commented to Collalto, "They thereby do mischief and know nothing of the craft." Others, though, suspected him of deliberately prolonging hostilities for his own base advantage, one illustration among many of the gift for creating totally unjustified mistrust which was conferred on him at birth by an evil fairy. In fact he counselled peace feelers whenever he thought the moment half-way propitious. Thus, after the battle at the Dessau bridge, "The Emperor has not the means to wage war and without money this business can have no duration." Two months later he was writing to Ferdinand that this was the juncture at which to negotiate from a position of ascendancy and high standing, a circumstance on whose continuation no reliance could by any means be placed. Similar examples exist in plenty. In contrast is cited a strange sentence to be read in a letter of 21 December 1625 to Privy Councillor von Trauttmansdorff. Tilly, he wrote, had secured the Weser, he the Elbe; to the Danes, the Swedes, the English, and the Dutch remained the sea. "That is why the war will have to be fed with gold and silver from the Indies and perchance continued for thirty years before something salutary may ensue." The foregoing means that Wallenstein correctly foretold the duration of the Thirty Years' War and desired this? Sheer misinterpretation! For in the same letter he reiterates that the means for a "lingering war" are lacking. That the Spaniards were niggardly in their disbursement of "gold and silver from the Indies" he knew all too well. The sentence containing the "thirty years" aphorism is therefore nothing but bitterest irony, with the figure chosen at random. If you have the funds to wage war for thirty years, well and good. For the time being, including the current month, I see no prospect of any. . . .

His efforts to have peace negotiated and his toying with his own resignation sprang from one and the same motive – his wish to extricate himself, his longing to be at rest again.

To his bad temper, ill-health and gloom he owed his facility for falling into dilemmas. Forced to make a choice, he would see both solutions as equally dangerous. "If I march, if I do not march," was the tenor of his vacillation in July, when he had to decide between staying

by the Elbe and moving to Silesia. He was faced with similarly distasteful alternatives in the planning of the south-eastern campaign. "Should
I reach the enemy before them [the Hungarians] and do nothing, I
discourage the army and dissipate its strength, but if I venture it is
precarious for both because Bethlehem [as he always called him] will
bring with him a great quantity of cavalry." The receipt of depressed,
depressing letters of this kind from his headquarters encouraged doubts
at Vienna about the commander-in-chief's suitability for his appointment. In addition there were embarrassing incidents which made good
tale-bearing, reports about outbursts of rage inappropriate to a man of
his position and dignity. The Elector of Saxony's attention was drawn
to one of the ugliest episodes. It occurred when Wallenstein's army was
crossing Lower Lusatia on its way to Silesia. Saxon commissaries had
been charged with the provision of victuals. One evening these failed to
arrive at the little town of Forst. The reasons were perfectly valid and
the fault was not the commissaries'. Their account to the Elector was as
follows: "Regardless of all that, the highly esteemed Lord General
would not listen to our explanations, but had us summoned before him
and at the sight of us" – *primo intuito* – "in the presence of the Lord
Field-Marshal Don Balthasar,* large numbers of noble cavaliers and
the common folk running together in the street, impugned us with
words wounding to our honour, saying 'How, by the Holy Sacrament,
comes it that you have not had delivery of the victuals made to the
billets?' Whereupon I, Veit Kracht, sought to relate the circumstances
and to show how far our order gave authority. . . . He none the less,
without allowing hearing or excuse, continued to rail at us, took the
account from the Land Delegate and wrathfully tore it to shreds, calling
us mean curs, sluggards, brutes, and rascals, and continued so until at
last he himself wearied and bade us leave." Such violent proceeding,
added the aggrieved commissaries, had not been at all to the taste of the
officers on hand. No less a person than Field-Marshal Marradas later
sent them a message that they should forget the happening and behave
as though they had heard nothing. The scene can serve as proto-
type for many. Wallenstein had been seized by his "perversity", as
his rages were called, and had raved until he reached a point of
exhaustion.

Vexations blurred his achievements. Of one, the most striking, he
was well aware – he had maintained and vigorously increased the strength

* A field marshal was at this date subordinate to a commander-in-chief
(translator's note).

of the imperial army at no cost whatever to the imperial Exchequer. Another was his instinctive as well as thoroughly trained strategic eye for the right spot, rivers, bridges, passes, at which to employ his army. He sensed in advance the moves that the enemy would make. For example, he guessed with almost uncanny accuracy the route which Mansfeld would take through Silesia and Moravia. In moments of depression he thought everything gone to the devil. In more serene ones, poring over Mercator's projection and as though drugged into a state of dizzy elation, he would evolve the boldest, most spacious plans. Plans realized in part at a later date.

THE OFFICERS

The Field-Marshal posted to him in October 1625 in answer to his own urgent requests was Count Ramboald Collalto, President of the imperial War Council and a soldier of distinctly political character. At first Wallenstein showed complete satisfaction with the appointment, several times a day dashed off messages to his assistant, indulged his habit of seeking to exchange ideas on every conceivable topic, and shifted as much work as possible in his direction. "Count Collalto helps me immeasurably and I could certainly not have been sent anyone whom I would have preferred, for he lifts much care from my shoulders." Barely three months later Collalto forsook the army, asked highest authority for his release, and returned to Vienna. The background was as follows. Wallenstein had given the Duchess of Brunswick a permit for the transport of twenty barrels of wine and a quantity of merchandise. The safe-conduct, meant as a talisman against pillage by his own soldiers and on occasion effective as such, failed in one particular instance. The lieutenant-colonel of Collalto's own regiment (about which he, as a courtier resident at Vienna, bothered but little) raided the baggage-train and had the goods seized. Whether on his own behalf or that of the Field-Marshal, fond of a good drop and quality wares, is a moot point. Wallenstein intervened, compelled restitution of the booty – which in similar cases he was rarely able to do – and dismissed the thief from his command. Collalto took grave offence. He, as the officer's immediate superior, had the right to discipline him, not the General. Words were exchanged, but they were succeeded by a month of tranquillity during which everything continued as before. Then there occurred Collalto's sudden defection. Wallenstein, livid at this reticence and trickiness on the part of his assistant, completely lost his self-control. "If the Count was able, as he says, to tolerate the situation for a month and offer me fair phrases, God preserve me from dealing further with one who is such a dissimulator and, when time has passed, so precipitately absconds. I imagined him to be my best, most trusty friend; he is my worst enemy. Wherefore I can no longer harmonize with him and His Majesty's service must severely suffer." Never, he could swear to God, had he evinced a person greater courtesy than Collalto. "For him it was a matter of wine and victuals, for me that of my word." A tissue of lies? Sham indignation? Only poor judges of human nature will pronounce that verdict on a man who was not a good one either, simply lonely, first confidently seeking help, now rampant in his disappointment. He really had wanted to keep his word to the Guelph princess. He sincerely had pinned his hopes on Collalto, always addressing him as "My Lord Brother", an honour he extended to none of his other officers. The shock led to the hatred which seared the letters to his father-in-law. Never, never again will he have anything to do with Collalto. "I see that he is a false, wicked creature." Were the Emperor to hold Collalto's mischievous, evil practices in higher esteem than the reputation of one who laboured day and night on his behalf, he would immediately petition to be relieved of his command. "Collalto, in summa, is a great schemer but no soldier, and his valour is best passed over in silence." If the War Council's President had anything he wished to explain, it would be better for him to visit the camp in person than to send others. "I shall deal with the poltroon as he deserves." For six months he continued in this key, and on an ever shriller note, until a return to reason prevailed. "I would also ask my lord that, if he sees a way to reconcile Collalto, it be done, else he will constantly work against me." The time would come when they would correspond as formerly and get on well together.

For the present the problem was who should succeed Collalto. He must, Wallenstein insisted, be capable of commanding an army, a gift not vouchsafed to any and every colonel. The Field-Marshal was the General's senior assistant and, in virtue of that status, responsible especially for discipline. He could however also be placed at the head of a corps in order to operate almost independently in the field at great distance from the Commander-in-Chief. To the Duke the number of suitable candidates seemed small. He proposed Count Friedrich Solms, a Protestant whom Vienna on that account did not want. The imperial army had an excessive quota of Protestant colonels. Wallenstein, on the other hand, hesitated to take old Don Balthasar Marradas, he who in the preceding year had been so angered at his supersession. "Don Balthasar is a sound *cavaliero*, but this business is too big for him." Finally he did accept him, and soon he was as satisfied as he had initially been with Collalto.

No officer, though, could rest assured of the Commander-in-Chief's continuing good opinion. Coincident with his personal liking, it was easily liable to capsize into scorn and fury, a process not entirely excluding the possibility of a second metamorphosis.

There was the case of Colonel Wratislaw. In the summer of 1625 the General was lavish with praise of him, wanted to see his services financially rewarded, and in the autumn recommended his appointment as Major-General over all infantry. What a very different situation six months later. "Let my lord tell the Emperor that I can bear witness before God never in my life to have met with a more useless military individual." "He lacks valour, experience, and discernment." Maybe, apart from more serious flaws, the Colonel's face had something to do with his ill-fortune, for the General once wrote about Wratislaw's "long nose" and his objection to irregularities of physical appearance applied equally to all anatomical features. He always referred, even in letters to the Emperor, to Count Jakob Fürstenberg, Major-General in Tilly's army, as "hunchback Fürstenberg", blaming him for most of the troubles he encountered with the rival Bavarian army. "If it had not been for hunchbacked Count Fürstenberg, the enemy would have suffered a fine blow . . . *in summa*, beware of those on whom nature has put its mark."

At their first meeting Lieutenant-Colonel Christian von Ilow – sometimes called Illo – was repugnant to him. "Ilau [*sic*] was here only a few days, but caused me plenty of mischief among the commanders. . . . I do not like him for many reasons. First, he is a proud, puffed-up fellow. Secondly, he enjoys stirring up intrigue among the commanders. Thirdly, as I can with good conscience aver, none among the commanders in Holstein is as extortionate as he. Therefore I like him not a whit." That would change. He allowed Ilow to rise to Field-Marshal and then to something more.

Another instance, his long resistance to the move to have Count Wolf von Mansfeld, one of the court officers, promoted to field-marshal, underlines his lack of use for braggartism and predacity, traits often met in common. "Were he as sick as he is puffed up, he would long be dead. . . . From the Empire has come a letter about Mansfeld that the Wolf is at the door, very hungry and grabbing with both paws. It is the only task he does not neglect."

His relations with Aldringen fluctuated. The Luxemburger had a talent for being indispensable. About his capacity alike as collector of contributions and as commander there could no longer be any question, least of all since the battle at the Dessau bridge. Nevertheless Aldringen was an intriguer, an incomparably more skilful one than Ilow. Already astonishingly far up the ladder, he wanted to climb still farther. Where the Duke now stood? He served him and he served others. Reports to Munich, transmitted by hunchbacked Fürstenberg, as well as to Vienna flowed fluently from his pen, allowing Elector Maximilian to be informed as he would not otherwise have been about the frame of mind current at Wallenstein's headquarters. Abbot Antonius of Kremsmünster was the recipient at Vienna, communicating the Colonel's "charming notes" to quarters where they were read "with favour and especial satisfaction" – by the Emperor, in other words. Wallenstein was aware of Aldringen's espionage activities. Once he upbraided him caustically on the subject, but he took no further action. "My lord knows people's humours," ran Abbot Antonius's consolation, "knows how to keep his temper, and can dissimulate, wherefore this will come more easily to him. . . . Let us meanwhile not fail to continue our confidential communications and correspondence." The broad smile spreading over the cleric's features as his raven's quill sped scratchingly across the paper can be imagined. The sticky net being spun from the capital, for all its distance, around the imperious General can be surmised. As at the beginning, so it was at the end.

For all his own complexity, soldiers of a plain, matter of fact, rugged, straightforward cast of mind were Wallenstein's favourites. "Pechmann will do very well there. He is a good fighting man and will have credit with the ranks." "Lindlo is a veteran and good fighting man. He does not make many speeches, but he knows his task and is diligent." Still higher was the estimation in which he held Count Heinrich Schlick. "If His Majesty has a good officer, then he is Count Schlick," he who had at such a very late juncture, after the battle of the White Mountain, rowed his pinnace away from the fleet of the Bohemian rebels and must have possessed no mean diplomatic qualities to enable him to thrive under his new master. In 1627 he was appointed Field-Marshal on Wallenstein's warm recommendation at the same time as Marradas became Lieutenant-General – a satisfaction to Wallenstein since it signified that this rank, formerly the highest possible and rarely conferred, was now far below his own. He was also not averse to seeing members of the old princely families serving under him: three Saxe-

Lauenburgs, a Holstein, Anhalt, Brunswick-Lüneburg, Baden, Brandenburg, Nassau – Protestants, one and all.

There were officers like Aldringen who corresponded in four or five
languages while others could not write their names. There were Catholics
and non-Catholics. There were Germans (barely half the total), Spaniards, Italians, Walloons, Danes, Scots, Irishmen, Frenchmen. There
were princes, townsmen, peasants. Their common denominators were
egotism, brutality, lack of friendships, and the absence of even such
chivalric bonds as existed between brigands. They competed for place,
emulated one another in intrigue on behalf of or against their
Commander-in-Chief, and were rivals in pillage. At the outset Wallenstein was, it seems, on a comparatively familiar footing with his senior
officers, issuing informal invitations to share a meal with him at which
they could talk freely and he for his part conversed without constraint.
That is what Gualdo Priorato says. He was on the scene and he is at his
most reliable in description of the General in his military setting. The
degree of comradeliness he initially permitted among his entourage was
on a par with his asperity when uttering a reproof. Then dignity was
thrown to the winds. A colonel, and a prince of the empire at that,
whom at an inspection he had shrilly denounced for his men's poor
equipment, noted next day that although the General was already sorry
"to have in his perversity spoken such words, . . . I shall not so soon
forget the sermon".

He had no love for the bandits among his followers. He was against
the rapine and martyrdom of the peasants, the robbers of citizens. On
practical grounds, not from compassion. The soil must provide a living
next year as well as this. If merchants could not prosecute their commerce with some security, they would be unable to pay contributions.
A host of orders and angry passages in his letters attest to this attitude.
"That De Fur [Colonel Desfours] is a pest. He promotes every sort of
disorder and spoliation and has done more damage than the whole
army . . . He is a Fur [y]* in name and fact." Desfours had a Lieutenant-
Colonel Höffer who wrought still worse havoc than his master. Wallenstein once ordered him to be brought under heavy guard to his headquarters for trial. Desfours was full of arguments why it could not be
done, not omitting the impossibility of sparing the necessary mounted
escort. He had more horsemen than enough, Wallenstein retorted. "Let
him therefore cease his superfluous, shameless reiterations and *in*

* Or, a more accurate and abusive pun on the Latin word *fur*, a thief, rascal,
rogue, knave (translator's note).

continenti bring Lieutenant-Colonel Höffer well-secured hither. Since otherwise he assumes the grave responsibility for all that Höffer has done, he will know how to comply." Another letter shows that Höffer's successor was no improvement. "Wherefore it is Our wish to have admonished and ordered him a last time to heed and to see that what has been forcibly removed from the poor be restored to them and the criminals arrested and punished with life and limb who, contrary to Our positive injunction, have unabashedly ventured such disorder and acts of insolence. Failing his obedience and the arrival of further complaint, he can rest assured that We shall undertake such example as shall be reflected throughout the army because We are immutably resolved neither to let pass nor to permit such inexcusable exorbitancies. He will conform accordingly." Do such incensed, almost browbeating threats hold up a mirror to inability to impose his will? He was indeed as little able to protect the poor as was the Spartan veteran Tilly. Distances were too great. The officers, far removed from the Provost-Marshal's sword, did as they chose. Discipline prevailed in the gilded isolation of army headquarters and its vicinity. Beyond those precincts rapacity, murder, and thievery were the order of the day. Execution of the majority of commanding officers would have been the only way to quell the chaos. How could they have been replaced, replaced with such as would have behaved better? A colonel had to be guilty of outsize atrocities before Wallenstein was in a position to have the sword so swung as to sever head from torso. "That there shall not be complaint of me in the Empire that I do not punish transgressors, I have today had von Gürzenich's head hewn from his body. True, he was sentenced to the wheel, but in my opinion one can content oneself with this." Gürzenich, a Friedland liegeman of Wallenstein, had gone too far, particularly inside convents.

THE ANGUISHED FLOCK

The scene was anything but peaceful when for the space of a day and a night Wallenstein's army, its throng of hangers-on trundling ahead or behind, passed through the countryside either to the clamant call of drums and trumpets or, probably still more sinister, in complete silence if the General had just held a court-martial among plunderers and the corpses of throttled men and boys were strung from trees along the road. "God give solace to the place where *they* go and make their winter quarters!" exclaimed one who watched its passage.

Let the reader not expect highly detailed descriptions of atrocities.

In the first place the same could be repeated about contingents under Mansfeld, Tilly, Spinola, Bethlen, or any other commander. During later stages of the war, when Wallenstein had disappeared from the scene, matters did not improve. On the contrary, frightfulness increased disproportionately. Whatever we could offer by way of gruesome, nightmarish, sanguinary tales would not particularly set apart the personality of our hero. Occurrences of this kind have so often and so readily been narrated since their happening three hundred years ago that nowadays critical writers suspect some robust exaggeration. Certainly nothing has been omitted in the telling. The sum of sufferings, were they capable of being catalogued, may in all great wars have come to more or less the same, however differently compounded. Perfection has been accompanied by horrors which did not attend the seventeenth century's clumsy, extremely imperfect conduct of hostilities, although it had its substitutes. Lacking in Wallenstein's day, as compared with later times, was *esprit de corps* amongst officers; the sense of duty wrung from other ranks by drill and discipline, not to mention such reputedly compulsive emotions as patriotism; and the organization which knows how to distribute the greatest possible burdens between the greatest possible number with the greatest possible efficacy. Wallenstein made a start along these lines. But because it was the beginning of a start amidst a society not structured for war, an inorganic polity, his system remained one of wild irrationality.

Here is one example, from October 1625. Wallenstein's troops have occupied Halle, a town within the archdiocese of Magdeburg. During the operation a number of regiments invaded neighbouring Saxon territory. An official reports to the Elector: "The cavalry, including many Frenchmen and Croats, disported themselves like bloodthirsty madmen down on the hill among the draught animals, riding at and shooting the sheep, despoiling the shepherds and cowherds of their food, their money, and whatever they had, stealing too the swineherd's new hat, and laying about them with blows so that the herdsmen fled with the animals into the wood. Whereupon the soldiers descended upon the village, tyrannized it, seized its cattle, drew the horses out of their shafts, robbed the villagers, scoured cupboards and chests, broke everything in two, beat and thrashed the peasants, ravished the womenfolk, all as though this were Hungarian borderland and they the Turks." The official's protest that this was the Saxon Elector's territory only received the reply, "A fig for Electors! I must eat, my horse must eat!" and still worse behaviour. In the meanwhile, though, one of Wallenstein's colonels,

Beckmann or Pechmann, had noted the tumult in the village. He dispatched a trumpeter "who arrived just as they were making the most of the hay and who bellowed, 'Swing, swing, swing, you shall swing for it!' And with these welcome tidings I could remain master of the place. . . . The Colonel also sent me a message that if birds of the same feather came again and would not be repelled, I should have their heads severed from their shoulders and I should tell this in the villages to the elders. Whereto I answered him that the means were good and, had I but orders from Your Electoral Grace, I would soon render the peasants willing enough to act." The episode is a bad one. Yet, as long as the swineherd's new hat is thought worthy of reference, no peak of atrocity has been attained. It is moreover a notable point that the colonel scatters the marauders not merely by threats of hanging, but has the peasants positively encouraged to adopt measures of self-defence against his own men. The will to impose discipline has not at this point been extinguished amongst the officers.

Now another example, from 1633. The scene is Goldberg, the town where Wallenstein went to school and with whose inhabitants he had had not unfriendly dealings in 1626 during his pursuit of Mansfeld. The present case was different. Goldberg had been in the hands of the Saxons, currently the Emperor's enemies. It had not played at politics, it had been occupied through no fault of its own, it had done nothing to deserve the tribulation described in a book entitled *The Dreadful but Truthful Narration of the Exceedingly Barbarous, Verily Satanic Devastation by the Imperialists on 4th October 1633 of the Town Goldberg in Silesia. Told from Authentic Written Accounts and Circumstantial Reports of Those who experienced the Tyranny at That Place. Compiled by a True Patriot.* Wallenstein soldiery, in this instance preponderantly Spaniards, smashed with axes the town-gates closed against them and proceeded to slay, wound, torture, rape, and sack in the most ghastly fashion. "The officers began the lootings, for the officers were the vilest, most godless and base miscreants. The officers chained the town councillors together and forced them to hold their horses while they entered their and their friends' houses, outraged women and maids, ill-treated children. . . ." When the obvious possibilities for plunder had been exhausted, "they had recourse to what had been carefully hidden or buried. The soldiers were given permission to seize the citizens and harrow them to their hearts' delight so that they should divulge where any goods and money lay concealed. Many had ropes placed around their necks, others were dragged naked about the streets, heads down upon the cobbles, blood and brains alike bespattering the stones. Others had their bones and skulls smashed with hammers until they sank dead upon the ground. The foreheads of others were ground with stones and knotted ropes, screwing their heads together with knotted ropes that the eyes started from the sockets and blood poured from mouth and nose. Yet others had burning pine-splinters thrust beneath their nails, while naked bodies were sprinkled with boiling brimstone or hot brimstone beads were dropped slowly and at intervals upon men's and women's bodies in order that the torment should be right prolonged." So the tale continues for seven pages more. The Patriot's narrative seems in substance likely to have been true. There exists another which more or less corroborates its details. During the past eight years the depravity engendered by the war had made progress and in the next eight years would increase still more. These were the officers, these were the men whom Wallenstein now had under his command.

What passed through his mind when he heard of their infamies is unknown. Probably not much. War and the profession of arms were like that. If there were princes, including the guiltiest, who in letters screechingly vented their distress at the sufferings of their subjects, he had too much good taste for that. Better to demand obedience and maintain discipline as well as he could.

He imposed penalties. He had frightful punishments promulgated. Whoever demeaned himself in a neutral country such as Saxony after the manner ascertained by the electoral official was not to be treated as a soldier, but to be broken on the wheel like a "common footpad". Occasionally too this was done. Recitals of the Duke's horrid justice were declaimed by those, especially those, who were anything but well disposed towards him. The Venetian ambassador at Vienna, for instance, recounted how he had individuals executed without conceding them time for final absolution, this being one of the reasons why his soldiery so frequently deserted. He was nicknamed "Gibbetstein" and, by the Hungarians, "Gallows-Duke". The question is what effect such deterrent measures had. Borne on his golden isle through a sea of filth, rewards or retributions were the sole alternatives he offered, a man contemptuous of the human race, at one remove from it, and unapproachable. The facts, though, as they have come down to us, are inconsistent. It is said that the soldiers ran away from their commander-in-chief because they found his tyranny unendurable. It is said to the contrary, and the Elector of Bavaria pitched a pitiful story of woe about it, that Tilly's mercenaries flocked to the imperial colours because they manifestly expected a pleasanter life under Wallenstein. Both assertions will be true enough. The liberties life takes with consistency are stainless. Nevertheless the second allegation will be truer than the first. Later events furnish evidence for the taking.

He forbade, as we already know, and forbade in his most intrinsic self-interest, that his army reduce the peasantry to despair. Count Khevenhüller, in his *Annals*, establishes that Wallenstein maintained "notable discipline" in territories occupied by him "that the land should not be laid waste and reduced to ashes, nor the people driven from their houses and holdings, but everything cultivated and harvested. . . . And although the Empire was hard pressed, soldier and peasant lived side by side and all commanders learned this manner of conducting war from the Duke of Friedland." Khevenhüller, for all that he was no friend to Wallenstein, none the less did not suppress the truth in so far as it was repeated to him, not even when it was painful for his own party. The most sickening description of the sack of Magdeburg stems from his pen.

The obverse of the coin, a tolerable co-existence between soldiers and peasants, was the principle. The reverse, martyred peasants, burnt-out farms, cattle dispersed, shows the principle rent on the resistance of savage reality. To what degree it was rent, to what degree it was of beneficent consequence cannot be exactly determined. For of course the chroniclers primarily recorded the spectacular and the horrendous, not the half-way normal and frictionless state of affairs which did not furnish them with much material.

THE CONTRIBUTIONS

The costs of the wars fought between 1618 and 1648 under the Emperors Matthias, Ferdinand II, and Ferdinand III are said to have amounted to 110 million gulden in all. Of this total 28 million gulden fall to the share of the seven years' period of Wallenstein's twofold generalate. Provided that the basis of the laborious calculations is reliable, their result signifies that Wallenstein spent no more, or slightly less, than his successors. Nevertheless the lay economist may remind his readers that the sum of 110 million gulden by no means represents the full outlay on hostilities. The expenditure of the German princes, allied or opposed to the House of Habsburg, could easily double the figure. If the question were asked whether a society numbering more than twenty million individuals could not within thirty years afford 200 or 250 million gulden without bringing about its own destruction, the answer would be that the constantly increasing ruin derived not so much from the expenditures on the combatant armies as the grimly concomitant circumstances. Production did not, as in the wars of later ages, rise. It dropped, dropped in wide tracts of territories to almost nil. The burdens of material sacrifice were scattered here and there entirely at the whims of martial fortune. This city prospered; its sister was burned down. And who can set a price on what soldiers demolished from sheer lust of devastation or the desolation caused by epidemics, the cost of civil slaughter and rout?

We are not, by the way, altogether happy about the figures named. We are told that approximately 500,000 gulden was the annual outlay on a regiment three thousand strong. That holds water if the monthly wage of a mercenary is put at ten gulden and allowance is made for commissioned and non-commissioned staff pay, from colonels down to provost-corporals and whoremasters, as well as expenditure on artillery, munitions, transport, and what not. Wallenstein had on average at least forty regiments under his command, while there were years when his army rose to more than a hundred thousand men. Simple arithmetic insists that such a year must have consumed at least twenty million gulden instead of the four million calculated. We hear of a regiment which received nine thousand gulden for a month's maintenance. How could it have managed? In part the solution may have lain in the fact that its strength was always below establishment, but to this it can be objected that regimental and company commanders concealed such deficiency as long as possible in order to pocket the profit. It will never prove possible to throw complete light on a profoundly clumsy, and moreover camouflaged, economic system, especially when what remains of its records is fragmentary.

Now for the main problem. Who paid for it all? How was payment effected? Through subsidies from better-off allies? Hardly. The bounty bestowed by the Kings of Spain on their Viennese cousins totalled during those thirty years 1,700,000 gulden. So much for "Indian gold". The Popes at Rome? Urban VIII, with whom we are at this juncture concerned, energetically repudiated the notion that the war in Germany was any of his affair. Rome contributed altogether 900,000 gulden, a drop in the ocean. The Emperor, meaning his Exchequer and its financier-abbot, and the Hereditary Lands which he drained? There neither was nor could be much there. Carinthia and Styria, Ferdinand II's patrimony, produced barely enough to defray his immediate imperial pomp. The Tirol and the glacis lands, divorced, poor, and recalcitrant provinces, had their own courts to keep. Upper Austria was until 1628 in lien to the Elector of Bavaria who squeezed it lustily for his own benefit, not others', and the peasant war of summer 1626 had anyhow reduced its inhabitants to beggary. Hungary, the small strip where the imperial writ was deemed to run, is not worth mention. That left Lower Austria, Bohemia-Moravia, and Silesia. These really did pay, although once more only sums which seem paltry, however large they loomed in the eyes of the payers, in comparison with what was needed, and in the first year of Wallenstein's generalate they paid nothing at all. If, finally, the reader were to assume that recourse was had to the same means as in 1622, debasement of the coinage, he would be subject to correction. Inflation had been tried once, experienced, and was never tried again.

Here are extracts from letters by Wallenstein about the financial situation. "The other reason" – for his wish to resign his appointment – "is disgust, for I perceive that the court thinks I should both wage this war and furnish all its funds. In my view I have done more than too much in as far as I have set this army on foot, brought it into position, daily augment its strength, and have by several hundred thousand gulden plunged myself into debt. I had . . . a message from court that I should pay the sixty thousand tallies of corn. Now they write that I am to handle them in the most sparing manner. That means that in less than two months the army will have exhausted its rations. I have written for a thousand hundredweight of powder and I obtain no answer. I cannot take the field if the soldiery has not been paid a month's wage, whether I am given it or not. There are precedents for this treatment in the case of Count Buquoy, but at least he had a large region upon which the army could live; I lack all that. The court orders me not to impose taxes on the Princes of Anhalt and others, just as though I had fully paid the armada. From General Tilly I have no help at all, for he tyrannizes me as his master does our lord, the Emperor . . ." (16 March 1626). "If I am sent no munitions, I have but short time more for shooting. But if I am sent no money, I not only do not take the field, but it must cause anxiety whether the soldiery does not take a different direction of its own. I understand that Questenberg has reported to the Emperor as if no money were needed. I fancy he has done it to tickle the Emperor's ears, but thereby he performs a notable disservice . . ." (8 June 1626). "Now I beg my lord that he bethink himself of ways whereby I may take my quittance, for by the God whom I worship I am no longer able to remain the while I see myself scurvily used. Let the Emperor be satisfied that I have deployed him such a muster as he never before has had done for him and to this moment he has not expended a farthing upon. . . ." And so on, brimming over, with letters of not much different tenor to Collalto and Trauttmansdorff.

Certain points emanate clearly. For the whole of the first year he had not received from the Emperor, which is to say the Hereditary Lands, either money, victuals, or military supplies. Seeing that an army of sixty thousand men could not for twelve months live on air, he had taken these things from elsewhere, including, on the strength of his personal credit, his own pocket. This could not possibly suffice. Sums were involved which, as Harrach aptly put it, "no private person" could be capable of raising. The army was preponderantly fed and defrayed from the "contributions" of the occupied lands. Wallenstein mentions them far less often than they deserve, but it does emerge from his letters that they too could not to the full provide for the soldiers' pay, not even their food. Here (in the bishoprics of Magdeburg and Halberstadt) they have nothing more to live on, he writes. He would rather have twenty thousand paid mercenaries than sixty thousand unpaid ones. If he is not sent the hundred thousand taler promised for the past year, Trauttmansdorff is told, "the army will melt like butter in the sun". A hundred thousand taler mean no more than a trifling gratuity per head.

The contributions were not Wallenstein's invention. With precursors in the sixteenth century, they had come into fashion since the beginning of the Bohemian troubles. Buquoy and Spinola had levied them; Count Tilly had perforce to erect them into a system. In theory the Lands had to feed the army and the princes whom it served had to pay the Lands. That held water as long as the war-chest of thrifty Elector Maximilian was tolerably well filled. At the moment when Wallenstein appeared on the scene the demarcation between contribution to food and contribution to pay was in Tilly's practice becoming blurred and thereafter the difference between the two processes of exploitation ceased to be profound. Conditions dictated that.

Wallenstein added two points to the procedure. One was a matter of principle according to which the Lands had to supply the pay as far as they could. The other was a material factor, the amounts involved. His army was larger than Tilly's and would continue to expand. The material factor and the principle were linked. Because the imperial towns, bishoprics and monasteries, counties and principalities would only pay if the military power on the spot forced them, an increasing part of the army was needed for precisely this purpose, even there where at the time no war was in progress. The army grew upon itself. The duty of a portion not engaged in battle was to maintain itself and those who each year for a few months did engage in battle. The imperial army, in the eyes of the General, was entitled to be maintained by all, in any case by its allies and enemies and by neutrals as well. It was unsound imperial law, but he viewed the business from a practical perspective.

A historian who thoroughly examined the evidence came to the conclusion that "the Wallenstein method of military maintenance was by no means as disorderly and extreme" as is commonly thought. The General was conscious that land and people would have to pay for "this wearisome war" next year and the year after, which they would only be able to do if they could live, work, and feel that their toil made some scrap of sense. A man of keenly creative economic vision could not help but loathe ferociously stupid waste. The instruments at his disposal were the trouble. On the one hand an archaic civil service incapable of tackling new tasks; on the other, his mercenaries and subordinates. In the war-torn Empire it was impossible for matters to proceed as tidily as in the Duchy of Friedland.

"Ordinances" laid down what each, from colonel to private, was weekly entitled to obtain: five hundred gulden for the colonel, two and a half for the private. A disparity, it must be admitted, but officers participated in the war as a profit-making enterprise whereas rankers could look forward, unless they had bad luck and incurred a debt with death, to no higher dividend than the saving of their life. For, this was the joke, a debit was put on everything, sustenance and pay, with the value of the former supposed to be deducted from the latter. Two and a half gulden sufficed for barely more than keeping body and soul together, although these, as ration lists prove, were at any rate to be kept thrivingly together: two pounds of meat, two pounds of bread, and two quarts of beer daily. To this was added a free allowance of hay and oats for horses, salt, firewood, and candles, all to be drawn from those on whom they were billeted. That was the scheme, a framework within which details varied, the trend towards a lower than higher standard, depending on current conditions. The commander-in-chief granted Aldringen, his Commissary-General, and regimental commanders latitude here. Overtaxed as he was, "I lack someone to assist me properly on the economic side".

In the larger dominions, Brandenburg, Pomerania, Silesia, the governments of the princes or the Estates, or both, had the requisitioned victuals collected in depots while the incidence of the "military tax" was apportioned according to property or profession, raised, and delivered into the regimental tills. The governments were also supposed to be entitled to allot the units their quarters. It was a title with little or no power behind it because Wallenstein often, even during the bad season of the year, had regiments switched from one location to another in accordance with what he called *ratio belli*. And if, in consequence of sudden, savage invasion, rulers fled and their administrations broke down, with nobody on hand to collect the contribution except the colonels, then these openly showed themselves to be what secretly they always were – the masters in the land. To accept the sustenance whose value was meant to be deducted from the pecuniary contribution, but nevertheless to demand the whole, was a favourite practice. The contributors were always in arrears. Thereupon the "tribulation troops" were put into the towns to harass them until a certain amount had been amassed. Officers passed from house to house and seized "pledges" at random. Assessments as stated on paper varied by place and circumstance.

In 1627 Magdeburg laid down that its citizens would contribute a payment of ten per cent on their entire property, merely as a war loan and one which would carry five per cent interest, as the city fathers in a fit of foolish delusion promised. To convert into cash ten per cent of one's possessions, meaning house, furbishings, jewellery, real estate and cattle, is neither so easy to effect nor so easy to collect. The council had to take stern steps. A veto was imposed on the marriage of engaged couples till they had paid. Even by resort to such measures it managed to accumulate only one-eighth of the anticipated sum. In the Silesian dukedom of Liegnitz the tax rose as high as twenty-four per cent of all assets. Calculation of what would have remained to the inhabitants, had it continued for four years, is simple.

Neither the demands nor the numbers of the soldiery would have rendered the Lands miserable; it was the disorderliness and ferocity of their behaviour, the impudence and senselessness of their requirements. The harm done by them during a few months could not be made good by the time of the next plague's arrival. The arrival of Wallenstein's troops had usually been preceded by that of the League's, Mansfeld's, or the Danes'. The argument about how it was as impossible to stay at this or that spot as to move to another because the territory all around was ruined became repetitious. Eyes were continually kept open for fresh, unexploited pastures, but they grew in scarcity.

The problem of dealing with the big imperial cities was of a different kind. They paid lump sums in order to be spared the provision of billets. Nürnberg, for instance, contributed annually a hundred thousand gulden, an irksome but not ruinous tribute for such a well-to-do community.

Yet here too the employment of a sanction in the shape of the vicinity and threat of imperial forces was necessary. The cities, whether rich or poor, well or badly ruled, were always in arrears. That was something the General took in very bad part. As the emissaries of Magdeburg reported, "He is the kind of lord who in return wants promises kept and therefore every nerve will have to be strained to be punctual with the money." As its arrival was not so, the Duke demanded, as penalty, and to the horror of the emissaries, still more ("Had it been paid at the right time and I not led by the nose!") There was, though, apart from the obvious reasons, another, not unknown to the Magdeburgers, why he was adamant about prompt payment – he had long borrowed the amounts owed him and the interest on these advances was high The later the capital came to hand, the slighter its value to him. Should its receipt be all too protracted, the whole legerdemain numerical structure would collapse, bringing down his fortune, his credit, and the credit of his principal financier.

The latter was none other than Hans de Witte, he who in 1622 had been a member of the coinage consortium. In those days he had run a kind of private state bank; now he ran a kind of private ministry of war and finance. On the strength of the contributions to be harvested from the states, the cities, and the bishoprics, on the strength of the taxation to come in from the Hereditary Lands, or even on the strength of no well-grounded expectation at all, he advanced the General enormous sums, hundreds of thousands upon hundreds of thousands which snowballed into millions. Of course he did not have that much, borrowing from the business friends with whom he had connections in all the big cities of Europe. The amounts mobilized by him had to generate profit in the shape of interest and had to be repaid quickly, after a year or half a year, for money was scarce. And de Witte had to calculate his own reward, or the hope of it, and in the end was defeated. Occasionally he worked with the Bohemian money-men who had proved useful in the days of the consortium, Bassevi-Treuenberg and Michna. The Kinsky brothers too, for all that they were Protestant and teetered on the brink of emigration, did not disdain participation in de Witte's loan activities, thus indirectly assisting to finance the Emperor's war in Germany. The mediation of de Witte was essential. He, the banker of European standing, possessed the credit which the Emperor entirely lacked and not even the Emperor's General had. Let the President of the Exchequer visit the Hanse towns, Wallenstein jeered, and see what they would lend him. "His credit is presumably such that the merchants will immediately disburse a hundred thousand imperial taler." Yet de Witte's mediation was also a short-term expedient. His reputation depended on ready repayment. He therefore persistently importuned his exalted partner: "Hans de Witte pesters me perpetually." Maybe this system of private advance financing on war taxation raised by irrational, archaic methods and never received to the anticipated amount was expensive and wildcat, but no better was known. An army of the size and requirements of Wallenstein's had never been experienced in the modern age. No one was prepared for what it entailed and improvisation spiralled from one gossamer arithmetical web to another. For the present, thanks to de Witte's imaginative enterprise and Wallenstein's rigid determination, the net held. The ministry of finance proper, the Exchequer at Vienna, contributed desperately little to success. "The Exchequer remits words only," said Wallenstein. An atmosphere of nagging tension pervaded the undertaking. The most powerful man in the Empire had continually to wrangle over a few thousand gulden with crafty, tenacious if terrified go-betweens.

He never ceased to complain. He was, he groaned, up to his neck in debt (which was true), in an emergency he would not have enough to carry his wife into safety, he would finally have to pledge the shirt on his back. A good businessman likes to moan. He was moreover, and in spite of his wealth remained, nervous about money. Let his affairs suffer a small reverse and he had visions of himself as a beggar exposed to the cruelties of the world without benefit of the golden cloak he had acquired for his protection. The suggestion that there was not a word of truth in his remonstrances, and that on the contrary he had profited shamelessly by the contributions, soon sprouted. People were however quick to allege many a matter without foundation, especially in the case of one with a strange gift for attracting such slander. It will be recalled how exaggerated were the reports of his gains in the coinage consortium. Our impression is that he was not guilty of peculation, distinguishing carefully between his own and the Empire's business. He was neither the man to give away gold nor the one to belong to the vulgar pack of light-fingered gentry. He had an exact account kept of what he expended in the Emperor's service by way of money and materials from his own duchy. To this had to be added his general officer's salary, first three thousand, then six thousand gulden monthly, which was never paid and gradually grew to a tidy little outstanding figure. He was experienced enough to know that the Exchequer would never be able to liquidate the whole debt in cash. But, if not in cash, then in freshly extended princely power which, apart from the pleasure of ruling, would be capable of being turned into money. Extended power where? For the present that remained obscure. There were those who claimed to know that he had ideas about Brandenburg, possibly even the kingdom of the Danes.

The hundreds of individuals who constituted the court which travelled with him were treated as though they had collectively been an unassuming military headquarters. Its expenses were paid out of the contributions although its membership was in the main composed of appointees useless for fighting purposes. For as long as there was war, in other words, he lived in all his splendour for nothing. That too was simply a matter of book-keeping. He provided, and he lent, what his court dissipated, adding the amount to the final bill against which meanwhile Vienna closed its eyes. That could not continue eternally. What then? If the contributions did not suffice, there was still the shift employed in Bohemia after the battle of the White Mountain – confiscations, this time on the scales that the Empire had to offer. It was only to be hoped that plenty of princes in the Lower Saxon Circle, for instance, would behave so badly as to enable their properties to be regarded as forfeit to the Emperor. The alternative would be for the Grand Creditor to render himself culpable somehow. What a relief, in a purely financial perspective, that would be!

THE DIPLOMATS

Foreign diplomats at Vienna, with the Venetian Padavin to the fore and the Nuncio Caraffa as well as the Spaniard Aytona not far behind, were the source of insinuations to which the Bavarian Elector's man, a certain Dr Leuker, listened gladly. The details he forwarded to Munich were scrutinized with eager attention. Envoys like to serve up nonsense in the absence of anything sensible to say or they mix sense with nonsense, proving with a garnish of gossip how *au fait* they are.

In the late winter of 1626 Padavin was already declaring that anything and everything could be expected from the "singular character of this cruel man and his ambitious plans". "Nobody even wants to hear the name of Wallenstein." And, a little later,

> Complaints about Wallenstein arrive almost unceasingly from Spain, from the Infanta, and from Bavaria. There is dissatisfaction too with the army; its loyalty is in doubt. Consequently not only is a feeling of security lacking, but there is fear of mutiny and a joinder with the enemy. All of these days the discussion has turned

on how Wallenstein could be relieved of his command without having a presentiment of it and, learning of this intent, in his desperado humour perform some mischievous stroke of which he is in any case suspected.

Right from the outset these were the kind of accusations being bandied about, before the battle at the Dessau bridge, at a time when the new Commander-in-Chief identified exaltation of the House of Habsburg with his own interests and had no other thought in mind than to serve the Emperor, defend the externally and internally menaced Hereditary Lands, and impose peace upon the Empire. The Venetian envoy was however mistaken in his belief that he whose name recurred all too often in his dispatches had no idea of what was being whispered. Padavin's tittle-tattle was unknown to him, but his instinct was far too keen not to apprehend the atmosphere which gave rise to it. His depressions and the grievances expressed to his father-in-law attest to that just as, despite his powerful military position, they reflect his feeling of helplessness in the face of such enmity. "*In summa*, if the wish is to maintain my appetite for matters, then let them leave me alone, for assuredly I neglect nothing that may be of use to His Majesty. Were I to think as much of my soul's safety as of the Emperor's service, I would of a surety pass through no purgatory, much less suffer the pains of hell." Never was Wallenstein, in his domineering, brooding, sensitive mind, more convinced of his own loyalty than at this period.

His knowledge of Germany was imperfect. His tempestuous student days at Altdorf and his visit to the imperial Diet at Regensburg in Emperor Matthias's day were long distant events. They had by no means been sufficient to endow him with spontaneous understanding of the imperial constitutions, sprouting from deep layers of tradition and subsisting in a rarefied atmosphere of legalism. Bohemia he knew well. There he had witnessed and profitably tested how power knew no limits. In the Empire a different situation, complex and artificial, yet stubborn and efficacious, prevailed. He was quickly enough conscious of its existence, but disconcerted by its bizarre quality. "They chatter to me about the recesses of the imperial Diet, about the Golden Bull, and the rest. When they parade them, I know not where I am." The Golden Bull had been promulgated almost three hundred years ago,* but princely

---

* A basic imperial law of 1356 which, among other important matters, apportioned the burden of imperial responsibility among the Electors and assigned them momentous privileges (translator's note).

privy councillors behaved as though the Emperor had set his seal on it the day before yesterday. Vienna sent him the legal expert for whom he asked, but the move could be of little assistance to him because he saw matters in their present context or as he thought they could and should be, not as what the centuries had made of them.

His judgement of the Empire's most important princes was swift and generally accurate. "The Elector of Saxony will adhere to us as long as our affairs prosper." "The Duke of Pomerania is an ingenuous gentleman." Later he called him a "poor ninny". "The Elector of Bavaria is better to himself than to us." As little as Wallenstein grasped John George of Saxony's bluffly patriarchal loyalty to the Empire, which merged all the more easily with his princely egotism for the Empire itself being an aggregate of princely territorial centres and ego-centrisms, as little did he discern the difficult seesaw in Maximilian's mind – how he was at once the Emperor's friend and foe, how he thought simultaneously in terms of his own state's and the ancient Empire's interests, how his haughtiness suffered pangs imparted by his sense of duty and his fear of God. Wallenstein, the complete contemporary untrammelled by his roots, regarded Maximilian as purely contemporary too, without historical dimension, and assessed him only as the ambitious intriguer "who does not like to spend money for nothing". He failed to understand that Bavaria, the outcome and heir of centuries, was different from Friedland and that therefore the ruler of Bavaria must view the world with other eyes than the ruler of Friedland. This is simply a more or less representative, although the gravest and most important, example of Wallenstein's misapprehension of German princes and German traditions as a whole.

Maximilian, for his part, did not understand the Emperor's Bohemian General at all, or understood no more than that here was the manifestation of a new, foreign, uncanny ascendancy in the old Empire. Moreover he and his rival in the power game remained the stranger to each other for never in seven long years meeting personally. Not that a few ceremonial encounters, like one which did occur towards the end, could have helped much. From the very first moment Maximilian's distrust was deep. Soon it grew into a hatred which never abated, for whereas most politicians constantly changed their estimate of men and affairs and shamelessly declared the precise opposite of what they had recently maintained, the Elector firmly, grimly clung to any conclusion that he had once reached. And a man who nurses a hate will believe all reports which confirm, gratify and increase it. Wallenstein had more than an inkling of the feeling nurtured against him and on occasion knew it in detail. Since he felt innocent of having given provocation and meritorious on his own score, he could not help but emotionally reciprocate what he had to endure by way of spiteful persecution. Perfectly clear to him too was that the courses of Bavarian and imperial policy, especially the imperial policy he proposed to follow, never really converged, however much they were said to correspond. On the contrary, the difficulty was to conceal their tendency to diverge.

With reference to military policy Maximilian used Tilly, his Lieutenant-General, as his link with Wallenstein. What strikes the observer is how different, how well disposed the latter's attitude was towards his Bavarian colleague for whom his favourite epithet was "the good old man". "He is assuredly honest and willing, but the instructions he receives from Munich are singular." "He is in bond to the Bavarian commissioners, must act against reason and waste his army. Not for nothing have his brave deeds earned him glory in the sight of this world, but for the patience he must exercise with those foul curs he will certainly attain *coronam martyri* in the next." I know of no letter wherein Tilly spoke in similarly generous terms of Wallenstein, but plenty of another kind. They are not abusive or slanderous, but they often contain complaints about lack of ready co-operation, hint at cause for disappointment, intimate enigmatic conduct, and vent embittered insinuations. The old war-dog possessed neither Wallenstein's sense of humour nor his intellect, but he had instinct, an instinct which rendered him aware of the elements of grandeur and instability in Wallenstein's character and led him after every encounter to feel outmanoeuvred, exhausted, confused. "For as long as I have to deal with the Duke of Friedland and keep a watchful eye on him, for so long too does he every hour cause me unrest, one excitement and turmoil after another." He, who for all his skill was no more than an artlessly honest fellow, could find no better words to describe his own reaction to the confrontation, late in life, with this specimen of high-strung superiority. The resplendence of Wallenstein's background did not escape him and he contrasted it with the greyness of his own headquarters. For those crooked times Tilly was a comparatively straight man, but in the closing years of his life he would have liked to enjoy riches, a taste sharpened by reports of his new colleague's fabulous wealth. A petition by the grizzled spartan to the Emperor has survived: seeing that he has so long ventured estate and limb, indeed life itself, for His Majesty's sake, next to that of God, has roved up and down the Empire on His behalf, and by the encompassment of many dangers is now come to this crowning action in land beneath the Great Bear constellation – Lower Germany – is there no possibility of recompense with one or another piece of enemy territory? Inconceivable that Wallenstein should have written such a begging letter.

Their difference in rank could not be other than doubly galling to Tilly who regarded himself as senior, in age in any case and in deserts too. Wallenstein was a prince; Tilly only a count. Wallenstein was the Emperor's General and shortly would be his Generalissimo; Tilly, merely an Elector's Lieutenant-General. If Maximilian was still reckoned to have the status to which the treaty of 1619 had raised him, that of the Emperor's prime representative within the Empire, Wallenstein was now in his own person the second; Tilly was simply a deputy for the first. It was a circumstance from which Wallenstein deduced a prerogative of precedence for his own envoys whenever they appeared with Tilly's before a third party. For imperial authority's sake, as he emphasized, because was not the problem of who was entitled first to pass through a door, put his hat on his head, be seated, a point of utmost political significance? In an exchange of letters Tilly could not refuse the younger man the dignity "Gracious Lord"; with the mode of address "Especially beloved Lord and Friend, Your Excellency" Wallenstein went as far in propitiation as it was at all permissible for him to do. Were they at the same place, sharing the same roof, we have witnesses to the delicate, almost affectionate consideration shown by the younger man for the older. The Nuncio Caraffa's assertion that the former once kept the latter waiting five hours in his ante-room is a downright lie. Regardless of Wallenstein's impulsively explosive though rapidly dissolved distrust and Tilly's embittered grousing, the rivalry between the two commanders would have been kept within tolerable bounds had it not been the reflection of a still deeper one, the silent struggle for power between Wallenstein and Bavaria which simultaneously was one between Bavaria and Habsburg, yet after such a fashion that Vienna's hydra-headed policy partly supported Wallenstein, partly adhered to Bavaria, and partly tried to tread a third, uncertainly traced path.

Since a common enemy always tends to bring people together, nothing was more natural than that those Viennese courtiers, including military men, to whom Wallenstein was a thorn in the flesh, should belong to what he called "the Bavarian faction": Peter von Stralendorf, a Mecklenburger by birth and President of the Aulic Council; Cardinal Dietrichstein and Wilhelm Slawata, his old personal enemies; von Meggau, the Governor of Lower Austria; and at one time or another Field-Marshal

Collalto and Commissary-General Aldringen. They muttered this and that, to one another and to Dr Leuker, the Bavarian envoy, too. They also allowed themselves to ascribe to the General a perfectly good capacity to collaborate more effectively with the Bavarian army if only he cared to do so. "These Master Pedagogues," retorted Wallenstein, "are well suited to framing precepts, but they are unaware that no means exist to handle in this way an imperial army which is unpaid. It would therefore be well if Lord von Stralendorf were not to heed what *should* be, but what *can* and *must* be. I await Count Trauttmansdorff with pleasure in order that he may comprehend all the difficulties, for assuredly I do more in the matter than many another would with an army that was paid." Privy Councillor Max von Trauttmansdorff was a man of independent mind without preconceived Spanish, Bavarian, or Wallenstein sympathies. It seems that on his visit in May 1626 to the Duke's headquarters at Aschersleben he did grasp the correctness of Wallenstein's strategy in the prevailing circumstances. Such investigatory calls by envoys from Vienna, Verda von Werdenberg, Trauttmansdorff, Gerhard von Questenberg, were frequent. Questenberg was one of three brothers – Gerhard, Secretary to the imperial War Council, Hermann, an Aulic Councillor, and Caspar, abbot of the rich Strachow monastery in the neighbourhood of Prague. Wallenstein did the abbot a favour with a valuable present – the bones of St Norbert which the Lutheran Magdeburgers, like it or not, had to relinquish. Gerhard von Questenberg he won completely over to his side, whether by power of personality or by playing into his hands the conferment of a barony and the means to sustain the rank. Intelligent, jovial, and industrious, Questenberg almost to the last remained one of his most useful connections with the court at Vienna.

Tradition says that the imperial War Council, the department whose minutes were kept by Questenberg, was always a source of vexation to Wallenstein. Prince Eugène of Savoy, his more fortunate successor in the appointment of Commander-in-Chief, commented on this institution, "Hitherto one of the main impediments to Austria's conduct of war has been the bad organization of the imperial War Council. Not only the establishment of a proper army, but even the leading generals and the most victorious campaigns have been hindered by it. The treatment of the great Wallenstein and myself attest to this. When I finally became its President, it consisted partly of envious individuals whose jealousy induced them to find fault with all my earlier operations and partly of excessively clever theoreticians who, although incapable of commanding a company, claimed nevertheless to know everything better." Wallenstein, it is true, experienced constant friction with "the court at Vienna", using this phrase as a vaguely collective term. Spitefulness was never lacking, particularly among unemployed would-be generals, and the pleasure was great if anything upset his plans. The facts do not however support the allegation that the imperial War Council, a body created in the previous century, laborious in procedure and perpetually expanding in numbers, could seriously inconvenience him. Prince Eugène saw matters in a different light because the days of his activity were two generations later in a more modern period when the imperial army really was imperial. The army that Wallenstein commanded was his own. He had mustered it and he financed it, in so far as anyone did, a fact to which he only too often made caustic reference. He felt altogether superior to the imperial War Council; its President, Collalto, was in his capacity as regimental colonel and field-marshal his junior officer. Wallenstein had direct access to his monarch whenever he wished (which he seldom did). His complaints were certainly directed against the "Master Pedagogues" and the "baldpates" as a whole, but rarely against the imperial War Council.

A somewhat similar situation existed as regards the Council's fellow-department, the Exchequer or ministry of finance. The War Council should have seen to war supplies and the major strategic design. It did neither. The Exchequer should have seen to the money supply and it did not. The first was bearable; Wallenstein was satisfied to be his own strategist. The second he found unbearable, and when in July 1626 the Exchequer saw fit to tell him that Silesia must not be touched by his troops because otherwise no taxes would arrive from there, he fell into a fury. "Now consider the Exchequer's well-considered instructions: the foe is in Silesia, the land leans more to his than the Emperor's cause, I am to remain outside its borders, the enemy will, exactly as they have set it down on paper, at once let himself be beaten, and I can march back and forth with the army just as they have a pair of horses put between the shafts, ride to court, and return home." This is the scorn of the soldier in the field for the courtiers, the "crawlers", who interfered in deadly serious business unfamiliar to them while themselves unable to perform what by their trade they should have been able to do. Such instructions, apart from the rage they provoked, had no upshot other than that the General simply ignored them. He could afford a lot of leeway and he knew it. Let him resign and there would arise the frightful perplexity whether the army would remain in being or scatter.

He had moreover reliable, influential friends at Vienna, the Harrach-Eggenberg clan. He had chosen his protectors well. "*In summa,*" wrote Dr Leuker to the Elector, "Eggenberg, Wallenstein, and Harrach are, I perceive, so triumphant at court and on such good terms with one another that whoever offends one has the others against him." In the autumn, when Wallenstein was accused of having proceeded too slowly and let Mansfeld slip through his fingers, when the battle against Bethlen had at the last minute not taken place and the Hungarian campaign vanished like a path in the desert, but the General demanded winter quarters for his troops in Bohemia, at this season even Eggenberg appeared at certain moments to be critical. So the diplomats contended, and they contended many another point too. The Duke was conceivably playing false, or at any rate his gamesmanship was indolent, impertinent, and intractable. Serious consideration was being given to relieving him of his command. On his part threats to resign were either to anticipate his dismissal or mere manoeuvre. The Emperor, normally so mild-mannered, had let Lord von Harrach have the rough side of his tongue when he tried to defend his son-in-law. "Your Electoral Highness will not credit how malicious and mocking the talk about the Duke of Friedland in general is," Dr Leuker gleefully reported. With Wallenstein's headquarters not all too far from Vienna, the exchange of embassies multiplied. His demand was for winter quarters immediately, in Bohemia, Moravia, and Austria. The questions on the other side were why so far everything had gone so slowly and why no winter campaign against Mansfeld or Bethlen was possible. His army, the General replied, was demolished, eaten up by famine and disease, the soldiers were dying all around, a sight he could no longer bear, and his resolve to escape from the labyrinth of his command was absolute. There was nothing inherently new in this answer. For almost a year he had been on the lookout for a way of decampment. Was the decision now final? "I am not to be moved from my *propositum,*" he wrote to Harrach, "for if I do what the court wants, I shall have lost for the Emperor his battle and his lands, but if I do what I think to be reason, I must myself be the loser." In his next letter there is a bitter reference to the "few hours remaining" to him as the Emperor's General. A comedy? Harrach refused either to accept the notice or the notification of it which must in any case imperil his own position. On 10 November he set out for Modern, the army headquarters in the vicinity of Pressburg. There he stayed a week. Then he and Wallenstein rode in the direction of Vienna to meet Prince Eggenberg at a half-way point. Here was the last effort to take stock of matters and clear the air. Not, as during the past eighteen months, through the mediation of inept negotiators, but through that of the First Minister in person. A last attempt, the outcome uncertain.

BRUCK-ON-THE-LEITHA

The castle of Bruck is situated on the edge of the town of the same name which lies by the small river Leitha. On the near side of its banks are Austrian woods, hills, and vineyards; on the far side begins the Hungarian plain. The castle still belongs to the Harrachs. In one of the galleries hangs portrait upon portrait of the family heads, from its founder in the fourteenth century to Baron Karl, the real originator of Harrach good fortune, and onwards to last century's military men and politicians. The gallery is, though, of later date and most of the building's arrangement is quite different to how things looked on that late autumn evening of 1626 when Eggenberg, Harrach, and Wallenstein warmed their gouty feet by the fire of a chimney-place in a room which remains unidentified. The castle was only half a day's journey from Vienna, where the meeting could just as well have occurred, but Wallenstein had no love for the city. Eggenberg's excursion was an act of courtesy.

No record exists of the discussions held on the evening of 25 November and the morning of the following day. Wallenstein's subsequent references to "what I agreed at Bruck with Prince von Eggenberg" are the most reliable source of indirect information. The diplomats' papers must be treated with care: the Venetian, the Frenchman, and the Bavarian always thought themselves in the know, they were always full of gossip, yet the fact that their dispatches agree at some point furnishes no certainty of its accuracy because it is perfectly conceivable that one of them may have whispered his secrets in the ear of the other. Furthermore we have a memorial by one who concealed his name, but who claimed to have every detail at his finger-tips, a claim taken seriously by his addressees.

Wallenstein did not come to Bruck to vindicate himself. Always convinced that he had been misunderstood and offence had been meant, always completely certain of the correctness of his actions, he came to obtain consent to his demands or to proclaim his resignation if these were not met. Eggenberg wanted him to retain his appointment, to hear his conditions, and to have the strategy or policy which lay behind them explained to him. He, for his part, could decide nothing; that was the

Emperor's prerogative. So it was a matter of provisional decisions, promises which must be ratified and on which Wallenstein harped in the days succeeding the conference. "I expected today the courier who is to bring the confirmation of my points, in the absence of which I cannot continue to serve," he told Harrach on 30 November. "I cannot contain my surprise that the courier does not arrive with the confirmation of the points which I presented to my lord and without which I neither can nor shall serve," he reiterated on 3 December. "It is time that I bethink me of means to take the field again next year and in what direction I shall turn, for the winter will soon pass." A mere week after the informal talk by the fireplace at Bruck he was impatient again. What were the points at issue?

In the first place, the matter of winter quarters. In so far as the troops could now no longer be sent back to the Empire, the problem of their location was practically settled. Their distribution over the Hereditary Lands had however to follow some plan. Secondly, the question of recruitments, not merely to restore the army to its former establishment but to expand it. He had, Wallenstein wrote to Collalto on 27 February, "previously expounded to Prince von Eggenberg" why the Emperor needed more soldiers. Next, the troops' pay. "To date I have replenished it from my own resources. In future I shall not do so, for thereby I ruin myself and my family, have no thanks for it, and in time of need shall not possess a groat." It is the old spectre of penury haunting the rich man, never rich enough, and entangled in dizzy business practices. What he demanded at Bruck was the levy of the "Bohemian contribution", a poll tax to be imposed on the subjects of the Bohemian crown; nobles, burgesses, and free peasants alike. For how long, in what form, and whether he should have at his disposal the whole amount or simply a part, that would prove a cause for argument in the following months, but at Bruck, it is clear, Eggenberg agreed in principle. Finally Wallenstein dealt with the problem of extending his own authority, his advancement from "Captain over the Army in the Empire" to Generalissimo over imperial troops everywhere, his investiture with rights which hitherto the monarch had reserved to himself. They were demands of a new category and not until a good twelve months later were they granted him in full. Nevertheless a start was made at Bruck, for shortly after the conference he began to sign colonels' commissions without reference to Vienna. So much for the "points" to be substantiated. Whoever, though, wanted to render comprehensible to the Minister why the Emperor should need still more soldiers must also have discussed the political situation and what were the conclusions expediently to be drawn from it.

After the meeting the French minister wrote that Eggenberg now was, or pretended to be, satisfied with the General's conduct of the war. To which the Venetian envoy added that Wallenstein as usual had at first feigned reluctance, then allowed himself to be persuaded to stay in command "for a year"; the court as well as the First Minister had formed a favourable opinion of the General's conduct of the war; and, in particular, everyone now appreciated the need to increase the army's strength to seventy thousand men. "With the negotiation on this single subject the meeting ended." From which it is obvious that these gentlemen knew little about Wallenstein's points, only really about the one on new recruitments.

Finally there is the memorial, in Italian, by the unnamed observer. Its date is 26 November. The author must therefore either have been in Vienna, where Eggenberg arrived late that evening, or indeed have been one of the party at Bruck. His report, sent in secret to the Elector of Bavaria, gives at any rate the impression of having been inspired by the Minister. If its contents can be believed, the General outlined his grand design as follows:

The Emperor's position was critical because the majority of Europe's princes were more or less hostile to him and he lacked money. From this arose the necessity to conduct a defensive war, keeping hostilities away from the Hereditary Lands but stationing so large and powerful an army in the Empire "that it would be the terror of all Europe. This army, since its purpose is not to take possession of anything in order to appropriate it to His Majesty, must in no circumstances be placed in any foreseeable danger of being either beaten or destroyed through sieges or similar operations. . . ." An eye would need to be kept on the movements of the Transylvanian and the Turk without being inveigled into distant, awkward scenes of action. Primarily however the Empire must groan beneath the burden of the army until it decided to seek an honourable peace and to pay the soldiers. Only thereafter would it be possible to undertake anything against other than German foes and raise the Emperor to the status he should properly enjoy, the real head of christendom. But why should the House of Habsburg not be allowed to make any new conquests? Because, the Duke replied, most of his soldiers would as Protestants not be prepared to slaughter their co-religionists. He had moreover intentionally entrusted a large portion of his regiments to Protestants so as to avoid every appearance of a war of religion. How was an establishment of seventy thousand to be paid without money? Nothing easier; as long as no injustice was inflicted on friends, it was possible to live on the land of rebels and enemies, this being for practical purposes the same as pay, and to do it for as many years as desired. "That is the tenor of what the Lord General said to His Highness the Prince von Eggenberg, and from which he assuredly recognized the principles on which the Lord General was conducting this war and that, with rare sagacity, he did not wish to make his victories dependent on chance but always repudiated any action which did not consort with his main objectives."

Shrewd, cowardly, and cruel, political and psychological warfare. Avoid battles, avoid wearisome sieges, and avoid every open breach of the imperial constitutions, but like a vampire lie with the heavy weight of the army upon the Empire and suck out its blood until it screams for mercy. Be raised to Europe's greatest power at no cost at all and then see what can be done with this new greatness. An accursedly clever report, cleverly reporting on a clever man. And cleverness too in the way each sentence, suggestive as it is of an initiate's knowledge, is yet ending with a word of praise. Whether the little dissertation was also meant to have its praise re-echoed is a different question. That was anyhow not the effect it produced. Another question – is it to be taken at face value?

Many historians have done so. For our part we cannot, but none the less believe that there is something to it. The Unknown may have known Wallenstein personally or he may have observed him at a distance with a trained eye. He saw very rightly that, besides other qualities, there was an element of timidity in the imperial war-lord, that his preparations for whatever he did were extremely circumspect, that he wanted "to hazard nothing", always fearing whenever he allowed himself to be seduced into mistaken measures "the ruination of the army", "the loss of the lands". He scanned all horizons, searching out not only present foes, of whom there were few, but potential, future ones, of whom there were many and from whom the few could at any moment anticipate help – Sweden, England, France, Holland. "We must regard it as a maxim that we may trust absolutely no one." It was also true that all he ever wanted, however great the force employed, was an "honourable", a "sound, lasting peace". Of course, that was what they all wanted. With Wallenstein exuberant hope of its achievement alternated with pessimism. The time came when, in his opinion, even ten victories would serve no durable outcome, but a single lost battle signify destruction. That was at the end of his life, not in 1626. The Unknown prodigiously overestimated the timidity and passivity of Wallenstein's conduct of war at this stage. In September Dr Leuker, the Bavarian, had heard a "noble Italian minister" openly proclaim in the Emperor's antechamber how "he would wager his head that were the Duke of Friedland with an army of a hundred thousand men and Mansfeld or Gabor with not more than ten thousand men to find themselves in *campagna rasa*, Friedland would not attack Mansfeld or Gabor but take a defensive stand". So ran the gossip, such were the misconceptions. The real Wallenstein warned that mere defence "discouraged" the troops and uselessly "consumed" them. The self-appointed purveyor of secrets had as hazy a crystal ball as the ambassadors. He knew about the army's expansion; everyone else did too. He knew nothing about the other points and wrote much about the new art of maintaining an army without pay. At Bruck the talk had been of money, lots of money, and which must now be provided. Therefore the Unknown was not at Bruck or, if he was, then far away from the room where the three great lords held their discussions. Nor did he, on the morning of 27 November, have an audience of the exhausted Eggenberg. What he reported was not the purport of the negotiations and agreements, but the notions he had formed, partly from observation, partly as a matter of speculation and exaggeration, about Wallenstein's way of waging war, the system which let the oppressed pay, pay for ever, for having to obey.

The report did not lack effect. Maximilian in his new Munich residence read it, read it again, and fell into feverish excitement. He found in it confirmation of what his suspicious, zealously pious, jealous spirit had long concluded. He understood that the Unknown's praise was sheer semblance and what was at the heart of the matter – overthrow of the Empire's old order through enervation, bleeding to death, horrible gradual subjugation, and that without harming a hair of a heretic's head. Express couriers sped to his Catholic fellow-princes. Invitations were issued to members of the League to meet in February at Würzburg. There the memorial was discussed in detail. Possibly everything contained in it was correct, or possibly not everything, but a comparison of the contents with what had happened since suggested unfortunately that most of it was indeed correct, and this all the more so for its derivation from an individual "who has knowledge of Friedland's affairs and intentions more than others and stands high in his confidence". That meant that the Elector knew who the Unknown was. We do not.

Meanwhile what had been dispatched under secret cover had become such public property that Wallenstein thought it necessary to employ

the services of a hack. The refutation was cast in the mould of a letter
by an "imperial captain" to his brother-in-law, circulated, and copied.
Specimens survive in various state archives. The "letter", in German,
is much longer than the memorial and much clumsier. Italians were far
better at this kind of thing. What, complains the alleged captain, are the
tales that this deceitful romancer presents and what are the inventions
that this poet concocts in order to gull the injudicious? "Now witness,
God help us, the captiousness of this fabulist!" How can he claim to
know what transpired between the two princes at Bruck? It so happens
that he, the captain, is completely familiar with all to whom the Lord
General entrusts his secrets, but they too were at the most only in a
position to learn of the conference's satisfactory result, not the course
that matters took. The captain did indeed raise with his brother-in-law
all the objections capable of being raised against the mysterious Italian's
report, but in a laborious, bombastic manner. His polemic appears to
have achieved its purpose with no one, whereas the Unknown attained
his purpose to excess. In this kind of business style, skill, and cleverly
calculated psychology count for more than truth.

As a whole the conference at Bruck had a conflicting, strangely sustained dual effect. At Munich the brazier of hate was replenished. At
Vienna the malicious, mocking talk about the Duke of Friedland stopped
in a flash. Instead, about nine months later, amazed admiration became
the fashion.

On 28 November the "resolution" about the Bruck "points" was drawn
up at Vienna. Comparatively quick work and manifestly not thorough
enough. Questenberg and Werdenberg, entrusted with its transmission
to army headquarters, had to compose many a wrangle with the Duke
or he with them. Dietrichstein, Governor of Moravia, wanted no billeting in his country, much less on his estates, an intelligible standpoint.
Slawata and Martinitz, the Defenestration survivors and Bohemia's
highest dignitaries, grudged the tax contribution, wanting to levy it for
only three months and then to deduct an amount, fourteen thousand
gulden each month. "That is a childish notion, for it cannot be," commented Wallenstein. "Let all be assured that not even fourteen kreutzer
can I afford to have deducted. I ask for nothing more in the world than to
have a pretext and withdraw my head from the noose," Harrach was told.

He was still toying, and continued until far into spring to do so, with
the idea of extricating himself through a kind of timely retreat from the
labyrinth and the toils of a power which was incomplete.

His officers saw matters in a different light. Franz Albrecht von Sachsen-Lauenburg, an impudent, intelligent young man, sent a comrade a copy of a letter from His Majesty with the words, "Here you can see what the Emperor writes to the Duke of Friedland. I account it for naught. . . . N.B. I console myself with the thought that the General is now as much as the Emperor himself."

Germany's Subjugation

SNOW on the fields, the roads, and the mule-tracks, on the roofs, on the head of the statue of Venus in the park. At the end of December many soldiers in Wallenstein's vicinity froze to death. A rich and powerful man was well off, though, in winter too. A certain snugness was not lacking – "I wish for nothing other than to stay at home." A certain pleasure in the new house which, without being finished, was tolerably habitable. Dalliance, after eighteen months of separation, with his wife, the fruit of which would appear late in the following autumn.

Business, vexation. Vexation concerning the winter quarters. "Not a single soldier who has been in Hungary is fit to take the field before June." The troops were exhausted and disease-ridden. They had to be allowed time, six months at least, to recover. But Bohemia, entering its tenth year of war or warlike affliction, was no nursing home; it was itself in need of nursing. Nor do mercenaries, however reduced in strength, ever behave like invalids. They take advantage of the fact that they are always one up on their involuntary hosts. The hungrier and the more woebegone they are, the greater the advantage that they take. "*In Summa Summarum,*" sighed Questenberg, responsible for settling the quartering problem in Bohemia and Lower Silesia, "I apprehend the direst poverty for soldiers and civilians alike. . . . I know no remedy." "Distress and indigence, neither is ever wanting," Wallenstein commented resignedly. True enough, whenever there is war, be it summer or winter.

In Moravia responsibility for billet allocation lay with the Governor, Cardinal Dietrichstein. He offered the stoutest resistance, as a matter of pastoral care and because he would have preferred to see his own, far from inconsiderable estates spared. And, as Wallenstein was aware, there was another motive too – the crusty loathing of the churchman for him, the all too successful upstart, a loathing which was mutual and created a tension that fed upon itself. On this occasion victory went to the worldly power and the worldly realism he could call in aid. Dietrichstein had to submit to billeting on his estates, billeting of a kind for which he would later present an account of astronomic proportions. Karl von Liechtenstein did no better. When in February he died, many asserted not only that he had departed this life out of grief at the ruin of his properties, but that Wallenstein had out of personal spite, not need, bedded his soldiers there. The tale is true to the degree that its two protagonists for long past had not been on the best of terms, at any rate as far as Liechtenstein was concerned. He had felt over-trumped by his former junior partner. On Wallenstein's side no letter survives in which he speaks badly of the Governor, as he did of Dietrichstein, Martinitz, and Slawata. Insiders moreover said that Wallenstein would gladly have added the dead man's titles to his own and to that end evinced financial generosity towards this and that imperial minister. Insiders knew so much which had no actual foundation. In reality no successor to Liechtenstein was selected. Vienna regarded conditions in Bohemia as sufficiently normalized to allow the vice-royalty to be dropped and the old hierarchy restored. Wallenstein's cousin or uncle, Adam, was appointed High Burgrave of Prague, previously the country's highest office.

Vexation also with Maximilian's Catholic League. It thought it had, and it did have, reason for shrill complaint. During the autumn campaign those of Wallenstein's colonels who had remained behind behaved in traditional fashion, especially Rudolf Maximilian, one of the Lauenburg dukes. His soldiers tormented the citizens of Erfurt regardless of the city belonging to the Empire's most pious, most loyal ruler, the Elector of Mainz. The sequel – a protest by the Elector to the Emperor, pleadingly grave remonstrances by His Majesty to Wallenstein that so very much depended on the Elector's goodwill, and Wallenstein's reply that he would, as always, try his utmost to restrain the military. He probably did what he could, but at the same time he wrote to Harrach, "Only Bavaria is responsible for this, because he does not wish the Emperor to have power in his dominion."

The suspicion did not lack substance. Maximilian, the new Elector, wanted power in the Empire to rest in the hands of the Electors, his own particularly. In the hands of the Emperor too, and in all honour, but held by him as the first among equals, not as that form of imperial power which Maximilian surmised Wallenstein to have in mind and which looked to him more of a Friedland than an imperial brand. The conference of League princes or their deputies that he had summoned to Würzburg in February was to assemble data on the excesses committed by Wallenstein's army. It was additionally to deal with the policy lying behind them because, so Maximilian instructed his representative to declare, "Numerous individuals at the imperial court and other places who understand these matters hold that Friedland seeks none other than to wear out all the lands through vast assemblies of armies and through such unheard-of harassments in order thereafter to arrange affairs with the one and the other at his pleasure." This was the secret report about Bruck-on-the-Leitha which had become lodged in the Bavarian's brain and burrowed away at it. The Würzburg conference decided to send an embassy to Vienna, vigorously to demand that all loyal Estates should be spared depredation, and to caution against fresh Wallenstein recruitments. Shortly afterwards there was even talk, in an exchange of letters between the Bavarian and Mainz Electors, about the desirability of a separate peace with the Danes, for if the worst came to the worst the Emperor would have to be protected against his own power and the League forces be required against the Duke of Friedland.

Wallenstein did not need confirmation of such letters to guess their text. Meanwhile he proceeded with precisely that which Maximilian wanted to prevent while, to be prepared for all eventualities, doing this himself – he continued with his army's re-equipment. The purpose, as defined in a recruitment proclamation: to accomplish His Majesty's peaceful intentions through the law's strong arm, to stifle the assaults of the rebels and those beyond the pale, to re-introduce prized peace into the Holy Roman Empire of the German nation. The means: good, able-bodied, well-qualified fellows. Not to mention powder, culverin bullets, muskets, as well as "mattocks, pickaxes, and spades" which he ordered from his duchy. Sooner or later the account for supplies from his own workshops would, like his advance outlays on recruitment, have to be settled.

With the sun bearing down on the severe frost, mild breezes blowing across the fields, and human beings emerging from the warm byres, the time inevitably came to decide what should in summer be done with the army, old and new. Wallenstein would have been best pleased to make his plans alone. That was not possible. He had devised a variety of schemes, "but the principal action must be resolved at Vienna". He dallied the first three weeks of March, pleading sickness, the urgency for a cure, and the time necessitated by this. Finally, on 25 March, he started. His intention was to put the distance from Prague to Vienna – 150 miles – behind him in two days so as at least to have done with the prologue to the disagreeable play as quickly as possible. He took nearly a month, coming no farther than Kolin on the first day and a desolate village called Habern, near Czaslau, on the second. There, at a wretched inn, he took to his bed, his gout worse than ever, as though he had never drunk the waters. At Vienna, where sceptics had long since questioned the Duke's arrival, jeering murmurs rose. The Venetian envoy spoke of "an excuse"; the Brandenburger commented that the General "may well be befallen by a fit of malingering". Truth salted this piece of sly falsehood. The euphemism "escape into illness" did not yet exist, but the symptom did and a glimpse of it was to be caught when Wallenstein wrote Harrach from his hovel, "I become somewhat better, but my desire to mend is poor, for then I shall meet with an illness that will pester me more heavily than the gout does. None the less, when 'tis better, I shall set out and betake myself to Vienna." On the evening of 20 April his litter, carried through the gates of the Harrach palace in Vienna, was gently set down by its red-and-blue liveried bearers at the entrance to the suite of rooms placed at the General's disposal by his hospitable father-in-law. He at once took to his bed again, remaining there another month. The bed was a bastion. The invalid had to be visited. He must pay no visits nor listen at endless meetings to Privy Councillors' prattle. His entourage included Valeriano Magni, the proud Capuchin and enemy of the Jesuits, father-confessor to the Archbishop of Prague. Wallenstein, it seems, trusted and talked openly with him. Others trusted him too. Isaia Leuker, the Bavarian envoy, for example, who on several occasions wrote to Maximilian that, when Wallenstein came to Vienna, he would need Magni's guidance and would during any audience behave as Magni advised.

Dr Leuker was a man who, as is proper for a diplomat, kept his ears wide open. He was also aware of what his master liked to read, a circumstance that somewhat robs his reports of their value. While Vienna awaited Wallenstein, the industrious official sent dispatch after dispatch to Munich. How bleak, he explained, the Emperor's situation was, seeing that he was certainly willing to redress the Friedland situation, but could not, must not. How no minister, except the venal Questenberg, wanted to have any more dealings with the Duke. How Marquis Aytona, the Spanish ambassador, had declared that his king would be lost if he relied on Wallenstein and confidence could alone be reposed in the League and pious Tilly. How the former Colonel Wratislaw was telling tales about his former commander fit to make one's hair stand on end (which is not really surprising). How Field-Marshal Collalto spoke in the most contemptuous terms about his companion-in-arms. In short, how on all sides mutterings were to be heard and perplexity prevailed. A reader of these dispatches cannot fail to feel that the General journeying to Vienna was about to step into a snake-pit. That was precisely the General's own view. Therefore the refuge that he sought in his bed, the site from which he subjugated the tongue-wagging opposition. "Before Wallenstein arrived at court, every man disparaged him," recorded the Venetian envoy. "Today not a voice is raised against him."

In bed he received affably enough the Bavarian representative, gave him his hand, and took a turn with him up and down the political horizon. The greatest danger, he descanted, threatened from the northeast. The King of Sweden's progress must be heeded. He had secured for himself every seaport from the Neva to Riga and then down the Courland coast, with the Prussian ports his most recent acquisition, so that he was lord and master from, or nearly from, the mouth of the Oder to where Muscovy bordered on Finland. His infantry was superior to the Polish. Moreover Poland was undermined from within. Poles were secretly sympathetic to the Swedish cause, a factor upon which Gustavus Adolphus counted, just as he incessantly wooed the Muscovites. No one could ever be certain what Brandenburg, to the west of Poland, was up to. At any time a thrust by Bethlen from the south could be expected. In Upper Silesia, half-way between Brandenburg and Transylvania, remained the remnant of that Danish–Mansfeld army which last autumn had declined battle and was daily increasing in strength. The Danish monarch was re-arming. How would it be if he were to seek contact with the advance-post of his power in Silesia, if he were to aspire to a link with Bethlen, as intercepted letters showed that he was doing? From all this ensued that a strategy which was responsible for defence of the Hereditary Lands, the Empire, and the Catholic cause must be very circumspect and must look preponderantly to the east. Therefore he, the Emperor's principal commander, must relinquish neither the Elbe nor the places in Brandenburg that he had occupied. He would gladly send auxiliaries westwards to Count Tilly, in the direction of the Weser, and he would do it as soon as he could vindicate such a move. Was however Tilly's strategic disposition quite suitable? Was not this brave general somewhat inclined to dissipate his strength on sieges of varying importance? And if he wanted to march down the Weser, could he be certain that the Dane would not give him the slip eastwards and do what Mansfeld had done last year, something which could have been avoided by adherence at the right moment to Wallenstein's plan and prosecution of the major offensive on both sides of the Elbe? In such perilous circumstances matters must be allowed to take their time. His own army must recover before it took the field again, a very wide field, whatever compass-point *ratio belli* indicated. Dr Leuker's suspicion had been bottomless when he entered the bed-chamber. Nevertheless he found it difficult not to be impressed by Wallenstein's calm, amiably extended argumentation, especially regarding Gustavus Adolphus. Had it not been so, he would not the same day have written to Munich in such detail on the subject. He closed his report with the statement that he had "used my ears, but been sparing of my tongue in His Princely Grace's presence, so as not, as is particularly easy in such places, to cause offence." Who knows? Perhaps he who lay in bed would even graciously have entertained objections from his conversational partner. Examples exist.

THEATRUM EUROPAEUM

Was Wallenstein sincere? It depends on what "sincere" in such a case means. He knew the Bavarian Elector to be his enemy, and consequently he was his too. More impulsive than Maximilian, less drilled by centuries of discipline and inbreeding, he allowed his frames of mind to be captured by situation. He told no lies. He believed the inspiration appropriate to the moment, deriving from it the persuasive force of conviction. Munich's worst fear was that he intended utterly to exterminate the League and its army in order to be the Empire's sole master. At the time with which we are dealing there is not a speck of evidence for that. Munich's next strongest censure was that he grudged Count Tilly any victory and refused him every help. But matters could be seen in this and in that light. Wallenstein was probably not quite clear on the subject himself. The misunderstanding which from the outset prevailed between him and Tilly was that Tilly had expected "succour" in the shape of a few imperial regiments more or less attached and subordinate to him. Instead Wallenstein arrived with an army larger than Tilly's, soon three times as large. For military and political reasons he wanted to keep it independent. In 1626 already he had aimed at a "conjunction" of the two forces, something different to division and transfer. From their combination he hoped for outstanding success, but it would have been a combination in which, thanks to superiority of numbers and his own superiority, he would invariably have been the stronger partner. Now, in spring 1627, Tilly alone was no match for the Danes. Given the Wallenstein regiments stationed in Brandenburg and central Germany for which he asked, he might have been. Supposing a purely Bavarian victory in northern Germany to have been feasible, was it desirable?

For Wallenstein patently not. That was regarded as the main point. Was it, though, not *ex officio* inevitable that the Emperor's commander-in-chief and effective master-politician must dislike a successful Bavarian initiative in the north? Experience, in the south, in the Upper and Rhenish Palatinates, had shown what Bavarian leadership in successful action signified. Maximilian played his own hand in politics. He hated what he called the "Spanish servitude" as keenly as what Wallenstein called the "Bavarian servitude". A member of the great Habsburg alliance, he none the less had always one foot in another camp, the centre of a third party uncertainly fumbling for a firm basis of reality. That was not something that Wallenstein did – as yet. His thoughts ran on imperial, solely imperial lines. Or, to phrase it more aptly, his line of thought was Austrian. His egotistic interests were unbridled, but for the present they were in harness with those of the Austrian House of Habsburg.

The catalogue of dangers which he had recited to the Bavarian doctor had not included those in western Europe. The perpetual menace of the States-General went without saying. The Dutch defence against Spain was successful on land, brilliant by sea. Without it many a dangerous element would not have existed. In the near future no major operation needed to be feared on the part of the two western monarchies, the Protestant and the Catholic which externally pursued a Catholic policy. The London government was a bad one, vain and vacillating, in bickering negotiations with a Parliament which kept it on an ever tighter financial curb. The country gentry and the townsmen cared little about the lot of the King's Palatine brother-in-law and lent no alert ear to the Continental confusions unless trade, and impediments to it through duties or blockade, entered the game. The war at sea against Spain was, or could have been, popular if conducted with greater success. King Charles had nothing more cheerful to offer his uncle, Christian of Denmark, than a piece of jewelry which no money-lender would accept as security and a few thousand soldiers. France, although ruled by a stronger hand, was not much more active. Cardinal Richelieu would have liked to have lured Bavaria's League out of the German war, arranged a separate peace between it and Denmark, and in some way have afforded the Palsgrave satisfaction. Denmark would have been afforded relief and the Habsburg cause weakened. The subject received sympathetic consideration, that was all, at the League's Würzburg conference. Maximilian did not want to venture the leap, to dissociate himself openly from Habsburg, and to make any acceptable overture to the Palatine government-in-exile leading an exigent, but tenaciously bustling, existence at The Hague. That France undertook nothing east of the Rhine except feeble diplomatic moves was due to the disagreeable domestic circumstance of a major Huguenot uprising not entirely unlike the Bohemian one of 1618 – anti-royal, religious, and feudal in spirit. The First Minister's prime duty was to see to order at home. Its accomplishment was the task that he had set himself before initiating a grand sweep around the country's glacis. In 1626, in order to be able to devote all his energy to the stubborn internal problem, Richelieu concluded a peace with Spain which left affairs in northernmost Italy, in the Val Telline and adjacent regions, much as they had been before.

If England and France had a foe in common, then it was Spain. It held the latter in a vice on land. Its claims to sovereignty over sea-lanes and insistence on superiority along the road to Heaven affronted the former. Yet hardly had France made peace with Spain than it occurred to the Duke of Buckingham that it would be no bad thing to encourage arson in the neighbouring property by support for the Huguenots and possibly a better temper towards his King among the Puritans of Westminster by simultaneous invigoration of the laws against the Catholics at home. Maritime hostilities between France and England were the result. To what purpose? Whoever asks that must believe that wars always arise from sheer necessity. Has the point been proved? Proved for Wallenstein's age? As long as highly placed subjects continued to feel loyalty to factors other than the state, to religion, to class, to local considerations, they could not without more ado be clear as to which sympathies and antipathies should be the guardian of the monarch's European policy. As long as the monarchies were not as yet completely identical with the state, kings and favourites had room for freely, arbitrarily selected enterprises, properly private wars, quickly begun, easily ended. That was here the case. The consequences were nevertheless significant, especially for Christian of Denmark. He should, and would like to, have been the spear-head of a great Protestant coalition. Instead he was now dependent on the resources of his own country where angry questionings could be heard in the Rigsraad: What concern of Denmark's were Germany's troubles?

Gustavus Adolphus, on the other hand, was actuated purely by reasons of state and the rationale of war. For almost twenty years the safety of the realm, commercial advantage, religion, the greatness of God, the greatness of Sweden, the fame of Sweden's ruler had been his guiding constellation. He was on good terms with the Muscovites; Wallenstein's claim to know it was no empty rhetoric. Having right at the outset of his reign relieved them of Ingermanland, at the eastern end of the Finnish gulf, as well as of a handsome territorial slice north of the Lake of Ladoga, he and they were provisionally reconciled. Now Gustavus Adolphus let it be known that he and they did have one mischievous enemy in common – Poland. Behind Poland, though, stood the House of Austria and all who in central Europe swore by the Roman faith. The Pope, the Emperor, and the whole Austrian dynasty had but a single aim, to dominate the world, and they were close to achieving their objective. When a house is on fire, those who live next door must carry water and help to quench the flames so as to save their goods and chattels. Tsar Michael Romanov, lobbing his very heavy sceptre from hand to hand and back again, listened amiably to this allocution. His answer sounded friendly too, but it did not contain much of substance. Provided the harvest was good, the Swedes could have grain duty-free and at reasonable prices. In the matter of the European war, Muscovite sympathies inclined more to the Protestant than the Catholic camp. Trade was carried out with the Danes and the Dutch, across the White Sea with the British. There was much talk about the Papists and about their evil intentions. Spain was very far away. So was the Pope. The Empire was nearer. By patient diplomacy the Muscovites had attained *de facto*, if not *de jure*, recognition of their newly elected Tsar as the "presently incumbent Ruler of All the Russias". To this, God knows why, they attached enormous importance. On the Emperor's part the formula constituted a discreetly mellowed offence to the dignity of Sigismund, King of Poland, who held his own son Wladislaw to be the true Tsar. There, for the Muscovites was the real enemy and the real Catholic. The only piece of Europe that really and seriously concerned them was the great Polish polity. For all its impractical structure and its monarch's impotence against his nobility, Poland was none the less at all times, as experience taught, better at war than the Russian realm which had nothing to oppose it with other than unfathomed depth. The Poles sat in Smolensk; the road from there to Moscow was charted. Emperor Ferdinand's occasional support for his co-religionist and brother-in-law Sigismund had not gone unnoticed. However, with an armistice subsisting until 1632 between the Russians and the Poles, and Habsburg aid applying only against the Swedes, the Tsar's councillors voted against intervention, content if Sweden and Poland tied each other down and mutually soured their existence. As long as that continued, let Prince Wladislaw call himself Grand Duke of Muscovy if it gave him pleasure.

His father clung unflinchingly to the designation "King of Sweden", an impediment to every negotiation between Stockholm and Warsaw since no agreement could be reached on respective styles. At Madrid too nothing was known about a King Gustavus Adolphus, simply about the "Swedish tyrant".

What difference did it make? In 1625 the tyrant had added the whole of Livonia, down to Riga and across the Duna, to his possession of Ingermanland and Estonia. For Poland the loss, outcome of a summer campaign which in those parts had to be even shorter than in more hospitable regions, was humiliating. Gustavus left a governor and garrisons in the conquered land. In autumn he was in the habit of returning to Stockholm as Wallenstein did to Prague and Gitschin.

The year 1626 witnessed a new development. Sweden carried its Polish war into Prussia, a step nearer Germany. It could not be treated as an attack on the Empire. Prussia was Polish foreland and a Polish fief held for the last eight years in fee by Brandenburg's Elector. To cast anchor with 125 ships in the Prussian port of Pillau and to land with fourteen thousand men was an ambiguous manoeuvre. Gustavus's choice and execution of it, performed with his customary vigour and customary good luck, created the potentiality of a link between two intrinsically distant theatres of war, the north-easterly European and the German. The royal strategist had precisely this potentiality in mind. The valley of the lower Vistula, dividing Prussia from German Pomerania, was not that broad. Alternatively a thrust was possible from Prussia through Poland to Silesia, that interestingly located territory, a bundle of German and Polish principalities, like Prussia not subject to the Empire but through chance inheritance to the House of Habsburg. It offered a capacious path to the fortresses of the Hereditary Lands, a bridge to Poland, an excursion down the Oder to Pomerania and Brandenburg. In Wallenstein's strategy Silesia always played a key part. For Gustavus Adolphus it was not that, but the conceivable objective of an expedition which would have brought him closer to Bohemia and his south-eastern brother-in-law and fellow-Protestant, the Prince of Transylvania. Colossal combinations, these, reckoning the distances to be overcome.

The King of the Waters was free to land where he would, given sound ships and men. Herein lay the superiority of sea-power, as Wallenstein well understood without currently knowing a means to meet it. Gustavus Adolphus's present choice of Prussia had however a particular reason. In 1625 he had stayed aloof from the big, delusive coalition because his conditions remained unfulfilled. Let Denmark, without getting too far, carry the burden of keeping the Germans or Spaniards or Austrians away from him. Denmark, left to itself, carried the burden badly. The great imperial, and Wallenstein's, war-machine aimed at the coast, a project which was not these landlubbers' alone. Obsessed by the passion to preserve or to revive the old universal monarchy and to eradicate the long-established fact of Netherlandish independence, regardless of half a century's history, the King of Spain's councillors had worked out that what could not be attained dry-shod might nevertheless be achieved by sea. To paralyse the Baltic trade of the Dutch would be to touch their wealth on the raw. Spanish warships in the Baltic forming a pack with Polish ones based on German harbours? In 1626 the plan was aired at Brussels, for example, and Gustavus Adolphus knew of it. He could not help but view it as inimical to himself, as well as to the Dutch, just as Wallenstein reciprocally construed the slowly creeping Swedish advance from Finland to the Vistula, pouncing upon province after province, harbour after harbour, as a major undertaking whose ultimate target must be his very own preserve. Where such construction is put on policy, a clash can be postponed, but not for ever.

Prussia was well off, still more through commerce than prosperous agriculture, and as un-warlike as conceivable. George William of Brandenburg found the breach of his neutrality all the more distressing for that neutrality having long been anything but genuine. He had, though, nothing but paper protests with which to counter his powerful, friendlily hostile Stockholm brother-in-law. His liege-lords, the Poles, saw matters differently. It was no joke for their nobility and merchants that Poland's main river artery, the Vistula, should be simply cut in two, all Prussian harbours other than Königsberg and Danzig belong to the Swedes, duties of impossibly high percentage be imposed by Swedish inspectors to assist in payment of the Swedish army, Axel Oxenstierna as Swedish governor have his seat at Elbing, and Swedish garrisons be scattered through the interior as far as Marienburg and Mewe. In Warsaw's view Prussia must not become what Estonia and Livonia had become, Swedish provinces. This was still a war purely between Poland and Sweden, but one which had an intermediately strong effect upon Germany, the Netherlands, and Spain.

Wallenstein understood Europe's unity. His conversation with Dr Leuker showed how familiar he was with the Continent's north-eastern geography. More precisely than his ally Tilly, the Bavarian of Belgian origin, whom no textbook had in his youth warned of the Swedish danger and who was in any case not disconcerted by any foe except the one immediately facing him. A question of different temperaments. From winter 1627 onwards it became Wallenstein's project so to preoccupy Gustavus Adolphus with hostilities in Prussia that he would not be able to stir from there. For nearly four years that purpose continued. As early as March 1627 he detached a regiment to Poland. It was only a start. He, Wallenstein, as well as the Emperor, would fall into the direst danger if Sweden sounded the general charge before Denmark had been eliminated. In his perspective the new order of affairs in Bohemia remained imperilled, a rule of naked force lasting just as long as the successful force which was its sanction. The Danish and Swedish courts crawled with Bohemian refugees. They would accompany the northern kings if they came into the land and would shriek after their own until such time as they had it again. He had little but contempt for those Bohemian grandees, Martinitz, Slawata, Dietrichstein, his fellow-usufructuaries, who never ceased to create quandaries for him on account of taxation and billets: "They never think of the future, only the present, and yet know that if the Emperor be endangered they are lost." Exactly. They sat in one boat, he and his native enemies, but he was aware of it and they were not.

Wallenstein's desire to help Poland brought him closer to Spain which desired by the roundabout sea-route to do the same. It was also one of the objectives which set a distance between him and Bavaria. The train of thought there ran along inland lines of communication, was of a Rhenish and western European calibre and, if necessary, wished to rely on France, not Poland and Spain.

ARNIM

Lieutenant-General Marradas – not longer much to the fore – Field-Marshal Count Schlick, Major-Generals von Schauenburg and del Maestro, and Paymaster-General Aldringen constituted the nucleus of senior officers who had been with Wallenstein a longer time. A number of new names came to be added: Torquato Conti, who exchanged papal for imperial service; Colonel von Mörder*; young Ottavio Piccolomini from Siena, who commanded the crack regiment of life-guards. The most important, though, was Colonel Hans Georg von Arnim, important alike for his personality, his past, and the part he was destined to play in Wallenstein's life.

* In German the name's enunciation is 'murder' and its meaning 'murderer' (translator's note).

Arnim's family was at home in the Uckermark, a north-eastern part of Brandenburg. Born in the same year as Wallenstein, he entered the service of Gustavus Adolphus in 1613 with the rank of colonel and acquired diplomatic as well as military experience. Scope for the practice of diplomacy was afforded by Gustavus Adolphus' wooing of the Brandenburg Elector's sister, a suit spiced during its five years' duration with a variety of journeys incognito, rejections, and renewed promises. Arnim, the native Brandenburger, fitted the role of lovers' go-between at Berlin. The match was hardly played and won before Arnim sold his sword to Gustavus Adolphus' arch-enemy, the King of Poland. As his enlistment was for operations against the Turks, his transfer was not much taken amiss at Stockholm. Whoever duly revoked his contract of service received his testimonial and was released from further obligations of loyalty. Brief as was the Polish interlude, that with Mansfeld proved to be briefer still and in 1624-5 a Swedish refresher course succeeded it. Arnim, who had helped to bring about the Brandenburg–Swedish marriage, supported the idea of a grand Protestant coalition headed by Sweden, Saxony and Brandenburg in the van. Denmark's prospects on its own he viewed pessimistically. In 1625-6 he was free again and in the military market. Bids for a man with his qualifications could not be lacking. One came from Brandenburg, but was as unattractive as the Elector's wretched situation. Another came from Denmark. Wallenstein's was the third. Although he opted for this, he did not, even after the Duke had in January 1627 invested him with the colonelcy of long-nosed Wratislaw's regiment, cease to toy for a while with the Danish offer.

From the foregoing the conclusion could be drawn that Arnim was one of the many who sought their fortune in war irrespective of where it took them. Nevertheless he was not one of the many. His conduct was so respectable that he was nicknamed the "Lutheran Capuchin". His comrades boozed; he did not drink. Others acquired immense riches; he did not feather his nest, or merely moderately. He enjoyed listening to his chaplain's daily exhortations, continued the habit that he had learned from Gustavus Adolphus of praying with his men before every passage of arms, and more than any other commander was a disciplinarian who enforced forbearance towards the suffering civilian populations. His education had an aesthetic flavour. His memory was stupendous and he could recite the most intricate treaties, article by article, in faultless Latin, Swedish, and French. His speeches were stirring. His frequent change of masters did not signify much. Of greater importance was that, apart from the spell with King Sigismund, he had hitherto only served

Protestant lords. At his own initiative he had become something of a private politician and general agent among the Protestant powers. He recovered his expenses, but no more. Considering this record, it must cause surprise that Arnim should enter Wallenstein's, meaning the imperial, meaning Counter-Reformation service. Perhaps, trusting to his diplomatic flair, he simply wanted to be close to the centre of affairs, no matter on which side. Indeed, why not try that opposite to his accustomed one and seek to gain influence over it? Did he sense that Wallenstein was not at heart an adherent of Catholic reaction? That Arnim, for all his respectability, had a streak of falseness at the bottom of his soul could not however be excluded. Unfathomable falsity, if old Count Thurn was to be believed. That was how the clever man looked to the stupid.

Why Wallenstein should have selected the Brandenburger is more obvious. He respected officers who were disciplinarians and who kept their domains clean. He liked to engage Protestants. As he told representatives from the Hanseatic cities, Arnim was a good fellow, a German and not an Italian, not simply a German but a Brandenburger, and not a Catholic but a Lutheran. If they could not make friends with him, then he was really at his wits' end.

A good fellow he had called him, treated him on that assumption, and in the coming years relied on him as on none of his other officers. He called him "soldierly", a high distinction in his eyes. "He is a soldier and on the ground will know how to have due regard for all." For the years 1627 and 1628 the three volumes of his correspondence with Arnim are the richest mine of information. On one occasion he wrote him no less than seven letters in a single day. For our part, if we were sound imperialists, we would hesitate to admit to our innermost circle a man who had long and valiantly served the Swedes. That was not the yardstick applied in those days. To allow a portion of one's sympathies to rest, in the middle of hostilities, with the other side was almost the normal condition of things. Arnim's familiarity with Gustavus Adolphus's ways of thought and disposition appeared to Wallenstein only an advantage. Arnim, whose shrewd memory was stocked with many a Stockholm secret, was now able to construct a confessional for Wallenstein's confidences, those of a man who always needed someone on whom he could lean and to whom he could unreservedly reveal his plans, hopes, fears, and embitterments. For a few short months Collalto filled the niche. For some years old Harrach had met the necessity, but he now fell into the background; his days were numbered.

The commission by which Arnim was accepted into imperial service has a postcript in Wallenstein's hand. "If 'twere possible, I would for many and divers reasons welcome his presence by me in Silesia at the beginning of May." That was the plan. His colonels, with a great part of the army, were in May to meet in Silesia, very close to the enemy occupying the Upper Silesian fortresses, and there receive their orders for the summer's campaign. On account of his month's delay at that wretched Habern, the date had to be postponed to June. On 23 May, after a first and last audience with the Emperor which is said to have lasted barely a quarter of an hour, he left Vienna and never saw it again. His position, according to the Venetian envoy, was more secure than ever, thanks not least to the juicy bribes enjoyed by Eggenberg, Werdenberg, Questenberg, and others. On 2 June he departed, with his usual splendour, from Prague. The column wound its way via Gitschin and the pass near Castle Nachod into the valley of the Neisse where the new regiments lay in camp.

THE 1627 CAMPAIGN: PART ONE

Who was the enemy? Denmark against Germany would sound somewhat odd and not indeed be the right answer. Germany as a political entity did not exist at all and Denmark only a shade more than that. It was the King of Denmark and Norway, Duke of Slesvig and Holstein, who was waging war in Germany in his capacity of greatest, wealthiest Danish noble, German prince (as the Danish Estates emphasized), and head of the Lower Saxon Circle (as he himself claimed). Precisely this gave the business its character of a cross between a foreign and a civil war. Not Germany, the majority of whose Protestant inhabitants sympathized with him and a minority of whose Protestant princes supported him either as allies or through some sort of help or at least passive toleration, was ranged against him, but the Emperor in the shape of an army scraped together here and there under his authority, and the Elector Maximilian as head of the Catholic League, meaning Bavaria plus a few appendages with impressive names but little real power. To them could be added the Spaniards who at this particular moment began to display a keen interest in the Lower German hostilities, not so much on account of Denmark as that of the salt waters surrounding the Danish isles and the Sound whose passage the Danish monarch permitted or prevented as he pleased, but for which, when he permitted, he charged highly vexatious dues. And the way that the Spaniards adhered to the

The campaign of 1627

imperial side was that adopted on the Danish side by the Swedes, the English, the Dutch, and the French, allies of potential rather than effectual character.

In spring 1627 King Christian had for practical purposes to rely on his own resources. The Germans lent him, partly because they liked him, partly because they had no choice, the soil trodden by his troops, but no more; the English, a few regiments; the States-General, a little money; Protestantism-in-exile, some senior officers. He had recently nominated as his lieutenant-general the old Margrave of Baden-Durlach, last survivor of the freebooters who in 1622 had fought for the Palsgrave. His field-marshal was none other than Count Thurn. That these two had only sustained defeat after defeat did their standing no harm. A reputation once acquired remained indomitable. Whoever had Thurn in his camp could reckon with the heartfelt good wishes of every Bohemian awaiting liberation. Thurn moreover was, although the most prominent, not the sole Bohemian in the King's service. Lord Ladislaus von Zierotin, last legitimate Governor of Moravia and nephew to Baron Karl Zierotin, Colonel von Bubna, Wallenstein's companion-in-arms during the Turkish campaign of 1604, and Hans Christoph von Waldstein, a close relative, commanded units in Silesia.

Why should the decimated Danish–Mansfeld force, which in late autumn 1626 had withdrawn from Hungary, have remained in Silesia rather than making a timely retreat northwards down the Oder, through Brandenburg into Pomerania, and thence to Mecklenburg? The answer is that its leaders did not regard themselves as beaten. In spring they hoped to resume the pincer movement, culminating in junction with Gabor Bethlen, which the previous year had gone awry. Since 1618 this grand will-o'-the-wisp of Protestant hopes had never lit the conflagration expected of it. Now too, especially as the Transylvanian was far gone in dropsy, it was an empty delusion. All the more ground, arm-chair strategists will argue, for Christian to have tried to establish contact with his considerable advance-guard. Considerable because this Silesian army had during the winter months expanded along familiar lines and finally attained a strength of seventeen thousand mercenaries garrisoned in the citadels of Leobschütz, Troppau, Jägerndorf, and Gratz, with Crossen-on-Oder as its main stronghold. But the King of Denmark's former energy seems to have been sapped. For no palpable reason he held back his troops on the Baltic coast, in the archbishopric of Bremen, in Lauenburg, in western Mecklenburg, a territory whose ducal over-lords were at first agreeable to this course but subsequently, fearing the Emperor's vengeance, put an ever more scowling mien on the matter.

Wallenstein acted faster. In April he ordered the regiments stationed in Brandenburg under the Duke of Lüneburg's command to occupy the lower reaches of the Havel, from the town of Brandenburg to Havelberg. Thereby the quadrilateral between Havel and Elbe was closed to movement by the Danes. The Lüneburgers seized the Domberg, a castle situated above Havelberg where the Havel flows into the Elbe.

Tilly and Wallenstein, each after his own fashion, were cautious commanders. Tilly tended to clean up his rear completely, besieging even the smallest fortress, storming and garrisoning it with his own men, before he moved forward. Wallenstein, during the apparent inactivity with which he was so often reproached, first made sure by way of recruitments and armaments that he was stronger than his opponent in order then to cut him off by means of widely spaced, gradually narrowing lines of march, to encircle and eventually catch him. His outposts along the Havel served just this purpose. So did the task entrusted in June to Colonel von Arnim. Elector George William and his First Minister, Adam von Schwarzenberg, had taken up residence in distant Prussia. The intention, apart from wishing presumably to be far from their country's sufferings, was to show the King of Poland how they could not be held responsible for the King of Sweden's actions in Brandenburg. Schwarzenberg, a Catholic convert, had long been at pains to give an imperial bias to his master's policy. The lower the Danish fortunes of war sank, the higher his influence rose. By May he had his master where he wanted him. George William, not long ago of Danish complexion, not long ago an even more Swedish than Danish partisan, not long ago still striving to help in the formation of a great Protestant coalition, now in a letter to Wallenstein abased himself to the degree of cursing his brothers-in-law, the northern kings, and requesting assistance against the Danish invasion. Henceforward his desire was, with all his heart and for the rest of his life, to remain His Imperial Majesty's devoted, faithful Elector. He wrote that for fear of sharing the Palsgrave's fate, yet at the very moment in which he surrendered Brandenburg to the imperialists he secretly promised the King of Sweden a free hand in Prussia. Brandenburg-Prussia was like a bisected worm whose two parts pitifully crawl in opposite directions. Such a distracted, defenceless state of affairs favoured Arnim's task to march with a number of regiments, an army corps, properly speaking, down the Oder into Brandenburg, capture the most important river passes at Crossen and Frankfurt as well as Landsberg to the east of the Oder, and in the west gain possession of certain key places along the Spree, but in such manner as to lend the occupation a cloak of legality. Arnim, Brandenburg subject that he was, fulfilled his mission with vigour and diplomatic skill. At Berlin he wrung personally from the Elector's deputy, grizzled Margrave Sigismund, formal agreement to what he had already begun to do. Within four weeks he controlled, through a chain of garrisons, the whole of the Oder valley as far as Pomerania. "I share your pleasure, Sir, that you with a handful of soldiers have achieved more than others who have five times their number," wrote Wallenstein. Then, with reference to the Danish cavalry in Silesia, "The opinion prevails that they wish to join the King [Gustavus Adolphus] by proceeding through Poland, but that hole is barred to them."

The implementation of Wallenstein's plan followed upon its broad-based preparation. His enormous superiority of strength – forty thousand men against seventeen thousand – was brought to bear in a southerly direction from Neisse. One Danish stronghold after another, Leob-schütz, Jägerndorf, Cosel, Grätz, Troppau, was seized. "*Con le arme e con le practice*", as he put it. The arms were shells, fire-balls, and pitch-rings, or, did the enemy venture a sally, muskets and partisans. The artifices consisted of messages wrapped around stones and thrown over the walls, their text promising the besieged attractive conditions if they would surrender. Psychological warfare, of a kind. Military captivity and prisoner-of-war camps were unknown. Only senior officers were kept in custody for subsequent exchange or ransom. The fate of a conquered fortress's garrison depended on circumstances. Did a commander capitulate in good time, he could obtain good terms for it, such as leave to depart unimpeded, in full panoply, and with drums beating if things were going well, or without arms, music and banners. Afterwards the majority, officers and common soldiery alike, enlisted more or less voluntarily in the ranks of the victorious army. Alternatively they had to promise not to serve against it for a specified time, possibly six months or the duration of a campaigning season, whereupon they dispersed to engage either in highway robbery or to find another master. Should the besieged not have given up until all was lost, too late and uncondition-ally, the harshness resonant in the professional phrase "Cut all down" often prevailed. Nevertheless soldiers behaved in general less brutally to one another then than in subsequent days. Rancour was confined to the thick of engagements, which were brief and rare. Why should they have hated each other? Companions in misfortune, it was pure chance on which side they stood.

In Silesia clemency was normally the rule. Garrisons were disarmed and, certain conditions accepted, allowed to disperse at large, a freedom from which many were only too glad to take refuge under Wallenstein's colours. From Cosel, the Danish forces' focal point – "How Wallenstein's supporters brag on account of Cosel," Dr Leuker exclaimed – the cavalry at first managed to escape, but its retreat to the west was cut short through Arnim's dispositions and its luck lasted only three weeks. Making their way northward on the right bank of the Oder, the runaways were overtaken near the Pomeranian border and overpowered by their pursuers. The prisoners included, in addition to the Danish Colonel Holk, Johann von Bubna. Wallenstein's practice, to treat emigrants in the service of the enemy as officers, not traitors, applied to this friend of his youth too. There were however exceptions. A bad one was that of Hans Christoph Waldstein, his cousin, caught at Troppau, whom he sent in irons as his personal prisoner to Castle Skal in Friedland. "I permit for his keep no more than two Rhenish gulden per week." Another case was more gruesome. The General had an old score to settle with Wenzel Bitovsky of Bitov, a distant relative of his first wife who thirteen years ago had proved a nuisance with law-suits about Lucretia's inheritance. Wallenstein had him, and only him, picked out from among the captured rebels and extradited to the Emperor's vengeful officials at Brünn where in the following year Bitovsky was beheaded. Whatever the explanation for this horrid business, he who brought it about was a man without pity, one untroubled by the question whether at some time he might not himself stand in need of pity. But then who believes in decline and fall while success is steeply ascendant?

Silesia was liberated or subjugated, the definition being a matter of choice. Lower Germany lay open, with the Danish king helplessly marking time, helplessly withdrawing. In a few days, wrote Wallenstein to Harrach, "I march against Germany. He of Bavaria has joined with the other Electors and would dearly like to have prevented it, though the trick will not serve him, for he would fain have been *dominus dominantium* in the Empire." The imperialists were to roll forward in three columns against what remained of Danish military: Arnim from the Oder and the Spree towards eastern Mecklenburg, Field-Marshal Count Schlick ("If His Majesty has a good officer, Count Schlick is the man") and a hundred cavalry squadrons via Frankfurt-on-Oder down a centre axis, and Wallenstein with fourteen thousand infantrymen in the direction of the Elbe farther west. His line of march led via Schweidenitz, Goldberg (the town of his boyhood days), Sagan, and Kottbus into Brandenburg. Nowhere was any resistance offered. That had been taken care of. The provision of supplies was the Brandenburgers' worry.

Wallenstein saw to his dukedom at the same time as his mind's eye roved over the war-map of Holstein and Slesvig. "The Governor of Friedland tells me that if one more iron works is established in that vicinity it will be burdensome to the inhabitants. Reflect well and thereafter determine what can be done. Methinks, if it falls hardly upon the citizens, horses could be employed." Again to Taxis, "I have oft told you to see that some Italians who will produce silken wares are brought to Gitschin. You have excused yourself on account of the war, but now, God be praised, no foe is left in the Emperor's lands and therefore I bid you act, cost what it may, for I shall not inquire into that. . . . Order water to be stored at Gitschin in all the houses and ladders placed by all the flues. Have the streets kept clean and enough water available in the town." From Sagan he wrote that he intended next year to build there. The architect should in autumn hold himself available with a plan as to how the castle could be made habitable; Gitschin construction projects would undergo reduction. The order is remarkable because Sagan, a Silesian duchy, did not at that date belong to him. It had however already entered his purview. During spring he had at Vienna begun negotiations about it. It was always the same: preoccupation with the practical and the beautiful, with surrender far away abroad to the illusion of enjoyment in home possessions.

This is the point at which to insert a word about Tilly's more modest achievements, more modest because that is what the means at his disposal were. In mid-July, after the capture of a number of strongholds, he too had taken the offensive, forced in the teeth of Danish resistance a passage across the Elbe from west to east in the region of Lauenburg, and thereby thrust a wedge between the hostile concentrations under Baden-Durlach and King Christian in the areas of Havelberg and Lauenburg respectively. Both recognized this situation to be so critical that they sought safety in withdrawal, the King in the direction of Holstein, Baden in that of the Baltic coast where the island of Poel lies opposite Wismar. When on 27 August Wallenstein entered Havelberg, no enemy was either there or practically anywhere between the Alps and the sea. Tilly laid no small amount of credit for this success to his own account, although with an admixture of bitter foreboding. "For a long time already I have observed that I can do nothing which will meet with approval in those quarters [Wallenstein's] so that, no matter how hard I labour, they will try to confine me to my old bounds and let me gnaw a few bones while others pass through the door pushed open by me and enjoy the meat." It is the old conflict, the querulousness of one who had so long been in first place and now barely retains the second, an embittered astonishment that the Bohemian newcomer should overshadow his fame through achievement which for his taste invariably has a slightly charlatan flavour. Nevertheless when on the last day of August Wallenstein sailed down the Elbe and landed at Lauenburg, Tilly awaited him with splendid military parade. The grizzled Spartan demonstrated who he too was and what at need he was capable of. The council of war was followed next day by political counsel: the two Commanders-in-Chief, hunchbacked Fürstenberg on the Bavarian side, the Dukes Franz Albrecht von Lauenburg and Georg von Lüneburg, Generals Schlick and Aldringen on Wallenstein's. Discussion turned on terms to be offered to the Dane. Strong meat. King Christian was to dismiss his army and disarm completely; renounce for ever the dignity of leader of the Lower Saxon Circle, cede Holstein, the territory which alone invested him with ostensible title to that imperial appointment, to the Emperor who would decide at his pleasure upon its disposal; the damage done to German princes and cities through the war needlessly conducted by him to be indemnified in full, meaning indemnity for the damage done by the other side as well; at no future date enter into any alliance directed against the House of Austria; free passage for shipping in the Sound so that it would no longer be impeded by dues. Wallenstein could not but know that Denmark was not yet ripe for the acceptance of such exorbitant demands, if indeed this sea-power could ever be made ripe for them. Tilly, a simpler nature, thought them equitable and conformable to the military situation.

The Danish negotiator, a Prince von Holstein-Gottorp, left Lauenburg in extreme gloom of mind immediately after he had been presented with the outrageous conditions. The signal was sounded for breaking camp and the preparation on all sides for the invasion of Holstein with an overwhelming superiority which would drive the foe like cattle before it. "Grease him down," as Wallenstein phrased it. "Have," he wrote to Taxis, twelve hours before the start of this second, presumably final campaign against the Dane, "about a hundred lime trees, still young, selected so that in spring they can be planted in the garden. Prithee, see that this really is done now, for if they are not all picked at this season, in spring you will not so easily be able to bring them together."

DEALINGS WITH DIPLOMATS

Envoys from the German princes to Wallenstein usually had unpleasant tasks to fulfil. Not for them the plums of policy-making like marriage projects, commercial treaties, or alliance arrangements, but raw realities like the wretched business of requisitions which it was desired to have reduced or the effronteries of this and that officer which it was desired to have punished. The diplomats arrived in a state of apprehension. However, bleak as their prospects of success might be, they had their duty to perform. The Duke, for his part, neither relished listening to their tales of woe nor saying no, far less than would have been supposed of his tart nature, yet he was unable to say yes because the army could not be paid other than by mulcting the defenceless territories. So, as a substitute for yes, he put off the petitioners with vague promises. In place of no, he would exclaim: "It cannot be", as though, rather than being an arbitrary decision, this derived from the intrinsic character of affairs, which basically it did. The process was a constantly recurrent one. His behavioural variations are what render it interesting.

He suddenly erupts. May 1627, Vienna. Two plenipotentiaries from the League are to obtain a suspension of the recruitments: in effect, a reduction of the Friedland army. The latter, they intimate, exists for the Empire's protection, a purpose hardly to be attained by the ruin of one Estate after another. Wallenstein becomes "somewhat impassioned". God and His Saints know how counter to his strictest orders the offences of his forces run; the criminals will be disciplined, the junior officers by loss of life, the senior ones by removal from their appointments; but a large army there must be because the perils to Emperor and Empire are too many. The envoys persist. They have to. Wallenstein "erupts". Do they perhaps suppose the Emperor is subject to moulding? Never, is the politic answer, would anyone venture to prescribe anything to His Majesty. None the less it would be well to bear in mind the Emperor's obligation to the Empire as much as those of the Empire to the Emperor. Whether they supposed the Emperor to be subject to moulding is a question worthy of attention. During his first generalate Wallenstein's trains of thought were on imperialist, strictly imperialist lines. But if it was not his intention, as has been alleged, to overthrow the Imperial Constitutions, neither was his interpretation of them identical with that of the Empire's major potentates.

He stops his ears. Vienna, in the same season. The Brandenburg representative is to wring concessions on his pillaged country's behalf. His elegiac theme will be re-echoed throughout the next few years. "But when," runs the report, "the formalities over, I began to touch upon the main subject, His Princely Grace hid his face in his pillow and stopped his ears with both hands, so that I had to relinquish my business altogether and begin another discourse." Expatiating on the weather, God, and the state of the world, the envoy finally succeeds in bringing his interlocutor, protected by the recesses of his bedding, around to the point he wants. Straightway Wallenstein goes over to the counter-attack. Elector George William is one of the Empire's guiltiest princes who last year rendered possible Mansfeld's campaign in Silesia, this year sanctioned King Gustavus Adolphus's landing in Prussia, and in any case is in conspiracy with Denmark and Sweden who may have no liking for each other but are nevertheless united in hostility to the Emperor. The occupation of Brandenburg by imperial troops is there-fore just and reasonable. The envoy tries to rebut the charges. Not having prior knowledge of the Swedish landing in Prussia, his master was in no position whatever to prevent it. Any leanings towards Sweden or Denmark are out of the question. Appearances are deceptive and in every instance explicable in terms of sheer necessity. "His Princely Grace could enter no demurrer," he comments complacently. In reality Wallenstein is likely to have wearied quickly of the arguments and hence his readiness to make at least verbal concessions. Brandenburg's ruin, he remarks, is to nobody's interest, least of all his own. If the country is sucked totally dry, there will be no more to be obtained from it. He will gladly order evacuation as soon as he can, namely, when he marches on Denmark. A castle in the air, this. His aim was not to let the envoy leave without a glimmer of hope. First evasiveness, then bickering and upbraiding, in the end a conciliatory word that cost nothing.

He is very gracious. The harassing problem of Brandenburg – the March – refused to disappear from his desk. He could not solve it because, irrespective of the dubious loyalty prevailing at Berlin and Königsberg, in 1627–8 the country was for him a main operational base. So he toyed with the problem, put it off, tried to elude it, and in personal negotiation was on one occasion frosty and proud, on another excessively polite. Adam von Schwarzenberg's experience, in June 1628 at Frank-furt-on-Oder, was the most pleasurable although its beginning was unpropitious enough. His personal assistant arrives with the news that Wallenstein is sick of the ague, has banished all secretaries, valets, and pages from his company, had all dogs driven from the streets, and gone so far as to forbid the ringing of church bells. Clearly, nothing to be done there for the moment. The more agreeable is the Minister's surprise when on his first evening Major-General del Maestro appears with a stately retinue and conveys an invitation to be received in audience on the following morning. Wallenstein's own coach, beset by lackeys, brings him at the appointed hour to the Duke whose courtesy extends even to meeting him at the stairway. Walking on his left, he leads Schwarzenberg into his closet where for two and a half hours they converse most amicably. The subjects are of course perennial points of complaint: the quarters which in the coming winter the March will simply not be able to provide; the colonels' statements of account, which are never correct, and their refusal to receipt what has actually been paid; as particularized items, the atrocities which Count Montecuc-coli's cavalry regiment has committed, the abominable harangues against the Elector held by a certain Lieutenant Schaffner; and so on, and so on. No sooner has the Minister reached the third point than he stops, mindful of how he has been told that the General is a bad listener. Is the recital becoming too long for him? Not at all; Count Schwarzenberg should kindly proceed. And then: he is doing all he can to make matters easier for Brandenburg, but there are limits to his capacity. "His Serene Electoral Highness's land lies too close to the scene of misfortune." Colonel Montecuccoli, though, shall be put through the hoops, the impertinent lieutenant have his head chopped off, as many soldiers as possible be withdrawn from the March. Thereafter the discussion shifts to political generalities until such time as dinner is served. Several imperial princes are at the table, but Schwarzenberg is seated in the place of honour. Another talk follows after the meal, and the meeting is barely ended before Wallenstein pays his return visit. That lasts no less than five hours, with his suite condemned to wait the entire time in the antechamber. Next day the same astounding tokens of graciousness are renewed. "At table His Princely Grace was very gay." Less gay afterwards. Pomeranian representatives are admitted and irritate him, partly by their obstinacy, especially by drawing his attention to the confidential to and fro between King Gustavus Adolphus and the Pomeranian seaport of Stralsund. "I am no Polack,* I fear not the Swede," Schwarzenberg hears his host shout. Later the Duke tells him that he was attacked by the ague. He had firmly determined not to let it get the better of him,

---

* 'He smote the sledded Polack on the ice' (*Hamlet*, I, I). Wallenstein's use of the term is however distinctly derogatory (translator's note).

but the Pomeranians were all too long-winded and vexatious. Could he turn his ague on and off, according to the convenience of the situation? Did it really get the better of him, against his will? That he sometimes turned to advantage what were called his fits of frenzy and black depression is not impossible of proof.

The marks of favour conferred on Schwarzenberg do not fail to make their impression on Wallenstein's officers. A buzz of amiable effusions tempered by a clink of spurs pours into the plenipotentiary's ears. This in turn encourages the citizens of the little town to ask their compatriot to intercede on its behalf. During their last visit to Frankfurt the Duke's entourage evinced but little friendliness; the Master of the Horse alone extorted nearly a thousand taler; here are the vouchers. The Minister shows them to Colonel Franz von Lauenburg who, being by chance not involved, offers to help by bringing the matter to the commander-in-chief's notice. At that very moment up runs the Master of the Horse, pale as a sheet, and beseeches that the business be, for the love of God, allowed to drop without another word, else it will cost the life of all. "He was, like every one of them, a fine fellow," reports Schwarzenberg, "and so I let the subject rest." Who, after this, is prepared to argue that Wallenstein did not punish the misdemeanours of his officers if he learnt of them and they had been perpetrated by those in his vicinity? That he should have practised his charm on Schwarzenberg is however explicable in terms of the Minister's position. At Berlin he had long been the leader of the anti-Swedish, pro-Habsburg faction.

More cheerless, and on more occasions than one, was the treatment undergone by another Brandenburg representative, Curt Bertram von Pfuel. Not that he had no talent for his trade; his reports reflect a scrupulous, shrewd spirit. Perhaps, though, he was ill-formed, too fat, too lean, too tall, too short, slightly cross-eyed, or singular in some other respect. Whatever the reason, he was always out of luck. In January 1628, at Prague, for example. We see him, on the Charles bridge, stationed in ambush for the Duke who is borne in his coach and the company of his brother-in-law, Cardinal Harrach, across the stone vaulting. Recognition of the skilfully sited suppliant is followed by stoppage of the coach and the question whether there is anything that he has to impart. Indeed, an electoral letter. In a second the Duke's feathered hat is briefly raised, his horses are on the move. Pfuel knows the Little Side. He dashes as fast as he can through its lanes to reach Wallenstein's palace before he descends. At the gate such a crowd of nobles hems the great man in that hopes of approach are in vain. It is dinner-time, but not for long, and then the Duke drives to the Emperor on the Hradschin where he remains for the rest of the day. Next morning Pfuel takes up his position in the Knights' Room of the palace, waits one dreary hour after another, but on the Duke's eventual appearance is noted, greeted, able to kiss hands. He presents his credentials. The Duke wards him off. Today impossible; tomorrow. Poor Pfuel is mistaken if he thinks that he has his bird in bush. At the very moment when next day he is about to re-enter the palace, the all too familiar coach emerges. Through the window Wallenstein calls out to him that he should have patience for a couple of days; there is so very much to do at court just now. A couple of days are a costly matter. Envoys owe it to their master to maintain proper state, a sacrifice they make the more readily for being unable to do so at home. Pfuel however assures his sovereign that his enforced leisure is repulsive to him. On the third day, the ninth of his Prague stay, an invitation to dine ensues on another urgent request for audience. In the great hall of the palace he is privileged to eat and drink amid a din of voices and beneath the ceiling's depiction of Mars, or maybe Phoebus, or maybe the Duke transfigured. However, upon rising from table, Pfuel really and truly succeeds in having a few minutes' conversation with his quarry. He senses only too keenly Wallenstein's craving to escape him. He is brief. So are the answers he receives. Remove a number of regiments from Brandenburg? Yes, gladly, but where to? The plea is repeated, likewise the reply. Reduction of the monthly contribution? Out of the question. Pay and provision only for soldiers on the ground, not for those merely existing on paper? Yes, that shall be. A rate of thirty silver groschen or one and a half gulden for a Brandenburg taler? Yes, that shall also be. A few more points, fleetingly listened to, and Wallenstein hurries away. Pfuel can regard his mission neither as fulfilled nor as utterly failed. He continues to pester ducal councillors and chancery secretaries. Again an appointment is made and again he sees the coach roll out of the palace portal. This time, though, the Duke permits him to sit beside him. Time is precious, but perhaps something can be agreed while the horses struggle up the steep road to the royal residence. Perhaps. Yet the instant Pfuel draws a paper from his coat-pocket the Duke demands what it can be. Something in writing? Oh dear, that gives him the ague, he cannot bear written business, and at present he is in any case surfeited with other preoccupations, a point emphasized with manual gestures and ocular expressions. The diplomat's uphill trundling in the red upholstered leather recess is as barren of result as his entire trip to Prague.

THE 1627 CAMPAIGN: PART TWO

To expel from the continent the Danish power, this sad remainder of the hoped-for European coalition, was now easy enough. It would not have been difficult even if King Christian had been in command of, and had commanded better, a less demoralized force. It was akin to the elucidation of a mathematical problem after all the equations are solved. Three columns, that of Arnim coming from Mecklenburg, of Schlick from eastern Holstein, and the main Wallenstein–Tilly body down the Elbe, drove the Danes and their scanty allies into an ever narrowing corner. A spirit of comradeliness had been meant to reign between the two commanders-in-chief, with the issue of the password daily alternating between them, a supreme command held in common. The plan was however doomed to frustration when, right at the beginning, Tilly was wounded in the knee during the siege of an unimportant little place called Pinneberg. He was carried back to Lauenburg in Wallenstein's special litter for patients with leg trouble. Elector Maximilian had cause for irritation. His lieutenant-general, he wrote, should in future take better care of his precious person. Wallenstein was left in sole charge and reaped the rich victory.

It was new, prosperous territory, unscarred by war, into which he came. Fields and meadows stretching to the horizon, cattle dappled black and white, scattered farmsteads, a fan-tailed play of the sun's rays behind banks of clouds. Now and again, slenderly infiltrating lanes of sea. Moated castles, manor-houses in the Italian style, tombstones with ancestresses, hands folded in prayer, carved in relief very like in the little church at Hermanitz. His coach ran between birch and bush. Yet he observed neither the scene nor the bluish and golden brown autumnal splendour. His head was too full of politics and war. "I am master of Mecklenburg and most of Holstein," he wrote to Collalto. "I hope this year still to have Slesvig and Jutland too, when I shall advise that peace be made, for then I shall be in possession of these. Not that I believe that we shall be able to hold them, but that thereby the foe will agree to *conditiones pacis* better for us." His absorbent eye was fixed on another slice of land, not part of the Cimbric peninsula, but in its eastern vicinity.

For some days he had his headquarters at Elmshorn and Itzehoe. The siege of Castle Breitenburg was stoutly resisted by its Danish garrison. News of a success farther east came to Itzehoe. Baden-Durlach had decided that he could not hold Poel against Arnim, withdrew from the island across Lübeck Bay to the Holstein coast, and there walked blindly into the trap set for him by Count Schlick. Twenty-seven companies of infantry and fifteen cavalry squadrons crossed unhesitatingly into imperial service. The old, ill-starred paladin saved himself by northward flight. A fresh local gain was the seizure of Breitenburg by storm. All too scornfully had its commander rejected the customary favourable terms of surrender. "Cut all down!" Aldringen consolidated his success in south-western Holstein. The rest of the Danish strongholds could be left to their own devices. The main force advanced towards Rendsburg, a fortified trading centre garrisoned by Englishmen, Frenchmen, and Danes. They proved, under the captaincy of a German, sager than their fellows at Breitenburg, after a fortnight capitulated, and were allowed with bag and baggage to join King Christian, if they could find him. He had fled to the isle of Fünen. No hold-up, no resistance any more. The residue lacked, for an experienced strategist of Wallenstein's calibre, even professional attraction. Mopping-up operations were left to Schlick. The long, pointed headland of the Danish peninsula was occupied by the imperialists almost as far as the Sound.

The outcome of a campaign begun barely five months ago in Upper Silesia was impressive enough. Abbot Antonius, his flow of correspondence with Aldringen uninterrupted, commented that "His Lordship's martial progress, amazing in so short a time, is so great that all are taken aback and say, '*Quid est hoc?*' Truly, beyond all human expectation and hope as it is, it will, it is to be trusted, achieve so long desired, reputable and durable peace. *Finis coronat opus.*" Forgotten were the views aired half a year back about Wallenstein's generalship. He, though, in whose mind the memory of all evil and all good were equally graven, had not forgotten.

At the end of September he wrote to the Emperor from Itzehoe a letter which amounted at once to a self-vindication and a political memorial. In style it was still terse as compared with contemporary prolix outpourings, but by his own standards, which kept also His Imperial Majesty on a tight rein, it was circumstantial. He justified the size of the army. "Had Your Majesty not been possessed of such strength You would upon the hour, if God had not performed a miracle, have been robbed of Your kingdom and lands, for all the adjacent Sovereigns were allied against Your Majesty and the Empire's princes conspired with them. The Catholics would not have numbered enough to resist them; the Lutherans who are deemed loyal would have excused themselves that they could not withstand such might. I had not only to keep watch upon the King of Denmark, but also on the Turks, Bethlen, and France." Had the army been no larger than the immediate Danish danger seemed to require, how would he have been in a position to feed it and to compel the provision of winter quarters? "For that purpose did I need all the time to have soldiery on the Rhine and in the Wetterau* – under pretext of the French, yet truly it was to cover the rear." "This great force possessed by Your Majesty will conduce within the Empire to a good and lasting peace, which I most humbly commend. . . . I believe that whilst the Electors are assembled at Mühlhausen they will strongly espouse the cause of peace, which again I most humbly beg Your Majesty not to reject." The concluding sentence explains, in part, this document. Its writer knew that the Electors, under the leadership of Bavaria, were on the point of holding joint counsel – the event took place in October – and that the business of this meeting would principally be directed against him. He forestalled the attack, not with spurious arguments, but by a policy proposal. To impose through overwhelming power a state of orderly peace on Germany such as had since time immemorial not existed there had always been his objective. To that degree the anonymous author of the report on the Bruck conference was right although, as had been shown, less in his assessment of Wallenstein's generalship. One who within three months had carried an advance from Troppau to Flensburg and conquered the major portion of a foreign state hardly needed to brook any longer the reproach of being unfit for offensive warfare.

Peace. Proscribed, long purloined, yearned after, deeply sighed for, regenerative, pleasing to God, highly esteemed, noble peace, as it was termed. And the cessation of that which too was talked of – the great and grievous disorder, the raging flame of war in the entrails of the Empire, the morass of woe and misery, the unheard of, terrible exactions, contributions and oppressions, the thieving, murder, arson, bloodshed, and devastation, this ultimate, agonizing, undeserved annihilation. Words did not fail people, wisdom rather, and there was no one to control what was happening in Europe. Not even Wallenstein, far though he had come along this road. Peace with Denmark would have been possible if the *status quo ante* had been proffered and nothing demanded except renunciation of intervention in German affairs. On this problem Wallenstein's views wavered. Eating creates appetite. In September he had dismissed the thought of retaining Slesvig and Hol-

* An area of low ground near the Taunus Mountains in western Germany (translator's note).

stein; they were simply pawns. Six months later he told Arnim that King Christian would take his time before accepting the peace offered him, "for he must not suppose that Holstein and Slesvig will be his again. Jutland, should he want to have it, he will have to redeem with sundry millions". There were indeed days when he contemplated doing away with the Danish kingdom altogether, but then he would revert to conditions of a more sensible order. At its best the concept of a peace treaty with Denmark never amounted to more than that of a separate peace whereby Denmark would drop out of the struggle. The coalition, whose temporary leader Denmark had been and which had so stupidly left it in the lurch, would then put another power in the front-line. The House of Habsburg in the Netherlands and on the Sound did not signify merely Wallenstein, merely Austria on the Sound. It signified Spain, and that was an enormity to which Protestant, sea-faring Europe would never become reconciled unless it must. Most humbly to commend the conclusion of peace was an excellent, wise move. To obtain peace after the events of the past summer and autumn was, if anything, more diffi-cult than before. There are situations in which defeat does not serve peace and victory, victory especially, does not help it either.

On the island of Fünen Christian passed his army, or rather, his officers, for at the moment he had no army any more, in melancholy review. Bitter recriminations were exchanged. The King wanted to court-martial his principal commander. Baden-Durlach in his quality of an imperial prince protested against that; Duke Bernhard von Weimar did likewise; and these two could not in all seriousness be held respons-ible for the disaster. They went to Holland. Durlach later returned to Baden to spend a saddened, albeit tranquil old age. Weimar, a young man, saw no reason for resignation, as by now Matthias Thurn, that tried and trusty loser of battles and revolutions, might very well have done. He, like Weimar and a number of Bohemian emigrants, would shortly enter Gustavus Adolphus' service.

For one man the torment of rout, humiliating wrangles, and vagrant penury; for the other, triumph. In order thoroughly to gather the harvest of this year Wallenstein applied and in October received, permission for three months' home-leave. The holiday would be prolonged to nearly eight.

SWEDES AND SPANIARDS

Luck rather than genius had enabled Wallenstein to keep Danes and Swedes apart. To do so was axiomatic. The Danes had been trouble

enough. Danes and Swedes together, under the leadership of Gustavus
Adolphus, would loose in central Europe a storm of an entirely different
order. What was now to be done with Denmark? Neutralize it by way of
a favourable peace? In the coming year overrun its appurtenant isles
and topple the King, of whom it was said that his own subjects had had
enough? Who should have the crown in his place? The Emperor had
offered it to him, Wallenstein told Arnim in a letter, "but I declined
with great thanks, for I would not be able to maintain myself". Whether
the offer was meant seriously or not, he did well to reject it. Had he been
allowed to discard the impossible Lauenburg conditions, he would probably have been able to conclude a creditable peace treaty right away in
autumn 1627. For anything of wider scope, the subjugation of Danish
power at sea after that of its power on land, he needed ships, "for what
we should do now must take place at sea". But were the ancient kingdom
to be dissolved or receive treatment analogous to that of Bohemia, it
required an understanding with another power.

No consequences arose upon the episode about to be narrated. It is
none the less worth narration if for no other reason than the light that it
throws on the political habits of the age. Wallenstein, however singular
he appeared to his contemporaries, was not left unaffected by those
usages. Because they, precisely they, and only they, enable his end to be
understood, their manifestation cannot in a biography of him be left
until that end, as if what was practised in 1633 was then practised for
the first time. It was constantly practised, by one and all; it was one of
the fine arts. On this occasion the initiative, so Gustavus Adolphus'
historians assume without more ado, was Wallenstein's. I do not know
whence they derive their certainty except from Gustavus Adolphus's
own report to the King of Denmark. Lies however formed part of this
fine art just like the game of alliances suddenly reversed; they belonged
to it like the cleverness and hyper-cleverness of leaving in the dark who
was the tempter and who the tempted. Wallenstein at any rate was
agreeably surprised and soon became very thoughtful when in November
Colonel Arnim transmitted a letter from Oxenstierna, the Swedish Chancellor. Although, it stated, the Swedes had reason to complain of the
help extended to the Poles by the Emperor, they nevertheless desired
nothing other than friendship with His Imperial Majesty and would
gladly learn, best through a discussion with Arnim in person, how such
could be attained and strengthened. Although the affair seems to have
been started by Arnim, Oxenstierna's friend, it does not follow that he
had orders from Wallenstein. The latter wrote to Arnim that to raise

the Swedes' hopes would not be stupid since they might thereby be brought to desist from alliance with Denmark. Three weeks later he said that he had once again studied Oxenstierna's letter more closely and found it interesting. "My opinion is that he [Gustavus Adolphus] should in every way be treated with, for if he wishes to attack Denmark on the other side and to occupy as well as Norway, the places pertaining to Denmark where they abut on Sweden, I deem that the Emperor will make no difficulties." In such circumstances it would be easy to negotiate a peace between Poland and Sweden. Right outside such arrangements, though, would have to be left the nations troublesome to Christendom, like Turks, Tartars and Muscovites. The Dutch too, "who to me are *destructores regum et principum*". On the other hand it would be advisable to bring Spain into the confederation. Meanwhile Arnim should assure King Gustavus Adolphus of Wallenstein's long-standing particular esteem and should keep on the whole to generalities. Three months later he even thought it possible to include the States-General in an overall peace deal. "If the Dutch do not wish to play the buffoon, I repose trust in my ability to compose the differences between them and their King [the ruler of Spain] whereby they would have freedom of religion and upon certain conditions also in other respects relating to political government, *in forma rei publicae*." Did he believe that the House of Vasa would abruptly join hands with the House of Habsburg? What is definite is that he took the project more seriously than the coolly calculating, deeply experienced Oxenstierna and the King, already determined upon a major war with the Papists. Throughout the winter of 1627-8 he kept returning, with brooding naïvety, to the subject and left Arnim an astonishing amount of play. He should see "in whatever ways the negotiation can be undertaken with Sweden, for if it doth not profit us, so it cannot harm us either. . . . I leave it to him. He knows the Swede and therefore he shall do whatsoever he presumes to be best for His Majesty and Christendom because I will gladly have the Swede for friend, only that he shall not be all too mighty since *amor et dominium non patitur socium* [love and domination are bad bedfellows], but the negotiation must by all means proceed."

To the art of negotiation belonged the secondary, sometimes primary purpose that, were nothing else gained, the partner or opponent should at least be compromised, a trick not altogether despised by statesmen even in our own enlightened century. The ruse was no stranger to Wallenstein either. In 1626, for example, he had at the outset of his generalate tried it on the Danish commander Fuchs. "If nought other

ensues, I intend to see that I discredit Fuchs with the King." Now it
was the Swedes' turn. Gustavus Adolphus communicated to King
Christian with marked exaggeration how the Emperor had offered him
no less than the Danish throne, and he subsequently informed the
Riksdag officially and in opprobrious terms about this Wallenstein
intrigue. The war would not have lasted thirty years if negotiation itself
had not degenerated into a hollow game of dangling false hopes.

Wallenstein, however much he might surrender to feverish fancies
about all to be won by alliance with Sweden, was sceptical enough not
to accept the risk of being exposed as the Serpent deceived. "I know
full well," he wrote to Arnim, "that the Swede enters upon no negotiation out of love and affection and that he is no more than his brother-in-
law Bethlehem [*sic*] to be trusted. That is why I commit the matter
entirely into your hands. But the ships must be set on fire where they
are." In Wallenstein's correspondence throughout late autumn and
winter this notion of the need to incinerate the Swedish fleet is a curious
concomitant to that of a deal with Sweden. One, he is convinced, will
do the other no harm. "The poorer and weaker the Swede is, the better
for us. The negotiation must nevertheless proceed nimbly along one
path and the other, despite that caution behoves." Nothing came of
either the negotiation or the incineration. The Duke seems to have
envisaged an operation by commandos with special rates of danger-pay
and incendiary torches to be attached to Gustavus Adolphus's armada
in Prussian, and possibly Swedish, harbours. An order easier to issue
than to execute. He knew nothing about ships and seafaring. Now he
was expected, or had to, acquire maritime knowledge in as many months
as he had applied decades to learning the art of war.

Precisely the opposite picture to that of the Swedish alliance project
was presented by a publicly proclaimed plan of stately proportion – the
creation of a Habsburg ocean power, "Habsburg" in this instance meaning Spanish–Austrian–Hanseatic. Or, omitting the Spaniards, German
and Habsburg. It would in any case bear the Wallenstein stamp. Whoever the initiators might be, to circumvent the commander of the host
and coast was not possible.

The idea had its antecedents. That flourishing commerce is at the
heart of all things, including war, was an axiom already learned. Dutch
shipping prospered, from the North Sea and Baltic to the Cape of Good
Hope and as far as the Spice Isles. The Dutch, the Danes, and the British
had moreover imposed a kind of blockade on Spain and confiscated or
sank every German ship nearing the Iberian coast. This scandalous

condition gave rise to speculation in Spanish quarters on whether the King's martial interests and the Hanseatic cities' mercantile ones could not be merged in a maritime defence community. The Germans, that is, the Hanse, would be offered a monopoly of Spanish foreign trade, protected by cannon-mounted men-of-war, and encouraged to lay down naval shipyards. Spain would in exchange have one or more German ports, in east Frisia perhaps and Pomerania, placed at its disposal and from these wreck Dutch shipping activities, build a bridge to the King of Poland, and paralyse Sweden's communications with Prussia. The design should not however be launched under Spanish auspices, seeing that no one had any illusions about Spain's popularity among German Protestants, but indirectly in the name of the Emperor who, after all, was a German and legally still suzerain over Bremen and Hamburg, Wismar and Stralsund. Ferdinand's Privy Council decided that the plan was good and should be realized if the Hanse's cities were prepared as a matter of genuine conviction to co-operate. Compulsion would be impolitic.

Envoys sallied forth. Ludwig von Schwarzenberg, the Marshal of the Court and principal opponent of the scheme, was detailed for Lübeck. Conde Sforza and Señor Gabriel de Roy, servants of the King of Spain and credited with knowledge of maritime matters, were sent north to investigate possibilities and arrange essentials with the Emperor's General. They were all enchanted by him, especially Schwarzenberg who met with him in October at Rendsburg. Neither Bavaria nor the Electors, hostile to Spain and jealous of the House of Austria's new greatness, should have their backing, he wrote to his friend Khevenhüller at Madrid, but simply and solely Wallenstein. The Infanta at Brussels heard from Sforza that never yet had there been in the Empire a commander so devoted to the cause of Spain as Wallenstein. He had turned on his charm and once again manifested the personality his reputation belied, a man whose swift, imaginative breadth of intellect grasped the other speaker's flight of ideas. Had the Spaniards been told that he was simultaneously treating with Sweden, they would have been thunderstruck. The fact did not appreciably oppress Wallenstein's conscience. What of it? What would emanate from the Swedish contacts? Probably nothing. But if something did, provision for Spain's possible participation had been made by him. As a matter of fact the large-scale maritime design in some degree suited his own notions. He had quickly enough attained the limits of what land-power could achieve. What now? Go to sea, conclude peace, or so strengthen the conquered coastline as to render it invincible to attack from the water. This last was by far the most difficult alternative. For war at sea he needed ships. For the conclusion of peace too because the conviction that the foe would only be persuaded to choose peace by reason of superior power, the possibility of worse to come, was a thought uppermost in his strategic and political deliberations. Were the Madrid salt-water zealots to supply him with ships, he would gladly accept them. He imagined that vessels could be constructed and a fleet worthy of the name be fitted out as speedily as in 1625 he had drummed together his regiments. To Count Sforza he was expansive and impressive about his plans for the coming year. He would have at his disposal four armies; one for the subjugation of the Danish isles, one for the protection of Pomerania and Mecklenburg to prevent the Swede from playing him any tricks there, one for Slesvig and Jutland to act as a land-bridge between the two fleets situated either side of the peninsula, and the fourth for the siege of strongholds still held here and there by the Danes. Additional cavalry units were stationed throughout the Empire. In summer moreover he would have a canal dug from Kiel to the North Sea, allowing Spanish men-of-war who during winter had been anchored at Dunkirk to glide without ado across the peninsula and avoid the dangerous passage of the Sound. He estimated the outlay on this project at a hundred thousand taler or somewhat more, should Madrid care to advance the sum. On a sudden inspiration he conjured up the vision of a mighty counter-Dutch move, as active and progressive as they were, but imperialist, although based on the Protestants of Lower Germany. The Infanta interpolated some questions. Would it not be cheaper to subdue both shores of the Sound and fortify them? And, were the Emperor to make peace with Denmark, was the intention to include Spain and Holland? What the Infanta meant, without any precise notion as to how it could be formulated, was a Dutch submission. What Wallenstein visualized, equally vaguely as to the modalities, was a sensible compromise.

Nothing came of it all. Neither of the twenty-four ships the Spaniards proposed sending to the Baltic nor of the Emperor Ferdinand Canal* (to which Wallenstein's imagination clung rather more stubbornly than the rest of the details) nor of the armed Spanish–German trading company.

The Hanse would not be persuaded. Ludwig Schwarzenberg appeared before the League's members in Lübeck's town hall and spoke with the

* The Kiel Canal was opened in 1895 and named the Emperor-William-Canal (translator's note).

tongues of angels. It was no good. For too long the Emperor had in the eyes of the Hanse become a vile enemy with whom its ties were purely nominal. Its cities were crowded with *émigrés* and from its pulpits preached clergy who formerly had done so in Bohemia. The persecutor of their co-religionists was suddenly to be their great protector? A little late for that. An aide of Schwarzenberg, more percipient than his master, wrote to Vienna that in reality the Emperor lacked a single friend in northern Germany. Thoughts ran along every conceivable line, Danish, Swedish, Dutch, other than Spanish or Austrian – a piece of straight-forward perception for which he asked to be forgiven. The delegates of the Hanseatic cities who on 28 February met at Lübeck did what had ever since ancient times been done in similar delicate situations: they excused themselves on the score of inadequate instructions, on the score of poverty, on the score of love of peace inexorably dictated by their weakness, and they postponed until another meeting further discussion of the subject. The King of Denmark had not left his finger out of the pie, undermining Schwarzenberg's efforts with a message to the Hanse. Luck, partly as a matter of providence, partly as a matter of the paltriness of his German allies, might not so far have been much with him. Nevertheless he was in confederation with Sweden, with England, with the States-General, and he was still strong enough to safeguard or utterly to ruin the commerce of the seafaring cities, should they become impudent. True, the Papists had reached the salt-waters, but they lacked ships, and those waters were tolerably broad. That was Christian's message to the Hanse, a message to which it lent its ear.

Meanwhile Wallenstein and Ludwig Schwarzenberg, until recently good friends, thought nothing, nothing more whatsoever, of one another. The charm had been turned off; the ague had broken out. Why? Perhaps Wallenstein learnt how Schwarzenberg in his correspondence criticized his lethargy and the indiscipline of the army begot by a state of war in winter, criticism which he did not relish. On top of this came the political differences of opinion. The failure of his angelic eloquence at Lübeck to carry the day in any respect angered the Marshal of the court. In the wake of his pleading followed threats. He recommended the use of force – Lübeck should have its port of Travemünde, Hamburg its Krautinsel, and both cities their ships seized. Wallenstein never cared to have more enemies than were inevitable. To force at a single stroke the German maritime cities, one and all, into the opposite camp he regarded as a most injurious piece of tomfoolery. "From His Majesty's letter can be seen what milk Count Schwarzenberg has spilt," he complained to

Collalto. "Prithee see, my lord, that he be recalled, for he will do no good and by his intemperance drive all to desperation." Schwarzenberg's venom, crazy concepts, and utterly impossible projects, addressed to the most various audiences with the demented obstinacy peculiar to him, enjoyed free rein until Wallenstein presented the Emperor with an ultimatum: either Schwarzenberg was removed or he, the General, would not return to the army. The threat worked. Schwarzenberg was summoned to Prague on an excuse which he recognized, not without embitterment, as a relegation. Here was the reward for all his troubles? Ah, but he knew who was responsible for the blow, and why.

Thereafter not much remained of the "armada-at-sea", the great Hispano–German war-and-trade association. In so far as it had been intended to be Spanish, nothing at all. A German or Fleming, scion of the ramified Mansfeld family, was appointed admiral and given the Mecklenburg port of Wismar as his base. There he was either to have keels laid or to purchase as many ships as possible before summer came. Gabriel de Roy was made his assistant, but, a point to which Wallenstein attached importance, simply as a technical expert in the imperial service. For the time being land-power must repel invasion by hostile fleets. "It has been reported to me," said a dispatch from Wallenstein to Arnim, "that Pomerania has twenty-eight harbours. That is a comparatively large number. However, be that as it may, they must be occupied and fortified." An impossible order by one who understood nothing of naval affairs. To Arnim's relief doubly impossible, because Pomerania's harbours certainly did not amount to twenty-eight.

THE ZENITH OF LIFE

The day on which Wallenstein decided to acquire the duchy of Mecklenburg is almost impossible to determine. Such ideas crop up first in the night as forms of wishful thinking, then become a realistic possibility, and gradually assume certitude. The possibility and certitude were founded on the fact that Ferdinand II was financially in the hands of his general, owing him what in cash he would never be able to repay. The cost of the Bohemian war had been met with the estates of rebels. Why should the process not be repeated in the Empire and all the Empire's appurtenant territories?

The concept could hardly be termed sound. Put into effect, it could only cause entanglement and prolong the war. Therefore it was unsuited to one whose wish was to disentangle matters and shorten the war. It was equally inappropriate to the Empire's affairs. Had Wallenstein had any feeling for the power of tradition, had he had any intuition about the nature of this strange political entity with its stubborn will to survive, he would have pondered his project twice. Were it to be said in palliation that something very similar, the divestiture of the Winter King, the transfer of the electoral dignity to Bavaria, had happened but shortly before and for the same purpose of discharging an imperial war-debt, the answer would be that Frederick's crime had been incomparably more flagrant than the Duke of Mecklenburg's and the beneficiary of the spoliation a kinsman, not a nobleman of foreign stock. The elevation of Bavaria had moreover done ineffable harm. Wallenstein was well aware of this since he was capable in an ill-humour of writing that it was Bavaria who could be thanked for all these horrors of war. Just as, barely over a year ago, he had warned against expropriation of the Duke of Brunswick because such methods would lead to perpetual war, "a war which it would be impossible for me to support". In fifteen months convictions easily change, especially when convictions are not really held. Let fantastically splendid advantage beckon and everything looks different.

If Wallenstein wanted pacification of central Europe, he now had to do what Maximilian had not wanted to do after the battle of the White Mountain – practise magnanimous renunciation, acquit the Emperor of his debts, and be satisfied with what he possessed. With ready money lacking, his demands could only be met by way of land, by way of land belonging to others, by the commission of injustice. Injustice and peace go badly together. He chose injustice. What probably clinched his decision was not so much the ruling passion for power peculiar to him as the standards prevalent in the society in which he lived.

On 2 October 1627 Wallenstein wrote that he would know how to stop Tilly's regiments from making their winter quarters in Mecklenburg. Seeing that "the Dukes had transgressed against the Emperor", there was reason, he indicated, to suspect that the Elector of Bavaria wanted to "pluck them a feather", meaning to govern there at his pleasure. He was not yet saying who actually wanted to do that. Four weeks later, though, he secretly admitted it to Colonel San Julian, his representative at the imperial court:

I have changed my mind about Sagan and I desire nothing more in His Majesty's lands, for I perceive that large tracts are difficult to obtain and insecure to hold. I propose again Mecklenburg. . . .

If the Emperor wishes to sell me the land in its entirety, I shall be the better pleased. If not in its entirety, I propound a part of the elder's portion and a slice of the younger's, who was a moiety better than the elder. *In summa*, I would have it so that the younger will regard that as an act of grace, whereas we shall satisfy the elder with a number of localities which will allow him sufficient to live. . . . You must however see that this negotiation about Mecklenburg goes no farther than between Prince Eggenberg, Lord Verda, and yourself alone. The Prince must meanwhile prepare the ground so that upon my arrival the members of the Council themselves shall make this proposition, when in the beginning I shall deprecate somewhat but at the last accept it. As for Sagan, hold back at present, for the one is better than the other.

The same letter drops a hint, to animate the Privy Council members, about the possible endowment of Jesuit seminaries in Mecklenburg. The lordship over Sagan had been conceded to him as long ago as spring.

"I propose again Mecklenburg." In other words, this was not the first time. For the present the proposition is meant to be known only to his greatest friends at court, Eggenberg and the Chancellor Verda von Werdenberg, is to be cautiously propagated by them in Council, and then to be suggested by the latter in such fashion that it will come to Wallenstein as a surprise which he asks time to consider and he can pretend to accept with reluctance.

The Mecklenburg brothers, when they attained to the duchy's government, had divided the land between each other in a manner which retained its main legal and representative institutions in common. Adolf Friedrich, decidedly the more intelligent, resided at Schwerin; Johann Albrecht at Güstrow. What was their crime? In essence that of having chosen the defeated, the Danish, side in the war. Had King Christian won, nobody would have questioned their behaviour. They had done what other estates too had done – voted for defence of the Lower Saxon Circle, re-armed a little, permitted the Danish army to march through and to occupy certain places, and contributed to its maintenance with victuals. In summer 1627, as soon as Wallenstein's approach showed where success lay, they became incontrovertibly loyal and humble. Too late. For a while the conqueror accepted receipt of their letters and acknowledged them politely, briefly, and vaguely: he would do what he could to spare their land. "But that evil tongues allege Your Dilection [Johann Albrecht] to be in ill-repute with Us is surely that these are themselves wrongly instructed." A week earlier his mess-age to Arnim had intimated, "It would be becoming for a mutation to take place shortly in the land of Mecklenburg." Of what kind we already know. On this passage followed the order, henceforth frequently reiter-ated, to keep the duchy as far as possible free of billeting burdens and to confine occupation of the cities to those with harbours. The land was in his mind already his and his subjects were to fare as well as could be.

The time had come to take up his own winter quarters in his native Bohemia. The November journey proved to be a slow one with many halts and the receipt of many letters on the way. At Frankfurt-on-Oder it was Arnim's correspondence with Oxenstierna that delayed him. At Sagan in Silesia, having after all decided to pocket the miniature capital with his left hand, so to speak, he made his entry as its Duke, although the dignity had not as yet been formally conferred on him. From Sagan to Gitschin the road was strewn with his own princely mansions much as fashionable Romans had their overnight villas strung along that which led to their country seats. On 7 December he arrived at Gitschin. A fortnight earlier Duchess Isabella had borne him a son, Albrecht Carl. This was happiness, in so far as an individual like Wallenstein is capable of ever experiencing happiness. To the north lay the great duchy about whose acquisition he had no doubts any more. At home there was the fledgeling heir to beget the House of Wallenstein and Friedland, a great Bohemian–German dynasty. A new one, admittedly. But had not all dynasties once been new? The baptism was performed by his brother-in-law, the Cardinal. Guests in the palace and the neighbourhood; festivities; congratulations; endowments; divine services daily – "I must be pious". A moment of comparative rest for one who knew no rest, but year in, year out spent his whole long day in the dictation of stern, fastidiously precise letters, in negotiations in dealing with bills and holding inspections.

On 19 December he left Gitschin for Brandeis, on the Elbe, to meet the Emperor. The court had been at Prague for the coronation of the Emperor's son, the younger Ferdinand, as King-designate of Bohemia. Wallenstein had stayed away from the ceremonies, which had perhaps been one of the grounds for the protraction of his wintry journey. He did not care for ceremonies, least of all ceremonies in celebration of others, and instinctively did not care for the heir to the throne. There could however be no thought of avoiding throughout his furlough a meeting with his exalted employer. Off to Brandeis therefore. Reluctance at rubbing shoulders with the throng of courtiers is not unmixed with pleasurable marks of recognition. At the levee it is he who, after the ritual lavation, is permitted to hand Their Majesties the towel. During the performance of this duty he is invited to cover his head, refuses twice, which is presumably part of the ritual, and the third time complies. The same happens at table. His immediate acquiescence gives rise all round to jealous whisperings. To place their hat on their head in the imperial presence is a prerogative of imperial princes. This new privilege proclaims, should hitherto his princely dignity not have been completely unexceptionable, that his person henceforth constitutes an Estate of the Empire as much as does that of Bavaria's Elector. "In a few days," he writes to Arnim, "a mutation will be undertaken with regard to that same territory [Mecklenburg] as everything is already agreed." In other words the interval at Brandeis has not been spent only on courtly ritual, hunting and banquets. Return to Gitschin; Christmas service in the new cathedral; prayers in particular for the health of little Albrecht Carl. Rumour runs that his birth was premature and that he labours from "organic defect". On 8 January a journey to Prague. Six days later news of the boy's death. Neither charitable deeds nor punctilious piety nor the hum of priestly chants have helped. No word of complaint. A man in Wallenstein's position does not bewail death, and at the moment the press of business is such as to leave no proper space for ruminative sorrow. Whether later, looking back, thoughts of gloomy character descended on him must be left to conjecture. We could in any case guess their shape. Is the zenith of life indeed a point which has position but no magnitude, barely reached before passed? The birth of an heir at the exact moment when the most dazzling, delusive prospects unfurled before him was the zenith; his heir, only a fleeting visitant. As for dynasty, the propagation of his House, resignation gradually supervened. Duchess Isabella would seem to have exhausted her fecundity with the bearing of two children – a daughter, Maria Elisabeth, was already there – and Wallenstein to have known it. So his young brother-in-law and cousin, Count Max, who at least bore his name, would be the beneficiary of all the grandeur, the most recent as well as the old. Not that it was the same as the education of a son would have been, as working for that son's greatness. Daughters hardly count. A modest settlement is arranged for them, like widows.

The winter months are spent at Prague. The Emperor with his court is in the castle on the hill. Below, perched on its flank where the lanes steepen, is the Duke in his palace, a rival princely household. How different is the mood from just a year ago. Now nobody would dare openly to challenge Wallenstein's capacity for his task. In secret all kinds of things are doubtless said, written, and put down in journals.

The conservative party in the Emperor's vicinity made a last effort on behalf of Mecklenburg's legitimate rulers. Its expert advocacy survives in the record of Count Khevenhüller, Privy Councillor and enemy of Wallenstein. It would be worse than questionable, the document stated, to expel without more ado, unheard and without real conviction of the iniquities laid at their door, princes whose ancestors had for eight hundred years been established in the land. Such a procedure would increase the general lack of confidence inside the Empire, all the more for the Duke of Friedland having been heard to say that in Germany there must now be, as in France and Spain, a single ruler. An act of monstrous injustice in the north would bar the way to peace with Denmark, bring the Swedes into the land, and perpetuate the hostilities; the fortunes of war were fickle. Did Wallenstein deserve such extravagant bounty? Were the figures brought into play correct? Was it not much more a fact that, on precise calculation of all the contributions, the General owed the Emperor money instead of the other way about? Was it wise to endow a man "whose thoughts fly so high" with power to such degree that, should it in future appear desirable, nevermore would it be possible to be rid of him? Let the Emperor, if condemnation there must be, impose pecuniary penalty on the two Mecklenburgers and give that money to his principal commander. If a magnanimous gratification did not content the latter, why should he be content with Mecklenburg, content indeed with anything on earth? A warning: there were examples enough that "when sovereigns have granted their servants more authority than is meet, they have oft regretted it with all too belated remorse". The style of this paper is Wilhelm Slawata's; he liked to lard a text with learned insinuations. Others who may have collaborated on it are Cardinal Dietrichstein, that other ancient enemy, as well as Privy Councillors Stralendorf, Meggau, Max von Trauttmansdorff. We can only guess and, incidentally, should not dismiss the authors' argumentation out of hand, at least not as regards the probable reactions of the Electors and the northern kings. Alas, that always there are reasons to be found as easily for one point of view as for another. It was specifically the threat presented by the maritime powers from which Wallenstein deduced the need to be strong on Germany's coast, with *his* command, combining rule of the land and military overlordship, more reliable than administration by petty, now presumably more chastened but also more compromised and connubially northern-implicated princes. His friends,

Eggenberg at their head, adduced further grounds. The guilt of the Mecklenburg brothers was as patent as Wallenstein's achievement. Who had put an army of a hundred thousand men into the field at his own expense without reward and remuneration? Who, when all seemed lost, had made the Emperor master from the Adriatic to the German Ocean? Wallenstein alone enjoyed confidence, commanded love, inspired fear among officers and men alike. "Should he be lacking, none is known who could take his place and it would not transpire without mutiny and total ruin of the imperial army." The alleged evil consequences of his elevation? The Electors should not be overrated; they would, as in the past, write letters and leave it at that. Sweden was amply engaged in Poland. Denmark ("as the Duke of Friedland affirms") would make peace and, provided that it received return of its own possessions, not trouble greatly about Mecklenburg. The fulfilment of all the splendid possibilities, mastery of shore and sea, the Spanish–German trading association under the Habsburg eagle's protective pinions, the propagation of Catholicism, punishment of the mischievous and recompense of the good, and, by no means least, solution of the grievous financial problem, everything depended on this one decision. Who was right? A lazy individual like Emperor Ferdinand faced by a difficult choice does not follow the better counsel; he follows the more convenient. The matter had gone too far to allow a retreat to be sounded without the most excruciating embarrassment. He decided on behalf of the gentleman with a hundred thousand soldiers.

Wallenstein's investiture with Mecklenburg travelled along two lines, one public, the other secret. The world at large was only told that the Emperor had given the duchy in lien to his general until such time as his outlays on the war, the outlays on this bloody and unnecessary war which had been forced on the Emperor, had been met. A temporary, not final, expropriation therefore of its previous possessors. The secret truth was that the sequestration was permanent. Two deeds, known merely to the innermost circle, had been drawn up prior to that of the lien. One was a regular contract of purchase by Wallenstein, leaving the precise price to be fixed later. The other, a letter of investiture, gave him the right to name his successor. They were discreet provisional measures, anticipative of the public, ceremonial investiture eighteen months after. Wallenstein, as was his habit, took these unofficial agreements enormously seriously, insisting on corrections and obtaining them. "This must not be . . . for otherwise I would procure for myself but suits, not the land itself." "This, I pray, shall be omitted." The contract of purchase was simultaneously a letter of donation in so far as the value of the property was split into royalties, respectively the income derived from sovereignty over the land and the domains which were ducal, private property. The income derived from his sovereignty over the land was, as an act of favour, made over to him. He rendered payment for the ducal private property, but with deduction of 700,000 gulden as another token of imperial favour. A complicated transaction made even more complicated because payment did not of course take place in cash but was set off against accrued claims. Although it happened in secret, people none the less knew and Wallenstein, superficially only lien-holder, forthwith began to establish his position on a permanent basis. He already did so from Bohemia where, stretching his three months' leave of absence to much over half a year, he remained until June 1628. His two main purposes, entrenchment of his sovereignty and the country's military defence, merged.

His keenest wish was to hasten the departure of those two nonplussed unfortunates, Dukes Adolf Friedrich and Johann Albrecht. We have at least ten letters on the subject addressed to his temporary representative in Mecklenburg, Colonel San Julian, and as many to Arnim. On one occasion he is politely tactful: "Let them not request to see me there where once they ruled." On another the tone is sharp: "The Princes must be sent off. Two cocks on the same dung-heap is no good." To which he adds one of his favourite Latin tags, *Amor et dominium non patitur socium.* On a third he becomes frankly brutal: "Let him see to it that the Princes leave the land *per amor o per forca,* for all courtesy must in such instances be set aside *quia salus suadet*" (since the good of the state demands it). He allows them a fortnight for their departure, but he then prolongs it or has to tolerate its prolongation, seeing that he is not on the spot and his representative hesitates to use force. There is also the Dowager Duchess Sophia. "As to what touches the old Duchess, I leave it wholly to your discretion. I would far rather that she too left, but, if you think it not possible, let it be." That was what the Colonel thought. The old lady was allowed to stay.

Next came the act of subjugation by the Estates, consisting of the knights and towns – the performance of their homage. Wallenstein sent two personal representatives and two jurisconsults, the Emperor two commissioners on the Empire's behalf. At the beginning of April the Estates were ordered to present themselves at Castle Güstrow to learn what they already knew. They wriggled and writhed, singing the praises of their native dynasty. What commutation, they asked, was at stake?

Within their capacity they were prepared to pay if only they were allowed to keep their good overlords. On that point the commissioners lacked instructions. They had brought decrees, not proposals, and after a certain amount of discussion hither and thither the Estates were not spared the act of homage. Only then did the Dukes accept the inevitable and, with their ladies, leave the country.

That formally settled the Mecklenburg affair. Sagan, a trifle, succeeded at a stroke. Henceforward Wallenstein signed himself "Duke of Friedland and Sagan". He became a member of the Silesian princely Diet. Sagan was a sorry principality. He who had made of Friedland the best-administered territory in Europe could however also manage something with Sagan.

To the increases in status of political feudal character were added military ones. That Wallenstein had the unprecedented rank of "General of the Oceanic and Baltic Seas" bestowed on himself was a draft upon things to come: *were* there to be an imperial fleet and *were* an admiral to command it, fleet and admiral would be subordinate to him. Land, harbours and sea, maritime and continental trade, naval and coastal operations were in his view inseparables. If the Sovereigns of the Seas chose to fight inland, why should not the great land power one day soon venture on the waters? A single mind must moreover be the driving force behind whatever happened beneath the Emperor's colours on *terra firma*, whether at a distance from Germany or not. In Italy, for example. The scope of his command had originally been restricted to Germany, but in summer 1626 he had been obliged to proceed to Hungary. Since then, without ever having really been awarded the designation, he used the title "Supreme Commander in the Field". Now, in April 1628, he became "Generalissimo". Again a new creation, just as the powers attached were unexampled. He took good care too that there should be no deficiency in their definition. "I must tarry here several days," Collalto was told, "until my appointment is properly indited . . . but, from what I saw of it, I saw that it answers not at all, wherefore I have sent it back." The move was on a par with his attitude to the Mecklenburg documents – he would countenance no attempt to leave out what he wanted in nor to put in what he wanted left out. The product was a species of dictatorship in the military sphere whereby the Emperor abdicated his rights in favour of Wallenstein. The General is empowered "to ordain and command, orally and in writing, ordinarily and extraordinarily, even as if We in Our Own Person did ordain and command such". He is to exercise plenary justiciary powers over the army and to pay it according to need – which implies that he can also expand it according to need. The soldiers' equipment and provisioning are entirely his responsibility. He is to commission all officers with the exception of general officers; they alone still require the Emperor's confirmation. This "plenary power, authority and mandate" is to hold good everywhere and always. Was anything higher possible? As a military man, hardly. What did it mean? Policy would in principle continue to be laid down at Vienna and thereon would depend whether Wallenstein's tasks were reasonable or unreasonable, realizable or unrealizable.

> The Duke is powerful and clever, it's true,
> But like us all, say what you will
> He remains the Emperor's vassall still.*

His Majesty's henchman, that was what he remained, even as possessor by imperial grace of Mecklenburg. An open question was how all these new endowments, honours, and appointments would be interpreted and with what feelings they were engrossed. No cheerful ones, if the Spanish ambassador is to be believed. He found the Emperor at this time to be in a state of melancholy, "extremely apprehensive on account of the Duke of Friedland's capricious disposition. I was grieved that, notwithstanding his knowledge of Wallenstein's character, he has not dared to wrest his command from him. He opines that this would have for its consequence greater evils than if for the nonce a good mien is shown him." Two parties at court, the Emperor in two minds, and gloom cast over the one by what the other does or lets be done.

The same could not be said of Wallenstein. It was his best period. No complaints any more of tiredness or illness, and that in spite of 1628 not passing without two severe bouts of gout. No threats any more of resignation. The disdainful epistolary protests against the behaviour of the imperial War Council and the Exchequer disappeared. What he wanted, he attained – nearly always. Granted, he had not yet tamed the Electors, Bavaria, Saxony, the lords spiritual on the Rhine, and he knew it. But Brandenburg and Pomerania had to obey and northern Germany he held in his hand, the only query how harsh or cunning and pliant that hand would prove to be. In Prague and Vienna he could fancy himself master. He demanded the relegation of the impossible Schwarzenberg, architect of the grandiose Hanseatic Trading Company design, and he prevailed. He wanted Philipp von Mansfeld, the Flemish sailor,

* Schiller, *Wallenstein: A Historical Drama in Three Parts*, tr. Charles E. Passage.

as his successor and obtained him, regardless of Mansfeld once having been in Swedish service. He desired the promotion of Colonel Arnim, his military intimate, to Field-Marshal rank and this was done. "I cannot recall whether last year I adumbrated to you how I and Count Schlick deemed advisable, whilst the army is so large and must be divided into a great number of corps, that an establishment of four field-marshals, as is wont in France, should be created, whereby when one of them is dispatched with a big force he shall have the greater authority over such troops." Well, Arnim was to be one of the elect and the letter transmitted his commander's heartiest congratulations. The other three were Count Schlick, Collalto – who had already held the appointment – and Wolf Count Mansfeld. The last, the "hungry Wolf", Wallenstein had *not* wanted. His acceptance is evidence of the constraint to practise occasional accommodation which, notwithstanding all else, he could not escape.

His prolonged months of leave were no holiday. Whether at Prague or Gitschin, his sway over an unruly army and turbulent politics had to be upheld. His surviving letters number hundreds, if not indeed thousands. Those of a personal nature he wrote in his own hand, those of official character he dictated and had placed before him for final revision. War department bureaucrats were in attendance on him in Bohemia too. Thanks to the discipline he imposed, the drafts of those letters still exist, a part of them in print, the texts of most still in manuscript. Wallenstein's working day cannot be visualized other than, after his morning ride, a process of sitting hour after hour in his study, dictating and reading, then receiving in audience, again dictating, sometimes in the presence of visitors. His memory was good. It had to be. The map of Germany as well as central and eastern Europe was kept in his head. Recently he had added that of the northern seas and islands. Who, at the moment, was where and with which regiment? What had he promised this and that prince? How much and with what maturity date did this and the other city owe him? He had to know, for, if he forgot, his debtors would not recall themselves to his mind.

The troops had to have room and they had to have something to eat. Neither cattle nor corn was allowed to be exported, but had to stay for the soldiers. Interknit with the problem of quarters was always that of money because quarters intrinsically signified money unless a city or district chose to purchase with money its freedom from quartering.

There was the problem of money in general. At the peak of his power, for all the glitter of his wealth, money was no easier to scrape together than at the beginning. It was, if anything, more difficult. The construction of ships, the buying of timber, canvas and hemp, the establishment of foundries, the recruitment of sailors – where was the money to come from? In January Madrid notified a first, meagre support of 200,000 crowns. They did not arrive until summer. He needed the Silesian contribution for 1628, a total of 600,000 taler, and was promised it by the court. A pledge was not cash in the war-chest. The Nürnbergers had engaged themselves for 100,000 gulden. Where were they? Magdeburg owed at least 75,000 taler to the Duke or his banker, de Witte, which was the same. The city sent a delegation to Prague to haggle. That alone cost 15,000 taler because "all palms" at court "have to be greased. If we are to achieve anything positive, a few thousand more will have to be stood." To punish the city council for its tardiness, Wallenstein demanded 12,000 taler extra. "We shall not gain much here," ran the Magdeburgers' report home. "Sometimes we quake in our shoes when we are to go and endure one tumble after another. . . . His Princely Grace stands in high esteem and 'tis strange to see how he is maintained in favour."

On top of the financial problem was the strategic one. The seaports had to be occupied in defence against the sea-borne foe. The ports were of two kinds: the great free imperial communities like Hamburg, Lübeck and Bremen, and towns subject to a territorial sovereign like Wismar and Rostock in Mecklenburg and Barth, Greifswald, Stralsund, Kolberg and Stettin in Pomerania. In practice the difference was not rigid. Stralsund and Rostock belonged to the ancient Hanse (long in decline, but still on account of its legendary quality a formidable alliance) and their tie with their overlord had slackened.

In the case of Hamburg and Lübeck Wallenstein experienced a totally new world: politically, republican in form although predominantly aristocratic; economically, commercial and international. A new world with which he had first to become conversant, an achievement not possible without paying for the apprenticeship. But the better he knew it, the more skilful would be his manipulation. As early as April 1628 he was writing to Philipp Mansfeld, his freshly acquired naval expert, that caution was needed in negotiation with the maritime cities in order not to render them desperate and drive them into the arms of Denmark or Sweden. Ludwig Schwarzenberg's all too clumsy final conduct at Lübeck was the reason why he had chased him away. In dealing with the Stralsunders he himself made a mistake because Arnim informed him wrongly. They were to accept an imperial garrison; they did not want to. An all-Hanseatic delegation appeared in Prague to plead the defence of its city members' neutrality and, in particular, to put in a good word for Stralsund. Wallenstein received the representatives in his palace. Seated on green-and-gold velvet stools, they faced the Duke. There would be peace with Denmark, he explained, if its King was willing. He must however ask for it. If he did not, means would be found to smoke him out of his island den. He could at any time be ruined by confiscation of all Danish goods in German ports. He, Wallenstein, did not want the Stralsunders' money. He wanted to put a garrison inside their walls. They should either come to an agreement with Arnim or be prepared for a horrible ending. He also knew the means to peace between Spain and the Dutch – King Philip should license them to go to the Devil. Upon which he laughed, adding in a good-natured tone that there he had spoken like a Catholic. The black-gowned legal experts were dismissed. The scene deserves mention because a year had scarcely elapsed before he had quite other ideas about the Dutch and about maritime commerce in wartime too.

Slowly, against stubborn resistance, the visionary imperial fleet at Wismar began to assume some shape. Wallenstein regarded it as primarily directed against Denmark. That was the opposite to the view held by the Spaniards. They, in Madrid and in Brussels, as well as Señor de Roy, supposed naval expert on the spot, had their eye on the one eternal enemy, the Netherlanders, with their commerce and their fishing. Denmark was of no interest at all to them. That was why Wallenstein and de Roy could not brook one another. But was he serious about invasion of the Danish isles? Was it not much more a matter of tactics, boasting, feints? Basically he knew that peace with Denmark was now possible, although not on the conditions that, incited by the court at Vienna, he had last September expounded at Lauenburg, neither by the confiscation of Slesvig and Holstein nor by the election of the Emperor through the Danish Estates as their King. Those were fanfaronades trumpeted into the air to cause someone or other pleasure. He had surmised it long ago – only one kind of peace was possible with Denmark, a peace of *status quo ante*, at best with the qualification that Christian IV must renounce interference in German affairs. He knew it as well as, deep inside him, he knew that one day Madrid would have no choice but to be reconciled with the "rebels", the States-General. If time is requisite to attain clarity about what is already apparent deep inside, still more time is required to render it apparent to allies. For they are stupid, these allies, and are conscious of nothing else than that battles gained must also bring them gains by way of land or gulden and kreutzer.

Well, he already had his highest gain, Mecklenburg. Whatever the concessions that would have to be made to the Dane or anyone else, it would not be *this*. "Certainly my desire is to assist peace hand and foot, but Mecklenburg I must retain and have. In contrary case I desire no peace." He was writing to Arnim.

An Adversary

FATHER ALEXANDER VON ALES, alias Francesco Rotha, merchant, was one of those Capuchins whom Elector Maximilian liked to employ for his secret diplomacy. Ardently pious men, they yet had a leaning towards arcane intrigue and lacked any firm terrestrial ties. It constituted part of their own and their patron's cover that they made their highly political journeys to Paris, Brussels, Rome, or London at their own initiative and in conjunction with other members of their Order in such a way that Maximilian, a lover of twilight, was afterwards in a position to maintain that he had been able neither to promote nor to impede their endeavours because he had known nothing whatever about them. Endeavours, incidentally, which usually remained unsuccessful, illusory, artful, and shadowy. The mission that in April 1628 took Father Alexander to Prague was entirely independent of the tasks performed there by the accredited Bavarian agents. It sought to obtain from a "Great Personage", whose identity nobody besides the Elector was allowed to know, for once really solid information about Wallenstein, his character, his methods, and his plans. The monk stayed a few days, conferred several times with the Great Personage, and returned to Munich. On 26 April he signed his report, penned in Italian, for the personal attention of His Serene Highness. A detailed stocktaking. None the less, for all its nuggets, Maximilian's greed was not sated and Father Alexander had to resign himself to repeating his journey. This time, though he could not add anything substantially new, he reproduced the Great Personage's own words. *Il personaggio grande*, at one point referred to as *"il padre"*, a careless slip, had on the first occasion said all, or a little more than, he knew. On the second he could only rearrange the material. His analysis proceeded systematically, like a schoolboy writing an essay. First, Friedland's disposition. Secondly, his manner of acting. Thirdly, his plans.

His disposition. A man of unbelievable cunning. A seasoned dissimulator. Where others pretend to be more stupid than they are, he assumes an even more eccentric, tyrannical air than comes natural to him in order to keep people at a distance, frighten them, and above all spoil any desire to pry into his secrets. "All this is done with consummate artistry." He has ripe judgement, iron determination to fulfil any decision he has reached, and does not care at all whether he treads on anyone's toes as long as he achieves his purpose. "What an almost royal state he has created in his behalf, ruthless of the hatred of so very many that he has thereby drawn down on himself. Withal he is a great economist" [*un grand economo*]". That does not stop him from being immensely liberal where it is to his advantage. "He is accounted a man of his word." His tokens of thanks and the bribes by which he renders the Privy Council tractable to his wishes, so that no one dares to gainsay him, always number a round thousand. Should however His Imperial Majesty seek most humbly any kind of concession from him, for example, the evacuation of Saxony which, scoffing at Elector John George's loyalty, he has occupied with several regiments, he has but one answer: It cannot be – *non si può*. It is Friedland's nature, this passion to have the upper hand. Nothing is more difficult for him than to subordinate his will to that of another. He is correspondingly touchy.

> The violence of his temper which many are daily made to feel also breaks out against such as, without doing Friedland any wrong, are merely possessed of such innate failings as do not please his humour. He openly admits that he cannot master his irascibility. Still less does a feeling for religion, a timid conscience, et cetera, restrain him and no manifestations of such, other than hypocritical ones, emanate from him notwithstanding the many alms which he gives, when he shows clearly enough that this is for reasons other than pure piety. . . . So much of his disposition which reflects incarnate the picture of one of those ancients like Attila, Theodoric, Berengar, amazing to history, who as simple leaders of armies attained through the benefaction of others to kingdoms and (so adds the Great Personage) strove after the imperial dignity.

From the subject's disposition result his methods. Wallenstein, it must be granted, has proceeded thoroughly systematically, step by step, from assistance to Tilly to independent command and then to absolute military authority. His tricks are familiar. The briberies. The flattery of Father Lamormaini, the Emperor's influential father confessor, as well as of the Jesuits in general. The constant threat of resignation although he has not the slightest intention of implementing it. The pretence in his camp at being the disciplinarian indifferent to hatred whereas in reality he does all he can to acquire popularity with the soldiery. The preference for the appointment to colonelcies of Protestants because they are the most accommodating to him. How his mind works in regard to major strategic moves is as plain as it is in the smallest details. Never to do battle with Denmark is deliberate. To have let Mansfeld in 1626 escape to Silesia and Hungary was deliberate, enabling him in the course of the pursuit to become established in the Hereditary Lands. It would be quite feasible for him to obtain money from the Emperor for the army's maintenance, but that he does not want; the army is to remain *his* and he be able to drain the Empire with it. The remonstrance was often made that an army of such size could not be maintained without money: "at which he laughed and said that in many cases where it had been alleged that wars could not be continued experience had taught the contrary". Only deliberate cunning prompted him to ask at the start for Count Collalto as his field-marshal in order that he could pick a quarrel and induce him to leave in disgust, which occurred soon enough. Absolutely nothing happens in Friedland's proximity that he has not devised.

> To all this comes his small respect for the entire court. He holds all in contempt and quarrels openly with the ministers. Towards the Emperor he behaves as though 'twere he who is Emperor. . . .
> He insults ruling sovereigns. He has said in the presence of the Spanish envoy that the King of Spain has his wits not rightly about him. Of the King of Poland he has said the same. Of the Pope he has spoken with disrespect and remarked that there are twenty-five cardinals who should be put to the galleys in chains. On the same day as the Friend' – Father Alexander's designation for himself – 'took his leave of the Personage, Minister Eggenberg observed to that same Person, 'Truly, this Friedland is a Scourge of God, a true scourge'. . . ."

Thus his disposition, thus his means. And his plans, his objectives? "Either, without open resistance to His Majesty, he will tyrannize the Emperor and all other imperial princes as though he were King of Germany . . . or he will, if resisted, play the offended party and do yet worse." His one unalterable main purpose remains to ruin the sole rival in the Empire that he still has, the Catholic League, for "Friedland fears above all Bavaria". One reason more for Bavaria to operate diplomatically and cautiously. It may show the Duke no enmity, but must secretly incite it among others, foremost among the Spaniards at Brussels. The road to Madrid leads through Brussels. Let Spain be won over and it will be time for the Electors to proceed openly against Friedland. They must catch him in his own trap. Let his exorbitant demands be for once rejected and, as so often before, he will threaten to resign, an offer that will on this occasion be accepted. The principal command will be transferred to Tilly, unreliable regimental commanders relegated, the stores of arms and victuals accumulated by Friedland at various points within the Empire simply be taken over. The whole must happen at a single blow and soon, very soon.

The "Friend" asked questions. Whether the court altogether lacks anxiety and does not ponder the character of such a man? Not really, because the Emperor relies implicitly on his father confessor. In the case of Eggenberg and Collalto matters stand differently, but the former is indolent and never takes preventive action, at the best only after damage has been caused. The loyalists, those who worry, have their best ally in the Spanish ambassador. Recently he ventured to lay his warnings directly before the Emperor. Unfortunately in vain. The Emperor's view: there we go too far. "The envoy has therefore reported to Spain that Friedland has so far divested the Emperor of his power as only to leave him with the name." Whether there exists a secret understanding between Wallenstein and Spain? Absolutely none. What is the position as regards the ostensible plan for a major campaign against the Turks? Nothing but an excuse to remain in a state of armed readiness. The same holds good for the disturbances which are again on the point of eruption in northern Italy. Wallenstein behaves as though he intends to intervene there with great force; that is simply sham. He will "never surrender certainty for uncertainty, which is why at present he thinks neither of the Turks nor of Italy, but is indeed of a mind to skin the German princes and alone in the Empire stay under arms". Last question: is Friedland inclined to break with the Dutch? "The answer was absolutely in the negative." "Finally the Personage sets forth two more points for consideration. First, without detraction from all that has been said before, Friedland is by nature very timorous of those who show him their teeth and this is a postulate upon which plans can safely be laid. . . . The Personage has infallible proofs of that." Secondly, a warning must go to the Pope of the danger that Wallenstein represents and, even more urgently and in utmost secrecy, to Count Tilly "on whose goodheartedness Friedland much counts in order to be able to deceive and soon to destroy him".

The Elector had hardly read the last sentence before he ordered his commissioner at Tilly's headquarters to return to Munich as quickly as possible "because such important matters come to pass that We regard it as of the highest, indispensable exigency to furnish Our Lieutenant-General Count von Tilly with news thereof and with suitable circumstantial instructions on that score". From which it can be seen that the Elector believed every word passed to him by the Great Personage and was only avid to learn yet more.

At the end of May arrived the second report containing the Personage's own words. His statements sounded even more dangerous than as quoted in the first, and decidedly more speculative. The unnamed individual probably felt compelled, so as to continue in the role that he had assumed, to paint the picture in ever stronger tints. What is Wallenstein's ultimate objective? No less than to become Emperor or at least King of the Germans, *re hereditario*, two titles between which the Personage made no precise differentiation. He does not, it should be noted, propose to intervene during the lifetime of the present Emperor, but definitely after the latter's death which could if necessary also be hastened. Then he intends to show "of what Germany, united under a single ruler, is capable". His public assertion that neither the Diet nor the Electors are essential renders the point perfectly clear: he does not want the Emperor's successor, the younger Ferdinand, to be elected King of the Romans in the elder's lifetime, and why he should not want it is perfectly visible even to the blind. He has his eye on Charlemagne's crown. Any prince or any count is eligible for election to the imperial throne. If however the Electors do not choose to elect him, he will manage the business without them in the way that the Roman soldier-emperors did. Nevertheless he will always retain a semblance of legality because the spirit of the new Attila is so constituted that for his peace of mind he requires the support of both power and legitimation. What happens while Ferdinand II remains alive? For that duration the great hereafter will be prepared bit by bit. Wallenstein is now master of Lower Germany, a broad territory which he will render docile as the grand dukes of Florence rendered Tuscany docile to themselves. Denmark will be allowed indulgent terms. He will come to some settlement with the Mecklenburg dukes. With the Palsgrave, so near despair that he is prepared to accept whatever he may be offered, too. There is indeed no European problem which Wallenstein as Generalissimo, later as head of the united Empire, will not be in a position to solve. At any rate that is what he thinks. The impediments to him? He knows them – the League, the powerful Hanse confederation, the great free imperial cities. The League he will hamper, harass, try to involve in foreign conflict – that with the Dutch – until it is in a condition to be attacked by him. He is already proceeding militarily against a "Hanseatic town in Pomerania", meaning Stralsund; "the Emperor's pleas were impotent to restrain him." He is expected to deal with the free imperial cities after the same fashion. Finally he will bring the whole of Germany under his sway. Rule by an absolute monarchy, asked the Friend, in place of the ages' old aristocracy? How in the world could that be prevented? "As an incontrovertible fundamental," answered the Personage, "must be assumed that Friedland will scoff at every hindrance to his intentions unless it exists in the shape of an efficacious, powerful army. . . . That is why in the hour of decision Friedland will not desire to make his fortune dependent on the fortunes of war, all the less because it is certain and confirmed that he is as cowardly when he feels weaker or no more than equally strong as he is bold when he knows himself vastly superior." Equally sure is that he will not fear any force, for all that it may be his equal, if it does not give him ground to regard it as hostile and capable of any hostile action. Alas, the Elector of Bavaria and General Tilly do not give him such ground. Moreover "the conviction is justified that never to the end of his days will the Emperor be in a position to wrest from this man his weapons except by force". The inference is palpable. The army of the League and the Electors must be strong, so strong as to enable it soon to send to Vienna or Prague a message of the following kind: "Since the Electors see that the army is not in the Emperor's hands, but those of Friedland whom they consider their enemy, they demand that this man be deprived of his authority, in default whereof they would be constrained," etc, etc. . . . At the same time it would be a good thing to enter secretly into relations with a number of Wallenstein's senior officers. Had Friedland, the Friend inquired, furnished the Infanta with any troops against the Dutch? "Yes, but only a few horsemen of whom he has more than enough. That he will not embark against the Dutch, either little or much, can be taken as quite definite. When the Spanish ambassador spoke to him of this, he derided him with sneering words and gestures." How, the Friend wanted to know, do things stand with regard to the Spanish ambassador? Extremely well, but Olivares, the Minister, perhaps for reasons of private interest, does not think along the same lines and Señor Aytona cannot report in as free terms as he would like. At Madrid it is not the King who rules, but quite other individuals. Consequently it is all the more important to draw the Infanta at Brussels into their confidence, a purpose for which Father Filippo, "a very zealous, capable and astute" monk, could be employed. On this the incensed Elector commented in the margin, "Why does not the *Personaggio*, who at the outset much encouraged Friedland, do it himself?" "Finally the Personage says that Friedland assuredly turns over in his mind the idea of changing Germany's form of government, that he has always mocked and held in contempt the imperial Diets and assemblies, and that he hates the clergy" – *gli Ecclesiastici* – "and burningly desires to reform them (which here means their abolition). Let action against this man be taken speedily, for he is like the cat which springs into its opponent's face ere it has received a blow."

Thus far the memoranda. What was their source? That has been a puzzle ever since the documents again saw the light. In one passage the Great Personage is called, as though inadvertently, "the Father". It immediately confines to a very small circle the number of those among whom the Personage can be found. A cultured monk and a dabbler in politics. He speaks perfect Italian, seeing that all his comparisons are taken from Italian history he is probably Italian by origin, and when he says that Wallenstein will one day "through a medley of undertakings show what great strength is immanent in Germany if it is united under a single suzerain" he echoes the fear of the Latin *vis-à-vis* the Teuton. A monk with a most intimate knowledge of Wallenstein – that is indisputable – who "at the outset much encouraged" him, indicating a former assistant or ally, and yet simultaneously maintains good relations with Bavaria. A monk very critical of the court at Vienna – "*quelle corte venalissima*" – he is probably not a member of it. None the less he conducts conversations of considerable candour with Eggenberg, the First Minister. There cannot have been many personalities combining all these qualities. There was in any case one.

In the summer and autumn of 1629, eighteen months after the material here under examination, Elector Maximilian conducted a correspondence in code and in Italian with Count Valeriano Magni, a Capuchin resident at Vienna, a correspondence which shows Magni to have been familiar with the state of court affairs and intrigues. Familiar too with Wallenstein's plans. The Duke was not on the spot, but Colonel San Julian disclosed the most confidential matters to the priest. An astrologer, the former reported, had just told him how he had received the ducal commission to cast the Emperor's horoscope for the coming months, which gave food enough for thought. A few weeks ago Wallenstein had warned Lamormaini, the Emperor's father confessor, against the war in Italy and had described France's position there as good in law. (A memorandum to this effect was indeed written.) The General's main objective always was to see the League disarmed. And so on. He, Magni, was on good terms with the new Spanish ambassador just as with the old. In August Maximilian expressed his thanks for earlier secret services. "It is true that we are not yet out of the dangers arising on the Duke's activities, yet I hope that he will not forget his bounden duty." Maximilian exercised in his letters the most scrupulous prudence over his utterances. How was he to be quite certain that Magni would not divulge their contents to one of Wallenstein's confidants? For the Capuchin was engaged in a double game, allowing himself now as heretofore to be employed on diplomatic missions for Wallenstein. He belonged to that class of secrets' barterers who in the end no longer know for which side they are spying.

This Valeriano Magni is the "Great Personage" precisely as he was the author of the secret report on the Bruck-on-the-Leitha conference. Where it was a question of adding fuel to the fires of dispute between Wallenstein and Bavaria, Wallenstein and the League, and of trapping the General in a skein of suspicions, there he performed wonders. Wallenstein did not know. As late as the second generalate he tolerated Magni in his company.

The following furnishes proof of the monk's complicity. The report on Bruck was composed by a cultured, clever Italian for the Elector of Bavaria who passed it to his League friends with the comment that it came from one "who knows of Friedland's business and intentions before others do and who is greatly in his confidence". Its contents were a miscellany of genuine and pretended confidential knowledge. The author claimed to have learned the essence of the matter directly from Prince Eggenberg. Wallenstein was still accorded hypocritical praise. The writer must, though, have known that it would be anything but to Maximilian's taste to hear how the Duke's strategy consisted of avoiding battles and his policy envisaged an inundation of the Empire with troops, sucking it dry, and compelling it to obedience.

A couple of months afterwards the Elector sent one of his diplomats to Vienna for delicate negotiations. He advised him to make use of Father Magni as a man who was in good standing with the General, could achieve much with him, and knew him through and through. Another two months and Dr Leuker promised in forthcoming negotiations with Wallenstein "to take Father Valerianum as guide and to let myself be governed in all my suits by his advice". There lies revealed

Magni's link with Wallenstein on the one hand, with Bavaria on the other. He plays the go-between and recommends how properly to treat the eccentric General whom he knows so very, very well.

The "Tales of a Capuchin" again derive from a cultured Italian. More detailed and discursive than the Bruck report, the basic theme is identical – Wallenstein's hair-raising rational programme for Germany's subjugation through enormous military superiority and the avoidance to every unnecessary military risk. Again Eggenberg is one of the author's informants. Again Maximilian calls the author "a Person who is in Friedland's confidence, wherefore he has knowledge ahead of others". And that is not the same man who had previously puffed himself up with what he knew about the Bruck conference? Not the same person who a year later, signing himself Valeriano Magni, once more made a show of his court connections, emphasized his intimacy with the Spanish ambassadors old and new, and was on terms of utmost intimacy with Wallenstein's agents while simultaneously warning Bavaria against Wallenstein? The man is always the same – the monk, the Italian, the Great Personage, Count Valeriano Magni. It is he, beyond all doubt.

Wallenstein had probably known him since 1604. His first campaign, initially against the Turks, then the Hungarians, had also been Magni's first. The former went through it as an ensign, the latter as a minister to the sick. During the course of the adventure all of them, at least all those from Bohemia, formed a single family. The height and the haughty bearing of the young noble turned monk, his ascetic features and glowing eyes, his Italianate aristocratic manners must have struck the observant ensign. Notwithstanding that he had been born at Milan, Magni had spent his youth in Bohemia and spoke Czech and German as well as he did Italian. A variety of glittering careers are said to have been open to him due to the patronage extended to his family by Pope Clement VIII. He preferred to join the Mendicant Order and rose to eminence at Vienna and Prague. A saintly man and a man of prayer, a helper of the poor, a proselytizer of the genteel. The Emperor submitted to his sermons. Ambition is however known to wear many guises. That Magni was an argumentative theologian, argumentative particularly as regards the Jesuits, has been mentioned. He did battle against their greed for power. In the process he gained a kind of power himself. At an early stage moreover he allowed himself to be employed on political missions. In 1622, for example, he went to Paris as agent for the Duke of Bavaria. He was not merely to effect recognition by France of Maximilian's electoral dignity, but to forge a downright Franco–Bavarian alliance. He did not succeed, but he performed the mission with great astuteness, discretion, and a store of ingenious wiles. His trump card was the peril to the Bourbons presented by Habsburg predominance. Would not an alliance of France with the League be a useful counterweight? This friar, it is clear, was not bound by any ties of loyalty. He played at politics. He could identify himself with French or Bavarian interests just as closely as with those of the Austrian and Spanish Habsburgs. Our interpretation is that he had no other than his spiritual home. Politicians bound to no terrestrial land could exist more easily then than later when the character of states had stiffened into absolute rigidity.

At Prague the Archbishop, Wallenstein's brother-in-law, appointed the Capuchin to be his confessor, meaning his senior adviser. Thereby Magni obtained entry to the Wallenstein circle. Its atmosphere did not lack tension. Whereas the Duke of Friedland was accounted patron of the Jesuits, the Cardinal let himself be persuaded by Magni to fight hotly for his rights, especially as regards rule over Prague's university, against the Society's imperialist leanings. The internal conflict was reaching a fresh climax, with the dynasty entirely on the side of the Jesuits, to such a degree that Wallenstein advised his brother-in-law's confessor to withdraw from his difficult office, promising to find a more fruitful field of activities for his capacity. But behind Magni stood Rome, the Congregation De Propaganda Fidei, and, armed with a papal testimony as to the great satisfaction he had given, he retained his post and his positions. This was in 1628, precisely the year of the "Tales of a Capuchin", intrinsically a colossal accusation albeit full of admiration for the accused. It was a game. Father Valeriano derived exquisite pleasure from living in closest proximity to a great man and turbulent personality of the kind normally only met in ancient writings, winning and breaking his confidence, whereby he, the monk, became the superior's superior. The more he magnified his subject, the greater his own magnification. That was why he exaggerated and romanticized. "None but God penetrates to the depths of his soul" – none but God and Valeriano Magni, the Great Personage, Counsellor of the Mighty. Were the Electors to follow his counsels and consummate Wallenstein's dismissal through the tricks he inculcated into them, how proud the killer of the Bengal tiger would be of his trophy.

The prospects were not bad. Never had Maximilian been in a state of more harried fear than after receipt of the first and second Capuchin Tales. Couriers were sent flying in all directions – to Tilly in northern

Germany, to Mainz, Dresden and Cologne. The perilous, until now covert designs of the Duke of Friedland had been disclosed, ran the message to Mainz, and it was impossible to tarry any longer without incurring the utmost danger. Precisely this had for long past been his anxiety, replied the Archbishop of Mainz, but to mobilize his fellow spiritual Electors he needed more exact details. Maximilian complied by sending a translation of the initial report accompanied by the request that his name should not be mentioned in the matter as otherwise yet greater malevolent hatred, danger, and trouble on Wallenstein's part would dog him. Regiments under Friedland's command were marching through the Eichsfeld, Mainz's property, and plundering on the way, which was presumably the start of Wallenstein's aggression, came the answer. His fellows at Trèves and Cologne were told by the Archbishop that the Duke of Friedland's threatening projects were bearing fruit, the beloved German fatherland was mortally menaced, a conference of the Catholic Electors must be immediately convened. "Most heartily beloved Lord Brother, 'tis time to awaken from sleep," Cologne's Archbishop expounded to Bavaria's Duke, "for our downfall is closer than we had thought." Another ten weeks of inactivity, Maximilian told Mainz, and all faithful Electors would be lost. And so on, in ever rising excitement. They disputed which of them had first seen calamity coming. They regaled each other with recipes for dealing with the emergency – Tilly's army should be moved to the south-west to be ready in any eventuality. They really did summon a League congress to Bingen-on-Rhine. The Bavarian representative's instruction speaks for itself – the problem was principally whether Wallenstein's troops should be attacked at once or whether their attack awaited. The Emperor should at any rate be presented with an ultimatum – were the Duke of Friedland not dismissed, were the army not reduced to the strength of a few thousand men and incorporated into the League's force, then they would be free to take any, even an offensive move in exercise of the perpetual right to self-defence. In the heat of a Rhineland summer the hills heaved and brought forth a protocol of 134 pages. We envisage the grizzled Privy Councillors wanting action and yet not wanting it, hesitating and warning of the dangers of hesitation. Open war between the League and Wallenstein would be a catastrophe, particularly on account of the gloatingly undertaken intervention to be apprehended on the part of foreign powers. On the other hand to do nothing and wait would perhaps have still worse consequences. For the time being the following should at least be done – a demand put to the Emperor by a collective electoral deputation to dismiss the insufferable General. Were the accustomed procrastinative answer to be received, then it should be bluntly declared that, in view of the distressing fact of His Imperial Majesty being unable any longer to issue orders to his own commander, the faithful imperial Estates had no choice other than to resort to self-help. The resolution comprised, almost word for word, Valeriano Magni's proposal.

Temporarily nothing came of the matter. To the difficulty reflected in the fable of the mice, their bell, and the cat was added that of Wallenstein's behaviour during the current year and the next: it did not really fulfil the Capuchin's warnings and therefore hampered the conspirators. Another impediment was that Maximilian always wanted to maintain the pretence that he in no wise belonged to the conspiracy whose true mainspring and driving-force he was. In the weeks when he was preparing the Bingen Conference he sent his chancellor to Vienna to tell Prince Eggenberg how he had had no suspicion whatever of what Father Valeriano had of his own accord secretly discussed with Rotha – Father Alexander's alias – and then told Eggenberg. It had happened entirely without any instruction from him. A misinterpretation of this occurrence could not but incur for him the utmost odium. An equivocal procedure, harmful to one's cause, never to accept responsibility for what one does. Magni remained in Wallenstein's vicinity. Maximilian and Wallenstein continued to exchange the politest messages. The time would come when the Electress of Bavaria would write to good Father Valeriano that never, but never, had her illustrious husband had other than trust and affection for the Duke of Friedland nor had he truly had ground for anything else. If certain people had agitated against the commander-in-chief, Bavaria had regrettably been unable to prevent it. The letter was specious. Meant for Wallenstein, he read it and even then, in 1632, was not yet aware of the game played four years earlier between Elector and Great Personage.

We, who do know it all, find the situation not lacking in irony. People in politics were dishonest with one another, so unspeakably dishonest, so dishonourable, so enwrapped in secretiveness that probably it was impossible for anything better than infinite perniciousness to ensue. Who emerges as relatively the most honest among this batch of lying knaves? More to the point, how accurate is the portrait of Wallenstein painted underhand by Father Valeriano Magni?

The godly man had first-hand knowledge. That he mixed with guess-work. Friedland would never allow himself to be drawn into Spain's war with the Netherlands and the help he lent the Infanta was merely a matter of form. True, less so as regards the Duke's contemporary utterances than as seen in the constant trend underlying his policy. He launched an attack on Stralsund in the face of the Emperor's humble plea to desist. True, such a letter on Ferdinand's part exists. He spoke contemptuously of the Pope. Probably, judging by his private letters. And of the King of Poland. Nothing to that effect has been transmitted, but because we are familiar with Sigismund Vasa as a silly old pedant we incline to a view which fits. Aytona, the Spanish envoy, reported home that as affairs regrettably stood the Emperor possessed ultimate power in name only. Correct, the dispatch has been found. And so on. Valeriano was by no means a confidence trickster. Is that surprising? Maximilian knew his informants. In the Father's ascent from fidelity via the half-way plausible to the chimerical, he could at all times quote from examples of his own observation. There was something to the allegation that Wallenstein felt Bavaria and its League to be a cause of chagrin to him. To describe him as "fearing it above all else" amounted to strong exaggeration. The claim that he would not rest until the League's forces had been destroyed lacks not only written proof – that would probably in no case whatever be available – but lacks confirmatory actions. The perpetual squabble about billets was no such action, simply a banal bit of business inherent in the nature of affairs. If the Duke felt the Elector to be an adversary and he instinctively disliked him, the question should be asked who began this mutual frolic, the newcomer and intruder into the Empire, Wallenstein, or the old-established owner of the *supremo dominio*, Maximilian. The annihilation of Bavaria as an idea pre-eminent in Wallenstein's mind was nothing else than a suspicion emanating from his personality – he must with inflexible determination want this, that, and the other. The world is not fashioned thus, or at least it is only *extremely* rare for a person to be in a position to succeed in all his desires or in the teeth of the world, and that with the most thoroughgoing consistency. In respect of Bavaria the conclusion drawn was dubious, in respect of the Hanseatic cities it was flatly wrong. As soon as Wallenstein had been able to form an understanding of the coastal republics and their commercial activities, of which at the outset he had none, he treated them with incomparably more considerate and liberal circumspection than any other power, whether Denmark, England, or Sweden, let alone Spain. More of that shortly. His policy towards the Hanseatic cities in 1628 and 1629 gave the lie to one of Magni's forecasts just as his strategy had given the lie to an earlier invention. What an inanimate object will do in a given set of circumstances can be foretold. To predict what course will be adopted by a human being moving through the world's turmoil is impossible.

Sheer fraud, the oracle decided, was Wallenstein's plan for a large-scale war against the Turks, simply a move to arm and arm again. The verdict has never been refuted. The war against the Turks was never fought. It *could* never be fought as long as matters between Habsburg on the one side and Denmark, Sweden, England, Holland, and France on the other stood as they did. To deduct from this non-event the mendacity of the project or expressed wish would be hasty. Valeriano Magni knew that Wallenstein was only pretending war against Turkey. We, 340 years later, do not know.

Not long ago, between 1614 and 1624, say, the notion of a crusade stirred many a European mind, furnishing a link with the distant past and a presentiment of the future. The issue would have been less the redemption of the Holy Places than liberation of the Balkan peoples from the infidel barbaric yoke, particularly the Greeks, as well as maybe the securing of strategic bases in Egypt or elsewhere. Father Joseph, Cardinal Richelieu's adviser, a Capuchin whose influential secret task Valeriano Magni would only too gladly have undertaken, warmly propagated the idea at Paris, Madrid, and Rome. The world was indebted to him for the hortatory poem in 4500 Latin verses entitled *La Turciade*. An Italian–French grandee, Duke Charles of Gonzaga and Nevers, sacrificed his fortune for this shining objective, bought ships, and founded to the applause of three Popes, including the regnant Urban, an Order of the Christian Militia. Admittedly all these magnanimous preparations silted up. Although small as yet in comparison to what was to come, the division of Europe into states had solidified too greatly for it to be able to act as an unselfish religious whole – Madrid had no wish whatever perhaps to assist its French neighbour to Egypt. Presuming that Wallenstein had been serious about the Turkish war and presuming that he had put the project into practice, the character of the enterprise would, whether deliberately or not on the part of its leader, have been different from that visualized by the Duke of Nevers – not an enterprise launched by European christendom, but by Austria, the rising great power. It would have been something of the kind that two generations later Wallenstein's more fortunate successor, Prince Eugène of Savoy, had the good fortune to accomplish. That in 1629 the time was too early for what in 1697 was ready to be plucked is a fair conclusion. Wallenstein, whose brooding spirit sensed much, here sensed something too – he had been born too soon, for this accomplishment. An alternative explanation is that he deceived people about what he knew that he would never do. Can a man be such a consistent liar? If yes, was he the man? "Certainly my desire is to assist peace hand and foot, but Mecklenburg I must have and retain. In contrary case I desire no peace." So he had written, the century's most artless, brutal, and honest statement. Permanent war, death, and affliction for hundreds of thousands rather than loss of his new toy. The same letter mentions war with the Turks. "The Emperor and the Ministers would afterwards" – after peace with Denmark – "gladly turn the forces against the Turks." This is but one of innumerable examples from his correspondence with Arnim at the time of the Tales of a Capuchin. "From your letter I note what you write relating to peace in the Empire and imperial war against the Turks. I assure you that I shall concern myself as avidly with this enterprise as any in the world." A year later, to Collalto: "I have discoursed at length with Count Tilly upon the Hungarian war and finally came to our proposal to war against the Turks. He leapt in, hands and feet, exclaiming that it would be a sacred, glorious, easy, and useful undertaking." Four years later he told negotiators in a totally different setting that when at last there was peace, he wanted to "march against the Turk" with the united imperial and Protestant armies and "take back from him all that of which he has deprived Europe". Very well, it was deception, as Magni thought, practised throughout six or seven years. If his letters contained truth in starkest terms, then it happened that truth and deception were all too craftily mingled. What is assumed, whether anything is assumed where nothing can be proved, depends in the end on individual taste. Is the entire problem one devoid of meaning? It postulates that Wallenstein was clear in his own mind about the seriousness or the frivolousness, the mendacity of his proposal. As the issue was a proposal currently incapable of fulfilment, one that had not even to be begun to be put into train, contingent on a nebulous hereafter, what was the onus on him to be clear about it in his mind? But caution, indecision, or a shrug of the shoulders when contemplating an imaginary set of circumstances were traits ill-adapted to Valeriano Magni's firmly drawn, zestful character-picture.

From it followed the inference that Wallenstein wanted to become Emperor. True enough, he felt an "irresistible urge to be supreme". How could that be satisfied other than by obtaining the imperial crown, an imperial crown moreover, now that its aura left much to be desired, mightily enhanced through deeds performed by a unified German

Empire of a kind calculated to freeze the smile on the faces of Europe's rulers?

Elector Maximilian believed that immediately. The Emperor believed it six years later after the soil in the exiguous garden of his mind had been carefully turned, planted and watered. Late in the nineteenth century a historian believed it who in other respects was no poor expert on the subject. He proved to a nicety that Wallenstein, in the case of a speedy demise by the ageing Ferdinand, would have had no choice but to grasp at the crown, even though reluctantly, because without possession of the highest office he would have been left simply as the ringleader of a stray band of brigands and would have had to expect the gravest difficulties with the two imperial proxies, Bavaria's and Saxony's Electors. The foregoing illustrates how one man proceeding by strict logic came to his conclusion as a corollary to character, another proceeding by strict logic reached his solution as corollary to a situation which never arose, and both of them arrived at one and the same piece of arrant nonsense.

We do not, incidentally, make every self-contradiction in Magni's psycho-analysis a subject for reproach. Any psyche becomes a bundle of self-contradictions the moment that an effort to portray it is undertaken. Wallenstein is supposed to have been of extremely violent temper, raging also against those who without offering provocation were by some innate condition a source of irritation to him. It fits exactly what is known about him and to which the experiences of hunchbacked Colonel Fürstenberg and long-nosed Colonel Wratislaw attest. At the same time he is supposed to have used the violence of his demeanour for political purposes. It is, within limits, possible. It can indeed happen that nature is given its free rein cognizant of the effect it will produce. The truth in this instance weighs heavier however in the other scale. Wallenstein was not playing a part when he cursed and raged. Where he concealed his true self was in ceremonial restraint on his behaviour. He was sometimes, not always, shrewd enough to adapt his deportment to that of his company of the moment. We have had examples; there are more to come. He seldom indulged in pure play-acting, and then usually to his peers. A gilded phrase about peace between Christian brothers, hand on heart, eyes raised to heaven. That type of performance on his part creates a particularly distasteful impression precisely because it was so foreign to him. The mouthing was in line of business.

He had no respect for the court at Vienna whose venality and imbroglio he saw through. That is correct. His manner was abrupt even with Ferdinand. He felt respect for nothing that was stupid, weak, or both. He was like a burglar testing the doors and windows of a house. If easy of access, he breaks in. If not, he passes on. That was what Magni meant when he spoke of Wallenstein's secret cowardice: self-assured with those inferior, cowardly with those no more than his equals in strength. *Vile* is cowardly, but it was an unhappily chosen word. Wallenstein had, after all, made his way in the army as a cavalry leader. Nevertheless we know his anxiety about his acquisitions, the eternal money phobia of the multi-millionaire. And we know the bent of his strategy, imposing yet circumspect, "nothing hazarding", audacious when he felt strong, retractive when he met dangerous resistance. The "infallible proofs" for his deeply hidden lack of self-assurance, which Magni claimed to possess, may in fact have been carried around in his head. Lack of self-assurance could be why this man of power always needed the crutch provided by feeling that he had the law on his side. He had to tread the path of legality and be "in order". All the same it was only naked power that he took seriously and those who, possessing it, knew how to employ it in the shape of levies, quarter-cannon and money. He despised everything void of power – the dusty lumber of the Imperial Constitutions, written protests, long-winded loquacity, assembly voting. We grant the self-contradiction; it is a human factor. The General, Magni maintained, wanted to hinder the meeting of the electoral Diet responsible for selecting the Emperor's successor. From this he deduced that Wallenstein had in view to use the interregnum to become Emperor. Another version circulated too and was a degree more plausible – the Electors were to be disfranchised, the House of Habsburg invested hereditarily with the imperial dignity. None the less the one rendering is probably as mistaken as the other. He took little interest in constitutional questions. He had small taste for entering upon enterprises steeped in unforeseeable difficulties and whose profit to him was not plain to see. The dispute with Bavaria, he wrote good-humouredly in the following summer, was settled. "In short, they were anxious lest the Emperor desire to make the Empire hereditary." It is not the tone of a man who seriously contemplated such a venture.

Now we come to the totally exorbitant, nonsensical claim by Magni whereby Wallenstein's career is not allowed to contain any occurrence unless it has been planned and contrived through unfathomable cunning on his part. Thus it came about that he permitted Mansfeld to escape to Silesia and Hungary so as to be able in pursuit of him to distribute his troops over the Hereditary Lands. Thus it was that of malice aforethought he requested to have Count Collalto as his field-marshal for the purpose of picking at the first opportunity a quarrel with him. Great heavens! The letters of the time, those wherein he gives vent to his feelings, have to be read again to judge that – the initially incredulous stupefaction, then disillusionment and embittered fury. It needs reading again what he wrote before taking the decision to follow the freebooter to Silesia: his perplexity, his near-despair; his impression that he was in a situation where whatever he did must go awry. It was all planned beforehand and slyly brought about? It has to be read again how bitterly he waged from Bohemia and Silesia a constant battle for money, money from the Exchequer, money for the army. Reading it again and listening to the informer's whisper that he could have had money enough from the Emperor if he had only wanted, how can such interpretations be taken seriously?

The past is innocuous: it cannot hit back and it can with impunity be blethered about. The future is different. Falsely foretold it compromises the teller. We have already encountered deplorably wrong predictions by Magni. Here is a final one. "The conviction is justified that never to the end of his days will the Emperor be in a position to wrest from this man his weapons except by force." The conviction was justified until proof to the contrary two years later. The fear and trembling of the imperial ministers before they dared to send news to the commander-in-chief of his deposition was inspired by Magni and Magni's allies. All the greater the surprise when Wallenstein accepted the order with composure, bowed and went. Was there at that juncture one single person who said to Magni, "Most Reverend Sir, you have erred in this very important question and hence is it not probable that you have erred in others too?" No, no one said it, that conclusion was drawn by nobody. Correct predictions stick. Wrong ones are passed over.

Scanning the Tales of a Capuchin brings to mind again Kepler's horoscope of long ago. In certain respects the two documents resemble each other. The astrologer willy-nilly and the insidious monk painted character portraits strange enough but, regardless of incompatibilities, intrinsically consistent. Portraits of an imposing and a wicked man. Insatiably ambitious, egotistic, taciturn, nefarious and never still, calculating, daring (as Kepler underlined) and at the same time timid (as both emphasized). Kepler did not know his client even if he had personally known him because there was nothing yet to know. Valeriano knew very well his betrayed well-wisher, down to such details as that he habitually refused a request with a hoarse "It cannot be". What never-theless renders us sceptical of both delineations is that they reflected types and to that degree were brain-children rather than compiled from reality. Kepler clung, although with caution, to the astrological tradition. Magni is likely to have read what Machiavelli wrote about the Borgia offspring and will surely have been familiar with Plutarch, Suetonius, and the chapters on Tiberius in Tacitus' *Annals*. From them he took as much as, if not more, than from his own observation. Which does not go so far as to assert that everything borrowed by him from literature was necessarily unsuited to an understanding of the living man. As periods of history always resemble one another if they are only quarried deeply enough, so individuals too are always similar somehow and those out of the common rut, rulers, tyrants, more than simply somehow. Similar, but not identical. Historians must beware of formulating equations, of equations between one figure and another as of equations between type and individual. The individual never conforms to type.

There were three Wallensteins. First the man of flesh and blood, with the sombre groundwork of his soul, his harshness and greed, his secret-iveness and his copious candour, his dreams and his sufferings. Lastly the image of him fashioned for themselves by his enemies, with exacer-bated suspicions and clumsy determination of the indeterminable. "The common, false repute of this lord," Bavarian Field-Marshal von Pappen-heim wrote to Maximilian, "is so imbued into folk that I can oft only with difficulty prevent myself from believing all tidings of the like as are so circumstantially told of him, although I was by him at the very time and hour as that which is narrated as happening." And then, between these poles, was something else, something intermediate, an aura around the real person in whose creation his enemies participated and he too. After all, not every leader of his day was execrated, exalted, and intermin-ably discussed in this way. That was his fate, not that of his rivals. He provoked it without always being true to the aura.

Stralsund

OFTEN and gladly, with dramatic trimmings and enhancing its importance, have patriots told the tale that follows. "World-historic days", "the last bulwark of Protestantism"; the usurper's stealthy tiptoe withdrawal after venturing forward with dreadful oaths, a beginning to his end; David and Goliath. It was not quite like that.

In the first half of 1628 trace could be seen of what would subsequently be the predominant feature of Wallenstein's policy towards the German maritime cities – careful moderation. It was precisely because Ludwig Schwarzenberg's handiwork had been so rough that he insisted on the recall of this enthusiastic, hapless diplomat. In April he wrote to Philipp Mansfeld, the new admiral of his ghost fleet, that "great temperance" must be used towards the towns so that "they shall not peradventure be driven to desperation", meaning an alliance with the northern kings and a breach of their neutrality. The latter he recognized. He accepted Hamburg, Lübeck, Bremen for what they were, commercial republics with international interests especially in the direction of Scandinavia and only very loose ties with the Empire. He tried as far as possible not to damage their trade.

Alongside of this policy he differentiated between free imperial seaports and those subject to a territorial liege-lord, like Pomeranian Stralsund or the Mecklenburg ones, now his. Here he had a sound legal point. From Rostock and Wismar he demanded obedience in the shape of money contributions and the stationing of garrisons. This done, he was inclined to exercise paternalist care. At Wismar he went so far as to forbid his sutlers to pursue their activities so that the local shopkeepers should benefit from the soldiers' requirements. He also had hutted encampments erected in order to ease the quartering burden. All very sensible. Why did matters not work out that way at Stralsund? A number of factors were operative: the strategic situation of the city and the adjacent island of Rügen, "the best place in Pomerania", as he called it; conditions inside Stralsund as well as the relations between Stralsund and its weak-headed ruler, Bogislav XV; bad intelligence on the part of the Commander-in-Chief sending his orders from Bohemia to the distant coast; probably fits of ague and gout on days when a clear head was necessary; retardatory accidents, bungled mediations. As a pejorative term "Stralsund" is far less typical of Wallenstein than is usually imagined. It represents an exception. On no other occasion did he waste time and strength on the siege of a large town. Only once in his career did he allow "Cut all down!" when victory had been won. That was Tilly's method, which he criticized, not his.

Stralsund was really a republic, and of a fairly radical character at that. The Duke of Pomerania was not permitted to set foot on its soil without its Council's prior consent. Its aim, or that of its oligarchic leadership, manifestly was to achieve a status of direct fealty to the Emperor. The administration of church affairs lay in the town's own hands. Its representatives travelled as far afield as Moscow. Thanks to its strong merchant fleet it enjoyed a prosperity which it had no wish to share with its poverty-stricken compatriots. It was on close terms with Denmark and Sweden. To the Pomeranian ducal court at Stettin, Wolgast or wherever else it might be residing, this defiant civic pride had for long been a source of vexation. Some hope of cracking it was from time to time nourished by the social friction inside the republic. Its populace was hostile to the wealthy patriciate which had made government hereditary among its families. During the conflict which in the years 1611–16 troubled the community the party of ducal sympathizers sided with the poor, hoping to gain in the role of unselfish arbitrator a central position within the refractory free state. It did not altogether succeed, but it helped to weaken the oligarchy. The Council had to submit to the establishment of a popular assembly, the Commonalty, invested with the right to accept or reject what the senior body wanted. In the four city divisions, the "Quarters", there took place meetings of all citizens, assemblies at a basic level which in turn controlled and on occasions terrorized the Commonalty. In the days of Stralsund's approaching crisis the mayor who headed the Council was Dr Lambert Steinwich. Dutch observers reported him as being a "valiant, sensible man, well-intentioned for the defence of this city's freedom and privileges as of the whole Protestant condition. *Columna hujus civitatis*". His democratic rival and opponent was Jusquinus von Gosen, a lawyer and skilled agitator.

What had served the town well in its struggles with the Pomeranian dukes and would serve it well with another adversary was its physical situation, rather like an island, with the sea, the Strela Sund, on one side and a series of ponds and morasses encircling the remainder of its periphery. Five causeways, two of them relatively wide, three narrow and quickly cut, led to the mainland. Beyond the divisive waters were suburbs and a small forest, the Hainholz, where the villas of the rich and a number of hostelries stood. For centuries, in reliance upon natural advantage, not much attention had been paid to man-made defences, circular walls, earthworks and moats. In spring 1627 the democrats called, to von Gosen's beating of the patriotic drum, for two strong measures – the building of new fortifications, outworks, bastions, and the burning down of the suburbs which in a serious eventuality it would not be possible to defend.

The shrill demands were causally linked to the behaviour of Colonel, soon Field-Marshal, Hans Georg von Arnim. He had come to an agreement with the Pomeranian Estates and Duke Bogislav about an occupation statute. The ducal places of residence would be spared billeting, but this did not include Stralsund. The notion, even as mere rumour, that they would be expected to accommodate imperial troops had hardly reached the Stralsunders' ears before they noisily swore never to submit. "Better die honourably than plunge into shameful servitude!" A republican spirit of Dutch or, if preferred, Swiss calibre. The Stralsunders' strict, somewhat gloomy piety had indeed a streak of Calvinism deriving from Dutch influence. Straightway a start was made on throwing up entrenchments and destroying the defenceless suburbs, whereby the population of the fortified city was increased. Petitions for aid were sent to the leading Hanseatic cities, Lübeck, Danzig and Hamburg. The civil defence force, formerly furnished by the guilds and "Quarters", was reorganized on modern lines into companies, units with a strength of 350 men whose command distinguished members of the Council did not disdain. As this did not suffice, a recruiting drive was launched and brought in another thousand volunteers. The municipal artillery was overhauled. Munitions were purchased or were sought to be purchased; the sister cities were hesitant about delivery. A number of ships were manned and armed.

Arnim, whose spies roamed through Stralsund, knew all this. It may have been that the city's hectic activity, meant to fend off the enemy, worked like a magnet instead. Only now did it cross the mind of Wallenstein's deputy that commutation was not enough and that Stralsund must bow the knee. He had already seized the island of Rügen. To sail from there into Stralsund harbour took half an hour; Denmark was twelve hours away. That is, if ships were available, which to Arnim at present they were not. The incomparable benefits offered by Stralsund's harbour preoccupied imperial strategists even more than its citizens' fractious patriotism.

The Council, for all its boldly warlike measures, vacillated in the way that in similar situations the wealthy usually do. They were badly on their own. The Emperor, their legitimate overlord if only in theory and most of the time very far away, was through the latest turn in affairs anything but distant. In the person of Arnim, his general, he lay encamped in neighbouring Greifswald with sundry thousand men, was gradually moving his regiments on Stralsund, and threatened woe to the city if he entered by force. Should a reasonable concession be made? Should they buy themselves off? Arnim had demanded payment of a hundred thousand taler. The senators succeeded in persuading the irate Commonalty in principle to accept this demand and, as a sign of willingness, to pay a first instalment of thirty thousand taler. While emissaries travelled back and forth on this negotiation, the imperialists by a *coup de main* occupied Dänholm, an islet which dominated Stralsund harbour. At once, in spite of Arnim's soothing assurances, the Stralsunders threw up earthworks and emplaced cannon there. They were seamen enough to appreciate the true meaning of this breach of faith. What took place thereafter in the shape of pacificatory gestures, temporary promises, seven signed stipulations, simply served to gain time while both sides tried to improve their situation. After the occupation of Dänholm a state of undeclared war existed. There is no evidence to show that Wallenstein was behind this development of events. In view of the implicit trust reposed by him in Arnim, it is conceivable that the Colonel acted on his own initiative. At any rate the incident had occurred and one thing led to another.

At the beginning the Generalissimo had taken the Stralsund business as little seriously as Arnim did. Between New Year and the end of May he wrote his local deputy no more than five letters on the subject of this growingly malignant problem. An astonishingly small number in the light of his correspondence habits. Stralsund certainly cannot be said to have been causing him constant anxiety and rage. That came on suddenly, like a fit, and did not last long.

Meanwhile, and without his properly realizing it, the seaport acquired European significance. The reason was that general hostilities slumbered, Germany was conquered and tamed, and Denmark too with the exception of its islands. The northern kings continued to hold sway over the seas, lying in wait for an opportunity to land on the German coast. Stralsund, however, was offering resistance to the imperialists, the Spaniards, and the Pope, as common parlance loosely went. Stralsund alone. The city attracted to itself the Habsburg, or Wallenstein's, might and the fragmentary remainders of the great Protestant coalition. To its own, not altogether pleased, surprise it slipped into a partly real, partly symbolic major role. At Madrid the Duke of Olivares regarded the siege of Stralsund as a most highly welcome event. So did King Christian at Copenhagen and King Gustavus Adolphus in Prussia, although for the opposite yet inherently identical reason.

Early in March a Danish envoy visited the city. His message had a rough ring to it. Stralsund could have royal favour and in an emergency aid if it remained true to the Protestant cause; inexorable hostility by Denmark and Sweden alike if it betrayed it – as a year later Christian was to do – and granted the Papists fire and water. The senate wriggled. Thoroughly uncertain what to do, it was involuntarily forced into the posture of a heroic defender just as Wallenstein was into that of an aggressive attacker. The alternatives, it pleaded, were not intrinsically as stark as that. The situation, God be praised, was not quite the way it looked to Copenhagen. The envoy was treated to polite nothings. Nevertheless henceforward the Stralsunders, the rebellious democrats as much as the appeasement-minded Council, knew that Danish help was there for the asking. They only had to take the hazard and seek succour. The mere possibility strengthened the party of defiance. From the very outset of the Dänholm occupation it had been questionable who was being blockaded by whom, the city by the islet or the islet by the city. The latter would be the case if the city dared to take advantage of its superiority in ships. In March it did, allowing no Arnim vessel to approach Dänholm and starving out the occupiers until in April they were forced to retire. Nothing could have mortified more deeply Arnim's self-esteem, no less intense for being well-concealed. He had been made to look ridiculous in the eyes of the commander who had placed blind faith in him. Victory would have rendered him more complaisant than a defeat of this kind. At sea he was foiled. On land, with fourteen thousand men under his orders, he was much more than a match for the Stralsunders. He exploited the fact by drawing his noose tighter, surrounding the town with dams, and subjecting its post to strict censorship. Through skilfully positioned culverins he kept under control the narrow channels separating Rügen from the coast. His preparations to drain the ponds protecting Stralsund on the land side were plain. The result was that when in April and again in May fresh Danish emissaries arrived in the intimidated town, they were given less reluctant audience. Soldiers, ships, and even fortification specialists were, it is true, declined. Not only was everything possible already being done by hasty erection of bastions and lines of palisades, but the acceptance of manpower from Denmark would have meant an open breach with the Emperor. It was one thing to defend one's rights, another to admit the Empire's foe within the gates. On the other hand material support, guns, ammunition and other accessories, would be gladly received by the city fathers. They were moving by small steps along a path which they had not wanted to tread at all and whose end could now surely with a little sophistication be foreseen.

Where Denmark had a hand, Sweden could not remain behind. Gustavus Adolphus knew the strategic significance of Stralsund as well as Wallenstein. In accordance with the rules of the power political mechanism these two men were willy-nilly opponents. The Swedish monarch too was attracted by the strong though peripherally meagre magnet, the strategically important though otherwise petty place of eighteen thousand inhabitants. "We do not wish to let the Emperor have Stralsund if we can forestall him. Denmark and the Sound would thereby be lost and Sweden would be next, though for a time the peril might be averted." Still in Prussia and engaged in fighting the Poles, Gustavus Adolphus sent the Stralsunders five tons of gunpowder for which they had vainly asked their ally Danzig. No conditions were attached. The accompanying message stated that mutual help was customary between friends and asked why they had not in good season fully relied on him. Again, a tiny step. Surely in time of need it is permissible to accept a present, an unsought, disinterested present.

Now Arnim wanted to put an end to the matter before what was on the simmer came to the boil. From the middle of May he began by day to plague the town with bombardments, at night with surprise attacks. Neither obtained their overall objective, but they sufficed to stimulate a mood of desperation among the populace and leaders alike. Arnim, with religious as well as no doubt more mundane considerations in mind, proposed an eight-day truce for the Whit holiday. If the Stralsunders stopped first and for the period of the feast-days ceased all fortification work, he would follow. The city demanded simultaneity, not a first and an afterwards, and that Arnim should evacuate the positions just captured. The sham-humane scheme ran aground, the bombardments continued. Fervent supplications sped across the seas to the northern kings: a foe like this could not be withstood for long; materials were not enough, men were wanted, also demy-cannon royal, muskets, serpentine powder; and everything quickly, very quickly now. Danish help came even quicker than expected because it was under way before Stralsund had asked for it. A regiment of wild Scots which Copenhagen had been only too glad to get rid of, Danes, and Germans, a thousand men in all. Their commander was Colonel Heinrich Holk, of Slesvig origin. He was just twenty-nine, capable, brutal, and predatory. Edging past Arnim's coastal batteries, the flotilla safely made harbour. From that moment the Stralsunders were no longer captains of their political fate. They were free to continue the struggle, no longer free to relinquish it unscathed. Their abettors were the stronger party, a relationship which they would politely hide – although this was not a streak native to Holk's nature – for as long as their wishes coincided with those of their protégés.

At the moment there were no differences. Sombrely glowing enthus-iasm throbbed through the threatened community. A council of war was constituted. Its members were the senior Danish and Scots officers, Mayor Steinwich, a few Councillors, and the democrat von Gosen. Horrible penalties were imposed for defeatists, among them skinning alive and public exhibition of the trophy as deterrent to others. Death was the punishment for blasphemers. The most painful expiations lay in store for guzzlers, gluttons, and in short any who drew offensive attention to their person. Seeing that the alliance was a multilingual confederation, all derogatory talk between the nationalities, Danes, Germans, Scots, was forbidden. The defenders included Bohemians. These were never missing when anti-imperial business was to hand. New songs were composed, their authors barely known:

> Eyes open therefore Germany,
> Mark what this Wallenstein army
> Has up its sleeve.
> If unmoved you put up with it,
> The danger is to your gullet,
> Brain and heart shall heave.

A prose-writer composed the manifesto *Hanseatic Clarion* to admonish the cowardly sister-cities as to their true interest. The domino theory was spelled out exactly as it was done by the opposing side. Let Stralsund fall and the fate of all the Hanse towns was sealed, thereafter that of the Netherlands, Denmark, and Sweden, while finally the last of the Empire's Protestant Estates, Brandenburg and Saxony, would be finished off like fried sausage or gobbled instead of a sweet. It had begun in Bohemia, Moravia, Austria; there it would end. "Nothing is achieved by womanish wailings." There must immediately be common action, *nihil cunctando* (brooking no delay). The enemy's supplies must be cut. Re-arm. Trust in God, His Royal Danish Majesty, that valiant Hero and Gideon, Gustavus Adolphus, high and mighty, invincible King of Sweden. Stralsund pamphlets of this kind were matched by others which fluttered through northern Germany, harbingers and promoters of a sympathy and excitement incomparable to any since the Bohemian revolution. Did Wallenstein realize what a hornet's nest he had stirred up?

On 2 June, finishing his long and eventful winter vacation, he started from Gitschin with an escort of eight hundred horse. For where? Presumably Mecklenburg. Properly speaking, there was this year no campaign to lead. At the moment there was no one against whom it had to or could be led. He had had enough and the same held good for the imperial troops, encamped at various points from Jutland to Pomerania. Stralsund was an irritating side-issue. Presumably it would not need his personal attention.

He took his journey easily, making several days' stay along his route: Friedland, Sagan, Frankfurt-on-Oder, Berlin. From Sagan he wrote to Arnim. "As the Stralsunders have tolerably well had the lid closed down on them, an agreement should be concluded whereby if they wish to become bad boys again they will none the less not be able to." At Frankfurt he was without palpable reason befallen by a fit of ague and a heavy bout of depression. There were hardly any external causes to prompt it. No one, least of all he himself, could predict whether the ague would show retardative effects as was sometimes the case or prove grimly stimulative, as it did on this occasion. "I see that they of Stralsund persist in their mulishness, wherefore I am resolved to deal seriously with them." Orders were published for three regiments to march on Stralsund without a minute's delay. Brandenburg and Pomerania were imperiously bidden to contribute artillery pieces because "where there is enough cannon, there something can be done". As suddenly as they had infested his soul, as abruptly did the ravens fly away. At Berlin, the House of Brandenburg's miserable little capital, he was gay and enchanted the princesses with his company; the Elector was lodged at Königsberg. On 25 June, at Neustadt, he learned of Holk's arrival at Stralsund three weeks earlier. The news made him thoughtful. "It causes me anxiety that from day to day the scamps receive more help.

I have now through Duke Franz Albrecht [of Lauenburg] notified the Duke in Pomerania that if they will accept a garrison pledged in loyalty to the Emperor, the Duke, and the city, I am prepared to desist from the siege." That remained his stipulation, not really an extravagant one. He was not happy about this undertaking and he wanted a compromise. He no longer aimed at domination of the city – "domination" was anyway fairly meaningless as some form of agreement always had to prevail – but he wanted assurance of its neutrality. He gladly entertained Brandenburg mediation proposals.

The old Pomeranian dynasty had drunk itself to death and Bogislav XV was the last of the Greif dynasty.* Brandenburg had the best claims to the Pomeranian inheritance. This explains its stake in settlement of the squabble. The other mediator was Pomerania as represented by its knightly Estate, its court, its Privy Councillors. Their position was that they hoped to achieve through Wallenstein what had miscarried on account of the Stralsund democrats – a reduction of the city whereby it would forget its dreams of autonomy and become plain Pomeranian again. A haircut for Samson. On the strength of this speculation the Privy Councillors from the outset worked towards a compromise indirectly to the advantage of the Empire's highest authority, directly to their own, the dukedom's. They played the go-betweens for camp and senate. The latter they warned of dire consequences, the former they tried to inspire with kindly clemency. To be in collusion with them, and therefore indirectly with Arnim, was the accusation thrown by the Stralsund democrats in the teeth of the peace-party inside its walls, the rich and the timid.

Since the arrival of Holk and the Scots it was late in the day for any moderation. It became still later when on 30 June the Swedes arrived in eight ships. On board were six hundred soldiers, a Colonel Rosladin, a Lieutenant-Colonel Düval, ordnance officers, engineers, siege-works specialists, and a diplomat, Filip Sadler, Gustavus Adolphus' most experienced negotiator. He was the first to land. The ships were to await what he achieved before they disposed of their coveted cargo. This was Gustavus Adolphus' approach to business, a tactfully supple but clear diplomacy in contrast to Christian's alcoholic bluster. Sadler demanded a formal treaty of alliance, initially for twenty years, between Sweden and Stralsund. A few clauses prettified the connection for those who attached importance to prettiness. The alliance was to be defensive,

---

* *Greif*=griffin, the fabulous creature with an eagle's head and wings and lion's body (translator's note).

offensive only where this appeared necessary to the King. It was not to affect Stralsund's obligations to the Emperor, the Empire, and their own sovereign – whatever that may have meant. The Swedish auxiliaries were to remain under the general direction of the city's government – whatever that too may have meant. For political purposes, nothing. Mayor Steinwich, the patriot, had wanted to maintain the republic's independence against Emperor and northern kings alike. At this juncture when Wallenstein, the real man as well as the frightening phantom, was still a day's journey from Stralsund, Steinwich surrendered independence. He could at any time have had similar, better terms from the Generalissimo. What prevented such a compromise was the myth attached to his name, the reputation for bottomless wickedness and lust for power which preceded him, the bogy man of the Papacy, the whore of Babylon whose puppet he allegedly was although in reality that was anything but the case. Once again a tragicomedy of errors. The apex of error reached, the two parties with utmost bitterness succumbed to their respective suppositions – the Stralsunders that they were defending the freedom already lost to the Danes and Swedes, Wallenstein that he must "punish" the city and force it into an "obedience" of whose shape and outcome he had only the vaguest notions.

Four days after signature of the treaty with Sweden he arrived in front of Stralsund and made his headquarters in one of the Hainholz villas. In the end it had gone without saying what his destination must be. He too, the commander-in-chief, General of the Oceanic and Baltic Seas, had become irresistibly drawn to this ridiculous magnet. Shortly after arrival he is said to have exclaimed that the town should yield even if bound to Heaven by chains. The witnesses are trustworthy and the oath is not so terrible. A customary formula, rather. But people in his position should take care. In a later age he would have had a few hardened public relations men at his elbow to render him less vulnerable, write his speeches, deny or soften the tone of unreflected utterances. As yet the profession did not exist. His scribblers were clumsy dolts whom he rarely used because he regarded power as more important than repute. He who was supposed to be so taciturn and unfathomably cunning, weighing every word, let himself go without concern for the impression created by the swashbuckling phrases tumbling from his lips. When eventually the city would not let itself be torn down from Heaven, that single expression compromised him more than the business itself. Subsequently it was even depicted on canvas, the would-be all-mighty's arms strained high to the sky, his eyes glowing with rage and arrogance.

During his journey he had on several occasions received from the Stralsunders assurances as to their loyalty and declarations of their aggrieved
indignation. His reply had been that he required deeds, not words, and
that their link with the Danes, the Empire's enemy, seemed to him very
remarkable. If however they were truly repentant, it was his habit to
exercise mercy towards contrite sinners and they should send a delegation to where he would shortly be, in his forward headquarters outside
their city. On arrival he found no delegation awaiting him and decided
to attack at once. The redoubts, covered works, trenches were long since
prepared, the means assembled. Some 25,000 soldiers, including reinforcements, heavy artillery, quarter-cannon, and demy-quarter-cannon
were on hand in unrecorded number.

The occurrence of such an assault on a fortified place is probably
easier stated than visualized. In this instance it lasted two days and two
nights, with bombardments by day to break down the defences and
terrify the inhabitants, the serious attacks after midnight. Although
directed simultaneously against all four gates, the onslaughts concentrated on the Frankentor in the north-east and the Kniepertor in the
north-west. They opened on the two broader causeways and were
defended by the strongest outworks. Four assault columns of a thousand
men each pressed forward, one after another, were thrown back by a
hail of shot, and pressed forward again because they must. Hundreds of
horsemen on their flanks plunged through the water past the defences
to take the defenders in the rear. These launched counter-attacks. No
pike could pierce the steel of those whom magic protected, no bullet
harm them; they had to be struck dead with maces and hatchets.* The
shrieks of the dying mingled with the desperate cheers of the living.
Grenades exploded as they dropped in powder-casks. The Duke awaited
reports in the Hainholz, a little far from the fighting, it might seem.
The Swedish commander, Rosladin, was mortally wounded; his deputy,
Düval, a prisoner; Bubna, a Czech leader of the Scottish contingent,
dead; its chief, Major Monroe, was carried back on a stretcher. During
the second night the outworks fell into the hands of the besiegers. The
besieged retained only the gates and the ravelins, small artificial outward-
jutting mounds. Inside the city panic reigned. Exhaustion, hunger,
demoralization. A third night could mean the end, with vengeance to

---

* The superstition that certain individuals enjoyed such supernatural support
was very frequent among European soldiery. As will be seen in the penultimate
chapter (p. 840), the Irish dragoons who had to deal with Trčka credited him
with its possession (translator's note).

follow, the wolf inside the door. The senate with gall in its heart decided on a message: His Princely Grace, a very valiant imperial Prince, could not desire the further bloodshed of obedient subjects and Christians. His Princely Grace should for a space cease firing, making approaches, all other hostilities, and with an assurance of safe escort condescend to receive a deputation from the city. That was on 9 July, in the morning. On the same day a plea for additional aid, as swiftly as possible, went to the King of Sweden.

If Wallenstein wanted to quell the town, he should have continued his assaults; it was ripe to fall. His soldiery too is said to have suffered horribly and that a state of uproar prevailed among those sound in life and limb. Maybe, but that does not furnish the true reason for his attitude. Regardless of blood-steeped appearances, he did *not* want to quell the town, or would not have been glad to do so. To coerce it, yes. To take it by storm, no. He knew too well what would follow and the effect it would produce throughout northern Germany. An agreement, he wrote to the Emperor, was better "than if entry had been achieved by force. First, because of the blood-bath which would thereby have been inevitable, causing great bitterness among all and being condemned as a great tyranny. . . ." Making a virtue of necessity or sour grapes have been the comments, but it would be better to see it in the context of his policy. At any rate he answered the Stralsunders within the hour that he was ready for a discussion. He declined an armistice, agreeing only that fighting should cease for a quarter of an hour, or at most half an hour, along the road which the representatives would take. Bombardments during the succeeding days continued, but not the nocturnal attacks, and it is clear that while negotiations proceeded the battle lost any authentic fury.

The reception of the city fathers was gracious. They were allowed to be seated, which was thought an honour. He listened patiently to their long-winded speeches. He explained his position. If the town was honestly willing to return to its allegiance, a general pardon would be proclaimed and all forgotten. Dänholm had been the original issue, but he no longer cared about that and they could keep it. Nor did he insist upon an imperial garrison, only on one which had taken its oath to the Emperor, Pomerania, Brandenburg, and Stralsund itself. Money was also largely a matter of indifference to him, he had enough – a too rosy presentation of his financial state – but a hundred thousand taler once having been agreed, the outstanding seventy thousand must be paid. And let them not suppose that he did not keep his word with heretics, all his actions gave the lie to such a suspicion. He concluded with a paternal warning to take opportunity by the forelock. *Fronte capillata est, post haec occasio calva* (take occasion by the forelock, behind it comes the cranium).

This, badly as things stood on that 10 July for Stralsund, was unexpectedly mild behaviour on the part of the feared Generalissimo while the terms were unexpectedly moderate too. Essentially sensible, they were appropriate if the townsmen meant their offer honestly. At the moment they probably did. In the long run they were not in a position to do so if only because of their Danish and Swedish allies. Here Wallenstein's vision was blurred. He must either not have gone as far as during recent weeks and the last four nights he had, or he should have been ready to proceed with utmost dispatch right to the final horrors which he wanted to avoid.

Inside the city agitated debates ensued. The senate, discouraged and wavering from the start, would have preferred to lend its ear to the Roman's warning. More critical was the attitude of the Commonalty, the "Quarters". How large would the occupation force be, who was to be in charge, who was to pay? The Danes as well as the Swedish colonel on his death-bed implored the Council to stand fast. They could not accept responsibility and withdraw unless the imperialists were to evacuate the whole of Pomerania. Duke Bogislav's advisers, as always trying to derive some advantage on their suzerain's behalf, put in their oar from the other side. Their chatter served to aggravate instead of to assuage matters. It increased the resistance of those citizens who did not want to be degraded to the status of ordinary subjects. Their courage was cheered not only by the landing of four hundred Danish auxiliaries but invigorated rather than damped by the resumed Wallenstein bombardment. On its heels came a sudden offer of truce, stimulated, it seems, by two days' downpour which caused the imperialist soldiery torture. Advance posts stood to their hips in water. To the townsmen the offer was doubly welcome. First, as such. Secondly, it showed how uncomfortable their adversary felt. No longer quite so welcome was the return of Colonel Holk with a thousand Scotsmen and a plentiful load of ammunition. Shortly before Wallenstein's arrival and the culmination of the crisis Holk had left for Copenhagen to get married. Back again, his conduct was more that of a brusque superior than an ally. It gave the peace-party food for thought, but not such as they could any longer utter. The Council was past being able to insist with the Danes and the Swedes and their own radicals on what it really wanted. On 21 July the

Pomeranian mediators were told, in answer to their proposals, that without prejudice to honour and conscience the Council was ready to express contrition, to swear allegiance to Emperor and suzerain, and within practicable time limits also to raise some funds. The proviso about a garrison was not however capable of fulfilment because under such a requirement it would not be possible to disengage from the foreign levies. They were, it might have been added, allies from whom it would no longer be feasible to escape one way or another. Moreover no agreement would under any condition be ratified before the besiegers had withdrawn.

The next logical step for Wallenstein would have been to renew the assault. He did not. He longed to extricate himself from this business into which he had slithered and whose perilous complications were no figment of his imagination. A contemporary calculation claimed that he had lost twelve thousand men during the attacks and through sickness. Such estimates tended to be on a generous scale and in this instance may have been an exaggeration, but certainly the siege was having a poor effect on both the number and the morale of his troops. Gustavus Adolphus was said to be planning a sudden sally against the port of Kolberg. More reliable reports spoke of the troubles being prepared by King Christian, who was threatening Rügen and could any day prove a menace to the mainland, whether Pomeranian or Mecklenburg territory. This was the sore point which the obduracy of Stralsund underlined – the northern kings dominated the seas, now as heretofore. Consequently it was inadmissible to persist where persistence was already too protracted. What, Wallenstein asked Arnim on 19 July, did the strength of the garrison really matter? "What touches on the withdrawal, I too desire not to create any difficulties. . . . Therefore I bid you treat with them after such fashion that we can come out with honour and soon depart." Suddenly the substance had been surrendered. Preservation of appearances remained the sole issue.

Weak-headed Bogislav and his councillors would do for that. With the utmost speed Wallenstein concluded with Pomerania, its Duke and Estates, the treaty which he could not obtain from the Stralsunders. Pomerania stood security that Stralsund would perform all that was agreed, namely, to eject the foreign troops and in their stead accept a garrison sworn according to this and that formula, deliver up money, tear down the newly erected bastions, and so on, and so on. Were these conditions not fulfilled, the Emperor could at his own discretion seek indemnity from the dukedom. This, it must be emphasized, he could in any case do as Pomerania was and continued under occupation by imperial forces. The treaty was in this respect not much good and not much good in any other either. That Bogislav would without imperial aid be able to force the town into any action which with imperial aid had not proved possible was a ridiculous illusion which Wallenstein for his part never entertained. What he wanted, and nothing more, was some sealed compact to permit him to withdraw "with honour". On 25 July, that secured, he left, accompanied by his personal staff, eager to take possession of Mecklenburg and from there to reorganize the defences of northern Germany. For another week Arnim had to reap what he had sown. With Danish naval movements in the area of Barth and Warnemünde unequivocal, he received an order to break camp without the loss of a moment and move to Triebsee with everything capable of being marched or carried. Even without the loss of a moment it takes days to raise a siege on this scale. It requires "more time and trouble than just putting horses between the shafts to go for a drive", as Wallenstein had somewhat didactically told Duke Bogislav.

And now, though admittedly not for long, the jubilation of the townsfolk over their deliverance. The first careful, as yet incredulous jostling from out of the confining walls, the sniffing of the scent of those stolen away, the plundering where there was anything left to plunder. Upon the heels of the debouchment jeering jingles to replace the battle-hymns. Jeers against the Pope, however little he had to do with the imbroglio, jeers against Arnim the Lutheran apostate, jeers against Wallenstein, against him in particular:

> Thy God thou didst forget
> When thus thou wast so pert
> To tumble down the goodly town;
> Yea, though to High Heaven were it
> Bound with chains, 'twas thy lust
> To raze and ground it in the dust.
> 'Fore Stralsund did the bolt strike thee,
> Had ague but taken thee to sea,
> The bolt ne'er down had striken thee.

On damage followed derision. The damage was his, however he might try to screen himself against the fact, and the blame was his too. Had he treated the town, which was a rear vassal in name only, as he treated those other imperial seaports, Lübeck and Hamburg, had he left it in peace and quiet and required only peace and quiet from it, it is conceivable that it would have stayed neutral. Stralsund straightway assumed his demands to be more vindictive than he meant them. It reacted accordingly. He reacted in turn. It abandoned its neutrality to grow into the first Swedish base on German soil, a development that he had wanted to prevent and which the Stralsunders had by no means greatly desired. He allowed himself to be attracted by the false magnet, became stuck to it in front of everyone's eyes, tore himself free when it was late although not too late, and accepted the derision.

Something remains to be added. In the Stralsund affair Wallenstein did not have the imperial court behind him, at least not the party which sided with Bavaria and had long been fomenting trouble against him. Imperial Vice-Chancellor von Stralendorf went so far as to let the city *ex officio* know that in the highest quarters its acceptance of a garrison was by no means insisted upon and that the Generalissimo would be instructed in this sense. Thereby he gave the Stralsunders the chance to cite the imperial will against the imperial commander-in-chef. Stralendorf went too far, though. A later letter from Ferdinand to Wallenstein expressed doubts, no veto. To deduce from Stralendorf's opposition that trains of thought at court were more responsible and moderate, more pacific than at army headquarters is wrong. The matter is simple. There was a party which always passed hostile judgement on whatever course Wallenstein took. Let him do something provocative and its fault-finding was clamant. Let him object to much worse provocations and forthwith this same party would adopt, commend, and see them carried through. Professional politicians talk and act far less often by reason of a proximate cause than the decent man in the street fancies. They fulminate against an enemy or rival in the power-game as circumstances dictate and what they recently said is soon forgot.

For a few months Stralsund lay wreathed in a halo of European admiration. Thereafter life continued in the greyness of everyday reality. Such post-victory atmosphere is something of a disappointment. Heroic times are harder but finer. "Here," reported Sadler, the Swedish envoy, "the fruit of earlier action begins to ripen; the formation of cliques, distrust and antipathy between authority and the people . . . in such manner that ever since the departure [of Wallenstein] everything takes an evil turn." Striking a balance, the Stralsunders could draw no conclusion but that their independence had been saved and lost.

The Danish mercenaries disappeared. The number of Swedes rose until their strength was 5700. Their commander was nominated Governor, however Mayor, Council, and Commonalty cared to debate.

Soon the original treaty was in the eyes of the King of Sweden not far-reaching enough. He demanded "actual submission", the sheer incorporation of Stralsund into the Swedish kingdom. In theory it did not immediately happen, but it gradually happened in reality, and at the end of the great war it obtained formal confirmation too. The free city fell to the status of a small Swedish provincial town. That it remained for two hundred years. An epoch during which the Stralsunders were probably neither much unhappier than they would have been with a different outcome to the events of AD 1628 nor yet much happier either.

Mecklenburg

I was a well-populated land of about three hundred thousand inhabitants which Wallenstein in July 1628 entered. Incomparably more spacious than Friedland, the revenue it yielded was smaller because hitherto the resolute sovereignty capable of creating industries and ingeniously promoting trade had been missing. Perhaps too the Mecklenburgers did not much care for modern hustle and bustle. The territory, in spite of its much indented coastline, had something land-locked, remote about it and lacked proper links with the navigable rivers to east and west. Right behind the dunes and fishing villages lay fat pastures and meadows where black-and-white spotted cattle grazed. Spreading woods shadowed the waters of intertwining lakes. The nobility lived in unassuming castles, the peasants tilled acres which were still largely their own (a condition soon, though not in Wallenstein's day, to be changed), and the distantly scattered towns like Malchin, Plan, and Grabow with their single main street, square market-place, town hall, church, and cemetery did not look much different from Bohemian provincial townships. Often, as at Gitschin, their inhabitants were townsmen and peasants in one. Doberan, Dargun, and other ancient monasteries bore witness to Cistercian labours, but the monks were long gone. Sound Lutheran sermons were preached from the pulpits of the brick churches, rising like citadels in the better-off towns. Monuments of an even more distant past, heathen funerary mounds, and Cyclopean ramparts were there for such as had eyes to see. The duchy took its name from one of them, Micklinborg near Wismar, where presumably had lived the ancestors of the expelled dukes Adolf Friedrich and Johann Albrecht, direct descendants from Wendish princes and undeniably rulers with deep roots in their land although the claim to have two thousand years' royal blood running in their veins may be taken as a slight exaggeration. Their successor, he who had despoiled them, did not investigate the point.

In a category of their own were the seaports Rostock and Wismar. Theoretically obedient to their local suzerain, in practice pursuing an autonomous policy, their gaze was fixed northward and westward in the direction of Lübeck, Hamburg, and as far away as the Dutch. Their populations were a mixture of merchant community imbued with civic pride, refractory working class, and seafaring folk, rather as in Stralsund. These were towns whom Wallenstein, with the instinct of a feudal liege-lord and royal servitor, did not trust. Their profit-yielding activities, on the other hand, roused the respect of the economist in him. Rostock possessed a centre of higher scholarship, the oldest in northern Germany. That filled him with mixed feelings too. He did not at all care for the spirit of unrest which could emanate from such an institution, but the lustre attaching to an overlordship which numbered men of learning among its luminaries greatly appealed to him. He held the sciences in deep esteem. So far his dream of Gitschin university had borne no fruit. To have at least a famous foreign cultural establishment within his territory could only be a source of satisfaction.

Güstrow lay approximately in the centre of the country. Its palace, a modern building by a Lombard architect, dominated the town and, unlike Schwerin's island-fortress, was in an excellent state of upkeep. Its three-tiered arcaded courtyard, towers, and battlements closely resembled the great Bohemian houses. On 28 August 1628 Wallenstein, coming from the scene of his superficial defeat, Stralsund, arrived at the city boundary and tolerated the reception prepared for him by the Estates which recently had pleaded so loyally against the expulsion of their traditional masters. "'Tis true, ceremonies serve me little, but that they shall not take it for offence, I shall let it proceed."

The palace he found empty. Duke Johann Albrecht had on his doleful departure taken with him whatever was capable of being moved in order to turn it into money. Even if he had left his furnishings, they would hardly have sufficed the new tenant. Wallenstein, the mortgagor and not yet invested Duke of Mecklenburg, none the less behaved as if that was who he was. Orders went immediately to his always docile banker and buyer, de Witte. Fine Dutch bed-linen, damask table-linen, tapes-tries, and gold-embossed leather wall-hangings were to be shipped in thirty-five big sea-chests from Amsterdam to Hamburg. Also carpets from Venice; blue, gleaming, short-piled velvet from Lucca; thirty thousand taler worth of table-ware from Sepossi, Genoa's most famous silversmith. Equally imposing alterations were planned outside the palace. "It does not bid a very promising beginning," commented a patriot worriedly, "that Friedland now lets it be heard that he will not quit Mecklenburg unless he is driven away at the point of the sword."

What confirms this impression is the activity at many official buildings. In Güstrow the new church is almost demolished, the Chancellery, the riding school, the tennis court, and the nearby houses must also make room." The "new church", the Calvinist temple with a crude wooden table to replace the altar which Johann Albrecht had had erected from the stones of a dismantled monastery was, to the applause of the Lutherans, torn down and the stonework used for an annex to the palace. Three years later Johann Albrecht on his return dismantled the annex so that no trace of the usurper should be left. The bricks and mortar may truly be said to have experienced a political fate. I do not know the use to which they are currently put.

Wallenstein settled in, as he was accustomed to do, on a grand and permanent scale. The palace was quite incapable of accommodating all the eight hundred employees of his court establishment. Where they lived is unknown. Probably the best citizens' houses were rented on their behalf. A tower and observatory was hastily constructed for the ducal mathematician and astrologer.

The transformation of Güstrow, the sleepy little country town, into the residence of one of Europe's richest princes, or of one who at least led his life along the most splendiferous lines, was a spectacular occurrence but a side-issue. Wallenstein had begun to rule his new realm while he was still at Gitschin. Now he took the matter seriously in hand. From July 1628 until July 1629 it remained one of his three principal interests. The other two were the war and European policy in the narrower and broadest sense. The former could at present be conducted laxly and, so to speak, with his left hand because the enemy was busy celebrating. The latter remained intricate enough. The possession of Mecklenburg was furthermore inseparable from major policy factors. He had taken it because opportunity beckoned, but he had also taken it so that neither Danes nor Swedes should be able to have it. His possession was not secure until at least one of the northern kingdoms abandoned the dislodged dukes and recognized their successor. What, to mention a hopeful possibility, if old Bogislav of Pomerania should once again prove to be the fool for which Wallenstein held him by making common cause with the Stralsunders and waging war against the Emperor? Nothing could be more desirable. "I would that the fancy befell him," he confided to Arnim, "for then Pomerania would mighty plainly be Mecklenburg's due." Barely had he landed in the second before he was speculating on its expansion. Pomerania, meaning Cis-Pomerania with Barth, Stralsund, Greifswald, Wolgast, and the islands of Rügen and Usedom, would indeed have formed an entity, scenically and strategically. In this instance it did not come to that. By the time Bogislav perforce concluded an alliance with the King of Sweden, Wallenstein was no longer in a position to take advantage of his false step.

A foreigner who could not understand the local gibberish, he wanted to move carefully, availing himself of established institutions and office-holders in so far as they were serviceable and prepared to serve. The nobility, in particular. "I am willing to employ the nobility in the councils as well as on other business of the land and about my person more than the precedent dukes have done."

The nobility followed the call. Although at first hesitant and suspicious, they came and put themselves at his disposal. A Gebhard von Moltke accepted the presidency of the Privy Council. A Hans Heinrich von der Lühe became president of the Exchequer. "What touches on Hans Heinrich, I know not what to make of it that he hath so soon become a good Wallenstein man," one of the expelled duchesses complained bitterly. True enough, exiles do not understand such things. Those who had stayed behind saw things differently. The new ruler was on the spot, his determination steely, his power overwhelming, and the hope that he would quickly disappear again small. Provided that he was obeyed, his personality seemed to be extremely sensible, conciliatory. Therefore why not render the land the services which in the present cruel circumstances had to be rendered? Why not be paid for them? Court appointments as well as principal government posts were in part filled from local resources.

Matters would run even more smoothly with Mecklenburg's nobility if its rising generation were promptly taken in hand. A number of young knights were sent by Wallenstein to Gitschin to study under the tuition of the Jesuits and then to do service at his court. That the youngsters were led to mass is probable but not, in view of their tutors' shrewd broad-mindedness, altogether certain.

If young Mecklenburgers were transplanted to Bohemia, there was also a cross-fertilization of young Bohemians in Mecklenburg. Five Waldsteins and Harrachs, one of them little Franz whom the Jesuits had underhand tried to make one of their own, were placed in a boarding-school, a knightly academy, which Wallenstein founded at Güstrow on the lines of the Gitschin model. The "lords" came from Bohemia, for there was no such native Estate; the mere knights or esquires, twelve in theory but in practice probably only seven, came from Mecklenburg. The Güstrow academy was neither a myth nor merely a plan, as used to be believed. It flourished, albeit for only two years. Its governor was a Walloon. The staff consisted of a French language master, an Italian fortifications expert, a fencing master, a dancing master, a chaplain, a doctor, an apothecary, four servants for the lords, three for the knights, five grooms, and other ministering spirits. The annual overheads amounted to 6282 imperial taler. There is no evidence that, as at Gitschin, it was a Jesuit school. None the less it was doubtless Catholic-conducted and one of its purposes to befriend in a discreet way Mecklenburg's gentle-born youth with the Old Religion. It was also meant to help and create an international, so to speak Wallenstein, aristocracy. Had the founder been able to acquire a principality in northern Italy, a scheme with which he sometimes toyed, he would have arranged for Venetian youngsters to romp with Bohemians and Mecklenburgers. There was something of an educationist in him, linking up with his love of order and the pleasure that he took in organization. He enjoyed seeing boys brought up in accordance with his instructions and under his surveillance.

He left the Church undisturbed and unmolested under the supervision of its consistory. Pastors were appointed and paid as formerly – I have counted sixteen who were inducted under Wallenstein – and allowed to preach as they liked so long as they showed due respect to the suzerain. They readily did. For a Catholic, and the Generalissimo of Emperor Ferdinand the Protestant Exorcist at that, to rule a Lutheran land was not quite so topsy-turvy as it may seem. His predecessor at Güstrow, Johann Albrecht, had been a Calvinist. We know how envenomed were the relations between the two Protestant sects. The Calvinist chapel was replaced by a Catholic one consecrated for the Duke and his court. That was all. In Friedland he pushed forward the Counter-Reformation dilatorily and without zeal because he had to. In Mecklenburg he did not have to and was content. He kept his pledge to the Estates, made at the enforced ceremony of allegiance, that he would leave them their religion unimpaired.

Indeed his relations with the Estates, representing the knights and districts, were reasonably smooth. That political liberty struck no chord in him is well known. Such sympathy as he could muster for the concept of liberty comprehended at best the advantageous, adventurous free enterprise personified by his Hans de Witte. To the expelled dukes the Estates had frequently been a source of irritation, but Wallenstein transformed what had hitherto been a brake and an obstacle into an instrument of government. "From your missive I see what impertinences and protractions have been indulged by the Estates," he wrote to his governor. "Therefore I say that they shall not deal with me as they used to deal with the former Dukes, for I shall assuredly not suffer it, and for the first I shall distrain upon the goods of the reeves and gentry, their persons too." This expressed the position in a nutshell. The Estates had by their act of homage given his rule the air of legitimacy that he needed. Now he expected them to grant him money for the land's defence and to have its collection from the propertied classes undertaken by the reeves because, as a matter of good order, these alone were entitled to execute such a levy. At harvest-time they were peremptorily summoned to Güstrow. Wallenstein demanded fifty thousand taler per month, but acquiesced in a contribution of thirty thousand. This impost was worth while and not intolerably excessive.

For the short period that Mecklenburg was under Wallenstein's guidance it became another *terra felix*, a haven of peace. That was something which the Generalissimo was capable of bringing to pass if he really wanted, as he had done for his Bohemian duchy, although at the expense of other lands. When in winter 1627 he refused billets in Mecklenburg to the League army, he knew what he was doing. After that he sent off the imperialist, his own, troops into bordering Pomerania and Brandenburg. Specially appointed commissioners watched that regiments marching through Mecklenburg kept to previously fixed routes along which not a single day of rest was allowed. Woe betide them if they committed any act of pillage. Only six thousand infantrymen and five hundred horsemen were foreseen for the defence of the province's widely extended borders. The contribution extracted from the representative assembly was meant to ensure their prompt payment and the concomitant possibility of imposing strict discipline. In Mecklenburg law and order prevailed as long as the usurper ruled. It was worth more than the levy of 360,000 taler annually.

In addition the land enjoyed effective, uncorrupt administration and speedy judicial process, civic arts which Wallenstein had acquired in Friedland. Let us not exaggerate the blessings that he brought, in particular as they hardly had time to mature. Nevertheless they are characteristic and they achieved an astonishingly quick reconciliation of the subjects to their new suzerain.

It was during the Mecklenburg period that Wallenstein instructed his Friedland governor to take in hand the draft for a political constitution. Into it were incorporated northern institutions which appealed to him.

On the other hand he introduced Friedland institutions to Mecklenburg where, in late autumn 1628, the governmental machine experienced a total reorganization.

Hitherto it had been all too simple and therefore complicated. The Chancellor had, under the aegis of the Duke, been responsible for all public affairs – justice, administration, revenue, negotiations with the Estates, the towns, and foreign potentates. There had been only a single law-court holding quarterly sessions under the Chancellor, now at one place, now at another, and constantly with its files on the move. It did not feel competent to pronounce a final verdict in difficult cases. These were referred to a legal faculty, generally that of Rostock, a step involving the passage of years. If eventually a verdict was given, members of the knightly Estate were entitled to appeal against it to the *Reichskammergericht* at Speyer. The Estate set great store by this privilege because Speyer knew how to invest suits with perpetuity and thus to make a mockery of Mecklenburg justice. The new Duke cut this Gordian knot. He separated judicial from administrative affairs. Justice was constituted a purely Mecklenburg matter. That is, he requested and obtained from the Emperor the eagerly sought prerogative *de plane non appellando*, an award that he already possessed for Friedland and which was normally conferred only on the most distinguished Electors, those of Palatine–Bavaria, Saxony, and Brandenburg. The condition attached was that Mecklenburg should have three tiers of legal process. The Duke created them: the Court of Justice situated permanently at Güstrow, the Court of Appeal, and the Privy Council. This last body was also the top governmental authority where, it must be conceded, a division of power between executive and judicature was not operative. When the mood took him, Wallenstein presided. On other occasions, his governor. Three members, Gebhard von Moltke, Gregorius von Bevernest, Volrath von der Lühe, sterling Mecklenburgers all, were nominated to it. For administration of the revenues an Exchequer on the Friedland pattern was brought into existence. In lofty superiority over its president and members ranked the "regent", finance minister of all the Wallenstein lands. The Chancellery, former repository for all business, continued with a reduced but well-defined burden of duties comprising ducal rights, fief and boundary affairs, relations with the Empire, and diplomacy in the extended as well as original sense of the word. From the staff list – Chancellor, director, five members, archivist, pronotary, three secretaries, three senior registry officials – we infer a certain amplitude of business. Wallenstein was not the man to distribute sinecures.

Three institutions of a new character – Privy Council, Exchequer, Chancellery. Their presiding officers, the governor, regent, and chancellor respectively, constituted the cabinet with its own special secretary, a certain Heinrich Niemann, doctor of laws and subsequently captain of cavalry, who was also Wallenstein's private secretary. Neither he nor the holders of ministerial office just mentioned were Mecklenburgers. The first governor, Colonel San Julian, who had with Niemann been responsible for paving the way for Wallenstein's assumption of power in the land, came from Provence. Soon after Wallenstein's arrival he was sent to Vienna as ambassador or general agent. His replacement, Albrecht von Wengiersky, was a colonel of mixed Polish and Silesian origin. His chancellor, Johann Eberhard zu Elz, Wallenstein brought with him. This Lutheran from the Trèves Electorate should never, as ecclesiastical affairs now stood in Bohemia, have been permitted to be in the Duke's service. In Mecklenburg it was permitted; Mecklenburg was a stepping-stone to anywhere. The doctor of laws knew how to make himself so indispensable that both in Germany and Bohemia he stayed with his employer down to the last day although, as Elz informed the world the day *after* the last, it caused him agonies. A foreigner too, a Bohemian, was Heinrich Kustos, the regent and principal fiscal recipient. On the go between Friedland and Mecklenburg, his head full of the monstrous maze of credits and debits signifying Wallenstein's fortune, he carried a heavy load of responsibility. We do not envy him his task and, to forestall matters, he got poor thanks for it. Whereas Wengiersky and Elz escaped from Mecklenburg in time, Kustos left it too late. When he finally tried to flee, he was captured by the Swedes and handed to the restored Dukes. For two years they kept him in cruel custody to squeeze out of him whatever he possessed by way of money and knowledge. Then they used him as witness in a monster trial against native collaborators. That the Dukes on their return must rage against Wallenstein's Mecklenburg as a mound of corruption and despoliation was in the nature of the situation, but it corresponded badly with the truth. Whatever else in the Empire Wallenstein brought about, tolerated, or was unable to stop, in his own land he wanted and was able to stop it.

His government might come from above, be restless and impatient, but on the whole it was good government. Administration by nobles and Estates was transformed into streamlined bureaucracy. Justice was impartial and prompt. A nineteenth-century archivist who sorted the documents of the Güstrow court remarked with astonishment how thin was the bundle of documents dating from Wallenstein's day as compared with earlier and later periods. The fact is that often judgement was pronounced within twelve hours of a suit's presentation. As in Friedland, a postal service was established with Güstrow for its pivot, mounted riders and relay stations. "To promote the common weal," the Duke ordered "a single continuous uniformity for measures of capacity, area, length and weight," an anticipation of what subsequent rulers saw fit only 120 years later to introduce. As in Friedland, no poor, destitute or beggars were allowed in Mecklenburg. The draft of a Poor Law by the Chancellery did not satisfy Wallenstein. To his dictation the chancellor took down a revision, a cabinet ordinance in effect, as stern as it was clear and straightforward. The Duke moreover forbade the Estates assembled at Güstrow to disperse before they had passed a resolution on it in conformity with his wishes. Every town and every parish was within six months to set up and maintain a hospital or almshouse, the costs to be apportioned among the inhabitants according to a property scale. Mayors and pastors had to search their purlieus for indigent families. They found three hundred in all, which sounds a small number to us. This was a Wallenstein innovation which, like everything else he created, afterwards disappeared to give place to "beggary by divine providence". Not until the late nineteenth century was a workhouse erected again and then, of all places, in the palace at Güstrow. In the 'thirties of our century it continued to serve this purpose.

He travelled about the country, he made inspections. In December 1628 he went to Wismar to examine on the spot the feasibility of a canal leading from the port to the Lake of Schwerin and from there down the Stör and Elbe as far as Dömitz. We know his passion for canals. This one would have linked the interior of Mecklenburg with the Elbe and, by a roundabout route, the Baltic and the North Sea. It had in fact already existed since the preceding century, in part at least, but shallow, narrow, and with inadequate wooden locks. Hydraulic construction engineers, commissioned from Hamburg, submitted to the Duke a prodigious project. To render the canal navigable for merchant and naval vessels could not be done for less than five hundred thousand taler. The figure demonstrated how badly Wallenstein had underestimated the costs for the Kiel canal, an idea that he refused to relinquish. As to the new project, "the money should be available and the work should be done". Until a short time ago the northern outlet of the Lake of Schwerin was called "Wallenstein Dike", a vague memory of what had been intended, not of what was executed. A single word of command was not enough to raise five hundred thousand taler.

How much did Mecklenburg yield its new ruler? We can answer the question only approximately. All the more approximately because Wallenstein was there only a year. As soon as the terror of his presence was no longer felt, the flow of revenues ran down and soon ceased completely.

A difference should theoretically be made between the normal income of the state, or of the Duke who was the state in person, and the contributions. The latter were from time to time "granted" by the Estates and served the anomalous purpose of the war, payment of the army. That is, they were supposed to serve it.

The ducal income had in turn a twofold origin. There were the domains or princely departments, with their yields from corn, timber, and fishing, whether directly or through farming out; and there were the "royalties" or sovereign claims over customs duties, excise duties, tenure fees, licence fees, penal imposts. When Wallenstein was given Mecklenburg in lien, the capital value of the dukedom was estimated at 700,000 gulden. That would have borne, at the usual interest rate of six per cent, 42,000 gulden annually. The imperial commissioners instructed to fix the earnest money set the annual receipts at 86,000 taler (86,071 taler and a half, 19 schillings, three and a half pfennigs, to be precise), which was much more than 42,000 gulden. Wallenstein would in that case have purchased the dukedom cheaply. The commissioners' assessment was that in normal times the royalties brought in more than the estate. Out of imperial bounty they were allowed him free of payment – implementation of the 700,000 gulden agreed as a goodwill gift. If the royalties brought in more than the dominions, or at least as much, 86,000 taler, they would have corresponded to a capital value far in excess of two million gulden. But do we know whether the money actually came in? I don't believe that it did. The apparently so precise calculations were always riddled with illusions. Valuations were either much too low or much too high, depending on whose interest was being championed. It was pretended that times were normal. Unfortunately they were not. Wallenstein, since his tenure of the lien, might do what he could to breathe fresh life into agriculture and commerce, but in the previous year the land had been pretty well stripped alike by Danes and imperialists. Even the fact that "contributions", to a stately tune and a lavish accompaniment of lamentations, were "granted" by the Estates, was far from meaning that they were received.

Only in theory did these contributions flow into a special coffer. "Pray arrange matters so," wrote Wallenstein, while still in Bohemia, to his Governor San Julian, "that all Mecklenburg contributions remain for me, for I have no other money besides." The last phrase recurred constantly. This merger of funds can be excused on the grounds that he was simultaneously Mecklenburg suzerain and imperial Generalissimo, with Güstrow in 1628-9 at once his capital and his headquarters. Moreover, to add to the confusion, there existed an agreement whereby the contributions from his duchies, Friedland, Sagan, and now Mecklenburg, were to be "kept in" for him, that is, to be put directly at his disposal. We assume it to have been as a substitute for his pay, alone 72,000 gulden annually, as well as the outlays on court, headquarters, and other local and current costs. His qualities of general, suzerain, and private individual in one could, with the best will in the world, not have been strictly kept apart. It was done up to a point. De Witte, who advanced all the enormous sums and then recouped them in whatever way he could, kept separate accounts about expenditure by the suzerain, the general, and the army respectively. By background and training he was a sober man of business. Become rich with Wallenstein and drawn by him into ever more dangerous operations, he could not prevent in practice the submersion of what on paper he still held separate – personal purchases were covered from the official contributions because the official outgoings had been defrayed from private resources.

"I have no other money besides." Could Friedland no longer meet the bill? Friedland had produced, or helped to produce, possession of Mecklenburg. Corn from Friedland, arms and ammunition from Friedland, advances for regimental colonels from Friedland, all these had made of Wallenstein the Emperor's major creditor. Now Friedland was financing only the Bohemian part of his intricate, multifarious life – the building at Gitschin and elsewhere, the endowments, the horse-breeding, the court that Duchess Isabella maintained at Prague with undiminished magnificence. So strangely had the balance shifted that what had originally been Wallenstein's huge fortune only continued to furnish the wherewithal for its founder's immediate representation while he lived on Mecklenburg and the Empire, fancying himself beggared if the restive "golden ass" reneged. How easily and almost unobserved do we rise from a state of modesty to that of comfort, from comfort to that of splendour, from splendour to that of the bizarre. Descent from the bizarre to splendour or mere comfort is something different. It frightens and takes you by the throat.

He wanted to have his Mecklenburg revenues in a lump sum on which he could rely. "Tell Kustos that I request him in Mecklenburg to dispose of matters so that I can obtain from there twenty thousand imperial taler each month, for lack of which I shall else not have enough to live." Two hundred and forty thousand taler per year were more than the estimate of his normal income, including imperial sources, and much more than it was in reality. A part of those taler could therefore only come from the contributions, which for a time they did. With de Witte's help, they rolled in iron-hooped casks to wherever Wallenstein happened to be. But it became more and more difficult to scrape them together. For the last five months of 1629 the Duke prepared, or ordered Kustos to prepare, a budget. On the liabilities side it foresaw by the end of the year payment in three instalments of 130,000 taler to Hans de Witte or Walter de Hertoge, his business partner at Hamburg, and 12,000 taler reimbursement of expenses claimed by the imperial commissioners for the wearisome period of peace negotiations with Denmark. Total, 142,000 taler. On the assets side provision was made for 91,390 taler from the land contribution; 30,000 taler from excise duties for six months; 20,000 from the sale of timber; 10,000 from rentals; 6000 from licence fees. Total 157,390 taler. Surplus, 15,390 taler. To this would be charged outlay on the ducal academy as well as work on the palace and on certain fortifications. A budget that gives food for thought. In the first place there is no provision for the state's administrative costs; they would need to be furnished from elsewhere. Secondly, an item alien to the matter in hand is included. The diplomats dealing at Lübeck with the King of Denmark should by right have been paid from the Emperor's pocket, not Wallenstein's. Here he was once more extending a loan to his master. Thirdly, the preponderant part of the debit figure is made up of an allocation to de Witte, whether because of an advance or to draw the monthly 20,000 taler from it. Fourthly, it attracts attention that the contributions bring or are intended to bring in far more, almost two-thirds of the total, than the regular income. Finally, the entire calculation makes us dizzy. "In what way the Exchequer shall attain to the sum named is herewith displayed." Would it really and truly attain it? Could so many drops be squeezed from the drought as to fill the barrel?

The very first instalment promised the Hamburg banker did not arrive on schedule. De Witte wrung his hands. Wallenstein in his sternest tone called Wengiersky and Kustos to account. He had had enough "of being put off with words whereby our credit and fair name then suffers. We had expected better of you." Force must now be used against the Mecklenburgers, knights, townsmen, peasants, to extract payment from them. "It does not suffice me that summons are issued. Sequestrate. And heed not the Estates more than myself, which pains me in the highest degree." The order did not fail of its effect. The money was collected and by New Year's Day 1630 had gone via Hamburg to de Witte. This success may explain why Wallenstein often adopted such a hectoring tone towards his officials – he had to scare them so that they should scare the taxpayers. The question was how long ends could be made to meet. Our impression is that the richer he became, or the more titles to wealth he possessed, and the more he spent, the heavier the burden of financial worries bore down on him. His Bohemian wealth had been real, the income from lush estates and well-run enterprises. The Generalissimo's wealth was increasingly an illusion, a towering structure of prodigality, advances, debts, and afflictions. Even if Friedland, next to ensuring its own glittering representation, saw to the army's requirements, that, economically speaking, did not improve matters. For how other than by contributions and confiscations, afflictions again, should the Emperor pay for the Friedland armaments production?

He was, wrote Wallenstein, a friend of the nobility. So he was, as long as the nobility served and paid. He was at the beginning no friend of the great and wealthy seaports Rostock and Wismar which rounded off his territory. In autumn 1627, before he had acquired the duchy and precisely at the time of the impending "mutation", he was eager already to bring them under his control and for the next six months he did not cease to be preoccupied by this anxiety. He knew of only one method to dominate a well-populated city, the erection of a citadel at its centre, which was what in the face of stout resistance he had done as Governor of Prague. "A large town without a citadel is useless," he wrote to Arnim. To garrison and fortify Wismar and Rostock became his fixed idea. While still in Bohemia, he urged Arnim on nineteen occasions to undertake the business, then pressed it nine times on San Julian. "Make a start upon building the citadels at Rostock and at Wismar, for I can have no peaceful hour until the citadels have at least been begun." His intention was twofold – to fetter the restless inhabitants (or, as he liked to phrase it, "to put the bit in their muzzles") and to secure the harbours against attack by the northern kings. The two aims interlocked because inhabitants and seafaring folk alike sympathized with Denmark. In the case of Wismar the position was that it had in October 1627, that is, when the dukes still reigned, surrendered to Arnim, accepting occupation for the duration of the war by a thousand imperialist troops and placing the Wismar ships at the disposal of the imperial fleet against appropriate indemnification. Rostock proved, though not without reason, more perverse. The town had accommodated itself to payment of a considerable contribution. It could not, or did not care to, prevent San Julian from constructing an entrenchment north of the town by the Warnow estuary. As this made him master of Rostock harbour, the King of Denmark declared the city hostile and renegade to the Protestant cause, confiscated its ships lying in his ports, and had others seized at sea whenever he could catch them. The northern seaports were now in the wretched situation of having to choose between reprisals by the land power and reprisals by the sea power, while any postponement of choice would bring down on them the wrath of both. In Rostock tumult ensued. Townsmen and sailors were not prepared to tolerate unemployment and the ruin of trade. They banded together, raucously demanding alliance with Denmark. "Your letter from Warnemünde tells me what the rabble at Rostock dares to take in hand. . . . You will see to it that *in continenti* the citizens of Rostock are disarmed and work on a citadel is begun." For six months the matter remained in a dangerous state of suspense. In October 1628 the Duke of Friedland-Mecklenburg moved in force against the town. He threatened to carry it by assault. Hereupon a judicious settlement similar to that with Wismar was achieved. Rostock submitted to the installation of a garrison, simply as protection against outside enemies, it was emphasized. The Duke accorded the university a token of particular good will: the houses of its professors were spared any billeting. Wallenstein's growing broadmindedness in his dealings with the seaports, what he learned in his traffic with them, and how boldly sensible he was in applying the lesson is a factor which needs to be viewed in a context larger than that of Mecklenburg.

What was it that he had become? The Duke of Friedland, Bohemia's greatest lord? The Duke of Mecklenburg? An imperial prince like other imperial princes? Did he still know what he really was and wanted to be? I don't think that he did. Occasionally he said in conversation that as an imperial prince he must want the imperial princes to continue to play their important part and would surely be stupid if he were party to rendering Habsburg rule absolute. It sounded logical, but the tune was in the wrong key. It was thanks to the imperial power, his own military power, that he had in unlawful, unheard of fashion forced himself into the company of princes. His new fellows, keenly aware of their own interests and supercilious, would tolerate him reluctantly just as long as the anomalous conditions created by him prevailed. To be a major imperial prince, a Lower German politician in his own right, consorted badly in some degree with his military appointment. From this there was no freeing himself because he owed everything to it, yet it hampered his position as a ruler and the freedom of his policy inspired by his own genius. Did he want, not merely temporarily, to shift the pivot of his existence to Mecklenburg? It seemed so, for he made himself at home in Güstrow and the winter of 1628-9 was the first during which he failed to return to Bohemia. It did not seem so, for his wife and daughter remained throughout at Prague and his court at Güstrow was purely male, rather more like an army headquarters. Moreover while he was embellishing the palace at Güstrow with a splendour it never either before or after enjoyed, while he was seeing to it that work on the palace at Gitschin, a fortnight's journey away, continued busily and expensively, he was simultaneously putting into operation an architectural scheme which since summer 1627 he had had in mind for the small town of Sagan, capital of the duchy of the same name. What did he want of Sagan? To take up residence there? Facts speak against that. From the time he adopted the title Duke of Sagan until his death he spent precisely nine days there in all; once four, once three, once two. Compared with his other acquisitions, the dukedom was very small beer. Building there had none the less to be, a palace of incomparable magnificence, an eighth world wonder, according to gossip. To make room for it, no less than seventy citizens' houses were duly expropriated, assessed, and compensation paid, although the last in part only. Heirs and the heirs of heirs were at the beginning of the eighteenth century still dragging through the courts their claims for what Wallenstein's assigns owed them. It was October 1628 when the Duke, outside Rostock and trying to coerce the town into good sense, told his Sagan governor that the site selected for the zoo was useless, further steps for its establishment should be desisted from, he would do better instead to hurry along the construction of the palace.

As at Prague and Gitschin, he availed himself of an Italian architect's services. His first instruction ran that a plan should be made of the town and the existing palace. This it had originally been intended only to repair and render habitable. No, too mean, far too mean. Away with the old structure. Let everything rise anew above the gentle charm of the Bober valley. Tower above it, though, with anything but gentle charm – a baroque palace and castle of defiance with deep moats, bastions and walls wrought from prodigious four-square hewn blocks, then a first storey, a sheltered courtyard and arcades. Further the design never got. Decade after decade the neo-ruin stood there, monument to the strange outsider who had for no more than six years been Duke of Sagan, one among the many fragments of his life's work.

So much for Sagan. Friedland? Wallenstein, regardless of his elevation to Duke of Mecklenburg, continued work unceasingly on the rounding off and rationalization of his Bohemian property, selling estates which brought him little and bargaining for more lucrative ones. At the end of May 1628 San Julian was directed to hold the Rostock contribution at his disposal "because I owe Hans de Witte more than four hundred thousand imperial taler on account of sundry possessions that he has paid for me", meaning in Bohemia. Another example of how contributions had to fulfil his most personal ends, but *not* proof as to dishonest application of war-moneys. Simply perpetually the same circle: to pay his debts he helped himself out of the extorted taxes to what was his due.

What use this heap of castles? Wallenstein, on the search for what he would never find, had distended his identity to such a degree that it threatened to dissolve into nothing. The process would persist until a hostile, more stubborn power forced him to take stock and to climb down. Take stock of what? Climb down to where?

At this particular moment his most embittered foes were the expelled Mecklenburg dukes. Embittered but powerless. The times when great-hearted defenders and reckless adventurers jumped into the breach for the dethroned Palsgrave were long past. The dukes did not enjoy such international support as had the Winter King. Not that they totally lacked it. Sophia, Dowager Queen of Denmark, had been born a Mecklenburg princess. A close relative, she was a kind of ancestress to princely Protestantism – mother of King Christian and the widowed Electress of Saxony, grandmother of King Charles of England, Duke Ulrich of Brunswick, and Mad Christian. The hale and hearty old lady had spun a political web of which money constituted one strand. She had lent her cognate rulers considerable sums, at interest and against security of course – three hundred thousand taler to Ulrich of Brunswick, four hundred thousand to the Mecklenburg dukes. In the second case, with her collaterals threatened or lost, the change of government could not but appear especially vexatious to her. Nyköping, in Denmark, where she held court, consequently became a focus of agitation on behalf of the dispossessed.

The two of them had initially separated and taken their respective pitiful courses: Adolf Friedrich to Saxony where the Elector granted him asylum if not much else, Johann Albrecht to Magdeburg where he found "neither conversation nor pastime". In 1629 however, as they wanted to be as close as possible to their land, they settled at Lübeck, Adolf Friedrich travelling unrecognized through his stolen patrimony. Johann Albrecht was looking for a house with "at least four rooms". He was totally destitute. A plea to London for support seems to have come to nothing. His elder brother had an allowance of two thousand taler from King Christian. Two thousand taler; four rooms. How many rooms were there at Güstrow, Prague, Gitschin? How many taler did Wallenstein spend in a day?

In such miserable circumstances a government-in-exile on the Palatine pattern was out of the question. A few retainers nevertheless remained faithful to the dukes, among them the Privy Councillors Cothmann and Hagen. The princes, assisted by these jurists, deployed a despairing activity whose aim was to plead with Europe's dignitaries, all the Electors, the Regent at Brussels, the imperial ministers Eggenberg, Stralendorf, Trauttmansdorff, and others, to make "intercession". A stream of appeals was duly loosed. No less than three on the part of the Saxon Elector, while in June 1629 six Electors composed one in common. We know how glad potentates were to challenge injustice with a quill and to accord help which cost as little as it yielded. In summer 1628 the brothers were so naïve as to try an approach to Wallenstein himself immediately after the usurper had made his entry into Güstrow. Privy Councillor Cothmann ventured to set foot in the town and ask for an audience. That he obtained, but with what upshot! "Heed this well!" Wallenstein addressed the diplomat in a biting tone. "To pursue rebels, not to concern myself with intercessions, is why I have been sent into these territories by His Majesty. Come again on such a mission and I shall lay your head before your feet." And, interrupting Cothmann's excuses, "You have heard. Therewith you have your answer." "Wherefore," as Cothmann's melancholy report to his beggar-prince closed, "I had to take my leave, returning to my tavern in the town, and next day I betook myself again on my journey." "Therewith you have your answer" – the words became legendary. They severely ruffled the princely dovecotes. "The Duke of Friedland disgusts friend and foe, harries Electors and Princes most disgracefully," as Elector Maximilian exclaimed. "To many it appears intolerable that the Duke of Friedland harshly upbraided the Mecklenburg representative, when the latter with great moderation bade for intercession and wished to excuse his Prince, did not fully hear him out, but threatened the envoy to have his head placed between his feet." How Maximilian had attained his electorate and with what consequences is familiar to us. Better manners than Wallenstein he certainly had and he would never have handled an envoy so roughly.

Mecklenburg had created politically a new Palatine, less important than the original, affecting neither Spain nor France nor Holland nor England, but providing a parallel none the less. The Palsgrave had never been got rid of, he continued to cause a hubbub or let others cause a hubbub for him until he died. How were the Mecklenburg dukes to be got rid of?

Wallenstein hesitated. At the start he would have liked somehow to indemnify the victims so that they should "be able to live" and would keep quiet. As late as 1629 he was heard to say, "The Dukes of Mecklenburg must not be wholly dispossessed. We must grant them something and let each have fifty thousand taler until the bustle comes to its end." That sounds genuine. For years past one of his preferences had been for some kind of amicable settlement with those whose property he had acquired. Such a process would prove more lasting and in the long run more economic. But he was familiar with, and capable of implementing, the opposite principle too – there would be no trouble from anyone chased into Europe's farthest corner or lying dead beneath the ground. He had set a price on the head of Lord von Redern, Friedland's former owner. Such conduct was inconceivable in the case of the Mecklenburgers. That he could not permit himself *vis-à-vis* the body of German princes even at the summit of his power. What he would have liked to see would have been a formal trial of the brothers before the Aulic Council, succeeded by pronouncement of the *bando imperiale*, the imperial ban. San Julian pushed both these pieces of constitutional procedure without achievement of either. After more than a year's exertion, though, he attained the substance of his objective. In June 1629 the Dukes were declared finally devoid of all claims to their territory: "Imperial Manifesto or Well-Founded Deduction on the Causes for the Deprivation of and the Deposition from their Principalities and Lands of the Two Brothers, Dukes Adolf Friedrich and Hans Albrecht of Mecklenburg". Ten days later followed the bill of enfeoffment which raised Wallenstein to the status of hereditary duke. Only after it had been ceremonially handed to his representatives, Count Max and Colonel San Julian, did he sign with the initials significant of what he had in fact long been – A.H.Z.M., Albrecht Duke of Mecklenburg.*

* A[lbrecht].H[erzog].Z[u].M[ecklenburg].

The Imperial Chancellor, the Elector of Mainz, and all German princes were informed of the investiture, a step which again placed lords and councillors in a quandary. To address Wallenstein as Duke of Mecklenburg was to ratify injustice: imperial princes were not allowed without clearly proven guilt to be exiled from their land and people. To refuse the title was to invite the vengeance of him who carried it and of which his spitefulness was thought thoroughly capable. Recognition of the new duke never ensued on the part of the Electors and Europe's kings. The problem was spun out until it was settled automatically. The nearest move to discreet sanction was undertaken by two powers from whom it would hardly have been anticipated – the States-General and the Hanse. They had their reasons.

The Mecklenburg brothers retorted with a White Book of 1116 pages; the imperial impeachment had had twenty-two. The four main points of the impeachment were, albeit one-sidedly, rebutted in harrowing detail. The authors were however able to prove that their masters had incurred no greater guilt than the other Lower Saxon Estates and, whatever their secret sympathies, had outwardly acted according to force of circumstance. A verdict not preceded by trial and without a hearing of the accused was null and void. Quotations from the Bible and legal texts of ancient, medieval and modern times superabundantly verified the point. How basely had the Mecklenburg representatives been treated at His Imperial Majesty's hands, not even being admitted to audience. The experience of Privy Councillor Cothmann at Güstrow was not left unmentioned. Never before in the history of the world had anyone dared to display such disrespect to an envoy from princes of immemorial royal descent and to dismiss him with boorish, wounding invective and monstrously barbaric answer – Wallenstein was unsurpassably adept at furnishing his enemies with propaganda through impetuously passionate outbursts. The publication's most impressive achievement was the appendix, which contained a collection of 259 authentic documents and letters. A number, by no means unfriendly in tone, were from the Duke of Friedland to his future victims. All in all, the White Book was meatier than the Manifesto, not simply because it was fifty times longer. For the moment that could be a matter of indifference to Wallenstein. He was studying, very thoroughly and to the exclusion of all else, his bill of enfeoffment.

In July 1629, exactly a year after his arrival, he left the country as its fully invested suzerain. The new problems which imperial power politics had incurred for him necessitated a journey to central Germany, then farther south. His departure was as gorgeous and minutely planned as

his entry had been. Precise logistics were always required for the board-
ing of such a multitude in appropriate style. Wallenstein however upset
all calculations by staying a week at Schwerin instead of the planned four
days. Until now he had seen its residence only in the snow; he liked the
look of it in the July sun. On 20 July the train proceeded to Neustadt
on the Elbe. The Duke was quartered in the old castle. A new, uncompleted one stood nearby. Wallenstein had the main local official
brought before him, inquired the purpose of the building, and ordered
him to see to its completion. The castle stands today still. He inspected
the Elbe locks and thought that they needed improvement. At midday
he ate in his room, formerly Duke Adolf Friedrich's, and held a siesta.
Then, accompanied by the official, he visited the foundry. Everyday
utensils had been made there. Since the Duke ruled in the land its
production had been switched to cannon balls. Why was there only one
furnace and no sledge-hammer? The installation of another had been
planned, but the course of the war had unhappily prevented it. Let the
men get on with their work, and that under the sombre stare of the
Duke seated on a stool. He watched the flames leap out of the furnace
and the metal pouring into the circular moulds. For whom were the
cannon balls destined? Your Princely Grace, Field-Marshal Arnim, and
the Spanish ambassador at Wismar. "The devil he is the Spanish
ambassador," Wallenstein flared up. "He serves the Emperor." He
quietened down, beckoned to the official. "I will hear no more such
words. Who said that he in Wismar is the Spanish ambassador?" "The
overseer, Your Princely Grace." He fell into angry silence again. He
would on no condition allow Gabriel de Roy, furnishing moderate
assistance at Wismar in the preparations for an imperial fleet, to be
regarded as in the service of Spain when he was not even formally that.
After inspection of the foundry came an expert look at the state of the
environs. A two hours' drive through field and forest. Return to the
castle and dictation of a letter to the Exchequer at Güstrow on what was
to be changed and improved. Then fruit, his entire evening meal, was
brought and he lay down to sleep. Early to bed was the rule on such
summer trips when a start was made at four or five in the morning.
The train, moving across the Mecklenburg border, went in the direction
of Wolmirstedt and Magdeburg.

He thought that he would be back soon. He never returned.

Dialectics of Victory

JUNE 1629. Wallenstein is writing to the President of the imperial War Council: "I have thought about our affairs the whole of the past night and my conclusion is that we have such large forces tied down here and elsewhere that we shall not be able to invade Italy in such power as is supposed. . . . I have sent fifteen thousand men into Poland, seventeen thousand into the Netherlands. Fourteen thousand are wanted for Milan, but I must leave at least twelve thousand in Pomerania and Brandenburg, for my lord can rest assured that knaveries in plenty come to pass and that a rising will occur if the slightest opportunity offers. I have to leave six thousand men around Magdeburg, a goodly number in the Empire, and against Metz it is we, not the League, who must take up position. . . . Should Bethlehem stir, His Majesty would needs have in haste to recruit some cavalry in those lands. . . ." And so on. The letter is dated after the end of the Danish campaign, but reveals that the moment of apparent peace is not really such. The Generalissimo, a sleepless night behind him, adds up the resources at his disposal like a financier reviewing his investments. They are barely adequate, he decides, for his all-round defence and he excludes the possibility of any major enterprise. Up to a point too he is a financier. Money is the topic of his letters more often than infantry and cavalry, money that he lacks but must have, money worries which are rendering his banker de Witte ever more desperate.

A few months later he received in audience a man by the name of Lebzelter, Groom of the Chamber and favourite of the Elector of Saxony. To him he talked with the candour he sometimes practised, a compound of his real thoughts and arguments that he knew would make for popular hearing at Dresden. Never, he said, would he be party to the pillage, let alone destruction, of the Protestants. He had no liking at all for such Vienna-concocted schemes and was

> little in the habit of asking what were the opinions of Prince Eggenberg, Father Lamormaini, and others of that breed. . . .

Conscience was a matter solely between man and God. Everyone was answerable to Him for his religion. Therefore it was reasonable to live together in peace at any rate politically. His Princely Grace wished and craved for nothing more than that noble peace should be attained in the speediest manner, more particularly since he for his part would gladly be rid of the great burden, anxiety, trial, and labour lying upon him. For almost thirty years he had been immersed in the commotions of war and had achieved all for which he had striven.

There were however many enemies still about, the most dangerous, as the whole world knew, the Swedes, and a perilous venture had been launched in Italy. Against his own warnings, but a deed now unfortunately done, and the upshot was to have the King of France, the Venetians, even the Pope against the Emperor. Was it in those circumstances feasible to dismiss the imperial army? How willingly he would but the time to send home two-thirds of the swollen forces was not yet. He knew only too well what all its comings and goings meant to townsmen. . . .

For the twilight period about to be described the records of such conversations, surveys, and assessments of the current situation are many. The details vary according to the great man's mood and who his listener happens to be. On one occasion the Dutch are people with whom accommodation is possible while on another he condemns them as rogues. The Protestants are sometimes "heretics", sometimes as good as Catholics. Today the campaign in Italy is condemned as mischievous, tomorrow it will find his support. Nevertheless the tenor of thought behind the proliferation of kaleidoscopic ideas stays the same. What he wants is a peace founded on toleration, and he is honest enough to admit that he wants it on personal grounds. He has enough, the wars have brought him what they could, and during such years as may remain to him he would like to enjoy his acquisitions. Provided that he can keep Mecklenburg. Why should he not keep it? Is there anyone in the Empire more powerful than he?

More powerful than he, probably not. In no one else, neither in Ferdinand nor in Maximilian, is so much power of decision concentrated. That, though, is not the end of the matter. For every point where after immense trouble he has his own way, there are three where he has to submit and partake in something of which he disapproves. The most powerful man in the Empire is still an underling, a salaried

employee. His principality has made no change in that status. Father
Valeriano may allege that all the Emperor's ministers have been bought
by and are in bond to him, but it is not true. He has enemies, false
friends, sharp critics in distant Vienna, the city he now avoids. Individually they weight incomparably less than he, but together as heavy
or heavier. If only old Harrach were alive, his fond defender, the
Emperor's cherished counsellor. He had died in spring 1628 at the
Prague palace. In Friedland there had been six months' mourning and
a prohibition of all festivities, a tribute the more eloquent of the Duke's
sorrow for the loss in beer consumption that the veto must have entailed.
Eggenberg, lukewarmer, lazier, in the last analysis less loyal, is no
substitute for his father-in-law. To whom can he now address his
grumbling, his imploring, his mocking letters? Harrach had been at
once the Emperor's minister and Wallenstein's ambassador. Now he
keeps his own at court, San Julian, but he is like Count Max no more
than an opportunist and courtier. Needing someone at Vienna to whom
he can pour out his heart, he turns again to Field-Marshal Collalto,
apparently totally oblivious of his fury over this "false, wicked creature".
During the course of 1629 the flow of letters to Collalto, sometimes
three a day, is at the flood and they leave an impression of unrestrained
frankness. It would not have been so if he had been in a position to give
orders at Vienna.

In the Empire too, for all his regiments, the orders that he can issue
are within very narrow bounds. He has to treat the maritime cities with
consideration. In the first place he needs their money and is dependent
on their sufferance of the imperial fleet to which he attaches such
importance. In the second Stralsund has taught him that they are hard
nuts to crack. Dealing with small princes and counts in Lower Germany,
Thuringia, the Wetterau* is easier; they are defenceless. Leaving aside
Brandenburg, that does not apply to the Electors. Saxony, exploiting its
claim to be treated with forbearance, has the impudence to charge dues
on corn carried from Bohemia down the Elbe to the army in the north.
From Lutheran Dresden threads are spun to Catholic Munich. It was
already so at the time of the Bohemian troubles, it is so now. All Electors are basically against Wallenstein, the Catholics more menacingly
than the Protestants. He knows it. He knows that the former want to
rid themselves of him and that the topic is put on the agenda of one
conference after another, just as he knows that they simultaneously

---

* A small depression near Frankfurt-on-Main (translator's note).

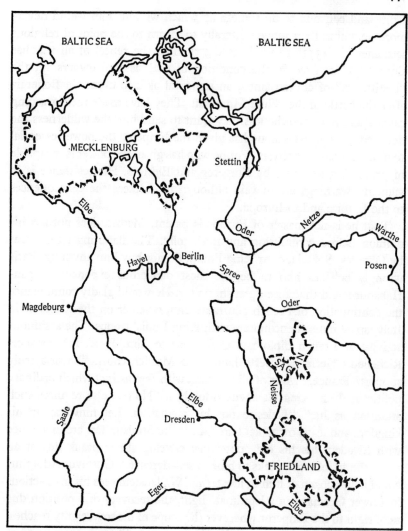

Wallenstein's Lands

aspire and conspire to do something which without him would never-more lie within their range – literally to return to the point of religious settlement in 1555* to work its destruction, the repeal of all that has since 1552 occurred in the condition of ecclesiastical ownership, the "restitution" of church lands, an upheaval akin to events in Bohemia after the battle of the White Mountain. They have made their grasping calculation, but none the less they want to send into the wilderness the detested sorcerer who alone has given the Emperor the power essential to unleash such a cataclysm. For he who has given the power is incapable of preventing its abuse by Emperor and Electors. His resistance is in vain, his warnings are in vain although he foresees the consequences to the Empire and to Europe.

That he is not master of Europe is patent. Madrid does not ask his opinion before committing any fresh folly. The flattering letters sent by Olivares, Spinola, even King Philip, do not buy him anything. Paris wrongly believes him to be the most dangerous exponent of pan-Habsburg, and therefore Spanish, policy. He would gladly countenance the continuation of French neutrality and, whether on the Rhine or in Italy, spare himself encounters with King Louis' troops. The assiduous activity of French diplomats is familiar to him. How, for instance, Richelieu's German experts haunt the Munich court. "Bavaria truly supports France." Most of all he fears, with the instinct which ordinary politicians lack, King Gustavus Adolphus. "No one else requires such attention as he." "I desire not his mediation. Let him stay in his kingdom and leave me to act here. . . . If the Stralsunders are in alliance with Sweden, 'tis his old subterfuge envelops their prank, for at all times the artful rogue seeks to hide in self-defence." Gustavus Adolphus could have spoken of him in like terms. Wallenstein sees his own actions in Lower Germany in a legitimate light, the recovery of a position due as of right to the Emperor wherever the scope of his sovereignty reaches, hence to the coasts, hence on the German seas. There is not a word of truth in the allegation that he has in view a hostile landing in Sweden, as Oxenstierna must allege for home consumption. One man's security is simply another man's menace. Gustavus Adolphus also fancies his stand at Stralsund to be fundamentally a safeguard because "nowhere are we so weak as in Sweden". Wallenstein in turn undertakes preven-tive moves attested by his effort to keep Polish–Swedish hostilities alive

* The Peace of Augsburg allowed each German prince to settle the form of Christian faith which would prevail in his dominion – *cujus regio, ejus religio* (translator's note).

for as long as the Poles will allow themselves to be persuaded and to be aided to that end. Precisely this is what Gustavus Adolphus conceives as unprovoked aggression.

Master neither of the play nor its replay, it is the only one left to him, the one on which his life is founded and from which he cannot cease even if he would. What, for example, would otherwise become of his Mecklenburg possession? Family no longer means much to him since the hope of a son has had to be abandoned. The princely sports of table, bed, and the chase are now, or always were, alien to him. The grandeur of his court has become habitual and his only fear is that he might have to reduce it. Power is his profession and, the more so as he chose it and none else, his pleasure, much as it is that of his one real rival in the realm, Maximilian of Bavaria. The latter, though, serves the Holy Virgin and the greatness of his ancient ramified House and the Empire too. He serves purposes extant long before and long after him. He stands on firm ground. Wallenstein does not. He is a stranger everywhere. He is only invested with power which he has himself created, but with which he is not durably identified nor it with him. To be able freely to play his lofty game of good sense he would need autonomy. Mecklenburg was meant to serve that purpose. Yet Mecklenburg is but small, and he is not sure of it, and besides it is again something owing to that imperial power which on the one hand is himself and on the other consists of a set of cliques – Austrian Privy Councillors and father confessors, Bohemian reactionaries, obedient Electors and other faithful imperial Estates, cardinals, Jesuits, Spanish imperialists, Italian marauders. Quite baffling is the character and substance of the power to whose stubborn resolutions Ferdinand II appends his name.

The years 1629 and 1630 show traces of a free and personal policy on Wallenstein's part. He ought intrepidly to pursue it, but it is impossible to see on what foundation and on the strength of whose authority, with whose identity for its authority. If he cannot, his downfall is simply a question of time.

THE ART OF MAKING PEACE

We have to go back a little, to the day when Wallenstein entered his capital of Güstrow. We have seen how he acted as Duke of Mecklenburg, exemplifying his policy within narrow range. The course of major political events did not meanwhile stop and the local suzerain continued at one and the same time to be the Generalissimo and European politician.

He had not abandoned the siege of Stralsund so hastily only because he wanted to divert himself with his new sovereignty. Whereas the danger of a Swedish landing somewhere in Pomerania or Mecklenburg proved as previously to have been an empty rumour, the Danish peril was real. On 11 August 1628 Christian with seven thousand men took the island of Usedom. Three days later he seized the town and fortress of Wolgast. The very next day Wallenstein was on the march. He came from Güstrow. Arnim with his luckless Stralsund veterans was on the way to meet him. The ensuing battle was his first full-scale engagement since he caught Mansfeld at the Dessau bridge in 1626, a moment of concentrated energy imbued with a conviction of success. "The King," he had said, "at present keeps to his isles, wherefore I cannot as yet approach him. But he is soused full every day and I hope to Heaven that in his cups he will one day venture something and creep out of his watery holes, when he will assuredly be ours." So it proved. The Dane did creep out, posted himself half a mile from Wolgast, relied on the protection afforded by a morass which was a vincible impediment, and had to watch the slaughter and disintegration of his army. At night he was able to save a few demoralized survivors by embarkation on his ships. The impression left by this encounter was telling on both Wallenstein's enemies in his own camp, especially Maximilian of Bavaria who after such a success thought it wise to talk no more just yet about the Commander-in-Chief's dismissal, and on Christian. The latter's war against Emperor and Empire was entering its fifth year. He had gained nothing and lost much. Wolgast proved again to him his inferiority on land. In November one of the two Holstein strongholds still in his possession was forced by Wallenstein to surrender. On the other hand the Danes did feel in a position to negotiate because their impotence on the mainland was compensated by their never truly endangered situation in the islands.

From the outset talk of peace had provided a reedy accompaniment to the martial music. Nobody was responsible for the state of war, nobody had wanted it, nobody had done more than defend his own lawful rights. To blame was the other party. To blame, in the eyes of well-meaning intermediaries like the Infanta at Brussels and the Elector of Saxony, were simply errors, misunderstandings, the distressing lack of mutual confidence. As long as the warring parties set their sights on a complete victory, Wallenstein on the confiscation of Denmark,

Christian on the *status quo ante* at least in Lower Germany, the efforts of intermediaries beat upon the air. However, as the years passed, the enterprise became less alluring to both parties, something that was carried on because it had once been begun, but carried on without hope.

One negotiator was more pertinacious than the rest – that Prince of Holstein-Gottorp who, it will be recalled, in September 1627 came to Lauenburg to be the recipient of the frightful peace conditions concocted at Vienna. He refused, since his own vital interests were at stake, to be completely discouraged. In late autumn he conferred a number of times with Wallenstein who, glad to display a more reasonable attitude than his principals, did indeed promise to reduce the terms somewhat. Holstein carried the news to the Rigsraad. That Estate of Danish nobility had always castigated their monarch's German expedition as an extraneous business and not properly Denmark's affair at all. In February 1628 the Rígsraad told the Emperor that the war was one of which they knew nothing, not Danish, and waged by their sovereign in his capacity only as President of the Lower Saxon Circle; they were its innocent victims and hostilities should stop. The protest and plea, appearing to indicate internal dissension, made the warriors at the Vienna court if anything more brazen. "On our side people are not lacking who would be pleased to see the war in the Empire prolonged," Wallenstein wrote to Arnim, "but by God's help I have crossed them and brought His Majesty to the point where he has agreed, as I have advised the Duke of Gottorp by letter, that a start shall be made on negotiations as soon as I shall have reached Holstein." Then already, not believing in a settlement with Sweden, he wanted such with Denmark. If on occasion the conditions formulated by him sounded savage, it was either a momentary delusion or a verbal obeisance to the talk in Vienna and Prague. Its inconsistency with the logic of his own outlook may only gradually have dawned on him.

That same February Wallenstein and Tilly were appointed peace commissioners for such eventuality. Henceforward the reedy accompaniment to the martial music had rather more body, even if it did not yet echo as loud as the roar of guns at Stralsund. In late autumn the old convention of wrangling about the site of negotiations was observed. Christian wanted neither Hamburg (ostensibly on account of the plague prevailing there) nor Lauenburg nor Kiel, but Lübeck. That was agreed. On 29 January the plenipotentiaries arrived – delegates from the King and the Rígsraad, representatives for Tilly and Wallenstein. Straightway an argument began about the wording of their respective commissions, with the Danes protesting particularly at being called the originators of the war and declaring Wallenstein's maritime titles unbefitting. Not the slightest ground for hope was given when the substance of the negotiations was at last reached. Both sides, again according to the rules of the game, thought it clever to behave as though each was the unqualified victor. The Danes demanded no less than immediate withdrawal from all their king's territories, German as well as Danish, indemnification for their war expenditure, restoration of all their rights and freedoms in the Lower Saxon Circle as they had formerly existed and in Mecklenburg too, a general amnesty, the inclusion of Sweden, England, France, and the Netherlands in the treaty's terms, and other points on a similar pattern. After a month the imperialists repaid them in their own coin: Denmark was to renounce all interference in imperial affairs, Slesvig and the Danish portion of Holstein should be ceded, a lien furnished for an indefinite time on Jutland, reparation made for the sufferings of Pomerania and Lüneburg, and money, money, and more money be yielded. This peace programme passed through Wallenstein's hands. He did not take it seriously.

Before its prolix conditions were revealed at Lübeck, he presented the Emperor with a secret statement which represented his real views. The situation, he explained, was not such as presumably it was at Vienna thought to be. Denmark was not beaten and for the future was unbeatable at sea. Regardless of victories won, the imperial position was fundamentally a defensive one and difficult because the long coastal line was exhausting to cover. "The King is probably fully aware of this." The Rígsraad wanted peace, especially the baronial Estate with properties in Jutland. Christian's standpoint was different. The ambassadors of France, Holland, Sweden, and England buoyed him up with extravagant hopes if he were to continue hostilities and threatened him with dire consequences if he were to give up. "The King, by nature proud and covetous, is become reckless on score of the scorn and hurt that he has sustained and he would like to enter into a new confederation with them. . . . I see clearly that as little as the King will attain from Your Majesty that which he craves, as little too will he agree to the proposals advanced by Your Majesty." Peace was not to be had without the surrender of Jutland, Slesvig, and Holstein. The rest of the business would cause small difficulty. "But everything depends upon knowledge in good time of Your Majesty's gracious resolve, for 'tis certain that the others will" else "bring him over to their side and hence this most important and necessary labour will not achieve its desired purpose." On the same day, 26 February, letters in the same vein but in even more pressing terms went to Trauttmansdorff and no less than three to Collalto. The prescience he revealed had obviously not been divulged to him all at once, but was a process long past at work inside him, a process which demanded closer attention to facts than to words and more concentration on words spoken last than first.

The reaction at Vienna was one of bewilderment and recalcitrance. One moment advocacy of a dictated peace appropriate to a victory such as modern times had never seen; the next, without anything in the whole wide world having been altered much, a renunciation of this kind? Not until 23 March did Wallenstein receive Ferdinand's answer. Judging by the acknowledgement to Collalto, it cannot have been what he hoped for: "I beg that it [the policy decision] be not postponed, for when hereafter we would have it, its implementation will not be possible. That the Prince [Eggenberg] intends after Easter to leave for Styria perplexes me so that I know not what to say." He had relied on Eggenberg's support, but the minister, jovial and lazy as always, insisted on a holiday before dealing with such crucial business. At Lübeck the negotiations dragged on. "Wrangling", as Wallenstein termed it, and wrangling in writing at that. The diplomats living cheek by jowl remained on strictly postal terms.

Wallenstein decided to substitute serious contact for the Lübeck skirmishings which could consume years. This round would need to be played on his own ground, around the fireplace at Güstrow, in secret, the players a very few elect. "My design is to send them [the conditions] to our representatives so that they can wrangle over them with the royal commissioners," he informed Collalto. "Myself, I shall in strictest secrecy investigate through Schauenburg whether means to conclude peace exist or not." Major-General von Schauenburg was King Christian's prisoner, but he enjoyed the freedom of movement allowed to distinguished hostages. It was precisely his prisoner-of-war status which enabled him to make himself at home among the Danes and to hear what did not come to the ears of the imperial diplomats. The Duke of Holstein's chancellor volunteered his services as a second intermediary. His report to Dresden, "Apart from the Duke of Friedland, no man knows of these secret negotiations other than Hannibal von and zu Schauenburg and I", did not lack self-complacency. The two visited Güstrow on several occasions at the end of March and the beginning of April. What emerged from their elucidatory discussions was passed to

two Rígsraad members whom they probably already knew to be pacifically inclined and who now surprised the King with this secret communication. The draft treaty was on the lines of Wallenstein's February
assessment of the situation and very much in tune with the Rígsraad's
views – the King should abandon his German policy, his kingdom should
be left unshorn. Kite-flying, a preliminary draft. Four personalities had
to be persuaded: King Christian, who was likely to have to comply;
Count Tilly, the other peace commissioner; most importantly, the
Emperor; and finally too Tilly's jealously vigilant master.

The Lieutenant-General had to be lured to Güstrow, entertained for
several hours a day, flattered, made to feel at his ease. Tilly came in
April. Hitherto he had propounded acting from strength and regarded
the official conditions as barely satisfactory. Inside Güstrow palace his
outlook was transformed with astonishing speed. Let it suffice to ascribe
this to the power of Wallenstein's personality. At a distance Tilly
invariably treated his superior to an old man's mischief-making. When
they met, he succumbed. Only conscientiousness constrains us to note
a subordinate motive to which historians give credence. For some time
past the Emperor had sanctioned the donation of four hundred thousand
taler to the meritorious League commander, although he was of course
unable to honour his pledge. The monkish Tilly itched to be a man of
property, at this moment presumably more than usual. The palatial
pomp amidst which he dwelt as a guest, the luxurious carpets and silken
hangings, the swarm of silently scurrying lackeys could not do other
than render him wistful. It so happened that King Christian had owing
to him by Brunswick-Wolfenbüttel a debt which corresponded approximately (precisely, it was thought, but the amount was only three
hundred thousand taler) to that rashly awarded grant. How would it be
if Denmark, otherwise not obliged to pay a penny, had none the less to
cede that Brunswick lien and it were then transferred to the Lieutenant-
General? This solution was so eagerly championed in messages to Vienna
by Wallenstein, busy courting his obtuse invitee, that the suspicion of
a link between the main purpose, winning over Tilly to the sensible
peace project, and the trifle of four hundred thousand taler cannot be
rejected out of hand. No one, though, should assert what they do not
know.

What we do know is that the trifle was simply the outcome of a larger
project which originated with Wallenstein, although not so entirely
unfamiliar and unpopular with Tilly as he subsequently claimed. The
issue turned in this instance not merely on the lien but the whole of

Brunswick. Its Duke was alleged to have had traitorous dealings with Denmark and thereby to have incurred guilt somewhat in the manner of the Mecklenburg brothers. Let Brunswick be sequestrated, whether according to imperial or martial law, and it would be available for distribution to none other than the two League generals Tilly and Pappenheim. The latter, Wallenstein's warm admirer, would only too gladly have become a participant Brunswick suzerain. At his own initiative he began proceedings against the Duke, cross-examined his privy councillors, and came to the conclusion that the dukedom was indeed ripe for sequestration. The next step was a pilgrimage to Our Lady of Loreto, with a stop at Vienna to prosecute his suit. Wallenstein's blessing was on the project. With Brunswick become another Mecklenburg and the fiefs composing it fallen into the laps of the Bavarian commanders, the Empire would possess an aristocracy of military men at whose head would still stand, not as lonely as before, the Duke of Mecklenburg. All the League outcry about the rape of Mecklenburg must then die away. The trouble was that Elector Maximilian was not the man to walk into such a trap. He intervened at Vienna on the Duke of Brunswick's behalf. To Pappenheim he wrote that it was surely inconceivable for a Bavarian officer to have presumed to such enormities. The wink was understood. Wallenstein remained the sole soldier-suzerain and Brunswick in the hands of Brunswick, albeit soon badly in arrears to General Tilly.

By 19 April, when the Lieutenant-General put his name to the expert opinion signed by both commanders-in-chief, Copenhagen was prepared to accept, the imperial court to allow conclusion of the Wallenstein peace proposals. How flighty Viennese policy-making was. An objective declared the best imaginable and attainable was a few weeks later condemned as inaccessible and its opposite hailed as better. Financier Abbot Antonius hurried to Munich to inform the Elector of the new situation. This, he lied, had from the outset been the policy really intended, but Vienna had wanted to proceed step by step, a method now no longer advisable. Maximilian listened, was surprised, and surrendered with a mutter of "war expenditure", the aspect upon which he could justly call himself a specialist, although ready at an extremity to agree even without a fee. So all of those on whom the matter depended were agreed. Or not?

Defection from the cause which Denmark and Sweden had and did not have in common was, in the eyes of Gustavus Adolphus and Oxenstierna, a catastrophe to be avoided at a high price. Denmark, as they saw it, was the last hurdle on Wallenstein's way to mastery of the Baltic and his path to Sweden. That country must at least be present at the negotiations in its capacity as Denmark's ally and a power involved through Stralsund in the German war. It also had to be there in order to transform a separate and sham act of peace-making into a genuine agreement or to rupture the negotiations. That is indeed what matters would have come to. The propositions to be put forward by Gustavus Adolphus's representatives, the dismantlement of all coastal defences, the evacuation of all northern Germany by imperial troops, were such as could only have been required from an utterly defeated foe, not of Wallenstein as he was placed in 1629. Perhaps they were the terms which Gustavus Adolphus had to exact in order to disinterest himself from Germany. Prior to a trial of strength, though, there could according to the rules of the game be no general settlement. It would not follow until two decades later.* A trial of strength had not yet taken place between Habsburg and Sweden, whereas that between the Emperor and Denmark was ended. Christian was himself now sullenly desirous of separate, not a collective northern, peace and he intimated his attitude by refusal to let the Swedish representatives travel through his territories. Wallenstein also pronounced to Collalto a veto on the presence of Swedes at Lübeck: "His Majesty shall deal alone with Denmark, and no other party, for they come not to compose but to disturb the business." When Sweden requested permission for the attendance at least of a delegation from Stralsund, he gave it to understand that any Stralsunder who ventured within the vicinity of Lübeck would be shot. He had not forgotten Stralsund. Gustavus Adolphus did not forget Lübeck.

French diplomats had for a long while been toying with a totally different concept of a separate peace, one not between the Catholic coalition and Denmark, but between Denmark and a splinter party of the coalition, namely the League, Bavaria. It was Richelieu's and Father Joseph's old idea, that of creating a third party, in Europe and especially inside the Empire, directed against Spain and Habsburg, stretching from France and the Rhine to Bavaria, inclusive of as many Protestants as cared to come in. Maximilian was not altogether averse to the scheme. He had tried it before, he would try it later. To collect around his person and to have guaranteed by the French a faction that would essentially be a party of imperial princes possibly also comprising Saxony, the Lutherans' leading power, was one thing: an alliance with international

* The Peace of Westphalia, 1648, ending the Thirty Years' War (translator's note).

Protestantism was another. Maximilian suffered under the load of his responsibilities and scruples. To this was added the factor that the moment of a collective Catholic victory in the north, wherein he held a stake and which was about to yield interesting fruit, was one unfavourable to Richelieu's fine-spun plans. His envoy, Baron Hercule Girard de Charnacé, expatiated on the possibilities of mediation between the League and Denmark, the imperilled rights of the Electors, the ancient German liberties, and the next imperial election which assuredly could for once, and in the present instance particularly, fall upon the Head of the Wittelsbach dynasty. He spoke with the tongues of angels. Maximilian, stroking his beard, lids lowered, listened without interruption very attentively. Finally he replied. Peace with Denmark was the business of the whole League, not Bavaria alone; he would allow his allies to express their views. Peace concluded, he would demand disbandment of the imperial army – a shot across Wallenstein's bows – and he would on no account agree to election of the imperial successor, young Ferdinand, without prior disbandment. Should however the Emperor engage upon an unjustified war against France, he would certainly remain neutral. This little and no more was at this juncture to be extracted from him, not enough ammunition for Charnacé when in April he reached Denmark. He did his best to goad fresh life into the King's pugnacity against the one enemy, Habsburg, less the other, the League. Maybe he would have succeeded if Wallenstein's common sense offer had not yet been on hand. He came too late. They all, it turned out, came too late – the Swedes, the French, the British, the Dutch – the last of whom suddenly signalled financial assistance which it had failed to pay in good time. Entirely too late, an ultimate gesture of rage when the temperateness of peace was prevailing at Lübeck, a snowfall in May, was Christian's impetuous attempt once more to prove his military expertise on Slesvig's periphery. "He has already forgotten Wolgast and I have to teach him a lesson again," commented Wallenstein. Shortly he was able to tell Collalto with an easy mind, "The King, I think, will by dinner-time have got over his sally". On 5 June treaty instruments were exchanged. On 30 June the imperial ratification arrived. It confirmed upright, steadfast, definite, perpetual peace between the parties and honest, untarnished amity on land and at sea, so that all past vexations should be not merely forgotten but regarded rather as lapsed, annulled, quenched, extirpated, dead and done. More specifically the King of Denmark promised not to interfere any more in the Empire's affairs and in particular to renounce on his beloved sons' behalf the claims to those imperial endowments formerly administered by Danish princes – Bremen, Verden, Schwerin. The last was of importance to Wallenstein who a year ago had incorporated it into Mecklenburg. The Emperor for his part swore nowhere to arrogate sovereign Danish royal rights and, should contrary to expectation a misunderstanding arise, to heed well arbitrational judgement.

That brought to a close what historians subsequently called the great war's Lower Saxon–Danish period. Extirpated and lapsed was the situation in which as long as four years ago Wallenstein had been appointed captain-general of all the imperial forces in the Empire. Where were the enemies of yesteryear? Mad Christian and Mansfeld were long dead; the Estates of the Lower Saxon Circle were all either loyal or subjugated; Denmark was back within the fold of peace. With this pressure relaxed, surely the counter-pressure should relax too. Had Wallenstein rendered himself superfluous? That was how the Electors saw and, with exasperated impatience, expressed the matter. He of course viewed it in a different light. Not that war had for him become an indispensable habit. Unlike Gustavus Adolphus, he was no perpetual youngster and reckless rider. It was not even that, conformable to popular belief, he was so attached to his generalship. A few months after the Peace of Lübeck he entertained the notion of shedding his generalate on land and contenting himself with a kind of coastal defence commission in such fashion that he would not at all time have to be "personally present". Six months in Bohemia, six months in Mecklenburg was, it may be guessed, what he had in mind. That was impossible. He could only stay Duke of Mecklenburg as long as he was Generalissimo. Both dignities, generalship and ducal status, rested on the power to which for the past decade he had helped the House of Austria, first in Bohemia, then in the Empire, and which was intolerable for Europe. The Peace of Lübeck was no restoration, although it seemed so. Whence, after such devious adventures, should restoration derive? To allow of it, Wallenstein would strictly speaking have had to repudiate himself and modestly return to the parental roof at Hermanitz. There is no such return, as little in the life of one man as in the fate of all. He could not be parted from the highly responsible, far-reaching and dangerous cause with which he had identified himself as long as that cause was prepared to allow such identification. Before the business at Lübeck had been concluded, the edict on the restitution of church lands, that inexpressibly spurious restoration, demonstrated that no restoration would in all seriousness occur.

Leaving aside border disputes and blemishes like Poland, Stralsund, Holland, northern Italy, seen moreover in the perspective of an international jurist, Wallenstein for the next eighteen months was a commander-in-chief without an enemy, a peacetime general. No unequivocal military task was on hand, no job that must be done. Resultant uneasiness, for the job that must be done can be of help, especially to those who always keep their eyes open all round and come reluctantly to a decision. Resultant leisure too, leisure to move more freely than was otherwise the case. What happened then, what was done, attempted and rejected, all happened simultaneously. Its narration, though, must follow step by step.

SEA AND CITY

In the course of his grand tour Wallenstein may have seen the sea somewhere along Italy's ample coastline. If he did, then never again, not even in Holstein, until July 1628. At that date the Grand Admiral's ignorance of maritime matters was indeed great. During his journey he had mistaken Oder barges for seaworthy vessels.

He learnt quickly. On arrival at the German littoral he regarded its cities simply as so many bases, money reservoirs, and proletariats in need of taming. Within a short while he had become their partner and patron. The relationship would probably have evolved still better if the mishap and mismanagement at Stralsund had not occurred.

To say that he only talked and did nothing for the naval project is wrong. He did what he could. He was its ardent supporter – for a time. However, as with all contemporary political enterprises and particularly those under the aegis of the twofold Habsburg power, resources were not commensurate with what was desired and imagination envisaged. Madrid's contribution of two hundred thousand crowns was a bauble. Wallenstein had asked King Philip for twenty-four galleons; they never came. He asked Infanta Isabella for ten; she offered excuses, such as expressing doubt upon the advisability of sending the precious craft through the Sound controlled by the Dutch and the Danes. King Sigismund was the sole Catholic ruler who ventured to unite his fleet, beggarly enough, with that of the Emperor. Since January 1629 Polish ships had ridden at anchor in Wismar harbour. There remained the possibilities of purchase, but the Hanse towns were mulish about selling because they safeguarded their neutrality like the apple of their eye, or of undertaking construction. Requisite for that were money, materials, and skilled shipwrights. Wallenstein tried to obtain them in Holland through the camouflaged agency of a Scottish merchant. The States-General saw through the deal and prohibited it. No less difficult was to find mariners for such a new, queer master. Infantrymen made shift as naval captains, at the outset understanding as little of the sea as the Generalissimo had. At best they were content to practise coastal piracy.

Since autumn 1628 the admiralty staff, with Philipp Mansfeld as admiral and Gabriel de Roy as nautical specialist, had been installed at Wismar. Wallenstein had successfully protested against de Roy's nomination as General Commissary for the imperial navy. He knew how loathed the Spaniards were in German cities and the vile pig-headedness with which they conducted their actions at sea. De Roy continued in an equivocal position – under the orders of the Emperor and Wallenstein an agent of Madrid.

By the end of 1628 about a dozen ships, half of them in fighting trim, are said to have been lying at Wismar. Next year they numbered twenty to twenty-five, including the Polish contingent. Mere figures tell little. The single-masted vessels which Mansfeld had had built at Lübeck, Wismar, and Rostock had a burden of about eighteen tons. The warships of the Spaniards, British, and Swedes carried as much as four thousand tons.

Prior to conclusion of peace with the Danes the intention had been to render possible, or to appear to render possible, an attack on King Christian's islands. As late as January 1629 that was the instruction issued by Wallenstein to his admiralty. How seriously he meant it, seeing that the inadequacy of his scratch half-squadron should have been obvious to him, is unknown. In any event the Danish objective constituted a conflict in embryo with the Spaniards. Their interest was not directed against Denmark, but as ever, as ever again, and forever against Holland. They pinned on the Habsburg fleet their hopes of ruining the rebels' fishing activities and Baltic trade. To that end they would very much have liked to establish an autonomous base on the island of Sylt. Wallenstein disliked the project. Falling out with the Dutch at sea meant falling out with the Hanse by land. After the Peace of Lübeck it would have been more difficult to explain the purpose served by the imperial fleet. Maybe to show the flag, impress the Swedes, and complement the coastal batteries through a more flexible defence mechanism. Gustavus Adolphus did in fact behave as though he were thoroughly frightened by it – what aim could this hitherto non-existent imperial German fleet have other than the invasion of his peace-loving country? Perhaps, in a period when so much was exaggerated, babbled about, inaccurately reported, and when so many fantasies of pride and fear prevailed, he did overrate it. He possessed only fourteen large men-of-war. There were said to be twenty at Wismar. In August he had the port blockaded. At the end of September the imperial ships ventured out. Shots were exchanged, the Swedes broke off the encounter, and de Roy proclaimed a notable victory. Wallenstein's governor, more sceptical, believed that the Swedish vessels had retired only two days later of their own free will. Their commander had indeed a royal order to the effect that, with the enemy locally in greater strength, no defeat should be risked. For the imperial naval enterprise it was a pinnacle of achievement, properly speaking its only one, a moment when this figment of imagination attained reality because the opposite side credited it with having such. De Roy took advantage of the situation to fly his true colours. During the succeeding weeks he allowed his officers to capture eight enemy ships, "enemy" signifying to the Spanish mentality whoever was not a friend, whether Swede, Dutch, Hanse, or anyone else. Wallenstein intervened. The ships and all cargo seized were to be returned forthwith "because no good would be done by impediments to commerce and it has never been Our intent to put to sea against ships of trade, but alone against any warships coursing before the port". The mariners and merchants were to be informed that the Duke of Mecklenburg would know how to protect the freedom of commerce on the high seas. One of Mansfeld's captains was severely reprimanded for having "borne himself more like a pirate than as behoved a soldier". The phrase concentrates Wallenstein's concept of soldiery. For his day it was not bad.

Not bad either was, or was soon to become, his whole commercial and marine policy. As early as 1628 he acquiesced in the principle that neutral cargoes carried in enemy bottoms should be recognized as neutral and not subject to confiscation, a principle fostered by Hamburg and Lübeck, liberals from weakness, and not the stronger maritime powers. He permitted Rostock, his own city so recently subjected and with a garrison imposed on it, to trade with hostile Sweden. Its merchants pursued their business at Rostock without hindrance. Rostock was allowed to make deliveries to the Swedish army in Prussia, important war materials excepted. But what did "important" in this context mean? He issued a number of orders to leave undisturbed Lübeck's and Hamburg's dealings with the east and the Netherlands. What was wanted of these towns "would probably be better attained through informal and private discourses than rigorous interrogations". Wise words so few days after Stralsund, a lesson learned. He forbade the export of victuals, cattle and corn. Those he needed for his own forces. Yet even here he granted privileged treatment in specific cases.

If such concessions on the part of one reputed to be arrogant and tyrannical created pleased surprise, Wallenstein's commercial practice after the peace of Lübeck developed in a manner which did not fail to arouse the interest also of the hard-headed Dutch. He had, he told a Lübeck representative, "no mind at all to do the slightest detriment to business, either at sea or on land, but much more to let it take its untrammelled course"; Sweden, not he, was destroying the freedom of the seas. He could prove it. Gustavus Adolphus thwarted every attempt at trade with Pomerania, which he regarded as antagonistic. He blockaded Danzig because it had declined an alliance with him. He inflicted horrific tariffs on Prussian ports. Stralsund, liberated and saved by the Swedes, miserably watched its commerce disappearing. Hamburg and Lübeck, whose neutrality Wallenstein acknowledged in full, and Rostock and Stettin, under his suzerainty, flourished. He had no objection to Rostock beer being carried in Swedish holds, to Sweden buying arms in Hamburg and unloading there its copper ore. The traffic between the Hanseatic towns and the Netherlands proceeded under his protection. He had a sharp brush with Brussels because the Spanish admiralty at Dunkirk suffered a Lübeck vessel destined for Amsterdam to be boarded. That, he argued, was unlawful; the ship must be returned. He had the Dutch informed that he would not tolerate any Spanish naval interference with their merchantmen inside the Baltic. Trade there would be free for as far as his power extended. Wallenstein's path, if ever it had run parallel to Spain's, now branched away and led him close to that of the rebellious Netherlands into the economic sphere where, contrary to the political one, reason is operative. More than the purely economic motive force tends, thereafter, to enter into play.

How could a feudal military landlubber come so quickly to practise shrewdness on the salt-water front? He might understand nothing of maritime commerce, but from his Friedland experience he knew a lot about commerce as a whole. What was lacking was complemented by those Hanse diplomats who, since he ruled in Lower Germany, frequented his court. They were in close touch with the Netherlands. Through them he came into contact with the enlightened rebels. The year 1629 saw the beginning of a lively exchange of letters with Foppius van Aitzema, the Dutch agent at Hamburg and a friend of no less than the celebrated jurist Hugo Grotius to whose recommendation he owed his appointment. Not for a moment do we believe that Wallenstein skimmed through *De Jure Belli*, gracing the Frankfurt Autumn Fair of 1625. None the less the treatise's ideas may have seeped through to him just as its author's fame will certainly have done. In his dream of a university of Sagan he wanted, among his other intellectual banner-bearers like Kepler and Martin Opitz, Gropius to hold a chair. Dutch and Hanseatic theories worked upon him as soon as he came within the radius of their attraction.

Add to this the sound, strong mental calibre of the man which enabled him quickly to master matter utterly foreign to him and season it with his sense of order. Piracy represented disorder, wanton waste. The Duke of Mecklenburg had an interest in the welfare of the cities as the Generalissimo had such in the peasants' peaceful sowing of their seed so that they should be able to harvest it, and as far as he could he protected both. The difference was that the high seas were relatively controllable whereas the land over which his regiments marched hither and thither was extremely uncontrollable. To release a captured ship was easier than to breathe fresh life into a burnt-down, depopulated village. Instead of driving them into the arms of the waiting Britons and Swedes, he did not grudge the maritime cities their cautious abstention from political partisanship. He hardly needed the precepts in this direction which during the Stralsund episode he received from Vienna. On the contrary it was Vienna and ever again Madrid who faced the Hanse with the crude alternative of being friend or foe. He wanted peace, peace at least in northern Germany, and practice of the peaceful arts there so long as peace could not be had everywhere. True, he was not prepared to relinquish Mecklenburg nor to budge from northern German soil.

He was too viciously entangled in a skein of irrational constraints to be able to struggle through to the freedom of good sense, an oarsman plying his sculls regardless of his skiff being tied to the bank. He continued in bond to the House of Austria and thereby, against his better instinct, to Spain too. The Hanse cities had a presentiment of that. To have transformed their neutrality into national loyalty he would have had to represent a nation like France or Sweden, a state demanding obedience because it could give protection. With the Empire that was not the case. When he talked of achieving what was not as yet in embryo and of teaching the Electors lessons, his eagerly repeated vaunts served to excite tremors of fear and hate at Munich, Mainz, Cologne and Dresden, but not much more. That he was German merely by option was an added irritant, not a crucial element. Any born German, whether Swabian, Bavarian, or Austrian, who navigated Wallenstein's course would hardly have fared better. By chance, or probably not so much by chance, none did so. Prince Eggenberg, for example. A clever man too, but restfully lazy, shy of venturesome enterprises, thoroughly enmeshed in conventional concepts. What did Wallenstein care for imperial tradition? He used his mind, therefore gave rein to his fancy. Untrammelled intelligence and play of fancy are near identical

Directly or indirectly he controlled the following regions: Holstein, Slesvig and Jutland, but only until the Peace of Lübeck; Mecklenburg, the great bishoprics of Halberstadt and Magdeburg, Pomerania, Brandenburg and Silesia. His sway over the last was imperfect in so far as he no longer had any regiments there, but the Silesians had to pay him contributions and he had a seat and a vote in the princely Silesian Diet. Then Friedland and Bohemia. Effacing the frontier familiar to us, it was a solid land mass encompassed and linked by the flow of Elbe and Oder. To the army these rivers became indispensable lines of communication. Horses, timber, arms and cereals were borne down them tariff-free. The privilege was meant to apply only to military stores, but unofficially it was exploited for other purposes by merchants and shippers, redounding not least to the advantage of Hamburg and Stettin. The army was the devourer of energies, the thieving guest, the incubus. That is well known. More rarely noted is its other function as a distributor of incomes, a mart for money and goods. The chronicles are silent about that aspect because people prefer to tell of their sufferings rather than their profits. The letters of enterprising producers extolling their goods to the Generalissimo blab the truth: "Your Princely Grace will not repent of the custom given me for I shall assuredly at one or another opportunity prove my gratitude." Wallenstein's court provided moreover a powerful spur, in Lower Germany as earlier in Bohemia, to consumption and the placement of orders. Its eight hundred adherents, with many great lords habituated under the one great lord to not wanting for anything, meant something to an economy indigent as a whole. It gave local traders as well as those from an area farther removed, the Netherlands, a chance to show what they could do. Alongside the main, plain business of consumption was that of reinvestment, whether for the iron foundries in Mecklenburg or the cattle traffic from Holstein and Mecklenburg to Friedland. The roads, at least within a very wide radius of the court, were "entirely clean and maintained secure and severe, inexorable punishment is imposed wherever anything occurs".

Because he needed them, Wallenstein was considerate to those who worked and were useful. He turned against them, terribly, only when they no longer wanted to be used and rebelled. For the rest he preferred the few rich to the innumerable poor. No wonder. He who lives in fine houses fears disorder and clings to internal as well as external peace and quiet. It had been the Stralsund patriciate, not the proletariat, which sought agreement with him. The same held good for Lübeck, Rostock, Magdeburg, cities where the preachers, often refugees from Bohemia and Austria, contributed their part to popular agitation. He was, he wrote in summer 1629 to the Magdeburgers, ready to recognize the difference between rabble and honourable citizenry. "We have observed the whole course of the disorder, not overlooking that this revolt has stemmed more from the own wantonness of the partly light-minded rabble. . . ." The trouble which in 1629 broke out with the great city of Magdeburg contradicts what has just been recounted about his caution and liberality in matters of municipal policy. He allowed himself exceptions when the ague took him. Against Magdeburg he set out to proceed on Stralsund, or near-Stralsund, lines. Yet in the end he did not. The affair ended with a gesture of generosity akin to a clap of stage-thunder.

MAGDEBURG

The populous Elbe community had, as elsewhere, three parties. A small minority, though not small of fortune, sought to please the Emperor in each and every respect. The majority of the Council and a portion of the citizenry, choosing the golden mean, wanted to defend the city's privileges but not to provoke His Majesty, to fulfil this fair and evade that unreasonable demand. The third party went all out for resistance, pinning its hopes first on the Danes, then, when the Danes succumbed, on the Dutch and the Swedes. Preponderant in numbers, it was composed of fishermen, barge crews, craftsmen – "the rabble". Its spokesmen were excitable divines.

Matters took their usual climacteric course. Fuel was added to the flames from within and without the walls. Wallenstein had originally been rather more sympathetic to Magdeburg than some other places. He afforded it considerable advantages. Now he wanted something in return – a lot of money, more than it could pay or than its citizens were willing to pay, for the claim that they were unable to muster one hundred and fifty thousand taler leaves us unconvinced. In any event they did not deliver the sum previously agreed. To the financial squabble was added a religious element. Long before the edict on the restitution of church lands was signed by the Emperor, the imperialists assumed possession of an old Premonstratensian monastery and re-introduced monks into this arch-Lutheran city. The monks preached, they offered all kinds of amenities to those ready to be converted, they were zealous, and they fussed. Rage on the part of the poor, rage on the part of the pious, flight on the part of the rich and imperially inclined, refusal on the part of the Council to admit a regiment as garrison. Wallenstein's customary summons to recusant towns. Magdeburg envoys at Güstrow. The Duke, preoccupied with many and important matters, terse. He had nothing against the city, but like all other cities it must pay; such was war.

It did not pay. Wallenstein passed the business to Aldringen, his most experienced debt collector. Aldringen ordered a blockade. Nobody was to enter Magdeburg, nobody to leave it, no ship to dock, no fisherman to cast his nets. The blockade was entrusted to tertiary subordinates, without much experience of politics but plenty of pillaging. Sorties by the imprisoned, counter-actions by their gaolers. Thieving by the Croats, mutual murder. The fishermen, deprived of their bread, robbed a nearby cloister and raided a ship carrying corn for the imperial forces. Instead of taming the city, the blockade brought to power the third, the majority party. Against that the Council might be helpless, but its judgement was sound: Magdeburg could not withstand prolonged siege because, unlike Stralsund, it had not the sea.

In this dilemma the Council asked befriended cities like Lübeck, Hamburg, and Brunswick to mediate on its behalf. Their representatives appeared before Wallenstein at his Wolmirstedt headquarters. This time he was gruff even to these Hanseatic intercessories on whose pacific neutrality he had come to rely so much. "You must know that it is His Majesty's General with whom you are dealing and not take me for a fool. I care not for the corn. It is the city of which I must be assured, else all my victories can redound to my humiliation." The petitioners repeated all that Magdeburg was prepared to perform. "It has but to accept a garrison," Wallenstein retorted. "That will be difficult to implement." "I can make it easy for them, and every other city too. They will not starve me out, I can starve them out." He desired moreover, to talk to the Magdeburgers directly.

They came, headed by the city syndic. "How have you conducted yourselves, you gentlemen of Magdeburg?" "Serene, high-born Highness," began the syndic. "I know well how it is," Wallenstein broke in, "Is it not wanton, dishonourable, oblivious behaviour to which your rabble presumes and thereby begets rebelliousness?" Possibly, indeed probably, he went on, the Council really could not help the mob's impudent proceedings. The city must however punish the lawbreakers because, apart from two principal felons, he did not wish to deal with the gallows-birds; and thereafter it must accept a garrison. "That is my intent." "Gracious Prince and Lord," again began the syndic. "We were not at that time there. . . ." "I let that pass," he was once more interrupted. "I cannot haggle, I am no trader." He reiterated the phrase, as also the statement that he had to have a garrison inside the town, "for I shall enter in despite, 'tis certain". "I shall enter in despite, 'tis certain," he repeated. "And that I want the rapscallions handed out, for I am resolved to have their heads struck off. . . . And I do not have both these heads, it shall cost two thousand. That is my intent." He waved his hand thrice, nodded. War Commissary von Questenberg, in attendance, made signs: the Magdeburgers, dismissed, should hold their tongues, do obeisance, and disappear.

That was in August 1629. The blockade was transformed into a siege according to the book of rules. Colonel Pappenheim, the expert who had disapproved of the Stralsund undertaking, thought this enterprise promising. The Hanse made fresh efforts at mediation, efforts supported by the leader of Magdeburg's expelled imperial loyalists. None the less a patriot, he sought at Wallenstein's headquarters mercy for his city. In October a fresh mass audience of Hanseatic and Magdeburg representatives was held at Halberstadt. Suddenly gracious, the Duke extended his hand to these delegates, an honour not conferred upon any and all. The conduct of the city against its sovereign, the Emperor, had been unheard of, but if it was repentant and would in future put a sharper curb upon its populace, then the past should belong to the past. Not a word more about a garrison. What he wanted was money – two hundred thousand taler. That, the Magdeburgers swore, was too much. The amount could not be raised. It could, though, because it had to be. They offered one hundred and fifty thousand, but in such manner that one hundred thousand would be reckoned as on account to the damage sustained by the city through blockade and siege. Whereupon Wallenstein: "Now, truly, because We perceive that Magdeburg and all the Hanse cities are determined to abide in allegiance to the Emperor, We are of grace prepared to remit the entire sum so that it may be seen how

We do not wage war for lucre but are alone concerned to maintain the obedience which is the Emperor's due." Among the delegates there was a rustle of joyful surprise. "We learn that the Hanse cities conceive that the imperial edict respecting the reformation of religion is to be prosecuted. That in no wise is our view, but rather that the edict cannot endure, and We promise the Hanse cities that not the least shall be demanded of them by reason thereof, for the religious peace cannot thus be overthrown." He would know how to protect them all in their faith, their commerce and their privileges. This scene of clemency came to be called the "Peace of Halberstadt".

It was not so altogether spontaneous, not so completely due to a flash of inspiration – first embittered wrangling about money and then, that conceded, its noble renunciation. Always worried, generally pessimistic, Wallenstein's analysis of the Empire's, or the Emperor's, position was gloomier in autumn than it had been in summer. In particular he expected an offensive move to be made from Stralsund – a premature anticipation, but with each month that passed less premature. He thought it better to come to an understanding with the Magdeburgers which would obviate uproar and an irksome tying down of resources, earning in their place the increment to be derived from a magnanimous gesture. All the same, just as in the dark depths of his soul a spate of predilections jostled for priority, so was the vexatious Magdeburg business contrary to the most fundamental tenor of his policy. He had indulged in an exception. He retrieved the situation, not too late as in the case of Stralsund, but in the nick of time.

And, while he was exhorting the Hanse to uphold its fealty to the Emperor, this war's sole purpose, at that very moment he retracted his own. "The edict cannot endure." The edict of restitution was however the heartfelt be-all of Ferdinand III's aspirations, "this glorious work of reformation", "the whole fruit of the victories hitherto granted Us by God".

THE EDICT

On 6 March 1629, while the negotiations with Denmark were still in train, the Emperor signed the tidings dearest to his heart, an involved composition full of historical references and legalistic deductions from the Peace of Augsburg in 1555 and notably larded with paragraphs beginning "On the other hand", "So that too", "In view of", and "But as long as". Its conclusion proclaimed that all the Empire's Protestant

Estates must, on pain of being put to the imperial ban, restitute the bishoprics, prelacies, monasteries and convents, charitable institutions, benefices, and other endowments diverted since the Passau Compromise of 1552 from their consecrated purpose. The authors of the edict doubtless had the law on their side in so far as it is still legal to restore a state of affairs which ineluctably leads to fresh inequity, homelessness, turmoil, fear and spiritual anguish, and in so far as that is still law over which seventy years have eddied as does the sea over flat land behind broken dikes.

Does the reader recall how in Wallenstein's younger days matters stood in Germany? They stood badly, close to a collapse of imperial law, fairly close to civil war or war between the Estates. The religious peace, false from the start, no reconciliation of ideas but a continued co-existence of powers, had not allowed antitheses to wither away. That process is something which men of good will certainly expect to happen and which in the end does happen, but after centuries, not decades, and its realization derives sheer from the passage of time, not good sense and brotherliness. It had therefore not been good sense that had temporarily inhibited the outbreak of civil war; it had been Bohemian unrest. In 1620, to forestall help by the Protestants, the Union, the Saxon Circles, to the Bohemians, the Catholic princes had agreed to abandon any resort to force; they would try and settle the problem of ownership in ecclesiastical properties only by legal process applied to cases individually. By the unforeseen overspill of Bohemian hostilities war had none the less come to Germany. Piety and greed fed on the triumph of Catholic arms and the eating created appetite. The year 1629 saw the claims for pilfered church possessions becoming more massive and daring. As yet the demand was not for a comprehensive solution, simply the revendication of this and that piece of booty. In Württemberg, for instance, no less than seventy rich monasteries and convents were the subject of suits. They represented claims totalling one-third of its territory and the main source for those ducal revenues on which promotion of the land's cultural progress, its schools, and its livings depended. Such were the fat spoils which engaged the zeal of southern Germany's bishops, those of Constance, Augsburg, Würzburg and Bamberg. Gradually they proceeded from case in point to principle. Many poor souls' irretrievable damnation was at stake, they asseverated. *Faits accomplis* must be created at a single blow before the humbled opposition set about its defence. What, Emperor Ferdinand wanted to know, did his faithful Electors think? A busy exchange of communications was loosed between Bavaria, Mainz, Cologne and Trèves. The planned restitution, wrote Maximilian, was indeed rather repugnant, but it must be. The Bishop of Bamberg, when everything had been decided, expressed somewhat similar sentiments – who would truly relish participation in such onerous, detested endeavours? The expert opinion sent to Vienna by the four Electors took the philosophic approach that there was more reason to lament on behalf of the Holy Roman Empire of the German Nation and strive with unabated ardour for the estimable peace pleasing to God than to give rise to yet greater lack of confidence and unrest. Verily! All the same, if the road to ruin is paved with finely phrased doubts, it will nevertheless be taken when, as well as bane, gain in goods and dominions beckons. Here it was taken all the more easily because the letter of the law was clear and the objective none other than fulfilment of the Peace of 1555, its demonstrably literal fulfilment as substitute for the subsequently befallen, wholly illegal accretion. Because moreover, as the Electors did not fail to indicate, the power to do so was available, for under the Emperor's authority the juncture was such "that assuredly no one will either dare, lust, or have any grounds insubordinately to resist Your rightful imperial decree". Equity and power, a splendid combination. The same Diet of princes where on 27 October the Catholics discussed restitution resolved that measures should be undertaken against the despotic conduct of the Duke of Friedland. The diplomat whom Maximilian of Bavaria shortly afterwards sent to Prague had two pieces of business to transact – the restoration of ecclesiastical property and the reduction of Wallenstein's military establishment. Ill-assorted bedfellows. Whoever favoured peace, which all did, was not at liberty to desire the restitution. Whoever favoured restitution was not at liberty to want demobilization. Politicians however seldom pin-point issues as precisely as that.

The year 1628 passed in correspondence, preliminaries, and the preparation of drafts. They were meant to remain secret and became public. There had come to his ears, John George of Saxony told the Elector of Mainz, projects of a most critical and dangerous nature. He recapitulated rumours which compounded what was generally held against Wallenstein, intent to transform the Empire into a "New Model", with intentions not in the least concordant with Wallenstein's aims, extirpation of the Protestant faith. Should, proceeding step by step, measures first be ventured against the puny and defenceless, the imperial counts and free towns, and for the nonce the bigger brethren, Saxony and Brandenburg, be spared? Maximilian regarded that as advisable in practice although dubious in principle. John George's predecessors had helped themselves all too profusely to bishoprics within their territory. Should that state of affairs continue to prevail? Possession of properties regained, what was in fact to be done with the enormous mass of holdings? Which dynasty, Habsburg or Wittelsbach, should have priority in occupation of the northern and central German bishoprics? Were there monks enough, Cistercians, Premonstratensians, Benedictines, and of good enough character to turn the neo-veteran institutions once more into centres *de propaganda fide*? Abbot Antonius, the finance man and Benedictine, thought yes. Jesuit confessor Lamormaini, his rival, thought no and he called timely attention to the greater effectiveness of his Order. Should not a part of the abundance, especially the convents lacking inmates, be used as boarding-schools and seminaries for the Society of Jesus? Did not the draft sent in October to Maximilian by imperial Vice-Chancellor Stralendorf, at the urgings of the Catholic Electors as he emphasized, really go rather far? Stralendorf's note of warning sounded as though he was not entirely standing by what his own department had concocted. The confiscation of the religious houses formerly owing direct allegiance to the Emperor would fall very hardly upon Saxony, and that the Calvinists should lose the benefit springing from the religious peace, while doubtless historically impeccable, was a trifle harsh in light of the Elector of Brandenburg's regrettable adhesion to Calvinism. And so on, back and forth. All was still in flux when the Emperor had the bugle blown for this Last Judgement. He did not want to wait any longer. Not that he was driven by greed, only secondarily at least. Primarily it was, as usual, his imperial missionary fervour.

Characteristic is that the mightiest man in the Empire, Generalissimo the Duke of Friedland, was never consulted about the edict. No expertise on his part has survived because he was never afforded the chance to formulate one. He was against it. Then why did he not prevent it? Because he was no politician, not as later ages understood the word, capable of manoeuvring parties and making masterly appeals to public opinion. Because unlike the Cardinal at Paris, that more fortunate contemporary pawn of destiny, he did not even sit as first among equals in the Council of a tightly governed monarchy. Germany's system of rule was not comparable to France's. On one side there were the Electors; on the other, the imperial ministers, corrupt, opportunist, always divided amongst themselves. Wallenstein was no courtier, no arch-intriguer, not even a passionate supporter of what he recognized to be right. Were wrong done, folly committed, risks run, his habit had ever been to scoff but to conform, above all when he was not at court in person. He never was, as people thought, the Emperor's Caesar.

Nor a stickler for principles. When in 1625 he set out to conquer Germany, there existed between him and Lamormaini a secret agreement that the two major endowments of Magdeburg and Halberstadt should be conferred as benefices on the Emperor's second son, not in vindication of the terms of 1555, with which Wallenstein was unfamiliar, but consistent with the laws of war. In the event he postponed indefinitely the young Archduke's assumption of the livings because he needed the income for his army. In Mecklenburg, though, he unhesitatingly incorporated the bishopric of Schwerin, administered by a Protestant Danish prince, into his duchy. That was not "restitution". He eradicated even the name of the old bishopric; Schwerin-Bützow became a plain Mecklenburg rural district like any other. And his position was such that no one ventured to employ the edict against him.

By now he knew Germany well enough to surmise the consequences which would transcend well beyond the edict's literal fulfilment, the despair which would grip the hearts not solely and not so greatly of the princes as those of their subjects, the anxiety which would be created whether a "universal reformation" on Austro–Bohemian lines was projected and, arising on that, the readiness to rush into the arms of any foreign saviour. The Swede, for example. Whoever wanted peace inside Germany, public peace and private peace of mind, was not free to want the edict. Whoever wanted the edict did not, a fig for all fine words, want peace. Wallenstein had the Elector of Saxony told that the edict thoroughly displeased him and that he would not let himself be used for its implementation, meaning that he would not send his soldiers to prise open monastery doors and chase away those living behind them. It amounted to a secret revocation of the obedience which was the Emperor's due. His pronouncement to the Hanse representatives, "The edict cannot endure", was a public one. Possessed of no forum from which his sentiments could be spread, he none the less saw to it that they were known at Vienna, for he must have supposed that the letter he wrote to Collalto, President of the imperial War Council, would also be shown others to read. "The edict is the motivation," a reference to the popular stir at Magdeburg. "All this is caused by the untimely and severe reformation, as likewise the imperial edict on the restitution of church lands and expulsion of the Calvinists." "For the imperial edict has turned all the non-Catholics against us ... the whole Empire will be opposed to us, the Swede, the Turk, and Bethlehem too." "The bitterness is so great that they all say, Let the Swede but come, and he can not help them, they will gladly perish with him." The Empire was ostensibly at peace. When however the effects of the edict began to become apparent, the victor and peacemaker took a more pessimistic view of its situation than at any period since his entry upon the general-ate. After all, he who rode in slow procession through the land and was everywhere accosted by emissaries could not help but be a little better apprised of common feeling than the Privy Councillors at Vienna. The edict agitated his shrewd, proud, and culpable spirit as it did that of a hundred thousand innocents. Six years later there was no more talk of any of this mischievous business, and never again thereafter.

The wheels of imperial justice ground slowly. As they began to turn, they met with passively stubborn resistance. An imperial commissioner, accompanied by a powerless escort, would appear before a town to requisition this monastery or that church. He was roundly refused admission. It would take time for a couple of companies of ruffians to follow, time enough to see what would happen then. A strength of one hundred and fifty thousand men – more precisely, so it is alleged, one hundred and thirty-four thousand men – was not very large to force Germany at every point, still less large if their commander-in-chief felt no inclination to apply that force. Even many members of the restitution committees displayed reluctance. Pappenheim, co-responsible in the Franconian Circle, first excused himself on the score of his wedding celebrations, which he wished to enjoy without interruption, and then by reason of his military duties. Others pleaded indisposition and had to be gravely, repeatedly admonished to discharge their delicate commis-sion. To this was added the complication that often the documents with the text of the endowment or the year of sequestration, on which everything depended, had disappeared along with the monks, so that the executors ought also to have been skilled antiquaries. In short, the edict in the first instance disturbed and did more damage by the mere fact of its existence than by the order for its effectuation. By early summer 1630, when Wallenstein came to Swabia, virtually nothing had been undertaken in the defenceless and, for the restitutionists, so exceedingly tempting duchy of Württemberg.

And again nothing happened. Two Lutheran Estate members who appeared at his Memmingen headquarters as petitioners sent back to Stuttgart a staggering report – the General had expressed himself in such fashion as to "render quite clear that His Dilection takes staunch displeasure in such highly hateful procedure". The Emperor had indeed imposed his mandate. Not, though, of his own free will, but at the insistence of his clergy. His Majesty was no longer his own master. For a few more months the Württembergers obtained a breathing-space, fancying themselves protected by none other than him who had previously been described as the Counter-Reformation's vilest tool: "For if he be not so disposed, all imperial ordinances count for naught." In July letters penned by the Emperor himself, strict orders really, arrived at Memmingen. Now, eighteen months after promulgation of the edict, the General gave way. Twenty-eight companies, under the command of Colonel Ossa, were launched into central Württemberg. They were to be on hand in case the inhabitants to be expelled should have the impudence to continue to offer resistance. In vain were the final pleas borne by a Stuttgart emissary to army headquarters. He was, Wallenstein declared, a friend of Württemberg. The reformation of the monastic establishments touched him deeply, he sighed, "but because all his warnings against it have been of no avail, he must let it happen and be glad that another hath been charged with the commission". He had reached the end, not only of his sabotage of the edict of restitution, but his generalate too, and he knew it. The mien of a regretful shrug of the shoulders was natural to him. Let others do it. It was no longer his concern.

COLLATERAL CAMPAIGNS

Power politics will possess precisely the strength lying behind the ultimate argument, open or concealed, always at the disposal of the politician who engages therein. If war is out of the question, there is no power game. If war furnishes a swift, incisive weapon – to the point, masterly, effectual – that will characterize the play of power. A slow, impotently drawn out and botched war will match a policy of similar sort. In Wallenstein's day travel was troublesome, public speaking unknown, its place taken by letters and files. They have survived in large numbers, but to sift there the relatively durable strands of thought from fleeting fancies is a matter of training. Wallenstein's cultivation of long-term perspectives is what distinguishes him from most contemporary politicians. They babbled this today, that tomorrow, bothering not at all about inconsistency and busying their heads with nothing other than tactics and momentary absorptions. He of course was also subject to moods. Those are the occasions when historians, treating much more seriously what he wrote in a particular letter than he probably did himself, claim that his policy took a fresh turn, whereas in reality he had already leapt in the opposite direction before the first letter even reached its addressee. Such expressions of sentiment were simply reversals from one path of impracticality to another. Wild-goose chases. He had moreover to appear to obey, by way of words at least to bow to the will of his employers, for all that in fact he failed to comply. He had to find excuses. Urged by Vienna at last to undertake something in Italy, he emphasized the need to assist the Spaniards in the north-west so that the Dutch should not become altogether too impudent, and he would thereupon indeed inaugurate some trifling activity. Requested to do the opposite, to switch the main weight of operations in the direction of the Netherlands, he declared his readiness to follow in the immediate future the road to Italy in person, though he never did. It was an exhausting, irritating war of movement on paper which soured his temper. The Swedish–Polish hostilities were the only collateral campaign which he supported as a matter of sober reflection because his object was to tie down Sweden, year after year, in Poland.

In spring 1629 he used the opportunity afforded by a Polish request for aid to bring the issue to a head. Four infantry and five cavalry regiments, a small army of fifteen thousand men, were detailed for the Prussian theatre of war. Here was the harvest of Stralsund, the fear of what the Swedes would attempt from that accursed bridgehead if they were allowed to draw breath elsewhere. The expeditionary corps was under command of the officer whom he held to be his most efficient, Arnim. "Pray, let him lose not a moment, but move immediately upon Prussia, for this is no unconsidered enterprise." The Polish nobility flinched however at imperial help which was thought, not wholly without reason, to be capable of harbouring intentions against the duchy of Prussia. They were not even comforted by the notion of a brilliant victory in the Swedish campaign. Wallenstein, generally well informed, believed that he knew why. "The Poles are by nature hostile to the Germans. The *Proceres Regni* [the kingdom's magnates] deem that the more powerful the Emperor becomes, the sooner they will be quelled by their King and, as they opine, reduced to servitude." Such a frame of mind among the Republic's potentates augured badly for the campaign. The Seym, Poland's parliament of nobles, had sanctioned an auxiliary contingent ten thousand strong. It now denied ever having acquiesced in a figure above six thousand, let alone fifteen thousand. The King, for one reason and another, did not want Arnim as commander-in-chief. The Polish commissioners who were to meet the Field-

Marshal at the Prussian-Pomeranian border in the first place failed to arrive and then brought unpalatable tidings – for the time being no Germans were desired inside the country. That put Arnim in a quandary, for where he stood his troops lacked victuals. With raging impatience Wallenstein told him that he had orders to march into Prussia and that that was what he should have done. He would be good enough to cross the border without loss of a further minute. "While Gustavus negotiates only to gain time, let this my ordinance accordingly and truly be fulfilled." The column therefore rolled across Polish territory without the royal permission and had the success which comprised its purpose – Gustavus Adolphus, hearing of its approach, temporarily postponed the liberation of Germany because a state of peace in Prussia and the security of his left flank were essential to him before he hazarded the German adventure. At the end of May he landed once again in his Prussian port of Pillau instead of Stralsund.

He met with an unexpectedly strong opponent. Notwithstanding their baneful sidelong glances and the vexatious mutual pinpricks they inflicted on one another, the allies earned a few spectacular laurels. Convergence of the German with the Polish corps downstream of the Vistula; an unplanned encounter with Gustavus Adolphus's cavalry coming from the north; a skirmish that led to a battle, a battle that deteriorated into a defeat for the Swedes, retreat of the latter into strongly fortified Marienburg; in Arnim's hands precious trophies, especially a number of light field-pieces called "leathers" on account of their casing, used by Gustavus Adolphus to good effect, and now capable of undergoing appropriate scrutiny at Güstrow.* Marienburg besieged. At that point stagnation set in. Superiority of the defenders in their stronghold. Lingering mortal agonies of Arnim's mercenaries through artillery exchanges, even more through illness and hunger. The commander tendered his resignation.

He had already drawn it up on the evening of the day which saw his triumph, reporting sick. The real reason was that he got on all too badly with the Poles. What particularly envenomed him, a born Brandenburger, was the open secret of Polish intentions against Brandenburg–

* A three-pounder gun with an extremely thin barrel bound with rope and mastic, the whole covered by a sheath of hard leather. Far lighter than the common piece of field artillery, its mobility was a military sensation although the use of a special powder and much reduced charge was entailed. Invented at Zurich ten years before, an Austrian officer obtained its secrets and at a price revealed them to Gustavus Adolphus. Only one specimen survives and X-ray techniques have been applied to the penetration of its composition (translator's note).

Prussia and its capital, Königsberg, plans hatched in Warsaw and Vienna, plans likewise disapproved by Wallenstein. Adding another element of confusion to the north-eastern theatre of war, they would have finally driven Brandenburg into the arms of Sweden. That was Wallenstein's comment to the Polish monarch and to Arnim too, but he drily accepted his resignation: "We are heartily sorry that he seeks his resignation by cause of indisposition. Since no man can be held against his will, We must let it proceed." To Collalto he wrote, "I swear before God that never in my life did I use any man with as much patience as him. Hardly a month, though, as soon as the slightest tremor shook his mind, but that he thought to show the Emperor the door, and therefore I put an end to the matter so that he should not suppose His Majesty incapable of waging the war without him." He disliked wilful playing at politics on his generals' part except in so far as he was engaged in most highly wilful politics of his own. He disliked the frequent resort to thoughts of resignation except in so far as he was the pastime's most frequent exponent. Nobody, beside or below him, should imagine that he was indispensable. His letters to Arnim became friendlier again as soon as his initial irritation passed. There was no parting these two.

If the move across such a wide board had forced Wallenstein's opponent to make the desired counter-move, it shortly gave rise to another, totally undesired – a long-term armistice, practically amounting to peace, between Poland and Sweden. The encounter with the imperialists, the brief, dangerous summer campaign of 1629, induced in Gustavus Adolphus a greater readiness for compromise than he had hitherto displayed. The military situation argued in its favour. The Swedes were still holding more or less what they had held for the last three years, the coast and the delta. They could not be dislodged. More far-reaching objectives of a hardly vital character seemed unlikely to prove attainable during the next four years. The Poles could in turn regard their most precious possession, honour, as saved. This was the juncture at which French diplomacy intervened in the guise of mediator. During the previous spring Baron de Charnacé had vainly tried his best in Bavaria and Denmark, but returned home empty-handed from his Greater European mission. He had been supposed through Bavaria's neutralization to free Denmark's hands and to goad it against the House of Habsburg. Could the same be done with Sweden through the neutralization of Poland? Forthwith Richelieu's wily agents lent their support to the Brandenburgers. These could not be other than most deeply interested in peace in those distant parts, peace between their Swedish semi-ally and their Polish liege-lord. Compromise followed the usual haggling over precedents and titles, the usual propositions and scornful audience of prolix, unreasonable demands. An armistice for no more than six years. What, though, could not happen in six years? Experience taught that protracted armistices were kept to their last day. There currently existed a Polish–Muscovite one, as there had formerly been that between the Spaniards and the Dutch. In a chaotically treacherous world reliance upon a piece of legality, especially of provisional character which at more opportune time it would be possible justifiably to revoke, was in the interest of all. By means of an intricate, triangular, Swedish–Brandenburg–Polish agreement Gustavus Adolphus obtained what was of keenest interest to him, control over Courland and its lagoon, the ports of Elbing, Pillau and Memel, as well as the port dues which filled his war-chest. No later than 21 October Wallenstein knew about the shipwreck of his so long pursued, "not unconsidered" eastern policy. Poland had dropped out. Sweden would all the sooner take its place. "I cannot move on account of the Swede, Lord Tilly not on account of the Dutch, and because His Majesty's enemies see how our affairs stand they no longer seek peace," he confided to Collalto. The Polish expedition had been rightly conceived in so far as anything which cannot succeed is right. For it to have succeeded, Wallenstein would himself have had to set out for Poland with a hundred thousand men, as he occasionally boasted that he would. Having driven the Swedes off the mainland, he would have had to occupy the entire Prussian coast like the German littoral of the Baltic. That, if we are not going to be lax in following our train of thought, would have necessitated not merely the expulsion of the Swedes, but the overthrow of the Polish aristocracy, the Polish kingdom, and what not as well. Neither his military nor his political means were anywhere near enough when it was a matter of taking Habsburg power politics to their logical conclusion. Only one alternative remained – to stop short of such conclusion.

The reason why the French should have so much more eagerly than hitherto sought to free Sweden's arm for the scrimmage in Germany lay in Italy. We marvel as we set down the words, seeing how far Italy is removed from Poland and still farther from Stockholm. None the less the moves all fitted together. Politicians did not permit themselves to be abashed by distances which took three months to cover, although the process looked more comfortable on Mercator's projection than in its reality of dust and sweat, hunger, murder, and pestilence.

Hostilities in Italy had begun as a succession squabble. Duke Vincento of Mantua was the last of his line in the House of Gonzaga. He ruled over two territories, Mantua at the eastern end of the Po plain and, squeezed between Savoy and Spanish-held Milan, the margraviate of Montferrat in the west. Wallenstein's Prague mansion was a superior farmstead in comparison with the palace at Mantua, a town within a town, five hundred rooms with precious furnishings for every season, twelve inner courts, three big squares, galleries embellished with statuary from ancient Greece and paintings of modern masters such as Raphael, Leonardo, Titian, Tintoretto, and Rubens. This Arabian Nights castle had cost a great deal of money. For recent Gonzagas, political vexation had been added to the irritation of pecuniary difficulties. Who was to be the successor on old and sick Vincento's decease? He had appointed a cognate, a distant relative yet indubitably his nearest too – Charles of Gonzaga and Nevers, a French grandee, a romantic and a crusader whom we have once already met. As Wallenstein referred to him as "poor Nevers" and openly took his part, he may have known him. Father Joseph, that other crusader and politically preoccupied mystic, Richelieu's adviser, certainly knew him, and very well at that.

The ailing Vincento's testament was of a political character and the terms which flowed from his quill had been at the bidding of France, one of whose pre-eminent noblemen was to acquire dominion at the centre of northern Italy, a Frenchman and decidedly no Spanish sympathizer like another candidate for the inheritance, the Duke of Guastalla. On Spain's side too was Duke Charles Emmanuel of Savoy, he who eight years ago had wanted to become King of Bohemia, a restless, disloyal individual. In December 1627 Vincento died. Straightway Savoy and the Spanish governor of Milan fell upon Montferrat, a petty piece of predatory warfare ill-disguised by legal pretensions. Somewhat later, after an incognito journey through southern Germany and Switzerland, Nevers appeared at Mantua to take possession of his heritage. Mantua and Montferrat were both imperial fiefs. At this date it was a formal rather than a material point, but he who craves new wine can put it into old bottles. The dispute about Mantua was the Franco–Spanish dispute focused on two landmarks, the dispute between the dynasties of Bourbon and Habsburg which lies behind so many apparently meaningless tales. Could Vienna remain aloof? The love prevailing between the illustrious members of the House of Habsburg was not altogether so unadulterated and true, but neither could they turn their backs on one another. Let Madrid become busy in Italy and Vienna had to be of the party in rival collaboration. For such purpose fusty imperial law was serviceable. At Prague, where in winter 1628 the court resided, it was intimated to someone in the Duke of Nevers' employ that his master had been in no position simply to assume succession to the fief. He should have awaited investiture, a procedure demanding close prior investigation into the suit. The Aulic Council, ever susceptible to political influence, could not find otherwise than that Mantua should be subject to imperial sequestration. Nevers was to renounce castle and demesne. But, unless compelled, that was something which he would not do. Compulsion would therefore be necessary, meaning by force of arms and, in practice, siding with the Spaniards.

Wallenstein was against this new undertaking. He told the Spanish envoy and the imperial ministers to their faces that "if they wanted to wage war against Mantua and the Duke of Nevers, the thought of procuring a single soldier from him should not enter their minds, even though the Emperor in person were to give him the order. It would be an unjust war, for all the justice in the world cried out for Nevers." So diplomats reported, and in this instance their accuracy can unquestionably be acceped. Fifteen months later, with reference to his attitude at the outset, he told Lamormaini, "I have never regarded the hostilities against Nevers as just and I still do not regard them as such." Lamormaini had never considered it just either, more particularly since it was taking place solely between Catholic rulers. Wallenstein and Lamormaini, the Generalissimo and the father confessor to the most pious of pious monarchs, were reputed to be what is called all-powerful. A double dose of all-powerfulness was against the war in Italy, yet they could not prevent it. It is another example of alleged all-powerfulness's impotence.

Why did this unlike pair hold so like an opinion? With Lamormaini loyalty to Rome and to the Pope may have played its part. Urban VIII was for Nevers. If he must choose, he would rather have Frenchmen than Spaniards in Italy, seeing that the former were, or for the time being seemed to be, less mighty and pleasanter in intercourse. That was Italian national instinct, shared by the Venetians. The outlandish Spanish rulers were popular nowhere in Italy, and the German ones not much more so, whereas the French had the advantage of being least in evidence. Let us therefore assume that Lamormaini whispered, however vainly, into his master's ear as a Roman. What about Wallenstein? Maybe that once upon a time he really had known and formed a liking for the Duke of Nevers and that he had indeed studied the genealogical tables, reaching such and such conclusion. The possibility is improbable; his jurisprudence never earned him a degree. But his mobile intellect apprehended much, including no doubt the difference between justice and injustice. When later he wrote, "God is punishing the Spaniards because they attack poor Nevers without reason," he must have meant it. It is arguable too that power politics, that entirely different element, and justice hang together. As long as right prevails, there can be no war and, if there is, its extension is inadmissible. The inequitable dispute about Mantua extended the war by drawing in France although "to begin with, before the Spaniards attacked Nevers, France did not intervene in these matters". Wallenstein was against the Mantuan venture because he was afraid of France, and of France as Germany's neighbour on the opposite bank of the Rhine more than as Italy's neighbour. This was 1628, Wallenstein's great winter and spring in Bohemia. No peace as yet with Denmark, Stralsund in its upstart condition, the Dutch in any case in such state, and the Swedes anything other than agreeable. Should France needlessly be rendered hostile?

The year that we already know, but only from the northern German scene, slipped by. In the Italian business it was frittered away except for the Spaniards wreaking havoc in the petty principality of Montferrat and besieging Casale, its mountain stronghold. The court at Vienna negotiated with Nevers, who rejected the proffered abatements of its sequestration process. Madrid negotiated with the Emperor. How was the Frenchman to be driven out of Mantua, how should the occasion be used to undertake a *jornada secreta*, to veer towards the secret tack of settling accounts with Austria's perpetual adversary, Venice? It was to be mainly a Spanish enterprise, reinforced by imperial troops. With the King victorious in Italy, he could surely be relied upon to do whatever was dear to the Emperor's heart. Its success, let alone its beginning, depended on a prior armistice between Spain and the Dutch. The subject was clandestinely ventilated between Madrid and The Hague, and it was one of the concepts which enjoyed Wallenstein's strong backing although he would no doubt have still preferred a final settlement to the stealthily discussed armistice. Simultaneously Paris negotiated with Nevers and Venice. The justice of the cause was patent, so was Spain's insidious intent, and if only they would prosecute their part vigorously the King of France would not leave his friends in the lurch. For the present the whole business consisted of mere penmanship, an inchoate matter of notions built on premises whose validity had still to be proved and conducted through correspondence carried back and forth over distances always months apart.

Real impact was made on 28 October 1628 by the capitulation of La Rochelle, the Huguenot citadel on France's western coast. No comparison is drawn between the fall of La Rochelle and Stralsund's successful resistance in the same year because it is one which has so often been attempted and which does not hold water. The fall of Stralsund would not have made the Emperor master of Germany as Louis XIII was now master of France. The Cardinal, his minister, exploited the situation. He proclaimed Italy's freedom, or what remained of it, a vital French interest and that action must be taken accordingly.

In January 1629 the disputatious churchman himself led a winter campaign. He headed a large army of forty thousand men, marched across the mountains, overthrew Savoy, retook Montferrat, liberated Casale, and put in a French garrison. Then cessation of hostilities. Combining moderation with energy, Richelieu was too careful to push at this season of the year towards the interior of Italy. For the moment he was satisfied to dominate its point of entry while talk was heard of increased French diplomatic activity in southern Germany, Denmark and Poland. The alliance between France and Holland was renewed. French tentacles stretched eastwards in the direction of Verdun, Metz, the dukedom of Lorraine, all formerly imperial possessions. Here it was, Wallenstein complained, trouble knocking at the door. Without the Mantuan issue, which could so easily have been avoided, France would have remained neutral.

In April 1629 another blow fell. The Dutch, puffed up with the triumphs of their half-century's war of independence, switched to the offensive. With cavalry, infantry, and artillery they assaulted the Flanders frontier fortress's Hertogenbosch. Wallenstein's name for it was "Bolduk" and the attack on it, he wrote to Collalto, depressed him more than if his own port of Rostock had been besieged: "Bolduk burdens my mind day and night." Why? Because he worried that with this bastion the whole of Flanders would fall, because he knew that the Spaniards in the face of spectacular discomfitures would neither want nor be able to conclude the peace or at least prolonged armistice which he wanted, because he thought the Dutch likely after the fall of Bolduk to be inspired by such overweening presumption as to put any more agreement with them beyond discussion. The Netherlands had become far more important than Italy. Desirable, now as heretofore, was peace or truce between the Spaniards and the Dutch. This was the policy which he beseeched his correspondents at Vienna to pursue while he for his part promised "to scare the Dutch resident rigid". Intimidation too was the purpose of the three regiments dispatched on his own authority in the direction of Holland, with others to follow. Their task was not to annihilate the United Provinces, only to dampen their self-assurance. As for Mantua, his admonitions and calls for peace were unceasing. "I beg my Lord Brother to help that the Italian fires be not kindled again" (April); "I like not at all the Italian dispositions" (May); "Let there be peace in Italy and there will be peace with France" (October); "If there can be peace, I entreat yet again that it be not declined" (November). We know that his inclination was to fret and to inflate such fretfulness into panic. It is exemplified by a "candid assessment", a deep humiliation for this proud man, in which he appealed to Father Lamormaini. The letter creates an almost nauseous impression. There is talk in it of "heretics" whom there had been good hope of utterly destroying if only the Devil had not made a last effort and incited the Catholic monarchs of Austria and France against one another on poor Nevers' account. Meanwhile there was danger of the entire Netherlands being lost as well as non-Catholics and Catholics rising in arms against the Emperor. Not like previously, one after another, allowing their easy suppression, but all at one and the same time; France, Sweden, the Empire, Holland, the Swiss, and "the whole of Italy". If only means could be found to maintain the imperial authority and leave Nevers to his own affairs "before mutual bitterness is properly engendered, for afterward all will proceed more laboriously". Heretics, the unity of all Catholics, the beloved Deity, not to mention gratification at the surrender of La Rochelle, a source of no gratification to Wallenstein as statesman. This is not his language. It is that of the imperial father confessor, and in politics people have to be taken as they are. But all his trimming was of no use. The "candid assessment" simply served to cause a scandal at Vienna and, since Lamormaini handled it indiscreetly, to estrange Wallenstein from Eggenberg, proponent of the Mantuan enterprise.

Wallenstein, about whose paramountcy spies then and historians for centuries thereafter talked nonsense, had, like the hireling that he was, to send troops to Italy, whether he wanted or not, troops who subsequently would be missed in the Netherlands, let alone in another crisis which could be foreseen. "The Swede . . . is turning this way. I do not know how I shall meet him, for I cannot take the field with more than six thousand men, on horseback and on foot." To clear the mist from

Vienna's eyes, he had to paint the picture in garish colours. He tergiversated, he pleaded for a respite until the following year, urging that the present one was too far advanced and winter quarters would be very difficult to find in so poverty-stricken, over-populated a country as Italy. He had several regiments switched from the Elbe to the Weser. From there they could be moved either against Holland or to Swabia and on to Italy. The decision was thus left open, though not for long. Letters from the Emperor forced him to choose the southern theatre of war. He promised "to comply obediently" with the all-highest order, but he asked His Majesty to have a care that the Spaniards kept their pledges and were on hand in Italy with victuals and artillery "because for lack of them the army would founder, whereby Your Majesty would lose more than You have gained in all these campaigns and the damage would be irreparable". Here at least was plain speaking. Ferdinand banished his annoyance at it with boar-hunting and stuck to his decision, disregarding his Generalissimo's warnings and, as is obvious, totally indifferent to the sufferings which these new hostilities must again entail for the people of northern Italy.

Two hundred years later a Lombard of well-born family, Manzoni described them.

> There were 28,000 foot-soldiers and 7000 horsemen. . . . A great part of the population fled to the hills, taking with them their most treasured possessions and driving their cattle before them. Others remained behind so as either not to leave some sick person in the lurch or to keep an eye on valuables which they had hidden or buried. Yet others had nothing to lose or counted indeed on gain. As soon as an advance section arrived in a village selected for rest, it immediately set about thoroughgoing pillage there and in the neighbourhood. Anything capable of being consumed and abducted disappeared. Everything else they ruined and smashed. Furniture became firewood and dwellings were turned into stables, not to speak of the thrashings, injuries, and rapes that were inflicted.

The novelist was a great reader of ancient reports. His description is assuredly accurate, as also that of the plague which the German mercenaries brought with them and which provided Wallenstein with a convenient excuse for not going to Italy. Nor was this condition of things confined to Italy. It applied to the whole of the long trek by the picked regiments and squadrons, especially in such areas as west of the

Arlberg and the Grisons where the routes left little leeway for persecutors and persecuted respectively. "The people neither can nor are of a mind to suffer it any more," ran a report in September 1629 from the Vaduz strip of territory. "With those of Balzen 'tis all over, as unhappily with others too who will hardly be able to survive this winter."

The Commander-in-Chief in Italy, with the rank of Lieutenant-General, was Rombaldo Collalto. His subordinate commanders were Aldringen and a certain Gallas or Gallasso, born at Trent and until recently in Bavarian service where he had risen to field-marshal. His enlistment in summer 1629 under the imperialist colours vastly annoyed Elector Maximilian. Wallenstein contended that the fault was not his: he had accepted Gallas only after the latter had asked Munich for his release and therefore been in the market. The price was high. Gallas demanded "to be the third person in the army", ranking after the Generalissimo and the Lieutenant-General. This Wallenstein conceded. He must have had a high opinion of him and since he was a good judge of military qualities there must have been, at the beginning at any rate, something estimable about the puffed-up drunkard. When Collalto fell ill – most senior officers were almost always sick – Gallas and Aldringen held joint command. Nor far removed from them was Ottavio Piccolomini, the Sienese colonel of Wallenstein's bodyguard. The Italian war was in essence conducted by Italians. Aldringen, the polyglot Luxemburger, had no difficulty in dealing with them on equal terms.

Autumn 1629 witnessed two collateral campaigns, in the Netherlands and in Italy. Those whose duty it would have been to make provision for them had not done so. Nothing was on hand. As a result pillager and pillaged suffered to the same degree. Distances were too great, capacities too small. Petty jealousies and scornful mistrust troubled relations between the allied commanders. What a few months ago had happened between Arnim and the Poles was repeated between Count Nassau, Wallenstein's representative in the Netherlands and Count Berg, the Spanish commander there and between Collalto and Spinola, the Spaniard posted from Flanders to Italy. The temptation would be to tell them all: those who cannot wage war should keep their fingers out of the martial pie. Pretty well precisely that was what Wallenstein, who could wage it, had been saying for the past five years.

In the Netherlands the allies made a successful foray as far as the neighbourhood of Utrecht. The objective had been to lure away the besiegers of 's Hertogenbosch, but the Prince of Orange would not be lured. One of his commanders manoeuvred past the Germans, crossed the Rhine, took the fortress of Wesel, then Duisburg, Essen, and Ruhrort, not without the approbation of their townsfolk. "The edict is the cause. . . ." The allies were forced to abandon their gains and make for the Rhine, whereupon the defenders of 's Hertogenbosch completely lost heart and surrendered. Nassau, with the remainder of his hungry corps, had to seek winter quarters on German soil. The Dutch, eager to repay his visit, pursued him, spread themselves in the area of Jülich and Berg, and roamed as far as Paderborn. The expedition had proved even more fruitless than the Polish one.

Apart from what Manzoni thought worthy of mention, the winter in Italy passed as war winters do. Spinola besieged Casale; Collalto besieged Mantua. As the French intervention in the preceding year had not been for fun, it had to be repeated. The French on the border of Italy. Eastwards the Spaniards. Beyond them the imperialists. Everywhere the plague. Wallenstein, in spring 1629 at Karlsbad for the cure, analysed the southern situation perfectly correctly. Events in Italy denoted a struggle for hegemony between the Spaniards and the French. The Emperor should never have intervened. He had unfortunately done so. What was essential now was to adhere strictly to the point in legal dispute, the fief of Mantua, the ostensible issue. There should be no stepping over borders, no molestation of Venice as long as it made no move. The Italians did not care for the strangers in their land, neither the Spaniards nor the imperialists nor the French, for all that they liked the last relatively best. They had however realized that for the French the Duke of Nevers was simply a stalking-horse. "While they do not gladly see anyone powerful in Italy, they would fain have held the business in balance so that we and the French would have become weary, made peace, and left them in their earlier state," Wallenstein enlightened Collalto. "Wherefore I beseech my Lord Brother . . . not to provoke the Venetians, since thus he deprives other princes, yea, the whole world, of the opinion that it is not solely His Majesty's intent to administer justice, but rather to ruin them. In such manner shall we soon be quit of the French in Italy." To pacify Italy, neutralize it, if possible render it friendly – alas, the means at his disposal were not such as to make practicable anything of the kind. In July 1630 his generals stormed the citadel of Mantua. With the most exquisite courtesy the Duke of Nevers was escorted to the southern boundary of his land, as chivalry and regard for his cousin, the Empress, required. But the sequel! Gallas, Aldringen, and Piccolomini had the fairy palace surrounded by three thousand men in order there to indulge themselves, eyes glazed with drink, undisturbed. The treasures collected in the course of three hundred years were divided as among brothers: the paintings and the statuary, the stately furniture, the carpets, the tapestries, the jewellery, the golden dinner service, the silver table-ware. All was loaded into wagons allegedly destined for the Emperor. They arrived elsewhere. What was in excess of the transport available to the senior warriors was next day seized by their juniors, dancing around fires in the raiment of the Gonzaga ladies, throwing into the flames the library's precious manuscripts or huckstering them for a few pence to those who knew better – a cousin of Aldringen is said to have had the best bargains – wantoning in the cellars in rehearsal for worse, to which churches, monasteries, wealthy private mansions, banks, and the ghetto later attested. Never did Wallenstein do anything of the kind. He would not have done it although opportunity beckoned. Nevertheless we possess no word of criticism by him of his officers. When in July the news arrived at Memmingen, he had other worries. Nor did he have any illusions as to what his commanders expected from the conduct of war. For our part, let us at any rate note the names of those three at Mantua – Gallas, Aldringen, Piccolomini.

The victory atrocity had no aftermath other than that Nevers upon his return to Mantua a little later found it in a sad state. With the French in Savoy, the plague consuming the army, the King of Sweden at last and in earnest involved in his invasion of Germany (now was happening, Wallenstein commented, "what I have long predicted"), Vienna lightly abandoned what it had lightly begun.

Grand political strategy, it must be said, and Elector Maximilian sneeringly said it. What was it that the Duke of Friedland had really achieved with his thunderous beating of the recruiting officer's drum and his exorbitantly swollen legions? Stralsund? Poland? The Netherlands? The criticism was to the point. But Maximilian himself had formerly advocated very vigorously the Polish expedition. That the Dutch after fifty years of provocation had for their part proceeded to provocation and that the House of Austria's two branches stemmed from a single trunk was not Wallenstein's responsibility. He was loth to subjugate the Dutch, only wanted to bring them to reason, and might have succeeded if the greatest part of his potential had not been tied down, first of all in Germany through Maximilian's very own work, the edict, and secondly by the Italian campaign against which no one had warned with such despairing insistence as he. In spring 1630 matters did not stand well with imperial or Austrian affairs. If, as reputed, he possessed paramount power, the blame was his. Torn hither and thither by the caprices of a sovereign authority, imperious for all its amorphousness and the many voices with which it spoke, the culpability lay superficially at his door for an overall situation that a year ago, after the triumph over the German Protestants and Denmark, had looked right favourable but now was woebegone.

Let however no one reproach the narrator with keeping something back. Wallenstein too had not always been against a "diversion" in Italy. He was not so at the close of 1628 and a little later, namely, for as long as the French had not stirred. Epistolary cocoons had been spun between the two branches of the House of Austria, although without upshot. Madrid toyed with the notion of a war of aggression against Mantua and Venice, Spain's enemy and also long past the Emperor's. The prerequisite was a long-term truce between Spaniards and Dutch. Nothing came of the truce and consequently nothing of the expedition against Venice. Moreover King Philip and his politicians viewed Wallenstein's whole-hearted participation as a desideratum. The General's weakness for principalities had been remarked. Earlier, when the King wanted to win him over to the idea of a large-scale maritime effort against Holland, he had had the title of a Duke of West Frisia offered to him. This time it was to be a principality, Verona, it seems, at the expense of Venice. Wallenstein was a Bohemian and a north German prince. No doubt he would have been pleased to become an Italian one in addition, to introduce his model economy into the garden of Europe, and to have new subjects to bully in the "rascally Italian language". If he could not shun performance of the two major potentates' wishes, why not accept the proffered price? And Venice, as it had been ten and twenty years ago, was indisputably a vexatiously impertinent neighbour to His Majesty. Punishment for Venice, reward for him who imposed it. But Richelieu's winter journey to Savoy moved war in Italy, which must henceforth be a war against France, into an unfavourable light. From this moment forward, and not an instant sooner, Wallenstein advised abstinence. A brief pleasantry and dream, hardly worth mention. Hardly worth the profound investigation devoted to it by a historian in order once more to prove Wallenstein's "boundless territorial greed". In history, in this one particularly, deeds are what count and, if anything else, then those judgements and attitudes in which a certain consistency can be traced, not the innumerably multifarious mental gambols which disappear like footprints in sand.

THE DUTCH RESIDENT

Seed will not prosper in too sandy a soil.

The ambivalence of Wallenstein's relationship with Holland is familiar. The republic was a source of disquiet to him. It proved once and for all that rebellion could be successful and that a polity without princes was possible, or almost possible. In a bad temper he would say that the Hanse was "the Empire's Holland and the incipience of all evil and insubordination". But in the way that, for the sake of peace, he tried to neutralize the Hanseatic cities, so in the last analysis he also and always dealt with the Dutch. Whatever he undertook against them derived from compulsion, was insignificant, and remained unsuccessful. What he attempted for their pacification sprang from his own free will as a piece of entirely personal empiricism. It could only succeed if Madrid at last condescended to recognize its seceded subjects for what they had long ago become or if imperial policy were to render itself wholly independent of Spain. Both were intrinsically desirable. Both were impossible because of human nature. The free-roving intelligence of the merely demi-puissant could not breach that barrier.

We see him, in winter 1630, exchanging courtesies with Prince Frederick Henry of Orange and doing the Stadtholder favours. The Emperor's Generalissimo is beneficently disposed, or he would be if there were signs of reciprocity.

For some time already they had been given by Foppius van Aitzema, the Dutch resident at Hamburg. The diplomat should not really have been there at all, for the Emperor had the Hamburgers warned that under the semblance of commercial promotion Aitzema was pursuing all kinds of practices inimical to the Empire and doubly dangerous in so famous a mart where diverse nationalities met. He should be expelled. Wallenstein was however not at all insistent on the point. Quite to the contrary. He saw to it that Aitzema was furnished with safe conducts for travel between Hamburg and The Hague, effected his release when he was none the less arrested by Tilly, and exchanged with him letters of a highly confidential nature. They held identical views about the freedom of maritime carriage, the scandal of Swedish tyranny at sea, the common interest of all weaker nautical powers against the stronger. Their contacts continued regardless of the siege of 's Hertogenbosch, the invasion of Gelderland, the Dutch counter-raid across the Rhine. Did the Dutch want to end the undeclared war? Or did they only want to keep the enemy in suspense and with kind words paralyse his efforts until the Swedes had come? On this, as on so many problems relating to the intricate, cryptic diplomacy of the day, no light can be thrown. It may be that Aitzema, with his lively imagination and his admiration for Wallenstein, set his sights higher than his employers and that these used their representative's credulity for less creditable purposes. He belonged to the class of men who interpret their duty with a latitude which verges upon the venturesome and who create policy on their own. Which was precisely what Wallenstein did in grand style. Their taste for experimentation attracted them to each other. Wallenstein made no secret of his correspondence with Aitzema. He told the Infanta Isabella and de Roy, the Spaniard, about it. In March 1630, when Aitzema's visit to Gitschin was imminent, he asked the Regent's government to send him someone who could attend the talks – there was "no little involved". He wanted, it is clear, to cover himself: there was to be no conspiracy, no secret manoeuvre relating to separate peace. But no witness came from Brussels nor would what Aitzema was told at Gitschin have fallen pleasingly on Spanish ears. He had learnt, the Dutchman after his visit informed the Prince of Orange, that Wallenstein was no friend to the King of Spain.

These discussions took place in the palace where Aitzema was allowed to lodge with the higher-placed of his retinue while some servants were housed at an inn. At the palace the etiquette of visits and return visits was observed. When Wallenstein did the envoy the honour of calling on him, a chamberlain first arrived to inspect the walls and carpets because not a speck of dust must be perceptible. "They say that he is more feared and better served than any prince in Europe. His court and palace are as clean and well-ordered as only a house in Holland can be. When he drives abroad, people jostle from afar to see him. In the vicinity of the palace however no sound of man or beast may be heard." Out of the stillness of the dust-free rooms we catch something like the following snatches of conversation.

Wallenstein complains that in Holland and on its borders his best troops are perishing from hunger. In Italy, where none of his officers can stand the Spaniards, he suffers from the same source of vexation. King Philip writes rarely and patronizingly; Olivares, the royal minister, denies him his proper form of address, *Altezza*. He really wants nothing else than amity with the sovereign States General. Aitzema: That too is the wish of the sovereign States General. Wallenstein: Yes, but with their billeting and other affronts they regrettably place him for practical purposes in a distinct dilemma. Is theirs perhaps a two-faced game? Aitzema: On the contrary, they sincerely wish to be the Emperor's good neighbour. Previous Emperors treated them as such. Why not now? Wallenstein, reminiscently: "When war began between Spain and the States General, there was Emperor Maximilian, who in his heart of hearts was a Lutheran. The Emperor Rudolf lacked any faith. When it came to Matthias's turn to rule, the long truce subsisted. Our present Emperor is a very mighty suzerain. He has sufficiently proclaimed his love of peace and, in particular, his readiness for peace with the States General. It is the Dutch who deal with him in such manner that he has been forced to war upon them." Aitzema seeks to rebut the charge and deviates from the main issue by reference to certain misunderstandings that have occurred between the Duke, Lord Tilly, and his own humble self. Wallenstein, laughing: "He puts that very civilly. The Dutch are subtle. My cousin Slawata, who last year wrote to me about Tilly, was far too blunt. They are gross fellows, the Bohemians, and they lie much too grossly. I regard Tilly as my friend." The allusion requires explanation. Michael Slawata, Bohemian *émigré*, had in the preceding summer warned Wallenstein from Amsterdam how he knew from some important people that Tilly had orders to arrest or, should this not be feasible, have him murdered, a fact of which the writer desired to apprise him because he would be much pained if His Princely Grace were to depart the world in that way. Wallenstein's reply ran:

> Your letter dated Fourteenth of June has today reached me. From it I perceive Your affection for my person and thank you for this same, notwithstanding that I must much marvel how You can choose to engage Yourself with such childish matters. The Roman Emperor, my lord, is a just and grateful master who recompenses faithful service in a fashion different from the one of which You write me. Lord Tilly too is a gentleman who understands how to get the better of rebels, but not how to arrange assassinations. The masters of the place from where You write have always been concerned with lying vapourings and stratagems.

Wallenstein, reverting with contented merriment to this old, groundless, not even *completely* groundless tittle-tattle, proceeded to ask the Dutchman whether he was aware of having certain compatriots who aimed to ruin him? They had spread the tale that none other than Mynheer Foppius van Aitzema had indicated to him the sorry financial plight of the States General. Aitzema, boldly: And what had he replied?

Wallenstein: "I said that 'tis true that the States General are not simply very deeply, to the neck and head over ears, in debt; but to declare Foppius Aitzema to be my informant were to lie." Back to the more serious topic. Wallenstein: No matter whose the responsibility, it is the Spaniards who are now pressing the Emperor to play the mediator in their quarrel with Holland and particularly to act as such at the forthcoming Regensburg electoral Diet. There he will sympathetically bear in mind the cause of the States General and counsel moderation. Better still would be if Holland were to send a representative to Regensburg. Indeed – genially – would not Aitzema care quite simply to stay with him so that they could then set out on the journey together? Aitzema: That he must humbly decline. In other words he will not bind himself where the other is prepared to be bound. Leave-taking in Aitzema's apartment on the eve of his departure. Once again Wallenstein protests his love of peace in all that concerns Europe: his dearest wish is to lead the Emperor's army against the Turks, which can only be if peace reigns amongst the Europeans. He brings news of a complimentary nature. At his request the Emperor has raised a certain van der Mylen, a compatriot of Aitzema, to the baronage. Aitzema expresses his thanks for an act of graciousness by His Majesty towards the Dutch. Wallenstein, grandly, "Mynheer must know that I am a soldier who cherishes honesty and worth. It was I who recommended van der Mylen to the Emperor. I am, so far as my duty permits, the sovereign States General's and the Prince's servant." This declaration closes the discussions.

It was a peak in Aitzema's diplomatic career. So much is manifest. He kept his ears wide open. He drank deeply of the atmosphere. He was astounded at the exemplary hospitality steeped in the chilly discipline of Gitschin and at his host's freedom of speech. Not that his visit had much practical result. As far as that goes, during these years hundreds of encounters occurred from which nothing emanated. Aitzema at any rate thought that he now knew Wallenstein's views. He exaggerated the importance attaching to them because, like most observers, he regarded him as almost as good as independent or as almost all-powerful in the imperial camp. Did the one deceive the other? If so, then the little fish the big one. He knew from other sources that Wallenstein's outlook was basically peaceful and by this time heartily anti-Spanish. He showed himself for what he was, trusting. And Aitzema? He may in his personal policy have backed Wallenstein and even Vienna, but it did not mean that his masters did. Soon after his visit he wrote to Wallenstein. The Hague was against, indeed feared, a Swedish invasion of the Empire. This was at its best his own wishful thinking, not the outlook of the States General who were diligently working for revival of their old alliance with Sweden. When Gustavus Adolphus did in fact come, not much more was to be heard of contacts between Holland and Wallenstein.

From afar the episode recalls one previously mentioned, the negotiations between Arnim and Oxenstierna in the winter of 1628. Then too Wallenstein had been the credulous party because he held the endless hostilities to be senseless. Relying on his own mental calibre and uninhibitedly feeling his way, he plainly exceeded what properly speaking was his authority. A subordinate of Ferdinand II, for instance, should not have talked to a Dutchman in contemptuous terms about the King of Spain. Just as he should not have talked disdainfully about the edict of restitution, the Pope, the Jesuits, Habsburg policy in Italy, and the whole bloody confusion in which he half-participated and which he half-resisted.

Belief in The Stars

FOR year after year now we have told the tale of this one man, of the dim spark that burst into flame, blazed, shrivelled, and was extinguished, but we have for the most part only done it in the way that historians treat a subject, be it what it may, personage, power among powers, monarch, state or statesman. He did this; others did that; confusion was the outcome. He listened, he thought, he was plagued by doubts; he planned, he foresaw, he commanded; he was not used to having to issue an order twice. The manipulation of an abstraction. Is a closer approach, quite close, so as to enter within and not forever remain without, forbidden when preoccupation with the subject has been so sedulous?

Night Thoughts (January 1630)

Where is this darkness? What night is this? Porca Maria, *collect your wits! Yes, that's it, yesterday we left Halberstadt. . . . My heart still beats from the chill of waking. It always beats now when I lie abed. How oppressive the air is. Dust. They did not sweep properly before I arrived. I shall have to make an example of someone. Unless the rabble is hectored every day, it does nothing. . . . What frets me? I know not. I do know. That letter from de Witte. Can he not leave me in peace? Am I to travel in my litter to Silesia and see that they pay? Dohna treats them too leniently because he has his eyes on the Breslau principality. They would all imitate me. I must write to him that the Silesians, if they cannot raise the three hundred thousand, should borrow from old Zierotin. Bravely saved his fortune by fleeing to Breslau, is good for a million Rhenish gulden, and glad to lend against good interest and security. . . . Why do they hate me in the Empire? Simply because I have served the Emperor all too well against the will of many, and have no thanks for it. . . . I'll bowl no skittles with him this winter. Let him not think to see me in Vienna. In summer at Regensburg, yes, if the Diet comes to pass. With him and his son. And the Bavarian. No, not him. If they want me to wage war in Italy, I cannot go to Regensburg and exchange compliments. . . . My leg. That open sore yesterday. It nauseates me when I see it. Can I no longer ride, life holds nothing. . . . Let the horses I ordered Piccolomini to buy in Italy be at Gitschin when I arrive. They must stand high. A charger is better than a dozen skittish fillys. Those I can obtain in Bohemia. . . . I must congratulate the nuncio upon receiving his red hat. No, I shall let it be. The fellow addresses me as* Excellenza, *not* Altezza, *as other Eminences do. It is time to reject receipt of such impertinently inscribed epistles. . . . That old Trčka is offering me Smidar or one hundred and sixty thousand taler. A gesture of friendship, she writes. Has she forgotten that this must be nearly the thirtieth occasion that she touts it, procuring it from the Emperor for one hundred thousand, if as much as that? Let her cozen someone else. Is fit for commerce. Had I met her in Lucretia's stead, her help would have been other. Away, Lady Lucretia! I don't need your money. I have acquired twentyfold what you brought me. . . . Adam Trčka, now that he is in charge of my regiment's eight companies, must have a colonelcy. That will please Maximilian and my wife too. . . . Isabella understands nothing of commerce. Is true and dear. . . . I feel as though I were a child again. How long in all has it been? Thirty years, thirty-five? Life's main course, 'tis run. What comes before is brief, what thereafter unknown. Teeth drop out, feet ache, voices have to be raised because you are hard of hearing. Turn your back and, pointing, they'll laugh at you. Bethlehem, they say, at the last was swollen like a barrel, flowed from every pore, drowned in his own water, as it were. Now his toes are turned up, good riddance to him. Hush, the day comes when they'll talk of you like that and, even if they don't dare speak it aloud, then think it in the night. . . . Eggenberg. He still begot at fifty-eight. My respects to him. Perhaps someone who takes care of himself and need not drudge like I can do it longer. O I know the whore-mongers' question, How does he manage? Shut your mouths or I'll shut them for you! I employ my time on other matters. And that of the inky-cowled brethren too – What is it that he believes? As for those bald council-board coots, And what may be his mark? They all fain would know me.* Un poco di prudencia, signori, *for I would make away with him who knew me. . . . Jaroslav snores. Infringement of orders. Should have his hands smashed. Let be. He has served me faithfully. Guards enough, farther without. . . . If I go to Regensburg and meet the King of Hungary there,* I must know first how our nativities stand. Who told me that they are not well conjoined? Pieroni? No, Kepler. Then it was Pieroni who made the calculation; but Kepler's judgement is keener. Let him explain it to me at Sagan. Not obscurely, though, as his practice*

---

* The Emperor's son, Ferdinand (translator's note).

is. . . . *Gitschin. I want to have everything completed there now. The two chapels, for me and my lady. The altars in the churches. The loggia. That must be embellished with* lavor di stucco. *In front of it a grand fountain, with water piped to it from all parts and then out again into the fountains to right and left. If 'tis not done this year, Taxis shall learn that I am a bad one to foil. Yet what benefit me all my endowments? They'll not let me enjoy them. No, be just; they would. There are many who would be glad to see me lock myself in Gitschin and nevermore emerge. Can I? From where take the money for me and de Witte? Max is the only one whom I can trust. He has a way with him, friendly and at the same time shrewd, that succeeds with all. I know what it is that he wants of me. Peace. Remain alive and you shall have it. . . . A son! Why have I no son! Had he been hale, he would now have begun to speak, German and Italian, and after another fifteen years to help me. Was God's wish to scourge my wife? For what, I wonder. Me? . . . Farther away from Mecklenburg with every day that passes. If Gustavus descends, the dukes will fall upon my houses and despoil all that I have created there. How am I to hold Mecklenburg and Pomerania with less than thirty thousand men? Conti is valorous, but, with Collalto sick at Reggio, he should be dispatched south. Whom to send to Pomerania? Or nobody to Italy? Then Aldringen and Gallas must act together. They'll wrangle. Aldringen. Not that I like him, the poltroon. Writes like a hack. But he knew how to make himself indispensable. Unbearable and indispensable. . . . Suppose that you do them the favour, ask for your release, receive it. They'll see how far they'll get with the Dutch, the Swedes, the Turk, all Italy, and in the Empire too. Who there is for me, who for us? Not the Catholics. They would have the Spaniard away from the Rhine, they were against the war in Italy, and they fear that the Emperor will subdue them all to his single rule. Not the Protestants, because of the edict. . . . France looks ugly in the saddle, nature's misfit, but a great monarch all the same. He must be watched, not teased. His chief pontiff knows his handiwork, and when he says that something is to happen, it does. His case is other than mine. When I say, and I write my fingers sore, that something is to happen, it does not, but what I say that shall not happen, it does. . . . I shall recruit because I must. They insist that more soldiery be enlisted. How many are stationed on the Upper Rhine, how many by Metz? Fourteen companies of infantry, as many troops, or somewhat less; unpaid. But there, not in Italy, lies the danger. We should bring back those in Italy, not send yet more. If the Frenchman attacks in Lorraine, our bully boys will melt away like butter in the sun. I cannot go bail for everything. If they would but believe me, how weary I am of it all. . . . The priest says that when sleep escapes me I should pray. Then the Devil always comes, laughs, and asks, Do you really believe that old fool? I begin again, he comes again. . . . Sometimes Hell is here already, but it cannot be, for Hell lacks consolation, and I have at times had consolation. If it is Hell, then why the pleasure and the pride? If it is not Hell, then why the torment? But if 'tis neither Hell nor yet not Hell, that would be Hell's worst pang. . . . Harant's face. I cannot forget it, when I took him prisoner at Pecka, and later they struck off his head. He could not believe that it was going to happen. That was his fault. I counselled no one to rebel. Had I behaved like the Bohemians, the Moravians, what would I now be? A lieutenant-colonel with the Swedes, poorly paid, suspect as a stranger; or I would have rotted like Harant. Then I would have had peace. Peace. I cannot imagine what it is like and the clerics chatter fiddle-de-dee about it. . . . Hell. I can envisage it. I don't want to think about it. Nevertheless I must. Like someone on the wheel, knees, arms, chest broken, mouth open like an oven-door, and utterly alone, lying there, for ever and ever, and time standing still. This is too long, no room for raillery. Light! Ký cert! Where is the bell! – "Your Princely Grace?" – "Put wood on the fire and light the candles!" – "Does Your Princely Grace require another beaker of Perlenmilch?" – "No, let be. If the first did not help, neither will the second." – "Does Your Princely Grace require Dr Stropherus?" – "The Doctor? Let him sleep. In the morning, at six, to bandage me. . . ."*

That Wallenstein lay under the spell, and a deleterious one at that, of belief in the stars is a tradition supported by both contemporaries and historians. What good was to be expected, asked the Elector of Bavaria in 1633, of a general who "governs his actions and the welfare of the Catholic religion more by deceitful astrology than faith in God"? The question is whether for practical purposes the difference was so very great. Maximilian, that is certain, relied on God and the Holy Virgin. However when real issues were at stake he guided his conduct by reasons of state even when these did not entirely square with Divine behest. If Wallenstein allowed the information of astrologers to influence his policy and strategy, it can only be remarked that their information must on the whole have been sound, for his judgement in such matters was excellent. Presumably, though, the planets had little to do with the conclusions he reached about the Swedes and the Dutch, the French and the Poles. The recognition that Rügen was a site of capital strategic importance on the edge of the Baltic and that the campaign in Italy was a perilous folly did not depend on the stars. What, then, is the explanation for his traffic with astrologers, his considerable outlays and the waste of his time on the study of stellar subjects?

Intuition can teach much. Additional knowledge remains none the less acceptable. Wallenstein never visited either Spain or Sweden, the states which preoccupied him most, and he never beheld with his own eyes their kings and ministers. He had to depend on others' multifarious, vague accounts. Madrid, Paris, Stockholm, even Munich and Vienna, were unbelievably far away for someone sitting somewhere in Lower Germany. What would happen next year? What, on receipt of a three months' old missive, had happened in the meanwhile? There were no public debates and disputes from which to make deductions about the future. Everything was as secret as it was slow. Astrology, a kind of foreshortened intelligence service, held out hope of help when it was essential at least to perceive clearly the personalities to be dealt with. Superstition? For the period which we are contemporizing it was a matter rather of tentative rationality to interrogate a mathematician about men and events. Wallenstein is by now thoroughly familiar to us as a sane thinker free from the transmitted religious lumber and other mental impediments of his day. Astrology was a form (or pre-form, as later ages would say) of science and not an intellectual disease like the belief in witches which, precisely at this juncture, was levying a horrid blood-toll in Germany and to which Maximilian shamelessly subscribed. To interpret the constellations demanded considerable arithmetical erudition. That Wallenstein did not possess, but he associated with those who did and he understood their ciphers.

His collaborators in this darkly glittering sphere were mainly individuals with solid professions – Giovanni Pieroni, employed principally as his architect; the Mecklenburg doctors Herlicius and Fabricius; Father Sebastian Forteguerra, chaplain-general to his forces.

Among the foregoing only Pieroni, who in 1627 left his service for that of the Emperor, held office as court astrologer. The rest were called upon as occasion required. Herlicius, for instance, was selected to cast Gustavus Adolphus's horoscope, but he had only to undertake the calculations; interpretation was left to another. "Not that so much depends on it, but I want those who elucidate it to be divers. He is to pass no judgement, but simply to trace the figure." That was his suspiciousness. Several should try their hand independently so that the fitting together of the parts and the conclusions should be reserved to himself.

After autumn 1629 there was, as the outcome of a freshly established relationship, once more an appointed court astrologer.

A recommendation by Aytona, the Spanish ambassador, had served to introduce Colonel Ottavio Piccolomini. Of noble family, first in Spanish and then Florentine service, he was twenty-nine when Wallenstein accepted him, handsome before he grew fat and coarse, a cavalry leader of dash and skill. Piccolomini was in turn patron of an unemployed mathematician and alchemist, Giovanni Battista Senno, whom he had got to know in his native Siena. He took this also still youthful specimen of depravity with him to Germany and arranged for Wallenstein's eye to fall upon him. No doubt but that the Duke was mightily pleased by the appearance of them both. The sidereal adventurer was given bread and pay. He was with his master when in autumn 1629 Wallenstein lay sick at Halberstadt, in January 1630 when he slowly took his way to Bohemia, in early summer when he travelled to Memmingen, and in October of the same year when in different circumstances he left there again for Gitschin. Expensive observatories were constructed at Gitschin and Prague. Wherever Wallenstein was, there could be found Senno, with five servants and eight horses of his own in the train. To Wallenstein's misfortune. Senno, research has proved it, was a false, corrupt creature. Which does not mean that Piccolomini had already surmised the fact and made plans accordingly. Wallenstein never surmised it at all.

If astrology had any disruptive effect on his mind, then at the earliest it occurred after Senno's arrival, not before. It is moreover hardly likely that the young man will have accomplished such a change. For that he lacked the strength of personality. But if the spirit is ripe for temptation, opportunities will not be lacking.

That deals with Wallenstein's much discussed belief in the stars as objectively as the records permit. Anything else is necessarily speculation and, if indulged, could be along these lines: identity does not depend only on the individual. To be content to be himself, man needs society with its complex of duties and loyalties, straightforward relations with fellow-men, religion. Fortunate enough to enjoy such supports, each in his own way, were those of Europe's rulers to whose actions Wallenstein had to react. He himself was not so fortunate, possessing neither country, station, nor God of his own. Loyalty of service to the Emperor, the Empire, and Catholicism was surely a self-induced illusion. Ever and again the moment arrived when the arbitrariness of, and the flaw in, such a link were openly revealed. In the end he sought to depend only on himself. Weighed down with dignities and responsibilities, yet none the less solitary, a lone wolf, Wallenstein looked to the planets for the support he could derive from neither men nor God and His angels, to the one great Other to whom he trustingly bent the knee. It was not necessarily so, but it could have been so.

KEPLER'S LAST CASTS

Alongside the others, in position far superior to the others, there was still Master Johannes Kepler, an old man now, as people in those days were old when they reached the end of their fifties.

The Duke invited the astronomer to settle in his newly acquired Sagan. He would have an annual salary of a thousand Rhenish gulden, doubled in effect by a weekly allowance of twenty gulden for the cost of printing his writings. Decidedly more favourable conditions than had ever been offered by the Emperor and incomparably more favourable because the terms were honoured. In summer 1628 Kepler journeyed with wife and child to Silesia. Henceforth he signed himself "His Imperial Roman Majesty's, likewise Princely Friedlandic Mathematician". He declined, though, the small estate with which Wallenstein exuberantly proposed to endow him. He gave this and that reason. In fact he was inspired by his permanent distrust of mankind, his grumpiness, and his genius for acting against his own advantage by telling himself that he was on the look-out for precisely that.

Wallenstein obviously expected services in return. He may in addition have viewed Kepler's presence at Sagan as the first step towards the elitist university that he had in mind. Should it be founded, one pillar already stood there in the shape of him who "has precedence among the mathematicians" and whom he was pleased to honour so highly with the address "Especially Beloved Sir and Friend". Kepler guessed something of the sort when he said in a letter to a colleague at Strasbourg that, if his patron's luck held, this friend could hope for a Wallensteinian professorship.

For his own part, although he now had hearth, home, and a snug income, he was not happy at Sagan. Whoever is always in search of good fortune never finds it, but in its stead grounds for why he does not succeed. Sagan was small, off the main highway of events, and strange to the stranger. Apart from Boccacci, the ducal architect, and possibly von Nechern, the governor, he had none who constituted tolerable company. Moreover he complained bitterly about the "sharp Reformation", or Counter-Reformation, whose fangs Wallenstein could not draw and which rendered the atmosphere spiteful.

At the beginning of April 1630 Kepler paid a visit to his lord's principal Bohemian seat, the freshly erected Smiřický palace. If, as may be assumed, he met there Senno, the young ne'er-do-well and his rival, he let slip no words about the encounter. On his scientific discussions with Wallenstein he reported rather loftily, "I am just back from Gitschin where my patron forced me to stay for three weeks, a waste of time for him and for me." His protégé refused, as he had done five and twenty-five years earlier, to furnish the Duke with clearly outlined, practical data. Such he presumably obtained from Senno.

The fact remains that before his death Kepler finally had the protector who made it feasible for him peacefully to complete and to set up in type his *Ephemerides*, those astronomic tables with advance calculations of the stellar movements for every single day until 1636. He could have stayed quietly at Sagan, but he was seldom there and after two years had altogether had enough. He saddled his mare once more and betook himself to Leipzig, Nürnberg, Regensburg, eternally chasing those 11,817 gulden, the treasure which the Emperor, as heir to Rudolf II, owed him – "my entire fortune earned in thirty years". Wallenstein however paid his widow what he still owed her matrimonial master, regardless of the fact that the lack of money he so dreaded was already straitening his path.

The Dismissal

As it happened, Wallenstein had never set eyes on an Elector of the Holy Roman Empire. Ordinary princes, yes, in plenty. One of these "highest, most intimate and most privy councillors", no. It is moreover difficult to imagine him at Dresden, still more difficult to envisage him at Munich, he who during the last seven years of his life did not once appear in Vienna. A freakish situation, this – the Empire's Generalissimo, in constant negotiation with the Emperor, for seven years never visited the Empire's capital. The imperial commander-in-chief and leading imperial politician criss-crossed the Empire, but on no occasion made for those who called themselves the pillars of the imperial state. The loss was his. Non-appearance increased his reputation for singularity, abstractedness, weirdness. What caused him to give the Electors a wide berth may however have been their difference in status. In his own opinion he was far superior to them in intellect and purposiveness, but in the hierarchy he stood far inferior to them, these demi-kings. He would have had to approach their persons with a series of bows, most probably to kiss their hands, and altogether to behave precisely how he fancied that cardinals spent their days at Rome. He disliked such ceremonies even when they were in his honour. Forced to perform them himself, his loathing knew no bounds.

To the disinclination to expose himself to the Electors' gaze was added political disagreement. From the very outset they had been against him. With every passing year the urge to be rid of him became stronger. And as they reacted to him, so he to them. A normal process. "Often enough we make an enemy and active foe of one who could be our friend." An excellent sentiment, uttered by Maximilian, though not in reference to Wallenstein. That the latter was his natural, eternal enemy on whose side lay all the blame, none on his, he held to be certain, a certainty shared by his spiritual co-Electors and allies of Trèves, Mainz, and Cologne. The last, as his brother and a member of "Our Worshipful House", was in any case aligned with him. To say "Bavaria" was not merely to think of the land between the Danube and the Alps, territory recently increased by the Upper Palatinate, but equally to mean the entire Wittelsbach dynasty, a shoot like the Habsburg family tree and inclusive of Cologne, Liège, Munster, and other wealthy bishoprics.

It was these four Catholic leaders and not, as might have been expected, the two Protestant members of the Electoral College who stoked the fires of opposition to Wallenstein. Dresden scarcely differentiated between the pious Emperor and his blasphemous commander-in-chief, as Munich was at pains to do. Apart from Lusatia, Saxony had largely been spared Wallenstein's billetings. Of these Brandenburg knew a frightful tale to tell and a dizzying bill to present: the forty million taler calculated by its bureaucracy were more than the whole Electorate was worth. Let it nevertheless be noted that Wallenstein's troops did not alone shoulder the responsibility. The Bavarians under Tilly were alleged to have conducted themselves no more amiably in the March. Therefore, when the crisis arose and the general attack was sounded against the General, Brandenburg declined to participate. "Should Our delegates observe that the Catholic Electors aim at the abrogation of the Duke of Friedland and seek to obtain the direction of hostilities for themselves, they shall have no part therein. . . . For on the one hand it will patently offend His Imperial Majesty and not be achieved, while on the other We do not see what it should profit Us or any other Protestant Estate. . . ." This constituted a glimmer of recognition that Wallenstein was not the Protestants' enemy and that there existed a more ruinous element of dogmatism in the Bavarian than the Friedland camp.

After 1627 Maximilian and his allies incessantly demanded a reduction in the numbers of Wallenstein's army. Although partially attained in the summer of 1628 through the dissolution of a few cavalry regiments, this was largely a matter of appearances. The succeeding winter heard talk of the need for fresh recruitments. With reason. Even after the conclusion of peace with Denmark, Wallenstein had still to attend to the secondary theatres of war – Poland, Holland, Italy – and to secure the northern littoral against Sweden, tasks for which there were never enough men available. Reasonable too was the counter-question put by the Vienna Privy Council whether the League had no inclination to diminish its own strength somewhat. Wallenstein, like it or not, had to conduct a handful of collateral campaigns. Since the Treaty of Lübeck two years ago Tilly had done literally nothing because it was his master's policy to remain strictly neutral towards the Dutch, the French, and the Swedes for as long as the Empire was not the victim of unequivocal aggression. There was only one answer, occasionally furnished in a roundabout way, why Tilly's army continued in being – it could in an emergency be turned against Wallenstein.

The flow of correspondence between Munich, Mainz, and Cologne was constant. Repetition of forever the same arguments, dissemination of foolish rumours, exchanges of embassies. Wallenstein does not want peace with Denmark – while he was forcing the pace of negotiations and accusing Bavaria of the same fault. Wallenstein wants to drag France into war in order to make himself master of Italy as of Germany – whereas he was afraid of, and tried to appease, it. He is sending troops to Swabia because he has to supply them for the Italian campaign. No, they are intended for an invasion of France. No, still more dangerous, they are meant completely to subjugate the Electors and either to prevent or to disrupt the much resolved electoral Diet. "League Days", conferences of electoral representatives and allied lords spiritual, were held. At Heidelberg, February 1629, resulting in a joint embassy to Vienna. Why is there not at last disarmament? Why are there so many Protestants and foreigners in the imperial army? Why is Wallenstein requisitioning quarters in Upper Germany too? Against whom is this move directed? At Mergentheim, December 1629. This time an imperial minister, Abbot Antonius of Kremsmünster, is on hand. The League's diplomats keep him however at arm's length, communicate with him only in writing, refuse him what he has instructions to obtain, military assistance against the Dutch, but they are obliged to phrase their answer as vaguely and obliquely as possible because, dangerous though it may be to engage in war with Holland and even more to do so in a circuitous way via Holland with France, it would be equally dangerous to break completely with His Imperial Majesty and with Spain. The League army is indirectly an imperial one, was indeed the only imperial one before Wallenstein appeared on the scene, and at least the pretence of its existence on behalf of Emperor and Empire must be continued. Another Mergentheim resolution: Wallenstein's title to the Mecklenburg duchy will not be recognized. Protest will once more be raised against the army's swollen numbers, against the effronteries of its officers, against the totally intolerable Friedland tyranny. Will Wallenstein's dismissal be flatly demanded? The Elector of Mainz supports such a move: Wallenstein, scenting his jeopardy, may now play the moderate, but he will not concede a whit of his plans to place all Germany beneath his yoke. Maximilian, more impatient than any other for his hated adversary's elimination, none the less hesitates and gives tongue to his fears in

German and Latin alike – *est valde pericolosum* (it is intensely hazardous), especially if Wallenstein were to learn of the attempt. In the background lurks the hope pinned on the forthcoming large-scale electoral meeting, including perhaps the Protestants too, where it will be possible through the collective presence of the Empire's ruling heads to impose upon the Emperor many a matter unattainable by means of missive and mission.

This electoral Diet, normally held in the city of Regensburg, had long been under discussion. The Emperor urged its convocation. So did the Catholic Electors in so far as they accused Ferdinand, or at least a certain dominant party at Vienna, of obstructive postponement manoeuvres. The truth was that both sides wanted it, but for different reasons. The main target of Viennese policy was election of the Emperor-designate, the "King of the Romans". Ferdinand II was ageing and in poor health. The time of the Bohemian rebellion had taught the dangers harboured by an interregnum. Later came the lesson of what splendid potentialities for extension of power the phantom of imperial dignity still signified for him who knew how to exploit them. Somewhere, not precisely identifiable, hovered the threat that another name – Wittels-bach, for instance – might mar the long imperial Habsburg list. Better once and for all to extirpate all doubts about the succession. The Elec-tors moreover should at last show their hand on European problems, the Dutch, the Franco-Italian, the Swedish, and help to achieve peace if they could or, if they could not, regrettably a more than probable contingency, then help to defend imperial right under its sole legitimate leadership. The Electors' ideas ran along quite different lines. The collateral campaigns were none of their affair because no one, contrary to the imperial Constitutions, had asked for their opinion before they were launched. The succession was indeed their affair. They would not however have an election forced on them nor would they elect anyone prior to the satisfaction of their long-standing demands – abolition of the military impositions, reduction in the army's strength, and change in the command, seeing that real change was impossible for the duration of *his* command. They intended this session of their College to become the occasion of their onslaught. The topic of the King of the Romans' election should furnish them with the long coveted means of exercising pressure not merely to topple Wallenstein, but to have the relationship between the two components of the Empire's government, the Emperor and themselves, newly defined in their favour. It was easy to forget how glad they had been of Ferdinand's illegitimately enhanced authority when he signed the restitution edict. Not that the two Protestant members had forgotten. That was why the Electors of Brandenburg and Saxony watched the approach of the event with bad-tempered equanimity. The tension attendant on it was to them a factor appurtenant to the Catholic element as a whole, one which had become ever more alien, ever more hostile to them.

Had the court at Vienna any inkling of what was being concocted in Bavaria and on the Rhine? Judging by the impressions shortly to be gleaned from the course taken by the Diet, there existed no suspicion whatever of a superbly self-assured march towards a sizeable defeat. On the other hand signs, partly hearsay meriting scepticism, partly reliable too, are not lacking that during the interval Wallenstein's position at Vienna was deteriorating. After the Mergentheim League Day the imperial Chancellor was sent to Gitschin to discover whether he could not be persuaded to make some concessions to the Electors – reduction in the number of regiments and their costly staffs, evacuation of Brandenburg, and other gestures of good will. Nothing precise is known about the mission except that it occurred in February 1630. Only rumours, "advices" dispatched to Cologne and Munich, sometimes by acknowledged agents, sometimes by anonymous busybodies. For example, Wallenstein upon being politely requested by the Emperor somewhat to curtail the scope of his generalate flew into such a rage that he tore his hat from his head, threw it to the ground, and stamped on it. Or, just the opposite, he had meekly, sadly announced his readiness to acquiesce in anything and everything. If it was resignation that His Majesty wanted, he herewith offered it. If it was desired that he should abase himself to the Electors, he was ready to do so. This was because he knew that the Emperor, at the end of his angelic patience, was determined to send him into the wilderness. In fact, though, Wallenstein's belated diffidence was mere play-acting; he and his friends were covertly working with feverish activity to preserve his power, bribes flowed in as in the past and any attempt at cajoling the Electors was simply in order "to lead them by the nose". His Grace of Cologne credited such "advices". The moment, he wrote to his brother, was on hand to push forward and insist on dismissal. "Let him venture it who cares to have a flea in his ear," retorted Maximilian. He was not convinced that the Emperor had been sapped to that degree. Of the rest of the report's accuracy he was however firmly persuaded. He repeated the alleged expression "lead them by the nose". He never doubted that Wallenstein was out "to show still less respect for the Electors and to proceed in the

Empire in accord with his pleasure and own will". "Affairs cannot be helped without his discharge, for he does not keep his word."

Nothing is less probable than that Ferdinand should during the spring have been toying with the notion of Wallenstein's discharge. As late as early summer he was buoying himself up with quite other plans. Yet trouble was again brewing at Vienna. The faction, Slawata, Meggau, Trauttmansdorff, Stralendorf, and their fellows, which had from the start of his generalate cavilled against Wallenstein and kept quiet only during winter 1627-8, the brief peak period of his influence, again raised its voice. They were behind a Privy Council recommendation that steps, real steps should be taken – mere words could no longer achieve anything. The faithful Electors must be relieved of the fear that Wallenstein exercised absolute dominion in the Empire, that he no more paid any heed whatever to His Majesty's orders, that the sword had been placed in the hand of a *furioso*, a madman. Such intelligible anxiety must at last be dispelled by a tightening of the military chain of command and the initiation of other than simply verbal reforms. Nor should it be beyond the wit of man to make the General understand that such measures lay in his own most intrinsic interest. On an earlier occasion Stralendorf had told the Saxon chargé d'affaires that it was the Duke of Friedland alone, not the Emperor, who was responsible for the irksome billetings and "it was manifest how matters stood with this gentleman". They stood strangely with him. He fascinated them all. They were all afraid of him. Many were attached to him with blind conviction. Others hated him with blind conviction. For the latter it was a truth as palpable as that day follows upon night that no venture could be more hazardous than to stage the downfall of this fiend. What friends and enemies had in common was their constant preoccupation with the man. The fault must have been his, the intensity with which he imbued his life, its active and passive sides alike.

Had Wallenstein, the members of the court at Vienna, the Catholic and Protestant Electors been the sole participants in the forthcoming tussle, the issues would have been multifarious enough. It was however also a continental one. What European sovereign could fail to be interested in the answer to the question, as it was conceived, whether Germany would become a unitary state under the fictitious sway of its Habsburg Emperor, but really that of Wallenstein, or return to its old pattern of a republic of princes? In fact this way of looking at the problem contained a misunderstanding. The antithesis was by no means so clear-cut and smooth. None the less a round of mutual wooing was begun: by France of Bavaria; by Spain of Bavaria; by Holland of Bavaria and the League, in order to detach them from Habsburg leadership. and occasionally too of Wallenstein; by Sweden of the entire Electoral College, with the same purpose as Holland. The international body politic was, or appeared to be, so flabby and disordered that it was hoped to be able to knead it into the most various shapes. To the last it remained a matter of un-certainty as to who would be for whom. No one knew everything about anyone else, and nothing with complete certainty, an intrinsic impossi-bility in the course of such confusedly fluctuating negotiations, but always something. The diplomats, the "advice"-mongers, and the travelling gossips took care of that. Richelieu, on such deeply confidential footing with the Dutch, can hardly have failed to hear how freely Wallenstein had spoken to Foppius van Aitzema by the fireplaces Halberstadt and Gitschin. For the nonce French policy was anti-Wallenstein because it was anti-Habsburg and anti-Spanish, but more particularly because it was reasonably well informed about the Elector's hatred of him and intended to use it to blast apart the Catholic German and Austro-Spanish bloc. Not in order to ruin the House of Austria, an evil design in no way harboured by Louis XIII, but because "he could not watch how the selfsame so exceedingly waxes and seeks to sub-jugate almost one and all". That was how M. de Marcheville, the Car-dinal's envoy, phrased it. In autumn 1629 and winter 1630 he journeyed back and forth between the Electors with letters from his master, ampli-fying their sentences somewhat in his exposition. What is it that Their Electoral Highnesses should demand of the Emperor? That he remove from the Empire the Duke of Friedland who is a foreigner and has no business in Germany, that he make peace in Italy and menace none of his neighbours with sinister troop concentrations, that he compel the Spaniards to abandon their positions on the Rhine. If the Emperor does not do these things? Then King Louis will be glad to know against whom the Electors will turn their armed might. Against Wallenstein? Very good. Against the Spaniards? Good luck there too. In both instances reliance can be placed on vigorous French military aid. A rash promise. Richelieu himself did not go so far. He restricted himself to advice. It could surely not be that the Electors would venture upon an assembly at Regensburg overshadowed by the coercive presence of Wallenstein soldiery and let themselves be lulled by the Emperor's constantly reiterated arguments about the Swedish, the Dutch, the French threat? Europe had undertaken nothing, absolutely nothing, against Ferdinand as long as he had remained within the limits of his rights. For such time he had enjoyed the approbation of all, the Lutherans not excepted. Germany's misfortune and the danger to all friends of peace lay in his degradation to the status of slave to Spanish passions. A few more steps along this evil road and the Turks, Transylvanians, Muscovites, Swedes could truly prove Austria's undoing, weakened as it was by the "general discontent against Friedland and the Spaniards", "Our purpose is freedom for all". The Electors had, though, nothing to fear from Sweden or Holland if they threw off the grip of Habsburg imperialism. France would see to that. Bagno, the nuncio at Paris and utterly seduced by French policy, embellished its siren song. Was Bavaria going to be so undiscerning as to wage war against Sweden in order to secure Wallenstein in his duchy of Mecklenburg and render his presumptions still more intolerable? Then, while the League bled to death, he could at his leisure overthrow Italy, France, and Germany. The captious question, this prickly political notion, originated with Bagno's friend and Richelieu's ambitious, alertly imaginative, influential specialist for German affairs, Father Joseph. In this light Bavaria had nothing to fear from Sweden unless it acted indiscriminately against its own interests. Gustavus Adolphus's grand German campaign (in spring 1630 a foregone conclusion in almost everyone's view) would be undertaken against Austria's and Wallenstein's outrages, *les violences de Volestein*, not against its victim, the League. That way France would be assured of Germany's neutrality at a single stroke.

Was anything better than mere neutrality obtainable? At Munich M. de Marcheville raised the matter of a Bavarian-French defensive alliance. Maximilian thought the proposition interesting. His councillors were instructed to examine in strictest detail the pros and cons. The alliance would be against a single individual, Wallenstein. An individual could die or otherwise become harmless. To what purpose then the alliance? It could serve to alienate France from its Protestant ally and in a sense invoke it to do, in place of Spain, its duty as Europe's leading Catholic power. The Elector wavered. It would in this perilous world have been pleasing to find in France a protector; to give Vienna the impression of having "gone along" with France would be displeasing. The problem was how to square the circle. He wanted to join France, yet he could not tear himself away from Austria nor, in the nature of links, from Spain either. Put differently, the French aim was to lead the League, the alliance of German Catholics, by straight or crooked path into the Protestant camp; the Bavarian one was to abduct France from it. Such was the divergence of objectives which once again caused the negotiations to founder. Richelieu and his Capuchin were capable of cleanly keeping apart terrestrial and celestial goals; Maximilian was incapable of becoming the ally of the Swedes and Calvinistic Dutch. This Rubicon he could not cross. The animated talks between the Bavarians and French consequently remained for the present without any upshot except that those at Munich and Mainz felt encouraged in their resolution at last to chase back to Bohemia one, the illegitimate and unsufferable one, of the two emperors ruling contrary to the natural order of things in Germany.

"Against Friedland and the Spaniards" was how Richelieu understood the Electors' vital interest because that was how he understood his own. A comedy of errors? Was Wallenstein not an enemy of Spain, in northern Germany and Italy? He would have been, and it would have been clear that he would have been, had he really had the position that he was thought to have, that of the second, the real Emperor who could do as he wanted. Had it only been appreciated how he had to manoeuvre and maintain a balance, give this promise because he was not keeping that and concede here in order not to surrender there! He wanted, regardless of all temptations and sufferings, to remain commander-in-chief as long as there was nothing better on offer. The imperial commander-in-chief who was the Spaniards' general could not pursue a policy unequivocally opposed to Spain. Not to pursue such also meant not to have such in mind. Unequivocal is only what materially emanates. How can that apply to thoughts billowing back and forth? Antithetical thoughts, though, colour what materializes and render it equivocal, jagged, opaque, and retractive of itself.

In winter 1630 he let the Spaniards know that he would be prepared to undertake a tremendous campaign against the Dutch once there was an armistice in Italy and if he were given an enormous amount of money. As much as Madrid would nevermore be in a position to raise. At the Escorial there was pleasurable excitement. At Brussels the news was greeted more sceptically because by now his tactics were known there. These were crumbs cast upon the waters so as for a few more months to be left in peace. He sent troops, or rather he did not prevent their dispatch, to Alsace and Lorraine. The move came from Vienna. To what end? "I am desired to create a diversion in France. That cannot be," he told Collalto. "Let it however be disseminated that I shall proceed there." It was agreeable to him that the Spaniards should believe the rumour and its circulation might prevent the French from hitting on mischievous ideas. He repeatedly emphasized how he feared French action in direction of the Rhine. What is impossible to tell is whether he genuinely took this danger so seriously or simply used it to persuade the imperial court of the need for a cessation of hostilities in Italy. While he talked of a major blow against Holland, he withdrew his last regiments from there; he required them against Sweden. He did indeed make threatening speeches to tickle the King of Spain's fancy, he remarked to Mynheer van Aitzema at Gitschin, but his position imposed that task on him and he assumed The Hague to be capable of distinguishing between talk and action. Although historians have concluded from his speeches and letters that, in spring or early summer 1630, he had again wheeled towards Spain, away from France, this is a view supported only by his words. With approach of the crisis, the important Regensburg meeting, he had to stand, or appear to stand, by someone since he could not stand by himself. France would not help him. Maximilian claimed that Wallenstein made through middlemen an altogether roundabout last effort to propitiate Bavaria, "if he could but be sure to ingratiate and dispose Us thereby to his intent". The bait was the Rhenish Palatinate, the overture supposed to have come from Vienna but the all-powerful Friedland to be the inspiration behind it, and Maximilian was proud to have spurned the squalid proposal. There was truly no more to be done here. Not even in a personal encounter would the Elector's petrified hatred and suspicion have been dispelled.

There was many a point on which these two, sensible politicians, well above average in intelligence among princes and born bringers of order, thought alike. Maximilian was against the Italian war; Wallenstein too. Peace with the Netherlands was Wallenstein's aim and that of Maximilian, who knew what was Wallenstein's wish. Their views of the dangers to the Empire arising on Spain's imperialism were almost identical. Both had done something to impair the imperial peace by appropriating to themselves the rights of other suzerain lords: Maximilian, those of the Upper Palatinate and the electoral dignity; Wallenstein, in Mecklenburg. At a distance their intermediate status had moreover somewhat in common – great princes because of their vigour, their circumspectness, their wise and distinguished management of means, not on account of inherited resources. Bavarian sovereignty was too limited for the power politics which its Elector sought to found upon its strength; Wallenstein was always something of a king without a kingdom. Yet what they had in common created no bond of sympathy between them. The Elector's eyes would have dilated with surprise if he had been told that even in the slightest detail he called to mind the upstart Bohemian, the tyrant, the blasphemer. The one wanted to be in the other's place. They were in each other's way. Maximilian at any rate saw the General as standing ever more menacingly, ever more hatefully in his path. Incited by the French, vainly sought to be retarded by the Spaniards, they would collide and their trial of strength occur at the precise moment when finally the major crisis talked about for years erupted – the German invasion, that contest between Gustavus Adolphus and the Austro-Spanish party, wherein Ferdinand II would need Wallenstein's army and Wallenstein's organizational gifts more urgently than ever before. So would the Elector, if he could not absolutely rely on French protection.

MEMMINGEN

In July 1629 Wallenstein left Mecklenburg. From August until beyond the close of the year he remained in the northern half of central Germany. He reigned from Halberstadt, in so far as it is possible to reign without sovereign appointment. He received military and political visitors; he organized, he made dispositions, he struggled for money without which dispositions are impracticable; he fretted, he warned, he gave way. Troops for Italy, but reluctantly and at His Majesty's trenchant order, with the Spaniards never fulfilling their concomitant promises of food, artillery, and ammunition. Troops to Holland, quite in vain. Distribution of the remaining regiments over Mecklenburg, Pomerania, and Brandenburg, very thin on the ground because their strength on paper of fifty thousand was actually hardly more than thirty thousand. Bad news: 's Hertogenbosch capitulated, the Dutch crossed the Rhine, and Sweden concluded a truce with Poland which meant that Gustavus Adolphus could now be regarded as a declared enemy. Tilly came to heckle him about winter quarters. The old man's closest collaborators were complaining that he was becoming ever more difficult and muddle-headed so that soon there would be no getting along with him. Hannibal von Dohna, Burgrave of Breslau, arrived to relate the doleful reasons for the province being unable to render payment, which earned a sour reception. Aitzema stayed and inspired hopes which Wallenstein took more seriously than did the Dutch diplomat's superiors. Masses of letters were dictated or written in his own hand, even on Christmas Day. Overwork and vexation affected his stomach as well as his legs. The doctor recommended a cure at Karlsbad. In mid-January he travelled from Halberstadt to Gitschin. There he remained until the end of April. Visitors included Werdenberg, Aitzema for the second time, and Kepler. He signed letters patent for the establishment of new regiments and the expansion of existent ones. He might think that necessary, but those who had to answer for the need, the Privy Councillors at Vienna, did not. They insinuated that, to put the Electors into better temper, there should be 'reformation', a euphemism for disarmament. "The Court urges large-scale reformation. In a few months they will see how that will place them," he told Collalto. "One pulls this way, one pulls that. When our enemies are all astir, each will try to gloss over his present opinion as best he may." Which was precisely what happened. From Gitschin he proceeded to Karlsbad for a three weeks' business-bedevilled cure. Then from Karlsbad to Memmingen in Upper Swabia.

Why did he not return to Mecklenburg? Did he overlook that the Swede, the "uncanny guest", was finally about to pay his call on the Empire and that, much more obviously than in the two preceding years, the place of Germany's commander-in-chief was on the coast and nowhere else? Politics, not his own, furnish the solution to this puzzle. The focal areas of Habsburg imperialism were currently Italy and the area west of the Upper Rhine. The main theatre of war, no longer simply a collateral scene of action, was sited around Mantua. What would shortly prove to be the principal campaign, conducted on quite different lines, was still conceived as being manageable with something less than a hold of the left hand on the reins. Hitherto Wallenstein had exercised control over the Franco-Italian devilment at long distance, from Halberstadt and Bohemia. Memmingen, whether taking the route via Bregenz and the Grisons or that over the Gotthard Pass, was on the road to Italy; in a westerly direction it pointed towards Constance, Freiburg in the Black Forest, and Breisach on the Rhine. That he would be in a position to go to Italy and with a mighty effort put an end to matters there was what he promised, or practically promised. Provided that the pest was not raging, provided that the Spaniards kept their pledges. Two provisos impossible of fulfilment. Simultaneously he let it be believed that he was ready to launch a campaign across the Rhine. His position in Upper Swabia served him as a profitable jumping-off point even if he did not know down which particular course he would take his leap. Faced with such a variety of perils not yet come to fruition, he was fundamentally at a loss. That it was also feasible to reach Regensburg in four days from Memmingen seemed another ominous feature, albeit only in the eyes of German enemies who thought him capable of performing a *coup d'état* and *coup de main* against the electoral Diet.

It could have been that he, who had for years warned against the Lion from Midnight, wished at the moment when the depredator was slinking through the front garden to surrender to illusions. He spoke, in reference to Sweden, of "a few months' time". Yet, because whatever has to be done is not certain until it has in fact been done and because the Swedish invasion with its inevitably climactic effect on the entanglement of his own affairs was repugnant to him, he hoped against hope that matters might just once more rest with the threat proving to have been no more than a threat. Moreover his wishful thinking seems less unintelligible when it is known that Gustavus Adolphus could not until the very last moment decide whether this biggest throw of his life was altogether ineluctable. He hesitated, but, hesitant, he acted. Negotiations for some compromise were supposed to take place at Danzig between the King and the imperialists. The intermediary was Christian of Denmark, who disliked the idea of his powerful neighbour's German campaign. The talks would have had an onerous task to find a formula if they had taken place. They did not. The imperial representatives arrived punctually; the Danes, late; the Swedes, never. Had Wallenstein pinned any hopes on the outcome, he was not for the first time Gustavus Adolphus's dupe. One riddle remains, for it appears as though his interest in the high seas and northern Germany, in all that he had in years of assiduous activity promoted and attempted, flagged just at the moment when his work underwent its crucial test. His communications with the Hanse cities and his Mecklenburg governor grew sparse. The fleet, the fortresses and fortifications, formerly favourite topics, were hardly mentioned. It was as if a disappointed, weary indifference in relation to his own creations had supervened. Nothing auspicious, he once wrote, was any longer to be anticipated from the Hanse cities. Were that true, it amounted to a collapse of his policy of order in northern Germany.

It was a foregone conclusion that in such circumstances the General would hurry to Mecklenburg – so thought the Elector of Bavaria. For Wallenstein to appear at Regensburg (he wrote) would be vexatious because he would probably bring off the knavish feat of vindicating himself and winning the majority over to his side. To prevent his advent was hardly practicable, but, thank goodness, he would meanwhile have his hands full with the Swedes and therefore be found on the coast rather than the Danube. An error. Wallenstein's progress took him neither to the coast nor to Regensburg, but via Nürnberg – a wrangle there with the city fathers about their monthly contribution of twenty thousand gulden – and Ulm – a reception and presentation of handsome gifts including a silver basin and bowl, wine, fish, oxen and sheep – to Memmingen. On 9 June he made his entry with accustomed pomp: red upholstered coaches, standards sewn with costly threads, a bodyguard of six hundred strong in brilliant uniforms and carrying pikes whose tips were silvered. The Fugger mansion,* a lumpish grey building on the edge of the little town, served as his residence. Bells were at once silenced and the night-watchman's intonations forbidden, a state of affairs that lasted for the period of his four months' stay. What did he do during these long summer and early autumn days?

Not much. Even if he had been driven by a spurt of energy, which would then again have subsided amid illness and melancholy, there was no direction into which it could fruitfully have been channelled. On 19 June the Emperor, accompanied by his wife and son, arrived at Regensburg and was followed by the Electors, one after another. On 6 July Gustavus Adolphus landed with thirteen thousand men on the island of Usedom which commands the mouth of the Oder. In the following week he was reinforced by arrival of his Stralsund garrison. The first half of the month saw his first capture of a mainland site. On 20 July Stettin, capital of Pomerania, capitulated. That decided whether there could any longer be any serious talk of what had, though never with decisive seriousness, certainly been talked about – that Wallenstein should go to Italy. At the end of August he wrote of the Italian campaign as a business capable at this precise juncture of being profitably promoted. They were the most senseless words that he ever uttered, barely passable even as tactic. As for Regensburg, if he had been the man that his enemies thought him, a vicious and arch-subtle schemer, he could surely have intervened in the intrigue spun against him. Tilly was there. Why should he not be? Yet again it is difficult to envisage his participation in this princely Vanity Fair, an inferior among superiors, appearing before the Electors as defendant and assuming the role of his own counsel. He would have had to say in public what he had so often said in private, how he had been against this, and that, and never all-powerful. What an oration, historically sweeping, studded with the most intricate arguments and compromising for both sides, the Emperor as

* The Fuggers were a famous Augsburg family of merchant bankers whose activities began in the sixteenth century with mining and wholesale trading (translator's note).

much as the Electors, it would have been. Out of the question. He felt
in the right. Let those do him justice to whom he lent his services. Had
it existed, this would have been the moment to set in motion that
machinery of personal support, the ministers and courtiers bought by
his millions, whose crafty creation was such a matter of common
reproach to him. Instead he looked on. He is alleged to have obtained
through his cousin Max the most exact details of all that transpired at
Regensburg. Probably. On one occasion he crossed into the Tirol to visit
Archduke Leopold, the Emperor's brother who had as a blustering
youngster caused at Prague such horrid tumult. During the intervening
twenty-eight years he may have matured somewhat. Impossible, wrote
Leopold to Maximilian, to peer into anyone's heart, but this man,
Wallenstein, seemed to him thoroughly open to being put on the right
road, provided that he was correctly handled. At Regensburg the meeting did not go unremarked. Rumours being gladly given credence, the
tale of how the Emperor's brother hoped to be chosen as successor in
place of the Emperor's son and to employ to that end the Duke of
Friedland's aid found popular hearing.

Another, indirect and uncertain means of self-defence was discourse
with distinguished guests who stopped at Memmingen on their way to
the congress. Rocci, the Nuncio, was the first to lodge within the walls
of the overcrowded little town. He echoed the impressions already
familiar to us – how splendid the court, how polite the Duke, and how
sensible his views. "His Highness is inflexible, proud, and exceedingly
shrewd, but his behaviour to me was marked by extreme modesty and
courtesy. . . . He told me that he had, at least as much as anybody,
always desired peace in Italy. . . ." At the end of July the approach
was signalled of Brulart, the French envoy to the Helvetic Confederation, accompanied by no less a person than Richelieu's pious, seasoned
adviser, Father Joseph. The representatives of a power in a state of undeclared war with Austria, they applied from Constance for safe conduct.
Wallenstein's reaction was flattering. He immediately sent his Lord
High Steward on the "three days' distant" journey to the diplomats.
That must mean to Constance itself. It takes one day to sail the length
of Lake Constance. Another couple of twenty-four hours cycles should
suffice for the heaviest coach to lumber from Memmingen to Lindau
at the Lake's opposite end. The extension of this high honour evinced
how eager he was to receive the Frenchmen, especially the Capuchin
who so recently had thought necessary to draw the Electors' attention to
les violences de Volestein, and to show them the mettle of which he and

his mind were made. The opportunity of sitting twice for several hours in sheltered quiet face to face with the much discussed tyrant cannot have lacked piquancy for the churchman either. For his interlocutor who, though not familiar with the details of what had of late passed between Richelieu and Maximilian of Bavaria, did know the tenor of those communications, just as he was of course aware of what part his guest played in the determination of France's German policy, the prospect must indeed have had attraction.

No description of the encounter exists in the principals' own words. True, Wallenstein thought it desirable to let Archduke Leopold have news of it on the very day that the Frenchmen took their leave. "Father Joseph, the Capuchin, and the French ambassador resident at Solothurn have been with me. Today they travel to Regensburg. I observed from all that they said and did not say that the French long for peace, which is why they are being sent to His Majesty." But that is all. It reflects the habit of the day to tell in good time those concerned about a half permissible, half inadmissible conference, yet not how much there was to it. From Father Joseph's contemporary biographer, who obtained his information from a friend of the ecclesiastic, we know that there was more to it than the mere fact of its occurrence. According to this account, Wallenstein, as he liked to be with strangers of distinction, was expansive and spoke freely, freely in the direction in which he suspected that the Capuchin's dreams and sympathies lay. Of crusade against the Turks and the conquest of Constantinople, once there was peace in the Empire. Had it not been the noble objective of the Duke of Nevers whom imperial policy, contrary to all justice, was seeking to dispossess of Mantua? The Emperor was pious and peace-loving. Unfortunately it could not always be said of his Spanish or pro-Spanish advisers. The Emperor's Generalissimo was in no position, as he would like, to prevent every thorough-paced piece of Viennese nonsense and would continue not to be so until such point where he was wholly his own master, a suzerain and no servant any more. Father Joseph may have pricked up his ears at this last phrase. The Electors' indictment against Wallenstein read that he wanted to overthrow the Imperial Constitutions and render the Emperor as absolute as the King of France. The General had certainly spared no effort to frighten the Germans. Hearing him speak, though, did not the matter have a different ring? Was he seeking to aggrandize Ferdinand's power in order to make it his own, to turn it equally to grandiose and rational schemes? Was his aim, if occasion arose, to attain such position by quite other, intrinsically incongruous means? To found a European principality as of his own right was not a path that would lead to a unitary imperial entity. On what piece of territory did he then have it in mind to base his paramountcy?

From Memmingen the ambassador and his more important fellow-traveller continued to Ulm where they embarked for Regensburg. The instructions they carried, probably drafted by Father Joseph, contained counsel of European good sense. The Emperor was to be persuaded to conclude peace in Italy and detach himself from the Spanish mischief-makers. Should he prove impervious, the Electors must be induced to see where their salvation lay – that they would have nothing to fear from Sweden, that the Dutch would evacuate all German regions if the Spaniards did the same, that they could count on France's stalwart help if they resisted imperial usurpations. The document embodied no direct injunction to prosecute Wallenstein's downfall. The intention may be read between the lines. For that purpose the emissaries were in any case no longer necessary.

Ulrich, a son of the King of Denmark, was for seven weeks a guest at Memmingen. He was shown handsome hospitality and returned the kindness as behoved a person of his station. Tournaments were held, a cheerful way of passing the time in contrast to the political sultriness and tension of this summer. The populace was allowed to attend. They did well during these months. The way that prices were not only kept stable but actually forced down, in spite of the soldiers' presence and the inordinate consumption of Wallenstein's court, cannot be ascribed to other than the determined will to good order prevailing at the palace. The townsmen had no idea of the threats hanging over the head of their foreign master nor, regardless of his bodyguard's silver-tipped halberds, of the money worries which plagued him. Whatever the reasons that had induced him to come to Swabia, an additional one can be surmised. Northern Germany was by now terribly impoverished and, its gaze fixed on Gustavus Adolphus, more refractory than usual. From the towns and lordships in the south-west there was still hope of squeezing the money urgently, so very urgently needed. The financing of a major war without a regular system of taxation and with, properly speaking, no state behind it, an improvisation carried on since its institution five years ago, had come or nearly come to its end, and that before Ferdinand II had even announced to the Electors his decision to make a change in the army command.

DE WITTE'S DOWNFALL

For nine years they had done large-scale business together, the General and the financier. De Witte provided for Wallenstein like a genie out of the Arabian Nights. He plied him with all the splendours of the world, delivering the possible at once, the impossible a little later. Powder and lead, tapestries, silken stuffs and table-silver, real estate, money, and money again. Demand was made, acceptance taken as a matter of course. When the final crisis supervened, the customer owed his purveyor quite an amount for personal services. Nevertheless Wallenstein's purely personal needs, for all their magnificence, represented a trifling fraction of what had changed hands. Were it to be suggested that he might in 1629–30, when the overall financial situation became ever more alarming, have slightly restricted those household outlays which were added to military expenditure, it has to be allowed that the two hundred and forty thousand taler did not count for much in the martial budget. His whole court cost scarcely more than two regiments. The army consisted of almost fifty. The thrift of rulers moreover does not impress their subjects. This particular ruler was out to impress. His last progress from Karlsbad to Memmingen was said to have exceeded every previous display of luxury.

Certainly it revealed nothing of the confusion worse confounded behind the show nor echoed de Witte's cries for help, muted in 1628, next year increasingly clamant, eventually striking notes of desperation. The system invented by Wallenstein was no doubt the most rational that could be found. For the enterprises required of him it was however far from rational enough. Constant operation wore it thin, rendering it limper and less effective. One aspect of its irrationality was that a part of the army, nobody knew how large a part, was employed simply to exact the costs of the whole. Such administration swallowed too much of what it fetched, and it fetched to a constantly diminishing degree. To put it in language anachronistic to his age, Wallenstein's investments, his expenditure on behalf of the Emperor and his realm, had not been converted into hard capital but into debts whose collection together with the anticipated profit depended on physical strength, coercion, rapine. What would happen if the strength flagged or there was no more money to be coerced? The boundary cannot be drawn between genuine inability to pay, poverty, sterility on the one hand, reluctance to pay, and a perversity manifested as soon as the shock of the

harassment troops' immediate presence had faded on the other. The
two motives were interwoven, one able to plead the other. At any rate
neither the great cities, Augsburg, Nürnberg, Magdeburg, nor the
bishoprics nor the Lands, Bohemia, Silesia, paid any longer what they
had promised or anything approaching such a figure. By the end of
1628 de Witte had not received one hundred and fifty thousand taler of
the six hundred thousand taler contribution due from Silesia for the
year. Next spring half was still missing. The Estates' new pledge of
another six hundred thousand taler in 1629 and 1630 respectively
merely increased the aggregate of indebtedness. The contributors' debts
to de Witte, signifying Wallenstein, signifying the Emperor, crowded
one side of the ledger. Debts by de Witte to those from whom he had
borrowed in order to be able to lend crammed the other. His creditors,
stony-faced, expected punctual repayment plus interest. Already de
Witte had to negotiate for twelve per cent bills whose cover consisted
of contributions not yet due or which, perhaps due, would only trickle
in. With the approach of every spring and autumn fair he saw the breakdown of his credit, business, honour, and existence coming closer.
Matters went so far that he who handled millions (for proper appreciation we must think of them as thousands of millions) begged and
borrowed puny amounts down to a few hundred gulden. Under the
pressure of maturity dates he sold what land he owned for the most
miserable petty cash. In heart-rending tones the baited banker implored
his protector and pillager to help him. He had, he recalled, only ventured into these deep waters on his behalf and at his incitement, relying
on his might, which he had regarded as the Emperor's might and therefore boundless. As he no doubt retained the memory of an emperor to
whom the merchants of Prague had declined to sell bread or meat, it
will not however have been the imperial authority in which he so
blindly reposed his faith. It was Wallenstein whom he had backed and
who had put on him this spell now turned into a whirlpool sucking him
down to perdition. If only he had never met the Duke of Friedland! He
could have continued what he had been, a tradesman blessed by fortune, carefree, a subject of envy. Instead he must see consternation
furrowed in the faces of his employees, pestered days succeeded by
sleepless nights. Not that Wallenstein omitted to do what he could.
That is to say, he dictated letters, darkly menacing and imploring in
turn, letters to his regimental commanders, the Silesian princes, Eggenberg, Collalto, Ferdinand. Yet when he tried to spur his colonels to still
more merciless requisitions, the answer was that the bottom of the

barrel really had been scraped. When he wanted to hurl a thousand mounted men into Silesia to stimulate local alacrity to pay the magnates managed to repulse him with a veto in their favour surreptitiously obtained from imperial sources. Vienna always lent a kindlier ear to great gentlemen than to burghers and peasants. "... for *non datur medium* [no other way exists]. If they want to wage war, contriving affairs so as to give the Empire pleasure rather than displeasure through quarterings, then let them seek Our Lord God for their general, not me," he raged to San Julian. The old song, sung by him since 1625, but with more success at the start. The contraction of his authority inside the Empire corresponded to the situation in Vienna. The process was reciprocal.

In the late summer of 1630 de Witte was at the end of his tether and told Wallenstein so. His letter was full of dismaying figures and "dismayed beyond all measure" was how its writer defined his own state. He described what he would need and be unable to pay at the forthcoming autumn fairs as well as what was owing to him, which included among much larger items an amount of more than a hundred thousand gulden expended on the Duke's private business. He appended reports from officers which revealed how hopelessly matters stood in central and northern Germany. In the area of Magdeburg and Halberstadt townsmen and peasants were becoming more brazen, so that he who would try to extract more money from them must fear for life and limb. On the coast the Swedes, extending westward in line from Pomerania and Stralsund, had recently captured Kustos, Wallenstein's principal finance official, at the very gates of Hamburg. And precisely because nothing more was coming nor could for the present come from Mecklenburg was why he, de Witte, must as from 1 September cease the monthly payment of twenty thousand taler on which Wallenstein's court subsisted. De Witte's fateful letter was dated 14 August. It was quite impossible for him to have already received a report of the decision taken at Regensburg on the previous day. Premonition would be something different, for the crisis of the electoral Diet increased his fears. Defiance? He was too wretched, too deeply disappointed to be defiant, and therewith Wallenstein's spell over him was broken.

Wallenstein received his message at Memmingen ten days later. The time factor has to be exactly observed. By 24 August, although he pretended to the contrary, he very probably knew the course of events at Regensburg on 13 August. He may therefore, immersed in the bitterness of tidings which he still concealed from his immediate entourage, have perceived in de Witte, who had more than grounds enough to regard himself as utterly abandoned, betrayed, and lost through no fault of his own, one of the many now hurrying to forsake him. Never, ran the Duke's reply, had he broken his word. True, there had of late been delays, but their causes were or would shortly be removed. He would write to His Majesty for a more rigorous dun to be dispatched to Silesia. More to the same effect, as though such measures had not all too often proved their impotence. A postscript in Wallenstein's own hand dealt with the monthly payment of twenty thousand taler. "Master Hans de Witte. I shall see to it that he is honourably and honestly paid what I owe him. I shall assuredly do what I can on account of the Emperor's debt. But let him not leave me in the lurch in the matter of the monthly twenty thousand Rhenish taler, else I have no wherewithal to live, and I shall assuredly send in September to Augsburg for them. Should something that I do not expect yet happen. I would needs avenge myself upon him and those with him. None the less I affirm to him upon my honour that I shall not desert him." Again the old fear of suddenly impending poverty. Not a thought wasted on how the ruined man, tormented by his creditors, should rake up the gigantic sum. He would manage somehow if he was threatened and the threat linked to some vague pledges. On 2 September Wallenstein told Colonel San Julian, "I advise him that Hans de Witte behaves infamously towards me in that he does not deposit the money as is proper. Let him therefore see to it that of the money assigned for him [de Witte] none is paid. Let him see to it that he appoints another merchant to whom the money can be paid, for I will have no more to do with a knave oblivious of honour. . . ." Thus the end of this long connection.

Not a word of sympathy was heard from him when the news of de Witte having sought release from all his torments at the bottom of his garden-well penetrated to Memmingen, first as a rumour, and the pitiful act revealed what had ultimately been the state of the banker's affairs and mind. "The tale passes current here that Hans de Witte has hanged himself," he told Taxis. "See what things of mine there are with him and fetch them as speedily as may be, in particular tapestries, gilded leather, and other things. And he owed my lady ten thousand ducats. See that they too are paid without delay. Make use in all matters of the High Burgrave's assistance." The Emperor let it be known that he was deeply moved by de Witte's suicide. So was the world at large, in an economic sense if not in fellow-feeling. Not so, not for a moment, the man of whom it could have been most readily expected, for a decade his partner in all ups and downs, who had lifted his son out of the font, who might have been called his friend. His sole concern was to lay hands on the heritage as quickly as possible before the mass of those defrauded could fall on the remains. While it is not evident how the Duchess should have become de Witte's creditor, it is perfectly clear that, even if she was, a balance still existed in favour of de Witte's heirs. Nevertheless Wallenstein continued tenaciously to insist that matters stood the other way about – "because Hans de Witte is dead and We are in no wise indebted to him, but he to Us. . . ."

REGENSBURG

Once again, as long ago, we take a look into the diary of young Christian von Anhalt, now not so young any more. He had come to Regensburg to attend the Diet, defend his abbeys from seizure, and if possible, since his means did not meet his ends, corner an imperial appointment. Always a shrewd observer, he wrote down day by day what he heard and saw. The spectacular banquets of Their Majesties when magnificent music accompanied the meal and wine flowed from fountains. The processions to vespers headed by the temporal princes, the young King of Hungary and Bohemia following, flanked by the Captain of the Archers on his right, the Captain of the Halberdiers on his left, then the Emperor and Empress, finally the senior lords spiritual. The knightly ring-tilting where, to nobody's surprise, the Emperor's son won the first prize. The wolf hunts and the hare courses. The general topics of conversation, such as the chase, the Swedish invasion, the seventy thousand gold crowns brought with him by the Spanish ambassador for current expenditure; the precedence squabbles, someone having through trickery squeezed ahead of somebody else; the great heat, with the philosophical reflection that while in Italy it might on occasion be hotter, it was hardly likely to be as persistent; a Jack-of-all-trades called Schilpke who amazed the assembled personages by both his dentistry and his mnemonic feats; and the housing problem. This was irksome to a degree. The city's closely built houses had to lodge almost twenty-five thousand guests, far more than twice its population. The bishop's palace, the monasteries and convents could find room only for the most distinguished notabilities. The remainder had to make do with the citizens' age-old dwellings and allow themselves to be fleeced. Prince Christian, lodged with Sperl the merchant, had his sleep disturbed by hobgoblins and a ghost in a shroud. The Emperor arrived with a

retinue of more than three thousand. The tale went that he had borrowed six hundred thousand taler from Wallenstein to cover his outlay
and that the cunning Friedlander was delighted to lend them so as once
more to fetter his master with golden chains. Although credited by
subsequent historians, the story is too ridiculous to merit detailed
contradiction. Notwithstanding that currently he lacked the sixty
thousand taler for which de Witte piteously pleaded in order to postpone
bankruptcy, he is supposed to have raised ten times the amount with a
flick of his fingers and sunk it in the bottomless imperial well.

At Regensburg the great made play with the wealth which generally
they did not possess; the poor, a display of their poverty. More than
half of the twenty-five thousand intruders were probably quite indigent,
professional beggars, expellees who in consequence of the restitution
edict had had to abandon the former spiritual properties to their ancient
owners. They had come to show the world how matters stood with
them. For the city council they constituted a sanitary and social problem, the type of individual easily likely to prove a source of plague. This
did indeed begin to spread and distressingly disturbed the golden way
of life. A relief fund was founded to which those of the galaxy contributed according to name and rank. No exemption, like it or not, for foreign
diplomats.

These were to be met by scores. The French contingent we already
know. The Spaniard, Carlos Doria, Duke of Tursi, was instructed to
support Wallenstein and to counteract Bavaria's ambition. Rocci, the
Nuncio, in closest conjunction with Bavaria directed his influence
against the General, therefore indirectly against Spain and on France's
behalf. The Venetians, Mantuans, Savoyards, and Tuscans concentrated on the question of the Italian campaign. A latecomer was Sir Robert
Anstruther, an Englishman experienced in German affairs who had in
his suite a representative of the outlawed but forever hopeful Palsgrave.
Envoys from smaller and smallest of potentates were innumerable. The
electoral Diet, originally intended simply as a meeting of the Electors
with the Emperor, had grown into a European peace congress on
hitherto unparalleled scale and comparable with that which fourteen
years later was convened at Münster. The time was however not yet
ripe for peace; that is, human insight was still too blind.

The plethora of bigwigs as well as controversial questions was
mirrored in the multiplicity of committees: the six Electors by themselves, albeit the two Protestants had with bitter complaint begged to be
excused and their representation was confined to officials; the Catholic

Electors alone or closeted with other League members; the imperial advisers alone; the imperial and electoral advisers in joint session; the imperial and the French delegates; the French, in greatest secrecy, with the Bavarians; and so on. Since our concern is with biography, not historiography, we must omit mention of much that flew back and forth in the shape of repartee and written exchange.

On 3 July Ferdinand handed the Electors a formal statement for their deliberation. The paper, protractedly progressing from the fall of man at the time of the Bohemian troubles whence all this present misery had twelve years ago begun without the slightest fault on the part of His Sacred Majesty, culminated in six questions. By what means could a magnanimous, perpetual universal peace be attained or, if such was impossible, how should the Emperor's defence be conducted in upright unity? Whether it was not appropriate finally to break completely and settle accounts with the Palsgrave as an inveterate rebel? How should concerted action spoil the pleasure of the Dutch at campaigning on imperial soil? What was to be undertaken against the Swedes if the phantom Danzig negotiations brought no compromise? Supposing that the French continued to violate the Empire's, and therefore the Electors', right in Italy, what counter-measures should be effected? Finally and incidentally could perhaps anything be done to create a more orderly state of affairs in the transaction of military matters? The programme packed into these questions signified an imperial war against Sweden, Holland, and France under the Emperor's leadership and with the command in Wallenstein's hands. The Electors were invited to place a stamp of legality on what had hitherto never been so entirely legal, to give their blessing, and at most to subscribe a few practical suggestions.

For the next five weeks business proceeded, as in the previous year with the Danes, by pen-pushing. Discussions in this camp and that and another; documents shuffling backward and forward; replication, rejoinder, surrejoinder.

On 10 July the Electors began their deliberations. They considered, the Catholic majority considered, that Point Six should be settled first. Bavaria's postulates were that the strength of the imperial forces should be fixed once and for all instead of alternating between reduction and fresh recruitment, the chaotic contributions system should be replaced by regular grants from all Estates, a field commander "indigenous to the Empire" and enjoying the confidence of the Empire's representatives should be appointed. In other words, a change at the top. Saxony vainly raised its voice against these axioms, stressing that war was war and the lamentable atrocities a part of it, the edict of restitution was what must be done away with, if peace was made no military system at all rather than an improved one would be needed. Brandenburg argued along similar lines. The Protestants were however in a weak position, in the minority in so far as the Electoral College as an institution was taken seriously, their delegates mere officials, and as powers alienated equally from the Catholics and the Emperor. For a time they continued half-heartedly to partake in these counsels, acceded feebly in this or that resolution and then again withdrew their agreement, and finally lapsed into a condition of embittered observers. Real clash and concurrence was confined to the Emperor and Catholics.

The answer to Point Six, to which all others were subsidiary, was drafted while the rest were under discussion. The States General's activities, declared Mainz, must be seen in the context of Spain's. Let the Spaniards evacuate the Empire and doubtless the Dutch would do the same. The King of Sweden, Brandenburg emphasized, should on no account be underestimated. He had successfully done battle against three great powers, Poland, Muscovy, and Denmark, when young. His experience had matured since. His device of paying for war through dues imposed on the traffic of goods in conquered territories was excellent. He never ceded what had fallen into his possession. All the same, Bavaria objected, the alleged grounds for war put forward by Sweden made a distinctly thin impression. If King Gustavus could not otherwise be brought to reason, it would in this conflict, but only in this particular conflict, be the Electors' duty to stand by the Emperor. The situation in Italy, ruminated Mainz, was indeed in a thorough state of confusion. Through whose fault? The Electors never having been consulted before that campaign was frivolously launched, it was unreasonable to demand their advice on how its flames should be quenched. And so on. The Catholic Electors were at least unanimous about the Swedish problem. To that degree French blandishments had been of no avail; those with regard to Holland and Italy were crowned with more effect. On them unanimity ruled the other way about. And always a preponderant unanimity on the last point. On 17 July a memorandum delivered at the imperial headquarters depicted luridly the plight in the German Lands for which one man, one alone, bore responsibility. From the bottom of their loyal hearts the Electors beseeched His Majesty to place at the head of his army "such a captain-general as is indigenous to the Empire and an eminent representative of it, respected and recognized as such by the other Estates, and in whom the Electors and Estates alike shall have beneficial, firm confidence". The formulation was Bavarian and manifestly intended to intimate the qualification of Elector Maximilian as imperial commander-in-chief. What other "representative of the Empire" could have been a candidate?

If the Emperor's advisers felt surprise at this answer, then Vienna's intelligence service for all its eavesdropping and reporting had worked badly. Meetings reflective of disconcertment took place in the presence of both Majesties. After three days rejoinder was made. Their Highnesses the Electors were in error. The true captain-general was the Emperor, not the Duke of Friedland. The Emperor had never failed to punish the soldiery's excesses and the future would witness the maintenance of discipline on an even better footing. Were there complaints against the commander in the field, they should be specified.

The Electors were not this time going to be shaken off as easily as that. They had come to Regensburg with one principal purpose which for three years they had discussed and not attained because at a distance it was unattainable. Now they were all gathered together and had the Emperor on the same spot too. They would not let him escape before he did as they wanted or, with such unforeseeable consequences as adherence by the whole of Catholic Germany to the King of France, it came to an open breach. On 1 August the Electors' reply was carried by the four Catholic Electors in person, not by a messenger. Their rendezvous was at Mainz's lodging. From there they drove – it must have been a tight fit – in a coach to Ferdinand's residence. They watched him while he read. In principle his reading contained nothing new. Stale stuff, gruffly expressed, spiced with reminiscence. In 1625, without knowledge of the Electors, a large army had been set up "when no enemy was any longer on hand" and a field commander appointed, without financial resources but with unparalleled powers of authority. These he had used to treat the Empire's poor, the territories of the spiritual princes not excepted, abominably and like captured serfs, to impose pecuniary penalties and seize moneys without receipt, and to overthrow the exalted Imperial Constitutions. For himself, and to the wonderment of one and all, he created a household unprecedented by the courts of emperors and kings, a state aped shamelessly by his officers. There was no need to be specific; the ruin wrought was as overwhelming as notorious. No reproach fell upon His Majesty, whose fatherly disposition it was far from intended to grieve. The entire censure was incurred by this one man. Which was why he must away, now and forthwith, and in his place be found a field commander German-born, familiar with German views and habits, esteemed as one of theirs by the imperial Estates. The document's arguments were vigorously phrased. When, Ferdinand's study of it complete, the Elector of Mainz emphasized them yet more vigorously, the Emperor began to waver. He would, he is supposed to have said, consider the matter. That would take time, but something would indeed have to be done.

The Privy Council too began to waver. Its innermost circle, named the Confidants, next day already held a meeting. Each member, it was resolved, should set out his personal opinion on this extremely delicate topic fraught with peril in all directions. The multiform views were then merged as well as possible – but it was not very well possible – into an opinion presented on 5 August to the Emperor. What was the sum of its sentiments? The Emperor had no cause for complaint against his commander, quite the contrary. Many of the Electors' grumbles could easily be rebutted. For instance, the declared superfluity of the army and its general at the start, especially at the start, inferring that the Electors had forgotten the gravity of the peril personified by the King of Denmark and concomitant circumstances. The claim that an incompetent personality had been appointed general and that His Majesty had been ignorant alike of what he had done and failed to do was as incorrect as offensive. A matter of concern was that Wallenstein, having created the army by his own financial means and bound its officers to him, being in fact the owner of this military potential, could use it to dangerous ends of vengeance if the Emperor dropped him; history did not lack examples. Consequently it was better for the Duke to remain in office. No, it was better that he should not remain in office because worse was to be anticipated if he did. The Swede was on the march. That Protestants would swarm to his side on account of the edict – this so incontrovertibly equitable edict – was to be feared, signifying the menace of a highly dangerous new war of religion. How would the undisciplined, unpaid, largely non-Catholic Wallenstein rabble behave? Perhaps it would go so far as to erupt into and ravage the Hereditary Lands worse than the Turk? What if the Catholics, in the face of Swedish invasion and Wallenstein's continued command, were to make common cause with the non-Catholics? Although the worst of evils and no war of religion, it was not for that reason impossible; there hung a whiff of something like this in the air. On the other hand an untenable situation was reached by examination of the conditions under which Wallenstein could be retained. Thorough reorganization of the military financial system, agreed payments by the Estates or imperial Circles in lieu of the contributions? Not at all a bad idea, yet, in the light of how the Electors thought about the General, incapable of implementation under his command. Should he be summoned to Regensburg in his own defence? That would be detrimental to him, incompatible with his honour, and, given the prevailing temper, perhaps a threat to his life. In this distressing state of affairs what else could be recommended than closest contact with those Electors with whom the Emperor was relatively still on the best terms, the Archbishop of Mainz and the pair of brothers, Bavaria and Cologne? It would admittedly leave hard nuts to crack. Who, were the General relieved of his duties, was to be his successor, since the generalate must not remain an hour unfilled? From where, after abolition of the contributions, would the successor obtain his money? If moreover ("although Your Majesty does not expect this on his part") the Duke of Friedland should refuse obedience, draw the army to his side, and join with the Emperor's enemies, what aid were the Electors prepared to furnish in such undesired eventuality? Thus far and somewhat farther went the collective assessment of the emergency. Clearly it was a blend of distinctly different outlooks. To make the best of it was the task of him to whom it was submitted and who may well have felt queasy from its impact.

For a whole week he made nothing of it. On 7 August a fresh document, testy in tone and without any mention of the command problem, was borne from the imperial to the electoral camp. If the Electors wanted meetings about army reform, common strategy and war finance at experts' level, they could have them. If they wanted to know who the enemy really was, they could be told without any obfuscations – it was he who had without cause attacked the imperial Lands, who had fought in open battle with His Majesty's forces, and who had impeded the administration of salutary justice. This applied to Sweden, as the Electors admitted, and it applied equally to the Dutch as Estates disobedient to their hereditary liege-lord, to France, and to Venice too. What should be done to counter such imperial enemies was business for consultation and resolution. Someone reading this text unaware of events behind the scene must have fancied that negotiations had come to a dead end. As is usual in such situations, rumours of impending departures began to circulate. Play-acting.

The imperial party had believed itself to have the better hand and the time arrived for it to collect its winnings. Gradually it dawned that things stood differently. Dissociation from the League would have resulted in ominous isolation for Austria. In an emergency, Ferdinand hinted, an approach by him to the German Protestants could not be discounted. It would have been possible only by surrender of the edict, ultimately the surrender of all that he had in ten years achieved and in his piety held dear. For that he would have had to have been another, from some other House, and with another past. Far rather was Elector Maximilian in a position to seek new connections, whether with the Protestants through his Saxon fellow-dignitary (he had always been careful to cultivate an intimate link) or with Sweden via France. The smaller power had more leeway than the greater. Relative military weakness meant nothing in this instance. Wallenstein's troops kicked their heels from the northern littoral down to Italy. Even had their concentration been feasible, not for a moment did the Emperor's councillors entertain the idea of a *coup de main* against his loyal Electors. Nor did it for a moment enter Wallenstein's dreams, notwithstanding that he was thought liable to do it, or only in dreams of which we have no knowledge. Had he visited Regensburg, who knows what might have happened. It had however so transpired with his affairs that he had to stay away and remain wrapped in silence.

The nets cast at Memmingen for important visitors had been too wide-meshed. Father Joseph, settling down at Regensburg among the princes and diplomats, stirred passions, increased fears, and appealed to political motives, patriotism, love for the old German liberties as well as love of gold. If, as it seems, he failed to touch on the command problem, it was because matters were anyway taking the course desired by Paris. For the Capuchin's encounter with Wallenstein to have altered French policy was out of the question. So deeply ingrained prejudice is not so swiftly uprooted. The same held good for the nuncio and the Emperor's father confessor. During the animated discussions in Ferdinand's circle between 5 and 12 August Father Lamormaini threw his weight into the scales against Wallenstein. He did it in spite of knowing better than anyone Wallenstein's view of the Italian campaign. Father Joseph knew it too. By that token the target at Regensburg was not the real Wallenstein, the man above party who in the no-man's-land of his untrammelled intelligence had tried to pursue a policy beyond his strength, but an abstraction, the personality imagined in the plots and counterplots of the powers. Vainly had he preached peace with France, vainly wooed the Protestants, vainly courted the Jesuits and even tried for a tolerable footing with Bavaria. At the moment of crisis they were all against him.

On his side he had only Spain, whose influence in Germany he had so long secretly withstood.

At Madrid the reports from Regensburg, for all the weeks' distance at which it lay, were read with poignant anxiety. The desire to dominate events was, as always, stronger than the weakness promoted by remoteness. The Elector of Bavaria, Olivares lectured the Council of State, was a malevolent, mulish man, full of dark designs and in complete bondage to the French, while the Emperor was feeble to the point of piteousness. "This meeting was summoned solely to strengthen the might of France. The Electors are showing their true visage. They turn audaciously against His Imperial Majesty." Spain's greatest interest was to erect barriers against Bavaria's ambitions. Oñate, former ambassador to Vienna, agreed. Let Wallenstein fall and the German branch of the Habsburg tree was lopped. On the spot King Philip's representative felt obliged to adopt a more discreet attitude. Only after 13 August did he loudly and publicly intervene to thwart at least the transfer to Bavaria of the overall command. After 13 August, the day on which Ferdinand for a last time received the Electors and drily told them that "he purposed a change in the direction of his armed forces".

Another three weeks passed before the decision was implemented because first the succession problem was meant to be solved. The assumption of Wallenstein's functions by Tilly was regarded as no more than a temporary emergency measure. Maximilian was now, ostensibly with reluctance but at the insistence of his fellow-Electors, aspiring to the command and all the privileges with which its preceding holder had been invested. Anything less, it was indicated, would be wounding to the honour of one who incorporated the dignity of an imperial Estate. Wallenstein had never enjoyed such far-reaching rights as the Electors imagined, the imperialists replied, and it occurred to them to compensate the loss of face that they had just sustained by a merger of the two armed forces. That would have amounted to dissolution of the League, an attempt to regain surrendered ground from the rear countered by Maximilian's determination to exploit his victory to the full. His heart was set on becoming the Emperor's General, as Wallenstein had been, while at the same time remaining head of the League. He would concentrate in his own hands and enjoy the power of both positions without relinquishing his own creation. Such an accumulation of appointments, the Confidants with reason feared, would make him Caesar's Caesar to a degree that Wallenstein had never been. The situation once more led to argumentation as time-wasting as it was acrimonious. Meanwhile Wallenstein sat in the Fugger mansion and exacted contributions of which, for reasons already familiar to us, he was also in urgent need at present for his own subsistence. Had, in the event, his discharge not been seriously meant? The Electors shrilly asserted it in as much as, unmoved by the immense concession they had extorted, they piled up fresh difficulties.

A concurrent anxiety was how to acquaint the choleric subject of the change with what had been decided. Without insult, perhaps combined with reparation, and in any case in such manner that both sides would feel secure – the Emperor against an act of desperation by Wallenstein, the latter against electoral vengeance. Very wearisome were the discussions on this point held within the Privy Council as well as between imperial and electoral representatives. The Electors failed to perceive the problem. The General had but little force in his immediate neighbourhood and was in no position to set on foot any mischief; it was simply a matter of effectual deprivation of the command at the moment of its announcement. A servant must at any time be prepared for dismissal. This one had moreover practically every year applied for it. Why not at last hand him the physic he craved? The advice came from apothecary Valeriano Magni, the Great Personage, iniquitous Magni whose whispers and hisses could be caught at Regensburg by whoever thought it worth the trouble to listen. They knew of no peril, the Electors claimed, in which Wallenstein might stand. His liege-lord's protection had not been withdrawn from him. They would not however allow themselves to be deprived of their right to bring special suits against him. As regards honours and solatia, he had, were his rank and riches contrasted with his provenance, received enough. He could, as far as the Electors were concerned, retain his acquisitions. Not Mecklenburg, though. Coolly left in the lurch by his princely auxiliaries, cousins, friends, and rivals for power. Ferdinand had to come to a decision in a more intimate circle. The lot of conveying the repugnant news fell to Gerhard von Questenberg and Privy Councillor von Werdenberg, the two at whose hands it was thought that he might accept it with least aversion. How were they to phrase the message? Somewhat on the following lines. The Emperor, yielding to vehement representations on the part of the Electors, had had to undertake army administrative reforms of so extensive a nature, circumscribing the General's power and rendering it subservient to the Electors to such a degree, that it would assuredly appear impossible to Wallenstein to continue to hold such a

hamstrung appointment. Not a word, not a single word, on the relationship between the monarch and his general.

> Thus We, Who at all times remain with abiding favour attached
> to His Dilection, holding his merits in high esteem, have been no
> less intent on how the safety, honour, and good name of His
> Dilection, Our highest commander in the field, shall in such
> change be most equitably heeded. Wherefore We have deemed
> this a favourable dispensation to learn from His Dilection's self
> what expedient means may be propounded for his safety and
> credit . . . .

Not a hint about discharge, only a request for his opinion. Yet even if
the message had been contrived in Heaven, its thorns were there to
prick and sting. We readily believe the chronicler who relates that the
closer Questenberg and Werdenberg came to Memmingen, the hollower
each felt in the pit of his stomach.

They felt better when it was all over. The great gentleman who had
had time to compose his features as well as his phrases, not the bogy of
secret reports and lying inventions, that was the man they had encountered. His remarks were calm, polite, submissive, even cheerful.
"Gladder tidings could not have been brought me. I thank God that I
am out of the meshes." He gave the emissaries a message for the
Emperor, expressing his gratification at the trust reposed in him, and is
also supposed to have requested that no ear should be lent to his detractors, that he should be protected in his imperial princely dignity, and
that no obstacle should be laid in the way of his personal defence of
Mecklenburg against the Swedes. The message may have contained all
that. As it has not survived, it is impossible to tell, and perhaps it was
only to be communicated verbally. Ferdinand at any rate was very
agreeably affected by his former commander's behaviour.

The world at large, in its turn, was so much surprised by such calm
dignity, such loyalty above all suspicion, that it could hardly credit it.
How useless the weeks at Regensburg, how mistaken the years of discussion among his German enemies about the General's possible reaction had been. Not even Questenberg, warmly as he admired the
attitude of the fallen, could resist some small doubt: "Does he in his
innermost being hide other intent? Pshaw, am I an explorer of souls?"
To render the unintelligible intelligible, a story went the rounds that
he had smilingly interrupted the emissaries' nervous address and
shown them an astrological tract from which he had already gathered

everything – how at this season the spirit of Bavaria held the Emperor's in dominance and out of this the content of the imperial message had inevitably ensued. Transmitted by innumerable writers, the tale does not deserve a moment's belief. Whatever sway astrology may have exercised over Wallenstein, he kept it to himself. He would never have introduced the matter into so down to earth a scene of high politics. People needed an explanation – astrology, wizardry – for a riddle which, had they understood him better, would have puzzled them less.

What went on inside him? Lebzelter, the Saxon groom of the chamber, a man of more than ordinary knowledge, reported from Regensburg that "the General displays excessive melancholy, admits none to his presence, treats his servants and attendants badly beyond bounds, dismisses the greater part of them, and gives them no pay". He was eating practically nothing, sleeping little and constantly in pain. That sounds likely. He will certainly have had money worries, in any case since de Witte's bankruptcy and suicide, now all the more for his military entourage being no longer a levy on the Emperor's and Empire's account. "As the famine is past and this is a fruitful year, bread may no more be baked for the poor," went an instruction from Memmingen to his Friedland governor. "You will therefore cease it everywhere. See that the money is expended thriftily since you know that much is spent upon the court and none comes from Mecklenburg because of the war." A series of carefully considered orders followed: to buy quantities of wine, in Austria where it was better than in Bohemia; to keep toils on hand for boar-hunting; to see that the guest-rooms were spick and span. Not that he mentioned the reason – henceforward he would reside at Gitschin.

Perhaps he would have told old Harrach, had he still been alive, how he felt. Now there was no one to whom he could talk. His renewed friendship with Collalto had been no more than a firmly political move. In any event the Field-Marshal lay at death's door. His coffin, carried north through the Grisons, was borne through Memmingen soon after Wallenstein had left the little town. No question, as a point of pride, of allowing either Eggenberg or Count Max to look into his heart. Nor of telling the world, like the Bohemians in cowed apology after the battle of the White Mountain, what he had done, had wanted to do, only to incur misunderstanding. It could not indeed have been told. His design, though grand, had never been wholly clear, empiric rather, torn this way and that. But now everything must be kept gulped down, mortification, retrospects, blurred truth.

He had learned the limits of his power, the impotence of a regent's retainer, and (he could not see it otherwise) how ingratitude was the world's guerdon. He pondered the lesson. Almost all historians maintain that after 6 or 7 September, the day on which those two birds of ill-omen arrived from Regensburg, he brooded on vengeance. That was in fact assumed beforehand, causing the Privy Councillors to tremble when his deposition was resolved. Posterity, credulous, stuck to the notion. He was thought capable of taking revenge. Subsequently it was traced in his actions because previously the capacity for it had been ascribed to him, and from time to time he may himself have allowed the belief to infiltrate his mind and influence him, conformable to the character defined in Kepler's horoscope. The desire to repay tort with interest would never have needed to go beyond the person of Bavaria's Elector. Nevermore would tolerable terms be possible between him and Wallenstein. That Maximilian knew, although later he tried to forget it. As for the Emperor, Wallenstein was too penetrating not to perceive in what thrall Ferdinand had taken his decision. They were both equally in thrall, equally defenceless, equally constrained. As little as Ferdinand could at Regensburg employ Wallenstein's armed power, as little could Wallenstein seriously harbour thoughts of an uprising on his own authority. Given a meed of reason, and that was intrinsic to the man, revenge on Habsburg was not for him.

What was for him, though, was to feel released and rid of all responsibilities. Thirteen years ago he had voluntarily enlisted in the service of the Archduke Ferdinand, and voluntarily again at Olmütz when the Archduke had become King. However dense the hail of compliments, he had been dismissed from long service. The choice of his future lay open to him. A source of bitterness and relief. Suddenly to be supplanted from habituated high place and the centre of the scene was bitter. Nevertheless at a stroke he was out of a labyrinth of perplexities and worries – military, political, financial. In the last analysis there was something agreeable about being at liberty to take offence when compensated by such relief.

He remained at Memmingen another month. The dissolution of a general headquarters on the scale of his takes time. Tedious were incoming inquiries from commanders at a distance and not already apprised of developments. Probably too he was waiting for money from Hamburg or Friedland. In the meantime the first condolences arrived. Officers placed themselves at his personal disposal. "No ruler in the world shall I more gladly serve than Your Princely Grace," wrote

Colonel Goetz. He had immediately resigned his appointment, Quatermaster-General von Sparr announced, for there was no commander in view in whom he could repose the confidence which he had felt for the Duke. Arnim, unemployed and always playing politics, made overtures: might he not visit His Princely Grace at Gitschin? Rumours that the dismissal would shortly be retracted, if that was not yet the case, were unfounded but continued into the winter. Evidently there was difficulty in comprehending the reality of the great, almost silently transpired transition.

At the beginning of October he broke camp to make his way home with his procession of horses and riders. The journey via Nürnberg, Eger and Prague was interrupted by a severe attack of gout. At Sulzbach he spent six weeks in bed. To his Principal Chamberlain went orders not to await him at Eger, but, having deposited ten thousand taler, straightway to return to Gitschin with the coaches carrying coin and silver. "Furthermore We desire that on your arrival at Gitschin you shall diligently consult with Our Governor and have a care that all is ordered for the best, no superfluous or double outlay being spent upon Us and Our Spouse, as also that none of the moneys on hand shall be further spent, but these be carefully secured." His entry into Gitschin, regardless of all these severe resolutions, proved as splendid as had six months ago that into Swabia. His subjects, at least, should not observe any change.

The change went deep. If he brooded on it, he could not but acknowledge to himself that he had failed. In what respect? Through what?

Accepting challenges, seizing opportunities, he had created power and expanded it. The moment however that the question arises as to whose the power was, the scene becomes nebulous, and it was in this nebulosity that he ran aground. It could not be German power, for Germany as an active political entity did not exist, only for a brief period the fact of power over Germany. King Louis was France. Wallenstein called him so. He would never have called Ferdinand "Germany". Even when his troops inundated the north and he ruled in Lower Saxony, Holstein, and Slesvig as an Emperor had never ruled there before, the identification of the House of Austria with the Empire, of the Empire with Germany, was arbitrary and fluctuating. He spoke of "We", but he could not have said who that really was. "We" was the abstract of power, power as such, exercised by himself in the Emperor's name.

An age of greater powers, he sensed, was dawning. In central Europe too a great power must evolve if everything was not to fall apart and succumb numbly. Therefore a steeling of German energies under the Austro-imperial, the sole practicable agency, possessing constitutional, although restrictedly constitutional, claims to the role, was necessary. As he attached small importance to those constitutional claims, any serious intent on his part to capsize the German constitution is unlikely. There was, while keeping up appearances, a lot that could be done with constitutions, particularly such a chaotic, worm-eaten one as the German. He may have uttered threats against the Electors, but there is no such written word on record.

From closer acquaintance with the Germans he discerned, willing as ever to learn, that there must be toleration between the denominations if there was to be a measure of unity, efficacy, and internal peace. That insight again brought him, not altogether consciously, nearer to the principle of confederacy between Estates. Obedience to the Emperor; below him, autonomy for the imperial Estates. Lutherans and Calvinists should be left to be whatever they wanted to be. Had he wanted to turn Ferdinand II into suzerain over Germany, as Louis XIII was suzerain over France, he should not have repudiated the restitution edict because no other act was so effectually appropriate to imperial paramountcy. Its uncompromising application could not result in other than the economic, then the political ruin of the Protestant princes. Eventually that would have rebounded to the disadvantage of their Catholic fellows, who could not exist without them. Their desire for the edict was blind greed, not enlightened self-interest. Wallenstein's resistance to the edict refuted the myth that he aspired to absolute Habsburg hegemony over Germany. Religious toleration and the structure of Estates harmonized. Support for the one automatically signified support, albeit with modifications, for the other.

This sensible objective was jointly spoiled by his master, the Emperor, and the Catholic princes, and that thanks to the power which he had won for them.

The matter of external peace stood differently. He wanted an Empire stretching to uncircumscribed limits, orderly and subject since to him orderliness and subjection were identical. The Electors did not destroy his concept of external peace. Had he been on a footing of confidence with them, a surprising affinity of outlook would have come to light where Holland, France, Italy, and Spain were concerned. But they did not want to know anything about his views, so that such coincidence remained sterile. Vienna's policy, indissolubly tied to Spain, destroyed for him his concept of external peace. Wallenstein, reputedly Caesar's Caesar, could not breach the link, only delay or hamper its effect. Thereby he did himself harm without benefit to the cause.

Austria's connection with Spain led to the smouldering conflict with the Pope and all papal sympathizers, to the open conflict with France. The Electors by themselves would have been the losers against inflated Austrian power and unable to topple Wallenstein. French intervention, actually provoked by the policy of Vienna and Madrid, superficially provoked by Wallenstein in person, rendered that possible.

Why did they want to topple him? Allegedly because of his barbarity within the Empire, the gruesomeness with which he waged war. As the sequel shows, that was hardly the true reason. Nothing improved after his first disappearance from the stage, everything became only incomparably worse after his second. At Regensburg the comment that war and atrocities are inseparable came from the sober Saxons. They did not know that they were repeating what Wallenstein had year after year tried to din into the court at Vienna.

The Electors wanted to topple him because they envisaged him as seducing the Emperor into an imperial revolutionary policy. This policy was new and outlandish, he a foreigner. On that they laid emphasis. In reality only a foreigner could try and effect a German power policy. There were no German politicians and there could not be any. Only princes, self-seeking, at best able to conceive of a common princely interest, and their officials. Similar held good for Austria. The Emperor's advisers too were in the first place egotistic in their ideas, secondly Habsburg Austrian. Notwithstanding that Ferdinand had a high-souled concept of his imperial responsibility, especially as regarded its religious aspect, the confluence of his care for the Empire was muddied by his instinct for sovereign Habsburg power. Wallenstein, the Bohemian, hardly possessed this instinct at all and, whatever his personal creed, altogether lacked that for religious policy. Consequently his actions did not go far enough and went too far for the court. Not far enough in that he tried to blur the evil outcome of religious zeal and to check the influence of Spain, the detestation for which he had observed in northern Germany. Too far in that what he tackled on the Baltic went beyond the capacity of sovereign Habsburg power. His actions there manifested, fleetingly, splendidly, spectrally, something that, had he been mindful of theory and idiom, he could indeed have labelled imperial policy or, plainly and better, a policy of law and order. It provoked Sweden. He had no wish for that. There was nothing that he desired less than to clash head-on with Gustavus Adolphus – "Let him stay within his realm and leave me to act here." To act freely and rationally as local advantage demanded. The religious rigour and greed of his employers rent his fabric of good sense. Gustavus Adolphus would possibly never have launched his invasion of Germany without the restitution edict. Without it the Swedish campaign would certainly not have snowballed into the avalanche that then happened. Only the most extreme threat to their creed could have driven the Protestants into the arms of the King. Against that Wallenstein had warned.

Afflicted by his dependence, which stifled the offspring of his liberal wit, he tried to create his own sovereign power. It explains Mecklenburg. If however he fancied that as an imperial prince he would be able to reassure the imperial princes on the future, he deceived himself. They saw in him none other than the military usurper of princely estate, in his dukedom the impudent specimen of imperial, signifying Friedland, abuse of power, significant of worse to come. As a German prince he had not become one of their stock, but more than ever a warlock.

Only a foreigner could have tried what he did and as a foreigner he failed. Back therefore to the native heath, foreign to him since his start five years before, and make it now his home. The end, it would seem, of his remarkable career. Yet he lived, and for that very reason very few believed it.

At Regensburg the season of cosmopolitan theatre continued until the middle of November, almost five months in all. Wallenstein soon ceased to be the topic of the day. "After it had been bruited at the Collegial Diet that the Duke had complaisantly agreed to his discharge," reported a contemporary, "none gave him another thought." There was still enough to settle. There was still everything to settle. His downfall solved nothing, or barely anything. Catholic Germany did not downright abandon Austria. After long squabbling the succession was entrusted to Tilly. A compromise. Maximilian relinquished his claim – Tilly was his servant, for all that his unvarnished mental processes might not always precisely conform to Bavarian precepts. The reduction of both armies, that of the imperial one by nearly two-thirds of its establishment, was accepted. Reductions really took place, even if probably not to the extent specified. It was the fulfilment of an old, in the light of the Swedish invasion wholly outdated, electoral programme point, doubly maladroit because the dismissed soldiery could in its need do no better than to flock to Gustavus Adolphus. Money grants by the Circle Diets were to be substituted for the levy of contributions. Nevertheless provisionally, until such time as the beneficent innovation could be implemented, the old system would regrettably have to be kept in being. It continued of course as the sole practicable one. Who could amidst the tempest of Swedish hostilities think about Circle Diets, scanty grants, tardy payments?

The vain hope had been nursed that the King of Sweden, as soon as he heard of Wallenstein's downfall, would turn back. Gustavus Adolphus ignored such subtle quibbles. Maximilian decided for his part to see in Sweden a principal enemy eager to repeal in Germany, and perhaps even in Bohemia, all the changes imposed since the battle of the White Mountain. His decision may have sprung from a correct assessment. In any case consequences ensued.

The alliance of German Catholics and Lutherans was rendered impossible. It would have required, and there was babble of this at Regensburg, abandonment of the restitution edict. The concessions reluctantly offered by the Catholic Electors not only did not go far enough in any direction, but were illogical and lacked any foothold. It was possible either, like Maximilian, to adhere to the edict or to surrender it, but impossible to have anything of substance between. With the edict maintained, and (in spite of specious reforms) the imperial-Bavarian war machine too, the Lutherans had to seek Swedish protection. They did not want to, they postponed the grave decision as long as they could, but they had to, for they were manifestly and utterly lost, even if the Swedish intervention were still to miscarry. Everything hung together. To make peace in Germany, the Catholic imperialists would have had to renounce the edict. That would have meant complete renunciation of their overlordship in northern Germany, which had for its basis the edict's juridical element. The observance of this condition might have persuaded Gustavus Adolphus to return to Stockholm. As it was not heeded, Swedish hostilities instead grew, acquiring the properties of a magnet which tore both parts of Germany completely asunder.

The fact that even now John George of Saxony wished not to admit the compulsion inherent in the situation did not make away with it. This conservative, xenophobic, sluggish, callous ruler undertook moreover the first step in the direction where others followed. The Electors had not concluded their sessions before he determined to hold in the coming winter a convention for all German Protestants at Leipzig. The signal for a separatist league, like the Union had once been, but this time German Lutheran, not Calvinist and with its eyes fixed on Holland.

Wanton folly must indeed have been the order of the day for the Saxon, bluffest among the crafty and betrayer of Protestant Bohemia, to venture on a project so contrary to imperial law.

French diplomacy's vigorous, all too cunning encouragement of Gustavus Adolphus's campaign deprived it of long sought profit. France had wanted to divide and to neutralize Germany, real, non-Habsburg Germany, from Austro-Spain. That required harmony between Catholics and Lutherans. An intrinsically difficult undertaking, more and more difficult to achieve with each succeeding decade, the Swedish invasion finally blasted any hope of it.

Hereupon the tenderly fostered secret relations between Bavaria and France lost their usefulness. They might continue to be fostered, and next spring were in fact laid down in a treaty of alliance, but France was also Sweden's ally whereas Bavaria, clear enough on this one issue, proclaimed its allegiance to Emperor and Empire. General Count Tilly had moreover the imperial in addition to the Bavarian command, making it impossible to tell what he did in which capacity. Maximilian's Regensburg triumph bound him to Ferdinand, Germany's fate to Austria's, something that ran diametrically opposite to Father Joseph's sophistries. For the King of Sweden the price of pleasing the French, a promise of peace for Bavaria if it conducted itself everywhere, directly and indirectly, peacefully towards him, was cheap, but the postulate for its fulfilment was lacking. The Franco-Bavarian alliance, however seriously the parties had wanted to take it, was rendered helpless and nonsensical. To be simultaneously the ally of two warring powers is not feasible and at the moment Sweden represented to Cardinal Richelieu the more interesting piece on his board. One dexterous triumph was, with electoral assistance, attained at Regensburg by French policy – the Emperor's renunciation of Mantua and Montferrat. The recognition of "poor Nevers" had been Wallenstein's consistent counsel with a more far-reaching objective in mind – "Let peace reign in Italy and peace with France will reign". Electoral pressure and the new Swedish danger inspired the imperial ministers to try and contrive a general settlement with France. They held, they believed, one trump – the military situation in Italy favoured the imperialists, not the French. None the less they allowed themselves to be cheated. An armistice concluded, it was used for two purposes, by the French commanders in Italy to refresh and concentrate their troops, at Regensburg to inaugurate negotiations which were protracted till October, partly on account of bagatelles, partly on account of a particular demand ultimately conceded by Brulart and Father Joseph. Louis XIII undertook henceforward not to intervene in German conflicts, supporting neither rebels nor external enemies of the Emperor. And yet did not undertake the obligation. The envoys had no plenary power to give so extensive a pledge. They knew it. Richelieu left the agreement unratified. It had all been a game, to delay, to improve the French situation in Italy, to gain time for the destruction begun in northern Germany by Sweden. This political calculation came out right in a way that is seldom the case with political calculations. In the following year affairs went so badly for the German branch of the Habsburg family that in Italy it had to sound a retreat without any solace of French promises. The Mantuan war was ended. Peace with France there was none.

The story is sad to tell. What still remains to be told? That an Anglo-Palatine pair of envoys returned home empty-handed because Ferdinand's and Maximilian's unswervingly harsh conditions left no room for compromise? That nothing changed in the relations between the Dutch and the Emperor, the Empire, and Spain? That a principal secret purpose, settlement of the imperial succession with the selection of young Ferdinand, could scarcely be brought into play at all because Protestant and Catholic princes declined in like cold tone to make use of their electoral right? In high spirits had Lords Eggenberg, Trauttmansdorff, Stralendorf, Meggau, and Werdenberg come with their Capuchins and Jesuits to Regensburg. They slunk home defeated. The congress, this long desired, discussed and prepared electoral Diet, had deprived them of the dominant position in Germany and Italy. Their gain had been nought. The leadership of German affairs lay once more in the hands of the League, of Bavaria, as they had prior to Wallenstein's appearance. For the Electors it was a sour victory. Sweden was a foe of different calibre to the Bohemian rebels, to the Palsgrave, to the freebooters. Behind Sweden stood France, and shortly the Protestants. Obduracy and blindness, craftiness and fear and pride. Calamity upon calamity. Who would assert that the blame was Wallenstein's, his above all?

Restless Retirement

mor et dominus non patitur socium or, as he put it more crudely,
"Two cocks cannot crow on the same dung-hill". About Gustavus Adolphus, "Let him stay within his realm and leave me to
act here." Of ambition the German poet Hallmann said in a contemporary drama, "Heaven gives a single sun its share. Neither throne nor
bed has place to spare." Consciously, unconsciously, or half consciously,
Wallenstein was a prince such as the poets wanted him to be.

In at least one point all his fellow-princes corresponded to the part.
An unlimited amount of cerebral energy was expended on upkeep and
increase of personal honour, aura, and distance. Letters were returned
unopened because they had not been inscribed with the correct forms
of address. Treaties, however urgent their content, were for weeks
revolved this way and that until the formula was found whereby neither
sovereign was accorded precedence over the other. Gustavus Adolphus,
powerful, of high intelligence, but nevertheless merely the grandson
of a petty nobleman, went to the same, if not more extravagant extremes
as his crowned brethren. He declined to receive an ambassador when
the credential did not include among other titles that of "Most Puissant".
Proximity of relationship made no difference. Wallenstein never
addressed Max Waldstein, his brother-in-law, cousin, and heir other
than as "High and Well-Born Count". The salutation of young Ferdinand, King of Hungary and Bohemia, to his father ran "Most Serene,
Most High and Mighty Emperor, Most Gracious Lord". He signed
himself "Your Most Humble and Obedient Servant".

So much for dignity. That alone was not enough. Strife with grim
foes, challenges to destiny, lonely loftiness, brooding defiance, fateful
decisions were the stuff of princeliness. Tragedy, taught the Silesian
Martin Opitz,* had no room for the lower orders. Its subjects must only
be individuals on the top rung of the social scale and its themes deal

---

* His *Büchlein von der deutschen Poeterei* (Little Book of German Poesy),
published in 1624, for the first time offered in German a general view of the
chief categories of literature (translator's note).

with sovereign will, death by violence, despair, infanticide and patricide, fire, incest, war and uprising.

The truth of the matter was, though, that Europe's monarchs did not really live "tragically". The Stuarts, at a pinch, yes. Philip II too, on account of his gloom, and the late Emperor Rudolf in the light of his madness and fraternal feud. But the others? Pious, jolly, lazy, obstinate Ferdinand; Philip IV, an art collector, Nimrod and womanizer, no more; King Louis, stunted, ugly, sober and dutiful in everything – they were unsuited to royal drama. Gustavus Adolphus glittered and raged through a series of wars, but he was too sound in wind and limb, too straight from the shoulder, to satisfy high-flown requirements. The great ministers were another matter. The role of prince had, properly speaking, passed to them. The Duke of Olivares, with the conduct of Spain's fortunes in his hands, stalking through dreams of the most exalted imperial ambition, of enigmatic character, sometimes gay, sometimes mortally dejected. Cardinal Richelieu, the planner and with steely determination the executor of his own plans, constantly threatened by conspiracies, struggling for France's unity, high priest of Moloch, great speaker and writer, and in addition immeasurably rich. Here were heroes to poetic taste. Wallenstein fitted. He did not, for familiar reasons, possess as much political power as Richelieu nor probably quite as much money, and the Friedland palace at Prague is modest against the Palais Royal. He was however one step ahead in that, as regards origin and status, he seemed the greater anomaly. Neither like Olivares born to govern nor like Richelieu shackled by mitred standing, his lineage was of faint lustre, his religion of dark hue. He was a prince other than they, a prince regnant, almost independent, a prince out of no-man's-land. A bizarre tyrant, his head full of gigantic projects. In this sense Valeriano Magni's portrayal of his character was dramatic too, just as was the rumour of his having sent a man to assassinate the King of Sweden.

His fall did nothing to diminish myth. Quite the contrary. Wallenstein resided in Bohemia with Asiatic splendour, servant no longer, an entirely exceptional blend of private individual and prince. Hardly anyone cared to doubt that he was contemplating frightful plans of vengeance and that his scrutiny of the stars was more diligent than ever. There seems to have been some truth in the latter. One of his officials complained that it was impossible to have audience of His Princely Grace because he spent his day among papers without food or drink and the hours of the night mostly with the astrologer Signor Battista. It may of course have been that this man, too, had let himself be influenced by the gossips. Our mistress is scholarship, not poetics, and that is why this is the place to steer the story of Wallenstein's retirement back a little to the realm of facts.

The dismissal became effective at the beginning of September 1630. During the winter the Emperor began to ask his former Generalissimo's opinion on all kinds of aspects relating to the military and political situation. At the end of March he commented with a sigh to Questenberg that all this would not have transpired if only Wallenstein had stayed in the north rather than going to Memmingen. But, demurred Questenberg, Memmingen is on the road to Italy. Then why did he not go to Italy? Well, Your Majesty's strict order to the contrary was on hand and he surely had to heed that? Questenberg took the opportunity to point out how everything premonitorily predicted by the Duke was now happening. Tilly, dependent on and simply loaned by Bavaria, was a good soldier but in political and economic affairs a child for all his seventy years. By April it was an open secret that nothing was more ardently desired than to regain Wallenstein's services. "I have expressed considerable doubt," wrote Questenberg to his patron, "whether You will come, on account of Your disinclination, indisposition, and fear of again being asked to serve, and for the rest on account of Your natural bents and humours which are passably known to me." In May Ferdinand personally beseeched him to set out urgently for Vienna, or at least the vicinity of Vienna, as so many matters could so much more easily be settled in direct discussion than by protracted correspondence. Henceforward Wallenstein knew that the generalate was once more his whenever he wanted and made his wish plain. He did not. In summer no more than non-committal exchanges passed. Negotiations proper began in October. In December they attained their consummation, although in the first instance this was of a peculiar provisional character. The retirement could be said to have lasted a year and four months. By the leaves of a calendar the calculation is correct. The ebbing thunder of the first period merged, however, in the lightning of the second.

Exile it never was. His correspondence remained as massive as before. Imperialist officers, Aldringen, Gallas, Goetz, Ossa, Cratz, Holk, Piccolomini, Pappenheim, Virmont, sent him reports, confided in him, and were insistent (particularly Pappenheim) in expression of their desire that the great military father should as soon as possible resume his orphans' care. At the Friedlandic court appeared envoys from foreign potentates, Poles, Danes, Britons, and flattering letters were received from kings. During those sixteen months he was not a great but lonely man, much less a forgotten one. A shrewd historian has hazarded the guess that basically he never felt happier than during this intermezzo: wooed without for the time being forced to choose, a personality of immense renown with concomitant political power and opportunity, un-burdened by the pangs of responsibility.

Yet, pleasant as the leisure and freedom to choose might be, they could not last. Their end was a built-in factor. The same course of events which caused Wallenstein to be wooed compelled him to reach a decision. If the Swedes won, without him, against him, and were they to start a revolution in Bohemia, he was lost. He must therefore either conclude a pact with Sweden and the revolution or again throw his weight into the other, the imperial half of the scales. The logic of the situation was, whether he knew it from the start or not, inescapable. It can moreover be viewed from a less self-centred perspective. With the interest in the fate of Europe which he had accustomed himself to take, he could not remain an inactive observer at a moment when events were daily assuming a more unprecedented turn. "Let me be left to act. . . ." To have a share in affairs and, according to his lights, to create order out of chaos was his craft. Had he in his Memmingen hours fancied that he must or could forthwith renounce it, that had been an illusion.

WHAT HAPPENED WITHOUT HIM

Gottfried Heinrich von Pappenheim, recently and at Wallenstein's recommendation appointed Field-Marshal, was a cut above the squalid military average. Swashbuckler and theoretician, dashing and reflective, he liked to describe himself as an admiring pupil of Wallenstein. He set up propositions such as that nothing is more dangerous than to conduct a defensive war in open country and be kept helplessly and desultorily on the move under enemy pressure until finally encircled and captive. "The sole reason for this war's long duration is thrift and loss of time." Never had a victory been exploited promptly and with utmost exertion to force the enemy into conclusion of the desired peace. A momentary advantage and already contempt for the other side supervened. Troops were dismissed in order to save money, but simultaneously the common people were impoverished by contributions and pillage, reducing them to a state of despair upon which old and new foes could play and ensuring that there should never be an end to hostilities. "Examples of this are so many since the battle at Prague that there is no season wherein a few of them cannot be detected. But the last, with the Swedes, has of all been the worst." Why had not the army in Pomerania been made as strong as possible? Why be scattered all over central Germany instead, while there was time, instead of marching with concentrated strength against the enemy? "Let Your Excellency forgive my tedious chronicle. A trusty adviser must, regardless of person, speak the truth. And good advice must have its beginning in recognition of causes." The Excellency so addressed was Tilly. The date, January 1631.

Pappenheim's criticism was to the point. The good old war-horse, stationed with his League troops between the Weser and the Elbe, did not do much with the remaining months of 1630. Nor did he have any idea of what he would do at winter's end. On the coast the condition of the imperialists, freshly under Tilly's command, was pitiable. The Swedish spark needed to be trodden underfoot the moment that it fell to the ground without allowing it a second to catch flame and for the flame to spread. Tilly pleaded the soldiers' state of neglect, an excuse which is always true but never of help. He might equally have pleaded the policy of his two masters. The Elector of Bavaria had no wish for a quick, decisive battle with the Swedes. Had it been possible to harmonize the incompatible, loyalty and neutrality, he would gladly have done so. He would rather have seen his forces near the Rhine and Danube, where his vital interests lay, than on the Oder.

On the other hand Gustavus Adolphus's leadership lacked as yet the lightning quality attributed to it as characteristic because of subsequent achievements. Fifteen months would pass before, still in northern Germany, the first major clash of arms occurred. His "staggering ebullition" (Archduke Leopold's expression) had not yet been unleashed.

To be far from his home base, incomparably farther than Christian of Denmark in his day, was for Gustavus Adolphus nothing new. Neither was slowness and uncertainty of supplies nor the failure of reinforcements from overseas to arrive nor the arrival of far fewer than ordered. At the beginning outstripped in sheer numbers by the imperialist coastal defenders, it took six months before he had the forces necessary to make a serious start. Right away too the wretched contemporary rule of thumb became operative: lack of military stores, lack of money, lack of discipline. The Swedes wanted to be liberators, but, as had always been the case with Wallenstein, they had to levy contributions from the liberated populations and they had to burn down villages. They could later be rebuilt, Gustavus Adolphus consoled himself; war was like that. The King's ideas were one thing, the methods by which and the material with which he wanted to implement them were another.

The Empire too was not Poland and not Muscovy. Much more tightly organized and much more familiar to him by reason of religious, cultural, and princely relationship, it was in turn stranger to him precisely because he thought that he knew it better. For he did know it better than it knew itself. Very probably they understood something of the Empire's affairs as they had once been, he told the Nürnbergers on a later occasion, but nothing of how they were now. He did, and therefore he did not care to hear people continue to prattle about their Gracious Emperor when that selfsame Emperor was breaking the law, persecuting them with his soldiery, depriving them of their goods, offending them in their faith. It was beyond him that they should slaughter each other, but *vis-à-vis* non-Germans regard themselves as belonging to one and the same nation, and be distrustful of their foreign saviours. He envisaged his undertaking as a highly political business incapable of being effected other than by Swedish armed force. The German Protestants should come to him and, inspired by the energy imparted to them by him, contribute something to their salvation. Princes should act from above, their subjects from below; a matter of alliance and revolution. For a long time, basically always, this was the hope which misled him.

That there was no revolution is partly explicable in terms of German character and political condition, partly as outcome of the King's not altogether skilful psychological approach. A manifesto called on the Mecklenburgers to slay all officials and supporters of Wallenstein the Usurper. If they did not, he would hunt them down as faithless perjurers, punishing them with fire and sword worse than his enemies. That is of course not the way to encourage insurrection favourable to one's own side. The Mecklenburgers stayed quiet and obedient. If the King wanted to restore the dukes, he would have to do it himself. There was indeed a certain amount of disorder where until recently order had reigned; imperialist soldiery located there for the duchy's defence, not the peasants, devastated Wallenstein's farms. "I cannot believe that it is His Majesty's will that this should be so," he complained bitterly to Questenberg, "for I have deserved much better at his hands." Were no redress given, he would have to take his own revenge on the shameless scoundrels. Redress, how? Revenge, how? On the heels of the imperialists followed the Swedes. They were no gentler.

Only one ally joined Gustavus Adolphus voluntarily and early – the Elbe fortress of Magdeburg. In summer 1630 the great city, which Wallenstein thought that he had pacified, concluded a treaty with Sweden.

The latter's sanguine leader was however mistaken if he believed that the torch lit by Magdeburg would be borne from imperial town to imperial town. Isolated through its rashness, the municipal republic became a magnet for both sides. Tilly had the advantage of proximity. He could, by threatening Magdeburg, hope to force the King in its direction. Its conquest would put him in possession of the most splendid possible base and act as a warning to all those who might be tempted to copy its example. Gustavus Adolphus, for his part, undoubtedly played with the idea of using the Elbe, via Mecklenburg, as his main military highway instead of the Oder. It would however have meant an advance through neutral territory, Brandenburg, which would not have been so tragic, and Saxony, a more delicate matter because Saxony must be allowed no excuse for protest. He would moreover have been moving far from the security furnished by Stralsund and Stettin and moving between undefeated enemy columns on both flanks. For the present he decided in favour of the Oder and the east.

In this warfare there was no question of fronts. Forces were either concentrated in strongholds and pockets of resistance or they would trundle by one another without contact or crouch in improbable closeness to one another. That happened to the imperialists under Colonel Schauenburg situated, a few miles south of Stettin and the Oder upwards, in Greifenhagen and Gartz. Gustavus Adolphus launched an attack on Christmas Day 1630. In icy cold and amidst frightful carnage he won his first victory. The pursuit spread as far as Landsberg terrain. Now he dominated the Oder territories and had nothing more to fear from the east. At Augsburg, where the Catholics became markedly subdued, and at Vienna the news made a deep impression. Ferdinand, for the first time rudely awakened to the bane in the north, asked his former commander-in-chief for advice. Wallenstein replied promptly. The Swedes would try and gain control of Frankfurt-on-Oder and Landsberg, important places, both of them. They would hardly in winter, though, seek to penetrate Silesia, particularly as then they would have Tilly in their rear. Consequently there was a space to repair the defences of that Hereditary Land, gateway to other Hereditary Lands, and permit the troops to recover, acquire fresh courage, and be reinforced. Silesia must provide the basis, as in 1627, for the creation of a new imperial army. Recruitment and the establishment of additional regiments, he amplified in a second expert opinion, were inevitable. Although during his generalate the danger had never been so acute, he had always maintained at his disposal a force of sufficient strength to keep careful watch in all directions and ready to strike at the right moment. A concise self-vindication and an oblique taunt at others, to be sure, but sound, straightforward counsel.

Tilly, learning of the Greifenhagen débâcle, set off north-eastward from his camp at Halberstadt with one cavalry and three infantry regiments. In ten days he put two hundred miles behind him – an awesome achievement in wintry conditions. That gave cover to Frankfurt and Landsberg, but the grizzled warrior was despondent as never before in the course of his hard life. "Your Princely Grace," he wrote to Wallenstein, "can account Yourself fortunate that You have riddance of this heavy toil and great burden." Arriving at Frankfurt to find the Swedes withdrawn north-west with Mecklenburg for their next objective, he panted after them. Too late. The fortresses of Neu-Brandenburg, Malchin, Treptow, and finally Castle Demmin, where the imperial commander took refuge with 1800 men, had fallen. Mecklenburg was lost, or nearly lost. Rostock, Wismar, and Güstrow temporarily held out, but they were a mere vestige, Tilly's re-capture of Neu-Brandenburg a feeble counter-blow. Wallenstein's dominion was shattered. His principal officials, such as Moltke and von der Lühe, who had done no more than loyally serve their legal albeit new suzerain, suffered adversity. Their estates were plundered and on the King's order donated to Swedish officers. Again a few formerly happy individuals, reduced to beggary, learned the way of the world. After the just cause had won, ran Wallenstein's message to them, everything would be restored. They would rather have had a snug appointment at Gitschin and the money to make their way there, but from Bohemia came no invitation. Only Wengiersky, the governor, with heartfelt relief was able to accept one. His successor was Colonel Berthold Waldstein, brother to Count Max, whose part was no longer that of a regent, simply of a last defender and liquidator of the heritage. In May he left Güstrow for Rostock, dragging with him what he could of the castle's splendours, and until October he held out there. In July the former dukes re-entered the capital accompanied, or led, by none less than the liberator in person, the Lion of the North. The celebration was perfectly arranged. Initially tolling of bells, a final swift commemorative taste of the afflictions of usurpation, then metamorphosis into peals of jubilation. *Ein' feste Burg ist unser Gott* (A safe stronghold our God is) still blared from every steeple. A procession of princes including Bogislav of Pomerania, nobles, guilds and schoolchildren. Throngs of horses, velvet coats, plumed hats, broadswords. Divine service in the cathedral, the text from Psalm 126,

"They that sow in tears shall reap in joy." On the market-place twenty barrels of wine and forty barrels of beer to refresh the rescued subjects who would soon have to pay for the present in the shape of severe taxes. The new Chancellor was Privy Councillor Cothmann whom Wallenstein had once treated so roughly. Left open was the question who was to replace the property of the pillaged pillager with what? The problem would prove a sharp encumbrance during the time that remained.

The return of the dukes was a triumph for Swedish policy. It could show how he who adhered to the King did well. Gustavus Adolphus had need of such successes.

He wanted allies, allies who would give him guarantees and be compliant. In this adventure he wanted no neutrality and he said so from the start. "Such is nothing but a mass of *quisquilae* [rubbish] which the wind scours along and sweeps away," he asserted to a Brandenburg negotiator soon after his landing. "What kind of thing is it, neutrality? It surpasses my understanding." Again, "Here God and the Devil are in strife. If His Dilection desires to side with God, let him join me. If however he desires to side with the Devil, then verily he must fight me. *Tertium non datur* [Third course there is none]." Assurances inked on paper did him no service. He wanted realities, like fortresses and passes. His hands had eyes: they saw and believed what they grasped. The only way "once and for all to break the Spanish and Austrian yoke weighing down on Germany's neck" and to redeem the people from "papal, soul-defiling horrors" was, he wrote to John George, manly unity. Saxony however was reluctant to conclude an alliance, either in the summer or in the following winter. An instinct for power, the advantages of tradition, and the national cause may have played a part in the slow workings of John George's mind. What were the foreign monarch's intentions? Why had he come? Hardly for the sake of the Germans' blue eyes, of religion pure and simple. That did not happen. Unselfish motives blended with others which could hardly have been less unselfish. Religion and power – who could separate these sisters? He must want security for his northern realm, and whoever sought security aspired automatically to more than he already had. He wanted satisfaction too, indemnification for his military outlay because as the party attacked – no, because he had taken the field on behalf of co-religionists. But nowadays, with the scarcity of money, such was gladly claimed in the form of land. Examples existed. The treaty of alliance which Gustavus Adolphus had forced upon old Duke Bogislav could easily be interpreted as though Sweden had cast an eye on Pomerania. Were his arms to prove triumphant, there would be no more riddance of him. Were he to lose, and never yet defeated Tilly was still undefeated, it would be better not to have been one of the party. Hitherto Saxony had been spared the miseries of war. They would in any case afflict Gustavus Adolphus's German allies. The duty of a faithful father of his country was, if possible, to save his children from such miseries. Preferable therefore the neutrality despised by Gustavus Adolphus. Armed neutrality, unity of the Protestants among themselves, independence of Sweden. That was John George's line of thought when he pulled his wits together to think. He was encouraged along it by the Lutheran professional soldier who could not stop playing politics, Field-Marshal Hans Georg von Arnim. Notwithstanding his habit of changing his contracts of service like his shirts, Arnim struck the attitude of German patriot. Perhaps he really was one. We cannot see to the bottom of that strange heart. At Berlin, and of new at Dresden, the born Brandenburger's political sagacity was held in high regard. He travelled back and forth between the two Electors, he brought them together, he listened to and he prompted them. In spring he took over command of the army which John George had decided to assemble for all eventualities.

Arnim's policy ran athwart that of France. The Swedish invasion was indeed for Richelieu the fulfilment of a long-felt wish and on 31 January he did indeed conclude with Gustavus Adolphus a treaty of alliance and financial support. He would have preferred to keep it secret, but the King, to reap its psychological harvest, busily had the news spread. Close co-operation between Sweden and the Elector was not however what Paris, still nursing the hope of talking Protestants and Catholics together into a third, purely German power, wanted. In May the Franco–Bavarian treaty, a slap in the face for the Franco–Swedish one, was safely brought into port. Here was the fruit of Father's Joseph's contorted diplomacy. The Swedish avalanche had been released. Now its movement was meant to be kept under such control that it would drop in no spot other than, nor beyond, where France's advantage was best served.

During the late winter the Protestant Convention met for two months at Leipzig. A prince and a half with pitiful Lutheran pups scrabbling for a scrap, according to a Catholic squib. The princes in fact totalled thirteen and the towns were numerously represented. Because these were still equestrian times, we know the exact complements of their entourages and horses. The Elector of Brandenburg arrived with 178 attendants and 107 horses. The contingent from Augsburg's Protestants amounted to a delegate, his servant, and two horses – deliberate demonstration of how badly off the Augsburgers were.

At the outset a sensation was created by the sermon, subsequently published "at earnest solicitation and demand", of Matthias Hoë von Hoënegg, Doctor of Divinity and Senior Saxon Electoral Court Chaplain. For his text he took Psalm 83: "O God, keep not Thou silence: Hold not Thy peace, and be not still, O God. For, lo, Thine enemies make a tumult: And they that hate Thee have lifted up the head. They take crafty counsel against Thy people." The eloquent speaker left no doubt about the contemporary identity of God's tumultous enemies. They were the Papists, the Jesuits who day and night sought to subdue the Evangelists and cunningly to complete their ruin, the Congregation for the Propagation of the Faith, the clericals, and the Catholic League too. There followed talk of the Saviour, the Messianic and valiant hero Gideon, and the worshippers listening with knitted brows or nodding did not remain in the dark about his identity either. "What," retorted a Catholic polemicist, "was it that Doctor Hoë said about the King of Sweden? He is a true Gideon and butter will not melt in his mouth, eh?" Hoë von Hoënegg, a mischief-making specimen of humanity, had formerly been a good Austrian and spat upon the Calvinists. Of late he had become a friend to the Swedes, or, rather, had been bought by them.

Those who heard him presumed his "high-flown ditty" to be a political proclamation: it must surely have passed electoral censorship prior to being trumpeted upon the air. They were mistaken. John George, as emerged from the ingeniously balanced composition of his proposals, still did not want to make the leap into the Swedish camp. The Emperor was affronted to find no word therein about Gustavus Adolphus, against whose hostile conduct he was entitled to help from the Electors, but the King could have had more reason for indignation. Dresden was acting as though he were not on the scene at all. The intention to arm, with the Elector raising more than ten thousand men, was plain. Let his fellow-Estates do the same and there would be an overall strength of pretty well forty thousand. In the first place however such an association would be peace-loving and defensive except that resistance would forthwith be offered to the Edict's implementation. Secondly its organization would be very loose, each Protestant Circle looking to its own defence and a co-ordinating committee coming into action only in extreme emergency. Thirdly the hope persisted that the bark of the resolution would render its bite superfluous and that well-disposed negotiation would achieve the objective of imperial peace. That, the relief of so many thousands upon thousands of wailing, weeping individuals in direst need, distress and misery, surpassed all else in importance. For two months to have been spent on the discussion of John George's proposals surprises us. The problems, after all, were urgent and the dangers, like, for example, Tilly's siege of the great Protestant city of Magdeburg, mortal. The parties were assembled in a single spot. Speed would not have come amiss. The dreadful slowness of the age, manifest in its communications, movement, campaigning, infected minds too. Besides, the conferences by day were not helped by electoral beer-hall nights. The living at the host's expense was good while the search for heart-rending phrases to describe the wretched plight of the German nation proceeded. Arnim, protagonist of a third party, angrily abandoned the Convention. So, in even worse temper, did Bernhard von Weimar, a young prince eaten up with passion for speedy exploits.

The Leipzig Resolution, feeble yet equivocal, a half-way house wherein it would not be possible to stay for long, conformed to John George's proposals. Vienna none the less reacted as to a threat of revolution. The tenor of Ferdinand's reply was as usual a mixture of doleful and venomous pedantry. To Gustavus Adolphus the resolution was of little use, a promise of a Protestant army, inert, scattered, and lacking in co-ordination, which would moreover probably exist, apart from the Saxon contingent, solely on paper. The longer he lived among them, the more gratingly incomprehensible the Germans were becoming to the King. That was why he had to act on his own initiative, forcing the hand of individuals, Brandenburg's in particular, and substituting victorious battles for diplomacy. On 3 April, the day after the Leipzig delegates had limned their signatures in hierarchical order, he stormed Frankfurt-on-Oder. The troops garrisoned there by Tilly were slaughtered or captured, including their commander, Schauenburg, and cannon as well as victuals were seized in abundance. The citizens, for once, greeted the Swedes as liberators and shot out of windows at the imperialist defenders. Not that this prevented them from being victims of the succeeding atrocities. Misunderstandings like that happen. Was it feasible to demand of blood- and mud-stained pike-bearers the most subtle differentiations between assault and liberation? Two weeks later Landsberg fell. Silesia lay open and defenceless.

The news was serious. "Let the Court believe it or not," Tiefenbach, Schauenburg's successor, advised Questenberg from Silesian Glogau, "but it is very certain that affairs stand perilously. Comes the King into this land, one and all will receive him with a thousand huzzas, thence to

Bohemia, and thereupon to Austria." The Court believed him. Questenberg wrote to Wallenstein:

> Now the motto is, Help, help, and *non est qui audiat* [never mind who hears]. ... Our traps are down to the water-line, we now believe and recognize the injustice that we committed, and methinks that we do repent. ... Now it can be seen whether Your Princely Grace was right with Your inordinate recruitments and what in such short time our parsimony and thrift has yielded. Now I can and may speak openly with divers where it would not have been possible before and am accorded right in all.

Ferdinand repeatedly asked him whether he had no missive from Wallenstein, whether Wallenstein was coming, when he was coming. Questenberg felt a mixture of worry and triumph, triumph and derision. To find his own wisdom confirmed, even through catastrophes, could not but be some satisfaction, just like watching his own, the Wallenstein party growing like a tree by a brook.

Circumstances made of Wallenstein's retirement a condition more interesting than comfortable. Reports from the theatres of war arrived daily at his palaces in Prague, Gitschin, and Smřkowitz. They included bitter complaints about the lack of decision characterizing Tilly's senile strategy. The confusion, said Pappenheim, was so great that he had absolutely no idea where Gustavus Adolphus and his army were. The fundamental trouble was absence of the authority and resolve "which Your Princely Grace had ... God help us". Wallenstein in Bohemia was better informed than Pappenheim in his camp outside Magdeburg. He knew the whereabouts of Gustavus Adolphus; he was thoroughly familiar with the course of the Oder and its tributaries; and he considered the invasion of Silesia probable, that of Bohemia possible. He learned too how the Bohemian refugees were beginning to create a hubbub and heard how Redern, the poor fellow whom ten years ago he had driven out of Friedland, was busy with plans for the recovery of his lost property. Friedland, castle and town, received a garrison of musketeers. He collected provisions for the rank and file of the defeated eastern army descending upon Silesia. Quarters and food would be furnished by his principality of Sagan. Instructions, trenchant in tone, were issued to the governor there. A mere 1000 men would cost the poor little country 231 tallies of corn, 140 oxen, 45 barrels of beer, 525 tallies of oats, and what not, the governor remonstrated. He did not possess such quantities, and there was the palace construction too. In vain. Wallenstein, who ordinarily, prudently spared his territories the sacrifices of military exigency, was inflexible. In so far as they had ever slumbered, his energies were aroused. Now, with his very own realm threatened alongside the Hereditary Lands, he assisted the defence, and how very glad everyone was to subordinate themselves to him, the feudal lord, the preceding, and, it was to be hoped, prospective Generalissimo, to his unwritten, personal ascendency.

For the present these preparations proved premature. Gustavus Adolphus's business in Germany was unsettled and he could not yet leave.

The ugly war game always turned on who drew away whom in what direction. Through his diversion against Frankfurt the King had wanted to relieve Magdeburg's torment by forcing the imperialists eastward. As in January, Tilly broke camp, but he left behind more than half his troops under Pappenheim's orders. Told of Frankfurt's fall, he halted in Brandenburg on the banks of the Havel. His junior commanders, Pappenheim and Tiefenbach, as well as Questenberg in Vienna thought that he should continue his march, pursuing the King wherever he turned. Why did the Good Old Man keep on dallying with this damned Magdeburg? Tilly, though, had no desire to go farther east, let alone south-east, and he could cite in support of his reluctance Wallenstein's experience in 1626. He returned, very slowly, to Magdeburg. Should the Oder be lost, the Elbe must be secured by elimination of its greatest central bastion to which all Protestants looked with hope and fear. On this point Tilly sturdily resisted his critics, and in the immediate future he proved right. Magdeburg's danger compelled the King to march on Berlin instead of forward to Glogau and Breslau, Sagan, Friedland, and Prague. His columns were badly reduced, for some troops had always to remain here and there if gains were to be more purposeful than stones thrown into water. At this juncture his strength would hardly have been equal to that assembled by Tilly around Magdeburg, almost thirty thousand men and eighty-five guns. He stopped at Berlin so as finally to put matters in order with Elector George William, by forging an alliance or at least obtaining the fortresses of Küstrin and Spandau, as well as to address clamorous letters to Elector John George, seeing that if he wanted to reach Magdeburg he must cross Saxon territory. "At the Last Judgement," he thundered, "You Evangelists will be arraigned because You would not act upon the Evangel, and reprisal surely awaits You here too. Let Magdeburg be gone, and if I withdraw, then look to it how You will fare!" Magdeburg was gone on 20 May, taken by storm, its population massacred, its buildings burnt to ashes. Barely five thousand of its thirty thousand inhabitants were supposed to have survived.

"When Friedland was notified by a groom of the chamber that Magdeburg had been captured by Tilly," the Bavarian agent at Prague informed Maximilian, "he seized from the table a small silver bell and in fury threw it after the chamberlain, shouting that it was not true!" Wallenstein, in other words, was thoroughly enraged by Tilly's victory or Gustavus Adolphus' defeat, or both. We don't believe a word of it. In the first place he will certainly not have received the news from a personal attendant, but in a sealed letter. Secondly he had long been prepared by Pappenheim and Questenberg as to the inevitability of the city's fall and he can therefore not have been surprised by the event. That the catastrophe, an atrocity unprecedented in centuries, should have caused the Catholics to jubilate or incite them to ribald doggerels was a bad sign. A new verb entered the German language: "to Magdeburgize". Spirits had undergone some brutalization during the past twelve years. On the Protestants the effect was ambivalent. If *this* was possible, something similar, they feared, could happen in any of their own parts, for contrary to expectation the Catholics had proved the stronger and gave no quarter any more, while the deliverance promised by the Lion from Midnight had not matured. In an apologia Gustavus laid the blame on the Magdeburgers, which was mean, and with justification on the two Electors of whom to the last he could never be sure whether they were friend or foe. Horror at the occurrence was however paired with redoubled bitterness capable of reverting into fresh courage. "Magdeburg has been taken, but yesterday I apprised the Emperor that in my opinion our antagonists may be thereby the more incensed and on its account fly into a great passion," Questenberg wrote to Wallenstein.

Not that Elector George William could ever be provoked into a great passion. What in mid-June finally coerced him into a passive, timidly concealed, but nevertheless full alliance with Sweden was the rhetoric of force. Gustavus Adolphus had now to be certain of Brandenburg, its fortresses and approaches, the quarters and the soldiers available for recruitment there. He issued an ultimatum, threatened to do his worst, and had his way. The mediator between the princely brothers-in-law was Arnim, freshly appointed Saxon Field-Marshal, believer hitherto in a third, German party, at the moment unable any longer to believe in it. Hesse-Kassel had joined the Swedish side, under the influence of young

Prince Bernhard von Weimar, Mecklenburg and Pomerania were on it in any case, and now Brandenburg. In a theatre of war at one remove matters proceeded the other way about – Protestant Swabia was once again lost to the imperialists. The forces rendered free through the conclusion of peace in Italy trundled back the way that they had come, debouching via the Grisons and Lake Constance into southern Germany under the leadership of Gallas, Egon Fürstenberg, and Aldringen. They licked into shape those impudent imperial towns as well as the counts and princes who had adhered to the Leipzig Resolution. They pushed farther north in very considerable numbers, Fürstenberg with fifteen thousand men, Aldringen with seven thousand, and soon they would be drawn into play. Nobody of the co-signatories to the Resolution really remained except the Elector of Saxony, indubitably by far the richest and busy emptying his money-bags for mercenaries, of whom he soon had twenty thousand together, yet quite palpably ever more isolated.

Tilly had wanted to have Magdeburg as a lesson to all rebels and as a stronghold in central Germany, but the living city, not the mound of corpses and ruins. The fire, whatever its cause, had not been his fault, and afterwards he again did not know what to do or how to use his victory. Launch into Brandenburg and hurl himself on the King? The latter would inveigle him into inhospitable country drained dry, towards impregnable positions and traps along the Oder. Turn on Saxony and put a speedy end to the danger brewing there? Not exactly like the King in other respects, Tilly also did not think much of individuals who were neither friend nor as yet foe, but in a state of armed readiness. The atrophying Leipzig Resolution was in his eyes a veiled declaration of war. Maximilian's view, following French advice, was different and he still wished to spare his fellow-prince rather than to drive him into the arms of Sweden. Therefore Tilly, to the despair of his impetuous second-in-command, continued irresolute in the neighbourhood of dead Magdeburg. "This is none other than the enemies' accustomed style," growled Pappenheim to Wallenstein. "As often as we have beaten them, as often have they retarded *fructum victoriae nostrae* [the fruit of our victory] with false negotiations and won time to regain their strength. . . . I know not what else to write to Your Princely Grace than that, with this powerful host, we stay quiet without cause."

Movement by both sides up and down and across the wide board, the furrowed, burnt soil. Tilly to Hesse, to bring to reason the Landgrave of Kassel – a gesture dictated simply by his own dilemma. Thereupon a shift by Gustavus Adolphus north-westward to the Elbe with a strong encampment at Werben where it is joined by the Havel. Tilly back north again, into the Magdeburg region and past the murdered city in the direction of Wolmirstedt, Burgstall, Tangermünde. Contact with the enemy, a skirmish, a major encounter within hand's breadth, then retreat by Tilly without venturing upon a real clash. Fifty miles farther south-east, at Eisleben, his strength was augmented by Fürstenberg's corps. Due east lay the road to Saxony. That was what he had in mind. The plain, pious soldier *per se* was now playing politics crucial to the next five years, and that for purely military reasons. Saxon pseudo-neutrality must not be tolerated any longer. John George's army must be dissolved and its component parts absorbed by him, Tilly, before it reinforced the Swedes. The notion was his own brainchild and he urged the Emperor to obtrude upon His Serene Electoral Highness "to request a categoric declaration as to whether he wishes to be friend or foe. Then it would be possible to be guided thereby and to arrange matters accordingly. Now however there is cause for constant anxiety and never knowing whereat one does well or rightly." Bavaria did not at any price want to make trouble, and Vienna wanted at least to postpone such, but the old warrior forced the pace. His talks with Saxon delegates were grim and bad-tempered – times had altered, the Protestants no longer held the upper hand, the religious peace had never been more than makeshift, Saxony would do better straightway to relinquish its stolen bishoprics, injustice brought no blessings. His letters to the Elector eventually assumed the character of ultimatums. He hoped once more to achieve Saxony's deflection into the imperialist camp. What he failed to understand was that precisely this was for Saxony no longer possible without total dishonour and total exposure. He was, in other words, imposing on it the course which he was trying to forestall. At Dresden, the political tension was of a tautness rare at German courts. In print the scribblers declared this, that, and the other: joinder with Sweden was inevitable or else all lost, or joinder with the Emperor, or else a third choice. But scribblers carried no weight and, when Tilly's regiments invaded Saxony, seized Merseburg and Leipzig, then proceeded after their ferocious fashion to do themselves well in the lush land, John George took the step for which he had months past been preparing without any certainty whether he would take it. Twenty years' government conducted with loyalty to the German cause and abounding in deeds whose usefulness was known to the world would have deserved better thanks, his last appeal emphasized on a sorrowfully embittered note. To remain in the spirit of the Imperial Constitutions faithful to his beloved Emperor was his desire, but against barbarities of the kind now being perpetrated on his soil he must avail himself of the resources furnished by nature and tradition. His hastily concluded compact with Sweden for the term of the common danger – a vague provision – left him more independence than was customarily enjoyed by Gustavus's German allies. The King did not trust the Elector, with reason; the Elector loathed the tie with the foreigner. Compulsion, not affection, was its inspiration. The magnet had at last exercised its attraction to the full. Protestant Germany, which betrayed the Bohemians and left the Danes in the lurch, had become Swedish.

The Swedish–Saxon alliance was the direct harbinger of the military crisis, being indeed created to this end. As happens in games, war games not excepted, after prolonged to and fro, after fifteen months during which onlookers were beginning to become bored, the crisis was at hand. This time none of the opponents, conscious of its inevitability, sought to avoid the issue. Its initiation was a well-arranged, polished piece of play, the concentration of forces. John George's raw recruits, some eighteen thousand of them, marched from the east towards Düben, a spot on the map to the north of Leipzig. Swedes, twenty thousand on foot, 7500 mounted, crossed the Elbe at Wittenberg to proceed south-wards with the same objective. Infantry, cavalry, artillery. The lightest of the guns drawn by eleven, the heaviest by thirty-one horses; the King with his regiment of guards and black-gold banners; the King's steed without its rider; more cavalry, with blue, red, white, yellow, and green colours; the King's chariot; ammunition carts, baggage wagons, pack-horses. An order of battle in motion over a river. A fine sight. Rather less fine after the battle.

That started, slowly, during the morning of 17 September between Düben and Leipzig on the Breite Feld ("Broad Acre"), developed its full fury towards two o'clock, and ended in the dark. Forty-five thousand Swedes and Saxons, the Bavarians and imperialists slightly fewer, but with seventy-five guns against a mere twenty-six. So much for the numbers involved. Tilly's soldiers, in large measure Wallenstein's under the command of Wallenstein officers, were war veterans. The Saxons, newly drummed together, understood nothing of their business although Arnim, their commander, may have understood it well enough. The imperialists had moreover the protection of the large city, Leipzig, as well as the sun and the wind behind them, which was accounted an advantage. By evening the alleged advantages were gone and Tilly's troops in disorderly flight, captured or killed. About ten thousand are said to have been left over. The Swedes took the entire enemy artillery, their ammunition, war-chest, and colours. The last can today still be seen in the Riddarholm church at Stockholm. What happened is known in broad outline. How Pappenheim, sweeping out to the left in order to outflank the enemy front wheeling to the right, moved too far away from his centre and fell into the clutches of Gustavus Adolphus's reserve, his "second line". How Tilly, with his marching fortresses, the "tercios",* dispersed the Saxons who composed the enemy's left wing, but thereby exposed his centre so that the more mobile Swedish brigades caught him in the flank, with their musketeers and light artillery having an all too easy prey in the heavy masses, and cavalry squadrons approaching from all sides charged with perfect confidence against the leviathans helpless in the defensive. The scene's particulars have been reconstructed and described. In our narrative only one battle will be delineated in detail, and that is yet to come. Suffice it that Breitenfeld in a matter of five hours altered the situation militarily, politically, and morally as deeply as a battle is capable of doing.

Wallenstein received the news from Aldringen who on that day was stationed with seven thousand seasoned Italian campaigners at Jena. "Your Princely Grace will already have heard what a defeat Lieutenant-General Count Tilly sustained on the seventeenth of this month between Leipzig and Eilenburg when he lost all his artillery, and the entire army, horse and foot, was so to speak severed and slain. . . . I had in the meantime dispatched to the Lieutenant-General an officer who returned on the eighteenth and reported how he had found all in flight and been hard put to it to save himself." Questenberg commented from Vienna, "God punishes us perhaps not . . . *propter nostram salutem,* but *proper nostram ingratitudinem* [for the sake of our salvation, but on account of our ingratitude]". No letter from Wallenstein in which he comments directly on the event, sneering perchance at Tilly, has been found. What he felt, thought, and planned may for the present be left open. A flood of other embittered communications is extant. The severer the shock, the less it was possible to do at the moment, or even to know how matters actually stood, the more people wrote to each other. Maximilian told Ferdinand that he had always been against the breach with Saxony. So had he, retorted Ferdinand, but it was Bavaria's very own general who had insisted. To Tilly, a week after the battle, Maximilian expressed himself with magnanimity. "We have learned

* Originally a Spanish formation which combined musketeers and pikemen in a strength of two to three thousand (translator's note).

with particular grief from Aldringen and others of the misfortune You and the army under Your command have sustained at the enemy's hands, and whereas 'tis well to ponder that this like all other things must be left to and be enjoined by God's inscrutable Will, yet You will on this score be in no little distress, wherefore We have for that reason desired herewith to condole with You." The true state of affairs and what should be done now was not however something that he could well assess from Munich. . . . The Catholic camp's wallowing in woe on the great disaster, the grievous defeat, *la disgrâce du Comte de Tilly*, the grave and afflicting condition, met response in a Protestant paean drenched with derision and elation. Even in distant Moscow bells were rung in honour of Breitenfeld, for the Muscovites were against the Poles, consequently against the Emperor and for the Swedes.

What would the victors do? Probably best for them, following Pappenheim's principle, to exploit their victory forthwith and to the full, pursuing Tilly mercilessly on his north-westward flight and preventing any rally, any fresh concentration by the imperialists. For of course there were still imperialists. "Annihilation" is a relative word. No army is annihilated in open battle. A good third of that involved at Breitenfeld may have been saved, no doubt over a widely scattered area, but capable of re-assembly. The smaller the number of troops, the quicker it was feasible to complement them. A quota of commanders had moreover not participated at Breitenfeld at all: Ossa, on the Rhine; Aldringen, Fugger, Gallas in central Germany; Tiefenbach, holding Silesia with the rest of the eastern army. The amalgamation of these corps would result in a force larger than that which had just been dispersed. Amalgamation would be practicable only somewhere in the middle, for which Tilly's personal authority and the remainder of his effectives were necessary. Could such amalgamation and reformation be prevented? Gustavus Adolphus thought not. Seeing that we understand less of the art of war than he did, let us allow his judgement to stand.

Another course would lead from Saxony to Bohemia, from Bohemia to Austria, to the heart of Habsburg power. That the King should have headlong taken it while panic still blazed in Prague and Vienna was a subsequent verdict, even on the part of his Chancellor, Oxenstierna. The pros and cons are in balance. Other enemies, it could be objected, had faced Vienna and failed. The allied council of war at any rate decided on a third way. The Swedes now felt strong enough to control northern Germany with two armies and to set out with a third, under the royal command, for the south-west, in the first place towards Thuringia, then

Franconia. Inside the Empire were the allies, already won or still to be gained as such, but who remained to be rescued – the Brunswickers, the Hessians, the Swabians; and in the Empire was the main body of the enemy. The Saxons could for the time being attend to Silesia so as to keep Tiefenbach's army in check and repledge the Silesians their formerly broken word. John George, it should be noted, wanted matters to proceed the other way about, he marching into the Empire, the King into the Hereditary Lands. The Elector's wish was however exactly what the King did not want. The Saxons' presence in central and southern Germany would produce, if anything material at all, a revival of the third, the German party. Better to constrain the vacillating Elector through undisguised conflict with the House of Habsburg. Since the Swedish will carried more weight than the Saxon, the decision taken accorded with the King's inclination. He marched from Halle to Erfurt, from Erfurt into Franconia; Arnim, the Saxon Field-Marshal, through Lusatia against Silesia. But he did not enter Silesia. He crossed the Elbe upstream and, to everyone's surprise, on 1 November the border of Bohemia. The Saxons had been there once already, in 1620–1, as oppressors. They would have had to have changed radically for them now to come as liberators.

HE DID NOT HELP

The melancholy Breitenfeld dispatch sent by Tilly to Vienna – "ill-fortune finally ruled more than good fortune" – contains a hint that he had had to march against Saxony in order to find victuals for his poor soldiers because there, where they had previously roamed, between the Weser and the Havel, they had had nothing to eat. It was a complaint which throughout 1631 was reiterated in the correspondence of the Good Old, Poor Old Man. "All the days of my life I have never yet seen an army suddenly and totally deprived of all its requisites, great and small. . . . And I am to the utmost surprised that the poor soldiers have in such great exigency stayed so long." They did not stay permanently though: they fell ill, they dropped out, they died. Whether His Princely Grace the Duke of Mecklenburg and Friedland could not make alternative, better dispositions? Wallenstein, as Generalissimo, had been the army's grand provider. He was no longer either one or the other. "Forces' sabotage" has been the phrase used summarily to describe his new management of matters, a source of such deep disappointment to his successor. Did he in fact mean to do harm? Verifiable is only that he had no intention of serving the general cause at his own expense. Supplies to the army were of advantage as long as he headed it and sooner or later could menacingly present his bills. Now they would have been a dubious investment. Why risk it when better offered? His identity with Emperor, Empire, and army, intricate from the start, was severed. He stood alone, or he fancied that he stood alone. Perhaps this barren freedom, concentrated in a single aspect, was a greater evil than the intention, ascribed to him, of helping the Swedes by letting the imperialists starve.

Precision is however essential. His most flagrant sabotage of Tilly's mandate, and therefore of his country's defence, is alleged to have occurred in Mecklenburg where, as long as his underlings had any say, he sold surplus grain on the free Hamburg market instead of distributing it among the regiments. His governor did in the first place provide very well for the military, to the value of fifty thousand taler from the 1630 harvest. Nevertheless, as if it were not enough that the soldiers should behave, especially on Wallenstein's own estates, as if they had been quartered in enemy territory, the local commander did not even let them have what he received on their behalf, but had the cattle – Wallenstein's herds – driven out of the province in order to sell it elsewhere and set an example which his officers followed. Could this be a clue to understanding, as least as far as Mecklenburg is concerned, the forces' sabotage? What grounds had the hard-headed economist to sacrifice his harvests to the enrichment of pillagers? An additional element was his pressing need for cash. The governor had to tell him that both, victuals for the troops and remittances to Bohemia, were not possible. There ensued the order to convey everything saleable to Hamburg, and when as little as three thousand taler had been secured, these should with the assistance of the banking-house Heinrich Schmit immediately be transferred to Gitschin. Such paltry sums had become a source of satisfaction to him. Gone the days when he calculated in hundreds of thousands. Need any more reasons be adduced? To look for them where they do not exist, or at least *need* not exist because there are enough others about, has been a favourite sport with this subject's biographers. What was for Wallenstein more palpable than that he should extract from Mecklenburg what he could as long as he could? He was too old a military hand not to know that in any case matters would soon be done with there. The exact moment when he came to regard Mecklenburg as lost is difficult to pin-point, but it will certainly not have been later than spring 1631.

The argument that he could have saved northern Germany by being more generous, at least with clothing and boots, powder and lead, will not hold water. More was required. Lacking was the discipline which he alone had created and, had he remained in charge, might have been capable of upholding. Material aid without licence to control its disposal would have been to stop a vessel permanently holed.

Supposing, against all probability, that it would have helped? What advantage to himself could he have anticipated? For this eventuality let us note an additional, conceivable albeit supererogatory, motivation on his part. The Electors had sent him packing out of the Empire back to Bohemia and had gainsaid him Mecklenburg. Tilly's victory would have been Bavaria's victory. If during this year of gloom he at all knew what to wish himself, it cannot have been Bavaria's triumph. Expelled by the Electors, he kept out of affairs. Even when hostilities moved southward in the direction of Magdeburg, so conveniently linked by the Elbe to Bohemia, he did not allow the produce of his duchy to avail the army. Friedland bakers had to buy his flour at fixed price rises. The surplus was sent to Prague, northern Bohemia and Saxony. Not until Silesia, Sagan and Friedland were directly threatened did he change his policy.

That was the way of that world, his position in it, and how he was himself. No pity for the soldiers who so recently had been his nor for the commander-in-chief, operating under such difficult circumstances, with whom he had after all been for a long time on passably good terms. "What concerns his own person, he is indubitably amiable and tractable ...." With empty promises he kept the Old Man in suspense, not, in our view, out of cruel delight, but simply so as to be able to do one thing and another too, simply to be rid for a few weeks of his importunities.

Neutral, undecided, he felt himself capable of being influenced in any and every direction.

THREADS IN THE DARK

The Trčkas of Lipa were among Bohemia's wealthiest families. Their estates at Nachod, Neustadt, Opočno, Hermanitz, Kaunitz, Smiřice, and Dymokor amounted to about half the duchy of Friedland. Only a smaller portion of these possessions derived from inheritance. The greater part had been booty cheaply bought and bartered during the confiscation proceedings of 1621. The Trčkas had feathered their nest and grown fat on their country's catastrophe in the way that Wallenstein had done. If they were well off before the battle of the White Mountain, they were far better off thereafter. They should have been content with their new, greedily exploited condition.

They were not. Old Rudolf Trčka seems to have been a man of no importance. His wife Magdalena, born Lobkowicz, was cast in stronger mould, a constantly busy woman of business, astoundingly grasping, and a patriot. What, though, can "patriotism" signify here? Not kindliness towards the peasants who constituted the preponderant majority of all Bohemians. Lady Magdalena treated those on her estates even more cruelly than the Bohemian nobility in general did. No, patriotism with the Trčkas was purely pride, pride in a lordly status which was of most recent acquisition and which the Habsburgs had shorn of its prerogatives. Religion, since it also furnished an element of pride in race and caste, may have been a contributory factor. After the battle of White Mountain Lord Rudolf went to mass. So did his son Adam Erdmann. His wife, more stiff-necked, remained Protestant. The authorities winked at the fact. Another son emigrated.

In summer 1627 Adam married Maximiliana von Harrach, sister to the Duchess of Friedland, and became brother-in-law alike to Cardinal Harrach and Wallenstein. Spoiled, gay, and foolish, but with good looks and manners, Adam appears to have been a solace to Wallenstein's lonely temperament. In winter 1630 he promoted him to a colonelcy and saw to his elevation to the dignity of count. With Bohemia once more his focal point, he entered on closer relations with the Trčkas who were anyway his neighbours. Adam he made his personal assistant and instructed in deep political secrets.

By honouring the Trčkas with his friendship, Wallenstein came into touch, at least indirectly, with a totally fresh circle. Notwithstanding its affiliation to the Eggenberg-Harrach clan by conversion and marriage, the family had connections with the Bohemian émigrés through Adam's refugee brother as well as Wilhelm Kinsky, his sister's husband, who lived at Dresden. Another sister had moreover been betrothed to Matthias Thurn, the giddy firebrand and ringleader of the great rebellion; she died before the wedding.

The sly, tangled web of intrigue, against one side and on behalf of another, and the other way about, or for both or against both, spun with such delight by the Kinsky brothers in the days of Emperor Rudolf and Archduke Matthias, will be called to mind. Cleverer than the Trčkas they filled with gossamer political cocoons the vacuum of boredom suffered by the rich. Thus it had been twenty years ago, thus it still was. Of the four brothers, Ulrich, one of the wildest defenestrators, had been killed in the war; Radslav was in exile; Wenzel, formerly the central figure in very motley goings-on, was on cordial terms with the imperial court, while Wilhelm enjoyed a strange intermediate position. Declining to become a convert, he had in 1628 to accept a lenient relegation to Saxony, being allowed not only to retain his estates but to derive so handsome an income from them that his household at Dresden rivalled the Elector's in splendour. Indeed the exile, member of a politically badly implicated family, was, and again at Wallenstein's instigation, made a count by the Emperor and frequently allowed to visit his home. He was half in, half out. Any presumption, though, of gratitude to the Emperor for such good-natured, illogical generosity would be mistaken. Kinsky used his status of semi-*émigré* to establish contact with full-blooded *émigrés* like Thurn, Ruppa, Kapliř, Velen von Zierotin, Johann von Bubna, and it is unlikely that this intriguer's sojourns in Bohemia were of an altogether harmless variety. The lemon-juice rather than tongue-wagging ink used by Countess Kinsky in her lively correspondence with her mother, old Lady Trčka, required the letters to be held over a fire in order to let her writing appear upon the paper. Their contents, this suggests, cannot have been harmless. Post between refugees and those who had remained behind passed as a rule unmolested.

The refugees – there were about 150,000 of them. Poor people who had a trade and exercised it to the benefit of the host-country. Poor people who had no trade and lived by begging. Rich people who would not share their wealth with the poor, but instead were on occasion robbed by their new rulers and led by the nose during unending legal suits. The rich, like Kinsky, and the veteran leaders, like Thurn, would give up neither hope, hope of restoration of the old Bohemian civil rights which had constituted their privileges, nor playing politics. Thurn, after the 1620 disaster first in Venetian, then Danish, was now in Swedish military service. What inspired the anti-Habsburg powers ever again to entrust the Count with important tasks is not easy to understand. It cannot have been his martial successes; he never had any. His endowments were inflexibly sanguine convictions, ingenuous confidence in others, and mightily inflated self-confidence as well as an inexhaustible urge to action. Having at some stage appointed himself chief spokesman for the refugees and uttered solemn declarations in the name of "the Kingdom's three Protestant Estates", as though these still existed, he was recognized as such both by the Protestant monarchs and in Bohemia by those who still had the courage left to hope.

Gustavus Adolphus's German campaign caused the refugees' hearts to beat fast and gladly. The farther he penetrated into the Empire, the gladder. A couple of hundred Czech officers, some of general's rank, served with the Swedish army. Countess Kinsky sent her mother a portrait of the Lion from Midnight framed in a gold medallion. The wicked old woman always carried it in her bag; the King had no more ardent admirer. In her husband's study hung a painting of Wallenstein. "How high he has mounted," murmured Rudolf Trčka, "and, who knows, how high he will yet mount!" Meaning the throne of Bohemia. That was father's and son's wishful thinking. Adam would never have ventured to inquire of his great brother-in-law what he thought of the idea. Had he done so, and this is as certain as the uncertain can be, his answer would have been a surprised, repelled "no". However, as long as they did not ask, the Trčkas were at liberty to nurse their fond secret. Wallenstein did not spoil their sport. He was given no cause. He may have guessed. As a surmisal, a fantasy indulged by others with his name, it may have appealed to him. As a sober consideration it did not arise. He knew the specimen of hollow shadow-kingship erected in 1619 by the Bohemian lords. In their pride they were not even now prepared to abandon the scheme. He had observed the Palsgrave's fate with contempt. Was he to assume such puppet dignity? Should the émigrés return as victorious kingmakers, what was to happen to Friedland, his anything but shadow-commonwealth compounded of rebel estates? Exchange his beloved duchy, his life's most solid achievement, for a shadow-crown? That he should have entertained the notion lacks plausibility, is out of keeping, however twisted and turned. On a more modest scale the Trčkas were of course in the same situation. Their intrigues with the émigrés sowed mines beneath the legal structure that they inhabited so handsomely. Or, to use a more familiar metaphor, they were lopping off the branch on which they sat in the vague hope of leaping to a higher one at the moment this dropped to the ground. Comparatively small fry and mentally less gifted, the Trčkas can and must be credited with such ideas because proof is on hand. Totally incapable of proof is any dream of royalty on Wallenstein's part. As for the office of Bohemian viceroy, which Gustavus Adolphus is alleged to have offered him, the tale is utterly absurd. Wallenstein as mere deputy to Palsgrave Frederick whom Sweden continued to recognize as King? He, who owned approximately one fifth of the land and was uncrowned master of the rest? A beggarly bribe like that is supposed to have been deemed enough to decoy him? If the Swedes came to Bohemia, and in their train the *émigrés*, he could watch his magic castle evaporate in front of his eyes, land and money and reputation disappear. As in 1619, he would be able to escape with nothing save his life. With Habsburg he had risen, with Habsburg he must fall. "I know the Bohemians all too well . . . the knaves think of the present alone, not the future, and yet they know that, if the Emperor is imperilled, they are lost." His old warning. What held good for the Bohemians – he meant Martinitz, Dietrichstein, Slawata, who owed their grandeur to the White Mountain and would indeed be lost if the Emperor were imperilled – applied however to Wallenstein too. The Habsburgs were in peril. As never before, the order established in 1620 was in peril. He had to see to safeguards for himself. That argued the need for links, no matter the type, to the side which possibly, indeed probably, would be the stronger, the Swedes and refugees. ". . . because I consider playing for certainty to be at all times best," he wrote earlier in another connection. He adhered to his principle.

With the *émigrés* his relations had always been ambivalent. He, accessory to their distress and second to none in its exploitation, should have been the object of their hatred. They did not hate him. Partly because in his situation they would probably have done much the same since in this harsh world it went without saying that everyone ruthlessly acted to his own advantage. Partly because they were also a little proud of the European position attained by one whose roots were theirs. When those of them who fought under enemy colours fell into his hands, he was forbearing with them. At least on most occasions, though there were ugly exceptions. With Johann von Bubna, a Danish, then Swedish officer, and in days long past his tutor in the art of war, he was on terms of friendship. One in a position to know, Matthias Thurn, let slip that Bubna had "for years been the Prince's confidant". Gifts of money went to Ruppa, unfortunate head of the 1618 rebel government who lived at Berlin. Benevolence? Wallenstein was not benevolent, although inclined to benevolently sensible compromise provided that he was not the loser. Only Valeriano Magni had realized this characteristic. There would, he maintained, be no European problem which Wallenstein would be incapable of solving or believe himself to be incapable of solving. The *émigrés*, as long as they existed, hoped, and burrowed, represented a European problem. If they could be appeased by means of some modest solatium, so much the better. And might not their goodwill prove useful some time? The scene was set.

On it appeared Jaroslaw Sezyma Rašin von Riesenburg, refugee third class, impoverished petty noble from the Trčka ambient. At the time of the Bohemian revolution no one heard about a Rašin. He was not the man to have been on a level to negotiate with the Duke of Friedland. No more than a secret letter-carrier, and that probably for jingling coin. Had patriotism been his motive, he would not four years later have sold his secrets to the Emperor. His report, written in 1635, became the Viennese prosecution's most cherished document, its chief testimony to Wallenstein's treachery. His evidence is to be treated with reserve. Writing for the award of a general pardon supplemented by a fee, Rašin was sly enough to understand what Vienna wanted of him. Whenever he was not quite sure, Wilhelm von Slawata, Wallenstein's archenemy, on his own admission "reminded" the spy of this and that which Rašin had forgotten and Slawata was in far less position to know. Not that the report was wholly without foundation. Between lies, partly capable of proof, partly capable of divination, he told the truth, but truth only to be believed where backed by the witness of other sources not relying on mere rumour.

For what was not said of Wallenstein, this prodigious phenomenon steeped in legendary lore? To quote just one example, he was declared, in 1628 when he was waging war against Denmark and already feared Swedish intervention, to have had the King of Denmark's seal and writing forged in a letter to Stockholm, stating that Christian was strong enough on his own and neither required nor desired Swedish help. Gustavus Adolphus, puzzled, doubtful of the letter's authenticity, sent a courier to Copenhagen. His suspicion substantiated, the King informed the imperialist emissary disguised as a Dane that he would spare his life if he returned to his master and gave him the following message: Wallenstein, to be sure, viewed himself as an imperial prince, but in the sight of the King he was a coward and a rogue. Which annoyed the recipient to such a degree that for three days he neither spoke nor admitted any to his presence. The sight of the false emissary, a musketeer or lieutenant, reporting to his commander-in-chief has to be envisaged: "His Royal Majesty of Sweden conveys to Your Princely Grace. . . ." Such basically idiotic yarns were none the less believed and peddled in the correspondence of experienced diplomats whose credit was at least as good as that of Rašin von Riesenburg. Care is therefore requisite. Rašin was an agent of Count Thurn. He travelled back and forth between Bohemia, Dresden, Berlin, and wherever else his employers were to be found. He saw Adam Trčka often, Wallenstein seldom.

That much is certain. Most obscure of all, what Wallenstein's purpose with him was.

He is conjectured to have wanted vengeance, vengeance against Bavaria and against the Emperor who in 1630 had sent him packing, and vengeance only. This assumption was ubiquitous from or before the day of his dismissal, and its embellishment knew no end. In winter 1631 the French gazettes reported the Duke of Friedland to be extremely vexed at the displeasure which he had incurred. The Kings of Great Britain and Sweden had seized the welcome opportunity, inquiring whether he sought revenge. Would he not care to take up arms against Austria and Bavaria? If yes, he could be assured of Swedish, English, and French aid. The offer had been music in Wallenstein's ears. On its bearer he bestowed a golden chain and a thousand taler in cash. "This," the writer closed, "I learnt from gentlemen of honour and degree, *grands mignons* [great favourites] of the Kings of England and Sweden." Admirable inside knowledge. Tilly, reading the article, took it seriously enough to send copies to Maximilian, Ferdinand, and Wallenstein, that to the last accompanied by a note mingling chivalrous concern with malice. No credence would he ever again lend to stuff of this sort. Impossible that the Duke should requite the imperial favours with such noxious designs. Notwithstanding that it gave food for thought. ... Wallenstein replied disdainfully that tattle of this quality could not upset him. It made not bad listening, but laughter was the answer. To Questenberg he expressed surprise that jokes of this silly calibre should take in persons with general officer standing.

Two weeks earlier, at the Trčka castle of Opocno, the christening of Adam's baby son had been celebrated with the exotic pomp of feudal nobility. A family party – Lord Rudolf and Lady Magdalena, the High Burgrave of Prague Adam Waldstein, Archbishop Harrach, Wallenstein. Old, obstinately Protestant Countess Trčka cannot have been present in the chapel nor the mini-Protestant Sezyma Rašin on display at the festive board. Trčka had probably arranged his visit and concealment so as at a suitable hour to bring him and Wallenstein together. Nothing came of that. Rašin talked only to Count Adam, who asked how the King of Sweden was and whether Count Thurn was with him. There was hope yet of making a good Swede of the Duke, but the initiative must come from the other side in a way that would seem fresh, unusual to Wallenstein. That was the condition. Rašin's report is at this point credible and easy to see through. The Trčkas, Adam and the old pair, were playing at conspiracy. The opposite side was to behave as though it was setting the pace. That is, it was really to do so, for until then Wallenstein was unaware of the project. In May the scene was re-enacted at Castle Dymokur. The Swedes had taken Frankfurt-on-Oder, panic reigned at Vienna, and letters were passing between the Emperor and Wallenstein, supplicatory on the part of the former, sensible, advisory, but cool as regards the main issue on the part of the latter. Again Rašin talked only to Trčka, again Trčka demanded a first move by the King and the *émigrés*, but he allowed it to transpire that he was speaking on highest instructions. So the Trčkas had meanwhile informed the Duke, who had told them to continue their course. It could indeed be that one day he would do something of the kind if Swedish successes persisted so. What benefit he proposed to derive, how he visualized a new order in Bohemia and central Europe, that remained in the dark. Sezyma travelled to Berlin where Count Thurn had of late been made the Swedish representative. The two of them went to Spandau for an audience with Gustavus Adolphus. The King was first amazed, then interested. Who was this Trčka, how old, how judicious? The Duke's brother-in-law, Thurn replied, and influential. Still cleverer was his mother, a distinctly intelligent woman, a zealous Protestant and very patriotic. Rašin was once more, in the name of the King and of Thurn, dispatched to Bohemia: Count Adam should see how he could bring over Wallenstein to the Swedish side. "With heartfelt longing I await Rašin who is conducting this so highly important negotiation in Bohemia," Thurn wrote to Gustavus Adolphus in June, and that agrees with Rašin's report. On 18 June he was back in Prague. This time he met the Great Personage himself. He would do everything agreeable to His Majesty, Wallenstein affirmed, but only when the time was ripe. Lubberly blundering in so momentous a matter was not his habit. First, for instance, the compact between Sweden and Saxony must be sealed. And, added Trčka, it would be well if the King were to write to the Duke, in his own hand, so as to have his agreement in black and white. Return of Rašin to northern Germany. Authorization from Gustavus Adolphus to Thurn to deal with the gentleman in question (an oblique allusion to Count Adam) as he saw fit and, through him, to win other true patriots to the cause. Letter by Gustavus to Wallenstein. The letter is lost, but it existed. Wilhelm Kinsky read it so often and liked it so much that he could reel it off from memory. The text contained what Trčka wanted: Since Wallenstein with all too good reason was so very irate at the House of Austria, the King desired to succour him against his enemies and lend him "support in everything". In what particular of "everything" was imprecise. The Duke liked the letter and became more forthcoming. Impossible, because too dangerous, to express his thanks on paper, but answers carried in the head sufficed. He would need ten to twelve thousand Swedish soldiers; the rest he would manage. The item about twelve thousand men is confirmed in a letter by Thurn. Seeing that Rašin was Thurn's emissary and Thurn believed all that he said, the conformity lacks any attribute of unforeseen corroboration. From Wallenstein not one authenticated word has been found. From Trčka there is a single letter to Thurn, asking that his gracious cousin, the friend whom Thurn very well knows, shall be excused personal acknowledgement because he has the twitches. From Gustavus Adolphus an authorization to Thurn and a lost letter to Wallenstein elicited from him by the reports of Thurn and Rašin. Everything else is the tale of third parties who were not on hand and transmitted by fourth parties who were not present either: Arnim and Kinsky disclose their knowledge to the Swedish envoy at Dresden who, for lack of more solid material, refers it to the King's secretary. And so on. In an epoch when tall stories and fantasy were given free rein with special pleasure and when conjecture, lying, concealment were prosecuted with special artistry, such testimonies suffice for little more than a very leaky thriller whose central plot is not even implemented. Wallenstein may have talked of twelve thousand men that he would need or Rašin may, on Thurn's instructions, have insinuated to him that he could need them. At any rate they neither ever arrived nor did he make the slightest preparations to receive them, although as the most experienced military organizer of his day he knew that ammunition must be standing by, money in plenty, and stores from which to feed them. As for the King, was he unhesitatingly to divide his always inadequate army in order to entrust the one half to a leader utterly unknown to him except for his extreme eccentricity and former hostility? Ultimately it was all simply talk, Wallenstein making conditions impossible of fulfilment, the King sending missives which cost nothing. The only man never plagued by doubt was Thurn. "No instance exists," he wrote to Gustavus, "that this princely personage has at any time undertaken anything traitorously oblivious of honour, but, as say friend and foe, has been faithful and staunch." This was the same Thurn who in 1619 had branded and cursed Moravian Colonel Wallenstein: "There sits the insolent brute, hath lost his honour, goods and chattels, besides his soul, and doth he not do penance is like to go to Purgatory." Decent, forgetful, foolish, constantly duped creature!

Rašin's next Bohemian visit, in September, was protracted. Consequently conveyer and recipient of the secret mail were in one and the same place taken by surprise at news of the Breitenfeld battle. "You know," Wallenstein is supposed to have addressed the agent, "that Tilly has been struck upon the head at Leipzig? A terrible thing has happened, how mighty is God. How wholly unblemished was Tilly's name and how hath he lost his entire repute. If it befell me, naught is possible other than that I should take my life. But 'tis well for us." At least that last word is a lie. Wallenstein could not say "us" to the little sharp-eared man because he was himself not "we"; he belonged to no party. For the rest he viewed Tilly's defeat with the most mixed feelings. A weakening of the Spanish-imperialist side might be in his interest in so far as he had at all defined his interest, but not this weakening, this catastrophe. The weights in the scale had not simply been shifted, but the entire balance destroyed. Every road and every possibility lay open to the Swede, this uncanny visitor. Count Thurn was quickly taught the aftermath, Wallenstein a little later. In the second week of October the old rebel and his errand-runner overtook the King in the Thuringian forest. Their reception was indifferent. He was on his way to Franconia and had, Gustavus stated, no twelve thousand men to spare, 1500 at the most. The enemy was in the Empire, not Bohemia, and he must concentrate his strength on the former. Thurn during his return journey inscribed a very bitter letter to the King: 'I have grown old in honour, I have lived righteously and honestly, and I am not so advanced in dotage that I would mislead Your Majesty with my all too excessive trustfulness. . . ." All had been at trigger readiness, with Wallenstein prepared to assume the vice-royalty in Bohemia and the imperial forces in Silesia, Bohemia, Moravia, and Austria able to be routed. And now, how did he stand before those brave and noble individuals, his refugee compatriots? Nothing whatever had been at trigger readiness. All that had happened, as so often, was that letters had been written, talks held, whisperings taken place, non-committal and to no point. Wallenstein had never known what it was that he wanted and would do. Nevertheless the two principals in the negotiation, and Wallenstein more strongly than Gustavus, must have sensed in the depths of their souls that they were unsuited and could not become allies. Wallenstein as an assistant and dependant of the King of Sweden was an impossibility. Why did he engage in the shady game at all? To hear what he was offered. To be of the party, as an active participant and not as a passive victim, were anything transcendent to happen in Bohemia. To hedge his bets, as he later put it. This real motive he could never confide to the emigrants. Therefore he named that with which all the world credited him and repeated so long until he may at moments have given it credence himself: "The Emperor and his whole House should be made to feel that he had affronted a gentleman."

Wallenstein's earlier contacts with Gustavus Adolphus, those in late autumn 1627, also conducted indirectly and insincerely, were of a substantially different character. At that time the objective would have been to demarcate spheres of power, with Norway for the King, northern Germany for Wallenstein, the sea common to them both. Now the power spheres would have been a mixed brew, the King's infusion the incomparably stronger. This Wallenstein rejected. What was it to be then? He could not stay inert in the great crisis. He could not stay neutral, as little as the German Protestants had for all their writhings been able to do. Probably he had a presentiment all the time of what he would ultimately do. Without much gladness. Because he had to.

UTTERMOST CONFUSION

"For finally," Wallenstein wrote in December to Field-Marshal von Arnim, "when most lands will be lying in ashes, peace will have to be made, as the examples of fourteen years' continuous warfare render sufficiently visible to us." That was how he felt and that was what he wanted. He had gained enough by war, he was tired, and his gout tormented him worse than ever. Tranquillity on his own and others' behalf. To extricate himself alone was quite impossible. Consequently there had to be peace for him to have peace.

We know already what a difficult business it is to conclude peace. The best chance is when one party has to some degree, but not greatly, the edge on the other and both know that they cannot finish each other off. Then there is meeting half-way. The Swedes were however more than half-way. As Oxenstierna retrospectively remarked, "His Majesty's intent was to secure his kingdom and the Baltic. . . . [He] did not initially suppose that he would come so far." The occasion occurred, the enemy drew the King on, and the very expanse evacuated by the enemy too. At the end of December, after the capture of Würzburg, Aschaffenburg and Frankfurt-on-Main, he held his court in Mainz, he had become a neighbour of France. Plans to overrun Bavaria in the spring, and then

Austria after all, had no longer anything implausible about them. Eating feeds appetite. The restoration of German affairs, Bohemia included, to the state of 1618 was the minimum that the King must now demand because he appeared capable of obtaining in the field what could not be won across the conference-table. Exactly that was why he had again and again to resort to arms. His opponent would not submit until total defeat had been witnessed and sustained. But were Emperor Ferdinand and his councillors at last ready to listen to reason as regards the edict, they would with bag and baggage rather have fled to Italy than surrender their principal achievement, the Catholic Reformation in Austria, Bohemia, and southern Germany. The shattered political balance would need to be repaired if there was to be a peace tolerable to all. Failure to act on the necessity before the Swedish invasion, when in terms of power it would logically have been attainable, was the reproach that Wallenstein cast bitterly, haughtily, contemptuously in the teeth of the imperialist Spanish party. And of the Spaniards too. His wrath was directed not at his dismissal, which the Spaniards had tried to prevent, but at the policy of the Habsburg dynasty as a whole. That priest-ridden lot, as he epitomized it to a Danish envoy.

His secret relations with the Danes had Vienna's blessing. The capacity of King Christian, who observed without pleasure his northern neighbour's victorious German advance, to prove useful in recovery of the political balance, by mediation if not intervention, was conceivable. Wallenstein therefore accepted, and interpreted after his own fashion, this commission. He proposed to Denmark the purchase of certain Mecklenburg areas which were in any case lost to him and which Sweden would otherwise acquire. In addition Christian could have the bishoprics taken from him by the Peace of Lübeck. To the first bait Ferdinand agreed. The second ran counter to the edict and the bishoprics were at the Holy Father's disposal. Tonsure twaddle, Wallenstein commented irritably to the Danish envoy. The Emperor was at the moment in a rather delicate position; Denmark should simply take what was not amicably offered. Disloyalty? If loyal means obedient, Wallenstein was no longer that and he never would be again. Were his services wanted, those of a prince and a European politician in his own right, he must be permitted to go his own way.

A more interesting possibility than Denmark was presented by Saxony. The Swedish–Saxon alliance, not Sweden alone, had been what upset the political balance. To compensate this factor by splitting Saxony from Sweden was a notion positively crying out for attention. The alliance existed, and had had Breitenfeld for its sequel, but all the world knew its lack of animating ardour. Hans Georg von Arnim, that pious intriguer, was conducting Saxon affairs. Germanic in sentiment, intent on the German Protestants' and perhaps the German nations* independence, he served Germany's most xenophobic, Europe's most conservative ruler. Ferdinand's ministers recalled Wallenstein's old friendship with Arnim. They wondered whether "an attempt at, and at least a beginning to, cordial negotiations of such kind" could be made through the Duke of Mecklenburg and Friedland. He undertook this assignment also, giving it his own gloss, asked for a passport to allow Arnim to visit him unmolested, rejected a first draft as "too coolly couched", and received a second which referred to Arnim in more amiable terms. Questenberg brought the document to Prague towards the end of October. His main purpose was of course to persuade the Duke into resumption of the generalate. He encountered resistance, a plea of invalidism and listlessness in matters appertaining to war, a request not to incommode Prince Eggenberg on a subject whose discussion could only prove painful to both parties. . . . The arrival of this message at Vienna caused consternation to descend into despair. "Upon my return the day before yesterday I related immediately to His Majesty how the discharge of my business with Your Princely Grace at Prague had transpired. He attended with great dismay and was so afflicted that no human soul but could rightly feel compassion . . .. I pray that the Paraclete may at last inspire You to a better course." Questenberg's tactic in his communications with the titan was on the one hand to pour scorn on the guilty court party, on the other to exaggerate the Emperor's distress. This time he was barely guilty of exaggeration. Ferdinand drained the cup of humiliation to the dregs. He could, he wrote to Prague, not regard this decision as final; he simply could not. If only the Duke would come a little closer to Vienna so that it would be possible to talk to him. "I strive to repose confidence in the hope that Your Dilection, perceiving me amidst the present emergency, will not leave me empty-handed, far less abandon me." If Wallenstein thirsted after satisfaction for his abasement at Regensburg, which is solely tradition, could he desire anything more pitiable?

Questenberg's visit to Prague coincided with another from Sezyma Rašin. As they did not know each other by sight, they may have met in Wallenstein's palace. Its master, according to the secret agent, told

* "The Holy Roman Empire of the German Nation" was the Empire's title in full (translator's note).

him straightaway that the military conclave had failed. "Lord Questen-berg," he wrote to Thurn, "sought through the most stirring, promising words to prevail with the acceptance of the generalate by His Princely Grace who excused himself that on pain of his soul, oath, and conscience being forsworn he cannot do it, albeit he will take upon himself to negotiate with Field-Marshal Arnim." This was set down at the time. Four years later he added how the Duke had told him that, as Gustavus did not wish to act with him, matters must proceed otherwise – he would yet achieve the Saxons' enticement to Bohemia. Of all Rašin's lies this is the most impudent.

Arnim's move on 1 November across the northern Bohemian border, not as the bearer of Wallenstein's safe-conduct, but with his troops, as a conqueror, came as a complete surprise to all – Wallenstein, Gustavus Adolphus, the *émigrés*. The decision was entirely personal to the Field-Marshal, an amalgam of military and political motives. Saxony's situation had become somewhat less rosy after the King, without much attention to the remaining imperial army, had turned south-west. Tilly felt strong enough to detach two corps, under Gallas and Aldringen, in the direction of Bohemia where its border marches in part with Saxony. In Silesia, even in portions of Lusatia, was Tiefenbach's force. To thrust between these threats from east and west by seizure of the powerful Bohemian mountain spur was a daring, strategically rational step. Downy winter quarters and fat pickings were to be had there too, whether he made his entry as an enemy or, so to speak, as a liberator. For this was the question: in what character did he come? Not really that of liberator. With the Saxons pledged to the Swedes and the Swedes to the *émigrés*, the first and the last should have been good friends. At most they were so on paper. John George had no wish to promote a fresh Czech revolu-tion. Bohemia had since 1618 been written off by the German Protes-tants and acknowledged as within the Habsburg sphere of power. That was where it should remain, suffer, and keep quiet. Only Thurn, because of his thick-headed optimism, for a time misconstrued such flint-headed policy. He had a warrant from Gustavus Adolphus as his commissary-general to recruit troops in Saxony. With them he proposed to liberate Bohemia. He had collected funds among the wealthier of his fellow-sympathizers. Calculating old Countess Trčka had offered him fifty thousand gulden, as a strongly secured loan and on condition that subsequent to the liberation the rebel estates which she had sharply acquired must remain hers. The assembly areas required for the recruit-ment of mercenaries were however refused him on the thinnest of excuses, and Arnim had notified the Elector that Thurn's designs seemed highly suspicious. When the Saxons invaded his beloved country without one preparatory word to him, the rebel leader quivered with incandescent rage and despair. "Woe to us honest folk who have suffered so much for Christian religion! Are we to be robbed in this wise and the glorious kingdom to be despoiled? Had parley been held with me, in such manner as was enjoyed upon me by Your Majesty, a form pleasing to God could have been agreed . . .. The poor and the discouraged would have come into their rights, the godless traitors been punished, the tyrants suppressed." Deceived, once more deceived. He was allowed to accompany the march, or did so uninvited, along with well-known *émigrés* like Bubna, Velen von Zierotin, Ruppa, Colonna von Fels, Ulrich von Ričan, Alexander Kapliř, and a few hundred unknown ones. Partly they mediated between the Saxons and their countrymen, partly they caused all kinds of emancipatory disorder. Seeing that many of them bore Swedish titles of appointment, Arnim could not, as he would have liked, stop them altogether. He energetically thwarted, though, that on which most depended, the formation of an indigenous army on Bohemian soil. Poor Thurn, foiled again. How well, he at least thought, all had been got ready. How throttled was the great hope by the superficially friendly, insidious intervention of the Germans.

Arnim's original objective was only the northernmost region. Learning that Marradas, the imperial commandant at Prague, with his sparse garrison, had taken to his heels and Wallenstein too had hastily withdrawn, he saw no reason why he should not occupy the city, an event occurring on 15 November. Again it was supposed to have been Wallenstein who, in a handwritten note, prompted this step. Again the existence of such a plot was believed by his accusers. Again it was a piece of fiction invented out of the blue. Arnim did not need Wallenstein to tell him that Prague lay open. Any spy or any peasant told it by someone from there was enough for that. Just as easy is to guess why he took the city. Prague was Bohemia's noblest military and political pawn, densely populated, rich, and a place very different from Leitmeritz or Melnik to fleece. A conqueror who failed to seize Prague when it was to be had so cheaply would have been a fool. Wallenstein, for his part, had no inclination to meet his former subordinate as one of the defeated, a prisoner-of-war, however chivalrous his treatment might be. He therefore retreated to Pardubitz, two days' journey east of the capital. He had recommended a withdrawal by the imperialists to Silesia when Arnim was still in Saxony and Tiefenbach in Lusatia. With Vienna heeding the advice of the deposed Wallenstein far more keenly than ever that of the Generalissimo, Tiefenbach had to his disgruntlement to obey. If the mischievous purpose of the advice was to give the Saxons a free hand in Bohemia rather than the one alleged, to leave them in peace so that they should keep quiet, the sequel becomes unintelligible. For, with Arnim in occupation of the capital, it was Wallenstein who inspired the imperial commanders Marradas and Tiefenbach with the idea of a two-pronged approach, from south and east, saying that Arnim had inside Prague only seven thousand men who could be chased away as quickly as they had come. Was he on 10 November in a traitorous frame of mind while seven days later loyally imperialist? Was he like the god of the philosophers who simultaneously supports opposing sides? People seemed to think it. Whatever happened, good or bad, especially bad, the Friedlander was responsible, for inexplicable, inexplicably knavish reasons known only to his dark soul. As Laurens Nicolai, Swedish representative at Dresden, remarked, "Sundry believe that Wallenstein is the powerful spring in this mechanism and everything dependent on secret communications with him."

After eleven harsh years of exile the *émigrés* were back in Prague. Not quite so proud of the fact as they had expected to be, but proud enough, and as though in a dream, a dream dreamt so often and this time true. They had the skulls affixed to the bridge-tower after the executions in 1621 removed and, in solemn procession, interred in the Teyn church. That appealed to the citizens, but not to Arnim. As in 1618, they chased away the Jesuits, "these bloodthirsty, throughout the world justly abominated disturbers of the public peace and through their lethally indited scrawls more than all too well-known windbags", "these peace-hating and more than viperish slanderers", as though they were already the government, the kingdom's "three Protestant Estates". Arnim, who in his own eyes was the governor, liked that still less, the citizens still more, as also that in the market-place they were allowed to mock a wonder-working image of the Virgin. Protestant clergy came back in droves; the Consistory was re-established; close on fifteen thousand constrained Catholics proclaimed what their true faith had secretly always been. Matters went however rather far when the returned refugees requisitioned the best billets and did themselves well without paying. Was their Christian magnanimity weaker, had they become more alien to their country than they knew? They spread themselves in their former properties and such as they had hastily sold prior to departure, arguing that the sales had been forced and disadvantageous to them. A number took an even more extreme course when, hazarding what they had not cared to hazard eleven years ago, they incited the peasantry to form gangs against their new masters. On Friedland territory raids took place in the lordships of Münchengrätz, Leipa, Hauska, and Neuschloss. Castles were stormed, counting-houses and wine-cellars pillaged, violence was done to men, particularly priests, and beasts. As a result the flow of money and victuals to Gitschin stopped. At that point things had gone too far.

During the last eighteen months Wallenstein's finances, so important to this lonely man as a shield against the world, had experienced nothing but deterioration. De Witte's breakdown, his own dismissal, the loss of Mecklenburg were contributory factors. In October Tiefenbach's army moved from Silesia into north-eastern Bohemia. For the first time Friedland, the *terra felix*, savoured the medicine which its founder had administered to so many, coolly regretful that war should entail its bad taste, but which none the less proved astonishingly bitter to the palate when swallowed at home. The reports from his local authorities were frightful: whole villages laid waste, the poor people slaughtered, the Duke's noblest horses stolen, his mills burnt down, not even the churches spared, and the plague in the land. The Devil in person could not act worse than these Polacks, Hungarians, Croats! It was the usual shrill exaggeration of what without exaggeration was foul enough. The Duke reacted comparatively calmly. The governor at Friedland was told to behave like a man, and an honest one at that, to do what he could to succour the people, "Whatever else, be not faint-hearted". He interceded with Tiefenbach that the march in direction of central Bohemia should in so far as possible skirt the duchy, a detour of not many miles, "because my other estates are spent to such degree that I cannot in the least have benefit from them any more and I shall not in future be able to have means for my subsistence . . .." On top of this was the trouble from the *émigrés* and the peasant gangs inspired by them. He did not conceal from himself the seriousness of the situation. From his refuge at Pardubitz went orders to set up a body of cavalry to afford protection at least to Gitschin. An extra irritant was his deeply ingrained distrust of his own tax-collectors and officials. He constantly suspected them of using any excuse of disorder either to be idle or to line their own pockets. And, after all, he knew the men with whom he was dealing. His old relationship with Gerhard von Taxis, his senior administrator, broke over this. Taxis, caught between the emergency of the peasant rising and the censures of the Duke who wanted money which was not on hand, lost his head and fled. Once more Wallenstein's pitilessness, his sombre severity, came to the fore. By his action Taxis had perjured himself and amidst the present adversities left in the lurch those below him to whom he owed counsel and support, worsening an already desperate condition. Let him be found and his life was forfeit, his possessions in any event sequestered – a repetition of how he had dealt with de Witte. Gone, both of them, Taxis and de Witte. For twenty-three years, since he had managed the affair with Kepler's horoscope, Taxis had been his faithful, able retainer.

His tone to Taxis' successor and the officials under him became more than ordinarily rasping. "Your excuses are nothing but lies and inventions. As dear as your souls' blessedness is to you, see that you do not seek to lead me by the nose. For as true as there is a living God, you shall pay me with your heads if you do not each month deliver me the quota. I have long enough said naught to your procedures, but, mark me well, I shall assuredly not jest with you." We can apprehend the panic felt by the recipients of such messages, and they laid the burden of their tribulation on the shoulders of those who implored postponement of dues. "No more plaints of this kind are to reach His Princely Grace. In a word, he wishes not to hear of such, for if they [the officials] approach him with more of them, His Princely Grace intends to hack their heads off." Not that there are reports of such executions really occurring.

A bad case of excessive strain. Gout in his toes and fingers, an ache in his chest from unknown causes. Money so scarce that the senior officers of his court were no longer paid and the lackeys starved. Awareness that in central Europe's increasingly virulent crisis some resolution must be come to. Somewhere around 10 November his decision, the fruit of long internal debate, seems to have been taken. On 17 November he sent news to Vienna that he was ready to meet Prince Eggenberg. Prior to this conference, so ardently desired by the imperialists, there occurred another – on 30 November, at Castle Kaunitz close to Prague, with Field-Marshal Arnim.

It was the talk projected for October, but now held under totally different auspices. The imperial instruction to treat with Arnim on a separate Saxon peace was in Wallenstein's pocket. Count Thurn's unflinching faith in Providence permitted him to regard this as a "handsome pretext" under whose cloak it would prove possible to secure his own hectic hopes, plans for revolution and treason, the Rašin scheme. The situation lay the other way about. During four hours of secret discussion

Wallenstein and Arnim were able, under the cloak of dealing with the *émigrés'* dreams, to ventilate a variety of entirely different topics – probably the future of German Protestantism, the revocation of the edict, terms for a sensible compromise. Refugee representatives, Johann von Bubna, Sezyma Rašin, were in the castle, but not at these confidential deliberations on which the Saxons subsequently rendered a report to Gustavus Adolphus. There had been nothing, they claimed, except generalities about the desirability of peace. No doubt they had to play the matter down since one of the principal themes had been a separate Saxon or German peace arrangement. Eggenberg, Wallenstein later informed Arnim, had been extremely satisfied with the Kaunitz negotiations because peace and unison must at last have their place in the Empire again. It can be inferred, seeing that Wallenstein afterwards reproached him with breach of his pledge, that Arnim undertook to intervene more sternly against the sack of Friedland properties by the *émigrés.* That is all of what we know about this conference – except one more thing. The Duke bluntly told the Field-Marshal that he was on the point of resuming his imperial generalate. He is supposed to have adduced as his reason that his traffic with the King had been running well, but a ghastly indiscretion on the part of Count Thurn and Countess Trčka had brought it to light. The Jesuits at Prague, the very urchins in the street, had known of it. Had the intent been to ruin him? There was absolutely nothing that he could do other than in hot haste to resume the generalate and thereby absolve himself. Arnim, under the seal of topmost secrecy, in due time acquainted Nicolai, the Swedish envoy, with this version. Nicolai passed it to his superiors. His comment: Wallenstein's assurance that his sympathies for Sweden remained unaltered was probably to be understood as arising from his fear that Gustavus Adolphus could feel offended and publicize the whole business. We prefer to leave the question open. He presumably had to proffer some explanation for what must seem to his partners a sudden *volte-face.* But they all lied, Arnim included. He may simply have seized the chance to compromise Thurn. Whatever else the history books say about happenings at Castle Kaunitz is third-, fourth-hand tittle-tattle, not worth investigation.

Shadowy though Wallenstein's dealings with the enemies of the Habsburgs during spring, summer, autumn, and late autumn had been, a trace remained. Torn strands in the sky. Clouds high above the earth, asunder but sailing so close to one another that they could be viewed as one or many, according to circumstance. Separate peace with Saxony and Protestant Germany in general; peace with Saxony, Sweden, and the *émigrés*; peace with the Habsburgs' enemies as a whole, including undeclared ones, France and the Dutch. All had been touched on, and all was so stubbornly integral that definition of the complex would be difficult. The same applies to the character of the peacemaker. In the period drawing to a close everything that Wallenstein attempted politically seemed outside the rules because, except that he had been commissioned to incline Denmark, and later Saxony, to a favourable frame of mind, he held no official position. It was different as soon as he was the House of Austria's Generalissimo again. At that point he could, as he had done since 1629, but more strongly now, legitimately throw his weight into the scales of peace. He had the choice of dictating peace to his own party discreetly, whereby the Vienna court could make a virtue of necessity, or of exercising pressure openly, indiscreetly. Or he could, as Count Thurn never ceased to hope, go over to Austria's arch-enemies. Between these conceivable patterns of behaviour, the last radically divergent from the first, there existed links and delicate shades of difference, just as there did between the objectives.

GENERAL *PRO TEM*

By the beginning of December Vienna regarded Wallenstein as Generalissimo, or else it was that Ferdinand dealt with him as though he were so in order to promote the realization of his dearest wish. On 2 December Wallenstein wrote to High Burgrave Adam, his cousin, that "never less than now" had he had war in mind. God knows why. On 6 December he left Pardubitz for Znaim, fifty miles from Vienna. He is said to have spent two days with the old Trčkas, hardly a suitable sojourn in the light of what he was proposing to do. The report also surprises us because, if correct, the invalid must have completed the winter journey from Pardubitz to Znaim in only two days. It is one of those petty riddles about which his accusers never bothered when a testimony fitted their purpose. A day later Eggenberg arrived. He had recently asked whether Wallenstein's timorous avoidance of a confrontation with him meant that he thought him a sorcerer. The Znaim meeting had nothing of sorcery about it. Both parties had decided on their course before they sat down at the fireplace. Eggenberg brought with him an impossible condition – the supreme command should go to the young King of Hungary, with Wallenstein as his assistant – which could at best serve as ballast to be thrown overboard at the right moment. The minister's

instructions had been drafted by an expert, Questenberg. They therefore contained what was calculated to put the Duke in a good mood.
Never again would "the father confessor and other divines" with their
"ill-founded maxims" nor secular opponents and "vexatious individuals"
at court exercise any influence over the Emperor. Henceforth nothing
but kind words and affection would emanate from Vienna. The proposal, a favourite with the Spaniards, that he should serve under the
Emperor's son was rejected by Wallenstein as out of the question. That
settled, he agreed to accept the generalate for three months and to reorganize the army.

A ruse, of course. A cruel ruse to let three drops slide down a parched
throat and, on the emission of groans for more, to raise counter-claims
to a monstrous degree. That is how this has been interpreted. Our reading is another. The three months' condition, thought out at some point
in November, was a compromise between readiness and reluctance. He
took one, a fairly large step forward without being irrevocably bound. Or
at any rate he could pretend to himself that he continued unbound. For
a few months he was spared from the torment of reaching a final
decision. He would use the time to restore the military balance of power
which had been lost but which was essential if anything was to be
achieved, whether with German Protestantism or Sweden. Lost too had
been his own economic security, the preponderant part of his income,
and that touches on a motive which may have influenced the Znaim
decision. Not the amount of his general officer's salary, but the fact that
his court would be transformed into his headquarters, a charge on the
imperial Exchequer, the moment that he was again the senior military
personality in the field. However tight money from official sources might
in accordance with tradition prove to be, it would at least suffice for
that.

Finance must have been discussed at Znaim, and in better defined
terms than in 1625. The potentialities of the contributions system had
been exhausted. Hans de Witte, that helpful wizard, lay in his grave.
Therefore those who had an interest in revival of the squandered imperial
power would need to pay in cash. The King of Spain transmitted
410,000 gulden, the Elector of Bavaria 300,000, "Vienna" added 205,000;
Moravian taxes furnished 37,000; and so on. Small change, manifestly
inadequate even for a start. Wallenstein is said to have added something,
as in 1625, but his money-chests were notoriously depleted. From
whom should he have borrowed? The appointment was dated 15 December. All concerned were duly informed. Bohemia, where the Saxons

were holding their winter games, not being a suitable place for the commander of an army still to be stamped out of the ground, the three-months-Generalissimo remained at the castle in Znaim.

Couriers carrying congratulations in their knapsacks dashed along snowy roads. Colonels jubilated, or claimed that they did, "because the rightful shepherd, so long desired by us, returns to his abandoned and scattered flock". Tilly, his imperial command politely withdrawn, felicitated Wallenstein. Himself too, as being extricated from a tricky labyrinth. The expression was identical with that used by Wallenstein at Memmingen, and consequently in so ticklish a situation presumably the appropriate one. Pappenheim, shrewd as ever, prophesied that Wallenstein's reputation would of itself bring a turn for the good. Pope Urban gave his paternal blessing and 27,000 gulden, which reminds us of an utterance made many years before: "Should the Pope wish to achieve anything in this business, let him give money and hold back his crew together with his indulgences." Wallenstein thanked the Cardinal Secretary of State in elegantly turned Italian, adding that his health would on no account permit an extended tenure of his appointment. Concisely, coolly he acknowledged all congratulations, and the allusion to the temporary nature of his activity never failed to recur.

Disquiet reigned among those who at Regensburg had pushed matters to an extreme. The Elector of Mainz did not now wish to be included among them. He put the blame on Bavaria, Bavaria on him. The Emperor was told by Maximilian that he was "no little weighed down" by the Duke of Friedland's unanticipated re-appearance. Perhaps the great danger justified his step, but at the very least the approval of the Electors ought to have been obtained. Rather an illusory expectation. Two Electors were allies of Gustavus Adolphus; Trèves, the protégé and vassal of the King of France; Mainz, on the point of losing his territory and people. Only the two Wittelsbachs were standing against the Swedish storm, and Maximilian was looking for help in quite another direction. ... Wallenstein, in magnanimous mood at his moment of triumph, sent a personal emissary to Tilly, assuring him that he was "His Electoral Highness' faithful Servant, had sincerely forgotten what transpired at Regensburg, and been, as it were, coerced into this appointment", in addition to other aphorisms honeyed for consumption at Bavarian headquarters. Consolatory messages of a similar nature were exchanged between Vienna and Munich. Wilhelm Slawata, High Chancellor of Bohemia, took objective note of his hated cousin's augmented power: "What the Prince wishes, that *has* to happen."

Father Lamormaini, henceforward supposed to be forbidden the slightest political influence, was the one who pocketed least pride.

> I hear [he wrote to Wallenstein] that evil things have been whispered to Your Highness about me. I neither ask nor do I concern myself about that. I am a man of the Holy Church whom it behoves to attend more to the voice of God than the chatter of mankind. ... In July and August, when the state of affairs was otherwise, totally different from now, I was of opinion that it was inadvisable to burden Your Highness again with this office. What sensible person can make of this a reproach to me?

With what feeling the Duke read his words we do not know, as little as we know whether it gave him any pleasure to be once more at the narrowly circumscribed centre of affairs or whether he fancied that in future he would be able to accord better with Lamormaini, the Jesuits, and his enemies at Vienna and Munich. Probably he too was not sure. Moods do not last, but come, go, and return. This, though, was hardly the time for them. Never yet had he trodden the boards of so dangerous, so glaringly lit a stage. The world's staring audience expected miracles of him.

The Duel

MANAGING his estates as a young married man, Wallenstein had contracted the habit of quietly accumulating sufficient funds to enable him to travel to court and for a few months to live there in a certain state. His money spent, he went home. His wars were fought along the same tidy lines – in winter and spring rest for and expansion of his forces concomitant with the replenishment of stores and the laying in of money, arms, munitions, horses; in May or June the opening of a campaign not meant to be prolonged beyond late autumn; then back into winter quarters. He transformed into unswerving practice what was a contemporary military principle. But a principle not followed by Gustavus Adolphus who, among other things, derived his outstanding superiority from his contemptuous disregard for these seasonal rules. Was that Wallenstein's inferiority? We think not. He attached importance to his men's morale, which must be based on their physical well-being since it could not be rooted in anything else. Setting out with his massed strength so very late in the year, he had conducted those operations from Upper Silesia to the Sound, the most remarkable of his age until the King accomplished more remarkable ones still. Well-rested, well-armed, relatively well-fed soldiers can, incidentally, be supposed to have gone about their business rather less terribly than hungry, neglected ones.

Now his task was once more to build from the ground up. It was exactly what at Znaim he had promised to do. Not to assume the command. Only to reorganize and, his work performed, to withdraw to Gitschin. Whether from the start or when exactly he surmised the illusory nature of his restricted acceptance cannot be determined, but illusory it was. Merely preparatory, static strategy could clearly not be separated from strategy of movement. The organizer was instantly the Generalissimo too, keeping a watch on events from Alsace to Poland, from the Baltic to the Tirol. His interest in affairs, which had never really slackened, during the course of his labours tautened to the utmost intensity. Out of the question to lop it on a certain, randomly selected day. From the role of general *pro tem*, Wallenstein slid of his own accord into that of the Generalissimo. He probably made the arrangement simply to spare himself the agony of a quick decision.

In September 1630, when he had relinquished his command, matters superficially stood well with the cause that he served and which, for brevity's sake, was called the imperial one – the Austrian, the Austro-Spanish, the Catholic cause. To the eyes of the perceptive they no longer stood so well. During the succeeding fifteen months the gathering clouds had burst in a thunderstorm whose violence effected a metamorphosis exceeding the extent of Wallenstein's prediction. Protestant Germany was under arms and, with a single miserable exception, under Swedish sway; Catholic Germany partly conquered, partly on the brink of seeking refuge in foreign protection; France in Lorraine and advancing on the Rhine without war being declared; the Spaniards, practically chased out of the Palatinate, under accustomed pressure from the Dutch, unaccustomed pressure from the Swedes; Bohemia and Silesia, two lush Hereditary Lands, half occupied by the Saxons, with the *émigrés* back home and the peasants in rebellion; the Swiss unofficially allowing the King of Sweden, but not the Emperor, to recruit inside their territory; the French in the Grisons and in greater strength than heretofore in northern Italy, with Mantua and Savoy their pawns; the Pope cool to the point of hostility, rendering the religious character of these tangles an enigma; Poland hampered by its armistice with Sweden and the resumption of its war with Muscovy which would so gladly have relieved it of Smolensk and White Russia; Rácócsi, the Prince of Transylvania, inclined to follow the example of his predecessor Bethlen, just like the Turks who would have made themselves altogether differently at home in Hungary if their main might had not been needed on the farther side of their empire against Persia. The picture drawn by the historian Count Khevenhüller in his annals could afford no pleasure. The Spaniards had among Viennese diplomats none more friendly to them than Khevenhüller. He promised carefully to keep the letters, with their frequent, prophetic prognostication of the Swedish danger, received by him at Madrid from Wallenstein and to use them in his chronicle. They are not however to be found there.

In winter, when the martial sport of kings came to a standstill, its political counterpart stirred into an activity particularly hectic on this occasion because the prospect for the coming year was indeed frightful if the fronts remained in their present state. Negotiations between the

League, France, and Sweden about a separate Bavarian peace; negotiations between Austria and Saxony about a separate Protestant German peace; efforts to merge these two corresponding complexes and to superimpose on them the longed-for universal peace. The three-month general had to be as alert to such paper projects as he was to the direction taken by boots marching along the highways. He had to know whom he – or was it his successor? – would in future have for or against him. The separate Saxon peace seemed to him desirable in the highest degree. Universal peace too. When, since the beginning of his first generalate, had he not advised it, provided that it was to be had? That it was not to be had now, not even given the greatest, most clement wisdom on the part of his master, he knew. The King had come too far to enable him to be sent home with an "All forgiven". The situation had to be resolved and it had to be resolved between him and himself. Ordeal by arms, of the severest sort. Did he set his strange period of limitation because, at one and the same time, he craved and feared this trial?

After the Regensburg Diet a change is said to have come over him whereby he, who had until then been loyal, was henceforth a lonely traitor racked by thirst for vengeance. Contemporaries believed it, posterity embalmed the tradition. We reject it. Personalities of such a strong stamp do not alter. At the most, in such circumstances deeply ingrained tendencies come to the fore. He had always wanted to be independent and chafed at the yoke of others' wishes. Seeing that everything, more than everything, against which he had warned had now come to pass and the militarily incompetent Viennese war clique had in direct emergency recalled him, he regarded it as manifest that he would henceforward conduct the war, and politics too, as he saw fit. He told a representative of the Curia that he had not the slightest intention of fighting the Protestants as such; the fact of their immense preponderance in Germany was inescapable. To Gundakar von Liechtenstein, brother of the late Prince Karl and a politician fallen from favour at Court on account of his freely expressed opinions he said that a creditable peace as soon as possible was the desirable, sole attainable objective. At the time of the edict he had struck the identical note. His train of thought was coherent throughout, there were no changes, simply sharper contours. His second generalate would consequently present a repetition of the first, at once a continuation and a repetition, to the point of positive monotony, concentrating into two years what had formerly taken five. Alike as regards affairs in general and personal affairs. Overall political ambition never succumbed to that directed at his own interest. Through his passion for genuine independence it stayed with him always. Earlier it had focused on Mecklenburg. Now it would be a substitute for Mecklenburg, or something more. Where?

This winter too the auspices were unfavourable. Blood instead of water suddenly flowed from a pond near Leipzig. A child with four hands, two heads, and three feet was born in Vienna, and in the self-same city the towers of the Jesuit church abruptly toppled down as though they had been sliced away. A storm raged over the Baltic with thunder and lightning of an intensity neither heard nor seen before but portentous of Judgement Day. The most terrible report came from the region of Naples, so richly endowed with fine cities and sites, palaces and villas, vineyards and orchards – an eruption of Mount Vesuvius, spitting rocks and glowing ash, destroyed the Earthly Paradise and killed eighteen thousand souls, as though nature wished to show mankind that it, too, could stage a Magdeburg. It happened on 16 December, the day after the Emperor had appended his signature to Wallenstein's new appointment, but it was late January before the news reached Znaim. Eyebrows were raised, a few questions were asked, work was resumed.

THE WORK

An army, the situation being what it was, could be raised only in the Hereditary Lands; in Austria, Moravia and Bohemia. Mention of the last may cause surprise, seeing that it was under enemy occupation. We know, though, what a limited connotation in this period the word "occupation" had when applied to a whole country, how much remained unoccupied, and how close to each other opponents kept house. Moreover, in that they sporadically negotiated, there existed between the Saxons and Wallenstein an undeclared truce, often broken, but never for the purpose of large-scale operations. There was no front line, whether of natural obstacles or of artificial construction, between them, and thus it came about that the Saxons made themselves at home in, around, and to the north of Prague while forty-five miles westwards Colonel-Quartermaster Gallas laboured with splendid calm to put his corps into better shape. Wallenstein at his Moravian headquarters felt in no danger whatever. He was determined to proceed with his business from the bottom up and to take his time over it, however shrill the shrieks for help from the Empire.

Of a sumptuous turn always, he aimed at a force of a hundred thousand men in addition to those already or still available. His objective, impossible of achievement without assistants, entailed the creation of a hierarchy between the captain-general and the colonels responsible for the individual regiments. He had formerly done the skeleton-work on this concept, novel but appropriate to the army's new dimensions. Now he clothed it with flesh and bones. Introduced were the ranks of Major-General, Lieutenant-General,* Colonel-Quartermaster, General of the Horse and General of Ordnance (two branches of fighting to which he attached the highest importance), as well as Deputy Commander-in-Chief. There was to be only one senior deputy to the Generalissimo although in the past Collalto and Marradas had simultaneously been such in name. Collalto was dead. Marradas was "Commander-in-Chief for the Kingdom of Bohemia", an appointment approximating to that held in the early 'twenties by Wallenstein in his capacity as Commandant of Prague. The problem of military leadership by him beyond the borders of Bohemia did not therefore arise. The post of, properly speaking, deputy field commander was not again filled until 1633 when Gallas became its holder. Wallenstein must have regarded him as his most capable or as his most loyal officer, or both, in spite of his rodomontades. In the course of the winter he had promoted him to Colonel-Quartermaster. Soon he made him, like Aldringen, General of Ordnance. The two were as close as military men could be, had together led the campaign in Italy, plundered Mantua and concluded the paltry peace

* The whole range of military appointments and designations was at this time still very fluid and in an evolutionary stage. The basic traditional concept was that the command over any ruler's army lay in his hands and the title "General" was applicable to him alone. If a deputy was entrusted to take the field, then, by the end of the sixteenth century, he was termed "Lieutenant-General", like Tilly in charge of Maximilian of Bavaria's forces. A less strict application occurred when the commander of a corps operating independently came to be temporarily invested with this appointment, the case quoted by the author as happening to Collalto and Marradas.

The highest attainable rank had long been that of field-marshal, who used to act as the ruler's deputy in affairs relating to military administration and justice. In the seventeenth century it came to be applied to officers, like Pappenheim, in command of independent corps. They always remained subordinate to the General, i.e., the ruler, or whoever might be his formal deputy.

Included in the new hierarchy created at the outset of the second generalate was the rank of *Feldmarschall-Leutnant* or "lieutenant-field-marshal", the revival of an extinct title which was retained in the imperial, subsequently Austrian army until 1918. For this the historically accepted English-language rendering of "lieutenant-general" has been used. To avoid confusion, "deputy commander-in-chief" has been adopted for the appointment which Wallenstein termed "lieutenant-general" and which, as stated by the author, could be held by only a single officer (translator's note).

treaty with France, and they were married to a pair of Arco sisters. In spring he raised Colonel Christian von Ilow, that "proud, puffed-up fellow", the intriguer whom at the start he had so thoroughly disliked, to Lieutenant-General. Ilow was a Brandenburger, but because he held a little western Bohemian place in lien and was husband to a more or less Austro-Bohemian member of the Fürstenberg family, Czech historians have fancied him to have had Bohemian sentiments. A piece of nonsense, surely, for we possess no evidence whatever of Ilow having had sentiments of any kind. What attraction he had for Wallenstein must be a matter of pure conjecture. He may have been zealous and expeditious, qualities to which at the top level great importance was attached. He had performed his duties as had been expected of him – determinedly, brutally, fearlessly. Wallenstein, deep and many-faceted, liked to associate with those of plain character. It happened in the case of Ilow and it recurred in that of Colonel, newly Major-General, Heinrich Holk.

Holk the Dane, Holk the unpopular but sturdy defender of Stralsund. Wallenstein could be imagined as never forgiving him the part which he had then played. Not at all. The mercenary, his allegiance successively sold to King Christian and the Emperor, would serve this new lord with strictest scruple. For Holk, it is evident, soon admired the Duke as warmly as Pappenheim did. In time he was downright in thrall to him, simulating in his orders the very words of his master's biting, menacing tone: "In contrary case, and if on that score something should be left undone, he would needs have to vindicate himself to the General or whoever deputizes for him. This he will heed and know how to observe unerringly." The slowness of subordinates he described as their unfortunate inborn *motus Saturni* (saturnine state) – precisely Wallenstein's expression. He threatened, like Wallenstein, "to have him by his head". He held his herd together with grim severity: "I would sooner not be with the army than that anything of the General's rigour should go forfeit." Wherever a Holk document crops up, it is his pungent management of men and means, his struggle against all presumption, profusion and parasitic proliferation, including officers' packs whose permitted volume and weight he cut to a modest maximum, which springs to the eye. These qualities, his capacity for work, his vigour, his stringent sense of duty, induced Wallenstein to use him as his right hand, an individual to shoulder portions of his burden. For the time being he employed him as his itinerant Inspector-General. The legend which has survived about Holk is indeed very different, giving him the reputation of an iniquitous, bloodthirsty oppressor who with his one remaining eye sharply scrutinized his mercenary rascals as to their suitability for midnight arson and rapine. Such he was too, or could be, but incidentally to the blind obedience which he rendered in equal measure as he demanded it. Ordered to undertake a "visitation", as it was termed, on a strip of hostile territory and repay one set of atrocities with another, he performed it as he performed every task, thereby helping to produce the popular tale of Holk the robber, Holk the godless, devilish devotee of Wallenstein. Akin to other traditions, it contained something of truth, much of misunderstanding. In sober reality Wallenstein, the man of order, had placed his faith in another fanatic for order.

The Generalissimo, we know, did not much believe in fire and the sword as a method of procedure, but sometimes he had to apply it. In reprisal, for example. He then had not only the common soldiers who would do it with pleasure, but commanders too, like Isolani, whom he appointed "Senior Commandant over All Mounted Imperial Troops of the Croat Nation and Light Horse" (in other words, general of the irregular cavalry), Holk the Dane and Pappenheim the Bavarian, the last far superior to the foregoing in strategic ability and political perception.

Pappenheim, always avid for an independent command, remained at a distance and tried to influence the course of affairs through shrewd epistolary advice. Ilow and Holk were on hand and indispensable. To this trio was added, as the most indispensable of all, Adam Trčka, colonel of two, then four, finally seven regiments of foot and horse before in 1633 becoming lieutenant-general. If Ilow and Holk served as supervisors and emissaries in military matters, Trčka acted in that capacity as regards the political scene, initiated into all that transpired, the permissible, the half-permissible, and the impermissible. "We apprise You herewith that We now have high need of Your presence here in as much as We have resolved to let Field-Marshal von Arnim be informed through You of certain business of close concern to His Imperial Majesty," wrote Wallenstein in December 1631. Left unmentioned is just why it should be this debatable, volatile, simple young man who was needed. With his choice of Holk, the right man had been selected by Wallenstein for his purpose; with that of Trčka, the wrong one. The fact did not remain without consequences. His heir, Count Max, henceforward faded into the background as compared with Ilow, Holk, and Trčka, a fact that had consequences too.

So much for the closest assistants. Neither the bevy of junior general officers, whether taken over or freshly appointed – Virmont, Monte-cuccoli, Cratz, Merode, Desfours (the "thief" of years gone by), Traun, Schaffgotsch, Rudolf Colloredo, Hieronimous Colloredo, Ottavio Picco-lomini – nor the incomparably larger body of mere regimental entre-preneurs is as yet worth discussion. When Wallenstein's work was done, Arnim knew that "the Duke of Friedland has expended money on 130 regiments which neither the Emperor nor the Empire nor half Europe can pay." The figure was absolutely right. One hundred and thirty thousand colonels in addition to a good couple of dozen general officers. Their duty was to run the machine and maintain it according to the wishes of Znaim headquarters.

From there an icy blast of authority caught any who might prove guilty of presumption: "That he should dare to instruct Us, as it were, what We must do, surprises Us no little." The threats issued upon news of pillage by the soldiery were comprehensive in their brevity: "Let him remedy it or I shall." Hints dangled rewards: "If he expects further promotion in His Majesty's service, he will attend to good discipline, bring his companies up to strength, and, NB, arm them well, where-upon he can rest assured of my entire amity and good will." Occasionally, although rarely, there was an inflection of gratitude and almost tender solicitude. A case in point was his letter to Colonel Ossa, whose property fell into the hands of the Swedes: "I note how his possessions are ruined on account of the enemy's progress and I recognize how through his faithful, diligent service to His Majesty and the House of Austria he now undergoes divers vexations. Wherefore I proffer him my goods and chattels, let him but come with kith and kin. I assure him that I seek no advantage, simply to share with him what I have, of movables and immovables, so that he may as I truly enjoy them, which his services verily merit." What is to be made of that? Was it written in the small hours of the night so that, gentle from sheer weariness, for once the affection imprisoned in a deep recess of his hardened heart erupted? He must have had exceptional esteem for Colonel Ossa, a ruggedly loyal and intelligent man. We prefer to leave open what would have happened if the Ossa tribe had taken his offer literally and settled in the palace of Gitschin.

Such regiments as had been reduced to a tenth of their strength were increased to their full complement. Regiments whose morale was in utter ruin were dissolved. Entirely new regiments were established. The main business, enrolment of recruits, had to be effected by the colonels, with Wallenstein promising to pay them their outlays. Recruitment had become more difficult. The word had gone the rounds that the soldier's lot was but a gilded one. The wooden-legged beggars, the blind, and the frightfully maimed throughout the lands saw to that. Landlords too were reluctant to let their vassals leave even when they had received their muster pay, the sole prize for their poor souls that they would see for a long time ahead. Recruitment was undertaken in the Netherlands, always a source for good soldiers, and Major-General Merode was sent there for the purpose; in south-western Germany; in the Hereditary Lands as far as Dalmatia, Croatia, Hungary. At Vienna hitherto unheard of measures were introduced when commissions went from house to house and inquired into young men's calling and trade. Those who could prove none were led off to the nearest recruitment collection-point and, to their stupefaction, found themselves mariners on the seas of fortune, fighters for their fatherland, like it or not. Seasoned deserters, of whom there were thousands, had an offer of free pardon if only they returned to the colours. All these auxiliary methods could not however rival the rise in price of human military fodder. The muster pay, purchase pay really, reached fifteen to twenty taler. Not until the following summer did it fall to its accustomed level of four to five.

In principle a regiment of foot, divided into ten companies, consisted of three thousand men; a regiment of horse, arquebusiers, cuirassiers or dragoons, of a thousand. When Wallenstein began work, he found the most unimpaired infantry unit reduced to 620 rank and file. He unremittingly drove the numbers up and spurred on the colonels to bring their companies to established strength. At best that was achieved to half, on average barely better than to a third. By summer 1632 his command consisted of more than fifty-four regiments of foot, seventy-five of horse, and in addition the Poles. Had the norm been fulfilled, it would have signified a total of more than 237,000 men. Intricate, and always unreliable, calculations have shown that the figure actually reached only around, or something less than, 100,000 although twice as many if the camp-followers, women and boys, are included.

Human beings, whatever their numbers, make by themselves no army. Discipline, an old word familiar to Wallenstein, does. And logistics, a new one old in what it concerns. The Grand Organizer had primarily to concentrate on that. Quarters, until such time as the army would take the field. Victuals. Boots and clothing, which for certain favoured bodies like the Croats had already assumed the dignity of colourful uniforms. Arms, defensive and offensive. Funds, without which all else was not to be had. He had to be more thorough than in

1625, with less of *"capite, rapide"*. He had learnt much since those days. What puny opponents had Mansfeld, Halberstadt, and the King of Denmark been in comparison with his present one.

A hundred thousand men, an army of a size that christendom had seldom seen, an army of new character thanks alone to its numbers, and an army which would really have required another form of governance which in times to come would be dubbed the state. This, the state, did not exist. There was only on the one hand the Emperor as the patrimonial ruler, no, the ruler of his patrimonies, with his court, his Privy Councillors, and his empty coffers, and on the other the Lands with their power groupings, the Estates, a kind of passive governance check. "Estates" and "state" derive indeed from the same verbal root, but it is all that they have in common. War on the present scale could only be waged by the state, just as it was this new war which later made the new state. As yet matters had not proceeded so far. The funds for this new war, directly and indirectly, depended on the Estates of the individual Hereditary Lands. They, the Estates, were however from the start distrustful and displeased because it was solely their suzerain and his councillors who had concocted and determined on the war, proclaiming it to be unfortunately one of highest exigency imposed by law-breaking enemies. No Estates enterprise was at stake. Simply its victims, they wanted to come to grief as little as possible. Should it be argued that ten years before the Habsburg had in Lower and Upper Austria, in Bohemia and Moravia quelled the Estates' presumptions, the objection has to be seen in proper perspective. Their Protestants, radicals, and near-republicans might be dispersed abroad, but Catholic prelates, nobility, and city fathers were very like Lutherans in that they also did not relish giving away their money and having their possessions ruined through billeting. If the regents wanted to play at war and politics, they should themselves see how they defrayed their game, which of course they could not. It had been so during Wallenstein's first generalate and it was so now. The army's creator had in his own lonely person to substitute for the state which did not exist, a harassment which was always to a large degree of no avail.

Imperial commissioners were responsible for extracting locally as much as humanly possible from the Estates – Count Michna von Weizenhofen (son to Albanian "Inflation" Michna of 1622) in Bohemia, Questenberg in Lower Austria, Cardinal Dietrichstein in Moravia, others in Silesia, Upper Austria, Styria. His supplies requisition, Wallenstein wrote to Questenberg, was the most modest that he had ever issued and therefore *must* be fulfilled. After two years' incessant active service the veterans needed, as well as food and drink, money for fresh clothing and decent quarters for proper rest. He could not remit one iota. "To have the money yielded is difficult but not impossible," answered Questenberg, half pessimistically, half consolingly. "Anguish is better than ruin." Precisely, for what the Estates did not want to face was that they, not merely the imperial court playing at politics, would suffer havoc if the Swedes conquered the land. The comparative comfort of correspondence with the commissioners was not enough. Wallenstein exercising the most impatient patience, had himself to exhort the Austrian and Silesian Estates. On the Emperor he impressed that, if nothing whatever else would help, he must intervene with military sequestration.

He attained his goal, though, and resurrected his headquarters on an even more complete and grand pattern than before. It included the Friedland Chancellery, a structure containing the archives and capable of being erected anywhere because, when dismantled, it could be loaded on two wagons under the supervision of its director, Dr Balthasar Wesselius and his twelve officials; the field printing-press; the command quartermaster and paymaster, the transport and communications sections; the field hospitals, with their surgeons; the chaplain-general for the maintenance of spiritual order, the provost-marshal and the riot master as his mundane counterparts; the accountancy directorate to keep the most meticulous record of the Duke's imprests so that these should be equally exactly reimbursed. For of course his duchy was again making what deliveries it could: wheat, gunpowder, entrenching tools, clothes. Cuirasses he bought in Trieste, muskets in Danzig and the Netherlands, horses everywhere. He attended to the artillery, and here his leanings to the large-scale sometimes misled him. When he demanded mortars able to launch a three-hundred-pound shell, Gallas protested that such monstrosities could be neither hauled nor handled. Even church bells were sacrificed, if not this year then next, to the casting of cannon. The preoccupation with discipline, to the accompaniment of courts martial and penalties "to forestall much trouble", was constant. He knew no antidote other than setting "severe example" and "daunting the rest", insisted and persisted, inquired whether justice had been done and to how many, praising the number when it was large. Neither disciplinary terror tactics nor his legendary appearance, wrapped in a scarlet cloak, would intrinsically have sufficed to endear him to the lower ranks except that now and again he broke the spell surrounding his person, received deputations of soldiers who had a complaint to lay, listened and made rejoinder. The letters which during his three months – they became five – he wrote and received at Znaim ran into thousands. Their long-range effect – the army whose components in late spring moved concentrically on central Bohemia was without any doubt the most serviceable in men and equipment that the Emperor had ever had. The sorcerer had kept his word.

Never, while he was spurring on his officers with doses of astringency and kindness, read reports, and did his calculations, was his own empire, his duchy, forgotten. Or it would suddenly spring into his mind, over-burdened with other cares, and four letters be dispatched to Gitschin in the course of a single day. How did matters stand with the newly founded urban quarter of Reichenberg? The shingles for the roof of the palace at Gitschin were no longer required as the architect had a sufficient stock of tiles, but pray suggest alternative use for them. The palace was by no means complete, must however be so within four years at the most, and therefore: "See that not a minute is lost, for there will be enough to do to finish [on time]." For its pictorial embellishment the painter who had given satisfaction at Prague was to be engaged at twenty gulden per month and an allowance of forty gulden for travel expenses. He had agreed to grant the Jesuits four thousand gulden annually for the building of their college, a sum which should continue to be paid on condition that they contributed four thousand of their own, not otherwise; the fathers' habits were known. Twenty citizens' homes and the leather factory must be torn down to make room for the pleasure-grounds, the factory and houses reconstructed elsewhere, the citizens furnished with materials, and money too, but only when construction really began. If "that Wallenstein" – a relative, "Christian" by first name – did not at last clean his house, not merely the main rooms, but the back ones and attics also, in a manner befitting a man of his estate, let him be jailed at Castle Skal. . . . So it went on, even while he was preparing to depart on his dangerous duel, his eyes roaming ever and again back to his beloved dreamland which one day, later, eventually he hoped to enjoy in peace.

THEY CANNOT MAKE PEACE

Wallenstein's new tenure of command rendered null and void the Regensburg Diet's sole substantial decision. It was popular with the Spaniards who had tried to prevent his deposition and continued to regard him as the champion of their cause. It was unpopular with Elector Maximilian.

The Elector now stood in a status of alliance to France. The Treaty of Fontainebleau was supposed to shield him against Sweden and Spain alike. Of a purely defensive nature, it afforded during 1631, the year of Swedish successes, no help because Bavaria of its own initiative set itself in Sweden's path. Cardinal Richelieu's intimation that no cause existed for calling the treaty's mechanism into operation was formally correct. Simultaneous support for two actively engaged opponents would have trespassed from the chaotically fine distinctions customary with European foreign policy into the sphere of the illicit and non-sensical.

After the catastrophe of Breitenfeld, and when on top of the Swedish threat there arose in November the Wallenstein menace, the Elector looked with growing anxiety for a loophole. As France could not assist him for so long as his Commander-in-Chief was fighting the Swedes, escape lay only in withdrawal into the neutrality abandoned twelve years ago. Not an easy achievement. Maximilian, always conscientious and pious, first consulted his theologians as to the propriety of such a course. The celestial will and the terrestrial situation having been probed by the experts, they declared that it was not only proper but imperative – the palpably imminent destruction of the Catholic religion would benefit none, neither Europe nor God. His general, whom in December he met at Donauwörth, supplied supporting facts. Tilly, according to the conference record, was "entirely perplexed and, as it were, defeated, altogether irresolute in counsel, without any notion how to succour himself, and passes from one proposal to another, reaches no conclusion, sees the great difficulties and extremities but openly admits that he is at a loss for ways and means." He had been in tears. The old warrior's emotion fortified Maximilian in his decision. Allowed tolerable conditions, he must extract himself from the war, secure his winnings, and leave the House of Habsburg in the lurch. He had long regarded its one half, the Spanish, with antipathy. While feeling bound by strong bonds to the other, the Austrian, he was not so entirely whole-heartedly attached to it. "The Elector of Bavaria is a better friend to himself than to us," Wallenstein had discerned early on. The issue was therefore that of a separate peace, or better still a general peace, or the separate peace as impetus to a universal peace.

At Paris nothing would have been more welcome than Bavaria's neutrality, then that of the German Catholics as a whole, thereafter that of the German Lutherans. Father Joseph, the specialist for German affairs, had a different, more cynical understanding of the matter than Maximilian. The Swedish campaign, whose lightning successes had taken him aback as much as everyone else, was not to be discontinued but re-directed, away from inner Germany and concentrated against Austria. A neutral Germany would hedge in Sweden, a fighting Sweden contain the House of Habsburg, and France be able to draw breath in its smouldering conflict with Spain as well as to play the arbitrator all round. A very mundane plan, the Capuchin's, clever, far-sighted. The Swedes, he enunciated, must be turned to advantage like those toxins which, enjoyed with moderation, act as anti-toxins, but are fatal if taken immoderately. The reveries of desk-work are not however always capable of implementation at the point where a dozen powers are in frenzied struggle, each with many alternatives to consider, each jostling, each jostled. France too was jostled in so far as its King was to play the role on the European stage which, according to the convictions of his First Minister, was appropriate to him. In a fine state of order if compared with the Empire, it was by no means in a fine enough state of order for what Richelieu intended its performance to be on the world's wide boards. Feudal magnates, governors, and demi-kings in their provinces, were in dispute with the central government. On its eastern flank, in the vicinity of the Rhine, lay lands which approximately appertained to the sphere of French dominion, not to its sovereign territory. Lorraine, for instance, was a German Estate. Its duke, Charles IV, one of those restless, opportunist petty princes already familiar to us as trying to play a hand of their own between France and Germany, leant to the Habsburg side because it appeared less dangerous to him. In 1631 he even brought into the field a phantom army; it soon vanished. He corresponded with the French opposition, led at this stage by that pair of brainless intriguers, the King's mother, Marie de Medici, and the King's brother, Gaston of Orléans. The latter was staying at Nancy, the capital of Lorraine. To examine the motives of these princely politicians is supererogatory. Let there be unrest at home against the harshly exercised, absorptive royal power solely augmentative of royal greatness and Marie as well as Gaston would have in mind, no, not the distress of the royal subjects, but simply their own glory. There existed moreover the tradition that dissentients in neighbouring, potential, or actual enemy countries should be helped so that internal strife would cripple external effectiveness. Wallenstein was barely back in the field before, however badly he could spare any troops, he thought it prudent to encourage the Duke of Orléans with eight thousand Walloons (who had still to be recruited) because "it was of utmost consequence to affairs in general". Not that such quarter-interventions had ever paid off. They were undertaken out of weakness, had occurred previously and would occur again, without anything being learned from their outcome.

In late autumn 1631 Richelieu dispatched an army eastward. He and the King followed, their residence established at Metz. The intention was to recall the wayward princes to their senses. For the present success was confined to the Duke of Lorraine. He promised better behaviour and to allow the French as of right to traverse his territory on their way to the Empire. Orléans fled to Brussels where he placed himself under Spanish protection.

The presence of the French court and army in Lorraine grew in significance when Gustavus Adolphus crossed the Rhine to annex rather than merely to occupy places like Mainz and Speyer. He was now the Elector of Mainz, he announced, and he proposed to remain such. This was a dose of Swedish toxin in excess of Father Joseph's prescription. France wanted neither such a neighbour nor the eclipse of the spiritual Electors. The secret covenant, the Cardinal reminded the King of Sweden, provided that everything which lay within the borders of ancient Gaul should be a French sphere of influence. What business had Sweden in Mainz? The answer given his envoy was trenchant. If the French contemplated a breach of agreement, His Majesty would soon be treading on their toes. Richelieu's advisers suffered in such an explosive state of alliance severe temptation, if Germany was to be auctioned, to make a strong bid for Alsace or Baden and Württemberg. The Capuchin inveighed against this, invoking the King's duty to be the arbitrator, mediator, and protector of German liberty, not its subjugator. He had his way after a heated debate during which anxious participants asked what the position would be if it occurred to Gustavus Adolphus to make common cause with Austria. The question shows how little nations and their politicians, for all their travels and correspondence, knew of one another and how each at any time thought the other susceptible to any wanton change of side. If Richelieu feared that the King of Sweden wanted to become Emperor, the King of France was suspected in western Germany of the same intention and other Frenchmen suspected Bavaria of nurturing the identical ambition. Why not? There could hardly have been any flight of fancy which would not have borne some relation to degenerate reality.

Father Joseph's policy had its feet closer to the ground, though not close enough. With a heavy heart Maximilian agreed to neutrality, but under conditions to which, again except by reason of complete ignorance of Gustavus Adolphus's mentality, he could never have supposed that the King would accommodate himself. Were the Swede ready to relinquish all Catholic territories, cease the molestation of every orthodox German Estate, and allow the imperial troops unimpeded withdrawal into the Hereditary Lands, Bavaria would retire from the war. He meant, be it noted, the new Bavaria, in its entirety, including the Upper and Lower Palatinate, concomitant with his retention in perpetuity of the electoral dignity. Intercepted documents promptly informed Madrid and Vienna of Maximilian's game. To the Spaniards, whose declared enemy he had long been considered, the news came less as surprise than confirmation. Ferdinand pretended to be bitterly disappointed. His Privy Councillors' deliberations concluded that Bavaria had neither reason nor right on the side of its extremely dangerous practices. What should be done? The imperial ministers were in a quandary. Could not perhaps King Louis be reminded that the heresies and rebellions in his own realm continued to be stirred by the German Protestants whose excessive increase of strength he must therefore fear? Or the Pope's memory jogged on the mortal threat to the Catholic religion? Or the Spaniards induced to evacuate the whole Rhineland Palatinate, thus propitiating at last the King of England? Wallenstein's officers thought that they had long observed how Bavarian strategy had been aligned to nothing but pro- tection of Wittelsbach properties. "I am astonished," stated Colonel Ossa, "that people can still be found to try and dissuade HIM* from recognition of this evident deception, painting a different picture. . . . There is much talk of alliance, but I see none." A fortnight's armistice between Bavaria and Sweden provoked in Colonel Sulz the notion that "there must beneath this act be hidden more clandestine matters". Such was always the belief, that the visible was but the tip of an iceberg of totally different dimensions. The visible was at any rate enough to cast strong aspersions on the Elector's reputation for loyalty to his allies. Did he not intend to dodge the deluge, with all that he had acquired in this war for which he was culpably co-responsible, and to leave the Emperor under the downpour? To do so moreover with the assistance of a power about whose friendship for the House of Habsburg not even the credulous could have any illusions?

The damage was Maximilian's without any compensating advantage. Gustavus Adolphus contemptuously rejected his conditions and put his

* His Imperial Majesty.

own instead. No, or practically no, evacuation of conquered Catholic territories, and certainly not of the prosperous ones bordering the Rhine and the Main on whose exploitation he depended. Evacuation, on the contrary, by the League of the northern German fortresses still in its occupation and a reduction of its army to ten thousand men stationed in various garrisons. The future of the Palatinate would be decided at a future overall peace settlement. Richelieu's diplomats tried vainly to mediate. Maximilian, so much was clear, would find safety only by rendering himself defenceless as well as by the surrender of what he wanted to save. He turned about, seeking salvation anew with the party which he feared because at its head again stood Wallenstein and which he had been on the point of consigning to disaster. The truce arranged at a late, already hopeless stage of the negotiations was broken by both sides before it expired. A Bavarian official sent to Vienna to vindicate his master's actions met with an icy reception, but by the middle of February was able to strike a different note – Bavaria was loyal, had always been so, and, because it was loyal, deserved and needed military aid, now, at once, as much as at all possible. Wallenstein, rather good-naturedly, declared his readiness to regard Bavaria's attempt to abscond as null and void. "Pray see how good relations may be maintained between His Majesty's and the League army," he instructed Gallas. "As long as the League does not seek to engage in neutrality, we must support it with all the strength at our disposal." Thus on several occasions. None the less the preceding episode had furnished the final evidence that Maximilian was "a better friend to himself than to us". Wallenstein was not the man to forget it. Among the League princes the Elector of Trèves successfully crossed the enemy lines. He delivered unconditionally into French hands his fortresses and the city of Coblenz with its dominant position over the Rhine and the Moselle, a transaction beneficial both to the Archbishop and France.

The negotiations between Bavaria and France were paralleled by those between the Saxons and Wallenstein. If Bavaria dropped out, there was no longer any room in Germany for the House of Austria. It could only see to the unpropitious defence of its Hereditary Lands. If Saxony dropped out, Sweden's very advanced and broadly extended German front would be in an inauspicious, almost hopeless position, for it was the Saxon alliance that had turned the King's wary strategy into the "incredible fury". The Bavarian effort failed because France, faced with choosing between the League and Sweden, had for the moment to give preference to the stronger power. Saxony likewise did not venture on detachment from Sweden, only played with the idea. During the current winter and spring Wallenstein's peace policy foundered on this lack of firm decision. Nevertheless, regarding his policy as sensible, he relinquished it neither now nor in principle ever, just as Richelieu, ignoring his temporary set-back, continued to throw out bait to Bavaria. Both attempts at separate peace went awry because the conditions for a universal peace did not exist. The attempts led by association to an idea of it, but then to recognition that it could not happen. Imperial obduracy at Vienna and Madrid had before the Swedish invasion been the insuperable obstacle. Vienna had meanwhile lost its wanton bravado and would have been ready to grant concessions, possibly even the repeal of the edict, which it had not wanted to offer in good time. Ready, because the Swedes stood on the banks of the Rhine and in southern Germany. Precisely for that reason such concessions were no longer enough. The Swedes would not even have been content with a return to the *status quo* of 1618. All the misery had arisen on that. Why should it not re-arise if there was a return to the beginning?

Two fundamentally different peace aims have been attributed to Wallenstein, one of a revolutionary character wherein he relied on Sweden and the Bohemian *émigrés* for support, the other loyal and conservative in comparison to this, having for its objective a separate peace with the German Lutherans. The differentiation presupposes that he took little Rašin's cabal completely seriously and that he kept strictly apart what inherently was of a fluid, confluent character. The second theory is however scarcely more tenable. Peace is peace. He who desires it, desires it as a whole. Peace, including the Swedes, is what in retirement he had commended to the politicians at Vienna. If difficult in all events to maintain with Gustavus Adolphus, it would at any rate be easier if the latter had lost his trump card, the Saxon alliance. In the light of its perpetually fluctuating disposition, Saxony was the power most susceptible to peace-feelers. Successful, they could be a first step or remain the sole one. Why ponder more than the start since it was so tentative and everything beyond so obscure? At this time one of his favourite adages was that negotiations did no harm because, even if their main purpose was unfulfilled, secondary gains could be elicited. The opposing party might during their course relax his military effort and afterwards prove the easier to overwhelm, or he might be compromised and become an object of suspicion to his own side. Why not negotiate, especially during the sterile winter season when various advantages beckoned and of disadvantages there were none?

He wanted the war to stop. So did his old friend Arnim, Saxony's Field-Marshal and leading politician. "My heart goes out to that [the idea of a meeting with Arnim] as I aspire to naught else than the establishment again of peace, unity, and good understanding within the Empire." "What a grievous war is this," exclaimed Arnim, in an apology penned upon his machinations becoming known to the Swedes and a cause of scandal, "seeing that we Germans not only often slay our fellow-believers, but a brother his brother, a father his son, a son his father, and that, waged with greater success, it would make dear Germany prey and spoil of foreign hosts, a pitiful spectacle to the whole world." Honest words spoken with a national accent alien to Wallenstein. The German too did not inquire so exactly how Sweden could be fitted into his peace programme. He was equally conscious of secondary gains, more consistently and deliberately. The moment when he simply prolonged the contacts in order to contain his opponent and to delay Wallenstein's offensive against Saxony cannot be pinpointed, but towards the end he had surely nothing else in mind and was the deceiver, Wallenstein the deceived. Guile and two-faced intent belonged to the game. They were no impediment to subsequent endeavours in good faith. Politicians did not take them amiss nor that, amicability having reaped no harvest, frightful severity supervened. The atrocities then abruptly loosed on the land of the foe so recently a party to talks might be the outcome of sheer rage. It would shortly be the case with the Swedes whose excesses in Bavaria horridly surpassed all that had hitherto been experienced. More often, though, they were a means to constrain the opponent's return to the conference-table. As such their effect would have been prompter if the ruler in his panoplied palace, always well stored with meat and beer, had been made to feel them physically rather than manfully enduring his subjects' agonies in his mind alone.

Wallenstein and Arnim were on an odd footing. In 1629 the former had in a fit of irritation and haughtiness let the latter go from his service, but he never lost sight of him, felt well in his company, and somehow expected him to prove a source of benefit, of good fortune. An elective affinity, its working stronger in him than in Arnim. "I am," the Field-Marshal remarked complacently in his apologia, "reproached, as I hear, with the fact that the Duke of Friedland has been heard to say that he cares for me as for his own soul. That was so already four or five years ago. Had I not served uprightly, perhaps he would say it as little of me as of others." The links between them were not broken after the talks at Castle Kaunitz and Wallenstein's resumption of command. In Prague Arnim stationed a guard of honour at the Friedland mansion, from which not a silver spoon disappeared; the imperial palace on the Hradschin received less attention. He also tried to protect Wallenstein's Bohemian estates and humbly begged pardon when he did not quite succeed. For his part he received money through Wallenstein's mediation – pay still due from the days of his imperial service. The moment when as its subjugator he was in occupation of the Emperor's capital city, Prague, was admittedly somewhat ill-chosen for this belated remittance.

In January 1632 Arnim met Adam Trčka, advanced to the status of the Duke's political agent and confidant. What was discussed is unknown except to the degree that Arnim thought appropriate to tell the Swedish envoy at Dresden. Mere platitudes, he alleged. Trčka had asked whether the other side was still inclined towards peace. Arnim had answered that the question appeared to him difficult to understand as it was Sweden, the principal Protestant power, not Saxony, which adjudicated on peace or war. Finally, according to his account, he had sent his former chief the sour greeting that "he was sorry that he, hitherto Friedland's assistant, had now had to become his enemy". Formally he had already been such, whereas in the succeeding months he factually never was. Arnim softened his reports to suit Swedish sensibilities. The rest of the winter he spent in Brandenburg to attend to his estates. Breaking his journey at the township of Berlin, he met by chance a compatriot who held a Wallenstein colonelcy but travelled without let or hindrance through the territory of Elector George William, Sweden's ally. His name was Sparr, the man who had resigned his commission in protest at Wallenstein's dismissal and had re-enlisted on the General's reinstatement. A party man, a middleman. During the next half-year he bore offers from Wallenstein to Arnim and returned with replies which, if they contained no assent, cannot have been clearly negative since otherwise the exchanges would not have continued so long. Wallenstein's peace conditions, and whom they were to include, are pretty much known. They were not to include Sweden. It was to be a separate peace, and that was how Gustavus Adolphus's representatives at Dresden, alertly suspicious, understood the matter. That Wallenstein's authority extended only to negotiations with Saxony was not crucial. He considered himself master of Austrian policy and, had he seen any point to it, would have gone beyond the rights with which he was invested. He saw no point to it for at least as long as the big Protestant coalition had not been dissolved. Its dissolution must proceed via Saxony. To the leading Lutheran power, at heart loyally imperialist, conservative, and unhappy at its enforced foreign alliance, he offered the repeal of the Edict.

This much is certain and comprehensible, corresponding alike to his inveterate views and the reports, apart from Arnim's own, of various sources. Count Thurn had further details from a Saxon officer who had been present at the talks between Arnim and Sparr. Practice of the Protestant faith was to be free everywhere, in the Hereditary Lands too, whether the Emperor liked it or not, with the Protestants having their confiscated property restored and the General, as an imperial prince, knowing how to safeguard the Emperor's weal. "Prince Wallenstein, it is alleged, said that he well knew how the Pope, when he learned that the edict had been quashed, would promptly anathematize the Emperor, but he for his part would not let that go unpunished, even though he should have to expel the Pope from Rome." Here the record becomes uncertain again, involving indirect report, and at the hands of a chatterbox at that. Were the Bohemian landowners also to receive back their properties? Was Wallenstein so blind as to believe that he could compel Ferdinand to surrender his earliest and most pious achievement, the Catholic Reformation in Styria, Carinthia, and Austria above and below the Enns? What we are willing to credit is that he should have talked about Urban VIII in this manner. It was like him, and it is no objection to quote his coincident asseveration that with zealous ardour he kissed the Pope's feet. By letter, be it noted. Orally, never.

Arnim, whatever his views, accommodated himself to the party dominant at Dresden because the constantly vacillating Elector performed such accommodation on the plea that he was unable to act against the alliance fostered with His Royal Majesty. Henceforward his negotiation was no more than prolongation for military advantage's sake until such time as Wallenstein lost patience. The business could not be promoted by these means. The Generalissimo meant it honestly and honourably. In his view everything could be settled within an hour if the other side but cared. If it did not, placing more reliance on barb than benevolence, he had no reason not to rely on the barb of his own weapons. He bore Arnim, as the sequel showed, no grudge. Sparr was alone in feeling bitterly hurt – "Your Princely Grace meant so well that my heart aches to hear of Arnim's faithlessness." They lived cheek by jowl, faithfulness and faithlessness, probity and perfidy. All of them had meant well, and badly too, but Wallenstein better than his counterpart because once trust had anchored in the sombre shadows of his soul its moorings were firm.

Meanwhile, with plunderings, famine, and pestilence, matters stood ever more pitiably in the Saxon-occupied part of Bohemia, particularly Prague. A calamity, to be liberated. At any moment, without waiting for his new army in Moravia to be ready, Wallenstein could have ordered its counter-liberation, its reconquest, by the Gallas, Marradas, and Tiefenbach corps. Arnim knew that too. Until spring was well advanced, the Duke under the spell of his hopes for peace forbade any major operation.

Neither Bavaria nor Saxony dropped out. Nothing remained of the idle winter gossip about peace except the Electorate of Trèves' neutrality and a two months' truce between Maximilian's brother, Archbishop Ferdinand of Cologne, and the King of Sweden so as to allow the former a slight breathing-space. Universal peace? Neither of the main parties believed in it. There were indeed some German politicians at pains to accomplish it, like the homeless Elector of Mainz who had no more to lose and Landgrave George of Hesse-Darmstadt, a Lutheran youth of even ampler conservative and loyal imperialist leanings than his electoral Saxon father-in-law. He had particular reason for his adherence to Austria, being indebted to it for the booty which he had seized from his neighbour and relation, William of Hesse-Kassel. The latter was a Calvinist as radical as George was conservative, inside Germany Gustavus Adolphus's sole utterly reliable ally. The quarrel between the cousins reflected Germany's wretchedness. George, seeking audience of the Swedish court at Mainz, had to endure being told by Gustavus that the King could not abide Spanish-minded neutralists and that he should surrender his ill-gotten possession of Marburg: "He is a fine gentleman, beardless as yet, who would see himself used for peace negotiations." William drafted a programme of war aims for his great ally. The edict should be rescinded. So should the "spiritual reservation", in future allowing any abbot or bishop at will to enter, with his territory and properties, the Protestant association. The three spiritual Electorates were to be abolished altogether, the election of the Emperor so arranged that the Protestant party could always be sure of a majority. The "too sharp Jesuit herd and pack, with all its adherents" must be chased out of the Empire, care being taken that it did not slink back under another name. Protestants should in all Catholic localities, the Hereditary Lands included, enjoy full religious equality and freedom before the law, but not Catholics in Protestant polities. The Papists must pay with land, people, and money for the costs of the prolonged, horrible war, not merely as indemnification for those attacked but in order to deprive the attackers for ever of all military means. The Empire's most important rivers should be held by Protestantism's armed might, its fortresses and passes once and for all be occupied by the same, and the costs be borne by the Catholic party. If the discharge of such tributes left it any possibility to maintain forces of its own, this should be forbidden; it must render itself defenceless through disarmament. And sundry additional stipulations, all most ingeniously, rigorously devised. Why not, argued the Landgrave, impose those conditions on the foe which he had wanted to prevail when he had felt himself to be the stronger? His principle that treaties with heretics could at any time be broken was notorious. How should Protestant freedom be secured other than that its rancorous adversary was condemned to perpetual impotence? That took matters rather far. Indubitably such terms could be dictated only to an enemy lying broken on the ground, not to one in the process of making enormous efforts to regain its former strength. Wallenstein, ready as he was for peace and long since no friend to the Jesuits, would never have agreed, neither now nor later, to this solution of the conflict. He had in mind as a distant goal a fresh, more sensibly based balance, not total overthrow with unforeseeable consequences. What Landgrave William demanded was logical however in the light of the Swedish position. Precisely for that reason Wallenstein was at pains to attain a separate peace with Saxony. Had Gustavus Adolphus and his chancellor thought it worth taking the trouble to define them, the Swedish provisos would presumably have been still more lovingly spiced. George of Darmstadt received at Mainz only the vaguest of replies. No one there either desired or believed in universal peace; desire and belief amounted to the same. The Protestants, ran the argument, were as yet far too disunited and a long way from being well organized enough to render negotiations admissible at all – the sweet mirage of peace would simply scatter them in all directions. What, it was asked, should happen after the cessation of hostilities to the soldiers who for ten to twelve years had known nothing but war and were no longer suited to any other trade? Would they not willy-nilly desert to the Emperor or the Spaniards? What, in any case, was it supposed that the role of Spain, not prepared voluntarily to abandon its hold of the Rhine, would be? But, it was added menacingly, if the Germans thought to negotiate among themselves without their Swedish director and protector, they were making a mistake. Their saviour, who was staking everything for their sake, would have a word to contribute. In short, peace now was not possible.

"Therefore we must currently let the matter be, persuaded and observant that at this time Beloved Almighty God has (no doubt for reasons of sinfulness) not yet deflected the rod of His paternal wrath but reserves His punishment also for those who are the cause of this pitiful state," the Emperor told Christian of Denmark who too had feebly tried his hand at mediation. The other side was the cause, and God's castigation, while it would be visited upon them in particular, for the present fell indiscriminately upon all. What entered into none of their heads, except sometimes in their empty-headed phrases, was that God's rod did not fall at all, or rarely, and then comparatively mildly, on rulers, ministers, priests, envoys, guilty potentates, and their representatives, whereas it fell ever more dreadfully on the suffering mass of mankind who had no influence at all. Yet they were all so pious, so very pious: Ferdinand and Maximilian; Father Joseph and Father Lamormaini; Arnim, and John George as he articulated thickly, with much beer on his brain, "I'll not leave my Jesus"; Gustavus Adolphus too. The Emperor expected from his subjects mute endurance, the King an active acceptance of the sacrifices demanded by faith. He despised the Germans because he so seldom found them ready for that. "You knaves, oblivious of God and duty, who amidst divers religion disavow your faith and adopt the Papists' disgraceful idolatry! Shall you not have sufficient trust in God that, for the sake of His Divine Word, you will disregard and abandon house and home, wife and child? You wanton, recreant rascals! Therefore doth God punish you!" Citizens in the Upper Palatinate who did what the Elector of Bavaria ordered and went to mass had to listen to these wrathful outpourings from their deliverer. He saw to it that his soldiery sang Luther's hymns. He instituted days of fasting and of prayer in his camp. His enemies relied on the fact that on Sundays he would do no battle. On weekdays he forbade every kind of lamentation: "War is war and soldiers are not nuns." Among the swarm of those who determined destiny Wallenstein was by far the least pious, by far the readiest for peace.

THEREFORE THE WAR GOES ON

After Breitenfeld Gustavus Adolphus was regarded as the most dangerous strategist of his day. Tilly, a professional in his craft, seems to have felt almost superstitious fear of the Lion from Midnight. For his own part, Gustavus thought that he was a man of peace, but unfortunately, "God has provided otherwise for him and in general his neighbours have necessitated, coerced, and inflicted war upon him."

This was to throw dust in his own eyes. His vigorous, pious, wrathful soul was possessed by war and, had he lived longer, he would have continued to rove, in this direction, in that direction, and would never have ceased to fight.

As for his innovations, which Wallenstein observed from afar before he entered upon the duel, we must let experts have their say. From the Dutch he took over their discipline, their drill, their frequent exercises which, as one witness attests, made a single body out of a regiment, a single grip out of many hands. That was not possible without martial law. No less strict than Wallenstein's and penally more inventive, the Swedish was more systematic in its purpose, perfection of the military machine, while Wallenstein counted only on chill dread to constrain chaos successfully or not. From the Netherlands too derived the greater mobility of the Swedish order of battle, the broader, shallower, looser disposition with second and third lines of reserve. Conspicuous was the interest devoted by the King to firearms, from lighter muskets with more rapid discharge and quarter-cannon drawn by thirty to forty horses to those nimble field-pieces, the "leather cannon".* His massed cavalry charges were intended for close combat by sword. Whereas the Swedes employed flexible infantry brigade formations appropriately interlaced with cavalry and supported by throngs of musketeers, the imperialists relied on those enormous squares of tercios, with musketeers in the centre and pikemen on the flanks, the whole in such close detachments that the rear rows were able to prove effective through sheer weight, crushing the foe when matters went according to plan, but helpless when confusion reigned. On this difference in organization rested the victory of Breitenfeld in so far as temperament and the fatalities of chance were not the operative factors. The better, genuine morale of the Swedes, called to the colours under a kind of conscription process, is a point usually mentioned. As Gustavus Adolphus penetrated deeper into Germany and filled the ranks of his distending army with soldiers by trade, Germans and Scots, this special feature was lost. His host lived on the land and the towns by pillage as other armies did.

The King's generalship was as straightforward as that of his opponents. He knew the importance of harbours, mountain passes, and principal river-crossings. Everyone did. He went for places where there was something to gain, where he conjectured his enemy's wealth and

---

* A three-pounder gun with an extremely thin barrel covered with a hard leather sheath. Its lightness and consequent mobility rendered it a military sensation (translator's note).

sources of strength to be. He marched towards where his enemy moved in order to bar his way or he marched elsewhere in the hope that his enemy would follow him. His strategy was common property. Its distinction lay in the speed with which today he began to execute and drive to its completion what yesterday had been improvisation. The Elector of Bavaria was astounded. In two corroboratory letters to Wallenstein he wrote of their foe's "accustomed precipitancy" and the corresponding swiftness which it demanded. Precisely this was the conclusion which Wallenstein declined to accept. Once before, six years ago, he had allowed the enemy to force his hand and had undertaken a badly prepared, colossal sortie. Never since.

It was Gustavus Adolphus who allowed his hand to be forced, by old Tilly and the regiments which during the winter months he had scraped together in Swabia. Tilly's duty was to shield Bavaria. Maximilian thought that he could best perform it by taking the offensive. The King, when moving on the Rhine, had left behind him in Franconia a corps under Field-Marshal Horn. The latter not merely extended his position eastwards, but occupied, during the truce moreover, the bishopric of Bamberg. Tilly's comprehensive instruction was to expel him as well as to secure eastern Franconia, the Upper Palatinate, and the communication lines to Bohemia. He approached the task without Wallenstein's counsel or agreement although he relied on his help. Gallas, lodged at Pilsen, would join him, he believed, somewhere in the Palatinate. Whether Tilly was still equal to the enterprise and whether it was desirable to take the initiative in launching the campaign, to invite, properly speaking, the royal army to switch its operations from the Rhine to Franconia and Bavaria, was to Wallenstein's mind questionable. Had he been asked, he would rather have advised, as he shortly did when such inquiry was condescended to, defensive concentrations along the Danube and the Lech. He was, after all, only the three-months-general, the organizer, and the work of organization was not yet done. As was his habit with his subordinates, he left it to Gallas whether to advance as far as Eger, Bohemia's border, and thereby to act as a lightning conductor for Tilly, albeit with the caution befitting a sensible soldier. That he did not want to support Tilly and with concealed pleasure perceived Bavaria's impending ruin is not impossible. All that can be confirmed however is that this additional motive is unnecessary to explain his attitude. Another, perfectly adequate and rational, was on hand. He would not be ready until May, he would "hazard nothing" before then, and he would not allow a Bavarian project, decided in reckless desperation and without reference to him, to dissuade him from the procedure which he regarded as the only one justified. Aldringen's negligible contingent remained in touch with Tilly's, the man from Luxembourg mated to the end to the grizzled warrior from Brabant.

First, though, Tilly's luck held. He succeeded in throwing the Swedes out of Bamberg. An admirable achievement, six months after Breitenfeld, in spite of its evil consequences. The King's plan had been to operate Rhine-upwards from Mainz, to neutralize what Spanish and Bavarian troops were left in the Upper Palatinate, to proceed to Württemberg where he hoped for reinforcements from the Protestant population, and thence to take the road towards the Danube. Hardly had he heard of Horn's defeat at Bamberg when he entirely altered direction and was on his way from Höchst up the Main to Frankfurt, Aschaffenburg, Schweinfurt. There he merged Horn's corps and the regiments arriving from the north under the command of Banér and Wilhelm von Weimar with his own. Tilly shrank from risking an encounter in Franconia with an army far superior to his in numbers. He withdrew southwards through the Upper Palatinate, always hoping for help from Bohemia. Gallas's position at Eger was totally unavailing, he told him, and should be abandoned in favour of joining him as soon as possible with all the troops at his disposal. Southwards too went the King, not in direct pursuit of Tilly who was making for Ingolstadt, Bavaria's best fortified fortress, but farther to the right. He took in Nürnberg – on his triumphant entry followed a treaty of alliance with the important imperial city and the receipt of a contribution such as the citizens had never found possible to pay Wallenstein – Schwabach, Weissenberg, and Monheim before reaching Donauwörth, two days' march upstream from Ingolstadt at a point slightly westward from where the Lech on its northern course flows into the Danube. There the Swedes (or what were called such) freed from Catholic slavery the Lutheran citizens, killing many of them by mistake. On 4 April, the previous day, Tilly had entered Ingolstadt. Late in the evening the Elector arrived from Munich.

Maximilian recognized that the northern offensive had come off as little as the breakthrough to a separate peace. Nemesis was approaching his beloved Bavaria, for the past fourteen years spared from the enactment of hostilities on its soil. Salvation could derive from Wallenstein alone. From Munich already he had written him suppliant letters, page upon page, piteously delineating the peril and reminding him of a promise to help with five thousand horsemen of whom only two thousand had appeared in the Upper Palatinate. That was true. Hardly was he at Ingolstadt before his pleas rose to a heart-rending invocation:

> Wherefore with deep feeling I beseech Your Dilection that, in accordance with the kind affection and care ever displayed by You for Me and My lands as also in accordance with the manifold encouragements and pledges made to Me by His Majesty, You will at this present most dire pass and need not leave Me defenceless, but without any most destructive loss of time afford Me a truly helping hand . . .. Because I did not wish to abandon and to sever Myself from His Majesty, but to remain courageously by His side, I must now atone for this with the Swedes. I trust in God that His Imperial Majesty and Your Dilection will not let me be destroyed.

Reference to the affection always shown by Wallenstein for Bavaria and Bavaria's suzerain must not be construed as irony, simply unblushing reliance inspired by fright. Forgotten was all that during the last seven years had happened between him and Wallenstein, even what had occurred in recent months, what he had anticipated from the new Generalissimo, why he had tried to escape into neutrality. Without more ado he assumed that the other would do his part. Did he? The tone of Wallenstein's answers to Maximilian's resounding appeals was by comparison polite, sensible, concise, and cool. He had without knowing of the crisis on the Danube, advised that Tilly should adopt a defensive position somewhere, probably in the Upper Palatinate, "until our men can be assembled". He had moreover in good time and often pointed out the importance of Augsburg, southern Germany's richest town; it must be strongly garrisoned. Maximilian's shriek of distress from Ingolstadt elicited a rather more good-natured reaction: he would indeed not leave the Elector helpless, but succour him little by little with as many troops as humanly possible. The question was what little by little meant.

Orders had gone out to do what was possible for the defence of the Lech, Bavaria's border, a torrent at the time of the melting of the snows. All bridges were demolished as far upstream as Augsburg, into which soldiers were moved. That however the Swedes were to be stopped at the Lech was the decision taken at Ingolstadt. The encampment erected in the second week of April on the river's right bank at Rain is said to have been formidable, with artillery, entrenchments, six tercios (squares of a thousand men), and cavalry on both flanks, the whole laid out on a level higher than the left bank. To force a passage under the guns of a foe so posted was regarded as contrary to the rules. The King, after two years' warfare in Germany, proud, embittered, and unbridledly daring, broke the rule. Under the protection of a barrage by his batteries (three times twenty-four field-pieces) and the cover provided by bushes he had a wooden bridge built, so low as to present a poor target. On the morning of 15 April his musketeers crowded across the structure while his cavalry thrust through the waters either side of them. Bavarian historians deny that a proper battle occurred, and that Maximilian should at noon have inscribed a circumstantial description of the situation to Wallenstein, which is not practicable in the middle of an action, speaks for their argument. The Swedish monarch, he said, had with all his forces taken up position on the Lech and built a bridge above Rain. Resistance was being offered by the artillery and other arms, but it would not be able to continue much longer. Postscript: "Just now Count Tilly has had his thigh smashed in two by a double hook. It will, I fear, not be without danger to him. Aldringen has been shot in the head," and now he had no commanders any more. In the evening he sounded the retreat to the security of Ingolstadt, which he would have done better never to leave. Tilly's litter swung amidst the misled. The outcome had been that Bavaria, having unnecessarily exposed itself to the Swedish war-machine and then, as in Franconia, retreated, the land was open to Gustavus upstream as far as the mountains, cross-country as far as Munich, for all that he had not caught the army.

Soldierly tradition was rugged. What had happened to Tilly, this agonizing, probably mortal wound, could happen to anyone, old or young, at any time. None the less Wallenstein possessed enough natural chivalry to send his most courtly chamberlain, von Breuner, to express his condolence to the defeated. "We have heard in what fashion Your Excellency has recently been cruelly impaired. How this grieves Us in Our spirit," etcetera. Breuner, he went on, had instructions to convey this and that view held by the Duke about the war situation, and he would ask to be taken at his word. The nature of his views is unknown except that for the present he regarded Bavaria, its open country, as lost, a judgement that was militarily sound irrespective of whether it afforded him any worry or none. It had, after all, been a very late hour when he was called to put over the helm on a disaster for which others were responsible.

The most recent development was that he had slid from the role of general *pro tem.* into that of the Generalissimo. On April 13 the business had been concluded. Two days later, during the hours when Gustavus forced his crossing of the Lech and Tilly crashed from his saddle with a shattered thigh, Prince Eggenberg was carrying the agreed terms to Vienna.

THE GÖLLERSDORF CONDITIONS

All this time Vienna had been staring towards the last day of March like a soul sold to the Devil who awaits the moment of Satan's approach to claim his price. Were Wallenstein serious about the brevity of his service, the new army would fall apart. Its constructor was the one man who knew the machine's ins and outs, dominated it, and was capable of its employment. No one doubted the fact. "February is now almost gone, March will slip through our fingers unseen, and therewith the agreed three months end," wrote Eggenberg. "The fair wind promised by Your Dilection blows upon us, but who will maintain it, from time to time invigorate it, and finally steer us safely into *Portum Salutis* [the haven of safety] if Your Dilection after the expiry of three months abandons the ship?" His Dilection's hesitations, he continued, were of course understandable. None would wish in any way to exercise any pressure on his heroic disposition. Nevertheless it was to be hoped that his correspondent's reflections would lodge in some small nook of his addressee's far-sighted thoughts. The next step was the appearance as imperial envoys at Znaim of two Spaniards, the Capuchin Quiraga, father confessor to the Queen of Hungary, sister of King Philip IV, and a diplomat from Brussels. Presumably they felt qualified for their role of mediators because Spain had been anything but party to the Regensburg affront. They did not however manage to elicit the desired response. Wallenstein both knew his own mind and did not know it. He was too deeply immersed in his onerous, troublesome, pleasurable labour to part from it. He also wanted to leave an escape route open. He tricked himself and others into the belief that it existed. From about 20 March forward his letters dealt more and more often with future operations. On 28 March Abbot Antonius the financier, furthermore incumbent of the newly established bishopric of Vienna, set out for Znaim. The idea of bothering Wallenstein to come to Vienna occurred to nobody. The Bishop's mission was crowned with better success than the father confessor's. The Duke at least agreed to retain his appointment until he had met Eggenberg, suffering cruelly from gout in his hands and mysterious megrims. This was to forge his own fetters – encounters with

Eggenberg invariably brought positive results. Antonius must have done his task thoroughly, for when on 13 April Wallenstein left for Castle Göllersdorf, half-way between Znaim and Vienna, absurdly close indeed to the capital, and when the bows and embraces between the invalid general and the still more painfully afflicted minister had been perfectly performed, the settlement of their business took only a few hours. That would have been impossible without Antonius seeing to preliminary agreement on the stipulations. On 14 April Wallenstein was back in Znaim, Eggenberg in Vienna. He was so exhausted that he could not report to the emperor in person. The bishop explained on his behalf how Wallenstein was prepared on such and such conditions to carry on, thereby proving his ability not only to subdue those hostile to and envious of him, but his own scruples as well. Under what conditions?

A recurrence of events is a feature more frequent in the lives of strong individuals who place their distinctive stamp on their careers while remaining the prisoners of their personalities, self-contained, and without aptitude for fresh beginnings, than it is in those of ordinary men. The conference at Göllersdorf in 1632 was consequently a repetition of the conference at Bruck in 1626, the short session with the minister being preceded and followed by the more protracted negotiations with others of less weighty calibre. As was the case too after the meeting at Bruck, details purporting to be authentic accounts of what happened at Göllers- dorf were forthwith put into circulation. For four months the powerful, fathomlessly tyrannical, and territorially covetous general had spitefully drawn matters out, savouring the Emperor's desperation and driving the Elector Maximilian's to a peak. If he had finally accepted the supreme command, it could not be other than at a price in excess of anything that a servant had ever extorted from his master. A description of Wallen- stein's terms, his "capitulation", went straightway to Munich. Soon pamphlets with contents of similar kind were published in Protestant lands. Contemporary historical writings like *Theatrum Europaeum* and Khevenhüller's *Annals* accepted these versions. The historians of more enlightened ages followed in their footsteps. If we pick a favourite from the selection, then it would seem that Wallenstein had demanded and obtained terms on these lines:

He was to become Generalissimo on behalf of Spain as well as Austria. That sounds astonishing. Neither of the Spanish ambassadors at Vienna, Castañeda, later Oñate, were shown the relevant papers or told of their contents, let alone asked for their opinion. Spanish armies in Germany never came under Wallenstein's control before or after the

Göllersdorf meeting. He was to be Generalissimo in *absolutissima forma*. What does "absolute" mean?

The King of Hungary, young Ferdinand, was never to make his appearance in any part of the army, much less command it. He was, on the other hand, to take up residence at Prague when Bohemia had been liberated so that citizens should once more see that they had a sovereign. Another version alleged that it was old, tubby, ailing Ferdinand, the Emperor, who was never to be allowed to command or visit his army. Both variants are equally useless. The question of the imperial heir's command of the army had been settled in December, and he certainly did not reside at Prague after the reconquest of Bohemia.

Wallenstein's reward for his services was to be secured through, or to consist of, a Hereditary Land. In addition he should receive the "highest prerogative in the Roman Empire" in all territories to be occupied. What this "highest prerogative" was supposed to be, whether the electoral dignity, salt monopoly, or full governmental authority, has in the hope of making sense from nonsense been the subject of deep, vain researches.

The Generalissimo was to have unrestricted right of confiscation. The imperial judicial officials would not be allowed to intervene nor the Emperor, because he was all too clement and ready with a pardon for every petitioner, to exercise mercy without Wallenstein's authority. The grain of truth in this remarkable piece of information lay in the fact that the mass of properties penally confiscated would be used as a source of funds for the army's administrative costs instead of being squandered in the way that happened after the battle of the White Mountain. All else is false. Wallenstein could neither decree sequestrations, for which the courts continued to be competent, nor could the Emperor waive his prerogative of mercy.

During future peace negotiations Wallenstein's personal interests would receive appropriate recognition. In the question, for instance, of an indemnification for Mecklenburg. That appears obvious.

Whatever the cost of the war, the Emperor was to pay "all expenditure". "All" is improbable. Rather more than last time, though.

The Hereditary Lands should be open to the army for asylum. This again is self-evident, albeit that perhaps the evidence was not always palpable to the masters and beneficiaries of the Lands.

So much for these hot air tidings. Their author was as well informed about the Göllersdorf proceedings as the author of the secret report on the Bruck proceedings had been, which was not at all. His guesswork rarely approached the truth, and then clumsily. The frequently re-published "capitulation" is not Wallenstein's agreement with the Emperor, nor is it simply a draft, nor an Eggenberg memorandum, not anything whatever that those who want to save at least half the account's credibility like to believe. It rests on no better than rumour, rumour hostile to Wallenstein. That Valeriano Magni, his old adversary, had a hand in it is not susceptible of proof. Why should he not have had?

In all probability there never was an "agreement". Such an extensive document would have had to have been preserved in the Vienna archives, but it has never been found. The negotiations between Wallen-stein and Eggenberg were oral, Eggenberg repeated their contents orally to Bishop Antonius, and the Bishop reiterated these in the same way to the Emperor. What was subsequently settled and confirmed at Znaim between Wallenstein and the Bishop, Wallenstein and the Lords Questenberg and Werdenberg was again purely oral. The upshot of all the discussions was no general agreement, but a series of pledges which are partly extant and can partly be deduced from events. They are such as were in turn wholly unfamiliar to the taletellers. Wallenstein was invested with the overlordship of Glogau, a petty Silesian principality, no imperial Estate. A temporary indemnification for Mecklenburg, it could not in the remotest degree compare with the latter in status or pecuniary value, leaving open the disquieting question as to how at some future date Wallenstein was to be compensated for his northern duke-dom. He would make no gift of it. For all that at this stage he gladly accepted the Emperor's gracious donation of 400,000 gulden, he did not pocket them on behalf of Mecklenburg. Nor, of course, was it paid in cash. Where would it have come from? The sum was an amount still owed to the fiscal authorities by Wallenstein on the purchase of Bohe-mian real estate, a claim now waived. The beneficiary straightway asked his receipts office at Gitschin whether he had really been indebted for a total of 400,000 gulden. Only 339,429 gulden, 45 kreuzer, and 2 pfennig was the answer, the difference therefore standing to His Serene Highness's credit. For the moment therefore his reward consis-ted of Glogau and money. Whatever the other forms of requital, they remained in the dark. Less wool-gathering than seven years earlier was shown in the vexatious matter of war costs. Wallenstein was not promised the reimbursement of "all expenditure", an impossibility, but the pay-ment of regular, sizeable grants from the taxes of Bohemia, Moravia, Austria, and Styria. He addressed a concise, polite request to the Emperor that these subsidies should, as arranged with Questenberg, "really ensue". He seems to have counted on 200,000 gulden monthly from the Hereditary Lands plus 50,000 from Madrid, 3,000,000 per annum in all, still far too little to maintain a large army, but a basis such as in 1630 he had lacked. Its uncertain increase was to be effected from the funds and assets of subjects in the Empire and Hereditary Lands who were of recent date in a compromised position. Excluded from the procedure were persons in Wallenstein's realms; their properties fell into his hands. He immediately, amidst preparations for the spring campaign, ordered his Gitschin officials to inquire "in all secrecy" who might have unlawfully had dealings with Saxons and émigrés, what they possessed and its estimated value. In all secrecy – the victims' suspicions should not be aroused as to their forthcoming robbery. Not a thought for the fact that he himself had not been altogether innocent of dealings with émigrés, not one iota of a scruple on that score. Ever and again to seize from others, if it was within the letter of the law, and to line his pockets with what was theirs, the habit never died in him, despite sickness, despite a mountain of work, despite the military and political prospects now in view. Confiscations, in 1621, 1623, 1633, 1634, and he their perpetual participant. Imperial and Swedish diplomats later gossiped about plenary power over war and peace. He did not have it. He was again furnished with such as regards Saxony, and it applied via Saxony to the other German Protestant powers, but not to the Emperor's enemies as a whole. Nor did it signify that he could conclude whatever peace he wished. He was to be the imperial delegate, the Emperor's senior deputy, as he had already been at the Peace of Lübeck, and there was nothing new about that, just as there was far less fresh content in the entire Göllersdorf stipulations than people pretended to each other. With a few improvements the business was a repetition of the 1628 provisions. He was reinstated in former privileges such as the right to appoint regimental commanders and to put forward proposals for the conferment of general officer rank on "suitable individuals". Nothing exceptional was added. Wallenstein confined his demands to pertinent points. They were by no means humiliating to the Emperor and the mood at Vienna in those April days did not suggest that any horrible humiliation had occurred. Ferdinand II, tough, instinctively shrewd, thoroughly conscious of his own dignity, would never have renounced his sacred imperial rights. What the gazetteers propagated in this sense was downright invention.

Invention, that is, deduced from the situation. In the actual condition of things lies the truth behind the fable. No agreement made Wallenstein sole master of the army or arbitrator over war and peace. None the less he could fancy that to be his position because he had seen how in gravest emergency his standing as the one indispensable personality was unique, and what cannot he who is indispensable permit himself? In subsequent correspondence between Wallenstein and the Emperor, Wallenstein and ministers, there are tones indeterminately implying unexampled authority: "inflexible confidence", "altogether in Your discretion", hopes of a good outcome now that he was again at the head of affairs. His position was far stronger than in 1629 and, what stood in no agreement, it presented far greater opportunities. During the next eighteen months no order arrived from Vienna of a kind that had definitely come in the days of the Italian campaign and the edict of restitution, only timid proposals, meek questions.

Wallenstein cannot have become "general for life". There was no such command, nor would he, shying away from all ties and enjoying quiet as well as work, have wanted its tenure. Guarantees against a second dismissal were different. Those he must have obtained, orally, like most other points. For instance, the one already promised in the previous year that the father confessor should not again mix in politics or that his enemies at court should not again be given audience. They are matters promised without asking how the pledge is to be kept and without fear of appearing later to be guilty of a breach of faith. By what means could born politicians like Father Lamormaini and official advisers like Slawata and Trauttmansdorff have been reduced to silence? This news species of dictatorship survived no longer than the fright out of which it was born. If he thought that on this occasion it would last as long as he wished, it was Wallenstein who was gulled.

Richelieu, to whom political experience will not be denied, was among those who at the time and later believed in the "capitulation". "It would be difficult," he commented in his memoirs, "to decide whether these conditions were an outrage perpetrated by the servant against his master or of dire need in the Emperor's interest. It has as yet in extreme situations always been regarded as inevitable that the monarch who is unable to act for himself shall entrust all his affairs to another and place his destiny wholly in his hands."

BETWEEN BAVARIA AND BOHEMIA

Collateral theatres of war were so numerous, so kaleidoscopic that an observer becomes dizzy: in the south-west, Upper Swabia, Württemberg, Alsace; on the middle reaches of the Rhine, in Lorraine, at Trèves; in northern Germany, between the Elbe and the Weser, and in the Netherlands. Dutch, Swedes, Frenchmen, Spaniards, Germans were involved. From Champagne the French took charge of matters in Lorraine whose duke, in conjunction with Orléans, the rebellious royal brother, had become impertinent again. They also invaded Alsace, which they were not entitled to do because Alsace was imperial soil and no war subsisted between France and the Emperor. Wallenstein contingents under Montecuccoli, Fürstenberg, and Ossa were roving through Alsace with orders to keep an eye on the country east of the Rhine, Breisach, Freiburg, and Constance as well. A reversal of the situation took place in Württemberg, where Swedish sympathies prerailed. The Edict was overthrown, the monks were again dispossessed. Upper Swabia too was in a state of uproar, but, because the peasants were Catholics, against the Swedes. The Elector of Trèves had wanted to be neutral. The Spaniards, unaware of this, seized Coblenz and held it until thrown out by the Swedes, whereupon the fortress was correctly handed over to the French, the Elector's patrons. In the north, in the Magdeburg area, Count Pappenheim, the military virtuoso, had throughout winter and spring kept up a running fight against superior numbers, one small army against five small armies, two Swedish and three German, those of Hesse, Weimar, and Lüneburg. Their co-operation was as bad as their morale. Pappenheim, whirling here and there, divided one from another, defeated them individually, and disappeared, no one, least of all at Munich and Vienna, knowing precisely where. Mightily proud of his feats, he flatly declined to comply with Maximilian's order to return to Bavaria. He eventually allowed the Infanta Isabella to persuade him to shift the site of his activities to Flanders. The Prince of Orange was besieging the fortress of Maestricht, a fresh danger which impelled the Spaniards to withdraw from the middle reaches of the Rhine farther north. Enough of this. It belongs only marginally to the biography we are narrating, although it does belong there because Wallenstein, the Empire's Generalissimo, was unable to treat these collateral theatres as lightly as is his biographer. He had to be in constant communication with his distant deputies to hear what was happening and to give them exact instructions. Collateral scenes of war could suddenly coalesce. He who today was busy fighting in one region could four weeks later descend like an avenging spirit on somewhere totally different. As he wrote to the Emperor when the Elector of Mainz had also asked for Pappenheim's assistance, he was not surprised at the request since everyone thought first of himself, how he could recover his land and his people, but the General must keep an overall perspective in mind.

From April until July the main theatres of war were Bavaria and Bohemia. In Bohemia progress was slow. Central Europe's citadel had to be freed of its liberators, the Saxons and the *émigrés*, before Wallenstein undertook anything in the Empire, a principle from which he was not to be budged by any plea. He still regarded it as desirable and not impossible to win the Saxons over to peace, to a voluntary evacuation of Bohemia, perhaps to an overthrow of their alliance and a transition to his own side. On 23 April, ten days after the Göllersdorf meeting, he left Znaim in the direction of Tabor, Rožmítal, and Pilsen. Another month passed before conditions in Bohemia warmed up militarily, a month of bitter experience for the Elector of Bavaria, even more bitter for his subjects. The next month too.

"At Neuburg he crept with a stick around the church like a shadow on its wall," ran a report about Maximilian during the march back from the Lech to Ingolstadt, "so cast down that he could scarce be recognized." For almost a hundred and fifty years there had been no enemy and no hostilities in Bavaria. He had been instrumental in the country's betterment. Albeit strictly, he had, with the salvation of their souls in mind, reared to their advantage the subjects entrusted to him by God, even if they were not always duly grateful to him. Now Bavaria was at the mercy of a vindictive conqueror and he could do nothing to prevent it. His new alliance with France was no good, his old alliance with Habsburg had been no good. What had he done wrong? He continued his retreat with his demoralized regiments and the wounded Tilly, whose sufferings are said to have been unutterable. No doubt they were, but he was dying the death into which, year after year, he had led his men, who were worse rewarded than he, and at least he was receiving better, though equally helpless, treatment. It is not, however, possible to withold admiration for the manner in which he did not cease to attend to his duties, including the dictation of numerous letters to Wallenstein, from his bed of pain. On 30 April he passed from the unrest of his life to his rest, speaking his prayers as long as he could, his last look riveted upon a crucifix. "Our pious, worthy old Tilly," as Maximilian mourned. Wallenstein too is said to have been moved by the news. Moved or at any rate dejected, catching a scent of death. The King of Sweden had ground his old comrade in the dust, he is alleged to have commented, and he himself would probably be the next. . . .

The victor of the encounter at Rain proceeded to redeem Augsburg from the Catholic yoke, bully its authorities, and let them pay. The city which two years ago had not a coin to spare for Wallenstein thought a monthly contribution of twenty thousand tolerable. On 29 April the Swedes assembled in front of Ingolstadt. The Danube lay between them and the fortress. The bombardment began on the day that Tilly died. Ingolstadt's walls, redoubts, and outworks, the most modern in Germany, withstood the cannonade. Under cover of night and the protection afforded by the Danube, Maximilian, in obedience to Tilly's last behest, on 1 May left for Regensburg. In the fortress there remained a garrison strong enough to handle its defensive resources effectively. On 4 May Gustavus abandoned the siege because it would delay him too much and cost him too many men. His attempt to secure Regensburg through Field-Marshal Horn proved belated. The Elector arrived first. The imperial city might be of another mind, but he imposed himself on it as its lord and master. The real bolt in the door between Bavaria and Austria is Passau, south of Regensburg. The latter can be given a wide berth through the plain. Passau stands however where the valley of the Danube narrows to a defile which cannot be entered or penetrated without possession of this stronghold. Wallenstein had in good time secured it for the imperial troops. With Ingolstadt, Regensburg, and Passau in Bavarian and imperial hands, Gustavus's plan of campaign was crippled. Ravage Bavaria as he would, the King could neither cut it off from the north nor prevent Wallenstein's junction with Maximilian nor use the Danube as his path to Austria. This he knew. His dilemma can be guessed from the way that he described the new situation to his Saxon ally. Control of the Danube from Ulm to Regensburg, he claimed, had been his intent. Ingolstadt, without being worth much sacrifice, had unfortunately proved rather recalcitrant. He had therefore changed his concept and gone south. He would see to devastation of the whole area between Isar and Danube, hoping "thereby to deprive the enemy of the means which he otherwise derives from this duchy, and if Prince Wallenstein joins with the Duke of Bavaria, as is said to be in preparation, immediately to create such a *sedem belli* [seat of war] here that, with Divine help, we shall be able to arrest his power and do away with it in his own lands through their total ruin". How comforting that Bavaria was the life-blood of the League, and neither Bohemia nor Silesia the Papists' arsenal, but these priest-ridden rural territories and the rich cities to the south. Vienna would then be next year's objective. As for Bohemia, he hoped that the Saxons would be able to hold it:

Wallenstein's army was more a matter of smoke than fire. On 17 May Gustavus took Munich by arrangement. On his entry through the gateway across the Isar he was accompanied by a swarm of German vassal princes who included the Palsgrave, the poor Winter King, woebegone and still uncertain of his fate. The King took up his quarters in the Elector's newly built palace, exuding charm to the citizens and erudition to the Jesuits, his good humour a testimony alike to the clemency of his character and the greatness of his personality. Not that this prevented the Elector's *objets d'art*, his paintings and his statuary, and similar collections in the houses of the aristocracy from being plundered. Art dealers from Ulm, Nürnberg, and Frankfurt hurried to the capital to obtain the stolen goods at auctions at which the inhabitants of Munich also put in an appearance. Who can resist the opportunity to purchase beautiful articles cheaply and who then questions their origin? The city almost wore a mask of gaiety, but in the country east and west and south of it, as far as the Tirolean border, the occupation proved frightful. Burnt villages, market-towns, and monasteries; murder, torture. All according to plan. Gustavus put down on paper that, for reasons of higher strategy, he proposed to devastate Bavaria. When the French envoy made a feeble effort at intervention, he told him to his face that he wanted to scorch and ravage the land in order to teach the Elector what kind of an enemy he was. The blood-curdling accounts did indeed appal Maximilian, who hurried to transmit them to Wallenstein with reproach heaped upon reproach. The Swede "wreaks havoc with an excess of barbarity and his people say that they have orders to ruin the Bavarian land. Yr Dilec. perceives how I suffer, with naught other responsible than my constant allegiance to His Imperial Majesty and his House, for which I must atone." Peace? It was doubtful "whether 'twill be possible through amicable negotiation to achieve an equitable peace with the King of Sweden on account of his well-known arrogance enhanced by the advances he has made". To be forced to be a spectator was breaking his heart and, should Wallenstein delay much longer, he could not say what yet would happen. Maximilian did not inquire into the link between his own guilt and the chain of misery. That his soldiers had in other places long behaved as vilely, or nearly as vilely, as the Swedes in Bavaria was to him an irrelevance. Now he was the victim, the common folk with whom he identified himself were the victims, and a breeze which blew a fire-belching dragon's breath across his own house was a totally different matter. High-strung, vulnerable behind his outward austerity, and with an egotism which transcended his person and was concentrated on his one high, sharply contoured responsibility, the state whose name he bore, he could not understand why his ally did not abandon all else to hurry to his assistance. Wallenstein knew war better. Had it caused him suffering, he would have been as badly off as a doctor who feels the pains of his patients. Let the Elector compose his mind a little, he wrote, remain quietly in the neighbourhood of Regensburg, and await his coming. He would come, but first he must settle affairs in Bohemia. Meanwhile Bavaria's afflictions, on behalf of the common cause and capable of indemnification later, must not be too highly assessed. At Vienna the Bavarian lamentations did not altogether fall on deaf ears. Shoulders were shrugged, the reports discussed in low tones, letters carefully formulated. Undoubtedly it was inevitable that Wallenstein's advance into the Empire was taking so long, nevertheless regrettable too. Hardly six weeks had the saviour been appointed before the old doubts about him revived, albeit in muted tones because louder were not licensed.

The Swedish sojourn at Munich was more amazing to an inquisitively watching world than comfortable for its resident. Gustavus Adolphus's headlong penetration of Germany had brought him to its southern border and he no longer knew what he should do. Steering by no compass, he waited for what Wallenstein's reaction might prove to be. He learnt it at Memmingen, where once before someone had learnt something. On 25 May, a week after he had taken Munich, Wallenstein had re-taken Prague. The crowd of *émigrés* had scattered and Arnim's invading army was in retreat, revealing the truth of Saxon weakness. The King had assessed Saxon strength too highly while putting too low an estimate on Wallenstein's new force. Now he was certain that Wallenstein could, and would, turn against Dresden. Were the Lutheran Electorate lost to him, his position in northern Germany would collapse. Far to the south, he would be as in a cage. Back he went to Munich, back to Donauwörth, and divided the main components of his troops. Banér and Bernhard von Weimar were left in Swabia and Bavaria to hold, if possible, what had been won. The King, with only eighteen thousand men, left for Nürnberg and Saxony. Wilhelm von Weimar was ordered to proceed to Thuringia in order to hurry along the recruitments there and to be on the road to Saxony. The Swedes and their supporters must reach it before Wallenstein, or at least not much later. The erratic, almost overwrought return to the previous year's point of departure was a compulsive reaction determined by Wallenstein's Bohemian move, which was thereby vindicated, just as was his advice to

Maximilian to do nothing against the Swedes in his position of hopeless defeat, but to wait on events. Vindicated, that is, by the rules of his craft, a craft which has nothing to do with philanthropy.

Wallenstein could have been sooner in Saxony than Gustavus, for he was patently closer. He did not, though, want to be. The mere imperilment of Saxony had accomplished what he wanted and what amounted to an extensive Swedish discomfiture. Towards the Protestant princes he wished to display consideration. He had not relinquished his hope of entering into peace negotiations with them and he was not in the habit of giving up his ambitions so easily. He never gave up such things at all. He confined his activity to the dispatch of a few regiments into Lusatia, which was not Saxony, properly speaking, in order to show the enemy what he could do. The province bordered on his own Friedland. Therefore bread had to be baked and beer brewed in Reichenberg and in Friedland town and in Gitschin for the soldiers in Lusatia. A familiar routine.

He went about his business systematically and without haste, as he had always done. From Pilsen, Karlsbad, Eger, the north-west corner of Bohemia, the roads ran towards Saxony and the Bavarian Upper Palatinate. Gallas, on his orders, made sure of the area. On 21 June, four weeks after the capture of Prague, Holk drove the Saxons out of the northern border-point, Eger. Its inhabitants, he reported, had caused him more trouble than the foe and were an evil-minded lot. Could not the old castle above the town be converted into a citadel to tame them? His description was superfluous; Wallenstein knew the place. Was it not from here that seven years ago he had set out on his first German campaign? Troops began to concentrate on Eger. At the end of June the Generalissimo appeared in person. Signs that a new act was about to begin.

The Bavarians soon heard from prisoners and spies about the Swedes' new line of march. Aldringen, recovered from his wound and continuing in his capacity as Wallenstein's representative to the Elector, passed his information to Bohemia – Gustavus Adolphus had on 18 June been at Nürnberg, he would presumably move on Bamberg, then to Coburg, and, unless he was encountered first, on to Saxon territory. To encounter him was what they, the united forces of Wallenstein and Maximilian, wanted. The merger of their armies, which for months Maximilian had awaited with tremulous impatience, was impending, although otherwise and elsewhere than he had anticipated. He must go where Wallenstein was, not the other way around. With his shrunken regiments he peregrinated upstream along the Naab, through the Upper Palatinate, and through places which belonged to him but that he had never seen. Gustavus struck out eastward from Nürnberg for a reason immediately appreciated by the experienced Aldringen. "The King, it manifestly appears, intends to prevent the conjunction or to keep His Electoral Highness apart from YPG [your Princely Grace] and to encounter his army alone. None the less I hope that he will find himself deceived." So it transpired. When Gustavus reached Vilseck, the Bavarians were already gone in the company of Isolani's colourfully accoutred Croat riders and robbers whom Wallenstein had sent to meet them. The Generalissimo remained calmly at Eger while the armies converged under the July sun, and found time to turn his thoughts to Friedland. How building-work on the palace at Gitschin must once again be hastened. How the duchy's officials, from the highest to the lowest, when they took up their duties ought to be put on solemn oath in the manner common among sovereigns, not as at present be installed without ceremony and as though there were nothing to the business. That, the custom under the Bohemian lords who had possessed these territories, was inadmissible. He, Wallenstein, about to make the grand assay with Sweden's ruler, was a European suzerain, not a Bohemian baron. To enter his service differed from entry upon that of a country squire. . . .

We do not know where the Duke of Friedland's meeting with the Elector of Bavaria took place. Historians have claimed Eger or Tischenreuth or Neumarkt to have been the site, but they fail to mention their sources. Eger sounds quite improbable. For the Bavarians it would have been an altogether useless waste of energy to march so far north. Nor can we assume that the Elector would have undertaken the journey alone from his headquarters at Weiden. He swallowed many a bitter pill at this time, but he would hardly have been prepared to endure such a humiliation. Neumarkt lies far more to the south-west, in the vicinity of Nürnberg. Both armies passed through there, but after their merger. The scene may have occurred at Tischenreuth or else in the open countryside. A dangerous encounter, had the period not been provided with the safety valve of protocol. An ironic one, had its protagonists known the concept of irony. Enclosed at a distance by halberdiers, drummers, standard-bearers and flanked by straddle-legged senior officers, the two overlords strode towards one another, at the right instant stretched out their arms, at the next embraced. Discussion followed, at first merely polite, then polite and to the point. Accounts of the meeting circulated forthwith. All had gone smoothly, but keen-eyed observers had noted that "His Electoral Highness has learnt the art of dissimulation better than the Duke", and of course Wallenstein's eyes had at the very second of the ceremonial greeting gleamed with triumph and hatred. That was how he had to be, that was the image of him, that was "Wallenstein's insatiable ambition and absolute avidity for rule" as well as craving for vengeance. We do not believe a word of it. Even had he been agitated by exceptional emotion, he was too practised to reveal it and at this particular moment had made a visor of his features.

Not even now was he formally furnished with any supreme command over the Bavarians. In actual fact it went without saying that he would have such and that the Elector would in all decisions follow in his wake, him, the man with his dearly gained professional experience as against that of the amateur, the Emperor's Generalissimo as against the bounden ally, the possessor of the incomparably greater military power. The precise figures are not known, only the numbers of regiments and companies, which signifies little. Maximilian's contingent, 201 companies of infantry and 239 companies of horse, has been assessed as low as six thousand men. Wallenstein put the strength of the force under his command at forty thousand men, after its amalgamation with the Bavarians at a good fifty thousand. On 5 July he wrote to Colonel Montecuccoli, "To which Our answer is that We have already met with His Dilection the Elector of Bavaria and have together over fifty thousand men on horse and on foot. The King of Sweden is however at Nürnberg and has there entrenched himself. Therefore the day after next We shall set out against him and try whether he is to be brought to battle, whereby then many things will be transformed." So Nürnberg was where it would finally be. Gustavus decided however to remain on the defensive. He realized the mistake that he had again committed – Saxony was not Wallenstein's objective, but he himself, straightway, while still to be caught in Franconia. The combined armies moved southwards, on Amberg, Neumarkt, Roth, Schwabach. The last is today a mere suburb of Nürnberg.

At Vienna his moves were followed with indolently interested, always only half-stirred, subsequently surfeited curiosity, and were approved. His Majesty, he was told, and Prince Eggenberg admired his dispositions, the progress achieved, and his plans, recognizing "like all of us, that Yr P. Gr. has understood matters rightly and much better and *con vera ragion di guerra* [with true strategic appreciation] than the Elector, because in this wise the Kinndom of Bohemia and also the

Bavarian land have all at once been freed of the enemy". The decline, rise and decline again of his reputation belonged as much to the rhythm of Wallenstein's career as sleeping and waking.

NÜRNBERG

The King had manoeuvred himself into a trap and made the best of it. Had he marched farther in the direction of Saxony, the combined armies, incomparably stronger, would have barred his way. Had he, after so much strange hither and thither, tried to slip away to the west, his martial fame would have dissolved in dust and derision. So he remained where he was, adopting a defensive stance in conformity with the rules. In a few days "high and handsome" redoubts, deep ditches, and half-moon ramparts encircled Nürnberg, a feat achieved by twenty thousand soldiers, forced peasant labour, and enthusiastic young city volunteers under the supervision of the royal engineers. The ordnance is said to have numbered three hundred cannon, including the Bavarian pieces captured at Munich.

In Wallenstein's view so spiky a position should be left unattacked and instead blockaded at appropriate distance. What then? One day the enemy would have to emerge. Meanwhile he would attempt to bring relief forces on the scene, regiments from northern Germany, the Rhine, Swabia and Bavaria. Franconia would become the site of a twofold concentration. Ultimately it would witness the crucial crisis. Maximilian to the contrary, wanted a sharp passage of arms at once. During the succeeding weeks he never ceased to complain of his loathed friend's inactivity.

> I have indeed endeavoured to prevail upon the Duke of Friedland that with so stately an armament one should not tarry so long, but at some point proceed in earnest against the foe. To date I have, despite all assiduity, failed to prevail and the greater the passage of time the more must I perceive that the intent is to hold out against the enemy alone by procrastination and to await other un-certain opportunities to attack and do him injury. In the mean-while the most favourable season and occasion elapse, victuals and money are consumed to no purpose.

And so on. These were expressions of Bavarian fretfulness. What we have in black and white are proofs that the gradual evacuation of southern Germany and the Rhineland by Swedish troops, with their concentration in Franconia, was deliberate and planned on Wallenstein's part as previously Gustavus' retreat from Bavaria had been. To this there was a corollary. He hoped to intercept whatever forces came from the Main and from the Lech before they merged with the royal army. Therefore the encampment which he was constructing west of Nürnberg served a twofold purpose – the King's blockade and isolation.

In a matter of three days the landscape of this fortress, miles broad and deep, inclusive of several villages, was transformed from a prospect of pastoral peace into a place of human warfare through mortal masses and means. To the east the whole length of the position was protected by the Rednitz flowing from south to north and bisected by the tributary Bibert coming from the west. Trenches were dug, mounds thrown up, and bastions built along this river bank. Whole forests were pulled down to make room, furnish views, and allow timber to be sharpened into palisades. The rising ground to the north was embellished with a triple line of ramparts. Beyond these outworks a castellated ruin on a wooded hillock, the Alte Veste, was converted into a completely up-to-date defensive point with guns, ditches and entanglements. The improvised stronghold displayed, for intelligible reasons, its grimmest character to north and east. Rather less fierce was its appearance to south and south-west, but there too could be found quadrilaterals, entrenched batteries, and guard-posts. To how many did the encampment afford protection? Gustavus, inspecting his enemy's lair when no one was in it any longer, concluded that more than twenty-two thousand men could never have been there. Kings also err. Why, in the light of all that we can see and learn of the camp's size, should not forty thousand have lived inside?

A plan of this cantonment unprecedented in military history has survived. Made two years later by orders of the Nürnberg city council, it was compiled with a precision unsurpassed by any other contemporary work and gives the details as well as the overall picture. There can be seen the infantry's tents, the strictly marshalled swarm of hutments for horses and riders, the cookhouses and canteens, the munition stores, the punishment stations consisting of three gallows and a wheel on which, as a warning to others, hung a victim's quartered remains. He is said to have been a baker's boy, probably saucy and full of the joy of life. We do not know why he had to end it so horribly, but it is not beyond imagination that discipline had to be exercised even more harshly than usual amidst such crammed concentration. The Elector had his quarters close to the Bibert in the village of Altenberg, the most shady and pleasantest spot in the encampment, while Aldringen's were approximately in the centre at Kreutles, and Wallenstein lived on open ground to the south in a barrack which may have been the prefabricated structure used as his military chancellory. The latter was housed in tents around the barrack, as were also the senior staff officers and his doctor, with stabling for his horses close by. Not far off, right on the southern edge, was situated the hospital in five totally inadequate huts. There was also a well, a single one, for access to which the servants of the high and mighty squabbled; the common soldiery could avail themselves of a stream creeping turbidly on its course in the summer's heat. The encampment cannot have been conducive to salubrity. Was the air pure at least in the vicinity of the Duke's barrack? Did he have his accustomed herbal bath, for meals his partridges, his strawberries, his wheaten beer? Did he spend his days dictating, reading, issuing orders to officers and emissaries, cross-examining prisoners of war and roaming peasants? Did he ride with his entourage through the camp to address words of encouragement to the soldiers or point threateningly at a rampart which had not been mounted according to his instructions? How did he feel in Maximilian's company, did they now and again dine with one another? At any rate they signed orders together: By the Grace of God, Maximilian, Albrecht. The Bavarian's calligraphic artistry and Wallenstein's wildly sprawling strokes look strange in combination. Strange too were these July days and dog-days, with three warlords, and their armies, who had wanted to compose their quarrel and failed, facing each other so closely. "Now," Wallenstein wrote, "one has only to stand on one's own defence, for I hope that if the King receives here but a single blow, much in the Empire will be changed." He was the more patient, and never so patient, outwardly so much master of himself, as in front of Nürnberg. Much would be soon changed in the Empire? Changed in what sense? Was a complete defeat of the Swede really in his interest? His detractors claim that he did not wish for it. They regard it as the explanation for his spider's policy. Perhaps he did sometimes during the night ponder what would happen if Swedish power were no longer operative in Germany. Would the arrogance of the court at Vienna be revived, the hope of balance and compromise be lost, he himself become as expendable as he was in 1629? Night thoughts. In day-time the existing military situation was of more relevance than politics in an uncertain future. He remained under its spell for the rest of this year.

There were sorties from both camps, skirmishes, shots in the dark. One opponent would try, and sometimes succeed in, the seizure or burning of a provision train. The Swedes' advantage was possession of the great city with its storehouses and 138 bakers. To their disadvantage was that the world outside was less accessible to them than to the imperialists. Their stocks must in such tight quarters rapidly dwindle. As usual man had precedence over the poor animals, soldiers over civilians. The horses died first, then the citizens, 29,406 of them in all, a chronicler calculated, from disease and famine. Trouble is often the wages of ardour. For ardour to have been long spent alters nothing; immolation continues. Sickness proliferated in the other camp too. There it was however probably more to be understood as a matter of raw inexperience of living cheek by jowl, in terms of flies and vermin rather than deprivation. Sufferers were carried on bumping carts as far as Eichstätt and Regensburg. To set up hospitals for them, Wallenstein told the latter's civic authorities, was a Christian duty and imperial command. "I advise you," ran his postscript, "to rejoin me no more or something else will ensue." Victuals for those who remained in good health were mainly drawn from Bavaria, as Maximilian did not without bitterness fail to note – drained, reputedly so utterly ravaged Bavaria. Wallenstein acknowledged the point: the Elector was doing his best for the common cause, and consequently it was equitable for him to do the same. Behold, how just he could be.

To Wallenstein the union of Gustavus's army with the Swedish forces trundling forward from every point of the compass did not present itself as a practicable proposition. To prevent this he had only to interpose his own strength between Oxenstierna's approach up the Main and that of the generals Banér and Weimar from Swabia. To the despair of the Elector, to the delight and incredulous amazement of the Swedes, he did not stir. Oxenstierna, like a river into which tributaries debouch, drew corps after corps to his side, at Würzburg the Landgrave of Hessen with four thousand men, at Kitzingen Duke Wilhelm von Weimar with eleven thousand, at Windsheim Banér and Bernhard with seven thousand. By the end of August, when he arrived at Brück, between Erlangen and Nürnberg, his relief army numbered thirty thousand. Wallenstein's encampment did not enclose Nürnberg to the north. Since he continued to remain where he was, the two Swedish forces could merge in complete peace. What now? If Gustavus did not mean to raise the senselessness of his march on Nürnberg to a pitch of lunacy by decampment, a possibility open to him although it would have been perplexing to say where he should go, he had no choice but to bring matters to a head, all the more urgently because food and drink for an army of forty-five thousand men was utterly lacking. Wallenstein, as heretofore, declined battle.

The Duke's disquieting neighbour on the other bank of the Rednitz was not during these two months his exclusive preoccupation. How did matters stand with Grossglogau*, the most recent acquisition among his assortment of principalities? Max Waldstein, still his confidant in such affairs, had to organize on his behalf the receipts from the salt works and the sale of its products, from the mines, the customs, and the legal fees offices. Their prince would in turn offer his subjects regulation of the Oder river-bed to be undertaken at his expense, brick-kilns to serve for the construction and reconstruction of fine buildings, and as far as possible leniency as regards billeting. Glogau, hitherto of no concern to him, was now his city, and no city of his would be allowed to give an impression of unsightly neglect. Instructions on these lines sped from the camp. They availed nothing because at the beginning of August Arnim carried Sagan and Glogau. What his mercenaries did there, especially to members of the cathedral chapter, and what Wallenstein read in the reports of officials who had managed to flee to Polish territory, may have sickened even his hardened soul at the infamy that man can do to man.

The expedition was one of those diversions of which for the past fifteen years the war had in substance consisted, an undertaking which could just as well have followed another direction and would even better have never been started. Why Silesia? Why not Silesia? How many armies had in the past been impelled across the wooded passes between Bohemia, Saxony, and Silesia to the ruination of these lands? How many more would yet, century after century, be so impelled?

Arnim, jostled out of Bohemia, had expected a return visit by Wallenstein to Saxony. This his thrust into Silesia was intended to forestall. Moreover, so argued the Field-Marshal, the Swedish corps which was operating in Lower Silesia from a Brandenburg base could quite easily seize the entire province on the King's behalf. Better, in a German's eyes, for it to be in Saxon hands. The majority of its inhabitants too belonged among those who, according to current political theory, were groaning for liberation because, originally Lutherans, they had been coerced into idolatrous error through the Emperor's Reformation. Redemption from it was what they obtained for a while, and that was

* Greater Glogau.

the only stroke of good luck which Arnim brought them. All else that the Saxons understood by the word "liberation" had been demonstrated in Bohemia. Arnim, in his piety, was himself not wholly happy about the matter. German Liberty, God's Holy Word, a truly assured Christian condition of peace, these were indubitably fine things to strive for, but the way that his men behaved in Silesia was not to be put into words. "I have hangings nearly every day. It helps naught. They claim that they receive no pay and must seek their maintenance otherwise."

Wallenstein had some twenty thousand men in the east. Twelve thousand were in Bohemia under Marradas, the long-serving, useless old Spaniard. They were meant to police the country rather than to protect it. The force of ten thousand in Silesia under Colonels Goetz and Ilow proved incapable of stopping Arnim's advance up the Oder. Sagan, Glogau, Steinau fell, then Breslau, the capital. Once again an oft tried, always tempting, forever futile strategic notion reappeared – to proceed from Silesia to Moravia and to coalesce with the Prince of Transylvania. Although the latter was now named Rácócsi, not Bethlen, he also was not altogether uninterested in mirages of martial pan-Protestantism, and Buda's pasha too displayed partiality for the scheme.

The Duke never took amiss any of Arnim's actions for long, regardless of what the Field-Marshal did to him. His rage was therefore directed against Saxony as incarnate in its Elector John George, a contemptible creature, ever at the mercy of outside influence and giddily following the last counsel poured into his ears. After nine months of sincerely trying to achieve peace with Saxony, the time had come to bring the Elector to reason through "pillage, fire, cattle seizure and other spoliation". One diversion against another. What did not occur to him was that John George would suffer no distress, even if his person should sustain gilded imprisonment, only his poor subjects whose opinion as to the Silesian campaign had not been asked. In this respect his train of thought in no way differed from the mighty of his own and all other ages.

Lieutenant-General Holk, who until the middle of August was in a forward position farther north, was selected to be Saxony's scourge. He obeyed. He not merely suspended the iron discipline which on other occasions he maintained over his troops, but drove them to excesses of depradation that, not without a certain satisfaction, he reported to his commander-in-chief. "Colonel Corpus will tomorrow evening do his worst in front of Dresden's gate." "Colonel Corpus has set fire to and made incursions into the countryside as far as the outskirts of Dresden, burnt down three villages in the vicinity, reduced to ashes with all its denizens a town called Aitten as also various other market places besides cutting down some thousand persons." His final total was "five goodly towns and almost thirty villages, stripping the entire land this side of the Elbe". He was boasting, but barely exaggerating. Reports from Dresden, like those of the Swedish agent, sounded even worse. It was John George's turn, as in spring it had been that of his fellow-Elector Maximilian, to erupt into stereotype wails, "worse than the Turks", "as never before and nowhere", when in fact it was always and everywhere the same. Wallenstein mainly blamed Arnim. Holk's ferocious drive through Saxony would not have happened without Arnim's ferocious drive through Silesia and, apart from being designed as a spur to the Elector's love of peace, its concurrent purpose was to force Arnim to withdraw. If however war is generally a clumsy means to attain peace, this particular type, with its viperous tongues of fire, was clumsier than most. Court Chaplain Hoë at Dresden preached splendidly vociferous sermons against Papist tyranny. For the first time since the outbreak of hostilities prayers on the Emperor's behalf ceased. Vienna, though, very far from the scene, busied itself with the possibility of other diversions. Could not the Poles again contribute something to the cause by descent from the east upon the Protestant Electors? Wallenstein's relations with the Poles had always been at once close and tenuous. Close because the country's geographical situation as neighbour to Swedish, Brandenburg, and Habsburg territory as well as its suzerain's Catholic faith and affiliation to the Habsburg clan made them so. Tenuous because the kingdom's broad tracts were weak and imperilled, the position of its king even weaker. At the present juncture it was indeed non-existent. Old King Sigismund had recently died; Prince Ladislaus, his successor, was awaiting election by the magnates. An interregnum signified for the monarchy's enemies manifold temptations, as Ladislaus feared and Wallenstein, after discussion with a Polish envoy at his Nürnberg encampment, appreciated. As long as the Swedes had campaigned in Poland, he had been intent on keeping that war in being so as to keep them away from Germany. With peace between Gustavus Adolphus and Poland, or something like peace, and Swedish strife in Germany, Polish politicians desired precisely the same for the same reason. The difference was simply that in days gone by Wallenstein had done something of substance to prolong the war in Poland whereas Ladislaus was unable to undertake any corresponding action. The negotiations conducted by Wallenstein with Warsaw diplomats consequently remained of somewhat indeterminate character. What he gave them in writing was that "neither His Imperial Majesty nor His Dilection the Lord Elector of Bavaria nor We" were thinking of an armistice with Sweden and that further confidential correspondence between himself and the crown of Poland would doubtless be of service to christendom.

Word arrived, directly and indirectly, from even farther than Warsaw. The Transylvanian's pranks proved to be tomfoolery, no more. The Great Turk, though, could be terrible. That was a point taken into calculation by anyone who picked a quarrel with Austria. Gustavus Adolphus was no exception to this rule. The Peace of Zsitva-Torok, Cardinal Khlesl's peace of 1606, still subsisted, its duration incomparably longer than had originally been hoped. None the less the longer a peace with the Turks lasted, the more probable that it would not last much longer. Either external opportunity, as furnished by the Swedish monarch, or a shift of power at Constantinople could effect that. Such had occurred in May, as Wallenstein learned in July from a report by the imperial resident, orator, or internuncio to the Sublime Porte. The Grand Vizier had suddenly died. The Sultan's method of approaching the problem of how to shed his powerful minion had been shrewd. Of recent months he had displayed exceptional good will towards him, offered his own sister in marriage, and then, on the minister's entry into the Seraglio for audience, arranged for assassins to fall upon and swiftly strangle him. Murky justice of this kind was worth the trouble in more than one respect – his throttled victim's fortune in gold, gems, and other treasure, valued at three million ducats, fell into the Sultan's lap. The question was what the succeeding vizier's attitude towards the war in Europe would be. The imperial ambassador could furnish soothing tidings. The new man had at his first meeting made a favourable impression of moderation, underlined his adherence to the treaty complex, and explained to the Swedish representative that, while he held King Gustavus Adolphus's friendship in high esteem, he must not without cogent reason intervene in his wars. Wallenstein's reading of the report seems to have rendered him pensive. There had been the Grand Vizier, one of the mightiest personalities in the Ottoman Empire, probably one of the best endowed too, quite certain of his situation. Suddenly a second of shock, an icy clutch around the heart, ridiculous resistance, a few stifled cries, and he was gone, gone with him all that he had collected about his person, and promptly on hand a successor, probably chosen long before, but secretly, and everything else continued on its way. Turkish procedure. To the able ambassador, whose career had begun as citizen of a small Swiss town on the Rhine, Wallenstein wrote that he had read his report with interest and awaited his further news. More details (if here we may be allowed a guess) followed about the Grand Vizier's downfall as well as what was passing between Turks, Persians, Tartars, Muscovites and Swedes.

Four days after his relief army had joined him, Gustavus Adolphus went over to the offensive. In so far as the resultant wild manoeuvring remained under the control of its leaders and is capable of being described in professional terms, the following ensued:

On 31 August the King assembled his army in order of battle on the right bank of the Rednitz opposite the enemy camp. Artillery exchanges on this and the following day. Wallenstein did not stir. On this front his position, with the river and the morass on its right bank presenting impediments which acted as a defensive screen, was at its strongest. During the night of 1–2 September Gustavus marched his troops northward and crossed the Rednitz at Fürth. Wallenstein, for all his caution, regarded an open battle at the western end of his encampment and to the south of the Bibert as acceptable. On the morning of 2 September he led the greater portion of his regiments in that direction and waited; Aldringen was however left behind with a number of units. The King misunderstood the operation. Wallenstein, he fancied, had taken to his heels, departing south-west with the preponderant part of his army. He dispatched his cavalry in pursuit to where the enemy was not to be found and, imagining the encampment to be now but weakly defended, had approaches made to it. On 3 September he sounded the general assault, Bernhard von Weimar leading on the right, he on the left, the Finnish cavalry in the van, the white, blue, yellow, and green Swedish brigades, the Germans, and the Scots following. The objective was the Alte Veste and a wooded ridge opposite, parallel to the Rednitz. Whoever could mount artillery there would command the entire encampment. Straightway Gustavus's mistake was revealed. The line of the ridge was held in strength. The attackers had against them not merely Aldringen's contingents (their leader on this day performed sheer wonders), but the whole of the imperial and Bavarian forces. Streaming back into the camp from the west and taking up its long prepared emplacements, the combined armies were now able to fight under far more advantageous conditions than they would ever have done outside their stronghold. More advantageous conditions, yes, but we would not advise anyone not enamoured of such sport with death to venture upon such advantage. When Wallenstein's musketeers emerged from their sylvan ambuscade, the Alte Veste was turned into a flame-spewing knoll defended by eight thousand men who were relieved every two hours. "There was such shooting, thunder and clamour as though all the world was about to fall in. The noise of salvoes was unceasing," according to a contemporary report. Then Wallenstein's cavalry, stationed in the low ground of the Bibert, fell upon the attackers in the rear. Fighting was at such close quarters that Aldringen suddenly found himself alone among the Swedes and had to pretend to be a Swedish-German commander until able to extricate himself. At the Alte Veste control was assumed by Wallenstein in person, astride a charger, scarlet cloak thrown across his breastplate, peering through smoke and fire, shouting words of encouragement swallowed up in the din, and throwing handfuls of golden gulden among the soldiery. Almost sixty of his officers, some of notable birth, like Colonels Fugger, Caraffa, Chiesa, were killed. Their names are in the history-books. Those of the rankers sprawled twitching on the ground remained unrecorded. Towards evening heavy rain began to fall, on the wounded, on the Duke's beaver hat, on the slippery ridge which Bernhard von Weimar had wanted to crown with his field-pieces, a hope that had now to be abandoned. After nightmarish hours the King's council decided upon retreat.

> The combat started right early [Wallenstein reported], and lasted *caldissamente* [most hotly] all day. Many officers and men of Your Majesty's army are dead and wounded . . . but I can by my honour assure Your Majesty that all officers and men, on horse and on foot, behaved as bravely as I have rarely in my life experienced . . . . The next day the enemy stayed upon the hill until ten o'clock, but when hardly pressed he quitted the woods again with a loss of two thousand men (or, as I am told, more, for the woods are full of dead whom he could not carry away, and prisoners say that dead and wounded were borne back throughout the day) and withdrew to Korbach, where he remains . . . . In this encounter the King hath mightily blunted his antlers . . . and, for all that Your Majesty has dominion over soldiers of more than enough courage and valour, this battle has given them yet further confidence by seeing that the King, with his might all gathered together, has been repulsed and that the title "invincible" appertains not to him, but to Your Majesty.

The dispatch ended with a laudation of Aldringen, ascribing to him the principal credit for the defence of the Alte Veste. Written on the following day, three centuries have been able to subtract nothing from its contents and to add but little of substance.

Rewards were distributed to the wounded – four hundred gulden for colonels, three hundred for captains, forty for corporals, ten for the plain soldier. Wallenstein's old practice, *poena et praemium* [penalty and premium]. This occasion witnessed no penalties. Never before had he expressed himself so generously about those beneath him, never before allowed credit to another with such lack of jealousy as here in the case of Count Aldringen. The whole report radiates the best of tempers. The single word *caldissamente* achieves a degree of eloquence for which others later drew on a store of verbal tones, rhythms, and hues. He had attained what he wanted – to defeat the King, to deprive him of the aura which since Breitenfeld had attached to his name, and to accustom his soldiery to the foe.

The latter was in a dilemma, a great dilemma. Should he launch another attack? March away? Where to? The worst solution of all, it proved, was to stay and see what Wallenstein would do. Wallenstein did nothing. He knew how affairs stood in the Swedish camp. The King's army, he wrote, was dying away in swarms from hunger and disease or else absconding. It was not only absconding, but running across to the opposite camp, knowing where food was to be found. Within a fortnight Gustavus lost a third of his army, some fifteen thousand men, through illness and desertion.

We hear him complain how he is unable to understand the Germans – they continue to lavish affection on their Emperor in spite of all the tyranny he has exercised against them. We hear him talk of peace – it is possible at any time and what he demands is no more than right and modest. He must have Pomerania, Magdeburg and Halberstadt too, not for himself, but for the Protestant Electors. Wallenstein? Why should he not be ceded the duchy of Franconia (including Würzburg, whose prince-bishop can be indemnified with a sack of gold) as substitute for Mecklenburg? He will be prepared to restore to the Elector of Mainz his territory if the outlawed Palsgrave has his Heidelberg returned to him, though not the Upper Palatinate, far less Bohemia . . .. The tune was in a different key from that in the spring. As regards the "duchy of Franconia", it has to be realized that this was a whimsical product recently constructed from the bishopric of Würzburg and a miscellany of monastic, county, and manorial holdings along the Main, its overlordship reserved in the King's own hands. A rich tract of country, Franconia. Probably Wallenstein would not have been ill-pleased with it.

Colonel Sparr, that political soldier who had had the bad luck to fall into Swedish hands near Nürnberg, acted as royal emissary to Wallenstein. He transmitted three questions. Would an exchange of captured officers be agreeable? It would have been to Wallenstein's advantage because the Swedes, dating from Tilly's days, carried more prisoners in their train than he did. Could a system of "general quarter" be established whereby defeated parties would everywhere and at all times go unharmed? Wallenstein declined. He referred to the practice in the Netherlands. There it was customary that when fifty horsemen fell in with seventy, the former immediately surrendered. What would war come to? "Troops should fight or perish." Finally, and principally, whether in the light of so much innocent Christian blood already shed, etcetera, etcetera, would it not be salutary straightway to begin peace negotiations between delegated commissioners or the King and the Duke personally? With frosty correctness Wallenstein replied that he had no authority to deal with subjects of that sort, but he would refer the question to His Imperial Majesty. On receipt of this answer Gustavus knew how he stood. Decisions by the Privy Council at Vienna were delayed for months and, if ever taken, seldom had better to offer than platitudes and flourishes, endless historical lectures and dreary disputation. No second assault was feasible, peace talks were not to be had, withdrawal, no matter where, must end torment and destruction. He put the best face on it by drawing up, on 18 September, what was left of his troops – 27,000 men, it is said, but shortly before they had numbered 45,000 – in a challenging position opposite the enemy camp. Wallenstein watched from his high ground and made no move. Thereupon the Swedes wheeled away to the west. That they did so with such outstanding discipline must, in view of their physical and moral state, have cost their commanders enormous effort. Wallenstein noted the feat with professional administration "He [Gustavus] has performed a splendid retreat and I know from this and all his actions that, alas, he understands his calling well." He sent cavalry after the slowly disappearing columns, more to discover where their journey was taking them than to provoke another encounter.

This brought Elector Maximilian's impatience to the boil. Like it or not, he had so far participated. He had forced across his lips a few barren words of praise for the fight at the Alte Veste, although not without intimating that with a rather more active disposition probably more could have been achieved. Now, he was convinced, the departing enemy should be pursued with utmost vigour. He went in person to the Duke and addressed him with the most spirited oratory. "'Twas all to no avail," he afterwards bitterly complained, "and We had to experience how he gibed at Us, as though We had not experience enough in these matters, the two Field-Marshals Aldringen and Gallas equally agreeing with him." Hatred yearns for offence to be given. The bureaucratic Elector, with his suspicious character, was in any case at a disadvantag with military men. Hence we cannot tell whether he truly had to suffer gibes or was only driven to detect them in mildly-worded explanations.

Wallenstein had at any rate until 18 September been in the right. For the King of Sweden the outcome of his Nürnberg summer was worse than defeat in the open field. In numbers, in any case. In imponderables, more so. Last year's triumphal sweep had turned into disorder and dis-illusionment, purposeless hither and thither as enemy action dictated, death and scorched earth.

LÜTZEN

Since the battle of the White Mountain nothing conclusive had been effected. The war went on and on. The only conclusion that Wallenstein had already reached was that the Swedish intervention would prove as indecisive as had previously the Anglo-Danish-Dutch. That was a success, yes, but not one which intrinsically opened pleasurable perspec-tives. It would be possible to continue the war and to harass the Lands year after year with apparent advantage now to this side, now to the other, and so on back and forth.

Wallenstein's intuitive, wearied spirit was conscious of this possibility as something which should be avoided, and as such, in the long term, it continued to impress him. But there were moments when he thought otherwise and grasped at other hopes. Subject, like all of them, to the influence of news both false and true and the notions bred by it, he vacillated. During the succeeding, immensely bewildering seven weeks, crammed with events, there were hours of exaltation when he believed that he would be able "completely to make away" with the King of Sweden, that is to say, to defeat him so totally as to be able to conclude peace in his own way as he had previously done at Lübeck. Could it have been obtained, he would have been victorious over the most famous commander of the day, the new Alexander the Great, bringing his second generalate to a triumphal end and attaining satisfactory consequences for a number of parties, not least himself. Nevertheless the feeling that this was not to be, and the inevitability therefore of some accommodation with an exercise of moderation on both sides, predominated.

War could not be waged for ever. Or, at any rate, he could not wage it for ever, not in his condition of body and soul, and he was instinctively inclined to equate his inner mood with the outside world. Impelled by the desire to reach his objective, his current actions signified a frightful drain upon his resources.

Did Gustavus Adolphus find himself in similar predicament? Indications are not lacking that he, who had stood the test of many a scrimmage from Lake Ladoga to the banks of the Rhine, craved rest and would have been glad of extrication from the thickets of German perversity, trickery, and incomprehensibility. The schemes which he had evolved for the permanent unification of all Protestants under his leadership were no match for the bickering enmity that surrounded him. Yet both of them, Duke and King, were under constraint, that of affairs in general and that which the one imposed on the other. It applied to military operations too, and it was applicable to all participants in the war game. Every commander had an opponent whom he wanted to constrain, and vice versa; this one that one, that one this one. The martial dumb show became the more perplexing because mostly the other's goal was obscure and often even his location unknown. It could come about that in the expanse of the land sight was flatly lost of a captain and his ten thousand men until after a while he was lit on like a desert traveller gone astray. Strategy gave no unequivocal clues to intent. Moreover, after a long spring and a short summer, winter was in this instance impending, a season whose rules the King, with his worn-out army, would this time presumably have to observe more closely than a year ago. If anything was still to happen, it must be soon. Where?

For almost two weeks Gustavus stopped at Windsheim, north-east of Nürnberg and on the road to the Main. To Wallenstein it seemed the sensible, therefore probable course that to reach this river was his aim. Five days after the King's departure he broke camp and shifted slightly north without attacking the great city which had again sinned so severely against His Imperial Majesty and for whose protection Oxenstierna had remained behind with a few regiments. The King did not however proceed towards the Main. He chose once more to move south, and at that not to Bavaria but Swabia, the Lech, and Lake Constance. His reasons were trifling. Fresh troops could be recruited in Switzerland. The communications between the Upper Rhine, Swabia, and Bavaria should be kept open. The imperialists under Montecuccoli had had a success on the Lech. Swabia was, incidentally, the area least ravaged and consequently attractive as winter quarters. That was all, and it did not amount to much. Again, as in spring, he overestimated what Arnim could do to defend Saxony, which he must on no account lose and whose leaders never ceased to cast around furtive glances for a means of escape into neutrality. In case of a Saxon emergency, and not to have his path back to the coast cut, he relied on distantly scattered corps north of the Main: the Weimar dukes Wilhelm and his young brother Bernhard, the rising military star, in Franconia and Hesse; his General Baudissin and the Duke of Lüneburg, formerly in Wallenstein's service, who in Lower Saxony occupied some strong places like Wolfen-büttel, Hildesheim, Hanover, and Brunswick. How many soldiers did that make? Barely twenty thousand. Enough, he thought, together with the ten or twelve thousand under Arnim's command. The latter, though, was in Silesia and disinclined to leave. The truth was that the King was fumbling in the dark. His detour to Swabia was militarily senseless. Back to Donauwörth, back to Rain on the Lech, with repetition of his springtime victory. Did he feel the dreariness of the repetition? Many another did.

For almost two weeks Wallenstein, normally well informed about the enemy's movements, knew nothing of the King's southward trek. As late as 6 October he believed him to be in the neighbourhood of Würz-burg, beyond the Main, and Pappenheim's force to be his objective. Unable to save Maastricht from the Dutch, Pappenheim – this restless, recalcitrant warrior, this prima donna thirsting for action, this "swift and sly wit", as Oxenstierna called him – had left the Netherlands and was roving somewhere in the region west of the middle Rhine. Wallen-stein included, or he would have liked to have been able to do so, Pappenheim's eight thousand men in his calculations. With reason he complained, "There is no reliance on Pappenheim". A Bavarian as well as imperial field-marshal, at the head of League as well as imperial units, Pappenheim used his twofold position to do as at any given time he pleased. Wallenstein had disapproved of his fighting in the Nether-lands. "I am Pappenheim's good friend, but I cannot countenance such perilous and far-reaching improprieties." Foolhardy pleas by King Philip that he should himself undertake something against the "braggart Dutch" found their way disregarded into his files. As though he had no other concerns, as though it were his concern to drag the Dutch, cool in their attitude to Gustavus Adolphus, into the Swedish hostilities. After the fall of Maastricht he had sent his cousin, Count Berchtold Waldstein, with a trenchant order to Pappenheim to proceed up the Rhine to Bamberg: he needed him. Pappenheim had replied from Dortmund that he aspired to be in Thuringia in a fortnight although major obstacles in the shape of those non-Catholics, Baudissin, Lüneburg, and Brunswick, were seeking to bar his way. Wallenstein was not yet in receipt of this characteristically evasive message when, in the first week of October, he was hoping to join Pappenheim before the latter was overtaken by the King. That was why he marched on Bamberg, then Coburg. He was doubly mistaken – Pappenheim was not where he expected him, let alone the King. But a step like this always served several purposes. Were the main encounter with Sweden to be missed, Wallenstein's attack would be directed against Saxony so as to obtain winter quarters. There was another reason too.

Immediately after breaking camp in front of Nürnberg he had detailed Field-Marshal Gallas, with twelve thousand men and Holk for his subordinate, against Saxony. His task was "to attack the Elector in earnest". Holk's sally into the neighbourhood of Meissen had merely been a cruel frolic. Present strategy and politics were different. Saxony was to be occupied in its entirety and subjugated in such manner as to enable the winter to be spent there. Neither kindliness nor pillage, fire, cattle seizure or any other spoliation had, he wrote to Gallas, induced the Elector to change his mind, wherefore "now we shall no longer strike terror into, but wage war against him, and keep the land". The infliction of every unnecessary damage was therefore to be stopped forthwith and strictest discipline imposed. Occupation, this time, not a diversion. Let John George lose his land and, if he wanted it back, he would have to make peace. Brandenburg would follow. Gustavus Adolphus's whole system of princely alliances would founder. Because Coburg lay approximately on the road from Nürnberg to Saxony, his move was not in vain even if the principal foe was not met.

Nor was he, for at Coburg on 9 October at the latest Wallenstein obtained news of the King's real whereabouts. More than that, he learned of a fresh tack in the Swedish course. Gustavus, his misgivings aroused by Wallenstein's march to Bamberg, a direction he identified with Saxony, had decided to create a new diversion, against Bavaria, the Danube, Neuburg, then Ingolstadt or Regensburg, which was in fact the old one to the point of unqualified tedium. The imperialist reaction would however have been exactly what the King hoped if matters had rested with the Elector Maximilian. So far he had not ventured to part from Wallenstein, but had accompanied him docilely to Forchheim, Bamberg and Coburg. Now, overcoming his laboriously controlled tremors, he declared that he must with all his adherents instantly turn about to prevent the repetition of last spring's atrocities south of the Danube; the Duke of Friedland would do far better to come with him. The Duke refused. He wanted the crucial encounter to take place in Saxony, the place and time to be of his choosing, not his opponent's. He tried to render it intelligible to the Bavarian. Maximilian would not be restrained. A curious bargain was struck. The semi-Bavarian Pappenheim, provided that he could be found, should belong to Wallenstein whereas the wholly imperialist Aldringen with a few regiments was allotted to the Elector. Hereupon, after three months' intensive cohabitation, the two parted. Maximilian hurried southwards with his own troops and those provided by Wallenstein in advance. Hardly two days' journey away, he fell into his old vice of imploring the Duke for reinforcements, endeavouring to let Austria rather than Bavaria seem to be the cause of his anxiety. "Your Dilection will see that the foe will not allow himself to be drawn out of Bavaria by a diversion, but will want from there to carry war into the imperial Hereditary Lands with the intent thus far sooner to remove the imperial army and *sedem belli* from the Saxon again to the imperial Hereditary Lands." The warning written in hasty hand on one day was out of date the next, that on which Gustavus for the second, third, sixth time wrenched the wheel around and veered north. Donauwörth again, Nürnberg again – familiarity stales. The irony was that the northward hurrying King, the southward scurrying Elector passed pretty close to each other. Maximilian was ignorant of it, but, hearing subsequently of the Swedish ninety degrees deflection, he still tried to interpret this as an assault on Bavaria, for all that in such case it was being undertaken by way of a strange detour through the Upper Palatinate. Wallenstein, deep in Saxony, had to encourage his worried ally like an invalid: "In answer to the same I cannot conceal that the King's intent can in no wise be . . . to turn on . . . the Upper Palatinate and Bavaria." Maximilian had cried "wolf" too often, a habit irritating also to his own officers. "As regards our condition and conduct of war here," the Bavarian Colonel Otto Heinrich Fugger wrote derisively to Wallenstein, "it takes its *more solito* [customary way] and our moods vary according to each letter that arrives from the Bavarian land. If at one hour an enemy horseman lets himself be seen in the neighbourhood of Ingolstadt, then Ingolstadt is lost. The same holds good for Regensburg,

Munich, and Salzburg, and His Imperial Majesty at Vienna could be having his trunks packed."

Why Gustavus Adolphus should again have traversed lengthwise a large part of Germany – 380 miles in seventeen days – is not precisely known. Did the King know? One set of historians believes that a cry for help from the Elector of Saxony, an urgent petition citing "the alliance established between us", a reference to be understood in the sense that to leave Saxony alone would constitute a breach of it, furnishes the explanation. This is countered by the argument that the King had from the start envisaged Wallenstein's invasion and therefore, in the light of reason, could not have been unnerved by it. Is the light of reason sufficient to illuminate human reactions? Another group suggests that at the moment of his hectic change of mind he had no idea of Wallenstein's intentions and was more afraid of a north-west wheeling movement by the imperialists than a march eastwards. Were Wallenstein to occupy the passes of the Thuringian Forest, he would, together with Pappenheim, push a bolt across the wooded regions of central Germany. The Swedes would be cut off from the coast, from Stralsund, from the peninsular homeland. This anxiety, awareness that the way back lay through northern Germany, combined with a longing to escape from his present situation, is supposed to have been, as on a sudden panic, the mainspring of the King's action. We must leave his motives open, but the upshot had been foreseen by Wallenstein. "If the King does not mean to lose himself, he must succour the Elector." Both of them, monarch and duke, the latter, though, far ahead of the former, were on the road to Saxony.

Wallenstein's purposes in moving on Saxony were multiple and have to be differentiated. One was to subdue Saxony and force it to make peace. Another was to have the army provisioned during winter by the Saxons rather than the Bohemians and Austrians. A third was to fight in Saxony the decisive battle which would put an end to the Swedish mischief: "If we reduce and triumph over the enemy, as I hope that with God's help 'twill be, all his affairs in Swabia, Bavaria, and Franconia are lost." This third purpose did not square with the second. Winter quarters and a decisive battle are as different from one another as holidays and work unless the battle is regarded (as was done at various moments) as one for winter quarters. A fourth purpose was to coerce Saxony into surrender of Silesia: "I hope that Arnim will not be able to dally in Silesia, else his master's land will be lost." This did not fit in well with the expectation of a decisive battle. It would be fought under more favourable auspices if the Saxon army remained a distant spectator. Thought out in mid-summer, he now had this plan constantly before him. Let even the most robust of intellects try to introduce order into such a miscellany of arbitrary and accidental happenings, of roving armies, of feelers, plans, and counter-plans.

Wallenstein did try. The occupation of Saxony was the next step and must go ahead in tidy fashion. The country must be treated with consideration, as he repeatedly told his commanders. "Pray that he issue orders for the land to be conserved because this winter we shall have to live on it." The regiments carried their own livestock. Other victuals, particularly cereals, had to be collected in advance and stored in depots along the route. None the less if Saxony was to maintain the army in winter it had to be paid. New troops had moreover to be recruited, artillery, powder, and lead to be procured. The money could no longer come from contributions because by far the greater part of Germany, especially the imperialist towns, formerly the most useful source, was in Swedish hands. Wallenstein was more directly dependent than before 1630 on subsidies promised him from the Hereditary Lands, also on what Spain had agreed to furnish. The Spaniards made excuses. So did the Bohemian, Moravian, Austrian, Carinthian Estates. The Generalissimo had to beg, in the interest of "the entire Most Worshipful Arch-House and the universal Catholic body", for two hundred thousand taler, a paltry fraction of that to which he was entitled. The Commander-in-Chief of Catholic christendom was indeed to be found squabbling with Vienna over couriers' expenses – he financed the journey there and back for those dispatched by him and, he argued, it was improper that those coming from the capital should expect him to defray their return outlay.

During the second half of 1632 he was on a good footing with the Emperor. Good on paper, for it was almost five years since they had met face to face. Wallenstein's reports to Ferdinand were comparatively detailed as regards military business, their tone sometimes almost warm-hearted, and they were frequent. On occasion he would dictate three such letters in a day. From Coburg he sent, a courteous gesture, a pack of Saxon setters – he knew his sovereign's dearest care and passion. No one could maintain that Ferdinand left altogether unobserved the conduct of hostilities by the man who was allegedly supreme commander in the most absolute form. He meddled thoroughly. Was there not some justification for the Elector of Bavaria's fears? Did not appearances, and unfortunately far more reality, controvert Wallenstein's appreciation of the situation in Silesia? Nevertheless the imperial misgivings were delicately phrased and they would end with a hint, a proposal, a plea. Never friends, and more of strangers to each other than even during the first generalate, both behaved affably. They had need of one another and an enemy in common.

Bamberg, Coburg, Plauen, Zwickau, Altenburg, Grimma, Wurzen near Leipzig. This advance, in the second half of October, met with no resistance. He stayed in each of the larger towns for a few days, issuing information and instructions to the corps operating independently of the main army – Marradas and Ilow in Silesia, Gallas at Meissen, Aldringen in Bavaria, Montecuccoli in Swabia, Pappenheim somewhere. From there too went his orders to the duchy, never out of his mind. He intends to spend the winter at Gitschin; he wishes the Council Hall to be finished at last. Then it strikes him that he should lay down afresh and definitively the dynastic order of succession. First in line is to be Count Maximilian, his cousin, who shall already be allowed to call himself Prince of Friedland and is also to receive a monthly allowance of a thousand gulden. The condition is that during the Duke's lifetime he has no right whatever to interfere in government affairs. If Maximilian dies without issue and the Waldstein stock – on one and the same page it was written Waldstein and Wallenstein – becomes extinct, the Harrach family shall enter upon his rights. The details were formulated between two military and economic dispatches at a moment of approaching vital crisis. Astounding, unless it was the crisis which caused him to think of death. Perhaps he felt wearier, sicker, more afflicted than he let his entourage know. Formerly illness had heightened his value. Now it was advisable to conceal it as well as possible.

Forever the problem of the country's size, the country's poverty, in spite of which it must provide sustenance, through which it was necessary to scatter in order to obtain that sustenance; the slow back and forth crawl of news; the ignorance of the enemy's actions and reactions. And as a result of that, fluctuation in plans. Originally Wallenstein had wanted to march straight on Dresden. There Elector John George, formally responsible, sat in his castle calling for help. Help, the General calculated, must come to him from Gustavus Adolphus and from Arnim's Saxon army. Arnim was however at present deaf to his master's supplications. Were he to pull back to Saxony, the imperial corps under Marradas and Ilow which he was tying down in Silesia would follow. Nothing would be gained, but the liberated church would, amidst the tears of a hundred thousand faithful, crumble. Since it was however to be assumed that Arnim had co-ordinated his moves with the King, appearances spoke against a desire by the Swede to seek a decision in Saxony. Gustavus would, Wallenstein concluded on 3 November, turn on Bohemia from Franconia, merging his troops somewhere half along the way with the Saxons. Maximilian ought therefore to remain with his Bavarians in the Upper Palatinate, not far from Bohemia, while Aldringen should with his imperial units advance north-east so as to be on the spot in case of an emergency, whether in Bohemia, whether in Saxony. And this all the more because the barter transaction was not functioning – Pappenheim was still not at Wallenstein's disposal. Protests by Maximilian that this scheme was against the agreement and that he could not spare Aldringen. Diplomatic dawdling by Aldringen. Some twenty messengers were sent chasing after the roving or unreachable Pappenheim; he was to proceed to Saxony immediately, Wallenstein expected to meet him at Leipzig. No replies or evasive ones. The last was to the effect that he had seized Hildesheim, a town over one hundred miles northwards, extorting a month's pay for his soldiers. Were Wallenstein to send him a large number of troops and a large sum of money, he felt confident that he could lure the main body of the Swedish army to Lower Germany and finish it off there. On 29 October Wallenstein, not yet in receipt of this enthusiastic missive dated 13 October, became very impatient. He did not know whether Pappenheim was alive or dead, well or ill, and, if well, where he was. "That my lord should remain abroad so long and does not hasten his approach ... astonishes Us no little. Wherefore it is Our wish again to remind him to leave aside all other undertakings and to advance upon Leipzig at once ... My lord will know how to obey without an hour's fail." Two days later he had news from Holk. "Good tidings! Field-Marshal Pappenheim has been found. He besieges Erfurt." Erfurt was at least much nearer than Hildesheim. But why besiege this paltry nook on which, if taken, a garrison must be wasted? Wallenstein had always been opposed to long sieges. Years ago he had been critical of Tilly's leaning towards that form of strategy. He did not need Erfurt. He needed Pappenheim and his corps. That was the tenor of the message carried by his twenty-first express rider to the recovered paladin.

On 22 October he fell in with Holk's detachment at Brunn. Henceforward this capable commander remained as his chief of staff in his immediate or close proximity. It was Holk who prevailed on him to by-pass Dresden and march on Leipzig. From there it would be possible to reach and cross the Elbe farther north at Torgau. Gallas was to hold the Elbe front farther upstream, with Meissen and Pirna, north and south respectively of Dresden, as well as Freiberg, south-east of the Elbe and pointing to Bohemia. A reader looking at a map will from these dispositions gain the impression of large-scale strategy. Gallas's corps, widely fanned out, was an isthmus in the direction of Bohemia if Sweden and Saxony came that way, a bridge across the Elbe if Arnim tried a downstream Oder and cross-country approach. The main body of the army, for the occupation of Saxony, stretched farther north as far as or across the Elbe. The scattered corps none the less lay sufficiently close for them to be able within a matter of days to link up with one another. "Let things come as they may," wrote Wallenstein serenely, "the Elector is in a great labyrinth. The ice is beginning to break under him at all corners." On 1 November Holk occupied Leipzig in good – comparatively good – order, as reports by the citizens attested. No atrocities, this time. Within the limits of human capacity the General's intention was fulfilled.

His intention, not his plan of campaign, in so far as any such was feasible. He was issuing orders and countermanding them in accordance with the enemy's, no, the various enemies' moves. On 31 October an order went to Ilow to see to the co-ordination of his operations with Gallas. On 25 October Ilow was however still at Troppau, in northern-most Silesia, which Wallenstein could not know, and from there to the Dresden region is a far cry. On 1 November an order to Gallas to cross the Elbe and to find Ilow so that their corps should bar Arnim's way to Saxony. On 10 November an order to Gallas to wheel around imme-diately to Meissen. No, not Meissen, but in direction of the main army, and this to be performed by forced marches. It would not, after all, be feasible to impede Arnim's approach. Why not, so suddenly? There was a reason, but the letter passed over it in silence. The Duke of Lüneburg, Gustavus Adolphus's ally, moving up the eastern bank of the Elbe from Lower Saxony, had occupied the fortress of Torgau hitherto held only by weak Saxon units. To Wallenstein this was an unanticipated turn. Reluctant to undertake any serious engagement eastwards with a secondary adversary, he abandoned his advance on the Elbe. His reluc-tance had its real root in news, sent on 2 November, by Aldringen, always well informed and always a shrewd judge of situations. "The King marches against Schweinfurt and Königshofen with all the troops he was still able to collect in Franconia. 'Tis not to be doubted but that he will proceed through the Thuringian Forest to Erfurt and will seek to impede Your Princely Grace's design." The reading was plain enough – Gustavus, told of the imperial forces' extension and thinning out, was now seeking to force the crucial encounter on Saxon soil. As from this moment there must no longer be dispersal, no longer fragmentation, but concentration. A welcome start, precisely on the day when Wallenstein received Aldringen's fateful message, was made by the arrival in Leipzig of the long-lost Pappenheim, an accession of eight thousand men together with, for all his caprices, this masterly leader on a scene of battle.

That was on 6 November. Aldringen's message was already badly out of date. News travels faster than armies, but not that much faster. This had moreover had to double back upon itself – from northern Franconia to Regensburg, where Aldringen was, and from there back again to Saxony. On 3 November Gustavus was already in Arnstadt, south of the Thuringian Forest. A few days of rest, merger with Bernhard von Weimar's regiments. On 8 November the reinforced army entered Erfurt. On 9 November its advance-guard reached Naumburg on the Saale. The Swedish thrust, executed with "accustomed precipitancy", imperilled Wallenstein's position. He had meant to secure the passage of the Elbe at Torgau. He had failed. Thereby the link between Arnim and the Lüneburg–Saxon contingent at Torgau continued unbroken. Gallas's corps, at times envisaged as conquering the territory east of the Elbe, sufficed to make sure of the road to Bohemia, but no more than that. A withdrawal into the Hereditary Lands was not, though, if it could be prevented, admissible because that was the one point which, after all the planning and exertions of this year, must still hold good. The prospect of a battle somewhere in the plain between the Elbe and the Saale was unattractive, particularly if the King were to succeed in gaining numerical superiority by addition of the Torgau garrison, some six thousand men, or possibly Arnim's Saxons, twice that number. Wallenstein's instinctive preference was for concentration. The site of the crucial encounter would be wherever he stood, and the more soldiery he had in the immediate vicinity, the better. Nevertheless strategic, still more political considerations compelled dispersal. The imperial army's strength was theoretically supposed to be a hundred thousand men. In spring it had – perhaps – been that. A season's campaigning, with clashes, diseases, desertions, makes inroads. In September he had warned of daily increasing weakness. For more or less cogent reasons units, at the present of no help, were stationed from Alsace to the Upper Palatinate under Ossa, Montecuccoli, Aldringen, in Silesia under Ilow, in Lower Saxony under Gronsfeld. The troops directly under Wallenstein's command may have totalled 35,000. Whatever was about to occur between the adversaries would be between fragments of their two armies.

Naumburg lay on the right bank of the Saale. Colonel de Suys was sent with two regiments to make sure of this bridgehead. The Swedes were already there. At this point Wallenstein knew that he was caught between two fires. Better to smother that in the west before it spread to that in the east. He was coming too late, he wrote on 10 November to Aldringen, who had at last announced his approach: "We expect tomorrow already to meet the King." He marched on Weissenfels, also on the Saale and an hour from Naumburg, with both forces, Pappenheim's and his own. If Gustavus emerged, he would more than outnumber him on ground that he liked. Gustavus did not emerge. As in summer at Nürnberg, he hastily adopted a defensive position which used to advantage Naumburg's town-walls. How swiftly such fortification can proceed is well known. An assault, with the incalculably heavy sacrifices involved, was not Wallenstein's habit. Every single human life was costly, not of course because it was a human life, but because it was so difficult to replace. Was he, for his part, to repeat the Nürnberg procedure and build a counter-encampment? In summer that was practicable, not in late, dank autumn when the troops wanted firm roofs over their heads. Furthermore, were he to tie himself down on the Saale, the Saxons would the more easily cross the Elbe and Leipzig be lost. The tongues of flame would dart closer and closer to each other. He consulted his colonels, through Holk and Pappenheim. He decreed what they advised – the march back into the plain, peace and quiet. On 14 November he returned to his headquarters at Lützen, south-west of Leipzig.

The decision was subsequently construed as being dictated by traitorous intent or as evidence of at least indecisiveness. To act in the immediate proximity of an enemy always astir, always aggressive as though he were not there! "Although the Friedlander had a fine opportunity to attack the foe," snarled a lampoon two years later, "he thought that the foe too must conform to his wishes and likewise keep a truce with him." We grant that in the first instance the army's dispersal at the exact moment when the long awaited crucial encounter beckoned and threatened, the notion that this was the time for a cosy nook by the chimney-piece, strikes us also as odd. To be wise after the event is easy. The fact is that the situation was as in these hours it presented itself to Wallenstein, and he was by no means alone in the view that he took.

Had that energetic fighter Holk or that wily, mettlesome commander Pappenheim seen it otherwise, we would know of it.

From Holk's papers as chief of staff we do know that the concept behind the move was a large-scale dispersal rather than simply retirement into winter quarters. His own orders were to make a thrust towards Westphalia, taking in Minden, Osnabrück, Paderborn, Münster, Dortmund, and in the direction of Cologne. His note, "All enlistment officers to accompany me", is very revealing and paralleled by Aldringen's instructions to muster recruits in southern Germany. Pappenheim, with four regiments of infantry and five of cavalry, was to occupy the country between the Saale and the Weser, in the first place Merseburg and Halle, thereafter Aschersleben, Quedlinburg, and Halberstadt. This would not have been a matter of retirement into winter quarters in Saxony. Apart from the need for a bigger stretch of territory from which to squeeze food and money out of the towns, a bolt was to be drawn right across central Germany south of the main Swedish concentration of power. Saxony remained the focal point. Four regiments under Melchior von Hatzfeld were dispatched to Eilenburg, north-east of Leipzig, to keep an eye on Torgau; two, under Colonels de Suys and Contreras, to Altenburg; ten, under Wallenstein's direct command, covered Leipzig and looked towards Naumburg. Southwards detachments from Gallas's corps guarded the strongholds of Gera, Zwickau, Chemnitz, Freiberg, and Frauenstein. There lay the road from Leipzig to Bohemia, the road of withdrawal. What catches the eye is a gap from Leipzig to the Elbe between the two main chains of garrison-posts established to north and south. Were the Swedes to try and traverse it, Wallenstein meant to fall upon them from the north.

The troops were to be ready to start by seven in the morning on 15 October, "stand against the enemy in the field until nine", and then, under cover of a screen provided by the Croats and Trčkas' dragoons till dusk, scatter to all points of the compass. Pappenheim left for Halle, which he reached in the afternoon and immediately occupied. Colonel Hatzfeld and his four regiments made for Eilenburg. Major-General Rudolf Colloredo advanced with a few companies of infantry and Croats to the reinforcement of Weissenfels.

A stream called Rippach flows from the south on a north-westerly course towards the Saale and had bridges at the villages of Rippach and Poserna. At this time its narrow bed was full to overflowing, its waters percolated the meadows. Wallenstein knew this route; he had on the preceding day, during his march back, thought it bad. Now Colloredo

was scarcely across the brook when he encountered hostile units, with
more of them behind, and yet more on their heels – Gustavus Adolphus'
army. At four o'clock, before dawn, Gustavus had left Naumburg,
intending to slip past Wallenstein through the above-mentioned gap and
arrive within reach of the Lüneberg and Saxon forces at Torgau. Prisoners fell into his hands. From them he learned, though he could
scarcely credit it, that Pappenheim was away, other regiments under
Wallenstein's command were also gone, and that therefore if he made for
Lützen immediately he must be more than a match for the enemy. His
decision was instantaneous. Colloredo, for his part, fulfilled the duty that
chance had thrust upon him. As long as possible he and his preposterously
small force had to delay passage of the stream by the units of musketeers,
horsemen, and field-guns trundling towards him while messenger after
messenger was sent galloping to Lützen with news of how things stood
and what was at hand. Shortly before two o'clock the agreed emergency
signal, three cannon-shots, reverberated from the town: about turn,
hurry back, all who hear. The aide-de-camp who sped to Halle carried a
letter for Pappenheim from Wallenstein, and never had a missive been
composed in more pressing terms. "The enemy moves in. Let my lord
put aside all else and, with his men and pieces, take to the road so that
early on the morrow he can be with us. For my part I remain my lord's
devoted AhzM. Lützen, the 15th Nov. in the Yr of Our Lord 1632." As
with most of Wallenstein's letters, there was a postscript to this most
urgent dispatch: "He is already as far as where yesterday the route was
bad." The "bad route" was the marshy path across the Rippach in the
neighbourhood of Poserna. Thanks to Colloredo's resistance it was
four o'clock before the mass of the Swedes was across the stream, too
late in the day for them, since a battle could not be fought in the dark.
Wallenstein, with a few hundred yards between him and the enemy,
had gained the space of a lengthy night to make good his miscalculation.
Reinforcements were pouring in, first those from the immediate vicinity
between Lützen and Leipzig. On their arrival Holk conducted them by
torchlight to their stations. They had forthwith to dig themselves in
and throw up entrenchments with those sharp shovels called *reyč* in
Czech.

The relatively safest as well as the most natural strategy would have
been to hold a north–south position because the advance of the Swedes
was from the west. Had they won the battle, as the saying goes, that
would have allowed a withdrawal to the south where establishment of
contact with Gallas would ensure the line to Bohemia. The General

opted for an east–west disposition. That was the riskier alternative. Were the Swedes to attack the imperialists' left flank and turn it, their only way of escape would be in the direction of central Germany, the route taken by Tilly after Breitenfeld. The position was however tactically superior and its choice not a matter of improvisation. An operational plan has survived, allegedly drawn up in Wallenstein's own hand. This is not the case, as the writing is someone else's, but it was certainly drafted by him, one or two days earlier, seeing that regiments no longer present on 16 November play a part in it. Even in its blood-stained state it shows substantially the same grouping as that adopted during the night of 15–16 November. Perhaps Pappenheim had the document on him, together with the urgent summons to return, or possibly some other commander carried it with him. At any rate it proves Wallenstein to have studied the lie of the land in good time.

The ground was in fact as favourable as flat terrain can be.

On the right wing stood Lützen, a place with some three hundred houses and a strong castle in the middle. Adjoining it were the citizens' loam-walled gardens. Four windmills and their outhouses stood a little higher. From the town's northern end emerged the post-road to Leipzig, one of the best in Germany, with broad, deep ditches on either side. Beyond Lützen it made a shallow curve, then proceeded due east until it reached the so-called Flossgraben, a small canal used for timber shipments, of inconsiderable depth but with a firm, gravelly bottom. At this point the road rose and, together with the canal, furnished a ready-made defensive position. It would have been a good thing to extend the front to there, but the troops entrenching themselves behind the post-road were not enough for that nor, to Holk's regret, could they be spread as far as the Skölziger Wäldchen, a little wood in the east. "In Lützen castle and thorp," he reported, "were four hundred men, although the need was for a thousand. As many should justly have been in the wood on the left, had they been available." They were not. If all went well, it would be Pappenheim's cavalry, but not his infantry, who would before noon become available. A mile and a half was the widest front over which the order of battle could stretch.

For the imperialists their disposition was new. Wallenstein showed what he had learned from the Swedes. The tercios, those monstrosities of massed military squares, had disappeared. To give greater flexibility, and for fear of envelopment by the foe, files were nowhere more than ten deep. In the centre the first line was composed of five divisions, each a thousand strong. The second had two more of the same, separated

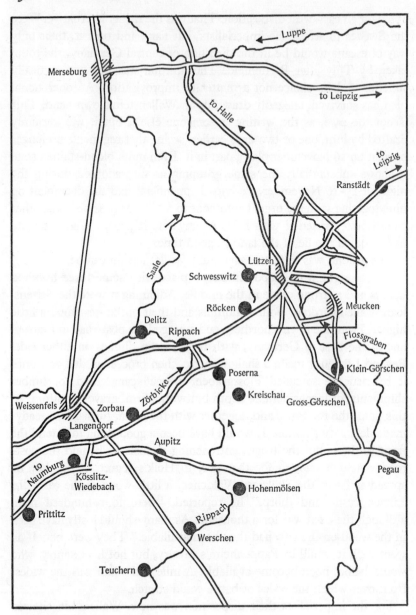

Lützen and Environment

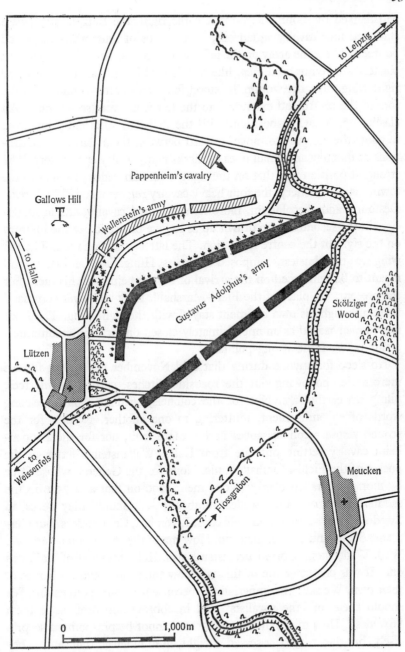

Lützen – Battle Plan

and flanked by mounted troops. On the right, the Lützen wing, were stationed four cavalry squadrons, with groups of musketeers dispersed between. The same array on the left. And there was yet a third line, with clusters of five hundred men, likewise flanked by riders. In front of the right wing, near the windmills, stood fourteen quarter-cannon. To the fore of the centre and extending to the left wing were seven more. An elastic, up-to-date disposition, with the divisions sufficiently far apart to allow the reserves to move forward between them; large concentrations of infantry and small ones of marksmen; cavalry everywhere. The strongest position was that on the right, with barricades reaching to the town, massed artillery, the four heavy cavalry regiments of Holk, Trčka, Desfours, and Piccolomini, more lightly armed cavalry, and arquebusiers in the second line so drawn up as to give protection to the infantry on the right of the centre formation. The latter was strong too. The left wing was the flimsiest, composed of Croats, Hungarians, and Poles, and meant to be reinforced on the arrival of Pappenheim with his men. For the present, "in place of the Field-Marshal", Holk took over command there although his own regiment stayed with the right wing. The front must be envisaged as an approximately closed one with intercommunication between the strong-points.

No sleep for anyone during that cold November night. Not for the mercenaries hollowing out the roadside ditches, cutting down trees, piling up earthworks. Not for the colonels, striding about, speaking words of encouragement, muttering to one another. Neither for the scouts, whose reconnaissances bore meagre fruit, nor for the Pappenheim cavalry setting out late from Halle, Wallenstein's letter in the pocket of the Field-Marshal's tunic. None for the General, whose force by morning totalled nearly 16,000 men, 8200 on foot and 7500 in the saddle. How many the Swedes numbered .. Should they be called Swedes? They were not only Swedes, Livonians, Courlanders, but Germans, Scots, and Frenchmen too. How many the Protestants were . . .. Well, Wallenstein sported Protestants also. Holk, his chief of staff, was one. It was characteristic of this war how the parties had no names of their own. We say "the imperialists" because it is more convenient. We should speak of "the royalists" and in abbreviation pronounce them "Swedes". How many the Swedes were cannot be pin-pointed so precisely, but they may be assessed at eighteen to nineteen thousand. They were at any rate more than the imperialists. In addition to their heavy guns they had what Wallenstein lacked, forty light, mobile pieces.

He saw the battle as a defensive operation. Not a foot, according to

Holk's report, did he mean to budge, but sooner be blighted on the spot. With the one minor exception of Wolgast, every one of his few battles had basically been defensive, with Nürnberg as the most recent and splendidly successful example. Defensive and, when all went well, followed up by an attack launched from the defensive, as with the sally across the Dessau bridge. His aim had been to inveigle Gustavus into Saxony and to destroy him. Now the King was here almost within gun-range, yet Wallenstein none the less found himself taken unawares. He assumed charge of the right wing. To be in charge signified in this context to be in close proximity to the mêlée, often amidst, and sometimes ahead of it. That was the only way for commanders to influence an action. It could not be achieved either from the rear or a strategic vantage-point. Such was in any case nowhere available in this flat country. Aching though he was, he abandoned his litter and planted his feet in velvet-wrapped stirrups. Some say that he rode from detachment to detachment uttering words of cheer, whereas others maintain that he vouchsafed his rows of gladiators no more than silent, gloomy looks. The latter seems more likely. Leading his men in prayer or inspiring them with oratory had never been his forte.

Taciturn or loquacious, for him the day ahead was onerous. At stake were all the fame he had accumulated against the northern intruder, the rival whom he would not abide in his preserve, the future of his plans, and whether he could make his winter quarters in Germany or must retire to the cramped, impoverished Hereditary Lands. This last factor may even have been sensed by the common soldiery, the sacrificial victims.

Gustavus, aware that the passing hours could increase the enemy's numbers, wanted to make an early start, but fog inhibited any move until past eight o'clock. Between nine and ten the artillery was stationed in the neighbourhood of the Skölzinger Wäldchen. From here the Swedes advanced upon Neuchen, the hamlet lying in a south-westerly direction, and later as far as the southern corner of Lützen. Shortly before eleven the battle proper began "with such a fury as no man hath ever seen or heard" and continued so. "Until deep into the night one encounter ensued on another, with the utmost resolution in the world, for whole regiments of the enemy that sustained the brunt of battle were slain, whilst on our side sundry thousand men too were left upon the field, most of the officers dead or wounded." Wallenstein's very own words, penned the following day. To be followed soon by more, much more written matter. From imperialist officers, Giulio Diodati, Holk, Desfours (of whose report only a fragment remains), and Gallas (for all that he was not there). From unit commanders, preachers, secretaries, court chamberlains, and gentlemen-in-waiting on the Swedish side. From journalists, present or nearby, and straightway ready with their veracious and correct narration of the bloody battle between His Royal Majesty of Sweden and the imperial army. Pamphleteers and chroniclers took their share from eye-witnesses of whom one had experienced this, another that, but none of them the event in its entirety and who were often unable, because of the gruesome chaos in smoke and fog, to discern what they did experience. These publications, brief, written under pressure, with omissions due to haste or concealments due to slyness, caused later researchers much trouble in reconstructing the con- current and successive order of events. How Gustavus directed his first, most powerful attack against Wallenstein's left wing as being the weakest, most promising target. How forthwith disorder spread there and infected the centre, the imperialists being driven out of the ditches which the Swedish cavalry, Finns, Ingermanländer, Småländer, vaulted, with Holk unable to prevent his men falling back. How at noon Pappen- heim arrived –

> Hey ho, there he comes ridden
> The mad Pappenheim right grim
> Fence and foss so quickly leaps
> That his hair behind him sweeps
> Hardly have I room for doubt
> That Old Nick himself rides out

– how he arrived at the right moment, with the Sparr, Bönninghausen, and Bredow cuirassiers, Lamboy's arquebusiers, and dragoons, and Croats, three thousand men in all, arrived and assumed command, ordering the Croats to disperse far leftwards in extended line and take the second Swedish line in the rear while he by frontal attack regained the ground already lost. A wire-mesh missile,* tearing open his whole side, soon made an end of him. His trumpeter dragged him out of the fray, but his people, seeing it, at once lost their stomach for the fight, as though this one man counted for so much. Senior officers, Colonel Bönninghausen, Lieutenant-Colonel Hofkirchen with the Sparr regi- ment in his charge, fled far behind and, hungry, looted their own side's

---

* A lump of molten metal strands, it could not accurately be termed a bullet or shell because it had no casing, a contributory factor to its vicious character which put it in the category of outlawed weapons (translator's note).

baggage-train on the way. Pappenheim, when his trumpeter told him that it was his cuirassiers who were fleeing, wanted to wrench himself free and return to the fight, crying, "O my brothers-in-arms, the Lord have mercy! Is there not one who will still fight loyally for the Emperor?" and then, "Is there none who can staunch my blood?" Not a soul, except the trumpeter Ehinger who bore him to his coach. Pappenheim took a ring from his finger, kissed it, and asked him to bring it to his wife. Wallenstein was to be told that he had died for the Catholic faith and he commended his widow and orphans to the Duke's protection. When he had kissed and bitten the trumpeter's hand, saying that he did it not to a trumpeter but a gallant man, he expired in Ehinger's arms, leaving later generations to see where his blood had seeped through to the urgent dispatch in his tunic. That was what befell Pappenheim. For the time being only the trumpeter and the page Holländer who rode beside the carriage knew it, but not those who ran away and not those who stood their ground, and not the hardly pressed infantry in the centre who bewailed, Where must Pappenheim be that he does not come to our aid with his cavalry? On the left the battle was downright lost. It would have been too in the centre, stripped now of its mounted flank support and with its battery, the seven quarter-cannon, despite grievous resistance wrested away, had not at that instant, shortly before one o'clock, fog fallen again, hiding the sun and the dead. To the far left moreover the Croats had fulfilled their task. The swift, motley rabble, surging beyond the Flossgraben and reaching behind the Swedes, blowing up ammunition wagons and plundering baggage, caused such disorder and rout that three regiments had to be thrown against them while the link between the first and second Swedish lines was torn apart. That proved to be the deliverance of Wallenstein's left wing which was soon to be restored by other, yet greater efforts.

It is possible to put together and establish beyond all doubt what was happening simultaneously in other parts of this horror-laden plain, with things developing quite differently from what has just been described, though in such a way as to cause events to interact upon one another, even when a thousand or two thousand yards lay between. How Bernhard von Weimar's attack against Wallenstein's right wing was broken by the hail of shot from the fourteen field-pieces near the windmills, by the smoke blown from the flames of Lützen in the faces of his German horsemen, and by the Holk, Desfours, Piccolomini, and Trčka regiments of cuirassiers led by Wallenstein in person. How they threw back Bernhard's cavalry, thrusting in southward and eastward among the infantry so that the struggle veered towards the centre wing and the imperialists there obtained relief from their right. How Holk, who on Pappenheim's arrival had relinquished his temporary command and galloped back, found his commander-in-chief amidst the Swedish infantry. "The Duke bore himself very bravely and skilfully, fighting two hours against the infantry with four regiments of horse ... and was entirely surrounded until Holk returned with the cavalry and seconded him." Holk's words are confirmed by the testimony of a Swede that he "was some four paces from Wallenstein, eight shots being fired at him, and he laying himself right across the saddle. Whether now anything struck him, no one knows ....." He became oblivious of his illness, his fatigue, his weariness of mind. Just once more he played at martial youth, as at Fort St Andrea, twenty-seven years ago. All of them, marauders, careerists, intriguers, became oblivious of themselves. In the fray a man of mettle, if he is a man of mettle, is that alone and yields entirely to the lethal frenzy, lust of battle, and the gasping strain. Certain others, though, who were not men of mettle, became oblivious of themselves in a different sense. More of that in a moment. Research has furthermore proved how the Swedish right wing, with Pappenheim wounded and the Croats not yet terrorizing its second line, was now crushing all resistance to its advance, in the centre too, but just the opposite was happening on the left. Weimar let the King know that he would not be able to hold his position for long, whereupon Gustavus, with the Småländer regiment behind him, left to go to his hard-pressed subordinate's aid. Spurring across the field, he reached the edge of the likewise badly mauled infantry on the centre's left and plunged deep into its ranks. The deference with which his own people let him by disclosed to the enemy that here was a personality of high distinction. A shot from a musket crippled his left arm. Amidst the smoke and fog the heavy, short-sighted rider could no longer control his steed. He bade his companion, Franz Albrecht von Lauenburg, to extract him from the turmoil. But, blundering helplessly, he met with a contingent of imperialists who killed him with pistol-shots and sword-thrusts in the head and in the back, then despoiled him, stripping him of watch and chain, silver spurs, hat, clothes, and boots, so that the naked corpse of the Lion from Midnight, the crusader and Don Quixote, lay upon the naked earth. That happened about one o'clock. Somewhat, but not much, later than Pappenheim's fatal injury and the flight of his cavalry, almost simultaneously with the flanking attack by the Croats. Historians know of the simultaneity. Those laying about one another in the tumult could not.

None the less the rumour that it was the King who had been slain soon spread among the Wallenstein soldiery on the right, and their leaders were inclined to lend it credence. "Inasmuch as his body was seen," wrote Holk, "the whole battle was on his side won." So it was, or appeared to be, on this side, at this moment. Wallenstein thinned out his right wing, which he regarded as safe, in favour of the left which he regarded as menaced. He dispatched there the Piccolomini and Goertz cuirassiers, Piccolomini taking over Pappenheim's command. Holk, the man whom the General did not want to do without, stayed on the right.

The Swedes, or at least those in the vicinity of the illustrious calamity, learnt also of the King's death. The soldiers surmised the omen of the riderlessly straying horse. Gustavus's equerry first brought the Duke of Weimar the news. One of the commanders, Knyphausen, was for breaking off the engagement if possible. Bernhard, ambitious and nursing a belief in the King's jealousy of his talent, wanted it to continue for his personal glory.

It lasted another six hours as against the two whose multifariously turbulent course has so far been described. These six hours have not been as thoroughly investigated as the two at the start. It has not been feasible, so wildly and more wildly yet, so blindly and more blindly yet, so desperately did matters now proceed. But approximately they went like this:

Left wing. On their way to it Colonels Goertz and Piccolomini meet with that waverer, Lieutenant-Colonel Hofkirchen, commanding the Sparr regiment in the Pappenheim contingent, and his cavalry. He has not run away as far as some others, Colonel Bönninghausen and Brevet Captain Count Louis Broglia, for instance, and he is slightly ashamed of himself. Indeed, if he did not feel so dizzy from fear, he would probably like to be one of the party. The officers appeal to him – the King is dead, the battle almost won, he should now remain with them and save his honour. Hofkirchen cannot steel himself to it. For a while he slinks with his people around the back of the front before eventually, and unobtrusively, attaching himself to the right wing. He imagines things to be less terrifying there. An error. The left can manage without, better without, him. Piccolomini, whatever else he may be, is what Wallenstein with respect terms a soldier. The charges by his cuirassiers, seven in number, became legendary. He led them, astride five different horses as one after another they in turn dropped wounded under him, and he himself is said to have been struck by six musket-shots which he simply

ignored. The infantry at the centre of the formation, believing Pappenheim to have at last arrived, supports his efforts with freshly revived
courage, and artillery fire from the windmills supports him too. The
Swedes have to relinquish the captured battery. Now, according to
Wallenstein's account, whole regiments who have borne the brunt of
battle are mown down, the Yellow Brigade and the Blue Brigade "which
in a moment is transformed into a mound of dead, a wonderful sight",
as Diodati wrote. Swedish cavalry is fleeing and seeks refuge "behind
the miller's cottage". So here, for a longer space than any during this
long time, all goes well if that expression is permissible for what men
are doing to one another and their poor animals. Victorious huzzas buzz
through the air.

For a time too all goes well on the right, else the interplay of support
for Piccolomini by the artillery at the windmills would not have been
possible. The fickleness of fortune in battle is proverbial. If before noon
it was the left wing which did not come up to expectations and almost
disintegrated, causing nervous souls to look for shelter on the right, in
the afternoon the shoe was on the other foot. This reversal and Gustavus's
death do hang together. Its effect on the Swedes is totally different from
that of Pappenheim's fatal injury on the imperialists or that which, say,
Wallenstein's death would have had on them. Wallenstein is a man to
be feared, not loved. His eclipse would have broken the spell, every scrap
of discipline would have been subverted into turmoil and *sauve-qui-peut*.
The hero and the man of prayer, the blue-eyed King, was loved, unequivocally by the northerners, even by the Germans. Young Weimar,
a sound psychologist, counts on that. He dins a longing for vengeance
into the soldiers' ears. They want to recover the corpse, somewhere
lying around. They want, despite their loss, to win the battle there
where it is most difficult to win. So Piccolomini's seven attacks are
matched by an untold number of Swedish ones at the other end of the
field. A hurricane of revenge. It sweeps them far forward. To the corpse,
which is found and borne to the rear. To the trenches, across the
trenches, to the windmills, taken one by one, and the quarter-cannon,
turned against their masters with consequences terrible for those in the
region of the ammunition stores established far behind. To quote Gallas,
"... and again they cause disorder among our cavalry, so that our
artillery stands exposed while our infantry, left uncovered by the cavalry,
closed ranks with their fellows ... and did not lose a foot of ground."
Obscure, at a first reading, as all these reports are. Revealing, at a
second, which renders manifest that the infantry of the centre formation

stood fast although let down by the cavalry on the right. "The Pappen-heimers, though, threw our right wing into confusion." The Pappen-heimers? What can Holk mean? He is referring to that bundle of nerves, Lieutenant-Colonel Hofkirchen, who now causes the same disaster on the right wing as during the morning he did on the left. We know it from the verdict of the proceedings against him. A reliable document, its evidence is that Hofkirchen refused to obey an express order of the Generalissimo, in the first instance indeed galloping senselessly at the head of his regiment towards the enemy, but looking round in fright when they came near, turning his horse's head away, and taking to his heels, with all his riders following him like sheep their bell-wether. This piece of deplorable insubordination was not without influence upon others. The arquebusiers of Colonel von Hagen, for instance, as emerges from the verdict against that officer. Had Hagen not run away, it says, the right wing would not in part have been broken and complete victory would not have eluded the Generalissimo. It truly was on the right, not on the left, that it eluded him, Piccolomini being unable to exploit his achievement on the left because he obtained no further back-ing there and the centre also becoming more isolated through events on the left. The semi-official report by Colonel Diodati conceals the fact by letting the heroism of the leaders glow resplendently.

> The Generalissimo was with habitual intrepidity everywhere at the head of his troops, and where rout had set in he brought back into action those who had given ground, joined in the hand-to-hand fighting with the enemy. . . . His Highness was struck in the left hip by a musket-ball, but he remained impervious to this shot, which did not penetrate the flesh, as to a thousand other cannon and musket missiles. Count Harrach, his Grand Chamberlain, close to him received a musket-ball in the throat which passed out by the ear.

How throughout the day Adam Trčka in the van of his cavalry wrought havoc upon the Swedes, a bullet tearing off his boot but not his foot, although another tore off the foot as well of Count Berthold Waldstein, commanding in the centre, and it was fatal to him, and General Breuner of the artillery and Major-General Colloredo were both hit in the head, and how altogether anybody could speak of luck who during these hours survived safely in spite of doing what in honour bound. And so forth. All that is to be learned from Diodati. Historians, however, have not been deceived.

The success of the Swedes at the Lützen end of the field was none the less not decisive. After some five or six hours their strength was spent. They came to a halt before darkness fell. Field-Marshal Holk, the one-eyed, the wild bull, used the break to round up the scattered cavalry and reorganize it. Consequently there was still fighting on the right wing too when on this late autumn day nightfall forced the end that neither side had the power to impose. What, then, did the half-accomplished dissolution of the right wing effect? Nothing, really. Nothing against the imperialists who, even had they defended themselves at all points, would no longer have been able to undertake a crucial counter-attack. Nothing for the Swedes either, because it is clear that at darkness, or indeed before darkness, they once more surrendered their bloodily earned gains and withdrew beyond the ditches to approximately their old positions. When now, during the first hour of the night, the Pappen-heim infantry, five regiments about four thousand strong, arrived from Halle, having started later than the cavalry and travelled much more slowly, it found everything quiet on the barren plain of death and the fourteen quarter-cannon by the windmills deserted. The Swedes are said to have passed the night on the battlefield. The proposition carries weight with those who believe in the illusion of their victory. It is how-ever incorrect. As the Swedes mounted the attack, the terrain defended by Wallenstein, which lay north of the post-road, must be called the battlefield. This they vacated. And they cannot have stayed the night near the road and the ditches, ground which had in any case become uninviting, for in that case they would at once have noticed Wallenstein's departure. Only in the morning did they discover it.

Colonel Reinach of the Pappenheim infantry declared his readiness to take possession of the battlefield with his men, still in the mood for action, and if he were given horses and harness to undertake recovery of the guns. "Lord von Reinach," Wallenstein replied, "we know some-thing besides – the Elector of Saxony and the Duke of Lüneburg are coming with sixteen thousand men. We shall be on the march forthwith. You must stay here, Sir, and take over the rear until all are gone except the Croats, twenty-five companies, who shall remain behind you. . . ." Severance of contact with the enemy, withdrawal in the first instance to Leipzig. The reason given to the Colonel was anxiety about the Saxon and Lüneburg forces, whose strength Wallenstein overestimated. Per-haps uncertainty as regards the whereabouts of Arnim's corps also played a part. Another explanation was that furnished next day in a letter to Aldringen: "Towards nightfall our people were so dispirited that the officers were unable to keep either the horsemen or the foot-soldiers by their units. So I resolved, after consultation with the commanders, to move at night here to Leipzig." Dispirited, at the end of his tether, for the past thirty hours without sleep, and now, with the tension relaxing, becoming conscious of his bodily pains, that may also have been the General's condition. What difference would it have made if a few of his units had spent the night on the battlefield among the dead and wounded? The battle of Lützen would have been a victory, according to the book of rules, just as comparing the number of captured colours was deemed significant. "I have obtained from the enemy more than thirty standards and pennants, he from me five or six at the most." What mattered the book of rules? Both armies had worn one another out, meaning that both had succumbed and could therefore equally well ascribe the melancholy victory to themselves. Weimar, Swedish commander-in-chief at the moment and because nobody disputed precedence with him, also led the remainder of his forces back whence they came, to Naumburg, not in the dark, but next morning. Holk's summary was, "The blood-bath lasted seven hours and, after both sides had suffered unheard-of ravage, the one withdrew along the one route, the other along the other route." The "unheard-of ravage" consisted of nine thousand dead and dying, among them more Swedes than imperialists.

This is the true course of events at the Battle of Lützen. Later Ottavio Piccolomini had it immortalized by Snayers, the most fashionable battle-painter of the day. The scene is the state of affairs as it was early on, around eleven o'clock, during the artillery duel. Everything is still very tidy. The swaying masses with their banners and lances and muskets and swords, down in the broad plain. The red jackets, the white and brown of the horses. Because the perspective is from north to south, the Swedes are in the background, the Imperialists occupy the centre. Discernible are Gustavus Adolphus, Holk, and Piccolomini. Only Wallenstein is missing. He, it seems, was never present.

The retreat proceeded in as good order as was humanly possible after the horrors of the day. Not a trace of pursuit. The Swedes lacked the capacity for that. Wallenstein mistook what they were still capable of, just as their leaders mistakenly feared a fresh imperialist attack. He reached Leipzig towards midnight and he stayed there for twenty-four hours amidst the soldiery, the women and boys, the baggage trains and the herds of livestock crowding the streets. An initial message was to Aldringen: "Tomorrow I march to Chemnitz to join Count Gallas and make head against the enemy. Wherefore my lord will put aside each and every business, no matter what its importance, and will proceed without pause to Eger with all imperial troops, awaiting there my further instructions which my lord will without fail and without any delay execute because I shall admit of no excuse, whatever kind it may be." In this letter, as in the last one sent to the Field-Marshal, ran an undercurrent of bitterness. Had Aldringen's eight thousand men been available at Lützen, its outcome would have been different. What, he had asked, could be the momentousness of any petty Swedish units which were agitating the Elector of Bavaria? Aldringen had, under the pressure of Maximilian's entreaties, wavered, and wavered again, until it was too late. From the dispatch it emerges that on the day after the battle Wallenstein still had it in mind "to make head" against the enemy in conjunction with Gallas. In other words, to remain on Saxon soil, probably between Chemnitz, Freiberg, and Frauenstein. In the evening of 17 December he left Leipzig via St Peter's Gate in a southerly direction. Evacuation of the city lasted the whole night. The wounded (they looked, according to the doctors, more ghastly than after Breitenfeld) were left behind.

Five days later, at Chemnitz, he determined to continue the withdrawal into Bohemia. Caretto di Grana, one of his most unpopular officers, was given the task of reporting on the battle at Vienna and expounding the ineluctable need to establish winter quarters in the Hereditary Lands for the recuperation of the exhausted troops and their expansion during the coming months. Caretto fell ill on the way. Another emissary, Giulio Diodati, travelled to Vienna bearing, in the form of a postscript by Wallenstein, the definitive news of Gustavus Adolphus's death. "The King is assuredly dead, having remained upon the battlefield mortally stricken with many wounds." Diodati arrived on 29 November. He was granted audience to tell in the Most Exalted Presence what he later put in writing, and we know how elegantly he fulfilled his task. He cannot in the course of his audience have left unmentioned the necessity for quarters, which involved lodgings, victuals, and money. A bitter pill indeed, but because his principal dish tasted so honeyed, Vienna was in the first instance disinclined to notice the acrid tang. A deluge of congratulations descended on the General. The warmest were in the Emperor's own hand – he felicitated himself as well as His Dilection upon this most happy success and on the Swede's death; God be praised and thanked. Letters followed from the King of Poland and the King of Spain, the Duke of Orléans (*"Mon cousin, c'est un ouvrage que le ciel vous réservait . . ."*), the Queen-Mother of France, the Holy Father ("*Dilecte fili, Nobilis vir,* Thy bravery has liberated not only Germany, nay, the whole Christian globe from its most dangerous enemy") – in respect of whom we prudently proffer no opinions as to what Urban VIII really felt about the King's death. Imperial Vice-Chancellor von Stralendorf had the presumption to asseverate that not for almost two hundred years had so valiant a victory been vouchsafed to christendom. He added that now surely a just peace would be achieved by – he underlined the name – a Duke of Friedland. The very next day, though, this same politician signed, with others, an expert view which put a damper on his jubilation – the victory of Lützen, in so far as it was one, consisted mainly in the death of the Swede, the like of whom, as an able, puissant leader, it was hardly probable that the foe would again find. But a complete victory, one on the basis of which a peace could be dictated, that, alas, it did not appear to be. . . . The sequel confirmed the assumption. The shock of it, however well he concealed the fact, shook Wallenstein to his depths. He could not overcome his mortification.

The Labyrinth

Who e'er did enter labyrinth
Whence outlet nevermore was found ...

COUNT AUGUST VON PLATEN (1796–1835)

THE outcome of the duel had been that the King was dead and the Duke lived. An ending of far-reaching significance, whatever its practical bearing, and not altogether a matter of chance. Gustavus would not have dared death so rashly if he had not sensed the battle at Lützen to be a mortal struggle. He died at a good moment. The aura surrounding his name was not dimmed. Had he continued to live, the light in which he appeared would have become ever duskier, more sullied and the German crusade would increasingly have disgusted him. This, at any rate, Wallenstein brought about. No more. On 2 December he entered Prague. From here he had six months earlier set out with such great plans in his head. If he had time to ponder – even now he did not have much – he could not but admit to himself that they had foundered. To make away with this one man had not been his object. He had wanted to "eat him up", to shatter the myth attached to his person, at some point to catch his armed might, to challenge and to rout it. He had wanted to remain inside the Empire this winter, in Saxony and far beyond the Saxon borders. The Swedish army had not been routed, only bloodily mangled, like his own. Had he expected at least to keep in pawn the captured Saxon fortresses, Pleisenburg near Leipzig, Altenburg, Chemnitz, Zwickau, and Freiberg, this hope was also disappointed. In the weeks after the battle they were lost, one after another.

To disperse the greater part of his army on the day before the battle was an incomprehensible error. To this it is objected that he had no other choice, if only on logistic grounds, when at Weissenfels he had proved unable to compel the King to offer battle. He had in any case weighed all the alternatives. On what basis? Gustavus left Naumburg on the morning of 15 November without knowing of his opponent's dispersal and simply intending to reach the Elbe somewhere. Had

Wallenstein retained his regiments for just one more day, and if his scouts had then brought him news of the King's hazardous venture, he could have fallen upon him from the north with an attack worthy of old Tilly. That would have been something different from the front which he had presented at Lützen, its task the purely defensive one of not yielding a yard. An ignoramus of war may here be allowed to suspect deficiency of foresight. Yet who could foresee what the Swedes would do, whether winter at Naumburg, whether march against Halle, the Elbe or Lützen?

Wallenstein was by nature a defensive fighter. The odds on a stout defence are always greater than on an attack, and he always liked to have the odds on his side. The masterliness of the defence at Lützen is undisputed. It would have been still more successful if from the start Pappenheim's and Hatzfeld's cavalry as well as Pappenheim's infantry had been available to him. As it transpired, the regiments were thrown in relays into the fight, not to achieve a breakthrough, but in order to restore endangered positions, which is a different thing.

Even victory at Lützen, mastery of the battlefield, would not have helped because he lacked the forces to exploit the situation. The Swedes had insufficient troops for that purpose; they would have been just as insufficient on the imperialist side. It would have required two armies, one to accomplish the rout, the other to undertake the follow-up. The forces at Wallenstein's disposal were equal to a battle, nothing more. It is why Lützen was his last battle, why after it he was tired of battles and ceased to believe in their efficacy. To stay in central Saxony amidst a hostile peasantry, with on the one side the Swedes who would reassemble and grow in strength and on the other the Saxons and Lüneburgers, what promise did that hold? Just as impossible as a pursuit of the Swedes was a wheeling movement towards the Elbe and Torgau. Lightning blows, first in one direction, then in another, a series of battles, were a feature of later wars. They played no part in the hostilities narrated here. Whether victory or defeat, with the battle of Lützen fought, further action did not come into question for Wallenstein's army. That raises the problem why he should have left Saxony in such haste.

Swedish specialists are of the opinion that the distance put between the opponents during the night of 16–17 November was unnecessary. To Wallenstein there appeared however no palpable advantage in staying where he was, even if at the moment it had been possible without any great danger. Should he have waited at Leipzig or in its neighbour-hood, awaiting developments, reinforcing his strength with Gallas's corps, the Hatzfeld regiments, and possibly the corps under Aldringen to whom he had issued a hectoring order to proceed north? We are trying to guess his thoughts. They sprang perhaps from something sounder than tiredness and panic. He feared the hostile spirit of the country which could be curbed only by superior power. He feared the fresh cavalry units at Torgau. He feared the corps under Arnim. Of the latter it has to be said that neither on the eve of Lützen nor in the days, indeed weeks, afterwards would there have been anything to fear from him if it had been known where he stood. On 16 November he was in central Silesia, about 150 miles from Lützen. Two weeks seem to have elapsed before he learnt of the King's death, for not until 30 November did he send Elector John George any letter of condolence. Although Arnim was far off, he was approaching. It was conceivable that he would assume a position in the Erz Mountains to cut off the imperialists from Bohemia just as the passage of the Elbe was barred to them. Put succinctly, winter in Saxony would at best have been an uneasy business with peril on all sides. Wallenstein did not believe that he should demand it of his soldiers, even supposing that it passed off well. What if it passed off badly?

In retrospect, the whole expedition to Saxony was incapable of success. The whole campaign in Germany was incapable of success. Germany was four-fifths Protestant; the Swedes had raised a stir there as never before. The Empire's overthrow had in 1627 seemed consum-mated. That condition was no longer operative and could not prevail again. The imperialists were not equal to the task. They would never again be equal to it. Fundamentally Wallenstein had known it in the spring. If he had in summer and autumn on occasion promised finer prospects, he had given way to temporary euphoria. Peace moreover, a peace satisfactory to all, appeared really impossible of attainment with Gustavus as victor, as saviour and master of the Germans. Now the King was gone. Yes, he would rearm. He would collect a force stronger than in the preceding year, one which would exceed the dream total of a hundred thousand men. To what end? "I crave peace," he told a Danish minister, "as keenly as my own salvation, notwithstanding that I make greater preparations for war than I have ever heretofore done. I hope to lay hands on those who reject the proffered peace negotiations, and have a taste for further blood-letting, in such tender spot as shall pain them . . . ."

OF MELANCHOLY

He was in his fiftieth year. Let no one imagine that this was the prime of life. At fifty a man was as spent and in decline as nowadays one in his mid-sixties – a snap judgement, applicable to ordinary individuals. The Emperor, for instance. Robust, pious by nature, leading the healthy life of a lazy-bones and sportsman, able to wake and go to sleep with an easy conscience, in his fifty-sixth year he none the less made so valetudinarian an impression that his early demise was anticipated. Wallenstein was no ordinary individual. He had not become a ruler, a king after his own fashion, thanks to any comfortable, innate advantages of birth, but through unceasing strain and effort.

It was the great of this earth who, when they began to age, took not kindly to melancholy, *atra bilis*, the black bile. A modish malady, and a mode which had prevailed pretty long. Dürer's picture of it, that brooding female figure, is well known enough. In 1621, just when Wallenstein was laying with youthful cupidity the foundations of his fortune, an English clergyman, Robert Burton, anatomized *melaina cholae* in a volume of nine hundred pages. It must, gauged by the frequency of its reprints, have appealed to his contemporaries. The vicar of St Thomas, Oxford, knew that the Black Fay had a predilection for leaping on the shoulders of the mighty when they grew old, they who neither loved nor were loved, who only exploited others, *sibi nati*, existing only for themselves, and who now felt their loneliness, how others deserted them to curry favour with their successor, how nothing gave pleasure any more, how it became much more difficult to retain what had been gained than formerly to win it. There was neither joy in living nor at dying: *vivere nolunt, mori nesciunt*. Anything done was soon regretted and sought to be undone. Yet anything desired was most furiously sought, *quidquid volunt, valde volunt*. Flying into a passion, touchy, always taking offence, prone to revenge, *injuriarum tenax* . . .. These were the traits of great lords in old age, as this scholar painted them. A general portrayal, a description not of a type, not a particular individual. The vicar was, with reservations, not unsympathetic to astrology: he who of his own free reason resisted the workings of the constellations could resist them. As for him who had Saturn predominant in his nativity, his characteristics were familiar – the profoundness of his cogitations, the burden that his persona imposed on him, his silence, brooding, cares, and fears – characteristics accompanied astonishingly by delight in horse-breeding, building, woods, gardens, rivers, ponds, pools, walks hedged with brick and stone . . ..

The dissector of downcast spirits was naturalist enough not to omit from his considerations, in addition to the stars, men's actions, and their spiritual lot, their physical states and the reciprocal effects of body on soul. How should men not be saddened by inflammations of the inner organs, haemorrhages, circulatory troubles, veneral putrefactions, gastric complaints and similar afflictions? How should they still be light-hearted when they could no longer do what formerly they had done so gladly and saw the others, the youngsters around them, doing so heart-feltly? . . . In his fiftieth year Wallenstein was a very sick man. He is described as totally emaciated and with features of so yellowish-green a hue sometimes tinged with black that he preferred to hide them behind a silken scarf. His hands were so cramped with gout as to render him often unable for weeks to append his signature to documents and letters. At Lützen he had still been able to mount a horse. Six months later he felt safe only in a litter. From the contemporary accounts experts have been unable to determine whether his affliction was gout *per se*, arthritis, some disease permeating all parts of the body, or a tertiary form of syphilis. To this constant condition was added an ague ailment called the "Hungarian complaint", probably a kind of malaria, which periodi-cally befell its victims with bouts of fever, cold fits, convulsive contrac-tions in the calves, painful twitches in the knees and ankles, symptoms associated with those already produced by his gout. This, if the genuine article, gave rise to such severe arteriosclerosis that eventually the heart muscles were affected, to the accompaniment of palpitations, angina pectoris. Gout moreover, in its most advanced stage, causes inflamma-tion of the legs which, if not properly treated, deteriorates into sup-purating abscesses. The treatment prescribed for their princely patient by his personal physicians was, in modern eyes, hardly apposite. He daily passed hours in vapour baths (whatever good that may have done him) and pieces of proud flesh were cut from his chapped feet. That, according to his coevals, was his physical state. Those who came after analysed it in their own way. One of them claimed to recognize traces of tuberculosis, the illness from which his sister had died early. At any rate he suffered not from a single disorder, but from a positive cluster. A man laid so low cannot have long to live; his driving passion will be for peace and quiet.

"Peace", a word henceforth recurring again and again, a word repeatedly on Wallenstein's lips, had a twofold meaning. It signified release from the bondage of responsibilities and life which, when it no longer gives pleasure, is pure torment. It signified, with an end to the great war, a general, political peace. He was egocentric enough to visualize these two longings as one – there should be peace because he wa tired of waging war and living. He was becoming old, he said, he was suffering, and the time had come to stop the slaughter. For the sake of peace he would be willing to relinquish something of his demands. He had been guilty of much evil, although unaware of the fact because he had stuck to the rules. Towards the end his wish was to undertake a last salutary achievement which would raise a monument to his name. To ask whether someone so culpable could really attain to that, even had he been a better politician less seared in body and soul, poses an admissible question.

THE BLOOD TRIBUNAL

For more than five months he remained at Prague, preoccupied with the business of rearmament. His correspondence continued to be pungent and multifarious, but he locked himself up in his Friedland palace and outwardly loaded the major part of his burden on Holk's broad shoulders. "His Princely Grace makes himself very rare," reported a Bavarian agent to Maximilian, "and the most senior officers are but seldom received in audience, like Colloredo who during several weeks was never able to penetrate to his presence." Holk was his factotum who saw to everything, whether artillery, victuals, or whatever problems arose.

As Field-Marshal and "captain of cavalry process", it fell to Holk to conduct the sad, inevitable matter of bringing to justice the Lützen deserters. Inevitable in the light of the law and the nature of war as it always had been and always will be for as long as it lasts. Most soldiers ventured their lives not voluntarily but because they must, their choice lying between possible death on a field of honour or certain dishonourable death by court-martial. Had desertion gone unpunished, the war machinery would have collapsed. In the long run it would not have been a misfortune, but it is impossible for generals to take that view. "I doubt not," wrote Wallenstein on 9 December to Gallas, "that my lord knows how evilly Colonel Hagen behaved at the recent battle near Lützen in that he and all his men ran away in a disgraceful manner. In as much as good must be rewarded, therefore wickedness must be punished . . ." and so on. Holk, Ilow, and Gallas had the guilty parties arrested, whenever these were clumsy enough to let themselves be discovered, and conveyed to Prague: Colonel Nikolaus von Hagen, Lieutenant-Colonel Albrecht von Hofkirchen, Captains Count Luigi Broglia, Suttel, Qualenberg, Staitz von Wobersnau – "a child, and only eighteen", as Holk extenuatingly termed him – along with others, twelve officers in all, five rankers. The court was composed of nearly thirty persons, as well as legal experts a number of officers particularly distinguished for bravery, like Rudolf Colloredo and Ottavio Piccolomini, and ranging in rank from colonels to sergeant-majors. Nothing was put into the indictment, nothing into the conviction which had not over and again been attested by witnesses and the accused had not of their own accord admitted. The outcome was obvious. An officer who, like Luigi Broglia, had ridden off the battlefield, far away, half-way to Halle, and, meeting the Pappenheim infantry on the march to Lützen, told it that all was lost, the Generalissimo in flight, the best to do was to turn around – what was to happen to him? That his judges should also have condemned the child, Captain Staitz von Wobersnau, whose noble bearing and overwhelming charm drew during the reading of his sentence tears from the eyes of the Provost-Marshal, speaks for rather than against them. To condemn him was not their wish. His guilt proven, it was their duty. There remained the possibility of reprieve, capable of being exercised on the child's behalf as on that of a grizzled artillery captain. Appeals arrived from Munich and Vienna for the highest born among those convicted. Wallenstein alone could exercise clemency. He did not.

The execution took place on the Altstadt Ring. A popular, sanguinary, sorrowful occasion dedicated to the restoration of divine right and Imperial Majesty's affronted authority. Common practice. Just about this time Hans Voppelius, commandant of the Leipzig citadel, was in the presence of the electoral family conveyed on the Neumarkt at Dresden from life into death for not having defended his fortress as stoutly as he might have done. Normal procedure. Except that here the number of victims was so large. And that it should occur on the Altstadt Ring which, twelve years ago, had been the scene of an identical event. And that Hilmar Staitz von Wobersnau made so touching a figure. He should, given his rank, have been the fourth to suffer at the executioner's hand. But Holk, flint-hearted Holk, placed him at the end of the line in the hope that a message of mercy might yet come. When it did not and the boy knelt down, a stir of protest, an outcry, surged through the crowd. The general officers on their tribune were not unaffected. Piccolomini, hero of Lützen, with a peremptory gesture and word halted the

process. Could not at least this youth be spared? The proceeding was
suspended. The youngster remained on his knees, sunk in prayer. Holk
mounted his horse to ride across the Charles Bridge to the palace. After
a while he returned, downcast. "It cannot be" had rung in his ears.
The boy-captain was put to the sword. He died "in so fair a manner", a
report of almost official character declared, "that all around were moved
to pity . . .. It cannot commensurately be told with what readiness and
submission this gentleman went to his death." Whether Wallenstein
believed that no exception could be allowed, whether he wanted a reputation for mercilessness or his reputation was a point of indifference to
him, whether he had lost all feeling for his fellow-men, it was not a good
start to a year meant to bring peace.

This winter he once again made his will. He obtained from the
Emperor a prerogative formerly enjoyed by the Bohemian nobility – if
ever a Duke of Friedland were to become guilty of treason, he should
suffer in life and limb, but his property would be permitted to pass to
the nearest agnate. He ordered a serious start to be made on the plans
for a Friedland university endowment, his long cherished dream. It was
to be an establishment meeting the highest standards set by the Empire's
oldest, most famous academies. During the whole of the new year there
was indeed no shadow of a sign that it may at any moment have occurred
to him to dissolve his dukedom and return it piecemeal to the previous
owners nor that he was not constantly pondering its expansion and
embellishment, a consolation on which he concentrated when so little
comfort was to be derived from any other source. Part of his time too
was spent in benefactions. The concern, for example, that he showed
on behalf of Countess Pappenheim was generous, detailed, and of the
most practical kind. Pappenheim, he let it be known, dying for Emperor
and Catholic christendom, had been unable to draw up a last will, but
he had appointed the Duke as his family's guardian. This duty he would
fulfil on his dead friend's behalf. He would not tolerate defraudation
of the widow and her orphans by any alleged collateral heirs and her
involvement in case-hardened lawyers' endless suits. For a start he sent
her five thousand taler – sorrowing survivors also need money – and a
letter of condolence couched in almost heartfelt terms. Severity against
the wicked, kindness to the good, God the Lord. Terrestrial rulers had
always fancied themselves as being in His likeness and following His
pattern. They had been regarded as such by their subjects. Which, for
all that it lasted so long, was probably not the right thing for either
side.

THE DESTINY WEAVERS

Our hero's life was political, which means that his strivings always concerned only the privileged few, whereas participation in politics by most of his contemporaries was passive. They were the victims of war when it rampaged through the land, the victims of levies, victims still worse victimized when war was waged, and the victims of loyalty when they were driven from their homes on account of their faith. For the rest their worries ran in other, naturally ordained channels.

There was no democracy except for a few passing revolutions in city republics. Everything was transacted by an upper class based on hereditary rights, money, and sometimes erudition. It was however a broadly based upper class, nowhere more broadly than in Germany with its major potentates and their privy councillors, military men, ecclesiastics, all busily delighting in the business of war and peace, secular boundaries and spiritual rules, as well as its minor lords paramount, down to counts and knights, not to mention the municipal patricians and gentlemen of the robe, the whole proliferating into a few thousand destiny weavers in all. The northern monarchs were in principle dependent on their feudal parliaments, their Estate assemblies. In Great Britain matters went so far that for practical purposes the King was in no position to have a policy towards Europe; his diplomats there became a laughing-stock. In Scandinavia a way had been found of circumventing the Estates either by telling them what they had no choice but to believe (a Swedish forest cottager could as little as a Danish burgess venture an opinion about the degree of danger looming from Vienna and Madrid) or by creating a set of belligerent facts which no conclave of sober-sides could revoke any more. French foreign policy, thanks to Richelieu's efforts, had arrived at a point where it was settled by the Cardinal and the Capuchin, with the backing of King Louis, almost entirely on their own. At Madrid things were not much different, to Spain's misfortune. In Holland two factions existed. The Stadtholder, the Prince of Orange, in alliance with the merchants of the East India Company headed the one which was militant and for the sake of various advantages wanted the war with Spain to continue even if a tolerable peace were to be had. Factions, although discreetly conducted and restricted to court circles, could also be observed at Vienna notwithstanding that they never questioned the authority of that mild old bogy, His Sacred Imperial Majesty.

Only the great powers could decide anything – Stockholm, The

Hague, Paris, Madrid, Vienna. In second line, and at a pinch, Rome and Munich. The Germans, alone the Protestants, could by sheer numbers probably have played a co-decisive role, a thought dear to such nationally conscious politicians as the recently created Lieutenant-General Arnim. An idea plausible enough on paper (let many small powers with a vital interest in common, loyally, honestly unite and they can represent an independent, estimable major factor among the great). The total of individuals' will-power rooted in age-old traditions unfortunately adds up less easily than the sum of their numbers.

With Gustavus Adolphus, it was thought, the strongest personality had disappeared from the Protestant camp. A fortnight after him died Frederick of the Palatinate, the Winter King, that bantam and emaciated former charmer who bore a heavy share of responsibility for the horrors amidst which he perished. Not through his actions, for he was scarcely capable any longer of performing any, but through his conscientious, conscienceless resistance as a point of honour abetted by multifarious international circumstance. A reasonable arrangement with his son, or the latter's guardian, would prove easier. One man less, and with him an era in this martial chaos came to an end.

Why not, for God's and humanity's sake, the war itself? Once more, as during every winter, philanthropists, putative peacemakers, raised the question. Among them was George of Darmstadt, whose philanthropy we are by degrees prepared to credit, and the King of Denmark. The former had barely heard of Lützen, this dreadful, shocking, almost unheard-of blood-letting among Christians, before he went to work. Speed, he felt, was of the essence. His letter to the Emperor is convincing. He had concocted a web of compromises to render acceptance tolerable to all. Christian IV, in a more diplomatic groove, offered his good services first to the Saxons, then the imperialists. No conditions were named. Both philanthropists presented their bill without taking Germany's most domineering guest into account.

Axel Oxenstierna acted as quickly, incomparably more effectively than the Landgrave. A statesman with twenty years' experience of office as Chancellor, he had been the King's friend, adviser and Estates' representative whose profound knowledge of jurisprudence and German theology had not robbed him of common sense. Rather did he assess very soberly and factually, soundly and with brilliant intelligence the personalities, the plans, and the conflicts which he encountered. Honest when honesty was politic, skilled in the art of lying when necessary, always possessed of the authority appropriate to a man accustomed to

command, Oxenstierna, superior, sagacious, and caustic, indulged in
none of the noble illusions about Germany which Gustavus had conveniently mingled with intentions of a less generous tenor. There was
no relying on the Germans, he said. They felt no gratitude towards
Sweden, not even the Mecklenburg dukes, and would gladly do without
their rescuers. They must not be allowed to. He contrived his own
investment by the *Riksdag* – for the present the throne was vacant –
with a species of local dictatorship that foresaw little or no expenditure
by Sweden and gradual withdrawal of the purely Swedish contingents.
A Germanization of the hostilities, although their leadership continued
to rest with the crown of Sweden in the persons of its Chancellor,
general, and diplomats, the Germans paying a good price. In what
manner? Observers who did not qualify as obtuse, Wallenstein, for
instance, knew very well that it would take the shape of "coastal places",
above all Pomerania. A grievously high price for a relatively right
moderate contribution. Still more grievous that a "mere Swedish
gentleman" should make bold to speak to German princes as no Emperor
had ever yet spoken to them. Nevertheless the situation was so contorted
that this had to be endured, or they thought that they must endure it.
That was why they always yielded when the Chancellor brandished his
freedom to leave them in the lurch, his freedom to ally himself with
England, Holland, France and to destroy the Empire utterly.

For the space of a winter extending almost into summer Wallenstein
made no move. Oxenstierna had time for what must be done in a hurry.
He concluded a fresh, stronger alliance with France, a blow to all who
hoped for an end to fighting. The French and the Swedes would hold
the Protestants in a pincer grip. Were they none the less to escape from
it, the danger was great that the war in Germany would be transformed
into a war in Europe with Germany and Spain on the one side, Sweden,
Holland, France on the other. Those blinded by the sight of conferences
did not see that or went so far as to regard the prospect as hopeful
because the Franco-Swedish alliance never lost its friend–foe feature, a
trait rendering it in their eyes always possible to seek protection from
one partner against the other. At Dresden the Chancellor responded to
the inflated misgivings of privy councillors with the haughtiest of
impatience and the most stinging raillery. Asked what really was the
object of the hostilities, he expressed profound surprise that this should
not be known when the war had been waged for so many years. Should
however Elector John George try any independent peace pranks, he
would set the German Estates on one another like a pack of vicious

hounds and with France, Holland, Poland kindle in the Empire such a flame as would not soon be quenched. Thereupon he left Saxony convinced that it had two aims, to put itself at the head of all Protestants and to make peace with Austria. This is what he said at Berlin where he felt more at his ease. He let himself be drawn after his own fashion into unconstrained colloquy. Yes, he knew precisely what France wanted – "What lies between Basle and the Moselle, that is what it would very much like." On his own country's behalf he inclined to a similar gain, he added, but for the present he did not disclose what its location might be. The object of the war, as he defined it, was to chivy the Emperor out of his territories so that subsequently he would be in no position to negotiate about anything except their restitution. Oxenstierna found the Brandenburgers more accessible to his views than the Saxons. Still more accessible than the Brandenburgers were the representatives of the Upper Rhine, Middle Rhine, Franconian and Swabian Circles whom in March he invited to a congress at Heilbronn. A significant move against Saxony. The members of the alliance about to be founded, called for short the League of Heilbronn, would be in the Chancellor's pocket, a situation to which after many weeks of heckling and wriggling the princes and their lawyers, the imperial counts and knights as well as the delegates from the towns submitted. The alliance was to be between all three parties, between them as a body and Sweden. The common war-chest would derive its funds from German, not Swedish, sources. The Supreme Council would consist of seven Germans, three Swedes, and a director, the Chancellor, who for the time being was alone to decide on military operations. Oxenstierna needed no more. The alliance, for "the restoration of the Imperial Constitution" (whatever that might mean) and the fulfilment of rightful Swedish desires, was a rickety pile of loose rock. It would be whatever the Chancellor wanted, it would furnish him with money and soldiers, or it would prove to be nothing at all.

A speech whose sophistication and elegant turn of phrase is hardly likely to have been observed by the Swabians contributed something to the congress's success. The speaker was the Marquis de Feuquières, the French ambassador, marshal of France, governor of Vic and Moyenvic, the King's Lieutenant-General at Metz and Toul. Soldier, diplomat, man of letters, he was a new star in the stormy German firmament. He had been dispatched in February in order at one and the same time to help and harm Oxenstierna. In his train he had a herd of attachés chosen partly for their knowledge of German affairs and partly for an ability to

hold their liquor which would even match the Saxon Elector's; a hundred secretaries, lackeys, and guards; flattering missives from King
Louis to the more important German princes, those of Saxony, Brandenburg, Weimar, Darmstadt, Kassel; much money to be used for gifts in
the right places or pledges of pensions, and a set of instructions from
Father Joseph which he speedily recognized to be unrealistic. The
Capuchin, obsessed by predetermined ideas, wanted to go on believing
in what it suited him to believe – in a true, non-Habsburg Germany
divided between Catholics and Protestants, in a unification of all Protestants under Saxony as a third power in alliance with France and
Sweden although in strictest dependence of course on France, in a
neutralization of Bavaria and the League which would leave Austria
alone and lost. The Protestants should have their German liberties, the
Catholics the preservation of their religion. John George would be
successor to Gustavus Adolphus, Maximilian successor later to Ferdinand. Simultaneously a diplomat should be dispatched to Vienna,
attempt to enter into discussions with the Emperor, and if he had no
success prove to the Germans how and why nothing had nor could have
emanated from the move. France would in any case be at the head of
affairs, in war the winner without openly playing a principal part, in
peace negotiations the main mediator instead of the Danes, let alone the
little Landgrave. "*Mon Cousin,*" wrote King Louis to Wallenstein, "I
have on every occasion attested to the Emperor, my dear brother, my
wish to achieve a good, honourable peace in the Empire", etcetera. The
letter's recipient repaid him in the same cheap coin: he had experienced
quite exceptional pleasure in the noble sentiments of an eminent potentate whom he had always·held in high estimation on account of his great
qualities .... It all constituted part of what was termed Richelieu's
"unspoken war". Clever, very clever, too clever by half. Matters did
not stand this way at all, Feuquières had to report from Heilbronn.
Because of his disgraceful mode of living, the fluctuation and vacillation
of his policy, his notorious sympathies for the House of Austria, the
Elector of Saxony was held in such contempt by the Protestants that
they would never accept him as their leader, apart from the fact that he
was far too crudely xenophobic as ever to render him of any use as a tool
of French policy. The Bavarian fraternal pair, Maximilian and Ferdinand of Cologne, were in turn the best hated princes in the Empire,
hated worse than the Emperor, they, rather than he, being accounted
authors of the ruinous Edict; the notion of their reconciliation with the
Protestants must unhappily be abandoned. It would be necessary to

proceed very cautiously because His Most Christian Majesty did not inspire the Germans with such confidence as was supposed. Feuquières journeyed from Heilbronn to Dresden to pay his respects to the Elector of whom he had meanwhile heard so much evil.

The amount of travel that was undertaken to no or pernicious end and at great expense, which in the last analysis the poor paid for, is astonishing. Much mental wear and tear as well as artfulness had enabled Feuquières to have a few articles inserted into a treaty with the Heilbronn League which dispensed with any relation to reality: freedom to practise the Catholic religion where before the outbreak of hostilities it had prevailed, recognition of Bavaria and its friends' neutrality if this were to be had. To finalize the useless scrap of paper two League envoys in October 1633 went to Paris. They enjoyed the privilege of hearing from the Cardinal, in more detail from his Capuchin, an exposition of French policy. The war, Father Joseph lectured, was a war between states, not one of religion. When it was done, let denominational disputants cavil to their heart's content. What mattered now was to unite against the Spaniards who would otherwise swallow everything. A start on this would be to ensure the neutrality of the German Catholics, a point whose good sense and advantage the King of Sweden had unfortunately not appreciated. Neutrality, with an easing of animosities, was a vital priority to peace. The Elector of Bavaria was an enemy of the Spaniards, hostile to Wallenstein, who must at all cost be incited against the Emperor. Thereafter it would be possible to do with him whatever was wanted. The Elector of Saxony was an enemy to the Heilbronn Confederation, he was toying with treason to the common cause. His son-in-law, the Landgrave of Darmstadt, was encouraging his bids for an independent peace. He must be provided with other counsellors, his drunken way of life must be turned to advantage, Arnim must be removed because his outlook was ambivalent. A quick review of the non-German powers followed. Nothing was to be expected from England with affairs there in their current condition. The Prince of Orange wanted a continuation of the war, others in the Netherlands did not; France would know how to thwart the negotiations between Spain and the States-General. Denmark was of a wholly imperialist mind and simply awaiting an opportunity to attack Sweden. To stand by Sweden was for German Protestants a duty imposed by gratitude and honour as well as a matter of interest. Admittedly it would be a source of satisfaction if Oxenstierna were to moderate his arrogant behaviour somewhat; Paris could tell a tale about that too. And were Sweden to set its sights on the Empire's ruin and partition, it would be an act worse than any by the Turks, that France would never tolerate . . .. Ah, yes, France, which wanted nothing of Germany, its exertions solely directed towards a healthy balance of power in Europe. Proof was its conduct in Italy where it could have taken so much and took nothing, a bagatelle excepted, and payment was rendered for that. Quite untrue was that France saddled its allies with the costs of the war. In the near future it would have eighty thousand men under arms to control the passes into Italy and the passage of the Rhine and the Moselle, to seize the fortress of Breisach, to make sure of Alsace. If that did not suit the Heilbronn League . . ..

The oration of this vividly imaginative, pious man included an observation about Wallenstein – an effort should be made to do something with the Duke of Friedland who was certainly no friend to the Spaniards. Cunning and enigmatic he might be, but he was only a mediocre soldier afraid of defeats. One day he would pay for his blowing hot and cold. His masters were of a type that stuck to what they deliberated and decided. At some time what he had only pondered aloud would be interpreted as treason . . ..

Had Wallenstein heard this address, he would often have nodded. At a certain stage he would probably have interrupted its flow to ask, "Is it not known that these are my intentions too?" The principle along which the ecclesiastic envisaged the evolution of politics was familiar to him – the state as it was to be and remain for a couple of centuries, one such entity among many, capable of waging war, keeping it under control, and concluding peace, externally sharply contoured, internally demanding obedience in secular affairs but tolerant in spiritual questions. Father Joseph's blunt antipathy to Spain, stemming from the instinct awakened by growing French royal power, would have found an echo in Wallenstein's high-strung aversion to Spain's imperial dream which was of another, an older kind. Yet Richelieu and Wallenstein could never come together, notwithstanding compatibilities hanging upon the air like gossamer threads, just as Arnim, so frightening to Father Joseph, and Wallenstein never came together despite a certain proximity of ideas. The similarities would have been easy for Wallenstein to identify, had he scanned the successive memoranda which Arnim during 1633 showered upon Elector John George's head, the expressions of his deep distrust vis-à-vis foreigners, Spaniards, French, Swedes, and his desire for peace along a straightforward course, not one as crooked as that of the

French. In all good sense Wallenstein and Arnim ought to have met; they never did. Opinion is one thing, individual character a second, the situation in which opinion can prove effective by constraint and modification a third, and the moment a fourth. Because always several alternatives beckon, thought inclines today this way, six weeks hence that. Let one man now be where six weeks ago was another, the latter is no longer to be found there although six weeks later back again. Thus, always close, it is possible to go on and on missing each other.

Here was no war of religion, the Capuchin with the modern outlook had warned. Ever since 1618 Vienna too had sworn, to the best of its belief and on the worst of premises, that none such was being waged. Precisely at this juncture the screw of Counter-Reformation was given another twist so tight that even foreign ambassadors serving Protestant princes had either to adhere to the true faith or leave the country within three days. Young Lutherans who had intended to seek refuge in the army as the only asylum left to them found their escape route barred. Wallenstein raised furious objections; his recruiting officers were anyway finding their business more and more difficult. Ferdinand II was not to be moved from the principle whereby he could do in his lands as he liked or was bound to do whatever his conscience dictated and which was no concern of any other power. His interpretation of the law of nations was correct. But how should much discussed, honourable peace be possible with a political entity that utterly, to the point of derangement differed and set itself apart from its neighbours? Not altogether easy to establish is who really drove the monarch into his religious excesses. It must have been his most trusted personal advisers, his father confessor Lamormaini, the Court pulpiteer Weingartner, Jesuits both of them, and members of the Old Spanish party, Martinitz, Lobkowicz, Wilhelm Slawata. Religious fanaticism was not to be found among his (in the professional sense) political advisers.

A memorial drawn up in January 1633 by Bishop Antonius, Vice-Chancellor von Stralendorf and Max Trauttmansdorff plainly shows that. They first listed, in accordance with the practice of all Privy Councillors, the arguments on behalf of new, ever more passages of arms. They did not, though, take any exaggerated pains over them because the available arguments were very weak. The death of the King of Sweden might produce favourable effects. The enemy was perhaps still more dispirited than the imperial side. The sacrosanct edict was incapable of implementation without total victory. And so on. Finally, in such a just struggle reliance could no doubt be placed on help from the Almighty, an ultimate hope adroitly trimmed by the memorial's authors to the advantage of their personal viewpoint with the remark that God's aid was not confined to fortune in war, but extended to the illumination of minds and the wisdom of His advice. The latter inspired the following analysis. Affairs stood badly with the Emperor's cause. His lands were so thoroughly devastated that at any moment a fresh outbreak of rebellion and anarchy must be feared. All of the battles won had helped not at all, but a single one lost, Breitenfeld, had involved the forfeit of almost all Germany, a fact connected with the regrettable truth that the Empire contained six times more Protestants than Catholics. The heart of the Germans was with the enemy, fear alone could impose obedience to the Emperor. For years, in spite of imperial successes, a miserable Christian von Halberstadt, Margrave of Baden-Durlach, and Ernst von Mansfeld had been able to keep alive hostilities. What, then, was the position now when the greatest powers had intervened and all German gates, towns and fortresses, rivers and seas were open to them? Would not the French pursue their centuries-old aim of reconquering those territories which once they had possessed as far as the Rhine? England, Holland, Denmark – they were all uncertain elements in the game. The imperial Catholic princes had either been dispossessed or had adopted neutrality or, as experienced a year ago, were keeping their weather eye open on neutrality – a slap at Bavaria. Spain was the one reliable ally, or would be if it could, but it could not. Incapable of achieving its objective even in the Netherlands, it could, thanks to the enemy's craftiness, be tied down at any time there or in Italy or in the West Indies. Austria stood alone. The talk was of religion and that without victorious force it would not prove possible to carry through the edict of restitution. The question was whether the Emperor's duty really was to carry it through if the price to be paid so much transcended the gain. What had, especially of recent years, been achieved by all the bloodshed on behalf of Catholicism's fortification? How much better had life been and how much more securely had the church flourished under the order instituted by Ferdinand I. Seventy years it had lasted until the unfortunate Bohemian war, source of all calamities. Was there no way back to the good old days, via the mediation of Denmark, Poland, and the Duke of Mecklenburg – Wallenstein? There should be no turning back now when victory for either side was still uncertain, in a state of suspense? This was always the best moment to negotiate "because", opined the Privy Councillors, sagely enough, "a dictated peace should be regarded as no peace".

The memorial is honest, sensible, worried; it is more appealing than Oxenstierna's cutting speeches and Father Joseph's excessively clever gyrations. Its origin can, incidentally, be traced to a letter received by Trauttmansdorff from Gundakar von Liechtenstein. Fallen into disfavour, he was living at a distance from the capital and he emphasized that he was not properly in a position to be acquainted with affairs. He was well enough acquainted. The prerequisite is only to have learned to think a little and to read the papers. It was what led the Privy Councillors to adopt, with a few exceptions, his thoughts almost literally. They omitted his remark that, were the Emperor to succeed contrary to expectations in once more subjugating the whole Empire, it would serve nothing because the rest of Europe, in the shape of England, France, Denmark, Sweden, Poland, Muscovy, the Pope – the Pope! – Venice, and the Turks would never tolerate such a concentration of power. Also that the conduct of war without Wallenstein was impossible and Wallenstein could die, as attested by the great peril in which he had recently – at Lützen – stood. And that the suitable mediator for peace was King Louis (a roundabout approach to him was feasible through Bavaria) because France, apart from the war proving a drain upon moneys needed elsewhere, was not happy about the state of affairs and its inability to secure anything, either by an imperial victory or a Swedish and Protestant one. On the last point we know that Liechtenstein's perspective, due to his isolation, was rationally out of focus. Richelieu's plans were bolder, more crooked, more ruthless.

In the same way a slight air of unreality hangs over the memorial of the three wise men. If only Vienna were to be serious on the subject, they believed a compromise peace possible. They were, we fear, ignorant of its enemies' virulent, obdurate determination. As regards their own camp, Antonius knew only too well that Vienna also had its war-party; he warned Landgrave George, the pacifist, against it. The two groups struggled in secret for the soul of the weak, tenacious, pious, individual upon whom the decision finally depended.

Prince Eggenberg was, in addition to the three personalities mentioned, the most important member of the peace party. The Questenberg brothers were a long step down in status, but they did not lack influence. Had Wallenstein been a politician among politicians, he would have put himself at the party's head and made it indubitably the stronger. It would have entailed travel to the capital he loathed, which for the past six years he had avoided. It would have necessitated a thorough discussion with Eggenberg, just as six and a half years ago at Bruck. He neither went there nor did he ask for such. He was obsessed by the idea that no business could be done with Vienna; he would settle matters alone. "Let me be left to act." He had no wish to be an Austrian Privy Councillor, albeit he bore the title alongside handsomer specimens, or a party leader. He wanted to be a one-man party, autonomous, lord over war and peace. His position, seen during this winter and spring from the outside, encouraged the dream. "The court of this prince is held in mighty respect," a report from Prague confirmed, "not only by all the imperial Estates, but by many foreign potentates too. Within two months two royal Danish envoys, a royal Polish, and a princely Savoyard embassy have been here. For the period of their stay they were His Princely Grace's guests and he entertained them generously. Similarly an imperial delegation was recently here."

An imperial delegation. If the gist was that he desired to decide the fate of central Europe by himself, this was none the less wrapped in many layers. He wrote letters to Vienna that no chance of peace should be rejected, recommending Danish mediation. He received politicians sent by Vienna, where care was taken to select those with whom he reputedly got on best, like Bishop Antonius. The latter, accompanied by Hermann Questenberg, passed through Prague in March on his way to the small northern town of Leitmeritz to confer with Landgrave George. Prior to the meeting he was to hear Wallenstein's opinion; he would afterwards report to him. Wallenstein, Bohemia's war-lord, was the Landgrave's host. The situation was not therefore that official negotiations were conducted between the imperialists and the Protestants from which he was excluded or he excluded himself. He was however irritated at not being the negotiator. The gentlemen from Vienna wanted merely his opinion. They would use, half use, or not use it at all. He knew how without him they would set about things. He had watched them in 1629 at Lübeck, how they squabbled with their negotiating partner, wasting time until he intervened. The real essentials would not be offered. That which in extremity they were allowed to offer would not be tendered all at once, simply bit by bit, first a ludicrous morsel, then a little more, and when it proved insufficient still something more so that the effect of concession would be lost, although this technique was thought consummate artistry. He had had enough of that; he was in a hurry.

Doubtless too the current gossip came to his ears. He was, they said, in bad odour at Vienna, suspected of unspeakably impudent notions, a hankering after the Bohemian crown not debarred. The chatter, probably, of a Trčka servant, according to which court circles were deeply embittered at his billetings and calls for money. Indubitably true, but how could he have acted otherwise? To place the army on a fresh footing of readiness cost money. With Germany under outside control, the Hereditary Lands alone could furnish it. The great lords had like the citizens to dip into their pockets. At Vienna a special tax was levied on equipages, token of wealth. The Moravians as usual did not want to pay; a "collection by the military" had to take place. Styria displayed reluctance not merely to pay but to accept billetings. Wallenstein argued the point with its governor, Eggenberg, "the best friend that I have", by letter. The war contributions, assuming that they were rendered, may have been ruinous. It would explain the irritability at Vienna as well as at Prague. Responsibility for all unpleasantness was always ascribed by one to the other, by the Duke to the court, by the court to the Duke, whose temper suffered accordingly. There is the testimony of his Friedland war chancellery director that since May it had struck him as very odd how Wallenstein received letters from His Imperial Majesty with a certain distaste, pushed them aside, often did not read them for days on end, and sometimes never replied.

Exact information about the talks at the close of March between the Bishop and the Landgrave is not on hand. Wallenstein did not have it either. Each came to Leitmeritz to discover what it was that the other wanted and what kind of peace he envisaged. The upshot was mutual probing which tied down neither party. Antonius, the Landgrave told Nicolai, the Swedish envoy, had spoken of the Emperor's heartfelt wish for a reconciliation, which did not derive from weakness but pity with afflicted christendom. As regards weakness, he would in the near future have two hundred thousand men at his disposal. (An exaggeration.) George replied that the Protestants too wanted peace, but it must be an honest, overall settlement and the satisfaction merited by Sweden was by no means to be left out of reckoning. Were the imperialists to fancy that they could divide their opponents, making independent peace with this one and that one, they must think again. The Bishop agreed that particularist peace-making only created fresh vexations. In respect of indemnification for Sweden, the imperialists' view was that they, as the affronted party, must claim such; but had agreement been attained on all other points, then, in Heaven's name, agreement on this would prove possible. "This," finished the Landgrave, "is the sum of the conference." From other sources it is known that there was something more. The Landgrave was in a difficult position. An unofficial envoy for the Electors of Saxony and Brandenburg whose attitude to the war aims problem was not at all identical, he was a harbinger of peace who had his very own ideas on the subject. Sweden, he proposed, should be indemnified with Pomerania, or a portion thereof. This would not suit Brandenburg, out to inherit Pomerania on the extinction of the present ruling dynasty. The Palatinate, the slice situated on the Rhine, should be returned to the Winter King's son while the upper part and the electoral dignity could remain with Maximilian until his death. Saxony wanted something, Lusatia, already in its possession, and the adjacent Bohemian district of Eger. The edict must be repealed; that was self-evident. The Calvinists and the Lutherans must be on a legal par. Both, representing the Protestants as an entity, must be represented on an equal footing with the Catholics in imperial institutions like the *Reichskammergericht*, the Aulic Council, and, better still, the Privy Council. Bohemia should have freedom of faith, Saxony's demand. Brandenburg's, on Swedish lines, went farther . . .. Had for the past ten years, and more, war really been waged for the sake of such trivial questions, such trivial solutions? Bishop Antonius, for all that he had been co-signatory to that serious memorial, was evasive, precise only on those points to which his principals would never agree. They would never allow freedom of faith in Bohemia. That was a matter for the Emperor, not in his capacity as the elected senior imperial authority, but in his personal sovereign right. Equal representation on the bench could be discussed. Discussed, yes, but it has to be admitted that Protestant Privy Councillors at Vienna would have appeared odd in days when the King of Great Britain could not have there any ambassador who was a member of the Anglican church. The Palatinate, or the Palatinate in parts, could also be a subject for discussion, but not without those whom it concerned, the Catholic Electors, in particular Bavaria. No talk about Sweden's booty at the expense of the Empire ought to be admissible, but maybe it would be allowed, at the very end. Silence about the Edict, as about Spain, France, the Netherlands. Saxony's territorial wishes, though, could expect to be treated with a certain magnanimity. The Bishop's attitude was not promotive of peace. Only a generous, precise, and overall offer could have been of assistance in the face of parties with such disparate ideas.

The Protestant coalition became even more sharply divided while the discussions at Leitmeritz were mistrustfully pursued. It was now that Oxenstierna succeeded in his political *coup* of withdrawing, by the

Treaty of Heilbronn, southern Germany from Saxony's sphere of influence and of tying it into that of the Franco-Swedish combination. Simultaneously the Chancellor cut the Palatine knot. He returned the Rhenish Palatinate to deceased Frederick's son under conditions which for the duration of the war transformed it into a Swedish protectorate. The government-in-exile, composed of pretty tired men, was in the following year allowed to return from The Hague to Heidelberg. A late act of justice, it may be said. Not one which facilitated negotiations about a general settlement.

The Danish mediation, discussed at Leitmeritz, was to be brought about by a conference of the interested parties. Months passed before there was agreement on the point of venue, Breslau. More months passed until the instructions had been concocted, the passports and letters of safe-conduct drafted, dispatched, returned for correction, and again dispatched. Then the imperial delegation waited somewhere in Bohemia for the Swedes, the Saxons, the Brandenburgers, or whoever else was due, and waited in vain.

It was not a way in which matters could profitably be conducted. It was the way that for another fifteen years they were conducted.

THE MAY NIGHT AT GITSCHIN

The game that eighteen months ago had been played in a rarefied abstruse atmosphere between Wallenstein, the King, Count Thurn, and the petty agent Sezyma Rašin was now resumed. In April a letter was brought by Rašin to Prague. The messenger did not satisfy Wallenstein. He wanted to see someone more important from the *émigrés*' camp, Johann von Bubna, Swedish major-general and friend of his youth.

On 16 May they came to Gitschin, Bubna and Rašin, arriving late in the evening in the square in front of the residence. Their passports examined, they were admitted. Adam Trčka led them to the Duke's study. Its candlelight fell on the features of an ailing man. No scent of spring here, but the visitors' reception was cordial.

Wallenstein, jokingly: "Are we friend or foe?"

Bubna replied in a businesslike tone that he had come at His Princely Grace's request to hear with what he wished to charge him.

Wallenstein: "Are we not arch-fools to knock in our heads for the sake of others when, since we have the armies in our power, we could arrange a peace to our liking?"

Bubna: "That would be easy of achievement if on the side of our adversaries all could be trusted as is Your Princely Grace. But" – a hint at his interlocutor's state of health – "Your Princely Grace too is mortal. The worshipful crown of Sweden, and therewith we, wishes neither to have anything to do with nor to hear from the Emperor. For" – the speaker's voice was brimful with bitter memory – "even though he wanted to keep what he promises, he is so smitten with his clerics that he must live according to their will and must do what they bid. We have more examples than one how the Letter of Majesty awarded us by the Emperor Rudolf has been kept. If however Your Princely Grace inclines to that which a few days past His Excellency Count Thurn communicated in writing and would assume the Bohemian crown, the person of Your Princely Grace would afford better access to peace. With the Emperor 'tis effort wasted. The late lamented, noble King of Sweden of blessed memory" – his inflexion here dropped to a pitch appropriate to the initiated – "wished that for You before aught else, to maintain and to uphold You therein, all which is known to His Excellency the Swedish Chancellor, Count Thurn, and myself."

Wallenstein, as though hearing about this for the first time, "What, the crown? That would be an arrant piece of knavery." Adam Trčka looked embarrassed. "The Emperor, 'tis true, is a pious gentleman, but he allows himself to be guided and led astray by every cleric and idle fellow. We must not let it come to that. We, who have the armies in our hands, can arrange between us a good peace and a peace which will conduce to the welfare of all, not simply one or another, but for all and each, not only to the great advantage of the Protestants, but also to that of the Catholics, and not only with identical right and prerogatives for the Catholics but also for the Protestants. What we who have the armies in our power negotiate and conclude, the others, even though 'tis not what they presently want, must accept and incline to. And that shall thus remain in full and indefeasible."

Bubna, sceptically: "To what end and aim is such subscribed if none the less the Emperor is to remain?"

Wallenstein: "The Emperor shall have naught to do with the matter, but we ourselves shall direct all the business and, whatever 'tis that we do and direct, thus too must it remain. The shavelings are coming down a little, have had enough and are tired of war; they must and will gladly hold their tongues." Fervidly, "It shall be a peace to the advantage and for the restitution of all whose lot is injustice! If I mean this not honestly, may God not suffer my soul to gain eternal bliss. I would not else speak to my lord so. He hath known me this many a year. . . ." The politician took his turn. "If you would wage war for long, you lack a head. The Elector of Saxony should in the Empire be your leader, but he is mere brute, and see how he lives. I tell it as avouched truth and promise you that the Elector has written to the Emperor how he proposes to contrive an assembly of the Protestants in the Empire, for all that he doubts the Estates' coming and does it only for appearance's sake, for if they come not he will have grounds to cross to the Emperor. 'Tis *pro forma* that he intervenes with the Emperor on the Silesians' behalf. And the Elector of Brandenburg is like inconstant. We hear that the Princess" – Gustavus's daughter – "is crowned Queen of Sweden, but the Empire's rule she will not be able to undertake. Shall you have fixed your sights upon the King of France, you will fare no better, for notwithstanding that now he too intervenes, he is as Jesuit as the Emperor cannot surpass."

Bubna countered that affairs stood by no means as badly as that. The King had provided for everything in case of his death. The Chancellor was regent and, with Sweden's sheer inexhaustible resources behind him, "holds command as the kingdom's legate".

Wallenstein, after praise for Gustavus Adolphus, returned to his theme that the prevailing state of calamity could only be brought under control by agreement between the armies and their imposition of a peace. Count Thurn, an old soldier, colonel already when he himself had been a young man of no standing, could become Lieutenant General – under himself as Generalissimo, it seemed, but this was not clear – while Duke Franz Albrecht von Sachsen-Lauenburg would be Field-Marshal. "The Elector of Saxony and the Bavarian will have to sweat money and be afflicted." The Swedish Chancellor was a man of great judgement who would assuredly strive for none other than freedom of religion for both sides as well as the restoration of ancient liberties and rights.

Bubna answered that his instructions did not go far enough to allow him to approve or disapprove such proposals. He would pass them to Count Thurn to be laid before the Chancellor.

Therewith the discussion closed. Next morning Adam Trčka called on the guest. His Princely Grace was anxious lest not everything had been rightly understood.

Bubna: "I have understood everything very well. The aim is that the Emperor shall after all remain. And even though satisfaction were to have been rendered us, his priests would incite him afresh, for they will not abandon their cozenage as long as this House rules." Trčka tried to pacify him, as Wallenstein had during the preceding evening. It would be of advantage for the points to be discussed to be told to the Chancellor by Bubna or Count Thurn. Rašin should convey his answer as speedily as possible to the Duke.

Bubna made his way to Frankfurt-on-Main, reported to Oxenstierna, and for greater clarity put his report in writing. The Chancellor listened, read the report, and, a past master in this field, immediately laid his finger on what was self-contradictory, enigmatic in Wallenstein's offer; he was always a friend of clarity and clean-cut alternatives. What did the Generalissimo have in mind? A peace treaty between all parties according to the rules or an arrangement between himself who had the imperial army in his hands and the Protestants in particular? Peace on earth, universal peace, yes, who was not in favour of it? But that required negotiations so wearisome and between so many potentates upon so complicated subjects that, alas, the business looked as good as hopeless. Precisely that was why the right way to peace was another. Let the Generalissimo take everything in his strong hand, let him promptly restore Bohemia's liberties – its political as well as its religious ones – let him bring home the exiles and in accordance with the ancient law have the crown of Bohemia set on his brows by the Estates, and he could be certain of Sweden's aid, provided that he undertook to support Sweden's rightful claims, when bit by bit no doubt general peace would blossom out of a cluster of individual agreements. What did this signify? The Chancellor was asking whether Wallenstein's intent was to be a loyal, albeit rather eccentric principal lieutenant of the House of Austria or a rebel. The first alternative did not interest him. The second suited him. There was no third.

At the end of June this Swedish answer was handed to Wallenstein in writing. He thought it sagacious and worth pondering. No reply ensued.

Three lines can be traced in the game which henceforward he partly played himself, partly permitted others to play in his name – *if* he permitted them. One, the Saxon–German–Protestant, was still just about within the bounds of legality. The other two, the Swedish–Bohemian and the French, were highly treasonable. Such a view is tenable, it is not devoid of logic. Yet even should it be true that most politicians follow Axel Oxenstierna's example and advance on their objective by conscious separation of the issues at stake, Wallenstein's lonely, visionary spirit no longer did so. He did not move along lines, he simply roved an entire field where one incongruity sometimes ran alongside another or took its own way. The sole immutable factor was that he wanted to be the arbitrator and peacemaker, and basically wanted to be it alone. How? He could not say. But he craved plenipotentiary power, not even precisely sure by which of the opponents, whether all or simply a selected few, he should be invested with such. At the zenith of his career he had been confident, without considering the details or difficulties of the task, that he could bring about peace between the Spaniards and the Dutch, relying upon his superior good sense to carry it off. He had, again at the zenith of his career, sworn to himself that he would thwart the implementation of the restitution edict and had failed to draw the inference – the edict could only be subverted through open disobedience to his Emperor and master. In a single instance, that of Denmark, a relatively modest affair, was he able to impose peace according to his own taste. Now, when the agonizing condition of his body and spirit rendered his holds on reality volatile, his self-confidence rose yet higher. And not even that states the case rightly, for if his self-confidence was great, so was the contrary too. Rigid good sense is not enough for the delineation of his last year. That is why so many diligent studies have intrinsically been in vain. They have entailed, presupposing a mental state which was not on hand and contorting brain and subject alike for the sake of finally finding firm, transparent truth, efforts to introduce reasonable order into what he said, what his admitted, half-admitted, not at all admitted but self-elected friends claimed that he had said, or what these said about him.

The problem is noted here once for all and it will be exemplified by this May night at Gitschin. Thereafter we shall not describe the twists and turns, the discontinuations, the resumptions, and the ambivalences of Wallenstein's end-game with the excessive wealth of detail lavished on it by others.

The discussion with Bubna moved along the outermost, the revolutionary line. Its prologue is not to be sought in the semi-licensed negotiations conducted in 1631–2 with Arnim, but in the wholly forbidden secret toils cast in Wallenstein's direction at that time by Count Thurn. Consequently it would be appropriate to hear of the most far-reaching radical schemes. What do we in fact hear?

There shall, Wallenstein proclaims, be a universal peace to every man's benefit and with equal rights for Catholics and Protestants. An amiable but vague assertion and for him not new, since he had always regarded the war of religion as mischievous. Practically nothing about the shape that peace shall assume, simply that all who have suffered injustice shall come into their own again. Where? In the Hereditary Lands, Austria, Carinthia, Styria? In Bohemia? He does not tell, does not bother to be so exact. It is Oxenstierna who, observing the lacuna, the point about where, whether Bohemia and the Hereditary Lands, underlines it in his answer. And if it is to be in Bohemia, how is the indemnification of the humiliated, the emigrated, the expatriated to ensue? Will Wallenstein dissolve his duchy and hand it over, bit by bit, to that "wanton knave, that von Redern", who awaits his return home in beggary, and to the others? Will those other beneficiaries of the battle of the White Mountain, the cognate Trčkas and Eggenbergs, do the same? It is regrettable that Bubna does not venture to ask. A few weeks later another émigré, Wilhelm von Ruppa, says that he knows Wallenstein and never will the grand robber part with his spoils.

A more astounding facet is that he was proposing to seize still more from the émigrés, at least the hitherto semi-pardoned semi-émigrés. Not on his own account, but to meet the army's needs. Those who during the Saxon occupation had displayed presumption were to have their estates confiscated. They included not only Ruppa, but little Rašin, with a tiny property left over somewhere, too. He signed the order which brought into being this new spoliation commission no more than a few days prior to his talk with Bubna and he did nothing to delay the process. On the contrary, he urged it along because he required the money. The result was that nine months later 15 Bohemian lords, 59 knights and 117 Prague citizens saw themselves condemned afresh to the loss of their fortune. Let the paradox at an extreme pinch seem resolved, let it be assumed that the Generalissimo had for the nonce to maintain the army by the evil means of times past and was striving towards better days, on what legal footing was the general reparation to be based? On an imperial act of pardon by means of a global amount? Not inconceivable, but not what the unflinchingly proud Bohemians wanted. Through a return to the old Bohemian political order via rebellion and revolution? That was what Bubna demanded, as Oxenstierna did in more detail – the Estates would have restored to them the right to free royal election and vote Wallenstein their king. That he rejected, as though startled by the notion: it would be "an arrant piece of knavery". So the Emperor was to remain – to Bubna's bitter disappointment. Not merely as ruler over the ancient Hereditary Lands, but also as King of Bohemia. He would just make a few sensible concessions. He would be compelled to do so, although Wallenstein did not think of using such a strong term. Or, if he used it, immediately moderated his tone by the intimation that no compulsion would be needed because the shavelings were satiated with war. Which he may have believed, for all that Vienna gave him no grounds for the presumption. Were the Emperor's spiritual advisers craving for peace and the party of good sense preponderant at Vienna, the arbitrator would eventually have to exercise no more than mild pressure. Why then a combination of the armies?

Which armies? This question too Bubna did not venture to put. Oxenstierna swept aside the preposterous idea. It can certainly not have been the Swedish army. Wallenstein had not gone crazy, in spite of rumours to that effect. Nevertheless, supposing the unimaginable, if Wallenstein's army and the main Swedish army merged, place would have to be given to the other side's principal commanders, Horn, Banér, in any event young Weimar. Wallenstein ignores these leading captains and proposes Count Thurn, with Duke Franz Albrecht as his subordinate, two marginal figures whose command lay in a marginal theatre of operations, Silesia. From which it becomes evident that he was thinking of nothing more than a combination of his own, freshly equipped army in Bohemia with that of the Protestants stationed in neighbouring Silesia.

This army of the Protestant allies, a strangely motley formation, originated in Arnim's strategy, the Saxon occupation of Silesia during the previous year which had been renewed in the course of this winter. Arnim, it will be recalled, had undertaken the occupation with several purposes in mind. (Everybody always had several purposes in mind.) One of them had been to stymie the Swedes by preventing them from doing the same. After Lützen Oxenstierna did the same. He sent into Silesia a miniature army, reputedly hardly more than six thousand men, with at least three purposes in mind – to support the Saxons against the imperialists, to control the Saxons and if need be (one never could tell) to fall upon them with cold steel, and to keep an eye on neighbouring Poland. This therefore constituted part of Sweden's daring, wide-ranging, always hazardous overall strategy, keeping the Danes in check from the south, the Poles from the west. The Saxon contingent in Silesia was the most considerable of the three Protestant corps there. The third, the Brandenburgers under Colonel Burgsdorff, was even smaller than the Swedish and prepared to be subservient to the Saxons. For the rest there was squabbling, not to mention general wretchedness.

The Dresden Elector, notwithstanding that he was partly too poor, partly too mean to pay his army, thought it a fine enough body of men to multiply its appointments. During the winter he raised its senior officer, Arnim, to the rank of Lieutenant-General and gave him a Field-Marshal in the person of Duke Franz Albrecht. The selection gave fully intended offence to the Swedes. This is the place at which to become more closely familiar with the Lauenburg prince who has on previous occasions already made his appearance. Clear-headed, impudent, filled with the joy of life, keen on every kind of adventure. Brave, as most of his kind were. A political dabbler, as many were. One of those young men who had the gift of briefly giving pleasure to Wallenstein's weary spirit. Oxenstierna judged him to be "wholly a creature of the Duke of Friedland", and he had indeed for ten years, five of them under Wallenstein, held the Emperor's commission. In 1631 he resigned it. Shortly before Lützen he was to be seen in the Swedish camp where two of his Protestant brothers had preceded him. Three others, converts in good time, served with the imperialists. During the battle Franz Albrecht stayed in Gustavus Adolphus's immediate proximity, made a gallant effort to save the wounded King, but nevertheless, besprinkled with his noble blood, had to leave the side of the dying or already dead monarch in order to escape his pursuers. The Swedes disliked his tale. How much they disliked it is evinced by the swift suspicion that none other than Franz Albrecht had killed the King. Although Oxenstierna did not downright assert it, the Duke seemed to him anti-Swedish, thoroughly unreliable, and all in all repugnant. To accord his Saxon appointment a deserving answer, the Chancellor hit upon the scheme of Count Thurn's nomination as, in turn, giving offence to his ally in general and Arnim in particular. How since 1631 relations were between Arnim and Thurn was common knowledge. As second-in-command Oxenstierna picked a certain Düval or Duewald who, he conceded, was in military matters a rash daredevil with excessive fondness for money and drink, but these, after all, were human qualities. Lauenburg spoke of "His Excellency the Brandy-Toper Duewald". Statesmanlike, philosophizing, sober Arnim, plagued by sad doubts and resentments; Franz Albrecht, compound of quicksilver and audacity; Thurn, grizzled idol of the émigrés, for ever jubilant, forever fooled, pig-headed simpleton; Duewald, the alcoholic. An ill-assorted quartet, and on the strength of its leadership only ill could have been predicted for the Protestant eastern army.

Starving, it lay during winter and spring opposite a number of imperial regiments under Gallas. Prudently neither did the other any harm. Wallenstein had planned to proceed to Silesia on the second morning

after that May night at Gitschin because he regarded this as the most
interesting theatre of war in the political, if not military sense. That is
the only explanation as to why he proposed Thurn and Franz Albrecht
as possible commanders of the combined armies. Empty talk to cheer up
somewhat Bubna whom he had so little positive to offer. The Lauenburger he might be able to use. Thurn assuredly not, he would nevermore be the man for his purposes. The man whom above all he needed,
the man with the greatest authority in Saxony and everywhere in Protestant Germany, the man who could in any case not be circumvented,
his name he could not divulge on account of the hatred between Arnim
and the *émigrés*. The report of the discussion during that May night at
Gitschin has to be most scrupulously analysed to separate sense from
nonsense, hidden meaning from hollow pretence. What Wallenstein
gave the *émigrés'* leaders to understand was as follows: you have nobody
else than me. You can build upon neither Sweden nor Saxony. (The
expressions of contempt for the Elector, the contempt of the austere
self-disciplinarian for the nightly soaker in drunken orgies, were heartfelt.) You cannot build upon France. Therefore you will do well to
entrust your fate entirely to me, and that without specifying what kind
of amends and satisfaction he was proposing. "We, who have the armies
in our hands. . . ." A screen too. He meant, "I, who have the army in
my power, and you, who are to play yours, the Silesian, into my hands,
so that I can accomplish my dream. . . ." That was the heart of the
matter. The rest was improvisation, conciliation, cowardly talk around
the subject.

Certain questions remain. Why, if he had so pathetically little to offer
the *émigrés*, did he summon them at all? He knew what they wanted –"to
deprive the Emperor of all". What did he want from or for them?
Formerly he had principally done them harm. This is to grope in the
dark. Better to refrain from pretending to have illumination.

The most rational explanation would pertain to the army in Silesia. If
he was planning to bring it over, he could not exclude its Swedish component. This, though, was really an *émigré* corps with Thurn as Oxenstierna's commander and surrounded by Bohemian gentlemen like
Bubna.

His dream concentrated moreover on the problem of peace as a whole.
The *émigrés*, implacable, constituted a part of it, just as did the quandary
of Bohemia's past and future. He did not have the answer, but the
question agitated him.

It could be that, old and sick, he recalled his youth, his earliest, betrayed ties, and that, while the identity worn for two decades crumbled, he was fumbling for a new one which would have been his original. Such things happen. Like, for instance, old people who in the end begin again to talk in the language of their homeland long left behind. In these months he was tenderly restoring his relations with Karl von Zierotin, husband of his long dead sister, his first patron. How far, since 1607, their paths had diverged! Now, when Zierotin, living at Breslau in exile, wanted for a last time to see his Moravian native heath, Wallenstein provided passport and ample protection "since it rejoices Us to assist in every possible way his purposed journey". Not that it proves much. We simply suggest that it sheds a little light.

Had he only wanted once more to hear what he knew? Had he only wanted to talk and to toy with the most extreme potentialities at no real risk?

Finally, had he let himself in so deeply with the Trčkas and Wilhelm Kinsky, Adam's brother-in-law, that he, the feared and exalted, no longer had the courage outright to say no when *émigrés'* chimeras were propounded to him? Demonstrable is that Count Adam, that utter nonentity, exercised growing influence over him. "No one," attested General von Scherffenberg, "schemed more with him than Trčka who was in his company almost every evening from eight until eleven."

FEUQUIÈRES AND KINSKY

Meanwhile the Marquis de Feuquières was travelling in stately manner between Dresden, Berlin and Frankfurt, absorbing whatever seemed to him of importance, semi-importance, or fractional importance, scattering pensions, promising loans at indulgent rates of interest, besieged by groups of petty princes hoping for favours from him, and setting down his impressions in letters to Paris which never properly ended because whilst he was writing them ever fresh impressions crowded in. The instructions he received in reply from the King, the Cardinal, the Capuchin and Secretary of State Bouthillier generally limped six weeks after events. They required altogether too much from him. He was to improvise on the basis of conditions as he found them and yet very exactly to follow a policy-line just as a violinist adheres to the harmonies and measures prescribed by a composer. In theory a harbinger of peace, he was in practice to work against Danish mediation because it inclined too much to the Austrian side. He was to co-operate on the closest terms with Sweden, and yet he was not to. Paris continued to believe in the

Roman Empire which was that of the German nation and sought to preserve it by severance from the House of Habsburg; Oxenstierna no longer believed in it. The ambassador was as far as possible to spare Bavaria's feelings as regards the Palatinate, but without offence to the King of England. He was to unite the Protestants among each other according to Swedish, no, according to French ideas and to let the Catholics have such guarantees of freedom and about their church's property as Oxenstierna was not prepared to give.... During the course of his journey Feuquières learned that implementation of a policy-line in a war of all against all is something different from playing music by sight. (Not that the lesson worried him.)

A great gentleman from a spacious land, he travelled through one which was spacious by nature but in a political perspective presented itself as a motley mosaic of miniature entities. In secret they were a source of amusement to him. Outwardly he was spirited in the assertion of whatever was requisite to the King of France's dignity. He relished it when for three weeks at Dresden he was invited to stay at the electoral palace with honours paid to him which in no wise lagged behind those appropriate to imperial envoys and were not enjoyed by the King of Great Britain's representatives. Dresden was for him an interesting place.

More interesting than was poor, remote, and insipid Berlin whose court, it seemed, stuck loyally by the Franco-Swedish alliance. Dresden, "Foe at heart, friend aloud", as a Swede conjectured, gave the diplomat something to do. Visits were exchanged and secrets swopped between French, Swedes, Britons, Saxons and Brandenburgers. Firm information, or gossip passing for such, was collected from adjacent territories like Silesia or Bohemia as well as from places as distant as Vienna. Especially satisfactory were the meetings between the Marquis, the Swedish envoy Nicolai, and Wilhelm Kinsky. Meetings always consisting of only one with another, never the three together.

Kinsky, fortune's favourite among the *émigrés*, held court on a scale equal to that of the Elector who hated him as an arrogant foreigner but tolerated him as a taxpayer. A part of this toleration extended to the right to play private politics. Here Kinsky held two trumps, his wealth and his relations with Wallenstein. How intimate were they? Assuredly not as intimate as Kinsky induced others to believe. To allege, as he did, that none knew the Duke better than he was to forswear himself. The three spies he kept in Wallenstein's entourage would have been superfluous if he had been allowed to tap at source. He admitted moreover to having been taken by complete surprise at certain of Wallenstein's moves. That he should have been very quickly apprised about a number of matters, for example, the course of the night-talk at Gitschin, is of no great significance because he could easily have learnt that from his compatriots, whether Thurn, Bubna or Rašin. During the summer Wallenstein issued an invitation through Adam Trčka – he never wrote to Kinsky himself – to visit his headquarters. What does it prove? No more than that something, probably of political character, was to be discussed, although we do not know what. The visit did not take place as Elector John George prohibited the Count's departure. Another time, and again indirectly, Wallenstein forbade him a continuation of his game with Feuquières and Nicolai. This too is not a sound indication since it is not impossible for a veto to be imposed where previously neither licence nor commission existed. Or Kinsky would pretend that he was acting on his own initiative and must first obtain Wallenstein's consent for the role intended for the Duke. But, again, it proves nothing. For my part I believe that Wallenstein knew of Kinsky's undertaking, more or less, but without actively fostering it, and that he derived a degree of pleasure from hearing how far Sweden, how far France would go to meet him in every, including the extreme and improbable, contingency. That does not amount to a firm relationship.

On 14 May Kinsky called on Nicolai. After introductory remarks he came to the point – whether Sweden and its allies still stood by what had earlier, in 1631, passed between Wallenstein and King Gustavus Adolphus? Did Wallenstein, countered Nicolai non-committally, still stand by it? Would the Bohemians accept him as King? They would jump at it, Kinsky replied. Wallenstein had the country anyhow in his power and was *de facto* Emperor, indifferent to religious problems, hostile to the Jesuits. He could no longer count on children, therefore the throne, if he accepted it, would soon be vacant again. He, Kinsky, believed the Duke capable of being ambitious enough to wish to be laid in the earth as a crowned head. When a few days later Feuquières arrived at Dresden, he could hear from his Swedish colleague of the wares that Kinsky was hawking, he could learn the same from the accredited French ambassador who had since January consorted in whispered conclaves with the exile, and soon he was able to have it from the latter directly. That he talked of Wallenstein as being entirely undecided in the matter emerges from the emboldening arguments with which Feuquières stimulated the style of a letter from Kinsky to the Duke. We know that from the draft which he carefully kept. Vaguely he claimed to be speaking in the name of a group which he termed Wallenstein's "most devoted friends and loyalest servitors". What had they to say?

These honest men could not believe that the Duke had forgotten the humiliating treatment dealt out to him at Regensburg as a reward for his salutary services. (Not a syllable as to the French having least grounds to be retrospectively indignant about that act of humiliation.) True, the House of Austria had restored his command. The Duke was however of too enlightened an intelligence not to appreciate that, his appointment having been taken from him on account of jealousy and distrust, his recall was due only to a state of extreme peril, and when this had passed it could well become convenient to send him into the wilderness again. His new command could not purge the ignominious ending of the old. The move was self-contradictory, not meant to last. Let the Generalissimo win Austria's cause and he was lost, for the Spaniards would not endure such authority as his a day longer than necessary. Let him lose and in the universal ruin he would be lost too. A soldier of Wallenstein's gifts would recognize the second possibility as the more probable. How formidable now were Habsburg's enemies, how strongly built was their alliance, and no longer did they need to shrink from a perpetual war along Dutch lines. As to Wallenstein's own army, his friends and assistants were under no illusion as to its deplorable condition, the rankers of base disposition, the officers of threadbare quality. Was his war-chest not exhausted, his credit spent? Did he not have to impose the whole burden of the war on the Hereditary Lands, thereby creating deep discontent at Vienna and in time making him as hated in the restricted territories remaining to him as he had been in the Empire? His most devoted friends and loyalest servitors consequently found it totally incomprehensible for him to persist in staying in a situation so hopeless on all sides, for him not to grasp at the handsome opportunity offered by becoming a partner in the most powerful alliance which alone was capable of upholding him on the position attained by him, no, of carrying him yet higher to a royal throne, ever higher. . . . It would be a pleasure to watch Feuquières striding up and down as he moulded these cunning phrases, in Italian, incidentally, because he knew no German, Wallenstein no French, and then to observe their recipient's face as he read them. Did the ambassador's courteous impudence anger him more than the flattering insinuations gratified him? No encouraging answer was elicited, and Kinsky never claimed to have obtained one.

The sophistication of the Frenchman's psychology is noteworthy. Father Joseph's prediction had been that Wallenstein's day-dreams would at some point assume reality, to his adversity, not his advantage. 160 years later Schiller expounded the argument in his own fashion:

> ... Must I act out the deed because
> I thought of it and did not shun temptation –
> Fed my heart on this dream, saved up the means
> On the uncertain chance of realization,
> And only kept approaches to it open? –
> By Heaven's mighty God! I never meant it
> In earnest, never fixed it as decided.
> I did no more than to enjoy the thought,
> The freedom and the capability
> Engrossed my fancy
>
> And now, farseeing, they will fit to plan
> What happened totally without a plan,
> And what my joyous spirit and my anger
> Led me to say from excess of emotion
> They will knit in an artful web against me
> And make of it a fearful accusation
> Which I must face in silence. . . .

The Marquis de Feuquières' wiles, his calls for belated vengeance, his baits to precipitous ambition are completely re-echoed in the scene where in Schiller's version Countess Terzky impels the hero towards his decision:

> And do not say the dignities restored
> Made up for that outrageous first injustice.
> Good will did not restore you really, no,
> The law of harsh necessity restored
> The office which they gladly would deny you
>
> Confess then that between the two of you
> There can be no concern with right and duty,
> Only with power and *opportunity!*
> The moment has arrived when you must strike
> The balance of this mighty life account.

Schiller knew neither the Capuchin's warning nor the Marquis de Feuquières's memoirs. The two contemporary politicians and, after more than a century and a half, the poet examined their subject and drew strictly the same conclusion. A solvable riddle. The gravity of reality merged here with its dramatic quality because Richelieu, Father Joseph, Feuquières, decidedly lettered politicians, in their actions felt themselves to be spectators of, or distant participants in, a play. Part of Wallenstein's doom was to be seen as a tragic hero while he was still a creature of flesh and blood, mostly on stage, always the focal point, and his end predetermined.

In Schiller the Countess wins. In history the serpent did not. He reported to Paris. With a commendation came the instruction to continue along his path. Soon there arrived a precise draft treaty, signed Louis, signed Bouthillier, for transmission to the Duke of Friedland, with the manner in which this should be done left to the ambassador's sagacity. To parade a treaty without Friedland having declared his hand against the Emperor was a delicate business, but it might be necessary so that he should declare himself. At all events he was to be offered the crown of Bohemia, a million livres annually in return for an army of thirty-five thousand men, and a permanent alliance to be dissolved only on agreement by both partners. His Majesty would do everything possible to render Germany's princes, Protestants and Catholics, amenable to Friedland's ideas. Including Bavaria. Were the latter to prove at the final opportunity incapable of being set right, Friedland was free to do as he saw fit. The "declaration against the Emperor" must consist in public, unequivocal action – the overthrow, no, more happily worded, the liberation of Bohemia, the invasion of the Hereditary Lands. French armies would co-operate appropriately, in the Grisons against the Spaniards, in Alsace and along the Rhine. Oxenstierna was to be included in the business, whether it pleased Friedland or not. Sweden must not be duped in an affair of such far-reaching consequence. Not duped, but an accent other than Swedish laid on long-suffering paper. What Paris concocted was Wallenstein's adherence to its wish-fulfilment of an overall Protestant–Catholic party. What Oxenstierna wanted, in so far as he took the intrigue at all seriously, was at one with Count Thurn and his radical visions – revolution in Bohemia, the Emperor chased into Styria or Italy, *no* peace concluded with the German Catholics. What Feuquières feared was that Wallenstein might come to an agreement with Count Thurn, that is, with Sweden, instead of himself. The Parisian draft treaty revealed of course none of these differences, underlying tensions, ambivalences. It contained precisely the provisions which eighteen months ago Gustavus Adolphus had accepted – the monetary payment, the size of the armed potential, the guarantee offered and required. If Wallenstein read the document – Kinsky will have seen to that – he must have found his dream pleasingly corroborated. He was being addressed as a third great power, *la France et la Suède et Friedland.* He gave no answer. He reminded silent. Even personal letters from Cardinal Richelieu and Father Joseph – we do not know their texts – did not move him to any reaction. What he did and said elsewhere had no bearing whatever on France's major offer. The result was that when, after repeated time-wasting conferences between Kinsky and Nicolai, Kinsky and Feuquières, the politician on his own account once again importuned the ambassador with idle questions, he had the following exasperated reply flung at him:

> The Duke of Friedland's game is too subtle for me [*il agit avec trop de finesse pour moi*]. From his silence in the face of all that I have let him have I can well guess what it is that he really desires, namely, strife between His Majesty and His allies. He is mistaken. His capers deprive him of the help with which the King, my master, and the whole union would be in a position to lend him against those whom he has most reason to fear and whom we also know to be his most dangerous enemies. With his methods he will neither regain their trust nor allay their jealousy and hatred.

Wherewith the Dresden plot pretty well came to an end.

How could politicians of the Cardinal's, the Capuchin's, the Marquis's calibre have taken Kinsky's hints so seriously? They drew their conclusions from Wallenstein's situation and, as they understood the matter, threatened interest. They knew what all the world knew, or fancied that it knew, of his insatiable ambition, just as to have doubted his demonic desire for revenge on the Elector of Bavaria would have been like doubting the sun's existence. Moreover they would probably not even have regarded the *coup d'état* of a Bohemian magnate, autonomous German regent, and army organizer on a European scale as "treason". Wallenstein, unifying in his person these three characters, was more than their sum, a power quantity of the most individual kind, *le Walstein,* as Feuquières often called him, as though his name signified at once degree and title. In central Europe the niceties of loyalty differed from those applicable in the continent's western kingdoms. This man was beyond the scope of standard definitions, and was it not plausible to assume until proof to the contrary was available that Count Kinsky, a man deeply versed in affairs and a member of the Duke's own clan, was manoeuvring according to his instructions? What, in the last analysis, did the whole shadow operation cost? Pen-pushing was cheap, the royal councillors were paid neither more nor less, the ambassador's outlay did not increase on the score of the hours he spent with Kinsky. If the venture succeeded, the advantage was enormous. If it miscarried, nothing was lost as long as the risk of deceit was guarded against. No, there was still something gained, namely, the dubious light in which the Emperor's Generalissimo would appear.

When the episode began to drag without tangible upshot, it escaped neither Nicolai's nor Feuquières's attention that Kinsky's wizardy was no better than most. What other conclusion could be drawn from the Count's sudden, unblushing predication that, who knew, perhaps, indeed probably, Wallenstein's interest was confined to an alliance with the Protestant Electors so as, with their assistance, to chase the French from imperial soil? That assertion brought him closer to the precarious truth than had all his preceding self-important talk. In so far as Wallenstein's policy was still imbued with reason, it was not pro-French. To avoid an open breach had been his aim in his most successful days. To avoid it now was his wish too, for the weightiest of arguments. Were France to proceed from half avowed to completely avowed hostilities, no end at all was any more to be foreseen. The King of France, Wallenstein told the Saxon Colonel Schlieff, must on no account be allowed to cross the Rhine. To have been the first among German princes to help the King to achieve that and to link the final remembrance of his name to this act ran counter to both his shattered statesmanship and unshattered pride. Not that it solved the problem, the frightful, insuperable problem, of how universal peace should be attained without Sweden, without France, without Spain.

The discussion during the May night at Gitschin is of greater importance than a dozen cabals of the three Dresden weavers of intrigue. At Gitschin we hear, for once, Wallenstein's own words, his words *against* the rape of the Bohemian crown as a piece of knavery, his words *against* the French arch-Jesuit, faithfully repeated by the disappointed Bubna precisely because he felt such disappointment. At Dresden we have a third party's observations on what an accessory said who for years had not seen the principal. And the accessory was a confidence trickster. The injury that he did Wallenstein, the waste of a great credit, nevertheless originated in the Duke's own soul. When he still more or less enjoyed good health, he maintained discipline over his friends, relations, political agents. Now he let their games run rampant.

AN ARMISTICE

During this winter conditions were not everywhere as comfortable as in Bohemia where Wallenstein and his assistants were continuing their improvements on the war-machine. Field-Marshal Gallas's regiments in Silesia faced their opponents in identical circumstances of putrid wretchedness.

> Since the Swede's death [ran the plaint of an anonymous Austro-Bavarian author], his Imperial Majesty has been made war upon by some few miserable princes and four Swedish nobles, Oxenstirn, Horn, Baudissin, Banér (who without a proper leader are to be regarded as robbers) to such extent that, aside from a very few strong places – Breisach, Philippsburg, Ingolstadt, Wolfenbüttel, and Forchheim – not only the whole Roman Empire, but the Austrian Hereditary Lands also have to a good part fallen into enemy hands.

The allegation about the Hereditary Lands was an exaggeration; what the writer meant was a slice of Silesia. "Some few miserable princes" referred in the first place to George von Lüneburg and Bernhard von Weimar. After Lützen command of the Swedish army had been divided between them, Lüneburg proceeded against Lower Germany, Brunswick, and Westphalia in order to seize the line of the Weser from the imperialists; Bernhard marched against the Main. South of the Danube was stationed an unimportant Swedish corps, remnant of the preceding year's campaigning. Alsace was almost wholly under the control of the "Swedish noble" and "mere robber" Horn. Farther down the Rhine prevailed the Palsgrave of Birkenfeld, another petty prince loyal to the Swedes. Weak though this strategic arrangement was, wide-meshed and characterized by flagrant flaws, it was none the less stronger than anything that Wallenstein, who in any case did not believe in military action during winter, had to offer against it. Bernhard, he thought, would stay in Bamberg, but the prince advanced on the Danube. He did not think that Horn would make an early move, but already in January the Swede crossed the Rhine and made his way through Württemberg to the Lech. Aldringen, on loan to the Elector Maximilian for the defence of southern Germany and previously in Swabia, retired to Bavaria. The unification in April of Horn's and Bernhard's troops near Augsburg was an unabashed repetition of the foregoing year's events. Repetition of Maximilian's embittered pleas to the Generalissimo: Your Dilection proposes to use Your good services for my later indemnification of the damage, but who will reconstruct my burnt cities for me? Repetition of the descent by Bavarian officials on Prague and Vienna and their empty-handed return. Repetition of the diffident hints from Vienna – were Wallenstein able to do anything on threatened Bavaria's behalf, His Majesty would undoubtedly be caused great satisfaction. Repetition upon repetition, but hardly anyone drew the obvious inference that, even though the Swedish invaders came as far as the King had in the previous year – albeit they did not reach Munich – they would still be no nearer their ultimate objective. By hardly anyone, with a single exception.

Seen superficially, Wallenstein's situation in spring 1633, was also very similar to that of 1632. He wanted to have his rearmament completed before launching any operation, thus adhering inflexibly to his principle not to allow himself to be lured into activity ahead of time. He wanted his first step to be the recovery of an imperial province, on the last occasion Bohemia, on this one Silesia. That done, he would move "into the Empire" and, once again, "rectify many a matter". As in the preceding year, he advised Elector Maximilian for the nonce to remain on the defensive. The difference, from a superficial point of view once more, was that now he could in effect issue orders to Bavaria because he had his own representative, Aldringen, on the spot with a force whose strength he gradually increased with draft from Bohemia. Not that he liked this, but he did it. The allegation that he neglected the south German theatre of war is therefore untrue although the instructions given Aldringen were not such as Maximilian hoped for – first, to seek refuge in the fortress of Ingolstadt, then, when Aldringen disregarded the order and established a position on the Isar close to Munich, "not to hazard anything" and, as Wallenstein later made himself even clearer, not to begin any attack except "at no risk". Perhaps his motive was sheer malice, secret satisfaction at Bavaria's devastation. It could however also have been an anxious, preventive strategy deriving from the overall military situation. For the imperialists, he claimed, a victory would not mean much, a defeat everything. It was an opinion shared by Aldringen, cool, critical, not imbued with particular loyalty towards Wallenstein, but at this juncture and in this instance decisively in agreement with him.

On 17 May the Duke at last departed from Gitschin, the splendour of his court refurbished like that of his army – a hundred and twenty servants in glittering liveries, forty court officials of noble birth, fourteen coaches drawn by six horses each. "A pretty train, a brave sight," was his pleased comment as he mounted, "but our return shall be with one far comelier!" So he was quoted as saying – one of a thousand poor inventions.

Holk's task, as last year, was to secure Bohemia's north-west corner, whether against Weimar, Lüneburg, or anyone else to whom it might occur (not that it occurred to anyone) to pay the kingdom a visit and stir up mischief. He had moreover to obey the restrictive order not to let himself be lured "into the Empire", the Upper Palatinate, by any impassioned appeal on Maximilian's part. Again Wallenstein's principle, as old as his command, that Bohemia, his Bohemia, must always be kept barred against intruders, a principle disregarded by others only when he was in retirement. More than enough, their numbers approaching thirty-five thousand, were the troops whom he had concentrated at Königgrätz for the expedition into Silesia. Their march took them via Smiřice and Nachod to a point half-way between the Bohemian border and the Oder. Arnim, Thurn, and their difficult colleagues totalled less than half, with their resources and their morale equally pitiable. Here, it seemed, an attack could be launched "at no risk" and a position of far-reaching importance be seized at a single blow. Experience taught the advantage to be had from domination of the Oder. But not a word was heard about attack. Word, very soon, though, of something different.

Adam Trčka appeared in Arnim's camp, conferred with him, and issued an invitation to a meeting with the Generalissimo. Arnim accepted. On 6 June he rode to Wallenstein's camp in the company of Colonel von Fels as deputy for Thurn (who was ill), the Saxon Colonel Vitzthum as witness, and the Brandenburg Colonel Burgsdorff. He met the Duke in his litter in an open field. With him were Field-Marshal Gallas and Count Trčka. There are reports as to what was said, the conditions formulated were disseminated in broadsheets hotly discussed in the streets of Dresden and elsewhere. They lack authority. The credence to be attached to their contents depends on taste or tact. The Brandenburger had ventilated the old, depressing argument that the Catholics did not feel bound to keep their word to heretics. Wallenstein countered with the question whether the Colonel wished so completely to cleave Catholics from Protestants. Not Catholics of the good old kind, replied Burgsdorff, but Jesuits. "God's profanation!" broke in Wallenstein. "Does he not know that my aversion to the scoundrels, these Jesuits, is such that I would that Satan had long taken the rogues? I have a mind to drive them all out of the Empire to the Devil!" He swore that, as truly as he wished to be reckoned one of God's children, yes, the Almighty should reject any part of his soul if in his heart he meant his words any other than they sounded.

> And if the Emperor will not make peace and keep the agreement, I shall force him to it. The Bavarian started this game. No assistance shall I render him, but would that his land were already ruined . . . would that he were long dead. If he make not peace, I shall myself wage war against him, for my desire is to bring about an honourable, honest, lasting peace within the Empire and thereafter with both our armies move against the Turk to seize from the knave all that of which he has robbed Europe.

Maybe, as alleged, those were his words, without much regard for the presence of Count Gallas, Ferdinand's loyal officer. Fevered utterance because his body really was riddled with fever, just as his fingers were so palsied with gout that another had to sign his letters for him. We shall however omit any recapitulation of the conditions bruited abroad. They are not merely inconsistent, but our single reliable account does not contain any conditions. He would probably not have been deterred from proposing inconsistencies, but who *could* have made proposals for a general peace which would present a pattern of consistency? Arnim, as an experienced man of business, was a friend of written records. Next day he therefore set down his version of the encounter and sent it to the Duke for confirmation. His understanding of the previous day's consensus was "that Yr Pr. Grace's opinion was that the hostilities between the two armies should cease and on both sides the weapons be turned, *conjunctis viribus* [with united strength] and without regard for person, against those who would presume to continue to disturb *statum Imperii* [the Empire's peace and order] and to restrict freedom of religion. Which I so interpret that everything" should be "within the Roman Empire brought to the condition that prior to this unhappy war prevailed in the year 1618". Arnim's phrase "which I so interpret" indicates that what was said in the open field cannot have been altogether so plain. Back came the answer from Adam Trčka, on behalf of his master whose bent fingers could not hold a pen, that it was indeed laudable for Arnim to have put matters in writing and laudable for him to propose to negotiate them with the two Electors; the Duke would for his part keep what he had promised. A careful reading shows this confirmation to be none. There was neither a word about the year to whose blissful condition it was proposed to return, the year of normality 1618, nor as to which regions, and to which not, its foundered normality should apply. The interlocutors had talked, magniloquently and without entering into any obligations, past each other. The most delicate points were left untouched. To Vienna, where rumours about the meeting and the year of normality 1618 were very soon rife, Wallenstein issued a denial: he had never proposed or agreed to any such thing. A most sensible, comforting communication, as Eggenberg commented in his letter of thanks. Had he scrutinized it thoroughly, he would not have been quite so comforted. By no means was "everything to be restored to the condition that had been in the year 1618". Not everything. Perhaps some things?

Arnim set out to meet, somewhere at some convenient country-seat in their respective territories, the Electors of Saxony and Brandenburg. The farther he was removed from Wallenstein's spell, the more dubious and bizarre may have appeared to him the message that he bore. His journey tacitly signified abandonment of the project in its original form, a peace concluded between and dictated by the army commanders. If Wallenstein, in dreams and a state of overweening pride conditioned by sickness, at moments saw himself as a man of violent political action which in fact he was not, level-headed Arnim never viewed his own person in that light. Generals could discuss peace in accordance with the mandate and along the lines laid down by their princes. Decision did not rest with them. For the period of Arnim's absence, in the first place a fortnight, then slightly extended, there was to be an armistice. It was badly observed. The forces were too close to each other. They clashed, if not for glory, at least for chickens and pigs.

While Arnim cantered from one Elector to the other, diplomatic hospitality flourished on Wallenstein's island of the blest. The other Saxon commander, Duke Franz Albrecht, paid a visit. He was thoroughly in favour of the armistice. For military and political reasons alike. All would be lost without it, he thought, so miserable were the circumstances right around his own headquarters. Count Thurn also put in an appearance. He found his reception flattering. "It would take too long to describe to Your Excellency how I was extremely handsomely received, profusely entertained in every way, and again escorted to the front. I shall await the first safe opportunity to relate the gratifying conversation. No change in what Lord von Bubna told Your Excellency. Everything remains well within bounds." The last phrase inspires alertness. This is the point, maintain Wallenstein's accusers, at which the two main lines of his traitorous policy, the German–Protestant and the Bohemian–Swedish, merged although the second was the one which he genuinely intended to implement and Arnim had only perforce been initiated. As chance would have it, Bubna had at this juncture just returned from Frankfurt with that clear, challenging rejoinder from Oxenstierna as to whether Wallenstein proposed to be rebel or imperial negotiator. The Duke, as will be recalled, regarded the letter as very sagacious.

If only words had carried any weight. If only Wallenstein's old proneness to tell people what they liked to hear, though his phrases constituted no pledge, had not degenerated into confusion and sickness. Thurn was on the spot. He was a Swedish commander. He distrusted Arnim. He shoved his way into affairs, blustering, blethering, bragging. He could be neither ignored nor informed, more particularly since four weeks ago an *émigré* had been received at Gitschin and fed on vague hopes, that Wallenstein's real objective was not agreement with either the Swedes or the exiles. To say as much would have represented an engagement, a delimitation which he did not have the courage to define. Perhaps in the last analysis they, the exiles and the Swedes, would after all be needed. And even if the intention was to turn against them, was it admissible to reveal this to the Saxons? Arnim might think what he would, but for the present his masters stayed chained to the Swedes. Wallenstein's German-Protestant line of policy was conceivable and inherently logical. Time would tell whether it was actually practicable. The Bohemian-Swedish-French line was a murky figment, but matters were now so frightfully tangled that there was no longer any escape from it. Deferment was therefore the order of the day and feeble-witted Thurn allowed to puff himself up. To the imperial court's intense annoyance. The Swedish commander was none other than the man of the defenestration, the most guilty of all the revolutionary leaders.

The senior allied controllers at Dresden and Frankfurt took care not to be deceived as Thurn's innocent stupidity rendered possible. What, Feuquières asked a Saxon Privy Councillor, was a general peace? Was it a peace negotiated by all the warring parties or was it one concluded by a few which thereafter the remainder had to accept unread? The latter was not unimaginable, replied the Privy Councillor. But, argued the ambassador, supposing that the rest did not agree? Would in that case the peacemakers proceed to war upon yesterday's friends? He hoped surely not, the Privy Councillor rejoined. Powers like France, like Sweden, like the States-General would assuredly not allow themselves to be trumped by Saxony, the ambassador intimated. That Wallenstein's aim was a separatist peace with the German Protestants was not only Nicolai's worry, which Kinsky's disconcerted, lying interpretation could do nothing to allay, but the worry of the more intelligent among the *émigrés*, like Ruppa and Ladislaw Zierotin, and the worry of Oxenstierna. "Some monstrosity is being hatched there," he growled at table. "'Tis so odious to me that I would fain be up and away!"

On 27 June Arnim returned to his Silesian headquarters after three weeks' absence. Brandenburg's politicians had shown interest, but a complete lack of instinct for the hidden properties of the proposal. Berlin was always slightly more sympathetic to Sweden than Dresden, slightly more radical, and it viewed the offer in that light, declaring it worthy of closer examination. How, for instance, did things stand as regards Wallenstein's own claims, the indemnification for Mecklenburg? Saxony's politicians proved suspicious. The armistice, they told Arnim, had already aroused all kinds of misgivings among the Swedes, the French, the British. It could damage the extremely valuable Danish mediation, in which Berlin did not believe at all. Was it advisable to make enemies of one's friends without by any means yet having made a friend of one's enemy? If the Duke of Friedland proposed to attack with their united forces those who wanted to continue disturbance inside the Empire, was it not palpable whom he meant? Namely, the Swedes, except that their name was not mentioned. A flat rejection of Wallenstein's offer, urged Arnim, contained two dangers. He could inflict terrible tribulation upon Saxony in order to silence his foes at the imperial court or he could, exactly the opposite, unite with the "stronger party" – namely, Sweden and France, though their names were again avoided. Moreover negotiations without Wallenstein or running counter to Wallenstein – the Danish mediation – were quite useless because the imperial army, its generals, officers, soldiers, were attached solely to his person. Empty talk would achieve nothing with the Duke. Some serious proposition, at the same time as innocuous as possible and without causing division in the Protestant camp, must be contrived. The result of these pros and cons was Arnim's receipt of an instruction whose usefulness was exiguous: the Elector's love of peace and his patriotism were proven, the prospects for the impending Christian peace congress at Breslau hopeful, whatsoever the Duke of Friedland could contribute to that same objective would be gladly awaited. Arnim would, it may be guessed, have had his way if he had displayed sufficient enthusiasm and if he had only been able to define his cause clearly. He did not and he could not. The paper he carried was too flimsy and full of riddles.

On his return he found the Duke "much altered", as he expressed it – cold, distant, majestic. Perhaps Arnim's prolonged absence and empty answers were offensive to Wallenstein's vision of being Europe's arbitrator. Perhaps he felt his position at Vienna to be crumbling – signs were not wholly lacking – and thought that he must now proceed more vigorously. Who, though, can look into a mind which revolved matters only within its own periphery, no longer within the compass of reality? At all events prolongation of the armistice was made dependent on fresh, harsh terms – he must be yielded the land as far as the Oder, he needed it for his army. Faced with a polite refusal, he denounced the armistice. They parted company. On the same evening he launched an attack on Schweidenitz, a fortress held by the Saxons. The attempt to catch the foe napping miscarried. The town was well defended. When next day Arnim hurried to the scene, its besiegers were forced to flee. The outcome of Wallenstein's first military effort in a year which had passed its zenith was not a happy one.

The armies continued to face each other from behind fortified positions, in the confined Silesian territory, in their common misery. Of action there was none.

THE SPANIARDS

At Madrid ministers clung to Wallenstein with the manic tenacity with which politicians believed in whatever they had once made up their minds to believe. They noticed nothing when, at the peak of his power, he worked against them in Germany. They cast the warnings and gloomy representations of their ambassadors to the wind. They loudly deplored the weakness which caused the Emperor at Regensburg to sacrifice his general, a sacrifice committed for the sake of Elector Maximilian whom they regarded as their unflinching, secret, and malevolent antagonist. Antipathy to Bavaria constituted a genuine common factor between them and Wallenstein, but it was not one to bear any fruit. Was there any other? The Duke of Olivares was not the champion of religion that, properly speaking, it would in his role of His Catholic Majesty's principal adviser have behoved him to be. What continued to happen to heretics on the Plaza Mayor was one thing; foreign policy was another. For instance, he viewed the edict of restitution as an error, much as Wallenstein did, and thought that its implementation should be indefinitely postponed in order to allay the wrath of the Protestant Electors. Not that Olivares' concern was for peace in Germany. He cared nothing for that, but a great deal for a more vigorous prosecution of the war against the Dutch and the French. His expectation that Wallenstein would do him precisely this favour caused him to work hard for his recall. When this had transpired, Doctor Augustín Navarro Burena was appointed standing representative to his headquarters so as to emphasize the good relations with Madrid. Navarro arrived as an admirer. The condition did not last. He was one of those outsiders in whose presence Wallenstein wagged his tongue, vented his rages, and extemporized his ideas all too unguardedly.

Castañeda, the new Spanish ambassador at Vienna, was a declared enemy. Strange how the situation prevailing during the first generalate recurred. For the royal ministers, Olivares and the Germany expert Oñate, both so very far away, Wallenstein continued to be the great indispensable personality. The man on the spot, though, sent the most sombre reports compounded of truths, half-truths, and lies. The Generalissimo, he alleged, neither made war nor wanted peace. He was about to sell his services to the King of England. At Vienna everyone trembled before him. Naturally Prince Eggenberg did not remain unaware of the ambassador's insulting impressions. On one occasion the two gentlemen had such an altercation as caused Castañeda to drive home and for a couple of days take to his bed. Questenberg, in a letter to his patron, is the gloating authority for that. Nevertheless until late summer 1633 relations between Wallenstein and Madrid, whatever Castañeda had to endure by way of vexation, were regarded as correct, more than correct. They were so regarded. Madrid believed them to be so.

At the beginning of 1633 a plan began to be put into operation which had been hatching for quite a while. A large expeditionary force was to move from Milan to Brussels under the leadership of Ferdinand, Archbishop of Toledo, the King's brother who was known as the Cardinal Infant. The warlike prince of the church would replace the ageing Infanta Isabella. Her days were said to be numbered; she died in the following November. The Cardinal Infant would with fresh troops and fresh energy at least retain Flanders for the Spanish crown and, it was hoped, accomplish rather more. The passage at sea being closed by Dutch ships and through France by the French, his journey from Lombardy would have to be made via the Tirol, Swabia, and down the

Rhine. Very tiresome, very dangerous. Never mind whether a province only capable of being reached by such routes could really be held or what advantages its retention offered. We know what power politics were, what the heirs to and upholders of an old power fancied that they owed either to themselves or to others. Philip IV wrote to Wallenstein about the protection needed for his brother's trek. He received the friendliest of answers. A message couched in similar terms went to the Duke of Feria, the Spanish governor at Milan. Aldringen had orders to afford the travellers all necessary assistance. Enemies were always amply on hand. Why should he add the Spaniards if it could be avoided at no great cost?

In spring, or rather, in early summer, because six weeks' allowance has always to be made for the post, the state of affairs at Madrid and in Wallenstein's camp respectively altered. The Flanders expedition lost in urgency, especially because the Cardinal Infant lay ill at Milan. What had been conceived as mere transit was transformed into unlimited military stay on the Upper Rhine, its object being to secure Burgundy against the French, expel the Swedes first from Alsace and then from Swabia and Franconia, free the road to the Netherlands, and link Germany with Italy through a chain of garrisons. One of those broad-based and actually quite impracticable pieces of strategy which would require German co-operation in as much as the manpower was only partly to derive from Lombardy. The rest was to be enlisted in the Tirol, Salzburg, or elsewhere, to a total of twenty-four thousand men. A new, large-scale Spanish intervention, in fact, with a Spanish attack on France from Germany supported by imperial arms. Full of confidence, as though it were all nothing, King Philip and the Duke of Feria, selected to conduct the scheme, applied to Wallenstein. He, already ailing, fell into a sick man's fury. Just as four years ago in the Mantua campaign, the Spaniards were on hand as trouble-makers. He never forgot the Mantua campaign, as he never forgot anything of that kind, events which seared his soul. The Spaniards had always been ill-advised, had unjustifiably launched an aggression against the Duke of Mantua, and in addition they had lost 's Hertogenbosch, Maastricht, and other places. He would know how to prevent a repetition of such events. Times had changed, thank God, and he had guarantees. Have a foreign general planted at his side? Let himself once again be driven into war against France by deluded armchair-strategists? Let his peace projects be torn apart? The more he revolved the matter, the more feverish became his reactions. As the director of his chancellery attested, "Advice arrived at the same time of the Spanish army's approach, whereupon the Friedlander's fulminations never ceased."

In a single day three messages followed on a first, stingingly negative assessment sent to Questenberg for onward transmission. The Infanta at Brussels was told that he was in no position to comply. The missive to the Cardinal Infant at Milan, to be expounded orally to His Highness by Colonel Diodati, was of the same tenor. To the Emperor he stated that he had more than once given his opinion on this tedious business, but could not refrain from reassertion. What was being concocted here would bring down on his head the whole powerful armed French potential. It would still more disastrously alienate the German Estates, Catholic and non-Catholic, from the House of Austria. It would bury the hope of peace currently hovering in the air. He entreated most humbly that the affair be most graciously brought to the point where the Lord Cardinal Infant's and the Duke of Feria's move into Germany be most promptly countermanded.

At Vienna his warnings did not meet with complete lack of understanding. Doubts of a similar nature were rife at the imperial court. Castañeda was astounded suddenly to encounter something like a German patriotism which did not wish to see Spaniards at liberty to do whatever they pleased in the land. The argument that they too were Germans to the degree that King Philip, in his character of Duke of Burgundy, was an imperial German prince appeared feeble, if not downright comical. At this juncture Trauttmansdorff revealed to the ambassador a state secret – when the Duke of Friedland again accepted the generalate it had been agreed that no one should hold a command in the Empire unless subordinate to him. The tale has been heard before. Spanish troops not subsidiary to the Generalissimo had long past been stationed on German soil. The Elector of Bavaria furnished a similar example. The secret was simply an excuse on Trauttmansdorff's part.

At the end of July the mood at Vienna veered, as was common there. Now it had become anti-Wallenstein. What was happening on the Silesian front created an ever more unfavourable impression because nothing was happening. Nervous glances were cast towards southern Germany where Bavaria's Elector was managing to keep the eastern part of his land free from the foe – his headquarters lay on the Inn – but where in western Bavaria, in Upper Swabia, and in Württemberg the Swedes were able to move without impediment. To look towards the Upper Rhine was to indulge in a twofold worry, especially as regards the fortress of Breisach on the right bank of the river. Talk about Breisach developed into and stayed the fashion. A turning-point in history, according to contemporary strategists. A last guarantee of the link between Burgundy, Alsace, and Upper Germany. An all-dominant situation on the Rhine. Admittedly the imperialists stationed there had failed to prevent the Swedes from liberating and ravaging to the north, to the south and to the east, let alone the west, and a layman can only with great difficulty resist the suspicion that affairs could have proceeded with or without Breisach. Be that as it may, the fortress was threatened, almost surrounded, and had to be saved. Wallenstein reluctantly bowed to the chatter about Breisach. One of Aldringen's officers, Scherffenberg, could make his way there with two thousand horse to encourage and victual the garrison.

Meanwhile Vienna had decreed that Wallenstein was not the right man to rescue the navel of the world. The Spaniards must do it. Ferdinand himself informed the Duke. Breisach lost, all lost. That was why he had with a heavy heart not only to allow the Spanish trek, but had also agreed to lend them Aldringen for their assistance. Aldringen must contribute five thousand men at least, apart from a few regiments under Colonel Ossa in the Tirol. His loss would be the easier to endure since Field-Marshal Holk could easily replace him with his corps at present inactive in northern Bohemia. A peremptory order. Strong interference in what after Göllersdorf had been the Generalissimo's undisputed domain. Manifestly not, however, a breach of *agreement*. The legal brains in the Emperor's entourage would not have left that unmentioned. Wallenstein, for his part, would have crowed about it. He kept silent. Not a word of protest was elicited from him. Valeriano Magni, the connoisseur of souls who claimed that the feared tyrant was fundamentally fearful and always gave way if the whip was cracked, may have accounted this as confirmation. Perhaps too in due course his wrath abated. Something none the less stuck. Again, as in 1629, his opinion had been slighted in what he felt to be a vital question. Nothing had changed in any respect. The old, injurious misery.

His reactions fluctuated strongly. On 1 August he wrote to Aldringen that since the Duke of Feria had undertaken the relief of Breisach no more help was required from the imperial side; General Scherffenberg should stay with his twenty cavalry squadrons where he was. After a week this countermand, dictated in anger and foolish because the Spaniards could not be in Germany before September, was revoked, leaving Aldringen free within his well-known discretion to undertake on Breisach's behalf whatever appeared right to him. Wallenstein allowed to happen what others did practically independently. At the end of October Breisach was relieved from its perilous situation by Feria and Aldringen. At the end of October. Does the late date signify that the danger had not been so pressing? Was Feria's expedition not alike overrated by the Spanish strategic visionaries who hoped that it would save their empire and by Wallenstein who expected the most catastrophic consequences to ensue? There is, for instance, nothing to show that French or Protestant policy was altered one iota by it. Much ado about little, when it came to the point. But what is point in politics? Point is what people say, believe, want, pretend to want, fear, pretend to fear, and one man thinks of another.

King Philip's ministers neither thought ill of Wallenstein nor had they any wish to impute ill-will to him. Some inkling that he was not the friend whom for the past eight years they had accorded incense now stirred their minds, but no more than that. His active enemies resided at Vienna, apart from Munich where such a state of affairs was patent. To call them the Spanish party, as was often done, would lack precision. Castañeda belonged to it, also that old Spanish brigand and ne'er-do-well Marradas, but alongside them sailed all kinds of dignitaries, Cardinal Dietrichstein, friend to Rome, Father Lamormaini, who shared Bavaria's pro-French sympathies, Count Schlick, the Bohemian, a number of officers left out in the cold and feeling correspondingly offended. Their connection with Spain was tenuous. If the decision about Feria had been a triumph for Spanish policy, it had equally been one for this heterogeneous group.

At some time during this midsummer a pamphlet was written by, so it is believed, Schlick, the President of the imperial War Council, and the Bavarian Vice-Chancellor Bartholomäus Richel. They concealed their identity behind the fictitious personality of a "Councillor". The imperial army, they asserted, slumbered. The enemy was constantly gaining in might and presumption. The Generalissimo did as he wished, which was nothing except waste time in groundless peace negotiations. First question: was he in the light of his increasing physical debility fit to fulfil his appointment? Second question: were there ways to induce his voluntary resignation? Third question: if not, what then? Fourth question: would it be better to bring down in ruin the House of Austria and shortly the whole of christendom rather than to hurt the Generalissimo's susceptibilities? Of these questions (the "councillor" continued) the third was the thorniest. Indubitably a couple of clever Capuchins or other acceptable fathers could be dispatched to the Duke to indicate to him the advantages of honourable retirement. More pressing, though, was to make sure of his senior officers so that, if need be, "they would no longer obey the Lord Generalissimo". As to who should succeed him, there was no dearth of suitable personalities. Why look farther than the successor to the imperial throne, the King of Hungary, as whose deputy Count Schlick was on hand. . . . On 12 August Count Schlick departed for the Silesian headquarters. The instructions which he carried, official and private, coincided in good part with the foregoing worried piece of pamphleteering. His official instructions were to investigate how things really stood, what was transpiring in the negotiations between Wallenstein and Arnim, and what could be done to promote the Spanish expeditionary force as well as a more active prosecution of the war generally. His private instructions authorized the Field-Marshal "so to dispose", as far as possible unobserved, "Counts Gallas, Piccolomini, and other excellent senior officers that His Imperial Majesty shall be assured of their steadfast loyalty and devotion in the case of a change pertaining to the Duke of Friedland by reason of his illness or otherwise."

By reason of his illness or otherwise. Sixteen months after Göllersdorf, a mere sixteen months after the saviour had responded to the cry of the drowning parties. Eleven months after Nürnberg. Nine months after Lützen. ("I felicitate Myself and Your Dilection upon this most happy success and on Sweden's death. God be praised and thanked.") During the second generalate everything went much faster than during the first.

A SECOND ARMISTICE

On 16 August Count Schlick arrived at headquarters, the "Camp at Schweidnitz". He found the state of affairs even more puzzling than he can have anticipated.

An unofficial armistice had continued to prevail in Silesia all the time. Contacts, with polite letters of regret about untoward incidents passing back and forth, had been maintained between the top commanders and those of lower echelons. Matters at this stage forbade, Wallenstein drily, tersely told Maximilian, larger-scale operations. None the less at the beginning of August he ordered Holk to inflict a fresh visitation on Saxony. Just like a year ago and with the same objective – through the agonies of invasion, by applying another twist of the screw, to incline the Elector to peace. The expedition had an element of urgency. Unless he made sure quickly of some advantage to himself, the forthcoming armistice would simply benefit his opponent. Holk therefore irrupted into the Meissen area with thirteen thousand men, repeated his performance of the preceding year with rather more horrors added, pushed forward as far as Leipzig, and again extorted seventy thousand taler from the sorely tried city. More was not to be squeezed out of it, and not much more out of the country as a whole except for the currently raging plague.

The ugly action was under way when Schlick reached Schweidnitz. New negotiations too had begun.

A few hours before the President of the War Council had sighted the tents, the colours, and the camp-fires from his coach, a discussion had taken place between Wallenstein and Arnim. Further meetings followed between them, Gallas, Duke Franz Albrecht, and Thurn. At one of the political talks, at least, Schlick was also on hand, most keenly observant, as can be imagined. On 22 August a second armistice was agreed. He had opposed it, Schlick claimed. He had no authority to prevent it. The terms, signed Duke of Friedland, Arnim, Thurn, bound the parties to refrain for a period of four weeks from any military operation in Brandenburg, Saxony – this involved Holk's recall – and the imperial territories, to obtain no reinforcements, and to send none elsewhere (to the Danube, for example), all this being acceded in the interest of bringing the peace negotiations loyally and without deceit to a desirable conclusion. Not a very revealing document. There exists a second, a draft by Arnim headed "Informal Reflections on how the Duke of Friedland can Formulate his Declaration relating to the Negotiations and his Offer so that No Suspicion may Arise among Others". He should say that he was determined "to enter into the alliance which the Holy Roman Empire has now for the best established between the Protestant Electors and Estates, the crowns of France and Sweden, and to work with them to the end that thereby everything within the Holy Roman Empire touching on secular and religious peace should be restored ·and preserved according to its former state". The historian who discovered this interesting document considers its signature by Wallenstein to have been probable. Nevertheless it is quite certain that he did not sign. "Friedland did not wish to negotiate in writing, so that it should not be possible to fasten it upon him," attested Duke Franz Albrecht von Lauenburg. "Although Arnim right often requested it, he was unable to attain this." So there was nothing in writing, no signature. He may once however have talked on these lines. Along quite others too, as evinced by Thurn's newly re-kindled belief and jubilation in a message to Oxenstierna: "Let Your Excellency entertain not the slightest doubt. It has been resolved to chase the Emperor to Spain."

The two Silesian fronts proceeded to indulge in a bout of amity marked by frolics and carousing. Count Schlick, a stern outsider, stalked through the imperial camp holding official talks with the Duke, most unofficial ones with Ottavio Piccolomini. Arnim was away on a political trip, his second but not his last, in the interest of a Wallenstein peace plan. He met the Elector of Saxony at Grossenhain, General Holk at Gera, the Swedish Chancellor at Gelnhausen near Frankfurt-on-Main. The Marquis de Feuquières was not far off, but Arnim avoided him. His love of the French was even less than his love for the Swedes. Left out, Feuquières felt that Oxenstierna mismanaged this important business.

How he managed it is recorded in a letter written on the same day, 12 September, to young Weimar. Oxenstierna reported to the Swedish commander-in-chief what Arnim said that Wallenstein had said to Arnim. Not a case of Wallenstein's own words.

The Duke and Arnim had talked about the postulates for peace, the expulsion of the Jesuits from the Empire, and the restoration of the untrammelled Bohemian royal election. The Emperor, according to Wallenstein, was prepared to conclude peace with Saxony, Brandenburg, and other Protestant Estates, but not with all, and in any case not with Sweden and France.

> After the Lieutenant-General had propounded this at length, he came finally to the main point, saying that the Duke of Friedland has not yet forgotten the affront put upon him three years ago, is not on the best of terms with Vienna, and is very violently vexed that the Duke of Feria has been summoned to no other purpose than to hold his own against him. Wherefore he is resolved, if he knows that he would in all eventualities be assisted by us, to revenge himself.

Wallenstein, the writer continued, thought that he could rely on Generals Holk and Gallas as well as the majority of his officers. Others, of whom he was not certain, were already or would still be relegated elsewhere. He did not regard all of Holk's regiments as trustworthy. That difficulty could be navigated by Oxenstierna's addressee, Duke Bernhard, marching in Holk's direction and, in an emergency, supporting him against his refractory underlings. Thereupon Holk and Weimar would together proceed against the Elector of Bavaria, Wallenstein against Austria and Styria. Field-Marshal Horn would need to attend to the Spanish army under Feria, and possibly too the French could once more make things warm for the Spaniards in northern Italy. "Were this matter to be taken seriously," summed up Oxenstierna,

> the game would, by God, be won. But I find it all too suspect and I know not what to pronounce. I discussed with him, Arnim, this and that in order to find the real reasons, but, as is his habit and nature, he was rather secretive although he went so far as to say that he cannot be without doubts, but 'tis certain that the Friedlander is distinctly displeased. . . . Whether he has the army as much in his hands as he fancies, he much questions.

The Chancellor closed his strange letter, of which it is not certain how far he coloured the contents for his addressee's benefit, with the remark that it was essential to remain preponderantly passive in this affair, to risk nothing, make no changes in one's plans for the sake of such shaky chances, but to take advantage of whatever was offered if indeed it came to a serious offer. This was the spirit in which he had parted from Arnim – non-committal encouragement.

Arnim continued his trip. He talked again to Elector John George and obtained an authority to act which went farther than he had had in June, but was none the less ambiguous. There was to be a "composition" between the imperial and Saxon armies – "composition" is something other than "unification" – in the interest of lofty peace and German liberties, an objective which (it was noted) happily coincided with that of the Swedish Chancellor. Of revolution in Bohemia and Austria, a *coup d'état* against the House of Habsburg, not a word. . . . Arnim talked once more to the Elector of Brandenburg. He left with a commission which repeated almost word for word his Saxon one. Not altogether astounding, seeing that he had drafted it. Again the reference to a "composition" between the forces "to help and promote the salutary work of peace", again the reference to the inclusion of Sweden which he had secured at Gelnhausen, again the reference to the expectation of a general treaty of peace to be slowly, thoroughly elaborated in conjunction with the Duke of Friedland. After four weeks' journey Arnim was back in Silesia, full of hesitant hopes. Wallenstein's change of front and accession to the Protestants was immediately impending, as dealers on the stock exchanges of Frankfurt and Hamburg were for hundreds of taler prepared to wager. Late in October – news from central Europe customarily became known in London only weeks afterwards – King

Charles remarked to the Venetian ambassador that merchants' letters reported Wallenstein to have rebelled against the Emperor. He had heard nothing, replied the ambassador, but it appeared to him "rather desirable than credible". The King agreed, adding "There are circumstances which give it some air of probability".

On 24 September, when Arnim met Wallenstein, the Duke demanded something totally different – their two armies, the imperial and the Saxon-Brandenburg, should combine to march into the Empire and throw out the Swedes because no firm peace was possible as long as they stood in Germany. To Arnim this change of outlook was incomprehensible, unbelievable, monstrous. Next day, to make quite sure whether it really subsisted, he sent his Field-Marshal, Wallenstein's "creature", quick-witted, youthfully zestful, and cynical, to try whether it was possible to reconvert his enigmatic negotiating partner. Franz Albrecht did his best. The late King, so his winged words sped, had never had any other aim than to achieve a just, lasting peace with freedom of religion and security of their prerogatives for all, and until proof to the contrary this must continue to be viewed as the Swedish policy. Granted, the saviour of German liberty had claim to satisfaction and must be offered it. If this power should then refuse to leave the Empire, time enough to coalesce against it.

> Thus I addressed the Duke of Friedland [Franz Albrecht reported], but he answered with great vehemence that all this was naught and he desired to proceed in no other way than that we should immediately unite with him, march into the Empire, and take by the throat the Swedes, the Spaniards, and the French alike, wherever they were encountered. He was moreover avid to possess absolute command. Because I had no instructions for such proposals, I said that the Lieutenant-General would assuredly not enter upon them. Whereupon he was seized by an ague and exclaimed, "So be it! The remaining three days of the armistice I shall honourably keep my pledged word, but I shall know what it is that thereafter I have to do."

He rose and, with "At Your service, Your Dilection", dismissed his guest.

The Protestants tossed and wagged their heads in bouts of indignation. Oxenstierna saw his notions of traditional papist ill-faith vividly confirmed. Elector John George swore a thousand "Zounds" and "Never Again". The most upset was Arnim: he had been thought capable of a piece of arrant knavery, of treachery to the blood of the martyred King. "However it may be," he wrote to Elector George William of Brandenburg, "what amply emerges is that nothing can be safely negotiated with this man, for reliance upon him there is none."

Thus ended the story of the second armistice as seen through the eyes of Arnim or those who had to believe whatever Arnim told them. In reality it was all quite different.

He was weary of the old ties, groping his way towards new ones, notwithstanding that he felt revulsion at the step and, as soon as any attempt was made to force them on him by reason of some random word of his, shrank back from it. The only tie which he could have endured, because it would have given him complete autonomy, was the "absolute direction". Something of the kind was what he dreamt that union with the German Protestants would confer on him. Then he would have been the third power, the arbitrator above party, and he would have dictated peace, his peace. Introversive and impatient as those obsessed by their dreams are, he was deceived as to the difficulty of the undertaking. The European war crawling from the chrysalis of Bohemian rebellion could not be stopped at a single stroke.

Even that blockhead Thurn sensed at the outset of this bewildering period, from June to September, how Wallenstein's wish was confined to an alliance with the Protestant Electors in order with their assistance to show the door to the Swedes. As at the outset, so throughout. There are records relating to this which weigh more heavily in the scales than that prize specimen of evidence, Oxenstierna's letter to Weimar, favoured by the Duke's accusers and those who adhere to the conspiracy theory. Franz Julius von Lauenburg, Catholic brother to Franz Albrecht and an imperial political soldier, was in October at Dresden. Saxon Privy Councillors and Arnim in person furnished him with the most motley information as to the background of the ruptured negotiations. It included talk of reconciliation between the Germans, between the Protestants and the Emperor, to be achieved with the help of the King of Denmark and the Duke of Friedland, of a conjunction between the armies, of an attempt to dislodge the foreign army – namely, the Swedes – from the Empire either by persuasion and with equitable recompense or, if not otherwise possible, by force so as then happily to restore affairs to the state prevailing before the Bohemian uprising. That sounds different from what Arnim said or, according to Oxenstierna, is supposed to have said at Gelnhausen. It has a more plausible ring. It confirms

incidentally that Wallenstein was very much against Arnim's visit to
the Chancellor. "The Duke of Friedland has not yet forgotten the
affront put upon him three years ago" and desired to slake his thirst for
vengeance by a revolution defying all calculable consequences – what
poor psychology this is, as seen through Wallenstein's eyes how unreal
is the policy which it propounded, how impossible if seen through
Saxon eyes. The German Lutherans, with Elector John George at their
head and arm in arm with Lieutenant-General Arnim, were conserva-
tives. The House of Austria, an Emperor from the Habsburg dynasty,
the religious Peace of Augsburg, and possibly freedom of religion in the
Hereditary Lands, these were constituents of the past's warm nest to
which they wished to return. Arnim neither believed nor wanted, nor as
a Saxon plenipotentiary would he have been entitled to want, what he
prattled to the Swedish Chancellor. And why did he add that he had
doubts on the subject? Is that the way to talk if one's objective is to instil
conviction? Was it not his purpose to instil conviction? What was his
purpose? To induce amiability in the mistrustful Oxenstierna – "I
think little or nothing of this Arnim business" – by the sheer extra-
vagance of the offer? Lies and quarter-truths have no long run. What has
to be dismissed is a predisposition to think of Arnim, the pedantic dealer,
the ever sober, the Lutheran Capuchin, as having been a politician of
logical consistency. He, as much as the rest, was addicted to talking,
writing, and chattering, one day this, one day that, about whatever
entered his mind.

Arnim's reputation was that of being hostile to the Swedes, a secret
separatist. The foreigners, he liked to warn listeners, had an easy hand
to play. If they lost, all they had to do was to return to their ships and
their respective countries, unharmed. If they won, they had their gain,
but Germany none. A reasonably coherent line of argument, and this
autumn too found him throwing suspicious, deeply angered glances at
the Swedes and the French. Precisely he should therefore have grasped
and promoted what lay at the heart of Wallenstein's policy, the policy
of a third, a German party. If however Wallenstein was never all-
powerful in Austria, Arnim was nothing less than all-powerful in Saxony
and Brandenburg. The Protestant Electors would at a certain stage,
indeed fairly soon, in one or two years, be ripe for separation from
Sweden and France, but they were not ripe yet. As they did not venture
the leap, Arnim could not hazard it either. As the Swedes looked on him
as their opponent, he had to pretend to be doubly loyal and to exaggerate
to the point of absurdity the pro-Swedish, conspiratorial aspect of

Wallenstein's offer and to seem thunderstruck when suddenly the Emperor's expulsion to Spain was cancelled.

The parties talked past each other and, just as in June, never dragged the essentials into the light. Wallenstein, apprehending that the big alliance could not be instantaneously blasted, pretended through cryptic phrases to be ready to join it. Time would tell how matters should proceed. To curse Spaniards, Jesuits, pulpiteers and Bavaria was agreeable to him. To speak with contempt of the court at Vienna was agreeable to him also. Duke Franz Albrecht reported how, when he had asked what purpose the unification of the armies would serve if there was to be peace, Wallenstein answered, "God's profanation! There may be disturbers of the peace, particularly the Spaniards, wherefore position must be taken against those who do not accept or will not keep the peace, an it were the Emperor himself!" This was in the early days of the negotiations. Towards their end, but prior to Arnim's return, Franz Albrecht recalled how

> ... the Duke of Friedland declared that the armies of all foreign rulers, like the Spaniards, the French, the Lorrainers and the Swedes ... who do not belong inside the Empire must be expelled so that the state shall again be reached which prevailed in the Emperors Rudolf's and Matthias's days. Whereupon I desired to know with whom a beginning would be made, and he replied, 'tis all the same to him on whom he turns first.

He would of course first turn on the Swedes, not on the Spaniards, and subsequently not on the Spaniards at all. Spaniards, French, and Swedes were fighting each other on German soil. Attack one and it was impossible to attack the others; they were on one's side, like it or not. The time was beginning when a feeling of hatred for all foreigners spread through Germany, a feeling that their presence, whether they were friend or foe, was equally noxious. Wallenstein, so proud of his imperial principality, was not immune to this new kind of patriotic sentiment. Mere wishful thinking. The Empire having once opened its doors to them as playground and laboratory for their enmities, there could be no national uprising against *all* entrants. Politically conceivable was only a link with Dresden and Berlin followed by an effort to be rid of the Swedes whether on amiable or unamiable terms.

Would that have been the third, the Wallenstein party, which was talked about? The pursuit of questions posed by such twilit circumstances is of limited use. Wallenstein had never been imbued with all the gifts appropriate to a statesman, only some of them, although those to a marked degree. The visions which rose and disappeared again in his chafed mind, his intuitions respecting peace and order and tolerance, his cravings for one last apotheosis, as well as his rage, distrust, and hatred no longer congealed into stable determination. To that extent Arnim saw correctly. Intrinsically he had always been a third party because he had not felt drawn to either, had always regarded himself as holding a central position, and had never in anything political subscribed to others' views. What is by no means the case is that his present activities remained wholly concealed from those around the Emperor's person or, in so far as they knew of them, met with their very severe disapproval. He constituted the central position. To that he wanted to bring over the German Protestants. On the flank stood the Swedes and the French. The lines which he threw out to them, *pace* Kinsky and Arnim, were of the most tenuous kind. On the other flank stood the power which, ever since 1619 when he had taken refuge within its orbit, had been for him the legitimate one of "Our Lord, the Emperor". He kept the court in some measure abreast of matters; he did not let contact lapse. Count Schlick was on the spot when the second armistice began and, subsequently returning to Vienna, he gave a tolerably satisfactory report. Wallenstein had promised him after his fashion what, if he could, he would do and what he would not. Soon, at one point or another, he would engage in major military action. In the coming winter he would spare the Hereditary Lands any billetings. He would at last place Aldringen under Elector Maximilian's command. Whether Schlick, now a skulking opponent, took such promises seriously must be left open. Ferdinand did. He took the prospect of a separate German peace very seriously. During September those politicians who would have represented Austria at the Breslau peace congress, Trauttmansdorff, Hermann Questenberg, and a political lawyer called Dr Justus Gebhard, stayed in Wallenstein's camp. Because the congress did not occur, they were unemployed and the more interested in what was happening at headquarters. Certainly the impression made on Trauttmansdorff, the party's outstanding member, was not predominantly unfavourable and neither did he advise Vienna in that sense. He also liked the prospect of a separate German peace. The vague tenor of everything heard was that all should again be as in the days of the good Emperor Matthias. That was what Questenberg told his brother, the abbot, while Piccolomini – of recent date Count Schlick's confidant – wrote to a correspondent that Catholics and Protestants would unite against disturbers of the desired peace. "There is definitely to be no negotiation between us and the Swedes because the opinion is that it would excite displeasure in the Empire and that it would not prove possible to persuade them voluntarily to renounce their power, but no readiness exists to tolerate a foreign nation with its army inside the Empire." This is what many, though not all, for there were sceptics, thought and what those in positions of influence expected. Wallenstein at any rate attempted to expand the scope of the armistice, a purely local one, by the adhesion to it of the Bavarian Elector and the achievement of a corresponding agreement with the Swedish generals who were harassing him. Maximilian bluntly rejected the proposal. His refusal corroborated what was in the nature of things. The issue was unfortunately not that of a peace but only a reversal of alliances, should the Swedes have no offer which would induce them contentedly to go home. During the succeeding January Wallenstein was inclined to extend such, but during September nothing was heard about that. Vienna was certainly not prepared to do it. A Privy Council opinion on what could possibly be conceded at Breslau for the sake of peace has survived. As far as the Germans and the religious problem was concerned, the attitude was sensible enough. Towards the Swedes it was harsh. As long as they retained a foot's breadth of German soil there would be no tranquillity, no safety. Vienna therefore preferred to speak of a unification of the armies rather than of peace. As he understood matters, Trauttmansdorff wrote to Wallenstein, the problem was no longer that of the armistice's prolongation, but the agreed conjunction of the armies and their march into the Empire. He was happy, the Emperor informed Wallenstein. Affairs either would be, or already were, settled with the Saxons and Brandenburgers, and now forward, quickly, to deeds of common glory! Were Wallenstein to succeed in this business with the Electors, his wavering reputation would be secured and the malice of his enemies reduced to silence. Did he not succeed, he was the man who had let slip the months from May to October, the whole campaigning season: deceiver or deceived.

He did not succeed. The contrivedly cheerful letters from Vienna were already out-of-date when they were penned between 21 and 25 September. Wallenstein allowed the illusion too long a lease of hope, first for himself, then for the others. The rupture of the negotiations may – perhaps – have come as a surprise to Arnim, but not to him. Ten days earlier he had added to an instruction for Adam Trčka a postscript in his own hand: *Z pokoje nebude niz*. Nothing will come of the peace. To express the most secret permutation in his design, he lapsed into his mother-tongue.

The poetess and historian* who looked most lovingly, most cruelly into his strange soul believes that hypertrophic intellect supervened over those vital energies from which action flows and in the end completely paralysed them. Diplomatic intercourse with him was always something of a torment. "During his second generalate matters had reached a pitch where deliberate decision and action became almost impossible to him. The swing of the pendulum to the extreme point where a conclusion ought to have been reached, then a return to its antipodal point, with the process repeated, followed a mechanical course, so that exact observation could probably have foretold when the revulsion must occur." Fine phrases, worthy of their subject. They are confirmed by the verdict of a contemporary witness. "Always," wrote Arnim, on 14 January 1634, "when the conclusion should have been reached, he has changed his persuasion. If it has happened from deceitful intent, he cannot be wholly trusted. If it is his instability, he cannot be built upon. Did his attacks of the ague intervene, then their renewal must be apprehended." The attacks of the ague, the mental debility – Smiřický heritage. The dramatist, whose purpose was not served by illness, made free, perilously wicked game with it:

> How do you know that I have not made fools
> Of them deliberately? That I have not
> Made fools of all of you? Do you know me
> That well? I don't recall revealing to you
> My inmost heart. . . .

Hegel, philosopher-critic, in turn regarded this as the pivot of Schiller's tragedy – the indeterminateness of a "noble, self-sufficient soul playing with the highest ends and therefore unprincipled", whose own end is finally determined by mean external constraint.

This is the peak of poetic interpretation. Perhaps it comes closest to the truth.

Contemporaries who could claim some, even indirect contact with Wallenstein thought that astrology was the key to the riddle. Adam Trčka, according to little Rašin, bewailed the variety of things that the star-gazers whispered into his great brother-in-law's ears. Nicolai noted

* Ricarda Huch, whose biography of Wallenstein was published at Leipzig in 1915 (translator's note).

in his journal, "Colonel Vitzthum reports that, while Arnim was at Frankfurt, an astrologer predicted to Friedland that in November 1633 he would fight a battle and win. And since he is so superstitious as to heed the influence of the stars and mostly to govern his actions by astrological reports, the opinion was that, even if at first he had been seriously inclined to the junction, this prophecy had led him to rue it." Arnim hinted derisively at a like cause. For no correspondence on astrological matters to have come to light during this last year of the Duke's life seems reasonable enough; Battista Senno, the bog violet, was constantly in the background. We do not however propose to avail ourselves of such dull-witted explanations. Had he really permitted himself to be guided more strongly than ordinarily by the planets, it would simply have been another indication of his decline, not its cause. He is the most traduced, the most highly misunderstood figure of authority in the realm of story. The belief that he was a slave to astrology stems from the character-study by Valeriano Magni, *il personnagio grande*, who blended so much falsity with so much truth into brilliant portrayal. Wallenstein was an outsider whose conduct was out of the ordinary. But people have no patience with what is strange. For its comprehension they adduced the dross familiar to them.

Yet other reasons were found. Field-Marshal Holk had died, very swiftly, during his withdrawal from Saxony and only three days after his meeting with Arnim. He suspected poison, an act of mortal spite on Arnim's part. Cowering in his coach, he had whispered to Colonel Hatzfeld, "Let him be gone, for I am truly sick," and was dead in the second night. Wallenstein heard the news before 14 September, the day on which he decided *Z pokoje nebude niz*. Is there any link between that and his utterance? Had not Holk been his pillar, his factotum, the man most deeply initiated into his political, treasonable projects? There is no proof of this last, although it was alleged, whereas against it speaks that Holk, eager and greedy for fame, neither understood the inactivity to which Wallenstein condemned him nor bore it gladly. Politics was moreover not the subject of discussion at the Field-Marshal's meeting with Arnim, when the lethal fever was already throbbing in his temples, only military affairs, the evacuation of Saxony and what Arnim was prepared to offer for it. He offered nothing. Holk's death explains little.

The metaphor of the pendulum whose rod swung from one extreme to another is spatial. Does indivisible ego have any spatial quality? In Wallenstein's case everything was concentrated and cohesive – the peace to which he persuaded the Emperor while acting in his name, the peace to which he constrained him, the struggle which he conducted against him in order to constrain him, the struggle which he conducted against him in punishment, the struggle which he conducted against the Swedes to drive them out of Germany, the amicable arrangement with the Swedes by the concession of a slice of land – everything focused on a single point, the freedom of his ego. During the period of the two armistices, four months, this was the operative condition. It had subliminally been so before. It did not subliminally change thereafter.

When the year drooped to its end, though, and his life too, he often thought back to the Schweidnitz negotiations with gloomy, self-interrogatory remorse. Then, then he could have had peace for the plucking.

STEINAU

He proceeded to demonstrate a truly hectic activity. "I am not here to carouse." An order went to Gallas, who had taken over Holk's corps of thirteen thousand men, to move into Saxony without exposing Bohemia. An order to Aldringen to make common cause with the Duke of Feria and, in God's name, save Breisach, but without relinquishing his independence and certainly not, as Feria craftily demanded, subordinating himself to the inferior position of a Spanish field-marshal. The order was of no practical importance. Since the beginning of September the troops under Aldringen's command had been merged with Feria's ten thousand starvelings – at the Emperor's decree. That put paid to the directive on which Wallenstein relied, which gave him, and him alone, supreme authority over the imperial army. He let it pass because he had no choice, but he laid counter-mines. One was the appointment of Gallas as Lieutenant-General, his deputy in the Empire, so that Aldringen should be under Gallas, and thus indirectly himself, rather than Feria, let alone Maximilian. Tricks which did not work. Aldringen, diplomatic in messages, did what Emperor and Elector required of him and was on his way to the Rhine before the Generalissimo's permission arrived.

Arnim, his worry about Saxony and Brandenburg well-founded, turned towards the Elbe. He left behind a number of garrisons in the Silesian fortresses. His allies, he hoped, would manage to hold the line of the Oder. For some distance Wallenstein followed him, then suddenly swung about and by forced marches reached the Oder at Steinau where Thurn and brandy-swiller Duewald were stationed with the principal part of their meagre resources. Colonel Schaffgotsch and a hundred and sixty companies of cavalry were sent across the Oder to bar the enemy's flight. The main body trundled against the defenders' walls on the left bank of the river. Wallenstein had thirty thousand men, Thurn less than six thousand. Wallenstein had seventy field-pieces, Thurn eleven. The Swedes could nevertheless have held out a while, Arnim complained, instead of straightway capitulating, as Thurn did, on conditions which are obscure. His soldiers were refused a free and honourable withdrawal. They had willy-nilly to enlist in Wallenstein's regiments. As for his two principal captives, Wallenstein acted oddly. They were threatened with instant death unless they sent instructions to the commanders of all Silesian fortresses to follow their example. This too Thurn conceded. Liegnitz, Glogau, Sagan, Crossen were handed over, one by one. Poor Thurn! Four months ago so cock-a-hoop with pride and splendidly received by Wallenstein. Now this inconceivable transformation. Whether the Duke's conduct was in accord with the established usages of war must remain an open question, its answer dependent on the unknown terms of surrender. Even though unconditional, the execution of general officers would have been an unusual step normally reserved for lower formation commanders who had unduly protracted the defence of their strongholds. At any rate it was an inhuman stratagem that he used, the inhumanity which he sometimes displayed when he felt himself five times superior.

For Thurn it was the end of his long, ill-starred career. He now disappears. Wallenstein, after successful, unprecedented exaction, let him go together with the flock of *émigrés* in Swedish uniform who must have fallen into his hands. Vienna took his magnanimity amiss. To have arraigned the father of the Bohemian rebellion before a belated court of justice would have given it pleasure. Scoffingly Wallenstein wrote that Thurn in the enemy's camp was of more use than on a scaffold. So Khevenhüller maintains. Neither the original nor a copy of this letter has been found although other reports about the Steinau affair, brief but proud, have been preserved. They went to the Emperor, the Electors of Bavaria and Mainz, to Feria, Trauttmansdorff, Questenberg, to the King of Poland at Warsaw, and to Dr Schmidt at Constantinople. Wallenstein was patently at pains to impress on friends and enemies the brilliance of the victory. And he was out to extract some material gain too. A few hours after the engagement he instructed Max Waldstein to see to it in the right places that a tax on alcohol in the duchies of Sagan and Glogau, hitherto not diverted into his exchequer, was ceded to him. He had surely earned a boon.

For the moment his effort to impress succeeded. Ferdinand had of recent weeks been besieged by Wallenstein's Bavarian, Spanish, Austrian enemies with increasing effrontery. If they did not yet dare to cast downright aspersions on the Generalissimo's loyalty, their back-biting about his incapacity, inscrutability, selfish malevolence became ever more savage. Now, late at night, arrival of the Steinau news. The monarch excitedly hurried from his bed to hammer on Eggenberg's door and let him share at once in his own delight. The minister, an invalid as much as Wallenstein, is said to have suffered a severe shock from being woken at this hour. There were tales enough of kings having their favourites put in chains after midnight and delivering them to the block at dawn. . . . In scale the victory at Steinau was not notable, but its effect might be far-reaching. The eastern part of northern Germany, apart from Saxony and Brandenburg, lay open to whoever controlled Silesia, and Wallenstein hereby controlled it almost altogether. Why should it not mean that Pomerania, Mecklenburg, and Stralsund, that sparsely defended Swedish treasure on the Baltic, were his to take? So late in the year, so late in life it could still have become a campaign like that of 1627.

Field-Marshal Wolf Mansfeld, the "rapacious wolf", pushed ahead as far as Frankfurt-on-Oder and Landsberg on the Warthe, places where we have been before. Wallenstein halted at Crossen. Neither the lowland nor the sea was his objective, but ever and again, ever and again, peace with the Protestants. At Crossen, on 20 October, ten days after Steinau, he met Duke Franz Albrecht.

Difficult to believe. Had they not barely four weeks ago parted in the worst of tempers? Had not Arnim sworn never again to negotiate, and Wallenstein too? "This piece of trickery," he had fumed to Trauttmansdorff, "is indeed not the first that I have suffered at their hands, but it shall certainly be the last." Yes, that is the way that people talk, yet do not relinquish what they have made up their minds to do because, compelled by good sense, they regard it as the only sensible course. As after the first armistice, so after the second the game of liaison between Wallenstein and Lauenburg never ceased to be played. Useless to ask who started it when there was no start. It suffices that the meeting took place. A noteworthy one. For here Wallenstein, on the first and last occasion in this labyrinth constituted by the year 1633, dictated and signed a draft agreement. Their Serene Electoral Highnesses of Saxony and Brandenburg of the one part and His Roman Imperial Majesty's Generalissimo of the other (so it ran) have had the present devastation, indeed destruction, of the Roman Empire under consideration. They have pondered ways and means whereby this may be remedied and Germany, rescued from spoliation by foreign nations, restored to its former flourishing and prosperous state.

> Therefore the two most highly esteemed Serene Electoral Highnesses and His highly esteemed Princely Grace the Generalissimo have agreed that their two Serene Electoral Highness's arms shall be joined with and put under the command of His Princely Grace the Generalissimo in view of the especial confidence reposed in him so that he will set on foot and attain the aforesaid intentions, and therefore with their associated power the re-establishment of religious and secular freedom, as it subsisted in the time of governance by Rudolf, Matthias, and then His present Imperial Majesty, shall be restored and upheld against those who continue to persist in its disturbance.

A straightforward text. Unification with the German Protestants, a common front against all the foreign armies eager for the plunder and havoc of the Empire, in the first place the Swedes, then the French, perhaps ultimately the Spaniards too – it was Wallenstein's dream from the outset, in June as in September, and whoever had not yet grasped that was beyond help. This time he wanted to put it plainly. He thought that his putative partners were, in the light of the emergency with which his Steinau victory threatened them, ripe for the development. A mistake. He thought that the Electors would blindly subordinate their armies to him because they must know him as he knew himself, he who followed a middle course, the only man whom they could trust, the man above party and with sovereign discernment. A second mistake. He thought that at his behest the Court at Vienna would accept without demur the *status quo ante* agreement. A third mistake. Its honesty is proved by his dispatch of the draft, immediately and proudly, to Privy Councillor von Trauttmansdorff. He had not wanted to enter into particular aspects of the peace; that would be a matter for the Emperor and the parties to the treaty. "If this comes to pass, I am of a mind to march with the electoral armies into the Empire and shortly to relieve our lands of all militant molestations."

On this occasion he concluded no armistice (which would have been welcome to the frightened Brandenburgers), but during the next two to three weeks, from the end of October to the middle of November, he did allow the new, never quenched hope to guide his policy in military matters. From a strategist's point of view they were precious weeks, for how many remained before snow and frost set in? He did not want to give up the concentration of his principal force in the area Silesia–Saxony–Bohemia. He was ready to receive the armies of the Electors with open arms if there came from Dresden and Berlin the news for which he longed. If it happened otherwise, he was prepared to give the screw a tighter turn. "Should the Elector [of Brandenburg] not make peace," he told Trauttmansdorff, "before Christmas he will lose his land."

Poor, dreaming Wallenstein. He and Arnim ran after one another in circles. At the best moment for the great deal, if a good moment ever existed, Arnim blew coldest. He had to. At this very minute the Swedish campaign against him was snowballing into the most virulent calumniations. Thurn's defeat, it alleged, had not merely been his wish, but the plan which he had secretly concerted with Wallenstein. That was the reason for the exuberance of his denials. The victory of Steinau, he wrote to Elector George William, was too poor a basis for the Duke of Friedland to rest such high demands on it and his offer void of content. It simply amounted to a claim that he must be taken at his word. Was that indeed feasible? Even supposing the time of Emperors Rudolf and Matthias were restored, what help would that be? Precisely out of these thickets had crawled the dragon of war. And so forth. Had Arnim advised acceptance of Wallenstein's peace terms, he would have weakened his position. He strengthened it by speaking against them because currently Dresden, and still more clearly Berlin, did not wish to relinquish the Swedish alliance. George William declared the draft agreement to be downright childish. His official answer to Lauenburg rang only a little more diplomatic. The Duke of Friedland's intention was regarded as laudable; the proposed manner of implementation was impracticable. Another fortnight passed before Franz Albrecht moulded the Brandenburg–Saxon message into less offensive shape and transmitted it to its addressee, adding that every man was mortal and with whom would it be necessary to treat if suddenly another stepped into the Generalissimo's shoes? "Duke Franz Albrecht shall have no reply from me," exclaimed Wallenstein bitterly, "for that appears superfluous. . . . All this stems from Arnim." Let the reader not fancy, though, that he had abandoned or parted company with his dream of winning over Arnim, ever again Arnim, to his purpose.

Confusion of minds and confusion amidst the war's chaotic reality. The armed masses lumbered past one another as their leaders talked past each other. Whereas Arnim thought that Wallenstein had his eye on Berlin and marched into Brandenburg, the Duke proceeded south-west, away from the Oder, into Lusatia so as to adopt his favourite position astride the Sudeten range. From there he could defend Bohemia and harass Saxony until it squealed for mercy. In Brandenburg and neighbouring Pomerania he left behind a corps under Philipp Mansfeld. "I now also hold Landsberg, and I believe that Stargart is in our hands," he informed Trauttmansdorff. "Therefore, apart from Stettin and Colberg, all Farther Pomerania is in our possession." His own progress was slow. The dragging move from fortress to fortress must have been deliberate. These were the days when he was on edge for Lauenburg's reply. Not until 13 November did it arrive. He tried to conceal the embarrassment in which it placed him by fresh, blustering threats that soon the Electors would have cause to rue their obstinacy. Uncertain is what he would have done if he had not within four days been forced to turn his attention in quite another direction. Oxenstierna, at Frankfurt-on-Main in the centre of his thin, widely spread Swedish spider's web, had ordered to Franconia a part of the troops who in summer had gained the line of the Weser. He wanted a diversion by Bernhard von Weimar against Bohemia. He feared that upon which Wallenstein's hopes rested – defection by the Electors. In this method of waging war all parties were always flurried. Everything was always thought possible, defence and attack, new coalitions and repudiations of old alliances, until somewhere someone did something quick and surprising that for a few months altered the situation.

THE FINAL CRISIS BEGINS

He no longer believed in the war, and that was why for six months he was so inactive in military affairs. Basically his strategy no longer served any other purpose than for the imperial side to preserve what it had until peace was made – the Hereditary Lands, Bavaria, and a few strongholds on the Rhine against France. The Duke of Friedland, complained Maximilian, always had only in mind the security of the Austrian hereditary kingdoms and territories. That was not enough. The Swedes and their adherents in the Empire must suffer confiscation of everything that they had won, cities and strategic sites, people and provinces. Had frank discussion between the two of them been possible – from the outset it never was possible – Wallenstein would have answered that Germany's liberation or overthrow for a second time was neither feasible nor yet desirable.

Had the experience of 1628 not sufficed? What success had it had? His military policy had a certain consistency as long as attention remained focused on it rather than the grand, tangled promises which he dispensed when Vienna put pressure on him. "Stand on your defence," "Hazard nothing." These were the precepts which he repeatedly inculcated into his commanders, Holk, Gallas, Aldringen. He no longer cared for spectacular gains. Berlin, the capital of Brandenburg, for example, when it was his for the taking, meant nothing to him. What purpose other than plunder would be served by the fleeting seizure of Berlin?

He was lucky that for a while such cautious, passive, unimpassioned strategy could suffice without serious disturbance by the other side. During this summer and autumn Oxenstierna, its principal planner, was puzzled what action to take because Wallenstein's failure to act presented a hurdle. A concentric assault on Bohemia, to ease Saxony's situation and to effect other schemes, was projected for August, then dropped; the second armistice had neutralized Saxony and Brandenburg. Movements back and forth, hurry and bustle, seizure of peripheral places followed, all of which demonstrated less of design than response to Wallenstein's quiescence. Day after day, week after week, the soldiers marched compliantly up and down the country simply in the hope of finding elsewhere what they no longer found where they were, bread, meat, and beer, and houses in which there might still be something left to pillage. The predatory swarm grew by ten thousand when the Duke of Feria appeared in Upper Swabia with his Spaniards. They were really Italians, a pitiable contingent without horses, wagons or ammunition for its artillery and totally without victuals. "In charge of this whole affair is a shaveling who should stay in his confessional," Ossa commented contemptuously. Ten thousand men were none the less ten thousand men, a figure larger than the fraction of the royal army which Bernhard von Weimar, Swedish commander-in-chief, during September dragged from the Saale to the Main, from the Main to the Danube, from the Danube to the Upper Rhine. In as much as Wallenstein was waiting at Schweidnitz for Arnim's return, the main emphasis of the campaign shifted south-west, in so far as "main emphasis" and "central theatre of war" can be applied to such martial bungling.

Aldringen continued in Elector Maximilian's proximity on the strength of the preceding year's exchange deal. Hitherto he had fulfilled the task, and no more, that Wallenstein had within strict limits imposed on him – to remain "in defence of Bavaria", that is, to keep most of Bavaria free from the enemy. In September he proceeded westwards from Upper Swabia to join Feria, whereupon the two of them set out on a long, skilfully executed migration. They skirted the Lake of Constance to the Rhine, the border of neutral Switzerland, followed the river to Basle where it wheels north, and marched downstream as far as Breisach. Its relief on 20 October, a week after the fall of Steinau, was an enormous success in the eyes of those who took Breisach enormously seriously.

The small repertoire of strategic manoeuvres, endlessly repeated, is by now familiar. Someone goes somewhere so as to draw somebody after him, like Wallenstein moving into Saxony in November 1632. Someone pursues somebody who does not wish to be pursued and he catches or does not catch him, as Wallenstein in 1626 dogged the freebooter Mansfeld as far as Hungary without entrapping him. Someone pursues somebody, or pretends to, suddenly turns aside and lunges into the weakly defended space left by the other, which, with Steinau as its upshot, was what Wallenstein had done on the Oder when he knew Arnim to be on his way to the Elbe. Variations on this pattern were possible. In the present instance the Swedish commanders Horn and Duke Bernhard tried farther north, along the Danube, through the Black Forest, and in direction of the Rhine, to parallel Aldringen's and Feria's westward progress. They did not reach the Rhine in time, they did not encounter the foe, and on a map the object of their operation is entirely mystifying. In October Oxenstierna, able to exercise only very remote control from Frankfurt, had a better idea. With Aldringen hurrying towards the Rhine, the road along the Danube, the road back, lay open. With Saxony and Brandenburg after the second armistice in fresh and acute danger, a diversion in the east was necessary. Bernhard should part from Horn, turn about, and "repeat his previous design" against Bohemia or Bavaria. He obeyed with the greatest alacrity. Nothing, he said, would assuage his men, his armed beggars, except money or action, meaning conquests and opportunities for booty. Such could be undertaken with fewer inhibitions in hostile territory, Bohemia or Bavaria, than in Protestant Württemberg. Whether the target should be Bavaria or the Upper Palatinate, signifying ultimately Bohemia, he temporarily left open; the trek was long. On 20 October, the day on which Aldringen entered Breisach, his troops were in Ulm and seized the city's ships. Nine days later they were in Neuburg, two days afterwards past Ingolstadt. On 4 November they sighted the outworks of Regensburg, as important as a key to the central section of the Danube as Breisach was for the Upper Rhine, the bulwark of Bavaria, the gateway to the Hereditary Lands. Tilly had in his death throes implored

Maximilian that Regensburg should be defended to the last. Gustavus
Adolphus had wanted to capture Regensburg and could not. Now it was
faced with Bernhard's army, swollen to ten thousand men and well
supplied with cannon, ships, horse-ferries. Conditions inside the walls
were not good. The predominantly Protestant population was leavened
with a large, rich Catholic priesthood. The Bavarian garrison which
monthly extracted forty thousand gulden from the lay, none from the
ecclesiastical community was loathed. The Elector had little love for
those whom he called the "Swedish Regensburgers". His care was for
the fortress, not its inhabitants.

More perceptive was his military judgement. From the moment that
Bernhard appeared at Ulm he predicted that Regensburg and Bavaria
as a whole were the target. His country was almost defenceless. For the
good of the general cause he had allowed Aldringen's advance to the
Rhine with his own as well as imperial troops. Now he was entitled to
claim aid for himself and the House of Austria. Whoever held Regensburg had Upper Austria at his feet, could for the fourth, fifth time rally
its Protestant peasants to his side, and, before the year was out, would
be able to knock on the gates of Vienna. With Regensburg lost, all would
be lost. Express couriers carried his cries for help to Wallenstein's headquarters and the Austrian capital, the dispatches shriller with every mile
that the Weimar prince put behind him. He wrote to the Emperor, to
Gallas, to Ilow, even to Adam Trčka whose rank hardly qualified him
for such an importunate mark of honour but whose influence on the
Generalissimo was by this time notorious. Vienna heeded Maximilian's
entreaties and transmitted them with the stamp of highest authority.
Very soon the number of couriers charging towards the headquarters
doubled. Letters from Ferdinand to Wallenstein on 28 October, 4
November, 9 November, 11 November. Utmost danger for Me and My
House, for My Hereditary Kingdoms and Lands, for the Catholic world.
Utmost urgency for reinforcements from Bohemia, regiments being
relinquished by Gallas, and placed under capable leadership, that of
Rudolf Colloredo perhaps. The Duke's presence on the site of the
emergency was not, however, demanded.

The Bavarian commotion interfered with Wallenstein's plans in the
most irksome way. Until 13 November he was awaiting, and with what
avidity, good news from Dresden and Berlin. It came. The disappointment was bitter. Not so bitter, though, that he gave up hope of bringing
at some little trouble the two Electors into the position allotted them by
his dreams. That required undiminished concentration of his military

might in Bohemia, Silesia, Saxony, Brandenburg. He did not moreover believe in the threat to Bavaria and Regensburg. Far more important than Bavaria was Bohemia. The centre of the war-scene was where he was in command, not where the Bavarian chose it to be. "I am prepared to pledge my honour that Weimar will not go into Bavaria, but to Meissen or Bohemia," he confided to Gallas.

On 9 November, to anticipate all eventualities or because he found it difficult to withstand the yelps from Vienna and Bavaria, he ordered Colonel Strozzi to proceed from Bohemia "with some twenty companies of horse and dragoons" in the direction of the Danube. Something of a concession to what was requested of him, but hardly made before he also curtailed it – Strozzi must not stray too far from the main theatre of operations, Strozzi must on no account cross the Danube unless Bernhard were to do so. At the moment where this was written, Bernhard had already done so. On 9 November at the latest Wallenstein had learned of Bernhard's camp outside Regensburg. On 14 November he still declined to believe in a serious imperilment of the city. The enemy, he maintained, had a totally different intent – to advance against Bohemia together with Arnim who, as he had just heard from Saxony, was already on the march. "I shall, with God's help, receive them in such manner that they will forget about an irruption into Bohemia." On the same day Regensburg surrendered and, amidst its citizens' cheers, Bernhard entered the city of the imperial Diets. On 18 November the news reached Wallenstein. He could not fail to feel embarrassment.

Meanwhile there had on his part occurred one of those swift changes of mind, a shift from dream to reality or into another dream. On 14 November he had manifested his determination not to permit Bernhard's wiles to divert him. On 16 November, before he knew of Regensburg's fall, he threw over his cherished plans and began to do what two days ago he had rejected. "I leave behind the baggage with the heavy artillery," he wrote to the Emperor, "and forthwith take the road for strenuous diurnal stages against Weimar. I pray to God that, if I am able to meet with him, I shall fetch him a blow. Count Gallas remains in Bohemia to watch Arnim." A lone decision, for we can perceive no one who could have influenced him. He felt that he must undertake the expedition to make good his error, and for a few days he seems to have espoused the new development with a certain enthusiasm. "I assure Yr Majesty that I shall hurry day and night to show Weimar his way back." There was no need to fear an invasion of the Hereditary Lands, he would see to that. He did so, effectively. His hand had not lost its cunning yet. Top priority, as two years ago, was to secure Passau and the valley of the Danube eastward of it, Upper Austria. Regiments were sent there under Colonel de Suys, victuals too. But, we wonder, was his own journey right across Bohemia necessary and proper? The future would show that, apart from making sure of Passau, nothing was necessary. The significance of Regensburg's fall, like so much else in this bloody tomfoolery was thoroughly exaggerated. Bernhard neither now nor later knew what to do with his triumph. It sufficed for this, for that, and thereafter, as usual, for no more. Wallenstein, urging his tired troops forward through Bohemia, seems gradually to have awoken again to this primary fact. His good spirits vanished as quickly as they had risen.

In seven days he had covered eighty miles. Given the conditions of the year's late season and the traveller's physical state, that must have been anything but a pleasure. At Pilsen he met, at his own request. Count Trauttmansdorff. A gloomy discourse ensued. He knew, said Wallenstein, that at Vienna everyone, leading ministers not excluded, talked mischievously, unjustly about him. His successes were discounted as mere luck, untoward events ascribed to his negligence. His officers, Aldringen, Strozzi, were given orders by the court behind his back. He, the Generalissimo, was ignored, for all that he had always fufilled the Emperor's wishes and never neglected to furnish a detailed explanation of his actions. Count Trčka's command of so many regiments was made a matter of reproach to him. Trčka did not indeed want the burden, he groaned under it, but he had the financial means for their support which others lacked and that must be turned to account. In short, never in his life had he felt as ill as now and he had no desire to retain his appointment. "I tried," reported Trauttmansdorff, "by sundry phrases to calm his emotion and, for the rest, let most of the fires quench themselves."

Wallenstein reviewed the general situation. Were the Emperor to win ten more victories, nothing would be gained. His Majesty had too many enemies and they would ever again mobilize fresh forces. Were he however to sustain a single severe defeat, then the game would be up. The army raised by him was the last to be had. He could no longer carry the responsibility. Were peace not finally to be made, he would rather betake himself with eight or ten followers to Danzig and there await the outcome. Let His Majesty disdain no opportunity for negotiations, no opening offered by his foes! Even at this moment there existed one, with Duke Franz Julius von Lauenburg as go-between.

Field-Marshal Ilow was summoned to assist in elucidation of the military position. Policy demanded that twelve thousand men remain in

Brandenburg. Count Schaffgotsch's command in Silesia would suffer no reduction; the country was hostile and could be held only by coercion. Gallas, on Bohemia's northern border, had no more than five thousand men, but Arnim, a constant threat, outnumbered him three times and could rely on Swedish reinforcement. This unfortunately meant that the strength of the attack against Weimar must undergo curtailment. Ilow, with the main body of infantry, would stay where he was, here in Pilsen. He himself would in the morning continue his march against Bavaria with a hundred picked cavalry squadrons, all dragoons and Croats, and eight pieces of light artillery. Perhaps some damage could be inflicted on the enemy. Useless at this season, though, to think about recovery of lost strongholds. The means were lacking, any attempt would result in the force's undoing. There was no alternative except, like last year, to seek winter quarters in the Hereditary Lands. Nor was there any hope of change in circumstances, at least no complete one, for as long as the war continued. Bitter, admonitory truth, and possibly Trauttmansdorff was not altogether unhappy to pass it on. We suspect that in the key-question he thought much as his interlocutor did although, being a courtier, he expressed his ideas circumspectly. In his report he did not, at any rate, suppress the observation that the motives for making peace delineated by the Generalissimo were identical with those which in spring His Majesty had been able to read in an opinion submitted by various Privy Councillors. Among those "various Privy Councillors" had been Count Trauttmansdorff.

Had Ferdinand II spent a night under the same roof as his command-ing officer, observed him at close quarters, seen his terribly altered features and his feverish eyes in their hollowed sockets, heard his groans in the night, some chord of sympathy would perhaps have been struck in him. The two had not however met for almost six years. The Wallen-stein whom he recalled was the newly created Duke of Mecklenburg, pitiless, high-spirited, triumphant, in the winter of 1628. Their contact since had been purely epistolary, sometimes in greater detail and agreeable in tone, but during this past year cooler and curter. The Generalissimo had been allowed to do as he liked. Here was the con-sequence. Probably Ferdinand had always known or guessed that Wallen-stein held him in low esteem. The dynast found no cause for pity. His answer was icy. He had never heard any evil words about the Duke, but let him be told the names of the speakers and he would investigate the matter. Orders issued over the head of the Generalissimo were likewise unknown to him, barring such as had in all cases been duly notified to him. He was moreover totally unaware of ever having rejected any peace offers. There had been none. The very first, albeit meagre, recently brought by Duke Franz Julius from Dresden, would be scrutinized. The Emperor personally added a postscript: "I should indeed like to know whether Mecklenburg-Friedland does not apprehend that Arnim has snatched many an opportunity from him and that he deceives him. I would also be pleased to learn with what vigour the Duke advances against Weimar." Not a scrap of confidence left, the last remnant dissipated through the Regensburg disaster. At the moment of crisis the pride, the archaic egotism of the hereditary monarch stood nakedly revealed.

Misunderstood, traduced, unthanked. Sick in body, sick in mind. Winter. Wholly without enthusiasm for the venture which he felt constrained to undertake. Wallenstein continued it with the growing conviction that he would not see it through. During the second half of the long march, from Pilsen to Neumark on Bohemia's western border and Furth im Wald on the Bavarian side, the tone of his letters, which for a few days had been full of hectic energy, dropped into a minor key. Bernhard was already with the main part of his troops thirty miles down the river and at Deggendorf, some ten miles farther on, across both the Danube and the Isar. Not much prospect of being able to do anything against him. Aldringen, returning from his so vital expedition to the Rhine, would have to be awaited. Without his corps the pursuers were under strength. Bad news too from Brandenburg. Had he not foretold trouble there if he strayed from Bohemia?

At Furth he held a council of war, as was his custom when he had an awkward decision to make. On such occasions he liked to have the support of his senior officers. Should the first step be to attack the fortress of Cham in the wooded hills south-west of Furth, recently occupied by the Swedes and furnishing a kind of flanking cover to Bernhard's troops on the Danube and the Isar? The majority of his officers, even including Trčka, were in favour. Asked for his opinion, the Bavarian commander in the Upper Palatinate commented that an assault on the fortress, ill-defended, was perfectly feasible, but that the most effective course would be to leave it on one side and make straightway for the passage of the Danube. Here Wallenstein lost his temper, put a curb on it, apologized that this was his habit and meant nothing. Infantry and artillery were lacking, he went on. They had had to remain in Bohemia at General Gallas's disposal. Too late to let them follow. To live in this mountainous country was impossible. It would be necessary to turn back. If however the Bavarian commander hankered after a few regiments, he should, in God's name, have the loan of them. "So this council ended," summarized one of the officers present at it, "and tomorrow, if things stay so, we shall be marching back without having performed even the smallest task. That the weather is excessively intemperate and that 'tis almost impossible to maintain a disposition, so much is unfortunately true." His council of war had not given him what he wanted. He made his own decision. On 4 December the march back began. The Danube could not be crossed and where he stood half the cavalry would within a week have perished from cold and hunger, he drily informed the Emperor. Frankfurt-on-Oder had meanwhile been retaken by Arnim (a mistake) and Knyphausen with his Swedish corps was a threat to Bohemia (something to this). "This force is not sufficient to meet so many enemies drawing in upon it, much less to dally longer in these inhospitable parts." Aldringen should never have abandoned Bavaria. Were he back at last, the situation could be reviewed.

Piccolomini, who had availed himself of the chance to commend himself to the Bavarian as one not unsuited to the appointment of Generalissimo in the event of any change, wrote to Gallas even before leaving Furth, "Your Excellency is free to judge how our withdrawal will be interpreted in Vienna and Bavaria. The enemy will no doubt be encouraged to make fresh progress." Postscript: "His Highness the Duke would like to make peace at any price, more particularly when at court he has caused such severe suspicion to fall on his person and fears some kind of action from there. More than ever the occurrences at Schweidnitz prey on his mind and their recollection renders him deeply dejected."

The return journey took time, a week where previously three days had been enough for the distance from Pilsen to Furth. From his sickbed Wallenstein wrote to the head of his duchy's administration that work on construction of the palace at Sagan must go ahead as soon as weather conditions permitted. Materials should be collected as quickly as possible, horses purchased in Poland or elsewhere. The world's eighth wonder must stand completed at the latest in three years. . . .

This withdrawal [exclaimed Eggenberg to the Bavarian envoy] is the most pernicious, the most perilous, the most heedless thing that the Duke has ever done. He will receive orders, stringent orders, to advance again. If he obeys, so much the better. If he does not obey, His Majesty will prove that he is the master, the Duke his servant. He will not allow himself and his House and His

Serene Highness of Bavaria to be ruined for the Duke's sake. I am looked on as a Friedland sympathizer. Yes, indeed, I have been and I am still the Duke's good friend, but the saying goes "*Amicus Plato, amicus Socrates, amicior autem religio et patria*". [Friend to Plato, friend to Socrates, but greater friend to country and religion]!

In what a hurry he was to abandon the sinking ship.

A grave mistake, granted, this grand-scale descent on Furth im Wald. Had the Generalissimo been less ostentatious in its announcement and content simply to send the auxiliaries requested, it would at a pinch have been swallowed. But to herald so much that now, for the very last time, was awaited with excited delight and then without compelling reason to retract his promise – who could defend such action? First to wave aside with cutting contempt all warnings about Regensburg, then to rush to make good the damage and yet fail to arrive – this was to take a vile pleasure in the Elector's destruction, to wreak late vengeance for another Regensburg occasion. Maximilian had always foreseen it. The occasion was at hand for its stentorian proclamation. He undertook it, his agents undertook it, with such vigour and such success that for a good three hundred years this is the explanation that has been believed.

It was false. At best it was a factor to be left in suspense, an additional factor, a factor unproven, a superfluous factor. If we were all to be weighed on the strength of this and that spoken word! "What concern is it of mine!" Wallenstein ejaculated furiously when a secretary read to him one of the Bavarian shrieks for help. More frequent are other utterances by him in respect of Maximilian – that the Elector constantly thought Bavaria threatened and that he equated Bavaria's welfare absolutely with that of christendom. It was how each saw the other, with Wallenstein able to quote the more convincing examples.

His disbelief in the threat to Regensburg had been in perfect good faith. Who voluntarily renders himself ridiculous? That he desired and craftily contrived the defeat of Bavaria is a nonsensical legend, born of misleading appearances. Even had he secretly wished that, it was at all times in his interest to chase the Duke of Weimar from the field. A victory by the Swedes' most capable, most ambitious general must, as part of the game in which he was constantly engaged, make the Protestant Electors more refractory, Bernhard's rout render them more complaisant. He hoped to inflict that rout, but in Bohemia. There he wanted to intercept him in his own fashion, which was different from going to meet him somewhere on German terrain.

He loathed having pressure put on him and, in spite of all experience and wariness, he continued to believe what he *wanted* to believe. Since the outset of his military career he had rejected a winter campaign as contrary to the nature of war. All his life the idea of suddenly having no money had frightened him. The same fear applied as regards soldiers. He looked on the army as his possession, difficult to raise, easy to destroy. And he kept it well together during the present winter. How well, spring would show.

Among the reproaches levelled at him was that after the minor success of Steinau he had extended his loose fronts all too far. What was his soldiery doing close to Berlin when the enemy was rapping on the gates to Austria? The eastern half of central Europe was where he was at home. Austria, Moravia, Bohemia, Silesia constituted to him a single bloc. Next to it lay Brandenburg, interesting to the soldier, doubly interesting to the politician in him. He knew the path from Upper Silesia to the Baltic, unlike the Bavarian stretch of the Danube where he had never fought. To render the bloc of the Hereditary Lands even more compact and to defend it against all outsiders while simultaneously putting military and political pressure on Brandenburg and Saxony, that was his real system, with Bohemia as its natural focus. There were too many enemies; it was impossible to be on hand everywhere. The various Swedish and Saxon forces manoeuvring through central Germany under Wilhelm von Weimar, Banér, Knyphausen, and Arnim, constituted a threat to unite at any moment for an attack on Bohemia or Silesia. This was an undeniable fact. Not, as Maximilian venomously asserted, sheer imagination.

There remains the charge that either he should not have undertaken the grand-scale incursion into Bavaria, if he felt it to be unsuitable, or he ought to have effected something worthwhile. Why not have waited for a few days to see what the foe was doing? And here was a further reproach which Maximilian did not fail to level: had Wallenstein held out no more than two days longer at Furth, he would have had Duke Bernhard on his side of the Danube in as advantageous a position for him as he could have desired. Perfectly correct. The Weimar forces on the banks of the Isar suffered as cruelly from the cold as the imperialists in the forests around Furth. The ground was frozen too hard for trenches to be dug. The environment was too barren and as far as Munich offered no rewarding objective. Bernhard therefore relinquished as quickly as he had formed the notion of conquering Bavaria, gave up for the space of this winter any more comprehensive projects, and crossed the Danube to consolidate his gains. What a splendid conclusion to the year it would be, were he to succeed in chasing Wallenstein back to Bohemia. The Generalissimo was however gone.

Where different arguments converge to bring a decision to a head, the quintessential one often hides behind the many. The latter are neither entirely superficial nor fundamental. They are allowed latitude because they serve convenience. Piccolomini was shrewd enough to appreciate that. Wallenstein had for a year not waged war in order that he should gain peace. He had not gained it. Twofold failure undermined his reputation, status, and power. Now, in panic haste, he once more snatched at the phantom of peace, his straw of hope. That was why he and his army must be in Bohemia, not losing time and men on wintry battles in Bavaria. He did not as in the past request long leave, and he went neither to Prague nor Gitschin. He settled in a citizen's house on the market-place of Pilsen, surrounded by his staff, a military and political headquarters, the eye of the approaching storm.

The Camp at Pilsen

WINTER, once again. For the past thirteen years the time for talking about the sublimity of peace. Summer was the season for fighting battles.

The to and fro of armies, whether friend or foe, had utterly ruined his country, lamented the Elector of Bavaria. Commerce had ceased. His impoverished subjects no longer paid taxes. Worst of all, his household could not meet its obligations and was deeply in debt. At Wallenstein's headquarters, the Friedland court in Pilsen, conditions were hardly more rosy. For months chancellery clerks, postmasters, doctors had not had a penny. "As magnificent as this court used to be, in as miserable a state is it now," reported Questenberg, "with nothing left except its deference and the old precision where obedience is concerned." In Bohemia buildings stood deserted and dilapidated, their inhabitants to be sought in the woods. The citizens of Prague, their hands raised in supplication and on bended knees, implored the High Burggrave to have pity. He could not help them, for the soldiers wanted to be housed and fed and the law was on their side. The great, living on the labours of the puny, were also affected, though less so. He was perfectly willing to contribute to war levies as long as he could, wrote Cardinal Harrach to his brother-in-law. For General Gallas to quarter three cavalry units on his last, not entirely devastated country property was however too much. The dragoons must go or, "Should I not be able to attain that from Your Dilection, You will assuredly cause me to abandon Bohemia altogether and force me to beg my bread elsewhere."

To complain about the soldiers was all very well, but on their side they and their leaders complained, with reason. Where should they go? Territories had become so poor that a province which had to furnish winter quarters for ten or fifteen thousand men was overfilled and drained to the dregs. Aldringen's corps, in December back from its Rhine migration, could nowhere find shelter. The Elector of Bavaria did not want it; Upper Austria did not want it; the Archbishop of Salzburg did not want it. Nevertheless the soldiers needed a roof over their head.

A third winter under canvas was out of the question. They were running around in rags and dying of hunger. The Swedes, with most of Germany in their hands, were, relatively speaking, better off. That did not hold good for the Saxons. "We are lying out here and suffering privation of a kind such as I have never experienced in any campaign," wrote Field-Marshal Duke Franz Albrecht von Lauenburg. "Schweidnitz was gold compared to this. If Your Electoral Grace is not of a mind to wage war actively, then in God's name do not decline peace, let it be as bad as it will."

Maximilian was another who would gladly have emerged from "this laborious and long-lasting labyrinth". The longer the war continued, he bewailed, the more hopeless became its termination by force of arms. Could not the King of France, a Catholic ruler, after all, be persuaded to play the mediator? He was not, he emphasized, asking out of kindly feeling for the Latin neighbour, but pure love of his native land. Did Saxony and Brandenburg not suffer at having a Swedish nobleman play the despot in a fashion that no Emperor had ever ventured? Even the Spanish ambassador, since November at Vienna to help in the disposition of some very delicate problems, advised the proposal of magnanimous terms in Germany – toleration of all denominations inside the Empire, a general amnesty, cessation of confiscations, and so forth. It sounds almost like a Wallenstein peace draft. The coincidence of three, and such inflexible, parties as Spain, Bavaria, Friedland, wanting the same thing did not mean that their motives were identical. Oñate wanted Germany sensibly united under Habsburg leadership in order that war against France should the more briskly be pursued. That was neither love of peace nor love of fellow-men, but straight political reasoning. And had Europe had but a single cause at issue, sweeping all others out of mind, Wallenstein and Maximilian could not have acted for that cause in common.

Not a new state of affairs. Simply worse than in the year before, when it was worse than in the year before that, and so on, right back to 1620.

GROWING DEFIANCE

On the very day when Wallenstein informed the Emperor of his withdrawal a delicate task was imposed on Questenberg in his capacity as member of the imperial War Council. He was to travel straightway to the Generalissimo and tell him that for this year His Majesty wished to have no requisition of winter quarters in his lands. They were no longer to be borne. There were plenty of other possibilities – in Brandenburg, in Lusatia, in Thuringia. Should Wallenstein refuse to envisage such positive possibilities and be adamant on the necessity for billets in Bohemia, Moravia, Austria, then the distribution of the regiments must be undertaken in agreement with the Emperor. The latter proposed, as in duty bound, to come to an understanding on the subject with his loyal Estates. Otherwise the impression might arise that he had a co-regent and no longer any say in his own realm. . . .

Wallenstein as co-regent. The Emperor, if matters continued so, robbed of his prime prerogatives. A new tone, indeed. Before Questenberg could fulfil his mission, a fresh dispatch with the General Staff's list of suggested quarters arrived. All-highest approval was requested – as a formality. The draft was final, with need for its driving force and Bohemia as foremost victim of a cruel calamity.

On its heels followed news of the abandoned Bavarian campaign. An ever deeper cloud of gloom descended. He had been very loth, wrote Ferdinand to Wallenstein, to take note of this move. He did not understand the reasons. The Duke would, without fail, turn about and proceed against Weimar. "This is my definitive decision on which I fully insist and to which I adhere notwithstanding that I have received another missive in this business from Your Dilection. . . ." Count Trauttmansdorff, still in the vicinity of Pilsen, was to discuss with the Generalissimo in detail and with great seriousness the Emperor's wish. "You will, my dear Trauttmansdorff, apply yourself with utmost zeal to My behest and know how to express it with emphasis. It is to be regarded neither as form nor as an inessential injunction, but as My full and definitive decision which I am in all solemnity determined to effect."

Suddenly Wallenstein was faced with what in this shape had never yet, not even during his more modest first generalate, manifested itself – his Sovereign's naked order. How did he react to the unprecedented experience? With the defiance of one who knows better and on the strength of experience, not of inertly inherited right, was himself used to issue commands. He said no. Conscious that he understood the problem more thoroughly than the Viennese ink-swillers, convinced that he had adequately seen to Austrian security, from the outset an opponent of winter campaigning because he knew what could be asked of soldiers and what not, he refused to obey his lord and master. Henceforward it was a contest in which one challenged the other, advanced, drew back, advanced again, as in a tussle between gladiators. A contest which at the start, as it seemed, was equally jeopardous to both sides. But care was called for. Had Wallenstein forgotten why, in 1619, he had gone over to the Emperor's side and what happened to those who would not follow his example?

Formally he took care. Instead of roundly refusing, he called a council of war attended by all general officers and colonels present in Pilsen. Field-Marshal Ilow read to the meeting Questenberg's billeting instruction and the demands transmitted by Trauttmansdorff. The opinion of the meeting was asked. Its opinion was that the impossible had been requested. To obtain winter quarters in Saxony, Thuringia, and Brandenburg was synonymous with a requirement to mount a winter campaign across territory where the ground was frozen and neither money nor victuals were to be had. Whoever furnished His Majesty with such advice would very soon, if he had to put it into execution, appreciate its hopeless nature. The same applied to the assault on Bavaria. The only result would be the army's destruction, with the soldiery driven to either despair or death, or first one and then the other. So on 17 December 1633, at Pilsen, the sense of the meeting. Its motion, strongly and lengthily worded, could be approved but not formulated by such a large gathering. Ilow proposed, and a certain Heinrich Niemann, formerly a Privy Councillor directly in Friedland service, of recent date at Adam Trčka's disposal as a modest captain, composed the text. He could wield a pen; Ilow had the knack in a hale, bluff way of sweeping along the officers with him and for the moment turning a minority into a majority, majority into totality. Covertly more than one of them was not, and for some time had not been, really happy at Wallenstein's strange strategy. Making war meant loot, loot meant recovery with interest of the outlay into which they had plunged. Stand still, no spoil, as Isolani, the Croat, bitterly noted. Wallenstein, isolated in his sick-room, was unaware of these feelings. He accepted the motion and sent it to Vienna accompanied by a polite letter. In such important business he had not, he stated, thought proper on his own responsibility to act contrary to His Majesty's expressed will. He had therefore taken this and that step. The outcome was contained in the enclosure. He begged obediently that his view and that of those responsible with him should be accorded approbation without delay.

The shot struck home, and it was not the only one loosed. Impelled by Wallenstein's inveterate critics who had become his open bitter enemies, the Emperor ordered Baron de Suys, in charge in Upper Austria, to advance to the Inn on Bavarian territory where he should liaise with Maximilian's troops. Part of Trauttmansdorff's task had been to make this also known at Pilsen, but only so as to suggest that the step was preliminary and not incapable of modification by the Generalissimo. In fact it was meant to be final, as Wallenstein understood perfectly well. Final too was his countermand, repeated two, three, four times – Suys was to stay in Upper Austria, increase his strength through recruitments, and let himself be deflected by no one, let him be whoever he might be, from his commanding officer's well-founded bidding. A most embarrassing situation for the colonel, particularly since the Emperor in a further letter added a handwritten postscript pointing in precisely the opposite direction: "Because this order serves My safety and that of My lands, he will immediately act upon the same (even when orders from elsewhere have been or are still issued)." Ticklish alternatives. Suys elected to obey the commander-in-chief in the field. He remained where he was. The Emperor's authority, expressed more bluntly than ever before, suffered affront as never before. During the first generalate Wallenstein had often submitted to it against his judgement and will. Not now.

He believed himself to be objectively in the right. Incidentally he suspected some intrigue at Vienna to undermine, slowly, step by step, his position; Colonel de Suys simply presented an opportunity. He is reported to have reproached Count Trauttmansdorff with the utmost asperity: "I see well enough with what a bandage you would blindfold me, but I shall tear it from my eyes. I observe the efforts that are being made to snatch the army from under my fingers." These words are not to be found in Trauttmansdorff's reports. There Wallenstein is quoted as once more defending his dispositions for the winter as having been the solely practicable ones because on the army depended Austria's salvation, but an army could be lost in three days and not reconstructed within the space of three years. He had had no choice but to hold the council of war and to produce the letters from Vienna. His authority with the officers, God be praised, was sufficiently strong that he could at any time tauten the reins. Would, asked Trauttmansdorff, a visit by the Spanish ambassador and perhaps Prince Eggenberg be agreeable? Not in the very least, retorted Wallenstein. Oñate would only come to try and draw him into Spain's eternal, hopeless war operations to which he would never be a party. As for Eggenberg, he knew in advance what he would propose – a division of command between the King of Hungary and himself. The King was his master, too good to be his fellow. He would readily, though, surrender the command as a whole, given honourable discharge and an indemnification "which would not however be onerous". If the gentlemen concerned thought that the consequences of his resignation would be simple, the error was unfortunate. For he, and he alone, had guaranteed the colonels their advances and on his personal credit rested the entire, so very fragile military fabric. What would happen, were he suddenly to disappear? "Peace," he concluded, "must be made, else all is lost."

Would he have done better not to decline a meeting with Eggenberg? Was not a talk, as in 1626 at Bruck on the Leitha and in 1632 at Göllersdorff, overdue? The rejection was another act of defiance. It was also a sign that if the whole cycle of events was undergoing repetition, there was none the less a difference; they had a much more malignant twist to them. Passages may recur in the book of life, but their length will be limited before a fresh leaf is turned. Wallenstein's relationship with Eggenberg was no longer the same. There had been an argument about the contributions to be delivered by Styria, the minister's own province. In the unspoken war which had broken out between him and Ferdinand, Wallenstein could not count on Eggenberg's neutrality or mediation. That he guessed. Had he had access to the dispatches passing between Vienna and Bavaria, the proof would have lain in his hands.

The audience accorded Questenberg two days after the discussion with Trauttmansdorff was still friendly in tone. Perhaps the former's lightness of touch raised Wallenstein's spirits. Perhaps too his constant consumption of analgesics produced in one or another instance euphoric side-effects. We do not know what most of these drugs were. In apothecary bills they are specified as no more than "potions" or "powders". To Questenberg, anyhow, his talk was neither of resignation nor of the crying need for peace, but of war in spring. The imperial army would be in good shape; that of the enemy, worn out from winter exertions, would not. His achievement would then be recognized for what it was. When had he ever left the Emperor in the lurch? Let His Majesty have confidence in him, not adopt bad advice from unqualified quarters, not contribute to the army's destruction through wrong orders. Was he lying? He never lied. At the moment of utterance he was wholly the man who said or wrote what he did. At a different moment, another.

Once more, as in 1626, he wanted to resign and be rid of his appointment's burden and torment. He wanted this now with a far, far more nagging longing than he had done then. Yet equally he wanted to retain his appointment in order to perform one last great act, and in no circumstances would he for a second time be harried out of it as at Memmingen. Not that. Anything, everything sooner than that. To make peace was what he pressed with care-worn urgency on those whom, had he wanted to do them harm or indeed ruin them, he should far rather have cunningly persuaded into wintry battles. It was *his* programme which he thrust upon them, which is no conspirator's method. If they accepted it, he wanted to be spared attention to details for which he lacked the patience, but to have some say on the main lines of the peace's conclusion and as a contributor to the Empire's pacification still win some affection there. Strange conspirator, strange rebel!

The Emperor whom we have become accustomed to term the institution's embodiment, the sacred phantom for whose sake victims had for thirteen years been in such quantities put to the fire and the sword, this synthetic figure behind which hid an ever more furious swarm of insinuators, Ferdinand II, in short, every day inclined more to see in Wallenstein a rebel and on ever fewer days one whom it might, with severity, perhaps be possible to tame. His answer to the council of war's motion and Wallenstein's accompanying letter was thoroughly ungracious. Never had it entered his mind to order a ruinous winter campaign. All that he had at last wanted to see was action, action against Bernhard von Weimar, and action, though slightly modified, was what he still wanted to see. Colonel de Suys's advance was to be forthwith set in motion and to be reinforced by a contingent of four thousand men from Bohemia. That, an absolute minimum, could do. As to Baron de Suys' insubordination, "it redounds to our no small excitation". Suys was to be called to order or replaced by a more suitable commander.

Wallenstein, as far as the last point was concerned, parried diplomatically by summoning the entirely innocent colonel to Pilsen and nominating Ottavio Piccolomini, general of cavalry and one of his loyallest officers, as successor. On the main issue he was again elusive. Enough regiments were available in Bavaria, particularly since Aldringen's return, in spite of the fact that his soldiers were in piteous condition. Enough regiments were stationed in Upper Austria. The enemy, if he had six times the number of troops, would be unable to undertake anything of consequence. To stay on the defensive until spring was essential. Bohemia was in any case worse threatened than Bavaria and Upper Austria. About the reinforcement of four thousand men, not a word.

At this juncture something ought to have happened. Nothing happened. It was Ferdinand who broke off the fight, suddenly climbed down. At such relative lateness in the season he would on this occasion acquiesce in Wallenstein's well-intentioned course. Moreover, since he was aware of the keen need in which the army stood, he had through retrenchment in his own household raised a hundred thousand gulden which, with corn, wine, and cattle, would soon arrive in Bohemia for the poor soldiers' delectation. "And remain, with imperial favour and affection, well-inclined. ..." A transformation. Why, at this time, such gracious transformation?

THE ENEMY NESTS, AND HOW BIRDS OF A FEATHER FLOCKED TOGETHER

From this winter have survived a series of thoroughly spiteful pamphlets about Wallenstein which derived from his own, if that is the proper term, imperial camp. They took the form of 'Discourses', 'Opinions', and fictitious sermons. Issued and distributed in secret, copied and eagerly read, they were probably all seen by the great panjandrum and arbiter of last instance, the Emperor. Today our approach would be different – speeches in Parliament and at public meetings, newspaper features, venomous squibs, purposive question-and-answer interviews on the air and across a screen. In those days none of these instruments was available except in the form of sermons which were often a lively jumble of politics and religion. Pastor Hoë von Hoënegg at Dresden is familiar to us as a master in this art. Another was the Emperor's Court Chaplain, Father Johannes Weingartner, SJ. The pamphlets to be discussed here demonstrate in outlook, violence of indictment, and sly suggestions for abatement of the alleged nuisance a similarity that would render it defensible to suspect a single propagandistic identity behind all, or nearly all, of them.

The initial publication constituted an exception. Dating from October it dealt mainly with military aspects. Historians, because a copy was found at Bamberg, have labelled it the "Bamberg Text". Certain, though, is that the author was not from that city; he wrote in Italian. Acquainted with the war's events over which Wallenstein during 1633 had direct control, he had not a good word to say for the Duke's conduct of these. Time lost, the finest opportunities for victory let slip again and again, the richest of provinces reduced to utter ruin without the slightest profit. A war "waged by post". Wallenstein was alleged to seek peace, but his own most personal interests were the impediment to peace, his own monstrous pretensions were what the Empire was incapable of satisfying. "Not (God forfend!) that I deduce from the foregoing a lack of loyalty on the part of the General, but that indeed his ambitious, roving thoughts are of a kind qualified to conduce to like effects and whereby he could be impelled to rest his hopes upon the non-Catholic Electors." What would otherwise remain a dark enigma and what threatened the House of Austria with a sombre fate found its explanation in Wallenstein's presumptuous, thoroughly selfish objectives. Let God assist His Majesty's wisdom with counsel on how to avert the calamity in good time.

Different was the tone struck two months later when the arch- and guardian angel for the Habsburg territories loosed in thunderous Latin a fiery blast against the pious: *Exhortatio Angeli Provincialis ad Imperatorem et Reges Austriacos* (Exhortation of the Angel Provincial to the Emperor and Austrian Regents). The Emperor was old Ferdinand; the regents, the rulers of Hungary and Spain, brothers-in-law. Divine reproof was their lot. They had chosen a commander whom they knew was vindictive, spurned by the church, sheer raving mad, blinded by arrogance, seeking not God's glory, no, his own alone, without respect for religion, allowing in Their Majesties' camps the heretics' false worship, asking not God for aid but magicians and soothsayers, determining the course of war and peace by astrologers' auguries, disgracefully neglectful of hostilities in order to pursue the phantom of a foolish peace. "I say no more. You know it and You hide it. . . . See how Your commander deceives You. . . . Salvation lies but one way: Expel Your commander and with a pure heart appoint King Ferdinand as leader of Your wars. . . . Thus speaks God, through Me, His Angel. Perform it swiftly. Follow His counsel or perish." Dr Bartholomäus Richel, the Bavarian envoy at Vienna, at once sent a copy of the angelic tract to Maximilian who, he knew, enjoyed such theosophic political disquisitions.

On its heels came three publications of non-celestial provenance. *An Expediat* (Whether 'Tis Expedient) asked "Whether 'tis Expedient to Remove Generalissimo the Duke of Friedland from his Appointment and to Place Ferdinand III at the Head of Military Affairs?" It purported to be an opinion given at a secret session of the imperial War Council. Although they try to outdo each other, these opinions of anonymous members of the War and Privy Councils cannot avoid repetition. They say the same as the archangel and the main difference between them is a point of chronology. While the first is as yet unaware of Wallenstein's withdrawal from Bavaria, the second has heard of the Pilsen council of war on 17 December. All three are strong on piety and craftily insinuative. The first, *An Expediat*, may have been one of several, the answer to a question put by Ferdinand to his ministers. The third is peculiar in that its author, without stating his name, reveals his identity. He knew, he emphasizes, the man in question as a child receiving instruction at Castle Koschumberg and who was later nicknamed Wild Waldstein. He had stayed wild all his life, an atheist, an inventor of vile blasphemies who shamelessly went so far in his favouritism of heretics as to build them a church at Glogau, in the power of the furies where ambition was concerned. Had he not often declared that he who controlled the army was paramount, as in Rome generals had become emperors? Long, long ago, in 1624, the author had, in a memorial containing forty items of accusation, warned His Majesty against this person. Unfortunately he had been told to hold his tongue. The time had come to wag it again, hard. The Generalissimo who in 1631 knavishly lured the Saxons to Prague and ever since, if not before, had practised treason, who recently had given Count Thurn his freedom transparently because he knew too much about his evil machinations, who openly presumed to seek restoration of the wretched conditions of 1612, who hated the pious Jesuits, this rival Emperor and rival King, this godless Duke of Friedland must be deposed. How? Transfer of command to the King of Hungary with Count Gallas for his deputy, briefing of the more senior officers by at least forty letters from the Sovereign, summons to Wallenstein to appear at Vienna and exculpate himself, force to be used if the summons was not obeyed. Everything must happen all at once, following this plan exactly, and being put into execution like lightning.

He who wrote this stuff was by his own designation Wallenstein's cognate "in the third degree". We know him – Wilhelm von Slawata, Lord High Chancellor of Bohemia, the jealous cousin, Slawata of the defenestration, true to his faith, true to his hatred, true to the narrow limits of his mind. Long had he forgathered in the snug nest which housed those others, the Old Catholics and Old Spaniards, sternly conservative-minded, Wallenstein's foes from the start. Cardinal von Dietrichstein was of the company; Conde de Marradas, titular Lieutenant-General, titular indeed since in 1632 he had been invited to relinquish his paltry command and temporarily transferred to the retired list, for which his military achievements offered more than grounds enough; Lamormaini, the imperial father confessor, and Weingartner, the court chaplain, not always at one because Lamormaini felt attracted to France and Weingartner did not, but completely seeing eye to eye on the main ecclesiastical problems and in the last analysis convinced that the struggle between the denominations must continue until one side was finished, confidently reliant upon God as to which that would be. Lamormaini and Weingartner corresponded precisely to the popular Protestant picture of Jesuits, precisely to what Wallenstein meant when he cursed the Order. Their influence over Ferdinand II was immense. None other than Father Johannes Weingartner, SJ, was Austria's arch- and guardian angel, author of the *Exhortatio*.

In another nest sat the military, unemployed, embittered members of the imperial War Council. There was Field-Marshal von Tiefenbach, in 1632 gently dismissed from the service. Or Colonel the Marquis Caretto di Grana, an ominous man of honour. "I swear," Wallenstein had written eight years ago, "that I would sooner bed in an infirmary than have him with me. From day to day I like him less." What he liked least of all was this officer's excessive rapacity. Never exactly to be ascertained was where the contributions went which he collected. When however he had seized hostages from a German town, promised to free them for a high ransom, yet after its payment demanded more, Wallenstein brusquely relieved him of his command.

The mortified commander requested that he should, as compensation, be entrusted with the fortress of Raab, Hungarian bulwark against the Turks. Wallenstein refused. "When I have regard to Grana's presumption, I am little surprised that he claims Raab; but when I have regard to his qualities, I cannot deem it other than highly disparate." The wonder is not that Caretto was hostile, but that with his notoriety he should have been a welcome ally to the pious, and shortly allowed imperturbably to offer advice to the Emperor. That Count Schlick, now active to great effect, was of the party hardly requires mention. Imperial War Council and churchmen – two nestsful whose inhabitants chirped at each other and met with mutual response. Who wrote what is not exactly known. A number of them may well have sat together for an interchange of arguments and secrets. Our narration has shown that to determine Wallenstein's character will always be difficult. Would one method be to scrutinize his foes? Here were his arch-enemies – confessional disputants who looked on compromise as diabolical dung, gentlemen of an old-fashioned feudal cut, bad estate managers and serf-sweaters, old-style imperialists, envious military bunglers, venal plunderers.

Bavaria, in the person of its Elector, had always been in touch with the churchmen. What passed in 1627 between Father Valeriano Magni, the Great Personage, and Maximilian will not have been forgotten. How did the noble Capuchin now? He does not seem to have been as active as formerly. At a first glance the delineation of Wallenstein contained in the "Opinions" resembles Magni's old character portrayal; the tricks devised for the preparation of his second downfall are a lively reminder of those which Magni commended for the first occasion. Latterly, though, everything was blunter, more militant, more undisguised, without a trace of the Capuchin's literary finesse. Magni was no longer needed. His wares had long past become more common property and coarser-grained, as happens when property becomes more common. Dr Richel negotiated directly with Schlick, with Caretto, with Eggenberg.

From his headquarters in the small town of Braunau on the Inn the Elector sounded the general attack. On 6 December he instructed Richel to work together with the two Spanish ambassadors and in utmost secrecy try to bring about Wallenstein's dismissal. On 18 December he wrote that it was time to take the lid off the pot and pay no attention any more to the Duke of Friedland's supporters. He must be removed, this man whose hateful, headstrong way of thinking, flights of fancy, outbursts of passion, and perfidious acts cloaked in every kind of reason threatened Catholic Christianity with destruction. Richel was not however to expose himself recklessly; the Elector would rather that matters should, in the light of Wallenstein's vengefulness, pursue their course without him. That was why Richel should seek to discover from those who did not belong to the Friedland clique, possibly Count Schlick and Father Lamormaini, what hopes of an early change existed. If there was one, good enough. Only if there was not, if the fire simply flickered and must be stoked, only then should the envoy, with all due restraint although with the utmost emphasis, impress on the Emperor how the Duke had contemptuously swept aside all the Elector's warnings and bore responsibility for all, all of the last two years' disasters, and that an end must be put to such intolerable subjugation. Maximilian enclosed a *Discourse upon Friedland's Actions and Contradictory Ordinances*, with close affinities to the "Opinions" of the War and Privy Councils' members as well as the archangel's. Richel was to present it to the Emperor, but again only if necessary. On 22 December followed another dispatch. Unheard of, the officers' meeting at Pilsen on 17 December! At variance, incidentally, with Friedland's habits, accustomed as he was to decide everything according to his own evil idea. Now, though, instead of repudiating the assembly's motion with a sharp rebuke, he had the impudence to quote it in justification of his conduct. As for the latter, did he not daily blaspheme the Almighty with old and newly concocted frightful oaths, setting the soldiers an example regardless of the death penalty on swearing, an offence which even among the enemy, the

Protestants, regularly incurred the severest punishments? Was it permissible for so pious a ruler as the Emperor to brook such any longer? Was he prepared to let the fortunes of his House depend indefinitely on the humours and moods of a single, self-willed, hot-tempered individual? The Elector had thought and felt all this in 1627, 1630 and eighteen months ago when he had embraced and lived in camp at close quarters with the subject of his loathing. The unsurpassably shrill key in which he pitched his tone was new.

Something else was new, too. Dr Richel, who performed his diplomatic task with sly, sturdy dexterity, was to enlist the help of the Spanish ambassadors. In 1630, at Regensburg, the Spaniards had acted on behalf of Wallenstein and against Bavaria. Not so now. Since summer their relationship to Wallenstein had been undergoing transformation. By the turn of the year it had become a complete reversal.

Here again a recurrence, up to a certain point and then no farther, of the previous pattern of events. During the second generalate the Spanish ambassador to Vienna, Castañeda, repeated the role played by Aytona during the first – gloomy dispatches to Madrid, whispering with Wallenstein's opponents, the young King of Hungary, Lamormaini. Castañeda was a channel for truthful, exaggerated, calumniatory information. He condemned the Silesian armistice and is supposed flatly to have told the Emperor that its sole purpose was the ruin of the Spanish venture, Feria's expedition. He anathematized no less furiously the rupture of the armistice: "Contrary to God, contrary to the good faith of pledged word and common sense." Madrid was still as far as ever from Vienna and the Duke of Olivares still believed in Wallenstein's power, indispensability, and genius. He still hoped to put into operation through him the unshakeable aim of his policy, a major war of Habsburg (meaning Spain and Germany) against the French and the Dutch, hand in hand with restoration of the dynasty's undivided imperial sway. In October, to circumvent the tedious Castañeda, he sent Count Oñate, the outstanding expert on German affairs, to Vienna as ambassador extraordinary.

Oñate came as mediator. The greater was his astonishment at no longer finding any real Wallenstein friends, only nervous former friends who lapsed into embarrassed silence and equally nervous adversaries who pressed him to take action. Initially therefore he adopted an attitude that, if not nervous, was at least circumspect. In such a fateful business it would be dangerous to throw the King of Spain's authority openly into the scales. What would happen if His Majesty's ministers declared against Wallenstein, but he none the less retained his position? On this account each set was goading the others so as to hide behind them; the King of Hungary, chafing at the bit as the sons of elderly paternal potentates are apt to do, was encouraging the Elector of Bavaria and the Spanish ambassador; the Elector of Bavaria incited the King of Hungary, the Spanish ambassador, and those imperial advisers who seemed to him the most promising for his purpose.

Oñate edged his way forward. He had an informant, Dr Agustín Navarro, who sat at the prime source of knowledge, and Oñate's conclusion was that Regensburg represented a case of error rather than ill-will on Wallenstein's part, adding in a postscript that, to be sure, more sinister constructions must be noted. On peace in Germany, Wallenstein's projected peace, he expressed himself to Eggenberg as befitted an important oracle, that was, if the peace were of advantage to the Catholic world, it would enjoy Spanish support, but if it was not, then Spain's whole German and Austrian policy would have to undergo very serious review. No threat of any ban on financial aid, should Wallenstein make any move to include France and Holland in his promotion of peace. Oñate was too well-bred for that. He had been but shortly in Vienna when news arrived from Madrid whose repercussion was better than anything else suited to put the Generalissimo to the test. Infanta Isabella, aged daughter of Philip II and Regent of the Spanish Netherlands had at last departed this life. Flanders was without a viceroy. The fear existed that it might incline to imitate the Dutch example and filch the House of Habsburg's most precious gem. The Cardinal Infant, for months inertly resident at Milan, must finally undertake the journey to Brussels. Anticipation of his approach, so it was thought, alone was able to discourage the Flemings and Walloons from the worst. His well-armed approach, be it noted. From Feria's force, wretchedly errant somewhere between the Inn and the Rhine, nothing more could be expected. The route down the Rhine also no longer commended itself. The French dominated the whole of Lorraine and could in the most unfortunate manner interfere with the Infant's train. The traveller was therefore to make a wide eastern detour and then to proceed diagonally westward, from Linz through Bohemia, Saxony, Thuringia, and Westphalia to Cologne. This would compel the Duke of Friedland to show his colours. Were he to contribute a contingent of six thousand mounted men to escort the prince through all the territories, each more dangerous than the last, he would at a single stroke have Spain on his side whereas the Bavarian–Spanish partnership evolving at Vienna would be dissolved as fast as it had come about. Already Oñate was strongly under the influence of Castañeda, Richel and Schlick, practically in the enemy's united camp, but he nevertheless waited on Wallenstein's decision.

The Spaniards, in Dr Richel's eyes, had reached the point of no return. Affairs stood better, he wrote to Maximilian on 14 December, than probably they looked from afar. Prince Eggenberg, reputedly the head of the Friedland faction, had put pen to paper and garnished the strict orders to Wallenstein with the most astringent phrases. On 21 December he quoted rumours to the effect that the Duke of Friedland was more or less lying at death's door; was solution of the problem through this portal conceivable? On 28 December he could report how Count Oñate had told him that there was no alternative to Wallenstein's complete relegation from the command and that he was on the quiet seeking to achieve this. Eggenberg was vacillating. The Duke of Friedland did not lack genius, he had remarked, but was far too scant of patience; he always heeded only his own ideas, would listen to no advice, and in consequence heaped error upon error. Change there would have to be, but this could perhaps consist simply in curtailment of the Generalissimo's plenary powers. Other councillors who meant well to the cause had warned Eggenberg to reflect that half-measures were no measures. On 31 December, in a first message: matters could not take much longer, the Duke's protégés and patrons had been reduced to silence and dared not defend him any more. The same day, in a second message: the goal had been reached, the Emperor was determined to bring the business to an end. A strongly guarded secret, but he had none the less penetrated it. Delay was engendered solely by the need first to win over the principal officers so that, when the moment came, they would behave as gentlemen. A sore puzzle was what should be done with the fallen idol. To leave him in freedom might be perilous. To take him prisoner would involve difficulties too.

THE PILSEN BANQUET

On the market-square of Pilsen resided the Duke and his staff, chamberlains, chancellery clerks, personal physicians, bodyguards, astrologers. There too resided Field-Marshal Ilow and Lieutenant-General Trčka with their officers. Constant were the comings and goings of mounted couriers and fur-covered sleighs sliding across the snowy space. On 27 December Ottavio Piccolomini travelled on secret mission from Wallenstein to deputy Commander-in-Chief Gallas, commanding on the

Silesian sector. On 5 January Questenberg left the town. On the previous day Don Diego de Quiroga, father confessor to the Queen of Hungary, had arrived. On 9 January Count and Countess Wilhelm Kinsky came from Dresden, in the company of Saxon Colonel Schlieff. Kinsky at once spent five hours with Wallenstein, Schlieff at least one hour. On 10 January Piccolomini returned. On 20 January Wallenstein received Field-Marshal Duke Franz Albrecht von Lauenburg who, after only a few hours, departed again for Dresden. On 24 January Gallas appeared. He had no compunction about supping straightway with Count Kinsky. There are plenty of witnesses to when these and many other personages were to be seen in Pilsen and for how long. Partly the reports stem from the travellers, partly from observers permanently attached to the head-quarters, like Rogge, the Bavarian military commissioner, and Dr Agustín Navarro, the Spanish representative.

The individual who was the focus of all this bustle lay between sheets. He was in a state where he could only for a few painful hours each day leave his bed. In spring 1627 it had been from his bed at Vienna that he had triumphed over his enemies at court. Now things were different. Questenberg's doctor told Rogge that he had had sight of the list of medicaments to be taken daily by His Princely Grace as well as the diet prescribed for him. As far as he could judge, a patient in such condition could not last long.

The Generalissimo received Quiroga on the evening of his arrival. He was very polite, listened attentively, and the audience lasted three hours. The subject was of course the Infant's northern expedition, more specifi-cally, the six thousand horsemen that he required in order to cut right across Germany. Never, the Capuchin pointed out, had King Philip held the Duke in other than very high esteem. He would continue to requite one service with another. The preservation of Flanders was dear to his heart, as was the speed with which it was undertaken since else it would be too late. He saw the compelling need, replied Wallenstein, and the impossibility of its fulfilment. From Eger to Cologne was 450 miles with not one place along the route that was not in enemy hands. Less than half the journey would have been completed before the whole train was either in captivity or dead. The route down the Rhine was no better. Better, indeed the sole solution, was postponement until spring of the plan's implementation. He advanced with great seriousness mili-tary arguments which, as far as they went, were difficult to rebut: Spanish ignorance had devised the project, but it was incapable of realization as long as the Swedes and their supporters stood undefeated in Germany. Don Diego heard, though, only the refusal. The King, his master, he remarked bitterly, could ask what he would, much or little, for he would not be granted either.

An accurate conjecture. The rejection of his request was on a par with rejection of the request to conduct a winter campaign in Bavaria. There were military grounds; they were sound; they sufficed. All the same, there was more to the matter than that. Wallenstein was against Spain. He hated what he regarded as Spain's intention to make itself at home in Germany and eternally exploit it for its own mischievous, unattainable purposes. He subsequently claimed to have flung that in the Capuchin's face. Yes, he had said to him, the allegation at Vienna that he had had the Dutch warned was correct. He would not tolerate the suppression of German liberty by Spain. At all times the Spaniards had fostered evil schemes. Without a vestige of right they had attacked the Duke of Mantua, and the outcome had been the loss of their best fortresses in Flanders. Did he really talk like that? Did he imagine having talked like that?

Quiroga, after two more useless bed-side visits, returned to Vienna. He had come as a friend, he had indeed been selected as such, and there is a good deal to suggest that his unsuccessful mission was not confined to the subject of the Infant's journey, but that it had been meant in addition or conjunction with it to achieve an amicable compromise between Wallenstein and the court. That was the view held by many. The Capuchin's report does not however indicate anything in this respect unless it is Wallenstein's assurance that he would be heartily glad to shed the burden of his appointment.

The Emperor's handwritten dispatch in strong support of the Infant's wishes, presented by Quiroga to Wallenstein, gave the latter cause to class the demand as a piece of all-Habsburg policy, an Austro-Spanish plot. His galled, brooding spirit needed no more. After his fashion he had been polite to Quiroga. Very soon he would speak about the demand for six thousand horsemen in different tones.

The decision to hold a meeting of the imperial army's general officers and colonels at Pilsen must have been taken in December. On 9 and 10 January, in accordance with the Generalissimo's instructions, they arrived. Forty-seven of them, from as far away as Austria, Silesia, Brandenburg, and Swabia. Ignorant as to why they had been summoned, they wandered about, rather at a loss, and asked one another what the reason might be.

Was Wallenstein the originator of the assembly? Was he sure what he was aiming at? We, for our part, know nothing. We can only guess, and our guess is this. The instigator was he who conducted and brought the meeting to its desired conclusion, Ilow. Brutal, wily Christian von Ilow, now the factotum that last year Holk had been, the strong-willed, base character upon whom a noble but broken personality leant because he had to lean on someone. Ilow had, with Adam Trčka, conceived the scheme. These two, Trčka, whose pride of birth was identical with patriotism in the peculiar way that the Bohemian aristocracy loved their country, and Ilow, with not a notion in his head other than more money, more possessions, and more high-sounding titles for himself, these two dunderheads were none the less not so dim-witted as not to appreciate that a far worse crisis than that of 1630 menaced their master's fortunes. They would fall with Wallenstein or rise still higher. He was becoming more and more ill, more and more idiosyncratic. He was visibly slipping from their grasp into incomprehensible regions of thought. Something must be done to hearten him, to bind him to the army through his officers and, reciprocally, the army to him through them. And Wallenstein let it happen, lacking the strength to see that it did not happen. Moreover the inclination to let it happen in order to observe what would emanate from it and how he would himself react to it, this interest was awake in him. Did he not, to attain his visionary objective, really need a new, clear-cut pledge by his officers as representing the army which since summer the court at Vienna had step by step been busy filching from his grasp?

It makes sense. Already three days later clever people thought, and their counterparts have continued to think ever since, that his resolution to resign was nothing but play-acting, and preconcerted at that. We are not so clever, more particularly because we do not credit mankind with being, everywhere and always, so clever in the handling of its affairs.

Ilow greeted the officers as they came. What, he asked Mohr von Wald, member of the Order of Teutonic Knights, did he, as the senior among the colonels, feel about the sharply worded communications the Duke was receiving from Vienna? What did he feel about the request to proceed in this icy winter against Regensburg? How was his response to this new demand to escort the Infant with six thousand mounted men? This was the tenor of his questions to them individually. Next morning, 11 January, the company assembled in his house and discussed the military operations enjoined by the Emperor. Although he had admittedly dropped the move against Regensburg, they unanimously dismissed them as impossible. After the midday meal Ilow gave vent to his gift for inflammatory rhetoric. Vienna was in the hands of the Spaniards and the Jesuits. Spain's policy was to put the Roman Empire in pawn to a monarchy of its own and to wage perpetual war. There was no money for the army, but plenty for other purposes. The Duke, with ingratitude and slander as reward for all his services, had had enough. He intended to resign his appointment. Would it be a good thing if the Duke departed? Good for the imperial service? Good for the colonels who had invested so much money in reliance upon Wallenstein's credit, upon the ducal guarantee, and were now faced with the prospect of losing their stake? Should not a last effort be made to alter the Duke's decision? The reply, emergent from the excited hubbub, was that such an effort was indeed urgently necessary. Colonel the Duke Heinrich Julius von Lauenburg, one of Franz Albrecht's innumerable brothers, was heard to declare that it would be easy for anyone to be Generalissimo and make his officers the most splendid promises if, when redemption was due, he could not be seen for dust. The point was well taken. Wallenstein really was under financial obligation to the regimental commanders. To have parted from them without more ado would have been equivalent to a form of fraudulent bankruptcy, and he would have been a defaulter with a very rough set of creditors. Led by Ilow, a delegation marched to the Duke's residence and was given access to his presence. He turned down their request. The delegation withdrew, pondered the situation, and, in accordance with Ilow's wire-pulling, again invaded the sick-room. This time the Duke said yes. He would, in God's name, for the sake of his colonels retain his appointment a while and see that they obtained their due, the army its victuals, the Empire its peace.

The delegation returned to its brothers-in-arms. Ilow talked and talked, and the drift of it all was that loyalty deserved reciprocity. If the Duke had pledged himself to them, then they should do the same, and the surer they would thereby be of him. That sunk home. Well enough, continued the Field-Marshal, but in writing was better than by word of mouth. He made a sign. Captain Niemann pulled a draft from his pocket and read it aloud. Any against? Consensus, of a kind, though hardly so enthusiastic as on the previous day.

On the following evening, 12 January, the Field-Marshal gave a banquet for the forty-seven officers. It was held in the Great Room of the town hall, a building which stands today, diagonally opposite Wallenstein's residence. With agonizing pains in his feet and knees, his hands, his heart, his throbbing temples and brain, he could not but hear what was happening in that Great Room, how the music blared, then after a time fell silent to give place to shouts and roars and crashes as of timbers shivering beneath an axe. They were among themselves, these overgrown, ferocious children, tempered soldiers of fortune, comrades of old, rivals of old, and they enjoyed each others' company. Flushed with wine, politics flushed their mind. The paper they were to sign began to circulate. What, some of them wanted to know, was it? Why was it needed? Was it in any way hostile to religion? Why was there nothing in it about loyalty to the Emperor? There had been plenty of talk on that, Ilow appeased them, and it was there, somewhere at the start, and that sufficed. It sufficed some of them, who limned their names, and others it did not. As the night grew longer, heads whirled and senses span. The scene became ever wilder. Contumelies were flung with stammering tongue against the Spaniards and the Jesuits, those two incarnations of evil, and were greeted with lusty laughter. Colonel Losy yelled that those who would not sign were scoundrels, the lot of them. Heinrich Julius von Lauenburg bawled in reply that Losy should be hurled through the window, whereupon Isolani, the Croat general, went for Lauenburg with drawn sword. Such incidents attracted as little attention as when Adam Trčka, with drawn sword too, threatened to kill anyone who was the General's foe and elicited from Ottavio Piccolomini a shrill cry of "*O traditore!*" Not much attention was paid to this outburst since Piccolomini, a second later, seized Colonel Giulio Diodati by the shoulders and leapt about the room with him. He was presumably in no state to be answerable for his actions and thoroughly merry on top of that. When the revellers finally reeled into the wintry night, they left the Great Room's tables, chairs, and fireplaces smashed.

Next morning Wallenstein received a report on the event. It was not the kind of occasion that he cared for. He ordered the forty-seven officers to present themselves. During the forenoon they appeared, bleary-eyed and with bloated features, but washed and attired as appropriate to such collective audience. Sash of rank across their tunic, hat under the arm, they crowded together, leaving a space between them and the Duke in his armchair. It was time for the invalid to exercise his legendary authority. He had learnt, he said, that there had been hesitations over signature of the document. That rendered it worthless. "I would sooner be dead than see myself living so; I shall withdraw and nurse my health." (Another tradition alleges, "shall spend the rest of my days in a cloister".) His intent was not, and God preserve him from it, to harm Emperor or Empire. As he spoke, he flew into a rage and entered upon details. There was the affair of the Infant's journey and the six thousand mounted men: "Were a schoolboy to crave this, he were fit for strokes of the rod. . . . When I do not obey such out of season orders, they seek to oppress me." There was the wretched money business. He received none, regardless of all assurances, neither from the Spaniards nor from the Emperor. A hundred thousand gulden was what Questenberg had brought, and he was supposed to be satisfied with such beggary. Where did the tax levies go? Why was war waged and the army grudged what it needed for that war? "Whither we come and ask for quarters, we are not wanted, as though we were Turks, demons, or Tartars." How did Vienna expect to end hostilities? "When we had flooded the whole Empire with our army, held all fortresses and passes", such attempt had proved unsuccessful. How was it to come to pass now? Peace, though, was not what Vienna wanted. They were besmirching the honour and reputation that in twenty-eight hard years of service he had won and they even were playing with the idea of hastening his end by poison. Were these the thanks for his achievements? Yet, for all that, he had yesterday agreed to the officers' pleas to delay on their account, and for the sake of peace, his retirement a little. Let them consider the matter once more. A nod of his head, signifying dismissal. Fresh discussion between the generals and colonels, and a fresh petition – the Duke should not take ill what yesternight had occurred in drunkenness. Today, in matutinal sobriety, they were all prepared to sign. And sign they did, five times indeed, for five copies were made, three to be kept by the senior commanders of the infantry, cavalry, and Croatian horse, two to be carried to Silesia and Austria for the appendage of outstanding signatures. Summarily the Pilsen Oath ran as follows: because of the highly painful insults offered to him, because of the refusal to the army of essential supplies, because of ruinous orders impossible of fulfilment issued by the imperial court, the Duke of Mecklenburg, Friedland, Sagan, and Grossglogau had decided to resign his appointment. His only too intelligible decision must redound to the undoing of His Imperial Majesty, the public weal, the army, and, not least, the army's commanders who in reliance upon His Princely Grace's word had ventured their fortunes. The Duke had heeded the suit and supplication of his officers to hold out with them a while and not, without their previous knowledge and agreement, to part from them. In the face of such magnanimity, the Undersigned had for their part sworn to stay honourably and loyally at their General's side, in no manner whatsoever to sunder or divide or let themselves be divided from him, but far rather to risk their lives and their last drop of blood for him. Let loss of goods and chattels, body and soul be the lot of him who, unmindful of honour's dictates, broke this oath. Approved: Heinrich Julius Duke of Saxony-Lauenburg, Ilow, Schaffgotsch, O. C. Piccolomini, Scherffenberg, Sparr, Trčka, Morzin, Suys, Isolano. Mohr von Wald, Bredow, Lamboy, Gonzaga, Beck, Wolff, Waevel, Wiltberg, de la Fosse, Henderson, Noyrel, Diodati, Burian von Waldstein, Prjchowycz, la Tornett, de la Mouilly, S. Piccolomini, Wangler, Schütz, Gisenburg, Salazar, Waldenfels, Notario, Balbiano, Corrasco, Rodell, Altmanshausen, Haimerl, Peukher, Butler, Gordon. In the afternoon of 13 January, the assembly ended and the officers dispersed to all points of the compass.

The authors of the document had no illusions about its being kept secret. There could not but be one among the forty-seven signatures who would gossip about the text and the concomitant circumstances. There could not but be several, not to mention the innumerable by-standers, secretaries, servants, inquisitive monks. One purpose of the undertaking, which had no plain purpose, precisely was to overawe Wallenstein's enemies at Vienna and Munich: here stood a wall, compact and without cracks, composed of the Commander-in-Chief, officers, rank and file. The court at Vienna was immediately informed of the events at Pilsen, and the surmises as to the significance of them were various. Some inclined to think that, as a whole, no great harm sprang from what simply amounted to an effort by Wallenstein to appease and to discipline army circles where rumours ran dangerously rife. Others denounced the happenings as unpardonable conspiracy. A third party concurred that unfortunately this was correct, but that it rendered action against the Duke more difficult. Richel, who analysed for his Elector these three classes of reaction, must have observed the eddies; the man had good sources of information. To be sure, just at this moment he lacked the best, the most direct.

To what use could the expositors, whether friendly or inimical – at Vienna we can no longer, in spite of Richel, discern any friendly ones – to what use could they put the Pilsen Oath? To what use could Wallenstein put it? Had the mountain heaved and brought forth a mouse?

The Emperor's officers had at all times to obey the Emperor's Generalissimo. That was inherent in the original obligation which they assumed and, as one of them subsequently maintained, required no corollary. Because the text was lacking in any straightforward motivation, very soon a special piece of news went the rounds. Earlier, it was claimed, the text had included the proviso "for as long as His Princely

Grace remains in the service of His Imperial Majesty or the latter shall for the promotion of His service use him". That was how the document had been read to the officers. When however it came to signature, the restrictive clause had disappeared. Mere legend. A gross confidence trick was beneath Wallenstein's dignity and incapable of implementation because such omission would have directed the officers' attention to exactly the problem which it was necessary to obscure. What emanated from the evidence of witnesses was no more than that during his speeches Ilow laid more emphasis on the Emperor and the imperial service than found expression in the oath itself, and that several officers challenged him on this point. Count Oñate had another version. The proviso had not, according to him, been wafted into thin air; Wallenstein had struck it out when the draft was submitted to him. This reading is psychologically rather more probable. The Duke was deeply convinced that officers and soldiers owed him personal loyalty, and loyalty to the Emperor at best through him, just as he is supposed to have told Father Quiroga that three-quarters of the army – namely, the regiments newly enrolled by him – were his personal possession. He would indeed have struck the proviso through, violently enraged if it had been presented to him and his approval expected. But that it happened – on what rested Oñate's claim to know this?

With or without proviso, the Pilsen Oath was not much use, at one and the same time sabre-rattling and timid, with many meanings implicit and yet unclear. Conspiracy, no. Conspiracies are not contrived in a crowd with the subject shouted at the top of one's voice, but among a few who are plainly told what is wanted. Wallenstein did not tell his forty-seven officers what he wanted. He simply assured them that he would try to satisfy their pecuniary demands and to alleviate the soldiers' needs, as well as that he was aiming at peace. The document lacked any precise indications or positive objectives. To give the oath of loyalty any substance, it would have had at least to envisage the possibility of the Emperor turning against the Generalissimo or the Generalissimo against the Emperor. Merely the slightest intimation of that, with all able to canvass their own interpretation.

What else is there to say? Not a great deal. Ilow and Trčka may have persuaded their master that now he was safer than before in his negotiations with the Saxons and Brandenburgers, with the Protestants as a whole. They may have persuaded him that now his foes at Vienna would not dare to oust him or, should they dare, he now would possess power to thwart them which at Memmingen he did not possess. They may have been content with their labour. He, and this we know, on the day after the Pilsen Oath felt wretched to the point of despair. Sooner than bind himself afresh, he would far rather have withdrawn his head from the noose, far rather have been released from the labyrinth and found rest somewhere. Yet he could not. Yet he would not.

FINAL NEGOTIATION ROUNDABOUT

While these things were happening at Pilsen, the dark comedy of negotiations had begun again.

On 26 December Adam Trčka wrote to his brother-in-law Kinsky at Dresden that all was now in readiness to settle terms not only with the two Protestant Electors, but also with France and Sweden. Kinsky's presence at Pilsen was urgently desired, and better still would be if Lieutenant-General Arnim came. ". . . are now resolved to throw off the mask entirely and, with God's help, to make a firm start upon the work. . . . If this opportunity is neglected, an eternity will pass before another such occasion recurs. This winter can see much good effectuated. Your lordship is ingenious. Do not omit to further the advantage of all Christendom."

"Are now resolved" meant "We have him now, if the right people nudge him." The letter, with its frequently quoted phrase "throw off the mask", was probably not seen by Wallenstein. Nevertheless it was a fact that he wanted to see Kinsky and he is said to have written to him in his own shaky hand.

Kinsky, for more than twenty years without any occupation other than that of arch-intriguer, felt his heart beat higher. Post-haste on New Year's Day he sent a message to the Marquis de Feuquières. The ambassador would recall their uncompleted Dresden business. Now the news was good, the moment at hand, and the principal personality determined to accept the proposals propounded to him in summer. Nothing more was required than a mandate for His Excellency to ratify the treaty between the King of France and the individual in question. Feuquières replied that he was enchanted and would not fail to instigate suitable steps. Admittedly they would take time. Count Kinsky should kindly continue to keep his friend in his prevailing frame of mind. To his staff, though, the diplomat described the business as delicate and dubious. In the light of his previous experience with the Duke of Friedland he did not even initially think fit to inform his monarch of the new development. Kinsky, his head buzzing with hectic notions of impending activity, had not the slightest suspicion of such muted reactions. An official travel permit in his pocket, he was received in audience by Elector John George and, we are told, touched on "strange projects". Then, safely ensconced in a column of sleighs, he hurried to Pilsen in the company of his wife, daughter to old Magdalena Trčka lying in her grave, and Colonel Schlieff, the Saxon military man with an inclination for dabbling in politics. Sezyma Rašin, errand-runner of ill repute, was also probably with them. Kinsky expected to stay several days. He stayed longer, too long.

The Count had talks with Wallenstein, Ilow, Trčka, and Gallas. Accounts by the participants are not available. Schlieff, who stayed a single day, has left the following testimony:

On instruction from highest authority he was conducted to Wallenstein's sick-bed. He must, the Duke said, talk to him. Last autumn there had been certain negotiations which had unfortunately come to nothing. Man proposes, God disposes. If the Elector of Saxony wished to conclude peace, good will was not lacking on his, the Generalissimo's, part. He would, as befited an imperial prince, have regard for the Empire's welfare. Spain was on the point of establishing dominion over Germany. That, as long as life was in him, he would not permit. He would help in person to drive the Spaniards out of Italy, Artois, Hennegau. The King of France, a powerful potentate, would clearly love to set foot across the Rhine. It must be prevented and seen to that France received satisfaction elsewhere. "The Tirol, and all that appertains to it, should remain forever imperially enfeoffed." Sweden? It wanted to keep the Baltic ports already in its possession, such as Rostock, Wismar, Stralsund, Kolberg, in which Brandenburg must be assumed to have an interest too. Ways would be found of conciliating both. The spiritual princes should have their territories again. Bernhard von Weimar, installed as Duke of Franconia by Oxenstierna at the bishops' expense, would be compensated elsewhere, in Alsace or Bavaria. Above all the Palatinate must be restituted. Was not a personal conference between himself and His Saxon Serenity possible? A delegate should be dispatched from Dresden to arrange such a meeting. Duke Franz Albrecht would be welcome, but he who must, first and last, be his negotiating partner was Field-Marshal von Arnim. The denominational dispute was not mentioned. Not everything could in the first instance be discussed. The problem, for example, of his own indemnification. He did presumably want some, a substitute for Mecklenburg. Where? To whose cost? Conjectures were rife, relating to Württemberg and Baden, the Rhenish Palatinate, even Brandenburg, impossible conjectures to which in moments of disequilibrium he gave sustenance. Others fancied, as they had long fancied, that he had his eye on Bohemia. He neither touched on this subject nor said a word about those hostile intentions which he was suspected of harbouring against the German branch of the Habsburg dynasty. "The Tirol, and all that appertains to it, should remain forever imperially enfeoffed." Detractors have understood this to mean that *only* the Tirol was to be retained by the Emperor. A senseless interpretation. If Ferdinand was to be degraded to the status of an innocuous princeling, he would in the first place have had to have been stripped of the imperial dignity and, secondly, isolated in an eastern corner of his former possessions, most conveniently in Styria, his native heath. "The Tirol" and all that appertained to it signified not the Alpine territory with its Italian passes, but connoted the Breisgau and Alsace, localities which linked the German Habsburgs to the Spanish branch and would, besides Bohemia, have been the most palpable candidates for forfeiture. The remark is just a scrap of dialogue, obscure as it stands, the work of a Privy Councillor detailed to take a minute of the Colonel's report.

Incomplete and indirectly quoted, what Schlieff heard at his bedside none the less constitutes the most detailed draft of Wallenstein's ideas that we possess. It is an improvement on that of the foregoing September because Sweden is included. The Swedes are not, as in the preceding year, simply to be ejected. They are to be propitiated by way of coastal territory. The point is crucial. Were the German Protestants, but not the Swedes, to make peace with the Emperor, there would be no more than a reversal of alliances and continuation of the war with a re-alignment of fronts. Would it not anyway continue? He wants, says Wallenstein, to help in person to drive the Spaniards from Italy and Flanders. That would entail another set of hostilities, on a large spatial scale, for the Spaniards would not disappear of their own. If one day, fourteen years later, the time was to come when the German Habsburgs were ripe for severance from the Spaniards, the time when they would themselves attack their Madrid cousins would never come at all. Consequently a war against Spain could not but be identical with a rising against the Emperor. That could not mean peace. The same applied to any "complete annihilation" of Bavaria, an objective not specifically stated by Wallenstein, but which Schlieff had the impression that he carried in his head. What are we to make of it all? How precise, how complete was Schlieff's report? How precisely, how completely was it taken down?

How much had Schlieff heard from Kinsky, not Wallenstein? If Saxony was not inclined to play its allotted role, Sweden and France could be taken into partnership – that momentary, lightning revelation of the antithesis between the two strands of the negotiations, the German–Protestant and the Franco–Swedish, was surely Kinsky's, criminally addicted as he was to intrigue from sheer pleasure in it and frivolity. How much had been plain chatter by Wallenstein, constant to his old habit of saying what he thought that the Saxons would like to hear? What portion of what he had uttered in pure rage against the Spaniards was empty of serious intent?

On Schlieff's return to Dresden he found the Elector drunk and incapable of giving him a hearing. Somewhat later he did show interest, an interest animated by the fact that this lazy, vain creature was more than ever resentful of Swedish tutelage. A keenly attentive listener was Field-Marshal Duke Franz Albrecht von Lauenburg. Matters stood extremely well, he told Arnim, who was killing time in Brandenburg besieging Frankfurt-on-Oder. The severity of the reproofs from Vienna, the attempts to steal control of the army from him, and other reasons had soured Wallenstein as never before. "He desires to avenge himself upon the Emperor. That is certain. Should I meet him, I shall soon see whether the business is firm and it is necessary for Your Excellency to visit him. Probably it cannot be otherwise if anything right is to come of the affair. I perceive well enough that he must have one who will help him." The writer's brother, Duke Franz Julius, he continued, had also arrived in Dresden on a mission from which it emerged "that the Emperor would gladly have peace, but not in the manner of the Duke of Friedland. . . . It [the Emperor's proposal] is an equitable piece of work, but nothing will come of it because the Generalissimo thinks very differently. . . . He [Wallenstein] is now so far in that he can no longer escape. . . . I entreat Your Excellency for the sake of Heaven to hurry and come here, else nothing will transpire. The business is firm and I learn constantly more from Schlieff. The Emperor and the Elector [of Bavaria] are to go." Wallenstein's words or words attributed to him, in this instance probably by Kinsky, and passed to third, fourth, fifth parties. Words, words, words. Not long ago he had accomplished deeds, raised armies, founded states. Now he was not much more than a skein of words woven by others. Franz Albrecht's letter was composed with a sore head because on the preceding evening he had "drunk myself half dead". Nevertheless there are two sentences worth pondering. "He is now so far in that he can no longer escape" and "I perceive well enough that he must have one who will help him". Franz Albrecht's alert eyes were the first which presumed to observe that the great, dreaded personality had reached the stage of helplessness and was himself beginning to be gripped by fear.

Precisely why the young Duke of Lauenburg staked so much on Wallenstein and why Wallenstein's ideas could be neither radical nor anti-Habsburg enough for him is not known. Franz Albrecht had suffered no injury at the Emperor's hands. Subsequently he was content to re-enter the imperial service. He had always been wealthy and had not, like others, been forced to hack his way with sword and scheming out of penury's shadows. Women were his greatest source of happiness, and his secretary attested that his duty almost exclusively consisted of "writing petticoat-letters". Next came politics, probably through a passion for play, akin to Kinsky's, although in this instance less malign, a sprightly way of deploying his personality to the full. He believed in Wallenstein and he was under his spell. Given the boldness to see what the dull-witted mass still failed to realize, he noted what he saw with the feeling that this was a situation which cried out for speediest help. On 14 January he set out with official permission for Pilsen, due to incessant snow-storms took five days for the journey, at Schlackenwerth received a transcript of the Pilsen Oath which he immediately sent to Dresden, conferred with Wallenstein, and on the same day started on the same arduous return road. His information hardly added to what Colonel Schlieff had reported. The Duke of Friedland would do everything to make peace "whether the Emperor would or would not". The case was urgent, very urgent, and the visit of Lieutenant-General von Arnim to Pilsen was ardently desired.

Arnim was the man who, even if it meant hard effort, ultimately decided what Saxony would do and what Brandenburg would do. Without his advice Elector John George was helpless. "God grant that he [Wallenstein] means honestly. Last year 'twas worth naught. In God's name, come. I await You fervidly," wrote the Elector.

Arnim was however of a different calibre from Field-Marshal the Duke of Lauenburg, vibrant with the joy of life. Slow-blooded, cautious, embittered by disappointments which in the final analysis he had himself invited, always deliberate, always didactic, he was never impassioned about anything, and never less so than about the present new yet familiar situation. Portents and miracles, he answered, were what he wanted, else he would credit nothing. How, in the face of what had been evinced last year, could any faith continue to be reposed in Wallenstein? The only point was that it might be better to concede him one tiny jot of belief because if no hope could be placed in Pilsen, then there was indeed none anywhere for their beloved Germany. The alternatives were to try once again with the Duke of Friedland or to persevere to the bitter end with the Swedes. "The first holds great danger, yet some little hope; the other contains yet greater danger and, to my mind, no hope at all." Let therefore in God's name the first be chosen, but care taken to become strong through great armaments because that would force the Duke to keep his ague under control and to behave with probity. As to Wallenstein's proposal to compensate the Swedes with a slice of German littoral, the German patriot could not stomach that. There were others with better claim to the ports and the foreign ally should be indemnified with money.

None the less Arnim delayed his departure for Dresden. Behind the threadbare excuse that he had prepared for Holy Communion on the coming Sunday and could not leave before Monday lay fresh reluctance and anger. Thanks to a political shot by Oxenstierna across his bows, he again felt his honour to have been painfully impugned.

The Swedish Chancellor had been watching with dislike what was on foot between Dresden and Pilsen, a dislike as keen as in the preceding year. To his cool brain only two possibilities existed – either Wallenstein was playing a game of deceit or he was trying to divide the Germans from the Swedes. A third, that Wallenstein could come to some agreement with himself, he dismissed. Had the Generalissimo been serious about that, it would have occurred in Gustavus Adolphus's lifetime. Against this fresh vexation there was only one convenient resource at hand – to compromise the position of the most important figure in Wallenstein's scheme through the widespread practice of compromising his reputation. Count Reinhard Solms, his chief agent for German affairs, hastened to Berlin and warned members of the Brandenburg Privy Council against Arnim. His master, Oxenstierna, could tell them many a thing about him, details learned in a roundabout way from no less an authority than the Duke of Friedland. Had not the Duke told a Swedish colonel that his compatriots had no more dangerous an enemy than Arnim? The previous autumn's negotiations had been wrecked solely by Arnim. Last October Arnim had of malevolence abandoned Silesia, condemning the Swedish corps to annihilation. The Duke had practically been forced to undertake the Steinau affair as he would otherwise have discredited himself all too badly with Vienna. He could really have done much more, like seizing defenceless Stralsund and

Stettin as well as other coastal places, but he had abstained in order to spare the Protestants. All this Wallenstein had confided to the Swedish colonel, the colonel to the Chancellor, the Chancellor to Count Solms who in turn confided it to Privy Councillor Goetze, the Privy Councillor to Colonel Burgsdorff, the Colonel to Lieutenant-General Arnim. The news relay accomplished its purpose. Arnim displayed emphatic repugnance to the resumption of a task which so far had earned him nothing but tedious travels, frustrations, and slander. Franz Albrecht, whose most crying anxiety was for Arnim's journey to Pilsen to take place, intervened to reconcile the parties. Wallenstein pledged his word in writing that every syllable of what had been alleged about Arnim and himself was entirely unfounded untruth and indemonstrable to the end of eternity. The question whether the poison from Oxenstierna's arrow was thereby effectively immunized remains open.

A further question is whether the Chancellor's imaginative assistants had invented the little tale. We suspect that at his headquarters there existed a centre of political warfare for the purpose of contriving the ruin of the one man who was regarded as Sweden's most dangerous opponent. Hardly by chance did so many strange stories of Wallenstein's treasonable intentions emerge from, of all places, Frankfurt-on-Main, the Swedish headquarters. The reasons for the deterioration in his reputation were however manifold. Given to babbling so lightly whatever appealed to a passing whim, had he really in a moment of blindness vented such utterly baseless expressions? Had Adam Trčka really boasted that the siege of Regensburg could of course have been raised if that had been wanted, but, in order to allow Bernhard von Weimar to gain a handsomely firm position close to Bohemia, it had not been wanted? Possibly, possibly not. Fatal damage to Wallenstein's standing was in any case ensured by the unbridled garrulity of his enemies, his friends, his semi- and quarter-friends, or his own. He had always been Europe's most slandered figure of power. Now the rumours, running right across the continent, ground him down irrespective of whether there was a grain of truth in them or not.

On 26 January Arnim arrived in Dresden. Only then could the cumbersome advisory machinery be put into motion. For the next seven days it trundled crunchingly along. Arnim argued strongly for his being spared negotiations at Pilsen. Three times last year he had had experience of the Duke of Friedland's fickleness, his honour had been affronted, and the task required such extravagant prudence that it entirely exceeded human capacity. Nevertheless because the Duke of Friedland set such excessive store by his humble person, because the Duke disposed of such a mighty armada and, were he repulsed, might commit extremely evil actions, because, in short, so much depended for christendom on the matter, he was, in God's name, ready to go if the Elector were pleased to send him. He must however have the most precise instructions. Was negotiation with the Duke, in as much as he was mortal and subject to many diseases, to be conducted as if he were an autonomous potentate? Or, as seemed more advisable, as a representative of the Emperor? Should he be required to produce an imperial power of authority? What was to be done if he had none? Or had one, but it was restricted? And what if the Duke had no regard for its restrictions? If he, but not the Emperor, were to accept the conditions posed by the Protestants? If, as in the foregoing year, he demanded a merger of the armies? If he harboured armed intent against the House of Austria on account of his private grudges? If he had plenary power from the Emperor, but not from Bavaria, from the League, which was equally a belligerent party? What was to happen to the soldiers after the conclusion of peace, how was the money for them to be raised, or was a campaign to be undertaken with them outside Germany, and against whom? A pile of questions, a pile of answers. An imperial authority, Saxon collegial wisdom decided, must be. Limited plenary power could not bring about unlimited effect, wherefore the Duke must not exceed his authority. But, objected Arnim, if this proved all too restricted, peace was out of the question unless Wallenstein did exceed it and the Protestants conformed. The Emperor, retorted John George, had left him, the Elector, free to deal with the Duke of Friedland. The purpose of the negotiations was peace. Whatever served that was permissible provided that the right of ratification was retained by the Emperor. According to the rule *Quod omnes tangit, ab omnibus debet approbari* (what touches all should be approved by all), a power of authority from the League was admittedly desirable but perhaps not absolutely essential. "His Serene Highness has no knowledge of the Duke of Friedland's private grudges and aversions." That was of no interest to the Elector. Talk turned to Sweden. Arnim remarked that the projected negotiations were very unwelcome to the Chancellor, but that was not his concern. Religion and German liberty were what he cared for. Talk turned on Brandenburg. Close collaboration, said Arnim, between Brandenburg and Saxony was necessary. Just at this stage Brandenburg was being sorely pressed by the Swedes to adhere still more closely to them by joining the League of Heilbronn. There must be a meeting between the Electors to prevent it and to concert negotiations with the Duke of Friedland. At what half-way castle could such a meeting be arranged? None, was the answer, because Torgau was completely stripped and sacked while at Annaburg death was stalking all around. Was not the best solution to send a Saxon representative to Berlin in the person of Lieutenant-General Arnim? This again required an instruction, one which emphasized how very warily and prudently it was necessary to proceed in so difficult, extremely important a matter, and it involved a journey which, sessions and audiences at Berlin included, could not take less than ten days. Duke Franz Albrecht should again proceed to Wallenstein in order to excuse the long delay. Colonel Schlieff had during these consultations at Dresden for the second time already travelled to Pilsen as a herald.

"Where," Wallenstein asked the Colonel, "does my lord remain so long? I had deemed him to have died." And then, "Where remains Lord von Arnim? Does he come or does he not?" Schlieff began a speech about how much His Excellency regretted having still somewhat to postpone his visit. As he spoke, Wallenstein's features began to twitch. His gestures altered as though he were beginning to suffer from the ague. Schlieff talked all the faster about the need for the journey to Berlin in the interest of the business as a whole, how it should not last too long, and, God willing, the Lord Lieutenant-General's arrival could be anticipated in ten to twelve days, but before that, indeed at any moment, the Duke of Lauenburg would be on hand. Wallenstein controlled himself. He even smiled. Yes, he commented, undoubtedly the journey to Berlin was in order and a good idea. Franz Albrecht was welcome, although admittedly he would have preferred Arnim. How were matters otherwise with the Elector? Would the wedding of the young prince soon take place? "At the beginning I observed him to be far gone in melancholy," Schlieff reported, "but, when I had finished my speech, his amiability was quite restored."

Two days later Franz Albrecht was in Pilsen, but during his first call experienced such fits of icy shivers that he had to retire. Henceforth communications continued from bed to bed. Daily, and several times each day, Wallenstein sent to ask whether there was news from Arnim and when he was coming. Almost daily a courier went from Franz Albrecht to Arnim or the Elector. Urgency, the urgency of the matter, was his sole theme. On 2 February, to Arnim, "For Heaven's sake let Your Excellency come soon." On 8 February, to John George, how the Duke of Friedland had complained bitterly about the dilatoriness with which a task was being treated where every minute was of moment.

There would be no difficulties after Arnim had appeared, but affairs had reached a pass when something untoward could easily happen. On the same day, to Arnim, why so late the departure for Berlin, why stay there so long? He had been expected in Pilsen on the 9th, in an emergency the 12th would just do. "His Dilection is anxious that something may intervene, for he is in very bad odour at court and the talk there about him and his people is very odd. If Your Excellency arrives, he will do whatever You wish." Whatever the route that Arnim might choose, sleighs and horses were everywhere provided. On 9 February and 13 February his messages to the Elector were in the same tenor, except that they were on an ever more urgent, ever more pressing note. "His Lordship the Generalissimo is aware that they are not idle at court and that is why not an hour should be lost in the business." Almost three weeks, he exclaimed on 17 February, had he now spent at Pilsen in the most nerve-racking impatience, an impatience even greater on the part of the Duke of Friedland. All the headquarters officers had been told of Arnim's impending arrival, but ever and again he failed to come. The talk on all sides was ever heavier with suspicion. . . .

Wallenstein lay and waited for Arnim. Why for Arnim? What had Arnim to offer by way of help and salvation? Not the astrologers, it would seem, were responsible for his pinning his hopes on Arnim. There are no indications to that effect. More likely it was Arnim's presence from which he expected comfort. Himself he was man and woman in one, Kepler had said; Arnim was devout, sage, a man, no more. Where Arnim was, rebellion had no place. Arnim meant a bridge from the inadmissible to the admissible, from highly treasonable to legitimate policy. Arnim at Pilsen would have furnished him with cover against the court at Vienna, against Kinsky's conspiratorial assiduity, against Trčka's and Ilow's wild talk. These two were constantly about his person, confined him to his bed, acted on his behalf, and he let them in spite of his surmise that they were bringing misfortune down on him. How agonizing the disappointment, the panic which preyed on him when now Arnim again failed to come and was far, far away. How his features began to jerk and a wild look to enter his eyes until he imposed control on himself, forcing a wan smile to wrap his loneliness and grief.

Normality still prevailed about him. The strict routine of camp and court, habits dating from better days, continued to be heeded. His duchy still produced and delivered what was needed. The Duke did not stir from Pilsen. The Duchess resided at the Harrach castle in Bruck on the Leitha. Her lady-mother was in need of money because old Harrach's heir, Count Leonhard, was a ne'er-do-well. Wallenstein had given instructions for her to be provided annually, in two instalments, with four thousand gulden from the Friedland treasury. As a New Year's gift the King of Denmark sent a team of noble steeds to Pilsen and was rewarded with a letter of thanks. From Sagan his principal administrator wrote that he was doing his best to comply with both his orders, to hasten completion of the palace and to feed Count Gallas's troops, but this winter it would not be possible and building would probably have to wait a while. Orders were issued, as normally. Missives were received, as normally.

The war too continued along its normal winter pattern. Wallenstein had seen to the defence of the Hereditary Lands and, despite all reproaches to the contrary, even to that of Bavaria. His regiments were stationed in Bohemia, Moravia, Austria, Bavaria, Lusatia, Silesia, Brandenburg. The eastern periphery: Inner Germany was dominated by the Swedes. The imperialists would be fools to leave the Hereditary Lands and venture a winter campaign in the Empire. That was Bernhard von Weimar's view, and he knew his craft. Opinion among the Catholics varied. In December Elector Maximilian had screamed for help. Now he wanted to be rid of the Aldringen soldiers who remained on his territory. In December the Emperor had demanded concentration in the west, on the farther bank of the Inn. Now he wanted deployment of the regiments as far to the rear as deep into Lower Austria. Wallenstein gainsaid him – the danger from the enemy required a massing on the borders, meaning Bohemia, eastern Bavaria, Passau, Upper Austria, and Salzburg, whose archbishop was against billetings. The usual awkward correspondence ensued. Finally the Generalissimo gave way. Aldringen was allowed to send a few thousand of his hungry, roofless troops to Lower Austria, but no farther. The Inner Austrian lands, Carinthia and Styria, were to render monetary contributions.

There was so much that was normal. What had he to fear from his monarch who often and graciously turned to him with letters which began "Well-born beloved Cousin" and ended "with imperial affection"? What had he to fear from a minister like Bishop Antonius who recently had sent such hearty greetings upon "the new-born Christ-child's" nativity?

Should none the less an unpleasant event transpire, a dismissal, say, more opprobrious than that of Memmingen, a breach, then he could be certain of his army. In any case of the colonels of his regiments; they had signed to that. Also of his most important generals – Gallas, Piccolomini, Schaffgotsch, Scherffenberg. He was on good terms with Ottavio Piccolomini, had done him good turns, in the past often enough and just now again, for in January he had had him created Field Marshal. The imperial commission was dated 1 February. Their farewells could therefore not but be of the warmest kind when, four days after the Pilsen assembly, Piccolomini took his leave to assume the command in Upper Austria and the instruction to sound out Count Aldringen, the only one among his senior commanders about whose attitude Wallenstein had any doubts, doubts of long standing. Lieutenant-General Gallas would do his duty. Had he not, through Piccolomini, conveyed a message that he was entirely in favour of putting the officers under oath? Had he not on 24 January come to Pilsen and stayed almost three weeks, bluff, bulky, jovial, mighty fond of his drink, and encouraging the rosy view on all sides? Had it not been precisely Piccolomini and Gallas who often had implored him to retain his appointment so that the Emperor should not become entirely dependent on the Spaniards and the Poles? At least he had no worries in that direction. He could talk to such loyal adherents without constraint, and act too, should action prove inevitable.

He groped for what was familiar to him, the condition of legality, or at least its sheen. He dutifully told Count Trauttmansdorff that Wilhelm Kinsky had arrived at Pilsen as a delegate from the Elector of Saxony, that Duke Franz Albrecht had come on Saxon instructions, that there would be negotiations with the objective of attaining the peace which was so essential, and that he should be sent assistance, preferably Dr Justus Gebhard. The Emperor replied in person. Peace talks with the Protestant Electors were wholly agreeable to him, court Councillor Gebhard would immediately leave for Pilsen to be at His Dilection's side and interpret the imperial wishes. Gebhard did indeed receive instructions steeped, as such instructions always were, in love of peace. On 10 February this indispensable treaty specialist, of whose documents it was said that not merely every word but every syllable of them must be closely scrutinized, reached Pilsen. It was all perfectly normal, a repetition of what had happened before. Or not? Not really?

"He is now so far in that he can no longer escape," Franz Albrecht had exulted. Nevertheless he wanted to escape. From the ghastly high treason wherein Kinsky, Trčka, and Ilow had involved him and with which he toyed in case the worst came to the worst. From having to take a decision. Back into the protection afforded by legality, outside whose shelter he did not care to live. Hardly had the Pilsen Oath been signed before he dispatched Count Hardegg, his Principal Equerry, to tell Vienna that he was prepared voluntarily to resign his office if he received assurances as regards his person, his honour, and 300,000 taler as indemnification. By this move he betrayed his colonels, for the obligation arising on the Pilsen Oath was mutual, as well as his revolutionary conspirators. The Emperor too? Does it make sense to speak of saving appearances when reality no longer had any footing? He had his offer repeated by Count Max, familiar with courtly ins and outs, proposing within four months to bring the army up to the mark again, then abdicate, help the young King of Hungary into the saddle, kiss the stirrups, and betake himself into retirement. We do not know what answer the Prince of Friedland on 12 February bore to Pilsen, but we must assume that it was cryptic in the extreme. Wallenstein had already let Prince Eggenberg know that "matters cannot continue in such fashion". They could not, in other words, go on as they were and a general accommodation must be attained. On that too we must assume that the minister simply shrugged and murmured, "too late".

The return of the dead is not desired even when they have been loved when alive. For Vienna Wallenstein was now dead. Loved he never had been. Rapacious successors lay in wait for the legacy.

For Vienna dead; at Pilsen a bundle of bodily pains and spiritual torment; for his friends a source of egregious hopes. Not that they sensed this. On the spot hardly, else they would promptly have abandoned him. At a distance, not at all.

Rudolf Trčka, a widower now, raised his glass to King Albrecht of Bohemia. "Brother," he said to his guest, a neighbouring estate owner, "abide with us. The Emperor's cause is lost and lost too is therewith all that you possess. On Friedland's side you can regain it and more." The guest demurred. Wallenstein was old, very ill. What would happen when he died? Provision was made, replied Lord Rudolf. The King of Poland would be elected his successor. Nevermore must the House of Austria be allowed to return to Bohemia. What, the old man's senior steward on another occasion asked him, if the émigrés came back? Would not the family have to restore to them many fine manor-lands? Indeed, and not gladly either, he replied, but his son assuredly knew what he was about. Adam had been promised the county of Glatz. What a magnificent slice of territory, together with Opočno and Smiřice, it would be! All those splendid stags in its woods! The steward persisted.

Would the Duke die a good death? Would he escape God's punishment? He had abandoned God and relied solely on his intelligence, status, strength, and astrologers. He was merciless, unjust, and had caused sorrow to many, many widows and orphans. True, granted Trčka, but none the less all was proceeding well with him. Agog with curiosity and scared wonderment were the conversations the steward held with Count Adam. He would become a great and rich man, the younger Trčka predicted for himself, as though he were not rich enough already. He would keep stables more splendid than any others, have twelve damsels in a bower, and acquire or exchange many estates to round his possessions finely off. He counted on Bohemia's new king for that. A king as strict as Satan, interjected the steward, and woe to him who sought to sin against him. On the contrary, retorted Count Adam, he would restore to the Bohemians all their liberties. He, Trčka, would know how to handle his humours. We have not been eavesdropping on father and son. It was their steward who heard them talk that way. We can decline to believe Rašin's reports because he was trapped in so many lies. We are not, though, entitled to spurn every testimony from individuals around this circle and we are at a loss to suggest how a simple steward should have been in a position to invent it all. Even Count Kinsky, incidentally, held his young brother-in-law in no high esteem. Trčka, he commented, was all too inexperienced, innocent as a lamb, and should learn a thing or two. Not that Kinsky was any better than Trčka, only shrewder.

It was he who lent impetus to the whole affair. Someone had to. Conspiracies do not proceed automatically. With the main conspirator not in the plot or at least contributing nothing, the sinister duty fell on Kinsky. He wrote to Bernhard von Weimar at Regensburg for a safe-conduct to visit him: an important deal was involved. We do not know what it was, but we are reminded of a point in the peace programme which, a few days before, Wallenstein had outlined to Colonel Schlieff – Bernhard must relinquish the Duchy of Franconia and could be compensated either in Bavaria or Alsace. The latter would have served to entice their most capable leader from the Swedes and transfer to him the watch on the Upper Rhine against both France and Spain. That the province constituted part of the House of Habsburg's lands troubled Wallenstein little. Bernhard sent the safe-conduct, but now Kinsky pleaded physical indisposition. He requested that a confidant be sent to Pilsen. Bernhard refused. Filip Sadler, the Swedish diplomat who reported on the subject to Oxenstierna, added that rumour declared

Wallenstein to be dead and that the whole business amounted to a piece of roguery. His verdict tallied with that of the Duke of Weimar who never abandoned his icy distrust of Wallenstein's peace plans.

The same was also true of Oxenstierna when he received our old acquaintance Sezyma Rašin in the capacity of emissary from Kinsky. Rašin, setting out on 4 February, routed his journey via Halle in order to meet another old acquaintance of ours, Major-General von Bubna, partner to the talks during that May night at Gitschin. Bubna was initially neither willing to listen nor to believe him – "The Prince is a liar." Then he did after all believe what he was told, whereupon the two cronies rode to Halberstadt, temporarily the Chancellor's residence. The Chancellor reacted as he had always reacted, only this time more brutally. When the Duke of Friedland rose against the Emperor, openly and unequivocally, the Swede would do everything on his behalf. In any other event, nothing. Not an encouraging upshot, but while he was still alive Kinsky no ιonger learned of it.

Little use that matters on the French side stood slightly better. Feuquières's scepticism had not abated, but after some hesitation he decided that it was wiser to inform his government of what on New Year's Day Kinsky had requested. Much less of a sceptic, obdurate rather in his projects and wishful thinking, was Father Joseph. A just peace, advantageous to the Germans, advantageous to the King of France, must, because it was potentially possible, be achieved. The third, supra-religious, solely German party independent of Habsburg must at least be formed. Why not with Wallenstein's assistance? A memorandum, drafted for the ambassador's illumination, envisaged two alternatives. Were the Duke of Friedland to perform a *coup d'état* against the Emperor, the first treaty draft could be employed although the problem of the Bohemian crown should be left somewhat in suspense. If he did not venture on revolution, his readiness for peace could nevertheless be turned to account. Wallenstein should force the summons of an imperial Diet where the King of France would be chosen as mediator and peacemaker with all the rights and dignities appropriate to such office. For the duration of the Diet's session Wallenstein should lend support to this French policy which would secure the interests of the Catholic church, tear from the House of Habsburg its pretence of religiosity, the loin-cloth of its lust for power, and know how to safeguard justifiable Protestant concern. The second alternative was indeed preferable because, were the Duke to proceed to open revolt, he would depend entirely on the Protestants. They were closer and could promptly help him, which France was not able to. Consequently Germany would be hacked to pieces by Sweden and its allies, a move not to the benefit of France. The ambassador should therefore discover Wallenstein's sentiments and the genuineness of his intentions through the dispatch to Pilsen of a confidant who would display sympathy towards both alternatives, albeit, if opportunity arose, tactfully laying emphasis on the second. While this well-meant political disquisition travelled slowly, very slowly, through France and Germany, a second Kinsky emissary was on his way to Feuquières, for Kinsky scented something of the disquieting urgency which Paris so utterly failed to feel. On 1 March, a date which really should have no place in this biography, the emissary met Feuquières at Frankfurt. Count Kinsky was impatient, he declared, and the Duke of Friedland too. The latter was befallen by such hatred of the House of Austria that he proposed not merely to drive the Emperor out of all his possessions, but to pursue him into the very mouth of Hell. Feuquières could not suppress a smile at this piece of rhetoric, but he had meanwhile received his instruction from Paris, taking the whole subject more seriously than he had himself meant to do. He therefore thought it as well to select one of the most experienced from among his swarm of attachés for a journey to Pilsen. The letters for Kinsky and Wallenstein were so formulated as to be mere replies to disclosures made at Pilsen and Dresden. Consequently they were incapable of being put to improper use by an enemy. Replies moreover which in turn required a reply, this time in writing, and penned by no less than the Duke of Friedland. Not that Feuquières anticipated the receipt of such solely practicable replies.

That was the trouble. Nothing was in writing. Kinsky's emissaries had their credentials from Kinsky, not Wallenstein. That is why we shall never know whether he acquiesced in Kinsky's figments or whether he in any way encouraged the Trčkas, father and son, in their greedy boastings. We think not, in so far as we can tell after such protracted preoccupation with him, but we gladly concede that belief or disbelief is here a matter of individual taste. If it is argued that the logic of things would have forced him to grasp at the Bohemian crown or, whether he would or not, to throw himself into the arms of the French and the Swedes, our answer is that logic's operation in politics is an uncertain factor. Many a lacuna occurs there, in fact and at least where reasoning is concerned, for all that the textbooks do not admit to this. Many an incompatibility passes muster there without veto. Were powers, and those who hold the reins of power, to pursue to its conclusion all that is inherent in the logic of a situation, our world would present an even odder appearance than it does anyway. How could he lie and wait for Arnim if he was on the brink of throwing himself into the arms of the Swedes and the French? Arnim most certainly wanted no revolutionary deal with Sweden, still less with France.

Wallenstein's final dreams had strands of sound intuition. Agreed co-existence of the denominations, toleration. Abandonment by the Habsburg dynasty of what rendered peace impossible and what it could no longer gain by war. Reparation, within limits. Reinstatement of the Catholic spiritual princes who had been expelled by the Swedes. Conciliation, somehow, very imprecisely, this, of Bohemia and the Bohemian émigrés. Indemnification for the Swedes, somehow, in the north. Indemnification for the French, somehow, namely, through the regions of the Netherlands bordering on France, at the expense of the Spaniards, so that the two of them, French and Spaniards, should leave Germany in peace. He was reputed to be ambitious enough to wish to lie in a royal grave even though he could for only a few months live as king. Others said so. The words were not his. There is not one written word, not one half-way reliably reported word of his which refers to Bohemia's crown. There is no trace of any incipient attempt to prepare for his ascension of the throne. Wallenstein's sovereignty would have signified restoration of Bohemia's ancient constitutional law. That, or nothing, would have been its implication. He could not therefore have become king by decree. He would have had to have been elected by the three Estates restored to their condition of 1618. Would they then have elected him? That would not have depended on the two Trčkas, but on several hundred electors who included a number of his bitter foes. Would he have sworn to observe the confederation statute of 1619, a republican constitution with a shadow-king? Had he, on the contrary, in mind to be more of a usurper than Ferdinand? Nowhere is there any answer to these questions, not even its slightest intimation. Empty talk, all of it. Smoke without fire. What we have heard him say is that he wished to take to the grave with him the reputation of a peacemaker. He had evolved an approximate programme for that. Difficult, difficult beyond description, to implement. Wholly impossible for an individual to attain. Its achievement, as was later to be seen, would have to be the labour of many, many wily negotiators, day after day practising for many years their wiles upon each other. Wallenstein had at his best been no negotiator, and he knew it. Dreamers are not such stuff as negotiators are made of. Invested with the necessary vigour, they put their dreams into effect by action and behest. He had once been invested thus. Friedland was the proof. Now?

His position, his past, the magic of his personality let him just once more be seen at the centre of the European conflagration, and that was where he dreamed himself to be. His ailing, already almost dissolved persona caused excrescences to exfoliate from the core of the visions that he carried in his head, excrescences attributable to the irresponsible dilettantes who were his advisers, to his friends, his foes, and those between, to politicians and to the scribblers on one side and the other. Shadows in the snow, dancing around a dying man.

NOCTURNAL REVERIE

Premonition, not cognition, was Wallenstein's portion. A judge of men he never had been, yet his present situation was all too human, of his fellow-humans' making. Fright, hatched from within, directed at none and nothing in particular, no more than tentatively against the court, the Spaniards, the priests, his enemies as a whole, possessed him. In his ears the noise beyond the doors, the coming and going of emissaries was indistinct. His spirit harboured fear, gnawing impatience, the tossing to and fro of antipodean possibilities. Heedlessly he suffered the visits of the two or three coarse-grained creatures into whose hands he, the finely attuned, had delivered himself. Harassment on all sides. Every word taken literally, and those uttered at some past moment brought against him. Gone the capacity to co-ordinate. Survival on the fires of old authority without ability to feed the blaze. Accompanying despondency. To keep all outlets open had been his aim and ended in the closest maze. Playing for safe stakes, he had hedged his bets too much and was become the wildest plunger. In quest of himself, the loser. Promoter of order, drowning in his own disorder's floods. All his life, under dreadful strain, he had mimed the disciplinarian to conceal the weakness in him. Now the mask alone was left, with agony to fill the void behind. The embers of his spirit exhaled no heat. In his extremity he was alone. Useless to have anathematized the Spaniards' imperial lunacy; it had brought the Protestants, the Swedes, the Dutch, the French, the other side, no nearer. For years he had trifled with them. Now they believed him no longer. Because he did nothing, they did nothing. Only talked. But he barely talked any more. He lay and waited for Arnim.

*   *   *

The light of the moon. The moon is sheer ice and snow. . . . The King of the Snowy Wastes had a hundred times the land that I had. Need he have interfered and spoiled my game? Had Aldringen been at Lutzen, I would have won and spent the winter inside the Empire's borders. The Bavarian prevented that, the Bavarian . . .. Ugh, that burning in the gorge. . . . Where is Holk? Dead, cried out and moaned for a priest, but there was none to hand. Dead, the lot, from the plague, from famine. Hidden in the woods, in terror of him. He needed them, and there was not one. . . . Why does Arnim not come? Now he needed them, and there was not one. . . . All gone, those I needed. Holk. Old Harrach. Pappenheim. Collalto. Left are the scoundrels. Could I but have the Bavarian by the throat, and stab him, like that fellow at Olmütz. So many years ago. Fourteen, fifteen. How the years roll on. . . . Peace, you will not use your steel again. You can no longer write your name. You can no longer hold your spoon. What harm did I do him? I wanted to do away with the Electors, they said. A lie. Do you do away with what you want to become yourself? True, you have to do away with him whose place you want to take. They would not leave me in peace. They did not want me because I was not born as they. What could I have made of the Empire, then! They would not have it because I was not born as they. Not one! Yet I meant it truly, honestly. That Lübeck syndic. A handsome man. Stood straight as a pike. In a black doublet, medallion dangling from his neck. His smile courtly as a count's. They are statesmen, these men of the Hanse. Not like Germans, more like Dutch. He did not trust me. Why did nobody trust me? When he needed them, there was not one. . . . Is it soon time for the purge? How it disgusts me. The doctor has promised that I shall have no more if only I take aqua sambuci* diligently. Every morning, every night I gulp it down and it helps me naught. 'Tis money tricked out of me when I pay these doctors and that apothecary on the market-square. Must learn to be my own apothecary. The last thing that I shall learn.* Unguentum altheae, electuarium hiera picra, tartarum crudum.† *It helps naught. You learn, you forget. You acquire it, you lose it. I learnt to deal with ships, I forgot again. Many the islands whose names I knew. Where are they? At mighty pains I was to bind the Swede to Polish soil. He would not let himself be bound. What, in a single year, I would have made of Mecklenburg! How I would have ruled it! Gone, over, and they are back again. . . . A wreck, swamped in draughts from the apothecary's shop. . . . That wreck, that*

---

* A remedy against dropsy (translator's note).
† A marshmallow ointment for sores and to encourage perspiration; an emetic with aloes in its composition used in enemas against gastric troubles; and potassium bitartrate also used as an emetic (translator's note).

stranded ship near Stralsund. I had all their goods restored to them, the merchants, and flayed the return of their pillage from those who had plundered it. In vain. They did not trust me. . . . That letter to the Stral-sunders, recently. They should throw out the Swedes. I would make a free imperial city of them. All for their benefit. It should not have gone. To this day they have not deigned to answer. Kings used to send me their ministers and fond greetings, fawning like dogs. The Pole, the Dane, the Briton, the Frenchman, Philip. Which of them is still here? Don Augustin. A spy whose head I should sever from his shoulders. I should have assented to what the Frenchman proposed. I shall agree, through Kinsky. A great man of business, Kinsky. One glance his way and he does what you want. What you do not want – I cannot! If I do, the French will cross the Rhine, annexe all terri-tories round about, and peace will not ensue. That is not something a Prince of the Empire may do, and a Prince is what I am. They shall yet see that that is what I am. I must write to Vienna, tell them not to believe all this evil chatter. They have not understood me. They never liked me, nor I them. But I shall send Max with the letter. He, with his suavity, can explain things to them. . . . If only Arnim came! Peace. I want to make this peace, withdraw thereafter. I shall make no peace, without recompense for Mecklenburg. I rightly acquired it. Let them make amends. The Palatinate or Württemberg. 'Tis all the same to me. Württemberg is fine country, they say, woods and wine. The Palatinate cannot be. No peace unless 'tis restored to the young Palsgrave. . . . Regensburg. Whose fault was that? Did I not warn them, again and again, that Aldringen should not move on the Rhine? Let him have stayed in Bavaria and Weimar could not have descended on the city. Now it is I who should have barred his way. Who is said never to have rendered any service. Who is responsible for all ills. Intolerable! Treacherous scorpions lie to the Emperor and he believes them! He believes them. Very well, let us do what he believes. . . . How they wrote to me. How they addressed and pleaded with me. After Lützen, the Emperor's handwritten note. How could there have been such a swift change of front? Those evil false wretches were at the back of it. . . . Arnim must still be in Berlin. If he leaves on the morrow, how long from Berlin to Pilsen? Seven, eight days, at the best. He will stop to see that oaf at Dresden. And the roads are full of snow. There is thaw here, but not there. How my feet hurt when it thaws! I could breathe as long as the frost was so icy, and my breast was less clawed by pincers. Now I am afraid to sleep, for my dreams show in what state I am when the air presses down. De Witte comes and complains. I jab at him, chase him away, and he dissolves. Kepler comes. With his papers, and his long fingers keep pointing at some date. He mumbles something, and points, *and points, but I cannot read it, and when I want to ask him, he is gone. Emperor Rudolf comes, panting, waving his arms in the way that I last saw him at Prague, the mannikin. No Spaniard, Rudolf. With him I could have come to an agreement. He was like Simple Smiřický, they say. Satan torments him as he torments me. But in my palace it is clean, cleaner than in the Emperor's. I dream of spiders' webs and fear and filth. That must be in men's souls, else I would not dream of it. 'Tis not God Who sends me dreams. Then they would be other and I would wake refreshed. How long is it since I dreamt so? Did I ever? The shavelings lie when they say that we dream so. . . . What was it that the preacher at Goldberg told me about the teaching of the Picardists?* Let a man be born evil and he cannot help it. Yet he can help it, and God punishes him for it, eternally, and it is all a matter of predestination. The Jesuits explained it differently. Let me endow monasteries and give bread to the poor, then I am devout. A doctrine that appealed to me, wherefore I accepted it. You are lying. You accepted it with another intent, and in your heart you never accepted it, but always adhered to the Old Faith, and not to that either, nor to aught else, from arrogance and fear wanted to know naught of God. Not like Holk who begged for a priest and writhed with remorse when told that he had the plague. Like a proud menial who despises his master, yet fears and hides before him. . . . O, to be so alone! God in Heaven, help me! God in Heaven, help me!*

Warning by Field-Marshal Ilow: the Duke no longer received visitors unless he had personally summoned them, and then hardly a dialogue transpired because, on account of his great pains, His Grace incessantly swore the most frightful curses.

Report by Don Diego Quiroga, Capuchin: Wallenstein had told him that, were he not afraid of Hell's perpetual punishments, he would swallow the most virulent poison so as finally to be released from all his misery.

Testimony by Scherffenberg, General of Cavalry: after conclusion of the business relating to signature of the Oath by the officers, he took his leave of the Generalissimo. Was the rumour true, asked Wallenstein, that Bavaria was again in correspondence with France? He was not, the general replied, acquainted with the practices of the Bavarian court where he knew not a single minister. "Hereupon the Duke lay a good while still, then started up and cried, 'O peace, peace, O peace, O peace!' And said not another word than 'God preserve Your Lordship'."

* In German *Picarden*, a corruption of the Dutch *beggaert* = beggar, and used as a term of abuse for various religious communities, especially the Bohemian and Moravian Brotherhoods (translator's note).

Piccolomini

THE letters patent which created General Ottavio Piccolomini Field-Marshal were drafted at Wallenstein's instance, but they were not in such terms as Piccolomini's patron had envisaged. The new Field-Marshal was subordinated to the new Generalissimo, Ferdinand, King of Hungary. The plenary authority for Dr Justus Gebhard was, unknown to the court Councillor, an empty form of words. The missives dictated by the Emperor to the Duke of Friedland signified, in spite of their friendly phrases, nothing. While Wallenstein lay inactive at Pilsen, altogether different things were happening, or being put into train, elsewhere. A plot existed. His, indeterminate, passive, mere dreams, did not deserve the name. The plot which existed was that against him.

Piccolomini, writing to Gallas at the beginning of December, condemned in a discreetly low key the withdrawal to Bohemia. Reactions at Vienna and in Bavaria, he sighed, could be imagined. Gallas replied in his good-naturedly pacificatory way. The weather was undeniably dreadful and unsuited to campaigning. If the critics knew what it cost to maintain such a war-machine in the face of such foes, they would strike a different note. What was the good of these bitter attacks? Ottavio's first, gentle hint had met with no success.

On 3 January he saw the Lieutenant-General, on Wallenstein's instruction, at Grossglogau. Also present was Rudolf Colloredo, general of artillery. A tripartite talk. What Piccolomini said is known, more or less, from the report rendered by him in March. Its tenor was that Wallenstein planned treason and rebellion on a scale hitherto unprecedented in the world's history. Ottavio had it straight from the Generalissimo. He proposed, the Duke had revealed, to lead the army over to the enemy, conquer the Hereditary Lands, capture the Emperor, and exterminate the Habsburg dynasty everywhere, not only in Germany. Then he would reorganize Europe. The Pope's offspring would receive Naples; Montferrat would be the Duke of Savoy's share, Lucca and Siena the Grand Duke of Tuscany's; Milan might go to Venice, perhaps to Savoy; France would have Burgundy and Luxemburg; Flanders was to receive independence. The King of Poland would be offered the bait of Silesia. Should he decline, his own Calvinists would be stirred up against him. Count Trčka's portion would be Moravia; that of Gallas, the duchies of Glogau and Sagan; that of Colloredo, the province of Friuli; for Piccolomini, the county of Glatz, the duchy of Teschen, and the lands of Wilhelm Slawata. "Thus quickly was the world divided." An excessively daring, difficult undertaking, Piccolomini had objected. Only its start, Wallenstein retorted. Nothing but courage and self-confidence were needed. If there were no other way, he would try his luck at the head of a thousand horse. This, then, was what Wallenstein had trippingly tattled on one of those December days when, according to Piccolomini's own account, he had been in a state of deep depression, ill in bed, and neither then nor evermore fit to mount a steed again.

Gallas seems to have had some doubts about Piccolomini's story. Not, presumably, because he thought him a liar, but because he knew Wallenstein's habit of inconsequential extemporization. Colloredo, on the other hand, appears not for a moment to have doubted the truth of the tale. He exclaimed that "this rascal" ought to be "swiftly strangled", a piece of advice not adopted. The three gentlemen concluded, or pretended to each other to conclude, that it would initially be better not to tell the Emperor at all, so that hasty measures should not accelerate the catastrophe which they were destined to prevent, but that Gallas should try to dissuade the Duke from his infamous plans. Piccolomini returned to Pilsen. He learnt from Kinsky what had already transpired with France, Sweden, and the Protestant Electors. He also fancied that Wallenstein was not only distant to him, but, contrary to his promise, did not keep him completely conversant with affairs. Hereupon he saw his duty in a different light from that which had been shed at Glogau. Secret emissaries rushed to inform the Emperor, Count Oñate, the Nuncio Rocci who later filled in the one detail omitted in Piccolomini's report – that Bohemia was to go to Wallenstein. The alleged division of the world in any case shortly experienced several additions and revisions. It proved quite impossible for Piccolomini to recall his invention in detail. The Tirol was now allocated to Field-Marshal Ilow; Luxembourg would be pocketed by Cardinal Richelieu personally, not the King of France; Salzburg would come into Duke Franz Albrecht's possession. And so on. Around 10 January Vienna was aware of the position.

What position? Had Piccolomini flatly forged the contents of his denunciations? If yes, why?

Probably he had not wholly and entirely forged them. That seldom happens. The lies of grown men are generally inspired by truth in a manner difficult to unravel. At first keeping rather close to earthy reality, they joyously soar higher and higher once they have learned to take wing. For Wallenstein to have erupted into abuse of the imperial court with someone whom he trusted is plausible. For him to have sworn to expel the Spaniards from Italy is indeed probable. Such wishful thinking on his part is familiar from more reliable sources. And if Piccolomini asked what was to happen to Italy, why should he not have replied that Naples would go to this individual and Milan to that? We also know that he proposed to keep France busy and to appease it with territory elsewhere than on the Rhine. In this connection he spoke of Artois and Hennegau. At some time he may have mentioned Spanish Burgundy. So far, so sound. The rest is imaginative superstructure. In that age the borderline drawn between reality and fantasy was not painstaking. "Discreditation" was part of the art of politics. Piccolomini, steering on a course which would on account of Wallenstein's universally believed vindictiveness constitute a life-and-death struggle, was bound to exaggerate. The venture on which he was about to launch would grow in greatness commensurately with the enormity of the danger that it was meant to deflect, and only the enormity of the danger would render it feasible because the Emperor's advisers would not be excited by distant, indirect threats. Can clear lines be traced here between half truth and downright mendacity? Piccolomini quivered with passionate longing for the important role of saviour. The harvest of the activity he subsequently garnered with cold, calculating, rapacious ingenuity.

At thirty-four he was well advanced in his career. With Wallenstein's support he rose in five years from colonel to field-marshal. The capture of Mantua brought him a fine store of booty. Lützen earned him fame. All highly estimable, but far too little for the ambition of this young man who had started in Germany with nothing but a resounding outlandish name. Wallenstein stood in his path. The summit could not be attained as long as he held his glittering position, all the less for Wallenstein's lack of lust for battle which paralysed warlike operations. Suddenly the opportunity to do away with him beckoned. In noble fulfilment of duty and to Piccolomini's own advantage. What a happy combination. Its apparent difficulty made the task all the more attractive. Was not Wallenstein the most impenetrable of men, the slyest of foxes?

What a degree of subtlety, dissimulation, and surety of aim in the most secret of strategy was required to ensnare and reduce him to helplessness. Anything like the outburst at the Pilsen banquet – *O traditore!* – must definitely not recur. In exculpation Piccolomini had (as he later claimed) straightway afterwards, in broad terms, initiated eighteen colonels and, regardless of their signature, pledged them to the House of Austria. They included a certain Walter Butler, an Irishman.

On 17 January Wallenstein had sent off his new Field-Marshal with his good wishes. Now Piccolomini sat in Linz and awaited further developments. At Passau, up the Danube, was Aldringen's headquarters.

THE SECRET SENTENCE

Bavaria's envoy extraordinary at Vienna, Richel, had but a single task – to prosecute the downfall of the Duke of Friedland and to learn, thanks to his connections with highly placed persons, what had already been contrived to this end. Count Schlick, President of the War Council, Father Lamormaini, the imperial confessor, and Count Oñate gave him what information they had, but at the beginning of January they were for their part thoroughly dissatisfied with progress on "the business known to you". On 9 January Richel reported the state of affairs to be poor and tepid. Wallenstein's supporters were still seeking useless compromises. He had heard the King of Hungary say that unless Bavaria took the matter in hand, no one would. Maximilian, as usual, weighed up every possibility and urged him on. The Elector was familiar with the tricks and dodges employed by Wallenstein to retain his appointment. Were his complete removal not possible, then a division of the command must suffice for the moment. If even this paltry satisfaction was refused, then, but only then, was he prepared to make an offer hard enough for his pride to swallow – his own army, the forces of the League, would be placed at the disposal of the King of Hungary provided that the latter became Wallenstein's successor. The painful production of this trump proved unnecessary. Maximilian and his agent overestimated the influence at court of the "Friedland faction". This in fact no longer existed. They overestimated the drive of Wallenstein's planning. Everyone did and always had done. They underestimated Ferdinand II's capacity for decision. He was thought weak, pleasure-seeking and lazy, qualities about which in better days Questenberg had often enough in letters to Wallenstein made fun. He was thought dependent on his advisers, a manner of ruling which in former times the Fathers of the

Society of Jesus had taught him to be the solely responsible one. He was thought dependent on his theologians, and he was. The mistake, though, was to suppose that therewith they had plumbed Ferdinand's character as a monarch. He was tenacious, thanks to his belief in God and the House of Austria, itself on such close footing with the Almighty. Often enough he had displayed the unimaginative believer's courage and in the most critical situations retained his head. And he had learnt to be perfidious, to practise the art of delicately malicious comedy if it served a good purpose. In 1618 he and old Archduke Maximilian had slyly entrapped Cardinal Khlesl by visiting, flattering, and tricking him into a return call during which he was arrested and abducted to a distant mountain-castle. Not because the Cardinal had done wrong, but because his peace policy did not suit the two imperial princes. That was long ago. Why should so plain-thinking, simple and self-confident a man as Ferdinand have changed?

He had indeed since the end of December decided to put an end to Wallenstein. For two more weeks he did not however regard the affair as so very urgent and visualized a cumbersome procedure as appropriate. At the beginning of January two imperial emissaries set out in different directions. Count Wolkenstein, author of the memorandum comparing the condition of Bohemia and *Terra Felix*, Wallenstein's forever expanding duchy, travelled towards Silesia and Gallas; Privy Councillor von Walmerode took the road to Passau and Aldringen. Journeys of this kind could not remain unconcealed. The reason furnished for public consumption was the problem of winter quarters and similar routine business. The secret instruction was to prepare both generals for a change in command.

Piccolomini's news precipitated a violent change of rhythm. Not for a moment was his account questioned. Laughingly Prince Eggenberg said to Richel that whereas hitherto he had been accounted Wallenstein's friend, now, when his estates were the very first to have been given away by the Duke, it could be seen what good friends they were. Oñate boasted how it had been he who had delivered the terrifying secret to its proper destination: "so it transpired that H.M. the Emperor learned everything from me." Many another claimed to have been the spearhead too.

The arrival of the Field-Marshal's red-hot warnings coincided more or less with information about the Pilsen Oath. That caused a far more devastating effect than Dr Richel knew. It fitted Piccolomini's tidings like a glove. Before Christmas the felon had announced the destruction of the Habsburg dynasty and the redistribution of the world. On 11, 12 and 13 January he had made a beginning. His officers had had to swear allegiance to him. It meant that the conspiracy had crystallized from the planning stage into that of materialization. During the subsequent legal proceedings the Pilsen Oath was declared intrinsically to constitute high treason and rebellion.

The gigantic ineptitude of the "Oath" is once more manifest. If intended to signify the starting-shot in a political operation to be implemented by violence, it should have been implemented in fact and immediately. If not, it signified nothing and ought never to have been allowed to happen. As it was, it signified almost nothing. To Wallenstein's mind it was simply a defiant, albeit empty, gesture without consequence. Upon its completion he took to his bed and awaited Arnim, the one man who could help, revolution's loyallest enemy. A mock alarum. In the imperial cabinet it had consequences. Nowhere else.

Excitement about the two sensations was not yet abated before a warning came from the Duke of Savoy. The Generalissimo was negotiating with Richelieu. He wrote to him weekly. Recently his envoy had spent seven whole hours closeted with the Cardinal. Again a titbit of truth: the shadowy relations between Kinsky and Feuquières as reflected in the distorting mirror of imagination.

Now Ferdinand's attention was drawn to a memorial that, written in December, had been received on 11 January prior to Piccolomini's hair-raising tidings. The memorialist was Prince Gundakar von Liechtenstein, a man of discernment and integrity. Was it not barely a year ago that he had issued the warning to make "peace as soon as possible" and that, if this was what the Duke of Friedland wanted, his view must be acquiesced in? Had he not long been in disfavour without much bothering to return to the Court's good graces? Of late he was heeded again and, as he emphasized, he expressed his opinion about Wallenstein without either disparaging the man's services or seeking to exaggerate his misdemeanours. The Duke was a danger to the Emperor, the imperial lands, and religion. He was so in the light of his character and his insatiable ambition, which was well-known. He was so in the light of his situation which must, even if it had hitherto not been the case, drive him into treasonable relations with France and the Protestants. He was so in the light of the acts which he had already openly committed, acts of public, insulting disobedience against his Emperor and master. That was why he should be relieved of his appointment and deprived of his capacity to do evil. Not that this was a step that could be taken at random. The first requirement was to make sure of his officers, meanwhile continuing to correspond as formerly so that he should not suspect anything. Should it unfortunately seem that deposition, arrest, and unbiased interrogation of the accused were impossible, a final move remained. Two or three of the Emperor's trusted councillors, conscientious individuals and familiar with legal process, must decide whether the Duke was guilty or not. If they concluded it not to have been clearly proved, there was nothing more to be done because the execution of an innocent man was in the eyes of God murder and trespass. Should however the verdict be "guilty", not to kill him would on the contrary be a sin "because *extremis malis extrema remedia adhibenda* [to extreme wickedness extreme corrective is applicable] and *pro conservatione statu* [for the state's preservation] everything should be done that does not run counter to God". And then? The new Generalissimo should, however disadvantageously, make peace because otherwise christendom was doomed.

It does Liechtenstein honour that he persisted in his pacific conviction. The measured, God-fearing and responsible tone of his memorial does him honour too. Nevertheless it is permissible to ask whether he was quite as impartial as he maintained. The Liechtenstein family was no friend any more to the Duke of Friedland who, beginning so far below it, had swung himself so high above it. Prince Gundakar had earlier been driven from his place as President of the Privy Council by Eggenberg, head of the "Friedland faction", and he was on good terms with the Spaniards, especially Oñate. At any rate if, for all his pious summing up, he had a clear objective in mind, namely, Wallenstein's judicial murder, he could not have argued more skilfully and comformably to Ferdinand's mentality. His proposals, previously drafted, resounded to full effect at the height of the crisis. The monarch followed them literally. The three judges were appointed. By 18 January their selection was already settled and, if all that was thought, talked, and written in the preceding days is added up, so was their verdict. On 24 January they met – Eggenberg, Trauttmansdorff, Bishop Antonius. They deliberated. Whether they once more passed Wallenstein's life and actions in careful review, as Prince Gundakar wished, or went briskly about their unpleasant business is unknown. The "best friend that I have on earth", the finance abbot with whom this poor "I", Wallenstein, had so often exchanged friendly, jovial letters, and Max Trauttmansdorff, less than two months ago the listener to his tragic monologues, reached a finding. Two findings.

From the one emerged a military order or proclamation addressed by the Emperor, with greetings and expression of his respect, to all his officers, senior and junior alike. For reasons of utmost and urgent importance he had been induced to undertake a change as regards his former commander-in-chief in the field. The officers were therefore wholly absolved from their duty towards the aforementioned and, until such time as the appointment was filled, should look to Count Gallas as the general holding highest authority. A number of officers, it was understood, had recently at an assembly held at Pilsen gone somewhat farther than they were legally entitled to do. As however such departure from the path of rectitude was caused through misrepresentation, and in order that those who had incurred guilt should not be driven to desperate decisions, all was to be forgiven and forgotten, a pardon from which none the less two other individuals besides the former commander-in-chief were to be excepted. In conclusion the monarch offered his suffering soldiery the solace that he would, in the future as always in the past, and indeed to even greater degree, do for them whatsoever in any way lay within his means. The proclamation was dated 24 January. Its announcement was within the imperial discretion left to a later occasion.

Complementary to this first finding was a second, temporarily still more secret than the first. A handwritten note by the Emperor reveals that Father Lamormaini was apprised of it on the selfsame evening. "The Bishop of Vienna will communicate to Your Reverence under the seal of confessional secrecy a matter of the greatest importance. Of its preservation on the part of Yr Rev. I know myself assured. Disclose to the Bishop your opinion without prolonged reflection, for in delay lies the utmost danger. With repeated reliance upon the reticence of him to whose holy prayers I commend myself, Ferdinand." From this message the conclusion could almost be drawn that above the three judges stood in the last resort the father confessor. For five weeks he kept the secret. Then, admittedly under very different circumstances, he passed it to the General of his Order. "The Emperor hereupon furnished several of the loyalest, namely, Gallas, Aldringen, Piccolomini, Colloredo, who pretended to be of Friedland's party, with plenary authority . . . to take prisoner the principal and the leading members of the conspiracy and, if at all possible, to bring them to Vienna or else to slay them as convicted felons" – literally, *e numero mortalium exturbare* (to eliminate them from the number of mortals). A guess can be hazarded about Lamormaini's answer to the Bishop.

Among the Jesuits in his province the father confessor instituted special intercessions and penances. By the indirect route through Rome he tried to have the same course adopted by all European centres of the Order "so that devoutness shall avert a terrible though unutterable peril". Ferdinand prayed throughout a sleepless night. He wrestled with himself, as the expression goes, as in 1621 he had wrestled before signature of the death sentence on the Bohemian rebels. He implored God for counsel. In such instances God rarely decides in favour of delay and mercy; He decides in favour of reasons of state. It is better, though, to give Him the chance of intervening on the side of deliverance rather than not to trouble about Him at all.

The findings were kept secret with astonishing, admirable discipline. For something like a week they remained buried in the hearts of the five original participants. On 25 January Richel knew nothing more interesting to report than that the campaign against the Duke of Friedland seemed regrettably to have come to some kind of a standstill. The first to be initiated into the secret, again with the injunction not to divulge a word, was the King of Hungary. Shortly before 8 February it was Count Oñate's turn. The rest of those eagerly attendant, the Bavarian, Schlick, Tiefenbach, were put off with such vague consolation as that salvation was on the way and soon, if they maintained themselves in patience, they would see. Oñate under laxer control than the Germans remarked to Richel that it would be as easy to kill Friedland right away as to drag him captive from place to place and less dangerous. Richel bowed. He understood.

Good-naturedly or sagaciously Ferdinand had nominated two members of the former "Friedland faction" as judges. But precisely they, the Bishop and the First Minister, had to exemplify inexorability so as not to fall together with their friend. Were they distressed, these hanging judges? Did Eggenberg at least feel a little distressed? We do not know. Did they act in good conscience? It would seem so. They behaved in accordance with their duty. They acquiesced in the picture of Wallenstein that for the past decade and a half the world had fashioned for itself, the picture of his unbridled pride, audaciousness, and in the frightful plenitude of power readiness to perform anything and everything as Satan's man. Before his first deposition they had been terrified whether he would tolerate it. He did. On the second occasion he would surely offer defiant resistance. This assumption was at all events well-founded. Hence dismissal on the Memmingen pattern was really out of the question. A different question is whether the readiness, which he intimated, to withdraw voluntarily and to retire in honour could not have been taken more seriously and even put to the test. Before 24 January there was hardly any talk of that. Thereafter, when he repeated his hints, still less. They probably knew without admitting it to each other that their decision really amounted to murder. Wallenstein could not, like a thief, be arrested in the middle of his headquarters. They washed their hands of this blood-guilt by leaving the decision to the selected executioners.

THE THREE EXECUTIONERS

Piccolomini was barely out of Pilsen before he wrote to Aldringen, hitherto uninitiated. "It is total rebellion against His Majesty. The Generalissimo seeks by every possible means an understanding with the enemy. I have come to an agreement with numerous others and we are determined to die in the loyal service of His Majesty and religion. Your Excellency will in your wisdom know what precautions to take. When we meet, I shall not fail to instruct you in detail of all things." This oral information was given on 26 January at Ennskirchen on the Danube. How attentively Aldringen listened. How pleasantly high did his heart beat in alternation with the fear which gripped it. A hectic correspondence between Passau and Linz, between Aldringen and Piccolomini, ensued. Gallas was the third in the game.

Because from 24 January onward he was for almost three weeks at Pilsen, because Adam Trčka no longer allowed anyone to leave the town without a permit issued by him, because a censorship of letters at some point was not inconceivable, for these and other reasons the Lieutenant-General's contributions were at this stage carefully camouflaged, hesitant, and sparse. The other two, only a day's journey apart, regaled each other with messages back and forth. The key figure, and proud of it, was Piccolomini. "The business is conducted in such a way that I alone bear the danger. With my upright designs I put my trust in God. Upon Him rest my hopes." It was he who was Wallenstein's favourite and therefore most admirably able to betray him. Aldringen was not so fortunate. The Duke distrusted him. However highly he assessed his abilities, a liking for this member of the "quill-driving profession" he had never had. Nor incidentally, had he seen him since their parting in October 1632. The succeeding year had, through the unlucky Spanish campaign in Germany and the problem of Aldringen's homeless, half-ruined army, caused all kinds of friction between the Generalissimo and his commander. Aldringen was in no position to become the mainspring of action in the plot. As far as words counted, he became such still more than Piccolomini by a display of piercing clarity of thought.

Gallas, brother-in-law to Aldringen, had for two years been a widower, a status from which he longed to escape. His desire for a regular bed-fellow did not cease while he sat entrapped at Pilsen and was weighed down with the gravest political anxieties. People are mistaken when they believe that politicians think only politics. Reports had reached him that the Archbishop of Salzburg had several eligibly marriageable cousins. With Aldringen's brother the senior assistant to this ecclesiastical dignitary, Gallas wished the fraternal pair to select the most beautiful of the brides-to-be and to play the matchmakers on his behalf. The contents of his letters to Aldringen, transmitted by Piccolomini, fluctuated between the crisis concerning Wallenstein and the anticipated nuptials.

Other subjects were also blended into the correspondence. There were letters carrying address, date, and signature, letters of a harmless variety which dealt with routine points about frontier-perils, billeting questions, and discipline. There were letters between Adam Trčka and Piccolomini, blind on the part of one, false in every facet on that of the other. There were letters in cipher, without address or signature, which dealt with the real issue. Wallenstein's name was never mentioned, reference being confined to *il* or *il personaggio*, whereas innocent communications always spoke of "His Highness". There were letters which were secret but not honest either. Perhaps they were allowed, indeed intended, to come to Wallenstein's eyes. It is not possible to tell. In this extremely parlous game it is not possible to tell how certainly Piccolomini staked his chances on Gallas. Initially no one could trust anyone else. And he who had set the machine in motion, Piccolomini, himself vacillated inwardly for a while. The business could end up very well for him. Equally it could end up very badly for him. He had to safeguard himself against that contingency.

Gallas vacillated even more. He, at the critical site, continued until some time in February to believe that the conflict between Emperor and Generalissimo was neither mortal nor incapable of compromise. "I found His Highness of such good disposition," he told Aldringen on 25 January, "that I need not expand on the subject. He said that he placed no reliance whatever on the enemy." To Piccolomini he wrote on 1 February that the Duke aimed at indemnification for Mecklenburg, security for himself "and for us all", and pacification of the army, meaning money. His demands went no farther. As for the negotiations with Saxony, the final treaties could wear a somewhat different look from the terms expected by their progenitors. At what stage Gallas learned of the secret finding, and therefore of his own new, flattering position, cannot be exactly established, but he was probably aware of it when he wrote the passage quoted because another in the same letter runs, "I must request that nothing be done too precipitately. Proposal 585 is good if it emanates from disinterested parties and if, in the first place, those to implement it are found. To tell a friend to act, when seated by a cosy fire, is easy." Gallas, as long as he remained at headquarters, constituted an uncertain ally. Not merely because he disliked the notion of "dead or alive", all the more for wishing to emerge from the affair alive, but because with the best will in the world he was at Pilsen unable to observe any dread danger to God, christendom, and Emperor. If Wallenstein was so profoundly perfidious as Piccolomini asserted, why should he allow the Lieutenant-General to take his departure?

He did want to keep him, but not as hostage. "Count Gallas is here and agrees to everything that we have decided," Trčka reported to Piccolomini on 1 February. "Arnim is expected hourly. The Duke will grant Count Gallas no leave before the negotiations with Arnim are ended, and Your Excellency will also be informed precisely." "Your Excellency may rest assured that His Princely Grace will transact nothing without the knowledge, wish and approval of the Lieutenant-General, still less terminate any matter." Piccolomini should moreover observe very closely the attitude of Master Aldringen as well as being so kind as to send the Duke "a small stock of Valtellina wine". Deceit was taking a hand in the game, Piccolomini complained to Aldringen – *il personaggio* was trying to deceive Gallas and himself too. In letters to Pilsen it would be prudent for Aldringen to hint how little he liked Piccolomini; it could have a positive effect. "Put briefly, dissimulation is the alpha and omega of this business." Accusing Wallenstein of the most studied hypocrisy, they wove a web of duplicity whose strands can scarcely be disentangled even by those who know the outcome.

For Piccolomini to have struck the most dulcet notes in exchanges with Wallenstein and Trčka is intelligible. This was of the intrigue's essence, at Vienna as at Linz and Passau. But why tell Gallas how pleased he was that His Highness was adopting such a sensible, understandable attitude since, having once been hoodwinked by the enemy, he would not afford him another chance of that? "If His Highness and Your Excellency wish it, I am ready to hasten to Pilsen. If His Highness follows Your Excellency's proposals, let us make the Duke great and beat the foe or else force him into the conclusion of treaties as His Highness desires." Was this in order to indulge the other's good-natured doubts? Distrust of Gallas? Fear that ultimately nothing might come of the pit that he had dug for Wallenstein? Why on 26 January expatiate to Aldringen, about whose outlook he could by now really have no doubt, "If the army receives satisfaction, if His Highness is furnished by the court with every kind of guarantee, then I verily do not know why he should descend into a labyrinth from which he could no longer emerge"? This letter, it may be argued, is dated and signed, therefore purely ostensible. Then why, four days later, in another, unsigned, does there occur the remark that *il personaggio*'s wicked chimeras *cannot* be brought to fruition? Was his conscience pricking him? I do not think so, for he had none. Was he spinning matters out, his ruminations genuine to the extent that of course he knew Wallenstein's conspiracy, with its planned annihilation of the House of Habsburg and re-distribution of the world, to be nothing but a chimera of his own? Until he had con-firmation of the imperial decision on which everything depended? A plausible explanation if, after the outstanding success of his mischief-making at Vienna, he had displayed an iron determination. Not even then, as will be seen in a moment, did he show such. The mind of this aspiring Machiavelli fluctuated like that of humanity's general run, today this way, tomorrow that way, and the day after back again. His bad luck was that statements which he meant only for the moment survived centuries.

Had Piccolomini wanted to delay or prevent the consequences of his grandiloquent indictment, he should have turned to Vienna. Admittedly it would have been embarrassing, had he had to intimate that his picture had been painted too black. The notion never crossed his mind. The latter half of January he spent listening with growing impatience for the reverberations from his bomb-shell. "I cannot disguise from Your Excellency," he confided to Aldringen, "that I am at an utter loss. I perceive that I shall be rewarded with ingratitude for the great services I am endeavouring to render the House of Austria." "The court leaves me without any news whatever." His political assistant, Fabio Diodati, brother to Colonel Giulio, was sent to Vienna. He returned as the bearer of good news from Count Oñate and the Emperor. The all-highest wish was to have the Duke seized, *per prigionar o per morte*, dead or alive. That should have pleased Piccolomini, yet it did not. "I cannot feel that our affairs stand dangerously enough to warrant so risky a resolution, not capable of being put into practice without the court previously taking steps to ensure the dissatisfied soldiery's loyalty and its toleration of this sudden act." Money, money, and still more money must be procured, a warning repeated in almost every one of his letters. He was palpably afraid of the operation which must, as night succeeds day, follow on his all too literally believed denunciation. Diodati had again to go to Vienna and, probably on 31 January, in complete secrecy met Count Oñate outside the city walls. How was implementation of the imperial instruction envisaged? They discussed the subject from nine o'clock in the morning until one o'clock in the afternoon. Oñate, according to the report next day to Piccolomini, declared there to be the utmost urgency. Although efforts had been made to conceal the "business", many already knew of it. The ambassador himself, for example, who at that date had not been officially told. The Duke's spy system, Oñate had continued, was perfect. (A mistake, seeing that Wallenstein had not the slightest clue.) Were he to learn of the rod in pickle for him, not only would he the more quickly go over to the enemy, but also seek the life of his executioners – Gallas, Piccolomini, Aldringen. "The Emperor will nevermore be able to trust him; Your Excellency will nevermore be able to trust His Highness." To send a minister, Eggenberg, say, to Pilsen – an idea which had been considered – was utterly useless. The plenary power of authority, the 24 January declaration, sufficed for all purposes. Money for the troops must be collected and held in readiness, but on no account whatever must any gleam of it be at present disclosed. Given to Wallenstein, he would use it for his own purposes. Given to other generals, the step would arouse the Duke's alert suspicions. Incidentally, added Oñate, there would soon be immense fortunes to be confiscated, the Wallenstein and Trčka possessions. That would do to satisfy the army and to reward all the faithful. Whatever unpleasantnesses the speedy execution might entail, they would be as nothing to the danger of total ruin which grew "with every day that this man is still allowed to live".

Vienna was of a much firmer frame of mind than prevailed in the general officers' camp. The perils of the undertaking were as usual underestimated, and for a change with good reason, though unknown to the imperial councillors. To fall upon Wallenstein, passive, lonely, unsuspecting, would prove gruesomely easy. The verdict uttered, no quibbles were admissible. The accused, now condemned, was afforded no opportunity to defend himself. That was in the nature of the case impossible. Qualms upon the point were set aside. The urge to vindicate God, christendom, and Emperor – a popularly invoked trinity – was backed by another to which Oñate first had the courage to refer – the immense fortune available for distribution after the deed. The imperial Treasury would be solvent as it had not within living memory been. The sequestration of Wallenstein and Trčka property would again bring a quarter of Bohemia under the hammer, with an inflow of income somewhere between ten and twenty million gulden. The tedious question of an "indemnification for Mecklenburg", as also that of imperial indebtedness to the Duke for deliveries since 1632 from Friedland, would be cheaply answered. All this was of course a purely secondary consideration, a concomitant. Purely secondary? At any rate a fantastically wonderful secondary consideration. Into whose lap would fall Friedland and Reichenberg, Gitschin, Nachod, Opočno, the marvellous stud-farm at Smrkowicz? From the start the conspirators' thoughts ran covetously on that. Oñate, regardless of such piquant reversionary anticipations, tried to tap other pecuniary resources. On his own authority he had Italian estates belonging to the Spanish crown sold. To pay the Emperor's soldiers a million gulden must be raised, he wrote to Madrid. With only 200,000 on hand, he rejected the most importunate petitioners. Later, not now, was the moment when the money would be needed.

Piccolomini continued to procrastinate. What was expected of him was that he should go to Pilsen, without funds, without arms, and have the Duke arrested or murdered. Failure meant his own certain candidature for death. If he succeeded, an uprising on the part of the soldiers could irreparably ruin his career along with many another prospect. Calculating politician that he was, he demanded two things – a direct instruction from Vienna instead of Oñate's exhortations as conveyed by Fabio Diodati and an order from Gallas which, dividing the responsibility, would allot the heavier share to the temporary Generalissimo. These calculations he hid behind a verbal smoke-screen. He was ready to sacrifice his life if his military superior required it of him. General Gallas's silence was a good omen that the crisis was easing or at least not increasing. Could not perhaps Gallas after all dissuade the Duke from his evil intents? Piccolomini, on the edge of the precipice to which his inflated self-importance had led his party, did not care to leap. Perhaps, he argued several times, Wallenstein could have the error of his ways demonstrated by simply hacking to pieces the Saxon negotiators, Arnim and Lauenburg. The proposal, not strictly comformable to international law, was dismissed.

In these circumstances the Emperor again sent Privy Councillor von Walmerode on his travels with the usual official, and the usual secret, set of instructions. On 30 January he started from Vienna, on 1 February he passed through Linz without calling on Piccolomini – afterwards pleading the clumsy excuse that he had simply forgotten – stayed with Aldringen from 3 to 6 February, and paid a lightning visit to the Elector of Bavaria. Maximilian was not initiated into the secret. Aldringen was, thoroughly, and he did not fail to let his neighbour at Linz know. "The Emperor's order is explicit and unconditional. The statement from the person at Vienna is so clear that I really do not see how postponement of the execution and obedience to the Emperor can be conjoined. . . . Herr von Walmerode, when he perceived that the will to implement the imperial order was lacking, was on the point of returning to Vienna. I held him back to await a reply from Your Excellency which, if I may request this, should arrive as soon as possible." Of course rivalry existed between the two friends. Let one be unready to act, the other would be ready – and to reap the harvest too. From the fact that Walmerode had avoided a meeting with him, Piccolomini could not but conclude that he, who had hoped to stand in such high favour, had almost fallen into disfavour. He was faced by the choice of subduing his fears or losing the hand. Informed officially, unequivocally by Walmerode, although in what manner is unknown, he willy-nilly declared himself prepared to do the deed. Nevertheless he insisted that he must await instruction by Gallas on how and when as well as have a second talk with Aldringen. On 5 February came from Gallas the news for which he longed. "His Highness thinks it desirable to discuss matters with Your Excellency." On 6 February he met Aldringen half-way between Passau and Linz. On 8 February they began the journey to Pilsen. Piccolomini meant to arrive. Not for the life of him his fellow-conspirator.

Yet Aldringen was the man whom Wallenstein had long wanted to see at Pilsen, "be it only for a day", either to win him over or to render him innocuous. Pains in his head, pains in his feet were the excuses in which Aldringen had persisted as best he could, with each evasion heightening anticipation. Vienna had forbidden him to make the journey without prior leave, an intimation that it would not be granted, probably in the interest of his own safety. Nor did he feel any inclination to make it unless in the company of several thousand horse.

Ilow had been able to talk Wallenstein into the first useless officers' meeting, Gallas able to win him over to the notion of holding a second. Into what did he not permit himself to be persuaded by those whom he trusted? He nodded, said yes, and signed the summons with a trembling hand. The first assembly, suggested the Lieutenant-General, had been an all too irregular affair. It should be repeated along better lines. Every colonel should be instructed to draw up a list of all his expenses and what the Emperor owed him. The total established, Vienna would be advised of the figure through a delegated emissary. This hint to pay could not be taken by Ferdinand, but it would furnish grounds for an open rebellion at the outset of which the properties of the highly remunerated idlers, the ministers and courtiers, would be seized. So Gallas claimed to have said. So Piccolomini alleged, and Gallas did not contradict him. The idea of a second officers' meeting will assuredly have been Gallas's. He wanted to have all the commanders already gained for the good cause, first and foremost Piccolomini, brought to Pilsen so as then to proclaim the Emperor's commands and proceed to arrest of the guilty.

On 11 February Piccolomini arrived with a retinue of stalwarts. Greetings between him and the Duke, first ceremonially, then as between friends. Greetings between him and the Lieutenant-General as between friends of a different calibre. Discussion of the situation. Agreement that their plan was incapable of fulfilment because the garrison on which they relied had just been relieved. The sentiment of the preponderant portion of the army was unknown. None of Bohemia's strongholds was in their hands. "We therefore decided to perform Your Majesty's command in a fashion that offered greater security."

These were the days, from 6 to 10 February, when Arnim was in Berlin. Elector George William's councillors proved recalcitrant and suspicious. Why should not Wallenstein, who had deceived them twice, do so a third time, Brandenburg's Chancellor wanted to know. The Generalissimo was simply aiming at division between the Protestants. What reliance could be placed on a man prepared to betray his own master? What security was offered for what would happen after the conclusion of peace? The Duke did not hold much with religion, but there were those on the Emperor's side who did and after the General's death conditions would be back to where they had been. That he was a crafty wretch not of untainted good faith, as another argued, had earlier had to be admitted by Arnim. Let the Protestant Electors once be divided from their allies and they might experience what happened in Polyphemus's cave. The objective was defined in honeyed terms, but the way to its achievement was distant, remarked Margrave Sigismund. For that reason the quarrel with the Catholics must be either tackled and resolved or abandoned, otherwise fresh causes for war would always be at hand. The only man to utter a condemnation of Sweden's reluctance to make peace and of its growing insolence, the only man therefore desirous of separate negotiations, was Adam von Schwarzenberg, that minister who had in 1628 at Frankfurt-on-Oder fallen under Wallenstein's spell. He was one against six. The answer given to Arnim was the usual love of peace and Christian piety hodge-podge with a spiky centre – no separate peace, no negotiations without Sweden.

Arnim did not give up. He requested an audience of the Elector in person. During the early hours of 9 February he was allowed to take a seat at his bedside and proceeded to deliver a harangue, learned and passionate, such as he alone among military men was capable of doing. The Swedes did not want peace, he lectured, and His Serene Highness knew it perfectly well. Why then say yes when this in fact meant no since it depended on the good will of those who had no good will? Whose will was much more directed at perpetual war in Germany just as for the past fifty years they had waged hostilities against the Russians and the Poles. Whose will was to reward their favourites with principalities here, collect taxes, humiliate the Electors, suppress the ancient liberties, and, in short, behave as absolute masters. Their design was to keep the whole of Pomerania and that portion of Prussia which they already had. The permanent war which they conducted at others' expense could prove only to their advantage, to the disadvantage in any case of beloved Germany, and to no part of it more than to Brandenburg. France? Everyone knew how His Most Christian Majesty and the Papacy's dearest son behaved towards his Protestants and his Estates. What was his rule other than the sheerest absolutism? What was at issue between the dynasty of France and that of Habsburg other than the conditions which would afford one or the other a finer prospect of dominion over Europe? That was certainly how France understood the matter and, even though Austria understood it so too, it was wiser to maintain a balance between the rivals rather than to help one, in the long run the more dangerous, against the other. In the long run the more dangerous because it must after all be said on Austria's behalf that for a long time it had in the most praiseworthy manner respected the imperial constitution. Only through the Bohemian unrest, through the temptation arising on good fortune, through an inference of divine destiny had it been misled into an abuse of power for which it had none the less on each occasion been able to adduce a superficial legality. So much for Sweden, France, and Austria. More about the misery in Germany, the whimpers, the lamentations, and the moans of the poor who day and night cried to God about the outrages of the unpaid, unreliable, ill-disciplined soldiery. More about the peril to the foundations of the Roman Empire. If the Elector lost his land and people, would his allies help him any better than England had helped the dead Palsgrave? Therefore peace! Therefore peace negotiations, separate peace negotiations, now and immediately! Tossing wheezily under the impact of so stern an oration, the Elector groaned, "in God's name, Lord von Arnim, I do not want to sunder myself from Saxony, but to conclude peace along with it." Arnim deemed that good, almost too good to be true, and he asked for written confirmation. The brief personal declaration which George William thereupon transmitted to him did not strike quite the note that he had wanted – close, friendly collaboration with Saxony as well as negotiation with His Imperial Majesty and his commander-in-chief in the field, the Duke of Friedland, were indeed accepted, but simultaneously emphasis was laid on the assumption that no other Protestant Estate – Sweden – would have any objection and consequently universal peace would still be the upshot. Had this come from anyone except His Serene Highness, exclaimed Arnim, he would have sent the letter back. He had the Elector told that he understood its contents precisely in the sense which they had worked out that morning, and none other. He took his departure. On 12 February he was back in Dresden.

On 12 February Count Gallas left Pilsen, without let or hindrance, with a coach and horses from Wallenstein's stables. His proclaimed intention was to return soon in the company of his good friend Field-Marshal Aldringen.

He looked for him at old Marradas's Castle Frauenberg, but did not find him as Aldringen was already on the way to Vienna. He caught up with him next day. How enormously Gallas was enjoying his new freedom of action. An order, dated from Pilsen, was sent to commanders regarded as reliable: "On the strength of the imperial authority vested in me and for the avoidance of His Imperial Majesty's displeasure as well as loss of honour, You will henceforth accept no orders given by the Duke of Friedland, Field-Marshal Ilow, or Count Trčka, but obey only such as either I or the imperial Field-Marshal Count Aldringen or Count Piccolomini shall issue." One of the elect was Lieutenant-Colonel Mohra who in the absence at Pilsen of his superior, Colonel Beck, held command in Prague. He was instructed to maintain strictest secrecy about the order. He complied, as the others did, until the bit of paper carried in their pocket was worn to shreds and totally illegible.

Gallas amended the Pilsen text in as much as Count Piccolomini was *not* to be obeyed "as long as he is with the Duke of Friedland at Pilsen, particularly as he may be forced to sign orders at the instance and will of the said Duke whereby many an honest colonel and officer could be seduced" from his duty. Piccolomini was however as little forced to do anything as, during his prolonged stay at Pilsen, Gallas had been. The warning was moreover at the moment of its utterance doubly super-fluous because Piccolomini was already out of Pilsen. His speedy departure, he had told Wallenstein, was essential. He must save Gallas who might be imperilled through Aldringen's cunning. He must per-suade him to return to headquarters. He must then himself go to Linz and make sure that the regiments in Upper Austria behaved loyally. Like Gallas, he had no difficulty in obtaining leave and one of Wallenstein's coaches. He had been meant to distribute the Lieutenant-General's secret order surreptitiously among the colonels arriving for the second officers' assembly. Again he lacked the courage. No trace in his conduct of treading any self-sacrificial path or risking any self-immolation. With other ideas in mind he hurried to Linz. Gallas was there – Upper Austria had to be defended against a fictitious uprising. To stir up the Lieutenant-General, hitherto rather mild and sceptical, he told him how it had been only too evident that Wallenstein had intended to have all three of them, Gallas, Aldringen, and himself, strangled. And Gallas, who did not care again to appear an ass, believed him because (as is well-known) the most expeditious way of strangling people is to give them transport and let them go where they want. Piccolomini was no longer lying like a full-blown intriguer, but like an immature schoolboy. Success no longer hinged on excess of effrontery. During the incipient hot-blooded man-hunt no questions were asked as long as hunters and dogs were duly stimulated by a scent. The word "belief" has therefore to be taken with a grain of salt. Who was, in all good faith, a believer? Certainly Ferdinand, given the limitations of his character. Certainly Maximilian, given the hatred with which since Father Magni's secret report he had swallowed everything. Presumably Count Oñate, given the slant of Spanish political thought. Aldringen undoubtedly had his own advantage, which would be immense, exclusively in view. Probably at Vienna and in Bavaria he mountingly exaggerated the danger so that victory over it should appear the more glorious. In discussion with his two friends he would suppress a knowing smile. The same holds good for Piccolomini. Dissimulation was the conspirators' highest trump and they dissimulated even among themselves. Gallas, the least intelligent and slightly less perfidious, had at Pilsen not grasped what was at stake. When he finally did, he participated all the more vigorously in the game in order not to be the loser. Henceforward he no longer spoke of "His Highness", only of "this criminal", "this traitor". As for the smaller and smallest fry, why should they not believe what the great, the initiated told them and what fitted the mythical Friedland mirage? Piccolomini was believed when he alleged that Franz Albrecht von Lauenburg and Arnim had conspired to divide Saxony and Brandenburg between them. Belief was not suspended when 26 February, 14 March, or any other fictitious, freely quoted date was circulated as that on which Wallenstein proposed to be crowned at Prague. General Johann Ernst von Scherffenberg was in command of the cavalry regiments transferred at the Emperor's own wish to Lower Austria. When on 17 February he arrived completely unsuspectingly in Vienna to discuss billeting matters, he was arrested during a meal, put in chains, placed under a constant guard, fifty strong, to ensure that he should be able neither to escape nor to commit suicide. Means would be found to make him speak. Part of the abominable conspiracy, his order from Wallenstein was to start conflagrations in all four corners of the city. The fires which on three successive nights occurred quite close to a munitions store constituted the beginning, the entire imperial family being meant to be murdered amidst the great blaze. Secret Protestants were in league with the arsonists. Shrill panic befell the capital's population. Everyone collected water for as long as the fountains flowed. Heavily armed military replaced the night-watchmen. In vain Scherffenberg protested that he no longer understood anything. He could reckon himself fortunate to be under lock and key. We must not allege that such lunacy was the direct work of Piccolomini and Aldringen. The ignition seems to have been the inevitable consequence of the mood which for weeks they had been stoking.

They proceeded to deploy their energies in comfortable safety from the reputed rebel who deployed nothing at all. Gallas's first task, to pledge the regiments in Upper Austria afresh to allegiance, was child's play. Why should they *not* obey the Emperor? They had never been taught anything else. What about those in southern Bohemia, Moravia, and Silesia? Aldringen, Marradas, Colloredo performed that duty. Colonel de Suys, appointed Lieutenant-General – loyalists were enjoying a crop of speedy promotions – was sent to draw the teeth of the regiments stationed in and around Prague. To Piccolomini was entrusted the splendid commission of marching with three thousand horsemen towards the headquarters at Pilsen "under the mask of friendship". A letter went to the Elector of Bavaria – he should be good enough to concentrate his forces on the Danube so that they would not perhaps sustain an unforeseen attack by Wallenstein's traitorous units. During the late evening of 17 February Aldringen came to Vienna. He immediately had discussions with Count Oñate who at midnight saw the Emperor. Next morning Aldringen was received in audience. What he said, in one of the languages over which he possessed such easy mastery, how eloquent he waxed about the bane of treason on the point of being spilt from Pilsen, about the time for dissimulation being past and the hour for major blows at hand, we can guess from what followed. On the same day the old Emperor and the young King resolved to proceed to Budweis where the sight of their sacred persons would spark the army's fealty (this charismatic northward strike soon proved unnecessary). On the same day a cascade of messages was showered by Ferdinand on senior commanders everywhere. They should no longer, for cogent, rightful reasons shortly to be divulged, accept any orders either from the Duke of Friedland, former commander-in-chief in the field, or from Ilow and Trčka, but only from this and that specified individual. Next day appropriate notification to allied personalities of sovereign status – the Electors of Bavaria and Mainz, the Duke of Lorraine, the Pope, the King of Spain. So many messengers were under way towards all points of the compass that Richel failed to obtain one and had to send his personal servant to Maximilian. Overjoyed relief at the Bavarian court. The Elector confessed that his disinclination to await the decision had been such as to lead him already on 16 February to inform befriended rulers. To his army he issued a manifesto bloated with secret bliss and righteous wrath. On 20 February the imperial proclamation of dismissal was affixed in towns like Linz and Budweis over which control seemed assured – and brought excitedly gesticulating citizens on the scene. One less. Serve him right. Always wanted to climb higher and higher. Supposing that he fights back? Supposing that he nevertheless becomes our Emperor? He will know what he is doing, the one we have. On the same day too Wallenstein was before the assembled Estates of Lower Austria declared by Counts Meggau and Werdenberg – an old friend, this! – a rebel and traitor. From the pulpits of Vienna's churches he was denounced as a tyrant and fiend. On that very day the talons of the imperial Exchequer snatched at his possessions. The estates of the former commander-in-chief in the field, the perjured rebel, wrote Ferdinand, were indisputably forfeit, wherefore the duchy of Friedland as well as the

Trčka estates were to be suddenly, stealthily seized. As many troops as necessary were to be supplied by Baron de Suys. No pilferings, no hurt to be inflicted on the inhabitants. A detailed inventory to be made of money, provisions, movables on hand at Gitschin, Nachod, and elsewhere. A letter by Ferdinand to the governors, officials, revenue officers, mayors, and judges of the Friedland and Trčka properties stated that those who would shortly visit them should be assisted with the utmost diligence. Deficient co-operation would entail the severest penalty. All this on the strength of allegations, no more, by Piccolomini and Aldringen. All this without the slightest sign from Pilsen of rebellion or treasonable venture.

O yes, there was one. The Pilsen Oath of 12–13 January. In the first proclamation of dismissal termed an "assembly" at which "certain colonels had gone rather far", in the second it was styled an "altogether dangerous, far-reaching conspiracy and association". This second proclamation, soon known as the "proclamation of proscription", the sentence of outlawry, was also the work of 18 February, drafted at the insistence of Aldringen, probably in his presence, after hearing the verdict of the three judges. Surely unparalleled for any man of his status had been the favours and the privileges, the investitures and the dignities conferred by the Emperor (so runs the text) on his former commander-in-chief in the field. What form did his gratitude take? His long-prepared resolution and his actions demonstrated it. According to the most reliable information "his design was to drive Us and Our Worshipful House from Our hereditary kingdoms, lands, and peoples, to usurp in breach of oath Our crown and sceptre, to which end he purposed to attach to himself Our faithful generals, colonels, and officers, to use these same for his wicked intent and thereby to deprive them of honour and reputation, lusting after the bestowal otherwise of Our faithful servants' properties, letting be heard indeed how he would utterly exterminate Us and Our worshipful House, and being at pains truly to perform with utmost assiduity this his perjured disloyalty and barbaric tyranny which before has never in kind been heard of nor is to be found in the histories. . . ." Whereon follows what already stood in the first proclamation, with a more precise roll of the commanders to whom obedience is owed until such time as a new commander-in-chief in the field is appointed. Wallenstein never saw this monstrous document. A sliver of luck in a mount of misery.

Wallenstein's Death

A STRAY and betrayed, he who two years ago appeared to pass so triumphantly along so broad a path. Jettisoned. Viciously and exultantly amassing an immense fortune, building his own kingdom, he had prospered. Bearing in mind the common weal, the whole, he had ever since lost his hold on success. The imperialists, the Protestants, the outsiders, they had given no thought to the whole, each only to his portion. That was why they had ever and again outdone him. That was why, reacting, he had constantly had to change his methods and to switch his immediate targets. That was how he had acquired the reputation of being a liar. He was the most honest of them all and, late in life, the better man among them too. He must have foundered, even had he not latterly picked Ilow, Trčka, Kinsky, those dolts, for his councillors.

"... declared his intention of utterly exterminating Our Worshipful Arch-House. . . ." It was Piccolomini who claimed to have heard it. Franz Albrecht von Lauenburg had in high spirits written to Dresden that it was all settled, "the Emperor and the Elector of Bavaria must away," and nowhere were political secrets worse kept than at Dresden. If Oñate referred to news from Saxony which reinforced Piccolomini's accusations, it may have been that Dresden gossip percolated as far as Vienna and into the ambassadorial listening-post. He had no choice but to treat such matters seriously. The danger to Habsburg's Spanish dominion, unable to survive in Flanders, Burgundy and even Italy if the German component was dissolved, would be grave. Bohemia was that component's focal point. Let it drop away and Austria could not be held, let alone the imperial sway, as 1619 had demonstrated by way of threat and near-realization. Sooner could the German dominion last without the Spanish than the Spanish without the German. The former was still the more artificially contrived, the more widely stretched and scattered. To its viceroys and grandees it had however brought wealth, power and splendour. Who voluntarily relinquishes dominion? At the beginning of the century they had striven for stronger links between Vienna and Madrid, had given help in carrying through the election of Ferdinand as King of Bohemia and, when the revolution there began, had contributed much to its suppression. That had then been their policy, the policy of Count Oñate. Fifteen years later he resumed it, against Wallenstein, who, in as much as he became a politician on a European scale, belonged to no party, or no party wholly, was estranged from the peers of his earlier days, the Neo-Bohemian nobility whom he had betrayed and the Old Bohemians of Spanish sympathies whom he despised, was alien from the German princes into whose circle he fancied that he had penetrated on equal footing, and a stranger to the imperial cities whose goodwill he courted, and was on terms with Rome, Warsaw, Madrid and Brussels, but also with Copenhagen, Stockholm, The Hague and Hamburg. An outsider, standing above the conflicts, an arbitrator – "Let me act. . . ." That was how in 1629 he saw himself, in 1633 all the more. Was there room for an arbitrator? Must not the parties, if sooner or later there was to be peace, come together on their own? Him at any rate they did not want, even where he and they had approximately the same goals in mind. A foreign intruder, he had rendered himself suspicious to them on many counts. More strongly than he imagined, his power rested on his imperial commission, his generalate. Let him overstep his position, or indeed abandon it, and he would tread upon a vacuum.

Had he been the right man for the task, could there have been a right man at all, there was much to suggest that the moment was right. Germany was beginning to become very weary of the religious strife. What at the outset of this war had stirred spirits, that now no longer stirred them. In its place was arising hatred of the strangers, whether Spaniard or Swede. The old Emperor would rather lose his terrestrial realm than his soul, but his secular, as opposed to his spiritual, advisers already took a different view. Ardently pious Elector Maximilian had never been other than prepared to put reasons of state before piety. The two most important German Estates, Bavaria and Saxony, longed for the old, cosy imperial suzerainty and peace. The Spanish politicians too. The latter's notion of peace, though, was simply of one between the Emperor and Germany, not between the Habsburg dominions on one side, the French and the Dutch on the other.

Younger and in good fettle, Wallenstein would probably have been keen enough on more war for his own purposes. The ego cannot, however, be severed from the moment in time. His tiredness and desperation coincided with that subsisting all about. The loneliest of men sometimes mirrors the broad sentiments of society. As he reflected the weariness with war, so did he reflect the chaos which a single, exhausted will-power was incapable of mastering. If he wanted to free Germany from Spanish dominion and to give it religious peace, he would have needed the majority of German Estates, at least the Protestant ones, behind him. Eighty years ago an Elector of Saxony had succeeded in a similar undertaking.* The long ensuing peace was owing to his efforts. A German, an imperial prince, a sagacious and daring politician was able to achieve that. Not one who was the House of Habsburg's Commander-in-Chief, and an outsider to boot.

In December and January Wallenstein's attitude towards the Emperor was one of defiance and rage. His dream was being spoilt. His strategy and policy were being undermined because he was being forced into inapposite campaigns. It was a breach of agreement, that agreement which Feuquières had predicted would not last one day longer than the emergency from which it arose. We do not know its conditions, but surely it will have stated that none of the vexations operative during the first generalate would be repeated – no interference by the imperial War Council members and military bureaucrats, nor the shavelings, nor Bavarians or Spaniards, no dismissal like Memmingen. Since summer the newly won influence of his enemies had every month become more apparent. By the end of December he knew that his second dismissal was at hand. It explains his reactions and the real conspiracy as against his unreal one.

Not that the real conspirators should be credited with especial anxiety on behalf of Europe's, Spain's, the Empire's future. They worried about their careers. They savaged Wallenstein like wolves falling upon a dying member of the pack. Aldringen's place, in the light of the frightful danger depicted by him, was in the field. Why he stayed so long in Vienna, from 17 to 24 February, was to make sure of being the first to obtain his spoils, and he immediately insisted that the military occupation of Friedland should be as forbearing as possible "in order that when, one day, the [duchy's] allocation is undertaken, each shall find his portion in a state pleasing to him". The conspirators may have harboured a vague feeling that the issue was between Germans and foreigners, with Wallenstein, who wanted to enforce peace, playing the

---

* Maurice of Saxony's rising against Emperor Charles V in 1552 led to the Peace of Augsburg (1555) and his abdication of the imperial authority. It passed to his brother Ferdinand to whom in 1521 he had ceded the Hereditary Lands. Ferdinand I's grandsons were the Emperors Rudolf and Matthias (see Chapters 2 and 3) (translator's note).

role of a German. Their correspondence was conducted in Italian and a small admixture of French. In the immediate future Scots and Irish would be drawn in. For all of them a Wallenstein peace could prove a nuisance, and soon the complaint would be heard that it was the outsiders who had prevented its fruition. Italians, Walloons, Britons. Germans and Bohemians too, but relatively few.

The sacrificial victim was blind to it all. He waited for Aldringen. He let Gallas go in order to fetch Aldringen, Piccolomini in order to fetch Gallas, and then he waited for all three of them. They enjoyed the joke hugely.

At this point the expression "deficient in knowledge of human nature" becomes a trifle thin. He must have been helplessly lost in his seclusion to allow himself to be deceived to that extent. Distrust demands an element of active participation, participation demands a modicum of animate energy. A few brief moments excepted, he was no longer a participant. Surrounded by traitors, he sensed nothing. One of them was Battista Senno, his astrologer, the bog violet from Padua, always in the Duke's vicinity, handsomely endowed with fees, horses, lackey, and consulted for the sake of his stellar knowledge. That is how his situation must presumably have been, although no evidence has survived. Secretly he was in the pay of Count Gallas, who for at least the past year had been making him pecuniary presents, three thousand gulden on one occasion. What were the services rendered? It remains unknown, but most likely they took the shape of reports from Wallenstein's innermost circle. At Pilsen a finance official, Putz von Adlersthurn, member of the imperial Exchequer, who was also a spy and kept a diary on the subject, was already quietly busy on an account of Wallenstein's treason. On completion it was published under the splendid title *Alberti Fridlandi Perduellionis Chaos*. On 13 January Councillor Putz was dying for a glimpse of a copy of what the colonels had sworn, the Pilsen Oath. Who offered him the state document for quick, unobserved transcription? Master Giovanni Battista Senno. Immediately afterwards he was back to his calculations, humbly, learnedly, solemnly furnishing interpretations when required by the Duke.

At Pilsen they were unaware of the machinery which had been set in motion against them. On 17 February, when Piccolomini was boasting of it, they were still unaware and continued their routine. On that day Wallenstein wrote to the Emperor that Swedish progress in the Upper Palatinate did not signify much, but he would consult his senior officers' opinion. Signed, "Your Imperial Majesty's Most Humble and Obedient Prince and Servitor". On the same day a dispatch to Questenberg referred to the arrival, as he had heard, in Vienna of twenty-five thousand taler from the King of Spain and His Holiness the Pope respectively. Out with it! The money belonged of right to the soldiers and to nobody else. Next day letters to two imperial officials, one in Bohemia, the other in Silesia: among the possessions of condemned *émigrés* there is a house in Prague which is to be conveyed to Count Adam Trčka, a property in the bishopric of Neyso which is to be assigned to Colonel Losy, both transactions in part-payment for what the Imperial Exchequer owes them. Ingrained habit, to confiscate something from the *émigrés* three weeks before he reputedly had it in mind to restore everything to them. Precisely two days before the rape of his own fortune.

Once again the generals and colonels were assembled in Pilsen. Not so many as in January, only about thirty, and with Piccolomini, Isolano, de Suys, Gallas missing. Gallas, Wallenstein consoled himself, would be coming. His absence must be involuntary. Gallas had suggested this meeting. Gallas did not come. Colonel Enkevort, sent after him on 18 February, did not return. On the previous day Colonel Giulio Diodati, who had been quartered in the town, disappeared with his entire regiment, which had lain outside. Disappeared without orders, without notice. Ilow sent an aide-de-camp after him. He never heard of him again, either.

Something was wrong. There had been a leakage. Ilow and Trčka must have perceived it sooner than Wallenstein, wholly dependent on them in the solitude of his sick-room. It did not escape Duke Franz Albrecht's vigilance. Pilsen began to give him an eerie feeling.

The same was true of the assembled colonels. They were better informed, had heard rumours, had guessed. Piccolomini had not dared to pass them Gallas' top secret order. Instead he forwarded it to their deputy commanders, the lieutenant-colonels stationed all about. It must not be thought that there were no means of communication between headquarters and the regimental emplacements in Bohemia. The officers strode about Pilsen in a condition of perplexity even greater than on the first occasion, waited, confided to each other that they would have done better not to come and still better to be away again. Some of them, Morzin, Balbiano, Lamboy, Beck, La Tornett, belonged to the trusty whom Piccolomini had initiated right after the first meeting.

Why in fact had they appeared a second time? Devotion? Alas, devotion was in those days a stunted growth. Wallenstein, an ever harsher, more bewildering, more isolated personality, had recently provided little reason for it. Fears for their money? Probably. Respect for long-established authority too. They did not as yet know of the deposition decree. And Gallas, as Deputy Commander-in-Chief, had, after all, supported the notion of this convocation. Distressing that he should be absent and unable to advise them further.

The talk of the colonels, as learned by Ilow and borne by him to the sick-bed, the absence of Gallas, the flight of Diodati cumulatively transformed Wallenstein's vague fears into awareness of the need to do something. But what? Dissecting that which in his mind was indivisible, we recognize three trains of endeavour. The first was to come to speaking terms with the imperial court and thereby to elucidate the serious misunderstanding that obviously existed. The last, to seek salvation in the enemy camp, in that of the Protestants, in that of Bernhard von Weimar, the enemy in closest proximity. Between these two there was an intermediate aim – to achieve a defensive position without the aid of either Emperor or enemy.

On 18 February he sent Count Max to Eggenberg. He never heard what, four days later, happened at Vienna. Eggenberg received the nephew; he declined to touch the missive which he brought. To Friedland's heir apparent it was intimated that his own position was not the most favourable. He quickly understood how he was no longer Friedland's heir apparent, but would have to use his wits to ferry himself and what was his, a by no means negligible quantity, safely into the future. His uncle, brother-in-law, major benefactor was best forgotten.

On 20 February – his anxiety had grown – Wallenstein sent Colonel Mohr von Wald after Max. In blind confidence he showed this long-service officer an admonitory greeting by Eggenberg, "not to espouse any other party", contained in a letter from Questenberg. He clung to this tiny guiding light in the gloom, this far too late, altogether too faint sign of extinguished friendship, as though his pride and defiance were broken. Never, Mohr was to say, had he intended anything against the Emperor. Were it agreeable to His Majesty, he was gladly prepared to resign his appointment of Commander-in-Chief in the field, albeit the forms must be observed and no duress employed. As soon as possible, too, a meeting with Eggenberg must take place, "because on account of such differences both His Majesty's service and the public weal must suffer". In addition to letters for Eggenberg, Ferdinand and Questenberg, Mohr carried messages for Gallas and Aldringen in case he fell in with them. Piccolomini, posted in the village of Horaždowitz, treated him friendlily enough, told him how things stood, presented him with Wallenstein's coach and horses, because whatever had belonged to the Duke now belonged to the Emperor and was at His Majesty's generals' disposal, and recommended him to travel in the direction of Gallas. The latter, whom he met on the road between Budweis and Linz, had him arrested, "as though I had known of Friedland's knavery and made myself accessory to it".

Efforts of this kind came indeed, since 24 January, too late. Which did not prevent them from being attempted with the utmost sincerity. Those were mistaken who then and thereafter, believed that he only wanted to gain time and to lull the imperial court. There was neither object left in lulling the court nor purpose in gaining time. He wanted to retract, to retain his dignity, to die in peace and honour.

That was his personal wish, not that of Christian von Ilow, who was too strong to give up and too obtuse to conceive of reconciliation with the Emperor. In such situations the obtuse are the more sagacious. The last of Wallenstein's three trains of endeavour, salvation through the enemy, was Ilow's expedient. He acted, arrogating to himself the *de facto* command. The sick man allowed him to take his course in as much as he evaded, now as ever and again, the appendage of his signature. Nothing paradoxical about this paradox to seek help simultaneously from Eggenberg and Weimar. Such was Wallenstein, such was the inferno into which, without knowing how, he had descended. Duke Franz Albrecht, Protestant, imperial prince, negotiator on Saxony's behalf, was ready to be the mediator. He was, he wrote on 18 February to Arnim, still waiting for him, and Wallenstein too, with great eagerness. Matters no longer stood quite as well as they had done recently. There was the abscondment of Diodati's regiment, the absence of Aldringen and Gallas, "and they are not altogether confident of Piccolomini". "The rest, though, wish to remain at the Duke's side until death." Yes, but because that could not be so completely certain either, Wallenstein was requesting the Lieutenant-General to assemble a couple of thousand horse at Meissen, near the Bohemian border, "so that, at need, they can come to his assistance". He himself would today fulfil another wish of Wallenstein by travelling to Bernhard von Weimar at Regensburg. He would tell him of the peace that Wallenstein wanted to make and that "the shavelings, Spaniards, and the like" did not want. He would gain Bernhard for an ally in case open conflict should break out between one part of the imperialists under Gallas, Piccolomini, Aldringen and another under Wallenstein. For, as the Lauenburger sanguinely emphasized, most of the regiments were still loyal, but "we must not, by God, abandon the Duke". Signed "In utmost haste". Then Franz Albrecht scrawled a few lines to Ilow – it was all of no consequence, vexations of this kind simply served to illustrate the conduct of mankind. He had no doubts about a happy outcome, at Regensburg he would take good care that his tongue did not wag aught that was not strictly useful to their cause – and he set off with eight horses into the frosty night. He remained faithful, this blithe spirit, after his fashion.

What should be done with the colonels on the spot, each of them concerned, with furrowed brows, for his future? On the morning of 19 February Wallenstein summoned them to his bedside, sampled them long and sadly, and spoke. It hurt to hear what was being bruited about him. "For myself I have as honestly upright a conscience as Colonel Diodati and I neither design at my advanced age to alter my religion nor have I ever had the intention of undertaking anything against my Emperor. That I have struggled hand and foot for peace, which some at court would not gladly see, is not beside the point. I mean to do so yet, and 'tis my opinion that His Imperial Majesty will have no happiness unless peace is made." "At court much is desired that the Empire cannot sanction." During the course of his peace negotiations he would call in representatives of his colonels so that they should constantly know what was happening. For the nonce he had the threat of something contumelious, disparagement and scorn, hanging over him. In self-defence he had ordered that the greater part of the regiments should be concentrated in the vicinity of Prague. How did the gentlemen view this move? Should they now refuse their adherence, they would have done better to have allowed him in January to take his departure when he had wanted to cast off all effort and care. On the principle that men always listened most attentively when talk turned on money, he added something about the financial situation. He had assumed the guarantee for all sums which the commanders had expended, or would still expend. How did matters stand? No money had since been received from the Emperor. This and that excuse was being pleaded. Presumably the cash went elsewhere. This too, how they were to obtain their indemnification and he the redemption of his pledged word, was a point to discuss with the Field-Marshal.

Conference with Ilow. Repetition, though in a more cheerless vein, of the January process. Incredible, the amount that was written and noted down then, surviving until the present day. Ilow and Trčka promised unconditionally to sacrifice life and property on His Princely Grace's behalf. Major-Generals Sparr, Morzin and Lamboy sounded the same note as those two had tried to strike. Lieutenant-Colonel Balbiano, of the Count Piccolomini Regiment, found an easy road to follow – his intention, he declared, was to serve the Emperor now and for ever. The rest registered their attitude cautiously. Because the answer under certain postulates prescribed by martial law was palpable, the question was essentially superfluous (Colonel Beck); loyalty unto death was due to the General who was striving so hard for a just Christian peace (Colonel Losy); undoubtedly, but to other senior commanders too (Colonel Adelshofer); nothing being against religion, the obligation assumed in January remained intact (the majority). Because he saw, said Colonel Butler, "that His Princely Grace seeks naught other than the army's conservation and the soldiery's contentment, he binds himself with other gentlemen to live and die at His Princely Grace's side." Without any delay the Bavarian Military Commissioner Rogge knew of Wallenstein's address, the discussion at Ilow's house, the vote, Trčka's question as to whether their promise held good in the event of a change in service by the Duke, and the answer – embarrassed silence. His informant was Colonel Beck.

An eerie piece of voting. From His Imperial Majesty those "other senior commanders" had received orders to kill the Generalissimo whenever it seemed expedient to them. Piccolomini was sitting in Horaždowitz, a day's ride from Pilsen, with a force sufficient to carry the headquarters by surprise. He made no move on 20 February, nor on the twenty-first, partly out of cowardice, partly to prolong the pleasure of the man-hunt which Vienna imagined as so excessively dangerous. It could not, though, last much longer. Prague, again only a day's ride from Pilsen, was firmly in the hands of Wangler, de Suys and Mohra, three of the earliest initiated officers. Gallas' order to the army, the obedience veto, was no secret any longer. It could not be, seeing the hourly increasing number of those who knew it. On the spot dismal portents accumulated. A warning arrived from old Lord Rudolf Trčka to his son: the most perilous developments were on foot, caution was imperative. Dr Agustín Navarro, Spain's long-standing resident representative, disappeared under cover of darkness. Only too gladly would Military Commissioner Rogge have done likewise. And here were the colonels swearing loyalty unto death to the former Commander-in-Chief whose life had been declared forfeit, some of them still dissimulating, God knows why, others uncertain what now, here, today, the right attitude was, all of them anxious to be more crafty, or at least no more stupid, than the rest. The outcome, during the morning of 20 February, was a new protestation, later called the Second Pilsen Oath, formulated in Ilow's mansion. On this occasion Wallenstein was the first to speak. To Us, Albrecht, Duke of Mecklenburg, etcetera, it has been a bitter surprise that diverse individuals should have distorted the meaning of the January document as though its intent had been contrary to the imperial suzerainty or to religion. No, that had not been its purpose. To resign had been what he wanted, but then he had agreed to retain his appointment for a while, a concession which entitled him to ask something from his colonels too, one act of loyalty deserving another, "so as, on account of the many machinations employed against Us, to preserve Us in sound security" – an admission, at any rate. However, because that mutual obligation had been so cruelly misunderstood, he released all the signatories to the oath from their pledge *if* he were to attempt, what was utterly remote from his mind, the slightest move against the Emperor. The officers listened to this personal statement without interruption, corroborated that their own loyalty corresponded to the General's, and, since everything was so entirely clear and blameless, repeated their oath to serve to the last drop of their blood with, by the side of and on behalf of His Princely Grace. Wallenstein put his shrunken, trembling initials to the document well above the others.

Had the First Pilsen Oath allowed for rebellion as an indeterminate possibility, the Second solemnly revoked it. That was one of its aims, to assist as a factor in the feeble counter-campaign now begun, and Colonel Mohr was to carry it to Vienna. At the same time Ilow and Trčka meant once more to bind the officer corps, which they felt to be crumbling, slipping through their fingers, by means of a piece of paper, and to the Devil with whatever was at hand. That did indeed not matter. Neither did the scrap of paper.

On 18 February Wallenstein had nominated Trčka as his deputy, the man from whom the regimental commanders would shortly hear the destination of their march, an order which they would obey as though it were the General's. Why from Trčka? Why, in this crisis, did Wallenstein not vigorously, directly take the lead at the head of the armed might which he continued to regard as his? To suspect trickery here is idle. Ilow and Trčka simply forced him to delegate the authority which he was too ill and too depressed to exercise. On 19 February, when he had first spoken to the colonels, he looked "like a corpse", as Colonel Schlieff, the Saxon whom on that day he received in audience, later attested. Even now his abettors had no thought for joining the enemy. That must have occurred in the Upper Palatinate or on the Saxon border. The grand rendezvous was to be on the White Mountain outside Prague. Trčka's argument was that the enemy threatened Bohemia. A piece of nonsense, and Bohemia's defence lay on its frontiers, not at its comparatively easterly centre. But in the centre was where they hoped to establish themselves. With the Duke of Friedland and his faithful regiments in Bohemia's capital it would be seen whether the Emperor would venture to act against him by way of dismissal or worse.

Beyond Prague their search for safety extended to Silesia, the campaign country so well known to Wallenstein of old. Field-Marshal Colloredo and Major-General Schaffgotsch had been in charge there since Gallas' recall. Colloredo had from the outset been regarded as the most hostile senior officer. Schaffgotsch, rich Silesian magnate and brother-in-law to the dukes of Brieg and Liegnitz, had shown readiness to participate. He was to bring the Silesian regiments into shape for the trial of strength between Emperor and General, secure the most important places, Glatz, Neisse, Troppau, Glogau, and prepare billets for imperial cavalry from Brandenburg which the Generalissimo under some excuse proposed to have closer to hand. On 19 February Schlieff was dispatched to Silesia with a secret message. Schaffgotsch's reply to Trčka, four days later, ran that he was doing all in his power to create a favourable atmosphere in this preponderantly Protestant land, but he felt himself to be impeded by Colloredo. "Pray advise me how affairs stand, particularly how negotiations with the Electors and the Swedes proceed, for if things lie aright there, the others present no difficulty." Postscript: "It gives me much food for thought that Diodati is gone. He will not have done that of his own accord. 'Tis time to keep our eyes open and not to celebrate." Next day Colloredo had Count Schaffgotsch arrested. His letter never reached Trčka. Unfortunately for its author, it fell into other hands.

On 20 February, after signing the Oath, the colonels left the headquarters and went wherever they chose. To Prague, most of them, and they knew why. Only two, Beck and Gonzaga, had to remain at Pilsen, allegedly to act as witnesses to the peace negotiations, in fact because they, though not the numerous others, were thought unreliable.

Trčka had arranged to travel to Prague on 21 February in preparation for the imposing junction between the forces. Wallenstein was to follow twenty-four hours later. Trčka fancied that Mohra, Beck's deputy, continued in command at Prague. He knew nothing about the presence there of de Suys and Wangler, much less of what these two had accomplished in a couple of days. He knew nothing. At Rokycany, ten miles out of Pilsen, Colonel Sparr, coming from Prague, taught him something. The Generalissimo had been deposed, nobody obeyed his orders any longer, everybody obeyed Deputy Commander-in-Chief Gallas and Field-Marshal Piccolomini, the capital was surrounded by troops. Trčka turned his horse's head, galloped back, dismounted in front of the Duke's house on the market-place. The haze which for five days had floated in the breeze now became fog. Ilow, Trčka, Kinsky, the blockheads, knew that they had lost. Wallenstein now understood to what councillors he had entrusted himself and that it was too late to disembarrass himself of them. Trčka was pale and agitated. Ilow did not lose his nerve. Kinsky laughed, his humour tickled by the imbroglio which he had helped to create. No record exists of how, at this very first moment, Wallenstein felt. In his sick-room the decision was taken to leave Pilsen forthwith, during the night if possible. From Prague or from Horaždovitz, where Piccolomini and Diodati lurked, an attack could hourly be expected. Let Eger, the north-west frontier fortress, be their objective.

For a few hours Wallenstein sought escape in activity. He sent for the director of his war chancellery and dictated instructions. To his governor at Gitschin: all the ducats in the ducal chests, whether of his own or other mint, must at once be conveyed to Rumburg and Hannsbach, where an emissary from Count Kinsky would take charge of them. Wallenstein's messenger reached Gitschin ahead of the confiscation order from Vienna, the order was executed, and the money, 39,000 gold ducats, the equivalent, after all, of 117,000 gulden, made its dangerous way as far as Saxony. To the regiments of Beck and Mohr von Wald, stationed in the vicinity of Prague: "With utmost surprise have We heard how divers have dared . . . to give orders that neither We nor Field-Marshal Ilow nor Count Trčka shall be obeyed anymore." Such orders were totally unlawful and the officers' duty was to comply with the behests of His Imperial Majesty's Commander-in-Chief in the field, none else, and now to march on Eger. . . . Hesitation, a gesture to the chancellery official, cancellation. No use. Only of use might be instructions to regiments encamped farther from the centres of the new imperial authority in Prague, Horaždowitz, Budweis, Tabor, than from Pilsen; those in Bohemia's extreme west. That applied to Colonel Walter Butler's dragoons at Kladrau, twenty miles away. Order to Butler: he and his men would leave that very night and wait in readiness on the road from Pilsen to Eger. It applied to the Count Trčka Regiment of Foot, which, under Lieutenant-Colonel John Gordon, a Scot, constituted the garrison of Eger. Order to Eger: Gordon would stay where he was and pay no heed to messages received from anyone else than the Generalissimo, Ilow and Trčka.

That much he did himself. The others did the rest. Or rather, they wrote letters, hopeful that these would have the effect of acts. Ilow to Franz Albrecht, who had presumably arrived at Regensburg: the breach was complete, at Prague matters stood thus and thus, the Duke of Lauenburg should be so kind as to persuade the Duke of Weimar to let his cavalry, in this emergency, advance on Eger. Kinsky to Arnim: the Generalissimo was going to Eger in person. Could not Arnim at last undertake his long-discussed journey and proceed there, "particularly as the business is at such extremity (but nevertheless of great importance) that there is not a moment to lose"? The "great importance" was meant to take the edge off "extremity". The notion that the business was no longer worth while should not occur to Arnim. Letters flung at an overcast horizon and at badly informed, flint-hearted individuals who would ask, What have you still to offer us? They had to be offered something, something more than Friedland's faded glory – soldiers, quarter-cannon, money. Where was the Duke's bodyguard, red-blue uniformed and with silver-tipped halberds, formerly commanded by Piccolomini? No one knew, but close by were five companies of a Trčka cuirassier regiment, the same number belonging to Colonel Heinrich Julius von Lauenburg and another couple of hundred infantrymen. They would all have to come along in the morning. Artillery? Quite an amount, in charge of the Master of Ordnance, Sparr, cousin to the Colonel. Its haulage required horses, specially strong ones, and time. A camp of this size could not be broken up head over heels. There was the Duke's baggage, in the shape of the luxury by which he was surrounded, the gold plate, cutlery, beakers, candlesticks, ewers, wash-bowls, as well as his wardrobe and his noble steeds. There was the court, or that part of it currently at Pilsen, with its lord high steward, lord high equerry and lord chamberlains, down to the coachmen and stable-boys, almost two hundred individuals in all. They had to come too, apart from those who ran away during the night, which some of the lower officials succeeded in doing. But where should its senior members, Lord High Steward von Scherffenberg, Lord High Equerry Hardegg, Lord Chamberlain Dietrichstein, the Chancellor, the personal physician, the astrologer, where should they have gone, who would have given them emolument and dignity, had they parted from Wallenstein? They did not feel happy in their shoes. They were not as blind as that, but the Duke's magic castle was their roost and under its roof they would shelter as long as it held. While Trčka's horsemen patrolled the approaches to Pilsen to avert an unpleasant surprise, the servants were busy with the chests and trunks.

Ilow and Trčka pillaged the town. They knew that for the time being they were rid of their possessions in Bohemia; the practice was familiar to them. They therefore recouped themselves while they could. At pistol-point, ran their instructions, was to be fetched from Pilsen's wealthy burgesses and patricians whatever was to be found – golden chains here, ten thousand taler there, whether on their own behalf or for the Duke's new war-treasury. Maybe Wallenstein knew. If he did, what did he think? Was he reminded of Olmütz in 1619? How he had threatened the Treasurer of the Moravian Estates, stolen the ready money and gone to Vienna with it? Robbery and flight were again the order of the day, but not on this occasion to the imperial court. Elsewhere, under another star.

At six in the morning he discharged Colonel Beck, his semi-prisoner, addressing him in an altogether unaccustomed tone. "I had peace in my hand. God is just." He came out of his dream and, with raised finger, frowned at the Colonel: "You deceived me. I know full well that you for ever warned against obeying me too far." "I crave Your Princely Grace's forgiveness. I know of naught," was the answer. "It does not matter. You promised me nothing, albeit I always deemed you an honest soldier and brave fellow. Mohr von Wald deceived me. I shall send you away with Dr Gebhard, who is on hand, but you will both have to wait a day on account of the mounted patrols." He sent for Lieutenant-Colonel Haimerl, commandant of the small Pilsen garrison: Beck was to have an escort of ten musketeers to facilitate his journey. They were all of them, Beck, Rogge, Gebhard, Sestrich (the army's auditor-general), who were now his open enemies, allowed freely to take their way. They would all of them declare that he had been the cruellest of tyrants who constantly compelled obedience by threat to life and limb. So would those, like Heinrich Julius von Lauenburg and Master of Ordnance Sparr, who currently more or less stuck to him. His actions did not conform to that pattern at all. A lonely man groped for human quality in a renegade, for soldierly reliability – many others betrayed me, but not you – sought a point of contact with him, and was rebuffed with icy coldness, and let him go wherever he would, a foe to his foes.

At ten o'clock in the morning the departure for Eger began. "In the greatest disorder", "in indescribable panic", as one who was nearby gloatingly put it.

That was Colonel Morzin, one of those who on Sunday 19 February had pledged themselves without qualification and on Monday had signed their name below the Second Pilsen Oath. Arriving in Prague on Thursday, he promptly poured his scorn on Wallenstein's "panic-ridden" flight. Had he but had a thousand horsemen at his disposal, how easily could he have seized the criminal by the collar. . . .

An example that serves for many. One example for all of them. Barely were they out of Pilsen than their eyes opened wide with fright. So it came about that they pleaded for gracious understanding as to how they had regrettably had to do this while not able clearly to know that, thus asseverating the loyalty of their golden hearts. Among themselves they cavilled, with some denunciation of one by the other, in the race for a sunny place in the imperial favour. That one there had talked too much, this one here too little. A third had acted mistakenly, or failed to act, when action should have served to save God, Emperor and christendom. It had none the less proved possible, Heaven be praised, but the direst danger could have been more quickly prevented. . . . Was it within two or three days that Wallenstein was deserted? That was how he saw it, what his feeling was, and wherein he woefully erred. Never, in the last resort, had these men viewed the matter any differently. The comparatively solid foundation of Habsburg power offered them a security which he could not provide.

This held good too for the lieutenant-colonels, the deputy commanders, of the six Trčka regiments which together formed a small army. Theoretically, through his brother-in-law, they were bound to the Generalissimo by a particularly strong tie. In practice Trčka barely knew his regimental staffs, probably paid them as little as other military proprietors did and was of little interest to them. More interesting were the offers and appointments dangled by Vienna – hitherto mere servitors of Count Trčka, they would henceforth be the colonels and owners of their regiments. That worked. If Baron de Suys, now the officer commanding at Prague, had initially distrusted the Trčka men, he was quick to recognize them as being just as complaisant as the rest. The ease of his task filled him with amazed pleasure. What was to happen after, the rewards, the punishments, already equalled in importance what was happening now. Fresh instructions from the Emperor ordered the confiscation of Ilow's and Trčka's estates, of the Sagan and Gross-glogau duchies, in particular of the Friedland mansion at Prague, including its legendary riches. War Councillor Caretto di Grana, travelling around Bohemia, was occupied to the exclusion of all else by the question of who should obtain what. His sound advice was not to reserve too obviously the best plums for Catholic rather than Protestant officers.

This worthy man alleged that as recently as three days ago – on Tuesday, 21 February – Pilsen had known perfectly well what Vienna was undertaking. Superfluously he added the question as to who could have been the source of information. He could have spared his breath. In Prague, on the other hand, at Piccolomini's headquarters in Horaždo-vitz, and at Frauenberg where Gallas and Marradas rode their high horses, everything that went on really was known, priority of knowledge by a matter of hours purely dependent on distance. On 20 February they knew of the grand rendezvous scheduled to take place on the White Mountain. During the afternoon of 22 February they knew of the flight from Pilsen and its direction. Piccolomini, making so bold, ordered the evacuated town's occupation and pursuit of the fugitives.

Under a grey sky the Wallenstein column moved westwards between scattered farmsteads, fields and pools along the road to Mies. The thaw had begun. Beneath the snow crust was heard the sound of gurgling. Over the uncertain surface the horses, a litter slung between them, slowly, slowly trod their way. Occasionally Wallenstein asked for his coach, was helped into it, then back again into the litter. Countesses Trčka and Kinsky, certain ladies of the court as well, followed in carriages. The gentlemen and soldiers, except for a couple of hundred infantry, rode. Suddenly cavalry appeared on the left flank, from a southerly direction. Shots were exchanged, the imperialists vanished. Presumably they had wanted no more than to reconnoitre. Thirteen or fourteen hundred individuals passing along a narrow path form a long train. To the military eye, though, they represent but an insignificant obstacle, and that was how they looked to Patrick Taafe, Colonel Butler's regimental chaplain, when he espied them at a distance – "several carriages, a moderate number of foot-soldiers and mounted men". Butler's dragoons were at their appointed place, in extended cross-country line, short of Mies. Convinced that it could only be them, Ilow galloped forward with one or two officers, found the Colonel and instructed him to join the column. If Butler had known that here was a fallen colossus and fugitive, he could, it may be assumed, have drawn aside somewhat, then taken to his heels eastward, escaping by force if need be. His regiment's strength was almost equal to the Duke's and in better fighting trim. Instead he followed and the whole convoy descended to the river, on whose bank nestled the small, walled town of Mies, a mere fifteen miles from Pilsen. The torture of recent days and the past night had been too great; the Duke was exhausted and in pain. Mies, in lien to Ilow, had a castle which could offer this guest all his accustomed comforts. Butler was told to establish his headquarters, with the regimental colours, inside the town. Caution prescribed that the companies of Captains Macdaniel, Burgh, Devereux and Geraldine should camp beyond the walls.

Letter-writing was resumed by candlelight. Kinsky wrote to Colonel Schwalbach at Dresden, urging him to do his best to persuade Arnim to leave for Eger immediately. His Princely Grace the Generalissimo, he added, would be prepared to come to Dresden with a very small retinue and meet the Elector. Could a passport be obtained? Ilow addressed himself again to Franz Albrecht. The Swedes and Bernhard von Weimar's troops should not merely approach the frontier, but should make an infantry invasion of Bohemia and occupy Pilsen. A valuable artillery park awaited capture. They should also seize Passau and incite the peasants in Upper Austria to rise. He himself would like to meet Duke Bernhard at some spot and negotiate with him as regards the Generalissimo. Another dispatch went to Colonel Ulefeld, known to be somewhere in Upper Austria. He should march with his regiment on Eger. Were this not possible through Bohemia, he must march up the Danube. Duke Bernhard would let him through, and if the Colonel could start something with the peasants it would be a good thing too. They were all of them, the Bohemians, the Danes, the Swedes, and now Ilow, always ready to use and sacrifice the peasants when it suited their purpose. In any case there was an atmosphere of desperation about his proposals and pleas, not least that he wished to visit Duke Bernhard. He, in place of his master.

Later an unexpected guest, Colonel Duke Heinrich Julius von Lauenburg, arrived. In the neighbourhood of Prague he had heard the latest news, but he had not seen anything authoritative in writing. He hurried to Pilsen and from there to Mies, since his own regiment, five hundred cuirassiers and two hundred infantrymen, was already there. Wallenstein invited him to supper, an honour which he would not normally have deigned to extend. He could not believe, he said, that the

Emperor had issued any such order against him. Some mistake had been made, a piece of deceit on Count Gallas' part. It would all be cleared up.

The nocturnal talk between Colonel Butler and his chaplain was of different tenor. Butler: This is a highly vexatious situation. Taafe: The best course, and possible too, would be to flee. Butler: No, that would not be the best course.

Thursday morning the journey was continued. Heinrich Julius, unconvinced, returned to Pilsen. Butler and his dragoons had to head the column, otherwise they might face about and disappear. The road led north-west, up hill, down dale, between darkly wooded knolls. It had been hoped to reach Eger, forty-five miles away, but only half the stretch was covered. A halt was called at Plan. Its castle had suitable quarters. Again nocturnal letter-writing, nocturnal discussions. Wallenstein, or Ilow, to John Gordon at Eger: the Duke wished on Friday to have word with Major Leslie, of Gordon's regiment, at a spot between Eger and Plan. To Margrave Christian von Kulmbach, the nearest German ruler, a member of the Heilbronn League and one of the Hohenzollern clan, went credentials from Wallenstein on behalf of the Friedland Chancellor, Eberhard von Elz. The latter would expound to the Margrave how the Duke of Friedland had wanted a just peace and had for that reason been traduced by treacherous individuals, indeed almost divested of his generalate, but how he continued unflinchingly to strive for peace, as undoubtedly Margrave Christian, an old and experienced ruler, did too. He should therefore kindly send Colonel Muffel, his military adviser, to Eger for an urgent preliminary conference with none less than Duke Bernhard von Weimar, Lieutenant-General Arnim, and the Duke. Distress signal wrapped in the dignity of the European position which until the day before yesterday had been his. To Count Max at Vienna went a message that Colonel Breuner, Wallenstein's chamberlain, would have various matters to explain. The message was for his heir, that is, via his heir for the Emperor. Breuner was once more to offer the Duke's voluntary resignation and to declare his readiness to pass the days left to him at Hamburg; he would nevertheless dearly like to retain his dukedoms. His third offer, and even more hopeless than the earlier ones. Yet he hoped. He could not grasp his downfall. If at the same time he sought salvation from the Protestants, it was not guileful double-dealing, but simply his old habit of "staking on a certainty", simultaneously to pursue incompatibilities. Ilow, with clearer vision, may have shrugged his shoulders at such illusions. They could not, particularly as Breuner's journey required money, three hundred gulden, be concealed from him.

Another mission could be concealed from him, and was. In the middle of the night Patrick Taafe disappeared from Plan, in his pocket a note in a foreign tongue and with an oral message for Piccolomini from Colonel Butler: he was following the former Commander-in-Chief in the field under coercion. He would rather lose his life a hundred times than break with the Emperor. Who could tell? Perhaps God had selected him for some specially heroic task.

Friday morning departure for Eger.

On this Friday the imperialists, the regiments commanded by Giulio Diodati and Tavigny, reached Pilsen. There had existed an agreement between Wallenstein and Lieutenant-Colonel Haimerl, the Commandant, that the town should be defended, but there had also been the ambiguous rider to stand "staunch to His Imperial Majesty". Haimerl interpreted it in the light of the situation. The valuable artillery park, with plentiful powder and lead, was on hand. The citizens were humble. "I am regarded as though I were the Messiah," Diodati wrote to Piccolomini, "and Your Excellency will be regarded as though God were come in person." Not a very amiable god. His soldiers rifled not only the remains of the ducal household, silver altars and table-silver, linen and Valtellina wine, but incidentally sacked the town as though it were a conquered enemy stronghold, which caused Gallas to furrow his brows. An order was issued for the pursuit of the fugitive traitor and, executed energetically, would probably have been able to attain its objective before Eger was gained. Energy was what was lacking, even now. Only greed, only cunning were on hand. "Gordon has instructions from me," Diodati cryptically informed Gallas. "I hope, and I believe it to be certain, that Colonel Butler will deal the blow, as he has had me assured through an infantry captain," Gallas even more cryptically informed Aldringen. With Pilsen theirs, all the main centres of Bohemia were in possession of the loyalists. No achievement, for, apart from Trčka, Ilow, and possibly Schaffgotsch, who among them had ever been other than a loyalist? Breuner, Wallenstein's emissary, got no farther than Pilsen, where his mission aroused nothing but laughter.

On this Friday Dukes Franz Albrecht von Lauenburg and Bernhard von Weimar attended divine service in Regensburg cathedral. Since Franz Albrecht's arrival on Tuesday they had seen each other a number of times, but Franz Albrecht had accomplished nothing. Sheer deception, like last year in Silesia, Bernhard had replied. He trusted in God and not the enemy, let alone an enemy who did not believe in God. He would not have a dog saddled for the Duke of Friedland. In vain Franz Albrecht explained, promised, implored. Now the two princes had listened to a stirring sermon on universal peace and were emerging from the church into the square when a messenger sprang from a horse and handed over Ilow's last letter from Pilsen, penned during the night of 21 February. Franz Albrecht read and passed it to Bernhard. Here was the open war between Emperor and Generalissimo. No, here was ostensibly open war. Here was deceit, again deceit. Were Wallenstein going to Eger, were he concentrating troops in that area, his intention certainly was to erupt towards the Upper Palatinate and thence towards Nürnberg, Bamberg, towards the Main, Schweinfurt, Frankfurt, towards wherever the Protestants lay scattered and were weak on the ground. A most perilous situation, all the more dangerous because a simultaneous offensive by the Bavarians from the south-east must be anticipated. Sound the alarm! Concentrate all available troops at a few points, at Bamburg, in the Upper Palatinate, on the Danube, to prepare an appropriate reception for treacherous Friedland. So wrote Bernhard on this Friday to Oxenstierna, to his brother Wilhelm, to his brother Ernst, to the city of Nürnberg. Franz Albrecht, sanguine as always and inclined to amiable misrepresentations, presented the picture differently to Ilow – Bernhard's concentrations, particularly in the Upper Palatinate, were meant for Wallenstein's deliverance. The letter never reached Ilow. His second cry for help, on Wednesday evening from Mies, only succeeded in further arousing Bernhard's suspicions. They wanted to lure him not merely towards Eger and Pilsen, but into the wooded hill-country of Passau too, out of secure locations into hazardous ones, to split up and fritter away the strength of his army, to drive him into a corner between Bavaria's Elector and Wallenstein, their precise understanding only too plain. . . . Until the moment when their downright ridiculous superiority was wholly and utterly assured, Ferdinand's loyal generals, and especially the Elector of Bavaria, had feared nothing more than Wallenstein's uniting with Bernhard. During this same time Bernhard prepared for a pincer movement attack by Wallenstein and his good friends Piccolomini, Gallas, and Maximilian.

In vain the final attempts to render himself intelligible to Vienna. No echo to the rapping on the door and the wooing of the Protestants. Calumny or blind mistakes on all sides. Sympathy nowhere.

*   *   *

Arnim? On this Friday he was still lodged in the palace at Dresden. The instruction which directed him to proceed forthwith – forthwith! – to Pilsen, to negotiate about peace with the Duke of Friedland as imperial plenipotentiary, and to accept the Duke's conditions even if they extended somewhat beyond what the Emperor wanted to concede, provided that they were to the benefit of the Protestant cause, this document was six days old. On Monday he had written to Franz Albrecht that he was, or had been, ill. On Friday he was still making no move. More haste, less speed. He believed Wallenstein to be at Pilsen and unimpaired in his appointment.

On this Friday morning Duke Heinrich Julius's five companies of cuirassiers, in obedience to an order received from their colonel at Pilsen, departed. Heinrich Julius now knew how things stood and had done a sharp about-turn, just as he spoke in the most contemptuous manner of yesterday's great friend. Nobody hampered his companies' withdrawal. Of the remaining troops Butler's contingent was by far the strongest and could easily have disappeared too; or, for that matter, have done something else. No such thought entered Butler's head. He accepted the honour of sitting for part of the way in Wallenstein's coach and listened with polite interest to what the General had to say. Unfortunately, Wallenstein observed, he had hitherto shown himself rather distant and ungrateful to so deserving an officer. The fault had not however been his – highest authority had refused the money to reward loyalty. He would know how to bring about a change. Butler would be invested with two well-paid regiments in place of his single unpaid one, apart from the plentiful funds at his disposal for recruitments in England, Scotland, and Ireland. Highly agreeable prospects, replied Butler. He was a free man and a foreigner bound to the Emperor by nothing more than his military oath. This he could revoke and be quit of his duty. He would know of no better service to enter than under His Serene Highness's colours, those of the most sagacious, victorious leader of this epoch. The colonel was a descendant of a large, noble Irish family. His inheritance had been a chivalrous manner and presence of mind, but little else, wherefore he had been compelled to seek his fortune abroad.

Of gentle blood too, and not without carefully nurtured connections to the imperial court, was Walter Leslie, the Scottish major of the Trčka–Gordon regiment whose salute Wallenstein received between Plan and Eger. The Duke did not question the loyalty of Gordon, whom he had done a number of good turns. About the garrison's second-in-command he felt not so certain. He wanted, probably on the advice of his henchmen, to cajole him before the drawbridge into the fortress had been crossed. Had Leslie heard anything of the confusion which had recently occurred in the army? No? Well, it had been like this. He had no longer had the resources with which to feed the army and to maintain it in good form. He had wanted to pull back. Those who had most ardently urged him to remain where he was, and not to leave the field to the Spaniards, had been Generals Gallas and Piccolomini. Then it had been precisely these two who had malevolently twisted the meaning of his contract with the colonels, winning over to their side the King of Hungary. Not, though, the Emperor. He had sent Mohr von Wald to His Majesty as well as, only yesterday, Breuner to learn whether the retention of his services was really desired or not. If yes, all right. If not, neither would he for his part any longer want the Emperor for his master. Doubtless he could find another, but he was thoroughly tired of being an underling. He would at last be completely independent and have his own soldiers. He was short of neither the money nor the credit nor the good friends, whether among the Protestants or in the imperial army. Many an officer who at present adopted a sound Austrian stance would at the first opportunity join him. He was going to await the outcome at Eger. Ferdinand would eventually realize that he would have done better to believe him than the Spaniards and their allies. . . . Leslie, his face a smooth reflection of deference, listened with riveted attention, noting every word of what was spoken with weary, blandly confident garrulity.

A moment of euphoria after moments of despair. He imagined that he was still rich when he had no more than those 39,000 ducats, should they reach their destination, and the golden baubles which he was hauling along. Imperial commissioners were rummaging through his castles, arresting his officials, studying the plans of his duchies for the purpose of their distribution. He imagined, or he wanted to imagine, that he had good friends in spite of the sheaf of disappointments just gathered. He felt in no imminent danger. He was too proud, too enfeebled, too despondent for that. Else he would, as Piccolomini expected him to do, have hurried past the fortress.

Eger lies in the extreme west of Bohemia, near its northern frontier, on the river of the same name, Agara, meaning a torrent. The Bohemians call it Cheb, or Heb, a bend, because the river at this point makes a slightly western curve before resuming its former direction towards the Elbe. Steeply above this curve and on a slope over the town stood the castle, a tower of black lava rock, a citadel within a fortress. Eger was wealthy, or it had been prior to contemporary troubles; the focal point of the mercantile routes Nürnberg–Prague and Prague–Leipzig; as the key to Bohemia, a sally-port and point of attack. In 1625 Wallenstein had marched as the newly appointed commander in the field from Eger into the Empire. In 1630, returning from Memmingen, he had come home via Eger. Less than two years ago Eger had been his head-quarters when he prepared to meet Maximilian and to go in quest of the King. The days here, with receptions by the town council and, amidst a swarm of lances and banners, exchanges of gifts in front of eagerly attentive spectators, had always been colourful and radiant. Now, when Eger's turrets and walls emerged out of the drifting mist, no deputation was waiting at the Lower Gate. Only Lieutenant-Colonel Gordon, the commandant, with whom a brief discussion followed. The cuirassiers and dragoons were to remain overnight on the outskirts in the open. The General, Colonel Butler, the court officials and servants would stay inside the walls, with the Duke's quarters in the house of Alexander Pachhelbel. The litter swung between the horses as they passed through the Upper Gate and Wood Lane into the Market Square. The towns-men looked the other way, as though nothing were happening, and busied themselves with their rattling hammers and screeching saws.

The ducal entourage was allotted various houses on the market-place or nearby. One report has it that the Trčkas and Kinskys shared a dwelling. That the most comfortable billet had been selected for the Duke is obvious from the fact that the commandant had lodged there until his removal now to the inhospitable citadel. As yet he respected the Generalissimo, rather more than was sanctioned, for he should not really have admitted him. This was his instruction, at any rate the initial instruction, from Giulio Diodati. Bitter indignation was expressed by Deputy Commander-in-Chief Gallas when he heard that Gordon and Leslie had cast away their honour by allowing the traitor refuge within their solid shelter. Good counsel had however been hard for Gordon to come by, more particularly as rumour claimed that the Duke was approaching with fifteen regiments. In this distant corner of Bohemia the new situation seemed more fluid than it did at the country's centre. The charisma of old authority did not fail of its effect the nearer the bearer drew.

On this evening Butler invited Leslie and Gordon to his lodging.

They did not know each other, but they felt a pressing need to become closer acquainted.

On this same evening Chancellor Elz set out for the Margrave of Kulmbach. Another messenger departed for Dresden or wherever Arnim was to be found. Towards eleven o'clock a horseman from Pilsen pounded on the town gate. At the Duke's order he was let in and conducted by Major Leslie to the Pachhelbel house. He had come from Haimerl, the Pilsen commandant. The Duke seized upon what he brought. Dated 24 January, it was the proclamation of dismissal. Had Wallenstein until this moment entertained a last few illusions, they were now gone. In his sickness of heart he relieved his feelings by harangue to the man who happened to be in the room, Leslie – abuse of the Emperor and the imperial House, how it was all over between him and its members, how in the immediate future Protestant troops, two thousand horsemen and one thousand infantrymen from the Palsgrave of Birkenfeld alone, would be at his side, and how those at Vienna would yet feel sorry for themselves. Leslie listened, took his leave, returned to Butler's table, and reported. To Butler the proclamation was nothing new. Thereafter they talked more frankly and in the language most conducive to mutual understanding, which was English.

On Saturday morning a conference was held in Wallenstein's room by his assistants and abettors. Whether, as on previous days, Count Kinsky continued to wear a smile is not mentioned. Afterwards Ilow summoned those three others, their counterparts and partners on whom everything depended – Butler, Gordon, and Leslie, the "three heroes", as later they styled themselves. This was the moment, thought Ilow, for cards to be put on the table. How long would it be before Piccolomini or Gallas was at Eger? Butler's dragoons were needed. The garrison's twelve hundred German infantrymen and Trčka's regiment (in name, Gordon's in reality) were needed. In such a situation, he had decided, there was nothing more to be concealed. And Ilow, when he had nothing to conceal, was accustomed to fly out bluntly. Did they not know, he demanded, how the House of Austria rewarded its faithful servants? With a golden key, a sword, and a lame, knock-kneed horse. Let someone gain a property or principality, though, and the sign was that he had not long to live. Nevertheless with the Duke, who had fallen into disfavour only because he had been so concerned for his army, matters stood differently. Were the gentlemen to pledge themselves to him as an independent prince and to renounce their allegiance to the Emperor, he would pay them not merely what the Emperor owed, but their reward would be the most splendid lands and highest commands. Could not a little time be allowed to pass, suggested the three heroes, until perhaps His Majesty and His Princely Grace were reconciled? Too late, retorted Ilow, nothing whatever more to be done. The Duke now was, and he would stay, his own master. The Swedes were very close, or Arnim with his Saxons, or both. To pledge their word was what they should do. To pledge their word was what they did. Hands raised, they stood there and swore to obey none other than the Duke of Friedland. Then they left and once more discussed the matter among themselves, at length and in detail.

Ilow, satisfied with this success, sat down with Trčka and Kinsky to the midday meal. Leslie re-appeared. He wished to ask, at Gordon's instruction, whether the gentlemen would not care to spend the evening with the Lieutenant-Colonel at the castle? Saturday before Lent was reason enough to celebrate. The commandant desired in any case to display hospitality to such illustrious guests. A token of newly plighted friendship. They gladly accepted. The invitation, for six o'clock, abridged the afternoon.

Wallenstein did not leave his room, let alone the house. The confines of his golden isle had narrowed, but they held. His Lord High Steward kept the servants in order from afar. His doctors mixed his potions, prepared his herbal baths, changed the bandages around his suppurating legs. His astrologer prowled around portentously. His chancellery was on hand with its director and its principal secretary, a pair of brothers. They were kept busy. The old discipline was maintained like an automaton which purrs away without concern. Letters were recorded and filed as they had been day after day, year after year. One was addressed to the Croat Colonel Corpus: "His person is required here for essential converse. We therefore admonish him upon receipt of this selfsame immediately to bestir himself and proceed to Us. Eger, 25 February 1634." It was the undying hope of still extracting from the clutch of the imperialists those troops stationed in northernmost Bohemia. Ilow's hope. Whether Wallenstein had not relinquished hope, seriously continued to hope, let others decide. What I believe is that his most nagging desire now was for revenge. No longer for peace in the Empire nor rest on his own behalf, but for revenge upon those who had done this to him.

Ilow laid down the lines for an army order that Captain Niemann set down on paper, an involved draft which again recapitulated all that had happened since January. Its culmination was a summons to the colonels not to let themselves be led astray by anybody or anything from what they owed the Emperor's commander-in-chief in the field anyway, and more particularly in the light of their oath sworn at Pilsen. They must march their regiments to Laun, the place selected for rendezvous, and at once betake themselves to Eger "since We seek to do naught other than to perform the service of His Imperial Majesty and the preservation of His Hereditary Kingdoms and Lands". At this stage a difficult pretence to maintain, as Wallenstein sensed when the chancellery director read the text to him. None the less even that official had never experienced such a shrill outburst of rage as ensued. The draft's final words pronounced, the Duke clenched his ailing hands and "with the most frightful maledictions and fulminations" shouted that the colonels owed their duty to him, not to the Emperor! *"Hisque verbis, omnibus furiis agitatus, me in malem rem abire jussit"* – tormented by all the Furies he shrieked to me to be gone to Hell. It is the last that we hear from him, assertion of the old, tragically mistaken belief that the army belonged to him, to him alone. It is almost the last. To say that he had retired and let himself be undressed early is wrong. He had remained retired all day, probably wearing nothing but a linen shirt and fur-lined robe. He knew that from six o'clock onward he would be alone the rest of the evening and night. His unloved henchmen, helplessly drunk, would not return before morning. At a late hour, it is alleged, his astrologer visited and warned him. A fabrication supported by no serious source. Four civilian guards patrolled below the first floor windows to keep away dogs, and humans too, the only sentinels in the direct vicinity of the house. A groom of the chamber sat, as usual, in the anteroom. Let the bell ring and he would inquire what his order was, whereafter the cup-bearer should come with hot ale in a golden beaker, or possibly the doctor. . . . The Duke lay and brooded, dozed, dreamed, harboured hatred.

Those three drove to the castle, squeezed into a coach with Captain Niemann, Trčka's indispensable adjutant who was allowed to join the party. The distance was not great, but the weather was disagreeable, with a rising, humid wind working itself into a storm. Well-bred people anyway went nowhere on foot. Their attendants, a few faithful followers of Ilow, Trčka, and Kinsky who never left their masters, did. Their masters began to use their legs only when the moat, facing the town and surrounding the castle to west and south, had been reached. They left their carriage and sauntered over the drawbridge through the outer gate, past the guardhouse, across the castle-yard to the inner gate, the entrance to the inner keep, where Gordon stood with his old friend Leslie and his new friend Butler waiting to welcome them warmly. They were led past the cold hall down a passage into an annex with a wainscoted, well-heated chamber, large enough for a celebration, neither too large nor too bare for so small a company. They were in a good mood, the guests, in genial anticipation of their first comfortably relaxed hours for a whole week. They hung up their swords, military trappings, mere signs of status, on the wall. They would not have been in such good mood if but one of them had observed what in the late afternoon had transpired inside and in the neighbourhood of the castle. Thirty-three of Butler's dragoons, admitted in small groups so as not to attract attention, were stationed in accordance with a predetermined order: twice seven in rooms to right and left, east and west, of the wainscoted chamber, nineteen of them in apartments round about. The guests neither knew that, nor could they hear how, after they were seated, another seventy Irishmen were led, softly, softly, across the drawbridge and, more than enough in strength, took charge of both gateways to prevent any undesirables from being able to enter or leave the citadel. To whom should anything of the kind occur when food (pike garnished with snails as well as other tasty morsels proffered by the townsmen of Eger) and wine began agreeably to effect a relaxation of all tension? Who could guess that their attendants, given a meal in the kitchen, were already under lock and key? That the drawbridge was raised, the outer gate barred? It made no noise, it did not disturb the merrymakers. They were truly merry and, among these newly pledged adherents, they merrily politicized. Within three days, boomed Ilow, the Duke would have a bigger, finer army than he had ever had before. Germany's freedom, Niemann saucily interposed, meant more to him than everything else, it was the House of Austria which wanted to crush it, and in Austria's blood he hoped shortly to wash his hands. A succession of such drunkenly frivolous utterances followed. They noted neither the watchful looks, the glances exchanged and those stolen towards the clock on the wall, nor the evil smiles suppressed into their hosts's beards. They did not observe that a sergeant brought Leslie something, the key to the outer gate. They made no remark when Leslie whispered to a page and the page disappeared, because at table it often happens that some minor instruction is given. On this occasion, though, the message to Major Geraldine, who commanded the one group of six dragoons, and for Captain Devereux, who led the other, was that the time had come. When, however, the fourteen erupted through both doors, Geraldine crying "Who is a good imperialist?", the three hosts springing up with a bellow of "*Vivat Ferdinandus!*", Captain Devereux chiming from the opposite side "And the

whole House of Austria", just as though the ditty's declamation had been
patiently rehearsed, while Butler, Gordon, and Leslie, snatching up
their swords, at once cut and thrust at their guests – when that moment
came there was no longer any secret for them to penetrate. Atrocious,
frightful horror. Kinsky, seated between table and wall, fell first, almost
immediately. Ilow was able to reach his weapon, Trčka too. They laid
about them, they defended themselves so fiercely that the table, with its
jugs, glasses, sweetmeats, tumbled over and all the windows were
smashed. Seventeen against four, or three, or two, made no sense, with
the majority fumbling in the dark and getting in each others' way.
Nobody counted the minutes that the fray lasted, but it lasted a while
because in the distant kitchen the attendants managed to break out of
their confinement and to hurry, at least two of them, to their masters'
assistance. They also were killed. Captain Niemann escaped into an
adjoining room, but he was caught. Ilow lay dead. The last was Trčka,
a giant of a man, protected by a doublet of elk skin. He broke a passage
through the throng, reached the corridor, the gate, the courtyard. He
was asked the password. "St Jacob!" "That no longer counts, Austria
is the answer!" The Irishmen, urging each other on, knew how to kill
one who, possessing the magic against thrusts and bullets, was immune.*
Done! The execution, ran War Councillor Caretto di Grana's subsequent laudation, could not have been performed more effectively if it
had been planned and practised for years.

Not for years. Not for half a day. This was how it had gone.

The three had first come to an understanding on the preceding
evening by way of cautiously exploratory discussion. Strange, Butler
said, that the Duke, normally not accustomed to advance upon the foe
with less than fifty thousand men, should now approach him with such
negligible numbers. The other two found it even stranger that he should
at this juncture have issued instructions to evacuate the frontier strong-
points of Joachimsthal, Elbogen, and Falkenau. This, they agreed,
should be prevented, and that was sufficient to establish understanding.
It rested on Butler's knowledge, and Gordon's too, of Gallas's proclamation of 12 or 15 February. Whether they were already familiar with the
proclamation of deposition or only received it on Saturday morning,
February 25, is immaterial. The former carried the same weight as the
latter. They must also since Friday or, at the latest, Saturday morning
have been informed of the secret sentence, "dead or alive", whether

* See p. 411 (translator's note).

through Diodati, Piccolomini, or Gallas. If not, Butler's step in sending a captain to Gallas with the message that he would arrest or kill the criminal, even though Arnim were within ten miles of Eger, would be inexplicable.

The triangular dialogue was interrupted by the midnight courier and Leslie's visit to the Pachhelbel house. His description of what occurred there raised the tension. At this point they rejected the notion of fleeing, which had previously been mooted, and decided to seize the rebels next day. Why not, asked Leslie, slay them at once? These three, to whom chance had allotted the role of the inferior but actual executioners, found themselves in the same dilemma as that in which for weeks their superiors had floundered. They knew the secret sentence, but only as a hint, a verbal intimation, unsigned, definitely lacking the imperial autograph. The Emperor had left the decision to the three major executioners, Gallas, Piccolomini, Aldringen. From the remoteness of Austria they shook off the responsibility onto the three minor ones within the confines of the fortress. Any further devolution was impossible. Wallenstein, though, was not just anybody. His murder could bring glittering reward or all kinds of trouble. What should be done?

Ilow was a bad politician, a bad psychologist. On Saturday morning he repeated the error that he had committed with the Pilsen Oath. Instead of treading carefully, he fired broadsides. He boasted of approaching Protestant aid, which was nowhere under way, and demanded the oath of fealty. He thought that he was acting under pressure of time. The three heroes sensed, however, a different time-pressure. This was what decided them upon slaughter. Like the three major executioners, they overestimated the difficulty. Butler was certain of his Irishmen, but of neither the Trčka cuirassiers outside the town nor the German troops inside it nor the townsmen, secretly Protestant sympathizers although subjugated and without hope. Wallenstein, though, had since the battle of Lützen lost all personal contact with his soldiery, content with the role of lofty, stern, ominous commander. At Eger, moreover, his adherents displayed the same lack of foreboding as at Pilsen. They did not even think it necessary to put the quarters of their sick master under a guard, for which Trčka's cuirassiers would have served well enough.

In such convenient circumstances the general staff work expended on preparation of the butchery was more precise than essential. The three heroes concluded that the three adherents should be reduced to silence simultaneously and, so as not prematurely to alarm the townsmen and the German troops, silently. Hence the rat-trap invitation to the citadel on its slope above the town. Hence the use of swords, not muskets. During the afternoon two companies were brought from the camp outside, dragoons for the castle and the operation, infantrymen to keep, if necessary, the main guard in check. Their officers were necessarily initiated into the plot – Geraldine, Devereux, whom we already know, and a certain Macdaniel who was entrusted with the external watch at the gates as well as over the courtyard. The duty officer at the outer gateway, a German, had to allow the dragoons to pass. It is no indication that he knew what was up. Perhaps he was merely advised to look away and not to bother his head about anything. If he understood his role, he was the only German who was allowed to play.

Later the heroes gave themselves, or had themselves given, credit for making so bold as to perform all this, forty individuals "against so heinous, vengeful a man, feared by all the world, who had by and around him so many soldiers, friend and foe alike, and more than two hundred servitors, and in a closed township where all are in the main more inclined to the adversary than to His Imperial Majesty and also hourly awaited the anticipated enemy!". Probably that really was how they saw the situation, just as Piccolomini had been wondrously convinced of the peril of his task. The upshot could have taught them better. The many had no idea or were indifferent, or both; the victims were blind.

The Three had successfully accomplished their project. It left them unmoved. The sight of the naked, bleeding bodies of dead generals was nothing extraordinary to old mercenaries. Leslie, by far the most intelligent and the bravest of the trio, went into the town to the main guard, had the loafing German officers and men assembled, barked at them an account of how this and that had happened on the Emperor's service, told them that they would be required again to swear allegiance to the Emperor, and bade them for the rest to hold their peace. Which they did. To obey murderers rather than the murdered is prudent. Then the energetic major let a second company of dragoons into the town, a step also previously agreed. Their task was to ride through the streets and make certain that no man left his house. All too punctilious a precaution. The townsmen knew nothing. Had they known anything, they would have snuggled all the more deeply into their beds. Back at the castle, Leslie could report that all was well.

Hereupon the question of "dead or alive" was once more briefly debated. Which solution served the House of Austria better? That is, which promised greater fame and reward? They could have argued that

Wallenstein was now forsaken and helpless as an exposed child, absurdly easy to transport to Pilsen as a prisoner. They resolved otherwise, because the enemy was so close, because only that morning Ilow had invoked the prodigious armed might which would stand ready within three days. Death, regrettably, it had to be. Gordon, who was thought the weakest, was left at the castle to oversee the dead. Leslie, to meet all eventualities, stopped at the main guard. Butler, Geraldine, and Devereux, with the already proficient dragoons behind them, continued to the market-place.

It was between ten and eleven o'clock and, with a storm raging wilder than any within living memory, must have been pitch dark. To have tried to light the torches would have been useless. The party fumbling through the dark heard from one house a wail of women's voices. Countesses Kinsky and Trčka had learned through one of the attendants, fled from the castle, the end of the banquet. We marvel that their frail lamentations were able to rise above the clamour of the storm. Butler, his mistrust as well as his pride aggravated by his responsibility, immediately sent Macdaniel back to the main guard with a message that the town already knew what had happened. A tumult was to be feared and must be nipped in the bud. He believed in numbers too, as regards the Pachhelbel house. Fifteen dragoons in front of the gate, fifteen in front of the courtyard door, as though the ailing man in his winding-sheet could still have escaped them. Nevertheless the Colonel preferred not to be present at the ultimate scene. He dispatched into the house the tried Captain Devereux with his tried number, the six.

They must have lit their torches under cover. Then they rushed up the stairs, Devereux with a partisan between his fists, shouting, "Rebels! Rebels!" They met the cup-bearer, at that moment carrying away the golden beaker, and struck at him. On the first floor landing they turned left towards the antechamber and the sick-room. Up sprang the groom of the chamber and gesticulated – this noise, for Heaven's sake, when the Duke was asleep! They slew him.

Wallenstein had dragged himself to the window, alarmed either by the howling of the storm or as the tumult in the house began. Now, when the yelling was quite close and blows swung like clubs against the barred door, he took a few steps towards the centre where a table stood and leaned against it. In the semi-darkness relieved by the torches he could neither recognize the men who burst into the room nor understand the insults – vile, perjured, rebellious scoundrel! – roared by the murderer to incite his own passion. He only knew, *Konec*, at last, 'tis here. From his throat there issued a rasp which sounded like the soldier's traditional plea, "Quarter!" A reflex, no more. He spread his arms wide. Devereux kept the distance that he needed for his weapon's impetus. He had to aim for the middle, a little below the breast-bone, and, one foot planted forward, guide his thrust upward. Diaphragm and stomach pierced, the major artery cut, the lung tattered, death's gigantic jagged blade ripped through four, five organs where one would have sufficed. Fire, choking pain, spiralling suction. Once more, a fragment of a second by human measure, consciousness may have awoken to that light of which none has ever told. Then, the body sinking to the ground, night, redeeming night.

A tall fellow took the corpse in his arms (it did not weigh much) to throw it out of the window. That the captain would not tolerate. The remains were wrapped in a red rug, dragged down the stairs with the head rebounding at every step, and taken in a carriage to the castle where the others lay. The storm had ceased. In the morning the bodies were borne to the chapel.

On this Sunday before Lent the news reached Dresden that Wallenstein had broken with the Emperor and was on his way to Eger – Kinsky's letters of Tuesday and Wednesday. John George of Saxony was so delighted that he invited himself to an evening's carousal with Lord von Arnim. That lasted until six o'clock in the morning. The two of them, as reported to Oxenstierna, "continually marched on Vienna". We can see the Elector, blue-red in the face, with stiffly swinging arms, stalking around the table – "To Vienna! To Vienna!" – and Arnim on his heels, a little embarrassed. We can see the servants at the door, grinning and whispering, see one of them leaping forward with the wine-jug when the Elector has flung himself into his seat and holds the empty goblet over his shoulder, see him drinking, laboriously rising, and striding around the table again: "To Vienna! To Vienna!" On Monday, late and with a heavy head, Arnim set off to meet the Duke of Friedland.

A Final Chapter

No sooner was he dead than all that had served him became a meaningless mass. The drops, the ointments, the potions in the chamber where he had been slain. The apparel chosen for its softness to his limbs. The gilded utensils. The court, its members flung into a precarious future, destitution. The possessions which he had so sternly cherished. Fending off clamour of any kind since his achievement of greatness and riches, he was extinguished amidst clamour. To shelter against the grossness of his fellows, he had built his own world, that marvellous structure, his duchy. Straightway it was torn apart, dissipated, handed over piecemeal to nincompoops, rendered worthless. To fasten upon these spoils was to snatch at substance. To try and pronounce upon him, demonstrate his guilt, show the world plainly what had been his aim was to fasten upon a void, to snatch at a phantom. On every side the consequences of his disappearance were understood, though there was hardly a man-jack qualified in his own eyes to judge who did not somehow understand them differently.

He foundered by letting himself be edged to the rim of the abyss, with finally too many enemies and no friends. His corpse was barely cold before his supporters were more numerous than his critics, whereby he once more held the centre of the stage.

THE MURDERERS AMONG THEMSELVES

That same night Butler sent a message to Gallas at Pilsen that it was he who had killed them all. Not Gordon, not Leslie, but he. A message to the Emperor expressed the hope that the execution had been both highly necessary and highly salutary, a word being added about how rigorous the Colonel's experience in His Majesty's service had hitherto been. Very soon Leslie was on the way to Vienna as spokesman for Gordon, Captain Macdaniel as spokesman for Butler. Gallas also contributed details. God Himself performed the task. The traitor had leapt to the window. (His gout, commented the General sarcastically, had not impeded him.) Then he had turned round, arms widespread, and had not uttered a word. When however the partisan penetrated his chest, a cloud of smoke issued, and there was a detonation as though a musket had been fired. "Presumably it was the Devil who departed from him." At a later stage Piccolomini, as a thrust against Gallas, disputed the point. "There were no supernatural noises. The common people believe this kind of thing. To them it seems evident that a perfidious creature with such heinous ideas should in life have been animated by satanic forces which also stigmatized his death by imparting to his abominable carcass this last testimony of shame."

Piccolomini, when on 27 February he received the news, was at Mies, where five days ago Wallenstein had rested. He was in any case closer than Gallas, but he hurried to Eger as fast as he could in order to make sure of being first. "I shall at once send the corpses of the evildoers to Prague for exposure at the most infamous sites," by which he meant the public gallows. Gallas, always a cut above him in taste, refused permission. For the present, at least. The Emperor should decide what was to happen to the dead.

On 2 March the news reached Vienna. The Bavarian envoy was officially informed. Next day more precise knowledge was obtained from Leslie and Macdaniel. While waiting in the Emperor's anteroom, Richel was proffered congratulations by dignitaries of such standing as Schlick, Meggau, and Trauttmansdorff. They were heartily glad that at last "he who had caused and occasioned Your Electoral Highness and Your land so much harm and suffering was undone. Everyone now speaks openly and without constraint of him, especially in the presence of those who used to be Friedland's patrons and creatures and who must not say anything to the contrary unless they would render themselves suspect." Maximilian at once instructed that a claim should be lodged for three hundred thousand gulden expended at Nürnberg for Wallenstein or on Wallenstein soldiery. Money, he presumed, would now be on hand. No, replied Richel, unfortunately there would again be none because, however extensive had been the traitor's assets, they were promised to far too many loyalists whose loyalty could not otherwise be assured.

Ferdinand raised Leslie on the spot to the rank and office of imperial count and chamberlain, putting the final seal of sanction on the murder. That was what he meant to do. He had honestly believed in Wallenstein's wickedness and he felt intense relief. That was what he had to do, irrespective of what his feelings were. The slightest manifestation of doubt, apart from rendering impossible the confiscations for the benefit of those supporters on whom he depended, would have created the most destructive confusion throughout the army. Nevertheless the secret sentence continued to be kept secret, as though the murderers had indeed acted properly and brought about a deliverance, but the initiative had been theirs.

Where it cost him nothing, the Emperor displayed clemency. The murdered, with the exception of Niemann, would be buried quietly in consecrated ground. Wallenstein's remains could be handed to the family, if it so wished. Not less than three thousand masses should be read for the departed, a number to be divided between Austria's churches and monasteries. Fifty were allotted to Lamormaini's Jesuit college and another fifty to Father Basilio, Cardinal Harrach's friend. The Cardinal, Wallenstein's brother-in-law, wrote to Ferdinand that his inviolable principle was to set public weal above private interest, or at any rate Eggenberg advised him so to write. At Bruck-on-the-Leitha the old Countess, mother of the Harrachs, was quite broken by grief and confined to her bed. The Duchess was in somewhat better condition, but always in tears. None the less she, or the lawyer who saw to her signature on the document, had already on the day before the murder put forward at Vienna her claims – through the will of God her husband had incurred guilt, but the lordships of Neuschloss, Weisswasser and Hirschberg belonged by deed of gift on his part to her personally and in no way constituted a portion of the confiscation property. News of the death had hardly come to Bruck before she ventured further claims on the strength of Wallenstein's last will and testament – she was entitled to have three hundred thousand ducats paid down, this sum to be followed by twelve thousand ducats, annuity and possession of the palace at Prague. The money should be transmitted as soon as possible to enable her to maintain her court establishment. Signed, Isabella, Duchess of Mecklenburg and Friedland. The lady did not understand her new situation.

Different was the line taken by Count Max. He knew immediately that no legal suit, only factual circumstance, could prevail when no rule of law obtained and that therefore his heritage was lost. He also knew that, provided he went about it properly, bold-faced and in good conscience, he would be able to retain the advantages accrued in his benefactor's lifetime. Although it was intimated to him that for the present he should not appear at court, he continued energetically to play his part as a member of the armed forces, a regimental commander and a principal royal equerry. In April, when Gallas and Piccolomini arrived in Vienna, he gave a banquet for these murderers-in-chief. The Venetian envoy thought it an unusual display of dissimulation, too gross to be in good taste. But Count Max proved right. That was the way of the world. Not outstandingly clever, he understood it well enough, and in the event slid over this vital crisis with gains instead of losses.

His conduct aroused the indignation of Ottavio Piccolomini, who would, in the nephew's place, undoubtedly have behaved likewise. He threatened to resign if Wallenstein's body was delivered to the widow, if Count Max was left in possession of the estates mortgaged to him by Wallenstein, if indeed severer measures were not instituted against the family and the guilty adherents. Generous treatment of the one side, he argued solicitously, would amount to base ingratitude towards the other, that of the executioners, the big and the little heroes, himself in particular.

At Eger the preoccupation was to secure and divide the spoils on hand. They were however rather disappointing, especially as officers and men had immediately after the murder carried away as much as they could hide. Rumours that Adam Trčka had had close on five hundred thousand ducats by him and the Duke barrels full of gold proved as reliable as such talk in such cases generally is. Gallas received back his silver service, but he kept Ilow's, found at Prague and allowed him in replacement, as well. War Councillor Caretto had to return the coach and horses of Count Schaffgotsch, arrested in Silesia, at an imperial wink that liberal reward was to be anticipated but arbitrary theft from highly placed persons would not be tolerated.

Then there was the business of the Wallenstein chancellery. During Saturday night Butler had promptly had it impounded and sealed. The secret correspondence would, it was hoped, elucidate the abominable treason. The major portion of this documentary treasure-house had been abandoned at Pilsen. Yet no initial scrutiny had been made either there or at Eger before Gallas insisted that the General had on the day before his death burned six hundred of the most compromising letters. Caretto followed with the charge that Countess Trčka, in all other respects undoubtedly a good and pious woman – she was a Harrach – had done the same with her husband's papers. How did they know that the figure was six hundred, neither more nor less? The chancellery's director, who soon testified against his dead master anything that he could, knew nothing about the matter. Yet Wallenstein, who would not have had six hundred letters about his person, could not have concealed this destructive activity from him. The selection alone would have taken days. When had he had these letters at his disposal? Difficult to see, too, which of them would have been candidates for destruction. He had never written letters on secret matters to Oxenstierna, Feuquières or Richelieu. Had he done so, they would have been handwritten, without a draft, and the archives at Stockholm and Paris would have been the places to look for them. Oxenstierna had had no direct correspondence with Wallenstein other than of a routine character, such as questions relating to the exchange of prisoners of war. Nor had Feuquières. Arnim often enough, and of his missives none or practically none are missing. One letter from Richelieu and one, truly most secret, from Gustavus Adolphus have not been traced. They were, I would assume, burnt immediately upon receipt, not on the last day.

A palpable inference is that Gallas and Piccolomini very carefully abstracted archive copies which implicated them. They had, after all, been on an intimate footing with the victim much longer than they now wished to let it appear, and they had been kept fully informed about the negotiations of the past year. Be that as it may, the executors knew Wallenstein's character and that of the alleged conspiracy. They knew that convincing evidence on that score would never emerge from the chancellery. The tale of the incinerated documents served a prophylactic purpose.

The initially expressed jubilation about the chancellery find, quickly quenched, was paralleled by another. Certain political prisoners looked like being a useful source of constrained information. Colonel Schlieff, during the very last days sent by Wallenstein to Silesia, was arrested at Prague. Three days after the murder Butler's vigilant dragoons caught Duke Franz Albrecht on the journey from Regensburg to Eger. The same happened to Chancellor Elz when he, in complete ignorance of what had transpired, returned from his mission to Kulmbach. Sharp-witted and bold as ever, not to be put down or abashed by anything, the Duke protested that he was Elector John George's ambassador travelling in connection with official negotiations expressly sanctioned by the Emperor. Formally correct, but of no help to him. Present activities lay outside the pastures of the law of nations. In princely captivity and a wealthy man, the Duke was better off than the rest, sending for servants and companions, a retinue numbering some fifty in all, and tender greetings to a certain I.S.: "I die her servant. Let things come as God wills. May write no more. *Patientia!*" Chancellor Elz protested too, more humbly. Never, as truly as there was a God in Heaven, had he known the least about Wallenstein's knaveries. "Because of his harsh treatment of us," he congratulated himself and the Duke's other servitors on the Eger murder. He was glad to be rid of his appointment and he would gladly find another less stringent, once he was released from this unjust custody. Caretto shrewdly asked the ex-chancellor whether he approved Wallenstein's execution. "Since I know not the cause," replied Elz even more shrewdly, "how should I judge the effect?" This evil-minded court councillor of Palsgrave Frederick, this intriguer who had led the Duke of Brunswick astray, destroyer of the 1625 peace negotiations, vicious chancellor to the King of Denmark, and finally soured minister of the former General – which was how one of Ferdinand's inquisitors described him – this slyest Calvinist in all Germany– another's description – quickly accommodated himself to changed conditions by a change of faith and flight into the lap of the Roman Church. His type does not go under.

Nor did Giovanni Battista Senno. During the night of the murder he had been locked up, but five days later he was set free. On 1 March, in his own carriage, with his instruments and papers, he formed part of the melancholy procession which departed from Eger for Pilsen. Headed by a well-satisfied, proud Piccolomini and a wagon with the bodies of the murdered in rough-hewn coffins, the Trčka and Kinsky widows as well as Lauenburg followed. At Mies the coffins were unloaded and placed in a vault of the Franciscan monastery until such time as orders came from Vienna. Senno continued to Pilsen. The Emperor, eager to hear the conspiratorial knowledge at the disposal of the man who for four years had been in Wallenstein's immediate proximity, demanded his closest custody and examination. Gallas made only a pretence of obedience. The astrologer was allowed to travel at his ease to Vienna. His interrogation took a fleeting, mild course declining into the downright ridiculous. Then we lose sight of him. Twenty-two years later, the story goes, he died at Genoa.

With the stately ship sunk, everyone tried to save himself, swimming wildly for land and claiming never to have been on board. Who can blame them? They reviled him who had lately been their lord and master, if not their benefactor. Such conduct was to trespass on the ground of those – Piccolomini, Aldringen, Beck – who would have the dead man's adherents as bad as possible so that their own virtue should shine the brighter. Simultaneously there was an outburst of quarrelling between the greatest paragons of all. Colonel Butler took offence because Vienna accorded the whole credit for the "Friedland execution" to Messrs Gordon and Leslie instead of the man who had accomplished the business entirely on his own. He threatened to exchange the imperial for Polish service. Piccolomini, on the other hand, was not only sensible of his own supersession by the duller, more decorous, luckier Gallas, but also of the displeasing subliminal mood prevalent in the capital and the army. Were there not individuals at Vienna who actually asserted that Wallenstein had been innocent whereas Gallas, Piccolomini, Aldringen had committed a gross deception? Was this shameless supposition not being inflated to nationalist dimensions by the allegation that the Spaniards had contrived the plot and the Italians performed the deed in order the better to crush the German nation? After so many years of hard service in Germany was it permissible, remonstrated Piccolomini in Italian, to call him a foreigner? Let those who raised the reproach that he had acted from sheer self-interest recall how he had not done so badly under Wallenstein, possessing position and wealth to a gratifying degree, not to mention what he could have acquired if he had trodden the felon's path. Rather than tolerate such insidious slander, he would resign his appointment and re-enlist as a common pikeman or for ever leave such an ungrateful land.

Worry that the major rewards could fail to materialize or that others might come off better. Accusations back and forth, rivalry for All-Highest favour. Irritation and impatience at Ferdinand's failure to reveal publicly his responsibility for the murder. Threats to take that step unless he did. Insistence on unequivocal statements, severer inquisitions and penalties to function as deterrents. As to the last, the generals' anxiety was not altogether groundless.

The major mutiny which in Wallenstein's lifetime they had feared and continued to fear did not happen, whether thanks to the energy of the leaders or the weariness and apathy of the led. Acts of rebellion occurred, not strong enough to merge into anything effective, but sufficient to frighten the new masters as symptoms. One of the two colonels who had first occupied Pilsen subsequent to Wallenstein's flight was soon afterwards shot by his soldiers. The circumstances remain unknown. Only little better known are those attaching to Lieutenant-Colonel Freiberger's attempted rising and revolution of no later than 2 March. Freiberger was a Lutheran from Brunswick, an assistant to and friend of Count Schaffgotsch. At his side stood an imperial war commissioner who was a Bohemian and returned émigré. Freiberger knew as yet nothing of Wallenstein's catastrophe. He imagined himself to be conforming to the Generalissimo's intent and the spirit of the Pilsen Oath when he published his manifesto to the Estates of Upper Silesia. That the Emperor meant to extirpate the Protestant religion, it ran, was now as clear as daylight. The Duke of Friedland's sole aim was the Empire's restoration to its ancient glory and the maintenance of every man's liberties. That was why he had joined with the King of France, the high and mighty United Netherlands Provinces, and the crown of Sweden. On the Germans, the Bohemians, the Silesians it was incumbent to do the same. Aid from the Saxons and the Swedes was on the way. To help with money, victuals, armed men and to pursue with fire and sword imperialist sympathizers as well as imperialists was the duty of the Upper Silesian Estates. Portions of five regiments, those of Schaffgotsch, Morzin, Böhm, Trčka, and Max Waldstein, participated. Hostages, nobles and burgesses who were suspect, were seized. There must have been others, Czech and German Protestants, nobles, burgesses, and peasants who could be relied upon. Long live Friedland, who was long dead. Long live the King of France, who was to become Emperor. Of course no aid arrived from anywhere. Of course the rising was an erroneous, blind, isolated, illusory undertaking. Of course the imperialists advancing against Troppau were the stronger. Until 18 March Freiberger managed to hold his fortress. Then he saw reason and surrendered. Vienna had been so shrewd as to repeat the clemency game previously played on a grander scale. The misled would be pardoned, though not the most wicked of their leaders.

A bagatelle. The tragedy of a few little men which no historian has thought worth investigation. Freiberger's quixotry was devotion to a Wallenstein mirage corresponding to his character as it now began to be delineated at Vienna. Had the Duke been the man that he was not, the great, loftily planning rebel, the rising of Troppau shows that he could have found a fighting following, in Silesia rather than in Bohemia. Bohemia was totally ground down and broken, but not as yet Silesia. That came later. It could have been too – what proof can there be in such matters – that the Silesians were more patriotic and true to their God than the Bohemians.

For the generals Troppau was a warning. Embers in the ashes. They visualized it as their most pressing task to pacify and pamper the army like an invalid, to obtain food and money, to silence the talk about the mischievous Spaniards. For the rest, the policy should be to stay on the defensive and leave the enemy alone if he kept quiet too. Wallenstein's strategy, recommended by him since December and conducive to his downfall, suddenly possible and quite satisfactory. And the enemy really made no move worth the name, either from the direction of Regensburg or anywhere else.

THE OTHER SIDE

With utmost speed Lord Rudolf Trčka had Wallenstein's portrait moved from his study to an attic. Old Karl von Zierotin, who had extolled his young brother-in-law's good qualities and in 1607 first introduced him to the court at Vienna, pronounced his own verdict. "As the tree, so its fruits. As the labour, so its reward. As the service, so its wage. We can be glad, very glad of that, but there is ground for sorrow too." What ground? To the end Zierotin remained an oracle and Solomon.

Lieutenant-General Arnim had hoped to be in Eger on 2 March. At Zwickau, fairly close to his destination, he met Sieur de la Broderie, secret emissary of the Marquis de Feuquières who was also on the way to Eger or, as he still imagined, to Pilsen. For the first time Wallenstein's two faintly discernible lines of policy, the German-Protestant and the French, to the annoyance of their respective representatives, crisscrossed. Vexation quickly gave way to common, dismal disconcertment when on the morning of 2 March they learned what had happened at Eger. De la Broderie turned back without loss of a moment. Arnim stayed for a few days where by chance he had made his overnight quarters. He was, it seems, as deeply affected as a man of his stamp and a politician of his age could be on the score of death and murder. Never before, he wrote, had so bloody a deed occurred under a Christian emperor. Henceforth he would have nothing whatever more to do with negotiations. Of the imperial government it would be said, "*Sanguine coepit, sanguine crevit, sanguine finis erit*" (Begun in blood, prospering in blood, its end will be in blood). The murderers tried to catch Arnim as they had caught Franz Albrecht. To speed his arrival, they sent him a trumpeter with a fictitious letter from Kinsky and sealed with the dead man's signet. Luckily for Arnim, the fellow came too late.

Bernard von Weimar was apprised of the course of events, convincing proof of his nonsensical mistake, at the same time as Arnim, possibly sooner. The Marquis de Feuquières, subsequently meeting the prince at Frankfurt, thought him not to be particularly distressed at Wallenstein's end.

Why should he have been? Why should the Swedes have been? They certainly had no cause. It was long, Feuquières claimed, since they had been so well pleased, an observation confirmed by Oxenstierna's private comments. Officially, icily, he condoled with the Elector of Saxony on the precipitate slaughter of his enigmatic Bohemian partner. The grievous ways of the Lord must be accepted and the best made of them, the confusions and perturbations turned to advantage, the readiest available fish drawn from the troubled waters. Oxenstierna, whatever else may be said about him, was no hypocrite. The murder had rid him of one of the dangers, difficult to define but considerable, for which in his extremely intricate position he was always on the watch. The danger of a third party. As Filip Sadler, one of his star diplomats, put it, the "third or Wallenstein party" had been "quenched through the massacre of its chiefs". A party which would have been neither Spanish nor Swedish, but German, of a Protestant, Saxon, Brandenburg hue, and, because such components did not suffice to constitute an autonomous power, relying on France. Precisely as the shrewd Marquis de Feuquières had understood the Swedes' fears, so he understood their relief. Father Joseph, who had for years pursued this objective and had seen in Wallenstein its appropriate promoter, is said to have been bitterly grieved. The third party was inherent in the logic of affairs, whether Wallenstein was conscious of it or not. Feuquières, as suitable for a man of letters, struck an emotional note. "*Une nouvelle bien tragique. Le pauvre duc de Friedland. Quelle pitoyable tragédie.*" Then, sharpening his pen for his future memoirs, "He did not succeed in persuading Duke Bernhard that he meant matters honestly. Hunted by the one, left in the lurch by the other, he was destroyed."

France's greatest man of letters waited a little while, though, before he spoke. Eight pages of Richelieu's reminiscences are devoted to Wallenstein's catastrophe, pages crammed with knowledge of affairs, insight, and thoughtful sympathy. "Finally suspicion gains mastery over the Emperor's feelings. It is the destiny of ministers that their authority fluctuates and usually does not endure unto their death, whether it be that monarchs weary of a man whom they have already granted so much that no more gifts are at their disposal or that they look askance at those who have to such degree deserved well of them that all and everything which still remains for bestowal is their due." That is the disaster which this author himself barely escaped, but the subject of his disquisition did not. He understood Wallenstein's fall with the penetration of a man experienced in all human turns of fate, viewed the Pilsen Oath as a mere act of self-defence which did not mean rebellion, and saw through the Italians' treachery. "He had raised Piccolomini from nothing to high military rank, heaped estates and honours upon him, wherefore he counted upon him and erred because not those whom we have put under the most generous obligation to us are loyal, but men of honour and virtue." About the murder: "Wallenstein's death remains a monstrous precedent, whether for ingratitude on the part of an inferior or the cruelty of a superior, for in a life fraught with perilous incidents the Emperor found no second servitor whose resourceful performance even from afar attained to the services rendered him by Wallenstein." "After his death he was reviled by whoever would have extolled him if he had remained alive. Let the tree fall and all will hurry to strip its foliage and hack it to pieces. Good or bad reputation depends on the bearer's end. Evil and beneficence are transmitted to posterity, and the wickedness of mankind inclines to the one rather than to the other."

So judged this prince of the church and statesman. Different at the moment was the opinion of him who, at present no more than a curial diplomat, was to become his successor, Giulio Mazarini, Cardinal Mazarin. He had known Piccolomini since the Mantua conflict, in the settlement of which he had been instrumental, and he extended to him his warmest congratulations on this new success – wonderfully pretty how he had managed this Wallenstein business.

On the first Thursday in April the curtain was raised in Madrid's theatre to present a piece dealing in a strongly heroic manner with Wallenstein's deeds and victories. A repeat performance scheduled for Sunday was abruptly struck from the bill. On Saturday tidings had arrived from Vienna. On 13 April the Council of State discussed the situation. "*Señor*," said the Duke of Olivares to the King, "a personality has been lost who, in spite of all, was of great merit and whom no other can possibly match." Remarkable, the tenacious conviction with which this politician clung to Wallenstein. Even his attitude to the tragic denouement, to which his compatriots had so assiduously contributed, was ambivalent. In part it had been desirable and necessary, he argued, but in part deeply deplorable. Only gradually did the former sentiment supervene as that solely valid, and then primarily thanks to the self-laudatory dispatches of Count Oñate. In November Olivares decided that the ambassador was an official endowed with the most brilliant qualities, who deserved favours and honours "because during this year he has served Your Majesty with great skill and credit in the Friedland affair". Later Oñate rose to be Viceroy of Naples, the most lucrative appointment the Empire had in its gift.

THE PEOPLE, THE TIMES, THE GAZETTES

The broad perspective of the mighty was not that of the afflicted flock.

For the Germans, that majority of them whose ancestors had repudiated the Pope, the murdered enemy became a friend. To be sure, propaganda by the mighty, in this instance the Swedes, worked in that direction. In his lifetime they had, by cunningly spread rumours, done the imperial Generalissimo damage as well as they could. Secretly they were pleased at his death. Publicly they exploited him to sow discord in the imperial army, to confuse minds, and to excite passions.

> How many an army did Wallenstein, with what unbelievable dispatch and at what cost, train and re-train for the Emperor's service! Who but Wallenstein broke at Nürnberg that most victorious and great force drawn together by Our Most Gracious King and Master, now resting in God? . . . Through Wallenstein we lost Our Most Beloved Hero, the King, and hereafter through Wallenstein suffered last autumn detriment on the Silesian border. . . . [Yet] I find not otherwise than that, though he was our enemy, he did not deserve such an end. . . . I gladly laud the enemy's virtue.

The Duke was the cause for the Emperor still being Emperor. God's punishment would befall the ingrates. Such testimonies to chivalrous impartiality, disseminated via broadsheets, were meant to be read by the imperial soldiery and to spur their imagination.

Broadsheets there were in plenty, plain reports at first, then garnished with items to tickle the reader's palate, make him lick his chops, appeal to his sentimentality. How Wallenstein, sword in hand, had resisted so desperately that he had to be run through three times. How the corpse was carried to the castle in a dung-cart. How the Countesses Trčka and Kinsky, amidst indescribable lamentation, had to wash the bleeding corpses of their spouses with their own hands. Welcome recreation speeding the wings of fancy, painful and splendid, was the decline and fall of the great to those who otherwise had so little to mark one day from another.

Derision was not wanting. A wide circulation must have been enjoyed by the ditty which began:

> The skin and bones here lie and rattle
> Of Wallenstein, great prince of battle . . .

Looking for his lucky star, far too long negotiation
Lost him much territory and population.
His Bohemian pate was all but shattered
When men's spurs clinked, clanked, and clattered.
Cocks, hens, dogs are driven away
Wheresoever he may stay. . . .

An accurate enough statement. The *Zurich Weekly Ordinary Gazette* printed another set of rhymes through whose jests ran a melancholy echo of the ambivalence, strangeness and misfortune of Wallenstein's life:

Here lies Friedland, of peace freed,*
Imperial prince, yet not imperial seed.
Admiral of ships and sailors short,
General without open battle fought.
Of ducal state inhabitant,
Ruler in mind of no one land.
In war and conquest man of peace,
Of kindly words held tyrant's lease.
Loyal Roman, foreign slave,
Upright, yet in falseness sheathed.
Would finally more than Emperor be. . . .

Such doggerels gained currency among the masses and were passed from mouth to mouth. They certainly did not originate in Habsburg chancelleries. Pictures, woodcuts, prints portraying the well-known, stern features of the victim and his last moment found a ready market which Eger actively exploited.

Soon politics, steeped in party and real or sham wrath, stepped in. Not since Luther's early days had Germany experienced such a squall of pamphleteering. By Protestants against Papist shavelings' modes and ways. By Germans against Spaniards. On Christian ethics' behalf against gruesome statecraft's reason. For truth against mendacity. Here is one example from the couple of dozen that have survived out of probably hundreds sunk without trace. *Report from Parnassus of the Advices Received and Relating to the Murderous Outrage and Assassination.* John Gordon, his unimportant cousin Adam Gordon, Butler and Leslie have to vindicate themselves before Apollo, chief judge upon Parnassus.

---

* The first syllable of "Friedland" signifies "peace". The literal translation of the line would be "Here lies Friedland without peace" (translator's note).

Prosecuting counsel is Themis, Imperial Chancellor Minos* is not afar and the denizens of Parnassus are on hand. The indictment is overwhelming, the defence feeble in the extreme. The accused are found guilty of perjury and "herewith handed to Nemesis, who shall dispatch them, one and all, from life to death as seems most expedient and appropriate, by means and method such as in the case of Ravaillac the Regicide.† And this judgement shall forthwith be proclaimed by Fame in all the world's public places so that everyman shall know how to preserve himself from such perjured, godless, disloyal, ignoble knaves and murderers."

Fame carried out her task. So-called epitaphs were her finest inspiration, scholars' sport, especially as they were composed in Latin, the language wherein at that time it was still best possible to give vent to clearest, pithiest, most memorable expression. *Caesarem cadentem erexit Valstein, Caesar erectus prosternit Valstein*, a neater way of saying, "Wallenstein put the falling Emperor back on his feet; the Emperor, back on his feet, prostrated Wallenstein." Or, as exemplification of human ingratitude, *Hispanicae libidini* – surrendered to the Spanish lust – he was slain to the Emperor's applause. The Spaniards were indeed pushed into the forefront, whether in prose pieces or in these Latin verbal felicities. With what justification is familiar. Protagonists A and B, the first asking, the second explaining, in *De morte Ducis Fridlandiae Dialogus* (Dialogue upon the Death of Friedland's Duke), came closer and closer to the heart of the matter until finally it was stated, "'Tis the ambition of the Spaniards to dominate all, to hold all. That none at Austria's court, unless he be Spaniard, shall dare to deserve well of Austria's House. Him they would not suffer, albeit that once to the best of his ability he did discharge affairs to Spain's benefit. For he was German. That was his crime. That was the cause. Thence flowed his affliction and all calamity."

He whom the Germans had in his lifetime refused to recognize as a compatriot was now adopted as almost a national hero. No more than six years passed before he was being compared with Arminius, Germany's liberator from Roman slavery. Not that Wallenstein deserved such a reputation. The current need was for a hero and saviour, even a failed one. In the absence of any other he was tried for the part.

* Themis was the goddess presiding over law and justice. Minos, King of Crete, became after death a judge in the infernal regions (translator's note).
† Ravaillac was the assassin in 1610 of Henry IV of France (translator's note).

Fame was meanwhile also performing its mission far beyond Germany's borders. Special issues of the Paris gazettes showed themselves well informed. The first, on 16 March, described the prelude to and the progress of the catastrophe, including Wallenstein's stubborn efforts to achieve peace and the crafty conduct of his enemies. "They were neither able longer to endure him in so powerful a position nor he to tolerate a second deposition. So accustomed had he become to be absolute in all matters that he ceased to rule only when he ceased to breathe." The writer, already at this stage, had no doubts about the order "dead or alive". In Italy, in as much as it was not under Spanish domination, the reaction was similar. Or rather, much more upset, much more indignant. At Venice the Emperor was the subject of so much slander that the Republic's ambassador at Vienna had to resort to diplomatic subtleties of elucidation: there were, alas, all too many of such evil-minded publications, but although their authors prudently employed fictitious names and imprints they in fact originated at Augsburg and Nürnberg.

These were the days at Modena of Count Fulvio Testi, poet and counsellor of princes. Testi had been in Vienna on one mission or another when the second generalate began. He was not to be deterred from dedicating to this turn of fate a sonnet, duly sent to the Duke. He certainly never saw him in person, for in 1632 Wallenstein avoided any visit to Vienna, just as he had done before and was to do thereafter. Did Testi admire him from afar, yielding to a childish worship of the great man, or was he on the look-out, as poets sometimes are, for opportunities to practise his calling? News of the murder received, he gave fresh wing to his rhythmic, rhyming fancy in ten verses of uneven length, 120 lines in all. Wallenstein, facing death, waxes eloquent. Others too, like Gualdo Priorato and Richelieu, were prepared to believe that he had uttered more than merely the exclamation "Quarter!", that he had briefly and with dignity defended himself. It would have been a splendid thing, but it neither was nor could be so. This had been no scene of parley, for all that the poet's radiant vision transformed it into one.

Hold hard thy sword, the mortally threatened hero bids. Knowest thou who I am? Laurelled victor over the Goths and Swedes, Albrecht the Great. Fearest thou not my name, not my guardian angel?

> Alberto il grande sono.
> E non temi il mio nome, anzi il mio nume?

On Ferdinand's brow, into his hand, amidst ruin and defeat, I pressed again the crown, the sceptre. (*He ponders.*) It is then true that Thou, my liege, hast my death Thyself commanded? Thou, to whom I restored Thy life? That an infamous murderer is the executor of Thy cruel will? O deceived Caesar! I am no traitor, though indeed betrayed—

> Io non so traditor, ma ben tradito!

During the succeeding decades Italian authors were nearly as much preoccupied by the subject of Wallenstein as were German ones, whether, as then was the fashion, in dialogues between celebrated dead or in historical essays. Mostly it was the victim who was displayed in a favourable light. There were also character delineations, such as *Il Volestano non poteva tollerar superiorità* (Wallenstein could not bear any power above himself), which testified to the enduring influence of Valeriano Magni, the Great Personage.

PUNISHMENT

Reactions of this calibre, not confined to Protestant Europe, embarrassed Vienna. Very soon an official declaration complained that untruthful statements were being circulated at every hand's turn. Yes, positively wicked ideas and utterly inadmissible flights of imagination which suggested that too precipitate justice, meaning injustice, violence indeed, had supervened in the case of the head of this disgraceful conspiracy and that His Imperial Majesty had been guilty of barbaric ingratitude. To make away with Wallenstein had been easy. A surprise. To convince the world of the righteousness of the act was proving difficult. Proper authority was being presented as a peace-hating, godless and tyrannical power. A second surprise, as distasteful as the first had been pleasing.

Lieutenant-General Piccolomini was summoned to help. He, at whose initiative the whole machinery had been put into motion, was to be brought forward as the man in possession of incontrovertible evidence. The material would be printed and published. In March Piccolomini really did put down a story on paper. It contained the lies which we already know and the truth which we likewise know. The lies were, however, incomplete. Essential components were missing. Irritable exchanges between the capital and the Lieutenant-General's head-quarters ensued. Amplifications and additions followed. In 1929 the report in its final form was discovered in the Vatican library. At the bottom left-hand corner of the last page is Count Gallas's seal and signature. The space to the right is empty. Piccolomini had declined to confirm what he had written, or his assistant Fabio Diodati had written for him. He declined because he wanted first to be certain of his reward, because he wanted to force the Emperor into revelation of the secret sentence, because he felt slighted, because he found fault with the trend of post-Wallenstein legal proceedings and policy. Without the principal witness's signature the testimony was worthless. The projected publication had to be abandoned.

A very muddle-headed, hasty, feverish investigation of the suspects and accessories now began. Its postulate was later defined by the "appointed Commissioners": there *must* have been more individuals involved in such a far-reaching, monstrous conspiracy than those few already executed, the murdered of Eger. Only they were not to be found.

Right at the beginning of March the examination had been undertaken in Bohemia of Trčka's personal secretary, Ilow's personal secretary, aide-de-camp, and personal servant, and of Senno the astrologer. At Vienna there followed that of Dukes Franz Albrecht and Heinrich Julius von Lauenburg, the former's personal secretary and aide-de-camp, of Generals Scherffenberg and Sparr, Chancellor Elz, Saxon Colonel Schlieff, General Count Schaffgotsch, imperialist Colonels Haimerl and Losy and others too. The yield was poor. How could it have been otherwise when the conspiracy, the abominable treason, was a pure mirage lacking tangible reality or nucleus? How should the little people, personal secretaries and servants, have known anything about this mirage? The highly placed parried skilfully enough. None more so than Duke Franz Albrecht, not one of the accused, simply an illegally held outsider whom it was hoped to coerce into face-saving information. What he revealed, particularly about negotiations in 1633, was in some respects interesting enough. Anything that could prove harmful to himself, if not to Wallenstein, he failed to reveal, confidently relying on the utter improbability of Vienna ever being in a position to read his letters to Arnim. Whenever the issue was "the groundwork of the conspiracy", those questioned replied with nice uniformity that they knew not a word about it.

The legal procedure reflected the Emperor's and his advisers' growing nervousness. A military court had been convened at Budweis. Wallenstein's movable chancellery had been taken there without anybody bothering to look into this mound of documents. Forgotten for ninety years, it was then, no one knows why, transported to the capital and rediscovered in the later nineteenth century. Vienna constituted an investigatory commission and another military court. In May a third and last was established with the army, busy besieging Regensburg. In

June that city was recaptured. Wallenstein had predicted that in good weather this would be easy. Any verdict was subject to review by the imperial War Council. The number of accused was miserably low, a total of six: Generals Schaffgotsch, Scherffenberg, and Sparr, Colonel Losy, Haimerl, and Heinrich Julius von Lauenburg. With the exception of Schaffgotsch, they had an easy hand to play.

The charge of having participated in the abominable conspiracy was at the outset abandoned. The indictment levelled only one, that of having subscribed to the first or second Pilsen Oath. Others had also done that, including some who sat on the board of the court martial. A general pardon had been issued for subscription to the first. Impeccable loyalty had been the tenor of the second. The accused were arraigned for having, the one in this way, the other in that, rendered obedience to the former Commander-in-Chief longer than their duty allowed. They excused themselves on grounds of compulsion and perplexity. They could adduce on their own score that they evaded Wallenstein's orders as soon as they had justification and opportunity for such action. They asked why they had not been initiated earlier by those who had been told of the Duke's evil intent and had carried the decree of deposition in their pocket. Duke Heinrich Julius, being an imperial prince, did not have to appear in court. Assisted by a wily lawyer, he refuted so cleverly the twenty-three counts brought against him that in his case no proper trial ever began.

Meanwhile the problem had been raised whether proceedings must not be instituted against and a valid judgement obtained in respect of the principally guilty party, the executed or felled or slain – the term gradually preferred – Friedland. Were, failing such, the confiscations legal? What answer should be given to Countess Kinsky who, in contrast to Wallenstein's family, had the temerity to demand prosecution of her husband's assassins? A most plaguy problem. The experts to whom it was passed, like it or not, had to confess that a mere recital of historical facts, no matter who composed it, was something totally different from a verdict. Nevertheless they urgently warned against undertaking retrospective judicial histrionics. There existed the imperial proclamations, especially the second, with its sentence of outlawry, made public in March, which contained everything. More important, there was the act itself, the execution, in this instance intrinsically equivalent to the verdict, because in the condemned's lifetime a trial had not been feasible. As such it conformed to natural law, the instinct for self-preservation, and reasonable political action. Examples could be quoted from the history of both Austria and France. *Silent leges inter arma* (in war the laws are quiescent), as Cicero taught. To start proceedings against the dead would be to throw doubt upon what had been done as though the matter were still open to question. Wallenstein's "interested parties and friends" would moreover have to be allowed to contest the indictment. Delicate, extremely delicate. How would the imperial Exchequer fare if sequestration of the Friedland fortune was postponed indefinitely? Wallenstein's crime, the experts put forward for consideration, was among all men of good will a settled fact. None the less precisely that to which "mighty much attached" and which had been confirmed by the Emperor's hallowed signature, the barbaric plan to conquer the Hereditary Lands, to distribute the ministers' properties, to eradicate the ArchHouse, that, alas, was so little capable of proof as to render any attempt to frame it in a formal impeachment an inadmissible risk. The consequences to the imperial reputation? Better, concluded the experts, to leave aside all juridical steps and leave the facts to speak for themselves. Ferdinand agreed. When, in autumn, his son and heir apparent once again pressed for posthumous sentence, he was not to be budged.

That notion abandoned, the task of propagandistic vindication became all the more urgent. Piccolomini's romance was available, provided that the Grand Calumniator was not quoted by name. A second, more knowledgeable and craftier taleteller, Anton Schlieff, the Saxon Colonel, entered the scene in the nick of time. No authorized negotiator like Duke Franz Albrecht, a mere agent, caught in Prague, frightened at the torture with which he was threatened, frightened for his life, he was at the greatest pains to achieve the object of pleasing his inquisitors. He informed them of his two missions to Pilsen and revealed what he knew about Lord Rudolf Trčka, Kinsky's dealings with Feuquières, and the threads spun in the dark between the King of Sweden and Wallenstein during the course of 1631. Not that Schlieff had participated in the latter events. What he had to offer was Dresden gossip. All found acceptance, not excluding the story that none other than Wallenstein had in 1631 lured the Saxons to Prague, and the material was resolutely turned into the *Detailed and Thorough Report of the Abominable Treason Planned by Friedland and His Adherents. . . . All Compiled and Abridged for the Instruction of Everyman from Trustworthy Relations Received as well as Original Writings from the Willingly Effected Depositions of Those Apprehended in This Case.*

This upshot was no masterpiece. For months a string of authors or commission members tinkered at it, confirming the rule that too many cooks spoil a broth. Its editor may have been a capable pedant in other ways, but he was no penman. Pitifully few Original Writings were available for inclusion – Franz Albrecht's letter to Ilow from Regensburg, if it was the original; Schaffgotsch's last letter to Trčka, if it had been accurately deciphered; Freiberger's proclamation at Troppau. That was all. Among the Trustworthy Relations was how in 1630 Wallenstein had left the Baltic coast undefended in accordance with a plan to facilitate a Swedish landing, how in 1632 the ruins of the Hereditary Lands by the imposition of so many mouths to feed had been the main purpose of the large and splendid army which he had indeed assembled, and how after the battle of Lützen he had needlessly, disgracefully taken to his heels. Had the General succeeded in anything, the help of God and the bravery of his soldiers had been instrumental. Had anything miscarried, it was what he had wanted. Without placing excessive strain on their arid imagination, the authors copied the material at their disposal – the Bavarian *Discourse upon Friedland's Actions*, Schlieff's oral and written statements, and page after page of Piccolomini's story. Only at the end did there occur to the editor a leading question which he thought would prove most effective. The Protestants, as long as Friedland had been loyal in his appointment, always described him as nature's greatest monster. How was it that they did not blush to change their tune to one of endearments when he had become a rebel to his Emperor? Already enemies to the House of Austria, should they not at least distinguish between treason and traitor in accordance with the very sensible heathen who had coined the phrase *Amo proditionem, non proditores* (I love treason, not traitors)? The admonished remained unmoved.

Incidentally and at an unobtrusive place in the text the state document included nine little words which told Habsburg opponents nothing new. They had never had any doubt about the admission there made that the Emperor had been forced to issue an order to arrest and put into custody the former commander-in-chief in the field, so that all the accusations laid against him should be able to be most punctiliously investigated, "or become possessed of his person, dead or alive". Stylists guessed that this last was a later inserted clause, turning the sentence into a monstrosity. Their surmise was proved correct when the draft was found and compared with the printed page. Here stood what Piccolomini had with stubborn, cold-blooded effrontery demanded: Ferdinand's assumption, finally and openly, of his no small share in the capital crime committed at Eger. In early autumn the inferior piece of work was set up in type, translated into Italian and Czech, and distributed as well as could be.

In spring 1635, nine months later, Schaffgotsch, Losy, Sparr, Scherffenberg, and Haimerl received their signed death-warrants. After the
verdict Count Schaffgotsch was subjected to torture. Since he could
already be regarded as a carcass, freely disposable, the hope was that
additional information might still be obtained from him. During three
hours of ingeniously intensified anguish nothing occurred to the unfortunate magnate which he could produce for confession. In the end
his tormentors desisted. The imperial War Council examined the verdicts in its capacity as court of higher instance – final authority lay with
the Emperor. It found the sentences to be just, yet not so just as not,
with a single exception, to merit modification into life imprisonment. In
July 1635 Schaffgotsch was beheaded. There had, for heaven's sake, to
be at least one accomplice deserving of death. For this and that reason
the Count was suited to the indispensable role. Perhaps also because in
his case, and in his case only, a large fortune was available for confiscation. Before the close of 1635 the remaining four were released from their
lifelong incarceration. Their promise that henceforth they really would
behave irreproachably enabled them to go wherever they would.
Possibly such rapid act of pardon can be viewed as fresh evidence of the
Emperor's clemency, and possibly as a mute avowal too. The trials had
proved worse than disappointing; they had proved a farce. Immediately
after the verdicts had been pronounced, the monarch ordered that
knowledge of them was "to be restricted and not made public". He
knew why.

AND REWARD

The renewed redistribution of Bohemia was no joking and no small-scale
matter.

Had Ferdinand been an economist, like his cousin from Bavaria, he
would have taken over Friedland as a whole, with its Chamber at
Gitschin, its governor, its estate administrators and travelling inspectors.
He would have ensured for himself annual revenues as handsome as any
from his finest provinces. He did not. The duchy's dismemberment,
resolved in January, was put into practice fast as possible. The marvellous machine, the one and only benefaction conferred by Wallenstein
on his country, was destroyed.

Instantly the contrast between *Terra Felix* and the rest of Bohemia
vanished. Billetings in the towns and on the properties, spoliations, and
lamentations by the victims, all on the familiar pattern. The servants of

the old order regretted its breakdown, for all that the former suzerainty had been severe. They obeyed in the hope of retaining office and their daily bread. They readily paid homage to their new masters, currently the imperial confiscation commissioners. The homage was like that once paid to Elisabeth Smiřický, then to the Slawata couple, thereafter to Wallenstein. They were used to being passed from hand to hand.

Only the Trčka possessions proved a source of vexation. It arose from the division of property between Lord Rudolf and Count Adam having been somewhat hazy, or at least capable of being presented as having been so, while proscription for the time being applied only to whatever concerned the dead son, not the living father. Nachod had indubitably belonged to the murdered man. Yet Rudolf, at the principal family seat of Opočno, bitterly disputed the fact. He even went so far as to block the imperial commissioners' entry into the castle with a guard ready to shoot, just as fifteen years ago lame Otto von Wartenberg had done at Gitschin. With a family fortune of four million gulden at stake, the imperialists had no small interest in rendering old Trčka ripe for its confiscation through a trial for high treason against him and his dead wife Magdalena. That was what happened, and happened easily enough, for we know the pair's political character. Lord Rudolf was lucky to die before the legal proceedings were in full swing.

How rich had the Duke of Friedland been? His cunning, his diabolical determination and firmness of mind, as well as his accumulation of wealth had always been overrated. The imperial commissioners, whose calculations were more exact than the Emperor was in his spending, assessed the assets at 8,661,000 gulden. This figure was offset by claims, genuine, exaggerated, or fraudulent, of 3 million gulden. A debit of 1,725,000 gulden was allowed as legitimate. The greatest expert on this subject has added to the assets a few additional millions, not capable of precise computation, in the shape of indemnification for Mecklenburg, claims on the Emperor for army supplies since 1632, and the value of cattle, very large stocks of grain, and goods and chattels of every kind with which the model estates were endowed. Only the third category represented any real, locally tangible item. The rest comprised a political receivable, an abstraction, a form of distant thunder.

The commissioners thought that there must be more. Buried treasure, though the officials swore that there was none. Bulging secret accounts at Hamburg (the city was sent a stern note), Venice, and Amsterdam; they did not exist. Whoever had anything material to report about hidden funds or moneys on loan was promised one tenth. Shrewd, nevertheless sterile bait. Those 39,000 golden ducats dispatched two days before the end could not but be somewhere. The search for them zealously pursued, the upshot was mortifying. Elector John George, as soon as he heard of events at Eger, seized the hoard from Kinsky's last dwelling at Pirna as a temporary, later permanent measure. In times of war the admissible and the inadmissible are not always easy to distinguish. The commissioners tried to recoup themselves by having recourse to Friedland's last governor. He should not at that stage any longer have relinquished his hold on the coins. The governor rejected the argument. The suit against him continued for fourteen years. In 1648 he was condemned to pay the whole sum plus accrued interest. Out of his own pocket. He could not.

Adding to Wallenstein's principalities and the Trčkas' enormous possessions the considerable properties of Count Schaffgotsch as well as the more modest fortunes of Ilow and Kinsky, fourteen millions remained to be given away. We know what the figure signified when we recall that all too often potentates lacked fifty gulden for a courier. It was a material upheaval similar to that after the battle of the White Mountain, but simpler. Then confiscation had had to be inflicted on thousands by way of carefully graduated penalties. Now only two parties were involved in total loss, the two who after the White Mountain had been the principal profiteers.

The bulk of the seized possessions was intended to be used for the army's satisfaction. The army meant the generals and the colonels. The generals and the colonels meant in the first place Wallenstein's murderers, the major and the minor ones, followed by the favourites at Vienna. There would, in other words, be dissipation, not rational utilization. The gifts were fundamentally pecuniary, but in property instead of cash. By the end of April it was known who would have the main morsels. Friedland and Reichenberg, worth 500,000 gulden, would go to Gallas; Nachod, assessed at 215,000 gulden, to Piccolomini; Teplitz, previously Kinsky-owned and put at a mere 94,000 gulden, to Aldringen. Piccolomini could feel that he had suffered discrimination as against Gallas, who in addition was given Kinsky's mansion at Prague, although enjoying preferential treatment as against Aldringen. The latter, the first to press his grasping hopes and the inventor of detailed distribution schemes, was not only reduced to third place among the major executors, but set far below the top level in the junior category. Hirschberg, valued at 225,000 gulden, went to Colonel, now Count and Lord Chamberlain, Walter Butler; Nové Město, at 132,000 gulden, to Colonel Count

Leslie; Smidar and Skřiwany, at 178,000 gulden, to John Gordon. Devereux, Macdaniel, and Geraldine received 40,000, 30,000 and 12,000 gulden respectively, in properties or parts of properties or money to be paid by those whose share had been assessed higher than the sum allowed them. Isolani, Caretto di Grana (he had to complain shrilly for five years before he got his award), de Suys, Morzin, Giuli Diodati – not one of them was forgotten. They saw to that, those who without clamorous self-recommendation might have been. Neither proud Count Oñate nor Father Lamormaini's Jesuit college nor the King of Hungary were overlooked. The latter was indebted to his father's generosity for Smrkowicz and its stud-farm. Thoroughbreds were always in demand. What happened to the bright-plumaged birds, whether anyone displayed interest in their appropriation or the soldiers killed and broiled them, is nowhere recorded. The Emperor's creditors joined the crowd of beneficiaries. Hereupon it became apparent that there was absolutely nobody, military or civil, within hailing distance of the court who did not have some claim or other. Loans, expenditure, arrears of salary, now or never was the moment for them to be paid and overpaid. The hands held high with outstretched palm could be counted by their hundreds. We want something, we want a lot, we want more. If so-and-so has received that much, why not we? At every turn yelps about slights put upon honour – as though honour had been the issue. A frenzy of rivalry for money and possessions such as that which in 1622 Wallenstein had experienced, except that this time it was a case of disintegration without a trace of Wallenstein's constructive urge. Generals Marradas, Goetz, Strozzi, Tiefenbach (he obtained the Aulibitz dominion, which included Gitschin), Lamboy, Beck (promoted to Major-General), Rudolf Colloredo (Trčka's castle of Opočno and its appurtenant properties were just good enough for him), Desfours the Thief, Mansfeld the Wolf, Hatzfeld (his share was Silesian Trachenberg which had been in Schaffgotsch ownership) and Privy Councillors Werdenberg, Meggau, Wilhelm Slawata, Walmerode, Stralendorf, Schlick, they all of them obtained "assurance", as the term was, of portions from the Friedland hoard. Had a higher assessment been placed on what they secured than their claims justified, so that they should have paid the difference, the debt was amiably allowed to lapse. Only Wallenstein's three judges appear to have been tactful enough not to ask for anything. They, and Gerhard Questenberg. In the end, too soon, no more was left. Limitless as the prize had seemed, large enough to render the House of Habsburg financially weather-proof for years ahead, it did not suffice to sate the rapacity of more or less useful parasites. Three years later 112 army officers were still vainly awaiting their money. The soldiers whom Ferdinand so warmly cherished probably had no greater benefit from the Friedland sequestration than that for a few months they could fill their bellies on the Friedland estates.

The frequent written objections raised by the widowed Duchess were systematically rebuffed. For more than a year the reply to them remained that first must be established how matters really stood with her. The lady fell into debt, penury, and ultimately despair. She abandoned the legal approach. That had been precisely the object of her treatment. No legal footing could be admitted here. When clemency was all that she sought, clemency was granted. Two and a half years after the Duke's death she was, out of Christian charity, awarded the domains of Neuschloss and Böhmisch-Leipa which Wallenstein had conferred on her. Not, though, the three hundred thousand ducats, not the annuity of twelve thousand, and not the palace at Prague. The principle ran that if the traitor's will held good in any respect, then it held good in all, and consequently it must hold good in none.

The magic castle had been wholly submerged. In vain all the invocations to hold it fast upon the ground, the far-sighted dispositions, the documents loaded with heavy seals and many handsome signatures. No ducal estates any more nor ducal towns nor feudal tenants. No chambers, no mint, no highest court of appeal. Neither a speedy postal service nor a planned and flourishing economy. Ill-gotten gain will not thrive, in spite of all? Easy come, easy go? The rule can be observed in operation when circumstances combine to make it so. When they do not, it is forgotten. Wallenstein had enjoyed his booty barely a dozen years. The heirs to the Wallenstein and Trčka–Kinsky–Schaffgotsch pillage, the Clary–Aldringens, the Colloredos, the Hatzfelds, the Gallas' or Clam–Gallas', remained the men in possession until such time as in Bohemia and Silesia landed property ceased to be. The Piccolominis would have done no worse if, towards the end of the eighteenth century, their Bohemian branch had not become extinct. By that time that which they held was no longer pillage, but property with ancient roots.

> Be in possession and you are law-abiding,
> The world will help to preserve your rights and titles. . . .

Law-abiding was Count Maximilian von Waldstein, Chamberlain to His Imperial Roman Majesty, Principal Equerry to the King of Hungary. What he had held in fee from his brother-in-law, cousin, and benefactor, overlordship of the monastery and town of Münchengrätz, as well as the properties of Zweretic, Swijam, and Studenka, he was now in the light of his loyal service, permitted to keep for himself and his heirs. A few more years passed and he purchased for fifty thousand gulden, a price that was a mark of favour, the last of what was left from the mass of seized possessions – the palace at Prague. Thereby the Friedland mansion at least remained within the family. Gradually it came to be known as the Waldstein Palace, a name, correct in substance, that until the middle of this century it continued to bear and still bears today although now the substance has been abstracted.

Count Max, with his knowledge of the duchy's entail, knew that, properly speaking, he was the heir and that no crime on Wallenstein's part, whatever it might be, gave the Emperor any right to extinguish the imprescriptible, perpetual Friedland donation. The privilege, initially granted in 1627 and subsequently renewed, was well enough known in court circles. Nevertheless for two hundred years the pretence was that it had never existed. Then, in 1842, late in the day, Christian von Waldstein, a descendant of Maximilian in the seventh generation, tried with the assistance of lawyers and historians, old parchments and unimpeachable arguments, again to raise the magic castle from the depths. In his suit before Bohemia's *Landrecht** he proved that his ancestral uncle, Albrecht, Duke of Friedland, had never been guilty, let alone convicted of the felonies with which he was charged; that even if legal sentence had been pronounced, such could never be directed other than against his person, and not against the entail; that here the principle of juridical limitations did not apply because the investiture had, *expressis verbis*, been for all time; that he himself, as the attached genealogical tree proved, was the present holder of the ducal Friedland entail and that it was incumbent upon him to demand the restitution within fourteen days of the degree and titles of which he was unlawfully deprived as well as its substance, this being the Friedland domains in their entirety. Within fourteen days. After two centuries. The case passed through courts of various instance, but the judgement was always the same: the execution of the Duke of Friedland with all its consequences had been an imperial penal act – an act, in the terminology of another age, of political justice or, more bluntly, a political act – in respect of which ordinary civil law judges had no competence. Presumably Austrian judicial civil servants could find no other mode of expression. Presumably they could not say to the eccentric Count,

* The highest court of justice (translator's note).

Your parchments are very interesting, but not so interesting as to have any topical bearing. Contemporary times have a justice of their own which they are not going to allow to be influenced by historians and ancient tales. A ghost cannot be clothed in flesh and blood. Go home, lock up your parchments in their chest, be content with what in your time, in your life you have and which, as we can see from these documents, enables you pretty well to enjoy life to the full.

THE THIRTY YEARS

It remains to recall how the war, this amorphously fluctuating, insane European war which after fourteen or fifteen years' duration Wallenstein had wanted to bring to an end, went on another fourteen to fifteen years, and to recall it with the brevity appropriate to a biography, the biography moreover of one who was left behind half-way and no longer witnessed what follows here.

During the winter months the Emperor's generals had attempted nothing whatever else than to keep an eye on and eventually to crush Wallenstein's alleged conspiracy. They had been able to afford to do so. In May the new Generalissimo, Ferdinand, King of Hungary, passed his new army, Wallenstein's army, in review at Pilsen and found it good. Now was decided the strategy which was the opposite of the Friedland strategy, to regard Bohemia, Silesia, eastern Germany and northern Germany as collateral theatres of war, but southern Germany as the main one. In June began the siege of Regensburg. The Swedes resorted to the old device of a diversion by invasion deep into Lower Bavaria. Landshut was taken. Lieutenant-General Aldringen, in command of the Bavarians, ingloriously lost his life as a fugitive. The diversion proved however of no use to the Protestants because four days later Regensburg, their principal gain in 1633, surrendered. Nor did it effectively help them that a more important, simultaneous eastern diversion, with the Swedes under Banér and the Saxons under Arnim, reached Prague on the day when Regensburg fell. Shadowy repetition of Arnim's campaign in 1631. The imperialists had only to hint at a move in this direction for the invaders to retreat. The chief reason was that the Swedes and the Saxons trusted each other as little as ever, still less than ever. Young Ferdinand and his deputy Gallas could let Bohemia be and drive the enemy, Bernhard and Horn, Danube upwards. They repeated what in the preceding year it had been Aldringen's task to attempt. As Aldringen had received reinforcement through the Duke of Feria's Spaniards, so did they receive more effectual, more fortunate reinforcement through the Cardinal-Infant's Spaniards. He was at last, with fifteen thousand mercenaries at his back, on the road from Lombardy and the Tirol. The battle of Nördlingen, at the beginning of September, exceeded in length and numbers those of Lützen, the White Mountain, and even Breitenfeld, raging for two days and ending in the Swedes' utter defeat. The imperialists had enjoyed a superiority in numbers such as Wallenstein in his few battles had never possessed. They displayed a tempestuous aggressiveness that Wallenstein never did. The outcome proved the Elector of Bavaria to have been right when he had so long argued in vain that the enemy, if it was really desired, could assuredly be expelled from southern Germany. Six months ago a threat to Austria, Bernhard could with the wreckage of his army and the hastily collected garrisons of surrendered fortresses just hope to reach the line of the Rhine and to maintain the link with France. The combined Spanish-imperialist soldiery debouched across Württemberg with a fury that had not as yet been experienced even in this war. Hitherto the land had comparatively been spared havoc, reputedly because it had been to Wallenstein's interest. During the next five years the duchy lost three-quarters of its inhabitants. Oxenstierna's Heilbronn League was in a state of complete dissolution.

Thus far went the triumph of Wallenstein's murderers, thus thoroughly were his war policy and his peace policy confuted. And were not. Ten victories, his warning had been, would bring peace no nearer. The battle of Nördlingen brought peace not a jot nearer. It postponed it until yet more terrible, more distant days.

This was so in spite of the fact that the breakdown of Sweden's venturesome position in southern Germany increased the pace of a process begun in the spring, dating back to 1632, and none other than the familiar Wallenstein plan for peace negotiations between the House of Habsburg and Saxony. The new Generalissimo inherited the plenary powers of his murdered predecessor. He very politely informed Dresden of the fact, the news was gladly received, and readiness to forget indignation at Wallenstein's end was on hand. Such smatterings of moral consideration generally do not last long when it is politics' turn to speak. There was certainly a lot to say. On the principle of power being capable of anything if it makes good sense, Wallenstein had believed that he could within an hour conclude peace with Saxony. It took a year. The talks began at Leitmeritz in Bohemia, shifted to Pirna in Saxony, and were then transferred to Prague. The imperialist representatives, Max

Trauttmansdorff, imperial Court Councillor Hermann Questenberg, and the hair-splitting lawyer Dr Gebhard, were the same as had long ago been appointed. The negotiations were not conducted as Wallenstein, to whom all pettifogging detail was abhorrent, had imagined that they would be or how in 1629 he had conducted them in front of his fireplace at Güstrow. Admittedly the issue with Denmark had been lightweight as compared with the venomous conflicts which for the past eighty years had been rampant in the Empire. Both sides stuck to the perennial rule of first demanding the utmost, retiring a few steps to a position nearer the middle, waiting to see whether the other would not approach rather closer, threatening to break off discussions, and, when the main matter seemed to have been settled, bringing up new conditions, qualifications, reservations. The middle, where after wearisome argument they met, was that the Elector of Saxony should conclude peace with the Emperor on behalf of himself and all, Germans and non-Germans, who cared to join, but that not a word was said about territorial or monetary satisfaction for the Swedes, let alone the French. Not a European gesture, in fact, only one directed towards Protestant Germany, and its conservative portion at that, the Lutherans, the "Augsburg religiously affined". To them it certainly looked tempting. The core was the repeal of the restitution edict. Not finally, because a concession made under the pressure of contemporary circumstances could only be temporary, but temporary for a long time, forty years, and with their passage the problem of former ecclesiastical possessions was nevermore to be solved by force. Emperor Ferdinand, who found it difficult to abandon the most blessedly Christian act of his reign, consented only after consultation with his theologians. Twenty-two of them, under the chairmanship of Cardinal Dietrichstein. A majority, members of the Dominican and Capuchin Orders, led by Don Diego Quiroga, inferred, as against a minority of Jesuits led by Father Lamormaini, that the sacrifice would not be displeasing to God if the politicians regarded it as absolutely essential, which in a manner of speaking was to leave men of the world to decide a worldly business. An amnesty for all felonies committed against the Head of the Empire should, it was agreed, date no farther back than summer 1630, the season when the Swedish invasion began. The restoration of all property into the ownership prevailing on 12 November 1627 was promised. The Saxons had wanted to go farther back. Wallenstein, we believe, had once proposed a return to the condition existing in 1612. Nevertheless 1627 remained the agreed "standard year". Friendly exceptions were straightway made. Out of innate goodness the Emperor engaged, for example, graciously to receive the homage of the Mecklen-burg brothers, provided that they truly and gratefully subscribed to the current conclusion of peace. Unfriendly exceptions were also made, as in the case of Württemberg and Baden, territories only just overrun by the imperialists who for their military purposes proposed thoroughly to torment them, and the list was long. The Saxons declined to coun-tenance the insertion of such vexatious matter into the body of the treaty. Only in an accompanying letter would they take cognizance of it as a unilateral declaration of imperial intent. Participants in the "Fried-land treason" were on the list, but who was meant by that is not to be elucidated. The exclusion of the Palatinate figured in the treaty itself. The onus for all the horrors of the past decades incurred by the deceased Palsgrave and the Bohemians was too oppressive to render it possible to meddle with what had earlier been decreed. The Saxons did not succeed in eliminating such unwise reservations, destructive of the amnesty's healing power, nor did they obtain the slightest alleviation for their co-religionists in the Hereditary Lands, especially Silesia. Would it be unfair, asked Trauttmansdorff, for the Emperor in his lands to enjoy the right which the Protestant princes thought reasonable for themselves, the right to dispose over the religion of their subjects? The Empire's future? Wordy paragraphs on that topic. All coalitions and special alliances inside its boundaries were forthwith forbidden. That was a blow at John George's Leipzig Resolution, the Palsgrave's long dispersed Union, and Maximilian of Bavaria's League too. There was to be but one army, to supervise the peace, under one supreme head, the Emperor, and it was in future to be known as His Imperial Roman Majesty's and the Roman Empire's Martial Force. A modifying rider stated that an ample portion of this army should be entrusted to the Elector of Saxony, which signi-fied an identical entitlement on the part of Bavaria and Brandenburg. This rider was in turn modified. Should the crowns of Sweden and France unhappily not adhere to the Peace of Prague, it behoved all Electors, indeed all Estates, Catholic and Protestant alike, in true Ger-man unity to render the Emperor aid until such time as the foreigners had been driven from imperial soil.

Was not all this what Lieutenant-General von Arnim – who was not present at these negotiations – had argued for years? That the foreigners, for all their friendly talk, did not mean well with the Germans, only with themselves, and would not shed a tear over the Empire's ruin? Had he not inculcated it, year in, year out? When however in the field of major policy that which we have wanted finally does happen, and happens without our being granted decisive influence over its form and procedure, then it is none the less not that which we have wanted. Arnim had striven for a third, German and Protestant party, in amicable agreement with Austria although not in subjugation to it, dissociated from the Swedes but not with base ingratitude stabbing them in the back. He cared deeply for the freedom of the reformed religion, everywhere, yet particularly in Silesia where he had once re-established it and the Papists could henceforth do as they pleased. He saw what was hidden from John George's imbecile gaze – that this treaty, for all that it read so bravely, would not bring peace. He protested. He resigned his commission. He was a virtuoso at quitting a master and retiring into the private life which he could never tolerate for long.

Arnim was still alive and able to express his opinion. Not Wallenstein. It is also difficult to draw comparisons between the compromises of Prague and the peace programme which he had carried in his head, mutable, simple, and imprecise, because detail of any kind irked him. A highly individualistic programme. Nevertheless a few points are clear. He had always been against the war as one of religion – "Conscience derives from God alone" – and always for separation of the political from the spiritual issues. If now, six years too late, the accursed edict was dropped into a drawer, that conformed to his ideas. Others, many of them, were missing. He had wished to extend the amnesty to all, to the Palatinate, to the Bohemian *émigrés*, had wanted to offer them at least propitiation of one kind or another. And, in the final phase, such to the French and Swedes too. He had wanted to tear apart the chains which made Austria–Germany the captive of Spain. This, notwithstanding its inauguration by unsuitable means and its infiltration by alien, morbid elements, had fundamentally been his policy. And indeed no European, consequently no German, peace was possible without pacifying Germany as a whole rather than a few privileged groups, without making the strangers who, like it or not, were on hand an offer of a calibre which would allow them to depart without loss of face, and without sending home the Spaniards who dictated Vienna's policy and forcing them to accept the new state of affairs.

In Germany there was joy at the Peace of Prague. The terms were read from the pulpits, bells were rung, guns were fired, and the night-sky was brightened by fireworks. The various parties subscribed to it astonishingly promptly – the large imperial cities, Lübeck, Hamburg, Bremen, Frankfurt, Nürnberg, Ulm, and the large principalities, Bavaria, Brandenburg, Brunswick, Mecklenburg – yes, the dukes at Güstrow and

Schwerin too, for all that they owed it solely to King Gustavus Adolphus if they could come home again. All the same, this belated spectacle of reconciliation was a delusion. Too many were excluded, the south Germans along with the Palatinate, the Calvinists in general, while others, Bernhard von Weimar, Wilhelm von Hesse-Kassel, George von Lüneburg, excluded themselves. They did it because they sensed that the war would none the less go on, a war now between European states in which they had allies superior in strength and the prospects of at last reaping some profit were sound. He was warning them betimes, Oxenstierna told emissaries from Mecklenburg: the Swedes, driven to the coast, would rear and savage those around them, the sufferers being those situated between the attackers and attacked.

No longer a war of religion. A war between states, although between as yet undefined, fledgeling states and correspondingly confused. The French had tried, in the style of the Marquis de Feuquières, to prevent the conclusion of the Peace of Prague. Somewhat like Arnim, but from a different perspective, they comprehended that it did not signify the creation of that third German party about which they had dreamt for so long, rather that of a Germany tied to Spain. Given their political outlook, that they would not tolerate. The battle of Nördlingen had forced them into open, more open intervention. The Swedish defeat might prove a direct threat to France, but it had the advantage that henceforth they would be the incomparably stronger partner in the alliance. They had organized an army, a group of armies, with a fighting establishment equal to any that Wallenstein had ever had under him. They sought allies in Germany wherever they could find them. Their troops marched on the Spanish Netherlands, into Alsace, into the Palatinate, across the Rhine against Heidelberg, down the Rhine as far as Coblenz. When on 19 May 1635, a week before the signing of the Treaty of Prague, a herald at Brussels proclaimed that war existed between the Kings of France and Spain, and consequently between the King of France and the Emperor, his announcement barely excited attention.

Desolation, through the years, through the lands, followed. A desolation during which the mercenary armies of Poles, Italians, Scots, Flemings, Croats, Cossacks, Greeks, Turks, as well as Germans, French, Spaniards and Swedes, marched back and forth on one long trail of plunder and on occasion against each other. Once, in 1636, the imperialists were at Compiègne and the Parisians in a panic. Another time, in 1642, the Swedes were in front of Vienna and the capital's great lords in flight along the road to Graz. In 1639 Ottavio Piccolomini at Thionville beat the French, commanded by none other than the Marquis de Feuquières who, his arm smashed, had time to learn in agony that it is pleasanter to prolong wars at the head of a diplomatic mission than to suffer a soldier's death. Emperor Ferdinand II died. His son succeeded him. The Electoral College functioned smoothly. Not that it made any difference. The war continued. Father Joseph, Cardinal Richelieu, King Louis, Pope Urban died. The war continued. In England and Scotland there was civil war, on one side the King, the nobility, the country people, on the other London, Parliament, and the towns. An unheard-of thing. Not that it much affected the European conflagration, for Great Britain had long been absent from the scene. And the war continued. The nameless were slaughtered in greater, far greater numbers than in Wallenstein's day. By soldiers who cried havoc far more courageously among the defenceless than among their enemy, by the plague and by typhoid, *morbus novus* (the new disease). His principalities were totally devastated, many farmsteads had not a living soul on them, Duke Adolf Friedrich of Mecklenburg noted. Where such still were, they subsisted on mice and other unnatural foods. Indeed parents ate their children and the other way about, as he had proof enough. That had not been so under Wallenstein. Privy Councillor Cothmann, the same whom the Duke had once threatened to lay his head before his feet, clamoured that there must be peace. In 1640 he travelled to the Regensburg Diet to use all his powers of persuasion to that end. The war continued. In addition to fleeting inroads, the Swedes three times more broke deeply into Bohemia and Moravia, seized Olmütz, besieged Brünn, and finally took Prague's Little Side and Hradschin by storm. Treasures were pillaged, high personages captured. Cardinal Harrach, Chief Burgrave Martinitz (whom thirty years ago the Bohemians had thrown out of the palace window), imperial court Councillor Walmerode, and Abbot Caspar Questenberg were among them. In 1637 Hans Georg von Arnim was taken, to the jubilation of vindictive old Count Thurn, by Swedes in his castle of Boitzenburg and incarcerated at Stockholm as a prisoner of state until, eighteen months later, he escaped by means of his valet's passport. The experience so deeply embittered him that he once more altered his political views and became the Swedes' most fanatical enemy. He hatched a large variety of plans for their injury and expulsion, such as inciting Stralsund against its tyrannical saviours, an attempt already made in autumn 1633 by Wallenstein. He died on the point of re-enlisting in the imperial service. Duke Franz Albrecht von Lauenburg had long since done this, as though he had forgiven and forgotten Wallenstein's murder as well as the unpleasantness to which he had thereafter been subjected. He was killed while fighting against the Swedes at Schweidnitz where in 1633 there had been the long armistice. The death of this high-spirited soldier is said to have been indescribably painful too. During the same year, 1642, occurred the second battle of Breitenfeld. Although the Saxons on this occasion supported the opposite side, they were beaten just as thoroughly as eleven years ago. They had been commanded by Ottavio Piccolomini who hereupon crossed into Spanish service. His enemy Gallas, in 1639 sent into early retirement on account of his intensely disappointing military performances, was brought back to replace him. Not that Gallas had any better luck than before. He had to pursue a Swedish corps under Tortenson who, engaged in a separate campaign with the Danes, had moved from Upper Silesia to Jutland. The pursuit was like Wallenstein's of King Christian in 1627. Tortenson was more skilful than the King. Escaping the trap presented by the narrow peninsula, he turned south again, Gallas on his heels, always on his heels. At Aschersleben near Magdeburg Gallas closed in and led his army to perdition. His irrevocable retirement ensued. His dipsomania and resultant corpulence were the joke of Europe. A French caricature depicted him pushing his swollen belly ahead in a wheelbarrow. Always, though, he remained the most delicate-minded of Wallenstein's three major executioners. The tale goes that, when he felt his end nearing, he implored Emperor Ferdinand III for an audience, if only for an hour. The monarch thought the plea unbecoming. He sent him his Privy Councillors Schlick, Khevenhüller and Kurtz, but Gallas did not care to unburden himself to them. He had a bundle of letters handed to him, burning them one by one. Nobody knows the subject of their contents or why these oppressed the dying man. It leaves us free to guess.

In that very April 1647, when Gallas passed away, the Elector of Bavaria, once more moved by the despair, and threats too, of his people, concluded an armistice with France, just as fifteen years earlier he had concluded one with Sweden. Old, spent and uncertain of himself, he six months later repudiated his neutrality again. The consequent behaviour of the French and the Swedes can hardly be epitomized as surpassing previous horrors because, as contemporary witnesses attest, such a pitch was no longer possible to attain. Brandenburg, of late under stronger rule, had in 1641 broken the Treaty of Prague. On its own initiative it proclaimed and defended its neutrality. Thus began the rise of Brandenburg-Prussia. The half-way point, and almost the culmination too, of Spain's downfall was when in 1639 the Dutch in English neutral waters sent to Davy Jones' locker the strongest fleet which in this century it had assembled, in 1640 the Catalans elected the King of France to be their King and the Portuguese deserted too, in 1643 its proudest levy of cavalry and infantry was annihilated by the French at Rocroy near the Netherlands border. In the same year the Duke of Olivares, imperialist visionary, departed from office amid the jeers and derision of all Madrid. Habsburg Austria could no longer look forward to help from Habsburg Spain. Nevertheless the war continued. There was almost incessant peace negotiation, yet it continued.

There had always been negotiation. The war of thirty years had been a misunderstanding which, had there been readiness to agree over petty differences of legal interpretation, could at any time have been resolved. Negotiation had taken place in 1618–19 between the Bohemian rebels, Matthias, and Ferdinand; at the beginning of the twenties between Vienna, the Palsgrave, and England; in 1625 between Wallenstein, the Lower Saxon Circle, and Denmark; between the Swedes and the Poles, and the Muscovites; between the Electors; between the Dutch and the Spaniards, the French and the Austrians, the Bavarians and the Swedes; between Wallenstein and Saxony and Brandenburg; between Saxony and the Emperor, on which the Peace of Prague followed. The latter constituted an offer, open to all, and the Saxons honestly tried to interest the Swedes in it. After five years a presentiment that the offer would not answer its purposes seeped through, first in Berlin, then at Vienna and Munich. There would after all have to be negotiation elsewhere between others. In 1641 France, Sweden, and the Emperor agreed about the site, Münster and Osnabrück. Three years passed before an understanding was reached about all the participants and the problems relating to participation. In December 1644 the congress of 148 delegates began. It lasted four years, the first of which was needed to establish why war had been waged. Eventually four main groups of reasons or subjects of conflict were enumerated – the complaints of the German Estates, principally against the Emperor, the problems of an amnesty more comprehensive than that of 1635, satisfaction for the Estates' allies or former allies, Sweden and France, indemnification for the dispossessed. The categories may seem to us a trifle inadequate in the light of such lengthy, destructive mischief. Who can tell? It has always been no more than a historians' postulate, credulously accepted, that mankind's bloody imbecilities require causes commensurate with their horror, or even causes at all. The atrocities prove nothing as to the purport of the imbecilities. The lasting profound consequences prove nothing as to the causes.

With the motives for waging war at last neatly extrapolated, another three years were expended on their settlement. No one will any longer be surprised at the pace. Two months had been necessary to achieve the Leipzig Resolution, the Little-Lutheran coalition under Saxon leadership, and a year for the Peace of Prague. Faster work at Lübeck in 1629 was solely due to Wallenstein. The notion that it is more practical first to conclude an armistice, then peace, was unfamiliar. In 1633 Wallenstein had tried it, unsuccessfully. Therefore the war continued during the four years of negotiation. Let one side once more gain some illusory victory somewhere and its representatives would raise its demands. The congress adhered to the baneful old custom, which had achieved institutional status, of the parties using the winter to set snares for each other in documentary counter-pleas and rejoinders and the summer to martyrize their lands. As for the Peace of Westphalia, the culminating labour by a hundred and forty-eight hard-headed, suspicious, vigilant, covetous diplomats in constant correspondence with their masters, some of Wallenstein's ideas could indeed be traced in its terms. Emperor Ferdinand III made peace with King Louis XIV at Münster. Not King Philip IV, though. Spain's hopeless war with France dragged along another eleven years, in southern Europe and in Flanders. The Peace signified the separation of German Habsburg from Spanish Habsburg, the final collapse of Spanish influence at Vienna. On the other hand the Spaniards condescended at Münster to recognize in perpetuity that the sovereign republic of the Netherlands, the United Provinces, existed. The duchy of Pomerania was divided between Brandenburg and Sweden, as was possession of the Palatine territories between grizzled Maximilian and the Winter King's son. The German princes' religious suzerainty – *Cujus est regio, ejus est religionis dispositio* – was again given statutory form, but not without beneficent protective clauses for dissenters. The Thirty Years War, if it originated in religion, may be said to have been Christianity's last war in Germany and Europe. Vestiges of Wallenstein's trains of thought can be found in all this. If they do not amount to much, then it is because his thoughts remained in his head. Mere forerunner and uncertain herald of things to come, he had not ground any material manifestations from them. During the negotiations prior to the Peace of Prague he was occasionally called to mind and there would be talk of "playing the Wallenstein game". In the bloody morass of the next decade and a half his name went under.

We have no wish to present him as an inspired pioneer. For all his originality of character he was no more than a man of practical good sense who knew how to seize opportunities. He had, it is true, wished to make peace, reasonable peace, with the German Protestants and the Dutch. If, however, a hope of predominance beckoned "for us", he wanted to see it realized without giving protracted consideration to whether such ascendancy would be of medieval or modern kind. "Let us have Electoral Bavaria with us and we are the masters, not only of Germany but of all Europe." The new principle of the balance of power introduced by France into the Peace of Westphalia, equilibrium in the German lands and throughout Europe, was a concept which he could barely have apprehended. Indeed it is not really possible to envisage what part he would have played on the boards of life's passing scene. How would he have reacted when, a mere fifteen years after 1634, a military leader of radically democratic leanings was responsible for the King of England's head being severed from his body beneath the windows of Whitehall Palace? Useless to ask. In our day we are, under ever increasing strain, at the head of the race or we fall behind. Those who can with wheezing breath no longer stay the course, the dead, drop away like stones along the roadside. We hardly grasp that but a short while back they were our fellow-creatures, fellow-runners too.

It was Count Max von Trauttmansdorff, the man ready to conclude peace in 1633, the man appointed judge of Wallenstein's life or death, who led the imperial delegation at Münster with praiseworthy skill. It was Deputy Commander-in-Chief Ottavio Piccolomini who conducted the subsequent, hardy less rugged, military negotiations on the imperial side, helping to lay down the stages of withdrawal from enemy occupied territory which extended over a period of six years, and settling the details of the troops' pay and release – who presided, in short over the demobilization and the real end of hostilities. When everything was done a banquet of great splendour, for military men among themselves, was held. Piccolomini had the scene painted, like that of Lützen and of Thionville. The pictures can still be seen in the "Spanish Hall" splendidly installed at his orders in his castle of Nachod, the Smiřický castle, the Trčka castle. Its cupola portrays his introduction, to the impotent fury of his defeated enemies, by Mars to the glories of a victor's Olympus. Inescapable reminder of another ceiling decoration.

For two years and three months Wallenstein's mortal remains were left in the monastery of the Franciscan Minors at Mies. Then, with gross lack of ceremony, the coffin was transported to the Carthusian monastery of Walditz near Gitschin. The monks, to their surprise, found that the corpse showed not the slightest sign of decay, even the mortal wound "offering neither to the eye nor to the sense of smell the offensive impress of putrefaction". In the Walditz vault the dead man lay beside the relics of his first wife, Lukretia von Landek, and his little son Albrecht Carl. It had all had to be *sine honore*. Not that the Carthusians literally obeyed that order – "In prayers and religious observances we shall be mindful of our greatest benefactor."

After the death of Emperor Ferdinand II rumour had it that "supporters of the murdered Wallenstein" had poisoned him. Khevenhüller, the chronicler, mentioned the tale, but he added that it had indeed been insusceptible of proof.

Emperor Leopold, grandson of Ferdinand, nourished doubts about Wallenstein's guilt. "Do you know for certain," he asked a courtier who at Prague pointed towards the dissident's palace, "that Wallenstein was a rebel?"

In 1647 Maria Elisabeth, Princess of Friedland, wedded a Count Kaunitz. The marriage was appropriate to the station of the Waldsteins as it had been before the Duke and as it was again afterwards. At the beginning of our century the last offspring of this alliance died. In the genealogical tree of the later Counts Waldstein the Duke nowhere finds a place. It is, and this is strange, Hans de Witte, that poor suicide, who does.

Dignified was the career of Count Max's descendants, each in their day. The Waldsteins had been Hussites and Czech patriots before all these events. Then they became Catholics, faithful vassals of the Habsburg dynasty, and what had initially happened through coercion or occasion was transformed into creed, standpoint, innate style. One of Maximilian's sons was Archbishop of Prague and a great builder of churches. Each generation produced at least one monk or priest. All Waldsteins acted as befitted landowners of their period – they served the state; they endowed learned collections, libraries, theatres, academies and scientific bodies of service to their country as well as founding factories and charities; they were patrons of talent and genius which needed help. Not that this activity was charged with the same ambition as had fired that great outsider, the Duke. It ran in more normal channels, had narrower bounds, followed a course more predetermined by their station in life, but it was fruitful. Terms like feudalism or exploitation are inadequate description.

The Carthusians had to leave their house when Joseph II, degenerate decendant of Emperor Ferdinand in the sixth generation, dissolved all contemplative monasteries in the Empire, a step that could not be taken without the destruction of many centuries' accumulation of treasures such as no barbaric onslaught could have effected more brutally. Henceforward the buildings at Walditz served as a place of penal servitude. As it would have been wrong for the coffins to remain in a prison church, Count Vinzenz Waldstein in 1785 was allowed by agreement with highest authority to have them borne to Castle Münchengrätz. Somewhat belatedly a ceremonial funeral now took place. A black-draped sleigh drawn by six horses; trumpet and bugle calls; nobles in mourning, Capuchins in prayer, soldiers; crowds to whom the Countess did not forget to scatter largesse; a sermon, solemn music. All this in piercing cold. A new lead coffin had been made, well-fashioned, but small, for there were not many remains to recover. In the lid had been engraved an inscription, pious and proud, with a not unequivocal final phrase – ". . . *dum pro Deo, pro Ecclesia, pro Caesare, pro Patria fortiter pugnavit et triumphavit*" – he triumphed *while* he valiantly fought for God, the Church, the Emperor, and the Fatherland. . . . At last God called him unto Himself and rewarded him with the Celestial Crown. The way in which He did this is not mentioned.

On the tercentenary of his death the family had a new marble plate erected on the wall above the vault. In the middle, larger than life, head and bust, armour-clad and with Field-Marshal's baton, in relief. Below, the coat-of-arms. Left, all his titles, including those of Mecklenburg: Prince of the Wends, Count of Schwerin, Lord of the Lands of Rostock and Stargard. Right, his dates. Bottom left, *Ecclesiastes XVII*, 31: *Quid lucidius sole? et hic deficiet.* What is brighter than the sun? Yet the light thereof faileth – a verse which echoes something of Bohemia's melancholy.

It is lonely in the Chapel of St Anne. The son's memorial is no more heeded than are the tombstones of the parents at Hermanitz.

Postscript on Annotation

In the original German edition there are 110 pages of small print where the author quotes his authority for all events and facts other than those met in any responsible account of the Thirty Years War. The annotations are linked to the seventeen pages of bibliography. In less than a dozen instances has the author added comment which might be of more than very marginal interest to the English-language general reader. There is however one important exception. For almost three and a half centuries the battle of Lützen has, with greater or lesser hesitation, been presented as a Swedish victory. On this the author says:

"My description of the battle of Lützen relies more on the work of Josef Seidler than any other writer.* Seidler, who is familiar with the entire literature on the subject, had the extremely fruitful idea of including among his investigations the verdicts pronounced at Prague against the deserters on Wallenstein's side. Thereby he succeeded in unravelling the frequently incomprehensible reports by Holk, Diodati, and Gallas. He can justifiably claim that, thanks to his labours, no 'Lutzen Problem' any longer exists."

* Seidler, Josef, *Untersuchungen über die Schlacht bei Lützen 1632.* (Investigations into the Battle of Lützen, 1632) Memmingen, 1954. Also, *Besteht noch ein Lützenproblem?* (Is There Still a Lützen Problem?) Memmingen, 1971.

Bibliography

In his introduction to the bibliography in the original German edition the author noted that there are probably some three thousand books and articles on Wallenstein and his times extant. Although he confined himself to listing such as had in one way or another proved useful to him and to which his text refers, his classified bibliography covers seventeen pages of small print. No more than five English-language sources are included. The rest are preponderantly in German, many in Czech, and a number in French and Italian. With the author's approval a dozen works have been independently selected for the general reader's interest. Nearly all are available in both American and British editions currently in print.

Encyclopaedia Britannica, 15th ed., 1974. The articles on the Thirty Years War and Wallenstein are by S. Henry Steinberg. That on the War gives a well-organized, vigorous, iconoclastic conspectus. Cf. also below.

LIDDELL HART, B. H., *Wallenstein – The Enigma of History*, in *Great Captains Unveiled*. Blackwood, Edinburgh and London, 1927.

MALAND, DAVID, *Europe in the Seventeenth Century*. London, Macmillan, 1966. New York, St Martin's Press.

MITCHELL, J., *The Life of Wallenstein, Duke of Friedland*. London, 1837. Reprinted 1968.

New Cambridge Modern History, Vol. IV, Chap. XI. Cambridge University Press, 1970. The chapter on the Thirty Years War is written by E. A. Beller, Professor of History, Princeton University.

OGG, DAVID, *Europe in the Seventeenth Century*. First appearance in 1925 as part of the *History of Modern Europe* series and in 1948 in separate volume form; the 9th edition was published by A. & C. Black, London, 1971.

PAGÈS, GEORGES, *La Guerre de Trente Ans, 1618–1648* (1939), tr. New York, Harper & Row, 1971.

POIŠENSKÝ, J. V., *Třicetiletá válka a česky národ* (1960), tr. Robert Evans, *The Thirty Years War*. London, Batsford, 1971. University of California Press, 1971. The work is interesting in as much as it deals with the subject from a Marxist viewpoint.

ROBERTS, MICHAEL, *Gustavus Adolphus. A History of Sweden, 1611–32.* London, Longmans, Green, 2 vols, 1953–8. An important work of scholarship interesting for its contrapuntal treatment of many events in the present biography.

STEINBERG, S(IGFRID) HENRY, *The Thirty Years War and the Conflict for European Hegemony, 1600–1660.* London, 1966. Norton, New York, 1967, paperback.

WATSON, FRANCIS, *Wallenstein, Soldier under Saturn.* London, 1938. The only other full-scale English-language biography, well-written, but not entirely free of inaccuracies.

WEDGWOOD, C(ICELY) V., *The Thirty Years War.* London, Jonathan Cape, 1938. Reprinted 1964. New York, Doubleday, paperback. A classic account of its subject.

Index